3 1310 00111 9128

P9-DEK-488

Psychology and Life

Twelfth Edition

Philip G. Zimbardo
Stanford University

Psychology and Life

Twelfth Edition

Scott, Foresman and Company
Glenview, Illinois
Boston London

To Christina Maslach Zimbardo, who has given new meaning to my life and new life to my fascination with psychology—in more ways than she realizes.

Credit lines for the photos, illustrations, and other copyrighted materials appearing in this work are placed in the Acknowledgments section beginning on page LVII. This section is to be considered an extension of the copyright page.

Library of Congress Cataloging-in-Publication Data

Zimbardo, Philip G.
Psychology and life.

Bibliography: p.
Includes index.
1. Psychology. I. Title.
BF121.Z54 1988 150 87-20612
ISBN 0-673-18938-4

Printed in the United States of America.
1 2 3 4 5 6—VHJ—92 91 90 89 88 87

Preface

This publication of the Twelfth Edition of *Psychology and Life* marks its Golden Anniversary! Fifty years ago Floyd Ruch created a unique textbook that changed forever the way college students would be introduced to the field of psychology. Before that time, psychology texts reflected the theoretical points of view (biases) of their authors and were primarily summaries of the state of psychological knowledge, written more for professional psychologists than for students. Ruch's goal was to make psychology accessible and interesting to students by presenting it in an unbiased, eclectic fashion and by balancing its scientific aspects against students' practical concerns—psychology and life.

Popularizing the subject without sacrificing the integrity of this still young field of knowledge was risky to attempt in 1937. Ruch succeeded so well that, since then, virtually all textbooks in introductory psychology have reflected the basic approach and pedagogical values of that first edition.

The current edition of *Psychology and Life* continues the tradition. It is student-oriented and eclectic in its presentation of theoretical perspectives, it provides an overview of the major field of psychological knowledge, and it attempts to be relevant to life concerns while being scientifically rigorous. In addition the text uses graphics and teaching aids creatively to engage the reader visually as well as verbally.

I came aboard this "ship of state" as consultant to the Seventh Edition of *Psychology and Life;* I then went on to assume full authorship for the next five editions. It has been a challenging labor of love to maintain the fundamental orientation that Floyd Ruch had so correctly anticipated would make psychology popular with undergraduates. It has meant keeping abreast of the dramatic changes in our field—the transfer of dominance from behaviorism and learning theory to cognitive psychology, an explosion of knowledge in neuroscience, an expansion of humanistic and social psychological contributions, a renewed interest in consciousness and mental processes, and the emergence of a life-span perspective on the developing individual and of the new field of health psychology. It has also meant keeping in touch with student interests and values, which I have accomplished by teaching an introductory psychology course for over thirty years.

One of my goals has been to use the privilege accorded me as author of this special textbook to go beyond merely documenting and summarizing the facts psychology has been accumulating and to try to *communicate* what psychology is all about. While many texts simply describe psychological phenomena, this edition of *Psychology and Life* explains *how* a process works, or *why* a theory or conceptual approach is or is not performing as envisioned. For example, the usual catalog of different behavioral functions for various brain regions is now complemented by new conceptions about the way nerve impulses are formed and transmitted at the molecular level of ion channels within nerve cell membranes. It is also augmented by descriptions of the research tools used to study the living brain.

One of the greatest challenges of psychology is the one that asks us to understand its diversity of topics and levels of analysis—from a concern for what is happening inside a nerve cell or a prison cell, to treating mental disorders in disturbed individuals or preventing nuclear war between hostile nations, to understanding how infants learn to make contact with their new world and how the elderly disengage themselves as they prepare to die. At one end of the continuum, psychology is allied with biochemistry and computer science, and at the other end with anthropology, political science, and research in ecology and industrial organizations. *Psychology and Life* has always been guided by the vision that it is possible to contribute to the further development of psychology by integrating and synthesizing knowledge across domains that are often viewed as separate, and by pointing the way toward promising new areas, conceptual breakthroughs, and "cutting edge" research. This new edition of an old classic challenges the reader to be open to new experiences, to adapt flexibly to these multiple levels at which psychologists study mind and behavior, and to explore psychological processes in depth and breadth.

On the psychology side the Twelfth Edition continues to be contemporary and comprehensive by including over 500 new references to research, theory, and practice. In addition there is a consistent effort to provide a historical context for the development of important ideas from psychology's major contributors. The text also presents "cutting edge" thinking and research that is changing some aspects of our field—most notably research in infant cognition, neuropsychology, vision, pain, memory, judgment and decision making, intelligence, and health psychology. Diagnostic categories for mental disorders are updated with the recently released revised edition of the Diagnostic and Statistical Manual (DSM-III-R).

On the life side, this text offers new or expanded coverage on topics such as coping with stress, lifestyles, and AIDS; becoming more perceptually creative; taking lie detector tests; improving memory; developing problem-solving and cognitive skills; and dealing with emotional and mental problems. It also offers information about sexuality and love, psychology and law, and peace psychology, and applies psychology to everyday life problems and their solutions. The *Opening Case* vignettes set the theme for each chapter by analyzing vivid individual stories that are centered on a variety of psychological issues. *Close-ups,* special sections set aside from the main text, present student-focused information in detail.

The metaphor that best captures my view of *Psychology and Life* is that of an adventurous journey, a journey that confronts some of the most complex puzzles about the causes and consequences of behavior—our own and that of others we observe. The text provides the road map into the mysterious realm of the human mind, with the author as guide and the course instructor as trip director. When traveled appropriately, this journey yields many benefits, among them an enhancement of critical thinking skills, a more solid foundation for understanding oneself and relating to others, a greater effectiveness in achieving one's goals, and a greater tolerance for the differences between ourselves and others.

Three final items of business before we start our journey: (a) an outline of the other parts of the total *Psychology and Life* program; (b) acknowledgments of each of the many people who have helped to make writing this revision a joy for me by sharing their wisdom, expertise, and special skills; and (c) some practical advice to students on proven strategies and tactics for getting the most out of this book (to help "ace" the course).

The Total Psychology and Life *Program*

To encourage greater efficiency in studying, learning, retention, and test taking, we have prepared two student-focused supplements. *Working with Psychology,* co-authored with Scott Fraser of the University of Southern California, will be a valuable aid for any student who wishes to improve his or her proficiency as a learner and academic performer. It contains many features (such as guided reviews and self-scored tests) that enable students to take better control of their education and gain greater competence in acquiring and demonstrating their knowledge of introductory psychology. *Working with Psychology* is also available in a computerized format.

The *Psychology and Life Unit Mastery System (PLUMS) Student's Guide,* prepared by Karl Minke of the University of Hawaii, provides a self-paced study program. It includes exercises for mastering chapter content and chapter specifics, as well as self-quizzes about each unit of material.

Giving Credit Where It Is So Well Deserved

I must begin by thanking all the students of earlier editions of this book who took the time to send me their evaluations, supportive as well as critical. Much of what is good in this edition is the direct result of that student input; I will read yours and perhaps it too will contribute to making the next edition better.

The enormous task of writing a book of this scope is possible only with the help of many colleagues, graduate students, and the editorial staff of my publisher, Scott, Foresman and Company. I thank them all collectively and individually.

Stephen Palmer (University of California, Berkeley) helped draft earlier versions of the sensation and perception chapters for the previous edition; many of his original contributions still grace the current chapters. This edition has also benefited from the input of Christina Maslach (University of California, Berkeley), research methods, sex roles, stress; Craig Smith (University of California, Berkeley), emotion; and Robert Arkin (University of Missouri, Columbia), self-handicapping. Invaluable assistance was also welcomed from my Stanford colleagues: Carlo Piccione, health psychology; Scott Plous, peace psychology; Terry Au, Kim Bartholemew, and Catherine Greeno, life-span development; George Quattrone, social perception; Lee Ross, judgment and decision making; Patricia Ryan, Morita therapy; Susan Brodt, organizational behavior.

Critical feedback, ideas for new material, references, stimulating discussions and other forms of assistance came from faculty and students in my department: Jeff Wine, Amos Tversky, Brian Wandell, John Flavell, Susan Nolen-Hoeksema, Sherri Mateo, Steve Tublin, Maggie Shiffrar, and Rose McDermott. A double thanks goes to Chris Dickerson for helping me get this new revision organized, while Zara Zimbardo came to my aid by preparing text materials that needed to be revised.

Having just learned how to type and use a word processor for the first time in my life, I can no longer thank Rosanne Saussotte for her decade-long tireless efforts in deciphering my illegible script. Now I can simply acknowledge that she is one of the most exceptionally sensitive, caring, and effective people I have ever been blessed to know. In that same category is Marguerite Clark who has been an eversmiling, guiding force behind many prior editions of *Psychology and Life,* supporting both Floyd Ruch's efforts and mine.

When it comes to the critical stage of editing an author's ideas and words so that a real book appears at the other end of the publishing pipeline, there are none finer at their trade than Betty Slack and Carol Karton. Their editorial skills were as welcomed as was Betty's tolerance when I fell behind the impossible production schedule by reading too much when I should have been processing new words. Credit for design and illustration goes to designer Debbie Costello and picture editor Sandy Schneider. At the head of the Scott, Foresman team is Scott Hardy, psychology editor, who skillfully orchestrated our work and that of the contributors to each of the components in the well-balanced, total teaching package that supports this text.

Finally, many colleagues from colleges and universities around the country aided and abetted our cause by reviewing chapters from the previous edition and suggesting improvements, or providing critiques of drafts of the present edition. I thank each of them deeply and hope that they will recognize how their input has improved the story of psychology that is told in the pages that follow. They are thanked in alphabetical order:

Jann Adams
Middle Tennessee State University

Tony Albiniak
University of South Carolina

John N. Bohannon
Virginia Polytechnic Institute and State University

Norman J. Bregman
Southeastern Louisiana University

Lynn Brokaw
Portland Community College

Frederick M. Brown
Pennsylvania State University

William Buskist
Auburn University

William H. Calhoun
University of Tennessee—Knoxville

Betty D. Clayton
Hinds Junior College

Nelson Donegan
Yale University

David Filak
El Paso Community College

Gloria Fischer
Washington State University

Donald G. Forgays
University of Vermont

Scott Fraser
University of Southern California

Nelson Freedman
Queen's University

John Grant
Merced College

Richard Griggs
University of Florida

James Haines
Indiana University—South Bend

Charles G. Halcomb
Texas Tech University

Larry La Voie
University of Miami—Coral Gables

Terry Maul
San Bernadino Valley College

Elizabeth McDonel
University of Alabama

David R. Murphy
Waubonsee Community College

Stephen Palmer
University of California, Berkeley

Margaret Phillip
Mankato State University

Steven Prentice-Dunn
University of Alabama

Edward Reid
Shelby State Community College

Catherine Riordan
University of Missouri—Rolla

David J. Schneider
University of Texas—San Antonio

Marvin Schwartz
University of Cincinnati

Milton Simmons
University of Tennessee—Martin

Anne Treisman
University of California, Berkeley

Phil Zimbardo

To the Student

Tactics and Strategies for Getting the Most Out of This Book

Certainly your goal is to get a passing grade, or even a good grade, in this course and ultimately to get your college degree. Hopefully your goal extends further to becoming an educated person—someone who is interesting to others because that person is interested in the world of ideas. By analyzing, thinking, and theorizing not only to satisfy your pragmatic objectives but also to enjoy the discovery of learning, you come into contact with the most incredible phenomenon in the entire universe—the human mind. So before we begin to examine specific tactics for getting the best return for the time you invest in studying this text and in taking this introductory psychology course, it is well to mention some general strategies essential for optimal learning.

- Adopt the mentality of the athlete who wants to function at peak performance and is not satisfied being second best or one of the "also rans."
- Just as an athlete prepares for competition by effortful practice, you prepare for competitive examinations by careful reading, notetaking, and active rehearsal of what you have read in this text and heard in lectures.
- Performance improves with effective practice, and practice always takes time and effort, so be prepared to put in the time and to put out the effort to achieve your optimal academic performance.
- Sometimes good athletes "run against the clock" and not against the competition; they set personal best goals that extend what they have done in the past. Decide upon the personal goals you want to achieve in this course (and in others), over and above examination grades. Psychology is an inevitable part of your life and will continue to be long after this course is over, so an understanding of the principles of psychology as they apply to everyday life is a permanent gift you can give yourself.
- There are many demands on your attention and time, so it becomes critical not to waste either. You'll do best when you allocate your time wisely. You'll be able to resist distractions and temptations when you know there is a job to get done.
- To do the job requires planning ahead—writing down your goals, schedule, means to reach subgoals and end-goals, and allowing yourself to become task-oriented. You can achieve the balanced time perspective of a future focus for tasks to be accomplished and of a present focus so that when they are completed you can reward yourself with partying, or whatever hedonistic delight is appropriate—until it is time to move on to the next task.
- In the process of mastering *Psychology and Life,* you will extend your mental functioning in many significant dimensions that will reap the richest dividends throughout your life.

To help you realize the potential excitement of this unique journey through psychology and life you will have to put in sufficient time and effort to master a great many new terms, concepts, principles, implications, and extensions of ideas so that you can fully appreciate the process of psychological discovery and not be concerned solely with the destination marked by an end-term grade. We offer some suggestions for getting the best return on the time you invest in studying *Psychology and Life.* They are intended to promote comprehension and efficiency, and make you aware of the features that have been built into each chapter to help you.

- Set aside sufficient time to study for this course; there is much new technical information that will require careful reading and reflection, at least three hours per chapter.
- Find a study place with minimal distractions; reserve this spot for study and do nothing there other than reading, note-taking, and reviewing your course material.
- Keep a record or log of the number of hours (in half-hour intervals) that you put in studying for this course. Chart it on a cumulative graph (one that adds each new study time to the prior total).
- Begin each chapter by reviewing its *outline.* It shows you the topics that will be covered, their sequence, and the way they are related to one another.
- Next, skip to the end of the chapter and read the *Summary.* It will flesh out the outline by indicating the important themes, concepts, and conclusions, as well as the sequence in which they appear.

- Read the *Opening Case* at the beginning of each chapter. It will give you a perspective on the central theme(s) in the chapter. (The *Close-ups* were the most fun to write.)
- Continue using the *SQ3R* method (which you've already actually begun):

  Survey: Skim the sections already mentioned to get the "gist" of the chapter.
  Question: Write out a brief list of questions you want to be able to answer about the content of this chapter.
  Read: Now dig in and read the chapter. Outline key points and paraphrase them in your own words. Become an active note-taker—the more active the better.
  Recite: When you finish each chapter, repeat *aloud* all the points you can remember.
  Review: After at least an hour, actively review all you can remember by writing out or reciting the major points of the chapter. Repeat and space these active reviews several times before an examination.
- Bear in mind as you study that the test questions that accompany this text ask you to demonstrate your mastery of the material in the following four ways:

  Definitions: recall or recognition of verbating statements, meanings of terms, concepts, and processes described in the text.
  Factual information: recall or recognition of information about different approaches to psychological issues, theories, models, research, and important individuals.
  Comparisons: recall of relationships between or among content presented at different points in the chapter, even though the connections may not have been made explicitly; ability to make judgments about differences, similarities, and contrasts of ideas.
  Extensions and applications: reasoning ability to go beyond what is given to form generalizations, to make predictions or derivations, and to illustrate some general principle or concept with a specific example.

Psychology and Life has been carefully designed to facilitate your learning experience. As you read, be sure to note these features:

- The different type styles of the four levels of headings indicate the structure of the chapter and show the relationships among the concepts. They should help you plan your reading and can serve as convenient break points for each period of study.
- The most important terms and concepts appear in **boldface type** and are also gathered alphabetically in the *Glossary* at the end of the book. (Each definition in the *Glossary* is followed by the number of the text page on which the term is defined and discussed in context.) *Italicized* terms are also significant.
- Detailed reports of particular studies are indented and italicized to distinguish them from the body of the text.
- *Close-ups* are set off by colored bands from the flow of the text. They contain ideas that extend the information being presented in special ways. Some are more in-depth presentations of research; others give applications or suggest items of possible personal relevance to you.
- When a name and date are given in parentheses after a statement or conclusion (Ruch, 1937), they identify the researcher and the date of his or her publication. (The word *see* before a citation indicates that it is a more general source of relevant information.) An alphabetical list of these authors and their publications, which form the scholarly foundation of *Psychology and Life,* is found at the end of the book. This enables you or your instructor to go directly to the primary source for more complete information on any of these ideas.
- The back of the book contains other useful reference information: a *Subject Index* of important concepts discussed in the text; a *Name Index* of all the individuals whose work is cited; and the *Glossary*—each with page references.

I value the opportunity your instructor has provided me by selecting *Psychology and Life* as a vital component of your introduction to the field of psychology. I hope you will find it a source of valuable new knowledge and maybe even find a new direction for a major and a career. Students typically report that *Psychology and Life* has been an excellent reference manual for term papers and reports in their later courses—a reason to keep it in your personal library of books that you will want to refer to even after the final course examination is long gone.

Overview

Contents

3 Life-span Psychological Development 57

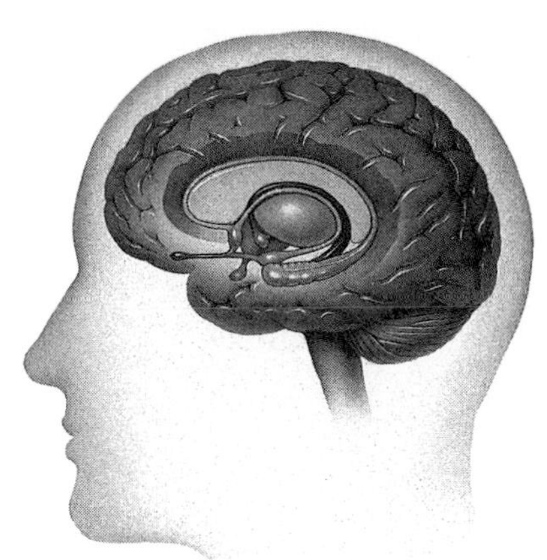

4 The Biology of Behavior 103

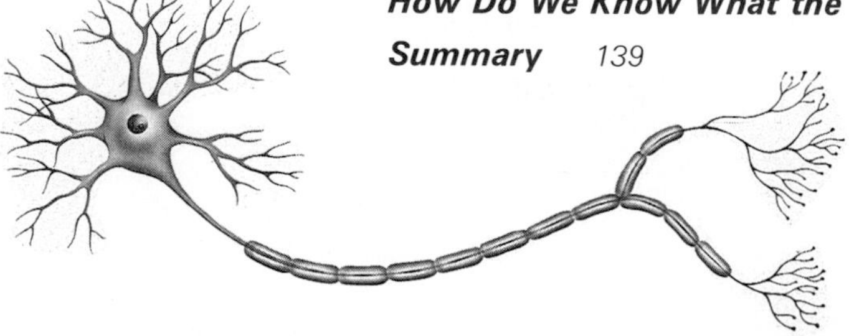

5 Sensation 141

6 Perception 183

7 The Nature of Consciousness 219

8 Conditioning and Learning 257

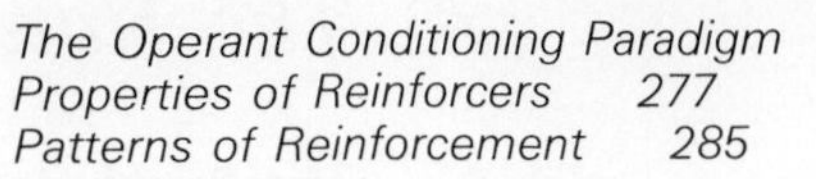

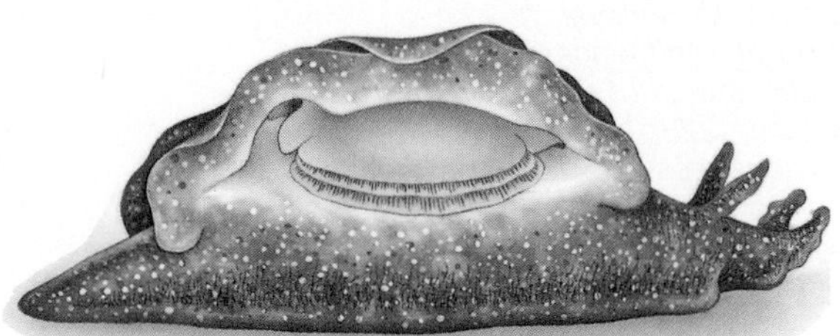

9 Remembering and Forgetting

13 Assessing Individual Differences 451

14 Health, Stress, and Coping 487

15 Abnormal Psychology 517

16 Therapies for Personal Change 559

1

Probing the Mysteries of Mind and Behavior

Welcome to the start of your journey into the realms of the human mind and the mysteries to be found in the behavior of all living creatures. You have accepted psychology's challenge to explore the many paths that must be traveled in order to understand more deeply "the nature of human nature." In doing so, you will learn *what* psychologists have discovered, as well as *how* they have discovered it. Perhaps one of those paths will also open up new visions into the workings of your own mind and behavior.

Your journey of exploration will take you to research laboratories throughout the world, to nursery schools and homes for the aged, to mental hospitals and prisons, and to factories and native villages. Sometimes you will follow paths that examine, in depth, many of the remarkable phenomena you usually take for granted: vision, hearing, speech, learning, memory, thinking, sleep, and dreams. At other times your route will turn toward the more exotic—toward hypnosis, romantic love, violence, and mental illness.

Reading *Psychology and Life* can do more than give you facts about psychological research and applications. It can enhance your critical thinking skills in a variety of ways—by sharpening how you frame questions so that they are answerable by data; by making you sensitive to sources of personal bias that distort what you see and what you conclude; and by showing you how to question generalizations from authorities and the media. Ideally, your greater curiosity about similarities and differences between you and other people can also result in a greater tolerance for a "deviation from the norm." Finally, by the end of this journey you will be a novice psychologist, better able to know yourself and be a source of psychological knowledge, and maybe comfort, to others.

Every scientific journey begins with uncertainty as its motivating force and a quest for understanding as its objective; and so we shall frequently ask questions like: "I wonder what made him act that way?" or "What could be done differently to prevent her from doing that again?" or "What would happen if that apparently crucial variable were changed?" In short, we will wonder *what, how, when,* and *why* about the human condition and the behavior of creatures large and small.

All persons are puzzles until at last we find in some word or act the key to the man, to the woman: straightway all their past words and actions lie in light before us.

Ralph Waldo Emerson, Journals

The following three *Opening Cases* offer a sampling of the adventures we will find in our exploration of psychology.

Why did Kathy quit her race?

She had it all. Kathy O. was a triple threat: top student, beloved friend to many, champion athlete. She was what a great many of us secretly dream of being when we indulge in top-of-the-line fantasies. Not only was she high-school valedictorian, but her high school held a day in her honor! In college, teachers and coaches described her as sweet, sensible, diligent, courteous, and quite religious. As an athlete, Kathy broke state high-school track records in three distances, and, in 1985, she set a new American collegiate record for the 10,000 meters.

Her parents usually came to see their attractive daughter (yes, that too) compete, but what they saw in her last race in 1986 left them totally puzzled. After having fallen behind at the start of the NCAA 10,000-meter championship race Kathy was a few strides behind the trio of leaders. Everyone assumed that, as the favorite in the race, she would soon bolt out ahead and be on her way, once again, to a new track record. Instead, without slowing down or missing a stride, Kathy ran from the track, climbed over a 7-foot fence, fled down New York Street, and jumped off the White River bridge (see the photo on page 3). She fell 35 feet onto the ground below.

Kathy's multiple injuries left her, at the age of 22, paralyzed from the waist down. She would never run again and might never even be able to walk. Nobody could understand why. Her father's explanation was that it resulted from "the pressure that is put on young people to succeed." Her teammates felt that the pressure came from within Kathy as much as from outside sources. "She was a perfectionist," said one of them. A "pusher" who would study even during team workouts, Kathy wanted to excel at everything.

And what did Kathy say about this strange, tragic experience? She later told an interviewer that she was overcome by a terrify-

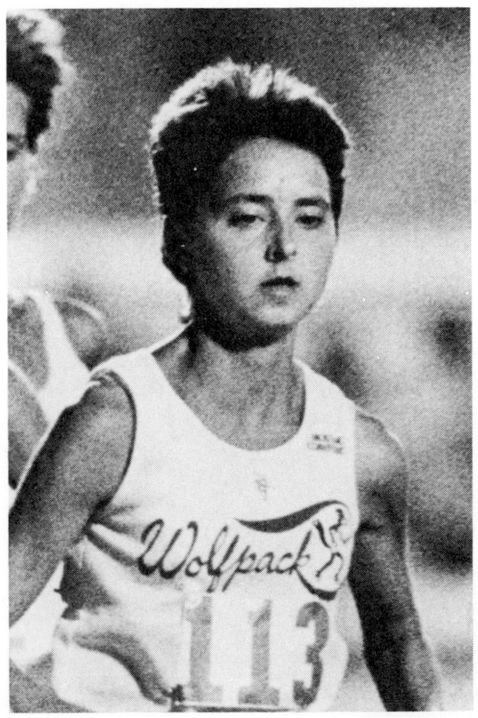

ing fear of failure as she began falling behind in the race and couldn't seem to catch up. "All of a sudden . . . I just felt like something snapped inside of me. And I was really angry. And I felt like it was so unfair. All of a sudden, I didn't feel like this was me because I didn't usually have reactions like that." Kathy couldn't face the embarrassment. ". . . I just wanted to run away," she recalled. "I don't see how I climbed that fence. Before that had happened, I felt like I couldn't run, and now I was running harder than I had during the race . . . I just don't feel like that person was me. I know that sounds strange, but I was just out of control. . . . I was watching everything that was happening and I couldn't stop (United Press International, December 22, 1986).

The case of Kathy O. raises many questions, because it violates our expectations about the behavior of someone like her. Nothing from her background would have led anyone to predict that this super-star teenager would have quit her race and tried to quit her life as well. Why had being Number One become so all-important to her that suicide was the alternative to losing a race? Can pressure to succeed cause such self-destruction even in those who have so clearly succeeded? In your role as "psychodetective" what factors would you investigate as contributing causes in this case? Are there any circumstances under which YOU might give up and quit as Kathy O. did? Is there a "person who is not you" who might show up to influence your behavior in some unusual situation, as Kathy claims happened to her?

Some of the fascination of psychology comes from trying to make sense out of cases like this one, which challenge ordinary conceptions about human nature. Not only is the motivation to satisfy our curiosity about

"what makes people run as they do," but it is also to help others and prevent such tragedies in the future.

Why did Tina kill her chicks?

Turkeys are generally good mothers. They spend much time caring for their young—cleaning, warming, and feeding them. Young chicks respond by chirping contentedly with a characteristic loud and clear "cheep-cheep" sound. One day a researcher, observing the behavior of turkeys, noticed that a turkey chick stopped making its usual sound; it still walked around actively, but it did not chirp. Tina, its formerly affectionate mother, stopped tending it, ignored it, and finally killed it! Why did this female turkey murder her own helpless chick? Could the maternal behavior of mamma turkey have been influenced by that "cheep-cheep" sound?

Yes, indeed; it has been found that this particular sound triggers an automatic reaction in all mother turkeys. To demonstrate how blindly automatic that response is, the researcher put a stuffed polecat near Tina. She furiously attacked this creature, who is a natural enemy. But when the stuffed polecat made the "cheep-cheep" baby turkey sound (from a tape recorder planted inside it), Tina gathered it to her bosom, giving it all the love that only a mother turkey can. Later, when the tape-recorded "cheep" stopped, Tina turned terrible, tearing apart the silent polecat (Fox, 1974).

Many other species also exhibit mechanical patterns of behavior during episodes of courtship, mating, maternal care, or aggression. Such unlearned behavior—which is released by some specific object or event in the environment, such as a particular color, shape, sound, or smell—is called a *fixed action pattern.* It is an inborn response to a given type of stimulation that is typical of a given species in its natural habitat. A blueprint for this instinctive behavior is genetically transmitted from one generation to the next, presumably because of its survival value among those animals who respond to the correct signals from nature.

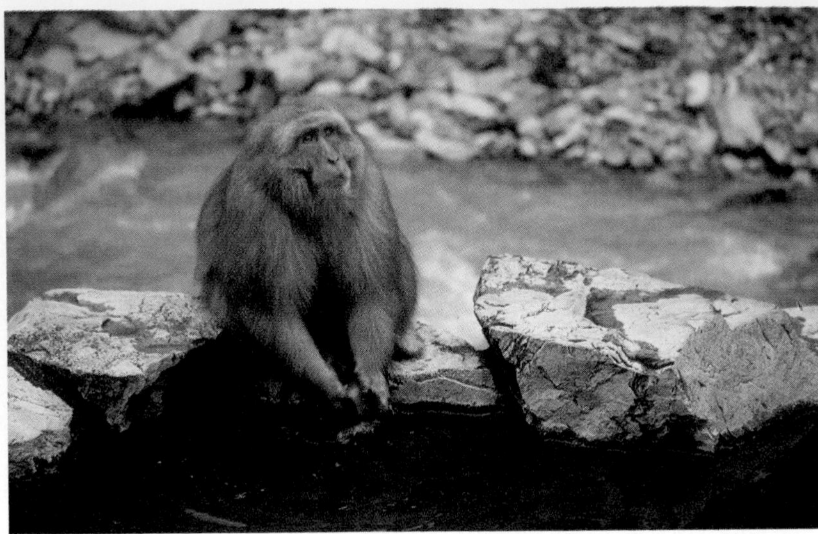

Why did Imo from Koshima wash her potatoes?

Much behavior is molded by basic biological needs for survival, but this is less so with animal species higher on the evolutionary ladder. When we observe primates such as monkeys, chimpanzees, apes, and people, we see cultural experiences coming to play a significant role.

Imo was a young female macaque living on the offshore Japanese island of Koshima. For years researchers had tried in vain to observe the life-style of her elusive troop of free-ranging monkeys. They finally enticed the monkeys out of the forest by leaving sweet potatoes and other treats as bait on an open beach, where observations could be made more easily.

Careful observations revealed that different subgroups had their own dietary preferences. Some ate meat, some fish, others roots; some ate fruit with the pit; others threw the pit away. Eating, then, was not a matter of simply using what was available to satisfy hunger. It was dictated partly by the customs of each monkey troop.

When the researchers' goodies were first put out, the older monkeys resisted sampling them at all. The younger ones were more adventurous and took the risk, after which the elders followed their example.

Then the young female, Imo, did something no other monkey had done. She began washing the sand off her sweet potatoes before eating them. In a few weeks her playmates began copying her; soon her siblings and other close associates regularly washed their potatoes too. After a while, Imo introduced a new ritual—taking potatoes that had already been cleaned in a fresh-water pool and washing them in the sea. Presumably the salt water added flavor or salt they needed in their diet. When the researchers returned ten years later, the habit of washing sweet potatoes in the sea had spread to two thirds of all the monkeys. This habit of sweet-potato washing had become "completely established as an element in the troop's cultural life."

In order to keep the troop in the open area for more extensive observations, the researchers now changed the diet to unhusked rice, since the monkeys took longer to sift the rice grains out of the sand before eating them; but the researchers had not reckoned with Imo's inventiveness. She scooped up handfuls of rice and sand and threw the whole lot into the water. The sand sank, the rice floated, and Imo skimmed off her fast-food snacks. Again, her discovery was copied by her companions, and this new eating habit soon became ingrained in the life of the group (Itani, 1961).

For reasons unknown, Imo was a more radical, creative thinker than her peers; but the ability of the others to learn by watching her resulted in shared skills, shared knowledge, and new ritualized ways of behaving for the whole group. What Imo and her monkey troop from Koshima had done was to create a simple culture, a prototype of human cultures, in which learned skills and preferences for particular ways of doing things were shared with others and even with later generations, supplementing inborn, genetically programmed abilities.

These three *Opening Cases* raise many puzzling issues. You will need to learn much more about psychology before having answers to some of the big questions, but you can discover answers to some of the smaller ones by reading this text. You will also learn that, although psychology still does not have all the answers to the basic questions about behavior and human nature, it is always trying to get them.

Psychology: Definitions and Goals

You now have a few clues about what a course in psychology includes. In this section we'll look at some formal definitions of psychology and preview the general goals of psychologists. We will then review some of the historical forces, ideas, and people who helped shape the origins of psychology.

What Psychology Is

Psychology seeks answers to the fundamental question: What is the nature of human nature? It does so out of the same curiosity and wonder that has motivated all thinking individuals throughout recorded history to ask why we do what we do. Our ancestors answered this question by creating mystical forces that controlled and governed human action. Psychology's answers come from different sources: from looking within individuals as well as from analyzing their immediate, personal environments.

Psychology is a behavioral science at the intersection of many other fields of knowledge; it is composed of parts from each. Psychology shares the interest of the new neurosciences, along with biology, physiology, and computer science, in the study of the brain and its mental activities. As a social science, psychology has important links to sociology, cultural anthropology, economics, and political science; and psychology retains its ties to philosophy and areas in the humanities and the arts, such as literature and drama.

Clockwise: melancholy patient suffers from an excess of black bile; blood empassions sanguine lutist to play; a maiden, dominated by phlegm, is slow to respond to her lover; choler, too much yellow bile, makes an angry master.

Early in the twentieth century, some American psychologists sought to break away from philosophy by developing a more objective science. They did so by investigating only outer actions (or behaviors) that were observable. For many years thereafter, *psychology* was defined as the scientific study of the behavior of organisms. Its subject matter was the observable behavior of both humans and other species. Therefore some of the precision and objectivity demanded in other sciences were demanded in psychology as well.

As the field of psychology has matured, it has become clear that we cannot understand actions without also understanding mental processes. Much human activity takes place as private, internal events—thinking, planning, reasoning, creating, hoping, and dreaming. As we shall see, psychological investigators have devised new techniques to study mental events, techniques that attempt to externalize the internal, to open to public analysis these private experiences. As a result, many psychologists now define **psychology** as *the scientific study of behavioral and mental processes.* This is the definition we will use throughout this text. However, that concept of mental processes, or "mind," is regarded differently by psychologists from different backgrounds. Its use is still somewhat controversial, with some preferring to avoid "mentalisms" in their analysis of behavior and others believing that mental processes represent the important stuff of psychological inquiry. The scientific-study part of the definition refers to the reliance of psychological conclusions on data and facts derived from research that satisfies certain rules of the scientific method. We will describe the methods and research approaches in the next chapter.

Although psychologists observe *specific* instances of behavior, what they are interested in discovering are *general laws,* principles or generalizations that describe how events, variables, or facts are related. When a relationship has been proved repeatedly despite attempts to refute or disprove it, and it holds across different conditions of testing, then it becomes a general law. For example, some researchers observed that children who got praised for asking questions did so more frequently; others recorded that hungry animals who received food at the end of a maze learned to run through it more quickly while reducing their errors on subsequent trials. From these and many other related studies, researchers could then propose a *"law of effect,"* which stated that a response followed by a reinforcement (a reward) was more likely to occur again. This general principle does not specify what kind of organism, response, or type of reinforcement, but extends to all varieties—until any limitations are shown by new research.

Before any broad general principles about human nature can be advanced, the relationship between the variables of interest must be stated in ways that can be tested and evaluated *empirically,* often in experiments. A **variable** is any factor that varies in amount or kind. **Empirical evidence** is evidence that is obtained through the observation of perceivable events, or *phenomena.*

A researcher starts out with a working **hypothesis,** an educated hunch about some phenomenon in terms of its causes, consequences, or events that co-occur with it. Often the hypothesis is stated as an "If . . . then" relationship. "*If* studying is spaced over an extended time period instead of 'cramming' or skipping it, *then* test performance will improve." In chapter 2 we will have much to say about the way hypotheses are tested in many different kinds of psychological research.

In its breadth of focus, psychology is without equal. Though the subject of its analysis is usually an *individual,* that individual might be a college sophomore, an aborigine, an infant, a grandfather, a chimpanzee, a white rat, a pigeon, a sea slug—or a computer simulation of the behavior of any of them. An individual might be studied in its natural habitat, be it forest or ghetto, or in the artificially controlled conditions of a laboratory. While often studied by itself, an individual may also be studied as a member of a pair (for example, a study of lovers' eye contact), a small group (a family conflict), a large group (a crowd baiting a would-be suicide), an institution (a person adjusting to a new role as prisoner or guard), or even a culture (members preparing to go to war). Finally an individual's behavior may be broadly investigated (studying violence at a *molar* level) or more analytically investigated (studying vision at a *molecular* level).

Modern psychology is a scientific discipline that is driven by the twin forces of theory and application. Its *theories* are attempts not only to explain the phenomena that psychologists study but to use those explanations as sources of new research. Later in this chapter we will preview some of the major theoretical approaches that will become important as we continue. But it is not enough to present theories and research methods; psychology must meet the challenges of *application.* It must pass the critical test of "So what good is it for me, my family, my community, my society?"

Many psychologists make careers out of applying knowledge, tactics, and strategies from research to everyday problems of living. They apply psychology pragmatically to solve problems for people, agencies, businesses, or governments. Some *clinical psychologists* help people cope with mental and behavioral disorders by using special tests that diagnose problems and evaluate people; many of them also use psychotherapies to try to alter the disorders. Much of what they do is similar to what *psychiatrists,* who also treat mental disorders, do. The major difference is that psychiatrists are physicians who can administer medication.

Unlike some other fields of knowledge psychology can be relevant for you now. It is hard to imagine that you will not be tempted to take some personal detours from our psychological journey into your own psychological functioning. Part of your task will be to discover how to make scientific psychology relevant to your life—to make it work for you. You can learn lessons that can help improve study habits, expand your memory, make problem-solving and decision making more effective, enhance self-esteem, cope with depression, and much more.

If the storehouse of psychological knowledge is filled with observations and research findings derived from tested theories, then the entrance key is shaped by good questions from curious minds, questions from serious "people watchers" and systematic "self-observers" who look at their own inner reactions and outer behavior. Their curiosity is then easily primed when they observe that something doesn't make sense, jars their expectations, or challenges their notions of how individuals ought to behave—as in the *Opening Cases.* They then begin to ask questions such as: What could have caused the behavior? How is it that similar people respond differently to the same situation? What are the circumstances under which someone might react like those who have done something "irrational, foolish, or evil"? How could a reaction be modified or prevented?

Perhaps your questions will unlock the door to future psychological knowledge. For now, try your answers to the questions in the ***Close-up:*** *"Commonsense" Psychology Quiz,* on the next page.

What Psychology Tries to Do

For the psychologist conducting basic research, the goals are *to describe, explain, predict,* and *control behavior.* For the applied psychologist, there is a fifth goal—*to improve the quality of human life.* These goals form the basis of the psychological enterprise.

Close-up "Commonsense" Psychology Quiz

Test your "commonsense knowledge" of psychology on the 15 selected statements below. Mark *T* before those you think are true and *F* before those statements you believe are false. Then check the footnote on page 8 for the answers (from Vaughan, 1977).

_____ 1. *To change people's behavior toward members of ethnic minority groups, we must first change their attitudes.*

_____ 2. *Memory can be likened to a storage chest in the brain into which we deposit material and from which we can withdraw it later if needed. Occasionally, something gets lost from the chest, and then we say we have forgotten.*

_____ 3. *The basis of a baby's love for its mother is the fact that the mother fulfills its physiological needs.*

_____ 4. *The more highly motivated you are, the better you will be at solving a complex problem.*

_____ 5. *The best way to ensure that a desired behavior will persist after training is completed is to reward the behavior every single time it occurs throughout training (rather than intermittently).*

_____ 6. *A schizophrenic is someone with a split personality.*

_____ 7. *Fortunately for human babies, human mothers have a strong maternal instinct.*

_____ 8. *Biologists study the body; psychologists study the mind.*

_____ 9. *Psychiatrists are medical people who use psychoanalysis.*

_____ 10. *Children memorize much more easily than adults.*

_____ 11. *Boys and girls exhibit no behavioral differences until environmental influences begin to produce such differences.*

_____ 12. *Genius is closely akin to insanity.*

_____ 13. *The unstructured interview is the most valid method for assessing someone's personality.*

_____ 14. *Under hypnosis, people can perform feats of physical strength which they could never do otherwise.*

_____ 15. *Children's IQ scores have very little relationship to how well they do in school.*

_____ *TOTAL CORRECT*[*]

Describe What Happens

The first task in psychology, as in other sciences, is to "get the facts"—to collect the relevant data. **Data** (the singular of data is **datum**) are reports of observations. A person's feelings of anxiety are not data because they cannot be observed by others. On the other hand, a person's restless behavior, oversecretion of epinephrine, or verbal report of anxiety can all be observed, measured, and reported by others, and thus can be data about anxieties.

Descriptions in psychology are statements about the behavior of organisms and the conditions under which the behavior occurs. Psychologists call the specific behavior being observed a **response** and the related environmental conditions **stimuli**

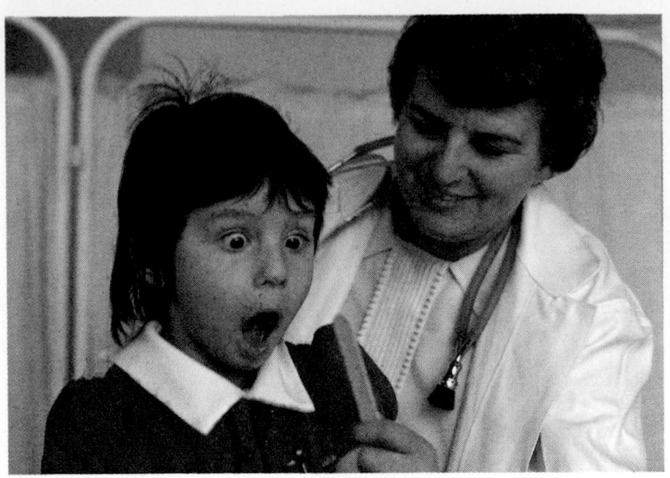

If you were to say that the doctor is happy or the little girl is fearful or anxious about the examination, you would be inferring what cannot be seen.

(the singular of stimuli is **stimulus**). A researcher may observe a sequence of ongoing behaviors, such as the development of the sweet-potato washing ritual by Imo and her troop, or only a single event, such as an infant's facial expression when a novel stimulus is presented. What psychologists look for are consistent relationships between stimuli and responses or between particular responses.

Describing events objectively is not as simple as you might think. For example, how would you describe the action in the picture on this page? In an objective description you would note gestures, facial expressions, objects and people present, actions being performed. But if you say that a person is showing anger, fear, arrogance, or timidity, you are inferring inner states, not simply describing behavior that you can see. Your descriptions of behavior—your data—can include only external features that can be perceived by others, such as what a person said, what movements were made, what score a person got, or how many people indicated agreement with a decision.

Explain What Happens

Though descriptions must stick to perceivable information, explanations deliberately go beyond what can be perceived to try to uncover principles, processes, or relationships that can account for them. In a mystery story, after you know who did it, you want to understand why—the reason that the killer committed an unreasonable act. Although inferences and speculations of inner states or underlying relationships are "out of bounds" during description, they are extremely useful when it comes to looking for explanations.

You wonder if two things you saw are related. If you find first-born children, as a group, are more intelligent than later-born children (on average they are), you start looking for reasons. If you learn that identical twins who have been reared apart from each other all of their lives behave more similarly on a test of intelligence than do siblings growing up in the same household, you want to know how to explain it.

For many psychologists the central goal of their field is to *understand* the lawful regularities in the causal mechanisms that underlie behavioral and mental processes. They want to discover "how behavior works," to find out how certain stimulus events cause observed responses. Sometimes the key to this understanding comes from careful observation and experience with many different instances of the same phenomena, as when Sigmund Freud explained cases of seemingly irrational acts and anxieties in adults as responses to their unresolved conflicts from childhood. It may come from research that systematically evaluates alternative explanations of a psychological event. But there is no better path to understanding than that of informed imagination. A well-trained thinker can entertain explanations that make sense of what is observed both by testing hypotheses and by insight into the human experience.

Sometimes researchers make an **inference**—that is, a logical judgment made on the basis of some evidence rather than on direct observation—about something that is happening inside an organism, something that makes the observed behavior more understandable. This inner, unseen condition is called an **intervening variable.** It may be a physiological condition (such as hunger) or a psychological process (such as fear). Intervening variables are *not* "interfering" variables, as some students might mistakenly think. Rather they represent inferred processes that are assumed to link observable stimulus input with measurable response output. Intervening variables are recognized as part of the explanation of the way stimuli and responses might be related.

Psychologists distinguish between overt and covert behaviors. **Overt behaviors** are responses that are visible to observers (smiling or crying, for example). **Covert behaviors** are unseen psychological processes such as expecting, interpreting, or dreaming; they may be postulated as intervening variables to help make observed behavior more

*The 15 items in the Commonsense Quiz were answered incorrectly by more than half of a group of introductory psychology students at the University of Pittsburgh. All items are false as stated, though many reflect widespread popular beliefs (Vaughan, 1977).

understandable. Many psychologists are primarily interested in these inner behaviors which can be studied only indirectly through inferences based on observation of some kind of overt behavior. Psychologists have been ingenious in developing procedures for studying many different kinds of covert processes, as you will discover in later chapters.

Predict What Will Happen

Predictions are statements about the likelihood of a certain event occurring or a given relationship being found. One form of prediction is based on a belief that a knowledge of the future is available through oracles, astrology, or psychic revelation; however, despite its popularity in the mass media, this claim to "read the future" is not substantiated. When it is stated in general and vague terms so that it cannot be proven true or false, it is rarely better than chance or guess. A more common form of prediction involves applying information about the past to future situations. If a situation is relatively constant, then knowing how people behaved before is a good indicator of how they will continue to behave in the future. You rely on such predictions every time you cross a street with the expectation that oncoming cars will stop at the red light, every time you expect that your professor will lecture and you will listen, rather than the reverse. Often the best source of prediction about your behavior in some future setting is knowledge of the base rate of that behavior among the majority of comparable people who have been in that situation before. A **base rate** is a statistic that identifies the normally occurring frequency of a given event. By contrast, a scientific prediction is more likely to be based on an *understanding* of the way events are related, on the mechanisms that link certain predictors to predicted events. Such a prediction is then able to take into account changes in a situation or other variables used to make the prediction, instead of blindly applying statistical probabilities.

Some of these predictions come from theories that attempt to explain how the events in question are related. More specifically, they come in the form of hypotheses that are derived from a theory. Recall that a *hypothesis* is a testable statement about the relationship between two or more variables; given certain conditions particular outcomes are expected. An experiment in psychology typically begins with a hypothesis to be tested. The hypothesis must be about conditions and outcomes that can be observed and must be specific enough so that the evidence obtained can, in principle, disconfirm it.

Once basic relationships are understood, other predictions can be made. The investigator's hunch that Tina's unmotherly behavior was related to the absence of the cheep-cheep sound led to the hypothesis that even a stuffed polecat would call forth maternal behavior if it made the right sound. A college admissions officer can predict students' college grades from their SAT scores; a public opinion polling agency can predict the winner of a presidential election from the opinions of an appropriate sample of potential voters; and psychologists can predict that students who define themselves as shy will show less self-confidence at social events than their non-shy peers.

The study of behavior gets added excitement when predictions are made about events that have never been observed previously or that violate commonsense expectations (the expectations of everyone's grandmother, called affectionately "*bubba psychology*"). Remember Tina Turkey's maternal behavior and the fixed action pattern released by the cheep-cheep sound? What is your prediction about the behavior toward her chicks of a mother turkey whose hearing is destroyed? If you predicted that she would probably kill them even if they were cheeping loudly, you might be right or wrong! It would depend on whether other non-auditory cues were also involved in triggering this behavior pattern.

An example of a *non-obvious prediction* is found in the relationship between attitudes and behavior. It has been assumed that the way to change certain social behaviors, such as discrimination, is first to change the underlying attitudes of prejudice. However, one theory predicted that the cause-effect direction should be reversed: change the behavior first and then the attitudes would fall into line with it (we will have more to say about this theory of cognitive dissonance by Festinger, 1957, in chapter 17). Empirical research then supported this theoretically derived prediction. (It should also be mentioned that it also supported the ancient saying that if you want people to believe in God, do not insist that they believe before praying; get them to pray and then they will come to believe.)

While some psychologists insist that explaining a relationship is the major goal of their field, others argue that if you cannot predict the conditions under which a given behavior will appear or change, you simply have not understood it. At least, they say, you cannot be sure your explanation is correct unless you can use it to predict what will happen or what will make it happen. When different explanations are put forward to account for some behavior or relationship, they are usually judged on the basis of which one can make the most accurate and comprehensive predictions.

Control What Happens

For many psychologists, control is the central, most powerful goal. Controlling behavior goes beyond predicting behavior by making it happen or not happen—*starting it, maintaining it, stopping it,* and *influencing its form, strength,* or *rate of occurrence.* The ultimate test of any causal explanation of behavior lies in being able to demonstrate the conditions under which the behavior can be controlled. Only by such demonstrations can it be established that the conditions thought to be responsible for a behavior are, in fact, both *necessary* and *sufficient,* and that other available conditions are not causing the observed effect.

The ability to control behavior is important not only for its validation of theoretical explanations, but because it gives psychologists ways of changing behavior to help people. In this respect, psychologists are a rather optimistic group; many believe that virtually any undesired behavior pattern can be modified by the proper intervention into a person's physical, mental, or behavioral functioning. Such attempts at control, in the form of intervention to change a destructive or unsatisfactory behavior pattern, are at the heart of all programs of psychological treatment or therapy.

Serious ethical issues can arise, however, when anyone tries to control another person's behavior. This is true wherever the attempt to control takes place—for example, in psychotherapy, in a psychological experiment, with prisoners subjected to behavior modification, or in a "societal experiment" such as a relocation plan that removes an American Indian tribe from its homeland to live in a city or on a reservation for the sake of "progress." It is interesting to note that *understanding*—rather than control—tends to be the goal of psychologists in many Asian and African countries.

As the field of psychology has grown, there has been, among psychologists, an increased awareness and sensitivity to the range of situations that can involve potential violations of ethical principles. Those working with clients or patients often draw up working contracts that explicitly outline the rights, obligations, and reasonable expectations of each party. In research, the well-being of those who participate as subjects in experiments—animals and humans—is now protected by formal ethical standards and committees of the American Psychological Association. Before any research project can be submitted for possible funding by a government agency, such as the National Science Foundation or the National Institute of Mental Health, its protocol must be approved by a local panel in a university or research center. The panel evaluates and minimizes potential *risks* to the subjects, weighing them against the potential *benefits* of that research to the subjects and to society.

Improve the Quality of Life

Many of the findings of psychology are being applied to the solution of human problems. Some of these findings have come from **applied research,** in which the goal is to find solutions to particular practical problems. Other findings have come from **basic research,** in which a phenomenon or process is studied for accurate and comprehensive knowledge without regard to its possible later applications.

Applied researchers have always had improvement of the quality of life as an important goal. Basic researchers, on the other hand, have generally felt that their responsibility lay in the scientific enterprise of getting objective facts and drawing accurate conclusions from them, not necessarily in putting their findings to use in the "real world." For basic researchers, often knowing an answer has been enough. Even though more psychologists have historically pursued basic, rather than applied, research, both approaches have yielded many discoveries of far-reaching importance to society. Indeed, many of our most important contributions have come from the unexpected practical relevance of what began as basic research. For example, when physicians rated the top ten advances that had done most to relieve the suffering of heart and lung patients and extend their lives, much of the essential research came from basic research laboratories. Forty-two percent of the 663 pieces of supporting research was from scientists whose goal was seeking general knowledge (see Comroe & Dripps, 1977).

Consider the remarkably potent role that the drug Chlorpromazine played in the treatment of schizophrenia—a severe mental disorder that afflicts 1.6 million Americans.

> *A short 40 years ago large mental hospitals throughout the world were places of horror and despair to patients, staff, and visitors. Screams, moans, obscenities, and the stench of feces and urine filled the air, and wildly hallucinating or violent patients wandered about. Many of the patients who would be condemned to spend the rest of their lives on one of these "back wards" were victims of schizophrenia, a complex psychotic disorder marked by a distortion of reality, isolation from social interaction, and disturbances in perception, thought, and emotion. It has all changed because of the discovery of*

Chlorpromazine. Now patients who do not respond to any form of treatment take a pill, and many of their most troubling symptoms are relieved! Even though the causes of schizophrenia are still not understood, a way had been found to control its devastating consequences.

Curiously, this "miracle drug" was discovered accidentally while developing a drug to combat surgical shock. The path that led to the practical use of Chlorpromazine in psychiatry is one filled with a variety of experiments that were "purely basic," exploring the unknown for its own sake. (see Swazey, 1974)

Over time, as awareness has increased that psychological findings can change people's lives, the demand has grown for psychologists to be more than just "objective" scientists. They now must make sure that their findings are not misinterpreted by policymakers, that they are used for socially responsible, constructive purposes to enrich the lives of those affected. In addition to investigators whose focus is either basic or applied research, there are many other psychologists who use the findings of both to try to improve some aspect of the human condition. Currently, about two thirds of all American psychologists work in fields that are applied—clinical work, counseling, education, law, business, consumer affairs, engineering psychology, military psychology, and more.

There are many different kinds of applied psychologists who work in a variety of settings. For example, clinical psychologists work in hospitals, clinics, or have private practices where they counsel or try to change the behavior patterns of people with mental and behavioral disorders. Industrial psychologists often work in organizational settings to discover ways to improve worker morale while increasing productivity and efficiency. Educational psychologists help design school curricula and child-care programs. Environmental psychologists work with architects and urban planners to design housing projects that facilitate the needs of the residents rather than just serve as spaces in which to "store" people. In addition, some are studying ways to promote behaviors that will conserve energy or reduce pollution.

Health psychologists are collaborating with medical researchers to understand better the ways behavior and life-style affect physical health. They also study the ways behavioral principles can be used to aid medical treatment—to get patients to comply with a doctor's orders and follow a prescribed routine, for example (see DiMatteo & DiNicola, 1982). Forensic, or legal, psychologists apply psychological knowledge to human problems in the field of law enforcement. They may work with the courts to determine the mental competency of defendants; counsel inmates in prison rehabilitative programs; or work with lawyers in jury selection and on problems such as the unreliability of eyewitness testimony. Psychologists are also working with computer scientists at both basic and applied levels in the area of *artificial intelligence* to try to better understand human problem-solving

Kristina Hooper, director of Atari's long-range planning lab, leads a search for new ways to link computers to human thought processes. In the photo she is monitoring a project aimed at enabling a computer to read and interpret facial expressions. Such a computer, she hopes, will some day be able to sense and respond to its operator's moods.

while developing increasingly sophisticated "thinking computers." For a schematic representation of the many fields and settings in which psychologists can work, see **Figures 1.1 and 1.2.**

With this brief overview of the definition, goals, and activities of psychology, we are ready to go *backward* to establish the intellectual origins of this discipline before proceeding to analyze the assumptions and conceptual approaches that characterize the major approaches in modern psychology. Let's examine the history of ideas that formed the intellectual foundation of psychology.

Psychology's Intellectual Origins

Psychology's long past stretches back through recorded history to the time when our ancestors thought and wrote about what made humans act and think as they do and how they might be made to behave differently; yet the history of psychology is short. The formal start to the discipline began only a century ago. John Dewey's text *Psychology* was published in 1886, followed the next year by *Elements of Physiological Psychology* by G. T. Ladd, and in 1890 by the grand work of William James, *Principles of Psychology*. The American Psychological Association was founded in 1892.

Figure 1.1 Specialty Areas of Psychologists
Shown are percentages of psychologists by specialty area (A) and work setting (B), based on a random survey in 1978 of 6551 members of the American Psychological Association holding doctorate degrees in psychology. (Based on Stapp & Fulcher, 1981)

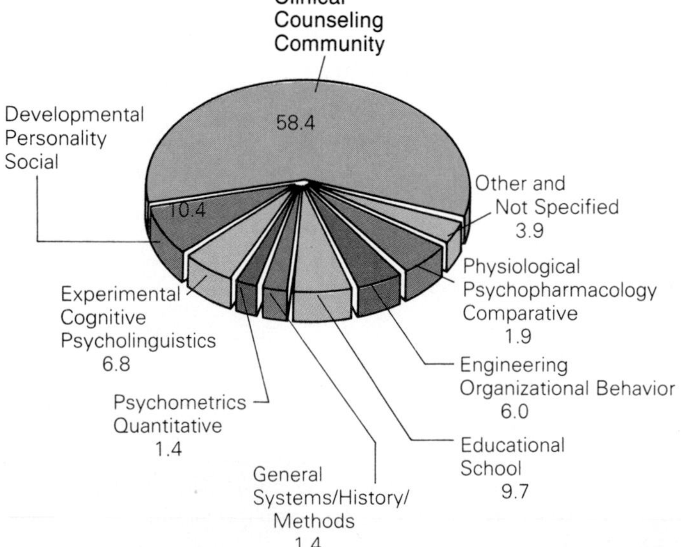

Figure 1.2 Work Settings of Psychologists

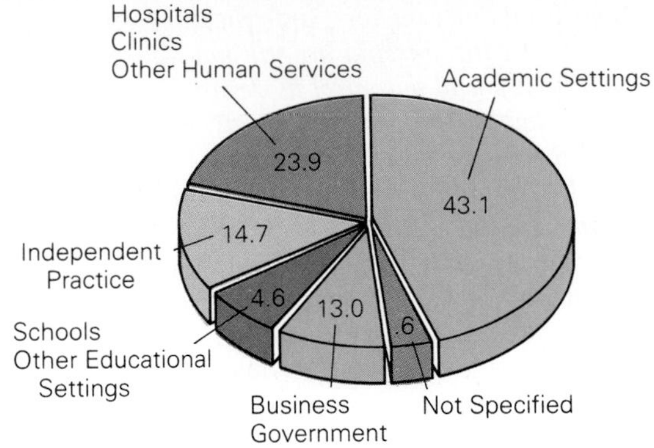

The year 1879 stands as a significant date in the history of psychology. It was in that year, in Leipzig, Germany, that Wilhelm Wundt founded the first formal laboratory devoted to experimental psychology. Soon afterward, psychological laboratories appeared in universities throughout North America, starting with the first at Johns Hopkins University in 1883. By 1900 there were more than 40 such laboratories (see Hilgard, 1986).

Ideas and intellectual traditions from both philosophy and natural science converged to give rise to the development of the new field of psychology. In its quest for understanding the human mind and human nature, it pursued a variety of approaches. The five foundation stones upon which American psychology was constructed were those of associationism; elementalism; evolutionism; experimentation, with a special devotion to method and quantification; and individualism (see Kessen & Cahan, 1986). The substance for these intellectual approaches came to America from Western Europe—notably, England, Germany, and France.

Associationism

For philosophers *ideas* are the basic unit of analysis. Plato, and later, French philosopher René Descartes, had proposed that the mind was composed of "innate ideas." The human mind came prepared with certain basic ideas that ordered all sensory experience, a view known as **rationalism.** In opposition to this doctrine was the theory that ideas arose from sensory experiences, and further, that thought and memory were composed of chains of these ideas that were associated with each other. This was **associationism.** Its seeds were sown by an equally impressive line of philosophers starting with Aristotle and Thomas Hobbes, but most fully developed by John Locke and others, known as the *British empirical philosophers.*

Locke's *Essay Concerning Human Understanding* (1690) proposed that experience was the necessary condition for the growth of the mind, for reason as well as for all knowledge. He proposed as the metaphor for an infant's mind a blank tablet—a ***tabula rasa***—on which experience etched its messages:

> *Let us suppose the mind to be, as we say, white paper void of all characters, without any ideas;—How comes it to be furnished? Whence comes it by that vast store which the busy and boundless fancy of man has painted on it with an almost endless variety? Whence has it all the* materials *of reason and knowledge? To this I answer, in one word, EXPERIENCE. In that all our knowledge is founded; and from that it ultimately derives itself.*

Psychology adopted the associationist view with its dual emphasis on experience, rather than heredity, and the "mental chemistry" of thought which consisted of simple sensations being compounded into complex ideas by their associative links. An example of an associationist principle is that of **temporal contiguity:** sensations, movements, or ideas that, occurring closely in time, become associated with each other. We will see in chapter 8 that this principle is important in the type of learning known as Pavlovian conditioning.

Elementalism

In an attempt to develop a science of the mind, early psychologists turned to models in natural science. What they found was the importance of analyzing a complex phenomenon by analyzing its smaller units: *reduction* of the whole to its parts. In biology it was the cell, in heredity it was the gene, in chemistry and physics it was the atom. The periodic table of chemical elements was seen as a model of how fundamental units explain the complexity of matter. In psychology the basic units began as simple sensations and reflexes (physical responses to specific types of stimuli, like the knee-jerk reflex). This approach has been followed most by physiological psychologists, whom we shall meet in chapter 4.

Evolutionism

A central topic in many areas of psychology is the contributions of **nature,** or hereditary influences, and **nurture,** or environmental influences to behavioral development. This issue has its origins in the evolutionary theory developed by Charles Darwin. His theory maintains three principles: (a) all species evolved over millions of years; (b) differences between species are because of hereditary differences; and (c) differences within a species are related to differences among its members in terms of their individual differences in fitness. Those most fit to adapt to environmental changes and challenges passed on their genes and reproduced more of their kind. These ideas were based on Darwin's careful observations of species throughout the world during his five-year journey on the ship *Beagle* and were presented in *Origin of Species* (1859) and *Descent of Man* (1871).

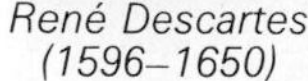

René Descartes (1596–1650)

Charles Darwin (1809–1882)

Evolutionary theory challenged the doctrine of *creationism,* which asserted that all species were created by an act of God, with humans being a special case of direct divine creation. Just as Copernicus' theory of the universe moved the earth out of the center of the solar system, Darwin's theory pushed man and woman out of the center arena of existence by giving them a common ancestry with animals. Darwin's doctrine further shook notions of homo sapien supremacy by dragging human origin down from the heavens into the muck of evolutionary slime. (It has been argued that the third blow to the collective human ego, after the two by Copernicus and Darwin, was dealt by Sigmund Freud's theory that unconscious, irrational mental forces often directed human actions.) The influence of evolutionary theory on psychology was seen in the study of the behavior of lower animals as part of the program of understanding people.

Experimentation

It was not until psychology became a laboratory science organized around experiments that its unique contribution to knowledge was established. Credit for that goes to Wundt and his German colleagues who pioneered an experimental tradition.

Wilhelm Wundt
(1832–1920)

In Wundt's laboratory, subjects made simple responses (saying yes or no or pressing a button) to stimuli they perceived under conditions varied by laboratory instruments. Since the conditions could be repeated and the data that were collected used systematic, objective procedures, independent observers could replicate the results of these experiments. An emphasis on experimental methods, a concern for precise measurement, and a need for mathematical, statistical analysis of data borrowed from physics and physiology characterized Wundt's psychological tradition.

Wundt's psychology was brought to the United States by Edward Titchener, who believed that psychology should be the study of the *contents* of consciousness, to be found by introspection, an examination of one's own thoughts and feelings about sensory experience. Titchener emphasized the *what* of mental contents rather than why or how the mind functioned. This view came to be known as **structuralism,** the study of the structure of mind and behavior.

Structuralism was associated with the work of Wundt and Titchener. It was based on the presumption that all human mental experience could be understood as the combination of simple events or elements. The goal of this approach was to reveal the underlying *structure* of the human mind by analyzing all of the basic elements of sensation and other experience which formed an individual's mental life. This system was attacked by virtually all psychologists because it was *reductionistic* (it reduced complex experience to simple sensations), *elemental* (it sought to combine parts to make wholes rather than studying complex behavior directly), and *mentalistic* (it insisted on studying only conscious awareness, ignoring the study of all subjects who could not verbally report their introspections, such as animals, children, and the mentally disturbed). However, the major school of opposition was that which reigned under the American banner of functionalism.

Individualism

The champion of American psychology was William James, a philosopher at Harvard who had studied medicine and physiology. James thought more broadly about a full range of psychological issues and wrote about them more brilliantly than any of his contemporaries at the end of the nineteenth century. Consciousness was central in his approach to the study of psychology, but it was not reduced to elements, contents, and structures—the stuff of interior decorators. For James consciousness was an ongoing stream, a property of mind that was in continual interaction with the environment. Human consciousness facilitated one's adjustment to the environment; thus the acts and functions of mental processes were of significance—not the contents of the mind. In place of structuralism, James' view of **functionalism** gave primary importance to learned habits that enabled organisms to adapt to their environment and to function effectively. The key question to be answered by research was "What is the function or purpose of any behavioral act?"

Functionalism was originally a general perspective about the way psychologists should study mind and behavior. Its emphasis was on adaptation to the environment and the practical utility of action which was studied by examining an intact, functioning organism interacting with its environment. Functionalists rejected the structuralist notion that the mind should be analyzed in terms of its contents; they sought instead to discover its functions, utilities, and purposes.

William James
(1842–1910)

Although James believed in the value of careful observation, he disdained the rigorous laboratory methods of Wundt, putting them down as arising only in a country like Germany "whose natives could never be bored." In James' psychology there was a place for the emotions, the self, the will, values, and even religious and mystical experience. His "warm-blooded" psychology recognized the uniqueness of each individual, a special individuality that could not be reduced to formulas or numbers from test results. Part of the study of personality psychology (see chapters 12 and 13) involves an attempt to capture this uniqueness that characterizes individuals. The concern for individuality has been one of the mainstreams of psychological thought.

With this brief historical excursion behind us we are in a better position to appreciate the roots of psychology's modern perspectives (see also Koch & Leary, 1985). To facilitate our journey, we will examine next the major conceptual approaches that characterize the thinking of modern psychologists about what is most important in the scientific study of mind and behavior.

Alternative Perspectives

There is such diversity in what psychologists study and the ways they study that it might appear their explorations of psychological phenomena are headed off in all directions at once. That is only partially true. Despite the variety of topics studied, types of organisms observed, and even whether the orientation is one of basic research or application, there are a set of common assumptions, approaches, and conceptual models. They serve as compass directions around which the major "breeds" of psychologists can be grouped.

Differing Assumptions and Approaches

All psychologists adopt philosophical assumptions which then influence the kinds of questions they raise, and the focus and methods of their research. Some of these assumptions are choices about enduring controversies: whether humans are inherently good or evil; whether they have free will or simply act out a script imposed by their heredity (biological determinism) or their environment (environmental determinism). Other assumptions are especially related to psychology: whether organisms are basically active or reactive, whether psychological and social phenomena can ultimately be explained in terms of physiological processes, and whether a complex behavior is just the sum of many smaller components or has new, emergent qualities. The assumptions psychologists adopt from among these and other options determine what they will study, what organisms they will use for subjects, the degree to which they will try to control what happens, and the level of analysis they will find most appropriate.

We discussed earlier that the level of analysis may range from molecular to molar. On the **molecular level,** psychologists study fine-grained, small units of behavior such as the neurobiology of memory or aspects of sensation in responding to a sound of a certain intensity. On the **molar level,** they study behavior of a whole functioning organism in a complex environment. This might include the effects on aggressive feelings of men toward woman, after viewing filmed pornography, or the conditions under which college students will blindly obey an unjust authority.

The level of analysis also varies in its *temporal focus.* Some psychologists focus on the present situation, observing the ways the behavior of organisms is shaped by rewarding or punishing their behavior or studying the expression of emotions. Others look to past experiences to explain present behavior, such as the influence of sexual abuse or divorce in early childhood. Still others study the importance of future events, perhaps investigating whether goal setting will influence sexually active teenagers to alter their risky behavior. Regardless of the way psychologists cut the pie, it is big enough and rich enough for all to enjoy.

Psychological Models as Maps

Most researchers base their work on a conceptual **model,** a simplified way of thinking about the basic components and relationships in their field of knowledge. A model represents a pattern of relationships found in data or in nature which it attempts to duplicate or imitate in some way. Some models are mechanical, as those created to represent how the ear works; others are mathematical, as those that attempt to mirror how certain kinds of decisions are made. Often a model is based on an analogy between the processes to be explained and a system already understood. Early psychologists used the *analogy* of a telephone switchboard as a model for trying to explain processes in the brain. Models are useful in any field where much remains to be discovered, because they provide a framework in which investigators can formulate new hypotheses to be tested, plan research, and evaluate their findings. The ultimate value of any model that serves as a minitheory in psychology is whether predictions derived from it are confirmed.

Among the current models being used by psychologists, five predominate: the psychophysiological, the psychodynamic, the behavioristic, the cognitive, and the humanistic. They vary in how specific and precise they try to be and in their dependence on research findings or theory. Also, they overlap at certain points, and most psychologists probably find useful concepts in more than one. But the five are based on quite different sets of assumptions and are distinct enough to have given rise to many lively controversies among psychologists. Research in a number of areas is organized around one or another of these general models, and you will be reading about their contributions at a number of other points in our journey. These broad conceptual models provide fundamentally different ways of approaching the study of psychology; they represent the big cuts in the psychological pie.

Because any model selectively focuses on certain content while ignoring other kinds of information, it sacrifices some of the richness of the remarkable creatures being studied. Analytic thinker Carl Jung, himself a creative model builder, had this to say about models:

> *Learn your theories as well as you can, but put them aside when you touch the miracle of life.*

The Psychophysiological Model

The word fragment *psych* refers to mental processes, *physio* to bodily ones. The **psychophysiological model** guides the work of most physiological psychologists as they try to find the links between the functioning of the brain and nervous system and behavior, both overt and covert. According to this biologically based model, functioning of an organism is explained in terms of the physical structures and biochemical processes that make it work. Visual sensation is explained in terms of processes in the eyes, optic nerve, and brain. Nerve impulses are explained in terms of chemical and electrical processes in and between nerve cells.

Four assumptions of this approach are (a) that psychological and social phenomena can be understood in terms of biochemical processes; (b) that complex phenomena can be understood by analysis, or reduction, into ever smaller, more specific units; (c) that all behavior—or behavior potential—is determined by physical structures and largely hereditary processes; and (d) that experience can modify behavior by altering these underlying structures and processes. The task of researchers is to understand behavior at the most precise possible *molecular* level of analysis.

Physiological psychologists are among a growing number of neuroscientists from many disciplines—including biology, chemistry, physiology, and pharmacology—all of whom do work related to brain functioning. Neuroscientists study subjects ranging from simple organisms like crawfish to complex organisms like human beings; and their research is conducted in both laboratories and clinical settings. For example, in a hospital they might study patients with brain disease or patients suffering a memory loss following an accident. Neuroscientists have won Nobel Prizes in physiology for illuminating how we hear (George von Békésy), how the retina of the eye is designed to allow perception of different features of the environment (David Hubel and Torsten Wiesel), and how the human brain functions when its two halves are split by surgery (Roger Sperry). We will have more to say about their discoveries in later chapters.

The Psychodynamic Model

According to the **psychodynamic model,** all behavior is driven, or motivated, by powerful inner forces. In this view, human actions stem from inherited instincts, biological drives, and attempts to resolve conflicts between personal needs and society's demands to act appropriately. We act because we feel motivational forces of various kinds. Action is the product of tension, and its purpose is

Roger Sperry (1913–   )

Nobel prize-winning neuroscientists David Hubel (left) and Torsten Wiesel have investigated the way the brain processes visual information.

to reduce tension. Motivation is the key concept in the psychodynamic model. As coal fuels a steam locomotive, so deprivation states, physiological arousal, conflicts, and frustrations provide the power for behavior. In this model, the organism stops reacting when its needs are satisfied and its drives reduced.

Psychodynamic principles of motivation were most fully developed by Viennese physician Sigmund Freud in the late nineteenth and early twentieth centuries. Freud's ideas grew out of his work with mentally disturbed patients, but he believed that the same principles applied to both normal and abnormal behavior. According to Freud's theory, what we are is fully determined by our heredity in combination with early childhood experiences. The infant, driven by unlearned instincts for self-preservation and desires for pleasure, experiences conflicts and traumatic experiences, such as parental taboos, that fully determine his or her personality thereafter. Often the early experiences continue to influence behavior in disguised ways that a person does not understand. This model was the first to recognize the irrational side of human nature; that actions may be driven by motives which are not in conscious awareness.

Sigmund Freud (1856–1939)

The psychodynamic view of Freud usually adopts a molar level of analysis, viewing a person as pulled and pushed by a complex network of forces. The nature of the human organism is seen as basically evil, with violence a natural means of expressing primitive sexual and aggressive urges. There need to be strong societal controls if people are to be saved from their own passions for pleasure and destructiveness.

Freud's ideas have had a greater influence on more areas of psychological thought than those of any other individual. You will encounter different aspects of his contributions to psychology as you read about child development, dreaming, forgetting, unconscious motivation, personality, neurotic disorders, and psychoanalytic therapy. His ideas will appear as frequent markers on our psychological journey. But you may be surprised to discover that these ideas were never the result of systematic research or experimentation. Instead they were the product of someone with a fertile mind who observed people and himself closely and well.

Many psychologists since Freud have taken the psychodynamic model in new directions. Notably, some theorists have moved away from a primary focus on the influence of instincts and drives on psychological development to a focus on social influences and interactions. For example, Erik Erikson (whom you will meet in chapter 3) theorized that certain developmental stages are based on psychosocial development. Karen Horney (pronounced Horn-eye) added flexibility to Freud's determinism by including an awareness of environmental factors in attempts to cope with conflicts. And Margaret Mahler has studied how children establish a sense of self separate from others with whom they interact.

John B. Watson (1878–1958)

The Behavioristic Model

The behavioristic model is *not* concerned with biochemical processes nor hypothetical inner motivations. Its domain is outer, visible behavior and its relationships to environmental stimulation. The behaviorally oriented psychologist uses data that are specific, measurable responses—blinking an eye, pressing a lever, or saying yes following an identifiable stimulus (a light or a bell).

The main objective of behavioristic analysis is to understand how particular environmental stimuli control particular kinds of behavior. What is studied are the *ABCs of psychology: antecedent* conditions that precede the behavior, the *behavioral* response, and the *consequences* that follow it. The level of analysis is thus molecular: the responses studied, such as learned habits, are broader than the responses of a neuron but narrower than the response of a person developing defenses for meeting inner needs.

According to the **behavioristic model,** behavior is assumed to be wholly determined—in this case, by conditions in the environment—and people are assumed to be neither good nor evil but simply reactive to and modifiable by the proper arrangement of environmental conditions. Though heredity may place some limits on what environment can accomplish, behavioral psychologists assume that what we become is largely the result of nurture (experience), not nature.

Behaviorists have typically collected their data from controlled laboratory experiments; they may use electronic apparatus and computers to present stimuli and record responses. They insist on very precise operational definitions and rigorous standards of evidence, usually in quantifiable form. Often they study animal subjects because control of all the conditions can be much more complete than with human subjects. Also the basic processes they investigate are assumed to be part of general principles that hold across different species, but occur in simpler form that is easier to study in subhuman species.

The view that only the overt behavior of organisms is the proper subject of scientific study is called **behaviorism.** It began early in this century with the work of John B. Watson. Watson was an American psychologist who was influenced by a concept of learning developed by the Russian physiologist Ivan Pavlov. Pavlov had discovered that, by using conditioning, a physiological response ordinarily produced by food could be elicited by the sight or sound of anything that was regularly followed by food. But whereas Pavlov's primary interest was in the physiology of the learned relationship, Watson's interest was in the learned relationship itself, the new relationship established between the response and the stimulus in the environment. He was reacting against the then-prevalent belief in the importance of *instincts,* unobservable hereditary mechanisms that were being postulated to explain personality and behavior. If behavior could be shown to be the result of learning, it would open up new possibilities for changing undesirable behavior. Watson established a new direction in psychology—a search for causes in the environment rather than in a person—and was the first to insist that psychologists study only observable behavior. Watson believed that mental events could not be studied scientifically. Other behaviorists went further, asserting, as does the leading behaviorist of our time, Harvard's B. F. Skinner, that no concepts about inner, unseen processes are needed to explain behavior.

For much of this century the behavioristic model has been dominant in American psychological research and thinking. Its impact, through its emphasis on the need for rigorous experimentation and defined variables, has been felt in most areas of psychology. Its contribution to our understanding of learning will be taken up in chapter 8, and many applications of its principles will be seen in other chapters.

The Cognitive Model

According to the **cognitive model,** *cognition*—the processes of knowing, which include attending, thinking, remembering, expecting, fantasizing, and consciousness itself—is not just an intervening variable linking stimuli to responses but is itself the key causal factor in behavior. We act because we think; and we think because we are human beings designed to do so. The ways we process the information we receive is believed to be as important in determining what we do as the stimulus input. Furthermore, we are not simply *reactive* in this process but also *active* in scanning the environment for what we need and transforming both information and physical objects to suit our purposes. We respond to reality not as it is in the objective world of matter, but as it is in the *subjective reality* of our own inner world. According to the cognitive model, our behavior is only partly determined by preceding events. It is partly a phenomenon that emerges because we can think in totally novel ways, not predictable from the past. Both inherited structures and environmental input influence us but neither one wholly determines the evaluations, definitions, and decisions that will be created in our experience. We start life as neither good nor evil but with potential for both.

In Wundt's laboratory a hundred years ago, conscious processes were studied by **introspection,** a method of gathering data in which subjects report their current conscious experience as accurately as they can. Wundt used the method to study sensations; he was trying to relate sensations to particular stimuli. This type of introspection is not widely used today, and the focus has shifted. Cognitive psychologists of the 1980s are interested in the way people *interpret* the stimulus environment and *decide* what to do, based on *memories* of what worked in the past and *expectations* of desired or undesired consequences. Instead of depending on subjects' own reports of feelings or thoughts, as introspection procedures would elicit, they look for outer behaviors that are indicators of inner processes. They create situations in which different responses will result from different thought processes and then record which response occurs. Their data are measures of these outer behaviors and thus verifiable by others who follow the same procedures; but their hypotheses and theories are about unobservable, covert processes.

Cognitive psychologists see thoughts as both results and causes of overt actions. Feeling regret when you've hurt someone is an example of thought as a result; because of regret, apologizing for your actions is an example of thought as a cause. Clinical psychologists study thought processes at both molecular and molar levels. They may examine the speed with which different types of sentences are understood (molecular) or a subject's recollection of an early childhood event (molar). Psychologist Herbert Simon won a Nobel Prize in economics for his cognitive theory and research on the way people make decisions under conditions of uncertainty—when they do not behave the way the predictions from rational analyses say they should, given the objective circumstances.

With the development of new, more objective methods for studying mental processes (which

Herbert Simon (1916–   ) is generally regarded as one of the fathers of artificial intelligence (AI).

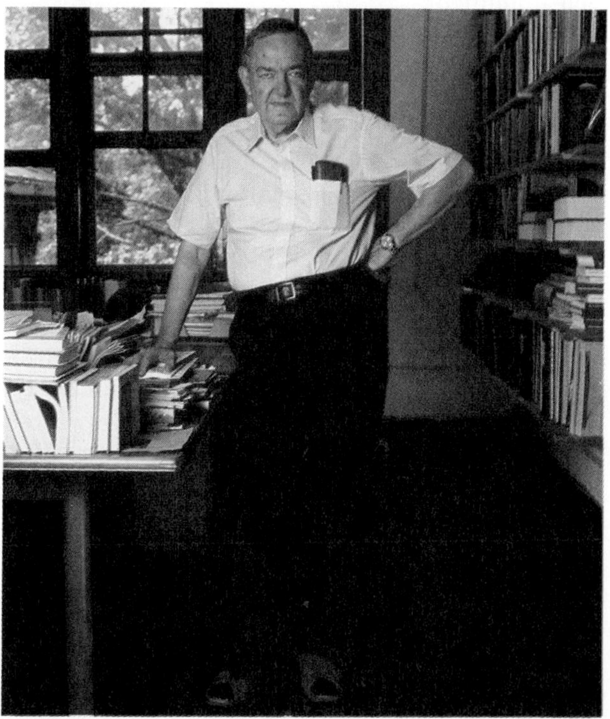

we'll examine in more detail in later chapters), some behavioristically oriented researchers have shifted to a more cognitive emphasis. Two of these are Albert Bandura, who incorporates cognitive events in his explanations of social learning, and Donald Meichenbaum, whose cognitive behavioral therapy trains people to see themselves differently and change the statements they make about themselves. The approach of these researchers weds the behavioristic insistence on rigorous research methodology and standards of evidence to the renewed interest in inner experience and even social foundations of thought (Bandura, 1986). Many psychologists see the new cognitive orientation as the dominant one in psychology today. Its contributions will be our primary focus in chapters 9 and 10 but will also figure prominently in other chapters.

Carl Rogers (1902–1987) emphasized an individual's tendency toward psychological health. Abraham Maslow (1908–1970) postulated a hierarchy of needs.

The Humanistic Model

Sometimes called the "third force," humanistic psychology evolved relatively recently (in the 1950s) as an alternative to the pessimism and determinism of the psychodynamic and the behavioristic models. According to the **humanistic model,** people are neither driven by powerful, instinctive forces nor manipulated by their environments. They are active creatures who are innately good and capable of choice. They strive for growth and development of their potentials, seek change, and plan and restructure their lives to achieve optimal self-fulfillment.

The humanistic psychologist studies behavior, not by reducing it to components, elements, and subprocesses, but by trying to see the *patterns in life histories* of people in their everyday environments. Thus the level of analysis is a molar one. In sharp contrast to the behaviorists, humanistic psychologists focus on the *phenomenal world,* the subjective world experienced by the individual, rather than the objective world seen by external observers and researchers. Unlike the cognitively oriented research psychologist who ties postulated inner processes to specific behavioral indicators, humanistic psychologists are more interested in the way these inner processes lead to new insights and value choices.

The humanistic model is less a research-based model, and it developed less as a theory to explain behavior in general than as an approach for helping normal people lead richer, more satisfying lives. It was this intent that gave rise to encounter groups and other types of personal growth groups in the 1960s and 1970s. Three important contributors were Carl Rogers, Rollo May, and Abraham Maslow. Rogers emphasized the individual's natural tendency toward psychological growth and health, and the importance of a positive self-concept in this process. May was one of the first psychologists to explore phenomena such as anxiety from the perspective of the individual. He also integrated some aspects of existential philosophy into this new psychological approach. **Existentialism** emphasizes an individual's personal decision making and free will in a world that is without reason or purpose. Maslow postulated the need for self-actualization and studied the characteristics of people he judged to be self-actualized. We will learn more about their ideas in later chapters.

The humanistic approach expands the realm of psychology beyond the confines of science to include valuable lessons learned from the study of literature, history, and the arts. In this way psychology becomes a more complete discipline that balances the empirical and the nonempirical, imaginative approaches (see Korn, 1985). This unification hopes to combine the two usually divergent human realms of the sciences and the humanities.

> *The sciences are the expressions and product of the rational understanding, employing concepts such as fact, law, cause, and prediction, communicated through an impersonal, referential, objective language; and the humanities, in contrast are the work of the imagination, which has its proper concern with the things of man through such concepts as appearance and reality, destiny and free will, fortune, fate, happiness, peace, tragedy, expressed in a language that is dramatic, emotional, and purposive. (Bird, 1974, p.1181)*

Using Psychological Models

Each of these five models rests on a different set of assumptions and implies a different way of looking for answers to questions about behavior, as summarized in **Table 1.1.** Let's briefly compare how psychologists using the different models deal with the question of why people act aggressively:

- **Psychophysiological**—study the role of particular brain regions in aggression by electrically stimulating them and observing when destructive actions are elicited. Also analyze the brains of mass murderers for abnormalities, such as tumors.
- **Psychodynamic**—analyze aggression as a person's reactions to frustrations caused by barriers to pleasure, such as poverty or unjust authority, or view it as a displacement by an adult of hostility originally felt by the child against parents.
- **Behavioristic**—identify rewards that may have followed past aggressive responses, such as extra attention given to a child who hit a classmate. Look for rewards the aggressive person is getting currently that maintain the aggressive acts.
- **Cognitive**—ask a person about the hostile thoughts and fantasies he or she experiences while watching aggressive scenes, noting the person's aggressive imagery and intentions to harm others.
- **Humanistic**—look for personal values and social conditions that foster self-limiting, aggressive perspectives instead of those that are growth-enhancing, sharing experiences.

All these approaches have been used in the effort to understand why people behave aggressively and how such behavior can be changed. In chapter 18 we will see what has been learned about the sources of aggression.

But it is not only professional psychologists who have theories about why people do what they do. Don't you already have some convictions about whether behavior is more influenced by heredity or environment, whether people are basically good or evil, and whether or not they have free will? As you read about the findings based on these formal models, keep checking the conclusions against your own views of behavior. In doing so, examine where your personal views have come from and think about some ways you might want to broaden or change them.

Plans for Our Journey

Although I have been teaching, conducting research, and writing about psychology for a quarter of a century, my enthusiasm for this journey becomes greater with each new venture. I hope that with the combined resources of this text as road map and your instructor as guide, you will emerge from this introduction to psychology filled with enthusiasm for further study and personal involvement in the field. First, let's contemplate the route we will follow together.

Table 1.1 *Comparison of Models*

	Psychophysiological	Psychodynamic	Behavioristic	Cognitive	Humanistic
Focus of Study	Brain and nervous system processes	Unconscious drives, conflicts	Specific overt behaviors	Mental processes, language	Human potentials
Level of Analysis	Molecular	Molar	Molecular	Molecular to molar	Molar
Predominant Research Approach	Study relationships between physiological and psycho-processes	Study behavior as expression of hidden motives	Study behavior as it relates to stimulus conditions	Study mental processes through behavior indicators	Study life patterns, values, goals
View of Human Nature	Passive and mechanistic	Instinct-driven	Reactive and modifiable	Active and reactive	Active and unlimited in potential
Predominant Determinants of Behavior	Hereditary and biochemical processes	Heredity and early experience	Environment and stimulus conditions	Stimulus conditions and mental processes	Potentially self-directed

Chapter 2 provides some tools and basic equipment you will need to appreciate better the research you will be reading about. It gives an introduction to research methods and ways to analyze data obtained from various types of psychological investigations. From there we are guided by the general strategy of first examining the whole, intact, functioning individual, starting at birth and going through the life span. In subsequent chapters, we take the organism apart, like "psychosurgeons," dissecting the whole into parts and processes. We do so to be able to examine, in depth, the facets of behavioral and mental functioning.

In chapter 3 we examine the psychological development of ourselves, versatile homo sapiens, over the life span—from infancy through childhood, adulthood, and old age. What transformations take place that enable a biological organism, starting with only a set of genetic blueprints, to evolve into a thinking, feeling person? The basic psychological processes, surveyed for their role in the development of the individual, will be analyzed in greater detail in subsequent chapters. Before getting into each of these specific processes, however, we will see how the structures and functioning of the nervous system are ultimately responsible for the wonderful things we can do and experience (chapter 4).

The first process we will examine in detail is sensation. How do we connect with the sensory world for nourishment and stimulation, as well as for pleasure and avoidance of pain (chapter 5)? The study of sensation helps us understand how we see, hear, smell, taste, and feel our way around. But we are not just sensation-programmed robots: our perceptions are interpretations of the messages from our environment based on our past experience, the current context, and our needs, goals, and expectations (chapter 6). Our ability to sense and perceive contributes to our uniqueness on a further dimension; we have a conscious awareness of ourselves and an ability to go beyond the givens of experience in extending the limits of our consciousness (chapter 7).

Whenever we learn something new, we are profiting from experience by changing our ability to adapt to our environment. We transcend our genetic inheritance by using our potential for a remarkable range of learning. Learning frees us from stereotyped automatic reactions (like the mother turkey's instinctive response to cheep-cheep sounds) by enabling us to develop adaptive, novel behavior sequences (like Imo's potato washing). We learn to predict what events tend to go together, as well as what the consequences of our actions will be (chapter 8). In fact, the nervous system is designed for learning, for being changed by virtually all that we experience.

We also need to keep a record of our experiences and anticipate the challenges we will be meeting. Memory is the living library of all references to our past (chapter 9). Much of it is available to help us deal with problems of the present or make future decisions—as long as we have access to the material that is stored there. When we do, we are able to go beyond what is given in our current experience to become powerful information processors—thinking, reasoning, judging, problem-solving, creating individuals (chapter 10). And when we add our unique ability for language, we can learn secondhand from the experiences of others and also communicate to others what's in or on our minds.

But our great potential for learning, remembering, thinking, and communicating did not develop just so we could sit under an apple tree and daydream. Humans are also designed for action, to survive by getting what they need, like harvesting apples to satisfy hunger, or by avoiding what is dangerous, such as getting out of the way of a falling branch. Like other species, we humans are motivated by basic drives like hunger and such (or is it sex?), but we are also motivated by personal and social needs to develop our potentials—to achieve, and, sometimes, to have power over others. Some of us develop such strong motivation for work that we become "workaholics." Accompanying these sources of action are diverse feelings, emotions, and moods that appear to be distinctly human qualities (chapter 11). The study of emotion ties together cognitive, physiological, and social factors as we prepare to meet the intact person again whom we left behind in an earlier chapter.

Up to this point, in looking at separate processes, we will have been searching for laws of uniformity—how different individuals respond to the same situations in the same general ways—through perceiving, learning, and remembering. Now our focus will shift back again to the whole functioning personality as we ask how and why people respond differently to the same situations. We'll look at several theories of personality (chapter 12) and then at how personality, intelligence, and creativity are assessed by psychologists and those whose decisions affect our lives—school administrators and prospective employers, among others (chapter 13).

Unfortunately, the circumstances of life are never completely ideal. We need to know what challenges are likely to upset our optimal functioning and how we can manage stress more effectively (chapter 14). When things are not managed well, we may become overwhelmed with extreme anxiety and tension, or we may suffer more serious mental disorders. The new field of health psychology will offer strategies and tactics for prevention as well as treatment of psychologically based illnesses and ways to maintain health of mind and body.

We will want to know the forms that major mental and behavioral disorders can take and the tolls they can extract from us as individuals and as a society (chapter 15). Can we ever fully understand what caused Kathy O. to engage in her self-destructive leap off the bridge? Maybe, but we also need to discover what kinds of therapy can help restore optimal mental health and how clinical psychologists go about their business of doing just that (chapter 16).

The final phase of our journey acknowledges that there is no such thing as an isolated individual. Each one of us exists because other people mated, nourished us, protected us, taught us, and gave us values, purposes, and goals. So we inquire into the social nature of the human animal (chapter 17) and into what aspects of the social environment can serve to impoverish or dignify the quality of human life (chapter 18). In examining social processes and social issues we will extend our focus to consider some of the ways psychology is being applied to important life settings, such as law, schools, and peace. Underlying these chapters is the fundamental concern about the way the bond that forms the human connection can be strengthened so that no person becomes isolated from the network of social support essential for individuals to realize their greatest potential. Answering that question will be a life's work for you, begun here but followed on new paths in other places.

Well, there it is, your itinerary for the trip. This is the travel plan I have arranged for you. Your instructor may schedule some detours or rearrange the sequence to match the course syllabus or to fit time constraints or a personal preference for an alternative route. But trust that, between us, we will get you there.

Many students have found it helpful to supplement this text with our student study guide, *Working with Psychology,* by Scott Fraser and me. If your teacher has assigned it, do the lessons and self-tests and you will get the most out of this course, including better grades. If it is not assigned, a personal copy in book or computer-disk format for the IBM-PC or the Apple is available.

The *Opening Cases* that begin the chapters serve to start you thinking about important concepts relevant to the core ideas of the chapter. These brief encounters along our psychological journey are meant both to pique your interest and to serve as a constant reminder that psychology is the study of the behavior of individuals, of living beings—not just abstract concepts or the numbers and variables in our experiments.

OK, then, you're on your way. I hope it will be a worthwhile journey. Be forewarned that, at times, the going will be a little rough and require that you extend yourself. If you do, the journey will become as rewarding as reaching the destination. Let's go, or as the Italians say, "Andiamo!"

Summary

- Scientific psychology started a little over a hundred years ago as an attempt to study elements of inner consciousness. Later, its focus was on outer, observable actions. Today, its subject matter includes the study of outer behavior, mental processes, and physiological processes.
- The goals of psychology are to describe, explain, predict, and control behavior, as well as to improve the quality of life.
- The objective data of psychology are observable stimuli and observable responses. Explanation identifies relationships and underlying processes that make sense of behavioral observations.
- The origins of American psychology are found in the intellectual traditions of associationism, elementalism, evolutionism, experimentation, and individualism.
- From the tradition of associationism, psychology adopted an emphasis on experience rather than heredity and the view that complex ideas arise from simple sensations.
- Elementalism contributed to psychology the importance of analysis, or reduction, of complex phenomena into ever simpler units.
- Psychology's concern with the nature/nurture question, the contributions to behavioral development of heredity and environmental influences respectively, derives from evolutionary theory, formulated by Charles Darwin.

- The development of psychology as a laboratory science began with the experimental tradition pioneered by Wilhelm Wundt in Germany and brought to the United States by Edward Titchener. Titchener's structuralism emphasized the study of the structure of the mind and behavior built up from elemental sensations.
- The tradition of individualism developed by American psychologist William James stressed functionalism—the view that the acts, functions, and purposes of mental processes are significant, rather than the structure of the mind.
- Five theoretical models cover much of the ground to be followed on our psychological journey. They have evolved from the work of investigators studying very different kinds of problems in diverse research settings.
- Psychologists trying to find relationships between behavior and brain mechanisms generally follow the psychophysiological model. It is based on the reductionist assumption that each level of functioning can be described more precisely in terms of the biological structures and processes that make it work.
- According to the psychodynamic model, behavior is driven by instinctive forces, inner conflicts, and motivation that can be unconscious as well as conscious. Early conflict experiences influence behavior throughout life, often in disguised ways. Social mechanisms are developed to restrain an individual's presumed selfish, sexual, and destructive impulses.
- According to the behavioristic model, behavioral actions are determined by external stimulus conditions. The psychologist's task is to identify the functional relationships between behavior and stimuli that elicit it or are its consequences. This model has been predominant in American psychology for much of this century.
- For psychologists who adopt the cognitive model, it is important to study the mental processes that intervene between stimulus input and response initiation. How information is processed influences the options organisms have in adapting to their environment and the symbolic ways they can transform it. Many areas of contemporary psychology now use a cognitive approach.
- The humanistic model is a perspective on human nature emphasizing an individual's inherent capacity to make rational choices. This approach suggests directions for therapy and self-improvement based on self-regulation of behavior and development of human potential.

2

Understanding Research

Prior to Valentine's Day of 1977, Fred Cowan, of New York, was described by relatives and acquaintances as a "nice, quiet man," a "gentle man who loved children," and a "real pussycat." But on that fateful day when ordinarily he might be passing out Valentine candies, Fred Cowan distributed death. He strolled into work toting a semiautomatic rifle and shot four coworkers, a police officer, and, finally, himself. In subsequent interviews, people who had known Cowan expressed shock and amazement at what he had done. One neighbor said that Cowan "belonged to the best family on the block." The principal of his parochial elementary school reported that Cowan had received grades of "A" in courtesy, cooperation, and religion, This quiet, kind, person "never talked to anybody and was someone you could push around," according to a coworker. But not on that day, the only truly violent day in the life of Fred Cowan, which ended with six senseless murders.

Stories like this lead us—lay people and research psychologists alike—to wonder about the meaning and causes of human behavior. How could a seemingly gentle man like Fred Cowan so lose control of himself? How could it be that the first aggressive crime he ever committed was mass murder? What kind of person can become a sudden murderer?

I'm sure that another question also comes to your mind: does this individual share anything in common with others who have also been suddenly transformed from gentle people into murderers? Indeed, later in this chapter, we will examine research data that shed some new light on this provocative question: but if you also secretly wonder whether *you* might ever behave similarly, probably you'd pose the issue differently. It is more likely you would ask yourself, "Under what *circumstances* might I take the life of another person? In self-defense? In my line of duty as a police officer or as a soldier in wartime? What if my life situation was blocking the attainment of important goals, making me extremely frustrated? Under such circumstances might I conceivably commit an act of homicide?"

"What if" is to research as a first kiss is to romance. It stimulates lots of action that hopes to replace uncertainty with new meaning. What also comes out of both adventures is excitement and a better understanding of ourselves and others. Psychologists love to think "what if" thoughts. What if that situation were changed; would he still behave that way? What if she were treated differently; would there be a corresponding change in behavior? What if I intervened with a particular kind of therapy; would it make a difference in their behavior?

Research is one way to answer such "what if" questions. While some researchable questions come from observing how we and others behave, many research ideas come from psychological theories and from reading research reports. When there are unexpected findings, contradictory results, or unexplained relationships that have been discovered by others, they act as catalysts for new research. The answers come from special ways of gathering evidence. In this chapter, we will focus on the kinds of evidence that psychological investigators seek, as well as the special procedures they use to gather the facts. Our interest will be on *how* we come to know the *what* of behavior and mental processes.

Recall the definition of psychology given in chapter 1: the scientific study of the behavioral and mental functioning of individuals. In this chapter you will see where the *science* part comes from in the definition. You will learn that it comes from adopting the principles and practices of the *scientific method* which govern research in all areas of empirical investigation. After that you will discover what is special about psychology's application of this general approach to its domain of knowledge. How do psychologists measure behavior and design their research? How do they analyze their data so that solid conclusions can be drawn?

Finally, you will broaden your perspective from lessons on the *hows* of psychological research to realize *why* this type of knowledge is personally relevant, even if you never perform an experiment. The mass media constantly bombard you with stories that begin with, "Research shows that . . . ." The stories often end with direct or implied calls for some citizen action based on that research. The action may be to stop doing something you do too often or too much of or to start doing things you ought to be doing if you value health, wealth, or the good opinion of others. The message of *Psychology and Life* is that, by understanding some of the basic principles of psychological research, you will develop basic skills in critical thinking that may make you a more sophisticated consumer of research-based conclusions.

Exploring Unknown Realms of Mind and Behavior

Where do your beliefs about physical reality and human nature come from? Some come from your direct observations of events, animals, people, and things in the environment around you; but much also comes *secondhand,* from the observations of others, and from what you read and are told by authorities who render "expert opinions" on various subjects. Both sources of knowledge may be less than perfect, because there may be hidden errors and personal biases present that distort the truth about the reality you believe you know. Since you may act on what you know, it is important to reduce those sources of error and have a realistic estimate of the confidence you can place in your beliefs.

It is easy to draw false conclusions about "the way things really are" when what we want to believe is "the way things ought to be *ideally.*" For example, the meltdown of the Soviet nuclear reactor plant in Chernobyl, Russia, in April 1986, was certainly not what the Soviets wanted to believe could ever happen. Therefore, consider this statement made only two months earlier (by the Minister of Power and Electrification of the Ukraine) about the virtual impossibility of such an unlikely event. Responding to the question, "How safe are the nuclear power plants being built close to big cities and resort areas?" the minister said, "The odds of a meltdown are one in 10,000 years." (Rylsky, 1986, p. 8).

It is also easy to get a false picture of reality by relying on faulty memory instead of checking out data. How much confidence do you put in the predictions of psychics and astrologers, especially in their big New Year's prognostications about disasters, the stock market, and the marriages and divorces of movie stars and other celebrities? Would

"How do you want it—the crystal ball mumbo-jumbo or statistical probability?"

you say these predictions were only "fairly accurate," maybe correct about 50 percent of the time? That's conservative, but wrong! A daily check, made of 550 specific predictions by 36 different astrologers and psychics in the nation's leading tabloids at the start of 1985, revealed that only 24 predictions were correct. That amounts to being wrong 95 percent of the time, yet psychics continue to make their predictions and many people continue to read them and believe that they are "pretty good" (Blodgett, 1986).

But such errors and fallacies are hardly new. Around the turn of the century one of the leading psychologists, Hugo Munsterberg, gave a speech on peace to a large audience that included many reporters. After reading their articles he was not sure what they were listening to or whom they really saw.

> *The reporters sat immediately in front of the platform. One man wrote that the audience was so surprised by my speech that it received it in complete silence; another wrote that I was constantly interrupted by loud applause and that at the end of my address the applause continued for minutes. The one wrote that during my opponent's speech I was constantly smiling; the other noticed that my face remained grave and without a smile. The one said that I grew purple-red from excitement; and the other found that I grew chalk-white. The one told us that my critic, while speaking, walked up and down the large stage; and the other, that he stood all the while at my side and patted me in a fatherly way on the shoulder." (1908/1927, pp. 35–36)*

Because supposedly credible interpreters of reality can be so wrong, and because even our own observations can be distorted by our personal biases, prejudices, and expectations we need ways to minimize errors in conclusion-drawing and to increase the accuracy of the evidence on which we base our generalizations. How can these objectives be achieved? Enter the scientific method and the research foundations on which most psychological knowledge is based.

Research in science involves a systematic search for reliable information about natural events. That search is guided by the **scientific method,** which is a general set of procedures for gathering and interpreting evidence that limits sources of errors and yields dependable conclusions. The scientific method demands special attitudes and values on the part of those who would earn the status of scientist. Psychology is considered a science to the extent that it follows the "rules of the game" established by the scientific method. What are the special attitudes and values of researchers who agree to use its procedures?

Scientists are motivated by a curiosity about the unknown and the uncertain. They seek to discover lawful, orderly patterns of relationships in the phenomena they investigate. Aware of the many disguises that Nature may wear in concealing truths, scientists are critical and skeptical of all conclusions until they have been proved repeatedly by independent investigators. Even then, there is a necessary open-mindedness which makes truth provisional, ready to be modified by new data, and never absolute. A respect for data as the ultimate arbiter of disagreements and as the cornerstone of knowledge is also a basic value. Secrecy is banned since all data and the methods for reproducing them must be *publicly verifiable*—open to inspection, criticism, and replication by others.

Scientific knowledge is built on a base of *empirical* evidence obtained by observation and measurement, rather than solely on the basis of "authority" beliefs and dataless experts. The data are collected using methods that eliminate or correct for the subjective influences of the researchers, increasing their objectivity. Inferences and conclusions about the meaning of the evidence are kept distinct from the description of the data and the methods for collecting them. Although the careers of individual investigators are enhanced by original research that offers new ways of looking at nature, science is enhanced by the *cumulative* building of its knowledge base. Each scientist stands on the shoulders of all those who have contributed previously—a lofty starting place in the never-ending pyramid of science.

The significance of the scientific method for any society that values truth and freedom was eloquently stated by philosophers Cohen and Nagel (1934) over 50 years ago. The force of their argument is even more powerful today as science and technology play ever greater roles in our lives.

> *Scientific method is the only effective way of strengthening the love of truth. It develops the intellectual courage to face difficulties and to overcome illusions that are pleasant temporarily but destructive ultimately. It settles differences without any external force by appealing to our common rational nature. The way of science, even if it is up a steep mountain, is open to all. Hence, while sectarian and partisan faiths are based on personal choice or temperament and divide men, scientific procedure unites men in something nobly devoid of all pettiness. Because it requires detachment, disinterestedness, it is the finest flower and test of a liberal civilization. (pp. 402–3)*

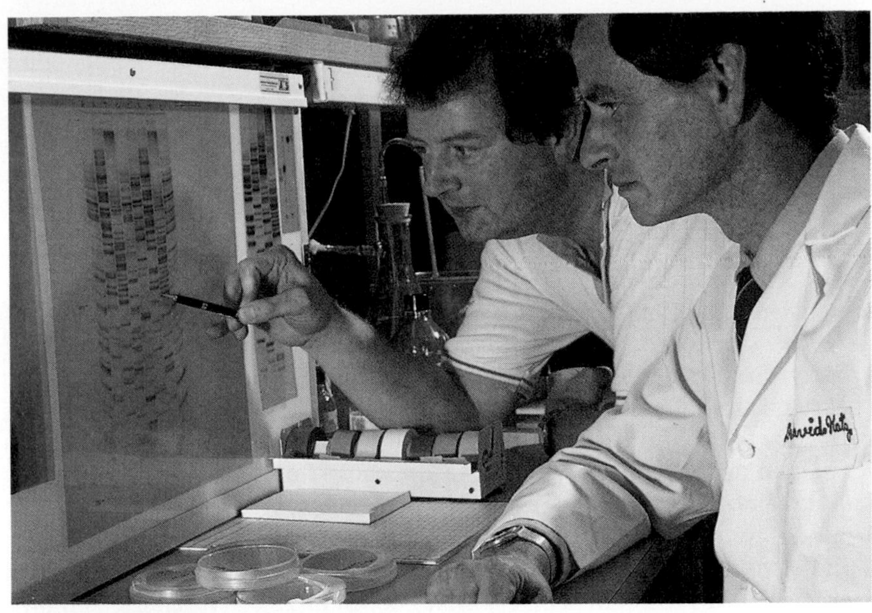

A controlled experiment conducted in a laboratory may involve the use of complex equipment for recording responses.

A Framework for Psychological Research

Psychologists ask the "big questions" that philosophers and others have posed for centuries, questions about reality, knowledge, the mind, and human nature. The answers psychologists seek come not from reasoned logic or expert opinion; instead, they rely on behavioral data from carefully controlled observations and experimental methods. Psychology is scientific to the extent that it uses the scientific method to collect empirical data on which to base its conclusions.

Psychological research is the *how* of what is known in psychology. Basic to research in psychology are (a) a reliance on empirical methods for investigating the "mysteries of human nature"; (b) systematic attempts to measure and quantify aspects of behavior and processes of mind; (c) adoption of procedural safeguards to increase objectivity and reduce the ever-present danger of personal biases; (d) the keeping of complete records of observations and data analysis in a form that other researchers can understand and evaluate; and (e) communication of one's findings and conclusions in ways that allow independent observers to **replicate** (repeat) the findings—or to reject the conclusions.

Strictly speaking, the empirical results of any research are limited to the reactions actually recorded from particular individuals in a specific context; but a researcher is always looking for *general principles* that go beyond these limits. The goal is to be able to discover *general laws of behavior* from the process of studying individual cases and observing only a selected portion of the behavior of those people or animals. Psychological researchers seek to observe a little and explain a lot. If the research has been conducted properly—observing and measuring a small sample of behavior from some individuals in sample situations—researchers can generate conclusions about a larger population.

We might say that there are two broad kinds of information that psychologists are seeking when they engage in the research enterprise. They want to discover the *structure* of behavior and psychological processes, as well as their *causes* or *determinants.* Explaining how different responses are related or what variables go together is one part of their quest; the other part involves asking what stimulus events cause a particular response to start, stop, or change in its quality or quantity. The way to get answers for the first kind of question about structure and interrelationships is to use *correlational* methods; the way to get answers about causality is to use *experimentation.* Each of these general approaches will be discussed in detail in a later section of this chapter.

Functional Analysis

Most psychologists conceive of behavior as a function of (caused by) two general classes of independent variables: one class includes the factors in an organism and the other comprises stimulus factors. Behavioral changes are thus dependent upon changes in one or both of these factors. Those who study only human behavior refer to the *person,* or *dispositional, factors* as **organismic factors:** personality *traits,* like extroversion; *states* of a person, like anxiety, drunkenness, or frustration; and other *status* characteristics, like gender or race. A special organismic factor central to the study of a developing individual over its life span is *time,* or the age of an individual when its behavior is studied.

Often researchers will study the influence of stimulus factors within particular *contexts* that may affect responses to them. For example, depending on the context, the same amount of money received for performing a task can be a reward that increases positive responding or a bribe that causes negative emotional reactions.

Functional relationships can be expressed in the following formula:

$$\mathbf{B = f\ (O_t \times S_c).}$$

It is read as, "Behavior is a function of organism factors at a given time in an organism's life interacting with stimulus factors within a particular context." This formula indicates that, to understand any behavior, we need to know about both dispositional and situational factors. Nevertheless, in different areas of psychology there is typically an emphasis on one factor only, with little attempt to study how the two interact. Traditionally, *O* factors have been the focus of research by those who study comparative differences between different animal species, individual differences in intelligence or personality, physiological or cognitive processes, and mental disorders. The emphasis on the *S* factors is apparent in behaviorally oriented research on learning and conditioning, and in social psychology. However, social psychologists would be quick to include context factors as well.

Suppose you were interested in discovering the determinants of Fred Cowan's aggressive behavior in our *Opening Case.* After defining what you mean by "aggressive behavior," which factors influencing aggression would you study? There are a host of them to choose from, depending, in part, on your theoretical orientation, as outlined in chapter 1. For example, you might select any of the following variables and factors for your human aggression research (see Konĕcni, 1984, for a discussion of the methodological issues in such research).

> **Organism factors:** Gender, race, ethnic group, traits of aggressivity, sociability, impulse control, frustration, emotional arousal, feelings of anonymity, altered state of consciousness, shyness
>
> **Time factors:** Children, youth, adults, elderly people
>
> **Stimulus factors:** Instigation by insult or prior aggression, witnessing an aggressive model in film or person, competitive play, presence of weapons, labeling a target as the "enemy" or as "animals"
>
> **Context factors:** The presence of a peer group, unfamiliarity of an environment, darkness, high ambient temperature

Your understanding of the determinants of human aggression involves knowing how these variables, and others in each of the four categories, function to generate the type of behavior that you can observe or measure in some way. In chapter 18, the social psychological analysis of violence and aggression will come into your focus of study.

Enhancing Objectivity

Three ways to enhance objectivity in research are to define variables clearly, to standardize procedures for data collection, and to use methods that avoid bias. When researchers use these procedures, they can detach their personal values and desires from the way their data are collected and have confidence that the data can be trusted as objective. They can also feel assured that the conclusions drawn from these data are, in turn, more trustworthy. This does not guarantee the truth of the findings, since researchers may make honest mistakes or purposely tamper with data to present fraudulent conclusions; but data are like heavily starched underwear—difficult to conceal for long from the gaze of careful observers.

Defining Variables Operationally

The variables in any study need to be defined in clearly observable terms. For example, if you want to study shyness, you might use one of the following observable behaviors as your definition: withdrawal behavior in a social situation, critical self-statements about one's social skill, or failure to make eye contact with friendly people. In a study of aggressive behavior, you might define aggression as either a behavior that injures another person or a score on a test of aggressiveness. This kind of definition is called an **operational definition,** because

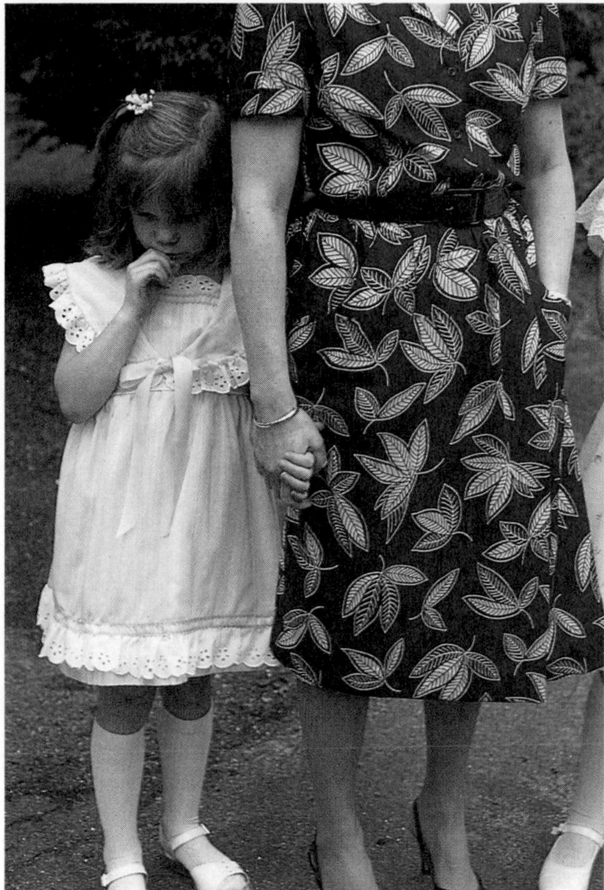

Shyness can mean different things to different researchers. An operational definition will allow an experimenter to precisely describe what is being studied.

it defines a variable in terms of specific operations an investigator uses to determine its presence. An operational definition avoids the ambiguity of everyday descriptive terms and ensures that both the stimulus variables and the response variables are observable events.

Even inner processes can be studied by defining them in observable terms. For example, hunger, an inner state, might be operationally defined as "24 hours without food," or "15-percent loss of body weight in a given time period." By defining hunger in either of these ways, an experimenter can then study its effects on various behaviors.

Sometimes when different researchers report contradictory findings about behaviors like shyness or aggressiveness, it turns out that they have used different definitions of the terms and, hence, have not been measuring the same behaviors. Operational definitions enable experimenters to precisely describe what is being studied. Then, when other researchers want to replicate the studies or build on their findings, they know how the variables were defined.

Standardizing Procedures

The technique of **standardization** employs uniform procedures to administer tests, interviews, surveys, and experiments. It minimizes *unwanted variability* in the behavior of research subjects. An investigator must always ask questions in the same way, replicate conditions exactly, and score responses in a uniform way so that all research participants experience exactly the same experimental conditions. As we shall see in chapter 13, standardization is especially important in both constructing and using psychological tests.

Avoiding Bias

Bias is an error in a particular direction that may produce misleading or erroneous conclusions. In scientific research it is likely to be unintentional, but, unless the research methods include ways of minimizing its potentially distorting effects, its presence can make a study scientifically worthless. The problem is similar to the one you face when you are ready to buy a used car: Do you put as much trust in the recommendation of a used-car salesperson as in the recommendation of an analyst hired by a consumer advocate company?

Even with standardized procedures, bias can inadvertently be introduced by either the subjects or the researcher. For example, a subject who dislikes females in authority can introduce bias by not paying attention to the instructions of a female experimenter, and, thus, can respond differently, under the same experimental conditions, from the other subjects. If a subject wants to make a good impression the subject can give the responses he or she thinks the experimenter wants and thus bias the results.

There are many examples of unwitting researcher-caused bias. Like the rest of us, researchers are human: they tend to see what they expect to see, despite their commitment to objectivity. Even worse, their expectations may prompt changes in the behavior of the subjects they are supposedly just observing.

> *In a study of unintentional researcher-caused bias, students were hired as "experimental assistants" to research how reliably "subjects" could determine the success or failure of people just by looking at their photographs. The subjects were to rate the expressions in the photographs on a scale from +10 (extreme success) to −10 (extreme failure). Actually, all the photos had earlier been rated as neutral. Half of the experimental assistants were told that the subjects they observed would give ratings that averaged about +5,*

while the other half expected average ratings of −5. Both groups then read the same instructions to their subjects.

As you can now probably anticipate, both sets of experimental assistants achieved the results they were expecting. In some subtle, nonverbal way, even though they had read standardized instructions and had just watched while the photos were being judged, they had communicated their expectations to their subjects and then observed them doing just as expected.

Similar results were found with rats as subjects. When experimenters were led to believe that one group of rats was smarter than another, they later reported observing superior performance by the supposedly smarter, but actually similarly ordinary, rodents. (Rosenthal, 1966)

"Find out who set up this experiment. It seems that half of the patients were given a plăcebo, and the other half were given a different placebo."

The unconscious biasing of data because of an experimenter's expectations is called the "experimenter expectancy bias effect." It has been studied extensively by psychologist Robert Rosenthal as an interesting problem in how subtle forms of interpersonal communication can lead to self-fulfilling prophecies. In one particularly dramatic demonstration, he told teachers that certain students would be "late bloomers." Sure enough, those students did do better as the year wore on; yet they were ordinary students who had been picked at random (Rosenthal & Jacobson, 1968b).

Researcher-caused bias can be controlled in several ways. Bias based on the expectations of experimenters can be eliminated by keeping both subjects and experimental assistants unaware of which subjects get which treatment. Bias based on the emphasis, tone, manner, or gestures of an experimenter may be eliminated by using standardized, impersonal testing procedures such as presenting instructions on tape or on computer consoles.

A special kind of bias exists when a patient improves after taking a substance, thought to be a therapeutic drug, for the cure of some ailment even though the substance is chemically *inert* (without any medicinal value). This clinically significant response to a stimulus or treatment that occurs independent of its actual physiological effect is called a **placebo effect.** In a more general sense, it occurs whenever a behavioral response is influenced by a person's *expectation* of what to do or how to feel, rather than by the specific independent variable employed to produce that response.

A placebo is one of the most powerful drugs that a physician can use in treating pain and sickness. A thorough analysis of nearly 100 studies of 29 different symptoms and sicknesses—including cancer, multiple sclerosis, alcoholism, migraine, rheumatism, and constipation—revealed that 27 percent of more than 4500 patients experienced pain reduction (Haas et al., 1959/1963). Another survey found that, among American patients in 15 different studies, about one third were "positive placebo responders." They responded to the chemically inert drug as if it were medically potent. In some cases it was as effective as morphine in relieving pain following surgery (Beecher, 1959). In one well-planned study, a sweet-tasting placebo was even more effective than a bitter-tasting tranquilizing drug (Baker & Thorpe, 1957).

The effectiveness of placebo treatments in medicine has a long history (see Shapiro, 1960). In ancient Egypt patients were often treated with medication such as lizard's blood, crocodile dung, powdered pig's teeth, donkey's hooves, and, for the wealthy, powdered remains of mummies. Some Egyptian patients got better—thanks to the power of placebos. In later times, doctors "cured" some patients by treating them with blood-sucking leeches, making them vomit, heating them, freezing them, and shocking them. Of course, many died, but those who survived despite what was done to them may have been the positive placebo responders who believed in the power of the physician to heal. In this way, suggestibility and faith may combine to produce a cure that is a "nonspecific placebo response" rather than a response to a specific treatment administered.

When placebo effects might possibly occur, researchers employ **placebo controls.** The effect of the treatment must be shown to be significantly greater for those who actually got it than for control clients who were merely expecting to receive it.

Another type of nonspecific response bias occurs when research subjects are affected by their participation in experiments—for example, if they are aware of being monitored by a researcher or feel special about being chosen for a study. An experimenter might then mistakenly attribute their reactions to the specific independent variable being manipulated instead of to these extraneous variables. When something other than what an experimenter explicitly introduces into a research-setting changes a subject's behavior it is said to be a **confounding variable**—it confounds the interpretation of the real cause for the observed behavioral effects. Simply put, people may change the way they behave when they know they are being observed.

This type of bias is called the **Hawthorne effect,** named after research done in the 1920s at Western Electric Company near Chicago, Illinois. In that study workers, who were selected for an experiment on the effects of lighting changes on productivity, increased their work output no matter what was done. The researchers concluded that the psychological element of feeling special about their participation in the research was more important to the workers than the physical variable being manipulated (for more details, see ***Close-up:*** *The Thorny Hawthorne Effect*).

Building Reliability and Validity

The goal of most psychological research is **reliability,** to generate behavioral data that are consistent and stable so that the same results will be found on repeated testing under the same conditions. A ruler will not give a reliable measure of height under all conditions. It will provide an unreliable measure if it is made of a material that expands or contracts according to temperature, or if, one time, a person is wearing shoes and another time is barefoot. The same rules hold for a psychological measure; reliability is enhanced when the research, test, or measurement conditions are standardized, sources of unwanted variability are controlled, and enough observations are made or responses measured so that atypical ones do not distort the overall effect.

Once we establish conditions for our ruler so that it gives reliable measures, it will be a valid instrument for assessing length or height; but it can be perfectly reliable and never give a valid measure of intelligence. For that task we need other measuring tools.

How about asking those who know you well, starting with your parents and best friends, to evaluate your intelligence? Their opinions will probably not yield valid measures for many obvious reasons, not the least of which is their desire to perceive you as special, thereby overestimating all your positive traits and abilities. In addition, their definitions of *intelligence* may not correspond to our definition. So how do we establish a clear, unbiased, external criterion so that we can assess your intelligence?

Validity means that the information produced from research or testing is an accurate measure of the psychological variable or quality it is intended to measure. It is built up on a foundation of good, conceptual analysis. For our example, we might choose a test to measure your intellect. On the basis of the scores it provides, predictions can be made about aspects of academic performance that depend on intelligence. The test would then be called valid for this purpose; but it would not be valid for many other objectives, such as your becoming a cheerleader, a marathon runner, or a college dean. In chapter 13, the concepts of reliability and validity will be discussed further in considering how tests of personality and intelligence are developed and used by psychologists.

Coincidence, Correlations, and Causality

There can be danger in making false inferences about the relationship between two events. Therefore it is of great importance to distinguish among the ways in which events may occur in time and place. First, one event may cause another; in this case the two events are said to be causally related. Second, the two events can be co-related, linked together by some relationship. Third, the two events can be related only by coincidence.

In dressing for a tennis match you happen to put on your left sock and sneaker before the right one. You win the difficult match, and thereafter, you develop a ritual of always dressing in a specific, left-right rigid sequence. You fear if you do not, you'll lose, so you don't take the risk. This coincidence has come to (superstitiously) control your behavior because it is being treated as if it were a meaningful correlation.

Close-up *The Thorny Hawthorne Effect*

The "Hawthorne effect" is a paradox in the folklore of the behavioral sciences. It reveals a tale of researchers who designed a simple experiment to measure the effects of *physical conditions* on worker productivity only to find out that they were really studying something else—psychological reactions to social conditions. From an experiment that did not work right, because uncontrolled, extraneous variables messed up the expected results, came new insights into the importance of the way research subjects interpret the nature of the research and their work context. Out of a failure to demonstrate a straighforward relationship between physical conditions of work and worker productivity emerged the impetus for the development of the new area of human relations in industry as well as a target for research by industrial psychologists. Although the research was conducted over 60 years ago, it is still being reanalyzed and reevaluated (Landsberger, 1958; Parsons, 1974; Schwartz, 1986). So what was this research all about, why is it so controversial, and why is it still of contemporary concern?

Between 1924 and 1932 seven studies were conducted in the Western Electric Company at Hawthorne, near Chicago, where telephone equipment was manufactured. The goal of this research was to find out what conditions would increase worker output, making employees more productive. The independent variables manipulated were changes in lighting, rest pauses, and hours of work; the dependent variable was the number of units per-hour that each worker assembled.

In the first studies, illumination was varied in the experimental group but not in the control group. Surprisingly, productivity increased both with good lighting and with bad. Equally curious, output increased steadily in the control group where no changes were made in lighting! What variables were influencing output since illumination obviously wasn't? One interpretation has been that this behavior change was because of the workers' knowledge that they were chosen for a research project, their pleasure in being treated in a special way, and as a consequence, being under surveillance. That is one of the origins of the myth of the Hawthorne effect.

A team of researchers from Harvard University, led by psychologist Elton Mayo (1946), designed the next series of studies in which output and worker fatigue were assessed as the length of the working hours and rest pauses were varied. In the company, workers received an hourly wage plus an added incentive based on the number of units produced by each department of about 100 workers. During the research, small groups of workers were selected to work together. Since their piecework pay was based on the total output of this group of 5 to 10 coworkers, individual effort was more clearly reflected in the team total than it was in the larger group.

In the "Relay Assembly Test Room" experiment, a team of five women workers were studied over a 5-year period during which there were 24 periods of variation in rest periods, working hours, and other changes. Again, the results revealed a rise in output regardless of the researchers' manipulations. "The general upward trend in output independent of any particular change in rest pauses or shorter working hours was astonishing." (Roethlisberger & Dickson, 1939, p. 86) This is the second locus of the myth of the Hawthorne effect. It was interpreted by Mayo as the consequence of group cohesion and morale among these women, caused by their privi-

While a coincidence is a chance or random association of events, a **correlation** is a consistent relationship between two or more variables. Much research in psychology is a search for correlations, for discovering what variables are associated and how strongly they are linked. Depression and suicide, anxiety and stuttering, viewing pornography and aggression against women, stress and job performance are but a few of the connections that researchers are trying to establish and understand.

If SAT scores of high-school seniors are *positively correlated* with their college grades later, it will

leged position as research subjects. Mayo went on to propose that what industrial workers really wanted was to live in social harmony with others and have the happiness and security that comes with "subordination of an individual to a common purpose."

While such social facilitation may have been operating at Hawthorne to boost productivity, other uncontrolled variables were also silently contributing to "the effect." The workers were aware of their output rates and knew that their pay would be more directly tied to the increased personal effort in this smaller collective unit than it was in their former company unit. Thus knowledge of the consequences of their behavior and reward for effort could account for the greater productivity, even without any social factors operating. This new method of payment increased productivity (about half as much) in another group that was given no other special treatment—supporting a reward interpretation for the rise in output. It was also true that the improved performance could be attributed to the workers' increasing skills over this extended time period, but there was no control group for comparison.

But the clearest evidence of the power of group standards, or *norms,* comes from the results with a male group that maintained a steady, but *low* output with the department-wide piecework incentive system, even though the group was put in a special observation room. Each operator restricted his output to keep it in line with what was regarded as a "proper day's work." Those who speeded up were brought into line by group disapproval and rejection, through tactics of humiliation, and by name-calling.

A careful reading of this research and its criticisms yields several revelations: there was a definite effect of uncontrolled variables on behavior; the experiments were poorly conducted, lacking adequate controls and standardized conditions; money did matter, not just good feelings among worker teams, in boosting work output; being treated in a humanizing fashion made people feel special and elicited job satisfaction and pride in the work; there appeared to be a naive capitalist bias in treating worker-management conflicts as resolvable through cosmetic changes in "job hygiene" factors and viewing workers as human machines. Despite the criticisms, this pioneering research will long be remembered as the experiment that succeeded as a "classic"—by failing to prove its point.

mean that students with high scores on the SAT will generally get high grades. If the reverse is true and they are *negatively correlated,* then students who get high scores on one measure will tend to have low scores on the other. You would expect a negative correlation between test measures of shyness and measures of assertive behavior, for example. The higher the correlation—either positive or negative—the closer the relationship and the more accurately you can predict one measure if you know the other. In both cases the two sets of measures will vary together in a systematic way.

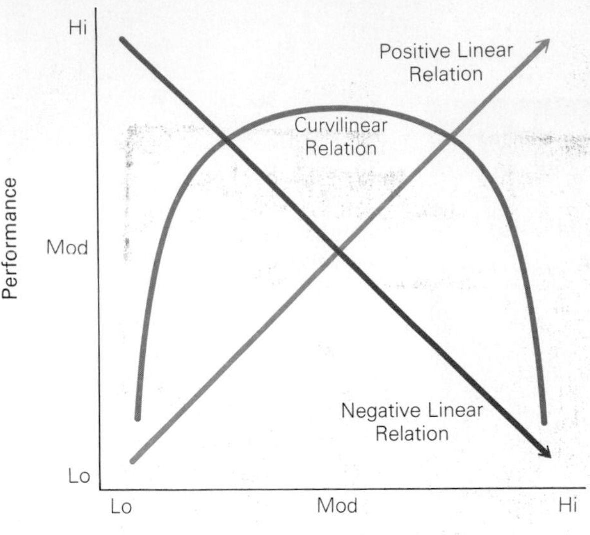

Figure 2.1 *Linear and Nonlinear Relationships Between Two Variables*

The solid line shows the curvilinear (inverted-U) relationship found between level of arousal and performance: performance is better at moderate levels of arousal than at either very low or very high levels. The dotted lines show the directions that either a positive linear or negative linear relation would produce, the kind of curve found when there is a linear correlation between the two variables.

Two variables may be related in yet another way; the relationship between them may be *curvilinear,* first going together in one direction and then in the opposite direction. The graph in **Figure 2.1** shows how these three types of relationships might look when performance scores on some measure are correlated with scores on subjects' level of emotional arousal. (Can you read the curvilinear relation, which is the one often found between these two variables?)

In correlational studies, where researchers are seeking consistent relationships between different sets of variables, both the independent variable (the predictor) and the dependent variable (that which is predicted) are responses. In contrast, in experimental studies, the independent variable is a stimulus condition from which predictions are made about the behavioral response.

Since correlations are relationships between sets of measurements, predictions based on them are *group* predictions; they are rarely accurate predictions for individuals (except in the rare cases where there is a perfect correlation). For example, the high positive correlation repeatedly found between heavy smoking and incidence of cancer tells us that there will be more cancer among heavy smokers than among nonsmokers. It does not tell us whether any particular individual will get cancer. Therefore some heavy smokers treat this causal relationship as if it were merely correlational—a deadly defense for many.

Did you know that there is a strong correlation between contraceptive use in Taiwan and the number of electrical appliances in Taiwanese homes? Given this finding, will contraceptive use increase if the government decides to give away free radios and popcorn machines? Only if the two variables are directly related causally. It turns out that a third set of variables—education and social class—is responsible for both of these events, not their relationship to each other (Li, 1975). Now try your hand at explaining the correlation evidence reported in **Table 2.1**

The ultimate aim of experimenters in psychology is to identify *cause-and-effect relationships*—to go beyond knowing just that two variables are related to knowing *how* they are related. But the correlation itself does not provide the causal information they seek; to get that requires a special set of research procedures known as the controlled experiment, to be discussed in the next section of this chapter. In order to demonstrate a causal relationship, the following conditions must be met:

1. The behavior can be started or stopped by presenting or withholding the independent variable (or the amount of the behavior can be changed by making corresponding changes in the amount of the independent variable).
2. These changes in behavior occur in this context only following manipulation of the independent variable. When the causal relationship between an independent variable and a dependent variable has been demonstrated, we can conclude only that changes in the first cause changes in the second.

Table 2.1 *Relationship of TV Viewing and Grades on Achievement Tests*

Hours of TV Watched Daily	Test Scores	
	Reading	Math
0–½	75	69
½–1	74	65
1–2	73	65
2–3	73	65
3–4	72	63
4–5	71	63
5–6	70	62
6 +	66	58

A consistent negative relationship is seen: The fewer the hours spent watching TV, the higher the grades in both reading and math. Does this prove that watching TV causes poor grades? How would you find out? What other explanations might there be for the correlation between TV watching and grades? (California Department of Education, 1982)

Providing Ethical Safeguards

Most psychology experiments carry little risk to the subjects, especially where participants are merely asked to perform routine tasks, but experiments that study subjects' emotional reactions, self-images, or attitudes, or use deception to conceal their true purpose, can be upsetting or psychologically disturbing. Therefore whenever a researcher conducts a study, it is important that he or she includes as a basic feature of the research process procedures designed to project the subjects' physical and psychological well-being (Diener & Crandall, 1978).

Typically all research done with human subjects begins with a full description of the procedures, potential risks and expected benefits to be experienced, and statements to be signed by the subjects indicating that they give their informed consent to participate. The subjects are assured in advance that they may leave an experiment any time they wish, without penalty. At the end of an experiment, they are given a careful debriefing, in which the researcher explains the hypotheses and purposes of the study and makes sure that no one leaves feeling confused, upset, or embarrassed. If it was necessary to mislead the subjects during any stage of the research, the experimenter carefully explains the reasons for this deception. In addition, subjects are reassured that all responses and records of behavior will be kept strictly confidential. Finally, they have the right to withdraw their data if they feel they have been misused or their rights abused in any way.

All universities and research institutes have committees that review every proposal for psychological, or medical, research before allowing the work to begin. Generally, if the review committee feels that an experiment involves some potential risk, the proposal will be approved only if the benefits of the research (to the subjects themselves and/or to scientific knowledge in general) outweigh those risks. In potentially "risky" experiments, the review committee may impose constraints, insist on monitoring initial demonstrations of the procedure, or deny approval (Steininger et al., 1984). Concerns for the well-being of animals used in psychological research have focused on ensuring acceptable living conditions, minimizing painful experiences, and treating them with respect during their participation, as well as providing appropriate care afterward. Because experimentation with animal and human subjects is essential for the development of psychological knowledge and its practical applications in our lives, researchers have become increasingly sensitive to the importance of establishing and maintaining ethical safeguards for both animals and humans.

Rats are often used for experiments because the experimental variables are easy to control and the genetic history of rats is known.

Conducting Research

Psychological research is carried out in a variety of different ways and in different settings. Some research is conducted in laboratories under highly controlled (and often artificial) conditions where a researcher systematically changes the stimulus variables and limits the responses that are possible. Other research is conducted in the "field," which is any setting outside a laboratory where there is ongoing, naturally occurring behavior. Whether in a laboratory or the field, all psychology studies involve the measurement of behavior. The types of procedures to make these measurements and the kinds of circumstances under which they are made will be discussed in this section.

Measuring Behavior

Although all psychological researchers are interested in behavior, the *kind* of behavior each is curious about may vary dramatically. For example, consider the differences among a motor behavior (such as a rat running a maze or a child drawing a picture), a cognitive behavior (such as someone memorizing a poem), and a physiological behavior (such as brain activity during dreaming). There are verbal behaviors (spoken or written language) and nonverbal ones (facial expressions or body movements). Some behaviors operate within a person's consciousness, while others operate outside of conscious control.

This variety and complexity of behavior pose major challenges to researchers who want to measure it. The first challenge is how to get access to the behavior of interest. Although some behaviors can be seen easily, many cannot. Thus, the task for a psychological researcher is to make the unseen visible, to make internal events and processes external, and to make private experiences public. Many methods are available to do this, and each of them has its particular advantages and disadvantages. We will consider three major methods of measurement—observations, verbal reports, and psychological tests.

Observational Methods

One of the primary ways in which to learn about others is to look at what they do. Researchers use observation as a scientific tool to learn about behavior, but they use it in a planned, precise, and systematic manner. They use observational techniques to measure behavior as it occurs.

A **direct observation** is one that can be made with "the naked eye." The behavior under investigation is clearly visible and overt, and can be easily recorded in writing or on videotape. For example, in a study of communication patterns, researchers might ask a group of subjects to discuss a controversial issue and then make direct observations of who started the discussion, who changed topics, who said nothing, and so forth. In a laboratory experiment on emotions, a researcher could observe subjects' facial expressions as they looked at emotionally arousing stimuli.

Observing some naturally occurring behavior with no attempt to change or interfere with it is called a **naturalistic observation.** For example, a researcher might sit behind a one-way glass and observe preschoolers at play without their awareness of being monitored. From the observations of each child's interaction patterns, the researcher might make inferences about popularity or social isolation. The *Opening Case* in chapter 1 describing Imo's sweet-potato washing was a field study carried out using naturalistic observation.

By standing behind a one-way mirror a researcher can watch a child at play and record his observations without influencing or interfering with the child's behavior.

Some kinds of human behavior can be studied only through naturalistic observation, because it would be unethical or impractical to tamper with the situations. For example, it would be unethical to experiment with the effects of severe deprivation in early life on a child's later development. Naturalistic observation is especially useful in the early stages of an investigation to discover the extent of some phenomenon or to get an idea of what the important variables and relationships might be. The data from naturalistic observation often provide clues so that an investigator can formulate a specific hypothesis to be tested by other research methods.

As opposed to direct, "naked eye" observations, **mediated observations** require the use of special equipment or instrumentation. Such equipment allows more precise measurement of an observed behavior. Suppose researchers wanted to see how quickly subjects can respond to a signal light. Although they can observe this behavior directly, they might not be able to detect small variations in speed. Therefore they might use stopwatches or computer-controlled timing devices to measure the behavior more precisely.

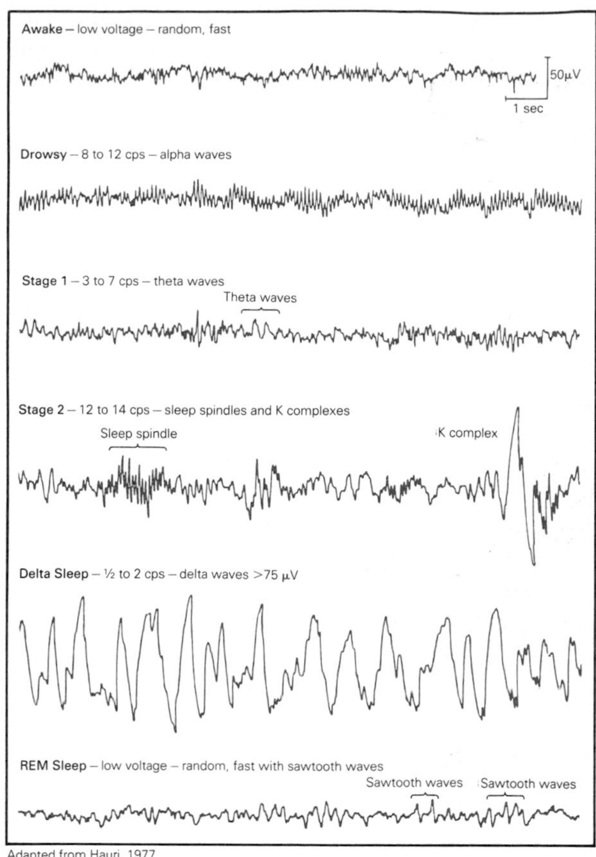

Adapted from Hauri, 1977

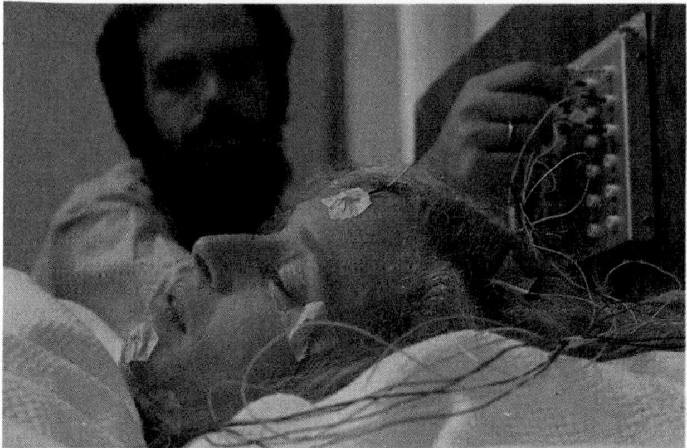
Subjects in sleep labs provide scientists with information about humans during sleep. By connecting the subjects to EEG machines, scientists can study the activity of the brain during sleep.

In addition to precise measurement, instrumentation can also help researchers to observe processes or events that are not visible to the naked eye. Just as you need microscopes to see the structure of a cell, or telescopes to see the characteristics of a planet, so psychological researchers need special instruments to see what is going on in the brain and body of an individual. For example, by using the technology of the *electroencephalogram* (EEG), researchers can record patterns of brain-wave activity and study how these patterns vary when subjects are awake, asleep, or dreaming. They can also observe the activity of the brain by using instruments that record the electrical activity in a single brain cell.

While some observations focus on the *process* of behavior, others focus on the *product* of behavior. In an experiment on learning, for instance, a researcher might observe how many times a subject rehearsed a list of words (process) and then how many words were remembered correctly on a final test (product). In some cases, researchers observe behavioral products that were generated in the past, rather than in the present, or that were generated for purposes other than research. Statistical records, such as census data, permit observations of family life, health, and job history. Personal documents (such as autobiographies, letters, and speeches) and materials in the mass media (such as television programs and newspaper reports) yield other information.

Verbal Reports

Sometimes researchers are interested in what people think and feel, as well as in what they do. They might want information about behaviors that are very difficult or impossible to observe (such as sexual activities or criminal acts). In these cases, investigations turn to the measurement technique of **verbal reports.** They ask their subjects a set of questions requiring verbal answers (either written or oral). Sometimes these answers are taken at face value, as in the case of opinion surveys; sometimes they are interpreted in terms of other information known about the subjects: nonverbal behavior such as fidgeting or giggling during clinical interviews or comparison of their subjects to others, as determined by the **norms,** or group averages, on tests given to many others.

Verbal reports are the primary, if not the only, method for getting information about subjects' beliefs, attitudes, feelings, motives, and personality. However, sometimes there can be problems with the validity of this technique. That is, verbal reports may not always be accurate and truthful. Subjects may give false or misleading answers for a variety of reasons—they may find it embarrassing to report their true feelings, they may want to "look good" and impress a researcher, they may not remember clearly what they actually did in the past, or they may misunderstand the questions. Thus, researchers make special efforts to ensure that the verbal reports they collect are indeed valid measures of the phenomena they are studying.

A **questionnaire** is simply a written set of questions, ranging in content from questions of fact (are you a registered voter?) to questions about past or present behavior (how much do you smoke?) to questions about attitudes and feelings (how satisfied are you with your present job?). The way in which questions are answered depends on how they are asked. *Fixed-alternative* questions provide a limited set of alternative answers, and the subject picks the one that best represents his or her own position. The alternatives might be yes or no, a 7-point scale from "strongly agree" to "strongly disagree," or a set of choices. In contrast, *open-ended* questions do not provide such limited alternatives, but simply ask subjects to answer freely in their own words. An example of an open-ended question is, "What do you like most about yourself?"

A questionnaire is used in an experiment to assess how subjects feel about participating, what their perceptions are of the other subjects or of the experimenter, and how they evaluate themselves. It can also be used in survey research, a way to efficiently gather information from a large number of people. In a **survey** a standardized set of questions is given to a number of subjects, either by mail or by having interviewers ask questions, face-to-face or by telephone. A *sample survey* collects information from a carefully selected group of people who are presumed to represent the entire population. (An example of a sample survey is a public opinion poll—its conclusions about "national opinions" are often based on a sample of about 1500 people.) There is always the risk of some error in sampling a population, however, and most polls carry a standard warning label about the margins for error (typically 3 percent).

An **interview** is a face-to-face dialogue between a researcher and an individual in order to obtain detailed information. Instead of being completely standardized, as a questionnaire is, an interview is interactive. An interviewer varies the questioning to follow up on what the individual says and is sensitive to the process of the interaction as well as to the information revealed. Good interviewers are able to establish *rapport,* a positive social relationship with the interviewee that encourages trust and sharing of personal information.

Psychological Tests

A **psychological test** is a measuring instrument used to assess an individual's standing, relative to others, on some mental or behavioral characteristic, such as intelligence, personality, vocational interests, aptitudes, or scholastic achievement. Each test consists of a set of questions, problems, or activities, the responses to which are assumed to be indicators of a particular psychological function. The use of group tests permits information to be obtained quickly from large numbers of people without the cost of trained individuals to administer the tests.

An interview is a face-to-face dialog between a researcher and an individual for the purpose of obtaining detailed information about the individual.

Typically, test performance is used to predict how a person will probably behave in a particular later situation. For example, your SAT scores were used as predictors of your grades in college (the decision about your admission to college relied, in part, on such predictions). Because psychological tests for measures of intelligence, personality, and vocational interest are so widely used in our society, we will study in chapter 13 how they are constructed, used, and, at times, abused.

Research Designs

The conditions under which an investigator measures behavior are critical parts of any research study. These conditions, known as the **research design,** determine what sorts of relationships can be studied and what sorts of conclusions can be drawn. There are several major types of research designs.

The Controlled Experiment

The observation of the silent turkey chick being killed by its mother, as described in the *Opening Case* in chapter 1, was an example of naturalistic observation, but when the presence or absence of the cheep-cheep sound was systematically varied, it became an experiment. The investigator intervened and changed the stimulus conditions instead of just recording what was happening naturally.

A **controlled experiment,** the cornerstone of scientific psychology, is a research method in which observations of specific behavior are made under systematically varied conditions. An investigator manipulates one or more stimulus variables and observes their effects on one or more behaviors. A controlled experiment permits a psychologist to test a hypothesis about the relationship between two or more variables and whether this relationship is one of cause and effect.

In the simplest experiment, the form or amount of one stimulus variable is changed systematically under carefully controlled, often quite restrictive, conditions, and a response variable is observed to see if it changes. The stimulus that is varied and used to predict the response is called the **independent variable.** The response, the unit of behavior whose form or amount is expected to *depend* on the changes in the independent variable, is called the **dependent variable.** In the turkey experiment, the stimulus of the cheeping was the independent variable; Tina's maternal or aggressive behavior was the dependent variable.

To determine that it is *only* the independent variable, and not other factors, causing the behavioral change, an experimenter attempts to control, or at least account for, the effect of all extraneous conditions. This can be done in three ways: through the use of experimental and control groups, by random assignment, and by using controlled procedures.

The *subjects,* or participants, in an experiment are the individuals whose behavior is being observed. They are assigned to either an **experimental group**—the group exposed to the independent variable—or to a **control group**—the group exposed to all the conditions of the experiment *except* the independent variable. Thus, a control group serves as a *baseline,* or *comparison level,* against which the effect of the independent variable can be assessed. The results of any experiment are always assessed by comparing them to some standard, some prior level of functioning, or to the behavior of those not subjected to the experimental treatment. In some experiments, subjects participate in both the experimental and control groups. In what is known as an *ABA design,* subjects first experience the baseline condition (A), then experience the experimental treatment (B), and then go back to the baseline again (A).

Subjects are assigned to experimental or control groups by a *chance* procedure called **random assignment** (similar to flipping a coin). Each subject has an equal chance of being in either the experimental or the control group. The purpose of random assignment is to make the two groups in the experiment as similar as possible before they are exposed to the independent variable. If behavioral differences are found between them, those differences can be attributed to the presence or absence of the independent variable and not to some other initial difference between the individuals in the two groups. *Randomization* is an essential feature of the experimental method. Without it results are open to alternative interpretations because of existing differences within the subjects rather than to differences produced solely by exposure to the experimental treatment—the independent variable being studied.

Another aspect of control in scientific experiments is the use of **controlled procedures,** methods that attempt to hold constant all variables and conditions other than those related to the hypothesis being tested. Instructions, temperature, time allowed, and how the responses are recorded—all of these need to be as similar for all subjects as possible to ensure that their experience is the same *except for* the difference in the independent variable. An example of a controlled experiment is outlined in the ***Close-up:*** *Aging, Health, and a Sense of Control* (p. 43).

Close-up Aging, Health, and a Sense of Control

It has long been assumed that the health problems accompanying growing old are genetically programmed into the species; but consider an alternate hypothesis—namely, that age-related decline in health is, in part, psychologically determined and not solely biological in origin. Can it, in fact, be shown that environment and psychological factors (psychosocial variables) play a significant role in the health of older people? If so, might biological declines in the elderly even be reversible by psychosocial intervention?

Clues to the likely answers to such questions have been provided by research showing that elderly people who see themselves as having choices about entering retirement homes fare better subsequently than those who see themselves having no choice.

In one carefully documented study of 40 people whose applications were received by a nursing home in Cleveland, Ohio, 23 died within a month of mailing the applications. It turned out that, of those who had died, the vast majority were applicants whose families had applied for them. (Ferrare, 1962)

This result is very provocative, but it is a correlational finding, showing the relation between two classes of responses. In order to demonstrate a *causal* connection between health and a sense of control, it is necessary to manipulate a stimulus condition that affects people's perceptions of their choices and control, and then assess the consequences on their health. Psychologist Judith Rodin (1983) and her colleagues have done just that in an extended series of studies. One of her experiments illustrates the sequence of events in a controlled experiment.

Rodin hypothesized that training which increased subjects' sense of control and reduced their feelings about lack of control would result in a variety of changes in three classes of variables: attitudes, behavior, and health status. Four months before the experimental treatment was to begin, 40 elderly female residents in a nursing home were selected and given extensive interviews covering issues related to perceived control, stress, and personal problems. In addition, behavioral observations were made, blood pressure and urine tests were given, and general ratings of health status were recorded. (None of the patients was acutely ill, and all were able to walk without assistance.)

The subjects were matched by age and length of residence and then randomly assigned to one of three groups: the experimental group, which would receive training; an "attention" control group, which would receive no training but spend the same amount of time with a psychologist just talking about problems of the elderly; and a second control group, which would receive no special attention. The training was the *independent variable;* perceived sense of control, a hypothesized *intervening variable;* and measures of attitudes, behavior, and health, the *dependent variables,* which were expected to change for the experimental group.

The experimental group received two sessions of training for three weeks by psychologists who were unaware of the pretest data. The training procedure taught these elderly patients to minimize negative self-statements and use positive self-statements. They were also given training in ways to be more active contributors to their

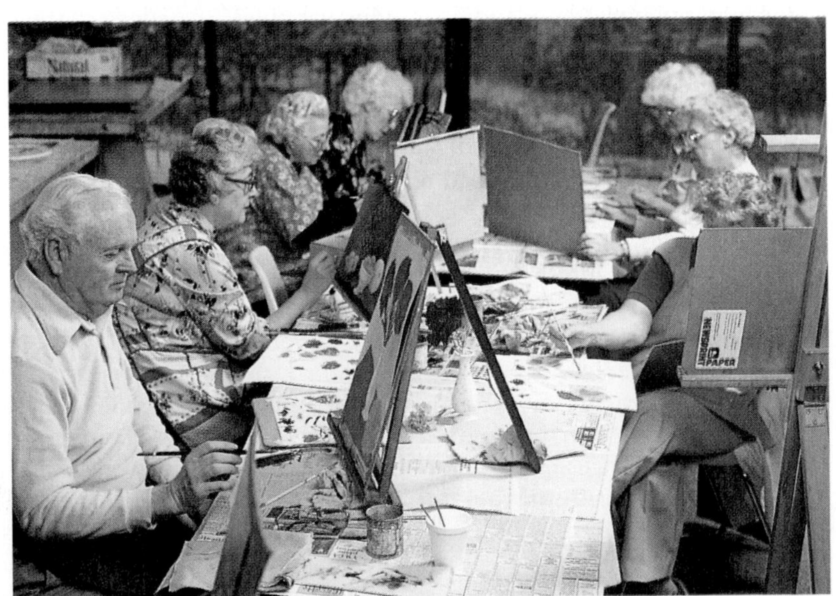

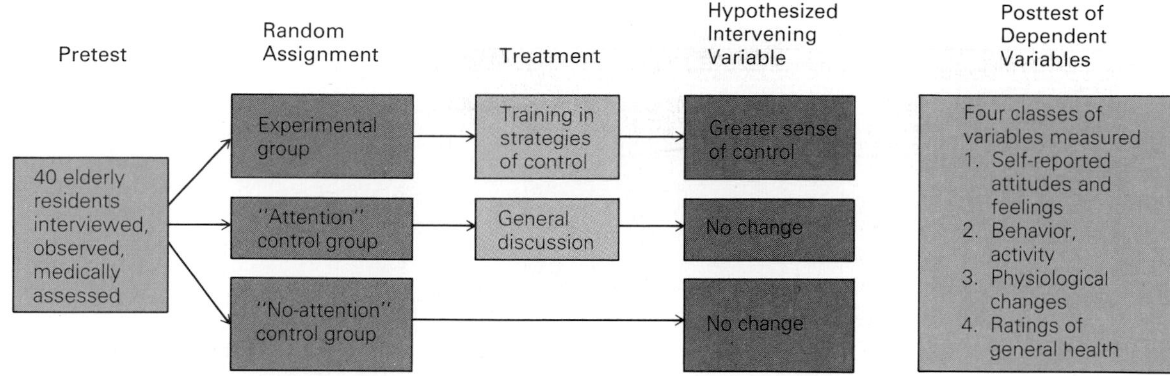

own experiences and in ways to solve problems about potential health hazards. It was hypothesized that this training would affect the intervening variable, *sense of control.*

One month after the experimental period, the pretest procedures were repeated as a posttest. An estimate of stresses that had occurred naturally in the residential setting was also made. As predicted, the women in the experimental group, on the average, were better able to deal with stresses in their environment and better able to modify conditions that gave rise to problems. They participated more in activities, were happier, more social, and more energetic, feeling that they had more freedom to effect change and determine relevant outcomes in their environment. Levels of stress-related hormones in the urine were also significantly reduced, and the general health patterns of the women in the experimental group were shown to be improved. On several of the posttest measures, the attention control group were slightly better than the no-attention control group, but the differences were not statistically significant. On measures taken 18 months later, the improvement of the experimental group had continued.

Some experiments include more than one independent variable, because there are usually many factors that can influence a complex behavior. Suppose a researcher wanted to know whether different learning strategies would lead to improved memory. One of the independent variables might be a strategy for learning a list of words: half the subjects would simply memorize the words (rote learning) and half would make up a story that included all the words (story chain). The second independent variable might be the time at which subjects were asked to remember the words: some subjects would be asked to recall the words immediately after learning them (immediate recall) and some would be asked sometime later (delayed recall). Such an experiment has a 2 x 2 design (two levels of one independent variable and two levels of a second one), as represented in **Figure 2.2A** on the next page. Thus, there are four experimental groups, and each subject is randomly assigned to one of them: rote with immediate recall; rote with delayed recall; story with immediate recall; and story with delayed recall. The dependent variable is, of course, recall of the word lists.

A. 2 × 2 Design for Hypothetical Memory Study

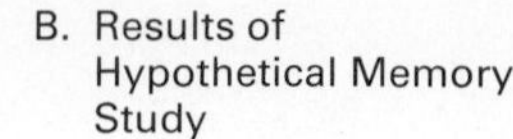

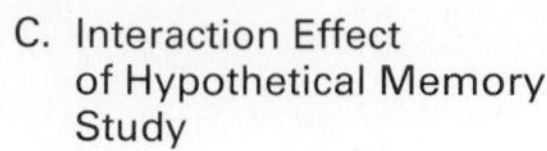

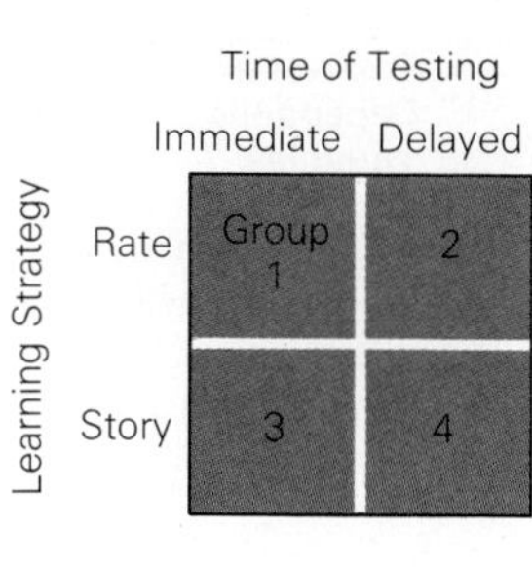

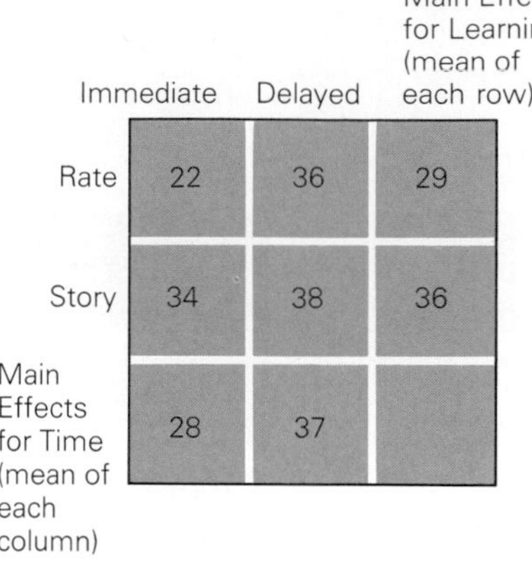

Main Effects for Learning (mean of each row)
Immediate
Delayed
Rate
22
36
29
Story
34
38
36
Main Effects for Time (mean of each column)
28
37

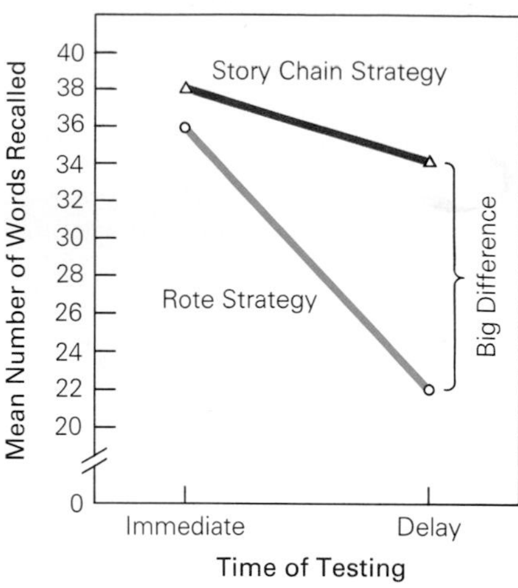

Figure 2.2 *2 x 2 Design, Main Effects, and Interaction Effect*
In the hypothetical study, subjects were given a list of 50 words to learn. Subjects in one group learned the words by rote memorization; subjects in the other group used the words to create a story chain.
Figure 2.2A indicates the design of the experiment; there are two levels for each of the two independent variables. The numbers in Figure 2.2B are the numbers of words recalled in each condition: rote + delayed, rote + immediate, story chain + delayed, and story chain + immediate. Memory is better for immediate recall than delayed recall and is better for story chains than rote learned items. These are the main effects. The figure shows the main effects for both the time variable and the learning strategy variable. Figure 2.2C is a graph showing the interaction effect. As clearly indicated on the graph, there was little difference between the two learning strategies when recall was measured immediately; however, when delayed, recall was far superior for the story chain strategy than for the rote strategy. The interaction specifies that the effectiveness of the learning strategy on memory depends *upon when the recall is measured.*

With this type of research design, a researcher can study not only the effects of each one of the independent variables, but also how they influence each other. If one independent variable has an effect on the dependent variable, regardless of the other independent variable, it is called a **main effect** (see **Figure 2.2B**). Thus, if subjects' recall is always better when it is immediate than when it is delayed, regardless of the learning strategy, then there is a main effect for the time-of-recall variable.

Sometimes, however, the effect of one independent variable depends on that of a second independent variable. This joint effect is called an **interaction.** In the memory experiment an interaction would exist if the rote memorization subjects showed better recall when it was immediate than when it was delayed, but the story chain subjects showed the same level of recall under both time conditions (see **Figure 2.2C**).

Subjects in the memory experiment experienced only one level of each independent variable—for example, they recalled the words either immediately *or* later, but not both. When comparisons are made between subjects in one condition (immediate recall) and subjects in the other (delayed recall), the independent variable is called a *between-subjects variable.* However, in some experiments subjects experience *all* levels of a particular independent variable. The memory experiment could be changed so that all subjects would be tested twice—immediately and later. The effect of the independent variable would then be measured *within* each subject, by comparing each subject's immediate recall with his or her own delayed recall. Such an independent variable is called a *within-subjects variable.*

After the manipulation of the independent variable has taken place, the dependent variable is measured. Although some experiments have just one measurement of the dependent variable, others have multiple measurements. In *pre-post designs,* the dependent variable is measured both before and after the occurrence of the independent variable. This allows a researcher to assess the amount of change that has occurred. For example, a researcher can assess the effectiveness of a persuasive communication, such as a political speech, by measuring people's attitudes both before and after they hear it. In *repeated-measure designs,* the dependent variable is measured several times after the manipulation of the independent variable, often as a way of assessing the effectiveness of the independent variable over some period of time.

Correlational Studies

It is not always possible to perform experiments to test hypotheses. Sometimes the phenomenon is too broad to be reduced to specific variables that can be manipulated by an experimenter, as in mob behavior or the cumulative effect of excessive environmental stimulation. It also may not be possible to manipulate the independent variable for practical reasons—for example, in studies of the effects of being in love or of being divorced. Finally, there are ethical reasons for not doing controlled experiments, as in the study of heredity in humans or reactions to extreme stress. To study such phenomena, investigators utilize other types of research designs.

The primary alternative design is the **correlational study,** which assesses the degree of relationship between variables. For example, a researcher might measure how much stress subjects are experiencing in their lives and how well they are performing at work. The researcher could then see if there is a relationship (a correlation) between stress and job performance, and, if so, how strong that relationship is. The researcher would *not* be able to establish what is cause and what is effect in such a relationship; as we said earlier in this chapter, *correlation does not prove causation.* The correlation could reflect any one of several cause-and-effect possibilities.

Suppose the researcher finds a correlation between stress and job performance: as stress increases, job performance deteriorates. One possibility is that stress causes people to do poorly at work. Another possibility is that people experience stress when they have difficulty handling their jobs. A third possibility is that a *third* variable is actually causing the other two. It may be that people with a certain personality style are more likely to experience stress *and* to perform poorly on the job.

Suppose research finds that, in classes where teachers ask questions to stimulate abstract thinking, students get higher scores on standardized tests than in classes where teachers ask questions requiring only rote recall. Should all teachers be encouraged to use abstract-type questions? What if the results were because students in the first classes *started out* scoring higher on exams, or that teachers with less-gifted students used recall instead of other kinds of questions?

Where there is no control over who gets exposed to an independent variable, and it is not systematically varied across subjects who are randomly assigned to experimental and control groups, we face the chicken-and-egg problem. "The trouble with correlational studies like these," concludes prominent educational psychologist Nathan Gage, "is that you wind up with a question of which came first, the chicken or the egg." He notes that the way out of this predicament lies not in studying the situation as it is, but in doing the proper experiment (Gage, 1986).

Correlations may also be *spurious,* biased or false, because the data are collected in a way that allows for a selection of cases in one part of the relationship to affect the data in the other part. For example Arizona and Florida have the highest incidence of respiratory illness and arthritis, not because of something in their atmospheres that is illness-producing, but because their populations include great numbers of elderly. Another example of a spurious correlation comes from recent research showing a *lower* cure rate for addicts who have had psychotherapy than for those who have not (Schachter, 1982). Is psychotherapy bad or ineffective, or is it that those addicts choosing to enter therapy are much worse off to begin with than the comparison group? (See Stanovich, 1986, for an excellent and detailed treatment of these and related issues.) Thus, although correlational studies have the advantage of being able to establish relationships between variables that cannot be manipulated in experiments, the interpretation of these relationships has to be done with caution.

Case Studies

A scientific biography of a selected individual is called a **case study.** It is a way to capture the richness and uniqueness of a human personality. The data may come from many sources, such as a person's own recollections, the researcher's observations, interviews with others who know the person, and any available information from psychological tests. This research design is often used with mentally ill patients by clinical psychologists interested in understanding abnormal behavior. We shall see in later chapters that it was the primary method used by Sigmund Freud. However, it has also been used to study the life cycle of normal individuals (see the classic case studies done by Robert White in *Lives in Progress,* 1966).

Longitudinal Studies

Many behaviors change with age. One way of studying these changes is through a **longitudinal study,** in which a researcher observes selected responses of the same individual at two or more different times in his or her lifetime. Some longitudinal studies have followed people's development over many years. Notable is the research of Lewis Terman, begun soon after World War I on subjects who were classified as geniuses when they were children. These subjects were followed systematically throughout their adult lives; some of the findings will be discussed in the next chapter.

Archival Research

Sometimes psychologists collect information by analyzing existing data or investigating products of behavior that were made at some time in the past. **Archival research** is the use of previously published findings or of data about behavioral processes or psychological environments gathered from books, documents, and other records or cultural artifacts. For example, in one archival study, the frequency of achievement-oriented themes in children's literature was assessed in different historical time periods. Relationships were then found between those themes and indicators of economic achievement in the society thirty years later (De Charms & Moeller, 1962).

Other Research Approaches

All of these research designs can be used, alone or together, to study a variety of researchable issues. Two broad and socially significant issues they are used to investigate are (a) the universality or cultural specificity of various behavioral patterns, and (b) the evaluation of the effectiveness of a given intervention in therapy, business, or government.

Cross-cultural research is used to discover whether some behavior found in one culture also occurs in other cultures. In cross-cultural research the unit of analysis is a whole culture or society rather than an individual, although the data are observations of individual reactions (Brislin, 1981). The cross-cultural method has been used to compare diverse sexual patterns, perceptual differences in reactions to illusions, and cultural factors that influence productivity (Hofstede, 1980). In one study, the researcher tested his hypothesis about the relationship between societal life-styles and conformity by comparing people from a hunting society (the Eskimos) with those from an agricultural society (the Temne, in Africa). There was more conformity on a standardized test in the agricultural society, where people had to learn to cooperate and depend on each other for their food, and less conformity in the hunting society, where food-gathering was done on one's own and required independence and self-reliance (Berry, 1967).

"We plan to determine, once and for all, if there really ARE any cultural differences between them."

An important new type of research in psychology, called **evaluation research,** judges the efficiency and cost-effectiveness of particular social programs or types of therapy. Do particular laws, regulations, or personnel practices have the hoped-for results? Are the benefits worth the costs, both financially and psychologically? How might a program be changed to function more effectively? Research results can be stated in terms of cost-effectiveness—how much a program costs in money and effort to produce a particular outcome (Kosecoff & Fink, 1982; Yates, 1980). A large-scale study that has compared the results of several alternative methods of treating clinically depressed patients will be described, in detail, in chapter 16 on therapy.

Why so many different types of research designs, you ask? Why so much concern for research methodology, you wonder? Two answers can be mentioned now and given substance later when you learn more about the field of psychology. The first is that the enormous variety of issues, topics, and kinds of organisms studied by psychologists requires multiple approaches to unravel their separate mysteries. Secondly, the complexity of the object of our study—an active, reflective, thinking, feeling, ever changing organism—poses unique challenges for a researcher seeking to analyze the processes that shape behavior and direct mental functioning. Unlike the stability and invariance of phenomena that are studied in natural science, the phenomena of psychology are more influenced by subtle, shifting, distorting factors. Sometimes they yield their secrets to improved technology for observing and measuring them, but often the key is found in better ways of understanding *how* to see them clearly, distinct from the background concealing them or from the filters of our expectations.

Analyzing the Data

Whatever the research design, and whatever the measures used, the outcome of a research study is always the same: a set of data. For most researchers in psychology, analyzing the data is an exciting step. They can find out if their results will contribute to a better understanding of a particular aspect of behavior or if they have to go "back to the drawing board" and redesign their research. In short, they can discover if their studies have worked.

Data analysis can involve many different procedures, some of them surprisingly simple and straightforward. In this section you will be led gently, step-by-step, through an analysis of some of the data from a study about "sudden murderers"—people like Fred Cowan, the man described in our *Opening Case.* If you have looked ahead, and if you are like many other students, you may have been "turned off" by the sight of numbers and equations. Your apprehension is understandable. In fact, many psychological researchers began their careers as dyed-in-the-wool math-haters. But try to keep this thought in mind: You do not need to be good in math to be able to understand the concepts we will be discussing. You just need the courage to see mathematical symbols for what they are—a shorthand way of conveniently representing simple ideas and arithmetic operations.

The raw data gathered from the 19 inmates in the "Sudden Murderers" investigation are listed in **Table 2.2.** The raw data are the actual scores or other measures obtained. As you can see, there were 10 inmates in the "Sudden Murderers" group and 9 in the "Habitual Criminal Murderers" group. When first glancing at these data, any researcher

Table 2.2 *Raw Data from the Sudden Murderers Study*

		BSRI	MMPI
Inmate	**Shyness**	**Femininity – Masculinity**	**Ego-overcontrol**
		Group 1—Sudden Murderers	
1	yes	+5	17
2	no	−1	17
3	yes	+4	13
4	yes	+61	17
5	yes	+19	13
6	yes	+41	19
7	no	−29	14
8	yes	+23	9
9	yes	−13	11
10	yes	+5	14
		Group 2—Habitual Criminal Murderers	
11	no	−12	15
12	no	−14	11
13	yes	−33	14
14	no	−8	10
15	no	−7	16
16	no	+3	11
17	no	−17	6
18	no	+6	9
19	no	−10	12

would feel what you probably feel—confusion. What do all these scores mean? Do the two groups of murderers differ from one another on these various personality measures? It is difficult to say. To help them make sense of the data they collect so that they can draw meaningful conclusions, psychologists rely on a mathematical tool called statistics. **Statistics** help us to describe what has been found in an objective, uniform way. They also enable us to go further by providing a sound standard (based on probability theory) for inferring if the obtained results are real or only because of chance.

Descriptive Statistics

Descriptive statistics provide a summary picture of patterns in the data. They are used to describe sets of scores collected from different groups of subjects and to describe relationships among variables. Thus, instead of trying to keep in mind all the scores obtained by subjects, researchers get special indexes of *the scores that are most typical* for each group and the way they are typical—whether they are spread out or clustered closely together. The pattern is important.

An updated sudden-murderer case, reported in the *New York Times* on August 22, 1986, began much the way that Fred Cowan's did. "To friends and neighbors, Patrolman Stephen Richard Smith seemed a polite, shy man with a taste for classical music, who liked to feed stray cats. Now that the 31-year-old officer is dead by the hand of his best friend and former patrol partner, the authorities say he may have been a brutal vigilante who had murdered or beaten several people. . . ." (Reinhold, 1986).

Is there a link between shyness, other personal characteristics, and violent behavior? A group of researchers thought that there might be and collected a set of data to analyze that relationship.

The researchers hypothesized that sudden murderers as a group had been typically shy, nonaggressive people who kept their passions and impulses in check. For most of their lives, they suffered many silent injuries—seldom, if ever, expressing anger no matter how angry they really felt. On the outside, they appeared unbothered, but on the inside they may have been fighting to control furious rages. Then, something exploded. At the slightest provocation—or with no apparent provocation at all—they released the stifled violence that had been building up for so long.

To test this idea about sudden murderers, the researchers obtained permission to administer psychological questionnaires to a group of prison inmates serving time for murder. Nineteen inmates (all male) agreed to participate in the study. Some had committed a series of crimes, while others had no criminal record prior to their first, sudden murder. All participants filled out three different questionnaires. The first was the Stanford Shyness Survey. The most important item on this questionnaire asked if the subject was shy; the answer was a simple yes or no.

The second questionnaire was the Bem Sex-Role Inventory (BSRI), which presented a list of adjectives, (such as aggressive *and* affectionate*) and asked how well each adjective described the subject (Bem, 1974, 1981). Some adjectives were typically thought of as "feminine," and the total score of these adjectives was a subject's femininity score. Other adjectives were considered "masculine," and the total score of those adjectives was a subject's masculinity score. The final sex-role score, which reflected the difference between a subject's femininity and masculinity, was calculated by subtracting the masculinity score from the femininity score.*

The third questionnaire was the Minnesota Multiphasic Personality Inventory (MMPI), which was designed to measure many different aspects of personality (see chapter 13). The researchers were most interested in the "Ego-Overcontrol" scale, which measured the degree to which a person acted out or controlled impulses. The higher the subject's score on this scale, the more ego-overcontrol the subject exhibited. It was predicted that, compared to murderers with a prior criminal record, sudden murderers: (a) would more often describe themselves as shy on the shyness survey; (b) would check more feminine traits than masculine ones on the sex-role scale; and (c) would be higher in "ego-overcontrol," as measured by the personality inventory.

Each of these predicted results was found. Among the general American population, 40 percent describe themselves as shy; 8 out of 10 of the sudden murderers (80 percent) described themselves as shy, while only 1 in 9 of the habitual-criminal murderers (11 percent) did so. On the sex-role scale, 70 percent of the sudden murderers chose adjectives that were more feminine than masculine, while only 22 percent of the habitual criminals said that the feminine adjectives described them more accurately than did the masculine ones. Finally, sudden murderers were higher in overcontrol of impulses than were habitual criminal murderers. (Lee et al, 1977)

Frequency Distributions

The shyness data are easy to summarize. Of the 19 scores, there are 9 yes and 10 no responses, with almost all the yes responses in group 1 and almost all the no responses in group 2. For the overcontrol scale, the scores range from 6 to 19, and it is harder to get a feel for how the groups compare by just looking at the numbers.

Now let's examine the sex-role scores, which reflect the difference in each inmate's ratings between his femininity and his masculinity. These scores range from +61 to −33. Of the 19 scores, 9 are positive and 10 negative. This means that 9 of the murderers described themselves as more feminine, 10 as more masculine.

To get a clearer picture of how these scores are distributed, we can draw up a **frequency distribution**—a summary of how frequent each of the various scores is. The first step in preparing a frequency distribution for a set of numerical data is to *rank order* the scores from highest to lowest. The rank ordering for the sex-role scores is shown in **Table 2.3.**

The second step is to put these rank-ordered scores into a smaller number of categories, called *intervals.* For this example, 10 categories were used, with each category covering 10 possible scores.

The third step is to construct a frequency distribution table, listing the intervals from highest to lowest and noting the *frequencies*—the number of scores within each interval. Our frequency distribution shows us that the sex-role scores are largely between −20 and +9 (see **Table 2.4**). For the most part, the inmates' scores did not deviate much from zero—that is, they were not strongly positive or strongly negative.

Table 2.3 *Rank Ordering of Sex-Role Difference Scores*

Highest +61	
+41	−7
+23	−8
+19	−10
+6	−12
+5	−13
+5	−14
+4	−17
+3	−29
−1	−33 Lowest

Table 2.4 *A Frequency Distribution of Sex-Role Difference Scores*

Category	Frequency
+60 to +69	1
+50 to +59	0
+40 to +49	1
+30 to +39	0
+20 to +29	1
+10 to +19	1
+0 to +9	5
−10 to −1	4
−20 to −11	4
−30 to −21	1
−40 to −31	1

Distributions are often easier to understand when they are displayed in graphs. The simplest type of graph is a *bar graph.* We can use a bar graph to illustrate how many more sudden murderers than habitual-criminal murderers described themselves as shy (see **Figure 2.3**). For more complex data, such as the sex-role scores, we can use a *histogram,* which is similar to a bar graph except that the bars touch each other and the categories are intervals—number categories instead of the name categories used in the bar graph. A histogram is a graph that gives a visual picture of the number of scores in a distribution that are in each interval. The histogram shown gives the sex-role scores (see **Figure 2.4**). It is even easier to see from the histogram than from the frequency distribution that most scores cluster between −20 and +9 and that there are only a few extremely positive scores.

Figure 2.3 *A Bar Graph Comparing Shyness for Two Groups of Murderers*

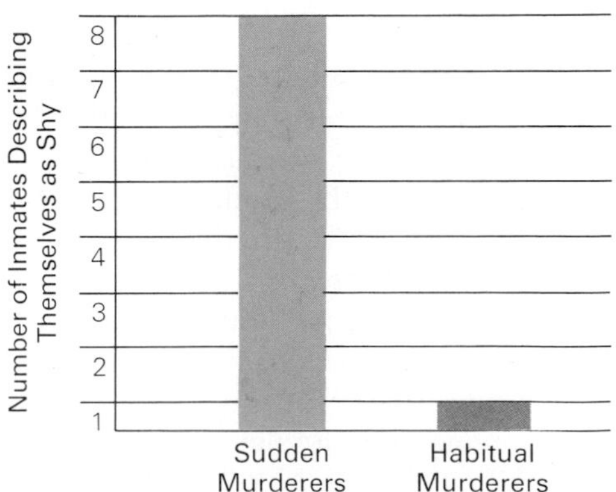

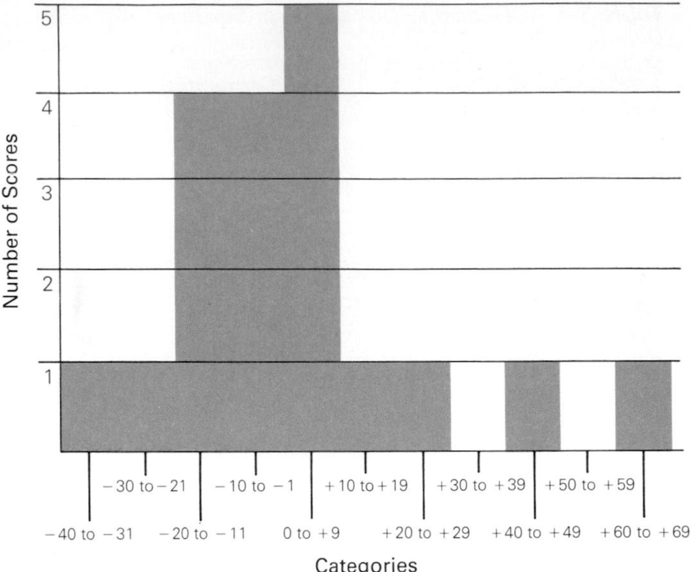

Figure 2.4 *A Histogram of Sex-Role Scores*

Central Tendency

What we have done so far has given us a general picture of how the scores are *distributed.* Tables and graphs increase our general understanding of research results, but we want to know more, such as the one score that is most typical of the group as a whole. This score becomes particularly useful when we want to compare two or more groups; it is much easier to compare the typical scores of two groups than their entire distributions. A single, *representative* score that can be used as an index of the most typical score obtained by a group of subjects is called *a measure of central tendency.* (It is in the center of the distribution, and other scores tend to cluster around it.) Actually, psychologists use three different measures of central tendency: the *mode,* the *median,* and the *mean.*

The **mode** is that score which occurs more often than any other. For the measure of shyness, the modal response of the sudden murderers was yes: 8 out of 10 said they were shy. Among habitual-criminal murderers, the modal response was no. The sex-role scores for the sudden murderers have a mode of +5. Can you figure out what the mode of their overcontrol scores is?

The mode is the easiest index of central tendency to determine, but it is often the least useful. You can see one reason for this if you notice that only one overcontrol score lies above the mode of 17, while six lie below it. Although 17 is the score obtained most often, it may not fit your idea of "typical" or "central."

The **median** is more clearly a central score; it separates the upper half of the scores in a distribution from the lower half. The number of scores larger than the median is the same as the number which are smaller. If you will rank-order the sex-role scores of only the sudden murderers on a separate piece of paper, you will see that the median score is +5 (the same as the mode). Four scores are higher than +5 and four scores are lower. Similarly, the median overcontrol score for these subjects is 15, with four scores below it and four above it.

The median is not affected by extreme scores. For example, even if the highest sex-role score had been +129 instead of +61, the median value would still have been +5. That score would still separate the upper half of the data from the lower half.

The **mean** is what most people think of when they hear the word *average.* It is also the statistic most often used to describe a set of data. To calculate the mean, you simply add up all of the scores in a distribution and divide by the total number of scores. The operation is summarized by the following formula:

$$M = \frac{\Sigma X}{N}$$

In this formula, M stands for the mean, X stands for each individual score, and the symbol Σ (the Greek letter *sigma,* used as a summation sign) means *sum all.* N, the number you divide the sum of all the scores by, is the total number of scores. So the mean of the sex-role scores obtained by the sudden murderers would be calculated as follows:

$$M = \frac{\Sigma X}{N} = \frac{115}{10} = 11.5.$$

Try to calculate their mean overcontrol scores yourself. You should come up with a mean of 14.4.

Unlike the median, the mean *is* affected by the precise values of all scores in the distribution. Changing the value of an extreme score *does* change the value of the mean. For example, if the sex-role score of inmate 4 were +101 instead of +61, the mean for the whole group would increase from 11.5 to 15.5. The pattern of mean scores in a research study is often easier to understand when it is displayed in an x–y graph, such as the one in Figure 2.1, on p. 36.

Variability

In addition to knowing which score is most representative of the distribution as a whole, it is useful to know *how* representative that measure of central tendency really is, to know whether most of the other scores are fairly close to it or if they are widely spread out. *Measures of variability* tell us how close together the scores in a distribution are.

Can you see why measures of variability are important? An example may help. Suppose you are a teacher of young children. It is the beginning of the school year, and you will be teaching reading to a group of 30 second-graders. Knowing that the average child in the class can now read a first-grade reading book will help you to plan your lessons. You could plan better, however, if you knew how *similar* the reading abilities of the 30 children were. Are they all at about the same level (little variability)? If so, then you can plan a fairly standard second-grade lesson. But what if several can read advanced material, while others can barely read at all (high variability)? Now the mean is not so representative, and you will have to plan a variety of lessons to meet the children's differing needs.

The simplest measure of variability is a range, the difference between the highest and the lowest values in a frequency distribution. For the sudden-murderers' sex-role scores, the range is 90 (+61 minus −29). The range of their overcontrol scores is 10 (19 minus 9). To compute the range, you need to know only two of the scores—the highest and the lowest. This is what makes the range so simple to compute, but it is also the reason why psychologists prefer other measures of variability—more sensitive measures that take into account *all* the scores in a distribution, not just the extremes.

One widely used measure is the **standard deviation,** a measure of variability that indicates the *average* difference between the scores and their mean. To figure out the standard deviation of a distribution, you need to know the mean of the distribution and the individual scores. The standard deviation is called *SD,* and the formula for calculating it is

$$SD = \sqrt{\frac{\Sigma(X - M)^2}{N}}.$$

This formula is a bit more complicated than the one used to calculate the mean, but the arithmetic is just as easy. As before, X is a symbol for the individual scores and M represents the mean. The total number of scores is represented by N, and Σ is the summation sign. The phrase $(X - M)$ means "individual score minus the mean" and is commonly called the *deviation score.* The mean is subtracted from each score, and each resulting deviation score is squared (to get rid of negative values). Then the mean of those deviations is calculated by adding: the squared deviations and dividing the sum by the number (N). The symbol $\sqrt{}$ tells you to take the square root of the enclosed value to offset the previous squaring. The standard deviation of the overcontrol scores of the sudden murderers is calculated in **Table 2.5.** Recall that the mean of these scores is 14.4. This, then, is the value that must be subtracted from each score to obtain the corresponding deviation scores.

The standard deviation tells us how variable a set of scores is. The larger the standard deviation, the more spread out the scores are. The standard deviation of the sex-role scores for the sudden murderers is 24.6, but it is only 10.7 for the habitual criminals. This shows that there was less variability in the habitual-criminals group. Their scores clustered more closely about their mean than did those of the sudden murderers. When the standard deviation is small, then the mean is a good representative index of the entire distribution. When the standard deviation is large, more individual scores are different from the mean, and the mean is "less typical" of the whole group.

Table 2.5 *Calculating the Standard Deviation of Sudden-Murderers' Ego-Overcontrol Scores*

Score (X)	**Deviation (score minus mean) (X − M)**	**Deviations Squared (score minus mean)² (X − M)²**
17	2.6	6.76
17	2.6	6.76
13	−1.4	1.96
17	2.6	6.76
13	−1.4	1.96
19	4.6	21.16
14	−.4	.16
9	−5.4	29.16
11	−3.4	11.56
14	−.4	.16
		86.40 = Σ(X − M)²

$$\text{Standard deviation} = SD = \sqrt{\frac{\Sigma(X - M)^2}{N}} = \sqrt{\frac{86.40}{10}} = \sqrt{8.64} = 2.94$$

Correlation

Another useful statistic is the **correlation coefficient,** which indicates the degree of relationship between two variables (such as height and weight, or sex-role score and overcontrol score). It tells us the extent to which scores on one measure are associated with scores on the other. If people with high scores on one variable tend to have high scores on the other variable too, then the correlation coefficient will be "positive" (greater than zero). If, however, most people with high scores on one variable tend to have *low* scores on the other variable, then the correlation will be "negative" (less than zero). If there is *no* consistent relationship between the scores, the correlation will be close to zero.

Correlation coefficients range from +1 (perfect positive correlation) through zero to −1 (perfect negative correlation). The further a coefficient is from zero, in *either* direction, the more closely related the two variables are, positively or negatively. Higher coefficients permit better predictions of one variable, given knowledge of the other.

In the "Sudden Murderers" study, the correlation between the sex-role scores and the overcontrol scores turns out to be +.35. This means that the sex-role scores and the overcontrol scores are positively correlated: in general, subjects seeing themselves as more feminine also tend to be higher in overcontrol. However, the correlation is rather low, compared to the highest possible value, +1.00, so we know that there are many exceptions to this relationship. If we also measured the self-esteem of these inmates and found a correlation of −.68 between sex-role scores and self-esteem, it would mean that there was a negative correlation: the male subjects who saw themselves as more feminine tended to be lower in self-esteem. But it would still be a stronger relationship than the relationship between the sex-role scores and the overcontrol scores, since −.68 is farther from zero than is +.35.

Inferential Statistics

So far, we have used a number of descriptive statistics to characterize the data from the "Sudden Murderers" study; this has helped give us an idea of the overall pattern of results. However, some basic questions remain unanswered. Recall that researchers begin with hypotheses. For our example study, the researchers hypothesized that sudden murderers would be shier, more overcontrolled, and more feminine than habitual-criminal murderers. Descriptive statistics let us compare average responses and variability in the two groups, and it appears that there are some differences between them; but how do we know if the differences are large enough to be meaningful? Are they reliable? If we did this study again with other sudden murderers and other habitual-criminal murderers, would we expect to find the same pattern of results or could these results have been because of chance? If we could somehow measure the entire population we are interested in—*all* sudden murderers and *all* habitual-criminal murderers—would their means and standard deviations be the same as the ones we found for these samples, giving us the same differences between the two groups? **Inferential statistics** are used to answer these kinds of questions. They tell us what inferences we *can* make from our samples about the population from which they were drawn and what conclusions we can legitimately draw from our data.

The Normal Curve

In order to understand how inferential statistics work, we must look first at the special properties of a distribution called the **normal curve.** When data on some variable (height, IQ, or femininity, for example) are collected from a large number of subjects, the numbers obtained often fit a curve roughly like that shown in **Figure 2.5.** Notice that the curve is symmetrical (the left half is a mirror image of the right) and bell-shaped—high in the middle, where most scores are, and lower the farther you get from the mean. This is called a *normal curve,* or *normal distribution.* (A *skewed distribution* is one in which scores cluster toward one end instead of around the middle.)

In a normal curve, the median is the same as the mean, and a specific percentage of the scores can be predicted to fall under different sections of the curve. In the curve shown in Figure 2.5, IQ scores on the Stanford-Binet intelligence test have been plotted. These scores have a mean of 100 and a standard deviation of 16. If you indicate standard deviations as distances from the mean along the baseline, you find that a little over 68 percent of all the scores are between the mean of 100 and one standard deviation above and below—between IQs of 84 and 116. Roughly another 27 percent of the scores are found between the first and second standard deviations above and below the mean (IQs between 68 and 84 and between 116 and 132).

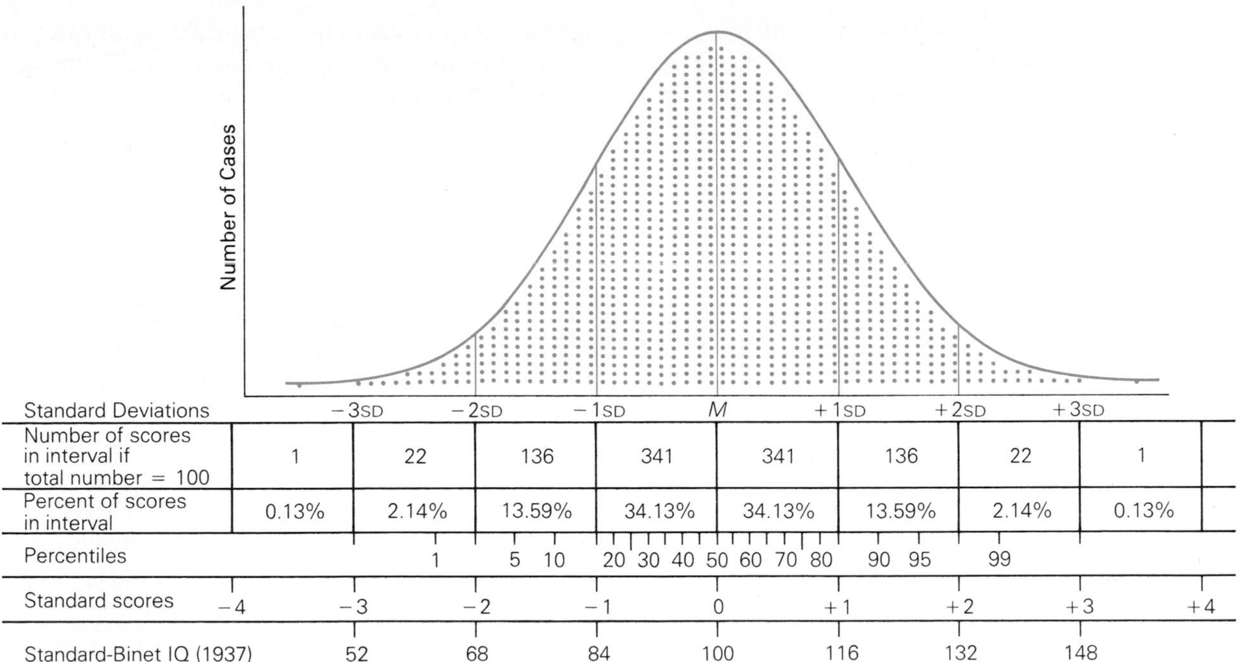

Number of Cases
Standard Deviations
−3SD −2SD −1SD M +1SD +2SD +3SD
Number of scores in interval if total number = 100
1 22 136 341 341 136 22 1
Percent of scores in interval
0.13% 2.14% 13.59% 34.13% 34.13% 13.59% 2.14% 0.13%
Percentiles
1 5 10 20 30 40 50 60 70 80 90 95 99
Standard scores
−4 −3 −2 −1 0 +1 +2 +3 +4
Standard-Binet IQ (1937)
52 68 84 100 116 132 148

Figure 2.5 *A Normal Curve*
The figure shows the distribution of scores that would be expected if 1000 randomly selected persons were measured on IQ or some other continuous trait. Each dot represents an individual's score. The baseline, or horizontal axis, shows the amounts of whatever is being measured; the vertical axis shows how many individuals have each amount of the trait, as represented by their scores. Usually only the resulting curve at the top is shown, since this indicates the frequency with which each measure has occurred. Actual curves only approximate this hypothetical one, but come remarkably close to it with very large samples.

This curve is very useful to psychologists because they know that in a large, randomly selected group, a consistent percentage of the cases will fall in a given segment of the distribution. For example, if the trait is one that is distributed normally, about 68 percent will fall in the middle third of the range of scores, between one standard deviation below and one standard deviation above the mean. Most of the scores in a distribution fall within three standard deviations above the mean and three standard deviations below it (but usually a few scores in an actual distribution will be lower and a few higher).

The distance of the standard deviation from the mean can be indicated along the baseline of the curve, as is done here. Since the standard deviations are equally spaced along the distributions, they are convenient dividing points for classification.

Less than 5 percent of the scores fall in the third standard deviation above and below the mean, and *very* few scores fall beyond—only about a quarter of a percent.

A normal curve is also obtained by collecting a series of measurements whose differences are due only to chance. If you flip a coin 10 times in a row and record the number of heads and tails, you will probably get 5 of each—most of the time. If you keep flipping the coin for 100 sets of 10 tosses, you probably will get a few sets with all heads or no heads, more sets where the number is between these extremes, and, most typically, being about half each way. If you made a graph of your 100 tosses, you would get one that closely fits a normal curve. (Try it.)

Statistical Significance

When a researcher finds a difference between the mean scores for two samples, the question is the following: is it a *real* difference, or is it simply because of chance? Because chance differences have a normal distribution, a researcher can use this normal curve to determine whether the difference found is likely to be a chance one or whether it is a real difference.

A simple example will help to illustrate the point. Suppose the professor in your class randomly varies the color of the paper on which quiz questions are printed. Half the quizzes are printed on white paper and half on pink paper, and the professor compares the mean score of the students using white paper to the mean score of the students using pink. The two mean scores would probably be fairly similar, and any slight difference would most likely be due to chance. Why? Because if only chance is operating and both groups are from the same population (no difference), then the means of pink and white samples should be fairly close most of the time. From the percentages of scores found in different parts of the normal distribution, you know that less than a third of the pink means should be more than a standard deviation above or below the real white mean. The chances of getting a pink mean more than three standard deviations above or below most of your white means would be very small. If the professor *did* get a difference that great, then he or she would feel fairly confident that the difference is a real one and is actually related to paper color.

Psychologists use a statistical inference procedure that gives them an estimate of the probability that an observed difference could have occurred by chance. This computation is based on the size of the difference and the spread of the scores. By common agreement, they accept a difference as "real" when the probability that it might be due to chance is less than 5 in 100 (indicated by the notation $p < .05$). A **significant difference** is one that meets this criterion, though in some cases even stricter ones, $p < .01$ (less than 1 in 100), or $p < .001$ (less than 1 in 1000), are used.

With a statistically significant difference, a researcher can draw a conclusion about the behavior that was under investigation. There are many different types of tests for estimating the statistical significance of sets of data. The one used in a particular case depends upon the design of the study, the form of the data, and the size of the groups. We will only mention one of the most common tests, the *t-test,* which may be used when an investigator wants to know if the difference between the means of two small groups is a statistically significant one.

We can use a *t*-test to see if the mean sex-role score of the sudden murderers is significantly different from that of the habitual-criminal murderers. If we carry out the appropriate calculations, we discover that there is a very slim chance, less than 5 in 100 ($p < .05$) of obtaining such a large t value if no true difference exists. The difference is, therefore, statistically significant, and we can feel confident that there is a real difference between the two groups. The sudden murderers *did* rate themselves as more feminine than did the habitual-criminal murderers. On the other hand, the difference between the two groups of murderers in overcontrol scores turns out *not* to be statistically significant, so we must be more cautious in talking about this difference. There is a *trend* in the predicted direction: the difference is one that would occur by chance only 10 times in 100, but that is not within the standard 5-in-100 range. (The difference in shyness, analyzed using another statistical test for frequency of scores, *is* significant.)

So by using inferential statistics, we are able to answer some of the basic questions with which we began—and we are closer to understanding the psychology of people who suddenly change from their mild-mannered, shy styles to become mass murderers. Any conclusion, however, is only a statement of the *probable* relationship between the events that were investigated, never one of certainty. Truth in science is provisional, always open to revision by later data from better studies, developed from better hypotheses.

Becoming a Wiser Research Consumer

Psychological claims are an unavoidable aspect of the daily life of any thinking, feeling, acting person in our psychologically sophisticated society. Every day you address the same issues psychologists do: you ask questions about your own behavior or that of other people, you seek answers from your theories or observations or what "authorities" say, and you check out the answers against the evidence available to you.

What authorities do you accept? How skeptical are you of reports in the press about what research has supposedly shown? Do you ask whether terms are operationally defined, observations standardized, the right controls present, or sources of bias avoided?

Because psychology is so sensitive to *how* we know something as well as to *what* we know, studying psychology will help you make wiser decisions that rest on evidence gathered either by you or by others. Some of those decisions are the everyday ones about which products to buy or services to use. Others are more substantial—affecting your entire life-style and perhaps even the life of this planet. Why shouldn't you smoke if it gives you pleasure? Should we try to combat the alarming rise in unwanted pregnancies among teenagers by spending more money for educational campaigns? Is it really hopeless to try to rehabilitate prison inmates? Can we reduce the incidence of heart attacks by attempts to change the dietary habits of entire communities? Do "self-help" books really help? Does psychotherapy work? How can the earth be protected from pollution and spared from war?

These and a host of other questions that rely on evidence for their prudent answers are better addressed by citizens with the ability to think critically. Some parts of this vital attribute include the ability: (a) to evaluate claims about what research shows about human nature and how to modify it; (b) to recognize inadequately founded opinions of so-called experts; (c) to distinguish between events that are only correlated from those that are causally related; (d) to identify and correct for the biasing factors in one's own judgments and in those of others; and (e) to be aware of the sources of error in thinking that make reasonable people act irrationally and smart people do foolish things (to be discussed in more detail in chapter 10).

When a product is billed as "37 percent more effective," do you ask, "Compared to what other treatment?" When "4 out of 5 doctors recommend *X*," do you question whether the survey included only 5 doctors—who might be prejudiced because they happen to be paid by the company that produces *X?* When someone presents you with "established conclusions" about the "obvious inferiority" of some social or ethnic group, do you ask to evaluate the evidence supporting such statements?

I hope that the things you learn from reading *Psychology and Life* will make you a more informed citizen, one who is sensitive to the pitfalls of erroneous reporting and conclusion-drawing. A goal for each of us is to develop a personal model of human behavior based on carefully weighed evidence. Since many of you who read this book will graduate to become leaders in our society, your decisions may even become part of public policy—or in opposition to the status quo which may be improved by appropriate challenges. Can the study of psychology as applied to life help in this regard? I think so, but let's check out the evidence a decade from now when you have had ample opportunity to test this prediction for yourself. Is the study of the ways we know about human nature of any value? We'll conclude this chapter by looking at the answer given by one of the most influential philosophers of our times, Sir Bertrand Russell.

> *In regard to human knowledge there are two questions that may be asked: first, what do we know? and second, how do we know it? The first of these questions is answered by science, which tries to be as impersonal and dehumanized as possible. In the resulting survey of the universe it is natural to start with astronomy and physics, which deal with what is large and universal; life and mind, which are rare and have, apparently, little influence on the course of events must occupy a minor position in this impartial survey. But in relation to our second question—namely, how do we come by our knowledge—psychology is the most important of the sciences. Not only is it necessary to study psychologically the processes by which we draw inferences, but it turns out that all the data upon which our inferences should be based are psychological in character; that is to say, they are experiences of single individuals. The apparent publicity of our world is in part delusive and in part inferential; all the raw material of our knowledge consists of mental events in the lives of separate people. In this region, therefore, psychology is supreme. (1948, pp. 52-53)*

Summary

- Psychological research is based on the scientific method, a set of attitudes, values, and procedures for gathering and interpreting empirical information in a way that minimizes sources of error to yield dependable results.
- Five basic features of psychological research are reliance on empirical methods, systematic attempts to measure and quantify aspects of behavior and mental processes, use of the scientific method to increase objectivity and reduce the danger of personal bias, keeping of complete records in a form that other researchers can understand, and communication of findings and conclusions in ways that permit other researchers to replicate the study.
- Objectivity in research is enhanced through the use of clearly and operationally defined variables; standardized procedures for giving instructions, presenting stimulus conditions, and scoring responses; and avoidance of bias through a variety of techniques including keeping researchers and subjects "blind" to which subjects are given which treatments, using placebo controls, and guarding against the influence of confounding variables.
- The goal of most psychological research is to generate reliable and valid behavioral data. If the test results are stable and consistent, the data are said to be reliable, and the same results will be found on repeated tests under the same conditions. If the test results are accurate measures of the variable the test was intended to measure, then the data are valid.

- Correlations are consistent patterns of relationship between two or more variables. The higher the correlation, either positive or negative, the stronger the relationship. However, correlations cannot be used to infer causality between the variables that are found to be related.
- A causal relationship is indicated if an investigator can stop, start, or change a behavior through manipulation of the independent variable and if the changes occur only under those conditions.
- Three major methods of measuring behavior are observations, which may be direct, naturalistic, or mediated (requiring the use of special equipment); verbal reports, which may be derived from questionnaires, surveys, or interviews; and psychological tests.
- The research design consists of the conditions under which an investigator measures behavior. The type of research design determines what relationships can be studied and what conclusions can be drawn. Types of research designs include the controlled experiment, correlation studies, case studies, longitudinal studies, and archival, cross-cultural, and evaluation research.
- A controlled experiment is a method in which observations of specific behavior are made under systematically varied conditions. An experimenter manipulates an independent variable and notes the effects on a dependent variable (some observable response). All conditions except the independent variable are held constant for all subjects. Subjects must be randomly assigned to an experimental group (which is exposed to the independent variable) or to a control group (which is not exposed).
- Psychologists use statistics to help them make sense of the data they collect and to provide the quantitative foundation for the conclusions they draw. Descriptive statistics are used to describe sets of data collected from different groups of subjects and to describe relationships among variables. Descriptive statistics indicate what scores are most typical for each group and how typical the scores really are.
- Frequency distributions indicate how scores are distributed. Measures of central tendency give a single, representative score that can be used as an index of the most typical score obtained by a group. Three measures of central tendency are the mode, the median, and the mean.
- Measures of variability indicate how close together or spread apart the scores in a distribution are. Two measures of variability are the range and the standard deviation, which indicates the average distance between the scores in a distribution and their mean.
- The correlation coefficient indicates the degree of relationship between two variables; it tells the extent to which scores on one measure are associated with scores on the other. Correlation coefficients range from +1 through zero to −1. The further a coefficient is from zero—in either direction—the more closely the two variables are related, either positively or negatively.
- Inferential statistics are used to determine what conclusions can be legitimately drawn about a given population from the sample data collected. The normal curve is a symmetrical distribution in which the mode, the median, and the mean all have the same value. A difference is statistically significant if the probability that the difference might be due to chance is less than 5 in 100—the acceptable standard in psychology.
- Becoming a wise research consumer involves learning how to think critically and knowing how to evaluate claims about what "research shows"; to recognize inadequately founded opinions of so-called experts; to distinguish between correlational and causal relationships; to identify and guard against bias; and to be aware of the sources of error in thinking and reporting about observations.

3

Life-span Psychological Development

Imagine that hunters have just captured a wild creature in a French forest. He communicates only by grunts, eye movements, and gestures. He runs on all fours and will bite or scratch anyone who gets too close. This *ferel*—uncivilized—creature, whose behavior appears more animal than human, is actually a boy of about 12! He is described by his caretakers as "equally wild and shy." He seems frightened and "always impatient and restless," continually seeking escape "back to the freedom of his forest home and family of wild animals."

Suppose further that you have been faced with the task the French government presented to young Dr. Jean Marc Itard: educate and civilize this savage child. Where would you begin? How would you discover what the child already knows? What would you try to teach him?

Dr. Itard eagerly accepted this challenge, in part, as a test of the "new science of mental medicine." The year was 1800 and psychology was not yet a formal field of study. The influence of the mind on behavior was a subject of great interest to educators, philosophers, and some physicians, but, as yet, there had been no research to test their ideas.

It was the time of the French Enlightenment, a time when philosophers were trying to ascertain humanity's true nature. The central issues of the debate revolved around (a) the fundamental differences between humans and animals, (b) the existence of innate ideas, and (c) the influence of society on human nature.

Humans had been put among the primates in the species-classification scheme of Linnaeus—to the outrage of many. This insult to human pride, compounded by Darwin's revolutionary findings, was the basis for the first topic of debate. The second issue, touched upon in chapter 1, pitted the French heavyweight Descartes as champion of the nativists against the Englishman John Locke, who carried the banner of the empiricists (remember his *tabula rasa?*). The final issue being hotly debated was associated with the name of Jean Jacques Rousseau and his "noble savage" view. He held that humans were corrupted by contact with society; it was only in a natural state that their inherent goodness and noble qualities were revealed. Others insisted that without society and culture humans would be nothing but wild beasts.

So Itard's frightened little pupil, covered with animal scars, became the test case for these lofty philosophical ideas about human development—as the French press proclaimed in regular news releases. Itard supported the empiricist view and designed a set of new educational and training procedures in the hope of demonstrating that experience could transform the "Wild Boy of Aveyron," who he named Victor, into a responsive, social, intellectual, communicative young Frenchman.

Success and enthusiasm filled the first years of Itard's patient and inventive tutoring. Victor learned to speak a few words—*lait* ("milk") and *O Dieu* ("Oh God")—and to comprehend many instructions and commands. He learned to keep himself clean and became affectionate and well mannered. But sadly, this initial spurt in Victor's cognitive and moral development sputtered and stalled. Five years later he had not progressed much further. Although he had learned to use symbols in thinking, to relate to other people, and to show pleasure in doing things well or show shame at mistakes, he had not learned to talk or behave in all the ways that would make him like other youngsters of his age. Most troubling to Itard was Victor's explosive, "uncivilized sexuality" with the onset of puberty.

Disappointed at the lack of progress, the teacher-researcher called off this "natural experiment." Victor spent his remaining years in Paris, cared for by Dr. Itard's housekeeper. He died in 1828 at the age of 40, 10 years before his teacher.

What can be concluded from this fascinating case study? Some have said that Victor was simply a retarded or autistic child, limited in his mental development by heredity. Others disagreed, contending that his survival alone in the woods for many years required skills beyond those of a retarded child. A careful reading of all the materials in this case has led a current expert to conclude that "man depends on society not only for morality and communication but even for the most rudimentary discriminations, concepts, and skills. Social isolation is disastrous, and if it is prolonged, its effects are in large part irreversible. Man outside of society is an ignoble savage." (Lane, 1986)*

*For more details about this unique student-teacher relationship, you might want to read the accounts by Dr. Itard, reprinted in 1962, or Harlan Lane's more recent analyses (1976, 1986).

The *Opening Case* of Victor, the "Wild Boy of Aveyron," offers a challenging start for our psychological journey. The basic questions it raised are still of fundamental concern to psychologists. To what extent is any behavior or characteristic due to heredity or environment? How important are early life influences in shaping our later development? Can some experiences come "too late" to be useful? For instance, would it have made a difference if Victor had been exposed to language at the age of 2 instead of 12? Is there a "developmental timetable" that regulates the appearances of particular aspects of functioning, without any practice or training? Are there behaviors that are not modifiable by education? And then there is the most profound question of all: How does a helpless, newborn baby turn into a sophisticated, complex adult capable of doing so much?

Think back to your first day of elementary school. Think of all the ways you have changed over the years since then—in size, body build, and strength; in what you can understand and do; and in your interactions with your physical and social environment. How might you be different today if you had grown up among a tribe of Amazon Indians, or in an urban ghetto, been adopted by a royal family, never gone to school, or been tutored from birth by a team of education specialists?

Consider two more questions. Is there anything about you that is still the same now as it was when you were 5 years old? How have your parents or guardians changed from your earliest recollections of them to your most recent? In each instance, you are dealing with questions of *developmental change*—how you and other organisms change over time.

To some extent, you are a unique creature without an exact duplicate anywhere—no one in the world has the same fingerprint as yours, and maybe no one in all history ever did. Yet your development has involved many systematic changes that were predictable for you and others of your species—culture, sex, and age.

In this chapter we will explore **developmental psychology,** the branch of psychology that is concerned with the processes and stages of growth, as well as with changes in physical and psychological functioning from conception across the life span. Though we will touch on the major psychological changes and challenges unique to each successive period of life, we will focus on psychological development, and primarily on the early years, when the transformations are so rapid and varied. Our plan is to see an intact, whole organism functioning and changing in many ways—acquiring language, learning to reason, and developing emotional and social patterns of behavior. These and other strands of development correspond to the separate content areas of psychology (such as learning and cognition) that will be our focus in subsequent chapters. We will return again to the whole person in chapter 12 where we'll examine personality in depth.

The Life-span Approach

Until recently, developmental psychologists limited their domain to three periods of major growth—infancy, childhood, and adolescence. Adulthood was considered to be primarily a period of stability between the growth of youth and the decline of old age; but this assumption has been challenged by a new view that development is a lifelong process, beginning at conception and ending at death (Baltes et al., 1980; Honzik, 1984). New tasks, different challenges, and characteristic sources of delight and frustration mark each period of our lives.

Methods for Studying Development

The research methods chosen by developmental psychologists depend on whether they are seeking to describe or explain the behavior under study. Descriptive information is provided by *normative studies,* while cause-effect information is provided by *experimental studies.* Each of these kinds of studies, in turn, comprise three types of time-based research designs: *cross-sectional, longitudinal,* and *sequential.*

Normative Investigations

The aim of **normative investigations** is to describe something that is characteristic of a specific age or developmental stage. By systematically testing individuals of different ages, researchers can determine developmental landmarks, such as those listed in **Table 3.1.** The data provide **norms,** standard patterns of development or achievement, based on observation of many children during the first 8 months after birth. They indicate the average age at which the behaviors were performed. Thus a child's performance can be diagnosed in terms of its position above or below a norm. In short, a norm provides a standard basis for comparison.

A good example of a normative investigation is a study conducted by Nancy Bayley (1969). She tested 100 infants, at monthly intervals from one month to two years, on a series of mental and motor development skills. From her findings she constructed a set of norms for infant development,

Table 3.1 *Norms for Infant Mental and Motor Development*

One Month	***Five Months***
Responds to sound	Discriminates strange from familiar persons
Becomes quiet when picked up	Makes distinctive vocalizations (e.g., pleaseure, eagerness, satisfaction)
Follows a moving person with eyes	Makes effort to sit independently
Retains a large easily grasped object placed in hand	Turns from back to side
Vocalized occasionally	Has partial use of thumb in grasp
Two Months	***Six Months***
Smiles socially	Reaches persistently, picks up cube deftly
Engages in anticipatory excitement (to feeding, being held and so on)	Transfers objects hand to hand
Recognizes mother	Lifts cup and bangs it
Inspects surroundings	Smiles at mirror image and likes frolicking
Blinks to object or shadow (flinches)	Reaches unilaterally for small object
Lifts head and holds it erect and steady	
Three Months	***Seven Months***
Vocalizes to the smiles and talk of an adult	Makes playful responses to mirror
Searches for sound	Retains two of three cubes offered
Makes anticipatory adjustments to lifting	Sits alone steadily and well
Reacts to disappearance of adult's face	Shows clear thumb opposition in grasp
Sits with support, head steady	Scoops up pellet from table
Four Months	***Eight Months***
Head follows dangling ring, vanishing spoon, or ball moved across table	Vocalizes four different syllables (e.g., da-da, me, no
Inspects and fingers own hands	Listens selectively to familiar words
Shows awareness of strange situations	Rings bell purposively
Picks up cube with palm grasp	Attempts to obtain three presented cubes
Sits with slight support	Shows early stepping movements (prewalking progression)

This table shows the average age at which each behavior is performed up to 8 months. Individual differences in rate of development are considerable, but most infants follow this sequence. (From Lipsitt & Reese, 1979, p. 18)

which are known today as the "Bayley Scales of Infant Development." This scale, and ones like it, can indicate to parents when they might expect to see certain behaviors in their infants. However, it is very important for anyone using these scales to remember that the figures are simply averages; in no sense do they dictate when a particular child *ought* to show a particular behavior.

Experimental Investigations

Many babies develop "stranger anxiety," a distress response to unfamiliar people. A normative study can show when this behavior most often appears—it begins at about 8 months and can last for some time—but a normative study can't explain it. To get at the causes, we need to conduct an experiment in which we systematically vary specific conditions hypothesized to influence this social-emotional reaction. For example, we might study whether the anxiety is a response to all strangers or only to those with certain characteristics.

One such study was done using as subjects 14 children between the ages of 1 and $2\frac{1}{2}$. In one experimental condition, a research assistant was trained to act either "positive-nice" or "negative-nasty" toward each subject; in another condition he was instructed either to make eye contact with the subject or to avoid doing so.

Under these varying conditions the subjects responded differently. The children avoided or reacted negatively to the "nasty" stranger and also to the one who ignored them—that is, their behavior was typical of a stranger-anxiety response; but they did not make this response to the unfamiliar "nice" person. In the situations when the stranger merely made eye contact with the children, this behavior opened lines of communication between them. Then, the children not only looked at the stranger but also vocalized, smiled, and approached. (Clarke-Stewart, 1978, p. 124)

With a better understanding of what causes particular behavior to occur or fail to occur, a developmental psychologist acquires new tools for improving healthy development and correcting or preventing unhealthy development. "Thus, where it was once necessary to chart the *typical*, the challenge for many has now become to discover the possible" (Lipsitt & Reese, 1979, pp. 22–23).

Time-Based Designs

Most research on development uses a **cross-sectional design,** in which groups of subjects, having different chronological ages, are observed and compared. A researcher can then draw conclusions about behavioral differences that may be related to those age differences. An *advantage* of a cross-sectional design is that an entire age range can be investigated at one time. A *disadvantage* is that, since the groups being compared differ by year of birth, differences in the social or political conditions they've experienced—rather than just their age difference—may be responsible for any differences found in their behavior. For example, a group of 16-year-olds who have grown up during a period of severe economic depression or political turmoil may reflect attitudes that are not typical of 16-year-olds born earlier or later.

In a **longitudinal design,** the same subjects are observed repeatedly—sometimes over many years. An *advantage* of longitudinal research is that since the subjects have lived through the same socioeconomic period, age-related changes cannot be confused with variations in differing societal circumstances. There are several *disadvantages.* First only individuals born at about the same time are tested; it is impossible to generalize the results to people born at some different time period. Second it takes a long time to complete a longitudinal study if the age span to be covered is large. Third it is difficult and expensive to keep in contact with the subjects for repeated measurements that can last a lifetime; they may move away, lose interest, or die—as can the researchers.

One of the most ambitious longitudinal studies was begun soon after World War I by Lewis Terman and is still being continued 60 years later by psychologists at Stanford University. Over 1500 boys and girls, in grades 3 through 8 (born about 1910), were selected on the basis of high intelligence scores (in the genius range). They have been tested at regular intervals ever since—first, to see how they compared to youngsters in general, then to see if their intellectual superiority would be maintained, and finally to discover the conditions and experiences that contributed to life satisfaction and to different styles of handling important life problems.

The first data were secured by survey questionnaires, interviews, and ratings by parents and teachers. Initial follow-ups used the same data sources, but after 1936, questionnaires were sent regularly by mail to the subjects themselves. In the 1940s the young adults were gathered at testing centers and given several kinds of tests. About 75 percent of those still living are returning questionnaires every 10 years.

Since Terman's death in 1956, the research has been carried on by Robert and Pauline Sears, now assisted by Albert Hastorf. Some of their findings about life happiness, assessed when the subjects were in their early sixties, will be described on page 101. (P. Sears & Barbee, 1977; R. Sears, 1977; Terman, 1925; Terman & Oden, 1947, 1959)

The best features of the cross-sectional and longitudinal approaches are combined in a **sequential design,** in which subjects span a certain, usually small, age range and are grouped according to year of birth; the groups are observed repeatedly over several years. Individuals born in the same year are said to belong to the same **birth cohort.** By choosing cohorts whose ages will overlap during the course of the study, a researcher avoids the problems of both the cross-sectional and the longitudinal approaches: age and time-of-birth effects, and lack of generalizability. In addition, overlapping the age ranges of the different cohorts allows a researcher to study a fairly broad age range in less time than would be required by the longitudinal method alone.

*In one sequentially designed study, four groups were selected: cohorts born in 1954, 1955, 1956, and 1957, who were 15, 14, 13, and 12, respectively, at the time of first testing. Each was tested for achievement motivation three times over a 3-year period. The design allowed the researchers to compare several groups at the same age and to follow the development of each group over the time period, while obtaining data covering the 5-year span from ages 12 to 17 (see **Figure 3.1**).*

These observations began in 1970, following several years of strong youth protest and the development of a counterculture that ridiculed the achievement orientation and rationality of the "older generation." The slogan of the counterculture was, "Never trust anyone over thirty!"

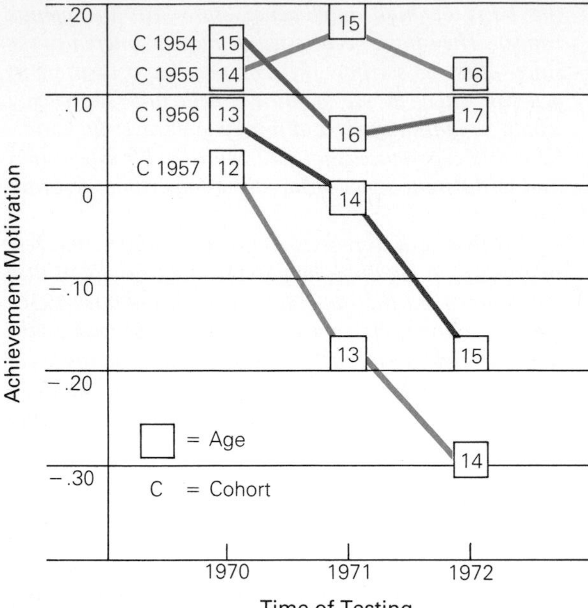

Figure 3.1 *A Sequential Study of Adolescents' Personalities*

Four groups of adolescents, born in successive years 1954 through 1957, were tested for achievement motivation in 1970, 1971, and 1972. The study followed several years of strong youth protest and the development of a counterculture that ridiculed an achievement orientation. The two later-born cohorts showed big declines in their achievement motivation, while the two earlier-born cohorts remained more stable. Differences among the fourteen-year-olds born in different years were especially striking. Apparently, even a two-year difference in time of birth can constitute a "generation gap" for some behaviors. (Adapted from Nesselroade & Baltes, 1974)

The two younger cohorts (born in 1957 and 1956) showed big declines in their motivation to achieve as they grew older, while the two older cohorts were more stable. Small differences between the cohorts at the beginning widened by the end of the study to become substantial. Some differences in this personality measure were even greater for groups of the same age (14-year-olds born in different years) than for the same groups at different ages (the 1954 or 1955 cohorts). So even a 2-year difference in time of birth can constitute a ''generation gap'' for some behaviors. (Nesselroade & Baltes, 1974)

Historical Analysis of Families and Life Stages

Membership in the Society for Research in Child Development has drawn investigators from many diverse fields, among them psychology, psychiatry, sociology, anthropology, education, pediatrics, nursing, anatomy, nutrition, social work, and home economics. Only recently have a handful of historians joined this influential research group. The reason for this is that only in the last ten years has the **historical approach** emerged as the third major way of gaining information about development. The approach is interesting, because *time* is the primary independent variable in the study of development, while *time perspective* is what historians are uniquely qualified to offer.

History puts human affairs into perspective. The child, ordinarily portrayed as a distinct, isolated entity for professional study by developmentalists, is placed, by historical analysis, in a social, economic, and political environment (Furstenberg, 1985). Family history includes both cross-sectional and longitudinal approaches to study the individual nuclear family and its relationship to extended kinships and the larger social community. Family histories demonstrate how families are influenced by major social forces at a particular historical period, and, in turn, how they become active agents of social change (Smuts & Hagen, 1985). An analysis of life history also reveals how society and science interact to define and institutionalize various stages of life while influencing family practices, such as "the proper place of the mother in the home" and the care of elderly parents at home or in nursing agencies.

With this perspective it is possible to see how social and legal policies that affect families and their members are themselves influenced by the historical circumstances of an era. Thus rigid, authoritarian child-rearing practices are traced to times of evangelical religious fervor, while the current phenomenon of "latch-key kids" who are alone at home for meals and other previously "family" activities, is a complex consequence of high divorce rates, smaller family size, absence of extended families, and working parents.

Two notable contributions of family history to developmental psychology are (a) its recognition that the transitions of individual life patterns—entering school, work, and marriage—are synchronized to collective changes taking place within the family, and (b) that such transitions of individuals and families are better understood within the historical circumstances of the time. For example, your decision if and when to marry, or to have children, will probably be made at a later time in your life than it was for your parents because of current social values. On the other hand, your decision to go away to college or to seek a job wherever the best one is located reflects individualistic and achievement values of American society—but creates the "empty-nest syndrome" for your parents in their middle age. Consider how the following 1986 statistics from the Census Bureau chart a new course for the American family.

1. One fourth of all children (over 16 million) live with only one or neither parent.
2. More than 10 percent of adults live alone.
3. Nearly 2 million couples living together are unmarried (4 times more than in 1960).
4. The average age of people marrying for the first time is more than 23 years, the oldest it has ever been since such records were started in 1890.
5. Divorces are occurring at the highest rate in history. Slightly less than one half of all marriages end in divorce.

The interplay of historical forces and society's definition of stages of life is outlined in the ***Close-up:*** *Discovering the Stages of Life* on page 64.

Basic Concepts

In studies of development, *age* is the usual independent variable; the dependent variable is the behavior whose changes are being studied at various ages. But age is really an indicator of underlying physiological and psychological changes that are presumed to be taking place and causing, or making possible, the changes in behavior. So age is also called an **index variable,** a variable that indicates the presence of other variables, but does not cause them to occur. It can be used in two ways—as a stimulus event, much like a blip on a sonar screen indicating the presence of a submarine or as a *response,* like a dream which can indicate unconscious wishes.

Psychologists make a distinction between **chronological age,** the number of months or years since birth, which they usually use as their independent variable, and **developmental age,** the chronological age at which most children show a particular level of physical or mental development. For example, a 3-year-old child who has verbal skills typical of most 5-year-olds is said to have a developmental age of 5 for verbal skills. As you will see in chapter 13, the familiar concept of IQ is based on the ratio of the overall mental developmental age to chronological age.

An important issue in developmental psychology is the extent to which development is characterized by *continuity* or *discontinuity.* Some psychologists take the position that development is essentially continuous, occurring through the accumulation of *quantitative* changes—steadily adding more of the same thing. According to this **continuity** view, we become more skillful in thinking, talking, or using our muscles much as we become gradually taller—through the cumulative action of the same continuing *processes.* In contrast, other psychologists see development as a succession of reorganizations with behavior *qualitatively* different in different *age-specific life periods.* In this **discontinuity** view, particular aspects of development are discontinuous, although development, as a whole, is a continuous process. Thus, newborns are seen not as less dependent than before birth on the mother (a quantitative change), but rather as dependent in totally different ways: a physical dependence that is different and a new dimension of psychological dependence (qualitative changes).

Psychologists who see development as discontinuous speak of **developmental stages,** qualitatively different levels of development. They believe that different behaviors appear at different ages or in different life periods, because different underlying causes are operating. The term *stage* is reserved for an interval of time in which there are some qualitative differences in physical, mental, or behavioral functioning from times before and after it.

The concept of *stages,* important in developmental psychology and appearing in several major theories we will study, also implies a progression toward an expected end state (Cairns & Valsinger, 1984). Developmental stages are assumed to occur always in the same sequence, with each stage a necessary building block for the next.

Related to the concept of developmental stages is that of critical periods. A **critical period** is a sensitive time during development when an organism is optimally ready to acquire a particular behavior; but certain stimuli and experiences must occur for this to happen. If they do not, and the organism does not develop the behavior at that time, it will be difficult, and perhaps impossible, to do so later. The question to be answered by research is whether certain experiences must occur in the early years for normal development to proceed. However, the answer to such a question, in any given area of a child's development, requires that major environmental changes occur in order to demonstrate that behavioral deficits or gains have taken place. A child must be reared under circumstances that prevent the normal emergence of some skills or behaviors and then must be given markedly improved circumstances to see if the initial loss is permanent or can be made up in a favorable environment.

Experimental evidence supports the idea that critical periods occur in animals and humans. For example, salamander tadpoles usually start swimming immediately upon birth. If they are prevented from swimming for their first 8 days by being kept in an anesthetizing solution, they swim normally

Close-up Discovering the Stages of Life

People have always started out as infants, become children, matured into adults, and gotten old. However, what is new are the stages of life corresponding to these different ages. It is only in recent times that "old age," "youth," and "adolescence" have been *discovered,* with "childhood" being found only a bit earlier.

Historical analysis reveals that the "discovery" of a new life stage is a complex process involving at least five steps (Hareven, 1985).

1. *First, individuals become aware of new characteristics in their private experiences;*
2. *Professionals observe this change and begin to analyze the conditions unique to it and write reports about it;*
3. *The popular culture and mass media recognize it publicly;*
4. *Public agencies then create legislation and establish institutions to deal with its "problems" and to safeguard the rights of this special category of citizens;*
5. *The circle is closed when individuals are ultimately influenced by all these public activities in their society, some of which create norms that prescribe the appropriate timing of their transitions into and out of any given stage.*

Applying this overview to American society one learns that childhood was discovered in the early 1800s among the newly emerging middle-class urban families. Its appearance was related to a variety of circumstances—the segregation of the work place from the home, the role of mother as custodian of the domestic front, smaller nuclear family units replacing the formerly larger units typical of rural and farm families, and the new importance of the sentiments of love and caring as the basis for marriage and family relationships replacing marriages by parental arrangement. Two other factors operated to make that time more child-centered than ever before. The decline in infant and child mortality (because of improved medical practices and public control of disease), and the practice of limiting family size (partly because of smaller living quarters in cities and other life-style changes). Soon there were books being written about childhood as a distinct stage of development and much literature offering advice to parents. Politicians entered with new legislation to regulate child labor and make school attendance compulsory.

It took almost another century for "adolescence" to be discovered in America. Although puberty is a universal, biological phenomenon, the psychosocial stage of adolescence came about when a culture of peer groups was observed in cities, especially apparent with the rising tide of immigrant children in the streets. School attendance was required through high school, and juvenile reformatories and vocational schools were created to give adolescents new places to congregate.

After the Second World War returning servicemen needed work, so women and adolescents had to get out of the work force. Women went home, and adolescents went to college or otherwise suspended adult responsibilities, including delaying the start of marriage and families (Keniston, 1971). Legislation then established the formal boundaries between adolescence and youth in terms of ages for voting, public drinking, military service, and auto driving.

Where youth ended was unclear until the past decade when "old age" was finally discovered—adulthood then found its place between the boundaries of old age and youth. Changing demographics in modern society are seen in the "graying of America," with an increasing number of aged people living longer, healthier lives, apart from their children. Psychologists now study them; books, movies, and TV sitcoms appear about these "golden years." Legislation sets 65 as the onset of this stage with retirement, social security, and other benefits available to this new breed of senior citizens.

Once any of these stages is institutionalized, then the people who grow up in that era get classified accordingly, treated differently, and begin to define themselves and their life options according to the norms established for someone at their stage of life. At that point the stages help create the psychological reality.

as soon as they are released. However, if kept in the solution 4 or 5 days longer, they are never able to swim; the critical period has passed (Carmichael, 1926). Likewise, dogs and monkeys raised in isolation for a few months after birth behave in bizarre ways throughout their lives, even if later reared with other normal animals (Scott, 1963).

Malnutrition can impair mental capacities permanently when it occurs shortly before birth and for a few months thereafter, when the brain is growing rapidly, but not when it occurs later in life (Wurtman, 1982). Children raised in institutions with minimal social attachments to adult caretakers show attentional and social problems in school even when they are adopted into caring families after the age of 4 years (Tizard & Hodge, 1978). From these and other studies, it seems reasonable to conclude that there are times in the early life of most organisms when optimum development is vulnerable to critical-period effects.

There is one startling exception to this rule in the area of *intellectual development.* Although children's intellectual development is sensitive to environmental change throughout childhood, there is little evidence that deprivation in early years causes permanent handicaps (see Rutter, 1979). A dramatic example is the case of Genie, a child who was isolated for years under the most "appalling" conditions. Although she was not rescued until she was 13, and was not able to talk, could barely walk, and performed mentally as if she were a 5-year-old, after 4 years of training she had improved and made up much of this deficit (Curtis, 1977).

Some children are able to experience the most terrible home or institutional life, filled with extreme stress, and are able to emerge unscathed, showing normal personality functioning. Children who do not succumb to extreme deprivation or disadvantage—and may even be the more hardy because of it—are termed **invulnerable children** (see Garmezy, 1976; Skolnick, 1986).

Developmental psychologists currently divide the human life-span into nine stages, beginning with the prenatal stage and ending with death. Death is included as the last stage, because it exerts a considerable influence on our earlier development and because adjustment to its inevitability is one of our major developmental tasks, especially near the end of our life span. **Table 3.2** lists all nine stages, together with their time spans and major characteristics.

In the remainder of this chapter, we will study the individual during different life periods and several basic psychological processes that change during the life span. We will begin with prenatal development and the activities of infants, and then examine, in some detail, the development of language, mental functioning, and social and emotional patterns. Finally we will discuss the later periods of the life cycle, focusing on the problems, choices, and satisfactions of adolescence, adulthood, and old age.

Table 3.2 *Stages in Life-Span Development*

Stage	Age Period	Some Major Characteristics
Prenatal Stage	Conception to birth	Physical development
Infancy	Birth at full term to about 18 months	Locomotion; rudimentary language; social attachment
Early Childhood	About 18 months to about 6 years	Language well established; gender typing; group play; ends with "readiness" for schooling
Late Childhood	About 6 to about 13 years	Many cognitive processes become adult except in speed of operation; team play
Adolescence	About 13 to about 20 years	Highest level of cognitive capacity reached; independence from parents; sexual relationships
Young Adulthood	About 20 to about 45 years	Career and family development
Middle Age	About 45 to about 65 years	Career reaches highest level; self-assessment; retirement
Old Age	About 65 years to death	Enjoy family, achievements; dependency; widowhood; poor health
Death		A "stage" in a special sense, see text

The Life Cycle Begins

An energetic sperm cell discovers a receptive egg cell; united, they follow a trail as old as life itself to become a newborn human being in a mere nine months. This marvelous transformation is guided by principles of evolution and shaped by individual genetic influences. We prefer to think of human nature as somehow above and free from the biological processes that so clearly direct animal behavior. Indeed, we tend to believe that each baby comes into the world totally unequipped to deal with its environment. Even William James, one of psychology's most significant early contributors, held the traditional view of the infant as a know-nothing, do-nothing organism. He wrote that the infant is so "assailed by eyes, ears, nose, skin and entrails at once" that it experiences its world as "one great blooming, buzzing confusion" (1890).

Research in the past two decades has challenged this view of the newborn. Babies start with remarkable know-how and can use many of their senses to take in information virtually from the beginning. We might think of them as prewired "friendly computers," well equipped to respond to the adults who care for them and able to interact with and alter their environment. We will review here some of the ways in which human development is influenced by the genetic instructions programmed into the genes, as well as some of the evidence that these genetic influences provide the potential for those little brains to start functioning much earlier than most adults realize.

Genetic Influences on Behavior

Our body build, behavior, and development were all determined, to some extent, at the moment the sperm and egg cells of our parents united in conception. Our genetic inheritance imposes certain constraints on our bodies, brains, and behavior—but it also makes certain behavior possible for us that is not possible for members of other species. Heredity provides the potential with which environmental influences interact to enable each species to adapt to its own habitat, but all we actually inherit are chromosomes and genes.

Chromosomes and Genes

Chromosomes are double strands of DNA (deoxyribonucleic acid) in the nucleus of cells. All normal human body cells have 46 chromosomes. As cells divide, each chromosome strand splits down the middle, with half going to each new cell. Each half then acts as a template for replacing the missing half out of materials in the surrounding tissue. In contrast to body cells, the **germ cells,** spermatozoa and ova, contain only 23 chromosomes, because they remain at half strength in their final division. When male and female germ cells unite, they form 23 pairs, to provide the 46 chromosomes that later will be found in a child's body cells. Thus the child receives half its chromosomes—a random selection—from each parent (see **Figure 3.2**).

The **genes** are segments along these chromosome strands that contain the "blueprint" for our development. They also set the timetables for different aspects of development. Genes provide the instructions for the development of our physical characteristics and even some of our psychological attributes. An amazing fact to consider is that a baby born with the normal complement of 46 chromosomes has somewhere between 30,000 and 100,000 genes in each cell.

An organism's full set of genes—all of the genes inherited from both parents—is called its **genotype.** The set of characteristics the organism actually develops—its observable features such as body build and eye color—is called its **phenotype.** A whole new field of research called **behavior genetics** is focused on attempts to identify the genetic bases of behavioral traits, such as intelligence, mental disorders, and altruism (Fuller, 1982; McLearn & De Fries, 1973).

Most human characteristics in which heredity plays a role are **polygenic** (*poly* meaning *many*); they are dependent on a combination of genes. Genes that are always expressed in an individual's development are called **dominant genes.** Those that are expressed only when paired with a similar gene are called **recessive genes.** All-or-nothing characteristics like eye color may be controlled by a single gene or by a pair of genes. Characteristics that vary in degree, like height, are thought to be controlled by several genes. Complex characteristics, including some psychological attributes such as emotionality, are believed to be controlled or influenced by many groups of genes.

Only about 10 percent of the genes we inherit will be used in the course of our lives. The unused genetic potential in our genotype is like a trust fund, available if our usually constant environment changes in significant ways. If that occurs those with the "right genetic stuff" will be able to adapt to the change and pass on those good genes to the next generation—of people or insects.

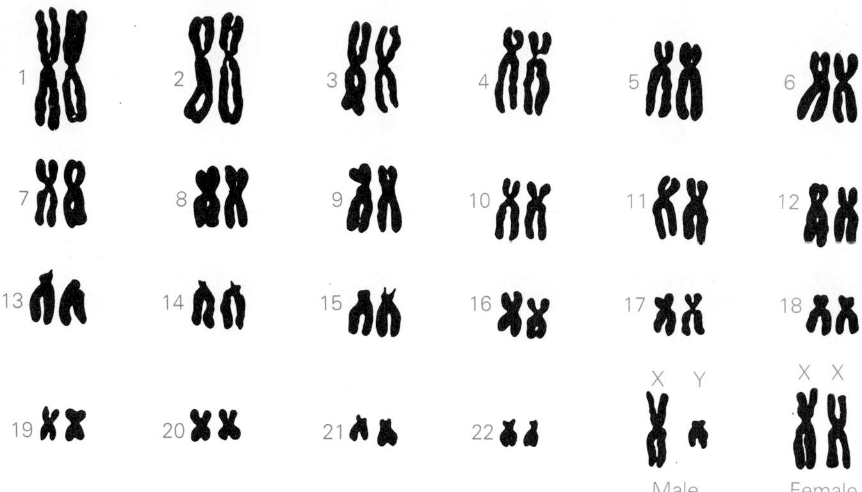

Figure 3.2
Shown are the twenty-three pairs of chromosomes each normal baby is born with. In both males and females, twenty-two pairs are the same. The twenty-third pair determines the sex of the child. Males have one X chromosome and one smaller Y chromosome, or an XY pair. Females have two X chromosomes, or an XX pair.

An interesting perspective on the relationship among genes, evolution, and behavior is provided by behavior geneticist Myron Hofer:

> *The genes that have been selected for us in the process of evolution are a series of hedged bets as to environments that may be encountered and the behavioral strategies that will be required to deal with them. The information is essentially historical—what worked in the past. . . . Not only does our genetic makeup contain hidden potential that awaits new environments to be expressed, but the behavioral capacities that we are predisposed to acquire also allow us different behavioral options at any moment in time. (1981, p. 191)*

When the environmental requirements are specific and predictable, genes rigidly program behavior. We then see stereotyped, unlearned behavioral patterns, such as the fixed-action patterns of Tina, the mother turkey, we met in chapter 1's *Opening Case*. Animals that are higher on the *phylogenetic* (animal development) scale face more varied environmental challenges and have replaced the stereotyped behavior patterns seen in lower animals with patterns that are more complex and changeable through experience. In the case of humans, an almost limitless diversity of behavioral traits can emerge as genetic predispositions interact with experience in varied physical, social, and cultural environments.

There are many steps between the action of a gene in organizing assemblies of protein molecules and the final structure of an organ or any behavioral function. At each of these steps environmental influences help determine the outcome. For example, at the very first step in the long process of development, neighboring genes regulate whether a particular gene will be turned on or off. In the following 2 or 3 months, environmental factors such as malnutrition, radiation, or certain drugs can prevent the normal formation of organs and body structures. A tragic case occurred in the early 1960s, when several hundred women had taken a tranquilizer called *thalidomide* early in pregnancy to prevent morning sickness and insomnia. However it had an unanticipated side effect: these mothers gave birth to babies whose arms and legs had not developed beyond stumps.

Physical Growth and Maturation

The blueprint provided by the genes directs the physical development of an organism in a predictable sequence. It is responsible also for the appearance of certain behaviors at roughly the same time for all normal members of a species, though there are some cultural variations. Some, like sucking, are totally unlearned. Others follow inner promptings, but need a bit of refinement through experience. For example, most children sit without support by 7 months of age, pull themselves up to a standing position a month or two later, and walk soon after they are one year old. Once the underlying physical structures are sufficiently developed, these behaviors require only a minimally adequate environment and a little practice for proficiency. They seem to "unfold from within," following an inner, genetically determined timetable that is characteristic for the species. **Maturation** is the name of the process of organizational changes in bodily functioning, through the continuing action of heredity. The characteristic sequences of both

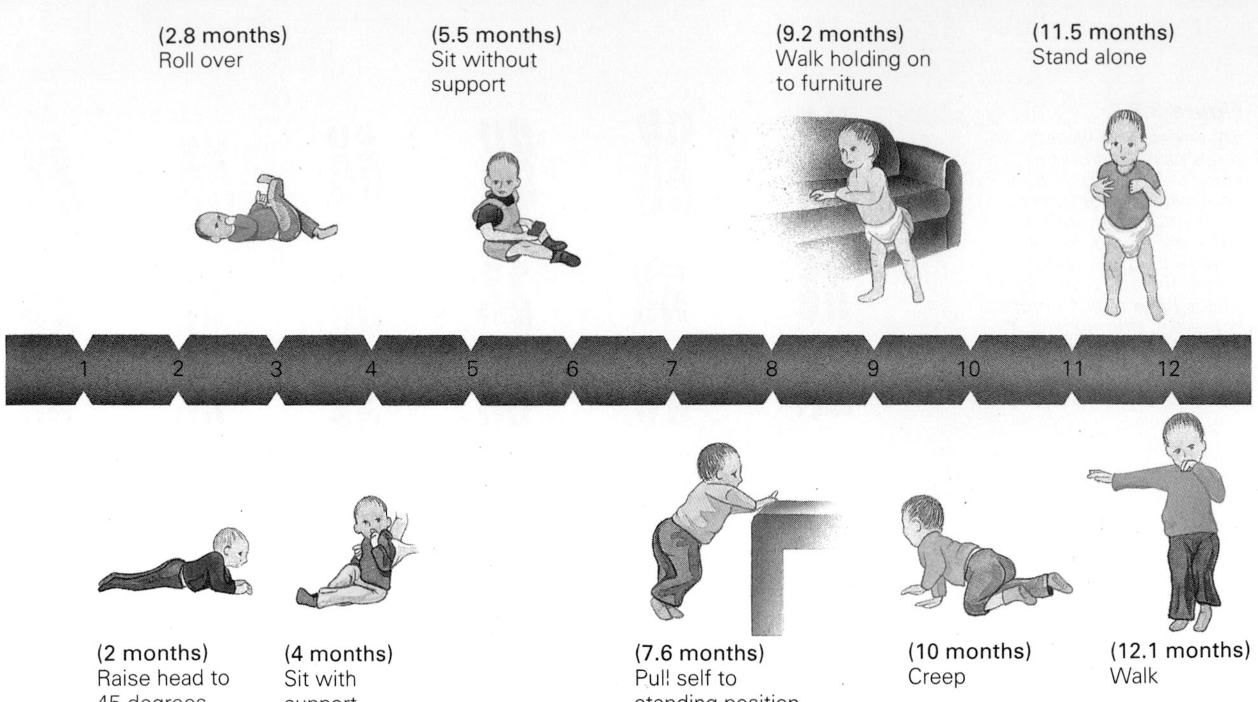

Figure 3.3

The development of walking requires no special teaching. It follows a fixed time-ordered sequence that is typical for all physically capable members of our species. In cultures where there is more stimulation, children begin to walk sooner. The Hopi Indian practice of carrying babies in tightly bound back cradles retards walking, but once the child is released, the same sequence is seen. What is remarkable about walking is that it occurs at all. The crawling infant successfully getting around must suffer frustation in the early attempts to walk; yet the effort persists. Ultimately the child reaps the evolutionary reward of greater flexibility and adaptability than is possible with "four-legged" crawling locomotion. (After Shirley, 1931)

physical and mental growth are programmed by maturation (see, for example, the sequence for locomotion in **Figure 3.3**).

Genetic factors are considered to be the instigators of the maturational changes which make an individual ready for new experiences and learning. It is also true, however, that certain kinds of experience may influence physiological functioning and thus biological development. For example, although no amount of practice or encouragement can teach children to walk or talk or read before they are maturationally ready, cross-cultural research findings reveal variations in the *timing* of some maturational changes. These differences can presumably be attributed to different cultural experiences. The influence of maturation is most apparent in early development, but it continues throughout life. It is maturation in the nervous system that changes the amount and type of sleep we need at different stages of life (chapter 7), maturation in the endocrine system that brings on the rapid development of the sex organs and secondary sex characteristics at puberty (for example, voice change).

Different aspects of development follow different maturational timetables. The earliest behavior of any kind is the heartbeat, the action of the heart muscle. It begins in the **prenatal** period, before birth, when the embryo is about 3 weeks old and a sixth of an inch long. Responses to stimulation have been observed as early as the sixth week, when the embryo is not yet an inch long. Spontaneous movements have been observed by the eighth week (Carmichael, 1970; Humphrey, 1970).

After the eighth week the developing embryo is called a **fetus**. The mother feels fetal movements in about the sixteenth week after conception, although they may be heard with a stethoscope a week or two earlier. At these ages, the fetus is about 7 inches long (the average length at birth is 20 inches).

Babies seem to be all head. At birth a baby's head is already about 60 percent of its adult size and measures a quarter of the whole body length (Bayley, 1956). The neural tissue of the brain (the total mass of brain cells) grows at an astonishing rate, increasing by 50 percent in the first 2 years, 80 percent above birth size in the next 2, and leveling off by about 11 years of age. An infant's body weight doubles in the first 6 months and triples by its first birthday; by the age of 2, a child's trunk is about half of its adult length.

Genital development has a quite different developmental program. Genital tissue shows little change until the teenage years, then develops rapidly to adult proportions. **Figure 3.4** shows the systematic, though different, patterns of growth for neural and genital tissues, compared with overall body growth. By birth or soon afterward, genetic and early environmental influences have resulted in the development of basic physical and psychological characteristics like body build, temperament, and even predispositions to certain physical and mental illnesses. These are called **constitutional factors.** They are presumed to be largely hereditary and remain fairly consistent throughout a person's lifetime. Even at birth, constitutional factors are apparent in a child's body type, characteristic physiological functioning, and basic reaction tendencies. For example, some babies are more sensitive to stimulation than others; some have a high energy level; some are placid, not easily upset. Basic reaction tendencies such as these, present at birth, may affect the way children interact with their environment and, thus, what they will experience and how they will develop (see for example, Kagan & Reznick, 1986; Miyake et al., 1985). It is still possible, however, for experience to modify the way a constitutional factor is expressed.

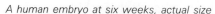

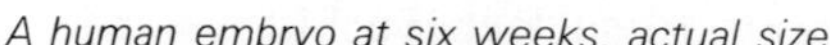
A human embryo at six weeks, actual size

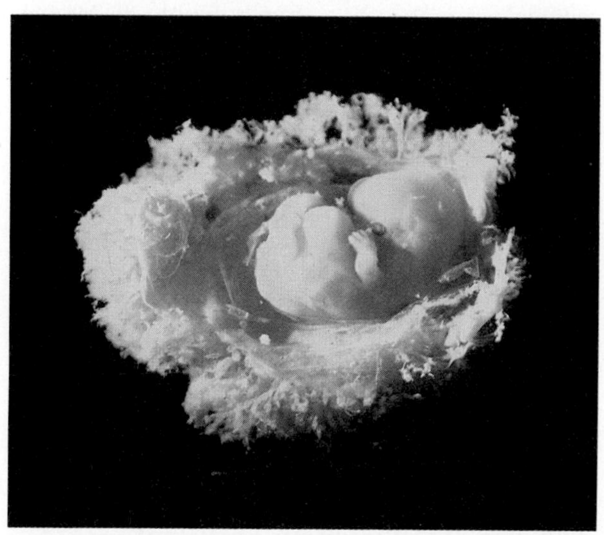

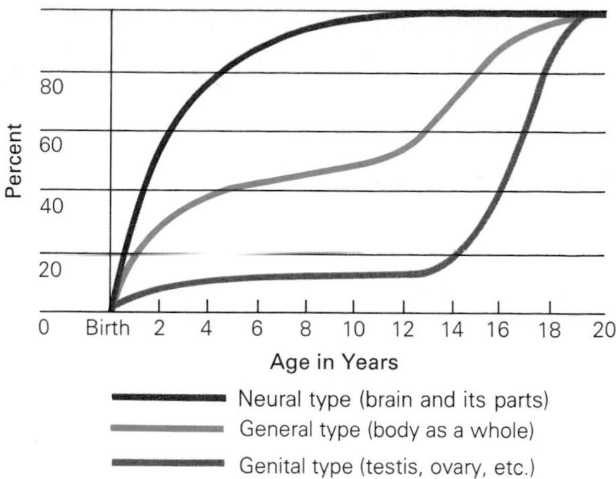

Figure 3.4

Neural growth occurs very rapidly in the first year of life, faster than overall physical growth. Genital maturation, by contrast, waits until adolescence. (Based on Scammon, 1930)

Nature and Nurture

To what extent is human behavior determined by heredity (nature) and to what extent is it learned (nurture)? The **nature-nurture controversy** over the relative importance of heredity and learning or experience has been of central importance in the study of development. Dr. Itard had hoped to shed light on this controversy by successfully educating Victor.

The extreme positions of Locke and Rousseau, described earlier, do injustice to the richness of behavior. Almost any complex action is shaped both by an individual's inherited biological influences and by personal experience, including learning. Also heredity and environment have a continuing mutual influence on each other, in which each makes possible certain further advances in the other, but also limits the contributions the other can make.

Heredity sets the upper limits of development; experience and practice determine how closely the limits are approached. For example, your heredity determines how tall you can grow; how tall you actually become depends partly on nutrition, an environmental factor. Similarly, your level of mental ability seems to depend on both genetic potential and environmental opportunity.

This interaction of nature and nurture is dramatically demonstrated in an unusual study in which "males like it hot." Although the biological sex of an organism is determined by sex chromosomes

(XX for females and XY for males), in one species heat changes how the chromosomes do their usual thing.

> *Among leopard geckos, when the temperature is moderate, half their eggs are hatched as females, the others as males. However when the temperature drops to a cool 25°C they all come out female; when it rises to a hotter 32°C only males are hatched. On the rare times when female geckos emerge from hot eggs they act like males during courtship and never lay eggs! (Kolata, 1986)*

A different type of interaction between physical and social aspects of behavior comes from something closer to home—the way people carry their books (when not using a backpack). Eighty percent of all college women carry their books cradled in front of them; 90 percent of the males are side-carriers. Observational research shows that both sexes start out as side-carriers, but, as they get older, males become even more so while women switch positions to be more up front (see **Figure 3.5**). The investigators conclude that these sex differences are attributable to a combination of muscle development, heavier book loads, and conformity to one's peer group (Jenni & Jenni, 1976).

Genetic influences have been found for many psychological characteristics. For example, certain reading disabilities appear to have a significant genetic component (De Fries & Decker, 1982). Some recent investigations suggest that heredity plays a larger role in shyness than in other personality traits throughout the life span (Plomin & Daniels, 1986). There is evidence that some forms of mental disorder, such as schizophrenia have a genetic component (discussed in chapter 15). Some traits of temperament found in one identical twin predictably occur in the other as well, even when the twins are reared in quite different environments (Floderus-Myrhed, et al., 1980). Findings with regard to genetics and intelligence will be presented in chapter 13.

Figure 3.5 *The Differences Between Males and Females Carrying Books*

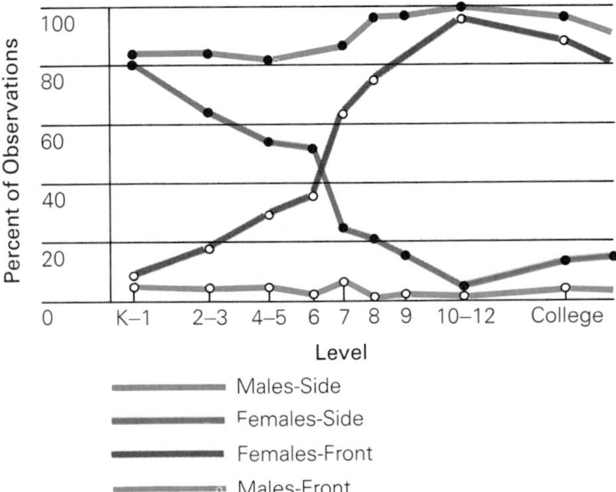

Although the debate continues, especially in some areas such as the influences on language acquisition, many investigators are even more interested in identifying *how* heredity and environment and their interaction contribute to development than in trying to weigh their relative importance.

What Do Babies Do?

How do babies organize their early experiences and what can they do? These questions are at the core of a virtual explosion of research on the **infancy period,** which lasts for about the first 18 months of life while the child in "incapable of speech" (the Latin meaning of *infancy*). Much of this research is focused on the **neonate,** the newborn baby up to a month old.

Responding and Adapting

Even within the first few hours of life, a newborn infant, given an appropriate stimulus, is capable of a variety of built-in responses. If placed upon the mother's abdomen, the baby will usually make crawling motions. The baby will turn its head toward anything that scratches its cheek—a nipple or a finger—and begin to suck it. Sucking is an exceedingly complex, but already highly developed, behavior pattern, involving intricate coordination of tongue and swallowing movements, synchronization of the baby's breathing with the sucking and swallowing sequence, and tactile stimulation from the nipple; yet it appears that most babies "know how to do it" from the start. Also, from the earliest moments of taking in fluid, sucking is an *adaptable* behavior that can be changed by its *consequences*—one definition of learning. The rapidity of sucking, for example, is dependent on the sweetness of the fluid being received. The sweeter the fluid, the more continuously—and also the more forcefully—an infant will suck (Lipsitt et al., 1976). In fact, the sucking rate even depends on the *pattern* of sweetness over time, rather than simply on the absolute amount of sweetness at the moment.

A group of newborns who were given a sucrose-sweetened solution through an automated nipple apparatus responded at the rate of 55 sucks per minute, compared with 46 sucks per minute for a group that received water. A third group, which had sucrose first and then water, matched the rate of the first group while they were getting sucrose; but when the sucrose changed to water, their rate fell below that of the water-only group. Not only did they respond differently to the different tastes, but the experience of the sweet solution in the preceding 5 minutes weakened their response to the water solution. (Kobre & Lipsitt, 1972)

Infants apparently come into the world preprogrammed to like and seek pleasurable sensations, such as sweetness, and to avoid or escape from unpleasant stimulation, such as loud noises, bright lights, strong odors, and painful stimuli. They also prefer novel stimuli to familiar ones (Cohen & Gelber, 1975). How these inborn preferences and response tendencies can lead to the learning of new responses will be discussed in chapter 8. For now, the important point is that they generate behavior that affects the environment (faster sucking produces more sweets), and this consequence, in turn, changes the subsequent behavior. Even an hour-old newborn is primed to interact with its environment and is prepared to learn from its experiences. It is through such interactions of inherited response tendencies and learned experiences that naive babies, in time, become worldly individuals.

Interacting Socially

Most of all, babies are designed to be sociable. They prefer human voices to other sounds and human faces to most other patterns (Fantz, 1963). As early as one week of age, a baby can distinguish its mother's voice from that of other women. In another week, the baby can perceive her voice and face as part of a total unit and will get upset when experimenters pair its mother's face or voice with those of a stranger's (Carpenter, 1973).

Babies not only respond to, but also interact with, their care-givers. High-speed film studies of this interaction reveal a remarkable degree of *synchronicity*—gazing, vocalizing, touching, and smiling of mothers and infants are closely coordinated (Martin, 1981). Babies respond and learn, but they also send out messages to those willing to listen and to love them. Not only have the behaviors of mothers and infants been shown to be linked, but their feelings are also matched. A 3-month-old infant may laugh when its mother laughs and frown or cry in response to her negative **affect**—emotion or mood (Tronick et al., 1980).

In general, developmental psychologists currently studying what babies can do are becoming ever more impressed with how *precocious* (smart for their a e) they are. They seem to come equipped to accomplish *three basic tasks of survival:* sustenance (feeding), maintenance of contact with people (for

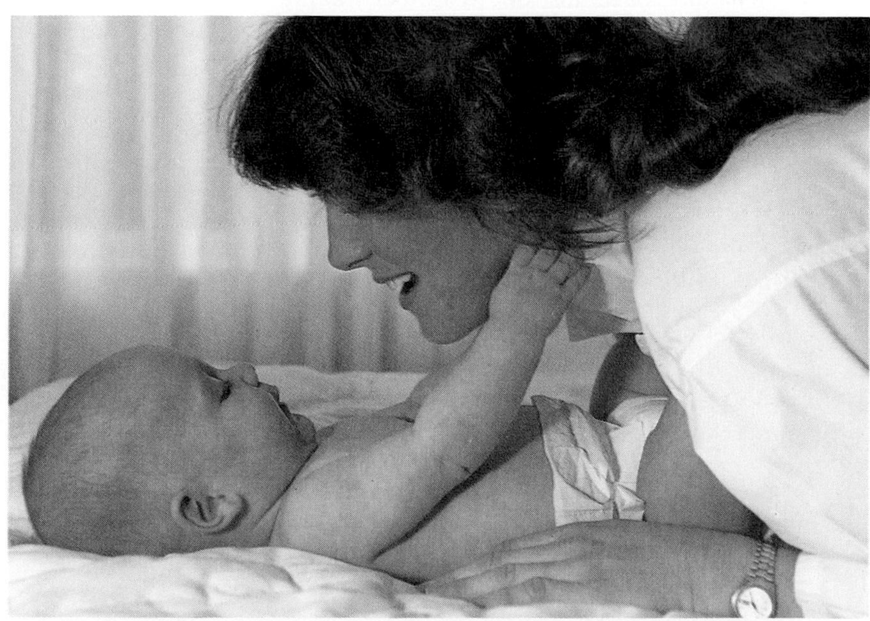

Newborns respond to the looks and vocalizing of their mothers. They also send out their own messages to these caregivers.

protection and care), and defense against harmful stimuli (withdrawing from pain or threat). To do these tasks requires perceptual skills, some ability to understand their experiences with people and objects, and basic thinking skills that very early combine the brain's information from different senses, such as vision and touch, to aid in grasping moving objects (von Hofsten & Lindhagen, 1979).

Some investigators have concluded that children are born with the ability to distinguish among things they experience and then to put this information into *categories.* This ability to categorize the flow on conscious experience is essential to build a knowledge base that grows by fitting the new into the familiar and adding new categories when necessary (see Masters, 1981). Given their limited education, infants are remarkably sophisticated young beings. (See also the article "Newborn Knowledge" in *The Best of Science.*)

The Beginning of Language Acquisition

Young children's acquisition of language is one of the most remarkable achievements of the human species. In the span of a few years, with little formal instruction, and often in spite of faulty information (parents talking "baby talk," for example), young children become superb linguists. By the age of 6, the average child is estimated to understand 14,000 words (Templin, 1957). Assuming that most of these words are learned between the ages of 18 months and 6 years, this works out to about nine new words a day, or almost one word per waking hour (Carey, 1978). Moreover, average 6-year-olds can analyze language into its minimal, separable units of sounds and meaning, use rules they have discovered by themselves for combining sounds into words and words into meaningful sentences, and take an active part in coherent conversations. Though language structure is not our focus, **Table 3.3** summarizes its various aspects so that you can appreciate better the complexity of what young children learn when they acquire language skills. How do they learn? How do they become able to express new ideas with word combinations they may never have heard? That is the test of true language mastery.

Stages in Natural Language Learning

The answer to the previous questions will come, in part, from a closer look at what a child does at each of four stages in language acquisition; the babbling stage, the one-word stage, the two-word stage, and the telegraphic-speech stage.

The babbling stage. Even before the vocal apparatus is completely formed, a baby begins to make vowel-like sounds. Cooing sounds begin in the second month, and babbling starts at 4 to 5 months. The onset of babbling seems to be biologically determined. Even a baby who is born deaf babbles until about 6 months; then the baby stops and is unable to speak without specialized intensive training.

Because babbling consists of syllable-like sequences such as "mamama" and "bububu," it sounds somewhat language-like. Indeed, some linguists have argued that babblings are the direct precursors of speech sounds. Specifically, they suggest

Table 3.3 *The Structure of Language*

Grammar is the field of study which seeks to describe the way language is structured and used. It includes several domains:

- **Phonology**—the study of the way sounds are put together to form words.
  - A **phoneme** is the smallest unit of speech that distinguishes between any two utterances. For example *b* and *p* distinguish *bin* from *pin.*
  - **Phonetics** is the study and classification of speech sounds.
- **Syntax**—the way in which words are strung together to form sentences. For example, subject ("I") + verb ("like") + object ("you") is a standard English word order.
  - A **morpheme** is the minimum distinctive unit of grammar that cannot be divided without losing its meaning. The word *bins* has two morphemes, *bin* and *s,* indicating the plural.
- **Semantics**—the study of the meanings of words and their changes over time. **Lexical meaning** is the dictionary meaning of a word. Meaning is sometimes conveyed by the *context* of a word in a sentence ("Run *fast*" versus "Make the knot *fast*") or the *inflection* with which it is spoken (try emphasizing different words in the phrase, "a white house cat").
- **Pragmatics**—rules for participating in conversations, social conventions for communicating, sequencing sentences, responding appropriately to others.

In recent studies, using imaginative video and computer techniques, babies have been shown to have an amazing language sophistication: a six-month-old can tell a vowel sound from a consonant.

that a baby babbles all sounds in all languages, and the repertoire is eventually narrowed down to the sounds to be found in the language he or she is exposed to (see, for example, Mowrer, 1960). This view, however, has little empirical support. For instance, a baby does not babble certain speech sounds (consonant clusters like *str* in *strong* and *xth* in *sixth*). Moreover, some sounds (*r* and *l*, for example) are present in babbling, but not in a child's first words. Rather than being the direct precursor of speech, then, babbling may be only indirectly related to speech. Perhaps babbling allows a baby to practice making sounds with the vocal apparatus, grouping the sounds into sequences, and adding "intonation" to those sequences (Clark & Clark, 1977).

Beyond babbling, infants also vocalize in response to the sounds made by their parents. Sometimes they do so simultaneously; sometimes they alternate their sounds with those of their parents, in a conversation without words. In doing this, the infants are learning sound patterns and intonations. When adults speak to infants and young children they use a special form that differs from adult speech—an exaggerated, high-pitched intonation than is usual in adult speech—known as **motherese.** It appears to serve a number of functions, among them to mark turn-taking in mother-infant dialogues, to help infants track and analyze components of speech, to get and hold attention, as well as to communicate affect. Mothers use a falling pitch to speak to distressed infants; they employ a rising pitch to engage alert infants.

How do babies like this motherese? New research demonstrates that they prefer it to other kinds of speech.

> *A sample of 48 four-month-old infants listened to tape-recorded speech samples of other mothers talking to their babies and also heard adult-directed speech by the same women. The infants' preferences were measured by the number of times they turned their heads in the direction of one of these types of speech stimuli. The majority of infants revealed a clear preference for motherese by turning more often to listen to its high intonation. (Fernald, 1985)*

As they near the end of their first year, infants begin to imitate the intonation pattern of their parents' language. Though no words are produced, the sounds of an American child are those of American English, while those of a Japanese child begin to sound Japanese (Glucksberg & Danks, 1975).

The one-word stage. The beginnings of patterned, "true" speech occur some time near the end of the first year, as the child's first recognizable words begin to appear. These first words are usually concrete nouns or verbs. They are used to *name* things that move, make a noise, or can be manipulated—*mama, ball,* and *dog,* for instance. For example, when the word *moon* first appears in a child's vocabulary, it may mean only a round thing; clocks, cakes, the letter *O,* or any other circular object may also be called *moon.* Gradually, the word is associated with other characteristics of the moon—its rising at night, its shining, its varying shapes—until the word is applied only to the moon (Clark, 1973). Children continue to overextend word meanings in this fashion well into their third year of life.

At the one-word stage, children use their first words for making both assertions and requests. They usually make assertions by pointing at an object and naming it. They seem to use such assertions to call an adult's attention to something they are interested in at that moment. They often make requests by reaching for an object and asking for it with a whining intonation. Thus, children seem to use language for communicating messages to others from their first words on (Greenfield & Smith, 1976).

Children not only are learning the meaning of single words, but they are also using them in a sequence of one-word utterances to convey more complex meanings.

A child hearing a car go by: Car.
Parent: What?
Child: Go.
Parent: What?
Child: Bus.

The parent interprets this to mean that the child is recalling a bus ride taken the previous day—a memory probably triggered by the sound of the car. In this one-word stage, the child is actively developing hypotheses about the way to combine words into sentences. Not used at this time are words for relationships, internal states, or passive objects that do not stand out in the child's perception.

The two-word stage. Children begin combining words into two-word utterances around 18 months of age. For adults to understand two-word utterances such as "Tanya ball," they must know the context in which the words are spoken. "Tanya ball" could mean "Tanya wants the ball" or "Tanya throws the ball." At this stage, children across widely differing language communities tend to express similar roles and relations with two-word utterances. For instance, 10 children speaking different languages (English, Samoan, Finnish, Hebrew, Swedish) were found to talk mostly about three roles: a mover, something movable, and location (Braine, 1976). An example of mover and movable is "Tanya ball" (when Tanya kicks a ball); while "sit pool" is an example of location (someone sits in a pool).

All children speak in one-word utterances before putting two words together, but they do not go through a three-word stage. After two words, sentence size varies considerably.

The telegraphic-speech stage. Beyond the two-word stage, speech becomes **telegraphic:** filled with short, simple sentences, using many content words (mostly nouns and verbs), but lacking tense endings and plurals. Telegraphic speech also lacks **function words** like *the, and,* and *of,* which help express the relationships between other words and which are added in a predictable order as a language user matures. "Bill hit ball window break" is a telegraphic message. The full message is, "Bill hit the ball that broke the window."

By the age of 2, English-speaking children have learned that word order is important—the three critical elements are actor-action-object, usually arranged in that order. They typically misinterpret "Mary was followed by her little lamb to school" as "Mary *(actor)* followed *(action)* her lamb *(object),*" ignoring the function words.

Around the age of $2\frac{1}{2}$, children begin to use words such as *dream, forget, pretend, believe, guess,* and *hope* to talk about internal states (Shatz et al., 1983). They also talk about emotional states with words such as *happy, sad,* and *angry.* They go beyond talking about the physical world and talk about the psychological world as well.

Language becomes more complex in maturing children for many reasons. They know more words (see **Figure 3.6**) and have mastered more grammatical devices; they have increasingly sophisticated memories, an ability to think about thoughts, and competence to understand abstract ideas. Furthermore, they discover that there is more to life than meets the eye—there are processes of change as well as objects that change. There are memories of the past and expectations of the future; there is also much that cannot be seen—like fear and trust—but which needs to be communicated.

Hypotheses and Rules

From a study of the regular error patterns of children at each stage of language development, it is apparent that they are trying out hypotheses about the way sounds and words ought to go together to convey meaning and about the rules of phonology, syntax, and semantics. Sometimes, of course, these hypotheses are wrong.

One of the most common errors is **overregularization,** in which a rule is applied too widely, resulting in incorrect linguistic forms. For example, once children learn the past-tense rule (adding *-ed* to the verb), they will add *-ed* to all verbs, forming such as "doed" and "breaked." As children learn the rule for plurals (adding the sound *-s* or *-z* to the end of a word), they will again overextend the rule, creating words like "foots" and "mouses."

Overregularization is an especially interesting error to psychologists, because it usually appears after children have learned and used the correct forms of verbs and nouns. That is, they first use the

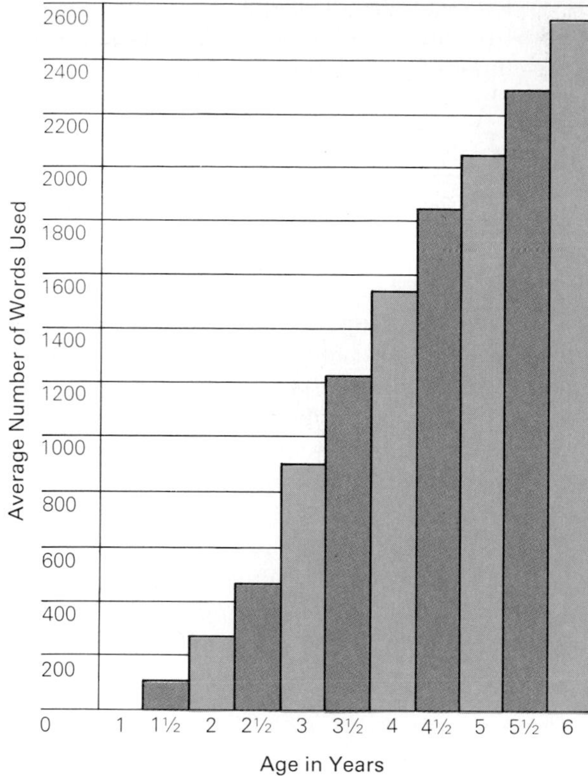

Figure 3.6 *Children's Growth in Vocabulary*
The number of words a child can use increases rapidly between the ages of 1½ and 6. This study shows children's average vocabularies at intervals of six months.

(From "The Acquisition of Language" by B. A. Moskowitz, *Scientific American,* Nov. 1978. Copyright © 1978 by Scientific American, Inc. All rights reserved. Reprinted by permission.)

correct verb forms (*came* and *went*), apparently because they were learned as separate vocabulary items; but when the general rule for the past tense is learned later, it is immediately extended to all verbs. The children say "comed" and "goed," even though they have never heard other people say such words. Such mistakes are evidence that language learning depends on acquiring general rules rather than just imitating what adults say.

Acquiring Language: Nature or Nurture?

Our discussion of *what* young children can do with—and to—language at different stages has not answered out initial question about *how* they acquire language. Do they learn it by imitating the sounds, words, and sentences they hear? Do they learn it because they receive praise and approval from adults when they speak grammatically, and gentle reproofs when they speak ungrammatically? This *nurture* viewpoint, argued by B. F. Skinner (1957), regards language acquisition as a *learned skill;* when examined closely, however, this view does not seem to fit the facts.

First, imitation is not essential to grammatical learning. While most preschoolers do not go around parroting what adults say, they, nonetheless, learn many new grammatical rules. One study detailed the story of a boy who could not produce speech, but was otherwise normal. Although he never could imitate an English sentence, he managed to understand a fair amount of spoken English (Lenneberg, 1962).

Similarly, approval and correction cannot fully explain the way children acquire grammatical rules. Parents tend to correct children's utterances on the basis of their *truth value* rather than their accurate grammatical quality. When a child says "One, two, I have two foots!" the mother may respond enthusiastically, "That's right! You really know how to count now." The mother is unlikely to frown and say, "No, you have two FEET, not two foots!" However, when children utter a grammatically correct, but factually incorrect, sentence, they are likely to be corrected. For example, when a child calls a muffin "a cookie," he is likely to hear his mother say, "No, that's not a cookie. It's a muffin" (Brown & Hanlon, 1970). Neither imitation nor correction, then, can explain grammatical development very well.

Environmental influences play a role in shaping language. The dependence of language acquisition on social interaction is seen in the case study of a boy with normal hearing born to deaf parents.

> *The parents spoke only in American sign language, but exposed their child to a daily diet of television viewing where he heard people talking; but because he was sickly and confined to his home, the only real people he had contact with were his parents. By the age of 3 he was able to use sign language fluently—but could not speak or understand spoken English. The reseacher concluded that a child can learn a language only if there are chances for interaction with real people who speak the language. (Moskowitz, 1978)*

Although imitation, correction, and environment influence speech acquisition, the bulk of the evidence, however, suggests that the primary role is played by nature, through maturation. According to these studies, children come to the language-acquisition situation with biologically predetermined mental structures that facilitate the comprehension and production of speech by limiting the hypotheses they generate about the grammar of language (Chomsky, 1965, 1975). As soon as their brains are sufficiently developed to send out nerve signals, children's language acquisition "programs" are partly written. Language emerges and evolves at particular periods that correspond more closely with physical and cognitive maturation than with particular learning experiences—always assuming opportunities to interact with speaking humans (Lenneberg, 1969).

Children learn to speak in a highly methodical way, by breaking down the language they hear into its simplest parts and then developing rules that put the parts together to communicate thoughts and feelings (Moskowitz, 1978). They produce words and sentences they have never heard according to these grammatical rules. Moreover, they usually receive very little systematic teaching from parents, tend to ignore corrections, and do not benefit much from additional practice (especially when they are taught grammar in school). All of this evidence seems to indicate that children are born to be competent in acquiring language.

Yet to say that language acquisition has a strong biological basis does not mean that children can achieve it without working. Quite the contrary, children seem to be forming and testing hypotheses constantly in learning new word meanings and new grammatical rules (Carey, 1978). Our affection for young children often leads us to overlook errors in their speech or to find the errors amusing when we do notice them. It takes great insight to realize that those errors reflect the hypotheses testing going on in the language-learners' heads and the active role it plays in acquiring language.

As children mature, they acquire many new language skills. They learn to use language to inform, to persuade, to flatter, and to conceal. They try to use elegant poetic variations, alliteration, metaphors; they invent new words and ways of expressing familiar ideas as well as give verbal expression to fears and fantasies. To carry on a simple conversation they master many skills: monitoring the sequence and pacing of conversations, interrupting, giving and receiving compliments, changing a topic, and paraphrasing. When these spoken skills are combined with the "body language" of nonverbal gestures, the complexity of message sending (encoding) and receiving (decoding) becomes enormous. But they do it, usually well—and without a single course in the art of conversational communication.

Life without language would be more than an inconvenient deficit. It would be life without connection to ideas and to people. Language meets the need to know, to belong, and to express what we know and feel. It is fundamental to our humanity.

Having outlined some aspects of early development, we next examine two of the major strands of development that continue throughout the life cycle: cognitive development—how we are able to use ideas and process information—and social-emotional development—how we form the bonds of human connection and become socialized.

Cognitive Development

The way in which the processes of knowing—perceiving, reasoning, imagining, and problem solving—evolve is referred to as **cognitive development.** Studies of cognitive development tend to focus on such topics as the kinds of things and the way children remember, the manner in which they develop expectations, the ways they distinguish the appearance of things from reality, and the ways they sort experiences into categories. Much of the current cognitive-development research derives from the pioneering work of the late Swiss psychologist Jean Piaget.

Piaget's Insights into Mental Growth

No one has contributed more to our knowledge of the ways in which children think, reason, and solve problems than Jean Piaget. For nearly 50 years he devoted his career to observing children's intellectual development. Piaget began by carefully observing the behavior of his own children from an early age. He would pose problems for them, observe their responses, alter the situations slightly, and again see how they would respond. In contrast to today's experimental psychologists who study information processing in laboratory settings by designing complex experiments that yield simple, specific conclusions, Piaget used simple demonstrations and sensitive interviews with individual children to draw complex generalizations.

Piaget was interested primarily in the changes that take place in a child's mental processes during the course of cognitive development. How does a child transform specific, concrete information gathered through sensory experience into general, abstract concepts that are not limited to any immediate stimulus situation? To answer this question, Piaget studied the ways children perceive certain situations and the manner in which they come to "think about" and "know about" physical reality. His interest was not in the amount of information children knew, but in the ways their thinking and inner representations of outer reality changed at different stages in their development.

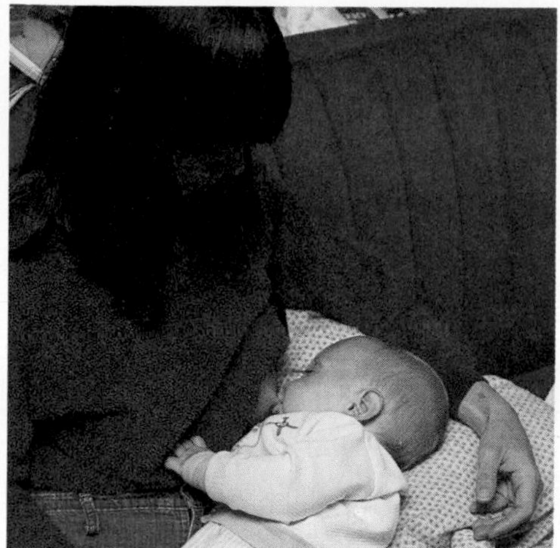

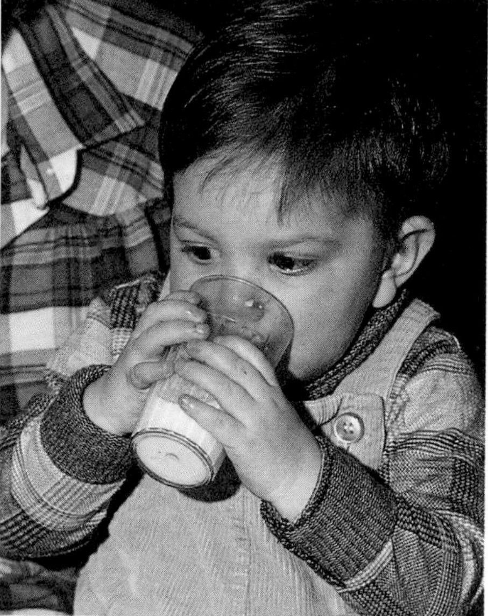

Although an infant will begin to suck a bottle just the way he or she sucked a breast (assimilation), the infant will soon discover that some changes need to be made (accommodation). The infant will make an even greater accommodation in the transition from bottle to cup.

Assimilation and Accommodation

According to Piaget, there are two processes at work in cognitive growth: assimilation and accommodation. In **assimilation,** we modify or change new information to fit into what we already know; in **accommodation** we restructure or modify what we already know so that new information can fit in better. For example, consider the transitions a baby must make in changing from a breast to a bottle and, finally, to a cup. The initial sucking response, as we have seen, is a reflex action present at birth. In adapting to a bottle, an infant still uses many parts of the sequence unchanged (assimilation), but must grasp and draw on the rubber nipple somewhat differently and learn to hold the bottle at an appropriate angle (accommodation). The step from bottle to cup requires more accommodation, but still will rely on earlier skills of sucking fluid in and swallowing it.

Piaget saw cognitive development as the result of the constant interweaving of assimilation and accommodation in an upward spiraling process. Assimilation keeps and adds to what exists, thereby connecting the present with the past. Accommodation results from problems posed by the environment, perceptions that do not fit with what we know and think. These discrepancies between our ideas and what we see are an important influence in cognitive development. They force a child to develop more adaptive inner structures and processes, making possible creative and more appropriate action to meet future challenges. So both assimilation and accommodation are needed, but in balance.

Through these two processes we become increasingly less dependent on perceiving and more dependent of thinking. Mental growth always includes going from reliance on *appearances* to reliance on *rules.* According to Piaget, the earliest mental structures, which he called **schemes,** simply guide sensorimotor sequences such as sucking, looking, grasping, and pushing, probably with little or no "thought" as we know it. These sensorimotor sequences are dependent on the presence of objects—things that can be sucked or watched or grasped, for example—but thereafter, mental structures increasingly incorporate symbolic representations of outer reality which, in turn, make possible increasingly complex mental operations (Gallagher & Reid, 1981; Piaget, 1977).

Stages in Cognitive Development

Piaget identified four qualitatively different stages of cognitive growth in the continuing upward spiral of assimilation and accommodation. He believed that all children progress through these stages in the same sequence, although they differ in their rates of development. He called the four stages the *sensorimotor stage* (infancy), the *preoperational stage* (early childhood), the *concrete operational stage* (middle childhood), and the *formal operational stage* (adolescence). Distinctive styles of thinking emerge at each stage.

The sensorimotor stage (roughly from birth to age 2). So many new cognitive achievements appear during the first two years that Piaget subdivided the **sensorimotor stage** itself into six substages. We will summarize only the two main trends in this period: the change in adaptive responses and the development of object permanence.

In the early months an infant "knows" only "in the sense of recognizing or anticipating familiar, recurring objects and happenings and 'thinks' in the sense of behaving toward them. . . in predictable, organized, and often adaptive ways" (Flavell, 1977, p. 16). During the first year the sensorimotor sequences are improved, combined, coordinated, and integrated (sucking and grasping, looking and manipulating, for example). They become more varied as the infant tests different aspects of the environment, discovers that actions have an effect on outer events, and begins to perform what look like intentional, cognitively directed behaviors toward clear goals. By the end of the second year, the capacity to represent absent events symbolically is clearly present, as shown by the child's ability to identify an object not present.

Part of the development of a child's adaptive responses is a gradual development of a concept of **object permanence**—objects are perceived as existing and behaving independently from the child's action or awareness. The child progresses from merely following a moving object visually (soon after birth), to continuing to look at the place the object has gone out of sight from (2–3 months), to watching for its reappearance at a different spot or visually searching for it (4–8 months), to retrieving it from out-of-sight positions under increasingly different and less vision-dependent conditions (8–18 months). By about age 2 the child "will grin with anticipation and then systematically search each possible hiding place. . . . [The child] may also spontaneously try the same game on you, with [the child] doing the hiding and your doing the finding . . . " (Flavell, 1985, p. 37). Clearly children at this age now have an internal symbolic representation of an object as independent of their perception of or action toward it.

The preoperational stage (roughly from 2 to 7 years of age). Young children start life as *naive realists.* That is, they believe in what they see. But like *scientists,* who look for regularities in the flux and variety of individual events, young children gradually become aware of **invariants** in the environment, things that do not change their identity even though they change their appearance. Their mastery of the concept of object permanence enables them to go on to discover that objects not only have continuing identity, but the same qualitative identity despite changes in appearance. Such thinking is characteristic of the **preoperational stage.** Early in this period, children may believe that a boy can become a girl if he plays with dolls or wears girls' clothes; by the end of the period, they are likely to know better. In one study, 3-year-old children who watched the hind end of a cat while a dog mask was put over its head thought the cat had become a dog; 6-year-olds were more likely to believe that a cat could not turn into a dog (DeVries, 1969).

Their previous mastery of object permanence also readies children for representative thinking during this period, thinking dependent on symbols rather than on sensorimotor relationships. Their thinking is still more dependent on appearances than on concepts and rules, which prevents them from carrying out certain mental operations; hence the term *preoperational* to characterize the thought processes of this period.

Thinking at the beginning of this period is characterized by **centration**—a single, central focus. A child cannot take more than one perceptual factor into account at the same time. One aspect of centration is **egocentrism,** which is not self-centeredness, but difficulty in imagining a scene from someone else's viewpoint. Piaget used a three-dimensional, three-mountain scene and asked children to describe what a teddy bear standing on the far side would see; his subjects could not describe the scene accurately until about age 7 (Piaget & Inhelder, 1967). In later research, however, looking at scenes more familiar to them, children of 3 and 4 were able to turn movable versions to show someone else's view, though they still did poorly with a stationary scene like the one Piaget used (Borke, 1975).

In general, **decentration**—the ability to take into account two or more physical dimensions at once—does not evolve until later. This ability is illustrated by Piaget's classic lemonade study: When an equal amount of lemonade is poured into two glasses 5-, 6-, and 7-year-old children all report that the glasses contain the same amount; but when the lemonade from one glass is poured into a tall, thin glass, they have differing opinions. The 5-year-olds know it is the same lemonade in the tall glass (qualitative identity), but believe that somehow it has become more. The 6-year-olds are uncertain, but also say the tall glass has more. The

7-year-olds "know" there is no difference. The younger children are still relying on appearance; the older ones now rely on a rule. They are also taking into account two dimensions, height and width, while the younger children are considering only height, a normally useful cue for "more."

Concrete operations (roughly from 7 to 11 years of age). The 7-year-olds in the lemonade study have achieved an understanding of what Piaget called **conservation.** This is the understanding that physical properties do not change when nothing is added or taken away, even though appearances change. The lemonade example showed conservation of volume. During the **concrete operational stage,** children develop other kinds of conservation, such as conservation of numbers and area. They are ready at last for what Piaget called **mental operations**—mentally transforming information and then mentally reversing the sequence. They can depend on concepts rather than on perceptual evidence gained from looking at and touching things.

Although these children become able to use logic and inference in solving concrete problems, the symbols they use in reasoning are still symbols for concrete objects and events, not abstractions. Their limitations are shown in the familiar game of "20 Questions," in which the task is to identify the object being thought of by asking the fewest possible questions. A child of 7 or 8 usually sticks to specific questions which, if correct, can give the child the correct answer (Is it a bird? Is it a cat?). A few years later the same child will approach the task systematically, going from general categories (Is it an animal?) to subcategories and then to specific guesses, which means asking several questions at first that cannot themselves answer the "What is it?" question (Bruner et al., 1966).

The formal operational stage (roughly from age 11 on). In Piaget's final stage of cognitive growth, the **formal operational stage,** logical operations are no longer bound by concrete problems. It is now possible to deal with abstractions, consider hypothetical questions (What if a man had eyes in the back of his head?), and design formal ways to test abstract ideas. Most young adolescents have acquired all the mental structures needed to go from being naive thinkers to experts.

The approach of adolescents and adults to the "20 Questions" game demonstrates this ability to use abstractions and to adopt an information-processing strategy that is not limited by the questions asked. They impose their own structures on the task, starting with broad categories and then formulating and testing hypotheses in the light of their knowledge of categories and relationships.

This five-year-old girl is aware that the two containers have the same amount of colored liquid. However when the liquid from one is poured into a taller container, she indicates that there is more in the taller one. She has not yet grasped the concept of conservation.

Modern Perspectives on Cognitive Development

There is no question about the importance of Piaget's contribution in focusing attention on the development of cognitive processes in children. The questions he asked, the phenomena he studied, and the conceptual insights he offered remain significant. His theory of the dynamic interplay of assimilation and accommodation is generally accepted as a valid account of the way a child's mind develops. The general developmental sequences he identified have also been supported by independent investigators. He became a model for psychologists' theorizing about developmental processes in terms of stages.

On the other hand, Piaget seems to have underestimated children's cognitive capabilities. Without the benefit of modern research techniques, he had to fall back on simpler methods of observing overt behaviors. For instance, in order to study infants' concepts of object permanence, Piaget examined if and how infants searched for hidden objects. Thus, to be credited with having object permanence, an infant not only had to "know" that an object continued to exist even when it was out of sight, but also to have the sensorimotor skills to search for the hidden object. The latter demand, which has nothing to do with the object concept, can lead to an underestimation of babies' knowledge about objects (see Gelman & Baillargeon, 1983).

With modern technology, researchers can now more accurately assess an infant's attention to, and interest in, a display by measuring the infant's heart rate, the time spent on looking at the display, and so forth. With the help of these techniques, researchers can capitalize on an infant's ability to show habituation and dishabituation of attention. **Habituation** is the adaptation of no longer paying attention to an unchanging stimulus. It occurs when an infant is shown the same display over and over: the infant attends to it less and less (spends less time looking at it)—as if bored by seeing the same "old" thing. When shown something different, the infant is likely to look at the display more—to show **dishabituation,** or a recovery from habituation.

With the means to measure infants' attention, researchers can now study infants' concepts of object permanence more directly.

> *In one study done with 6-month-olds the infants sat in front of a large display box. Directly before them was a small screen; to the left of the screen was a long ramp. The infants watched the following event: the screen was raised (so the infants could see there was nothing behind it) and then lowered, and a toy car was pushed onto the ramp; the car rolled down the ramp and across the display box, disappearing at one end of the screen, reappearing at the other end, and finally exiting the display box to the right (see* ***Figure 3.7A****).*
>
> *After the infants habituated to this event, they saw two test events. These events were identical to the habituation event except that a box was placed behind the screen: the screen was raised (revealing the box) and lowered, and the car rolled down the ramp and across the display box. The only difference between the test events was the location of the box behind the screen. In one event (possible event), the box was placed at the BACK of the display box, behind the tracks of the car; in the other (impossible event), it was placed on TOP of the tracks so that it blocked the car's path (****Figure 3.7B****). To adults, the first event is consistent with the* solidity principle: *the car rolls freely through empty space. The second event, in contrast, violates the principle: the car appears to roll through the space occupied by the box. (Baillargeon, 1986, p. 27)*

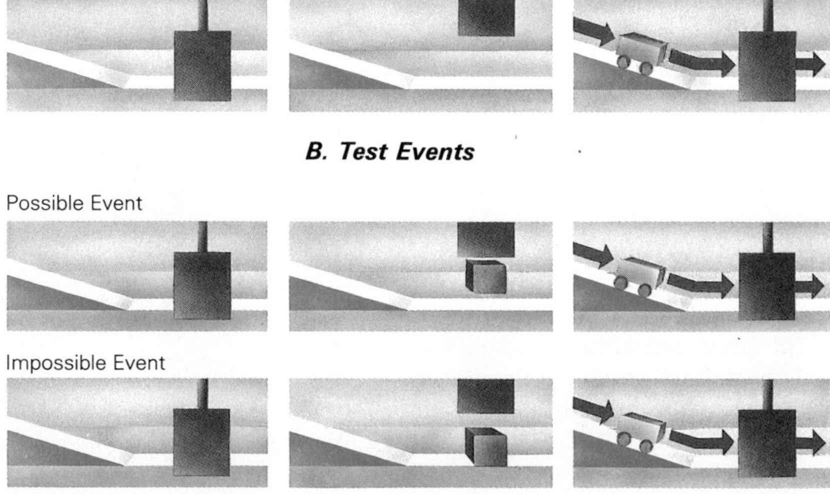

Figure 3.7 *A Schematic Representation of Habituation and Test events.*

The 6-month-olds in this study habituated to the initial display (a possible event). They recovered from habituation when shown the impossible test event, but not when shown the possible test event. Note that the only important difference between the two test events was that the impossible event violated the object concept: the car rolled through the hidden box. These infants seemed to find this violation interesting and surprising—suggesting that they expected objects (such as the hidden box) to exist and occupy space even when they were out of sight. Thus, in contrast to Piaget's claim that infants do not begin to develop object permanence until age 8 months or so, these findings suggest that infants already have some notion of object permanence by 6 months, if not earlier (see also Baillargeon et al., 1985).

Another reason for Piaget's underestimation of children's cognitive competence is that he relied heavily on children's descriptions of their thought processes; but children may understand something but not be able to explain it. It is not surprising that other researchers are supplementing and, in some cases, challenging some of Piaget's findings. For example, there is growing evidence that children possess some cognitive capacities earlier than Piaget believed possible (Selman, 1980). For example, when preschoolers can show their understanding of cause-and-effect relationships through nonverbal behavior instead of verbal responses, they display more sophisticated causal reasoning than Piaget's interviews with children would lead us to believe they have (Bullock & Gelman, 1979; Pines, 1983).

There is a bonus (unexpected, but nonetheless very big) for efforts to correct for Piaget's overreliance on children's verbal reports. Such efforts often alert us to discrepancies between children's verbal reports about their thought processes and their nonverbal behavioral performances. Understanding these discrepancies has become an important and exciting topic in the study of cognitive development: **metacognition,** or thinking about thinking—to be discussed in chapter 10 (Flavell, 1979; Schneider, 1984).

A third reason why Piagetian tasks may have underestimated children's competence is that those tasks almost always pit a conceptual reality against a perceptual appearance. Consider again the volume conservation task. In that task, the conceptual reality is that merely pouring a certain amount of liquid from one container to another should not change its volume. While pouring the liquid into a different shape container (from a fat glass to a thin glass) may result in a higher liquid level and, hence, a taller liquid column, such changes are irrelevant to judgment about volume. However, young children tend to judge volume on the basis of height, and they may be tempted to think that the thin glass contains more liquid than the fat glass. In order to be credited with understanding volume conservation, children not only have to master the conceptual reality, they also have to ignore the compelling perceptual appearance (Flavell, 1985).

When the compelling perceptual appearance is removed, children sometimes show greater understanding of the conceptual reality. One example can be found in children's conceptual development. When asked to sort objects by putting "things that are alike together," children often construct thematic scenes (for example, arranging a doll, a chair, a dog, and a tea set to form a living-room scene), whereas adults generally group objects according to their kinds (all dolls together, all chairs together, all dogs together, and so on). Piaget interpreted these findings as evidence of children's inability to organize objects according to their kinds. However, because children often are encouraged to construct thematic scenes with their toys, it is not surprising that they do so in sorting tasks as well. In a recent study where 3-year-olds were asked to put things that were alike together, some children were then told to put the things that went together on the same piece of paper; others were told to put things that went together into the same plastic bag. The task of putting things on sheets of paper allows children to construct scenes, whereas putting things into plastic bags does not. Indeed, when the temptation to construct scenes was removed, children displayed greater ability to organize objects according to kinds—as adults do (Markman et al., 1981).

In short, an important lesson to be learned from recent research on cognitive development is the distinction between *competence* and *performance.* To understand young children's cognitive competence, we need to use "child-friendly tasks" to minimize irrelevant demands.

Early cognitive competencies revealed by recent studies make us re-evaluate Piaget's stage theory (Gelman, 1979). If preschoolers have some rudiments of cognitive capabilities that Piaget reserved for older children and adults, do "preoperational" children really think in ways fundamentally different from "concrete operational" or "formal operational" individuals? Some argue that an important aspect of intellectual development consists of learning how to organize existing knowledge better, rather than the unfolding of new capacities. For example, a child may organize knowledge into subroutines—coherent units of information and systematic ways of using them. Subroutines increase the child's efficiency in carrying out arithmetical functions, comprehending stories, and other mental tasks. With practice, the child also develops greater ability to gain swift access to these stored subroutines (Case, 1985; Chi & Koeske, 1983; Flavell, 1985; Rozin, 1976; Siegler, 1983). Indeed, the emphases on information-processing capacity and domain-specific knowledge have generated much exciting research. They are forcing researchers to rethink beliefs about children's thinking and how it develops.

Social and Emotional Development

A child competent in language and cognitive skills would still be deficient without corresponding social and emotional development. Although developmental psychologists have tended to focus on the growth of mental processes, children do not thrive solely by becoming smart: they must form relationships with other people, and they must be in touch with their own feelings.

In this section we will examine some aspects of these strands of development: how children form relationships with others (parents most significantly), how parenting styles affect children's behavior and personalities; how gender roles develop. We will look at the development of moral understanding and end with a brief discussion of stages of sexual and social orientation, as described by two influential theorists: Sigmund Freud and Erik Erikson.

Socialization

Socialization is defined as the lifelong process of shaping an individual's behavioral patterns, values, standards, skills, attitudes, and motives to conform to those regarded as desirable in a particular society (Hetherington & Parke, 1975). Many people are involved in this process—mother, father, siblings, relatives, friends, and coworkers. Institutions such as the school, the church, and the legal and penal systems exert pressure to accept certain values and to comply with certain standards of conduct, but the family is the most influential shaper and regulator of socialization. It helps to form the basic patterns of responsiveness to others, which, in turn, form the basis of consistent styles of relating to other people throughout life.

Parent's goals in socializing their children range from the specific—saying "please" and "thank you" and not talking with a mouth full of food—to the general—being cooperative, honest, and responsible. Overall, parents are interested in fostering the optimal development of their children so that they will become well-functioning adults (see **Table 3.4**). In our society, one of the values associated with a desirable adult role is the ability to form bonds of intimacy and stability with others (Maccoby & Martin, 1983).

Attachment and Loving Relationships

Social development begins with the establishment of a close emotional relationship between a child and a mother or other regular care giver. This intense, enduring relationship is called **attachment.** For a child to develop attachment, sensory and response systems must be sufficiently mature, and there must be a close interaction with a parent or other care giver during the critical period of the first year. Attachment is usually apparent by the time an infant is 6 to 9 months old and is promoted by circumstances that extend the duration and/or frequency of close physical contact. It has been found that conditions for attachment are often best for first-born children and for infants who are "at risk" (premature or sick). Can you theorize why this is so?

We can infer a child's development of attachment from several behaviors. The child seeks to be near the parent (or care giver), resists separation, uses the parent as a secure base when exploring unfamiliar situations, and clings to the parent when afraid. Further, the child seeks both attention and signs of approval from the parent or care giver (Brackbill, 1979). The baby may gain closeness and attention through a variety of behaviors, such as smiling, vocalizing, looking at the parent's face, and crying.

Attachment behaviors occur in many species. In some, the forming of the relationship is aided by chemical effects from the mother's licking the newborn, eating the placenta, and giving off odors called **pheromones** that are attractive to the young. It is guided by a timetable associated with the stage at which the infant animal begins to move about. In some species, attachment takes the form of **imprinting,** the tendency of an infant animal to form an attachment to the first moving object it sees and/or hears (Johnson & Gottlieb, 1981). Usu-

Table 3.4 *Types of Tasks of Early Childhood Socialization in the Family*

Parental Aim or Activity	Child's Task or Achievement
1. Provision of nurturance and physical care	Acceptance of nurturance (development of trust)
2. Training and channeling of physiological needs in toilet training, weaning, provision of solid foods, etc.	Control of the expression of biological impulses; learning acceptable channels and times of gratification
3. Teaching and skill-training in language, perceptual skills, physical skills, self-care skills in order to facilitate care, insure safety, etc.	Learning to recognize objects and cues; language learning; learning to walk, negotiate obstacles, dress, feed self
4. Orienting the child to immediate world of kin, neighborhood, community, and society, and to his or her own feelings.	Developing a cognitive map of one's social world; learning to fit behavior to situational demands
5. Transmitting cultural and subcultural goals and values and motivating the child to accept them for his or her own	Developing a sense of right and wrong; developing goals and criteria for choices, investment of effort for the common good
6. Promoting interpersonal skills, motives, and modes of feeling and behaving in relation to others	Learning to take the perspective of another person; responding selectively to the expectations of others
7. Guiding, correcting, helping the child to formulate own goals, plan own activities	Achieving a measure of self-regulation and criteria for evaluating own performance

(From Clausen, 1986, p. 141)

ally this object is the mother—but not always. Young geese raised by a human will learn to follow that person instead of one of their own kind (Lorenz, 1937). A monkey raised by a dog will become more strongly attached to its foster mother than to other monkeys (Mason & Kenney, 1974).

In animals, this basic first attachment is the mechanism by which the young establish their identification as members of their species. Extensive animal research on attachment has demonstrated an upper age limit for developing a relationship, as well as the results of a failure to develop it. For example, puppies that do not form an attachment to other dogs by 14 weeks of age have difficulty ever doing so (Scott et al., 1974); however, even attachment to the mother is not enough for healthy social development. Young monkeys—despite the formation of a strong attachment to a mother substitute—have trouble forming normal social and sexual relationships in adulthood if they have been deprived of chances to interact with other monkeys in their early lives (see the ***Close-up*** on p. 84).

With human infants, the lack of close, loving relationships—on physical growth and even on life itself—has been shown in many studies. In 1915, a doctor at Johns Hopkins Hospital reported that despite adequate physical care, 90 percent of the infants admitted to orphanages in Baltimore died within the first year. Studies of hospitalized infants over the next 30 years found that despite adequate nutrition, the children often developed respiratory infections and fevers of unknown origin, failed to gain weight, and even showed signs of physiological deterioration, such as diarrhea, decrease in muscle tone, and eating difficulties (see Bowlby, 1969; Sherrod et al., 1978). Another study of infants in foundling homes in the United States and Canada reported evidence of severe emotional and physical disorders, as well as high mortality rates despite good food and medical care (Spitz & Wolf, 1946). This negative effect of early institutionalization holds also for families with high stress and low caring. In family environments marked by emotional detachment and hostility, children are found to weigh less and have retarded bone development. They begin to grow when they are removed from the hostile environment, but their growth again becomes stunted if they are returned to it—a phenomenon known as "psychosocial dwarfism" (Gardner, 1972).

John Bowlby (1973) proposed a theory of attachment in which early bonding of an infant to its mother was necessary for normal social relationships later. It now is known that the early proximity of mother to child is neither a necessary, nor a sufficient, condition for attachment (Rutter, 1979). Positive bonds can be formed with any care giver who is comforting, interacts actively, and is responsive to a baby's signals (Ainsworth, 1973). Indeed, the mother bond is strong when these "quality of care" conditions exist and weak without them. Children given high quality day-care benefit as much as those cared for entirely at home by their mothers. As summarized by one expert, "After 20 years of research on home versus day-care, we

Close-up *Attachment Is Not Enough*

An extensive program of research on the role of mothering in monkeys has provided intriguing and unexpected answers to basic questions about the mother-child relationship. Although the findings cannot be applied directly to humans, they suggest useful lines of human research.

The generally accepted theory at the beginning was that infants develop attachment and affection for a caretaker in response to having physical needs met, especially the need for food. But when macaque monkeys were separated from their mothers at birth and placed in cages where they had access to two artificial "mothers"—a wire one and a terrycloth one—the babies nestled close to the cloth mother and spent little time on the wire one, even when it was the wire one that gave milk: the one that provided contact comfort was preferred over the one that provided food.

The terrycloth mother was also used as a base of operations in exploring new stimuli. When stimuli known to produce curious and manipulative responses were introduced, the baby monkeys would gradually venture out to explore, then return to her before exploring further. When a fear stimulus (a toy bear beating a drum) was introduced, the baby monkeys would run to her; when new stimuli were presented in her absence, they would often freeze in a crouched position or run from object to object screaming and crying. When a cloth diaper was one of the objects, they would often clutch it, but it never pacified them (Harlow & Zimmerman, 1958).

Did the monkeys with terrycloth mothers develop normally, as it appeared? At first, the experimenters thought so, but a very different picture emerged when it became time for females raised in this way to become mothers. First, despite elaborate arrangements, it took many months to get any of them inseminated; success was finally achieved with only 4 of the 18.

After the birth of her baby, the first of these unmothered mothers ignored the infant and sat relatively motionless at one side of the living cage, staring fixedly into space hour after hour. If a human observer approached and threatened either the baby or the mother, there was no counterthreat. . . .As the infant matured and became mobile, it made continual, desperate attempts to effect maternal contact. These attempts were consistently repulsed by the mother. She would brush the baby away or restrain it by pushing the baby's face to the woven-wire floor. (Harlow, 1965, pp. 256–57)

When other "motherless" monkeys were artificially inseminated, most were either indifferent and unresponsive to their babies or brutalized them, biting off their fingers or toes, pounding them, and nearly killing them until caretakers intervened.

One of the most interesting findings was that, despite the consistent punishment, the babies persisted in their attempts to make maternal contact. In the end, "it was a case of the baby adopting the mother, not the mother adopting the baby" (Harlow, 1965, p. 259); and fortunately, with successive pregnancies, the maternal behavior of these mothers improved so that this brutal behavior was no longer the norm for this group of monkeys.

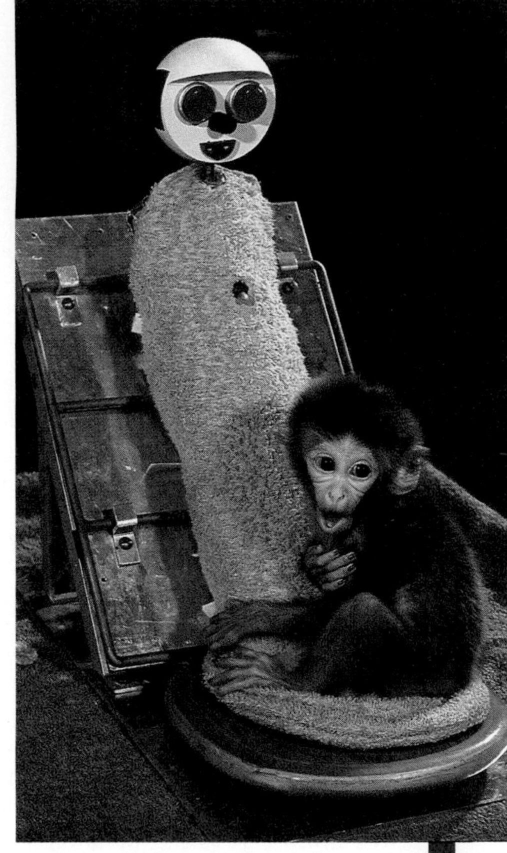

In subsequent studies, the researchers found that the monkeys who had only terrycloth mothers showed adequate, but considerably delayed, heterosexual adjustment if they were given ample opportunity to interact with other infant monkeys as they were growing up. As with human babies, the development of normal socialization and communication in monkeys seems to require experiences of *interaction* with other members of their species (Harlow & Harlow, 1966).

have found no reliable differences between children in quality day-care and those at home with mothers'' (Scarr, 1983, p. 6).

It seems clear that chronic early deprivation can slow physical, mental, and social development, producing lasting handicaps (Kagan & Klein, 1973); yet some children are resilient in the face of severe life stresses. Why?

A longitudinal study of a group of 690 Hawaiian children from very poor families followed their development from soon after conception to age 20. In their life of poverty, these children experienced many stressful events, and one in five developed serious behavior problems at some time during the 20-year period. Boys suffered most from illnesses, learning problems, and problems in controlling aggression; girls suffered most from dependency problems.

Those who were the ''invulnerables'' showed effective coping patterns, were physically robust, very active, and responsive to other people. Furthermore, they had developed a sense of self-confidence and coherence in their positive relationships with their families. Strong bonds had been forged between them as infants and their primary care givers. They were rarely separated from their families, were given much attention, and were part of a multigenerational social support network of family and friends. (Werner & Smith, 1982)

A close interactive relationship with loving adults is a child's first step toward healthy physical growth and normal socialization. As the original attachment to the primary care giver extends to other family members, they too become models for new ways of thinking and behaving. From these early attachments a child then develops the tendency to adapt to the needs of others in a socialized world.

Parenting Styles

''I am very pro-American. I have a small son and have hopes that when he grows up he will join one of the armed forces. To ensure this, I have thought of talking to him while he is sleeping—no great speech, but a little patriotism and the suggestion that an army career would be good. Can this type of suggestion help, or will it cause him to rebel?'' (Caplan, 1969, p. 65)

This father's request for advice, though unusual, highlights a central issue in socialization: How far can parents go in conveying their own values, beliefs, and even prejudices to their children? This concern raises a second issue: How does child-rearing shape and control what a child learns and does?

Ideas about what is required of a good parent have varied greatly at different times in our history. Today we have the advantage of being able to find out from empirical studies what results to expect from different kinds of parent-child interactions.

One variable that has been identified as promoting happy children and harmonious parent-child relationships is parental *responsiveness* (Parpal & Maccoby, 1985). Parents who are sensitive to their children's needs and who meet these needs relatively quickly are more likely to have children who are securely attached in infancy (Matas et al., 1978) and who are compliant in later childhood (Martin, 1981; Stayton et al., 1971). In later childhood, if parents are responsive and allow their children to have some measure of *control* over their environment it will have positive effects for the children (Carlsmith et al., 1974; Isen et al., 1971; Moore et al., 1973).

Some researchers, notably Diana Baumrind and her associates, go even further and suggest that particular patterns of responsiveness at certain ages comprise more successful styles than other patterns (Baumrind, 1967, 1973). They hold that, for children beyond infancy, the best kind of parenting is what is called **authoritative parenting,** in which firm parental control is combined with warmth and open communication. It is distinguished from **permissive parenting** characterized by little parental structure, and also from **authoritarian parenting,** characterized by parental structure but less responsiveness to children's input about decisions and plans. Baumrind bases her conclusions on extensive observations of families. However, some critics feel that her findings can be explained mostly by differences in levels of parental responsiveness (Lewis, 1981).

Parent-child interaction is increasingly viewed as a *circular* process; the child's behavior is very important in understanding the parenting style (Maccoby & Martin, 1983). It is important to accurately estimate a child's impact on a parent's behavior. For example, active, aggressive children may elicit quite different reactions from their parents than quiet, gentle children. In addition, the complex process of socialization is affected by many influences other than parent-child relationships—socioeconomic class, ethnic-cultural differences, mother's age, family size, and being raised by one parent instead of two.

Gender Roles

It is no secret that males and females are different. Not only do they have different physical characteristics, but they often behave in different ways and play different roles in society. While some of these differences are linked to biology, many are the

result of socialization. How do boys and girls grow up to learn their culture's different expectations and act in accordance with them?

Sex refers to the biologically based characteristics that distinguish males from females. The key characteristics are those that are necessary for reproduction. Males can produce sperm and ejaculate; females can menstruate, ovulate, gestate (carry a fetus), and lactate (nurse a child). Related to these characteristics are differences in hormones and anatomy. These differences are universal, biologically determined, and unchanged by social influence. They are the basis for some traditional societal roles, such as woman as homemaker or man as breadwinner and warrior (Rossi, 1984). Biological factors can also create *predispositions* to behave in particular ways (Maccoby, 1980). For example, boys are more physically active and aggressive than girls at all ages after infancy, a difference that is partly because of male hormones. Predispositions do not determine that all males will act one way and all females will act another; they just indicate the likelihood of these behaviors.

In contrast to biological sex, **gender** is a psychological phenomenon; it refers to learned, sex-related behaviors and attitudes of males and females. Much of what we consider masculine or feminine is learned, influenced, and shaped by the particular culture in which an individual lives (Williams, 1983). Cultures vary in how strongly gender is linked to daily activities and in how much tolerance there is for cross-gender behavior.

Gender identity is one's *sense* of maleness or femaleness; it includes an awareness and acceptance of one's biological sex. For transsexual individuals, there is a disparity between sex and gender identity; they feel they are one sex "trapped" in a body of the other sex. Once established, gender identity is difficult to change. For example, in cases where a child has been misidentified in terms of its sex (because of rare chromosomal and physical abnormalities), the attempt to change the child's gender identity can result in grave psychological damage (Money et al., 1957). A sense of gender identity is important to children's psychological well-being and can guide their choices of activities and interests. Some theorists believe that children inherently value things that are like themselves and seek out activities appropriate to their sex because they value them more than the activities for the other sex (Kohlberg, 1966).

Gender roles are patterns of behavior regarded as appropriate for males and females in a particular society. They provide the basic definitions of *masculinity* and *femininity*. There are many ways in which children learn these gender roles. First, they are rewarded for gender-appropriate behavior by their parents, teachers, and peers, and they are punished for actions which are gender-inappropriate. In particular, boys receive strong negative responses from their fathers when they engage in cross-gender behavior (Langlois & Downs, 1980). Second, when children look at what other people are doing, they see men, women, boys, and girls acting in different ways, and so they will imitate the appropriate group—even if there is no specific reward attached to doing so. Third, children also develop certain beliefs and formulate rules about gender roles ("girls can't play sports"; "only boys can be doctors"), and these beliefs may guide their own behavior.

Gender-role socialization begins at birth. In one study, parents described their newborn daughters as little, beautiful, delicate, and weak; by contrast, their newborn sons were seen as firm, alert, strong, and coordinated, even though the babies showed *no* obvious differences in weight, height, or health (Rubin et al., 1974). These different perceptions seem to be based on gender-role stereotypes, and they are important because they influence how parents actually treat their sons and daughters as they are growing up. They dress them differently, give them different types of toys to play with, and communicate with them differently (Reingold & Cook, 1975). For example, parents hold their sons more often, give them more physical stimulation, and pay more attention to their vocalizations and signals for food (Parke & Sawin, 1976; Yarrow, 1975). In later childhood, boys are given more freedom to explore and go a distance from home, while girls are encouraged to stay closer to their mothers and carry out more supervised activities within the home (Fagot, 1978; Saegert & Hart, 1976).

The result of gender-role socialization is that boys and girls grow up in different *psychological* environments that shape their views of the world and their way of dealing with its problems. A variety of socializing agents—teachers, peers, and the media, as well as parents—consistently and subtly reinforce these alternate conceptions of what is important in a male's and female's world view. For men, the unstated socialization goals are to be bold, to seek freedom, and to "dare to be great." For women, the goals are to be content with achieving security and a conflict-free life, while hoping to be good. It is in this sense that psychologist Jeanne Block (1983) concludes that parents give their girls "roots" to build homes and families, but give their boys "wings" to soar to new adventures.

Moral Development

Morality is a system of beliefs, values, and underlying judgments about the rightness or wrongness of acts. Morality ensures that individuals will act to keep their obligations to others in society and will behave in ways that do not interfere with the rights and interests of others. Babies are **amoral**—neither moral nor immoral, but simply lacking any understanding of people's responsibilities to each other. The development of this understanding is an important part of socialization.

Early Studies of Moral Development

In the 1920s a team of Yale University behaviorists set out to study moral knowledge and its relation to moral behavior in children aged 6 to 14. They administered tests of moral knowledge to large numbers of children and observed their behavior in situations where there was a chance to be either honest or dishonest. The data were unexpected. Most children were honest in some situations and dishonest in others. Instead of being guided by a general trait of honesty or dishonestly, behavior seemed to depend more on the situation—how attractive the reward was and how likely the children were to get caught. Also, moral or immoral behavior showed little relation to moral knowledge, which was generally high, and there was no evidence of greater moral development with age. These experimenters concluded that morality was not a stable quality in people, but a response that varied with the demands of the situation (Hartshorne & May 1928). Some recent researchers have found similar patterns (Mischel & Mischel, 1974).

Sigmund Freud (1913/1976) took a different approach. His interest was in the development of *motivation* for moral behavior rather than in the behavior itself. Freud believed that children learn to *internalize* certain moral principles that then guide their actions; they learn to act in ways that will not be punished or threaten their security. Freud argued that most people behave morally most of the time because of the inhibiting effects of their consciences or the guilt they feel when they do something wrong. Freud's ideas on this topic will be elaborated in chapter 12.

Piaget (1960) sought to tie the development of moral judgment to a child's general cognitive development, which we have already described. As the child progresses through the stages of cognitive growth, he or she puts differing relative weights on the consequences of an act versus the actor's intentions. For example, to the preoperational child, someone who breaks several cups accidentally is judged to be "naughtier" than one who breaks one cup intentionally. When the child is a little older, the actor's intentions will weigh more heavily in the child's judgment.

Kohlberg's Stages

The best-known psychological approach to moral development today is that of Lawrence Kohlberg (1964). Like Piaget, Kohlberg focused on the development of *moral reasoning* and proposes several *qualitative stages.* Each stage is characterized by a different basis for moral judgments. For example, at stage 2, a person's moral judgments tend to be based on a calculation of personal risks and benefits; at stage 3, moral judgments are based on a desire for acceptance from others (see **Table 3.5**).

According to Kohlberg's original formulation, people can fit into one of six stages of moral development. Since then, he has theorized that an even higher moral stage (stage 7) exists, although it is rarely found. To assess individual subjects, Kohlberg used a series of moral dilemmas in which different moral principles are pitted against one another. In one dilemma, for example, a man is trying to help his wife obtain a certain drug needed to treat her cancer. An unscrupulous druggist will sell it to him only for much more than the druggist paid—more money than the man can raise. Should the man steal the money? Why or why not?

An interviewer probes the reasons for a subject's decision and then scores the answers. The scoring is based on the *reasons* given, not on which decision is made. That is, a subject whose justifications concern meeting established obligations is scored at stage 4: the subject might say that the man should steal the drug because of his obligation to his wife, or that he should not steal the drug because of his obligation to uphold the law of society.

Kohlberg made four claims: (a) any individual can be at one and only one of these stages at a given time; (b) everyone goes through the stages in a fixed order; (c) each stage is more comprehensive and complex than the preceding; and (d) the same stages occur in any culture. All of these stipulations apply more clearly to the first three stages of moral reasoning than they do to the last four. Stages 1 to 3 are acquired by all people with normal cognitive development; almost all children reach stage 3 by the age of 13. The stages are acquired in order, and each can be seen to be more sophisticated than the preceding. Acquisition of these stages is roughly congruent with the development of stages of cognitive ability proposed by Piaget.

Attainment of stages 4 to 7, however, is not automatic; many adults never reach stage 4, and only a few go beyond it. The higher stages are not associated with any particular age or type of cognitive achievement. Movement from stage to stage is not always in order; sometimes adults who have attained a higher stage drop back a stage or two. The content of the stages themselves appears to be somewhat more subjective, and it is harder to understand each successive stage as more comprehensive and sophisticated than the preceding. For example "avoiding self-condemnation," the basis for moral judgments at stage 6, does not seem obviously more sophisticated than "promoting society's welfare," the basis for judgments at stage 5. In addition, the higher stages are not found in all cultures and appear to be associated with education and verbal ability in our own culture, features which should not necessarily be prerequisites for moral achievement (Rest & Thoma, 1986).

Kohlberg's stages of moral reasoning have been the center of considerable controversy. Some of this controversy has arisen from concerns about the universality of the stages, especially the higher stages, which sometimes are not found at all in cultures where a high degree of abstraction and education is not necessary (Gibbs, 1977; Simpson 1974). Especially controversial is the early claim made by Kohlberg that women lag behind men in moral development. Finally, many researchers have questioned the decision to study moral *reasoning* instead of moral *action;* they believe that what people *say* and what they *do* may not be closely related and that Kohlberg put too much emphasis on a certain way of talking, while caring very little about what people will actually *do* to behave morally (Kurtines & Greif, 1974).

Table 3.5 *Kohlberg's Stages of Moral Reasoning*

Levels and Stages	***Reasons for Moral Behavior***
I Preconventional Morality	
Stage 1 Pleasure/pain orientation	To avoid pain or not get caught
Stage 2 Cost-benefit orientation; reciprocity—an eye for an eye	To get rewards
II Conventional Morality	
Stage 3 Good child orientation	To gain acceptance and avoid disapproval
Stage 4 Law and order orientation	To follow rules, avoid censure by authorities
III Principled Morality	
Stage 5 Social contract orientation	To promote the society's welfare
Stage 6 Ethical principle orientation	To achieve justice and avoid self-condemnation
Stage 7 Cosmic orientation	To be true to universal principles and feel oneself part of a cosmic direction that transcends social norms

(Based on Kohlberg, 1964, 1981)

A Current Controversy: Are There Gender Differences in Moral Judgment?

There has been considerable controversy over the question of gender differences in moral reasoning. In early experiments, Kohlberg (1969) and some other researchers using his paradigms (Alker & Poppen, 1973) found that most men reach stage 4, while most women remain at stage 3. As you can see from Table 3.5, stage 4 has a law-and-order orientation, while stage 3 is based on living up to the expectations of others. Several researchers have recently taken issue with this claim. Most notably, Carol Gilligan (1982) has proposed that Kohlberg's finding that women develop less fully than men can be explained by the fact that his coding scheme is biased in favor of men. His original work was developed from observations of boys only. Thus, Gilligan proposes that women do indeed follow a different developmental path from men, but that they develop *differently,* not *less morally.* She proposes that women's development passes through reasoning based on a standard of *caring* for others to a stage of self-realization, whereas men base their reasoning on a standard of *justice.*

Other researchers dispute that gender differences in moral reasoning really exist; there is an ongoing and lively debate over the issue (Baumrind, 1986; Walker, 1984). In an extensive review of the empirical literature, Lawrence Walker shows that gender differences in moral reasoning are rarely found, and when they are found, they are explained by the male subjects in a particular study having a higher average education level than the female subjects.

The current controversy demonstrates the scientific method in action. Gilligan's work, which is based on the idea that gender differences do exist, consists of a plan of study rather than an empirical work completed (Greeno & Maccoby, 1986). At this time, studies are just beginning to appear which indicate that women may call more on rationales for their moral decisions that involve maintaining harmony and relationships. While men may call more on the need to maintain justice; in addition men may refer more to fairness (Lyons, 1983). These possibly different orientations do not necessarily correspond to women and men scoring differently on Kohlberg's, or other, scales (Gibbs et al., 1984; Lyons, 1983). The jury is still out on this issue, but its examination gives us the opportunity to see the ability of successive studies to build on, refine, and modify early conclusions. (See also the article "The Roots of Morality" in *The Best of Science.*)

Psychosexual and Psychosocial Development

Two other aspects of social and emotional development are the changes in a child's sexuality and the changes in personal and social orientations at different life periods. We will look at one theory regarding each aspect; again, the theories are cast in terms of qualitatively different stages of development.

Freud's Psychosexual Stages

Freud (1905/1976) postulated what he called **psychosexual stages,** involving successive ways of satisfying instinctual biological urges through stimulation of different areas of the body: the mouth, the anus, and the genitals. We will discuss the stages briefly; later, in chapter 12, we will see how they fit into Freud's broader theory of personality.

The most primitive stage of psychosexual development is the **oral stage,** in which the mouth region is the primary source of gratification—from nourishment, stimulation, and making contact with the environment. For example, infants and toddlers spend a great proportion of their time in nonnutritive sucking activities—thumb or finger sucking, and mouthing toys and other objects.

In the **anal stage,** which follows at about age 2, gratification comes first from elimination of feces and then from retention of them. Social demands in most cultures challenge a child's pleasure from both the process and the products of excretion. These societal demands eventually suppress and regulate the child's pleasure from this area of stimulation.

The **phallic stage,** from about ages 3 to 5, centers on the exploration and stimulation of one's own body, especially the penis or the clitoris. In Freudian theory, a child is assumed to experience sexual love toward the parent of the opposite sex during this period. During the **latency stage,** from about age 6 to puberty, satisfaction is gained from exploring the environment and developing skills. Puberty then ushers in the **genital stage,** which involves moving toward sexual—genital—contact with others.

According to Freud, either too much gratification or too much frustration at one of the early stages leads to **fixation,** an inability to progress normally to the next stage of development. Oral fixation is alleged to lead to a dependency on others, drug addiction, compulsive eating, and even tendencies toward verbal fluency and sarcasm. Anal fixation is presumed to result in a stubborn, compulsive, stingy, excessively neat individual.

Some clinicians treating patients with certain mental disorders have found Freud's concept of psychosexual stages useful. On the other hand, he arrived at his ideas through analytical introspection and through interviews with adult patients, not by studying children, as they actually proceeded through the stages. Attempts to find experimental confirmation for his predictions have had mixed results, at best; but we will have much more to say about Freudian theory in chapter 12.

Erikson's Psychosocial Stages

Also based on clinical observations rather than experimental research is a formulation of psychosocial stages of development by Erik Erikson (1963). **Psychosocial stages** are successive orientations toward oneself and toward others. Each stage requires a new level of social interaction; success or failure in achieving it can change the course of subsequent development in a positive or negative direction. Unlike Freud, Erikson sees development as continuing throughout life.

Erikson identified eight psychosocial stages in the life cycle. At each stage a particular conflict comes into focus, as shown in **Table 3.6.** Although the conflict continues in different forms and is never resolved once and for all, it needs to be sufficiently resolved at a given stage if an individual is to cope successfully with the conflicts of later stages.

For example, in the first stage, an infant needs to develop a basic sense of trust in the environment through interaction with care givers. Trust is a natural accompaniment of a strong attachment relationship with a parent who provides food, warmth, and the comfort of physical closeness; but a child whose basic needs are not met, who experiences inconsistent handling, lack of physical closeness and warmth, and frequent absence of a caring adult, may develop a pervasive sense of mistrust, insecurity, and anxiety—and be unready for the venturesomeness that will be required in the next stage.

With the development of walking and the beginnings of language, there is an expansion of a child's exploration and manipulation of objects (and sometimes people!). With these activities should come a comfortable sense of autonomy and of adequacy as a capable and worthy person. Excessive restriction or criticism at this second stage may lead instead to self-doubts, while demands beyond the child's ability, as in too-early or too-severe demands for toilet training, can discourage efforts to persevere in mastering new tasks. They also can lead to stormy scenes of confrontation, disrupting the close, supportive parent-child relationship that is needed to accept risks and meet new challenges. The 2-year-old who insists that a particular ritual be followed or demands the right to do something without help is acting out of a

Table 3.6 *Erikson's Psychosocial Stages*

Approximate Age	***Crisis***	***Adequate Resolution***	***Inadequate Resolution***
0–1½	Trust vs. mistrust	Basic sense of safety	Insecurity, anxiety
1½–3	Autonomy vs. self-doubt	Perception of self as agent capable of controlling own body and making things happen	Feelings of inadequacy to control events
3–6	Initiative vs. guilt	Confidence in oneself as initiator, creator	Feelings of lack of self-worth
6–puberty	Competence vs. inferiority	Adequacy in basic social and intellectual skills	Lack of self-confidence, feelings of failure
Adolescent	Identity vs. role confusion	Comfortable sense of self as a person	Sense of self as fragmented; shifting, unclear sense of self
Early adult	Intimacy vs. isolation	Capacity for closeness and commitment to another	Feeling of aloneness, separation; denial of need for closeness
Middle adult	Generativity vs. stagnation	Focus of concern beyond oneself to family, society, future generations	Self-indulgent concerns; lack of future orientation
Later adult	Ego-integrity vs. despair	Sense of wholeness, basic satisfaction with life	Feelings of futility, disappointment

(Based on Erikson, 1963)

need to affirm his or her autonomy and adequacy. The message being communicated is, "Don't treat me like a baby—unless I ask to be!"

Toward the end of the preschool period, a child who has developed a basic sense of trust, first in the immediate environment and then in himself or herself, has become a person who can now initiate both intellectual and motor activities. The ways in which parents respond to the child's self-initiated activities either encourage the sense of freedom and self-confidence needed for the next stage or produce a sense of guilt and a feeling of being an inept intruder in an adult world.

During the elementary-school years, the child who has successfully resolved the crises of the earlier stages is ready to go beyond random exploring and testing to the systematic development of competencies. School and sports offer arenas for learning intellectual and motor skills, and interaction with peers offers an arena for developing social skills. Other opportunities develop through special lessons, organized group activities, and individual perseverance in following an interest. Successful efforts in these pursuits lead to feelings of competence. Some youngsters, however, become spectators rather than performers or experience enough failure to give them a sense of inferiority, leaving them handicapped in meeting the demands of the next life stages.

Erikson's formulation has been widely accepted, because it looks at the life cycle as a whole, putting both the changes and the overall continuity into perspective. The first four stages are part of a child's socialization; the last four are landmarks in an adult's continuing socialization. These will be discussed in the next and final section of this chapter.

The Cycle Extends . . . and Ends

Though childhood years are the formative ones, we have a remarkable capacity for change across the entire life span (Brim & Kagan, 1980). The long-term effects of early infant and childhood experiences for different individuals are highly variable (Henderson, 1980; Simmel, 1980). Beyond childhood come choices about sexual partners, education, careers, marriage, family, and leisure time. Obligations and commitments multiply as time seems to become scarcer. We begin to "live for the future" and be nostalgic about the past. We lost the child's delight of being absorbed in the present moment, and stress becomes a more constant companion. In this concluding section, we can only consider briefly some theories and research about certain aspects of the human life span beyond the childhood years.

Adolescence

Adolescence is commonly defined as a stage of life beginning at the onset of puberty when sexual maturity or the ability to reproduce is attained. However, it is not so clear where adolescence ends and adulthood begins. Much of the difficulty in defining the span of adolescence lies in the wide variations between societies over the nature of adolescence. Although the physical changes that take place at this time are universal, the social and psychological dimensions of the adolescent experience are highly dependent on the cultural context.

In most nonindustrial societies there has never been an adolescent stage as we know it. Instead, many such societies have **rites of passage,** or **initiation rites.** These rituals usually take place around puberty and serve as a public acknowledgment of the transition from childhood to adulthood. Rites involving genital operations or forms of physical scarring or tattooing leave initiates with permanent physical markers of adult status. Separate rites are carried out for males and females, reflecting the clear separation of gender roles. The rites themselves vary widely from extremely painful ordeals (sometimes involving male circumcision) to periods of seclusion focusing on instruction in sexual and cultural practices. Whatever form they take, such rites are usually highly dramatic and memorable events in which the young initiates symbolically give up their childhood roles and accept the full privileges and responsibilities of adulthood. In many traditional societies, then, the period of adolescence as a transition between childhood and adulthood lasts for only the few hours to few months in which the rite of passage takes place.

There was no concept of an adolescent stage of development, even within Western society, before the nineteenth-century Industrial Revolution. From late childhood on, children worked alongside adults and were expected to assume adult responsibilities as soon as they were physically able. It was not until increased industrialization reduced the need for children as cheap sources of labor that adolescence was "invented"—motivated by a desire to keep young people out of a competitive job market (according to Krett, 1977).

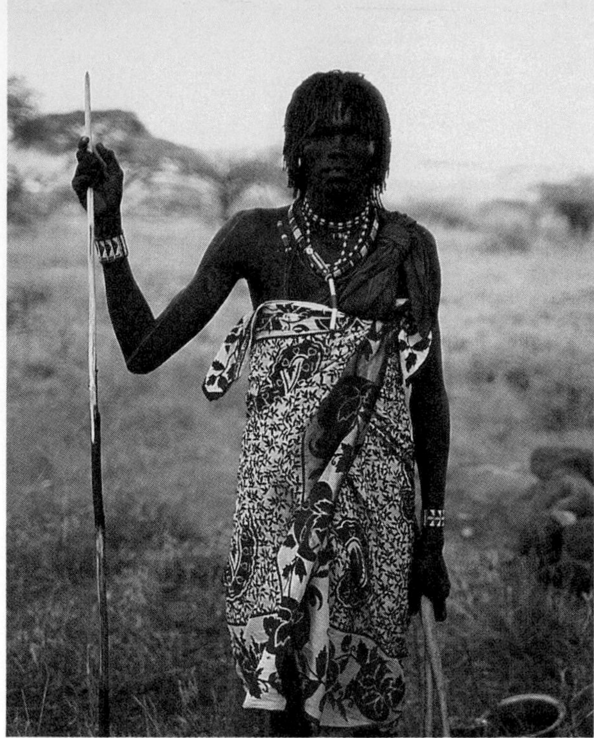

In many societies adolescents go through rites of passage to mark their entrances into adulthood. These ceremonies do not necessarily coincide with the time when these adolescents reach emotional and social maturity.

The adolescent stage is a time in which childhood dependence on parents and other adults is replaced by a growth in independence and self-definition. In our society it can extend for over a decade, through the teens to the mid-twenties until adult roles begin, and it has no clearly defined beginning or end. The legal system defines adult status according to age; but different legal ages exist for such "adult" activities as drinking alcohol, driving, engaging in sex, marrying without parental consent, joining the military, and voting.

Similarly, social events such as graduation from high school (or college or graduate school), moving out of one's parents' home, the gaining of financial independence, and marriage have variously been used to mark the beginning of adulthood. Even religious rituals such as confirmation or bar mitzvah are indicators of adulthood. Based on these examples is a single, 30-year-old student who is still financially dependent on his parents and who has not yet decided on his career aspirations still an adolescent? What about a 16-year-old who has left home, had a child, and attained financial independence from her parents?

Adolescents in modern Western society are faced with choosing among a wide variety of possible roles and values. Although they experience parental, peer, and larger social pressures to adopt certain roles, these influences may provide different and sometimes conflicting ideals. It is ultimately up to each person to forge a personal *identity,* to decide who he or she is as an individual and as a member of society, what he or she will stand for, and what life direction will be pursued. Given the complexity and rapid social change characteristic of Western society, it is not surprising that the formation of an adult identity can be a slow and difficult process. Recognition of these difficulties has contributed to a traditional view of adolescence as a time of inevitable stress and turmoil. While it is true that adolescence can be stressful, most adolescents are successful in making the transition to adulthood without undue trauma. (See ***Close-up:*** *The Myth of Adolescent Turmoil.*)

Adolescence is the first life transition that involves making important decisions which may influence the rest of adult life, but it need not be any more difficult than other transitions encountered throughout the life span. As we shall see when we discuss adult development later in the chapter, many of the issues first addressed in adolescence are similar to those that will be confronted in later stages of life.

Tasks of Adolescence

Of all the issues that are important in adolescence, we will focus on three developmental tasks that commonly confront adolescents in Western society: (a) coming to terms with physical maturity and adult sexuality, (b) redefining social roles, including achieving autonomy from parents, and (c) deciding upon occupational goals. Each of these issues is a component of the central task of establishing an integrated identity; and, consistent with Erikson's (1968) description of the social context of identity, each of these issues can be looked at as a different way in which young people define themselves in relation to others.

Puberty and Sexuality

The first concrete indicator of the end of childhood is the **pubescent growth spurt.** As shown in **Figure 3.8,** the growth spurt takes place about two years earlier for girls than for boys (Tanner, 1962). Two to three years after the onset of the growth spurt, **puberty,** or the attainment of sexual maturity is reached. For girls puberty corresponds to the onset of *menarche* or first *menstruation.* In the United States, the average time for menarche is between the ages of $12\frac{1}{2}$ and 13, although the normal

Close-up The Myth of Adolescent Turmoil

The Psychological Self of the Normal Adolescent

Item	***Percentage of Adolescents Endorsing Each Item***
I feel relaxed under normal circumstances.	91
I enjoy life.	90
Usually I control myself.	90
I feel strong and healthy.	86
Most of the time I am happy.	85
Even when I am sad I can enjoy a good joke.	83

(From Offer, Ostrov, & Howard, 1981)

The traditional "storm and stress" view of adolescence holds that this time is a uniquely tumultous period of life characterized by extreme mood swings and unpredictable, difficult behavior. This view can be traced back to Romantic writers of the late eighteenth and early nineteenth centuries such as Goethe. More recently, the storm and stress conception of adolescence was strongly propounded by G. Stanley Hall, the first psychologist of the modern era to write at length about adolescent development (1904). Following Hall, the major proponents of this view have been psychoanalytic theorists working within the Freudian tradition (for example, Blos, 1967; A. Freud, 1946, 1958). Some of them argue that not only is extreme turmoil a normal part of adolescence, but that failure to exhibit such turmoil is a sign of arrested development. Anna Freud writes that "to be normal during the adolescent period is by itself abnormal" (1958, p. 275).

In the early part of the century, cultural anthropologists such as Margaret Mead (1928) and Ruth Benedict (1938) argued that the storm and stress theory is not applicable to many non-Western cultures. They described cultures where children gradually take on more and more adult responsibilities without any sudden stressful transition or period of indecision and turmoil. It was not until large studies were undertaken of representative adolescents in this society, however, that the turmoil theory finally began to be widely questioned within psychology. The results of such studies have been consistent: few adolescents experience the inner turmoil and unpredictable behavior ascribed to them (Offer et al., 1981a; Oldham, 1978). For instance, Offer and his colleagues asked over 20,000 adolescents about their personal experiences. The researchers concluded that normal adolescents "function well, enjoy good relationships with their families and friends, and accept the values of the larger society" (1981a, p. 116). See the **Table** for a summary of some of the key findings of this ambitious project.

There also appears to be much more consistency in personality development from early adolescence to adulthood than the traditional turmoil theory would predict. Good adjustment in adolescence tends to predict good adjustment in adulthood; and although adolescence is experienced as a stressful period for many young people, those few adolescents who experience serious trauma are likely to continue doing so as they move into adulthood (Bachman et al., 1979; Offer & Offer, 1975; Vaillant, 1977). The implications of these findings are important: adolescents who are experiencing emotional turmoil or crisis should be taken seriously. Their problems should not be explained away as part of a normal passing "phase."

Unfortunately, mental health professionals may be especially prone to accepting the storm and stress viewpoint and consequently underestimating the seriousness of adolescents' problems. In one study, a group of psychiatrists, psychologists, and social workers were asked to fill out a series of questionnaires as if they were normal, healthy adolescents. On average, the professionals rated normal adolescents as being more disturbed and having more problems than did actual groups of delinquents and adolescents in treatment for psychiatric disturbances who rated themselves. Thus, these professionals' profiles of a "normal" adolescent were more extreme than true profiles of highly disturbed adolescents (Offer et al., 1981b).

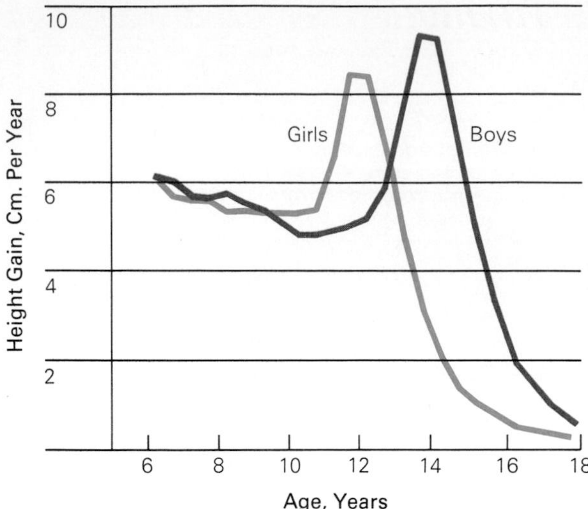

Figure 3.8 *Adolescent Spurt in Height Growth for Girls and Boys*
The curves are from subjects who have their peak velocities during the modal years 12-13 for girls, and 14-15 for boys. (Actual mean increments, each plotted at center of its ½-year period. Data from Shuttleworth, 1939, Tables 23 and 32.)

range extends from 11 to 15. For boys, the production of live sperm, accompanied by the ability to ejaculate, marks the onset of puberty. In the United States, the average age of this occurrence is about 14½ years, although again the normal range is considerable.

An individual attains a personal identity by coming to terms with him- or herself as a physical being, developing a realistic, yet accepting image of physical appearance. Although attractiveness has been found to have an influence on the way a person is viewed by others at all ages (Hatfield & Sprecher, 1986), during adolescence an individual becomes increasingly self-focused on appearance. The term **body image** refers to one's subjective experience of the way one's body looks. This image is dependent not only on objective body features, such as height and weight, but also on other people's assessments of one's body and how it appears to measure up to external standards of beauty. During adolescence the dramatic physical changes accompanying puberty and the increased emphasis on acceptance by peers, and especially peers of the opposite sex, can lead to an increased, if not excessive, concern with one's body image.

It has been found that approximately 44 percent of American adolescent girls and 23 percent of boys claimed that they "frequently felt ugly and unattractive" (Offer et al., 1981a). Even more striking, in another study physical appearance was, on average, the biggest source of concern for a group of 240 high-school students (Eme et al., 1979). Again, the females in the sample reported being particularly concerned with their appearances. The self-concepts of girls are closely tied to perceptions of their physical attractiveness, while boys seem to be more concerned with their physical prowess or effectiveness (see Lerner et al., 1976). Such a focus on physical appearance probably mirrors a cultural preoccupation with female beauty and male strength; and, since not all adolescents can embody the cultural stereotypes of attractiveness, it is not surprising that this can become a major source of concern. As you might predict, shyness zooms to its highest level at this time, up from a base level of 40 percent to 50 percent for adolescent males and 60 percent for females (Zimbardo & Radl, 1981). However, researchers find that young adolescence appears to be the peak of such concern, and, that over time, adolescents appear to become more accepting of their appearances. Nonetheless, the attainment of acceptable body images can be a difficult task, especially for adolescent females (as we will discuss again in chapter 15 in analyzing anorexia and other eating disorders).

Accompanying physical maturity comes a new awareness of sexual feelings and impulses. In one large study of American adolescents, the majority of males and females between the ages of 13 and 18 said that they often think about sex (Offer et al., 1981a). However, lack of knowledge and open communication about early sexual feelings and experiences can lead many adolescents to feel confused and anxious about their emerging sexuality. This can make it particularly difficult to integrate successfully their own sexual feelings with possibly conflicting peer and parental pressures and values. The development of a sexual identity that defines sexual orientation and guides sexual behavior thus becomes an important task of adolescence.

In early adolescence, sexual feelings are unlikely to find fulfillment in sexual relationships with members of the other sex. Rather, masturbation, or self-stimulation of the sexual organs, is the most common expression of sexual impulses in this period. One third to one half of boys and 18 to 37 percent of girls report masturbating by the age of 13, while 80 percent of boys and 69 percent of girls report masturbating by the age of 18 or 19 (Hass, 1979; Sorensen, 1973). Homosexual experiences are also not uncommon in adolescence. Fourteen to 17 percent of teenage boys report some homosexual experiences, although the actual rate may be considerably higher. The rate is about half as high for adolescent girls (Hass, 1979; Sorensen, 1973). The vast majority of adolescents who have homosexual experiences go on to an exclusively heterosexual orientation.

Exclusively homosexual feelings are typically much more difficult to resolve during adolescence. While most "gay" or homosexual individuals first become aware of their sexual orientation in early adolescence, many do not attain positive identities as homosexuals until their middle or late twenties (Riddle & Morin, 1977). The time lag undoubtedly reflects the relative lack of social support for choosing a homosexual orientation and exemplifies the importance of social setting in dealing with all aspects of identity development.

The proportion of adolescents engaging in sexual intercourse has risen substantially in the last 20 years. Most of this increase is attributable to a dramatic increase in the numbers of adolescent girls becoming sexually active. Concurrent with the increase has been a decline in the traditional "double standard," with a corresponding trend toward acceptance of nonmarital sex within romantic relationships. Recent figures suggest that about one half of all young people have engaged in intercourse before age 18 and about 75 percent have done so by the age of 20 or 21 (Chilman, 1983). There is evidence that initial sexual experiences of males and females differ substantially. The vast majority of females become sexually involved within love relationships. In contrast, for most males personal relationships appear to be secondary to the sexual act itself, with the average male reporting no emotional involvement with his first sexual partner (Miller & Simon, 1980). Most sexual activity in adolescence takes place within the confines of a romantic relationship, although relatively few adolescents actually end up marrying their first sexual partners. The average sexually active adolescent has been described as a "serial monogamist" (Sorensen, 1973).

Developing a sexual identity involves more than deciding upon a sexual orientation and gaining sexual experience. Adolescents are faced with deciding upon personal values to guide their sexual activity. This can involve an evaluation of both peer and parental moral values that may previously have been accepted unquestioningly. For those adolescents who do choose to become sexually active, the task becomes conducting their sexual relationships in a responsible fashion. Sexual responsibility entails taking into consideration the present and future consequences of one's actions, as well as being sensitive to the needs of one's partner as well as one's self. The high incidences of teenage pregnancy and sexually transmitted diseases suggest that many adolescents become sexually active before they are capable of shouldering the attendant responsibilities. For instance, it is estimated that more than one third of adolescent females who are sexually active outside of marriage become pregnant before the age of 19 (Zelnik et al., 1979).

Thus, it is apparent that one of the greatest challenges in the development of a sexual identity is to decide upon, and act in accordance with, a personally meaningful sexual ethic. Such an ethic should not only reflect one's personal standards, morals, and preferences, but should also be based upon a realistic understanding of the consequences of sexual behavior. While this task may take many years to complete, it is in adolescence that the foundations of a healthy sexual identity are established.

Social Relations

During adolescence family ties become less central as more time is spent outside the home. In our society, this typically means less structure and adult guidance, exposure to new and perhaps conflicting values, and a strong need for peer support and acceptance. Although an adolescent's role in the family may change at this time, family relations usually remain important. Adolescence thus tends to be a time of widening social contacts and the development of new social roles.

Much of adolescent identity exploration takes place within the context of peer groups. One study of the ways adolescents spent their time found that the most frequent activity was talking with peers. The adolescents not only reported spending more than four times as much time talking to peers as adults, but also preferred talking to their peers (Csikszentmihalyi et al., 1977). It is with their peers that adolescents refine their social skills and try out different social roles and behaviors. Through this process they gradually define the social component of their developing identities, including the kind of people they choose to be and the kind of relationships they choose to pursue. It is not surprising that peers take on a special importance at a time when adolescents are slowly relinquishing their childhood dependence on adults.

During adolescence, peers become an increasingly important source of social contact and emotional support; but it appears that as needs for close friendships and peer acceptance become greater, there is also an increase in the anxiety that may become associated with being rejected. Conformity to peer values and behaviors rises to a peak around ages 12 and 13. Concerns with peer acceptance and popularity are particularly apparent for females who appear to be more focused upon social relations than their male counterparts; but females are less likely to conform to antisocial behaviors than are males (Berndt, 1979). Loneliness also becomes significant at this age—between 15 and 25 percent of adolescents report feeling very lonely (Offer et al., 1981a). Adolescents who are not popular (sought out by their peers) may still enjoy at least one supportive friendship. Moreover, over the course of adolescence most individuals appear to become more comfortable with their peer relations. The observed decrease in levels of conformity during late adolescence suggests that, although heightened dependence on peers may be a "standard" phase, ultimately the task of identity formation requires a degree of autonomy from peers as well as parents.

A central element of adolescent identity formation is achieving some degree of psychological independence from parents; but, contrary to popular opinion, empirical research has failed to find support for the notion that a "generation gap" exists between adolescents and the adult world. The move toward greater independence need not, and usually does not, involve outright rebellion against parents or rejection of fundamental parental values (Kimmel & Weiner, 1985). Correspondingly, an increased concern with peer relations does not necessarily translate into alienation from parents. While conformity to parental expectations decreases over the adolescent years, intimacy with parents tends to stay constant (Hunter & Youniss, 1982); and most adolescents report surprisingly harmonious relations with their parents. The vast majority believe that their parents are presently satisfied with them and will be proud of them in the future. Conversely, few adolescents report having consistently negative feelings toward their parents (Offer et al., 1981a).

The process of deciding upon a personal identity is facilitated by a supportive family environment in which parents respect their children's needs for growing independence and continuing interconnectedness. This is confirmed by both empirical and clinical evidence suggesting that too little parental control and involvement may be as detrimental to the development of autonomy as too strict control and overinvolvement (Kimmel & Weiner, 1985).

Engaging in behaviors not shared or even approved of by parents can be a concrete means of establishing independence from them and affirming solidarity with peers. As suggested before, however, the influence of peers is typically not overriding or pervasive. While adolescents may differ greatly from their parents in preferences for music, fashion, and other issues of personal taste, their fundamental values tend to remain similar to those of their parents (Conger, 1977). When conflict does arise, it is often related to relatively superficial aspects of adolescent culture.

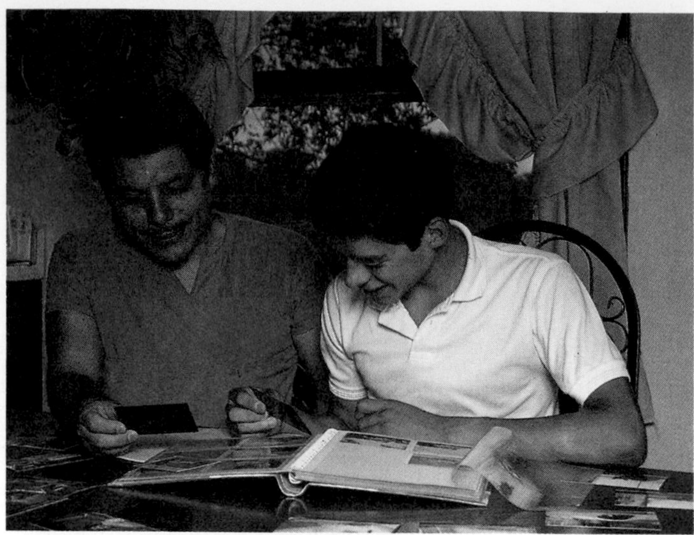

A supportive relationship between parent and child can facilitate the development of a healthy personal identity.

However, conflict sometimes centers on more significant "problem behaviors" such as drinking, illicit drug use, and sexual activity. Richard Jessor, a noted authority on adolescent problem behavior, suggests that "coming to terms with alcohol, drugs, and sex has emerged as a new developmental task that all adolescents face as part of the normal process of growing up in contemporary American society" (1982, p. 297).

The dual forces of parents and peers at times exhibit conflicting influences on adolescents, and this conflict can be interpreted as reflecting the dynamic process of separating from parents and becoming increasingly identified with peers. In general, however, parents and peers may be seen as serving complementary functions and fulfilling different needs in the lives of adolescents (Davis, 1985). Identity development ultimately involves establishing independent commitments that are sensitive to parental and peer environments, but are not mere reflections of either.

Occupational Choice

According to Erikson, deciding upon a vocational commitment is the hallmark of adolescent identity formation. The ubiquitous question, "What are you going to *be* when you grow up?" reflects the common assumption that occupation largely determines a person's identity. Occupational choice involves tasks central to all aspects of identity formation: appraisal of one's abilities and interests, awareness of realistic alternatives, and the ability to make and follow through on a "best" choice.

Prior to high school few young people are concerned with issues such as occupational choice. During the high-school years, concern with their future vocations and life-styles grows in importance. Through vocational choice adolescents can both differentiate themselves from, and affirm their acceptance of, parental and social values. This sense of continuity in time and connectedness to one's social environment is critical to achieving a sense of consistent individual identity. However, the task of deciding upon vocational commitments may be undermined by adverse social and economic forces not under their personal control.

Many personal factors have been found to influence vocational aspirations and achievement (Smart & Smart, 1973). Some of those that have been studied include intelligence, specific abilities and interests, academic achievement, birth order, and achievement motivation. The clearest factor, however, is socioeconomic background: the higher the socioeconomic status of adolescents' families, the more likely they will be to pursue and complete postsecondary education, and the higher their levels of occupational aspiration and achievement are likely to be. Middle- and upper middle-class parents tend to encourage higher achievement motivation in their children, but they also act as models of higher career success and have the economic resources to provide educational opportunities unavailable to children from less privileged backgrounds.

Unfortunately, many adolescents, and particularly those who are members of racial minorities and lower income families, will be unable to find jobs upon completion of high school. The unemployment rate among adolescents is more than twice as high as the national average (U.S. Bureau of the Census, 1985a). Furthermore, educational achievement is strongly related to occupational success as measured by income level. Of the approximately 85 percent of American teenagers who graduate from high school, only about one quarter go on to graduate from college (U.S. Bureau of the Census, 1984a). Thus, the stereotype of adolescents graduating from high school, freely choosing a vocational goal from a broad range of options, completing appropriate postsecondary training or education, and then going on to strive for success in their chosen field is simply not a reality for many of these American youngsters.

Educational and occupational choices made in late adolescence can have a profound effect on future options; but, as with all aspects of identity, occupational identity is best conceived of in the context of the whole life cycle. As many college students have already discovered, career choice is not a discrete event that is decided once and for all upon graduation from high school or upon selection of a major in college. Rather it is an initial and often tentative first step in a lifelong process which may include several job changes, periods of unemployment or retraining, and even complete occupational shifts.

Adulthood

The transition into young adulthood is marked by decisions about advanced education, vocation, intimate relationships, and for many, marriage. In the United States, where many students leave home to live in a college dormitory, they never really go home again, but set out on paths of self-determination. Erikson defines the major task of early adulthood as *intimacy:* the capacity to make a full commitment—sexual, emotional, and moral—to another person. Intimacy requires openness, courage, ethical strength, and usually some sacrifice and compromise of one's personal preferences. Intimacy can occur in other close relationships besides marriage.

Erikson paints a portrait of young adults consolidating a clear and comfortable sense of their identity in preparation for embracing the risks and potentials of intimacy; but the sequence from identity to intimacy may not accurately reflect present-day realities. Most individuals become sexually active and begin to explore intimacy issues in their teenage years. Moreover, there have been trends toward young adults living together outside of marriage and toward marriage at a later age than in the past (U.S. Bureau of the Census, 1985b). These developments suggest that individuals are often struggling with identity issues such as vocational choice in the context of intimate relationships and, conversely, beginning to deal with intimacy issues long before they have consolidated personal identities. Even marriage, the prototype of the successful resolution of the search for intimacy, is often more than a one-time task completed in young adulthood. In the United States, close to one half of all marriages end in divorce. Thus, many adults are forced to reexamine their conceptions of, and capacity for, intimacy at later points in the life cycle. This is another example of the way social trends affect the course of psychosocial development.

The alternative to intimacy, according to Erikson, is *isolation,* the lack of a secure sense of connectedness, a feeling of being essentially alone. Those who find a supportive partner with whom to share personal feelings, fears, and successes tend to be both happier and physically healthier than those who fail to do so. A common finding in many areas of psychology is that anything that *isolates* individuals from social support puts them "at risk" for both physical and mental problems.

For those who meet the challenges of identity and intimacy successfully, the next opportunity—and challenge—is *generativity.* The focus of concern becomes a commitment beyond oneself—to family, work, society, or future generations. This is typically a crucial step in development in one's thirties and forties. Those who have not successfully resolved the crises of identity and intimacy may still be trying to do so during this period, perhaps with an increasing sense of insecurity and failure.

Systematic studies of personality development in adulthood are comparatively recent and are still mapping unmarked territory. Two of the best known, by social psychologist Daniel Levinson (1978) and psychoanalytically oriented G. E. Vaillant (1977), studied only men (see the following study).

For men, the twenties seem to be a period of hope, optimism, and independence, with full responsibility for themselves and for their choice of life-style. Early in the thirties, there may be a period of reassessment, of questioning basic directions set in the twenties and either affirming them or "adjusting course" to follow new quests. The later thirties are often a time of consolidation and satisfaction. Between 40 and 50 what has come to be known as a "midlife crisis" may occur, in which their past choices, and present contributions and commitments, are questioned. Life is half over; has freedom been given up for security? Have they traded intimacy for career success? There is a new concern about genuine identity, a later version of adolescents' search for identity. Depending on the way they adapt to the stress of this inner turmoil, adults may renew commitments, make changes, or become resigned to unfulfilling life situations.

"It just doesn't look like the usual case of midlife crisis, Dr. Elmark."

The personality development of 95 highly intelligent men was studied through interviews and observations over a 30-year period following their graduations from college in the mid-1930s. The researcher found great changes in many of the men, often quite unpredictable from their behavior in college. The interviews covered physical health, social relationships, and career achievement. At the end of the 30-year period, the 30 men with the best outcomes and the 30 with the worst outcomes were identified and compared in a number of ways, including evidence of their maturity in terms of Erikson's psychosocial stages. ***Table 3.7*** *compares the scores of the two groups on several items that revealed psychosocial maturity.*

By middle life, the best-outcome men were carrying out generativity tasks of assuming responsibility for others and giving some of themselves back to the world. Even the adjustment of their children seemed to be associated with the fathers' maturity; the more mature fathers were more able to give children the help they needed in adjusting to the world. In a supplementary study of 57 members of the sample, the ongoing importance of the capacity for intimacy was confirmed. The purpose of the study was to predict psychosocial adjustment in middle age from measures of social motivation 17 years earlier. The best predictor of mental, physical, and social adjustment was intimacy motivation, "a recurrent preference or readiness for experiences of close, warm, and communicative interpersonal exchange" (Vaillant, 1977, p. 587). The two areas of adjustment that were most highly correlated with intimacy motivation were enjoyment of job and marital satisfaction. (McAdams & Vaillant, 1982)

As Freud wrote many years earlier, "Lieben und Arbeiten." Love and work appear to be central to mental health and happiness over the life span.

In general, even less is known about the adult personality development of women. In light of changing sex roles over the last few decades, a central issue for adult women has become the integration of occupational and marriage/family aspirations. Not surprisingly, greater uncertainty about vocational choice is expressed by women than by men. Among many of those whose vocation was exclusively homemaking, the interviewer (Sheehy,

Table 3.7 Differences Between Best- and Worst-Outcome Subjects on Factors Related to Psychosocial Maturity

	Best Outcomes (30 men)	Worst Outcomes (30 men)
Childhood environment poor	17%	47%
Pessimism, self-doubt, passivity, and fear of sex at 50	3%	50%
In college personality integration put in bottom fifth	0	33%
Subjects whose career choice reflected identification with father	60%	27%
Dominated by mother in adult life	0	40%
Failure to marry by 30	3%	37%
Bleak friendship patterns at 50	0	57%
Current job has little supervisory responsibility	20%	93%
Children admitted to father's college	47%	10%
Children's outcome described as good or excellent	66%	23%
Average yearly charitable contribution	$3,000	$500

(From Vaillant, 1977)

1976) found feelings of social isolation, with frustration and some guilt for not pursuing goals for which their education had prepared them. Other research has found that women who have a family and work outside the home tend to be more satisfied with their lives than either single working women or married homemakers (Crosby, 1982).

Behavioral options available to women are both supported by, and reflected in, changing societal values. According to a poll of women's preferences taken in 1970, motherhood was regarded as the best part of being a woman by 53 percent of young women; when the poll was again taken in 1983 only 26 percent of the young women reported this feeling. The later poll showed that a majority of working women regarded independence and being employed as satisfying and preferable to being at home. Furthermore, 59 percent of all women polled thought employed women were as good mothers, if not better, than women who stayed at home ("U.S. Women," 1983).

Carol Gilligan's challenge to Kohlberg's male-based theory of moral development was discussed earlier (p. 89). Gilligan holds that personality development through the adult years continues to progress differently for men and women because of their basically different earlier socialization—toward separateness for men and attachment for women. She sees both trends as one-sided and cites evidence that, in mid-life, many men and women try to establish a better balance, the men moving toward more attachment, the women toward greater self-identity (Gilligan, 1982).

The Later Years

One of the most significant changes taking place in American society is the aging of its population. As life expectancy goes up (currently approximately 78 years for women and 71 years for men) and the birth rate falls, a larger and larger proportion of the population is over 65. Old age often brings with it major life transitions including retirement, widowhood, decline of physical health, and a decrease in standard of living. In addition, a loss of clearly defined social roles and an increased awareness of death set the stage for Erikson's eighth and final phase of psychosocial development, in which the task becomes the attainment of a sense of ego-integrity. If adequate solutions are found at each of the preceding stages, older adults can enjoy a sense of fulfillment and wholeness, and look back on their lives without major regrets. On the other hand, a sense that one's life has been unsatisfying or misdirected may lead to feelings of despair and futility.

Increasing age brings sensory deficits and increasing health problems. Although adults over 70 represent only about a tenth of America's population, they receive nearly a fourth of all medical prescriptions, most frequently for tranquilizers. Bodily illnesses and mental deterioration are closely correlated, each kind of negative change being a catalyst for the other (Habot & Libow, 1980). On the other hand, the vast majority of the elderly describe their own health as fair to excellent compared with others of their age (U.S. Bureau of the Census, 1983).

Depression and social isolation are central problems for many older people. While the contributing variables to suicide are complex, suicide becomes more probable among older white males. Men also have a more difficult time adjusting to the death of a spouse than do women. However, women are most likely to find themselves living alone in old

The common belief that people lose many of their mental abilities as they get older is not true. Psychological research has found just the opposite.

age—there are over five times as many widows as widowers in the United States (U.S. Bureau of the Census, 1984c). It has been suggested that the superior adjustment of widows may be because of their greater capacity to maintain social ties with relatives and friends (Perlmutter & Hall, 1985).

Cognitive Functioning

On the positive side, there is evidence that some aspects of intellectual functioning are equal or even superior in older people, while there is little to support the stereotype of cognitive decline in the later years. For example, 70-year-olds score higher than college-age individuals on lists of vocabulary and information. They cannot recall lists of numbers as well, but they can still perform well on several other kinds of memory tasks.

Tests that involve speed of response, on the other hand, put the elderly at a disadvantage, and cognitive abilities are impaired by the presence of physical problems, such as cardiovascular disorders, or by living in unstimulating or socially deprived environments. Obsolescence can also handicap the elderly: in some kinds of problem-solving tasks they may do as well as they ever did, but younger subjects may do better because they have better backgrounds in current technology. A general conclusion is that, from the early sixties to the mid-seventies, "there is a normal decline in some but not all individuals for some but not all abilities. However, beyond 80 decrement is the rule for most individuals" (Schaie, 1980, p. 279). The following are additional conclusions, summarized by Bernice Neugarten (1976):

1. Old people who remain physically and mentally active perform better than those who become inactive.
2. Educational level predicts performance in old age; the higher the education attained, the better the performance.
3. Intellectual decline seems to be inversely related to longevity; the less bright die younger.
4. Intellectual decline is greater in old men than in old women.

Satisfaction with Life

Looking back, how do older people evaluate their life satisfactions, and what earlier factors are predictive of satisfaction with life? Some interesting answers emerge from longitudinal studies of men and women who have been investigated over much of their life span.

> *Among the wives in one study, marital compatibility and satisfaction with the husband's job at age 30 predicted (was correlated with) general satisfaction at age 70. Among the husbands the characteristics at age 30 that were predictive of general satisfaction later were good health, stamina, high energy level, job satisfaction, and having an emotionally stable wife. (Mussen et al., 1982)*

The longitudinal Terman study of high-IQ boys and girls (mentioned at the beginning of this chapter) explored affect and life satisfaction when the subjects had reached an average age of 62.

Among the men, affective qualities at age 30 that persisted for the next three decades of their lives were "optimism about life, an enjoyment of occupational combat, and a feeling of self-worth" (Sears, 1977, p. 123). Life satisfaction was assessed in relation to occupation, working into their sixties, family life, and broken or unbroken marriages. Most satisfaction was derived from family life and occupation. It was striking that "in spite of their autonomy and great average success in their occupations, these men placed greater importance on achieving satisfaction in their family life than in their work" (p. 128). However, satisfaction with family life was difficult to predict. Occupational satisfaction was not. It was related to several feelings expressed at age 30: ambition, liking for work, living up to one's potential, and having actively chosen one's occupation. (Sears, 1977)

Among the women, greatest satisfaction with their work was found among subjects who had had careers (whether single or married), but broader measures of satisfaction were reported among the homemakers. Earlier conditions that were correlated with high general satisfaction later in life for the group as a whole were positive relations with their parents, early self-confidence, good health, marriage, children, social contacts, community service, and work in a professional field. (P. Sears & Barbee, 1977)

Life satisfaction involves the fit between life aspirations and achievements within a specific time frame. All of these studies that followed subjects into their later years were undertaken long before the previously discussed shifts in employment patterns among women had taken place. Therefore, the effects of changing sex roles on life satisfaction may not be reflected in the results. However, these findings do indicate the importance of a combination of both satisfying intimate relations and personal achievement for overall life satisfaction. Moreover, there seems to be stability over time in general emotional-motivational orientation that can give direction and meaning to life—or, when negative or lacking, can lead to unhappiness and despair. (See also the article "The Good Die Younger" in *The Best of Science*.)

The Process of Dying

With old age comes the inevitability of death. The realization that life is finite and that one's days are numbered can have an important influence on mental health and behavior. Depending on the strategies developed to cope with the knowledge of mortality, there can be a renewed assault on life goals, an attempt to live the remaining time to the fullest, or denial or other defenses.

When death comes at the end of an illness, even the process of dying can be seen in terms of a sequence of stages that may include denial, anger, bargaining, and acceptance (Kübler-Ross, 1969). But other researchers studying the reactions of dying people have observed more fluidity and complexity than is suggested in Kübler-Ross' fixed stages. Some see "a hive of affect" with an interplay of hope and disbelief, of anguish, terror, rage, and envy, alternating with acquiescence, boredom, surrender, and even yearning for death (Schneidman, 1976).

After death, an individual's memory lives on in all those who were somehow touched by his or her presence during that lifetime. Handling that death becomes a new part of *their* developmental challenges—and, in that sense, the life cycle is never ending.

Summary

- Developmental psychology is concerned with changes in physical and psychological functioning across the life span. Some developmental psychologists study processes or strands of development, such as cognitive or social development; others study the challenges and characteristics of whole individuals at different life periods or stages.
- Normative studies are descriptive; experimental studies provide information about causes of observed behaviors. Each may involve cross-sectional, longitudinal, or sequential designs. Historical analysis of families and life stages allows developmentalists to assess the influence of historical circumstances on families and their individual members.
- Inheritance occurs through genes received at conception, half from each parent. Maturation programs many characteristic sequences of physical and mental change throughout life. Most complex actions are shaped by both nature (heredity) and nurture (experience and learning), as they interact throughout life.
- Newborns respond to patterns of stimulation, change their responses as a result of experience, and interact actively with their mothers or other care givers. Researchers are discovering that newborns come prepared with many cognitive, perceptual, and social competencies.
- Acquisition of language proceeds through babbling, one-word, two-word, and telegraphic-speech stages. Analysis of children's speech errors reveals that they actively test hypotheses and develop rules about language. Maturation plays a key role in shaping and timing language development.

- ▶ As described by Piaget, cognitive growth comes about through a continuing interaction of the processes of assimilation and accommodation. Assimilation fits the new into what is already known; accommodation changes the known to adapt to the new information or experience.
- ▶ Piaget, like Freud, Kohlberg, and Erikson, stressed the role of distinct stages in development. Each of these periods occurs in a fixed sequence that is qualitatively different from the others. Piaget proposed four stages of cognitive growth: sensorimotor, preoperational, concrete operational, and formal operational. Current researchers are exploring additional facets of cognitive growth and change throughout the life span that challenge some of Piaget's conceptions.
- ▶ A child acquires roles, behavior, and attitudes expected of individuals in a given society through the process of socialization. Normal socialization begins with formation of an attachment bond between the infant and the care giver. Failure to establish attachment in infancy is associated with physical and psychological problems. There are critical period experiences essential for the proper development of certain functions in humans and animals.
- ▶ Patterns of parental responsiveness in parent-child interaction affect parent-child relationships. A permissive parenting style is optimal during infancy. During early and middle childhood an authoritative style is more effective than either a permissive or an authoritarian one.
- ▶ Sex differences are physical differences; gender differences are psychological, learned differences associated with "masculinity" and "femininity." Individuals learn both a gender identity, a sense of being male or female, and a gender role, patterns of behavior considered appropriate for males or females in a given society.
- ▶ In Kohlberg's approach to moral development, each stage is characterized by a different basis for moral judgment, progressing toward greater concern for universal rights and abstract ethical principles, though men's and women's development may differ. Gender differences in moral reasoning appear to indicate that women make decisions based on caring, while men make decisions based on standards of justice.
- ▶ Psychosexual development, according to Freud, proceeds through an oral stage, an anal stage, a phallic stage, a latency stage, and a genital stage. These stages involve successive sources of gratification of instinctual urges. Failure to progress through this sequence is assumed to hamper personality development and cause specific psychological disorders.
- ▶ According to Erikson, there are eight stages of psychosocial development that extend throughout life. These mark changes in one's orientation to oneself and others; each represents resolution of a particular crisis and is essential for success in later stages. Adequate resolution brings trust, autonomy, initiative, and competence in the childhood years; identity in adolescence; intimacy in young adulthood; generativity in middle adulthood; and finally ego-integrity in old age.
- ▶ Adolescence is a period of growing independence and self-definition, during which a person begins to form an adult identity. Forming this identity involves developing a sexual identity, achieving autonomy from parents and greater identification with peers, and making choices about occupations and careers. Recent studies do not support the traditional view of adolescence as a time of "storm and stress."
- ▶ Middle adulthood and old age present new challenges and bring continuing change. Intellectual ability in the later years depends on an individual's past and present physical activity and on continuing mental involvement in life. It has been found, through longitudinal studies, that general life satisfaction of the elderly can be predicted from their emotional and motivational characteristics at around age 30, and that this satisfaction involves somewhat different factors for men and women.

4

The Biology of Behavior

Mickey Median was an average sort of a guy. On Sundays he'd be glued to the TV, watching football games with a bunch of friends whom he had known since high school. His job on the construction crew, the company's midweek softball game, and Friday night bowling all helped keep Mickey in top physical condition. Mickey's wife and teenage kids put up with this sports mania and his "happy-go-lucky" attitude toward life because it didn't interfere with his being a good husband, father, and provider. That is, until one day when Mickey's behavior began to change.

At first, the changes were welcomed by his family, but when they began to increase in intensity and frequency, there was cause for concern. His wife and kids didn't know what to do, because they didn't have the slightest idea of what had gone wrong. Indeed, it made them feel somewhat guilty to say that Mickey had become too religious, or too concerned about nuclear war and environmental issues, or that he spent too much time keeping a detailed diary and writing in notebooks about "Matters of Cosmic Significance."

When did it all begin? Perhaps the first sign of a behavioral change was Mickey's reaction to violence in sports. He argued with his friends that the hitting was just too hard and unnecessary—this from a former linebacker with a reputation as a fierce quarterback "headhunter." He gave up watching football games and now, on Sundays, went to church. He had found religion. Next Mickey went to his new church daily, then as suddenly, converted to another religion, and spent his spare time on street corners handing out religious leaflets.

He soon started writing his own religious and philosophical sermons—volumes of them—even though he had never written as much as a single letter since barely passing high-school English! He was consumed with the thought that it was his mission in life to write about all the truly significant things that he was now experiencing so intensely. In fact, with such lofty work to be done, Mickey had little sexual appetite left for "rendering his marital debt," as his wife put it. Their formerly good sexual relationship cooled, went cold, froze. No loss of love or respect for his wife, no other woman in his life, just no more urge for sex.

"And there's one more point I'd like to make," he'd say, after leaving the room and returning again and again. It seemed as if he couldn't end a conversation, but had to keep adding one more important fact. Mickey was "sticky" like flypaper and couldn't be shaken loose once he started on one of his all-important digressions.

This pattern of behaviors didn't come and go, wasn't tied to any particular event, situation, or season; it was there all the time. It was Mickey Median's new personality—one that certainly wasn't average anymore. Had he been single, without family obligations, or not been such a popular, fun-loving, "regular guy" before, Mickey's transformation might have gone unnoticed. His wife couldn't help noticing the new Mickey, but what she wanted back again was her "old man," the person she thought she had known so well after 20 years of marriage. No one she turned to for assistance was able to offer any explanation for this sudden personality change, and, without that, there could be no solution to the problem.

Just when Mrs. Median had almost given up, a chance event saved the day. Mickey had cornered a neighbor's boy, a young medical student home on summer vacation, and had proceeded to deliver his sermons on the evils of pollution, pornography, big business, drugs, football, and all-out nuclear devastation. Unlike everyone else who escaped these verbal barrages as soon as possible, the student was fascinated by the new Mickey. He told the family he had six questions for them, the answers to which might hold the clue they had been seeking.

"Had Mickey undergone a sudden religious conversion?"

"Yes."

"Did he have a tendency to write extensively with a content that was religious, philosophical, or cosmic?"

"Yes, again."

"And obviously, he took everything much more seriously than ever before?"

"Yes, indeed."

"Except sexual relations?"

"Well, yes, that is also true."

"Temper flare-ups?"

"He can become quite violent at times, yes."

"And my final question, does he get stuck on his conversations and can't seem to end them?"

"How can you know all that about Mickey from your brief encounter?" Mrs. Median wondered aloud.

The student said he had just finished an advanced course on brain functions in which he learned about a recently discovered syndrome that appeared to fit the facts of this case perfectly. Mickey's symptoms were not unique to him but were typical of most people's who had developed a particular kind of epilepsy. To be certain, Mickey would have to take a special medical examination, an electroencephalogram (EEG), in which his brain-wave patterns would be recorded and then analyzed.

Sure enough, the EEG recordings revealed that Mickey had a

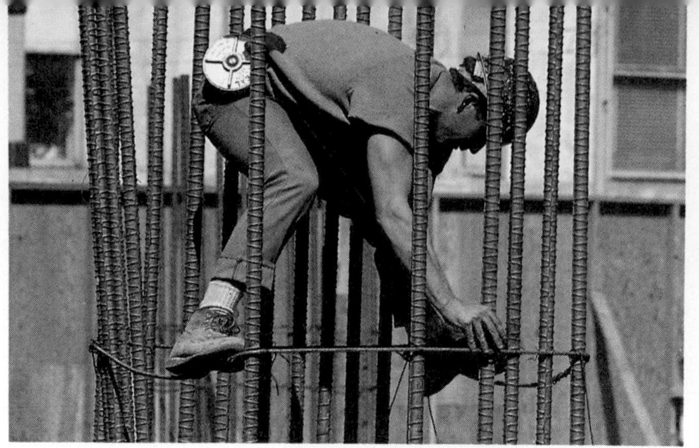

special type of epilepsy in which there were no fits or fainting, as usually occur; however, there was abnormal electrical activity in the left temporal lobe of his brain. For some reason, Mickey's brain was firing occasional impulses that stimulated the limbic system, a primitive part of the brain that is a center for emotional reactivity. The way it was being stimulated from within led to profound emotional effects that charged all events in Mickey's life, as well as his thoughts, with great importance. Paradoxically, when that same area of the brain was stimulated, sexuality was inhibited. The student told Mickey and his wife that this behavioral syndrome associated with temporal lobe epilepsy was just being recognized by psychiatrists and neurologists, (*neuro-* means relating to the nervous system, of which the brain is the central part). He assured the Medians that a treatment plan could be developed to modify that abnormal electrical firing of Mickey's brain. Whether he would become his old self again, or be a mix of his former and the "reformer self," would not be known for a while.

The new discovery of a syndrome of behavioral changes that occurs after the onset of alterations in a well-defined area of the brain is quite exciting for brain researchers. Such an occurrence in an otherwise normal, healthy person provides a unique physiological example of the links between brain mechanisms and behavioral processes (Baer, 1979; Geschwind, 1979, 1983).

Physiological psychology, the branch of psychology that studies the physical and chemical factors involved in behavior and mental processes, relates anatomical structures and physiological processes in the brain and other parts of the body to psychological experience and behavior. It studies humans as biological organisms who have much in common with other species. This is possible because research has demonstrated the principle of **conservation** of biological mechanisms across species. Apparently, nature and evolution used many of the same blueprints to design the "hard-wiring" of all animals. Thus, studies of simpler systems in lower animals are both valid and informative for humans. What is special about the human organism is its highly evolved brain and its more complex nervous system for communicating information within and between cells.

Neuropsychologists are physiological psychologists who investigate the foundations of behavior and mental processes as functions of the activity of the brain and nervous system. They seek to discover the **neural substrate,** or basis, of

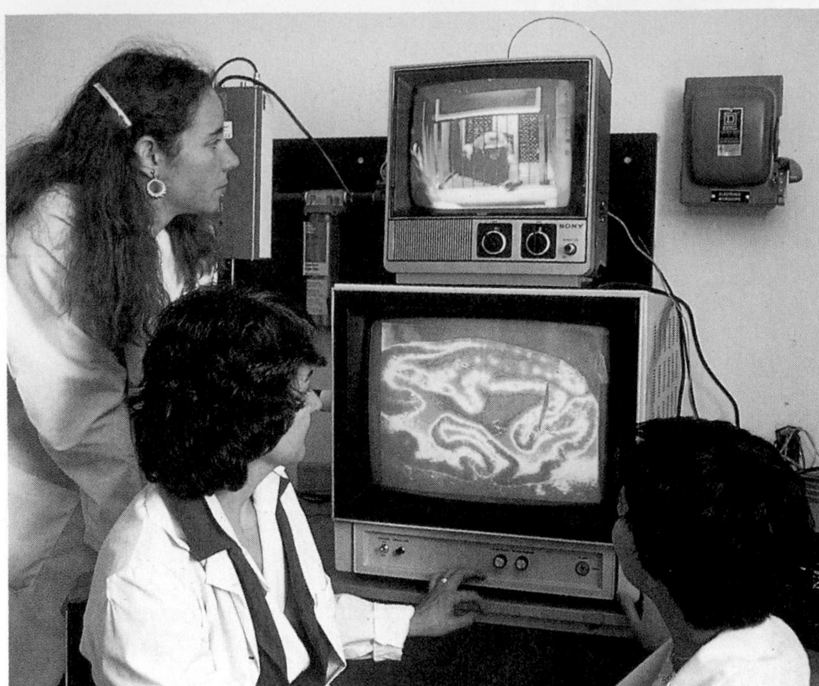

Psychologists often use neurobiology to study the effects of brain activity on behavior. In this picture the psychologists are studying the metabolic activity of a monkey's brain.

thoughts, feelings and actions. Their research, and that of other **neuroscientists** in biology, chemistry, and pharmacology, is on the brink of revealing how brain mechanisms are involved in the production of normal and abnormal behavior. Optimism is high that the coming decade will see many new discoveries that will enable us to understand better the neural basis of learning and memory, of pain and pleasure, of stress and well-being, and of many diseases, such as Parkinson's, Alzheimer's, and schizophrenia. As in the case of Mickey Median, once researchers have identified the link between brain activity and a complex system of behaviors, then clinicians and physicians can begin to treat the problem or modify the symptoms.

In this chapter we begin a general exploration of this exciting field within psychology, while in subsequent chapters we will examine selected aspects of the neural substrate of perception, consciousness, motivation, memory, and other psychological processes. Our venture into this domain is guided by the search for answers to four major questions: (a) What makes behavior "work"? (b) How do cells communicate with one another? (c) How does the brain control behavior? (d) How do we know what the brain does?

Francis Crick, who along with James Watson won the Nobel Prize for discovering the structure of DNA, believes that, "There is no scientific study more vital to man than the study of his own brain. Our entire view of the universe depends on it" (1979, p. 232).

What Makes Behavior "Work"?

This question rephrased in the current idiom of physiological psychology would be: What are the internal mechanisms and physical structures that determine how any given behavioral sequence operates? It is an old question, phrased differently in earlier times, yet fundamental to any basic conception of human nature. We will briefly examine how ancient philosophers and religious scholars asked what proved to be the wrong questions that led to false paths in understanding the "machinery" of behavior. We will see how a philosophical assumption about the link between mind and body initiated the scientific study of the nervous system, and what happened when conclusions based on facts from empirical research replaced alleged truths based on the power of authority or the persuasiveness of logical reasoning.

Mind and Brain

In prehistoric times, if one of our ancestors were acting peculiarly, that person might have an operation to insert a hole in his or her skull so that the evil spirits who were causing the person ill could escape. In prescientific thinking it was these inner spirits—some good, some evil—that caused behavior. (Could this have been the origin of the saying, "He's got a hole in his head"?) All human activities could be accounted for by the operation of one's *anima,* or life force, or by the demonic or divine possession of one's body. In this type of *animistic* explanation, the same kinds of spiritual forces thought to live in rivers and clouds were believed to guide living creatures.

The belief in spirits was in keeping with the early distinction by philosophers between the realm of the mind, where ideas reigned, and the domain of the body, where physical sensation and movements took place. The same separation of the nonmaterial mind and soul from the physical substance of the flesh was also assumed by early theologians, who searched for "the seat of the soul," the place within the human body where the divine spirit might guide bodily actions.

For the Greek philosopher Aristotle, the seat of the soul was the heart, the place where the mind's powers ruled the body's passions. The Greek physician Galen integrated Aristotle's notions about the importance of the heart with his own pioneering observations of the nerves of dissected brains. Because hydraulic models for pumping fluid through hollow tubes were popular in his time, Galen mistakenly assumed that nerves must operate on hydraulic principles. He decided that blood flowed into the heart where it was converted to "vital spirits," which were then pumped to the brain, and from there to specific muscles and sense organs.

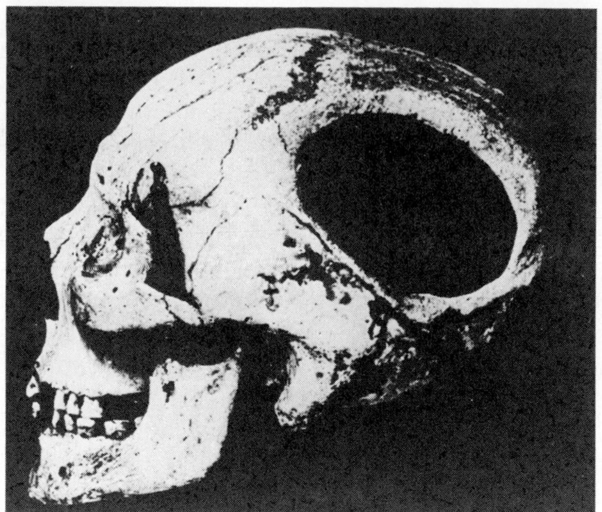

Trephination—perforating the skull with a sharp instrument—has long been thought to be a means of treating mental disorders. The process was thought to drive out the "evil spirits" causing the disturbance.

The Soul and the Machine

In the mid-seventeenth century the French philosopher and mathematician René Descartes advanced the theory that the body was an "animal machine" that could be understood scientifically—by discovering natural laws through empirical observation. He raised purely physiological questions, questions about the bodily mechanics of motion, that could be separated from philosophical questions about consciousness and perception. These, in turn, were separated from religious questions about the way divine laws govern human conduct. Descartes' insistence upon reducing complex sensory processes to their underlying physical bases has been termed the **mechanistic approach** to the study of physiological processes.

Descartes held that behavior "works" in the environment as a mechanical reaction to physical energies that excite the senses. Like Galen he believed that this excitation, flowing in hollow tubes as "animal spirits," was transmitted to the brain and then reflected back to contract specific muscles. This notion of a **reflex** in which an external stimulus leads to a physical response is still an important physiological concept, although we now know that nerves are not hydraulic tubes and that the incoming sensory signals and the outgoing motor signals to the muscles travel along different nerve pathways.

As a devoutly religious Catholic, Descartes could not, in his theory of bodily functioning, dispense with the soul, yet his belief in the mechanistic view of perception and other sensory processes prevented him from accepting the soul as the director of such processes. How did he resolve this dilemma? He postulated a **dualism** to separate the action of the mechanistic body and brain from that of the spiritual soul and ephemeral mind, each of them guided by its own principles. Still Descartes' religious beliefs required the soul to act on the body in some fashion; he theorized that the soul and body did interact, but at only one spot: the pineal gland at the center of the brain. He thought it was the only part of the brain with a unity that was not duplicated in its two halves (actually, the pituitary gland is another). His view was that the soul was not confined to this space, but could act upon the extended substance of the body only at this point.

Mind as an Evolved Ability of Brains

In the physiological research that followed Descartes' breakthrough, any ideas about the soul were quickly banished. In our own century, behavioral psychologists went further. They sought lawful relationships between outer behavior and external environmental stimuli, and disregarded what went on in the internal "black box" of the brain that lay between them. The behaviorists ignored the brain and dismissed the mind and the soul as nonscientific concepts.

Descartes' dualism has continued to the present, however, as the position of those who advance the doctrine of **teleology,** in which a purposeful, but nonmaterial mind acts upon a passive, reactive, and mechanistic brain to give behavior its direction (see Rychlak, 1979). Such an approach implies that the complex behavior of the whole organism can be understood only by starting "from the top down," from the higher order systems of control down to specific response units.

Physiological psychologists, by contrast, have tried to understand behavior "from the bottom up." Their hope is ultimately to understand complex mental processes by first understanding the biochemical processes that underlie both actions and thoughts. They reject Descartes' dualism in favor of **monism,** in which mind and brain are aspects of a single reality. In this view, also called **materialism,** the mind is the total of all possible mental states of our complex, physical brains.

> *Mind is the capacity for thought, and thought is the integrative activity of the brain—that activity up in the control tower that, during waking hours, overrides reflex response and frees behavior from sense dominance. . . . Free will is not a violation of scientific law, it doesn't mean indeterminism, it's not mystical. What it is, simply, is a control of behavior by the thought processes. (Hebb, 1974, p. 75)*

Reductionism and the Rush to the Molecular

Central to the theory of neuropsychology is the presumption of **reductionism,** the belief that observable phenomena at one level of analysis can be accounted for by more fundamental laws at a lower, or more basic level. Reductionism attempts to explain all biological processes, whether simple or complex, by a small number of laws. In this view, the basis of all behavior, including thinking and feeling, is to be found in the nervous system. All mental processes are assumed to be reducible to a neural substrate, even though they show characteristics that are not predictable by looking only at the level of neural functioning (Glassman, 1983).

The recent advances in neuroscience have been hailed as the "triumph of reductionism," replacing global, holistic conceptions of human nature with ever more specific and precise observations at the molecular and micro level of analysis—as we shall soon see in the next sections of this chapter. However, what is considered fundamental for one discipline might be considered highly complex for another. What neuropsychologists study is seen as more molecular than what most other psychologists study; where neuropsychologists stop is where other researchers, such as biophysicists, begin.

A word of caution is in order. Although thoughts are created by physical and chemical events taking place in the brain in some incredibly complex combinations we do not as yet understand, mental activities and neural events can be studied separately. If this were not so, then our study of psychology would stop at the end of this chapter. At this stage in the science of psychology it is difficult even to imagine how any rules for combining the activities of nerve cells could predict the content of your thoughts as you listen to a symphony, paint a picture, or play your favorite sport. Thus the enthusiasm for the gains in knowledge that have come from adopting a reductionist perspective should not be unlimited. The chief of the neurosciences branch of the National Institute of Mental Health recently reminded his colleagues: "It is necessary to caution, however, that the 'rush to go molecular' that characterizes much of this work must be tempered by a keen awareness of behavior" (Koslow, 1984, p. v). It is a reminder to all psychologists that the fundamental unit of analysis is the behavior of individual organisms, which must be understood, explained, predicted, and under some circumstances, controlled.

Nerve Energy

By the late nineteenth century, scientific observations and experiments had led to three general conclusions about the inner determinants of behavior:

a. The brain is the important center for controlling action.
b. This control is exercised through networks of nerves that transmit electrical signals from the brain to the muscles.
c. The functions of the brain and nerves are orderly and can be understood solely in terms of concepts and laws of biology, chemistry, and physics.

Scientists from many nations contributed to this enlightened view of "what makes behavior work." Five of the most important were Johannes Müller and Hermann von Helmholtz (Germany), Sir Charles Sherrington (England), S. Ramõn y Cajal (Spain), and Donald Hebb (Canada). Following is a brief review of their contributions to our understanding of nerve energy and the functioning of the nervous system.

Müller's **law of specific nerve energy** held that all nerve impulses were of the same form, but that different qualities of sensory experience were determined by the specific type of receptor that was stimulated and also by the location in the brain to which that input was connected. He hypothesized that the brain received a common kind of nerve signal regardless of the stimulus. Nerve signals were interpreted by the brain as light if they were transmitted by nerves from the eyes and as sound if the nerves were from the ears.

Helmholtz devised a simple demonstration to test whether nerve impulses were instantaneous (as fast as the speed of light) as many scientists of the nineteenth century believed. If so, then the "will to act" would be the same as the act itself. Helmholtz first stimulated successive points along a frog's nerve, then recorded the time that elapsed before the muscle contracted. He did the same with a man, electrically stimulating first his toe and then his thigh while observing any differences in time for his muscles to react. In both cases the results were the same: it took *time* for the stimulation to produce a reaction; and the greater the distance from point of stimulation to the muscle, the more time it took for the nerve impulse to show its effect. Moreover, the speed of transmission of a nerve impulse was rather slow for electrical events. It averaged only about one second per 90 feet in the frog's motor nerve, which is a little over 60 miles an hour—hardly the speed of light.

Of Helmholtz's experimental demonstration, the most noted historian of psychology, E. G. Boring, wrote: "To separate the movement in time from the event of will that caused it was in a sense to separate the body from the mind, and almost from the personality or self" (1950, p. 42). Helmholtz paved the way for research in cognitive psychology that uses **reaction time** to measure the duration of thinking and other mental events. In addition, he raised deeper issues; it was obvious that response to stimulation was being delayed in the nervous system, but where and how? Following Helmholtz researchers studying mechanisms of coordination and control within the nervous system asked a whole new set of questions.

To Sherrington (1906) goes the credit for showing that there are direct connections in the nervous system between nerve pathways carrying incoming sensory information and nerve pathways sending

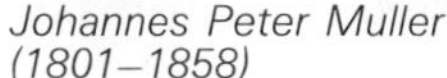

Johannes Peter Muller (1801–1858)

Hermann von Helmholtz (1821–1894)

outgoing motor signals (signals to muscles). These reflex arcs form the basis of survival behavior, where fast responding is essential: withdrawing a finger from a hot stove, or blinking an eye when an irritant gets in. Sherrington's study of reflexes also advanced the concept that the nervous system involves not just excitation but inhibition as well. While **excitation** of a nerve increases activity within the nervous system, **inhibition** of a nerve can reduce or even block activity. We now know that a major task of the nervous system is the continuing integration of a great many excitatory and inhibitory signals.

Around the turn of this century, Ramõn y Cajal (1933/1954) used cell-staining techniques, just developed by the Italian, Golgi, to identify individual neurons in brain tissue. He put forth the **neuron doctrine** which stated that all parts of the brain were composed of specialized cells called neurons.

While there are many others whose ideas and research helped build the foundation for modern neuropsychology, Donald Hebb opened the doors of this field to a host of new, energetic researchers in the United States and Canada. In his 1949 book, *The Organization of Behavior,* Hebb rejected the prevailing notion, put forth by Karl Lashley, that the brain was a "blob of homogeneous tissue," any part of which was interchangeable. Instead, Hebb argued that the brain was composed of **cell assemblies,** groups of neurons that acted together as a consequence of particular, repeated stimulation. The most important consequence of a cell assembly was its role in "central facilitation" which produced generalized arousal or attention. Disorganization in the functioning of cell assemblies resulted in emotional disturbance or forms of mental illness, according to Hebb's theory of the neural basis of psychological behavior.

Special Cells for Special Jobs

Did you know that your brain is "the most complex structure in the known universe" (Thompson, 1985)? Would you believe that "there are as many individual cells in your brain as there are stars in our entire galaxy" (Stevens, 1979)? The human brain is thought to consist of about 100 billion individual neurons (that's 10^{11} or 100,000,000,000 cells). What brought about this enormous increase in the number of cells that are required to make human behavior work compared to the number of cells in simpler animals?

More than three billion years ago a primitive life form existed in oceans of organic soup. In order to survive this one-celled creature developed a membrane that not only acted as a wall between its internal contents and everything on the outside, but also, through contractions, provided a means of moving about. However the cell also needed two other components: **cytoplasm,** which was the substance in which most of the cell's biochemical reactions took place and in which **metabolism,** the breakdown of nutrients into body energy, occurred; and a **nucleus,** which contained the genetic material, DNA, in chromosomes and directed the activities in the cytoplasm through the production of various nucleic acids. The cell was also able to divide to reproduce and perpetuate itself. With all this apparent self-sufficiency, why couldn't the one-celled organism endure without having to evolve into the many splendored, multicelled organ—the brain?

There are three reasons why a single cell was not designed to adapt to changes in the environment that interfered with its usual functioning. Its mobility was too limited when rapid motion was required; it had nutritional problems because it was not flexible enough to synthesize new substances when its regular food supply was unavailable; and the duplicates of itself that it produced were no better suited to a changing, hostile environment than was the parent cell.

Cell Differentiation, Specialization, and Redundancy

A multicelled organism with cells specialized to perform particular functions is the only way to achieve greater complexity and flexibility. Every cell in your body—and that of all living species of animals and plants—still has cytoplasm, a membrane, and a nucleus, which perform the general functions; but what the cells themselves do, and hence their makeup and ways of functioning, has become specialized. Within different body systems, the various cells have developed widely differing capabilities. Thus some cells can detect different kinds of sensory energy coming in from the environment; cells that form muscle tissue can transform chemical energy into physical energy (a process known as **transduction**) to get the work done; and nerve cells can transmit, throughout the body, information about what is coming in and what is going out—without themselves actually moving about.

These highly specialized functions of individual types of cells are duplicated many times over as a kind of "margin of safety"—guaranteeing that any specific job will get done even if some cells are damaged. This cell duplication, or **redundancy,** increases an organism's flexibility for dealing with extreme environmental assaults, while its cell specialization has increased the variety of environmental challenges to which it can respond or adapt. At what cost have the positive features been added? To gain these advantages, what price was paid?

The Need for Coordination

New problems arise from increasing the number of cells and give them specialized jobs. The major problem is that the cells can no longer work independently, but must operate in a coordinated fashion. While you are reading this, your eyes and head are moving; if you are taking notes (as you should be), your fingers and hand are working; you are also breathing, swallowing, blinking, and digesting food, while trying to memorize some of the printed information before you. Perhaps you are also squeezing in time for a little fantasy or two. This concert of separate functions must somehow be orchestrated into a coordinated whole if you are not to "go to pieces." Some actions are given priority over others ("keep reading, stop daydreaming"); sudden stimulus events must be attended to immediately while repeated ones can be put "on hold." How is this complex coordination and control of multiple inputs and outputs accomplished every moment of your life?

Effective functioning of any multicellular organism demands that its component cells coordinate their activities through some system of internal communication. How is this information transferred between cells in widely separated parts of the body? Two systems, often working together in complementary fashion, have evolved: in the *nervous system,* neurons send fast messages and produce transient, or short-lasting, responses; in the *endocrine system* hormones send relatively slow messages and produce more sustained, long-lasting reactions.

How Do Cells Communicate with One Another?

What a piece of work is man! how noble in reason! how infinite in faculties! in form and moving how express and admirable!

Shakespeare, Hamlet

The human nervous system provides for the flexible functioning of a biological organism that faces constant challenge from an everchanging environment. It can draw from past experience to respond swiftly to present demands while anticipating future possibilities—even its own eventual death. The human nervous system is the physical entity that makes it possible to flee danger or fight an adversary, to seek a mate and reproduce, and sometimes to build a better mousetrap, if not a brave new world.

The nervous system is the biological machinery for intelligent life. In humans this structure is remarkably complex. The complexity comes from the huge number of cells it contains, their diversity, the intricate ways in which they are organized into functional units, and the ways in which they can communicate with one another. We will first examine the basic unit of the nervous system—the nerve cell, or neuron. Our objective will be to analyze and understand how all the information available to our senses is ultimately communicated throughout our body and brain by nerve impulses. Then, we will outline the organization of the parts of the nervous system into its two subsystems, the central and peripheral nervous systems. Finally, we will consider the role hormones and the endocrine system play in regulating and modulating behavior and emotions.

Neurons as Building Blocks

All behavior begins with the action of neurons. A **neuron** is a cell specialized to receive, process, and/or transmit information to other cells within the body. Neurons, or nerve cells, form the basic building blocks of the nervous system. They vary in shape, size, chemical composition, and function; over 200 different types have been identified in mammal brains.

A typical neuron gathers information at one end and transmits signals at the other. The part of the cell that receives incoming signals is a set of branched fibers called **dendrites** that extend from the cell body. The dendrites spread out to receive input from hundreds or thousands of other neurons.

The cell body, or **soma,** contains the nucleus of the cell and the cytoplasm that sustains the cell's life. The soma combines and averages all the information coming in from its dendrites (or in some cases directly from another neuron) and passes it on to an extended fiber, the **axon.** The axon takes this combined signal and conducts it along its length (which can be more than three feet in the spinal cord and less than a millimeter in the brain). Axons end in swollen, bulblike structures called *axon boutons* or **terminal buttons.** These provide the mechanism for getting the signal across from the axon of one neuron to the dendrites or soma of neighboring neurons. The structure of a typical neuron is shown in **Figure 4.1** on the next page. Neurons transmit information in only one direction, according to the **law of forward conduction:** from the axon of one neuron to the dendrites or cell bodies of the next.

Three major classes of neurons can be identified according to the types of cells to which they send or from which they receive information: sensory, motor, and interneurons. **Sensory neurons,** also called *afferent* neurons, carry messages *in*—toward the central nervous system from cells in the periphery that are sensitive to light, sound, body position, and the like. **Motor neurons,** also called *efferent* neurons, carry messages *out*—away from the central nervous system to the muscles and glands. Sensory neurons rarely communicate directly with motor neurons, however. Between them is usually a third class of neurons called **interneurons.** The bulk of the billions of neurons in the brain are interneurons, which make many contacts with each other before reaching a motor neuron. For every motor neuron in the body there are as many as 5000 interneurons in the great intermediate net—the computational system of the brain (Nauta & Feirtag, 1979).

At birth, or shortly afterward, the brain of primates has all the neurons it is ever going to have. Unlike the brains of fish, amphibians, and birds in which new neurons appear and axons grow to distant destinations even in adults, the neurons of adult primates do not increase. This stable set of neurons may be essential for the continuity of learning and memory over a long lifetime (Rakic, 1985).

But our neurons die in astonishing numbers, estimated to be about 10,000 every single day throughout life! Fortunately, because we start with so many, we will lose less than 2 percent of our

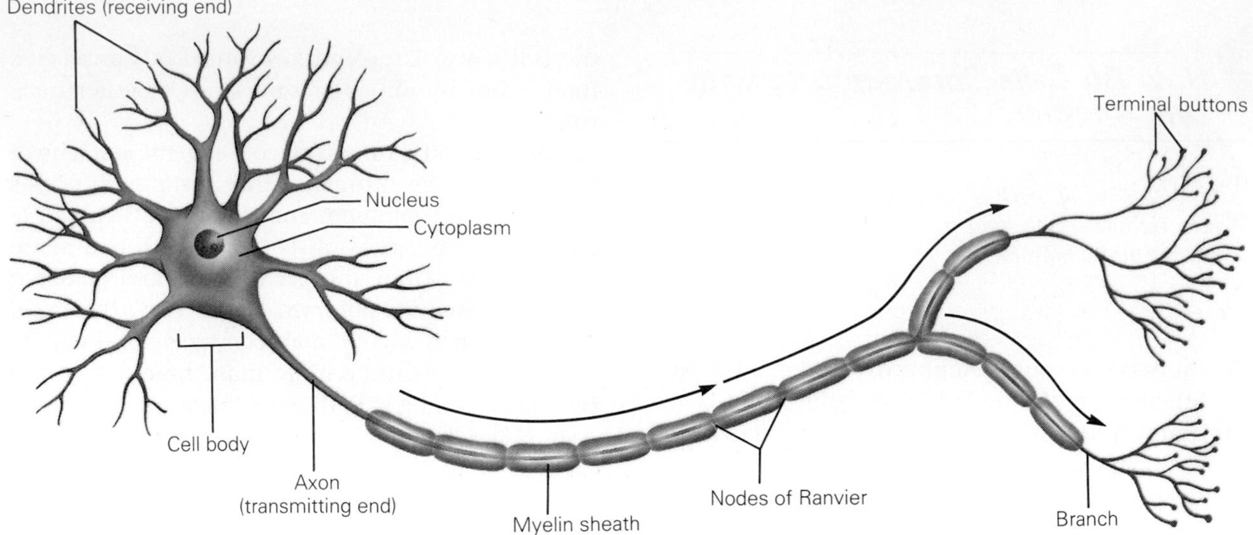

Figure 4.1 *The Neuron*
Shown is a motor neuron, one of the three main types of neurons in the human body. Nerve impulses are received by branched areas called dendrites and transmitted to the cell body or soma, where life-sustaining metabolic activity also takes place. The transmitting end of the neuron is the elongated axon, which is often enclosed in a fatty myelin sheath. Terminal buttons at the branched endings of axons transmit impulses to the next neurons in the chain.

original supply in 70 years, unless we suffer from a brain disease. The deteriorated brain functioning that sometimes comes in old age is usually not because of fewer neurons, but because of degenerative changes in the neurons themselves or in the chemical substances that carry signals between neurons.

Interspersed among the vast numbers of neurons are about ten times as many **glial cells (glia).** The word *glia* is derived from the Greek word for glue, and one of the functions of these cells is to hold neurons close to each other, though they do not actually touch. Although they do not conduct information as neurons do, they have three important functions: garbage removal, insulation, and poison control. When neurons are damaged and die, glial cells in the area multiply and clean up the cellular junk left behind. They can also take up excess chemical transmitter substances at the gaps between neurons. Their second function in a vetebrate brain is to form an insulating cover, called a **myelin sheath,** around the larger axons. Special glial cells, called **Schwann cells,** wrap themselves around the axons as the nervous system of the embryo develops. This fatty insulation greatly increases the speed of nerve signal conduction and is, thus, one of the great evolutionary advances of vertebrates.

The brain's constant activity and use of energy require enormous amounts of the nutrients carried in a rich blood supply and oxygen. (Though the brain makes up only 2 percent of the total body weight, it gets 16 percent of the body's total blood supply.) The third function of glia is to prevent poisonous substances in the blood from reaching the delicate cells of the brain. The *astrocytes,* another type of glial cell that comprise the **blood-brain barrier,** form a continuous envelope of fatty material around the blood vessels in the brain. Substances that are not soluble in fat do not dissolve through this barrier; and, since many poisons and other harmful substances are not fat soluble, they cannot reach the brain. Score another point for adaptive evolution!

Nerve Conduction: Sending the Message Out

What's similar about the violent discharge of an electric eel when disturbed by an intruder and the gentle lullaby of the mother putting her baby to sleep? Both are the outcomes of the same kind of electrochemical signals used by the nervous system to process and transmit information; both electrical messages involve changes in the membrane potential of a single cell. These changes are caused by the flow of electrically charged particles, called *ions,* through the cell membrane.

Think of a nerve fiber as a tube, filled with salt water and proteins, floating in a separate salty soup. Both fluids contain ions, atoms of sodium, chloride, and potassium that have either positive (+) or negative (−) charges. The cell membrane plays a critical role in keeping the ingredients of the two fluids apart or letting them mix a little; therefore the description of a cell's electrical state in relation to the outside fluid is called its **polarity.** When a cell is inactive, or in a *polarized* state, there are about ten times as many potassium ions (+) inside as there are sodium (+) and chloride ions (−) outside.

Because a membrane is not a perfect barrier, but "leaks" a little, some sodium ions slip in while some potassium ions slip out. To correct for this, nature has provided *transport mechanisms*—pumps—within the membrane to pump sodium out and potassium in (see **Figure 4.2**). Indeed, a great deal of energy is used to maintain this polarized state of readiness for every neuron in the body (Kalat, 1984).

When something happens to change the relative concentration of these ions so that they flow through the membrane, the cell becomes *depolarized* and capable of conducting electrical signals or nerve impulses. As the *permeability* of a neuron's membrane changes, ions flow through, in, and out of the cell, thereby creating the basis for all electrical signals in the nervous system. All nerve impulses in all organisms are started by biochemical changes in the membrane of nerve cells.

The universal language of nerve cells in all animals consists of two types of electrical signals: *graded potentials* and *action potentials*. **Graded,** or **localized, potentials** are passive signals, produced by the external physical stimulation of the dendrite or soma membrane, that vary in size according to the magnitude of the stimulus input. In sensory receptors, such as the retina of the eye, the physical stimulus of light, for example, is changed or *transduced* into a graded potential, called a *receptor potential* that carries information such as its intensity or brightness back to the brain. Thus the response bears a direct relation to the form of the eliciting stimulus. Graded potentials are only good for short-term, local signals, because they weaken over long distances and can be distorted. Graded potentials can influence distant parts of the nervous system when they are of sufficient strength to cause the cell membrane to depolarize suddenly to a certain critical level. The minimum stimulus energy sufficient to excite a neuron and trigger a nerve impulse is called the **threshold.** In chapter 5 a *sensory threshold* is defined as a statistically determined point on a stimulus continuum at which the energy level is just sufficient to detect the stimulus.

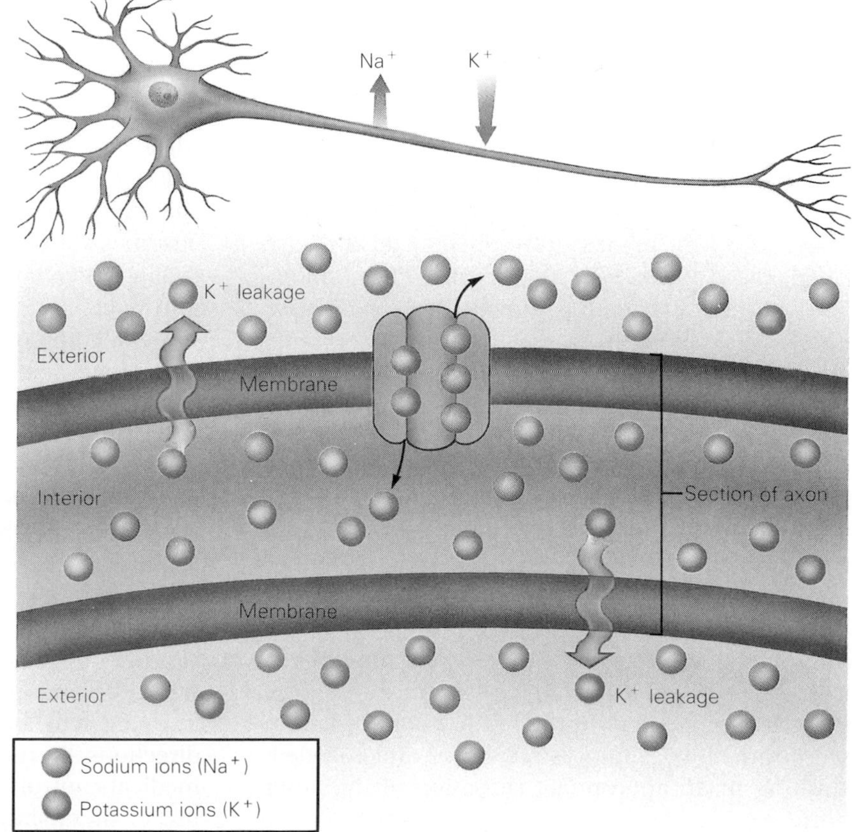

Figure 4.2 *A Sodium Pump*
This highly diagrammatic view of an axon section suggests the mechanism by which sodium pumps function to maintain the resting potential of a neuron. When the neuron is at rest, there is a high concentration of sodium (Na+) ions on the outside and potassium (K+) ions on the inside. Since potassium ions are continually leaking out through the membrane, a "pump" mechanism functions to exchange potassium for sodium, thus keeping the neuron in a state of readiness to fire. (For the sake of simplicity, the chloride ions which are also present have been omitted from the diagram.)

When that happens at the axon, a special event takes place; an **action potential,** or nerve impulse, is triggered. This second type of signal, arising from the dramatic release of the resting potential of the cell membrane, starts an explosive journey down the axon to its target cells. An action potential has the following characteristics:

a. It follows an **all-or-none principle**—once the threshold level is reached by the incoming, graded potential, a uniform and complete action potential is generated; if the threshold is not reached nothing happens.
b. The automatic, constant response bears *no* relationship to the form of the original stimulus.
c. Its speed or size does not decline with the distance it must travel.
d. It is *self-propagating;* it just keeps on moving until it reaches its destination at the terminal buttons.
e. It has a **refractory period** during which time a second impulse cannot be activated no matter how strong the second stimulus is and a later *relative* refractory period during which time only supa-threshhold levels of the stimulus will activate it.

Figure 4.3 illustrates both graded potentials and action potentials.

Different neurons conduct at different speeds; the fastest have signals that move at the rate of 200 meters per second, the slowest plod along at 10 centimeters per second (Bullock et al., 1977). The axons of the fastest neurons are covered with a myelin sheath, a covering that insulates the axon. The myelin looks something like long beads on a string. The tiny breaks between the "beads" are called *nodes of Ranvier.* In neurons whose axons have this myelin covering, the fast-moving impulse literally skips along from one node to the next like an express train passing local stations. Damage to this coating throws off the delicate timing of nerve impulses. Multiple sclerosis, for example, is a disease of the myelin sheath that results in double vision, tremors, and eventual paralysis.

You may wonder how a uniform, all-or-none action potential can transmit information about differences in intensity of stimulation. A more intense stimulus does two things to make its presence known. It triggers more frequent nerve impulses in each neuron, and it also triggers impulses in more neurons. Somewhere in the brain this information about rate and quantity is combined and encoded, resulting in an appropriate sensation of the outer world.

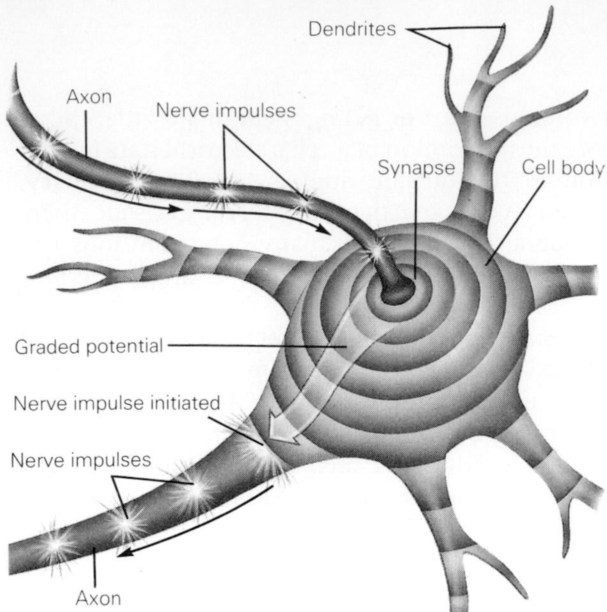

Figure 4.3 *Graded Potentials and Action Potentials*
An axon from one neuron is shown making a synapse on the cell body of another neuron. Excitation by the first initiates a graded potential in the second. This diagram also shows the two types of electrical potential changes which are the basis of all neural activity. Graded potentials develop relatively slowly and are local and varied in intensity; like ripples on a pond, they are stronger at their source and diminish with distance. Graded potentials are converted in axons into brief, all-or-none bursts of electrical activity called action potentials or nerve impulses, which travel all the way to the end of the axon. Axons in our bodies can transmit impulses at rates of up to a thousand per second. Normally, there are thousands of synapses on a neuron, but only one is shown here. Stimulation through the synapses is a common source of graded potentials, but some neurons generate such potentials spontaneously.

Ion Channels: For the Pores that Refresh

All excitation and electrical signaling in the nervous system involves the flow of ions through ion channels, which are as vital to nerve impulses as enzymes are to metabolism. **Ion channels** are excitable membrane molecules that produce and transduce electrical signals in living cells. They do so by opening or closing pores, tiny tunnels in the membrane, which causes ions to flow in and out.

Until recently, membrane permeability and the way it affected electrical signaling of the neuron was largely inferred, but in the last few years, neuroscientists have discovered how and why *cell membranes* are the key to the signals of all living creatures (Catterall, 1984; Hille, 1984). They discovered pores in the membranes that are designed to allow only specific ions to pass through. Not only does such knowledge allow us to understand the molecular basis of all electrical signaling in living cells, but it is beginning to open up new directions in the experimental modification and medical control of nerve transmission through the use of therapeutic drugs and genetic engineering.

Electrically Excitable Channels

When a channel opens briefly for only a few milliseconds, it is *selectively permeable* to specific ions, enabling only those with the "right chemistry" to flow in at an exceptionally fast rate (or greater than 10^6).

Each channel is, in fact, an elementary electrical conductor, which works with all the other channels to form an incredibly complex orchestra of billions of soloists shaping every signal and response of the nervous system to generate a harmony of behavior and a symphony of thought. All the known functions of nerve signals can be reduced to (or understood in terms of) the specific structure and activity of this tiny, liquid-filled pore. How tiny? If one square millimeter [▪] were divided into a thousand parts, there could be easily 10 to 50 thousand ion channels in this small area. Researchers have now developed experimental preparations that allow them to isolate and record the activity and effects of a single one of these pores! Their next step has been to identify and synthesize, in the laboratory, the gene that makes the sodium channel, which means they can systematically alter it at a molecular level.

The three positive ions of sodium, potassium, and calcium, and the negative ion, chloride, appear to be the ones selected to control the action in the membrane channel. The signal-processing property of neurons is determined by how many ion channels are packed into a given area of each part of the cell, along with the type of ion they select for and the kinds of signal that trigger their opening and closing.

Sodium channels are found in abundance in axons and muscle tissue, are fewer in neuron cell bodies, and may be absent in dendrites. The high density of sodium channels in the first part of the axon reduces the threshold for generating the action potential and typically starts the impulse on its way. The way is slow if the axon is not myelinated, because there are relatively few sodium channels operating; but it becomes speedy with myelinated axons because of their great density of sodium channels. Where are the most sodium channels found? Correct, at the nodes of Ranvier where the electrical signals literally jump from node to node (called *saltatory conduction*). Why? Because the great concentration of sodium channels at these nodes requires fewer ions to move into the cell in order to make a signal. Thus the action potential can buzz along with little time lost in ion exchange or cost in metabolic energy.

"The axon does not think; it only Ax." This statement reminds us that the basic function of axonal conduction is getting its all-or-none, simple impulse code from one point to another—swiftly and unconditionally. Since the information about the stimulus that is being carried by the action potential comes from the *frequency* of the impulses, the impulse has to come down quickly and be ready to refire immediately in a burst or train of impulses. That is one of the jobs of the potassium channels, more of which open *after* the action potential to let potassium ions out of the cell. These channels also regulate signals by delaying or extending action potentials.

The **sodium** and **potassium pumps** then work to push sodium out and potassium back into the cell, returning it to resting potential. These pumps are not ion channels, but transport mechanisms that use lots of energy to move the ions around. Because they do so slowly compared to the rapid flow in ion channels, nature has resorted to a "labor intensive" strategy of having as many as ten of these pumps for each ion channel.

Chloride channels also help return the cell to a resting state after being depolarized; one of their functions is to oppose normal excitability or to stabilize cell functioning by inhibiting the usual activity of specific neurons (Misgeld et al., 1986). Calcium channels are found in a greater variety of cell types than sodium channels, but they are less dense. They are called into action where the demand is for slower, longer, more sustained responding, as in the heart ventricle, the glands, and much enzyme activity.

Channels Not Excited by Electricity

The four channels already discussed are electrically excitable pores that open and close because of a change in membrane potential; however, they are only part of the story of nervous system communication. Other channels are specialized for signaling information coming from sensory stimuli, such as light, sound, pressure, and the nonconscious regulation of body temperature, blood ph levels, and other internal housekeeping. There are also many different channels that are activated by chemical transmitter substances released from the end terminals of axons. Let's briefly consider a unique feature of sensory-activated channels—the way their sensors open and shut gates at each pore—and then turn to the question of how messages get *across* the space between cells.

An ion channel that is activated by transduction of sensory input has three main parts: a *sensor* that detects the specific kind of stimulus and instructs the gate; a *gate* which opens or shuts the entrance to a pore; and a *pore* which conducts ions when the gate is open. Some channels have sensors built into the pore, while others have them at a remote distance. When a remote sensor detects a sensory stimulus, it releases a chemical substance, called a **second messenger.** This chemical substance flows to a particular pore where it fits into a second-messenger receptor like a peg in a hole. The message either opens the gated pore, and ions flow, or "instructs" the gate to shut, thus preventing ion exchange. Since it takes a while for the second messenger to arrive at the pore from the distant sensor and also some time for it to be replaced or inactivated, remotely gated pores are slow to signal the onset of a stimulus. They also persist in signaling its presence long after the stimulus is gone. Can you think of the kinds of signals for which such a slowpoke system is ideally suited? Signals in homeostatic regulation of the body and maybe some aspects of learning and memory may use second messengers.

Synapses and Neurotransmitters: Getting the Message Across

When an action potential arrives at the axon terminal, it cannot keep going because neurons never touch each other.

There is a gap between the end of each neuron and the start of the next. This junction, known as the **synapse,** is the space where evolution has etched one of its most significant contributions to humanity (Rose, 1973). Much of the complexity of human consciousness and intelligence may be traced to the remarkable activity that takes place at the synapse. To bridge the gap and get the neural message across to the next neurons in line, electrical conduction in the axon is changed to chemical transmission. The signal is carried by chemical messengers from one side of the synapse—the **presynaptic membrane** of the terminal button—across the gap to the **postsynaptic membrane** of the dendrites or soma of the next neuron. There it may initiate a graded potential, and the next electrical signal travels on to the next synaptic gap, and so on and on.

This process of chemical synaptic transmission is carried by messengers called **neurotransmitters.** When a nerve impulse reaches the end of an axon, precisely measured amounts of transmitter chemicals are released into the synaptic gap from **synaptic vesicles,** tiny sacs in the terminal buttons of the axon, as shown in **Figure 4.4.** The action potential opens calcium ion channels which admit positive ions into the terminal button. Their presence is

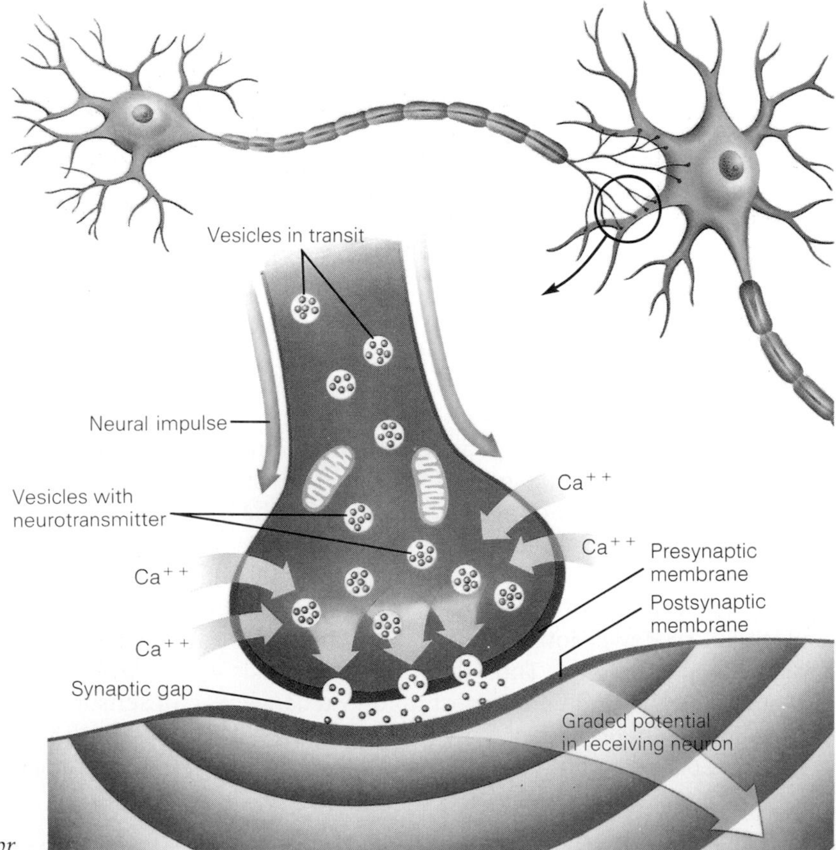

Figure 4.4 *The Synapse*
Activity at a synapse begins when a nerve impulse reaches the terminal button of an axon. The depolarizing action opens calcium ion (Ca^{++}) gates in the membrane of the terminal button, admitting the positive ions.

hypothesized to cause the rupture of the synaptic vesicles and the release of whatever chemicals they contain (Zucker & Lando, 1986). These neurotransmitter chemicals diffuse across the gap and attach to receptors in the postsynaptic membrane. In order to activate them there must be as precise a fit between them as between a key and the tumblers of a lock. The amount of chemical released corresponds to the number of incoming impulses: each impulse releases one vesicle. Thus, more frequent signals (from more intense stimulation) trigger a greater release of neurotransmitters. Then the neurotransmitter substance is either decomposed or reabsorbed into the terminal button, leaving the synapse ready for its next assignment.

Specific transmitter substances have been found in the brain, the spinal cord, the peripheral nerves, and even in certain glands. Some occur primarily in one location, while others are more widespread. More than 30 substances are known or suspected to be transmitters in the brain. Some of the chemicals believed to function as neurotransmitters are described in **Table 4.1.**

Some synapses are *excitatory:* the neurotransmitter causes the postsynaptic neuron to generate impulses at a higher rate. Others are *inhibitory:* the transmitter substance reduces the rate of impulses or prevents new impulses in the postsynaptic cell. For each transmitter there may be several different types of membrane receptors. It is the nature of the receptor channel, rather than the transmitter substance, that determines what the effect will be: the same transmitter substance may be excitatory at one synapse, inhibitory at another. It is the sum of all the excitatory and inhibitory effects acting on a neuron that determines whether it will fire, and, if it does, its rate of firing.

For the billions of neurons in the brain there are trillions of synapses. One estimate suggests that there are 10^{14}, a hundred trillion synapses (Hubel, 1979). A single neuron may share as many as 100,000 synapses with other neurons. Multiply this figure by the huge number of ion channels per neuron and the number of different neurotransmitters per neuron, and you can begin to see why the subtle modulation of behavioral response patterns results from overlaying these chemically coded systems on the neuronal networks of the brain (Iversen, 1979). (See also "The Way We Act" in *The Best of Science.*)

Table 4.1 *Chemicals Thought to Be Neurotransmitters*

For a chemical to be designated a neurotransmitter, several criteria must be met. It must be manufactured in the presynaptic terminal of a neuron and be released when a nerve impulse reaches the terminal. Its presence in the synaptic gap must generate a biological response in the next neuron, and if its release is blocked, there must be no subsequent response. Among the chemicals so far identified as neurotransmitters are the following:

Acetylcholine ("asséetil-cóleen")—found in many synapses of the central and peripheral nervous systems and the parasympathetic division. Excitatory at most central synapses and neuromuscular synapses; inhibitory at heart and some other autonomic nervous system synapses.

Serotonin—produced in the central nervous system, involved in circuits that influence sleep and emotional arousal. Can be either excitatory or inhibitory.

Catecholamines—three chemicals found in synapses in the central nervous system and sympathetic division.

Dopamine—found in circuits involving voluntary movement, learning, memory, and emotional arousal. Inhibitory.

Norepinephrine or chemically similar noradrenalin—both a hormone and a transmitter. Found in circuits controlling arousal, wakefulness, eating, learning, and memory. Can be either excitatory or inhibitory.

Epinephrine or chemically similar adrenalin—both a hormone and a transmitter. Either excitatory or inhibitory; actions include increased pulse and blood pressure.

Amino acids—widely found in brain.

GABA—the main inhibitory transmitter in the brain.

Glutamic acid—possibly the chief excitatory transmitter in the brain.

Neuropeptides—chains of amino acids found in the brain.

Enkephalins—mostly inhibitory, as in pain relief, but excitatory in some locations.

Beta-endorphin—the most powerful pain reliever produced in the brain. Mostly inhibitory but excitatory in some locations; contained in the stress hormone, ACTH.

(Adapted from Rosenzweig & Leiman, 1983, p. 159)

Drugs and Synapses: Messing with the Messengers

Many drugs exert their effects on behavior, mood, and thinking by influencing synaptic transmission. We know that venoms, food poisons, and certain herbs can affect the nervous system and cause paralysis, pain, convulsions, and hallucinations; yet, other chemicals can relieve our pain, reduce our depression, and transport some of us to alternate states of consciousness. How can such chemicals, found in nature or manufactured artificially, alter the way we function?

By now I'm sure you know the answer: Many of these drugs induce their effects by changing the usual action of ion channels. For every drug there is at least one corresponding receptor, and a single sodium ion channel may contain within it receptors for a variety of different drugs. The receptor is the sensor and the binding site for the drug. Drug action modifies the opening and closing of pores, and changes the nerve signal. A local anesthetic enters the membrane pore and plugs up the channel so that its sensitivity to stimulation is blocked. Some neurotoxins cause pain and even death by preventing a channel from closing, keeping the action potentials firing repeatedly; others do the opposite by closing an ion gate and blocking the nerve impulse.

Scorpion toxin binds to the sodium channels and prolongs the action potentials, preventing them from being turned off until the victim dies. Each year in Japan many people die from eating an improperly prepared delicacy, puffer fish, whose poison (TTX) blocks conduction of action potentials and causes paralysis of heart and lung muscles. Paradoxically, much of what is known about ion channels comes from research using radioactive forms of toxins whose action is highly specific to given types of ion channels—on tissue cultures and not people, of course.

You may have heard about the street drug called "angel dust" or PCP. It causes sudden increases in muscle strength along with bizarre changes in behavior resembling those seen in severe mental disorders—and can result in death. Recently the mechanism by which PCP affects the brain has been identified (Albuquerque et al., 1983). PCP binds to the potassium channel of the presynaptic axon membrane and prevents the sodium ion flow from being turned off. The axon keeps firing impulses and releasing transmitters into the synapse. In motor cells this produces extraordinary physical strength; in brain cells it can result in hallucinations and other abnormal mental functioning.

Many disorders of the brain are being traced to disturbances in the synthesis, release, or inactivation of specific transmitters, or in the receptivity of postsynaptic membranes. For example, in Parkinson's disease, the shaking palsy, there is a deficiency of the transmitter dopamine in the synapses of the part of the brain that controls movement. Administration of the drug L-dopa facilitates the manufacture of dopamine, which dramatically relieves the symptoms of this horrible disease.

Endorphins are a class of neurotransmitters that are involved in many reactions involving the most fundamental mechanisms of survival—pain and pleasure. Studying their action is providing researchers with a better understanding of how some of us become addicted to certain drugs (see ***Close-up:*** *The Keys to Paradise* on page 120). There is much hope among neuroscientists that when we really understand the biochemistry of synapses and neurotransmitters we will be able to unravel one of the profound mysteries of the human species, mental disorders.

Neural Networks: Acting in Concert

Up to now we have been looking at the way the nervous system *transmits* information within and between cells. Its other major task is to *process* information. The first level of processing is seen in the combining of graded potentials in the cell body and the modification of synaptic transmission that inhibits or increases nerve cell activity. Higher levels of complexity in information processing require *circuits,* systems of neurons functioning together to perform tasks that individual cells cannot carry out alone.

The simplest circuits are reflex arcs, which may involve only a sensory neuron and a motor neuron, or these two plus an interneuron between them in the spinal cord. **Reflex arcs** provide for automatic, rapid, simple responses—reflexes—to specific types of stimulation, such as the contraction and dilation of the pupil to light changes or the knee jerk in response to pressure below the kneecap (see **Figure 4.5**). The body's system of reflex arcs operates largely independent of brain involvement when the health and safety of the organism can benefit from a simple, swift response (Woolridge, 1963).

In addition, many reflex arcs contain interneurons that make connections with the brain. The brain is notified of reflex responses and can alter

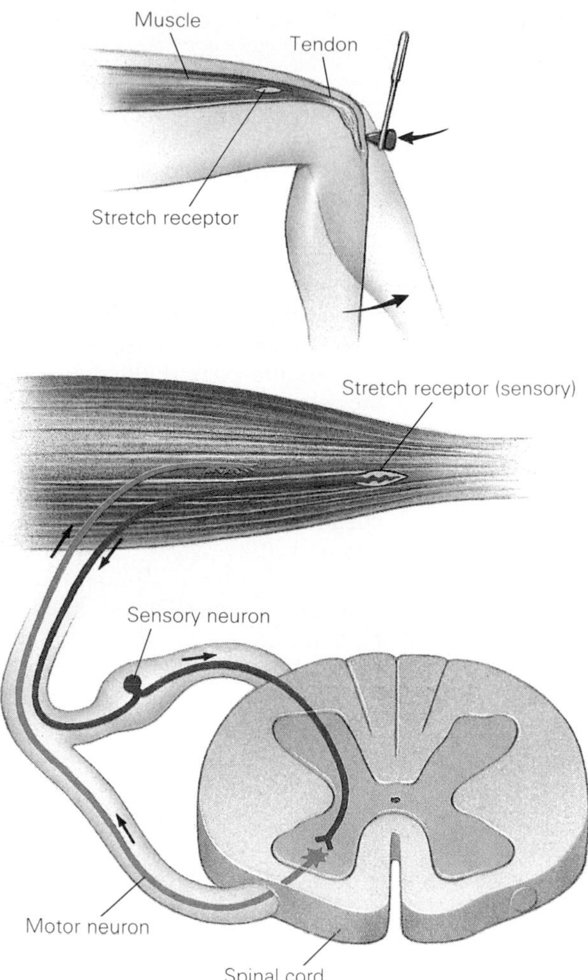

Figure 4.5 *A Reflex Arc*
Two kinds of neurons are represented in this simplified drawing of a reflex arc: (a) a sensory (afferent) neuron leading from a muscle cell and (b) a motor neuron with its long myelinated axon extending to the same muscle. Actually, a stimulus can excite many afferent neurons, each of which connects with large numbers of interneurons; many motor neurons will then carry messages back to the stimulated area. Other reflexes—for example, the pain withdrawal reflex—involve a third type of neuron, the interneuron in the spinal cord.

them to some extent. Though a single reflex arc is a simple mechanism, a reflex *action* involves many reflex arcs and other interconnections and may be quite complex. For example, the pupil-contraction reflex involves several interneurons before the information about light intensity even leaves the eye.

Neural networks follow a basic principle of nature: all life processes are organized *hierarchically.* This means that simpler units, structures, and processes are organized into levels of ever greater complexity, with higher ones exercising some control over lower ones. At each level of complexity there are limits and constraints that can be overcome only by a more complex system (Jacob, 1977). Just as new capabilities become available at each level from molecule to cell to organ to organism, new potential for information processing becomes available with increasingly complex neural networks. Thus, low level circuits in neural networks perform simpler functions of filtering signals, amplifying and modulating them, and calculating and storing information. (We shall examine these bottom-up functions in some detail in the chapters on sensation and memory.) At higher levels in the hierarchy, circuits combine many lower level processes for top-down functions of "recognizing," "evaluating," and "learning," as well as "thinking," and "feeling."

Because neural networks in humans are so complex, scientists trying to relate the structure and activity of neural circuits to the behaviors they control often study simple organisms such as invertebrates (animals without backbones). A favorite has been the large sea snail *Aplysia,* because its relatively few neurons are large enough to be identified so that their systems can be traced and "wiring diagrams" worked out for given types of behavior. For example, *Aplysia's* heart rate is controlled by a few cells that excite it to pump and a few that inhibit it. These are "command cells," individual cells at a critical position to control other cells and, therefore entire behavioral sequences. A neural circuit of only 70 cells is involved in *Aplysia's* reflex action of withdrawing its gill when its siphon is touched by a stimulus—a reflex necessary for its survival (see **Figure 4.6** on page 121).

One form of learning that *Aplysia* exhibits is **habituation,** a decrease in strength of responding when a stimulus that was originally new is presented repeatedly. Any novel, unexpected, or threatening stimulus elicits an **orienting reaction,** a complex physiological and behavioral response that maximizes sensitivity to environmental input and prepares the body for emergency action, but this lasts only while new information is being received.

Tactile stimuli applied to the siphon of *Aplysia* at first elicit an orienting reaction and gill withdrawal; but, with repeated stimulation, the gill-withdrawal response habituates: it becomes weaker and weaker until it is not made at all. Yet if a noxious stimulus is now applied to another part of the body, there is strong gill withdrawal. After an hour

Close-up *The Keys to Paradise*

The poet De Quincy wrote, "Thou hast the keys to Paradise, O just, subtle, and mighty opium." Those "keys" open the door to feelings of euphoria and analgesia (relief from pain). But opium—and its derivatives, morphine and heroin—can also open the way to addiction.

Opium, which comes from the juice of a poppy plant, exerts its powerful effect by acting on the central nervous system, but its derivative morphine comes in two forms: one, the powerful drug; the other, a totally inert and ineffective substance nearly identical in molecular structure. Somehow one can act on the nerve cells, but not the other. The question for researchers was how the nerve cells can tell them apart.

One hypothesis proposed specialized receptors on some neurons that can accept the active form of morphine but not the inactive one, much as a lock can be opened by the right key but not by wrong ones. But why should the brain have receptor sites to fit the juice of the poppy plant? One answer could be that the brain itself produces a similar key—its own opiates.

A search for these "keys" in the brain was undertaken, and in 1975, two pharmacologists isolated substances, called enkephalins ("in the head") in the brains of pigs that activate the same receptor sites as morphine and have a similar effect. These pain-relievers were produced by the brain itself (Hughes et al., 1975). Enkephalins were later found in the brains of other mammals and in many different brain regions. They act as neurotransmitters, and can increase or decrease the action of other transmitters—making them very powerful brain agents (Snyder & Childers, 1979). They occur in several amino acid chains which have collectively been given the name *endorphins,* a contraction of the words *endogenous* ("from within") and *morphine.* Like morphine, endorphins can be addictive, as well as relieve pain when administered from the outside.

The wide-ranging effects of endorphins have been studied by means of a research strategy based on the action of another chemical, *naloxone.* Morphine addicts suffering from near-lethal drug overdoses are helped instantly by injections of naloxone. In just 30 seconds naloxone reverses morphine's effects by preventing morphine from binding to its usual receptor sites—in effect, plugging up the locks so the opiate key can no longer get in. Naloxone has no other known effect on the brain's functioning.

Naloxone has been found to have the same effect in reversing the effects of endorphins. Pain relief usually brought about by endorphins following stimulation by acupuncture needles or electrical stimulation is blocked or reduced by naloxone. The presence of endorphins can thus be studied indirectly by observing the effects of naloxone. This means that if some procedure relieves pain but naloxone increases the pain, endorphins are the agent for this pain reduction.

Endorphins are now known to be stored in the pituitary gland. Besides relieving pain (to be discussed more fully in the next chapter), they play a role in the regulation of body temperature, respiration, hypertension, epileptic seizures, eating, memory, mood, and sexual behavior (Bolles & Fanelow, 1982). The most powerful analgesic produced by the brain, called *beta-endorphin,* has been synthesized by biochemists and given to human subjects to block pain.

Endorphin therapy is being developed to try to help drug addicts, chronic pain sufferers, and some types of mental patients. Perhaps some of the keys to human nature, if not Paradise, will be found in the mighty endorphins.

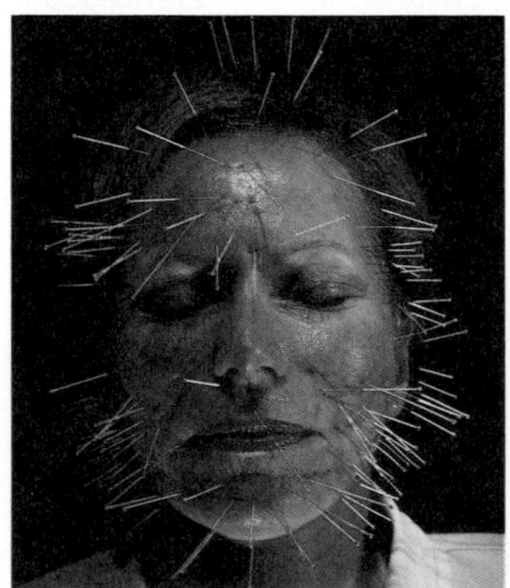

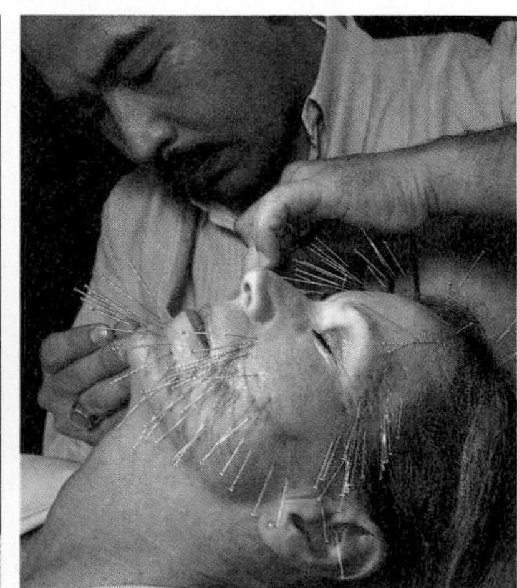

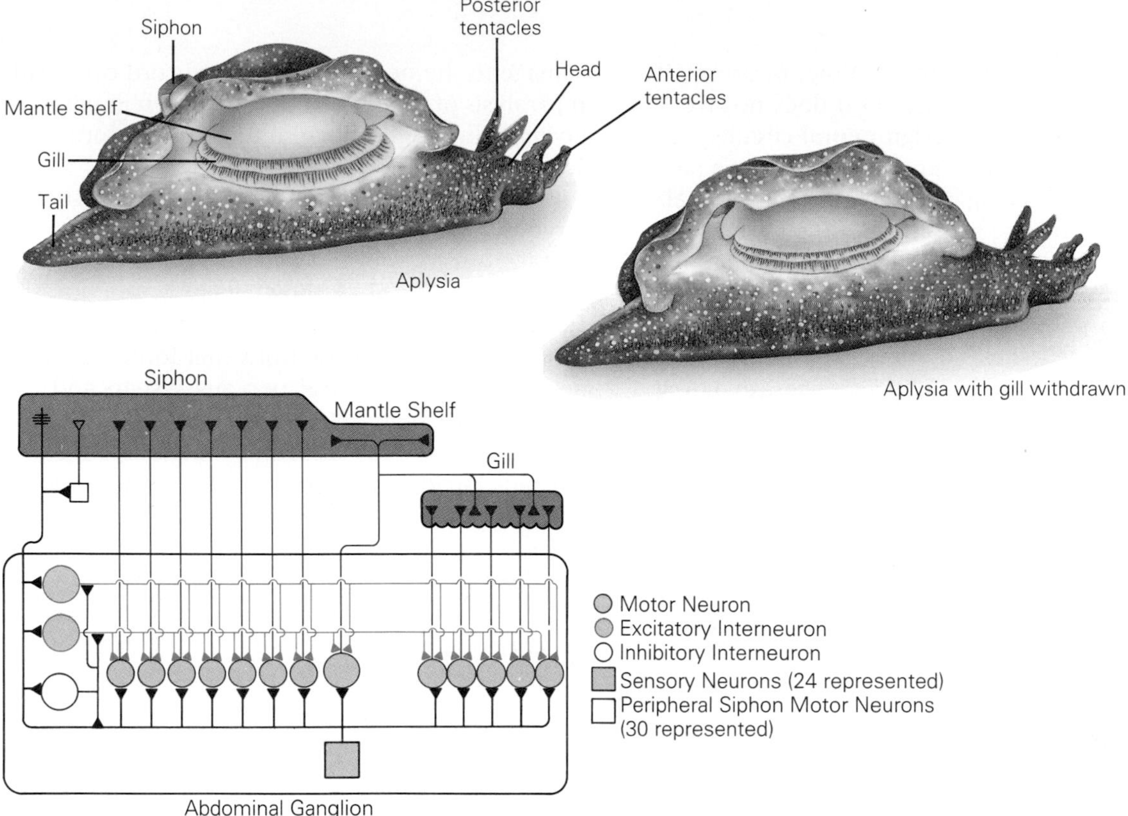

Figure 4.6 *Gill Withdrawal Reflex in* Aplysia

The sketches show Aplysia *in the normal state and with its gill withdrawn; The schematic diagram shows the abdominal ganglion with its sensory and motor connections. The 24 sensory neurons and 30 peripheral motor neurons are each represented by a single line, but the 13 motor neurons and 3 interneurons in this network are shown. Two of the interneurons are excitatory; the third, inhibitory.*

Adapted from Kandel, 1976.

of no stimulation, the gill-withdrawal reflex starts to return, and, after a day of no stimulation, recovery of the reflex is complete.

When the mechanism for habituation was traced by neurobiologist Eric Kandel and his associates, they found that during habituation a smaller amount of neurotransmitter was being released at the synapse, because of the action of an interneuron (Kandel, 1979). This finding is important because it identifies a specific biochemical mechanism that explains an observed change in behavior.

An Evolutionary Perspective: Nonadaptive and Illogical?

Studying simple circuits in invertebrates is a way to understand more complex systems, especially those in the human nervous system. It has been assumed that organizational principles can be found linking the properties of neural circuits to the behavioral functions that help the species adapt to its environment. This assumption is called into question, however, when we consider how neural circuits are shaped by evolutionary influences that were once, but are no longer, adaptive. Some characteristics that evolved as an adaptation to one set of conditions for a given era and environment have been chosen to perform new functions under changed circumstances. An example of this *preadaptation* is the change in the function of a bird's feathers, originally used for regulation of body heat and subsequently used for flight. Another example is the strange design of the neural network of the crayfish. When startled by an abrupt stimulus from behind, a crayfish escapes by activating its front neural circuits, causing a forward somersault tail-flip. Curiously, it also sends impulses to excite its rear segment, which would propel it backward toward the source of danger; luckily, inhibitory impulses are simultaneously triggered that weaken this fatal backup. These conflicting inputs have no current adaptive significance, but are embedded in the neural circuits that evolved from ancestors in whom front and rear neural circuits were identical and were flexed by excitatory impulses (Dumont & Wine, in press). It is important to note that evolution does not work on a long-range plan to design neural circuits, but selects behaviors that are most successful for a particular generation facing given environmental challenges. Our brains are so complex, in part, because they are overlaid with the effects of nonadaptive processes in evolution. We retain the old circuits even though they are of little use—exemplified by the sense of smell, once so important to our ancestors who survived by hunting prey and avoiding becoming victims themselves. "Our brains, which evolved under the selective pressure experienced by our prehistoric ancestors, have enabled us to conceive of our own deaths and compose music, functions that can scarcely have been selected for" (Dumont & Robertson, 1986). So we must ask not only how neural circuits work, but why they work as they do from an evolutionary perspective.

The Central and Peripheral Nervous Systems

The nervous system in all vertebrates (organisms with backbones or spinal columns) receives messages and transmits information to other parts of the body. It is made up of two major parts: the central nervous system and the peripheral nervous system.

The **central nervous system (CNS)** consists of the brain and the spinal cord. Its task is to integrate and coordinate all bodily functions by processing all incoming and outgoing messages. The CNS is the central control tower that directs the constant flights of stimulus input and the orders for response output. Since we will focus on the brain in detail in a later section, here we will outline only the role of the spinal cord.

The **spinal cord** is a trunkline of nerve cells that connect the brain with the rest of the body through pathways in the peripheral nervous system. It is housed in a hollow tube called the *spinal column.* Spinal nerves branch out from the spinal cord between each pair of vertebrae in the spinal column. They eventually connect with sensory receptors throughout the body, as well as with muscles and glands. The spinal cord also coordinates the activity of the left and right sides of the body and is responsible for some simple reflexes that do not involve the brain. For example, an animal whose spinal cord has been separated from its brain can still withdraw its limb from a painful stimulus. Though normally the brain is "notified," the action can be completed without directions from higher up. Damage to the nerves of the spinal cord can result in paralysis of the legs or trunk, as seen in paraplegic individuals who have suffered spinal cord injuries.

Despite its commanding position, the central nervous system is isolated from any direct contact with the outside world. It would be little more than stuffing in the "black box" were it not for the **peripheral nervous system (PNS),** the network of sensory and motor neurons that form the interface between the central nervous system and the surface of the body. The peripheral nerves located throughout the body have two functions: (a) some carry information from each of the sensory receptors (in the eye, ear, skin, and so on) to the brain, and (b) some carry messages from the brain and spinal cord to the muscles and glands (see **Figure 4.7**). The central and peripheral nervous systems are continually communicating with each other.

Figure 4.7 *The Peripheral Nervous System*
All main motor and sensory nerves in the peripheral nervous system are shown. Nerves in the spinal cord connect them with the brain.

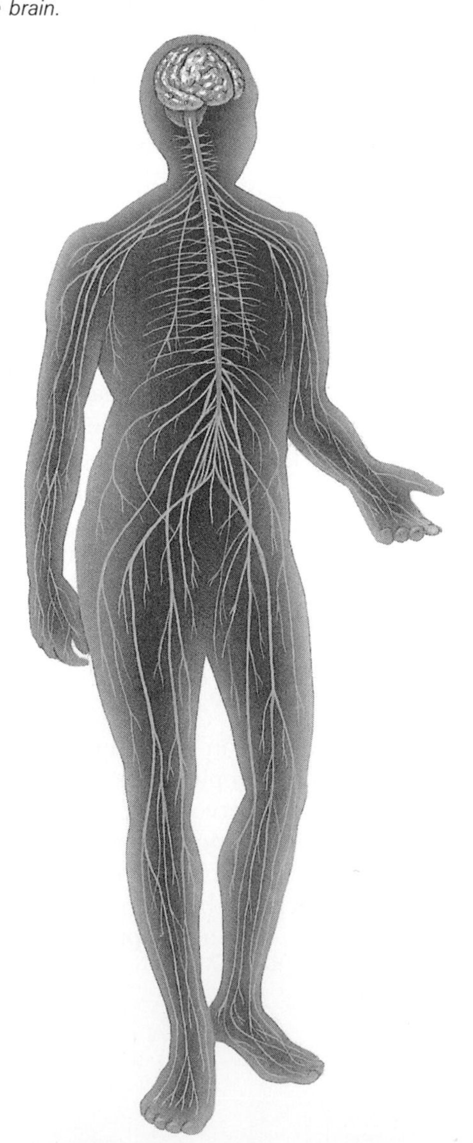

The first part of the peripheral nervous system, called the **somatic nervous system,** is under voluntary control. It controls the skeletal muscles of the body ("make a fist; now release it"). The **autonomic nervous system** is the second part of the peripheral nervous system; it governs activity not normally under an individual's direct control. It must work even when the individual is asleep, and it sustains life processes during anesthesia and prolonged coma states. The somatic and autonomic systems are directed by different structures in the brain.

The autonomic nervous system deals with "survival" matters of two kinds: those involving threats to the organism and those involving bodily maintenance. Two divisions within the autonomic system "work together in opposition" to accomplish these survival tasks. The **sympathetic division** deals with emergency responding, while the **parasympathetic division** deals with internal monitoring and regulation of a variety of functions (see **Figure 4.8**). The sympathetic division can be regarded as a troubleshooter: when you face an emergency or a stressful challenge, it mobilizes the brain for arousal and the body for action. Digestion stops, blood flows away from internal organs to the muscles, oxygen transfer is increased, heart rate increases, and the endocrine system is stimulated to facilitate a variety of motor responses. After the danger is over, the parasympathetic division takes charge to decelerate these processes so you can relax, calm down, and "mellow out." Digestion resumes, heartbeat slows, breathing is relaxed, and so forth. Basically, the parasympathetic division carries out the body's nonemergency "housekeeping chores," such as elimination of bodily wastes, protection of the visual system (through tears and pupil constriction), and long-term conservation of

Figure 4.8 *The Autonomic Nervous System*
This is a highly simplified diagrammatic portrayal of the parts of the autonomic nervous system—where the major nerves originate and what their main functions are. For simplicity, the system on only one side of the body is shown. Parasympathetic parts and functions are labeled in black and sympathetic ones in color. Note that the sympathetic nerves pass through or have connections in a chain of ganglia (clusters of nerve cell bodies) lying directly outside the spinal cord.

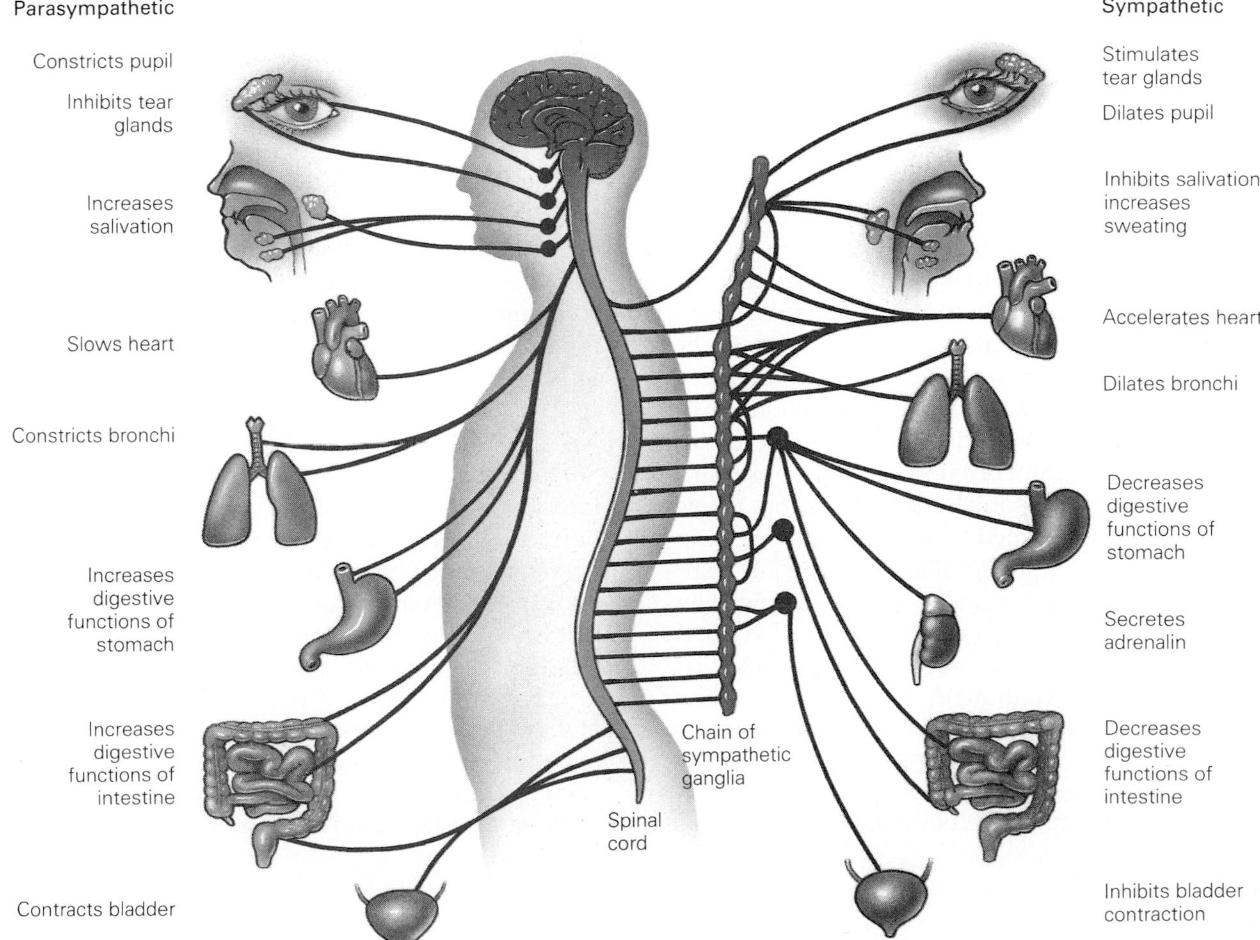

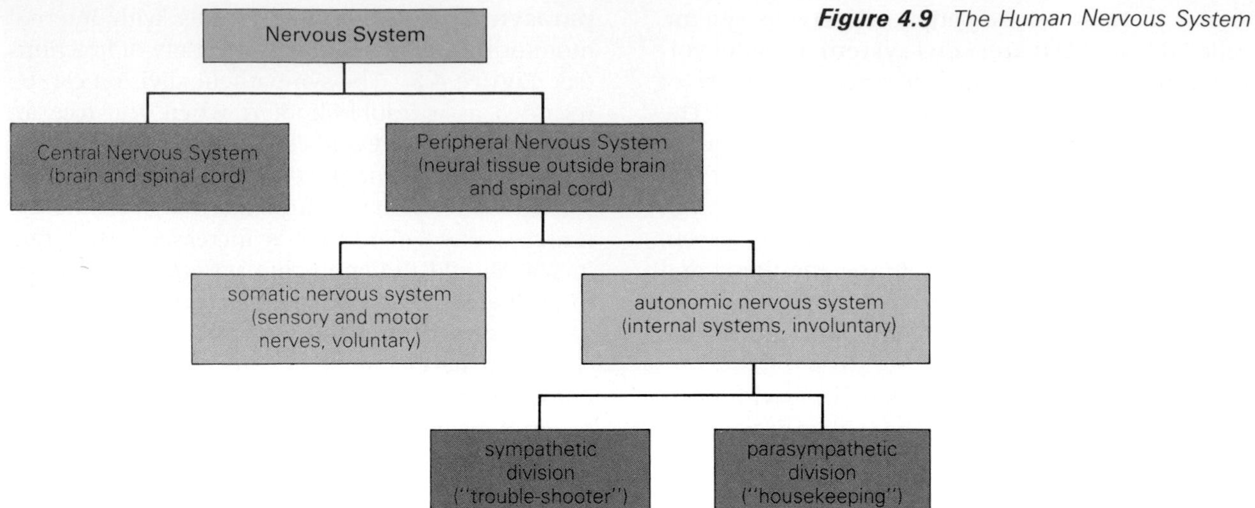

Figure 4.9 *The Human Nervous System*

body energy. **Figure 4.9** is a schematic representation of the components of the nervous system. Sometimes the sympathetic nervous system overreacts to a situation as if it were a threat requiring mobilization of flight or fight reactions—when it is not actually life threatening. (We will study this type of reaction in more detail in chapter 14 on stress and health psychology.)

Behavioral Regulation by Hormones of the Endocrine System

The endocrine system consists of glands (sets of cells), located in many parts of the body, that manufacture and secrete chemical messengers into the bloodstream (see **Figure 4.10**). These chemical messengers, called **hormones,** determine your growth, sexual characteristics, arousal, sexual behavior, reproduction, mood changes, and metabolism. They are carried by the circulation of the blood to distant target cells with specific receptors; they exert their influence on the body's program of chemical regulation only at the places that are genetically predetermined to respond to them. In influencing diverse, but specific, target organs or tissue, hormones can regulate such an enormous range of biochemical processes that they have been called "the messengers of life" (Crapo, 1985).

Hormones, once thought to exist only in vertebrates, have been found recently in lower species, such as worms, flies, protozoa, and even simple, one-celled organisms. Moreover, they seem to be made everywhere in the body, not only manufactured by glands. Endocrine glands respond to the levels of chemicals in the bloodstream or are stimulated by other hormones or by nerve impulses from the brain. This multiple-action communication system allows for control of slow, continuous processes such as maintenance of blood-sugar levels and calcium levels, metabolism of carbohydrates, and general body growth; but what about sudden crises? What happens to your body when you see a child in front of your car or bike? The system releases the hormone adrenaline into the bloodstream to energize the muscular system so that you can respond quickly to avert certain disaster.

The endocrine system also promotes the survival of an organism by helping fight infections or disease. It advances the survival of the species through regulation of sexual arousal, production of reproductive cells, and production of milk in nursing mothers.

Dual Chemical Messenger Systems

Some nerve cells make molecules that are secreted into the circulation and act on distant targets as hormones, while some hormones are made in nerve cells and then act as neurotransmitters. Again we see nature *conserving* biological mechanisms to reuse whatever systems work by refashioning them to fit the new circumstances.

It has been proposed that the endocrine system and the nervous system both evolved from a common ancestral system in which primitive cells used chemical messengers to signal neighboring cells (Roth et al. 1982); and hormones and neurotrans-

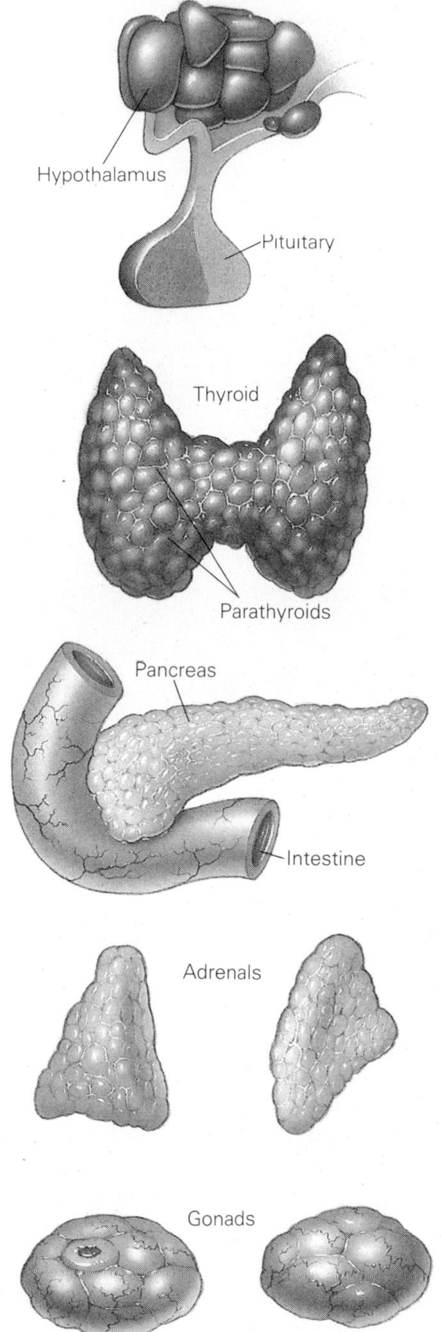

Figure 4.10 *The Endocrine System*
Shown are the major hormone-producing regions of the human body. All of these structures release hormones into the general circulation except the hypothalamus which releases its hormones into the portal circulation (arrow) connecting the hypothalamus to the pituitary gland.

mitters are alike in several ways. Both are chemical messengers that regulate communication between cells; both have specific receptors on target cells; and both work in synchrony to preserve the internal harmony of an organism, preparing it to survive and adapt to changes in the environment. They are also similar because many of these messengers are *peptides*—simple molecules made up of a linear sequence of amino acids. However, neurotransmitters influence nearby cells quickly, while hormones act slowly to influence distant cells.

Within a cell there are also many chemical messengers: messenger RNA (a form of ribonucleic acid) that regulates its genetic code; enzymes that regulate cell metabolism; and a chemical called *cyclic AMP* that regulates the enzymes of the cell. All hormones work by stimulating a change in these intracellular messengers. They do so by influencing the activity and rate at which enzymes and other proteins are manufactured, or by altering cell membranes, permitting or restricting passage of various substances into target cells. The influence of a hormone on the receptor surface of a target cell comes in two phases. When a hormone acts *outside* the cell to start a series of chemical reactions that result in the synthesis of cyclic AMP, it is acting as a *first messenger* system. However when the cyclic AMP, acting *inside* a cell, is a catalyst for internal chemical changes, it becomes the *second messenger* system. Do you recall another second messenger system that controlled the gates of ion channels when the sensor for the ion gate was remote rather than at the ion channel?

In addition to peptides, the other major type of hormones is *steroids.* Steroids are made from cholesterol and bind to receptors *inside* the cell to influence its genetic code. They contribute to mood changes associated with fluctuations of steroids during times of disease or stress (Majewska et al., 1986).

This "cross-talk" between the autonomic nervous system and the endocrine system contributes to the vital function of homeostasis. **Homeostasis** is the process by which constancy or balance of the internal conditions of the body is maintained. It is also thought of as the tendency of organisms to maintain their equilibrium and resist change. Homeostatic mechanisms are complex and subtle self-regulating mechanisms that keep many internal conditions within the limits necessary for the body's well-being, much as a thermostat in a heating system maintains a constant temperature.

Most hormones are produced in the nine regions of the body. These hormone-producing factories make a variety of hormones, each of which regulates a different bodily function, as outlined in

Table 4.2 The Hormones and Their Functions

Origin	Hormones	Function
Hypothalamus	Stimulators Inhibitors	Pituitary Hormone Regulation
Pituitary, Anterior	ACTH FSH GH LH Prolactin TSH	Adrenal Control Gonad Regulation Growth Stimulation Gonad Regulation Breast Milk Production Thyroid Control
Pituitary, Posterior	ADH Oxytocin	Water Conservation Uterus Contraction and Breast Milk Excretion
Thyroid	Thyroxine	Metabolic Rate Control
Parathyroid	PTH	Calcium Regulation
Gut	Gut Hormones	Food Digestion
Pancreas	Insulin Glucagon	Glucose Metabolism
Adrenals	Cortisol Aldosterone Epinephrine	Body Preservation Salt Conservation Stress Response
Ovaries	Estradiol Progesterone	Female Characteristics
Testes	Testosterone	Male Characteristics

Table 4.2. Let's examine what may be considered the most significant of the origins of hormonal influence.

At the pinnacle of the endocrine system reigns the *hypothalamus,* a gland which sits at the base of the brain. It is a central relay station between other parts of the brain, the endocrine system, and the autonomic nervous system. Neurosecretory cells in the hypothalamus get messages from brain cells to release at least seven different hormones to the pituitary gland where they either stimulate or inhibit the release of pituitary hormones.

The **pituitary gland** is called the "master gland," because it secretes about ten hormones that influence the secretions of the other endocrine glands, as well as a growth hormone that promotes protein synthesis and influences growth. The absence of this growth hormone results in dwarfism, its excess in gigantic growth (as we will see in the *Opening Case* of Keith in chapter 11). In males pituitary secretions activate the testes to secrete **testosterone,** which is responsible for such sex-linked characteristics of males as their beards, deep voices, prominent muscles, and broad shoulders. Testosterone may also have the behavioral effects of increasing aggression, boisterous activity, and sexual drive. In females another pituitary hormone stimulates production of **estrogen,** which is essential to the hormonal chain reaction that triggers the release of eggs from a female's ovaries, making her fertile. Certain birth-control pills work by blocking the mechanism in the pituitary that controls this hormone flow, thus preventing the eggs from reaching the stage of development where they can be fertilized. (See also "She & He" in *The Best of Science.*)

The time has come to move up to the top of the system where all of this molecular activity of ion channels, action potentials, neurotransmitters, and hormonal messengers get integrated, coordinated, and given a unified purpose in life. It's brain time.

How Does the Brain Control Behavior?

The universe exists for us only insofar as it exists in our brains. The brain is our three-pound universe. (Hooper & Teresi, 1986, p. 3)

In the hierarchical organization of the human nervous system, the brain represents the highest level of complexity. It coordinates information about the external world and an organism's internal state, controls our actions, and serves as a base for our higher mental processes.

It is the place where the endless stream of electrical nerve impulses and the constant flow of chemical transmitter and hormone messengers get transformed into our personal experiences, knowledge, feelings, beliefs, the consciousness of self, and all that goes into the making of "human nature." *How?* No one knows—yet.

One way of explaining something we don't understand is to use *metaphors* or *models* that try to explain it in terms of something we do know. Brain metaphors have typically been drawn from the most advanced technology of a given time period. For Descartes it was the machinery of complex water clocks; Sigmund Freud resorted to steam engines for his view of the brain as a hydraulic system of drives, actions, and reactions. With the invention of the telephone came the metaphor of the brain as a switchboard with some "hard-wired connections" put there by Mother Nature and newer ones put there by experience with Ma Bell! The latest model—the brain as biocomputer—describes the brain's complexities in terms of computer procedures. Other metaphors forego a mechanistic comparison to propose that the brain is like a *hologram* in which three-dimensional images are created by multiple sources of light input (Pribram, 1979). However none of these models comes close to answering the *how* question—how do all those molecular processes get orchestrated into a molar, sum total that comes out recognizing your mother, liking apple pie, saluting the flag, and believing in God? For now, we will rephrase the question to ask: how is the brain organized and what does it do for us?

Design of the Brain

The early stages of the development of all vertebrate embryos are quite similar: the primitive structure that eventually becomes the brain at first looks the same in a frog, rat, cat, or human embryo. The way the brain forms and separates into divisions is also the same across many species; but the higher the species, the larger and more complex the brain becomes and the more sophisticated functions it can perform. The development of the nervous system in members of each species follows genetic instructions that result in the "hard-wiring" of basic neural circuits. In the human brain, these instructions lead to a remarkably precise and efficient communication and computational system unmatched in many ways by any supercomputer. But heredity does not do it all. Stimulation and information from the environment are also needed to "fine tune" the brain structures to behave appropriately in each individual's particular environmental niche (Rosenzweig, 1984).

The various parts of the brain and nervous system develop at different rates, and the period of most rapid biochemical change for a given structure is a **critical period.** This is a biologically determined time when an organism is optimally ready to acquire new structures and processes. It is a "window" of maximum sensitivity to change.

Certain genetic and environmental influences must be present then, if development is to proceed normally; abnormal influences do their greatest damage to the brain at this time. Among the environmental factors that can prevent normal development of the brain are malnutrition, inadequate oxygen in circulating blood, infections, radiation, drugs, injuries, and inadequate stimulation.

Let's first look at the brain as if it were the site of some archaeological excavation, where many layers of ancient civilizations are piled one atop the other. In this way we will get a sense of its evolutionary development over millions of years. In the last part of this section, we will tour its present landscape, visiting the major structures that have been identified as the staging ground for various behaviors and mental processes of interest to us.

Brain Archaeology

Homo sapiens have three interconnected brains, identified as belonging to different epochs in our evolutionary past, according to Paul MacLean (1977). This "triune brain" (see **Figure 4.11**) contains deep within its recesses an ancient reptile brain, found in the part of the brain known as the *brain stem* and in the structures surrounding it. It contains many of the old behavioral programs that motivate snakes and lizards to act in rigid, instinctual ways by following "ancestral memories" that

Jimmy Tontlewicz, who had been submerged for nearly 30 minutes in the icy waters of Lake Michigan, demonstrated the remarkable recuperative capacity of the human brain when he recovered without suffering permanent brain damage.

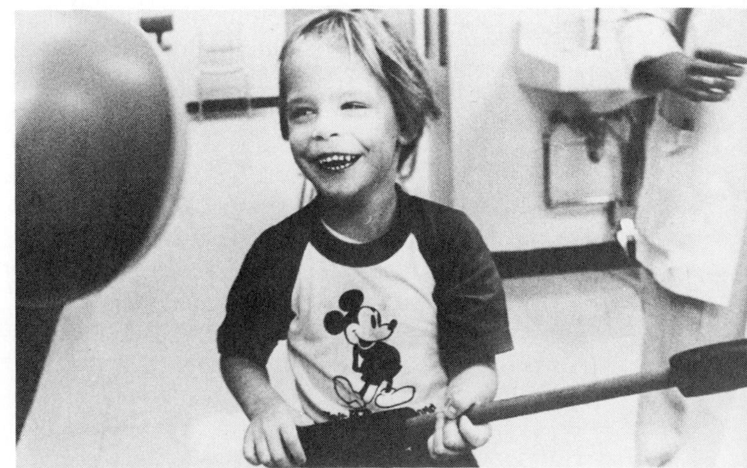

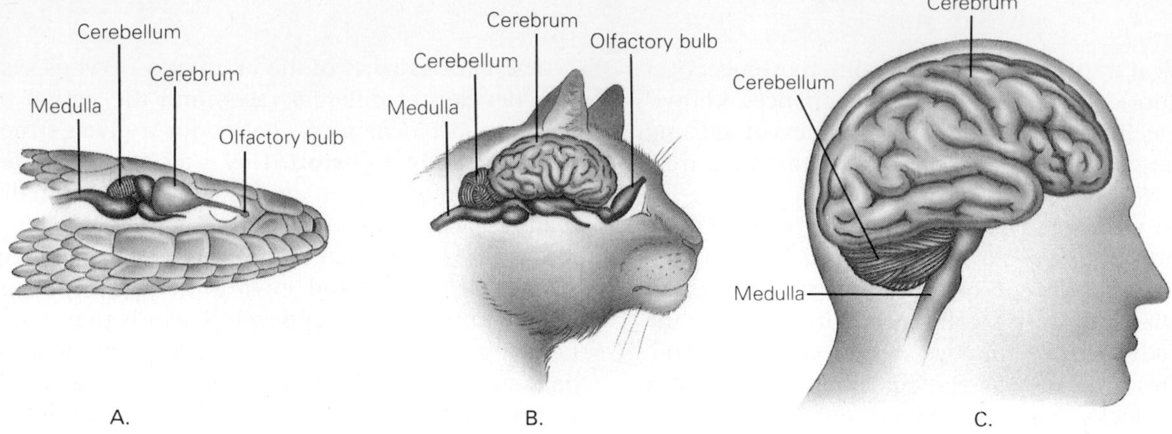

Figure 4.11
Cerebral development is increasingly more advanced in higher classes of vertebrates. A reptile has a somewhat large and smooth cerebrum and a reduced olefactory area. The brain of a cat is dominated by a convoluted cerebrum. The cerebellum, involved in coordination, is well developed in the cat as is the olefactory bulb. The human brain has a large and highly developed cerebrum.

are not changed by new experiences. On top of the reptilian brain is the old mammalian brain shared by cats, rats, and rabbits. Found in the brain area called the *limbic system,* this old brain is survival-centered. Its activities are geared toward survival of the species and the organism through feeding, fighting, fleeing, and sexual behavior. Wrapped around these two primitive brains is the new mammalian brain, the *neocortex.* Like a folded-up *New York Times* covering some small, sleeping animal, the neocortex has "all the news that's fit to print." The neocortex is "the mother of invention" and "the father of abstract thought." It runs the mind's show—but, at times, the sleeping animal stirs and then, "the primitive needs of mice may mess up the rational plans of man—and woman."

Brain Geography

The brain consists of three basic parts, each with subdivisions. Sitting atop of the spinal cord is the **hindbrain;** moving up and in we find the **midbrain;** and further up and all around is the **forebrain** (see **Figure 4.12**). The hindbrain includes two structures, the bottom of the brain stem and the cerebellum. The midbrain operates out of the top of the brain stem. All the rest is the forebrain: the diencephaion, the limbic system, the two halves of the cerebral hemispheres, and the outermost covering, the cortex. These Latin and Greek words were chosen by early anatomists to represent the familiar shapes they saw when they first began to look at brain matter: *cortex* to describe bark, *hippocampus* for seahorse, *amygdala* for almond, *sulcus* for valley, and so forth (see **Figures 4.13** on the next page and **4.14** on page 131).

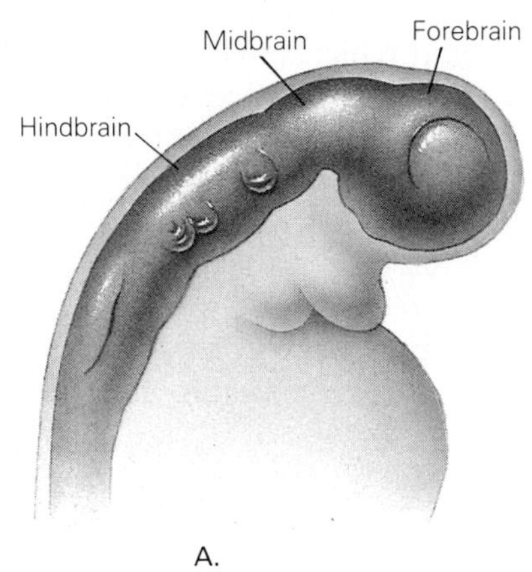

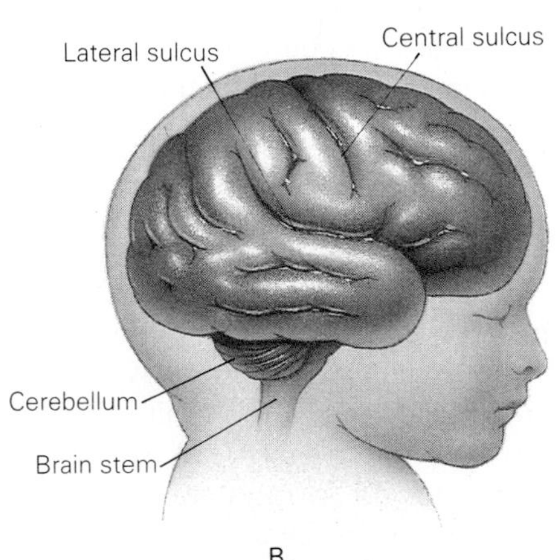

Figure 4.12 *Fetal Brain Development*
The diagrams illustrate the development of the human brain from the third week after conception to birth. A, 3-week embryo; B, newborn infant.

Figure 4.13 *The Human Brain*

Shown are two views of the human brain. The upper view shows an intact brain with the left cerebral hemisphere and some of the lower brain centers. Note that the cerebrum is divided into four prominent lobes: temporal, frontal, parietal, and occipital. The primary functions of the various areas are shown in parentheses.

In the lower view, the brain has been cut through the middle from front to back. Structures of the forebrain, midbrain, and hindbrain are shown, as is the corpus callosum, which connects the two hemispheres.

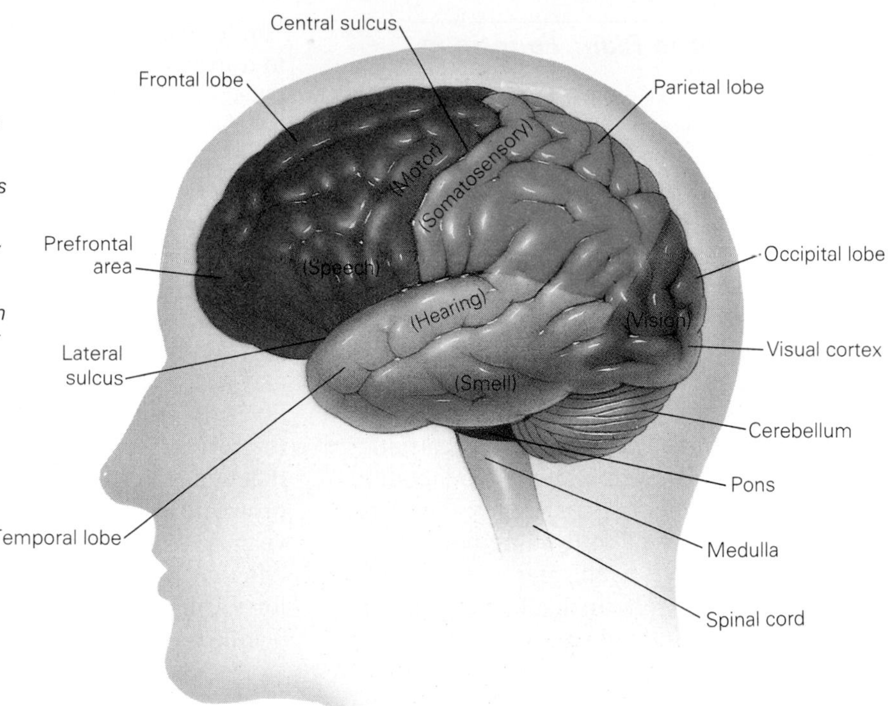

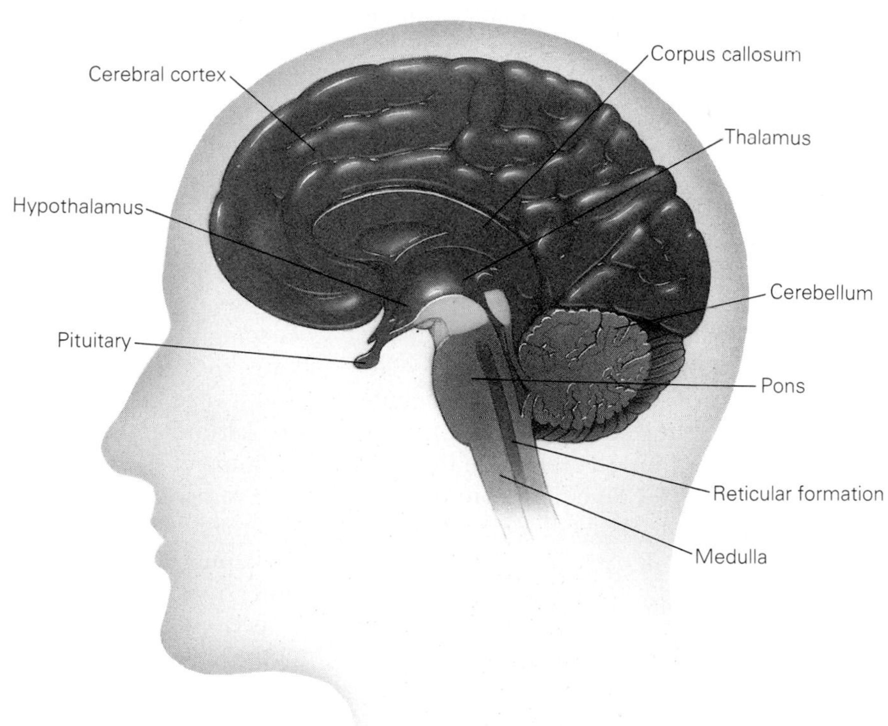

Forebrain

Midbrain (most not visible)

Hindbrain

The Brain's Game Plan: Functions from Structures

As students of psychology our primary interest lies in the brain's functions rather than its catalog of parts or structures. However, the two are correlated; the brain is organized into structures and regions that perform specific functions. Although it works in a holistic fashion with all parts interconnected, some brain regions are specialized for getting particular jobs done. What are those major jobs and where are they located?

The activities of the brain fall into five general categories: (a) internal regulation, (b) reproduction, (c) sensation, (d) motion, and (e) adaptation to changing environmental challenges. The first two are the brain's way of controlling bodily processes that keep it alive, well, and sexually prepared to reproduce and nourish offspring. In the third activity the brain makes contact with the world outside itself by processing sensory information from receptors throughout the body. It also monitors internal sensations that provide information about balance, gravity, movements of limbs, and its orientation in space. Some neuroscientists, such as Roger Sperry, believe that the fourth activity—motion—is the major role of the brain. It needs to get the muscles to move so that an organism can get around in and control its environment rather than be controlled by it. In this view, the brain is "a mechanism for governing motor activity, its primary function is essentially the transforming of sensory patterns into patterns of motor coordination" (Sperry, 1952, p. 297). The final function—adapting to the environment—is the brain's remarkable ability to *change itself* as it learns, stores what it has experienced, and modifies new actions (increases its flexibility), based on feedback from the consequences of its previous actions. With humans this function is elaborated into thoughts and plans to change the future, along with programs to modify the working of the brain through education, therapy, and medical procedures. Where in the brain are the centers for each of these basic functions?

Functional Organization

The **brain stem** is the center for basic life support: breathing, heartbeat, waking, sleeping. In rare cases, babies are born with only a brain stem and no other brain, a condition called *anencephalia.* The brain stem alone keeps their lungs and hearts functioning for a few days. Whether they are, in fact, "brain dead" is being debated by those who want to transplant their organs to other babies with birth defects and those who define life in terms of a beating heart (Herscher, 1986). The **medulla** is responsible for repetitive processes such as breathing and heartbeat. A special part of the brain stem is the **reticular activating system (RAS),** which is the brain's sentinel. It arouses the cortex to attend to new stimulation and keeps the brain "awake" even during sleep. Another region, the **pons,** connects to the cerebellum and is involved in dreaming and waking from sleep. The RAS has long tracts of fibers that run to the thalamus (in the oldest part of the forebrain). The **thalamus** is the relay station that sends on incoming sensory signals to the appropriate area in the cortex that processes them. A visual area of the thalamus would thus decide whether a stimulus was light, rather than sound, for example, and alert the visual cortex for more detailed analysis.

The **cerebellum,** attached to the brain stem at the back of the skull, has the tasks of coordinating body movements, controlling posture, and maintaining equilibrium. It appears to *limit* excessive movements by stopping them and setting boundary conditions.

When Karen Ann Quinlan remained in a coma for 10 years, her limbic system kept the internal machinery of her body working even though she had lost contact with the environment and could not move. The **limbic system** is composed of a group of structures that form part of the old mammalian brain found in all mammals. It helps maintain a homeostatic internal environment (in association with the autonomic nervous system) by regulating body temperature, blood pressure, blood-sugar levels, and performing other housekeeping activities. The limbic system also coordinates messages being sent to and from the cortex, and it regulates emotions and the powerful drives for self-protection and sexual desire.

Some of the most important parts of the limbic system are the hypothalamus, the hippocampus, and the amygdala. The **hypothalamus** (under the thalamus) does more in relation to its size than any other part of the brain. Weighing in at half an ounce and appearing smaller than a dime, the hypothalamus packs a powerful punch. It is the liaison between the body and the rest of the brain, playing a role in emotional arousal, appetite control, regulation of the internal environment of the body. As we noted earlier, it is the link to the pituitary gland and the endocrine system. The

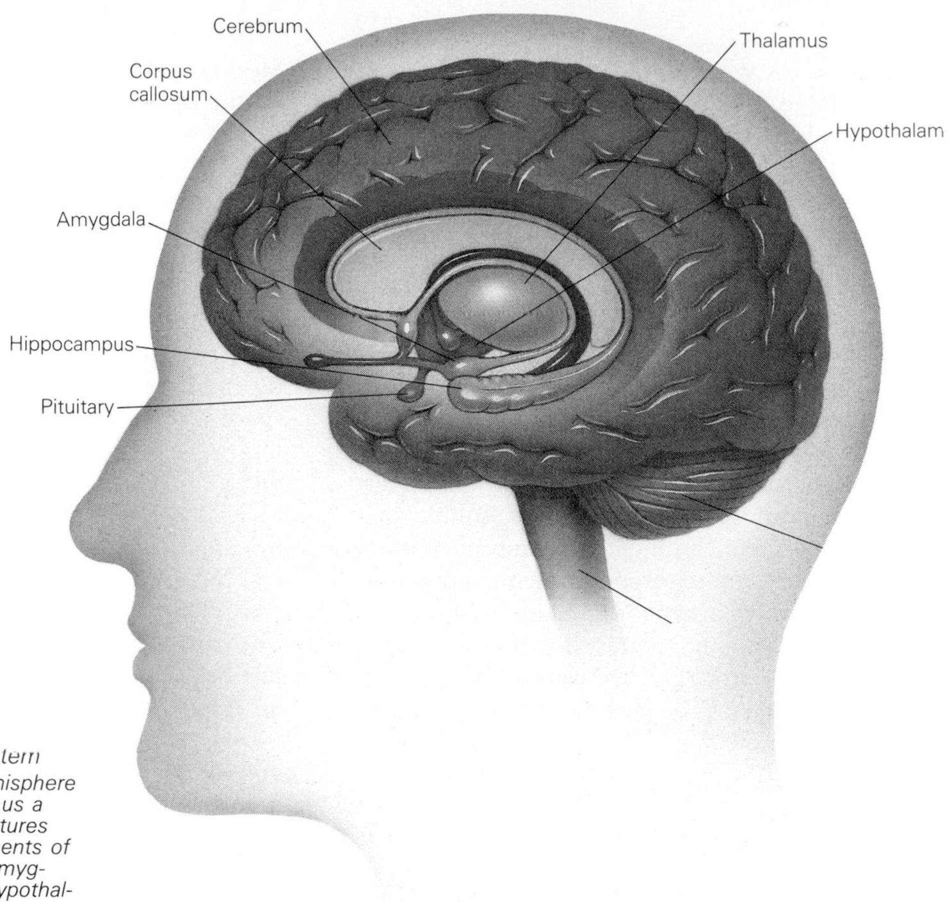

Figure 4.14 *The Limbic System*
The surface of the cerebral hemisphere is shown as transparent, giving us a view of the limbic system structures deep within. The major components of the limbic system include the amygdala, hippocampus, thalamus, hypothalamus, and certain parts of the frontal and temporal lobes of the cortex.

hippocampus performs three functions with incoming information: (a) matches incoming information to already stored information to determine whether it is familiar or new; (b) takes part in simple learning of associations; and (c) stores some kinds of information in memory. Aggressive behavior is, in part, influenced by the activity of the **amygdala,** which also functions in the gratification of some of our internal needs.

When someone says that you "really have brains," the reference is to your cerebral cortex. This newest addition is the crown of creation, also called the **cerebrum.** In humans it dwarfs the rest of the brain, occupying two thirds of its total mass. That mass means there are many neurons, glia, neural nets, and bundles of axons somehow responsible for organizing action and graded potentials into experiences, images, symbols, associations, memories, wishes, and fantasies. The cerebrum is where humanity lives.

Curiously, the cerebrum in all primates is divided in two halves, called the **cerebral hemispheres,** which are connected only by a white bundle of myelinated axons called the **corpus callosum** that carries messages back and forth. (In a later chapter we will learn that when this communication link is cut off during operations to treat epileptic seizures, the split-brain patient comes to have "two minds in one head.") The outer layer of the cerebrum, the **cortex,** is gray because it is made up of the cell bodies and unmyelinated fibers of billions of neurons. It is the part of the brain necessary for precise perception and conscious thought. It is also called the **neocortex.** The inner part of the cerebrum is white; it is made up of countless myelinated fibers which pass through the old brain on their way to and from the other parts of the body. The control centers carried over from the old **diencephalon,** the earliest part of the forebrain to develop, also contain the "gray matter" of many cell nuclei. The spinal cord has remained a tube; it and several cavities *(ventricles)* in the brain that are connected with it are filled with *cerebrospinal fluid.*

If the cortex were unfolded, it would be several times as large as this book. Why do you think that the cortex is so filled with folds? It is nature's way of economically packaging surface area that must perform a great many functions in the skull of a newborn baby and still help the baby survive coming out of its mother's relatively small vaginal opening.

Localization of Cortical Functions

The cortex of the cerebral hemispheres is the site of the highest level of neural integration. Its billions of neurons provide the mechanisms so that a series of yes or no electrochemical nerve impulses can lead to our recognition of a Beethoven sonata or a friend's smile. We can identify certain parts of the cortex that have more responsibility than others for particular control and coordination functions; but even when a particular part is shown to be essential for a particular function, we cannot say that part alone is sufficient. Ultimately the brain always works as a whole.

The outer part of the cerebral hemisphere is divided into lobes by a deep horizontal groove called the **lateral sulcus** and a vertical one called the **central sulcus** (see **Figure 4.13,** p. 129). Motor projection areas, devoted to sending messages to the muscles, are located along the two deep grooves; *sensory projection areas,* which receive sensory input, are located at the back of the brain. These two areas account for only about one fourth of the cortical area of the human cerebrum. The remaining three fourths of the cortex consists of *association areas* where sensory and motor messages are correlated and integrated. Such "higher" mental processes as analytical thinking are attributed largely to the association areas of the cortex's frontal lobes (Goodman, 1978).

There are more than six hundred voluntary muscles in the human body; their action is controlled by the motor projection area, or **motor cortex,** located along the front of the central sulcus.

Muscles in the lower part of the body are controlled by neurons in the top part of the motor projection area and vice versa, so that a sketch of the parts of the body controlled by each brain area (as in **Figure 4.15**) shows the body upside down. As you can see, the upper parts of the body can receive far more detailed instructions than the lower parts. In fact, the two largest motor projection areas are devoted to the fingers—especially the thumb—and to the muscles involved in speech, reflecting the importance of tools and talking in human activity. Messages from one side of the brain go to muscles on the opposite side of the body.

The sensory projection areas that receive messages from the various parts of the body are also called **somatosensory areas** (*soma,* you will recall, means "body"). These are the areas associated with feelings of pain, temperature, touch, and body position. The primary somatosensory areas are in the *parietal lobes,* just across the central sulcus from the corresponding motor areas. In these areas, too, the body is represented upside down and most space is given to the lips, tongue, thumb, and index fingers—the parts of the body that provide the most important sensory input. Like the motor areas, the somatosensory areas communicate with the opposite side of the body. In general, the parietal lobes integrate and analyze sensory input.

Auditory information is processed in the **auditory cortex,** which is in the *temporal lobes,* just below the lateral sulcus. Different parts of the area appear to be more sensitive to different pitch ranges. Each auditory area of the cortex, the left and the right, receives input from both ears. The temporal lobes are also implicated in perception, memory, and dreaming. Remember Mickey Median from the *Opening Case?* His temporal lobe epilepsy—neurons misfiring in this region—was responsible for the strange set of symptoms that transformed his personality.

The left temporal lobe handles language and speech, while the right temporal lobe contains systems for processing spatial information. This *asymmetry* in the functions of the two temporal lobes reflects a more widespread set of differences between the specialized tasks each hemisphere handles. In chapter 7, we will study how the language-dominating left hemisphere and the silent right hemisphere coexist—in a sometimes uneasy truce.

Visual input is processed at the back of the brain in the **visual cortex,** located in the *occipital lobes.* Here the most space is devoted to input from the center part of the retinas of the eyes, the area from which the most detailed visual information comes.

Finally, the largest of the four lobes of the cortex, the *frontal lobe,* is located just behind the forehead at the front of the brain. Its dominant position reflects the dominant role it plays in the cognitive activities of planning, making decisions, setting goals, and relating the present to the future through purposeful behavior. Accidents that damage the frontal lobes can have devastating effects on human behavior, as shown in the case of Phineas Gage (see the ***Close-up:*** *The Curious Accident of Mr. Phineas Gage* on page 136).

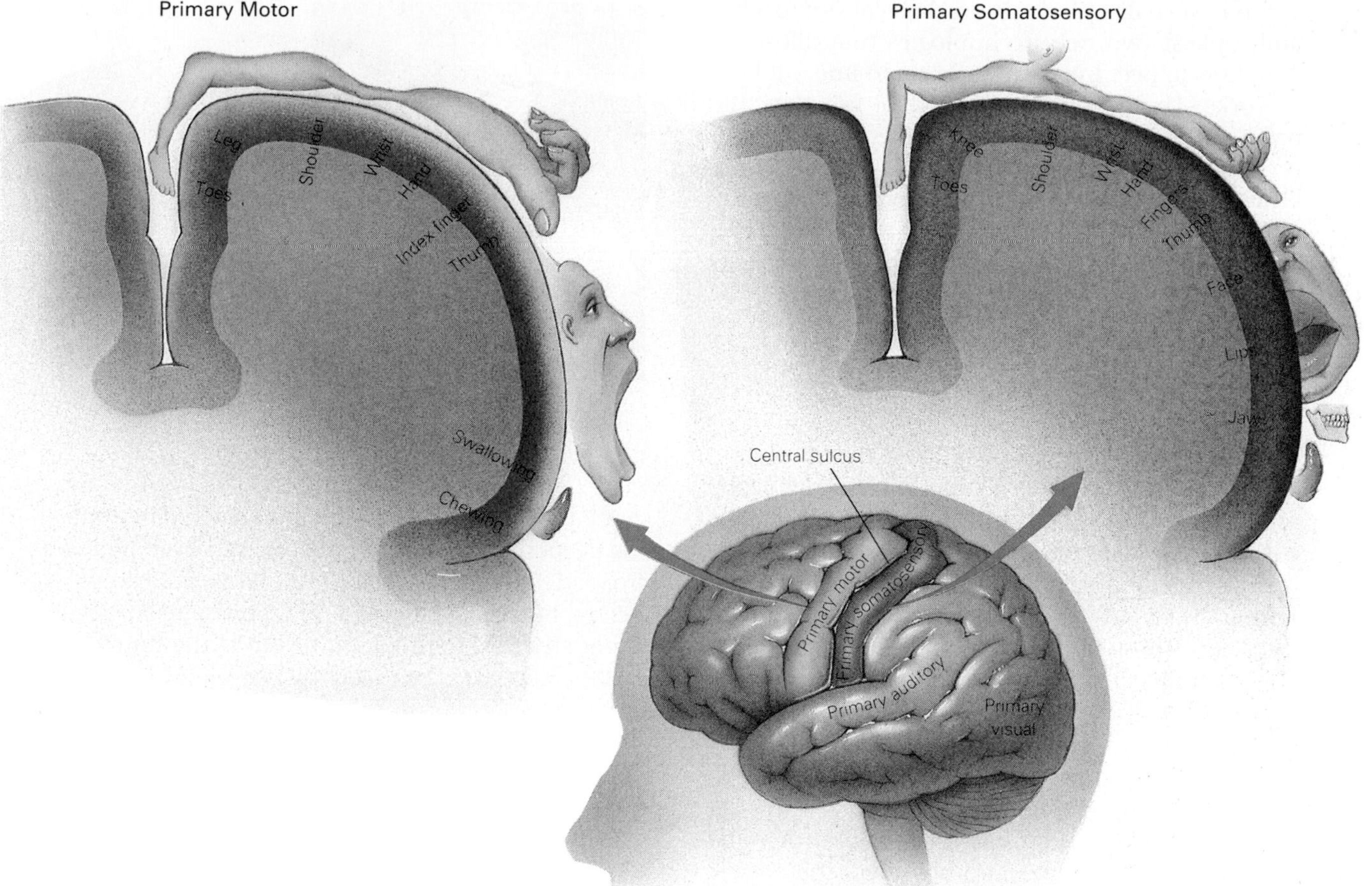

Figure 4.15 *Primary Motor and Somatosensory Areas*
The primary motor and somatosensory areas of the cortex lie along the central sulcus: the motor area just in front of it, the somatosensory area just behind it. Corresponding parts of the body are represented by points roughly across the sulcus from each other, and representation is upside down; that is, the legs and feet are represented at the top and around the inner surface between the hemispheres, hands and arms below them, and the head at the bottom. The greater precision of sensitivity and control in head and hands than in other parts of the body is reflected in larger areas of representation on the cortex. In the case of both the primary motor and the primary somatosensory area, communication is with the opposite side of the body.

Much of what an organism does may have a primary control center somewhere in the brain, but may also involve widespread activity of the whole brain. In this sense the preferred metaphor for the brain may be not an electronic computer, but a modern corporation that manages all its units according to the principle of participatory democracy. The success of the organization depends on many different groups, each performing a special task, but always communicating with top management about the process and products of its activities. Top management's evaluations and integrations of these various reports then become the basis for directing ongoing and future corporate ventures.

How Do We Know What the Brain Does?

In describing what is known about the functions of various brain structures, we have skipped over questions about the way that knowledge is learned. What methods are used to probe the secrets of the brain? Autopsies have provided some of the information we have about how damage to brain structure from injury or disease contributes to mental or behavioral disorders; but the three basic techniques most used in studying neural activity in *living* brains have been (a) stimulation, (b) lesions, and (c) the recording of electrical activity. In this section we will review these classical approaches and look at two new technologies that allow researchers to peer into a living brain to find out how it works. These studies serve a dual function: the basic science goal of understanding the structure, organization, and biochemical basis of normal brain functions; and the clinical goal of early diagnosis of disease and dysfunction of the brain, along with evaluation of therapeutic responses of patients to treatment.

Wilder Penfield (1891–1976)

Touching a Sensitive Nerve

Before neurosurgeon Wilder Penfield could operate on the brain of a patient suffering from epileptic seizures, he made a map of the cortex so that he could localize the origin of the seizures and leave unharmed other areas vital to the patient's functioning. His map-making tool was an **electrode,** a thin wire through which small amounts of precisely regulated electrical current could pass. As he touched one after another cortical surface with this surgical wand, the conscious patient (under only local anesthetic since there are no pain receptors in the brain itself) would react in various ways. At some sites there were motor reactions of hand clenching, and arm raising; at others there were "experiential responses" of vividly recalling past events or having sudden feelings, such as fear, loneliness, or elation associated with some sights and sounds, with a *déjà vu* familiarity about them. As if by pushing an electronic memory button, the surgeon touched memories stored silently for years in the deep recesses of his patient's brain (Penfield & Baldwin, 1952). In the final report of this pioneering investigation on 69 patients, Penfield concluded:

> *There is within the adult human brain a remarkable record of the stream of each individual's awareness or consciousness. . . . This demonstrates the existence of a functional system devoted to subconscious recall of past experiences and to the interpretation of present experience. . . . Final understanding of man's own brain and mind may seem very far away, but that is the ultimate goal of investigation. It may well prove to be man's most difficult achievement, to understand himself and the means by which this understanding is achieved. (Penfield & Perot, 1963, pp. 692–93)*

Penfield's explorations of the surface of the cortex, together with subsequent studies, have made it possible to draw precise maps of cortical projection areas. Stimulating the surface of the cortex, however, reveals relatively superficial information compared with what has been discovered by probing deeper into regions of the brain that are hidden from view. In the mid-1950s, Walter Hess pioneered in the development of a precise technology using electrical stimulation to probe the functions of the brain. Hess put electrodes deep into specific parts of the brain of a freely moving cat. By pressing a button, Hess could then send a small electrical current to the brain at the point of the electrode.

> *Hess carefully recorded the behavioral consequences of stimulating each of 4500 brain sites in nearly 500 cats. Electrical stimulation of certain regions of the limbic system led gentle cats to bristle with rage and hurl themselves upon a nearby object—which, in the early days, was sometimes the startled experimenter. Sleep, sexual arousal, anxiety, or terror could be provoked by the flick of the switch—and just as abruptly turned off. Sometimes complicated, stereotyped behavior patterns were turned on in the animals, as though the electricity were activating a prerecorded program. For example, cats have an unmistakable manner of stalking and capturing prey. This could be reliably produced, time after time, by stimulating a certain part of the limbic system. (Hess & Akert, 1955)*

Hess' deep stimulation electrode technique was like a beacon illuminating primitive brain regions for more detailed study by a host of other researchers. Investigators found that electrical stimulation deep inside the brains of rats would arouse them sexually and even result in a male's ejaculation without a female rat in view. Like addicts craving drugs, the rats would go to great lengths to manipulate an apparatus that would deliver a jolt of electricity to certain regions of their brains. Psychologist James Olds, who pioneered this aspect of the research, called these areas the brain's "pleasure centers" (Olds, 1973; Olds & Milner, 1954).

Lesions Are Forever

The **lesion** technique involves careful destruction (lesioning) of particular brain areas by either surgically removing them, cutting connections to them, or destroying brain tissue using intense heat, cold, electricity, or laser beams. Lesioning can reveal whether a brain region is essential to a particular physical or psychological function. Done in the laboratory and followed up by behavioral tests, it can produce known damage in particular structures that are correlated to observed behavioral reactions with greater precision than lesions caused by disease, accidents, wars, and other "natural," nonexperimental causes. (See ***Close-up*** on p. 136.) Our conception of the brain has been radically changed as the results of laboratory experiments with animals have been repeatedly compared and coordinated with the growing body of clinical findings on human behavior changes following brain damage.

Usually stimulation and lesioning techniques are used in combination in the laboratory: if one increases a reaction, the other will generally decrease it. This is a double check on interpretations of a causal connection between the activity of the brain region and a particular behavior. Lesioning, like stimulation, has revealed the brain to be a highly differentiated, complex, and precisely organized master control organ.

Knowledge of brain functions gained from laboratory studies has been supplemented by observation of the effects of lesions used as a therapeutic technique. A type of lesion used widely with epileptic and violent psychotic patients in the 1940s was the *frontal lobotomy,* which involved severing the nerve fibers connecting the frontal lobes with other brain areas. Though seizures and violent reactions disappeared, so—often—did the individual's emotional tone, sense of self, and sense of the future, so many of the traits that go into making us human. Because such lesions are irreversible, this psychosurgery little used today.

"Reverse" lesioning studies have allowed researchers to observe the *recovery* from brain damage. Philip Teitelbaum (1977) has found that when a part of the brain is damaged, the behavior it has been controlling may disappear completely or "decompose" into a less complex, fragmentary form which sometimes makes it easier to study. Then, as recovery takes place, the behavioral elements may be "put back in place," becoming integrated again in much the same way they developed the first time in the young organism. Teitelbaum's research has shown that redevelopment of behavioral coordination in cats with hypothalamic damage and human adults with Parkinson's disease is similar to the development of normal infants, both human and animal.

Recording the Activity of Neurons

Another way to understand how the brain functions is to record its electrical activity. Three types of records can be made: (a) records of activity made within a cell [intracellular]; (b) records of a cell's activity made from the outside [extracellular]; and (c) records of the action of many neurons at once through measuring brain waves and evoked potentials.

The tool used in the first two techniques is a *microelectrode,* a tiny needle made of thin metal or hollow glass filled with a saline solution. When placed in or near a neuron, this device detects electrical impulses, which are then greatly amplified so that they can be displayed on a screen or stored in a computer.

For *intracellular recordings,* the tiny microelectrodes are placed inside individual neurons. Usually invertebrates, such as *Aplysia,* are used in this research because their neurons are relatively few in number and large enough to be identified. It is thus possible to record the graded potentials within simple nerve cells. Such recordings may help illuminate the fundamental mechanisms used to process information in the brains of higher animals.

In *extracellular recordings,* the microelectrode is positioned to reach beneath the surface of the cortex, but outside a neuron. In a typical study, an electrode is placed in the visual cortex of a cat who is anesthetized but whose brain is still actively receiving inputs from the eye. Different visual patterns are then displayed. A given neuron will respond with a burst of impulses when a certain stimulus is displayed, but will remain inactive when another stimulus is presented. Researchers using this technique have been able to draw detailed maps of the stimulus "preferences" of different cells in the visual cortex (Hubel & Wiesel, 1979).

Besides responding to stimulation, the brain constantly generates electrical energy. Its signals, known as **electroencephalograms (EEGs),** can be recorded on the surface of the human skull. These brain-wave patterns show whether a person is alert, relaxed, asleep, or dreaming (see **Figure 4.16**).

Close-up The Curious Accident of Mr. Phineas Gage

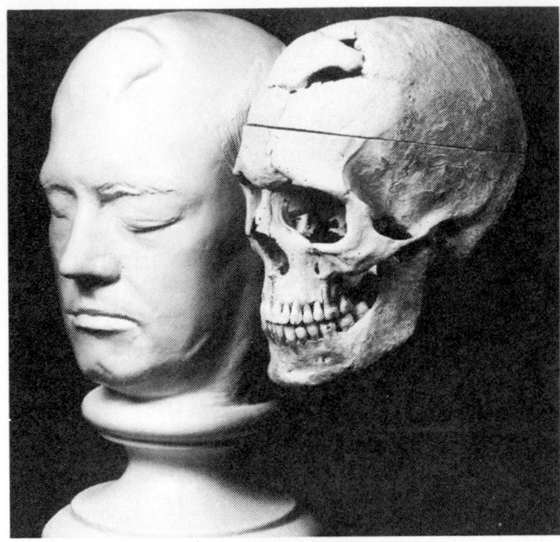

The cast of the head and the skull shown here are in the collection of the Museum of Harvard Medical School, a relic of a terrible accident. In September 1848, Phineas Gage, a 25-year-old railroad worker in Vermont, was tamping a charge of black powder into a hole drilled deep into rock in preparation for blasting. The powder unexpectedly exploded, blowing the tamping iron, over 3 feet long and weighing 13 pounds, through Gage's head and high into the air.

Incredibly, Gage regained consciousness and was taken by wagon to his hotel, where he was able to walk upstairs. T. M. Harlow, the physician who attended him, noted that the hole in Gage's skull was 2" by $3\frac{1}{2}$" wide, with shreds of brain all around it. He cleaned and dressed the wound, but two days later Gage became delirious and remained near death for the next two weeks. The wound became seriously infected, but eventually healed. In a month Gage could get out of bed without help; in two months he could walk unassisted.

Gage lived for over twelve years. Physical impairment was remarkably slight: he lost vision in his left eye, and the left side of his face was partially paralyzed, but his posture, movement, and speech were all unimpaired. Yet psychologically he was a changed man, as this summary by Harlow makes clear:

His physical health is good, and I am inclined to say that he has recovered. Has no pain in head, but says it has a queer feeling which he is not able to describe. Applied for his situation as foreman, but is undecided whether to work or travel. His contractors, who regarded him as the most efficient and capable foreman in their employ previous to his injury, considered the change in his mind so marked that they could not give him his place again. The equilibrium or balance, so to speak, between his intellectual faculties and animal propensities, seems to have been destroyed. He is fitful, irreverent, indulging at times in the grossest profanity (which was not previously his custom), manifesting but little deference for his fellows, impatient of restraint or advice when it conflicts with his desires, at times pertinaciously obstinate, yet capricious and vacillating, devising many plans of future operation, which are no sooner arranged than they are abandoned in turn for others appearing more feasible. A child in his intellectual capacity and manifestations, he has the animal passions of a strong man. Previous to his injury, though untrained in the schools, he possessed a well-balanced mind, and was looked upon by those who knew him as a shrewd, smart business man, very energetic and persistent in executing all his plans of operation. In this regard his mind was radically changed, so decidedly that his friends and acquaintances said he was "no longer Gage." (Bigelow, 1850, pp. 13–22)

Gage's case is one of the earliest documented examples of massive damage to the frontal regions of the brain, and it illustrates the great subtlety of the psychological symptoms that accompany such lesions. Indeed, it was Gage's family and friends, rather than his doctor, who noticed the changes in him. Gage's symptoms, such as "obstinacy" or "capriciousness," are hardly so remarkable that we would attribute them to brain damage in someone whose history we didn't know; yet it is interesting to note that they represent the very kinds of antisocial behavior that prefrontal lobotomies are supposed to *prevent.*

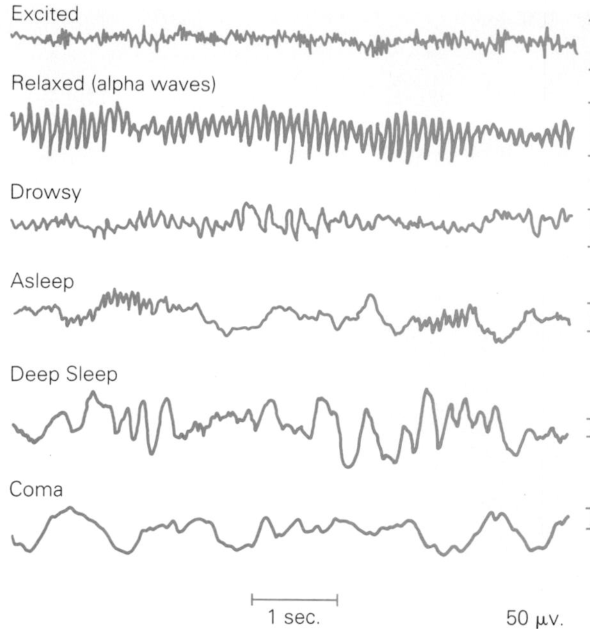

Figure 4.16 *EEGs Characteristic of Various States in Humans*

The patterns of brain activity caused by specific stimuli are called **evoked potentials.** To record them, the specific brain signals are usually extracted from the background "noise" of ongoing spontaneous brain waves. A researcher uses computer analyses to average out all the electrical activity that is unrelated to the stimulus—exposing the evoked potential signal. The characteristics of this signal have been shown to vary for different areas of the brain and for different stimuli and different mental processes (John et al., 1977).

The use of evoked potentials in studying brain processes is demonstrated by a study of reactions to unexpected events.

> *The stimuli were seven-word sentences, in some of which the last word was incongruous and hence unexpected. (Example: "He took a sip from the* transmitter.*") As sentences were presented, one word at a time, the subject read them silently. Every time a word was presented that did* not *fit what might be expected in the context, a specific type of evoked potential appeared. Some part or parts of the brain must have been set to assess and respond to the new stimuli in terms of previously learned information that formed a semantic expectation which was being violated. (Kutas & Hillyard, 1980)*

Each of these recording methods yields valuable information about the way the brain works to process information and to carry out its many tasks during normal and abnormal functioning.

Looking into Living Brains

Researchers have recently developed new techniques for obtaining detailed pictures of a living brain at work. These pictures help locate diseased tissue and also show where various brain activities take place as normal individuals are exposed to various stimuli. The biggest advantage of this approach is that it can show what is happening in different regions of a living, thinking brain at the same time.

One of these powerful new techniques is **positron emission tomography (PET).** This technique is based on the fact that a sugar called *glucose* is the main source of energy for the brain.

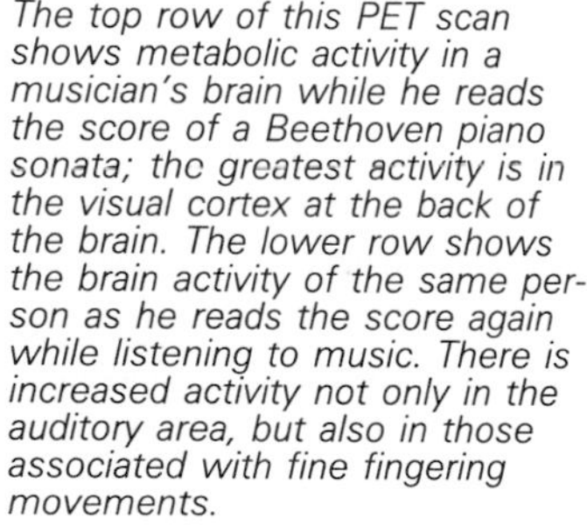
The top row of this PET scan shows metabolic activity in a musician's brain while he reads the score of a Beethoven piano sonata; the greatest activity is in the visual cortex at the back of the brain. The lower row shows the brain activity of the same person as he reads the score again while listening to music. There is increased activity not only in the auditory area, but also in those associated with fine fingering movements.

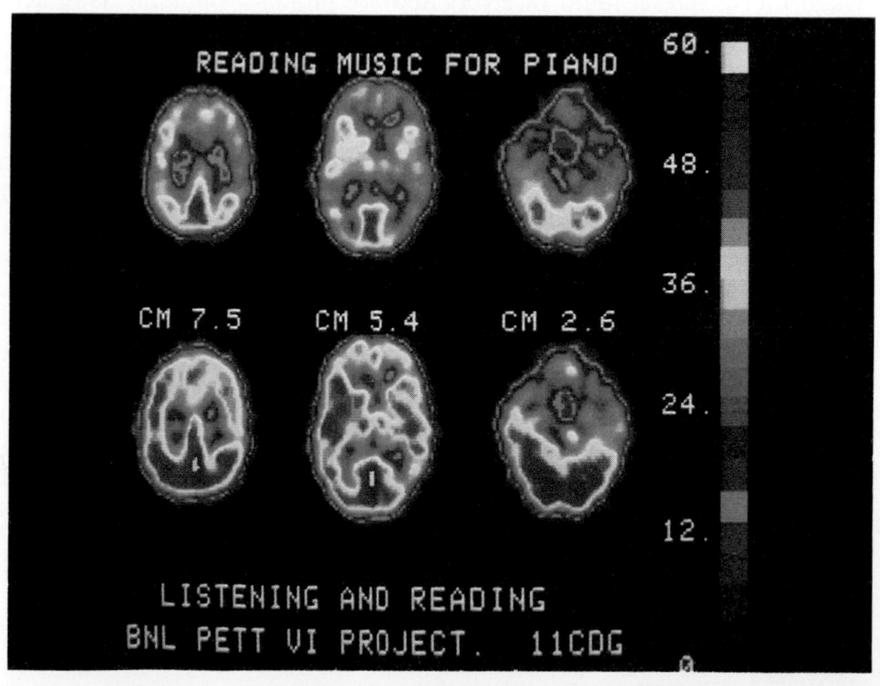

When brain cells are active, they increase their intake of glucose from the surrounding blood supply. In PET research, a radioactive substance similar to glucose is injected into the bloodstream. It, too, will be taken up by active neurons. Radioactive isotopes decay by the emission of positrons (or antielectrons) that give off gamma rays which penetrate the head and can be detected externally. Recording instruments outside the skull can detect the radioactivity emitted by over 200 biological compounds and keep track of the brain locations from which each came. A computer program can then be used to construct a dynamic portrait of the brain, showing where different types of neural activity is occurring.

Earlier we took pains to point out the significant role of biochemical processes at each level of nervous system functioning. We can now add the generalization that all diseases of the brain result from or produce biochemical alterations. Therefore, research and clinical study with PET that reveals biochemical cerebral activity is leading to a more comprehensive view of human functional brain systems in both health and disease (Phelps & Mazziotta, 1985).

Another new technology allows brain researchers and neurosurgeons to explore the living brain but without using X-rays or other substances that might pose risks. **Magnetic resonance imaging (MRI)** is a new technique for recording the activities of living brain and body tissue by means of signals *(images)* given off when a powerful *magnetic* pulse is delivered to an organ. By tuning the pulse to different frequencies, some atoms line up with the magnetic field. When the magnetic pulse is turned off, the atoms vibrate *(resonate)* as they return to their original positions. These vibrations are picked up by special radio receivers and are processed by computers. Maps are made showing the location of different atoms in the particular organ being studied. MRI signals from hydrogen atoms, for example, provide discriminations between moving and still tissues, and also between those rich in water and those rich in other substances.

These magnetic resonating images enable brain researchers to see where cells are processing oxygen normally and where there is abnormal functioning. In addition, they can examine the kinds of activity taking place in specific areas of the brain or the spinal cord in response to various types of physical and psychological stimulation.

You now have some of the answers from physiological psychologists to the general question, "What makes behavior work?" In addition, you can better appreciate how they study the complex relationships between physical structures, biochemical processes, and behavioral functions. As new technologies enable scientists to illuminate more of the darker, deeper recesses of the "black box" of the brain, we are witnessing a virtual explosion of knowledge about the ways the brain and nervous system influence our psychological development, daily actions, and disorders of functioning.

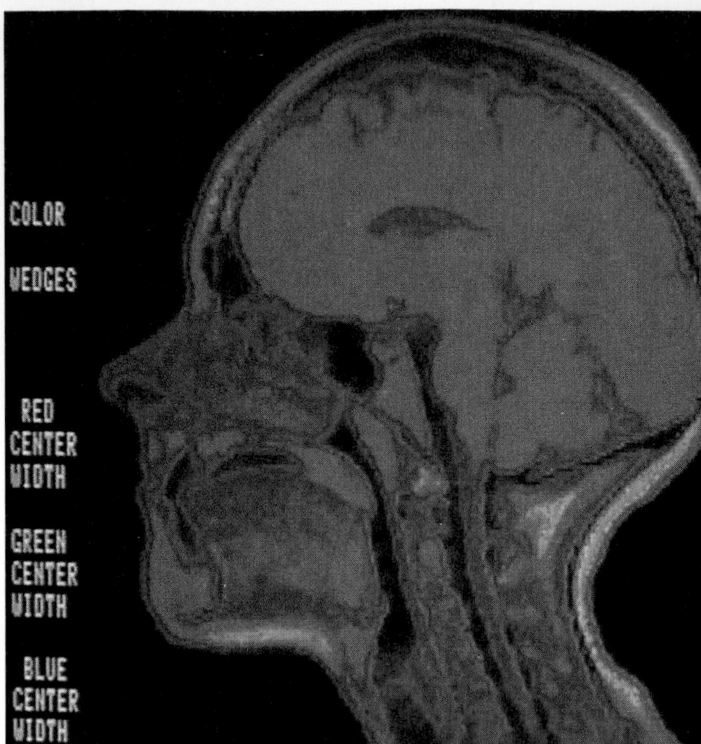

A color-enhanced profile made by magnetic resonance imaging (MRI) shows a normal brain. MRIs use a combination of radio waves and a strong magnetic field to view soft tissue such as the brain's. They provide truer images than other imaging techniques.

Wherever possible throughout our psychological journey, we will seek greater understanding of the various processes of thought, feeling, and action by considering what is known about their neural substrate. Of course, many of our concerns cannot be reduced to this molecular level, as when we ask about the way we solve problems, the way we make decisions, the causes of violence, or the origins of love. We will see that an ever increasing number of psychological problems are being probed at this molecular level of analysis—problems such as the brain mechanisms in memory, motivation, stress, emotion, and mental disorders. Learning and remembering, pleasure and pain, attraction and repulsion all begin as sensory stimulus events that must be detected and processed in special ways if our lives are to have meaning and direction. The study of sensation and perception, which follows in the next two chapters, helps us understand how we make contact with the world outside our brains, extract information from it, and transform the information into plans for appropriate actions. We will continue in chapter 7 to focus on one of the most profound issues of human existence—the nature of human consciousness and how it is altered.

Summary

- Physiological psychology is the study of the relationship between behavior, including mental events, and body processes. Researchers assume there is a biochemical substrate underlying all behavior, and they use a reductionist approach in their investigations.
- Historically mind and body were viewed dualistically, as separate entities. Today physiological psychologists view the "mind" as an integrative capacity developed by the brain that frees the organism from being controlled solely by sensory input.
- Cell differentiation and specialization create a need for communication and integration within an organism. The nervous and endocrine systems meet this need, sending neural and hormonal messengers throughout the body.
- Neurons are unique cells specialized to receive and transmit information to other cells. A neuron is made up of dendrites, a cell body or soma, and an axon that ends in terminal buttons. Sensory (afferent) neurons carry messages toward the central nervous system; motor (efferent) ones carry messages away to muscles and glands. The interneurons, which lie between them, make up the bulk of the neurons in the nervous system.
- Nerve conduction is an electrochemical phenomenon. In its inactive, or *polarized,* state, the inside of a neuron has a negative electrical charge relative to the outside. Changes in the permeability of the membrane *depolarize* the cell, allowing ions of certain chemicals to flow through, in, and out of a cell, thus creating the basis for all electrical signals in the nervous system.
- The two types of electrical signals in the nervous system are graded potentials and action potentials. Graded potentials, which take place in the dendrites or soma membrane, are good only for short-term, local signals. If the graded potential is above the critical level known as the threshold, an action potential is triggered. The action potential follows an all-or-none principle, does not diminish in size or speed, and is self-propagating.
- All electrical signaling in the nervous system involves the flow of ions through ion channels, excitable membrane molecules that produce and transduce electrical signals in living cells. Some ion channels open in response to changes in membrane potentials; others are controlled by chemical transmitter substances, and still others by hormones. The three positive ions of sodium, potassium, and calcium and the negative ion chloride appear to control all the action in ion channels, and, ultimately, all nerve impulses.
- At a synapse, the tiny space or junction of two neurons, electrical conduction becomes chemical conduction. Neurotransmitters are released from tiny vesicles in the presynaptic terminal button and travel across the gap to the postsynaptic membrane of the next neuron, inhibiting or initiating electrical activity in that neuron.
- In addition to transmitting information, the nervous system also processes information through neural networks, circuits of neurons organized hierarchically into levels of ever greater complexity. The simplest neural networks are reflex arcs, which may involve only a sensory neuron and a motor neuron, perhaps with an interneuron between them, in the spinal cord.
- Any novel, unexpected stimulus elicits an orienting reaction that maximizes the organism's sensitivity to stimulation. With repetition of the stimulus there is a reduction in response called habituation; it is a primitive form of learning that frees the organism to attend to more informative input.
- The nervous system is made up of the central nervous system, which includes the brain and spinal cord, and the peripheral nervous system. The latter includes the somatic nervous system and the autonomic nervous system, which is divided into the sympathetic division (which functions as a "troubleshooter") and the parasympathetic division (which functions as a "housekeeper").
- The endocrine system consists of ductless glands controlled by neural and chemical signals. The hormones of the endocrine system are chemical messengers that regulate many biochemical processes and help arouse the body for action in emergencies.

- Lower brain centers that control basic life processes have evolved similarly in humans and lower animals. Higher mental processes take place in the cerebral cortex, the outer layer of the brain, which is most highly developed in humans.
- About a fourth of the area of the cerebral cortex is devoted to processing sensory and motor information; the rest involves more complex analysis and synthesis. Although the normal brain always functions as an integrated whole, researchers have identified primary centers for each of the senses, motivational behavior, and other complex processes such as aggression and hunger. This is know as localization of brain function.
- The three classical approaches to studying living brains have been the techniques of stimulation, lesioning (destroying tissue), and recording electrical activity. Brain-wave recordings (EEGs) are records of both ongoing spontaneous brain activity and evoked potentials (specific neural reactions to particular stimuli). Positron emission tomography (PET) is a powerful new technique for monitoring the active brain by the use of radioactive particles. Another new technique, magnetic resonance imaging (MRI), uses magnetic fields to record brain activity.

5

Sensation

When he was 14 years old, Don began to have severe, prolonged headaches. Right before a headache Don would see a flashing oval light in his left visual field and then a blank white region with colored fringes around it. Within 15 minutes the headache would begin on the right side of his head, followed by vomiting, increased blindness in the left visual field, and up to two full days of no sleep. As he grew older, these attacks became increasingly frequent despite his doctors' attempts to treat them. Finally, when Don was 34, he decided to have an operation in which a neurosurgeon would remove a small portion of his right occipital cortex in an attempt to correct the problem.

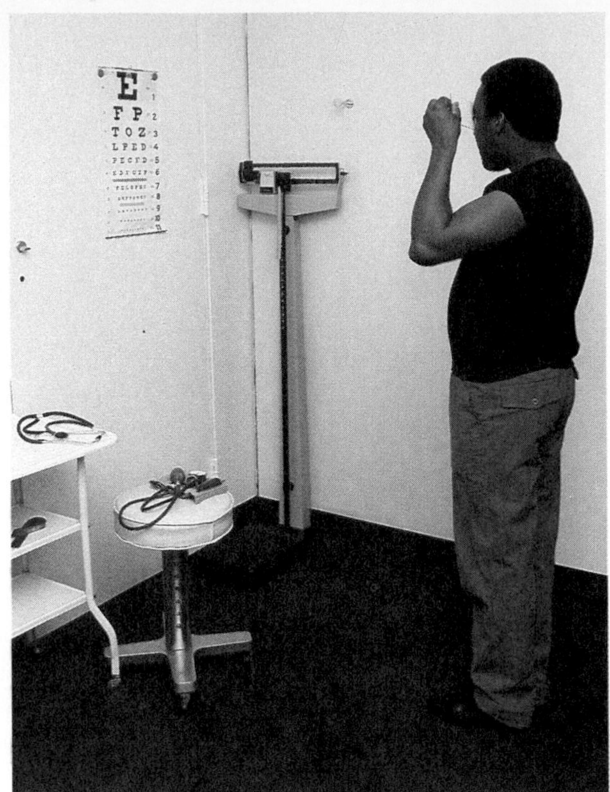

The surgery permanently cured Don's headaches. Unfortunately, because the region that had been removed contained the primary sensory cortex for the left visual field, it also left Don totally blind in the left half of his visual field—at least by all standard tests. For instance, when a bright spot of light was shown directly to the left of his fixation point, he was simply unaware of its presence.

On an informed hunch, however, a group of psychologists asked Don to "guess" the location of the spot of light by pointing with his left index finger. The results were remarkable; Don was nearly as accurate at locating the spot in this "blind" left field as he was at locating spots in the right visual field which he saw clearly! Further experiments showed that he could also guess whether a line in his "blind" field was vertical or horizontal and whether a figure presented there was an "X" or an "O." Throughout the tests Don was completely unaware of the presence of the spots, lines, or figures. He claimed he was merely guessing. When he was shown videotapes of his testing, Don was openly astonished to see himself pointing to lights he had not "seen" (Weiskrantz et al., 1974).

Don's "vision" has been aptly dubbed *blindsight,* visually guided behavior that identifies the location of stimuli projected to the blind area of an eye's retina without an individual's conscious awareness of seeing any object there. "Blindsight" sounds like a contradiction in terms, but we know that the detailed processing of visual input that occurs in the visual cortex is only the final stage of the overall process of converting light waves to conscious vision. An earlier, nonconscious stage of processing—and perhaps the place in the brain where it may occur—is revealed in Don's case. Comparable results have since been found in several other patients with similar damage in the visual cortex (Perenin & Jeannerod, 1975).

It is known that an animal can perform visual tasks in the absence of a visual cortex. It relies on a more primitive visual processing center below the level of the cortex. This lower center evidently developed earlier in the evolutionary process and still retains sensory abilities that were lost as humans developed more complex brains. It appears that this lower structure still contributes information about *where* objects are in the visual scene, but it does so below the level of consciousness.

Although there is currently a controversy about the nature of this blindsight phenomenon (discussed in the *Opening Case*), Don's experience raises a fundamental question about the way humans and lower animals make contact with their sensory environment. How does the brain, locked in the dark, silent chamber of the skull, know the blaze of color in a Van Gogh painting, the booming rich melody of Beethoven's Ninth Symphony, the succulent taste of cold watermelon on a hot day, or the pain that we all experience from accidents and disease? In this chapter we will discover how sense receptors are designed to detect what's in the external world and how the brain begins to make sense of the signals that are sent to it. In subsequent chapters we will learn how the processes of perception and consciousness add to this basic information to create our view of the world—and its events and objects—including us.

Sensory Knowledge of the World

Ordinarily, our experience of external reality is relatively accurate and error-free; in fact, it *has* to be so that we can survive. We need food to sustain us, shelter to protect us, interactions with other people to fulfill our social needs, and awareness of danger to keep us out of harm's way. To meet these needs, we must somehow get reliable information about the world we live in. All species have developed some kind of information-gathering apparatus. We humans lack the acute sensitivity to some signals that other species have perfected—such as the vision of hawks or the hearing of bats—but we have complex sensory organs and additional neural apparatuses that enable us to process a wider range of more complex sensory input than any other creature.

Because our experiences of the world can usually be counted on, most of us come to accept the notion that "seeing is believing." We automatically accept what we "see with our own two eyes" as existing out there in the physical structure of the external world.

An eighteenth-century philosopher asserted this "natural faith" in the reliability of the senses as "windows on the world" in this charming fashion:

> *By all the laws of all nations, in the most solemn judicial trials, wherein men's fortunes are at stake, the sentence passes according to the testimony of eye or ear, witnesses of good credit. . . . no judge will ever suppose that witnesses may be imposed upon by trusting to their eyes and ears. (Reid, 1785)*

Actually, the relation between what we see and what exists to be seen is not so simple. Our brains actively transform and interpret the information they receive from all of our senses. The process of gathering critical information about events in the world is the task of sensation. **Sensation** is the process of stimulation of a receptor that gives rise to neural impulses which result in an "unelaborated," elementary experience of feeling or awareness of conditions outside or within the

To hunt small flying insects at night, bats rely on a sensory system of echolocation, a kind of sonar. They give off high-frequency sounds and then locate insects by listening as the sounds bounce off them.

body. The elaboration, interpretation, and meaning given to a sensory experience is the task of *perception,* which we will investigate in the next chapter. The boundaries between these two processes are not distinctly drawn; however, most psychologists treat sensation as the more primitive, data-based experience generated by the activities of receptors, while perception is the more brain-based interpretation of that sensory input.

The study of sensation and perception offers "windows on the mind" that have been opened ever wider since their prominent place in the earliest history of experimental psychology. Recall (from chapter 1) that Wundt (1896/1907) had proposed sensations and feelings as the elementary processes from which complex experiences were built. E. B. Titchener (1898) brought this view to the United States, giving sensation a central place in his introspective analysis of the contents of consciousness. This position was known as **structuralism** since it dealt with the structure of conscious experience. It was opposed by William James, J. R. Angell, and others who advocated studying not the *what,* but the *how* and *why* of experience; their view was called **functionalism.**

The modern study of sensation has come a long way from those early days. Now sensory psychologists work along with physiologists, biologists, geneticists, and neurologists to map the process by which physical energy from the external world is transformed into sensations that result in our ten senses of vision, hearing, smell, taste, touch, warmth, cold, equilibrium, kinesthesis, and pain. Later in this chapter we will discuss the mechanisms of each of these senses, but first let's consider *how* sensation is studied by psychologists.

From Physical Energy to Mental Events

At the heart of sensation lies a profound mystery: How do physical energies give rise to psychological experiences? Stimulus energy arrives at our eyes (or ears, or other sensory receptors) as physical energy of some kind. There it is converted into electrochemical signals that the nervous system can transmit—still physical energy, but coded by our nervous system so that when the signal reaches the cerebral cortex, we have a sensation of a particular type color or sound, for example. The study of sensation is the study of the translation from physical energy to neural processes. **Transduction** is the process that converts one form of energy, such as light, to another form, such as neural impulses. Although the central mystery of this conversion remains, research has taught us a great deal about how and where it happens, and what physical and psychological processes can affect it.

The field of sensory psychology has two main branches: sensory physiology and psychophysics. **Sensory physiology** is the study of how biological mechanisms convert physical events into neural events. Its goal is to discover what happens at a neural level in the chain of events from physical energy to sensory experience. Sensory psychologists are primarily interested in discovering the way transduction works in the receptors themselves. They seek answers to questions such as: how does electrochemical activity in the nervous system give us sensations of different quality (red rather than green)? How does it give us sensations of different quantity (loud rather than soft)? We have already encountered some of the concepts and methods of sensory physiology in chapter 4.

There are four basic types of sensory receptors that are designed to detect a particular stimulus energy and result in a given sensation. *Photoreceptors* detect light and result in vision. *Chemoreceptors* detect the chemical stimuli that result in taste and smell. *Mechanoreceptors* detect movements of receptor cells that result in hearing and touch sensations, while *thermoreceptors* detect temperature changes and yield the sensations of warmth and cold. **Table 5.1** presents a summary of the stimuli and receptors for each of the human senses. In the next section, we will concentrate on the other major area of sensory psychology, called *psychophysics.*

Psychophysics

How loud must a fire alarm at a factory be in order for workers to hear it over the din of the machinery? How bright does a warning light on a pilot's control panel have to be to appear twice as bright as the other lights? How loud can a motorcycle be before its driver should be cited for noise pollution? These practical questions about sensation often arise in decisions about safety regulations, product design, and legal issues. To answer them, we must somehow be able to measure the intensity of sensory experiences—the brightness of lights, the loudness of sounds—by relating these psychological experiences to an amount of physical stimulation. This is the central task of **psychophysics,** the study of lawful correlations between physical stimulation acting on the senses of a living organism

Table 5.1 *Sensation*

The Stimuli and Receptors of the Human Senses

Sense	Stimulus	Sense Organ	Receptor	Sensation
Sight	Light waves	Eye	Rods and cones of retina	Colors, patterns, textures
Hearing	Sound waves	Ear	Hair cells of organ of Corti	Noises, tones
Skin sensations	External contact	Skin	Nerve endings in skin	Touch, pain, warmth, cold
Smell	Volatile substances	Nose	Hair cells of olfactory epithelium	Odors (musky, flowery, burnt, minty)
Taste	Soluble substances	Tongue	Taste buds of tongue	Flavors (sweet, sour, salty, bitter)
Body movement	Mechanical energy	Muscles, joints, tendons	Nerve endings	Position, movement, pressure, pain
Equilibrium	Mechanical and gravitational forces	Inner ear	Hair cells of semi-circular canals and vestibule	Spatial movement, gravitational pull
Organic sensitivity	Mechanical energy	Portions of digestive tract	Nerve endings	Pressure, pain

and the behavior or experiences it evokes. This attempt to measure and quantify sensation represents the oldest field of the science of psychology (see Levine & Shefner, 1981).

Gustav Fechner (1860–1966) coined the term *psychophysics* and developed methods that related the intensity of a physical stimulus, measured in physical units, and the magnitude of the sensory experience, measured in psychological units. Fechner was a mathematician, philosopher, and scientist who believed that psychophysics was the key to solving the mind-body problem. He provided an objective measure and a set of procedures that related bodily events (physical stimuli acting on sense receptors) to mental events (the reported sensation).

Fechner's psychophysical techniques measure the strength of sensations experienced by an alert, normal organism in response to stimuli of different strengths. Whether the stimuli are for light, sound, taste, odor, or touch, the techniques are the same—determining thresholds and constructing psychophysical scales relating strength of sensation to strength of stimuli. Two kinds of thresholds can be measured—*absolute thresholds* and *difference thresholds.* The first indicates the level at which a sensory system can detect the presence of a stimulus—the minimal amount of a physical stimulus required to produce any sensation at all. The second type of threshold is the smallest difference between two stimuli that a sensory system can detect.

Absolute Thresholds

What is the smallest, weakest stimulus energy that an organism can detect? How dim can a light be, for instance, and still be visible? How soft can a tone be and still be heard? These questions ask about the **absolute threshold** for different types of stimulation: the minimum amount of physical energy needed to produce a sensory experience reliably. According to the classical view of sensory thresholds, stimuli below the threshold amount produce no sensation; stimuli above it do.

Absolute thresholds are measured psychophysically by asking vigilant observers to perform "detection" tasks—trying to see a dim light in a dark room or trying to hear a soft sound in a quiet room. During a series of many "trials," the stimulus is presented at varying intensities, and on each trial the observers indicate whether they were aware of it. (If you've ever had your hearing evaluated, you were probably a "subject" in such a test.)

The results of such a study can be summarized in a **psychometric function:** a graph that plots the percentage of *detections* (on the vertical, or Y-axis) for each *stimulus intensity* (on the horizontal, or X-axis). A typical psychometric function is shown in **Figure 5.1.** For very dim lights, clearly below threshold, detection is at 0 percent; for bright lights, clearly above threshold, detection is at 100 percent. If there were a single, true absolute threshold, you would expect the transition from 0 to 100

Figure 5.1 How Absolute Thresholds Are Calculated
Since there is no point at which a stimulus suddenly becomes clearly detectable, a person's absolute threshold is defined as the intensity at which the stimulus is detected half of the time over many trials.

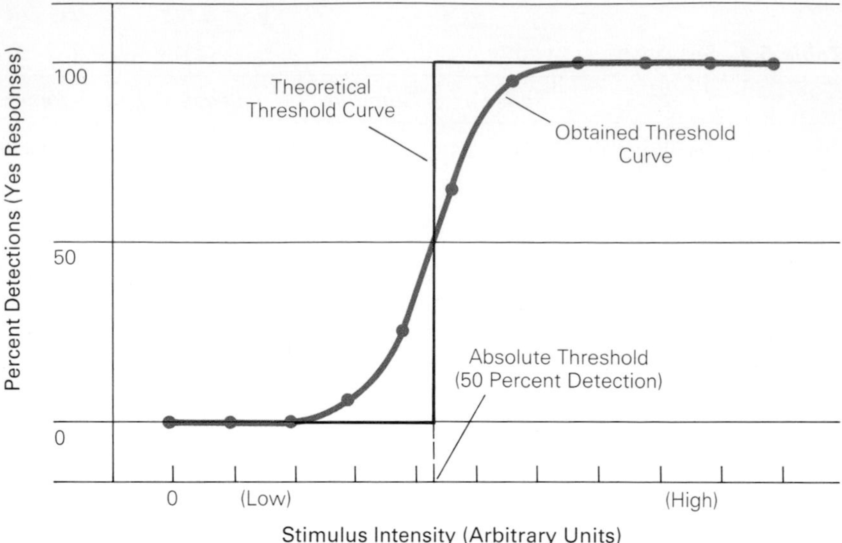

percent detection to be very sharp, occurring right at the point where the intensity reached the threshold; but this does not happen. Instead, the psychometric curve is almost always a smooth S-shaped curve, in which there is a region of transition from no detection to detection more and more of the time, finally reaching accurate detection all the time.

The usual practice is to define the threshold *arbitrarily* as the intensity level at which the psychometric function crosses 50 percent detection. This is an *operational definition* of an absolute threshold: the stimulus level at which a sensory signal is detected half the time. Thresholds for different sense modalities can be measured in the same way, simply by changing the stimulus dimension. **Table 5.2** shows absolute threshold levels for several familiar natural stimuli.

Table 5.2 *Approximate Thresholds of Familiar Events*

Sense Modality	Detection Threshold
Light	A candle flame seen at 30 miles on a dark clear night.
Sound	The tick of a watch under quiet conditions at twenty feet.
Taste	One teaspoon of sugar in 2 gallons of water
Smell	One drop of perfume diffused into the entire volume of a 3-room apartment.
Touch	The wing of a bee falling on your cheek from a distance of 1 centimeter.

(From Galanter, 1962, p. 97)

Is there really such a thing as a specific absolute threshold? Some psychologists think not. The smooth transition found from not detecting to detecting weak stimuli implies a *gradual,* rather than a sharp, change from absence to presence of sensation. In addition, there seem to be circumstances under which people behave as though they have seen or heard something even when their detection performance has indicated a stimulus below the sensory threshold (Dixon, 1971)—a phenomenon called *subliminal perception.* What may pass as subliminal perception may often be a matter of divided attention, which we will treat in chapter 7. (Incidentally, studies of the effects of subliminal stimuli on behavior have not yielded any conclusive proof to support the allegation, popularized in the mass media, that companies have increased their sales by using subliminal messages in their advertising.) Another problem for the classical concept of sensory thresholds is that *response bias* can affect threshold measurements.

Response Bias

A **response bias** is a systematic tendency, because of nonsensory factors, for an observer to favor responding in a particular way. After all, someone could respond "yes" in a detection task because that person wanted to be selected for a job requiring acute sensitivity. Response biases are most likely to arise in situations that have important consequences for an observer's life.

Why does someone's detection threshold become distorted by response bias? At least three sources have been identified: desire, expectation, and habit. When we want a particular outcome, we are more likely to give whatever response will achieve that desired objective. "I didn't see anything, officer" is more likely if we want to avoid getting involved; "Yes, I'm sure he's the one, sir" is a more probable response if we want to be in line for a reward.

Our expectations, or knowledge, of stimulus probabilities may also influence our readiness to report a sensory event. The same weak blip on a sonar scope is more likely to be detected and reported as a submarine if we are on a cruiser during wartime than if we are on a freighter on Lake Michigan during peacetime.

Finally, people develop habits of responding, individual differences to be "yea sayers," who chronically answer yes, or to be "nay sayers" or "don't knowers." This learned habit of biased responding means that under conditions of uncertainty some people will over-report perceiving the presence of a stimulus event (the yea sayers), while others will consistently under-report it (the nay sayers). How can this individual difference among perceivers be separated from the detection threshold of the stimulus?

Researchers use the technique of **catch trials** to find out whether response biases are operating in sensory detection tasks. *No* stimulus is presented on a few of the trials, to "catch" the subject who has a tendency to respond "yes." The threshold estimate of the real stimulus is then adjusted according to how often such "false alarms" occur. What would you do to catch a subject who overuses "no" when there is a stimulus present?

The Theory of Signal Detection

A systematic approach to the problem of response bias has been developed in the **theory of signal detection** (TSD). This theory is an alternative to the classical approach in psychophysics (Green & Swets, 1966). Instead of focusing on strictly sensory processes, signal detection theory emphasizes the process of making a *judgment* about the presence or absence of stimulus events. It replaces the theoretical concept of a single absolute threshold with two other ones: (a) an initial *sensory process,* which reflects the subject's *sensitivity* to the strength of the stimulus, and (b) a separate *decision process* later, which reflects the observer's *response biases,* those attitudes and beliefs that may influence what is reported. These biases are sources of "noise" in the system that lead to inaccurate estimates of the stimulus. This theory also replaces the procedure for measuring thresholds with a different (and more complex) one that can measure both the sensory and decision processes at once.

The measurement procedure is actually just an extension of the idea of catch trials. The basic design is given in **Figure 5.2A.** A weak stimulus is presented on half the trials; no stimulus is presented on the other half. On each trial a subject responds by saying "yes" if he or she thinks the signal was present, and "no" if it was not. As shown in Matrix A of the figure, each response is scored as a hit, a miss, a false alarm, or a correct rejection, depending on whether a signal was, in fact, presented and whether the observer responded that it was.

An observer who is a "yea sayer" will give a high number of hits, but will also have a high number of false alarms, as shown in Matrix B; one who is a "nay sayer" will give a lower number of hits but also a lower number of false alarms, as shown in Matrix C. By combining the percentages of hits and false alarms, a mathematical relationship that differentiates sensory responses from response

Figure 5.2 *The Theory of Signal Detection*
Matrix A shows the possible outcomes when a subject answers yes or no when asked if a target stimulus occurred on a given trial. Matrices B and C show typical responses of a "yea sayer" and a "nay sayer," respectively.

Matrix of Possibilities

A.

Stimulus Condition	Response Given: Yes	Response Given: No
Signal On	Hit	Miss
Signal Off	False alarm	Correct rejection

B.

	Responses of a "Yea Sayer": Yes Response	No Response
Signal On	92%	8%
Signal Off	46%	54%

C.

	Responses of a "Nay Sayer": Yes Response	No Response
Signal On	40%	60%
Signal Off	4%	96%

biases is achieved. This procedure makes it possible to find out whether two observers have the same sensitivity despite large differences in response bias.

According to the theory of signal detection, any stimulus event (signal or noise) produces some neural activity in the sensory system—perhaps the firing of some set of neurons. In deciding whether a stimulus was present, the observer compares the sensory value in the neural system with some personally set *response criterion.* If the response of the sensory process exceeds that critical amount, the observer responds "yes"; if not, "no." Thus, the discrete "threshold" appears in the decision process instead of the sensory one.

The response criterion reflects the observer's strategy for responding in a particular situation. By providing a way of separating sensory process from response bias, the theory of signal detection allows an experimenter to identify and separate the roles of the sensory stimulus and the individual's criterion level, or response bias, in producing the final response.

This approach has become the dominant one in modern psychophysics. Actually, it is a general model of decision making that can be used in contexts quite different from psychophysics. In many everyday decisions there are different rewards for every hit and correct rejection made, and penalties for making a miss and false alarm. Decisions are likely to be biased by the schedule of anticipated gains and losses in this way; such a detection matrix is called a **payoff matrix** (see **Figure 5.3**). If there is a potential big gain by saying "yes" (when a stimulus is really present) and an expected big loss by saying "no," if it is present, then a "yes" bias will rule. For example, a surgeon can be biased in favor of operating for a possible malignant condition by charging a big fee for the surgery and fearing the patients' possible death if the surgeon doesn't operate and the malignant condition were present; but the payoff matrix is different for the patient, since if the condition is really absent, then the decision to operate is a costly false alarm. Thus the decision is a combination of the available evidence, on the one hand, and the relative costs of each type of error and the relative gains from each type of correct decision, on the other.

A decision becomes more *conservative* when there is a high cost for a decision that can later be shown to be a false alarm, but less cost for a miss. A prison parole board must decide to release or detain an inmate on the basis of evidence presented at the parole hearing. If the prisoner is truly "rehabilitated," the correct decision is to vote for parole; if the prisoner is not rehabilitated, then the correct decision is no. When the evidence about the inmate's probable behavior after being released is ambiguous, what are the costs of making each type of decision error? Keeping a "good" inmate in prison costs the state money, and the inmate freedom, but these costs are not as evident as those that result from paroling a "bad" inmate who commits a major crime after being released. Therefore, when the fear of a false alarm offsets the concern for a miss, the decision will swing toward "no." Can you think of an example of a risky decision encouraged by the payoff matrix—taking a chance on "yes" when the supporting evidence might be absent?

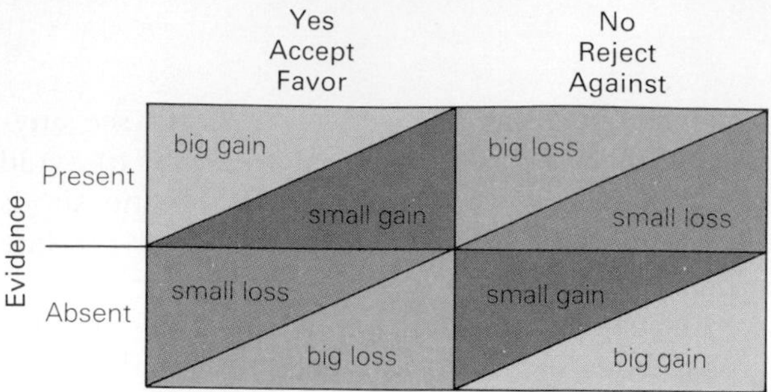

Figure 5.3 *Payoff Matrix*
The payoff in the top half of each cell in the matrix will generate "yes" biases, while the payoff in the bottom half of each cell will generate "no" biases.

Difference Thresholds

Suppose you are a programmer inventing a new video game. You have decided to use bars of different lengths to represent the friendly and enemy spaceships that have been destroyed; each time another ship is downed, the corresponding bar gets a little longer. You want the players to be able to tell which of the two bars is longer so they will know who is winning, but you want the additions to the bar length to be as small as possible so that as many spaceships as possible can be represented. What you need here is a **difference threshold,** the smallest physical difference that will be recognized *as* a difference.

You would find it in pretty much the same way you would find an absolute threshold, except you would use a pair of stimuli on each trial and ask your subjects whether the two stimuli were different (instead of just whether a stimulus was present). For this particular problem, you would show your subject two bars on each trial, one of some standard length and one just a bit longer. For each pair, the observer would say "same" or "different." After many such trials you would plot a psychometric function by graphing the percent of "different" responses on the vertical axis as a function of the actual differences in length on the horizontal

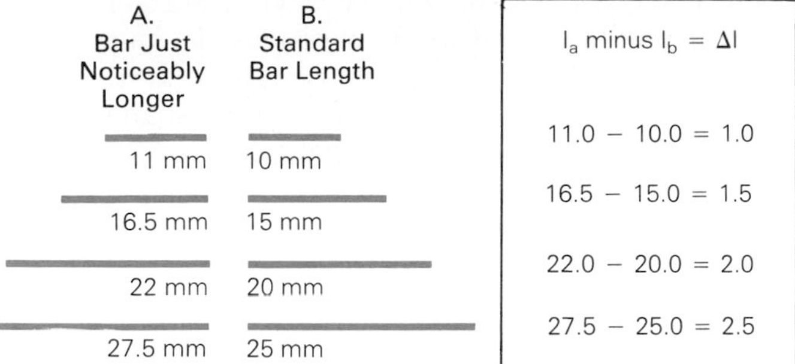

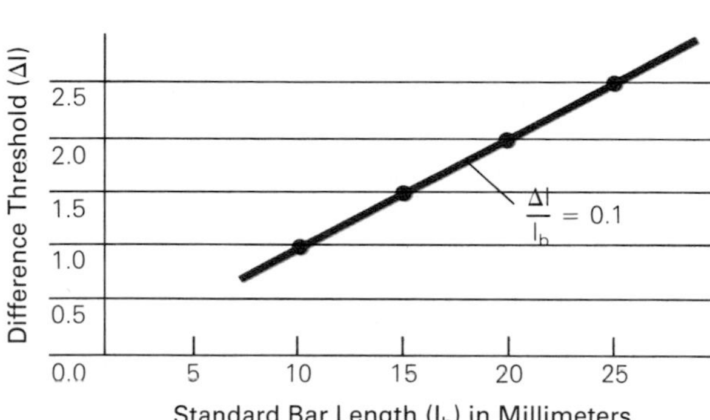

Figure 5.4 *Just Noticeable Differences and Weber's Law*

The longer the standard bar, the longer the amount you must add (ΔI) to see a just noticeable difference. The added amount of length that you detect on half of the trials is called the difference threshold. *When you plot these increments against standard bars of increasing length, the* proportion *stays the same: the amount that must be added is always one-tenth of the standard length. This relationship is a* linear *one, producing a straight line on the graph.*

axis. The difference threshold is the length difference at which the curve crosses the 50-percent value. Thus the *difference threshold* is arbitrarily defined as the point at which the stimuli are recognized as different half of the time (on 50 percent of the trials). This difference threshold value is known as the **just noticeable difference** or **jnd.** The *jnd* was Fechner's metric, the quantitative unit for measuring the magnitude of a sensation or the sensed distance between any two sensations. The psychophysical question asks how this psychological series of jnds changes as the physical series of stimuli change in intensity. What is the function that relates physical to psychological change?

Now suppose you have performed this experiment with a standard bar length of 10 millimeters using increases of varying amounts and have found the difference threshold to be about 1 millimeter; so you know that a 10-millimeter bar will be detected as different from an 11-millimeter bar 50 percent of the time. Can you go ahead and design your video-game display now?

Unfortunately, you're not through yet, because the difference threshold is not the same for long bars as for short ones. With a standard bar of 20 millimeters, for instance, you would have had to add about 2 millimeters to get a just noticeable difference; for one of 40 millimeters you would need to add 4 millimeters, and so on. **Figure 5.4** shows some examples of jnds with bars of several lengths: they increase steadily with the length of the standard bar.

What remains the same, however, is the ratio of the size of the increase that produces a just noticeable difference to the length of the standard bar. For example, 1 mm/10 mm = 0.1 and 2 mm/20 mm = 0.1. Ernst Weber discovered this constant relationship in 1834 and found that it held for a wide range of stimulus dimensions. The only difference between stimulus dimensions was the particular value of this constant ratio. He summarized all his findings in a single equation, now called **Weber's law:** the bigger or more intense the standard stimulus, the larger the increment you will need in order to get a just noticeable difference; or, the smaller or weaker the standard stimulus, the less the increase needed before you detect a jnd. A few drops of water added to a test tube are more likely to be noticed than the same amount added to a jug. This is a very general property of all sensory systems. The formula for Weber's law is the following:

$$\frac{\Delta I}{I} = k$$

Where ΔI is the size of the increase that produces a difference threshold or jnd, I is the intensity of the standard stimulus, and k is the constant ratio for the particular stimulus dimension (0.1 in our line-length example). Work through the bar length example plotted in Figure 5.4. to be sure you understand what a jnd is, what Weber's law is, and how they are related.

Constructing Psychophysical Scales

You are already familiar with physical scales—the metric scale for lengths and the Fahrenheit scale for temperature, to name just two. Could such scales be used directly for measuring psychological sensations? When you think about it, Weber's law suggests that they could *not* because the *psychological* difference between 1 and 2 inches is much bigger than the psychological difference between 101 and 102 inches; the *physical* difference is the same.

One approach to constructing psychophysical scales is based on treating just noticeable differences as psychologically equal intervals. After all, they are equal in the sense of being just noticeably different from neighboring stimuli, so why not just assume that jnds are the psychological units of sensation? Using our bar-length example, the 1 millimeter difference between 10-millimeter and 11-millimeter bars is taken as being psychologically the same as the 1.5-millimeter difference between bars of 15 millimeters and 16.5 and the 2-millimeter difference for bars 20 and 22 millimeters long. Together with Weber's law, this implies that equal increases in the physical intensity of the stimulus will produce sensations that rise rapidly at first and then more and more slowly, as shown in **Figure 5.5A.** This was the relationship proposed by Gustav Fechner in 1860; it is expressed mathematically in an equation known as **Fechner's law:**

$$S = k \log I$$

where S is the magnitude of the sensory experience, I is the physical intensity, and k is a constant for the dimension being scaled. According to Fechner's law, a person's experience of sensory intensity increases *arithmetically* (2, 3, 4) as the stimulus intensity increases *geometrically* (2, 4, 8). Thus, within limits, sensory experience is proportional to the logarithm of stimulus intensity. This *logarithmic* equation represents one form of mathematical relationship between psychology and physics—between sensory experience and physical reality. The Weber-Fechner law of psychophysics states that the intensity of subjective sensation increases arithmetically as the physical stimulus increases geometrically.

A hundred years after Fechner, psychologist S. S. Stevens devised a different method of constructing psychophysical scales, and he obtained a different answer. He asked observers to assign numbers to their sensations using a method called **magnitude estimation.** Observers were presented with an initial stimulus—for instance, a light of some known intensity—and asked to assign some value to it—say, 10. Then they were presented with another light at a different magnitude and told that if they perceived it as twice as bright, they should call it 20. If it were half as bright, they should call it 5, and so on. When Stevens constructed psychological scales in this manner, he found that the results could be described by a mathematical equation known as a *power function:*

$$S = kI^b$$

Where S is (again) the magnitude of the sensory experience, I is (again) the physical intensity of the stimulus, k is a constant (not Fechner's constant but a different one), and b is an exponent that varies for different sensory dimensions. **Figure 5.5B** shows psychophysical curves for brightness and electrical shock, where the exponents are very different. Doubling the physical intensity of a light *less* than doubles the sensation of brightness, which is qualitatively consistent with Fechner's law. As you

Figure 5.5 *Two Psychophysical Scales*
According to Fechner's equation, based on just noticeable differences, sensation units first increase rapidly with equal increases in stimulus intensity but then increase more and more slowly. (Adding one candle to two increases the brightness you see much more than adding one candle to 100.)
According to Stevens' equation, based on direct judgments of sensory magnitude, the psychophysical curve is different for different stimuli. For brightness, the curve is similar to Fechner's, but for a stimulus like electric shock, slight increases in physical intensity produce greater and greater sensations of pain. (From Stevens, 1961)

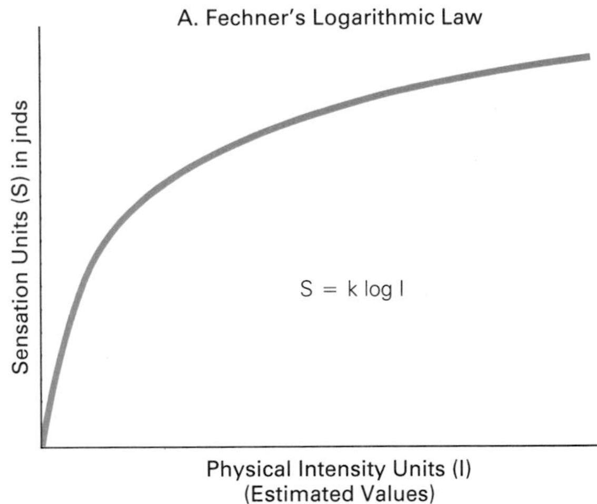

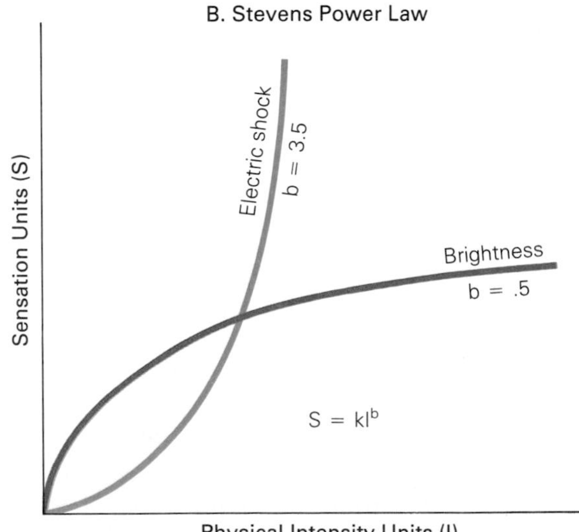

might guess, however, doubling the magnitude of an electrical shock *more* than doubles its corresponding sensation. Fechner's law cannot predict such a result.

Stevens' approach has proved to be very useful, because almost any psychological dimension can be readily scaled in this way. Psychologists have used magnitude estimation to construct psychological scales for everything from pitch and length to beauty, the seriousness of crimes, and the goodness of Swedish monarchs (Stevens, 1961, 1962, 1975). Stevens' direct method of magnitude estimation proved to be very convenient and more useful than the Fechner formula when adapted to data outside the province of purely sensory estimations; but it was not, as he claimed, a direct measure of sensation (Savage, 1970).

Although similar equations express the relationships between stimuli and sensations in the various sensory modalities, each sense responds to a different kind of stimulus energy, provides us with different qualities of sensory experience, and does so through the operation of its own ingenious physiological mechanisms. In the remainder of this chapter, we will look at the physical stimuli, psychological experiences, and physiological mechanisms involved in vision, hearing, the chemical senses, the body senses, and finally, pain.

The Visual System

Vision is the most complex, highly developed, and important sense for humans and most other mobile creatures, because animals with good vision have an enormous evolutionary advantage. As predators, they can detect their prey from far away; as prey, they can detect and keep their distance from predators. Vision also enables us to be aware of changing features in the physical environment and to adapt our behavior accordingly. With the help of microscopes and telescopes, vision allows us to probe the secrets of nature—from something as small as a molecule to something as large as a galaxy.

The Human Eye

Since the eye is designed to detect light, let us follow a ray of light into an eye to see what happens (see **Figure 5.6**). First, light enters the **cornea,** a transparent bulge on the front of the eye that is filled with a clear liquid called the *aqueous humor.* Next, it passes through the **pupil,** an opening in the opaque **iris,** a muscular disk that surrounds the pupil and controls the amount of light entering the eye by contracting or relaxing. The iris also has the pigment that gives the eye its color.

Just behind the iris, light passes through the **lens,** a structure enclosed in a flexible membrane capsule which, in most adults, is clear, transparent, and convex. In older people, the lens becomes flattened, more opaque, and amber-tinted. The shape of the lens is controlled by **ciliary muscles** attached to its edge. Light then travels through the *vitreous humor,* a clear fluid that fills the central chamber of the eye, finally striking the retina on the back surface. At the retina, light can be absorbed by any of the 125 million light-sensitive receptors. The **retina** is a complex membrane at the rear of the eye that has up to 10 different layers of cells.

Each of the eye's components performs a critical role in the eye's sensory capabilities. The amount of light striking the retina is controlled by the iris and

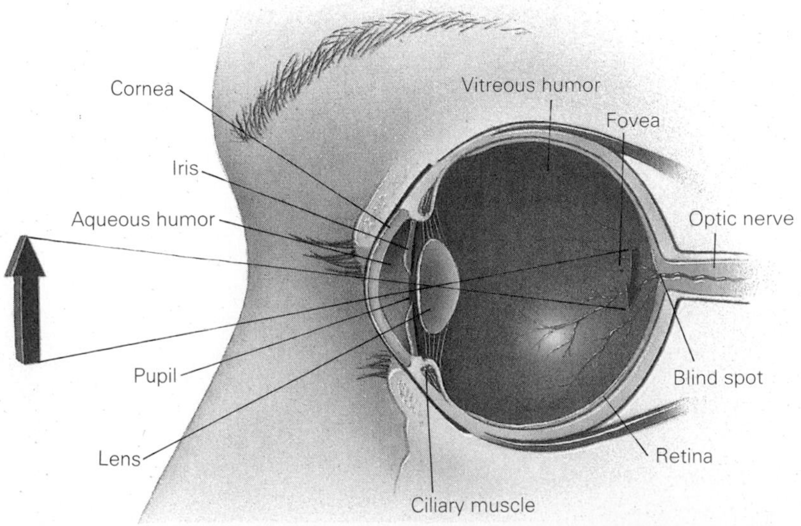

Figure 5.6 *Structure of the Human Eye*

the pupil. When illumination is dim, the pupil dilates so that more light enters the eye. In bright light, the pupil constricts, allowing less light to enter. Interestingly, pupil size also changes in response to psychological factors. For instance, positive emotional reactions dilate the pupil, whereas negative ones constrict it. Pupil size also reflects mental effort, dilating when concentration is intense. All of this is involuntary and occurs without your awareness (Hess, 1972).

Light entering the eye is useful only if it is focused on the retina in a reasonably clear image. For this to happen, light must be bent inward toward the center of the eye (see **Figure 5.6**). The curvature of the cornea does most of the job; the lens does the rest, reversing and inverting the light pattern as it does so. The lens is particularly important, however, because of its *variable focusing* ability for near and far objects. The ciliary muscles can change the thickness of the lens, and, hence, its optical properties, in a process called **accommodation.**

People who are nearsighted cannot focus distant objects properly, while those who are farsighted cannot focus nearby objects well. As people get older, the lens gradually loses its elasticity, so that it cannot become thick enough for close vision. After about age 45, the blur point—the closest point at which you can focus clearly—gets progressively farther away. When this happens, people who have never needed glasses before begin to need them for reading and other "close work," whereas people who already wear glasses may need to switch to bifocals (glasses that have a near focus in the lower part and a far one in the upper part).

Processing in the Retina

The most critical function of the eye is to convert the information about the world that is being carried by light waves into neural signals that the brain can process. This happens in the retina at the back of the eye, where integration of the input also begins. The retina can be divided into three major layers or zones of cells—from the rear to the front, they are the photoreceptor cells, the bipolar cells, and the ganglion cells (see **Figure 5.7**).

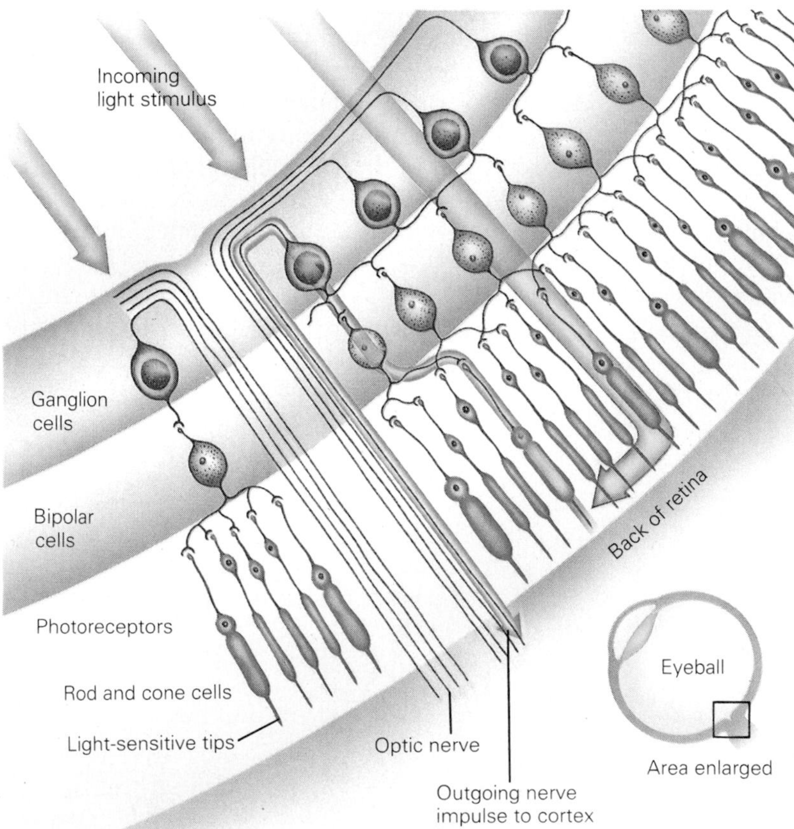

Figure 5.7 *Retinal Pathways*
This is a stylized and greatly simplified diagram showing examples of the pathways that connect three of the layers of nerve cells in the retina. Incoming light passes through all these layers to reach the receptors, at the back of the eyeball and pointed away from the source of light. Note that the bipolar cells "gather" impulses from more than one receptor cell and send the results to several ganglion cells. Nerve impulses (blue arrows) from the ganglion cells leave the eye via the optic nerve and travel to the next relay point.

Photoreceptors

The basic conversion from light energy to neural responses is performed in the retina by **photoreceptors**—receptor cells sensitive to light. There are two distinct types of these photoreceptors, called rods and cones because of their shapes. Rods and cones are uniquely placed in the visual system—between the outer world ablaze with light and the inner, dark world of neural processing and visual sensation. **Rods** are light-sensitive receptor cells concentrated in the periphery, or outer part, of the retina. The more than 115 million rods in the retina of each eye handle low-illumination vision. The 6 million **cones** packed into the center of the retina are responsible for our experiencing a world of colored objects.

In the very center of the retina is a small region called the **fovea,** which contains nothing but densely packed cones; it's rod-free. The fovea is the area of your sharpest vision: both color and spatial detail are most accurately detected there.

Bipolar and Ganglion Cells

The responses of many nearby receptors are gathered by the retina's bipolar and ganglion cells. The **bipolar cells** are nerve cells that combine impulses from many receptors and send the results to ganglion cells. They have a single dendrite with branched endings and one axon and terminal button. Each **ganglion cell** then integrates the impulses from many bipolar cells into a single firing rate. The axons of the ganglion cells make up the **optic nerve,** which carries this visual information out of the eye and back toward the brain.

Peculiarities of Retinal Design

Your eye seems to give you such clear and complete images that it is difficult to suspect some of the peculiarities present in the design of the retina. To start, you might expect that the receptor cells would be in the *first* layer of the retina that the incoming light would reach. Wrong! Actually they are in the *last* layer, as shown in **Figure 5.7.** This means that light delivers its message to the receptors only after it has passed through several layers of cells. Luckily, these cells are fairly transparent, so that the optical quality of the image does not suffer as much as you might expect. However, the blood vessels in the retina also lie in front of the receptors, and they are not at all transparent. Normally, you do not see them because your brain adjusts by "filling in" the image where their shadows fall.

To see the blood vessels in your own eye, try the following exercise: Look at a white surface (a plain wall or blank piece of paper) with one eye closed and shine a pen flashlight into the white of the open eye at the outside corner, gently shaking the pen light up and down. You will be able to see the blood vessels clearly because their shadows will be in front of different receptors, to which the brain has not yet adjusted.

Another interesting curiosity in the anatomical design of the retina exists where the optic nerve leaves the eye. This region, called the *optic disk* or **blind spot** contains no receptor cells at all; yet you do not experience blindness there, except under very special circumstances because: (a) the blind spots of the two eyes are so positioned that receptors in each eye register what is missed in the other, and (b) the brain "fills in" this region with appropriate sensory qualities just as it does for the shadows of the blood vessels.

To find your blind spot, hold this book at arm's length, close your right eye, and fixate on the upper square with your left eye as you bring the book slowly closer. When the dollar sign is in your blind spot, it will disappear. Yet you experience no gaping hole in your visual field. Instead, your visual system fills in this area with the background whiteness of the surrounding area so you "see" the whiteness, which isn't there, while failing to see your money, which should be headed for the bank.

To convince yourself that higher brain processes "fill in" the missing part of the visual field with appropriate information, close your right eye again and focus on the cross as you bring the book closer to you. This time, the gap in the line will disappear and be filled in with a line that completes the broken one. At least in your blind spot, what you see with your own *eye* may be a false view of reality. (Some people draw the analogy between this visual blind spot and the mental and emotional "blind spots" involved in prejudice; can you see any parallels?)

Pathways to the Brain

At the back of the brain is a special area to process information coming from the eyes, the part of the occipital cortex known as the primary **visual cortex.** Nerve impulses leaving the retina project to at least six parts of the brain, some in the cortex, some in subcortical regions. They first travel to the **optic chiasma,** which resembles the Greek letter X (chi, pronounced "kye"). In humans, the axons in the optic nerve are divided into two bundles at the optic chiasma; those from the inner half of each eye cross over to the other side to continue their journey toward the back of the brain, as shown in **Figure 5.8**).

From the optic chiasma there are two separate pathways on each side. A small one goes to the **superior colliculus,** a cluster of nerve cell bodies in the midbrain region of the brain stem. It has recently been discovered that the superior colliculus has a very important function that gives the organism flexibility in orienting to multiple sensory stimulation from its environment. It serves as a sensorimotor center that integrates sensory input of different types, such as sound and light, and motor responses that orient the eyes, ears, and head toward a wide variety of environmental cues (Meredith & Stein, 1985). In addition, this nerve cell cluster also controls the pupil to open in dim light and to close in bright light.

The other pathway, the major one, goes first to the **lateral geniculate nucleus** of the thalamus and then to the region of the visual cortex in each of the cerebral hemispheres at the rear of the brain. At the synapses in the lateral geniculate nucleus, influences from other brain regions, such as the reticular activating system, are believed to interact with the impulses coming from the eyes before they are finally sent to the primary visual areas in the cortex. Cortical processing of information from the two eyes gives us our perception of color, depth, shape, and recognition of known patterns. Researchers now think that only in humans does information going to the cortex ultimately become part of the conscious experience.

Recall that **blindsight,** described in our *Opening Case,* is visually guided behavior that is not consciously occurring in individuals whose visual cortex has been removed. The debate over its existence involves the hypothesis that there are two separate, but parallel, visual systems. Some investigators argue that these two systems are distinct in their functions as well as distinct in their location. The "first visual system" is concerned with *pattern recognition—how* things look. It is located in the pathways of the geniculate nucleus to the visual cortex. The subcortical activities of the superior colliculus are responsible for the "second visual system"—*place recognition,* or "*where* things are" (Bridgeman, 1983; Poppel, 1977; Schneider, 1969). It is in the superior colliculus that blindsight is supposed to take place.

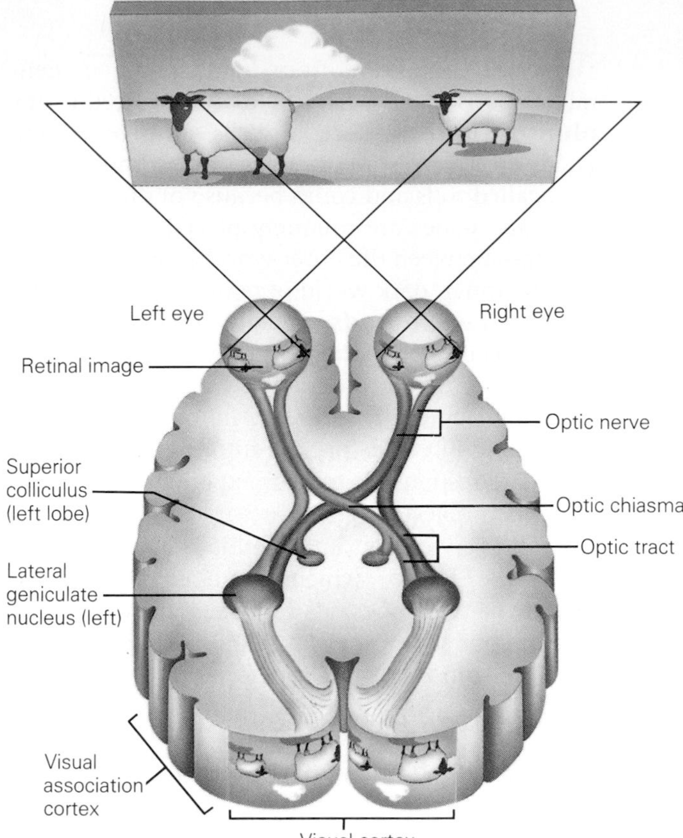

Figure 5.8 *Pathways in the Human Visual System*
The diagram shows how light from the visual field projects onto the two retinas and the routes by which neural messages from there are sent to the two visual centers of each hemisphere (based on Frisby, 1980).

Opponents of this dual visual-system hypothesis argue that the blindsight phenomenon can be attributed to factors other than subcortical processing of visual input (Campion et al., 1983). They claim further that visual information about *both* pattern and place recognition is processed in the human brain either by the visual cortex entirely or with the assistance of cortical mechanisms that operate after it, but not separate from it. This current controversy awaits new sources of data to resolve the issue of whether we "see" with one or two visual systems.

Dimensions of Visual Experience

One of the most remarkable features of the human visual system is that our experiences of form, color, position, depth, and other aspects of perceived objects are based on different kinds of processing of the *same* sensory information. If you observed the nerve impulses carrying these different kinds of information about the external world, they would be identical. How those transformations occur in color, contrast, time, and motion is our next concern.

Color

Physical objects and beams of light seem to have the marvelous property of being painted with color; but suppose someone told you that the red Valentines, green Christmas trees, blue oceans, and multicolored rainbows you see are actually colorless? Despite appearances, color does not exist in either the objects or the light. One of the first to say so was the great scientist Isaac Newton:

> *For the rays [of light], to speak properly, are not colored. In them there is nothing else than a certain power and disposition to stir up a sensation of this or that color. For as sound, in a bell or musical string or other sounding body, is nothing but a trembling motion, and in the air nothing but that motion propagated from the object, . . . so colors in the object are nothing but a disposition to reflect this or that sort of ray more copiously than the rest. . . . (quoted in MacAdam, 1970, p. 23, original 1671/1672)*

When you see color, it is a psychological property of your sensory experience, created when your brain processes the information coded in the light source. Although the processes involved are fairly complex, color vision is one of the best understood aspects of our visual experience.

Wavelength of Light: The Stimulus for Color

Any physicist will tell you that visible light is a kind of energy that is capable of being detected by our sensory receptors. In fact, the light we see is just a small portion of a physical dimension called the **electromagnetic spectrum.** This energy spectrum also includes X-rays, microwaves, radio waves, and TV waves, as shown in **Figure 5.9,** but we have no receptors that are sensitive to them. As a result, we cannot see or hear them without the help of instruments—X-ray cameras, radios, and television sets.

All electromagnetic energy comes in tiny, indivisible units called **photons.** The only physical property that distinguishes one photon from another is its **wavelength,** measured in units of distance of the wavelike propagation of a photon along its path. Wavelengths of visible light are measured in *nanometers* (billionths of a meter).

Photons with wavelengths ranging from about 400 to 700 nanometers are called *light;* they are the only ones that have any effect on your visual nervous system. As a result, any visible light can be completely described in terms of the number of photons it contains at wavelengths between 400 and 700 nanometers. For instance, "white" sunlight is the combination of all wavelengths of the visible spectrum in equal amounts. A prism separates sunlight into its component wavelengths, allowing you to experience a "rainbow" of different color sensations in response to the different wavelengths of light.

The important point is that light is described physically in terms of *wavelengths,* not colors. Colors exist only in your experience.

Color Space

To understand how you see colors from light of different wavelengths, we need to have a systematic way to describe different color experiences. Psychologists do this by representing each color sensation as a position in **color space,** using a three-dimensional model to describe a color experience in terms of its hue, saturation, and brightness. These represent the three basic dimensions of our perception of light. All the sensations of color that people can experience are located within this space, forming the *color spindle* (or color solid) shown in **Figure 5.10** on page 157.

Hue is the dimension of color space that captures what you might call the "essential color" of a light. In "pure" lights that contain only one wavelength (like a laser beam) the psychological experience of hue corresponds directly to the physical dimension of the light's wavelength, as we saw in **Figure 5.9.** In color space, the hue sensations produced by different wavelengths of light lie along the outside of the *color circle,* which is just the slice through the color spindle shown in **Figure 5.11** on page 157. The shortest (violet) and longest (red) wavelengths are shown as close together, reflecting the psychological similarity of violets and red.

Saturation is the psychological dimension that captures the purity and vividness of color sensations. In the color spindle, saturation is the distance

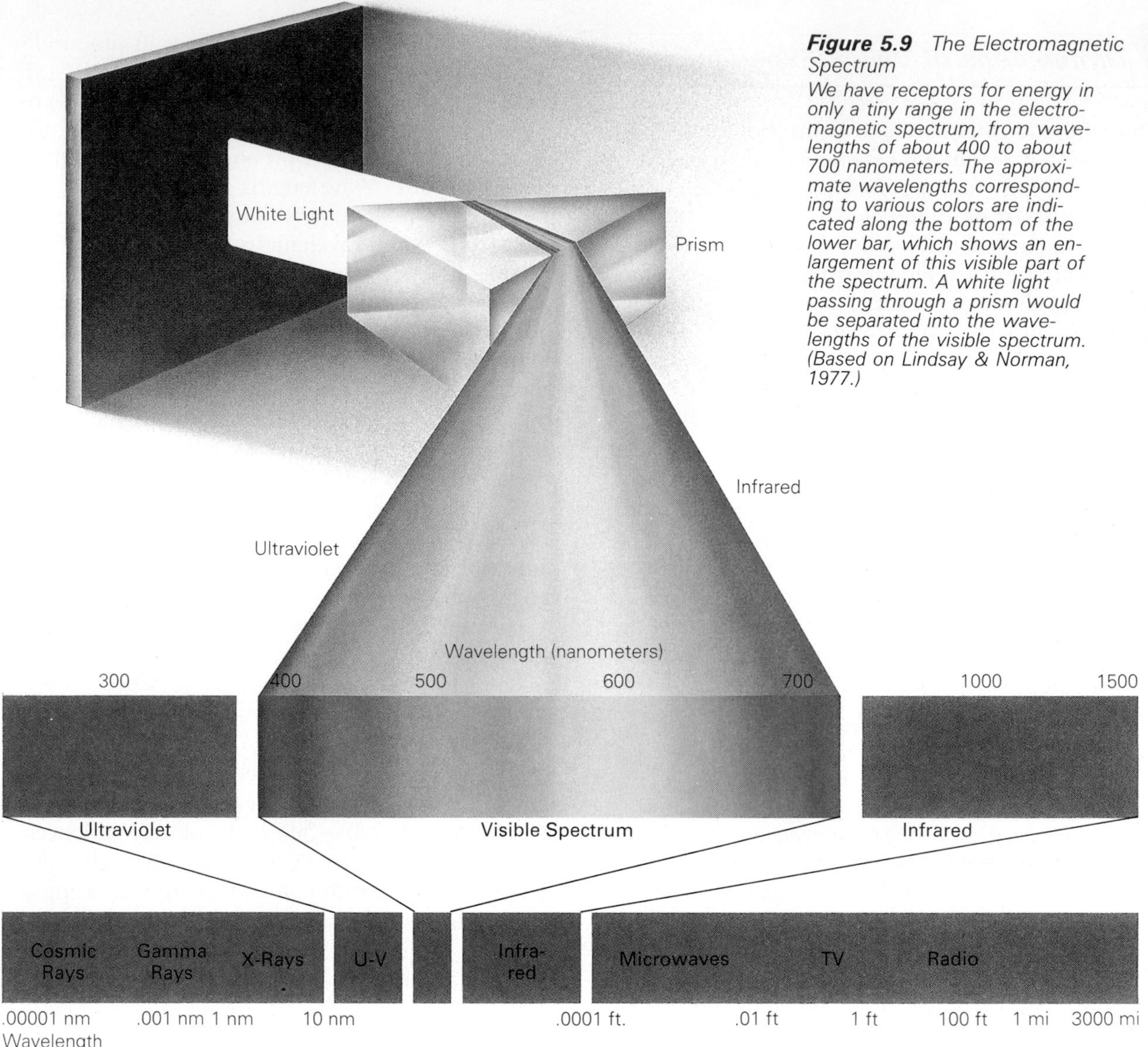

Figure 5.9 *The Electromagnetic Spectrum*
We have receptors for energy in only a tiny range in the electromagnetic spectrum, from wavelengths of about 400 to about 700 nanometers. The approximate wavelengths corresponding to various colors are indicated along the bottom of the lower bar, which shows an enlargement of this visible part of the spectrum. A white light passing through a prism would be separated into the wavelengths of the visible spectrum. (Based on Lindsay & Norman, 1977.)

outward from the central axis; the pure colors lying on the outer edge have the highest saturation, grays at the center have zero saturation, and the muted, muddy, and pastel colors with intermediate saturation lie in between, as shown in Figure 5.11.

Brightness is the dimension of color experience that captures the intensity of light. White has the most brightness, black the least. Brightness is the vertical dimension of color space with white at the top, black at the bottom, and all the grays in between. These "neutral" color sensations (sensations with no hue) lie along the vertical axis of the color spindle. All colors have some value on the brightness dimension—the brighter a color, the higher it is in the color spindle.

Figure 5.12 on page 158 shows a vertical slice through the color spindle that illustrates how the saturation and brightness dimensions for a blue hue form a *color triangle.* The grays, from black to white, form a vertical strip along one side, representing the vertical axis of the spindle. When colors are analyzed along these three dimensions of hue, saturation, and brightness, a remarkable conclusion emerges. Humans are capable of discriminating about 5 *million* different colors!

Complementary Colors and Afterimages

Colors opposite each other on the color circle are complementary colors (see **Figure 5.11**). Each hue gives its complementary hue as a color **afterimage**—an effect of a visual stimulus after that stimulus has ended. For an especially dramatic example of this principle stare at the dot in the center of the green, black, and yellow flag **(Figure**

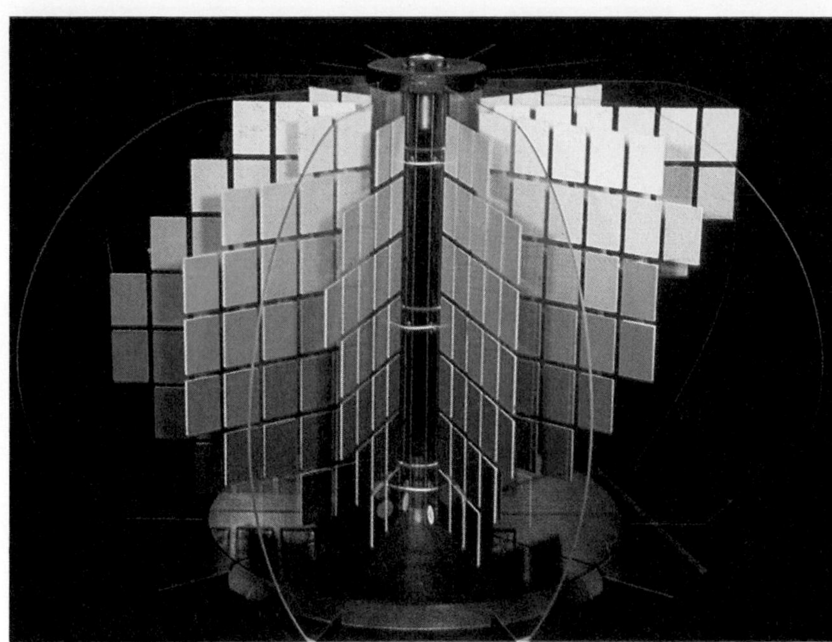

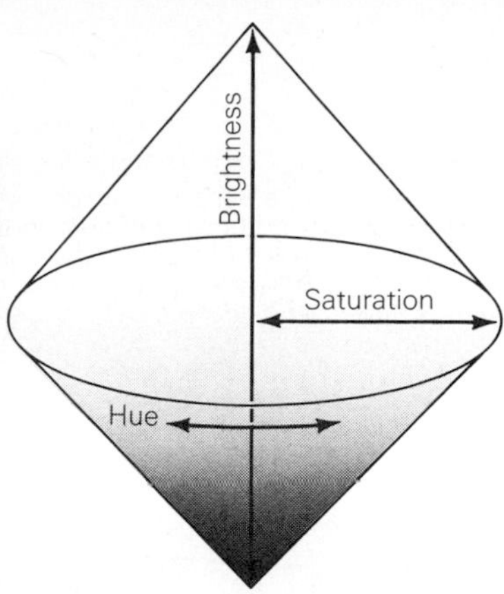

Figure 5.10 *The Color Spindle*
The color spindle (or color solid) shows each possible color sensation located somewhere within the three-dimensional color space whose dimensions are hue, saturation, and brightness, as shown in the schematic diagram. The values of a color experience along these three dimensions determine where it goes in color space; all color experiences together form the spindle.

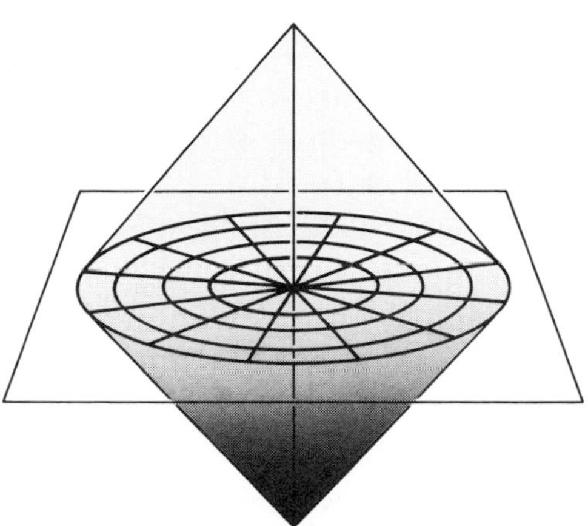

Figure 5.11 *The Color Circle*
The color circle shows the hues arranged in a circle, according to their perceived similarity. (The relation of this hue circle to the entire color spindle is shown in the schematic diagram.) Between the hues with shortest and longest wavelengths are the nonspectral hues, *which are not found on the electromagnetic spectrum but are created by mixing lights that are a part of the spectrum. (Based on Rock, 1975.)*

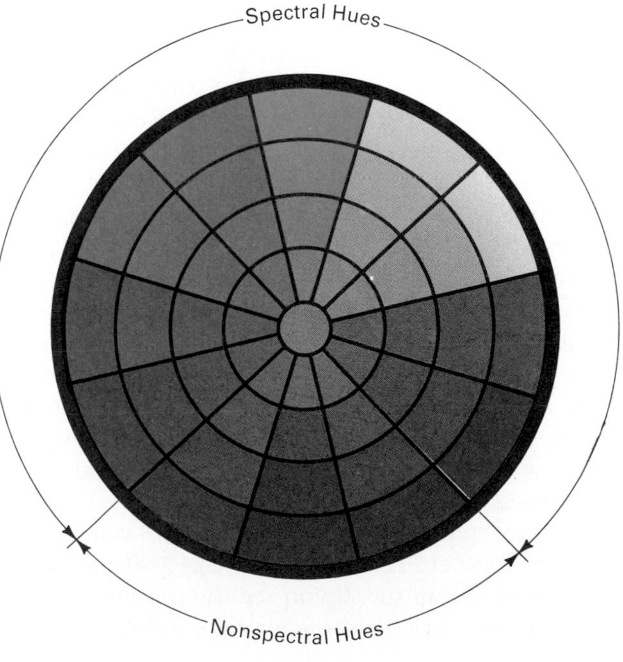

5.13 on page 159) for at least 30 seconds, moving your eyes as little as possible. Then focus on a white sheet of paper until an image forms. Were you surprised? Do you understand why you saw the colors you did? Red is the complement of green, blue the complement of yellow, and white the complement of black.

Afterimages (or *aftereffects*) may be negative, as in this example, or positive. Negative afterimages are the opposite or the reverse of the original experience and are more common and longer lasting. Positve afterimages are caused by a continuation of the receptor and neural processing following stimulation; they are rare and brief. An example is continuing to see the light of a flash bulb.

Figure 5.12 *The Color Triangle for Blue* *This triangle shows a variety of colors with the same hue that differ only in brightness and saturation. The schematic diagram shows how this triangle is related to the entire color spindle. Notice that along the right edge of the triangle are the "neutral" colors from white to black, which lie along the vertical axis of the color spindle.*

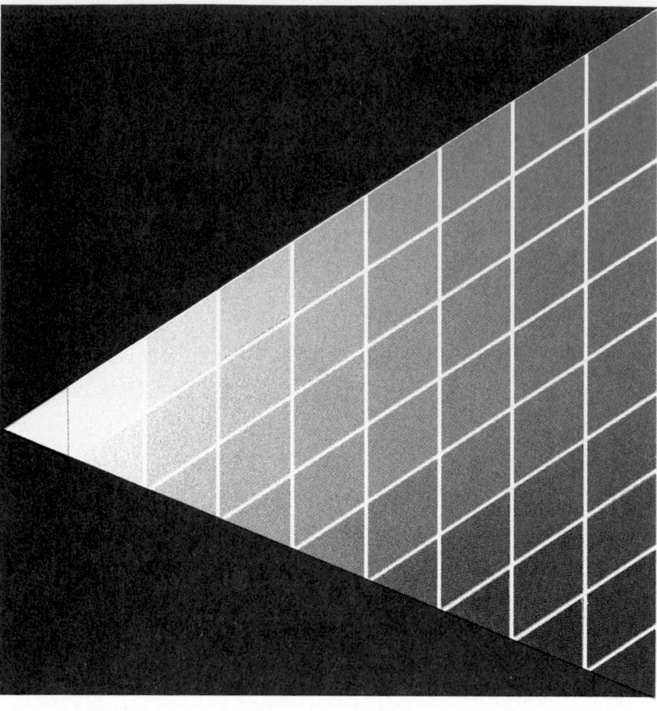

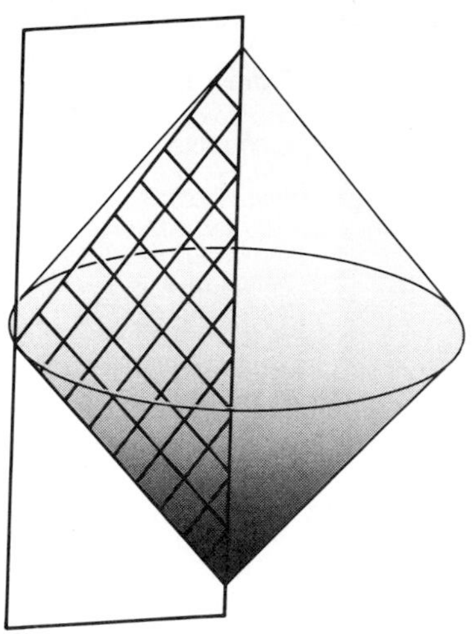

Color Blindness

Not everyone sees colors the same way; some people are color blind. **Color blindness** is the partial or total inability to distinguish colors. It is usually a sex-linked hereditary defect associated with a gene on the *X* chromosome. Males more readily develop this recessive trait than females, because if their single *X* chromosome has the defect, the trait is passed on; females would need it to be carried on both *X* chromosomes to become color blind. Estimates of color blindness among Caucasian males are about 10 percent, but less than .5 percent for females.

There are different ways of being color blind. People with *color weakness* can't distinguish pale colors, such as pink or tan. Most color-blind people have trouble distinguishing red and green, especially at weak saturations. Rare are those who confuse yellows and blues—about one or two people per thousand. Rarest of all are those who see no color at all, but only variations in brightness—a gray world. Only about 500 cases of this total color blindness have ever been reported.

To see whether you have a major color deficiency, look at **Figure 5.14** on page 160 and write down what you see. If you see the numbers 5 and 12 in the pattern of dots, your color vision is probably normal. If you see something else, you are probably at least partially color blind. (Try the test on others as well—particularly people you know who are color blind—to find out what they see.)

Theories of Color Vision

Now that we know something about the phenomena of color vision, let's examine how it happens at the neural level. What are the physiological mechanisms that enable us to see and distinguish colors? How do different wavelengths of light produce different color experiences?

The first scientific theory of color vision was proposed by Sir Thomas Young around 1800. He suggested that there were three types of color receptors in the normal human eye that produced psychologically "primary" color sensations—red, green, and blue. All other colors, he believed, were combinations of these three primaries. Young's theory was later refined and extended by Hermann von Helmholtz and came to be known as the *Young-Helmholtz* **trichromatic theory.**

Trichromatic theory was widely accepted for a long time, because it provided a plausible explanation for the production of people's color sensations and for color blindness (color-blind people had only one or two kinds of receptors); but other facts and observations were not as well explained. Why did adaptation to one color produce color afterimages that had the complementary hue? Why did color-blind people always fail to distinguish *pairs* of colors: red and green or blue and yellow?

Answers to these questions became the cornerstones for a second theory of color vision proposed by Ewald Hering in the late 1800s. According to his **opponent-process theory,** all color experiences arise from three underlying systems, each of which includes two "opponent" elements: red versus green, blue versus yellow, and black versus white. Hering theorized that colors produced complementary afterimages because one element of the system became fatigued (from overstimulation) and, thus, increased the relative contribution of its opponent element. In Hering's theory, types of color blindness came in pairs because the color system was actually built from pairs of opposites.

For many years scientists argued over which theory was correct. Eventually, it was realized that they were not really in conflict, but described two different stages of processing, corresponding to successive physiological structures in the visual system (Hurvich & Jameson, 1957). We know now that there are, indeed, three types of cones, each of which is most sensitive to light at a different wavelength, and they work very much as predicted by the original Young-Helmholtz trichromatic theory. One type of cone responds most vigorously to short wavelengths of light (seen as blue), a second type to medium wavelengths (seen as green), and a third to long wavelengths (seen as red). These correspond to the three primary colors in the Young-Helmholtz theory. People who are color blind lack one or more of these three types of receptor cones.

The retinal ganglion cells then combine the outputs of these three cone types in different ways, working in accordance with Hering's opponent-process theory (R. De Valois & Jacobs, 1968). Some cells in this system are excited by light that produces sensations of red and are inhibited by light that produces sensations of green. Other cells in the system do the opposite: they are excited by light that looks green and are inhibited by light that looks red. Together, these two types of ganglion cells form the physiological basis of the red/green opponent-process system. Other ganglion cells make up the blue/yellow system and the black/white system, by combining the outputs of the three types of cones in different ways.

Figure 5.13 *Color Afterimages*
Stare at the dot in the center of the green, black, and yellow flag for at least 30 seconds, then fixate on the center of a sheet of white paper or a blank wall.

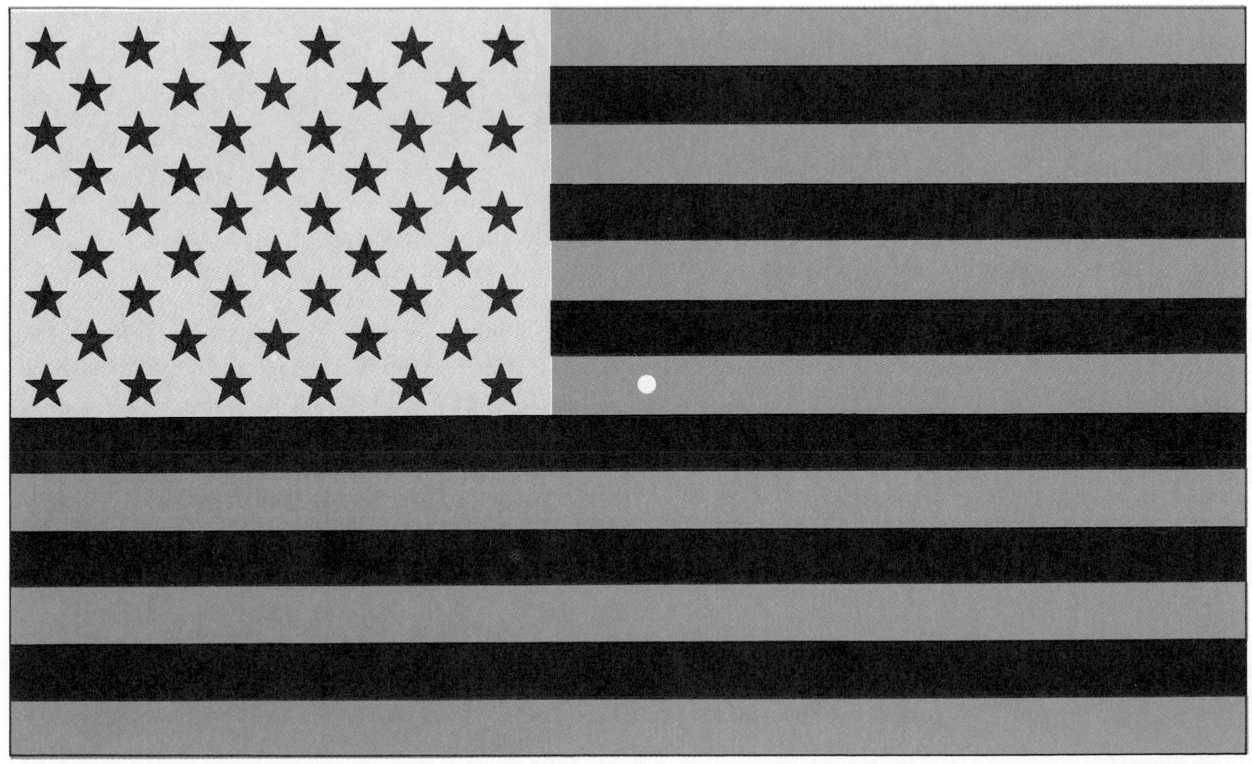

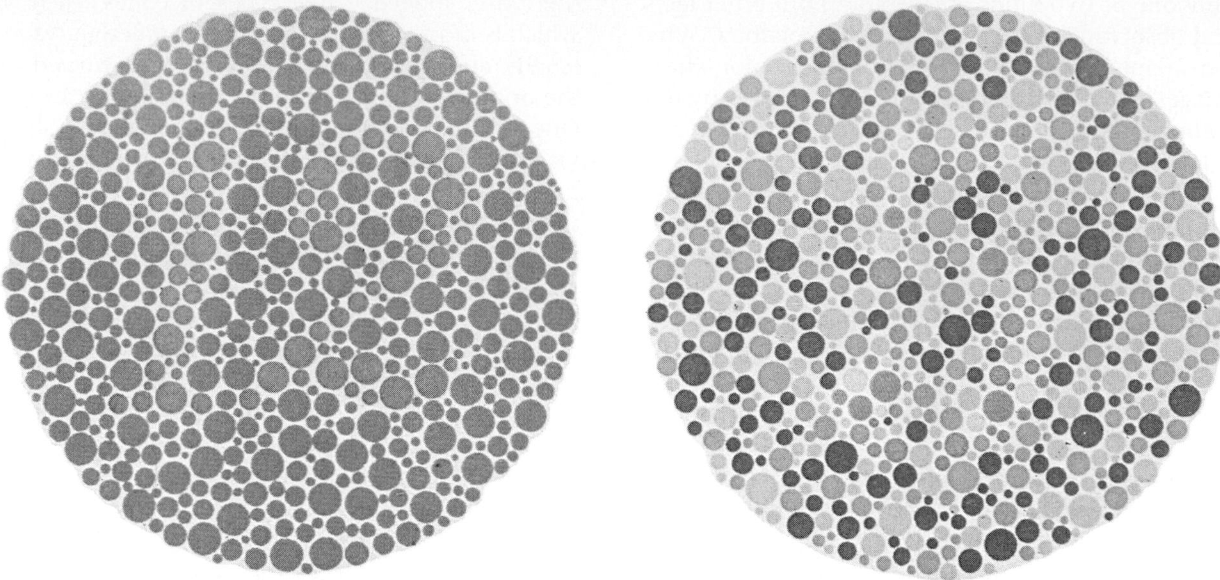

Figure 5.14 *Color-Blindness Tests*
What numbers do you see in these two patterns? Everyone will see 12 in the left one. People with normal color vision will see 5 in the right one, but people with certain types of color blindness will see something different. If you know people who are color blind, find out what they see. (Courtesy of Macmillan Science Co., Inc.)

Molecular Basis of Color Vision

Recent discoveries from genetics and neurobiology laboratories offer a solid, empirical basis for psychological theories about the way color vision functions. We perceive different colors by analyzing the three color inputs from cones that are sensitive to either red, green, or blue light. These cones contain pigments that detect one of these three kinds of light. The colors we see depend on how strongly light entering the eye excites each of these three types of cone cells. Theories and speculation now have been transformed into facts with the isolation and identification of three human genes that specify the three pigments responsible for color vision (Nathans et al., 1986). Using the powerful tools of molecular genetics, researchers have located the genes that direct the development of the three color vision proteins—red, green, and blue.

Other vision researchers have developed a technique for analyzing the electrical activity of a single cone cell from the retinas of macaque monkeys and humans, which are found to be quite similar.

> *Single cone cells are ''sucked up'' into a special hollow glass tube that is less than 1/25th the diameter of a human hair. Light of various wavelengths is shone on the tube and the strength of electrical signals emitted from the cone cell is amplified and measured. Using this technique, the researchers found that some cells were tuned to respond maximally to light wavelengths of 435 nanometers (''blue cells''), others to 535 nm (''green cells''), and a third group of cones were most sensitive to 570 nm (''red cells''). Now researchers are trying to identify the biochemical activities of these cells that are triggered by light and start the process of transduction of external energy into neural energy that underlies our visual sensation. (Baylor, 1987)*

Contrast Effects

In order to perceive different objects in space there must be contrasts in brightness to form boundaries and distinct edges to give objects shape, size, and orientation in space. Imagine what it would be like to live in the world as a partially blind person who saw no differences in brightness and no clear edges on objects. The image on the retina of a partially blind person is actually rather fuzzy and not at all sharp. This is because of some optical blurring caused by the shape of the lens and cornea, and the diffusion of light as it passes through the aqueous humor of the eye. How then does the visual system accentuate the edges between objects to make them stand out clearly? *Contrast* is nature's answer.

A patch of gray appears lighter against a dark background than it does against a light background, as shown in **Figure 5.15.** This *brightness contrast effect* makes the response to a constant stim-

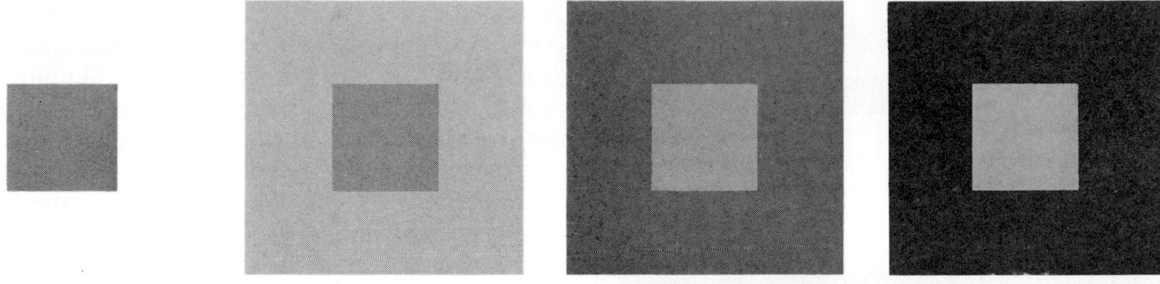

Figure 5.15 *Brightness Contrast*
Four (objectively) identical gray squares on different backgrounds. The lighter the background, the darker the gray squares appear.

ulus greater as the intensity difference between it and its background increases. In the retina adjacent areas are accentuated by this brightness contrast effect, causing perceived boundaries between surfaces to be sharpened. Sometimes there appears to be a distinct band that separates two neighboring patches of light—when, in fact, there is no physical difference between them. This illusion can be seen in **Figure 5.16** where a series of gray strips is arranged from darkest to lightest. Although the intensity of any given strip is uniform (as shown in the graph below it where the light intensity is constant for each strip), it appears as if there is *dark* band at the intersection where one strip borders on a lighter strip, but a *bright* band where it borders on a darker strip. The difference between any adjacent regions is thus accentuated by contrast effects. These bands are known as *Mach bands,* after the physicist, Ernest Mach, who discovered the phenomenon.

Another illusory effect produced by the tendency for edges to define a visual field is seen in the two rectangular surfaces in **Figure 5.17.** The top and bottom figures seem similar because they have dark left sides separated in the center from the lighter right sides. To prove that this perception is accurate, place a pencil down the center of the top figure and note the brightness difference on either side. To prove that your perception of the world can be distorted, lay the pencil down the center band of the lower figure. Voilà, like magic, the difference between the two sides has vanished! There is no contrast! A light meter moved by the researchers across the top figure recorded the sharp change in light intensity at the midpoint; but the bottom figure is shown to have two halves of the same intensity except at the midpoint region where there is a gradual shift toward brighter on the left side and darker on the right. This border imposes a false impression of contrast that spreads across the sides, making a difference where there is none.

Exactly how the visual system processes information from visual scenes to give the perception of spatial properties continues to be debated. Investigators have assumed that the overall process of spatial perception involves several basic stages: first, complex patterns are analyzed into small subunits, with each cell in the visual pathway, from retina to visual cortex, responding only to selected

Figure 5.16 *Accentuation of Contours by Contrast*
(A) The series of gray strips is arranged in ascending brightness, from left to right. Physically, each strip is of uniform light intensity. This is graphically expressed in (B) which plots stimulus position against the physical light intensity, showing a simple series of ascending steps. But this is not what is seen, for the strips do not appear to be uniform. For each strip, the left edge (adjacent to its darker neighbor) looks brighter than the rest, while the right edge (adjacent to the lighter neighbor) looks darker. The explanation is contrast. The edges are closer to their darker or lighter neighbors, and will thus be more subject to contrast than the rest of the strip. The result is an accentuation of the contours that separate one strip from the next. (After Cornsweet, 1970: Coren, Porac, and Ward, 1978)

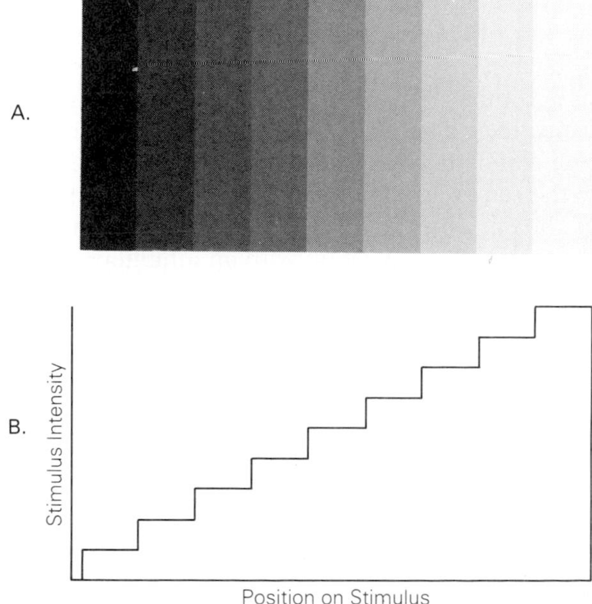

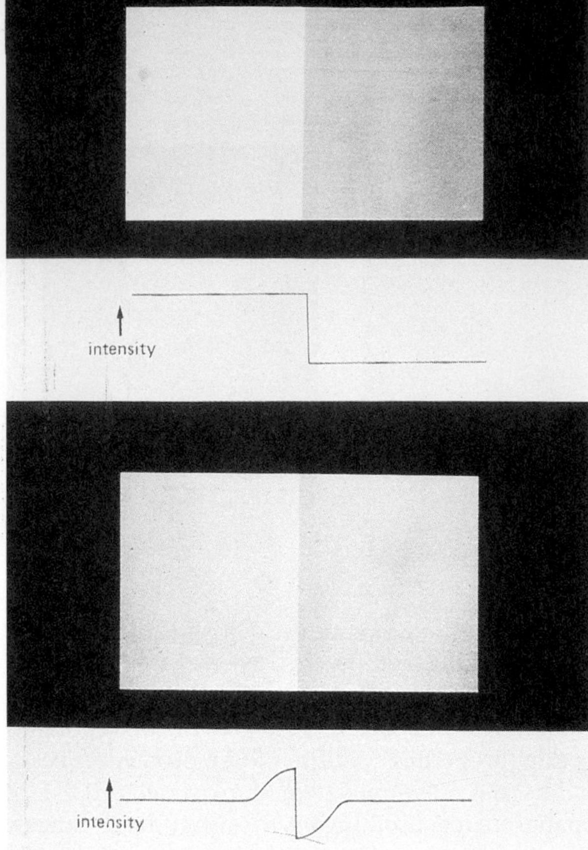

Figure 5.17 *The Illusion of Contour*

aspects of a part of the pattern; then the parts are synthesized back into a complex pattern in the brain. Little is known about the final synthesis stage, but we do know a fair amount about the early stages of analysis.

The Sensory Basis of Contrast

The cells at each level in the visual pathway respond to a particular part of the visual field. Each retinal ganglion cell integrates the information about light patterns coming from many receptor cells. When recordings are made of the electrical activity of single ganglion cells, the firing rate of some areas is changed by the presentation of a visual stimulus. This area is known as the **receptive field.** Receptive fields of retinal ganglion cells are round and of two types: those in which stimulation in the center produces excitation while stimulation in the surrounding part produces inhibition, and the opposite organization with an inhibitory center and an excitatory surround.

Research in sensory physiology reveals that ganglion cells respond to the differences in stimulation coming from their center and the surround. They are most excited by *stimulus contrast;* those with "on" centers fire most strongly to a bright spot surrounded by a dark border, while those with "off" centers fire most vigorously to a dark spot surrounded by a light border. Uniform illumination causes the center and surround to cancel each other's activity: a cell is not as excited by uniform illumination as it is by a spot or bar of light.

Some cells remain "on" as long as a stimulus is present; they are called *X* cells. Others respond strongly at first, then rapidly weaken with continued stimulation—the *Y* cells. These cells are believed to project different kinds of information to the visual centers in the brain. The *Y* cells may be more involved in the analysis of overall visual form, while *X* cells may supply the fine detail necessary for a high degree of visual acuity (Sherman, 1979).

When a receptor cell is stimulated by light it transmits information in two directions: upward to the brain and sideways to neighboring receptor cells. What is sent out to adjacent cells are impulses that *inhibit* their transmission. This sideways suppression of other receptor cells, called **lateral inhibition,** is the basis for the brightness contrast effect we have previously noted. As one receptor is excited by an intense amount of light it inhibits neighboring cells receiving less intense light. This exaggerates the difference between them—generating messages to the brain that there is more contrast than actually exists.

Additional inhibition will cause the retinal ganglion cells responding to the intersections to fire much less strongly than the others, producing the illusion of blurry gray spots. The spots disappear when you look directly at them, because, in the fovea, there are no receptive fields large enough to include parts of the black squares (see Figure 6.4 on p. 191).

The cells in the lateral geniculate nuclei have properties like those of the retinal ganglion cells; however, the cells in the visual cortex do not respond to stimuli that are effective at the lower levels of visual processing. David Hubel and Thorsten Wiesel pioneered the study of these cells in the early 1960s and in 1981 won a Nobel prize for their work. They recorded the firing rates from single cells in the visual cortex of cats in response to moving spots and bars in the visual field.

When Hubel and Wiesel mapped out the receptive fields of these cortical cells, they found both excitatory and inhibitory regions, as in the case of the retinal ganglion cells, but the receptive fields of the cortical cells were almost always elongated rather than round. As a result, these cells were strongly excited (or inhibited) by bars of light or by edges in their favorite orientation (Hubel & Wiesel, 1962, 1979). Because these cortical cells were simply and directly related to specific receptive fields, Hubel and Wiesel called them *simple cells.* Their output, in turn, is processed by other, even more complex types of cortical cells (see **Figure 5.18**).

Feature-Detection Neurons

When the electrical activity of single cells in the visual cortex was recorded in response to stimulation of different types, a surprising discovery emerged. Some cells responded to lines, others to edges; some responded to particular positions or orientations of a stimulus, others to particular shapes, still others to movement in a particular direction. Within their receptive fields these cortical cells did not respond to diffuse-light stimuli, only to patterns of specific shapes and angles of orientation.

One way to think about this finding is that the brain is designed to extract certain kinds of simple features from the complex stimuli that bombard the visual system. Lines, edges, angles, and corners are the effective stimuli for cortical cells. Thus, the visual cortex might respond to a triangle with *simple* cortical cells detecting the sides, some being "horizontal line" detectors, others being "straight line at 60 degrees" detectors. More *complex* cortical cells might detect "60 degree" corners. This separate information would then become combined as the stimulus that would activate a "triangle" detector somewhere in a higher level of brain processing.

Hubel and Wiesel (1962, 1979), in their research on the specialized feature-detecting properties of cortical cells (in the cat), called these cells **feature detectors** because they responded when specific patterns were present in their receptive fields. Each feature detector cell was assumed to abstract a particular aspect of a total pattern of stimulation to which it was specifically sensitive.

Based on this research, a hierarchical model of the visual system was proposed, in which cells at each of several levels were assumed to detect different features of the visual stimulus. This is called the **feature-detection model.** It suggests that individual feature-detector cells at every level successively analyze a visual pattern, each adding its input; all this information is then synthesized to form a total unit, enabling a viewer to recognize any known form.

The appealing simplicity of this model that shows the way the visual cortex analyzes and then synthesizes stimulus patterns is less widely accepted currently because of theoretical and empirical challenges to it. One challenge suggests that recognizing just one object like your grandmother, apple pie, or the American flag requires a huge number of cells, and processing separate features in successive stages takes too long. Another criticism of the feature-detection model of vision notes that the nature of any detector depends on the way it is identified experimentally. If a cell responds to a bar of light moving at a given angle, it is defined as a detector of that line orientation, in other words, its identity is defined solely in terms of its response to a single test situation. But maybe the cell would

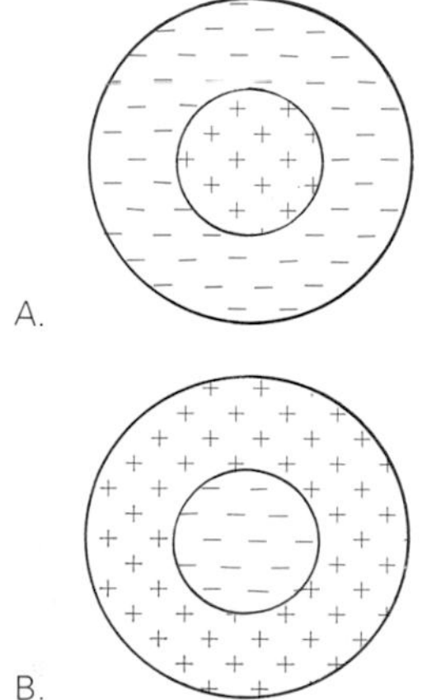

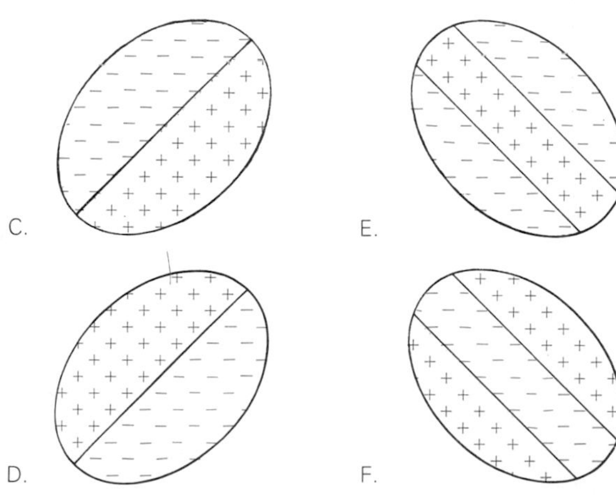

Figure 5.18 *Receptive Fields of Ganglion and Cortical Cells*
The receptive field of a cell is the area in the visual field from which it receives stimulation. The receptive fields of the ganglion cells in the retina are circular (a, b); those of the simplest cells in the visual cortex are elongated in a particular orientation (c, d, e, f). In both cases the cell responding to the receptive field is excited by light in the regions marked by pluses (+), while it is inhibited by light in the regions marked by minuses (−).

also have detected double lines or squiggly lines if the researcher had presented them, and not just the single feature. You can test this hypothesis yourself. Just pour a glass of water on a friend's head. If your friend screams, then you have discovered a "water detector." (See Levine & Shefner, 1981, for cogent criticisms. See also "The Instinct to Learn" in *The Best of Science.*)

The Spatial-Frequency Model of Visual Images

It has recently been discovered that most cortical cells are even more sensitive to successive, contrasting *bands of dark and light* than to simple bars of the same contrast. This research by Russell and Karen De Valois (1980) has formed part of the argument for a competing model of the way patterns and shapes are perceived. This **spatial-frequency model** suggests that our nervous system "thinks about" visual scenes by transforming visual images into an alternate representation that is mathematically equivalent to describing them in terms of light and dark. Any image that is composed of patterns of dark-light variations can be analyzed according to the number of its dark-light cycles over a given distance of visual space—known as its **spatial frequency,** (see **Figure 5.19**). These spatial frequencies can be analyzed mathematically by a procedure called *Fourier analysis;* they will yield a measure of the sensitivity of the visual system (Campbell & Robson; 1968).

Research evidence suggests that the human visual system may analyze visual scenes by actually performing some kind of Fourier analysis on the patterns of light-dark cycles it detects (Blakemore & Campbell, 1969). It is hypothesized that sets of cortical cells are organized into *channels* that are tuned to respond to different spatial frequencies. Some channels, specific to low frequencies, pick up blobs of light, others detect high frequencies, picking out fine details, while others are specific for frequencies in between. Together, they provide all the information needed to represent a visual scene by combining the range of spatial frequencies that define its light-dark pattern. Any two-dimensional pattern—from an American flag to a photograph of Groucho Marx—can be analyzed mathematically and broken down into computer codes as the sum of its many spatial frequencies (measured as *sine-wave gratings,* alternating light-dark stripes. See **Figure 5.20.** The low spatial frequencies are responsible for the overall shape (the "blurry" picture); the high spatial frequencies are responsible

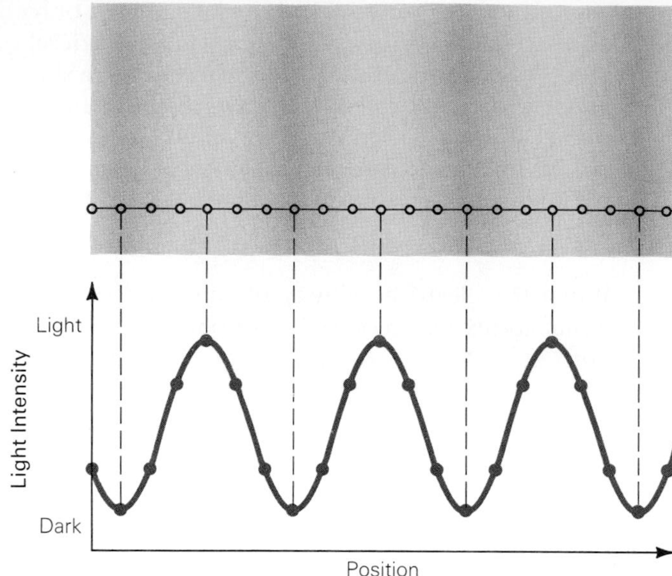

Figure 5.19 *Spatial Frequency Gratings*
The light intensity of the black and white stripes in a grating pattern is shown as cycles in a wave pattern. Spatial frequency is measured from peak to peak, reflecting the width of the stripes. Contrast is measured by the height of the wave from peak to valley, reflecting the brightness difference between the stripes. The length of these waves across visual space has no relation to the wavelength of the incoming photons of light discussed in the previous section on color vision. (From Levine & Shefner, 1981.)

for the sharp-edges and fine detail (the "outline" picture). As remarkable as is this technical achievement, consider that your visual system is doing it better, faster, and more reliably than the most powerful electronic technology.

Time, Motion, and Experience

The visual stimulation that gives us information about the world is constantly moving and changing over time as it falls on our retinas—and fortunately so. It turns out that changes in stimulation over time and space are essential for visual sensation to occur at all. Also essential is normal visual experience in the early life of an organism. When deprived of certain kinds of stimulation during infancy, the visual system is altered in abnormal ways.

Sensory Adaptation

After a period of unchanged stimulation visual receptor cells tend to lose their power to respond. This is called **sensory adaptation,** a phenomenon that occurs in other sensory modalities as well.

Figure 5.20 *High and Low Spatial Frequencies*
Detection of only the low spatial frequencies would give us the blurry view in B. Detection of only the high spatial frequencies would give us the outline view in C. Normal detection of all frequencies gives us the full view in A. (From Frisby, 1980.)

After prolonged exposure, colors seem to lose their intensity and tend to look gray; warm water feels less warm after a time; an odor that is noticeable when you enter a room soon seems to disappear; ticking clocks become silent, and rock music becomes bearable.

In chapter 4, we saw that organisms *habituate*—they stop responding physically to familiar stimuli that are no longer providing novel information. Sensory adaptation may be another part of their ability to ignore stimuli with reduced informational value, thereby freeing more processing capacity to attend to new stimuli that may have more significance.

A different type of adaptation—to darkness—results in an increased sensitivity to low levels of light. For example, you may have noticed that when you first go out of a brightly lit house on a dark, moonless night, you see very few stars; then, as you watch, the sky begins to fill with more and more stars. The reason for this is not that the stars get brighter, but that your eyes get more sensitive to the light that is already there. This process is called **dark adaptation;** the same process occurs when your eyes "adjust to the dark" in a movie theater.

Psychologists have studied dark adaptation by measuring subjects' absolute thresholds for light after different lengths of time in the dark. Two distinct phases occur: (a) the first ends when the curve levels off at an intermediate level of sensitivity after about 10 minutes; (b) in the second, the curve continues downward, leveling off about 20 minutes later at a point of much greater sensitivity. Try to figure out what is happening in the photoreceptor cells of the retina to produce this two-part reaction before you read the caption for **Figure 5.21.**

Did Anything Move?

Both frogs and rabbits need mechanisms for efficiently detecting motion in their visual world—frogs to catch bugs for food and rabbits to run swiftly from predators. Researchers have found that each of them has developed specialized retinal

Figure 5.21 *Dark Adaptation*
Changes in absolute threshold over a 30-minute period in darkness show this two-phase curve because rods and cones adapt at different rates and to different levels of sensitivity. Cone adaptation is rapid, but the threshold of cones never drops as far as the threshold for rods. When the cone adaptation curve is combined with the rod adaptation curve, the overall dark adaptation curve results.

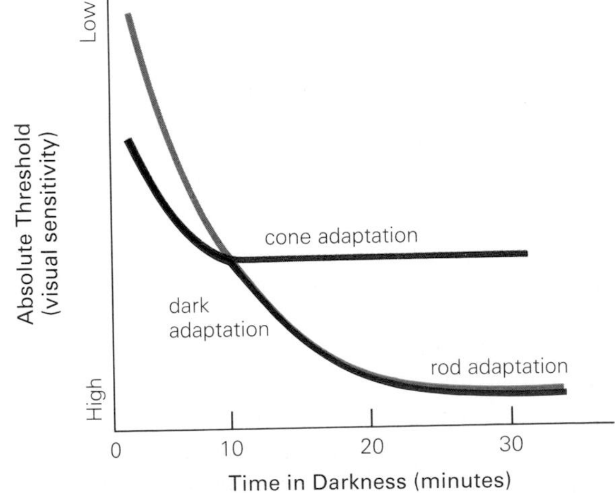

ganglion cells so that they can survive. Frogs have detectors that respond to the movement of small, dark objects into the receptor field. These *net convexity detectors* are nicknamed "bug detectors" since their activation may indicate the location of a tasty insect flying by (Lettvin et al., 1959). Rabbits have been found to have ganglion cells that respond selectively to the direction and speed of an image in motion (Barlow et al., 1964). Faster responses to these situational cues are accomplished by having this type of information processed at the retinal level rather than at the slower, more extensive level of the cortex.

Your visual system can detect only intermediate rates of continuous motion; you do not see very fast or very slow motion. If a light moves very slowly—as the moon does across the sky—you do not experience its motion; you notice, only after a time, that its position has changed. On the other hand, if a light moves too fast, you no longer see the spot, but instead experience a solid, motionless bar.

The most common neural theory to explain perception of motion states that the visual system contains *motion-detector neurons.* Recordings from single cells in the cortex of cats and monkeys have shown that there are indeed neurons sensitive to motion in a specific direction.

If there are special motion-detector cells, there should be negative aftereffects following prolonged viewing of moving stimuli. Sensory adaptation to motion produces negative aftereffects comparable to those you saw with color, where you looked at the green, black, and yellow flag and later saw a red, white, and blue afterimage. When receptors for motion in one direction are fatigued, your visual system gives you sensations of motion in the opposite direction from unmoving stimuli. A well-known example of this is the waterfall illusion: after staring at a waterfall for a time, people experience a rising motion when they look at stationary objects. The same thing occurs in the laboratory when a grating pattern is moved in one direction on a TV screen while an observer fixates on an unmoving point in the center of the screen. If the grating is stopped after a minute or more of adaptation, the observer sees the stripes drifting steadily in the opposite direction.

Yet motion-detector cells cannot be the whole explanation for our perception of motion. As we will see in the next chapter, experiencing motion is not simply a sensory process but also a perceptual one, in which brain processes interpret, and sometimes override, the incoming sensory information.

Effects of Deprivation

Is the ability of cortical cells to respond to selected features of the environment innate or learned? It appears that the most reasonable answer is, "Both." When newborn kittens and monkeys are deprived of any visual experience at all from birth, the cortical cells of these visually naive animals have the same properties as those of adult animals (Hubel & Wiesel, 1974). So it appears that the initial properties of the cells in the visual cortex are innately determined.

However, if the visual experience of a very young animal is *altered,* then these cortical properties are affected. The "plasticity" of these cells, when given abnormal visual input, has been proved in many studies. If a kitten receives stimulation to only one of its eyes at a time, by alternately depriving the other eye of stimulation every day for 6 months, it loses the ability to respond to normal binocular stimulation (Blake & Hirsch, 1975). As shown in **Figure 5.22,** receptor cells that have received only stimulation of a specific, limited kind, such as exposure to horizontal versus vertical lines, to stripes moving in only one direction, or to visual experience consisting of a succession of still images (stroboscopic illumination that eliminates movement), "learn" to respond only to that abnormal

Figure 5.22
A kitten is wearing training goggles similar to those used by Hirsch and Spinelli (1971). The horizontal and vertical stripes on the outside of the goggles are for identification purposes only; the actual stimuli are contained inside the goggles and are illuminated by transparent openings at the sides (out of which the kitten cannot see). The cardboard cone prevents the kitten from dislodging the goggles. (From Carlson, N.R. Physiology of Behavior, *3rd ed. Boston: Allyn and Bacon, 1986.)*

type of visual input (Cynader & Chernenko, 1976; Daw & Wyatt, 1976; Hirsch & Spinelli, 1970). The body of research on the effects of sensory deprivation clearly suggests that there is a *critical period* during which a maturing animal must receive normal visual experiences in order for its brain to develop normally.

Hearing

Like vision, **audition** (hearing) provides us with reliable spatial information over extended distances. In fact, it may be even more important than vision to orient us toward distant events. We often hear things before we see them, particularly if they take place behind us or on the other side of opaque objects like walls. Although vision is better for identifying an object once it is in our field of view, we often see it only because we have used our ears to point our eyes in the right direction.

Hearing also plays an important role in the understanding of spoken language; it is the principal sensory modality for human communication. People who lack the capacity to hear are excluded from much normal human interaction and may suffer psychological problems associated with feelings of frustration, rejection, and isolation as a result. Blindness is so obvious to others that they make adjustments for it; deafness often is not and sometimes goes unrecognized (even by the individual who is experiencing it if the onset is gradual). Depression and paranoid disorders may accompany undetected loss of hearing (Post, 1980; Zimbardo, et al., 1981).

The Physics of Sound

Clap your hands together. Whistle. Tap your pencil on the table. All these actions create sounds, but why? The reason is that they cause objects to vibrate. The vibrating objects then transmit vibrational energy to the surrounding medium, usually air, by pushing their molecules back and forth. These slight changes in air pressure spread outward from the vibrating objects as sound waves traveling at a rate of about 1100 feet per second. Sound cannot be created in a true vacuum (like outer space) because there are no molecules for vibrating objects to move.

Air pressure changes—changes in the density of air molecules in space—travel in *waves,* as shown in **Figure 5.23.** These particular waves are called *sine waves;* sounds produced by a single sine wave are called **pure tones.**

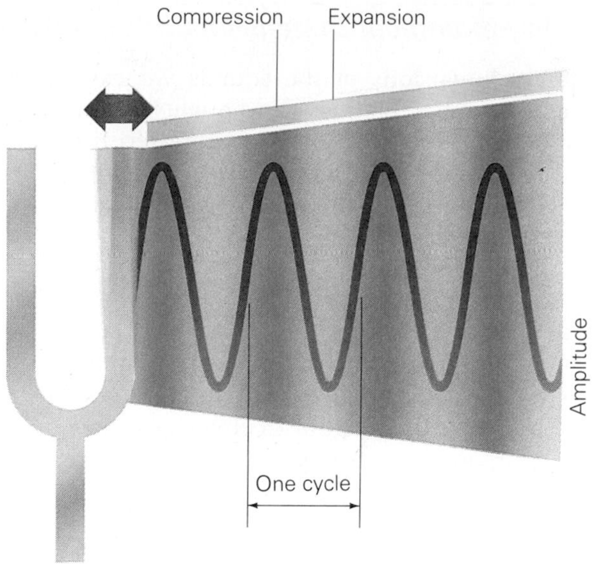

Figure 5.23 *Sound Waves*

A sine wave has two basic physical properties that determine how it sounds to us: its frequency and its amplitude. **Frequency** measures the number of cycles the wave completes in a given amount of time. One cycle, as indicated in Figure 5.23, is the left-to-right distance from a point in one wave to the same point in the next wave. Sound frequency is usually expressed in *cycles per second (cps)* or **Hertz (Hz).** The physical property of *frequency* determines the psychological property of **pitch:** high frequencies lead to experiences of high sounds, low frequencies to experiences of low ones.

Amplitude measures the physical property of a sound wave's *strength,* as shown in its peak-to-valley height. *Amplitude* is defined in units of sound pressure or energy. The amplitude of a tone determines its perceived *loudness:* sound waves with large amplitudes are experienced as loud; those with small amplitudes as soft.

A pure tone, such as one produced by a tuning fork, has only one frequency and one amplitude. Most sounds in the real world, however, are not pure tones, but are produced by complex waves containing a combination of frequencies and amplitudes. The differing qualities of the sounds we hear (clarinet versus piano, for example) are because of these differing combinations of frequencies and amplitudes.

Psychological Dimensions of Sound

Three dimensions of the sounds we experience, then, are pitch, loudness, and quality. Though you already know a bit about the characteristics of the sound waves that produce these experiences, we need to take a closer look at the way we sense these physical qualities.

Pitch

Paralleling the physical dimension of sound frequency from low to high is the experience of low to high pitches. The full range of human sensitivity to pure tones extends from frequencies as low as 20 Hz to frequencies as high as 20,000 Hz. (Frequencies below 20 Hz may be experienced through touch as vibrations rather than as sound.) Out of the full range of frequencies to which we are sensitive, the corresponding notes on a piano cover the interval only from about 30 Hz to 4000.

The psychophysical relationship between pitch and frequency is not a linear one: at the low end increasing the frequency by just a few cycles per second raises the pitch quite noticeably, but at the high end a much bigger increase is needed to hear the difference in pitch. To illustrate, the two lowest notes on a piano differ by only 1.6 Hz, whereas the two highest ones differ by 235 Hz—more than 140 times greater. This relationship between pitch and sound frequency is a case in which Fechner's logarithmic law holds.

Loudness

The human auditory system is sensitive to an enormous range of physical intensities. At absolute threshold, the auditory system is sensitive enough to hear the tick of a wristwatch at 20 feet; if it were much more sensitive, we would hear the blood flowing in our ears. At the other extreme, a jet airliner taking off from as far away as 100 yards is so loud that it is painful. In fact, the jet produces a sound wave with more than a billion times the energy of the ticking watch, in terms of physical units of sound pressure.

Because the range of hearing is so great, physical intensities are usually expressed in units called *decibels (dB)* that are logarithms of *ratios* rather than absolute amounts. **Figure 5.24** shows the loudness of some representative natural sounds in decibel units, with the corresponding sound pressures shown for comparison. Notice that sounds louder than about 90 dB can produce hearing loss, depending on how long you are exposed to them. (See ***Close-up:*** *Noise Pollution and Hearing Loss,* on p. 169.)

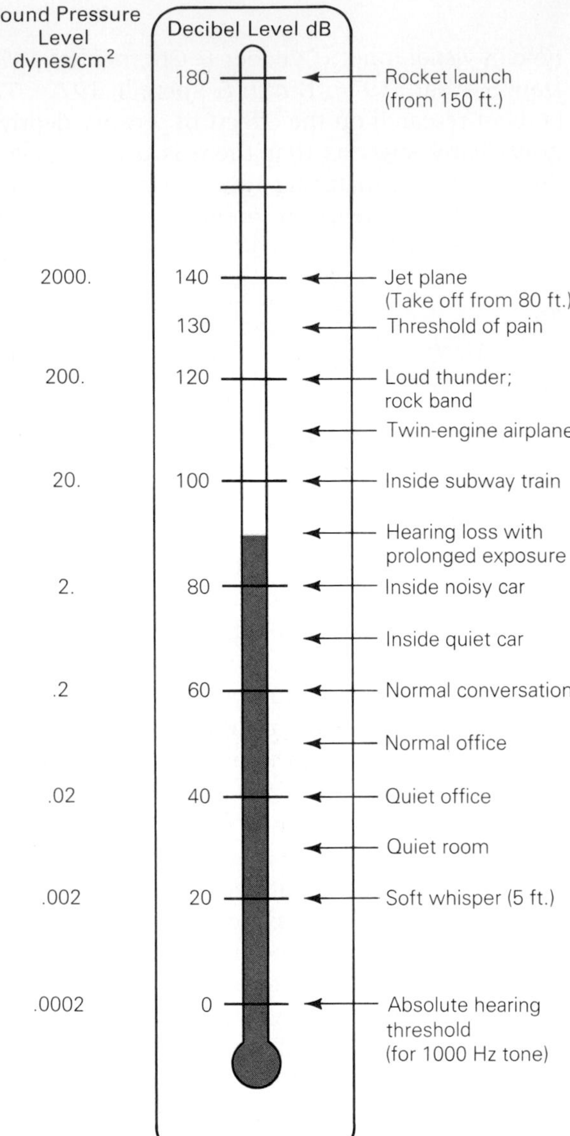

Figure 5.24 *Loudness of Familiar Sounds*

Timbre

Quality, the third dimension of auditory sensation, is called **timbre.** The timbre of a sound reflects the complexity of its sound wave. **Figure 5.25** on page 170 shows the complex waveforms that correspond to several familiar sounds. A complex sound can be analyzed as a sum of many different pure tones with different amplitudes and frequencies. The graph in the figure shows the **sound spectrum** for middle C on a piano—a graph of all the frequencies actually present and their amplitudes.

In a complex tone such as this, the lowest frequency (about 256 Hz) is responsible for the pitch we hear; it is called the *fundamental.* The higher frequencies are called *harmonics* or *overtones,* and

Close-up Noise Pollution and Hearing Loss

The typical urban environment is a very noisy place. Street traffic, jackhammers, jet planes, and even standard household appliances like dishwashers, radios, and telephones all contribute to the high level of noise pollution in our lives. Most of us are so used to it that we hardly give it a second thought. Perhaps we should, though, because prolonged exposure to very intense sounds can produce permanent hearing loss.

How high the intensity must be to impair hearing depends, to a large extent, on how long the exposure lasts. A sudden explosion at 200 decibels can cause massive damage in a fraction of a second; however, routine exposure to sounds less than 100 decibels can also cause significant hearing loss. Hearing loss from loud sounds is called *stimulation deafness.* Most people report such hearing loss for up to several hours after listening to a rock concert in an enclosed area. Not surprisingly, then, more permanent hearing loss is an occupational hazard for rock musicians, because they are exposed to such intense sound levels so frequently. It also occurs in many other occupations where people are exposed to loud noises for extended periods.

> *Stimulation deafness was studied in women who worked in a weaving mill where they were exposed to noises of 98 decibels for eight hours a day, five days a week. Hearing loss was measured by the rise in their absolute thresholds for sounds. For those who had worked in the mill for ten years or longer, the average absolute threshold was 35 decibels higher than for the new employees. (Taylor et al., 1965)*

With this much hearing loss you would not be able to hear people whispering just five feet away in a quiet room; you would just see their lips moving soundlessly.

The main damage caused by prolonged exposure to loud noise is to the sensitive hair cells that convert the motion of the basilar membrane into neural impulses (p. 170). When these hair cells are damaged, they do not regenerate, and they are so tiny and so inaccessible that surgery is out of the question. Damage to them is permanent.

Hearing loss because of loud noise is greatest in the high frequencies (at or above 4000 cycles per second). In fact, all people in our noisy society experience progressive loss of sensitivity to high frequencies

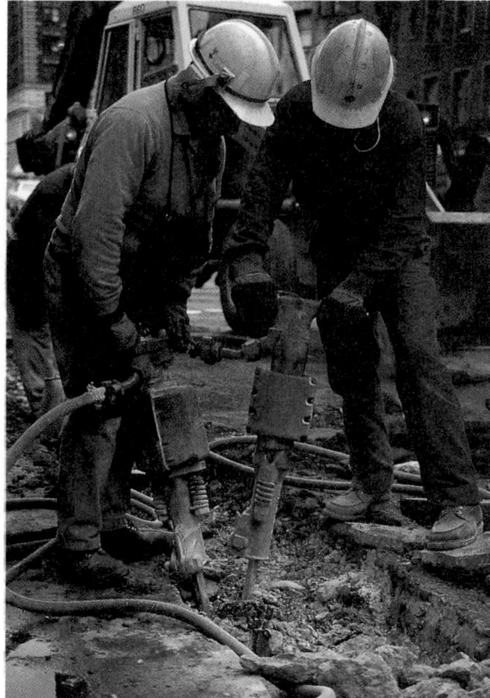

with age. It is not known whether the loss is due, partly, to the aging process itself or entirely to the cumulative effect of a lifetime's exposure to environmental noise. In any case, it is a good idea to avoid even brief exposure to excessively loud noise or prolonged exposure to moderately loud noise. If you must be exposed, wear earplugs or some other protective device.

are simple multiples of the fundamental. The complete *sound* we hear is produced by the total effect of *all* the frequencies shown in the spectrum. If pure tones at these frequencies and intensities were all added together, the result would sound the same to us as middle C on a piano. Amazingly, the human ear actually analyzes complex waves into these component waves.

The sounds that we call *noise* do not have the clear, simple structures of fundamental frequencies plus harmonics. Noise contains many frequencies that are not systematically related to each other. For instance, the static noise you hear between radio stations contains energy at all audible frequencies; you hear it as having no pitch because it has no fundamental frequency.

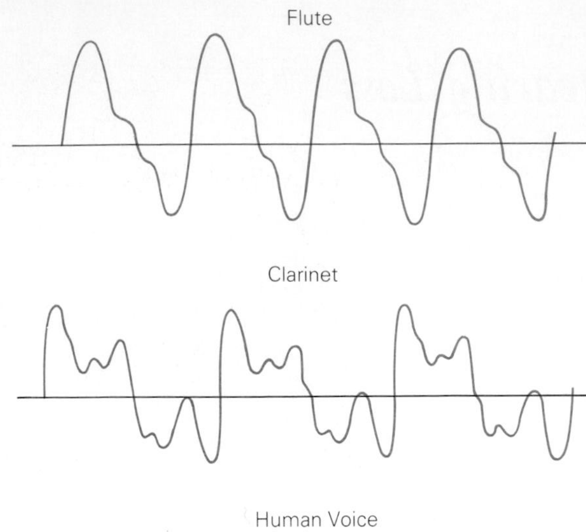

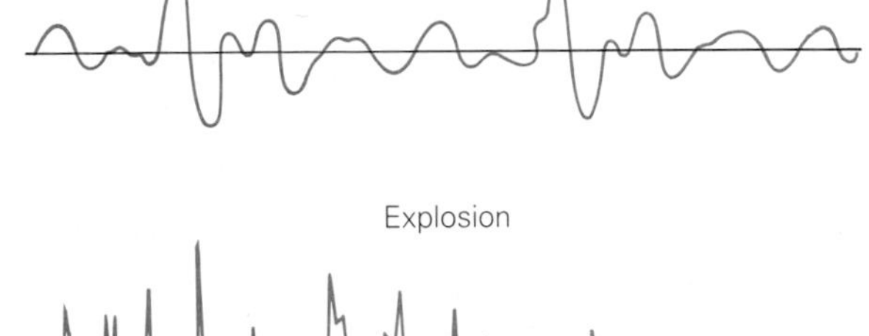

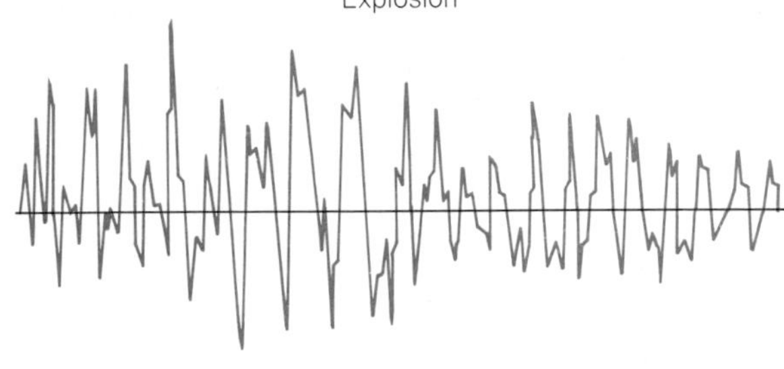

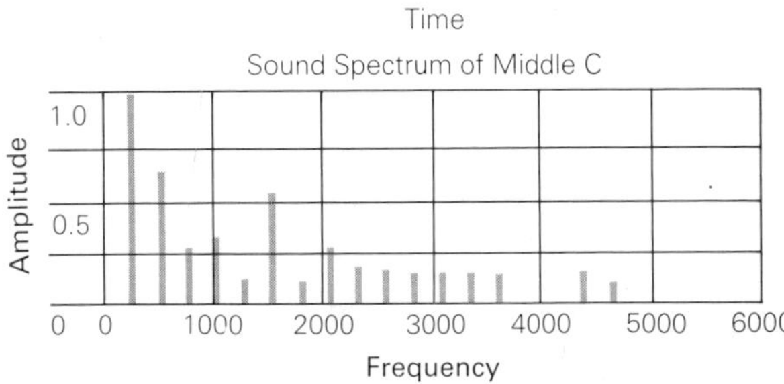

Figure 5.25 *Waveforms of Familiar Sounds*
Below the complex waveforms of five familiar sounds is the sound spectrum for middle C on the piano. The basic wavelength is produced by the fundamental, in this case at 256 cycles, but the strings are also vibrating at several higher frequencies, which produce the jaggedness of the wave pattern. These additional frequencies are identified in the sound spectrum. (Adapted from Boring, et al., 1948, and Fletcher, 1929.)

The Physiology of Hearing

Now that we know something about our psychological experiences of sound and how they correspond psychophysically to a stimulus, let's see how those experiences might arise from physiological activity in the auditory system. First we will look at the way the ear works; then we will consider some theories about how pitch experiences are coded in the auditory system.

The Auditory System

The first thing that must happen for us to hear a sound is that is must get into our ears (see **Figure 5.26**). Some sound enters the external canal directly and some after being reflected off the external ear, or *pinna.* At the inner end of the canal, the sound wave encounters a thin membrane called the *eardrum* or **tympanic membrane,** which is set into motion by the pressure variations of the sound wave.

The eardrum separates the outer ear from the *middle ear,* a chamber in the skull that contains three bones called the *hammer,* the *anvil,* and the *stirrup.* These bones form a mechanical chain that transmits and concentrates vibrations from the eardrum to the primary organ of hearing, the **cochlea,** which is located in the inner ear.

The cochlea is a complex and amazing organ. It is basically a fluid-filled, coiled tube with a membrane, known as the **basilar membrane,** running down the middle along its length. Fluid inside the cochlea is set into wave motion when the footplate of the stirrup vibrates against the **oval window** at the base of the cochlea. This fluid wave travels down the length of the coiled tube, around the end, and back to the base on the other side of the basilar membrane, where it is absorbed by the **round window.** As the fluid moves, it causes the basilar membrane to move in a wavelike motion; this motion bends the tiny *hair cells* connected to it. These hair cells ultimately change the mechanical vibrations of the basilar membrane into neural activity by stimulating nerve endings as they bend.

Nerve impulses leave the cochlea in a bundle of fibers called the **auditory nerve.** These fibers synapse in the *cochlear nucleus* of the brain stem, from which about 60 percent of the input crosses to the opposite side of the brain, the rest remaining on the same side. Auditory signals pass through a series of other nuclei on their way to the **auditory cortex** in the temporal lobes of the cerebral hemispheres.

In cases of deafness, some part of this pathway is impaired, and messages about pitch or loudness—

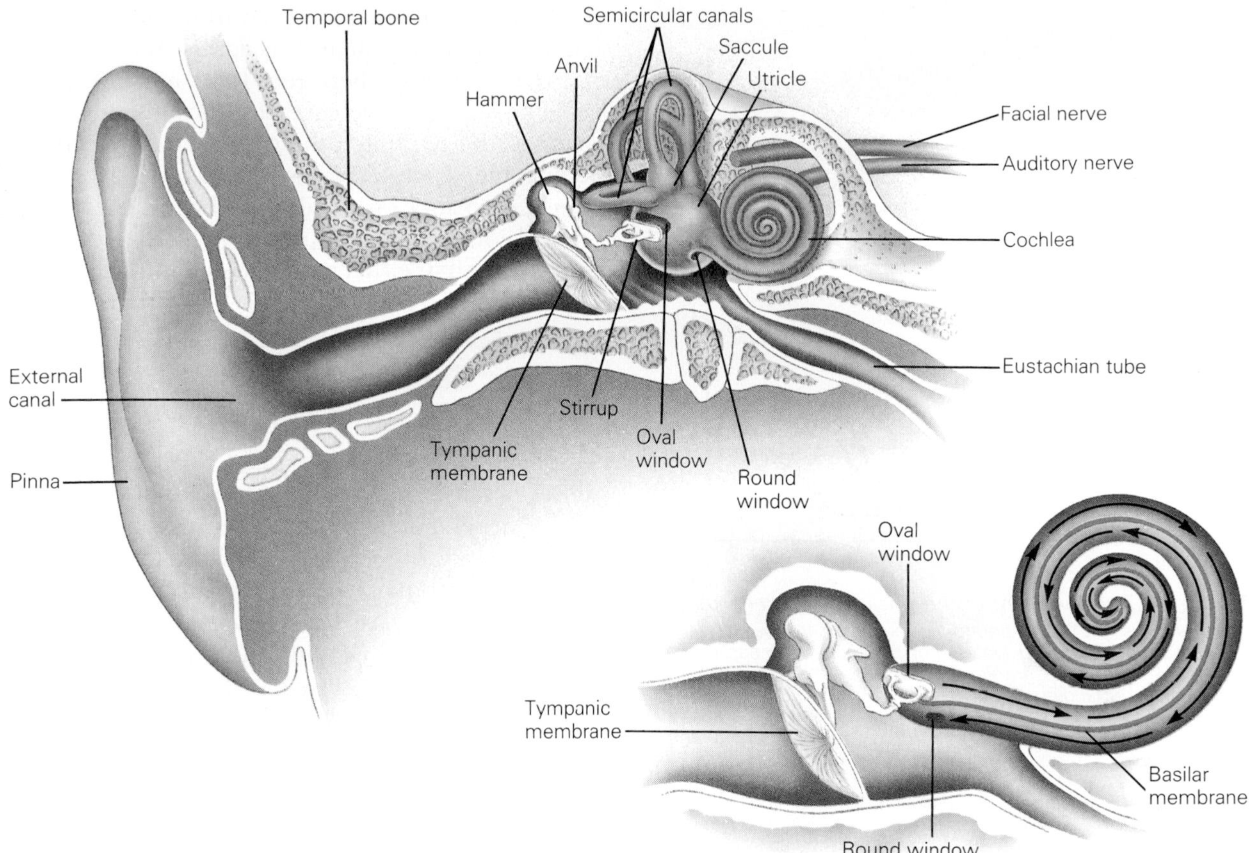

Figure 5.26 *Structure of the Human Ear*

or any sound at all—do not reach the brain. A remarkable device being developed to combat deafness is the "bionic ear." A removable microphone positioned behind the ear fits into an implanted plug that has wires leading into the cochlea. Messages picked up by the microphone are conveyed to a microprocessor (worn on a person's belt) which turns the sound waves into electrical signals. They are then transmitted to the plug and thence into the cochlea, which responds to the electrical signals and sends them on to the cortex. It is hoped that some people who do not benefit from hearing aids will eventually be helped by this new bionic ear, but much work must still be done to perfect it.

Theories of Pitch Perception

To explain how the auditory system converts sound waves into sensations of pitch, two quite distinct theories have been proposed: place theory and frequency theory. The first proposes that pitch perception depends on the part of the receptor that is stimulated; the second emphasizes how often the neural responses are triggered.

Place theory was initially proposed by Hermann von Helmholtz in the 1800s and was later modified, elaborated, and tested by George von Békésy, who won a Nobel prize for this work in 1961. **Place theory** states that different frequencies produce most activation at particular locations along the basilar membrane, with the result that pitch can be coded by the place where greatest activation occurs. The basilar membrane responds to sounds by moving in a traveling wave, as shown in **Figure 5.27.** For high-frequency tones, the wave motion of the basilar membrane is greatest at the base of the cochlea—the large end where the oval and round windows are located. For low-frequency tones, the wave motion of the basilar membrane is greatest at the opposite end. Thus the location of greatest movement *could* be the code for pitch.

The second theory, **frequency theory,** explains pitch by the *timing* of neural responses. It hypothesizes that neurons fire only at a certain phase in each cycle of the sine wave, perhaps at the peaks, so that their firing rate would be determined by a tone's frequency. This rate of firing would be

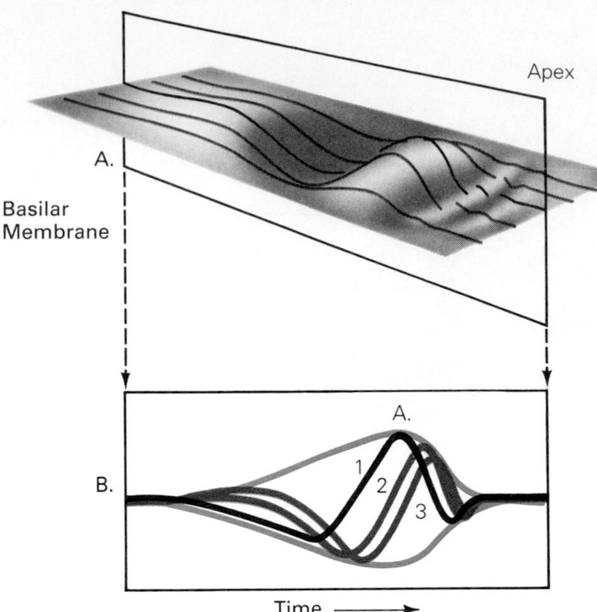

Figure 5.27 *Movement of the Basilar Membrane*
Part A shows the way a sound wave moves the basilar membrane in a traveling wave. (For simplicity, the basilar membrane has been "unrolled" from its coiled shape and shown as a rectangle.) In Part B, the same motion is shown in three "snapshots". The curve labeled 1 depicts the basilar membrane in the position shown in A. Later positions of the membrane are shown by the lighter lines labeled 2 and 3. The blue lines show the whole region taken up by the motion of the membrane—its "overall envelope" of motion. (A from G. L. Rasmussen and W. F. Windle, Eds., Neural mechanisms of the auditory and vestibular systems, *1960. Courtesy of Charles C. Thomas, Publisher, Springfield, Illinois. B and C based on Goldstein, 1980.)*

the code for pitch. An extension of frequency theory, called the **volley principle,** explains what might happen when the peaks in a sound wave come too rapidly for any single neuron to fire at each peak: as shown in **Figure 5.28** several neurons as a *group* could fire at the frequency of the stimulus tone (Wever, 1949).

As with the trichromatic and opponent-process theories of color vision, the place and frequency theories of pitch perception were long thought to be in direct conflict. More recently it has become clear that both are correct, with each working only for a portion of the audible frequency range. On the one hand, frequency mechanisms seem to account well for coding frequencies *below* about 5000 Hz; at higher frequencies neurons cannot fire quickly and precisely enough to code a signal adequately, even in volleys. On the other hand, place theory accounts well for our perception of pitch at frequencies *above* 1000 Hz: below that the motion of the basilar membrane is too broad to provide an adaquate signal to the neural receptors. Both mechanisms can operate between 1000 and 5000 Hz.

So again, as in the case of the competing color theories, the two pitch theories have proven to be compatible. Each explains part of the puzzle. A complex sensory task is divided between two systems, allowing greater precision in the resulting experience than either system could provide alone.

Other Senses

Vision and hearing have been the most-studied senses because they are the most important to us; but we depend on many other senses too, in which different kinds of receptors enable us to code stimulus input for flavors, odors, pressure, gravity, and temperature. We use them every day in eating, sleeping, working, playing, and keeping out of harm's way. We will close our discussion of sensation with a brief analysis of the chemical senses, the body senses, and sensitivity to pain. (See Table 5.1, p. 145, to review the stimuli and receptors of the human senses.)

The Chemical Senses

We have two senses that respond to the chemical properties of substances: taste, or **gustation,** and smell, or **olfaction.** These senses presumably evolved together as a system for seeking and sampling food. Taste is an "immediate" sense because

Figure 5.28 *The Volley Principle*
The total collective activity of auditory (black) nerve cells has a pattern that corresponds to the input sound wave (red), even though each individual fiber (blue) may not be firing fast enough to follow the sound wave pattern. (After Wever, 1949)

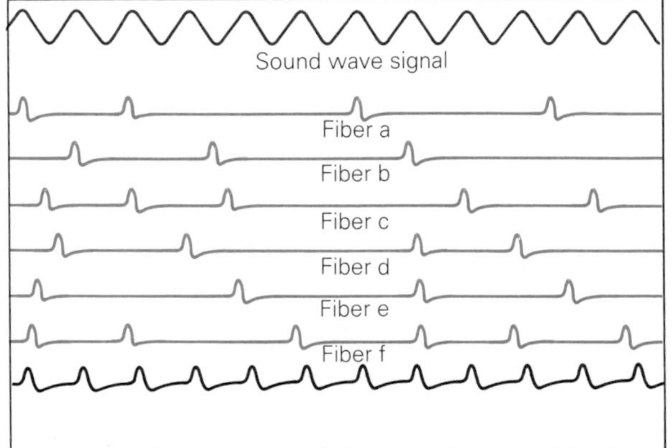

it operates only when a substance is in direct physical contact with the tongue and mouth. Smell is a "distance" sense for food—extracting chemical information from the air so that the organism can seek food in the right direction (Moncrieff, 1951).

Taste and smell work together closely when food is actually being eaten; in fact, the food you eat when you have a cold seems tasteless because the nasal passages are blocked so that you can't smell it. Demonstrate this principle for yourself; hold your nose and try to tell the difference between foods of similar texture but different tastes, such as pieces of apple and raw potato, or beef, pork, and lamb. Without your sense of smell to help you, it isn't easy.

Taste

There are at least four primary taste qualities: sweet, sour, bitter, and saline (salty). These are thought to define your taste space (analogous to color space), in which the primary tastes are positioned at the corners of a prism (as shown in **Figure 5.29**), and various taste combinations lie within its boundaries (Henning, 1916). There may also be a fifth primary taste, alkaline, but further research is needed to establish this with certainty (Shiffman & Erickson, 1971).

The receptors for taste are in the **taste buds,** sensory cells embedded in tiny structures called *papillae,* which are distributed in the mouth cavity, particularly on the upper side of the tongue, as shown in **Figure 5.30.** Sensitivity to sweetness is greatest at the tip of the tongue; to sourness on the edges; to bitterness, at the back. Sensitivity to saline (saltiness) is spread over the whole surface.

Figure 5.29 *Taste Space*

These four tastes—shown with the names of substances in which each taste predominates—are regarded as the primary ones. Although different parts of the tongue and mouth are more sensitive to one or another, individual taste receptors seem to respond to them all, but in varying proportions. (From Henning, 1916.)

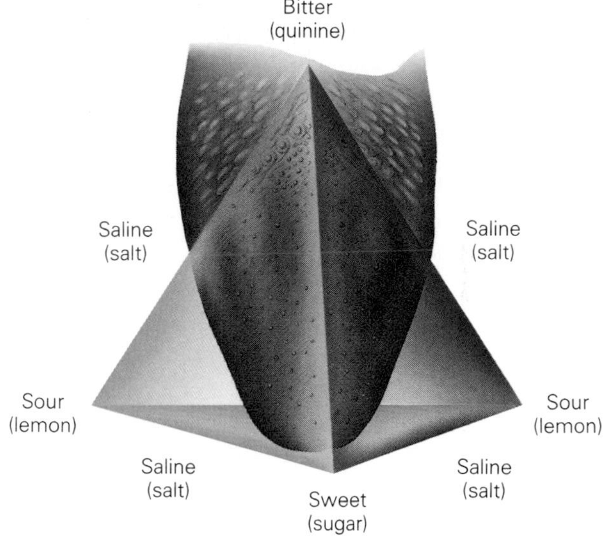

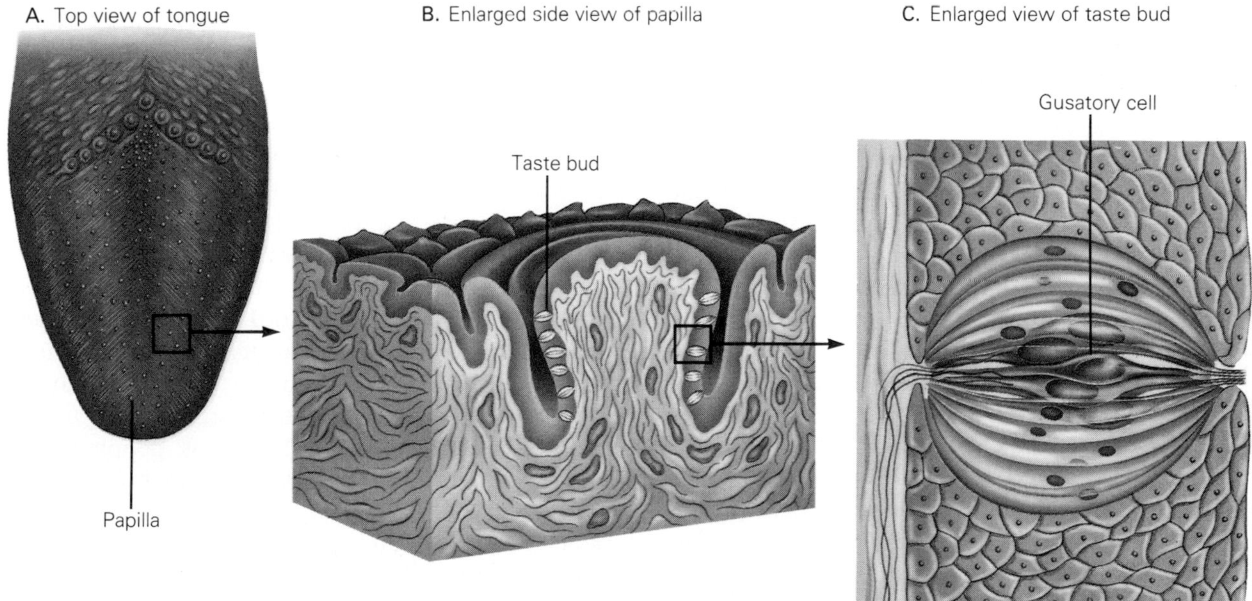

Figure 5.30 *Receptors for Taste*

Part A shows the distribution of papillae on the upper side of the tongue. Part B shows a single papilla enlarged so that the individual taste buds are visible; one of these taste buds is enlarged in part C.

Single-cell recordings of taste receptors in rats show, however, that individual receptors do not fire just to stimuli producing one of the four primary tastes. Rather, tastes seem to be coded in terms of *relative* activity in the different types of receptors, each of which responds somewhat to all the taste stimuli. For instance, all receptors fire to both salt solutions and sweet solutions, but some fire more to one, and some fire more to the other (Pfaffman, 1959).

Taste sensitivity is exaggerated in infants and decreases with age. Many elderly people who complain that "food has lost its taste," really mean that they have lost much of their sensory ability to detect differences in the taste qualities of food. A similar effect occurs in younger people who are heavy smokers; their taste sensitivity is impaired—another reason not to smoke.

Smell

Evolutionally important objects like food, predators, prey, and potential mates all emit organic molecules into the air. These molecules are physical stimuli for smell. They are important because they provide information about odor-producing objects at a *distance.* The significance of *olfaction,* the sense of smell, varies greatly across species. Dogs, rats, insects, and many other creatures for whom smell is central to survival have a far keener sense of smell than we do; thus, relatively more of their brain area is devoted to smell.

Not much is known about the physiological mechanisms of smell. The odor-sensitive receptors are located deep in the nasal passages, making them very difficult to study. Their sensory signals are sent to the olfactory bulb of the brain, located just above the receptors and just below the frontal lobes of the cortex. One hypothesis about the mechanism for smell is the **stereochemical** (lock-and-key) **theory** (Amoore, 1965). It suggests that receptor sites in the odor-sensitive cells have distinctive sizes and shapes corresponding to those of the chemical molecules that stimulate them (as in the case of endorphins). This theory does not have wide acceptance, but no alternative theory has fared better.

Members of some species communicate with each other by secreting and detecting chemical signals called pheromones. **Pheromones** are chemical substances used as communication within a given species to signal sexual receptivity, danger, territorial boundaries, and food sources. Worker ants and bees use pheromone signals to let others in their colony or hive know that they found a food source (Marler & Hamilton, 1966).

Humans seem to use the sense of smell in conjunction with taste to seek and sample food; but there are some hints that humans may also secrete and sense sexual pheromones. Particularly suggestive is the fact that, over time, menstrual cycles of close friends in a women's dormitory have been shown to fall into a pattern of synchrony (McClintock, 1971). Another suggestive fact is that sex pheromones of other mammals are used extensively in perfumes which are bought and used by humans to attract members of the opposite sex. See the ***Close-up*** on page 175 for a new look at human pheromones.

The Body Senses

To move around purposefully in our environment we need constant information about where our limbs and other body parts are in relation to each other and to objects in the environment. Without this knowledge, even our simplest actions would be hopelessly uncoordinated. In fact, we wouldn't even be able to sit or stand upright. The information we need to do these things comes from three senses that are grouped together by psychologists as "body senses": the *vestibular, kinesthetic,* and *cutaneous senses.*

The Vestibular Sense

The **vestibular sense** tells us how our bodies—especially our heads—are oriented in the world with respect to gravity. It also tells us when we are moving—or, more precisely, when the direction or rate of our motion is changing. The receptors for this information are tiny hairs in fluid-filled sacs and canals in the inner ear; these hairs are bent when the fluid moves and presses on them, as happens when we turn our head quickly or when a car or elevator we are in slows down or speeds up. The *saccule* and *utricle* shown in **Figure 5.26** tell us about acceleration or deceleration; the three canals, called the **semicircular canals,** are at right angles to each other and, thus, can tell us about motion in any direction. For instance, they tell us how our head is moving when we turn, nod, or tilt it.

The vestibular sense also helps people keep themselves upright. Those who lose their vestibular sense because of accidents or disease are initially quite disoriented and prone to falling, especially if they are in the dark or if their eyes are closed so that they have no visual information about their position and motion. They may also suffer from vertigo (dizziness) for a while. However, most eventually compensate by relying more heavily on visual information.

Close-up Sweaty Male Pheromones May Help Women's Sexual Health

Bees do it, maybe even educated fleas do it—and now it appears that we do it too. Like our lowly insect neighbors, humans give off scents—*pheromones*—that carry signals to other humans which affect their physiological responses. Recent research has linked male pheromones to the well-being of women's reproductive systems. An ongoing program of research conducted jointly at the Monell Chemical Senses Center and the University of Pennsylvania Medical School has found that women who have regular sexual activity with males are more likely to have normal menstrual cycles, fewer infertility problems, and a milder menopause than women who are celibate or have irregular sexual relationships.

It may be the sweet smell of male sweat, however, and not sexual activity that is the secret causal ingredient influencing the female endocrine system. An extract of male underarm secretions dabbed on women subjects shows effects similar to those of regular sexual intercourse.

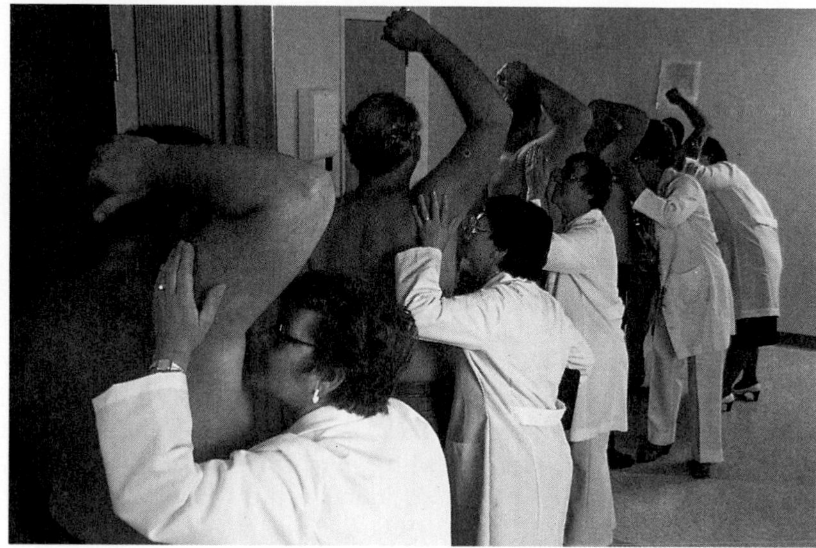

In double-blind experimental studies, underarm secretions were collected from men and women volunteers over a three-month period. These essences were mixed with alcohol and applied to the upper lips of female subjects. The subjects were college students with abnormal menstrual cycles (less than 26 days or more than 32 days) and no current sexual activity. They received three weekly treatments of either the warmed-up pheromone extract or only the alcohol application, depending on their random assignment to experimental or placebo control conditions. Over the 14 weeks of the study those women given the male pheromones speeded up or slowed down their menstrual cycles toward a normal 29.5 days plus or minus 3 days. This change was significantly different from that of the subjects in the control condition who continued to have irregular cycles. (Cutler et al., 1986)

In a companion study, ten women subjects who received similar applications of female *essence began to* synchronize *their menstrual cycles after only a few months. Those in a control condition showed no such changes. (Preti et al., 1986)*

The director of this research, biologist Winnifred Cutler, believes that the essence of "good sex" may be just that—the pheromones given off by the heat of passion. No research has yet been conducted with gay or lesbian subjects to test the generality of these findings.

The Kinesthetic Sense

Whether we are standing erect, riding a bicycle, drawing a picture, removing a splinter with tweezers, or making love, our brains need to have accurate information about the current position and movement of our body parts relative to each other. The **kinesthetic sense** provides this information by giving us constant sensory feedback about what the body is doing during motor activities. Without it, we would be unable to coordinate most of the voluntary movements we make so effortlessly.

We have two potential sources of kinesthetic information. The first is from receptors that lie in the joints. These receptors respond to pressures that accompany different positions of the limbs and to pressure changes that accompany movements of the joints. Evidence suggests that these receptors in the joints provide the main source of information about position of the limbs relative to each other (Geldard, 1972). The second source of kinesthetic information is receptors in the muscles and tendons that hold bones together. These receptors respond to changes in tension that accompany shortening and lengthening of the muscles and tendons. They are involved in motor control and coordination but tell us little about *body position.*

Obviously, athletes must rely heavily on feedback cues from their kinesthetic sense. One function of the extensive practice essential to improve any athletic performance is learning to monitor and memorize the subtle patterns of muscle movements and bodily positions associated with optimal performance. The next step in this nonconscious learning is being able to reproduce "on demand" those responses correlated with the kinesthetic feedback particular to an athlete's task at any given moment in a sport.

When athletes practice they learn the subtle patterns of muscle movements and body positions that are necessary for optimal execution. They then can reproduce those movements "on demand" during their performances.

The Cutaneous Senses

The skin is a remarkably versatile organ. In addition to protecting us against surface injury, holding in body fluids, and helping regulate body temperature, it contains nerve endings that produce sensations of pressure, warmth, and cold when they are stimulated by contact with external objects. Together these are called the **cutaneous senses** (skin senses). Their importance to an organism's survival is obvious.

The skin's sensitivity to pressure varies tremendously over the body. For example, we are ten times more accurate in sensing the position of stimulation on our fingertips than on our backs. The variation in sensitivity of different body regions is reflected in the density of nerve endings in these regions and also in the amount of sensory cortex devoted to them. In chapter 4 we learned that our sensitivity is greatest where we need it most—on our faces, tongues, and hands to provide precise sensory feedback from these parts of the body for effective eating, speaking, and grasping.

It probably has not escaped your notice that cutaneous sensitivity also plays a role in sexuality. Touch is the primary stimulus for sexual arousal in humans. *Where* you get touched or touch someone else makes a difference. Those areas of the skin surface that are especially sensitive to stimulation and give rise to erotic or sexual sensations are called *erogenous zones.* Exploratory research has found these zones generally in the body's genital, anal, and oral areas, as well as in the nipples of the breast. Other touch-sensitive erotic areas vary in their arousal potential for different individuals as a function of learned associations, in addition to the built-in greater concentration of sensory receptors.

It is possible for skin stimulation to serve in an unusual capacity as a substitute for a blind person's visual information. A visual substitution system has been developed that converts a visual image into a pattern of vibrations on the skin. A television camera records the image that is converted into electrical impulses which activate an array of 400 vibrators (in a 20 x 20 matrix). Practice with this system allows the blind to "see with their skin."

> *In a series of tests, both blind and blindfolded subjects were soon able to discriminate among simple geometrical shapes (like lines and curves) in different orientations. Then they learned to identify twenty-five moderately complex, three-dimensional objects, such as a coffee cup, a telephone, and a stuffed animal. With still more practice they were able to "see" these objects in relative locations in space as well. (White et al., 1970)*

Two different types of cutaneous receptors seem to work together to tell us how hot or cold something is. Some evidence for this is that small spots on the skin tend to be sensitive only to cold or only to warmth, except that the cold receptors respond when stimulated by objects *either* below the temperature of the skin or well above it (Hensel, 1968).

Curiously, the sensation "hot" has no special receptors but seems to depend on the joint activity of the cold and warmth receptors. The most striking evidence for this is the thermal illusion illustrated in **Figure 5.31.** When two tubes, one cool and one warm, are intertwined as shown, the sensation from holding them is one of burning heat, even though neither of the tubes is really hot at all.

Constant stimulation by a cold or hot stimulus produces sensory adaptation: the receptors stop responding to the constant temperature. When you dive into cold water or step into a hot bath, the temperature is a shock at first, but soon feels much more comfortable.

The intermediate point at which you feel neither warmth nor cold is called **physiological zero.** Normally, this is about 90 degrees, but it may shift temporarily as a result of sensory adaptation. Your adaptation to either warmth or coolness may become so complete that you are unaware of the temperature. That temperature has then become your new physiological zero, and new sensations of warmth or coolness will be felt relative to *it.*

Figure 5.31 *Heat Illusion Apparatus*

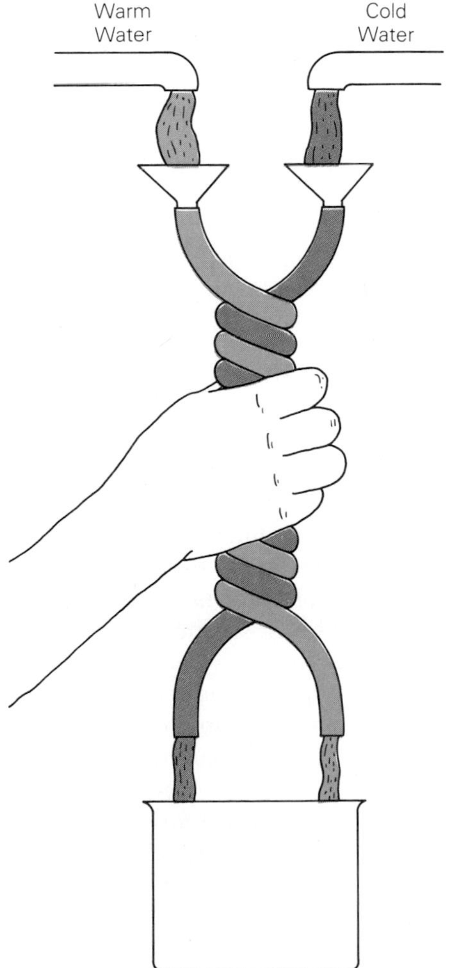

You can demonstrate this dramatically in the following way: put your left hand in a bowl of cool water (about 70° Fahrenheit) and your right hand in a separate bowl of warm water (about 100° Fahrenheit). Allow your hands to adapt for several minutes until they reach physiological zero, where you no longer feel any temperature. The put them both into a third bowl of water at an intermediate temperature (about 85° Fahrenheit). The very same water will feel warm to your left hand and cool to your right hand because the receptors in each hand are responding to the change from their own physiological zero, not to the temperature of the water itself.

Once again, we see that our senses, though often accurate in telling us about the physical world, can be led astray by adaptation, context effects, and stimulus patterns arranged to yield illusions of reality. In the next chapter we will study how sensory input can result in distorted perceptions known as visual illusions.

The Pain Sense

The final sense we will examine is the most puzzling of all—our sense of pain. Pain is the universal complaint of the human condition—from the pains of birth for mother and child, to those of teething, injury, sickness, and headache, the chronic pains such as arthritis, lower back pain, and pain with unknown origins that linger on for long periods, sometimes permanently. About a third of Americans are estimated to suffer from persistent or recurring pain (Wallis, 1984). The prevalence of pain for cancer patients is between 60 and 90 percent. The combined cost of medical treatment for pain and its resulting lost workdays is estimated to be more than $50 billion annually in the United States alone. Depression, and even suicide, can result from the seemingly endless assault of nagging chronic pain.

What is pain? If it is so awful, why do we need it? What can be done to control it?

Pain is the body's response to stimulation from *noxious* stimuli—those that are intense enough to cause tissue damage or threaten to do so. This complex response involves a remarkable interplay between chemical reactions at the site of the pain stimulus, nerve impulses to and from the spinal cord and brain, along with a number of psychological and cultural factors. Simply put, pain is a hurt we feel. "It is always more than a distressing sensation. It is useful to think of pain as a person's emotional experience of a distressing sensation; thus, morale and mood can be as important as the intensity of the feeling itself in determining the degree of pain" (Brody, 1986, p. 1).

Acute pain is studied experimentally in laboratories using paid volunteers who experience varying degrees of a precisely regulated stimulus, such as heat applied briefly to a small area of the skin. This procedure can test a subject's tolerance for pain as well as measure the sensory and subjective responses to it—without causing any damage to the skin tissue. In some cases a human subject's nerve impulses are monitored by passing a slender recording sensor through the skin into the nerve fiber itself. This enables the researcher to listen to signals being sent by the peripheral nervous system to the brain. Chronic pain is typically studied in hospital research clinics as part of the treatment program to find new ways to alleviate different types of enduring pain.

Almost all animals are born with some type of *pain defense system* that triggers automatic withdrawal reflexes to certain stimulus events. When the stimulus intensity reaches threshold, organisms respond by *escaping*—if they can. In addition, they quickly learn to identify painful stimulus situations, *avoiding* them whenever possible.

You might think that it would be nice never to experience pain. Actually, such a condition would be deadly. People born with congenital insensitivity to pain feel no hurt, but usually their bodies become scarred and their limbs become deformed from injuries. In fact, because of their failure to notice and respond to tissue-damaging stimuli, they tend to die young (Manfredi et al., 1981). Their experience makes us aware that pain serves as an essential *defense signal:* it warns us of potential harm. In this way it helps us to survive in hostile environments and to cope with sickness and injury.

The Anatomy of an "Ouch"

Despite the obvious significance of pain and much medical research to uncover the physiological processes involved, pain remains a scientific mystery. There are no specific receptors for pain such as exist for the other senses we have just studied, and no specific form of stimulation. Moreover, there are no known specific nerve fibers for sending only pain signals.

What has been discovered are powerful chemicals that are released at the point of intense stimulation (say, when you prick your finger with a pin). They are stored in or near free nerve endings and sensitize the nerves to transmit impulses from an injured area toward the brain. Let's trace the sequence of bodily reactions that erupt whenever your body is cut, burned, banged, infected, or damaged, and pain results (see **Figure 5.32**). In the seconds after an injury there is a cascade of chemical activities at the site, signals sent to the brain informing it of the location and extent of the damage, and white blood cells summoned to fight infection (see McKean, 1986). The following is a list of those activities:

a. Enzymes (called *kallikrein*) are activated that free the chemical **bradykinin** (BRAY-dee-kine-en) from its large precursor molecule, which is present in the blood and many tissues.
b. Bradykinin is the most potent pain-producing chemical known; it fits into precisely shaped receptors in several places, each of which starts a different activity.
c. It binds to receptors on the capillary walls of small blood vessels, allowing white blood cells and fluids to leak out to fight infection.
d. It binds to *mast cells* triggering the release of *histamines* which, in turn, open the capillary walls wider so more white cells, kallikrein enzymes, and bradykinin precursors can leak out.
e. It binds to other membranes causing another powerful pain-inducing chemical, called *prostaglandins,* to be released. (Aspirin and other popular drugs for pain relief work by inhibiting the production of prostaglandins.) This chemical does two things: promotes swelling in the area until healing starts; and binds to receptors on the nerve ending, sending additional pain signals to the brain.
f. Bradykinin also binds to nerve end receptors initiating afferent pain signals to the brain.
g. The brain or spinal cord sends back efferent impulses to the nerve end releasing *substance P,* which then also binds to the mast cell and releases more histamines.

The peripheral nerve signal is then transmitted to the spinal cord. From there it is relayed to the thalamus and then to the cerebral cortex, where the location and intensity of the pain are identified, the significance evaluated, and action plans formulated. Peripheral nerve fibers send pain signals to the central nervous system by two pathways—a fast-conducting set of nerve fibers that are covered with myelin, and slower, smaller nerve fibers without any myelin coating.

These different types of nerve fibers appear to be responsible for the two distinct classes of pain experience we have. The fast-conducting, myelinated fibers carry pain signals described as "bright" or "pricking" sensations, with a fast onset and quick offset. Such pain is caused by specific external stimulation, such as electric shock, and we can readily

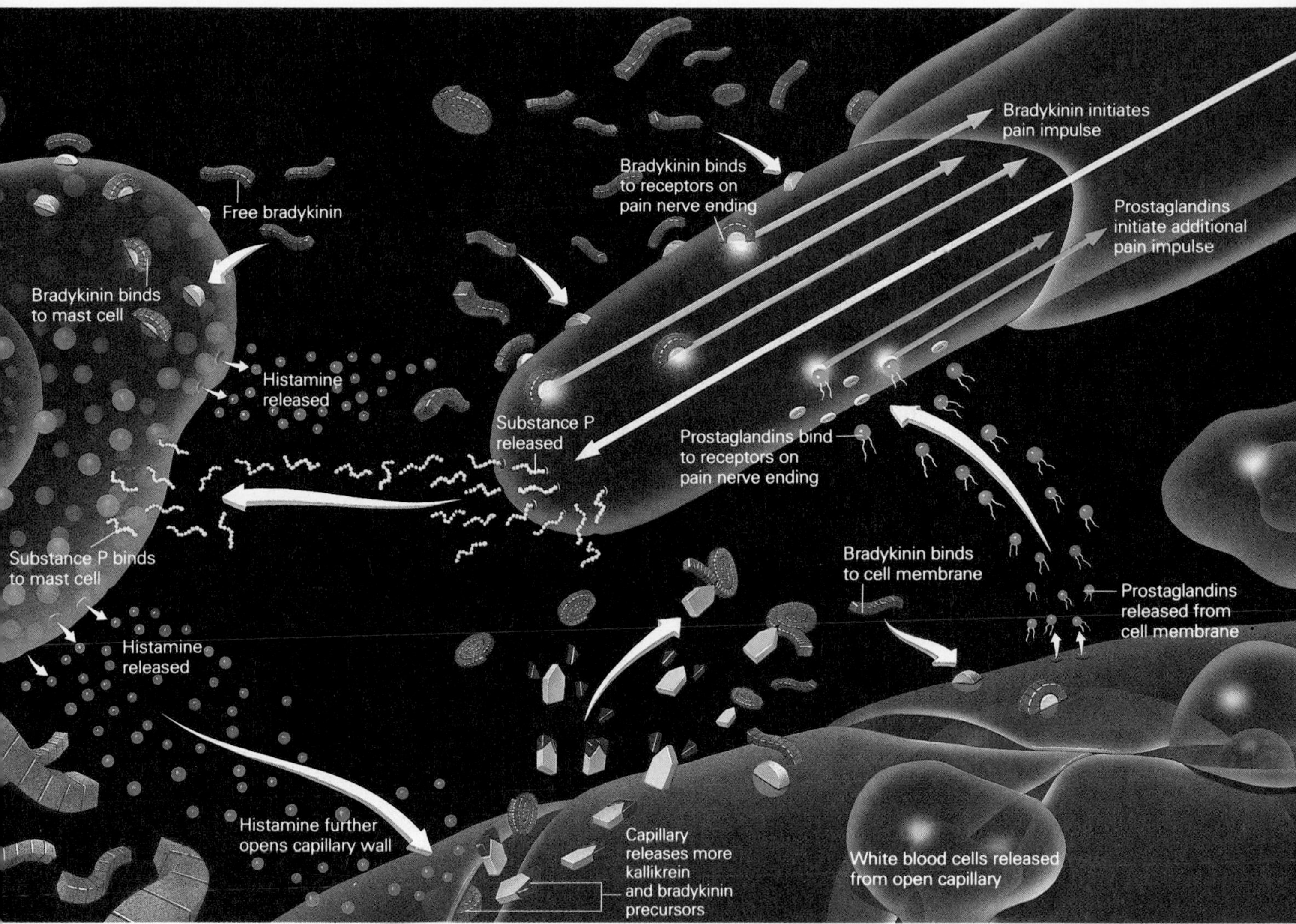

Figure 5.32 *The Aftermath of "OUCH"!*
Chemical activity intensifies in the seconds after injury, telling the brain how bad the damage is, summoning white blood cells, and setting the stage for healing.

localize the area of the skin affected. The slower, unmyelinated nerve fibers produce "burning" or "dull" sensations; they start more slowly, are diffuse rather than specifically localized, are more likely to be internal in origin, and last longer. When myelinated nerve fibers in the periphery of the body are destroyed, by poisoning or alcoholism, people can no longer experience the "pricking" pain, but only the "burning" pain.

One effect of these pain signals is to release *endorphins*—the brain's own morphine (see p. 120). Endorphins produce *analgesia* (pain reduction) by reducing sensitivity to pain stimuli. They appear to be responsible for the pain relief from stimulation by acupuncture needles, as well as from direct electrical stimulation of the brain stem (Hosobuchi et al., 1979) People who suffer from chronic pain that is not relieved by standard medical treatments have abnormally low concentrations of endorphins in their cerebrospinal fluid (Akil, 1978). The body has some other mechanism besides endorphins for producing analgesia, and researchers are working to discover this non-endorphin pain control system (Lewis et al., 1980).

One theory about the way pain may be modulated is the **gate-control theory** (Melzack, 1973, 1980), which assumes that the nervous system is able to process only a limited amount of sensory information at any one time. If too much information is being sent through, certain cells in the spinal cord act as neurological "gates," interrupting and blocking some pain signals while others are sent to the brain. Small diameter fibers in the spine open these gates when signals from injured tissues are received, while activity in the large fibers of the spine close the gates, shutting down the pain response. Treatment for chronic pain sometimes involves electrical stimulation designed to activate the "gate-closing" function of the large neural fibers. Other competing sensory influences that close the pain gates may come from massaging the hurt area, from emotional arousal of competition in sports or battle, or from engaging in distracting mental activities.

The Psychology of Pain

The pain response is a very complex one, because our emotional reactions, context factors, and our interpretation of the situation—factors depending on central processes in the brain—can be as important in determining the pain we experience and its relief as the physical stimuli. In fact, the sensation of pain may not be directly related to the intensity of the noxious stimulus at all—or even to its presence or absence.

The importance of central processes in the experience of pain is shown in two extreme cases—one where there is *pain* with *no physical stimulus* for it, another where there is *no pain* with an *intensely painful stimulus.* Up to 10 percent of those with amputations of their limbs report extreme or chronic pain in the limb that is no longer there—the *phantom limb phenomenon.* In contrast, some individuals taking part in religious rituals are able to block out pain while exposed to the intense stimulation of walking on beds of hot coals or having their bodies pierced with needles.

"Fire walking" on beds of glowing coals is still practiced in Sri Lanka and in many other parts of the world. Neither medical science nor anthropology have been able to account for the lack of pain or physical injury to its practitioners.

The *meaning* you attach to a particular experience can affect how much pain you feel.

In a classic study, men who were seriously wounded in battle were compared with men in civilian life who had received similar "wounds" with the same amounts of tissue damage in surgical operations. Only 25 percent of the soldiers wanted a narcotic for pain relief, while over 80 percent of the civilian men requested it. The difference in pain reaction was attributed to the significance of the wound for the two groups of men. For the soldiers, the wound was part of the expected context and may even have meant a ticket to safety, getting them out of battle. For the civilians, the surgical wound was more likely to be a disaster signal and a major disruption of their lives. (Beecher, 1956)

Although pain is a private, individual experience, the way people respond can become a habit learned from others, such as family members or ethnic groups (Weisenberg, 1977). One early study compared the responses of patients from four ethnic groups in similarly painful situations.

When surgical patients were observed and interviewed, ethnic group membership generally predicted how they would cope with the pain they were experiencing. The Jewish and Italian patients emotionally exaggerated the intensity of their pain and felt free to cry out to elicit support from family members or hospital staff. By contrast, Irish and "Old American" patients (Anglo-Saxon Protestants from at least three generations of Americans) adopted a detached, matter-of-fact orientation and inhibited any public show of emotion. When their pain became intense, the Irish patients would withdraw, but they would moan or cry out only when they were alone. (Zborowski, 1969)

This basic pattern of ethnic differences in response to pain was also found in a laboratory study of experimentally induced pain (via electric shock) to housewives from these different cultural backgrounds. (Sternbach & Tursky, 1965)

Another influence of learning on pain responses is seen in the differing effects of sympathy and attention versus withdrawal of attention on the part of family members. When pain complaints are followed by attention and social support, they become more frequent, whereas when they lead to withdrawal of attention and affection, they become less frequent.

In a study of 20 married patients, interviews were held with all the patients on the day of their admission to a pain-management program. Among other things, information was obtained about the patients' perceptions of their spouses' typical responses to their pain. During the study they reported their pain twice—once when they believed their spouses were observing from behind a one-way mirror and once when a neutral individual, identified as a clerk, was the observer.

Those who thought their spouses were not *sympathetic reported* lower *pain levels when they thought their spouses were watching. Those who perceived their spouses as relatively solicitous complained of* more *pain when they believed their spouses were observing them than in the neutral observer condition. (Block, 1980)*

Pain Management

Not only can we learn pain responses if they are rewarded by other people, but we can *unlearn* them as well. Discovering how to relieve the noxiousness of pain is a significant lesson for pain sufferers to learn from psychologists and medical therapy.

One clinic for chronic pain sufferers reported success using a three-part strategy: increasing a patient's activity level to ever more strenuous activities, giving analgesic "pain cocktails" randomly but never when pain was being reported, and training relatives not to respond positively to complaints of pain. Follow-ups showed that all patients made fewer pain complaints, were up and active for long periods, and showed greatly reduced dependence on medication. Almost all had returned to work. (Fordyce, 1973)

While scientists and pharmaceutical companies seek pain cures through drugs that block the action of bradykinin and others that stimulate the release of the brain's own nonaddictive opiates, pain clinics rely on other therapies as well. Extreme cases may call for surgery or the wearing of portable electrical stimulators, but pain is also managed by means of acupuncture, exercise, hypnosis, and relaxation or thought-distraction procedures. The Lamaze method of preparation for "natural childbirth" without anesthetics, reduces the intense labor pains by combining several of these methods. Lamaze breathing exercises aid relaxation, focus attention away from the pain area, and give a woman an activity she can control. The use of distracting, pleasant images, massage that creates a gentle counterstimulation, and the social support of a "coaching" spouse or friend all work to give a prospective mother a greater sense of control over this painful situation. Research has shown that such techniques increase pain tolerance when measured objectively by the longer duration these pregnant women are able to keep their hands immersed in a tank of ice water (Worthington et al., 1983).

Hypnosis can be quite effective in relieving the experience of pain. The intense pains women experience during the labor and delivery of their babies have been reduced, or even eliminated, by hypnotic suggestions. One obstetrician successfully used hypnosis as the sole form of anesthesia in 814 out of 1000 deliveries, some of them requiring Caesarian operations (Hilgard & Hilgard, 1974). Hypnosis will be discussed in greater detail in chapter 7.

Finally, one of the most potent of all treatments for pain is "placebo therapy" (Fish, 1973). As we noted in chapter 2, pain can be relieved by "drugs" *expected* to be pain-killers when, in fact, they are inert substances with no medicinal value—but lots of psychological value. Believing that a particular treatment will lead to pain reduction is thus sufficient to bring about major psychological and perhaps physiological relief. It appears that belief, as well as perception of pain, can trigger the release of pain-killing endorphins in the brain. Recent evidence suggests that the one third of the population who are "positive placebo responders" may have higher concentrations of endorphins than do other people (Levine et al., 1978).

So the way you perceive your pain, what you communicate about it to others, and even how you respond to pain-relieving treatments may reveal more about your psychological state—about the kind of inferences you are making—than about the intensity of the pain stimulus. What you perceive may be different from, and even independent of, what you sense. This paradox of the separation of physical and psychological reality provides the transition we need to follow another path in our journey, one that brings us to the topic of our next chapter: *perception*.

Summary

- The field of sensory psychology includes sensory physiology, the study of the way biological mechanisms convert physical events into neural and sensory ones, and psychophysics, the study of the correspondence between physical stimulation and sensory experience. Psychophysical techniques include attempts to discover absolute thresholds and difference thresholds, and to construct psychophysical scales for measuring and comparing sensations.
- The theory of signal detection (TSD) challenges the assumption that there are absolute thresholds. Instead it demonstrates how a sensory response continuum relates to stimulus variation. It overcomes the problems of response bias by providing separate measures for the sensory response and the decision criterion.

- The smallest unit of difference that can be perceived between a standard stimulus and a comparison stimulus is called a *just noticeable difference (jnd)*. This difference is a statistical estimate of the resolving power of a sensory stimulus.
- In the eye, light energy is converted to neural impulses by photoreceptors in the retina, the rods and cones. Ganglion cells in the retina integrate the input from several receptors; their axons form the optic nerves, which meet at the optic chiasma, where fibers from the inner halves of both retinas cross over to the opposite side of the brain. From the optic chiasma, a small pathway goes to the superior colliculus, where some information about the location of the stimulus object is processed. A large pathway goes by way of the lateral geniculate nucleus to the visual cortex, where information about color and detail is processed.
- The stimulus for color is the wavelength of light, the visible portion of the electromagnetic spectrum. Color sensations differ in hue, saturation, and brightness. Current color-vision theory combines the Young-Helmholtz trichromatic theory (receptor processing) and the opponent-process theory (ganglion cell processing). Researchers have now isolated and identified the human genes which direct the development of the three proteins responsible for color vision.
- Contrasts in brightness form boundaries and distinct edges that give objects size, shape, and orientation in space. Because of the brightness contrast effect, the distinction between a stimulus and its background increases as the difference between the object and the background intensifies. Cells in the retina as well as higher centers have receptive fields with an excitatory central area and an inhibitory surround, or the reverse.
- Researchers disagree about whether spatial information is detected by feature detectors or analyzed as spatial frequency patterns. Detection of spatial frequencies is studied by analysis of patterns of light-dark cycles, known as sinewave gratings.
- Changes in stimulation over time and space are necessary for sensation to occur; unchanged stimulation leads to sensory adaptation as shown in habituation and dark adaptation. Studies on the effects of sensory deprivation suggest that the ability of cortical cells to respond to selected features of the environment is both innate and learned.
- Audition (hearing) is produced by sound waves that vary in frequency, amplitude, and complexity. Our sensations of sound vary in pitch, loudness, and timbre (quality). Sound waves are converted to neural events in the cochlea, where tiny hair cells are stimulated by the pressure changes in the moving fluid. Place theory accounts best for the coding of high frequencies; frequency theory accounts best for the coding of low frequencies.
- Gustation (taste) is a chemical sense that works with olfaction (smell) in seeking and sampling food. Taste receptors are taste buds embedded in papillae, mostly in the tongue. They give us four primary taste qualities: sweet, sour, bitter, and salty.
- Olfaction (smell) is accomplished by odor-sensitive cells deep in the nasal passages. Pheromones are chemical signals detected by smell that indicate sexual receptivity, mark territory, signal danger, and communicate other information in many species.
- The vestibular sense gives information about the direction and rate of bodily motion. The kinesthetic sense, through receptors in the joints and muscles, gives data about the position of body parts and helps in motor coordination.
- The cutaneous (skin) senses give sensations of pressure, warmth, and cold. Sensations of heat are produced by simultaneous stimulation of cold and warmth receptors.
- Pain is the body's response to potentially harmful stimuli. The physiological response to pain involves a number of chemical reactions at the site of the pain stimulus and nerve impulses to and from the brain and spinal cord. The psychological response to pain includes emotional reactions, context factors, interpretations of the situation, and beliefs—factors dependent on brain processing—which can be more important than the physical stimulus in both pain and pain relief.

6

Perception

Marsha was a college student with a passion for photography. One evening in September when she was taking pictures outdoors in low light, she noticed something strange. When she first noticed the full moon as it rose over the horizon above the foothills, it was big and really imposing. It made a great picture! But as it rose higher in the sky it appeared to shrink, getting progressively smaller until it looked quite ordinary to her. She regretted not having taken more shots when it was so lush looking.

Although Marsha had casually noticed this change before, she had never really observed it so carefully, recorded it on film, or wondered why. Obviously the *actual* size of the moon couldn't change, only its *apparent* size.

The next day Marsha related her puzzling discovery to her friend Carlo. Together, they developed her photographic sequence of the rising moon to see if she had caught the moon's distortion in her photographs. Imagine her surprise when they measured the size of the moon's diameter and found it was *exactly the same size* in each of her two dozen photos. Her first thought had been that it was farther away from the earth when it was higher in the sky than when it was lower on the horizon. Not so, she discovered; the moon's orbit was circular. It was the same distance from the earth's surface at all times. Carlo had wanted Marsha to see for herself "the moon illusion" before he told her what he had learned in his introductory psychology course—that the change in the apparent size of the moon was because of processes taking place in Marsha's brain and not in anything out in the real world.

"Maynard, I do think that just this once you should come out and see the moon!"

The image of the moon on the retina was the same when it was on the horizon as it was in the equally distant overhead sky—as Marsha's photographs testified; but the brain believed one image was more distant. Therefore it "recomputed" the size of the seemingly more distant object. The eye and the brain put together present information with stored information from prior experiences—and came up with a *false* conclusion: "Hey, look at the big moon on the horizon!"

Carlo explained, in his best professorial tone that, according to the most accepted theory, the moon looks bigger on the horizon than overhead because the brain makes an error in estimating its distance. The brain uses information it receives from the eyes to judge the size of objects in space according to their perceived distance. Because we know from experience that the horizon is farther away from us, objects moving from overhead toward the horizon are not seen as smaller; their perceived size remains *constant.* Instead we see them simply getting farther away. The brain uses this visual evidence to conclude that the horizon is more distant than the sky overhead.

Marsha accepted that hypothesis as tenable, but asked Carlo to test it—by looking at it from a different position without familiar cues, such as looking at the moon between his legs. She predicted that the illusion of the moon's larger size on the horizon would be reduced if it were viewed in an unfamiliar position without the familiar cues the brain uses to estimate size and distance. Intrigued by the possibility, Carlo promised to do so with her on the night of the next full moon. (You might want to consider other ways of studying the moon illusion or to read more in Kaufman & Rock, 1962; Rock & Kaufman, 1962).

Marsha's experience is an example of the question to be answered in this chapter: How do we come to organize and interpret the stimulus input from all of our sensory systems into internal representations of external objects and events in the real world? The eye is more than a camera photographing lights; the ear more than a microphone recording sounds. Sensation gets the show started, but something more is needed to make it meaningful and interesting to us. We may look with our eyes, but we "see" with our brains.

Most of the time, sensing and perceiving activities are taking place so effortlessly and automatically that we take them for granted; and, most of the time, they work reliably to give us an accurate, or *veridical,* view of reality (Marsha's big moon being an exception to this rule). We never think of the enormous amount of physiological activity taking place in our receptor cells and sensory cortex cells just to recognize a friend's face in a crowded classroom, a lover's voice over the phone, or an insect's delicate touch on our necks.

In this chapter we will discover some of the ways that we make sense of the host of messages sent from sense receptors to the brain. We will also learn how the mind both interprets the givens of reality and goes beyond sensation to design new views of reality.

The Task of Perception

Look around the room you are in. Get a coin and examine it closely. Shut this book, rotate it and open it again. Did anything change its shape or size? Did any objects move? Probably not, but why are you so sure? According to the sensory information on your retina there were lots of things moving and changing. How can you be so confident that the movement was in your body or eyes and not in the objects out there? How do you "know" that the coin or book did not go through size and shape transformations that corresponded to the changing images they projected on the retina as they were moved? And during this exercise, the big question is the following: Were you looking out at the world, or was the world looking in at you?

The task of perception is to extract the continuously changing, often chaotic, sensory input from external energy sources and organize it into stable, orderly *percepts* of meaningful objects that are personally relevant to a perceiver. A **percept** is that which is perceived. It is *not* a physical object (distal stimulus), nor its image in a receptor (proximal stimulus), but rather the phenomenological or experienced outcome of the process of perception. You might say that the role of perception is to make *sense* of sensation. To do so involves many different mental processes that include synthesizing, judging, estimating, remembering, comparing, and associating. In this section we will distinguish among three different stages in the overall process of perception, examine how we interpret the images that appear unannounced on our retinas, and then play some tricks on our perceiving minds with ambiguous figures that make illusions of reality.

Sensing, Perceiving, and Classifying

The term *perception* is often used to mean the overall process of apprehending objects and events in the external environment. However the process is easier to understand if we divide it into three stages—sensation, perception, and classification.

Sensation refers to the first stage in which physical energy in the world—such as light and sound waves—is *transduced* into neural activity of cortical cells that codes information about the way the receptor organs are being stimulated. Even at this early point in the neurological journey there is stimulus selection and transformation going on. Retinal cells are emphasizing borders and differences in light, while not getting excited by unchanging, constant stimulation. Meanwhile, cortical cells are extracting features and spatial frequency information from the input they get from the ganglion cells of the retina.

Perception, in its narrow usage, refers to the next stage in which an internal representation of an object is formed, and an experienced *percept* of the external stimulus is developed. The representation provides a working description of the perceiver's external environment. Information from lower-order detectors is organized and modified by higher-order brain processes to convert stimulus features and elements into patterns and forms that are recognizable. For example, three lines, |||, that are identified by cortical cells soon become recognized as the percepts *H,* or a triangle, or a Roman numeral 3, depending on other information provided by the context. Or, as with Marsha's moon illusion, perceptual processes may involve our estimations of an object's likely size, shape, movement, distance, and orientation. Those estimates are based on mental computations that integrate our past knowledge with the present evidence received from our senses.

Classification, the third stage in this sequence, groups the qualities of the perceived objects into familiar categories. Circular objects "become" baseballs, coins, clocks, oranges, and moons; while human objects may be classified as friend or foe, pretty or ugly, movie star or rock star. At this stage, the perceptual question, "What is the object?" changes to one of classification, "What is the object's function? What is it good for?" The product of classification is a person's reported percept, which is the only data available to assess a viewer's experience.

The boundaries between perception and classification are not clearly drawn because these processes work so swiftly and seemingly automatically that they typically mesh smoothly together in our everyday lives, but conceptually they are different. Classification is based more on higher-order mental processing (past knowledge, expectations, inferences), while perception is based on a combination of sensory information and classification. The ***Close-up*** on Dr. Richard and the study of illusions on page 187 reveals other ways that these processes may be differentiated.

This division of the global process of perception into sensation, perception, and classification emphasizes the parts of this complex process. In the rest of this chapter we will use *perception* in its narrower sense (going beyond sensory information to provide a meaningful awareness and knowledge of the world of objects, actors, and episodes) and focus on the second and third steps in the overall perceptual process.

Interpreting Retinal Images

Let's suppose you are a man sitting in an easy chair with your feet up, looking at a portion of a room (**Figure 6.1A**). Light is reflected from the objects, and some of it enters your eye, forming an image on your retina. This "eyeball's eye view" of the room as it would appear to your left eye is shown in **Figure 6.1B.** (The bump on the right is your nose, and the hands and feet at the bottom are your own.) How does this retinal image compare with the environment that produced it?

One very important difference is that the retinal image at the back of your eyeball is *two-dimensional* whereas the environment "out there" is *three-dimensional.* This produces many differences that you may not notice without looking carefully. For instance, compare the shapes of the physical objects out there in the world with the shapes of their corresponding retinal images (see **Figure 6.1C**).

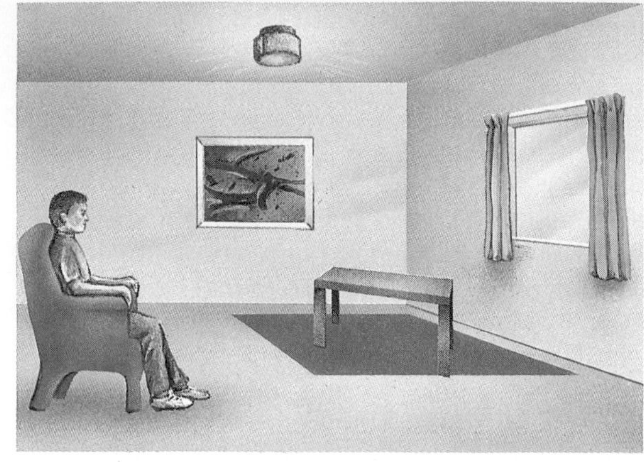

A. Physical Object (Distal Stimulus)

B. Optical Image (Proximal Stimulus)

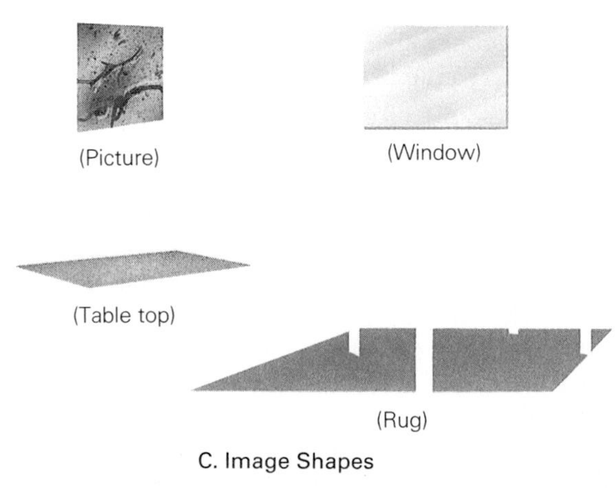

C. Image Shapes

Figure 6.1

Close-up Perceptual Glue

Dr. Richard was a psychologist with considerable training and experience in introspection. His special skill enabled him to make a unique and valuable contribution to psychology when, tragically, he suffered brain damage that altered his visual experience of the world. Fortunately, the damage did not affect the centers of his brain responsible for speech, and he was able to describe his unusual visual experiences quite clearly.

In general terms, the brain damage seemed to have affected his ability to put sensory data together properly. For example, Dr. Richard reported that if he saw a complex object, such as a person, and there were several other people nearby in his visual field, he sometimes saw the different parts of the person as separate parts, not belonging together in a single form; however, if the person then moved, so that all parts went in the same direction, Dr. Richard would see them as one complete person. Without some common factor—like motion—to help "glue" things together, he tended to see a confusion of separate objects, all of which were simultaneously present in his field of view, but which he did not experience as going together in the same way they would have before the neurological damage occurred.

Sometimes perceiving a common element would result in absurd configurations. He would frequently see objects of the same color, such as a banana, a lemon, and a canary, going together even if they were separated in space. People in crowds would "go together" if they were wearing the same colored clothing. At other times, however, Dr. Richard had difficulty combining the sound and sight of the same event. When someone was singing, he might see a mouth move and hear a song, but it was as if the sound had been dubbed with the wrong tape in a foreign movie.

Dr. Richard's experiences of his environment during such episodes were disjointed, fragmented, and bizarre—quite unlike what he had been used to before his problems began (Marcel, 1983). There was nothing whatever wrong with Dr. Richard's eyes or with his ability to *analyze* the properties of stimulus objects: he saw the parts and qualities of objects accurately. Rather, his problem lay in *perceptual synthesis:* putting the bits and pieces of sensory information together properly to form a unified, coherent perception of a single event in the visual scene. His case makes salient the distinction between sensory and perceptual processes. It also serves to remind us that both sensory analysis and perceptual synthesis must be going on all the time even though we are unaware of the way they are or that they are. For other cases in which neurological damage affects different aspects of perception, you may enjoy the superbly written "clinical tales" of Dr. Oliver Sachs in *The man who mistook his wife for a hat and other clinical tales* (1985).

The table, rug, window, and picture in the real-world scene are all rectangular, but only the image of the window actually produces a rectangle in your retinal image. The image of the picture is a trapezoid, that of the table top is an irregular four-sided figure, and the image of the rug is actually three separate regions with more than 20 different sides! How, then, do you manage to see all of these objects as simple, standard rectangles when your retinal images of them are so different?

Notice also that many parts of what you perceive in the room are not actually present in your retinal image at all. For instance, you perceive the vertical edge between the two walls as going all the way to the floor, but your retinal image of that edge stops at the table top. Similarly, in your retinal image parts of the rug are "hidden" behind the table, the stool, and your feet; yet this does not keep you from correctly perceiving the rug as a single, unbroken rectangle. In fact, when you consider all the differences there are between the environmental objects and the images of them on your retina, you may be surprised that you can see the scene as well as you do (and not as Dr. Richard would see it).

The differences between a physical object in the world and its optical image on your retina are so profound and important that psychologists distinguish carefully between them as two different stimuli for perception. The physical object in the world is called the **distal stimulus;** the optical image on the retina is called the **proximal stimulus** (see **Figure 6.2**). These names are easier to remember if you consider that *distal* means "distant," or *far from the observer* and *proximal* means "proximate," or *next to the observer.*

The critical point of our discussion can now be restated more concisely: what you *perceive* corresponds to the *distal stimulus*—the "real" object in the environment—whereas the stimulus from which you must derive your information is the *proximal stimulus*—the image in the retina—which is often quite different. In fact, *perception* can be thought of as the process of determining the distal stimulus from information contained in the proximal stimulus.

The distinction between proximal and distal stimuli applies to all kinds of perception, not just to vision. Auditory images—the patterns of sound waves that enter your ears—are different from the physical objects that produce them. Even tactile images—the patterns of pressure and temperature that you feel on your skin as you actively explore objects with your hands—are not the same as the physical objects that cause them. In each case, perception involves processes that somehow use information in the proximal stimulus to tell you about properties of the distal stimulus.

There is much more to perceiving a scene like this living room, however, than just determining the *physical properties* of the distal stimulus. You also see objects as instances of familiar, meaningful *types* or *categories* of objects: a window, a picture, a table, and a rug. Besides accurately perceiving the shapes and colors, you *interpret* them in terms of your past experience with similar objects. Classifying objects in this way allows you to treat many distant objects as being essentially the same in important ways: windows are for looking through, pictures for looking at, tables are for working or eating on, and rugs are for walking, sitting, or lying on. This process of classification is also part of what you do automatically and almost constantly as you go about perceiving your environment.

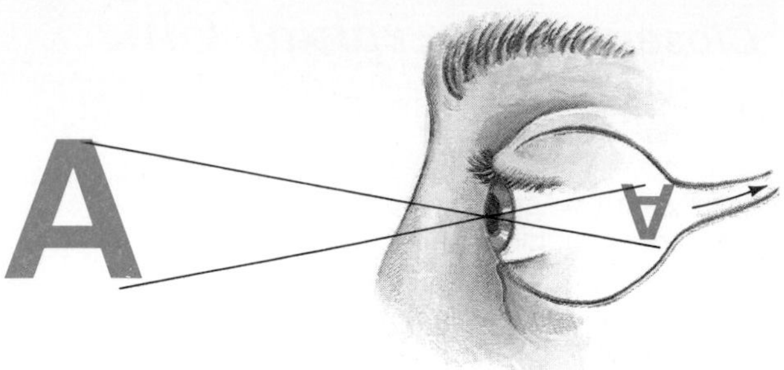

Distal Stimulus

Proximal Stimulus

Figure 6.2

To illustrate further the distinction among the three stages in perceiving, let's examine one of the objects in this scene—the picture hanging on the wall. In the *sensory stage,* this picture corresponds to a two-dimensional trapezoid in your retinal image, whose top and bottom sides converge toward the right and whose left and right sides are different in length. In the *perceptual stage,* you see this trapezoid as actually being a rectangle turned away from you in three-dimensional space. You perceive the top and bottom sides as actually parallel, but receding into the distance toward the right; you perceive the left and right sides as actually equal in length. In the *classification stage,* you recognize this rectangular object as a member of the category *pictures,* objects that are used to decorate walls of rooms.

Figure 6.3 is a flow chart illustrating this sequence of events. The processes that take information from one stage to the next are shown as arrows between the boxes. Taking sensory data into the system by receptors and sending it "upward" for extraction and analysis of relevant information, is called **bottom-up processes.** When a perceiver's past experience, knowledge, expectations, cultural background, and language feed down to influence how the object of perception is interpreted and classified, it is called **top-down processes.** Clearly, the two processes interact to affect the nature of perception of our environment.

The organization of our discussion in this chapter will follow the three-stage sequence outlined in this diagram. Since sensation was treated in chap-

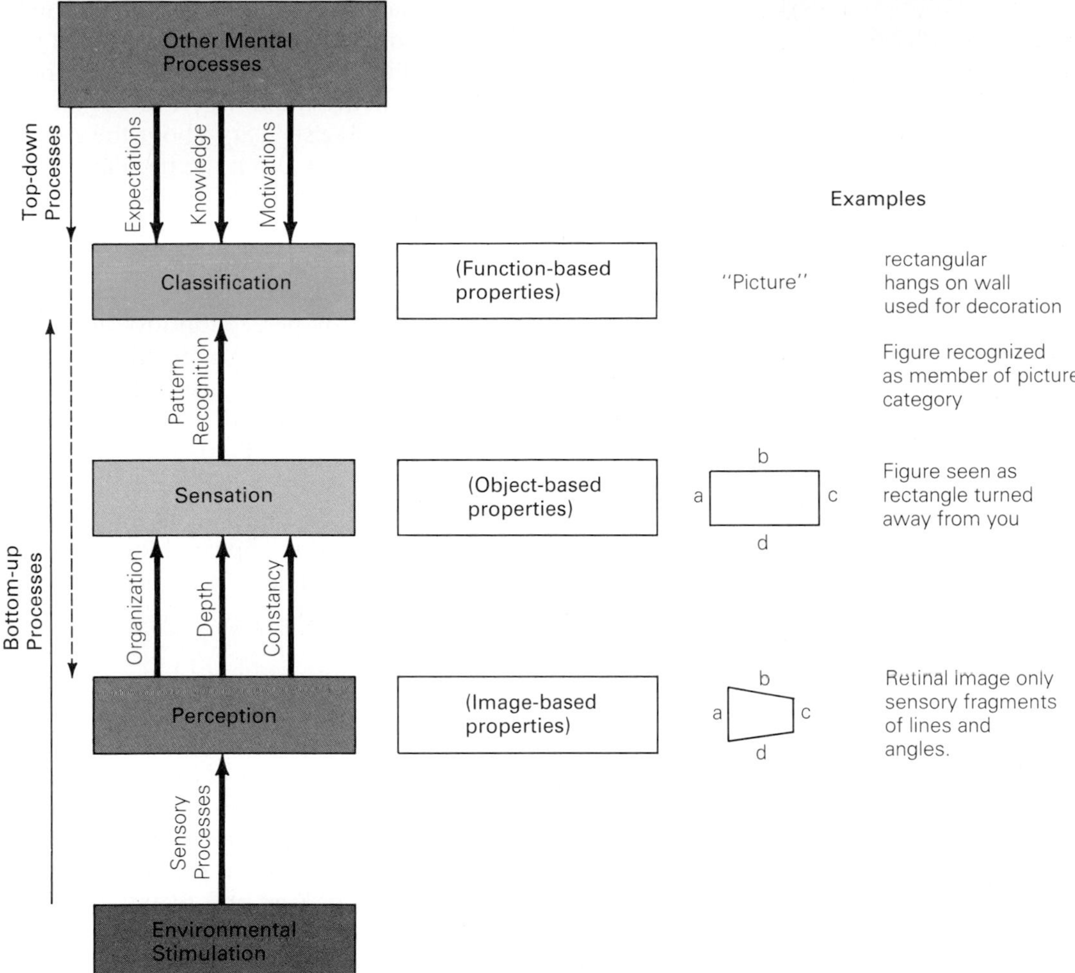

Figure 6.3 *Sensation, Perception, and Classification*
The processes that give rise to the transformation of incoming information at the stages of sensation, perception, and classification and the kinds of properties they generate are outlined in the figure. Bottom-up processes *are those in which incoming stimulus information is interpreted as coming from meaningful objects in the environment.* Top-down processes *are those that emerge from an individual's prior knowledge, motivations, expectations, and other aspects of "higher" mental functioning.*

ter 5, we will discuss how processes of organization, depth perception, and constancy lead from sensation to perception. Finally, we will discuss the processes that lead from perception to classification, and the influences of other mental processes on classification.

Reality, Ambiguity, and Distortions

A primary goal of perception is to get an accurate "fix" on the world; to recognize predators and prey, and sources of danger and pleasure that guide behavior in appropriate ways. Survival depends on accurate perceptions of objects and events in our environment; but the environment is not always easy to "read." It is filled with ambiguous data that lead to uncertainty, and, at times, confusion. Potential prey hide their vulnerability behind screens of protective coloration, just as hunters hide their lethal presence with camouflage. Some things taste good, like sugar or salt, but are not good for one's health; others look innocent, but can be deadly, like certain mushrooms, berries, and pretty colored snakes. So we learn not to trust reality entirely by appearance, but to supplement what our senses tell us with our other knowledge. In the photo on the next page the pencil appears divided at the surface of the water, but our basic knowledge of physical

Is the pencil really divided at the water's surface?

principles of matter tells us that can't be so—it's only an illusion. In this case it is a sensory distortion caused by the differences in the light rays given off by the parts of the pencil within and above the water.

When your senses deceive you into experiencing a stimulus pattern in a manner that is demonstrably incorrect, it is called an **illusion.** In this case, your misinterpretation of the sensory stimulus is shared by most people in the same perceptual situation. Your view of reality may also be distorted by three other processes in addition to perceptual illusion (about which we will have much more to say). A **hallucination** is a false perception that is idiosyncratic, not shared by others in the same situation. It is evidence of an altered consciousness caused by certain mental disorders, such as schizophrenia, brain diseases, alcohol intoxication, psychedelic drugs, hypnotic suggestions, and religious ecstasy (discussed in chapter 7). A **delusion** is a false belief, a distorted idea about one's self, others, or the environment that resists change despite evidence of its irrational basis. Delusions of persecution, jealousy, and grandeur are common in some paranoid conditions (discussed in chapter 15) as well as in some types of racial prejudice. Finally, a last type of reality distortion comes from the mind's tendency to filter out information that is threatening to one's self esteem. This **self-deception** may have initial benefits for maintaining self-image, but it can disguise real dangers to health and well-being that are better coped with by confrontation than denial (Goleman, 1987).

By studying hallucinations, delusions, and self-deception, psychologists learn something about the personality, conflicts, and motivations of the individuals who experience them. However, by studying illusions, psychologists learn about the nature of perception rather than about the peculiarities of the perceiver.

Lessons Learned from Illusions

Psychologists who study perception love ambiguities and the illusions they generate—in their professional lives, that is. Since the first scientific analysis of illusions was published in 1854 by J. J. Oppel, literally thousands of articles have been written about illusions in nature, sensation, perception, and art. Oppel's modest contribution was a simple array of lines that appeared longer when divided into segments than when only the end lines were present, as in:

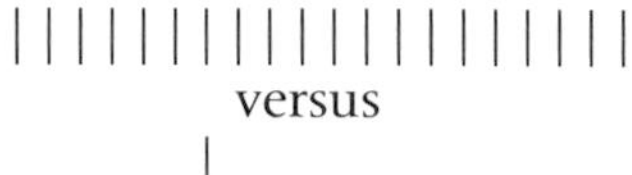

Oppel called his work the study of *geometrical optical illusions.* The word *illusion* shares roots with "ludicrous," both of which stem from the Latin *illudere*—"to mock at." What illusions do is to point up the discrepancy between percept and reality, between the marvelously complex sensory and perceptual processes that are evolution's masterpiece and the ease with which they can be fooled by a simple arrangement of lines.

Psychologists' interest in illusions goes deeper, however. Illusions can demonstrate the abstract conceptual distinctions between sensation, perception, and classification. They can even do more; they can help us understand some fundamental properties of perception (see Coren & Girgus, 1978).

First examine an illusion that works at the sensation level, the Hermann grid in **Figure 6.4.** As you stare at the center of the grid, dark, fuzzy spots appear at the intersections of the white bars. Now focus closely on one intersection; the spot vanishes (as in Lady Macbeth's fantasy). Indeed, as you shift focus, you transform the spots into little dancing dots. How did you do that, you wonder? The answer lies in something you read about in the last chapter (p.162): *lateral inhibition.* Assume this stimulus is registered by ganglion retinal cells, two of which have their receptive fields drawn in the lower corner of the grid. The one at the center of the intersection has two white bars projecting

Figure 6.4 *The Hermann Grid, with Two Ganglion Cell Receptive Fields Projected on It*

through its surround, while its neighbor has only one. It therefore receives more light and can respond at a lower level because of the greater lateral inhibition by the surround. Its reduced response shows up as a dark spot in its center. When you focus at the intersection, you place the image in the center of your fovea, which is where the retina has its maximum sensitivity (because of the concentration of cone cells). It also has many ganglion cells, but they are different from those elsewhere in the retina. Their receptive fields are smaller; hence, they will fall entirely within the intersection, both center and surround. There is no lateral inhibition caused by the surrounding black squares—therefore there are no more black spots. Mach bands (p. 161) are other illusions caused by the operation of sensory processes that distort reality. Illusions at this level generally occur because the arrangement of a stimulus array stimulates receptor processes in an unusual way to directly generate a distorted image.

To study illusions that reveal the operations of perception and classification, psychologists rely on *ambiguous figures:* stimulus patterns that can be seen in two or more distinct ways. Ambiguity is important for understanding perception, because it shows that a *single* image at the sensory level can result in *multiple* interpretations at the perceptual and classification levels.

Sometimes ambiguity arises because the same image can be interpreted as two or more different *objects* in the environment; this produces ambiguity in the *perception* stage. At other times, ambiguity arises because the object being perceived can be interpreted as belonging to different *categories:* this produces ambiguity in the *classification* stage.

Figure 6.5 shows three examples of ambiguous figures, with unambiguous versions of each. Look at each one until you see the two alternative interpretations. Notice that once you have seen both of them, your perception flips back and forth between them as you look at the ambiguous figure. This perceptual *instability* of ambiguous figures is one of their most important characteristics.

The vase/faces and the Necker cube are examples of ambiguity in the *perception* stage. You have two different perceptions of objects in space relative to you, the observer. The vase/faces can be seen as either a central white object on a black back-

Figure 6.5

Vase or Faces?

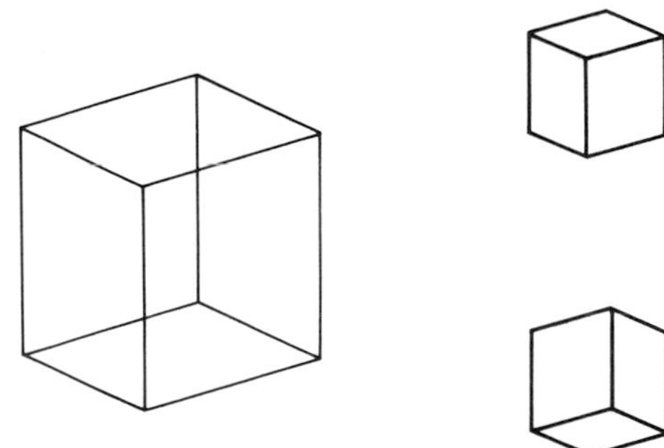

The Necker Cube: Above or Below?

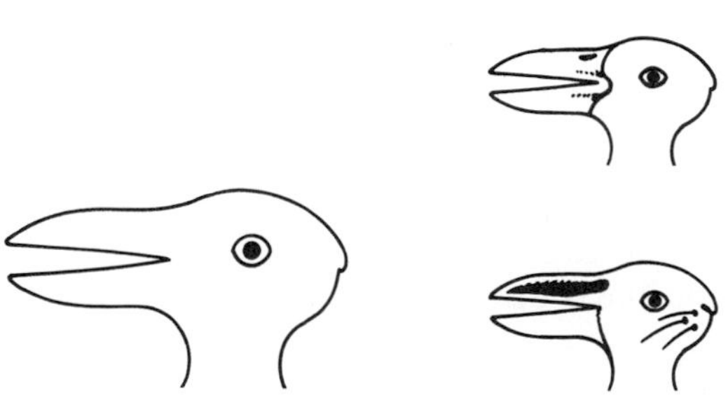

Duck or Rabbit?

Figure 6.6

Is the width of the brim the same size as the height of the hat?

Cut out the disk and pin it to the eraser of a pencil. Rotate the pencil slowly and stare at the center of the disk for 15 seconds. Then look at your palm. What do you see?

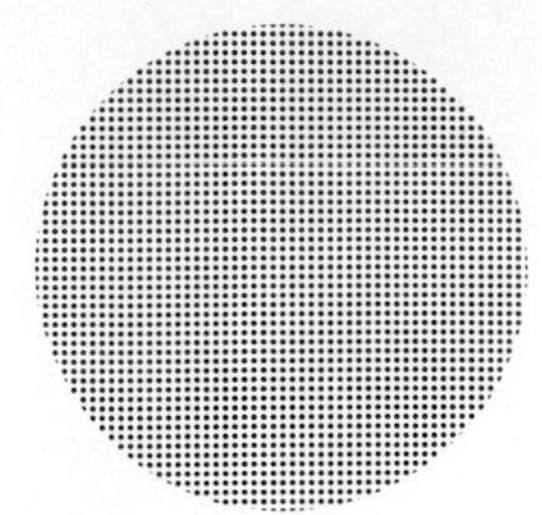

Are the upper and lower parts of the figure the same size?

ground or as two black objects with a white area between them. The Necker cube can be seen as a three-dimensional hollow cube either *below* you and angled to your left or *above* you and angled toward your right. In both cases the ambiguous alternatives are different physical arrangements of objects in three-dimensional space, both of which result from the same stimulus image—but not at the same time.

The duck/rabbit figure is an example of ambiguity in the *classification* stage. It is perceived as the same physical shape in both interpretations; the ambiguity arises in determining the *kind* of object it represents—a duck or a rabbit.

One of the most fundamental properties of normal human perception is the tendency to transform ambiguity and uncertainty about the environment into a clear interpretation that we can act upon with confidence. Dr. Richard lacked this perceptual mechanism: damage to his brain prevented him from organizing separate sensory inputs into perceptual wholes that were meaningful interpretations of the world about him. In a world filled with variability and change, our perceptual system must meet the challenge of *discovering invariance and stability.*

Perceptual illusions make us aware of two considerations: the active role the mind plays in structuring our view of the world and the effects of *context* on the way we perceive stimuli within it. Examine the classic illusions in **Figure 6.6.** Psychologists have discovered many such illusions, not only in vision, but also in other sensory modalities (see Shepard & Jordan, 1984, for auditory illusions of Western listeners). These illusions occur because, unlike Marsha's camera, the central nervous system does not simply record events. Rather, there are complex processes for detecting, integrating, and interpreting information about the world in terms of what we already know and expect; thus what we *see* goes beyond the present physical stimulus properties. The fact that these processes usually occur effortlessly and are helpful in decoding the world around us does not mean that they are simple or strictly error-free. (See also "Mindworks" in *The Best of Science.*)

Ambiguity in Art

The ambiguous figures that psychologists developed, although interesting, are rather simple and prosaic. However, they served as catalysts for several prominent modern artists who became fascinated with such figures because of the complex, dynamic visual experiences they created for the viewers. These artists have used perceptual ambiguity as the central artistic device in many of their works of art.

Shown are three excellent examples. The first, by Victor Vasareley, produces depth reversals like the Necker cube. The corners of the surfaces can be seen either as coming out toward you or going away from you. The next, by M. C. Escher (on p. 194) is based on "figure/ground" reversals like the vase/faces. In *Sky and Water* Escher has created

Which horizontal line is longer?

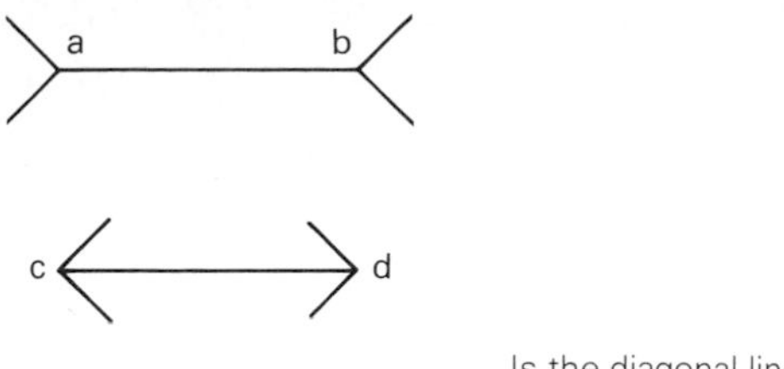

Müller-Lyer

Is the diagonal line broken?

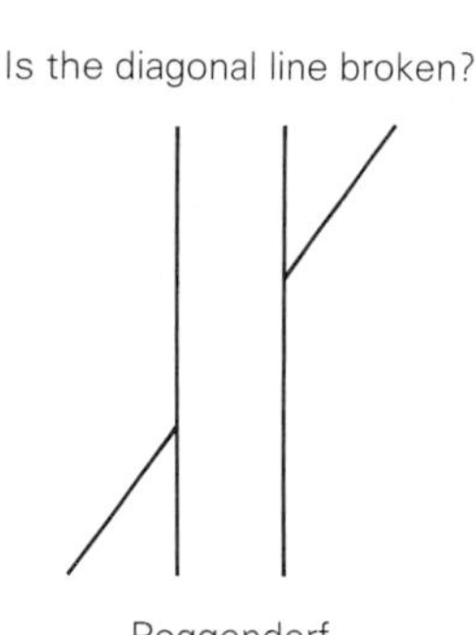

Poggendorf

Are the vertical lines parallel?

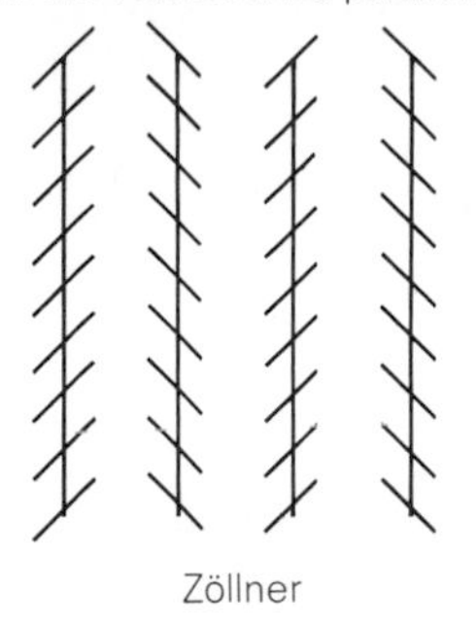

Zöllner

Which central circle is bigger?

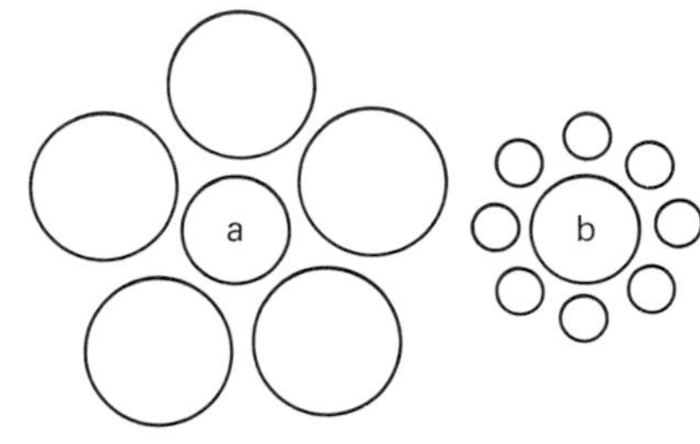

Ebbinghaus

an ambiguous mosaic of interweaving fish and birds at the center where you tend to see the fish or the birds, but not both. Toward the top and bottom the figures become gradually less ambiguous. Notice that when you look at the unambiguous birds at the top, you tend to see birds rather than fish in the ambiguous center section, whereas when you look at the unambiguous fish at the bottom, you tend to see fish rather than birds in the center section. This demonstrates the influence of context on your perception, a topic we will discuss later in more detail.

The final example (on p. 194) is *Slave Market with the Disappearing Bust of Voltaire* by Salvadore Dali. It is a more complex sort of ambiguity in which a whole section of the picture must be radically reorganized and reinterpreted to allow perception of the "invisible" bust of Voltaire. The white sky under the lower arch is Voltaire's forehead and hair; the white portions of the two ladies' dresses are his cheeks, nose, and chin. If you have trouble seeing him, try standing farther away. Squinting or taking off your glasses may also help. Once you have seen Voltaire in this picture, however, you will never be able to look at it without knowing where this French philosopher-writer is hiding.

Depth reversal shown in a painting by Victor Vasarely

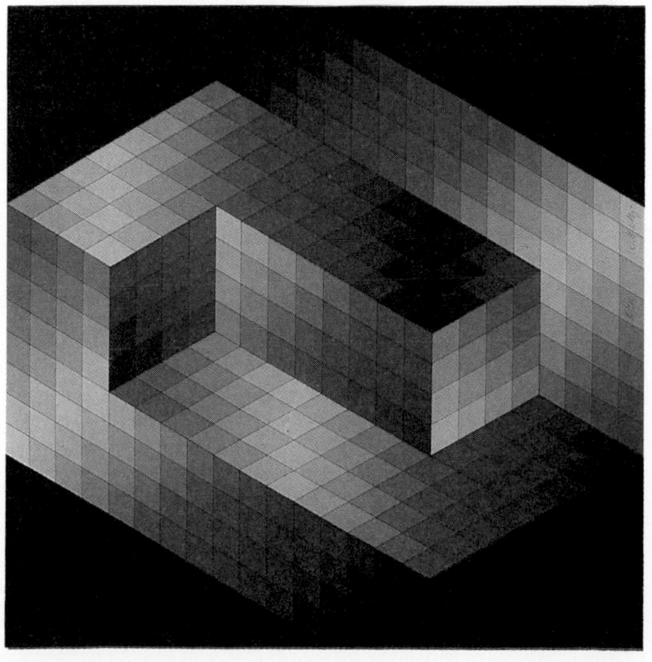

Illusions in Reality

Are illusions just peculiar arrangements of lines, colors, and shapes used by artists and psychologists to plague unsuspecting people? Hardly. Illusions are a basic part of our everyday life. They are an inescapable aspect of the "subjective reality" we each construct using our personal experiences, learning, and motivation to see the new in terms of old, familiar patterns and the ambiguous in terms of what others "see" or what we would like it to be. Even though we may recognize something as an illusion, it can continue to occur and fool us again and again.

Did you ever see the sun "rise" and "set," even though you know that it is sitting out there in the center of its solar system absolutely still? Can you appreciate now why it was such an extraordinary

Paintings by M. C. Escher and Salvadore Dali

feat of courage and wisdom for Christopher Columbus and other earlier voyagers to deny the obvious illusion that the earth was flat and sail off toward one of its apparent edges? A full moon on the horizon plays another trick you may have noticed. When it is overhead it seems to follow wherever you go and is always "right there." This "moon paranoia" exists even though you know that what you are experiencing is an illusion created by the great distance of the moon from your eye. Its light rays are essentially parallel when they reach the earth and perpendicular to your direction of travel no matter where you go—thus the moon seems to stalk your every movement!

Illusions can be utilized to achieve a desired effect, tricking the mind into seeing reality in a different light. Architects and interior designers use principles of perception to create objects in space that seem larger or smaller than they really are. A small apartment becomes more spacious when it is painted with light colors and sparsely furnished with low, small couches, chairs, and tables placed toward the center of the room instead of against the walls. Even more dramatic effects of purposely created illusions are the stock-in-trade of set and lighting directors in movies and theatrical productions.

The use of illusion to create everyday reality can be seen in our choices of cosmetics and clothing (Dackman, 1986). The multibillion dollar cosmetics industry attests to the extent we will go to create illusory appearances. We choose light-colored clothing to make our bodies seem larger and dark-colored clothing with vertical stripes to make our bodies seem slimmer.

The reality of illusions is also documented in other, more tragic, ways. An airline crash that killed 4 people and injured 49 others was caused by the pilot's misjudgment of reality, induced by a version of the Poggendorff illusion (see **Figure 6.6,** pp. 192–93). Two commercial passenger jets were converging on the New York area within 1000 feet of each other at altitudes of 10,000 and 11,000 feet. White cloud tops that protruded above 10,000 feet also seemed to slope upward in a northerly direction. The pilots of the two planes began evasive movements when it appeared the planes were about to collide; however, it was the direction in which the planes swerved that actually caused them to crash. The lower aircraft pulled up and the upper one rolled to the right and then to the left—just as might be predicted from the misjudgment of altitude separation induced by the illusion of the upward-sloping contours of the cloud tops (Coren & Girgus, 1978).

Thus, in the continual process of resolving the discrepancy between the distal stimulus ("external reality") and the proximal stimulus ("receptor reality"), we establish personal perceptions ("phenomenological reality") that guide decisions and behavior—for better or for worse. The way we go about resolving that discrepancy has been a source of controversy among psychologists for a long time.

The Nurture and Nature of Perception

Recall the debate between the *nativists,* who argued that all knowledge of the external world comes through the senses in a direct way that is interpreted by innate mechanisms *(nature,)* and the *empiricists,* who held that most perceptual knowledge is learned through experience with the environment *(nurture)*. These alternative views about the way in which a child's mind develops (chapter 3), have also played an important role in psychologists' theories of perception, and of learning (to be discussed in chapter 8).

Advocates of both the experience and heredity positions assumed that some perceptual attributes, such as color and brightness, were built into the sensory system. The disagreement has been over the mechanisms for perceiving *relational* qualities, such as the size and location of stimuli. Helmholtz (1866/1962) argued for the importance of experience in perception. His theory emphasized the role of mental processes in interpreting the often ambiguous stimulus arrays that excite the nervous system. An observer "makes sense" of the proximal stimulus by using prior knowledge of the environment. On the basis of this experience, the observer makes hypotheses, or inferences, about the way things really are. Perception is thus an *inductive* process, going from specific images to inferences about the general class of objects or events that they might represent. Since this process takes place out of our conscious awareness, Helmholtz termed it **unconscious inference.** Ordinarily these inferential processes work well and generate veridical perceptions of reality. However, when unusual circumstances in the stimulus array or viewing position allow multiple interpretations of the same stimulus, or favor a familiar interpretation when a new one is required, perceptual illusions result. The moon illusion is an instance of a faulty hypothesis about size based on prior information about the relationship of size to distance from the observer. This notion of "perception as hypotheses" is currently part of a general class of perceptual theories based on visual information-processing strategies. One version which stresses the importance of our transactions with the environment as the basis for developing these hypotheses is called, appropriately, **transactional perception** (Ames, 1951).

The modern nativists, following in the path of Locke, Berkeley, and Hume, argue for innately determined sensory processes that enable an observer to perceive an object's size, shape, and distance. One proponent of this view is J. J. Gibson (1966, 1979) who searched for those aspects of the proximal stimulus that provide information about the distal stimulus. His theory holds that a proximal stimulus is not an isolated image, but part of a *whole pattern* of proximal stimulation that the sensory system is designed to respond to as a *higher-order pattern of stimulation.* For example, objects in the environment have size, depth, and slant, which are properties of the distal stimulus. In the natural environment real-world surfaces of uniform texture that slant away from the observer, such as grassy meadows, cast an image on the retina that is not uniform. That proximal stimulus forms a **texture gradient;** images of uniform texture are smaller at greater distances because they are projected onto smaller areas of the retina (see **Figure 6.7**). Gibson identified such texture gradients not as inferences about size-space relationships, but rather as actual parts of the proximal stimulus.

Instead of trying to understand perception as a result of an organism's structure, Gibson proposed that it could be better understood through an analysis of the immediately surrounding environment (or ecology). As one writer put it, Gibson's approach was, "Ask not what's inside your head, but what your head's inside of" (Mace, 1977). In effect, Gibson's theory of **Ecological Optics** is concerned with stimuli for perception rather than the mechanisms by which we perceive. This approach was a radical departure from all previous theories.

Figure 6.7 *An Example of Texture as a Depth Cue*

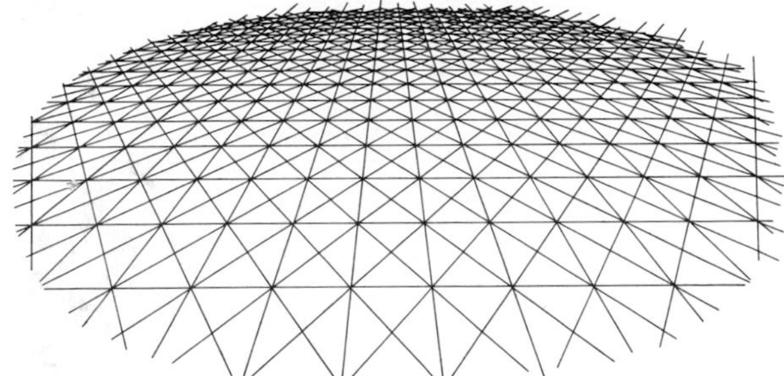

This wheatfield is a natural example of the way texture is used as a depth cue. Notice the way the wheat slants.

Gibson's ideas are also important because they emphasize perceiving as *active exploration* of the environment. When an observer is *moving* in the world, the pattern of stimulation on the retina is constantly changing over time as well as space. Gibson stressed the richness of this "optical flow" in perceptual events. Much of the earlier laboratory research on perception was based on having subjects sit in one place while viewing simple, unmoving stimuli under highly restricted and artificial conditions. Gibson and others argued that perceptual systems evolved in organisms who were on the move, seeking food, water, mates, and shelter in a complex and changing environment. The theory of Ecological Optics tried to specify the information about the environment that was available to the eyes of a moving observer. However, this emphasis on the stimulus side of perception clearly ignores an observer's mind and has little to say about the nature of illusions.

Another nativist approach which has had considerable influence on our knowledge of perception came from Germany in the 1920s—Gestalt psychology. Since it dealt primarily with the "laws of perceptual organization," we will consider next what this theory tells us about perception within that context.

Perceptual Processes

Vision is the most important and complex perceptual system in humans and most other mammals. In this chapter almost all of our discussion will be about vision, not because other perceptual systems are either uninteresting or unimportant, but because (a) vision has been more intensively studied than the other modalities, and (b) on the printed page it is easier to provide visual demonstrations than auditory or tactile ones. In the present section we will explore what is known about three kinds of processes that transform sensory information into perception of real-world objects: organization, depth perception, and constancy.

Organizational Processes

Imagine how confusing the world would be if we were totally unable to put together and organize the information available from the output of our millions of retinal receptors. We would experience a kaleidoscope of disconnected bits of color moving and swirling before our eyes. (Even Dr. Richard was somewhat better off than this, since he could put parts together, even though sometimes he did it incorrectly.) The processes that put sensory information together to give us the perception of a coherent scene over the whole visual field are referred to collectively as processes of **perceptual organization.** We have seen that what a person experiences, as a result of the perceptual processing, is called a *percept.*

For example, your percept of the two-dimensional geometric design in **Figure 6.8** is probably three diagonal rows of figures, the first being composed of squares, the second of arrowheads, and the third of diamonds. Nothing seems remarkable about this until you analyze all the organizational processing that you must be performing to see the design in this way. The organizational processes we will be discussing in this section include region segregation, figure and ground, closure, grouping, figural goodness, reference frames, spatial and temporal integration, and motion perception.

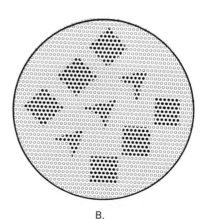

Figure 6.8

A.

B.

Region Segregation

First, consider your initial sensory response to **Figure 6.8.** Because your retina is composed of many separate receptors, your eye responds to this stimulus pattern with a mosaic of millions of independent neural responses coding the amount of light falling on tiny areas of your retina (see **Figure 6.8B**). The first task of perceptual organization is to determine which of these tiny areas belong with which others. In other words, the outputs of the separate receptors must be synthesized by being structured into larger regions that are internally uniform in their properties.

The primary information for this "region segregation" process comes from color and texture. An abrupt change in color (hue, saturation, or brightness) signifies the presence of an "edge" between two regions. Abrupt changes in texture likewise can mark edges between visibly different regions. Finding these edges is the first step in organizational processing.

Many researchers now believe that the cells in the visual cortex discovered by Hubel and Wiesel, discussed in chapter 5, are involved in these region-segregating processes (Marr, 1982). Some cells have elongated receptive fields that are ideally suited for detecting edges between regions that differ in color. Others have receptive fields that seem to detect little "bars" or "lines" such as occur in textures like grassy fields, wood grains, and woven fabrics. These cortical "line-detector" cells may be responsible for our ability to discriminate between regions that have different textures (Beck, 1972; Julesz, 1981).

Figure and Ground

As a result of region segregation, the stimulus in our example has now been divided into thirteen regions: twelve small dark ones and a single large light one. You can now think of each of these regions as a unified entity, like thirteen separate pieces of glass in a stained-glass window. Another organizational process now divides the regions into *figures* and *ground.* **Figures** are seen as object-like regions; **ground** is the background against which the figures stand out. In our present example, you probably see the dark regions as figures and the light region as ground. However, you can also see this stimulus pattern differently by reversing figure and ground, much as you did with the ambiguous vase/faces drawing and the Escher work. To do this, try to see the white region as a large white sheet of paper that has nine holes cut in it, behind which you can see a black background.

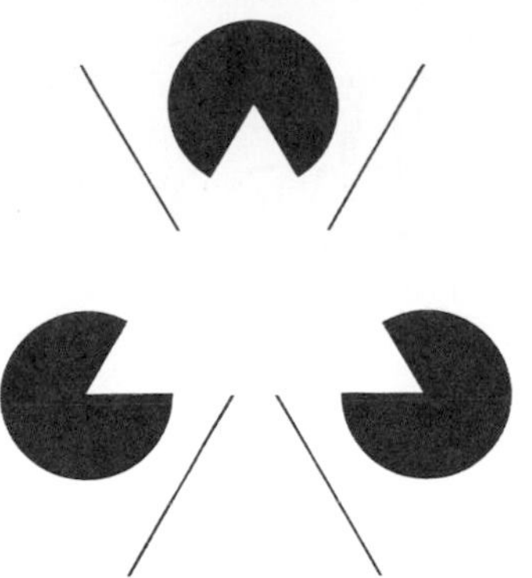

Figure 6.9 *Subjective Contours That Fit the Angles of Your Mind*

In perceiving these two interpretations, notice that when you perceive a region as figure, the boundaries between light and dark are interpreted as edges or contours that belong to the figure, defining its shape. In contrast, the ground seems to extend behind these edges rather than stopping at them as it actually does in the stimulus. Such facts suggest that this aspect of perceptual organization is related to depth perception, a topic we will discuss in the next section.

The tendency to perceive a figure in *front* of a ground is very strong. In fact, you can even get this effect in a stimulus when the perceived figure doesn't actually exist! In **Figure 6.9** you perceive a solid white triangle against a ground containing three black circles and a black X on a white surface. Notice, however, that there are really just three solid black figures and four disconnected lines in the stimulus pattern. You see the illusory white triangle in front because the straight edges of the black shapes and the interruptions in the lines are aligned in a way that suggests a solid white triangle covering parts of whole black circles and a complete X.

There seem to be three levels of figure/ground organization in this example: the top white triangle, the black circles and the X behind it, and the larger white surface behind everything else. Notice that perceptually you divide the white area in the stimulus into two different regions: the white triangle and the white ground. Where this division occurs, you perceive illusory *subjective contours* which, in fact, do not exist in the distal stimulus, but only in your subjective experience.

Closure

Your perception of the white triangle in **Figure 6.9** also demonstrates another powerful organizing process—that of **closure,** in which you tend to see incomplete figures as complete. Though the stimulus gives you only the three angles, your perceptual

Figure 6.10

system supplies the edges in between that make the figure a complete triangle. Likewise, in **Figure 6.10,** you have no trouble perceiving a horse.

Grouping

You also perceive the nine distinct figural regions of **Figure 6.8A** not as separate and independent items but rather as grouped together into three distinct rows, each composed of three identical shapes along a diagonal line. How does you visual system accomplish this **grouping,** and what factors control it?

The problem of grouping was first studied extensively by Max Wertheimer (1923), one of the founders of the Gestalt movement, along with Kurt Koffka (1935), and Wolfgang Köhler (1947). Before examining how this aspect of perceptual organization was studied, we will review some of the characteristics which set this German "school of psychology" apart from the behaviorist, atomistic, stimulus-response psychology that was then prevalent in the United States.

Gestalt is a German word that means, roughly, "whole configuration," or form. The rallying cry of Gestaltists was, "The whole is more than the sum of its parts!" They pointed out that whole patterns have *emergent properties* that are not shared by any of the component pieces. This idea can be illustrated by a line made up of many separate dots (see **Figure 6.11**). Alone, each dot has just two perceptual properties: its color and its position, but when they are arranged in a line, the line has additional properties such as length, orientation, and curvature that were not properties of any of the separate dots. These properties *emerge* only from the whole configuration. Similarly, a musical work like a Mozart sonata is much more than a mere collection of notes. Its greatness lies in the emergent properties of its melodies and rich harmonies rather than in the properties of the individual notes of which it is composed.

Gestaltists, therefore, studied and theorized about the perception of *whole figures.* They were particularly interested in the way in which the structure of the whole visual field *organizes* the parts within it. Gestalt theorists rejected empiricism and accepted nativism as the basis for perceptual organization. They believed that most organizational mechanisms were innate—"prewired" at birth in brain mechanisms and universal for the species, not learned from an individual's personal experience.

What Wertheimer did was to present subjects with arrays of simple geometric figures. By varying a single factor and observing how it affected the way people perceived the structure of the array, he was able to formulate a set of "laws of grouping." Several of these laws are illustrated in **Figure 6.12.** In part A, there is an array of equally spaced circles that is ambiguous in its grouping: you can see it equally well as rows or columns of dots. However, when the spacing is changed slightly so that the horizontal distances between adjacent dots are less than the vertical distances (array B), you see the array unambiguously as organized into horizontal rows; when the spacing is changed so that the vertical distances are less (array C), you see the array as organized into vertical columns. These illustrate Wertheimer's **law of proximity:** all else being equal, the nearest (most "proximal") elements are grouped together.

By varying the color of the dots instead of their spacing, array D is generated. Although there is equal spacing between the dots, your visual system automatically organizes this stimulus into rows because of their *similar color.* You see array E as organized into columns because of *similar size,* and array F as organized into rows because of *similar shape* and *orientation.*

These grouping effects (and more) can be summarized by the **law of similarity:** all else being equal, the most similar elements are seen as grouped together. Shape similarity was the factor responsible for your seeing the figures in Figure 6.8 as grouped into diagonal rows from bottom left to top right.

When elements in the visual field are moving, similarity of motion also produces a powerful grouping. The **law of common fate** states that elements moving in the same direction and at the same rate are seen grouped together. If the circles in every other column of Figure 6.12G were mov-

Figure 6.11

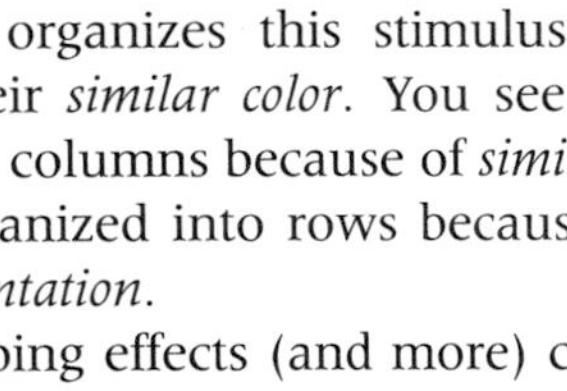

Perceptual Grouping

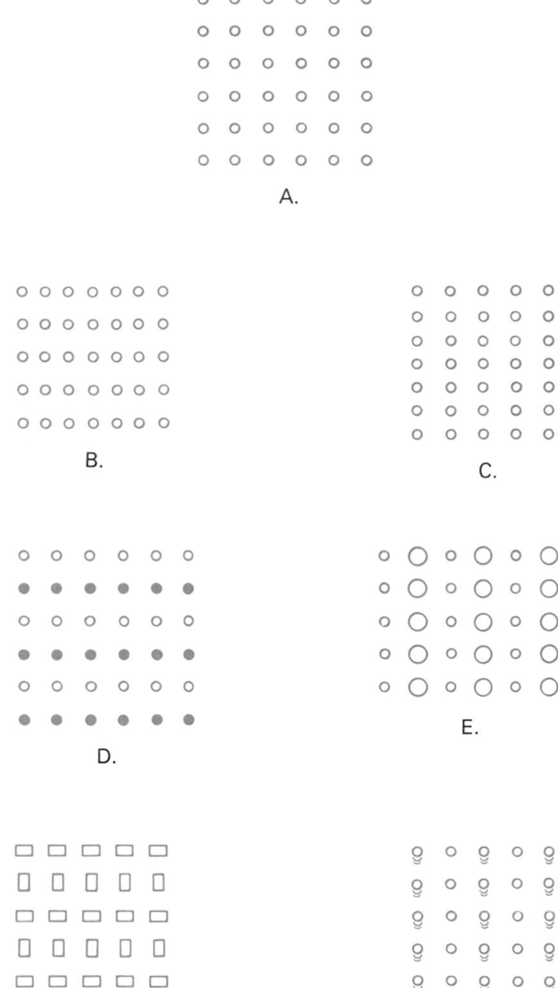

Figure 6.12 *Grouping Phenomena*

ing upward, as indicated by the blurring, you would see the array grouped into columns because of their similarity in motion. You get this effect at a ballet when several dancers move in a pattern different from the others. Remember Dr. Richard's observation that an object in his visual field became organized properly when it moved as a whole. His experience was evidence of the powerful organizing effect of common fate which, along with proximity, is subsumed under the law of similarity.

These effects show the principle we mentioned earlier, that perception depends on emergent properties of a configuration. The law of similarity operates only when two or more elements are simultaneously present in a visual field. The Gestaltists interpreted such results to mean that the whole stimulus pattern is somehow determining the organization of its own parts. They saw this as convincing evidence that the *whole* percept is *more than* and *different from* the mere collection of its *parts*. The strong argument was that perceiving the whole—the *Gestalt*—was itself more basic and took place earlier in the process than the perception of its elements.

Figural Goodness

Once a given region has been segregated and selected as a figure against a ground, with groupings among similar parts, the edges must be further organized into specific *shapes*. You might think that this would require simply perceiving all of the edges of a figure, but again, the Gestaltists showed that visual organization is far more complex. If a whole shape were merely the sum of its edges, then all shapes having the same number of edges should be equally easy to perceive.

Unfortunately this is not true. Organizational processes in shape perception are sensitive to something the Gestaltists called **figural goodness,** a concept which includes perceived simplicity, symmetry, and regularity. **Figure 6.13** shows several figures that exhibit a range in figural goodness even though they all have six sides. You will probably agree that Figure 6.13A is the "best" figure (or most standard-looking) and Figure 6.13E the "worst," (or least standard-looking) with the others falling between these two extremes.

Experiments have shown that "good" figures are more easily and accurately perceived, remembered, and described than "bad" ones (Garner, 1974). Such results suggest that shapes of "good" figures can be coded more rapidly and economically by the visual system than those of "bad" figures. In fact, the visual system sometimes tends to see a single "bad" figure being composed of two overlapping "good" ones (**Figure 6.14**). This example demonstrates that organizational processes provide the best and simplest interpretation consistent with sensory stimulation.

Figure 6.13

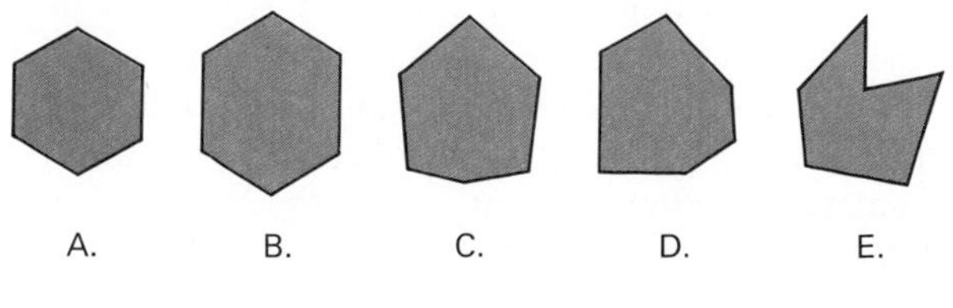

A. B. C. D. E.

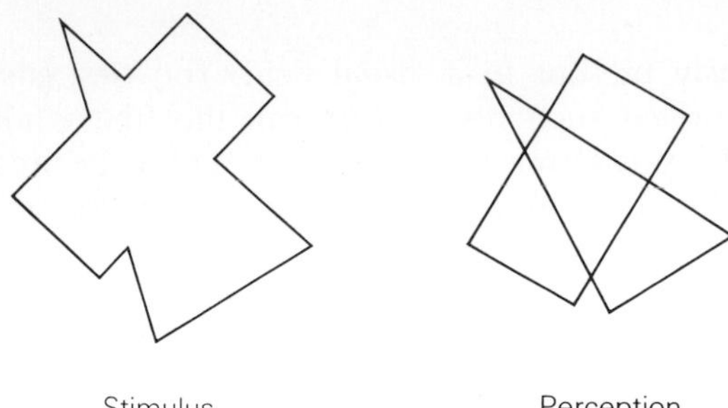

Figure 6.14

Reference Frames

Higher levels of organization are achieved when the shapes of figures are perceived relative to **reference frames** established by the spatial and temporal context. The perceptual effects of reference frames are also demonstrated in Figure 6.8: if you saw one of the upper figures by itself, it would look like a diamond, whereas one of the lower ones would look like a square (as shown in **Figure 6.15A**). When you see these figures as parts of diagonal rows, the shapes reverse: the line composed of diamonds looks like a tilted column of squares and the line composed of squares looks like a tilted column of diamonds (**Figure 6.15B**).

The shapes of the figures look different when they are in diagonal rows because the orientation of each figure is seen in relation to the reference frame established by the whole row (Palmer, 1984). In effect, you see the shapes of the figures as you would if the rows were vertical instead of diagonal. (Turn the book 45 degrees clockwise to see what this looks like. ↗)

There are other ways to establish a contextual reference frame that does the same thing. **Figure 6.15C** shows these same figures inside of rectangular frames tilted 45 degrees. If you cover the frames, the left figure looks like a diamond, the right one like a square. When you uncover them, the left one changes into a square, the right one into a diamond.

Spatial and Temporal Integration

Reference frames are just one example of the visual system's tendency to organize individual parts in relation to larger spatial contexts. In fact, even the whole visual field at any moment is seldom perceived as ending at the edges of our vision. Instead we perceive it as a restricted glimpse of a large visual world extending in all directions to unseen areas of the environment.

You must be able to integrate your perceptions from these restricted glimpses of the world from one moment to the next. As you fixate on different parts of the same figure, what you see in your present fixation is somehow properly integrated with what you saw in the last one, which was properly integrated with the one before that, and so on. If this were not true, you would not perceive the same objects in successive views; you would see a hodgepodge of unrelated and overlapping shapes.

The process of putting together visual information from one fixation to the next in both space and time is absolutely critical for useful perception. The world around you is so much larger than a single field of view that you could never know about the spatial layout of your surroundings without organizational processes that integrate the visual information from many eye fixations into a single continuing episode of related images (Hochberg, 1968).

Complex objects often require several eye fixations before you can build up a complete spatial interpretation even when they are small enough to fit into a single field of view. One interesting consequence of the way you put together the informa-

Figure 6.15

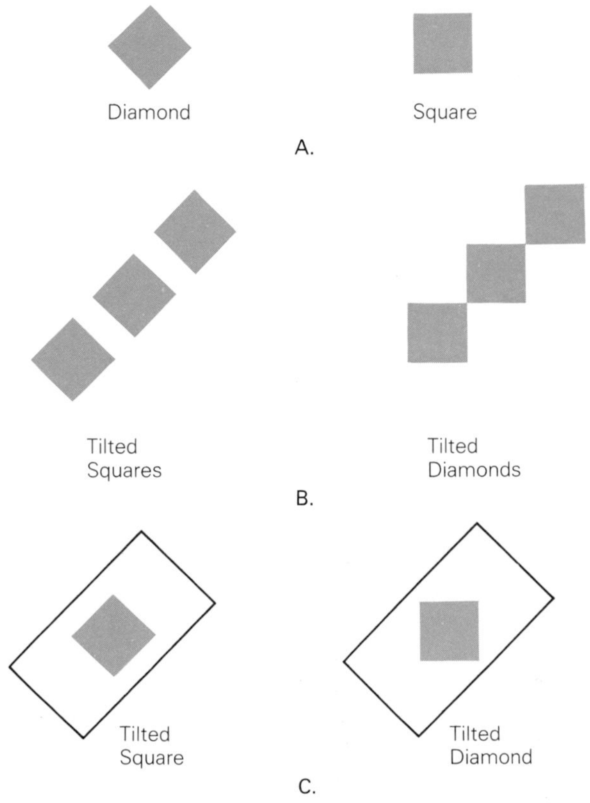

Diamond
Square
A.

Tilted Squares
Tilted Diamonds
B.

Tilted Square
Tilted Diamond
C.

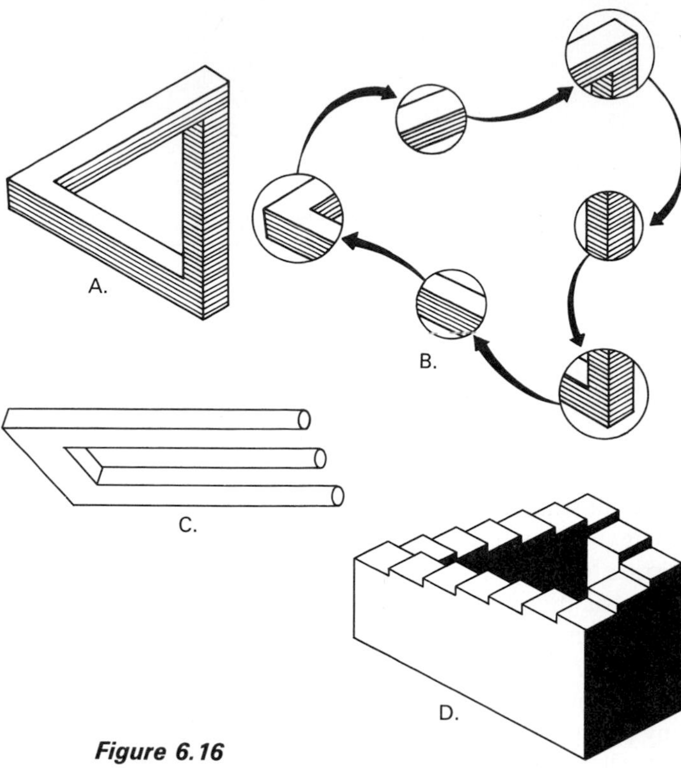

Figure 6.16

tion from different fixations is that you are able to perceive "impossible" objects such as occur in **Figure 6.16.** For example, each fixation of corners and sides provides an interpretation that is consistent with an object that seems to be a three-dimensional triangle (see **Figure 6.16A**); but when you try to integrate them into a coherent whole, the pieces just don't fit together properly. The structure in **Figure 6.16B** has two arms that become 3 prongs, and there is a perpetual staircase in **Figure 6.16C.**

Motion Perception

Although most of the visible environment is usually stationary, certain kinds of objects are not. The ones that move tend to be particularly important, since they are likely to be potential predators, prey, enemies, mates, or dangerous objects. Perceiving an object that is in different places in successive scenes as being a single object in motion is, therefore, critical for survival.

It is tempting to think that all of our motion perception can be accounted for by "motion-detector" cells in our brains, as described in the last chapter. Unfortunately, motion perception is a far more complicated affair, requiring higher levels of perceptual organization in the brain to integrate and interpret the responses of different retinal cells over time.

If you sit in a darkened room and fixate on a stationary spot of light inside a lighted rectangle that is moving very slowly back and forth (**Figure 6.17A**), you will perceive instead a *moving* dot going back and forth within a *stationary* rectangle. This illusion, called **induced motion,** occurs even when your eyes are quite still and fixated on the dot. In this case, your motion-detector cells would not be firing at all in response to the stationary dot, but, presumably, would be firing in response to the moving lines of the rectangle. To see the *dot* as moving instead requires some higher level of perceptual organization in which the dot and its supposed motion are perceived within the *reference frame* provided by the rectangle.

There seems to be a strong tendency for the visual system to take a larger, surrounding figure as the reference frame for a smaller figure inside it. You have probably experienced induced motion many times without knowing it. The moon (which is nearly stationary) frequently looks as if it is moving through a cloud when, in fact, it is the cloud that is moving past the moon (**Figure 6.17B**). The surrounding cloud induces perceived movement in the moon just as the rectangle does in the dot.

It is even possible for you to see motion in the visual field when it is you who are moving. Have you ever been in a train that started moving very slowly? Doesn't it look like the pillars on the station platform or a stationary train next to you are moving backward instead?

Figure 6.17

A.

Stimulus

Percept

B.

Another movement illusion that demonstrates the existence of some higher-level organizing processes for motion perception is called **apparent motion.** The simplest form of apparent motion, called the *phi phenomenon,* occurs when two stationary spots of light in different positions in the visual field are turned on and off alternately at a rate of about 4 to 5 times per second. This effect is seen in outdoor advertising signs and disco light displays. Even at this relatively slow rate of alternation, it appears that a single light is moving back and forth between the two spots. Another form of apparent motion is the **autokinetic effect** when a small, stationary spot of light viewed in a totally darkened room appears to wander about. In the *phi phenomenon* motion is perceived between still stimuli; in the *autokinetic effect* a single still stimulus is seen as moving. In the final section of this chapter we will see how the autokinetic effect has been used to study social conformity of individuals to group judgments. Can you anticipate how it could be used in that way?

All the organizational processes we have discussed so far are required to explain how humans can see a unified world from the successive, partial, and unorganized patterns of stimulation that affect our sensory organs. Unlike Dr. Richard, we are able to synthesize the many bits of sensory information we receive so that we can make sense of them. There is no question that our brain does it very well, but perception psychologists haven't yet learned how it does it.

Depth Perception

All the examples discussed thus far have been two-dimensional patterns on flat surfaces. Everyday perceiving, however, involves objects in three-dimensional space. Perceiving all three spatial dimensions is absolutely vital if you are to be able to approach things you want, such as good food and interesting people, and avoid things that are dangerous, like speeding cars. This requires having accurate information about *depth* (the distance from you to an object) as well as about its *direction* from you. Your ears can be used to help in determining the direction to an object, but they are not much help with depth.

Seeing how far away an object is may not seem to be much of a problem at first, but have you ever tried to figure out how the visual system might do it? The difficulty is that it has to be done using retinal images that have only two spatial dimensions—vertical and horizontal. There is no third dimension for depth.

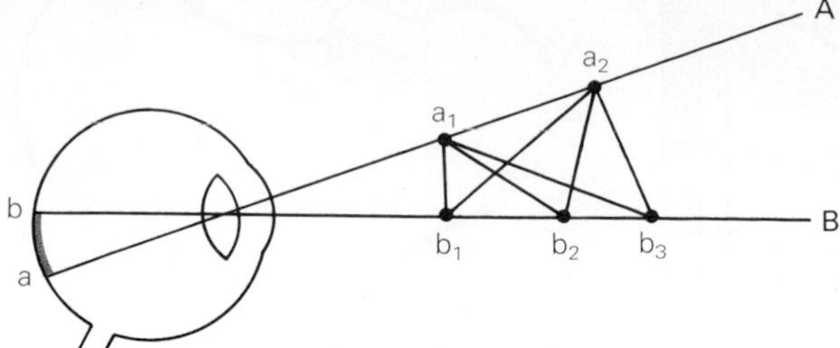

Figure 6.18 *Depth Ambiguity*

To illustrate the problem of having a 2-D retina doing a 3-D job, consider the situation shown in **Figure 6.18.** When a spot of light stimulates the retina at the point labeled *a,* how do you know whether it came from position a_1 or a_2 in the environment? In fact, it could have come from *anywhere* along the line labeled *A,* because light from any point on that line projects onto the same retinal cell. Similarly, all points on line *B* project onto the single retinal point labeled *b.* To make matters worse, a straight line connecting any point on line *A* to any point on line *B* (a_1–b_2 or a_2–b_1, for example) would produce the same image on the retina. The net result of all these possibilities is that the image on your retina is ambiguous in depth: it could have been produced by objects at several different distances. For this reason, the same retinal image can be given many different perceptual interpretations.

The ambiguity of the Necker cube (Figure 6.5B) results from this ambiguity in depth. Another interesting example is shown in **Figure 6.19.** The "Ames chair" looks like a normal, solid chair when it is viewed, using only one eye, from the one particular position at which all of its parts project onto the appropriate retinal locations. From other viewing positions, however, the "solid chair" is seen to be an illusion: it is just a suspended collection of disconnected sticks.

Fortunately, this illusion occurs only under these very unusual viewing conditions. Normally you would have both eyes open and would move your head while viewing the "chair," giving you more than enough information to see it accurately as a mere collection of sticks at odd angles in depth. Still, the fact that you can be fooled under certain circumstances shows that depth perception requires an *interpretation* of sensory input, and that this interpretation can be wrong. Your interpretation relies on many different information sources about distance (often called *depth cues*), some of which we will now examine more closely.

Figure 6.19 *The Ames Chair*
When viewed from the correct point (A), the chair is seen. When viewed from another position (B), the chair becomes a collection of sticks in space. From W. H. Ittelson (1968) The Ames Demonstration in Perception, *New York: Hafner Publishing Company, reprinted by permission.*

Binocular Cues

Have you ever wondered why you have two eyes instead of just one? The second eye is more than just a spare; it provides some of the best, most compelling information about depth. Two sources of depth information that are binocular (from *bi* meaning "two" and *ocular* meaning "of the eyes") are *binocular disparity* and *convergence.*

Because the eyes are about two to three inches apart horizontally, they receive slightly different views of the world. To convince yourself of this, try the following experiment. First, close your left eye and use the right one to line up your two index fingers with some small object in the distance, holding one finger at arm's length and the other about a foot in front of your face. Now, keep your fingers stationary, close you right eye, and open the left one while continuing to fixate on the distant object. What happened to the position of your two fingers? The second eye does not see them lined up with the distant object, but off to the side, because it gets a slightly different view.

This displacement between the horizontal positions of corresponding images in your two eyes is called **binocular disparity.** It provides depth information because the amount of disparity depends on the relative distance of the objects from you. For instance, when you switched eyes, the closer finger was displaced farther to the side than was the distant finger.

When you look at the world with both eyes open, most objects that you see are stimulating different positions on your two retinas, but you are not aware of this. The object you directly focus on projects onto the two foveae. Any others that happen to be at that same distance from you will also project onto corresponding retinal positions in the two eyes, but everything else will actually produce images at different places on the two retinas—because of binocular disparity. If the disparity between corresponding images in the two retinas is small enough, the visual system is able to "fuse" them into a perception of a single object in depth. However, if the images are too far apart, as when you "cross" your eyes, you actually see the double images.

When you stop to think about it, what your visual system does is pretty amazing: it takes two different retinal images, compares them for horizontal displacement of corresponding parts (binocular disparity), and produces a unitary perception of a single object in depth as a result. In effect, it interprets horizontal displacement between the two images as depth in the three-dimensional world.

Other binocular information about depth comes from **convergence.** The two eyes *turn inward* to some extent whenever they are fixated on an object (see **Figure 6.20**). When the object is very close—a finger a few inches in front of your face—the eyes must turn toward each other quite a bit for the same image to fall on both foveae. You can actually see the eyes converge if you watch a friend focus first on a distant object and then on one a foot or so away.

Figure 6.20

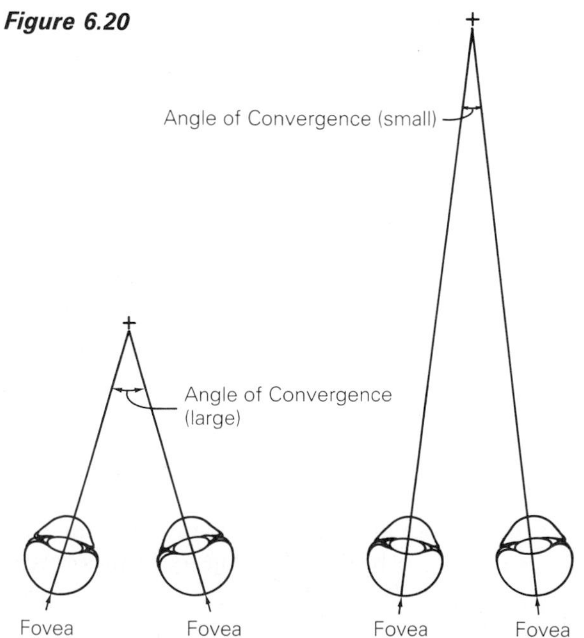

Convergence information sent back to the brain from the eye muscles is useful for depth perception only up to about 10 feet, however. At greater distances the angular differences are too small to detect, because the eyes are nearly parallel when you fixate on a distant object.

Motion Cues

To see how motion produces depth information, try the following demonstration. Close one eye, line up your two index fingers with some distant object as you did before, and then move your head to the side while fixating on the distant object and keeping your fingers still. As you move your head, you see both your fingers move, but the close finger moves farther and faster than the more distant one. The fixated object does not move at all. This source of information about depth is called **relative motion parallax.**

Motion parallax provides information about depth because, as you move, the relative distances of objects in the world determine the amount and direction of their relative motion in your retinal image of the scene. This relationship is illustrated in **Figure 6.21A** for motion along the line of sight toward the fixated object (as you look at the distant point toward which you are driving) and in **Figure 6.21B** for motion perpendicular to the line of sight (as you look out the side window).

Motion Gradients

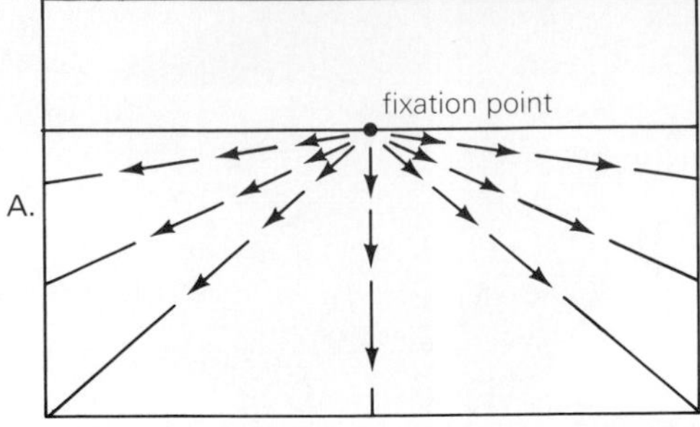

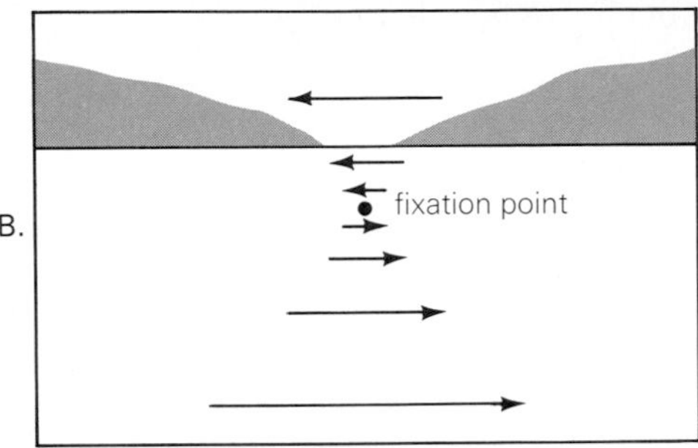

Figure 6.21 *Motion Gradients*
When you are moving in a stationary environment, the speed and direction of motion of points in your retinal image depends on their distance in depth relative to the fixated point (which does not move). Direction of motion of these points is indicated by the direction of the arrows, and speed is indicated by the length of the arrows. Part A shows the motion gradient (or "optical flow") of the image as you look at the point toward which you are moving (like looking out the front window of your car as you drive toward the fixation point). Part B shows it as you look at right angles to the direction of motion (like looking out the side window). (From Gibson, 1950)

Pictorial Cues

Further sources of information about depth are available even with just one eye and no motion of the head. These are called *pictorial cues,* because they include the kinds of depth information found in pictures. Artists who create pictures, in what appears to be three dimensions on the two dimensions of a piece of paper or canvas, make skilled use of pictorial cues.

Interposition or *occlusion* arises when an opaque object blocks the light coming toward your eye from an object behind it so that only the front object is fully present in your retinal image. This gives you depth information because the occluded object must be further away than the occluding one.

The fact that opaque surfaces block light produces additional depth information from shadows. *Shadows* provide important information about the three-dimensional shape of objects and about the position of the light source.

Three additional sources of pictorial information are all related to how light projects from a three-dimensional world onto a two-dimensional surface like the retina: relative size, linear perspective, and texture gradients. A basic rule of light projection is that objects of the same size that are at different distances project images of different sizes on the retina. The closest one projects the largest image and the farthest one, the smallest image. This is called the *size/distance relation.* The size/distance relation makes *relative size* a cue for depth perception.

Linear perspective is a depth cue that also depends on the size/distance relation—when parallel lines (by definition separated everywhere by the same distance) recede into the distance, they converge toward a point on the horizon in your retinal image. This very important fact was discovered by Renaissance artists, who began to use it to paint depth compellingly for the first time around 1400 (Vasari, 1967). Prior to that time artists had used only information from interposition, shadows, and relative size.

The last kind of pictorial depth cue comes from Gibson's *texture gradients* mentioned earlier (p. 195). The gradients result from the size/distance relation, but are applied to textures of surfaces rather than to edges. Although the texture of a surface, such as a rug or tile floor is actually uniform, the size/distance relation requires that its texture elements be drawn smaller and smaller in the parts that are farther and farther away.

By now it should be clear that there is not just one, but many sources of depth information. Under normal viewing conditions, however, information from many different sources comes together in a single, coherent three-dimensional interpretation of the environment. What you experience is depth "out there," not the different "cues" to depth that were in the proximal stimulus. In other words, you don't perceive double images, differential motion, interposition, shadows, relative size, or convergence of parallel lines, even though all these things are constantly present in the patterns of light that enter your eyes (unless you are an art student especially sensitive to drawing perspective). Rather, your visual system uses these sources of information "automatically," without your conscious awareness, to give you a perception of depth in the three-dimensional environment, and that is what you consciously experience.

It may even be true that your depth perception processes are at work when you don't consciously experience depth. This idea underlies the usual explanation of the Ponzo illusion (**Figure 6.22**). The upper line looks longer because you unconsciously interpret the converging sides according to linear perspective as parallel lines receding into the distance, like railroad tracks. You unconsciously process the upper line as though it were farther away and thus see it as longer, because a farther object would have to be longer than a nearer one for both to produce retinal images of the same size.

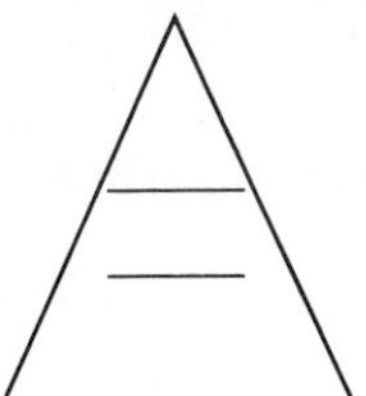

Figure 6.22 *The Ponzo Illusion*
The converging lines add a dimension of depth, and, therefore, the distance cue makes the top line appear larger than the bottom line even though they are actually the same length.

Perceptual Constancies

The goal of perception is to obtain information about the world around us, not about images on our sensory organs. We have already shown a number of ways in which the human visual system meets this goal by going beyond the information it is given directly. Another very important way it does so is by perceiving an unchanging world despite the constant changes that occur in the pattern of stimulation on the retina as the result of different viewing conditions.

Put this book down on the table, then move your head closer to it—just a few inches away—then move your head back to a normal reading distance. Although the book stimulated a much larger part of your retina when it was up close than when it was far away, you saw the book's size as constant.

Now set the book upright and try tilting your head clockwise. When you do this, the image of the book rotates counterclockwise on your retina, but you still perceive the book to be upright: its perceived orientation is *constant.* In general, then, you see the world as *invariant, constant,* and *stable* despite changes in the stimulation of your sensory receptors. This is a very general principle of perception—and a very useful ability to have.

Psychologists refer to this general phenomenon as **perceptual constancy.** Roughly speaking, it means that what you *perceive* are the properties of the distal stimuli, which are generally constant, rather than those of the proximal stimuli, which change every time you move your eyes or head. Constancy generally holds over almost all visible properties, but in this section we will discuss only three cases in which it has been intensively studied: size, shape, and orientation.

Size and Shape Constancy

What determines your perception of the size of an object? Part of the answer must be that you perceive its actual size on the basis of the size of its retinal image. However, the demonstration with your book shows that the size of the retinal image depends on both the actual size of the book and its *distance* from the eye. Because of this relation between size and distance (the same one we discussed in the section on depth perception), the perceptual system must determine an object's actual size by *combining* information from the size of its retinal image with other information about its distance. As you now know, information about distance is available from the depth cues of binocular disparity, eye convergence, motion parallax, and other sources. Your visual system combines them with retinal information about image size to yield a perception of an object size that usually corresponds with the actual size of the distal stimulus.

The two little men may not look it, but they are exactly *the same size. Most people see the little man on the right as smaller because they unconsciously use distance to judge the size of something familiar.*

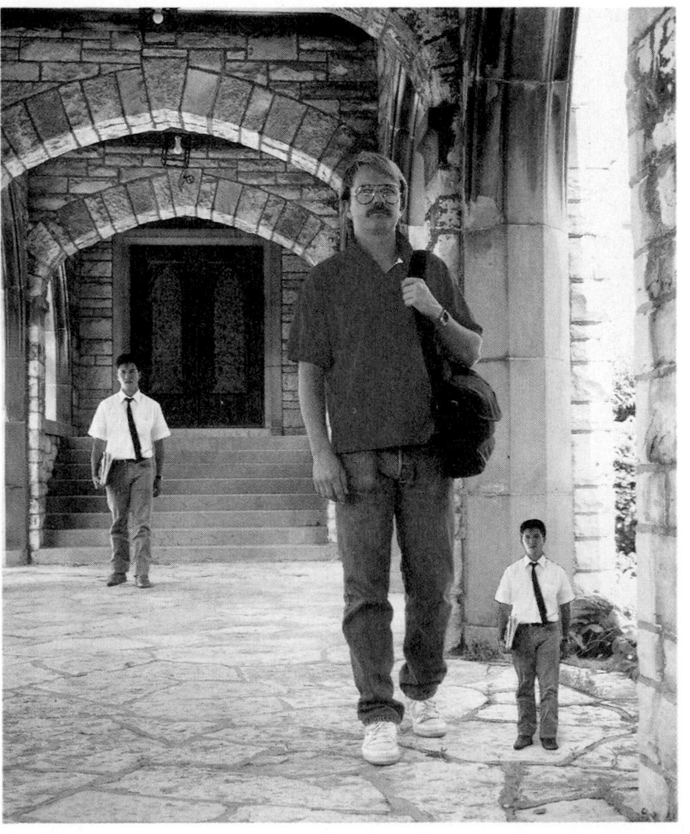

Size constancy refers to this ability to perceive the true size of an object despite variations in the size of its retinal image.

The theory that size constancy was achieved from retinal size by taking distance into account was first proposed by Hermann von Helmholtz (Cutting, 1987). He called the perceptual process that does this *unconscious inference.* It is a process of "inference" because the visual system must *figure out* (or "infer") the size of an object "out there" by combining several different kinds of information, sometimes including prior knowledge. It is "unconscious" because the observer is not *aware* of knowing the size/distance relation or of using it to perceive objective size. Unconscious inferences about the true sizes of objects seem to be made rapidly, automatically, and without conscious effort of any sort—a major achievement in our perceptual processing of information.

If the size of an object is perceived by taking distance cues into account, then we should be fooled about size whenever we are fooled about distance. One such illusion occurs in the "Ames room" shown in **Figure 6.23A.** Your six-foot-tall author looks like a midget in the left corner of this room, but like a giant in the right corner. The reason for this illusion is that you perceive the room to be rectangular, with the two back corners equally distant from you. Thus you perceive my actual size as being consistent with the size of the images on your retina in both cases. The bigger image corresponds to a bigger person. In fact, however, I am *not* at the same distance, because the Ames room, like the Ames chair, creates a clever illusion. It *looks* like a rectangular room, but it is actually made from nonrectangular surfaces at odd angles in depth and height (see **Figure 6.23B**). Any person on the right will make a larger retinal image because he or she is closer; but this larger image will be *perceived* as larger because the room—the reference frame—is seen as "normal" and the sizes of things inside are perceived relative to it.

Another way that the perceptual system can infer objective size is by using *prior knowledge* about the characteristic size of similarly shaped objects. For instance, once you recognize the shape of a house, or a tree, or a dog, you have a pretty good idea of how big it is, even without knowing its distance. Most of the time your perception is correct, but, as movie directors are well aware, you can be fooled by miniature scenery constructed to scale, which can give you a perception of normally sized real objects.

A.

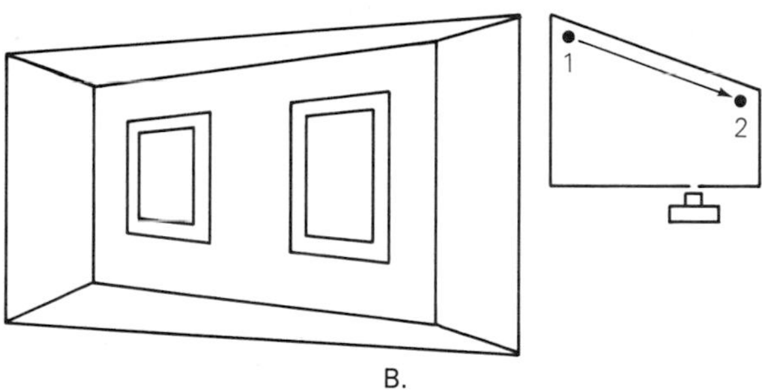

B.

Figure 6.23 *The Ames Room*

When information about perceived distance and prior knowledge of sizes are in conflict, the distance information is more powerful, as is demonstrated by your perception of Figure 6.23. Even though you know that a man's size does not change as he walks across a room, you *still* see his size as vastly different in the two corners. The depth information that makes the room look rectangular simply overpowers your knowledge that the room is, in fact, not rectangular. This is a case in which what you perceive wins over what you know. In the final section of this chapter, we will see when the reverse holds true.

Sometimes shape information is not sufficient to produce accurate perception of size, especially when past experience does not give you a knowledge of what familiar objects look like at extreme distances. This happened to a Pygmy named Kenge who had lived all his life in dense tropical forests using sound cues rather than visual ones to guide his hunting. Kenge had occasion, one day, to travel by car across an open plain for the first time with an anthropologist named Colin Turnbull. Later the anthropologist described Kenge's reactions as follows.

> *Kenge looked over the plains and down to where a herd of about a hundred buffalo were grazing some miles away. He asked me what kind of* insects *they were, and I told him they were buffalo, twice as big as the forest buffalo known to him. He laughed loudly and told me not to tell such stupid stories, and asked me again what kind of insects they were. He then talked to himself, for want of more intelligent company, and tried to liken the buffalo to the various beetles and ants with which he was familiar.*
>
> *He was still doing this when we got into the car and drove down to where the animals were grazing. He watched them getting larger and larger, and though he was as courageous as any Pygmy, he moved over and sat close to me and muttered that it was witchcraft. . . . Finally, when he realized that they were real buffalo he was no longer afraid, but what puzzled him still was why they had been so small, and whether they* really *had been small and had so suddenly grown larger, or whether it had been some kind of trickery. (Turnbull, 1961, p. 305)*

In this unfamiliar perceptual environment, Kenge first tried to fit his novel perceptions into a familiar context, by assuming the tiny, distant specks he saw were insects. With no previous experience seeing buffalo at a distance, he had no basis for size constancy, and as the fast-moving car approached them and Kenge's retinal images got larger and larger, he had the frightening illusion of the animals as changing in size. We can assume that with further experience he would have come to see them as Turnbull did.

Shape constancy is closely related to size constancy. You perceive an object's actual shape correctly even when it is slanted away from you, making the shape of the retinal image substantially different from that of the object itself. For instance, a circle tipped away from you projects an elliptical image onto your retina; a rectangle tipped away projects a trapezoidal image (**Figure 6.24**). Yet you usually perceive them accurately as a circle and a rectangle slanted away in space. When there is good depth information available from binocular disparity, motion parallax, or even pictorial cues, your visual system can determine an object's true shape simply by taking your distance from its different parts into account.

Orientation Constancy

When you tilted your head to the side in viewing your book, the world did not seem to tilt, only your own head. This perception was because of **orientation constancy:** the ability to perceive the actual orientation of objects in the world despite their orientation in your retinal image. This form of constancy, too, results from a process of unconscious inference. Information about the orientation of an object in the environment is inferred from the orientation of its retinal image. In addition *head tilt* is taken into account, which you know about largely through the *vestibular system* in your inner ear (as discussed in chapter 5). By using its output together with retinal orientation, your visual system is usually able to give you a perception of the correct orientation of an object in the environment.

Actually, there are significant individual differences among people in reconciling these contradictory data: some rely more heavily on this internal vestibular information, others more heavily on visual information from the external environment (see ***Close-up*** on p. 210).

In familiar environments, prior knowledge provides additional information about objective orientation. You know from experience that certain things are horizontal (the surface of a body of water, the floor of a room), and others vertical (trees, walls, hanging objects). Once you recognize them from their shapes, you know their probable orientation with respect to gravity. There is no guarantee that they are actually oriented in this way, however. When they aren't, your perception of orientation may suffer, as it did when you assumed that the floor of the Ames room was horizontal.

Perceptual constancy holds for many visual properties over a wide range of stimulus conditions. Under extreme conditions, however, it nearly always breaks down. For example, when you look at people from the top of a skyscraper, they look like ants.

The perception of constancy in the environment is one of our most important abilities. It is information about the *world* (the *distal* stimulus) that we must have for survival, not information about the retinal images (the *proximal* stimulus). It is critical that we perceive *constant* and *stable* properties of continuing objects in the world despite the enormous variations in the properties of the light patterns that stimulate our eyes. Without constancy, our eyes really wouldn't do us much good, because we wouldn't be seeing *the world "out there,"* but only the images on the backs of our eyes. It might be said that the task of perception is to discover *invariant* properties of our environment despite the variations in our retinal impressions of them.

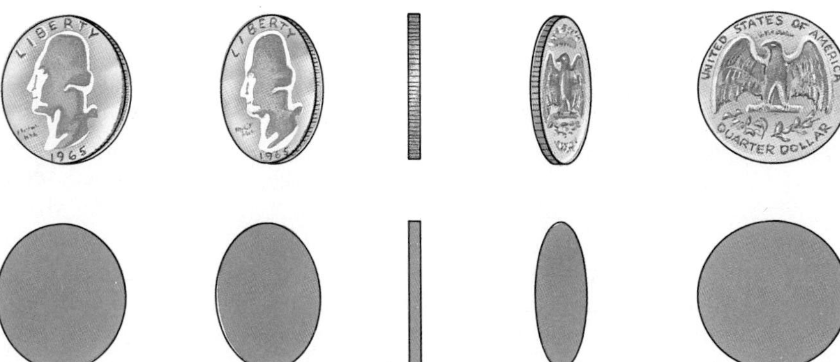

Figure 6.24 *Shape Constancy*
As a coin is rotated its image becomes an ellipse that grows narrower and narrower until it becomes a thin rectangle, an ellipse again, and then a circle. At each orientation, however, it is still perceived as a circular coin.

Classification Processes

You can think of all the perceptual processes described thus far as providing reasonably accurate knowledge about physical properties of the distal stimulus—the position, size, shape, texture, and color of three-dimensional objects in a three-dimensional environment. With just this knowledge and some basic motor skills, you would be able to walk around without bumping into objects, manipulate things that are small and light enough to move, and make accurate models of the objects that you perceive; but you would not know how the objects are used or how they relate to each other—or to you. It would be like visiting an alien planet where all the objects were new to you; you would not know which ones to eat, which ones were dangerous, or which ones you would need to do all the things you do every day.

To get this information about the objects you perceive, you need to be able to *classify* them—that is, to identify or recognize them as members of the meaningful categories that you know about from experience. Classification results in knowing that things are members of categories like dogs, chairs, books, people, and houses. Classification operates both at the perceptual level and at the cognitive level, to be described in chapter 10.

"Bottom-up" and "Top-down" Processes

Classifying objects implies matching what you see against your stored knowledge. The processes of bringing in and organizing information from the environment are often called *data-driven* or "bottom-up" processes, because they are guided by the sensory information—the raw data of direct experience. Sensations of visual features and perceptions of organized objects are largely the result of "bottom-up" processes. However, even at this level of hard evidence of sensory images, what your senses detect of all available environmental stimulation is heavily influenced by *attention*—you see and hear only those things to which you pay attention. In the next chapter we will analyze how attention controls what information gets into the system for later processing and what things "out there" in the environment do not have a functional existence if they are not noticed and attended to.

Processes that originate in the brain and influence the selection, organization, or interpretation of sensory data are called *hypothesis-driven* or "top-down" processes. Abstract thoughts, prior knowledge, beliefs, values, and other aspects of an individual's higher mental processes control the way incoming stimulation is managed—and even what qualifies as "relevant," to be noticed and dealt with.

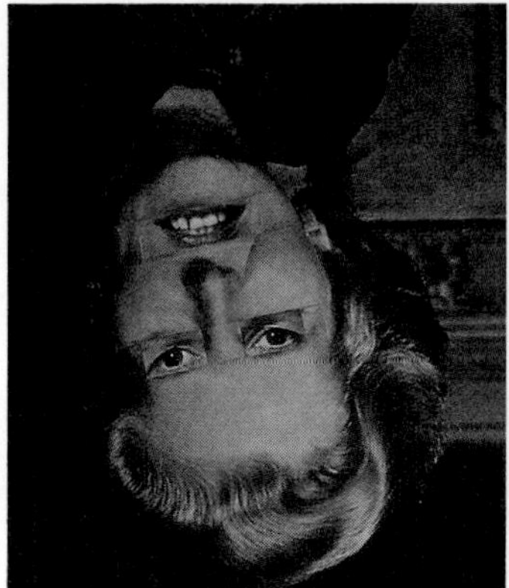

Figure 6.25

For a dramatic example of "top-down" processes at work, look at the two upside-down pictures of British Prime Minister Margaret Thatcher in **Figure 6.25** before reading further. You can probably tell that one of them has been altered slightly around the eyes and mouth, but the two pictures look pretty much alike. Now turn the book upside down and look again. The same pictures look extraordinarily different now. One is still Margaret Thatcher, but the other is a ghoulish monster that not even her mother could love! Why did you not see that obvious difference before turning the book upside down?

Through the vast experience you have had in socially important tasks like identifying people and interpreting their emotional expressions, you have become enormously sensitive to subtle differences in the shapes and positions of eyes and mouths—but only when they are in or near their characteristic upright orientation. In the example, you see the very same stimulus pattern as familiar or relatively unfamiliar just by changing its orientation. This demonstrates how greatly your experience with a kind of object can affect the way you perceive and classify it. (If you want to find out the exact orientation at which your experience with upright faces begins to affect your perception, rotate the face slowly from upside-down until you see it taking on its grotesque expression.)

Close-up Field Dependence in Perception and Personality

Are you the sort of person who has a strong interpersonal orientation and is emotionally open, or do you prefer nonsocial situations in which you can keep your emotions pretty much to yourself? Psychologists have found that your answer could probably be predicted from your performance on *perceptual* tests related to orientation perception. A personality dimension, called *field dependence,* has been proposed to reflect a person's preference for depending on external versus internal sources of information in *both* perceptual and social situations (Witkin & Goodenough, 1977).

The primary test for field dependence in perception is judging when lines are vertical (aligned with gravity) in situations in which there is conflicting visual information. In one version, called the *rod-and-frame* test, subjects are shown a tilted rod inside a tilted frame with no other visual information. They are asked to adjust the tilt of the rod so that it is upright with respect to gravity (A). Some people are able to do this quite accurately despite the tilt of the frame (B). They are called "field independent," because they seem to rely almost exclusively on *internal* bodily information provided by their vestibular and kinesthetic systems to define *vertical* (see chapter 5) and are able to ignore contradictory information from the visually tilted frame. Other people, however, adjust the rod so that it is strongly tilted toward the orientation of the frame (C). They are called "field dependent" because they seem to *depend* more upon the *external* field information provided by the frame and less on internal information.

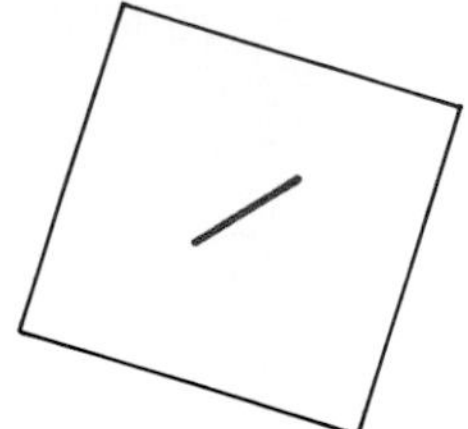

A. Initial Position of Rod and Frame Test

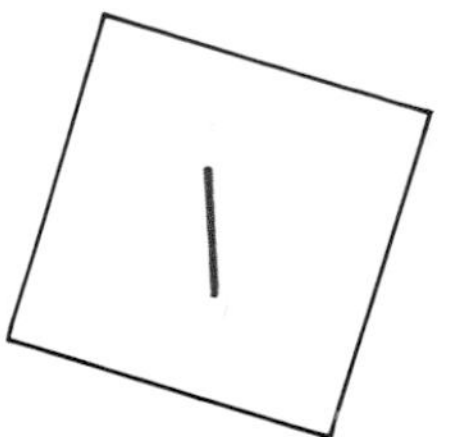

B. Field Independent Person's Response

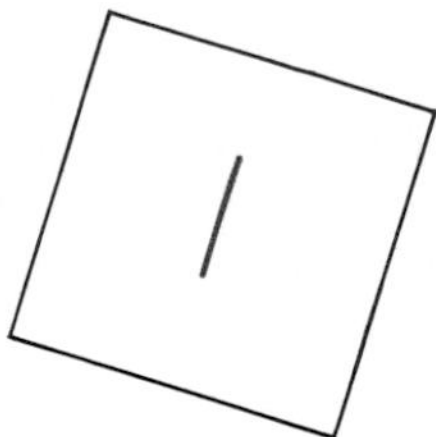

C. Field Dependent Person's Response

A number of studies have investigated the relation between "field dependence" and "field independence" in perceptual and social situations.

In one such study, subjects were asked by an interviewer to talk about a topic that interested them. In one condition, the interviewer kept silent during the subject's response; in the other, the same interviewer gave feedback ("uh hmm" or "yeah") during the response. Field-dependent subjects produced less verbal output in the silent condition than in the feedback condition, whereas field-independent subjects were not much affected by the interviewer's reactions. Later, in filling out questionnaires, field-dependent subjects more often agreed with the statement, "I think I might have done a little better if the interviewer had told me at times just how I was doing," whereas field-independent subjects tended to agree with the statement, "I don't think it made much difference one way or the other that the interviewer didn't tell me how I was doing during the interview." (Gates, 1971)

An interesting extension of this result to therapist-patient interactions is a finding based on analysis of therapy-session transcripts. Therapists ask more specific questions and give more support in sessions with their field-dependent patients than in sessions with their field-independent patients (Witkin et al., 1977).

From many such studies, it has been concluded that people shown to be *field-dependent* in a perceptual task tend to: (a) make greater use of social feedback in ambiguous situations; (b) be more attentive to social cues; (c) be more interested in other people; (d) be emotionally open; (e) like social situations; and (f) choose careers in welfare, humanitarian, and helping professions. *Field-independent* people tend to: (a) rely less on social feedback; (b) be generally less sensitive to social cues; (c) be more impersonal; (d) keep their emotions to themselves; (e) be less gregarious; and (f) choose careers in mathematical, scientific, and analytic professions (Witkin & Goodenough, 1977).

The correspondence between people's social preferences and their behavior on the rod-and-frame test suggests that we each have our own unique "cognitive style" that determines how we seek, acquire, and evaluate information about our environment, both physical and social (G. Klein, 1970).

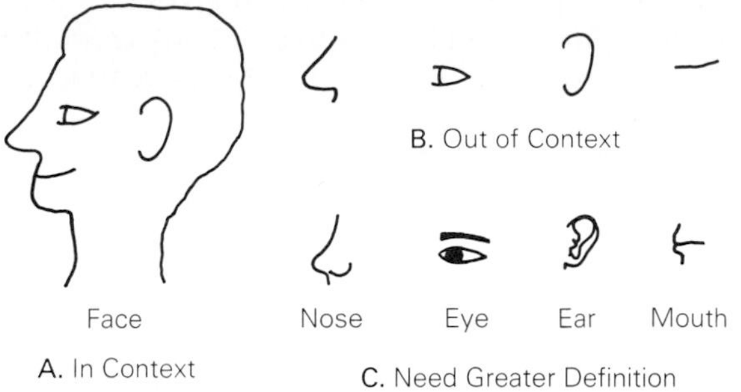

Figure 6.26

Classification—the third stage of perceiving—is a process in which memory, conceptual analysis, expectation, motivation, personality characteristics, and social experience are all brought to bear in comprehending what is being perceived. To *perception* it adds *conception*—mental activity; to *facts* it adds *meaning*. It is classification that gives our experiences continuity over time and across situations.

Three aspects of classification that psychologists have been interested in are the ways we recognize patterns as members of a particular category (to be treated in chapter 10), the way classification is affected by expectations, contexts, and personal and social motivation factors.

The Influence of Contexts and Expectations

Have you ever had the experience of seeing people you knew in places where you didn't expect to see them, such as in the wrong city or the wrong social group? It takes much longer to recognize them in such situations, and sometimes you aren't even sure that you really know them. The problem is not that they *look* any different, but that the *context* is wrong: you didn't *expect* them to be there. The spatial and temporal context in which objects are recognized provides an important source of information for classifying, because once you have identified the context you have expectations about what objects you are—and are not—likely to see nearby.

To illustrate how powerfully context can affect classification, consider the face shown in **Figure 6.26.** When the separate features are all shown together in the context of a head, each feature can be drawn very simply with minimal detail and still be recognized: the nose can be just a curve, the mouth no more than a line at the proper place. Out of this context, however, these same lines cease to be recognizable; substantially more accurate detail is needed before you recognize what they are. With a stronger or more familiar context, you need less information to recognize an object within it (Palmer, 1975a).

Examples like these demonstrate that perceptual classification depends on your expectations as well as on the physical properties of the objects you see. These expectations are affected by both the spatial and the temporal contexts in which the perception takes place. They demonstrate an important principle: *object classification is a constructive, interpretive process.* Classification can arrive at different results depending on what you already know, where you are, and what else you see around you. Expectations from context are an important element in "top-down" processing.

Context is sometimes so powerful that the same object is classified in different ways when it appears in different contexts. Read the following words.

THE CAT

They say "THE CAT," right? Now look again at the middle letter of each word. Physically, they are exactly the same; yet you perceived the first as an *H* and the second as an *A*. Why? Clearly your perception was affected by what you know about words in English. The context provided by *T E* makes an *H* highly likely (and an *A* unlikely), whereas the reverse is true of the context of *C T* (Selfridge, 1955).

Schemas

To explain contextual effects like these, it has been suggested that classification of perceptual data must depend on complex information structures in memory. Instead of storing information in memory in isolated bits, we organize our knowledge of the world into integrated packages, clusters of information that are called **schemas.** These are made up of information from different sources, organized around various topics, themes, and types. We have schemas about dating, college lectures, restaurants, good friends, and much more. Schemas may organize information according to objects, activities, people, or ideas that usually are found together or share some basic features.

Schemas not only are a source of factual knowledge in relevant situations but give us expectations. Once formed, they exert powerful influences on the way we classify the context and *predict* what objects are *likely* to be present in that context. We then use both these expectations and the sensory and perceptual information to classify the objects in the visual field. All this happens very quickly, automatically, and unconsciously. We will have a more detailed look in later chapters at the influence of schemas in remembering and thinking.

Perceptual Set

Another aspect of this influence of context and expectation on your perception (and response) is called *set.* **Set** is a temporary readiness to perceive or react to a stimulus in a particular way. There are three types of set: *motor, mental,* and *perceptual.* A *motor set* is a readiness to make a quick, prepared response. A runner in a 100-yard dash trains by perfecting a motor set to "come out of the blocks" as fast as possible at the sound of the starting gun. A *mental set* is a readiness to deal with a situation such as a problem-solving task or a game in a way determined by learned rules, instructions, expectations, or habitual tendencies. A mental set can prevent you from solving a problem when the old rules don't seem to fit the new situation, yet you retain and "force-fit" them to it, as we'll see when we study problem solving in a later chapter. However set does not necessarily mean inflexibility. It can facilitate responding when a person is prepared to make a correct response by inhibiting irrelevant or wrong responses. Game-show contestants who compete to answer first typically reveal the operation of this set.

A **perceptual set** is a readiness to detect a particular stimulus in a given context—a new mother is perceptually set to hear the cries of her child. Often a perceptual set leads you to see an ambiguous stimulus as the one you are expecting.

a. FOX; OWL; SNAKE; TURKEY; SWAN; D ? C K

b. BOB; RAY; DAVE; BILL; HENRY; D ? C K

If you saw the series of words or the pictures that represent them (without any labels) in row *a,* and a friend were given those in row *b* at the same time, and you both had to call out the missing letter in the same ambiguous stimulus D _ C K, would the differences in your perceptual sets make a difference in response? Definitely. Test it out yourself.

Labels can provide a context that gives us a perceptual set for an ambiguous figure. Look carefully at the picture of the woman in **Figure 6.27A** on this page; then have a friend, "a naive subject," examine **Figure 6.27B** on page 214 (don't you peek!). Next, turn to page 216 and both quickly call out what you see in **Figure 6.27C.** Did the prior exposure to the unambiguous pictures with their labels have any effect on either perception of the ambiguous woman?

You could also try this demonstration using the two labels on the ambiguous figure with each of two other subjects, who then call out what they see when the same unlabeled ambiguous stimulus is presented. This demonstration makes evident how easy it is for people to develop different views of the same person or object given prior conditions that create different sets. Mental and perceptual sets can also act as a part of social attitudes that bias how we interpret some part of our world. They can lead us to see attributes in others that are not "in them," but rather in our readiness to misperceive them as having those traits (to be discussed in chapter 17).

The Role of Personal and Social Factors

The way we perceive and classify something can depend on more than its physical properties and its context. It can also be affected by what we *want.*

Starting in the late 1940s, the "New Look" school of perception arose and raised the basic question, "Where is the *perceiver* in perceptual theory?" (Klein & Schlesinger, 1949). This approach attempted to integrate the ideas and methods of perceptual psychologists with conceptions of per-

Figure 6.27

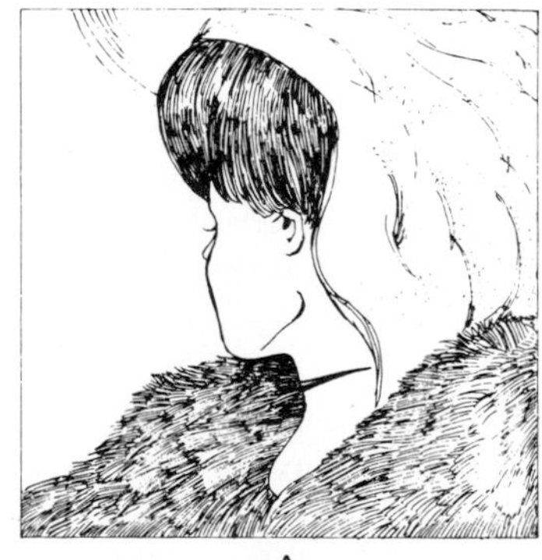

A.

sonality based on psychoanalytic theory and other person-centered approaches. Attempts were directed toward demonstrating that certain *organismic* variables (attributes of the perceiving organism) exerted consistent effects on perception.

One line of research was concerned with the effects of *need* on *thresholds* for perceptual recognition. A basic hypothesis around which this research was organized was that perception includes *psychological defenses* that protect a person from identifying stimuli that are unpleasant or anxiety-provoking. This view suggests a perceptual process called **perceptual defense.** It is similar to the process of *repression,* proposed by Freud, by which mental processes prevent painful perceptions from entering conscious awareness. (See ***Close-up*** on p. 215.)

Deprivation

Another series of studies showed the effects of motivation induced by hunger or personal and social motives in altering personal judgments and perceptions. For example, one experiment investigated the effects of food and water deprivation on word identification.

> *Some subjects went without food for 24 hours before the experiment, some for 10 hours, and some ate just beforehand. All subjects then tried to identify briefly flashed words, including words like* lemonade *and* munch, *that were related to their state of deprivation, together with neutral words, like* serenade *and* hunch. *Both of the deprived groups perceived the need-related words at shorter exposures than did the nondeprived subjects, but there were* no *differences in the responses of the three groups to neutral words (see* ***Figure 6.28****). Evidently, the deprived subjects' more rapid processing of the food-related words was influenced by their motivational state. (Wispé & Drambarean, 1953)*

Being hungry is usually a temporary motivational state, but more permanent deprivation seems to affect perception, too.

> *In a classic experiment, children were asked to adjust the size of a circle of light to match the sizes of several American coins—a penny, a nickel, a dime, and a quarter. Children from poor families tended to see the coins as* larger *than they actually were, whereas children from wealthy families tended to see them as* smaller. *This effect was explained on the grounds that the poor children were much more highly motivated with respect to money than were the richer children. (Bruner & Goodman, 1947)*

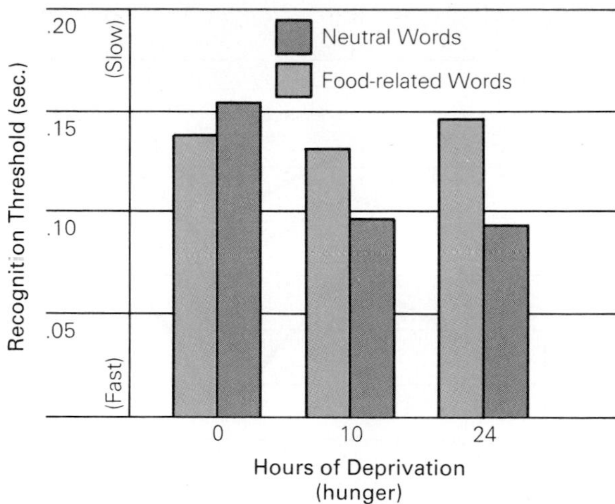

Figure 6.28 *Need-Related Responses*
While words unrelated to food were recognized equally fast by all three groups, need-related words were recognized more readily by food-deprived than by nondeprived groups. (Adapted from Wispé & Drambarean, 1953.)

> *Comparable effects were found when middle-class adults were hypnotized and given the suggestion that they were either "rich" or "poor" (see* ***Figure 6.29****). In this way, the researchers controlled for prior* experience *with coin sizes while varying only the subjects'* motivational level. *(Ashley et al., 1951)*

Personality

A second line of research coming out of the "New Look" approach to perception studied consistent *differences* between *individuals* in their perceptual-cognitive organization of the *same situations.* Tests were developed to identify people who were *high* or *low* on a particular personality dimension that was hypothesized to be associated with a distinctive perceptual-conceptual strategy. Then those two types of individuals were given a variety of perceptual or cognitive tasks to see if their approaches were, in fact, characteristically different. In general, more effects of these personality variables were found on cognitive tasks (for example, memory) than on perceptual ones (see Wolitzky & Wachtel, 1973).

One personality dimension found to influence perception was *field dependence versus field independence,* described in the ***Close-up*** on page 210. Besides the rod-and-frame test, this personality dimension shows up in tasks where subjects are asked to find simple geometric figures that are disguised by being embedded in a larger complex pattern. Field independent people do so easily: their

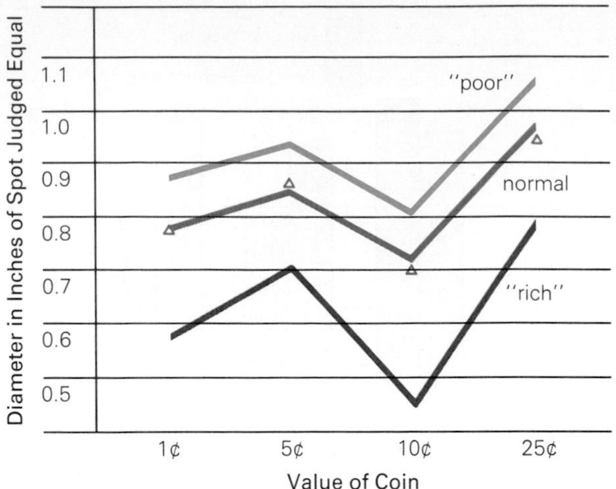

Figure 6.29

This figure shows the sizes of white spots judged to be equal in size to the four coins at the start of the experiment in the normal state and under "poor" and "rich" conditions when subjects were hypnotized. Triangles indicate the actual sizes of the coins. (From the American Journal of Psychology, *1951, 64, 564–72 by W. R. Ashley, et al. Reprinted by permission of the University of Illinois Press.)*

perception tends to be more psychologically differentiated than the perception of people who are field dependent (Witkin et al., 1962).

Another personality dimension that results in different ways of responding to a variety of perceptual tasks has been called *leveling versus sharpening.* They are two poles on the dimension of *cognitive style.* Levelers tend to smooth over what seems irregular, novel, or unusual, and omit details in order to give a more homogenous and less incongruous interpretation of the stimulus event. Levelers are also more likely to miss subtle differences since their perceptions are dominated by the similarities, apparently because their perceptual processing is too much influenced by memory of what has gone before. By contrast, when given a task with a sequence of gradually changing stimuli, sharpeners see the elements of each stimulus display as independent of what went before, accentuating and (over)emphasizing details. They tend to perceive the elements of a situation more accurately than do levelers, but they may miss the forest by focusing too closely on the trees.

People who typically deal with threats by denying their potential significance or who avoid noticing or classifying them as threats are termed *repressors.* At the opposite end of this continuum are *sensitizers,* who tend to be especially vigilant, perceiving subtle, disguised cues of potential approaching threats. This *repressor-sensitizer* continuum is related to a variety of cognitive-perceptual behaviors (Ericksen, 1966). For example, when shown very sexually explicit pictures, repressors look very little and recall much less than sensitizers (Luborsky et al., 1965). Such differences probably arise from the ways the two groups use attentional processes: the sensitizers have developed a more active scanning and searching attention than the repressors.

Although many interesting findings have emerged from these attempts to "put the person back into perception," there is yet to be a comprehensive theory that integrates the complex network of processes involved in perception, cognition, and personality.

Social Influence

One of the first demonstrations of the effects of other people on the perception of an individual—one form of social influence—used the *autokinetic effect.* This illusion of motion occurs when a stationary point of light is observed for an extended period of time in an otherwise completely dark room. After several minutes, most people begin to see the light wander slowly away from its initial position. Why this occurs is not understood, but Muzafer Sherif (1935) showed that people's reports of the direction and extent of movement can be systematically biased by the social context.

> *Subjects observed the light, for a time, by themselves, reporting what they saw. Then they performed the same task with several other observers present (actually confederates of the experimenter) who consistently reported movement in a certain direction. Not only did the real subjects' judgments change to conform to those of the other "observers," but later, when they were alone again, they continued to report that the stationary light was moving in the direction identified by the other observers. The social influence exerted indirectly by the others not only led to agreement by the subjects in their presence, but an internalization of the new way of perceiving even in their absence. (M. Sherif, 1935)*

B.

Close-up Perceptual Defense

Do you ever look away or shut your eyes at particularly gruesome moments in a violent movie? If so, you are engaging in an overt, conscious form of *perceptual defense:* doing something to avoid perceiving an emotionally aversive event. Psychologists in the "New Look" movement in the 1940s suggested that something similar might happen covertly and unconsciously during perception as a defense against the experience of unpleasant, threatening, or taboo events.

To test the hypothesis of perceptual defense, psychologists performed experiments to see how much time it took for subjects to identify "threatening" words such as *bitch* and *raped,* versus emotionally "neutral" words like *house* and *tree.*

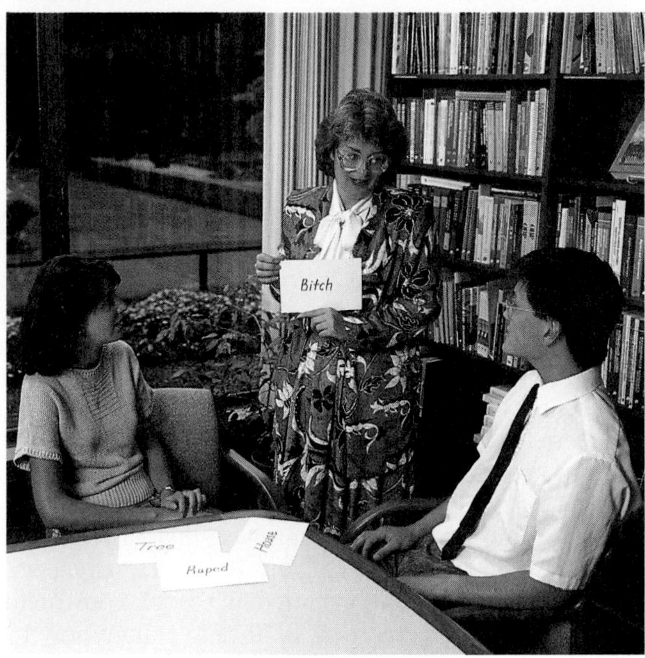

In one well-known study, words from two such lists were presented to subjects very briefly. The presentation time for each word started at .01 seconds and was gradually increased until the word was identified correctly. On the average, threatening words required longer exposures than did neutral ones. (McGinnies, 1949) This seemed to show that the visual system somehow tries to defend against consciously perceiving emotionally threatening words.

Researchers have objected to some of these studies, criticizing them because of possible flaws in their design. For example, in this case, it was suggested that the differences between the thresholds for reading threatening and neutral words could be explained because threatening words tend to be words that are less often used than neutral words. It might simply take longer to recognize seldom-used words. Later studies, however, corrected this problem by equating the two groups of words for usage—and generally continued to find evidence of perceptual defense.

Other researchers objected that the "defense" result might merely reflect a response bias *against publicly* saying *objectionable words. Their argument was that the subjects might have actually identified the threatening words at the same exposure as the neutral ones, but suppressed their responses to the threatening words until they were absolutely sure of what had been presented. This is the same response bias problem that was discussed in the preceding chapter (p. 146). Subjects might use a stricter criterion for responding to threatening words; as a result, they might seem to have a higher threshold for seeing them. Studies testing this "response suppression" hypothesis, however, have generally shown that at least some of the difference in response to threatening and neutral words is, in fact, because of perceptual effects and not response bias (Broadbent & Gregory, 1967).*

The concept of perceptual defense has also been criticized on purely logical grounds (Spence, 1967). How could a perceptual system defend itself against a threatening word unless it had already identified *the word as threatening? This objection suggests that perceptual defense is inherently contradictory. This would be true if conscious perception were a single process that happened all at once, but, as we have seen, it is a complex process that may have many stages prior to conscious experience. It is quite possible that an early unconscious stage may identify the word and its emotional tone. In this case, the identification that occurred in the early stage could, indeed, be kept from consciousness (Erdelyi, 1974).*

Not only can the majority affect an individual's perception, but a deviant minority can also influence it.

In another study, two confederates consistently identified a green color as "blue" during a color-naming task while the majority of the subjects identified it correctly. Later, when they were tested alone, some of the subjects who had been in the accurate majority shifted their judgments of the boundary between blue and green toward blue. (Moscovici, 1976)

These results indicate that both social majorities and minorities can influence perception and classification in other perceivers. *Response bias* (discussed in the preceding chapter) seems a plausible explanation for these findings, but the possibility of an actual change in experience is hard to rule out, especially where the subjects insist that what they reported was what they actually saw. In any case, the power of even a minority—or a persuasive leader—to change others' definitions of reality is very real. This effect was tragically demonstrated in 1978 when over 900 American members of the Peoples' Temple group committed suicide and mass murder in their jungle compound in Guyana in South America. They did so at the suggestion of their charismatic leader, Jim Jones. He had so distorted their views of reality that they came to believe they were about to be slaughtered by American military forces. Therefore, suicide was a "viable revolutionary option" for an allegedly oppressed people who had been shaped over the years to share their leader's paranoid view of persecution.

There are many ways in which social variables may influence perception. Broad cultural influences set basic, accepted social categories that determine standards for beauty, fear, appropriateness, or unacceptability. Socially learned attitudes can function as "anchors" or standards by which new inputs are often evaluated without conscious awareness of their biasing influence (Deregowski, 1980). It is not surprising that the way an individual classifies objects and events in the environment can also be affected by the ways other similar people are seen to classify the same things. After all, we humans are social creatures who depend on interactions with others for many of our most significant experiences and much of our information.

What each of us considers to be "reality" is determined in large part by common agreement. The notion that reality is a social construct based upon mutually agreed-upon ways of perceiving significant aspects of the environment within a given community of peers is termed **consensual validation.** In the next chapter, we will see that even as private a process as our consciousness is, to some extent, influenced by the actual or symbolic presence of other people. Our final chapters on social psychology will give many examples of this powerful effect of social forces on individuals' thoughts, feelings, and actions.

The important lessons to be learned from the classification dimension of the overall perceptual experience can be summarized broadly. The "top-down" effects of expectations, deprivation, personality, and social influence variables all highlight the same important fact—that perceptual experience in response to a stimulus event is a response of the *whole organism.* Besides the information provided when your sensory receptors are stimulated, your final perception depends on who you are, whom you are with, and what you expect, want, and value.

The interaction of "top-down" and "bottom-up" processes also means that perception is an act of constructing reality to fit one's assumptions about how it "probably is" or "should be." A perceiver often plays two different roles. As a *gambler,* a perceiver is willing to bet that the present input can be understood in terms of past knowledge and personal theories; but a gambler may not know "when to hold 'em and when to fold 'em," as the song goes. A perceiver can also act like a compulsive *interior decorator,* constantly rearranging the things that are there so that they fit better and are more coherent. Incongruity and "messy" perceptions are rejected in favor of those with clear, clean, consistent lines.

If perceiving were completely "bottom-up" processing, we would all be bound to the same mundane, concrete reality of the here and now. We could register experience, but not profit from it on

Figure 6.27

C.

later occasions, nor would we see the world differently under different personal circumstances. If processing in perception were completely "top-down," however, we would each be lost in our own fantasy world of what we expect and hope to perceive. A proper balance between the two extremes achieves the basic goal of perception: to experience what is out there in a way that maximally serves our needs as biological and social organisms moving about in a physical environment.

Creatively Playful Perception

Because of our ability to go beyond the sensory gifts that evolution has bestowed on our species, we can become more creative in the way we perceive the world. Our role model is *not* a perfectly programmed computerized robot with exceptional sensory acuity—but Pablo Picasso. Picasso's genius was, in part, attributable to his enormous talent for "playful perception." He could free himself from the bonds of perceptual and mental sets to see, not the old in the new, but the new in the old, the novel in the familiar, the unusual figure concealed within the familiar ground—or, of course, the reverse.

Perceptual creativity involves experiencing the world in ways that are imaginative, personally enriching—and fun (see Leff, 1984). This can be accomplished by starting a conscious program of directing your attention and full awareness to the things and activities around you. The goal is to become more flexible in what you allow yourself to perceive and think, while being constantly open to discovering yet one more alternative response to a situation.

I can think of no better way to conclude this rather formal presentation of the psychology of perception than by proposing ten suggestions for playfully enhancing your powers of perception (adapted from Leff, 1984).

1. Imagine everyone you meet is really a machine designed to look humanoid, and all machines are really people designed to look inanimate.
2. Notice all wholes as ready to come apart into separately functioning pieces that can make it on their own.
3. Think of your magical mental clock hooked up to a videorecorder that can make time move backward, fast forward, or freeze.
4. Recognize that most things around you have a "family resemblance" to other things that nobody has every noticed.
5. View the world as if you were an animal or a home appliance.
6. Consider one new use for each thing you focus on (ever see a tennis racket working out as a sieve for spaghetti?).
7. Suspend the law of causality so that things "just happen," while coincidence and chance rule over causes and effects.
8. Dream up alternative meanings for the things and events in your life.
9. Discover something really interesting about activities and people you used to find boring.
10. Violate some of the assumptions that you and others have about what you would and wouldn't do (the ones that are not dangerous).

With the new awareness of what can be "out there" comes a similar transformation of what can be "in here"—within you. The role of awareness, attention, and states of consciousness are at the head of the agenda for our next chapter.

Summary

- Our perceptual systems do not simply record information about the external world, but actively organize and interpret that information. Knowledge about perceptual illusions can give us clues about normal organizing processes.
- At the sensory level of processing, physical energy is detected and transformed into neural energy and sensory experience. At the perceptual level, brain processes organize sensations into coherent images and give us a perception of objects and patterns. At the level of classification, percepts of objects are recognized, identified, and categorized.
- Perception is a constructive process of going beyond sensory stimulation to discover what objects exist in the world around us. The task of perception is to determine what the distal (external) stimulus is from the information contained in the proximal (sensory) stimulus.
- Perceiving is a three-stage process consisting of a sensory stage, in which sensory information is coded and analyzed, a perceptual stage in which information is organized and synthesized, and a classification stage in which identification and categorization take place.
- Ambiguity sometimes arises because the same sensory information may be organized into different percepts. It is also possible for the same percepts to be interpreted and classified differently.

- Organizational processes provide the best and simplest percepts consistent with the sensory data. As a result of these processes, our percepts are segregated into regions and organized into figures that stand out against the ground. We tend to see incomplete figures as wholes, to group items by various kinds of similarity, to prefer "good" figures and see them more readily. Many of these organizing processes derive from Gestalt theory, which argues that whole figures have emergent properties that are not shared by any of the component pieces. The whole, according to Gestalt theory, is more than the sum of the parts.
- Perception of parts depends on the reference frame in which they occur. We tend to organize and interpret parts in relation to the spatial and temporal context in which we experience them. We also tend to see a reference frame as stationary and the parts within it as moving, rather than the reverse, regardless of the actual sensory stimulus.
- In converting the two-dimensional information on the retina to a perception of three-dimensional space, the visual system gauges object size and distance in relation to each other: distance is interpreted on the basis of known size and size is interpreted on the basis of various distance cues. Distance cues include binocular disparity, convergence of the two eyes, relative motion parallax, and pictorial cues such as interposition, shadows, relative size, linear perspective, and texture gradients.
- Despite the changing properties of retinal images, we tend to perceive objects as retaining the same size, shape, and orientation. Prior knowledge normally reinforces these and other constancies in perception; under extreme conditions, perceptual constancy may break down. Nevertheless, the study of perceptual constancies reveals that a major function of perception lies in discovering the stable, invariant properties of stimuli that may change in many ways.
- Classification, the third stage of perceiving, is the one in which perceived objects are identified and given meaning through "top-down" processes which may draw on memory, expectation, motivation, and personality characteristics.
- Expectations, schemas, and perceptual sets all may guide recognition of incomplete or ambiguous data in one direction rather than another that would be equally possible given the perceptual data. Personality characteristics, motives, and social influences all contribute to the meanings we see in perceptual data and may lead us to distort the information provided by the data.

7

The Nature of Consciousness

Karen wasn't worried about the operation because it was only "minor surgery" to remove an irritating cyst in her mouth. The nurse insisted on medication to help her sleep better so she'd be well rested.

"One hundred, 99, 98, 97 . . . ," Karen counted as the anesthetic was being injected into her vein. Wildly oscillating, vibrating geometric patterns flashed before her. "Ninety-two, 91, 9 . . . ." All dark, all sensation gone, awareness shut down.

Minutes into the operation, the surgeon exclaimed, "Why, this may not be a cyst at all . . . it may be cancer!" Fortunately, the biopsy proved the cyst was benign and the doctor's reaction just a false alarm. In the recovery room, the surgeon told the groggy, slightly nauseated Karen that she didn't have to worry: everything was fine.

But Karen had a difficult time falling asleep that night. She felt anxious. Tears rolled down her face, and she didn't know why. She dreamed about a puppy she had wanted, but wasn't allowed to have because of her allergy. She wondered if that was why she awoke feeling a bit sad, but she continued to feel depressed all day. Attempts to restore her usual good spirits were unsuccessful. The depression worsened and Karen sought professional help.

Under hypnosis, a therapist asked Karen to lift her hand if she felt that something was disturbing her, even if she did not know what it was. Karen's hand soon rose. When the therapist suggested that she report what was disturbing her, she exclaimed, "The cyst may be cancerous!" After being able to express her fear openly and being reassured, Karen's depression lifted. Was it really possible that in her unconscious, anesthetized state some part of Karen's mind had been able to comprehend the surgeon's frightening message?

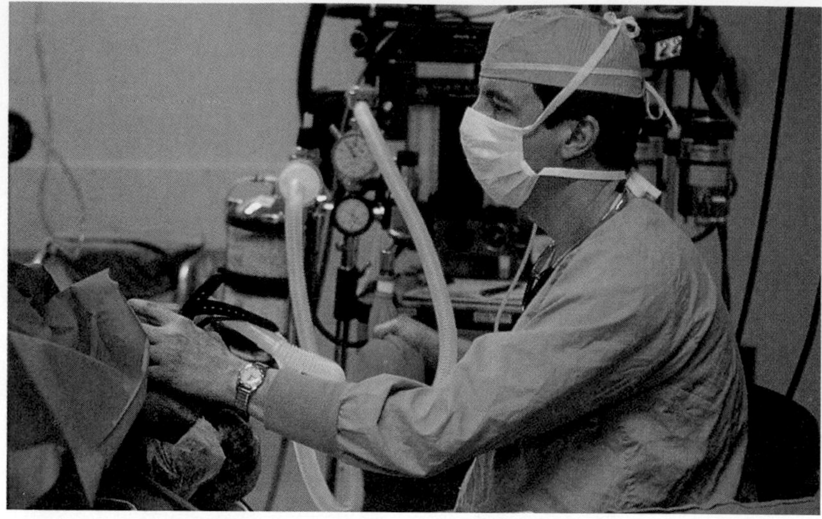

This possibility has been checked out in formal studies using both negative and positive messages. Ten patients were anesthetized and given negative messages. In each case, when recordings of their bodily functions indicated they had "lost consciousness," an anesthetist said in an urgent tone, *"Just a moment. I don't like the patient's color. The lips are too blue, very blue. More oxygen please (pause). . . . Good, everything is fine now."*

Upon awakening, not one of the patients recalled anything that had happened under anesthesia; but after entering hypnosis and being given the suggestion to reexperience their operations, 4 of the 10 were able to repeat practically verbatim the traumatic words used by their anesthetists. Four other patients displayed a severe degree of anxiety while reliving their operations even though they could not say why; and, at a crucial moment, each of the 4 woke from the hypnosis and refused to participate further. The remaining 2 patients, though seemingly capable of reliving their operations under hypnosis, later said they had not heard anything (Levinson, 1967).

In the second set of circumstances, recorded suggestions for quick recovery, given during general anesthesia, had positive effects. Patients who got those positive messages needed less postoperative pain-killing medication. They were even released from the hospital two and a half days sooner than control-group patients, who had been exposed to either soothing music or silence during their anesthesia (Hutchins, 1961; Pearson, 1961).

These early findings of the emotional and medical consequences of auditory awareness during general anesthesia stimulated considerable research among psychologists and physicians (see Agarwal & Smith, 1977; Bitner, 1983; Cheek, 1979; Cherkin & Harrour, 1971; Guerra & Aldrete, 1980; Millar & Watkinson, 1983). The phenomenon appears to be rather delicate, is not always replicable, and requires carefully designed controlled procedures to rule out alternative explanations.

Karen's case focuses our attention on the complex and fascinating manner in which human consciousness operates. Her ordinary state of alert, conscious awareness was altered in many ways—by sleeping and dreaming, by drugs, by hypnosis, and by such "unconscious" impulses as her frustrated desire for a puppy and her fear of cancer. Even when Karen appeared to be unconscious, deeply sedated by general anesthesia, her brain was apparently still processing environmental stimulations and extracting information from the situation.

What is consciousness and how can such a private event be studied scientifically? Our search for understanding the elusive nature of human consciousness will begin with rigorous, laboratory investigations of the nature of attention. Then we will consider the consequences of having two separately functioning minds in one brain, which happens when epilepsy patients undergo an operation that severs their corpus callosum, thus splitting apart the cerebral hemispheres. From this dramatic case of consciousness alteration, we will shift to the daily mental changes each of us experiences in daydreaming, fantasy, sleep, and dreaming. Planned interventions to alter consciousness through psychoactive drugs, hypnosis, and religious rituals will also be surveyed during our journey into the realms of consciousness and its various forms. These are some of the issues we will be examining in this chapter.

The Psychology of Consciousness

"A penny for your thoughts."

Before collecting, how can you be certain that they really are *your thoughts?* By what mental process did you separate your thoughts from *my* thoughts—some of which you also know and need to hang onto—at least until exam time?

Consciousness is the general term for *awareness*—including awareness of ourselves as distinct from other organisms and objects. Ordinary waking consciousness includes the stream of immediate experience comprising our perceptions, thoughts, feelings, and desires at any particular moment of awareness—along with our "commentary" on them and on our actions. Besides our awareness of some *content*—something we are analyzing or interpreting, including some sense of self—consciousness also includes the *state of being aware.*

Consciousness as an Aid to Survival

Consciousness probably evolved because it increased individuals' chances of survival by enabling them to base intentional, voluntary actions on an optimal interpretation of "reality"—to make sense of sensory and perceptual information at a level that was useful for their purposes at a given time and place.

Consciousness helps us in three important ways to make sense of the "blooming, buzzing confusion" that assaults our sensory receptors. First it reduces the constant flow of stimulus energy by restricting what we notice. We "tune out" what is not relevant at the moment—it becomes "noise"—to focus on what is relevant—it becomes a signal. Second, it enables us to segment the continuous flow of experience into *objects* (patterns in space) and *events* (patterns in time), following the laws of perceptual organization described in the last chapter. Thanks to our consciousness, we can pull out one thing at a time from life's endless conveyor belt of stimuli—to analyze it, interpret it, compare it to other things, and decide how to act on it (Marcel, 1983).

Third, it is our consciousness that enables us to draw on past memories to make the best sense we can of present input and plan the most appropriate actions. Instead of simply reacting to a present stimulus, we can recall similar events, acts, and outcomes from the past. We can also analyze causes, imagine situations and alternatives not present at the time, plan future actions, and direct behavior toward consequences we want.

Consciousness is the process that enables us to do these things. It is the ability to engage in an active, stable *construction of reality* through a selective analysis of ongoing objects and events in the context of our past experiences. Only in consciousness can the higher mental processes occur. Thus consciousness gives us a potential for flexible, appropriate response far beyond that of other species—aiding survival (Ornstein, 1986).

Cultural and Environmental Influences

Because all humans have evolved with similar sensory and nervous systems, there are many similarities in their constructions of reality. People tend to agree on a common view of reality, especially on the meaning of objects and events that are related to survival. Other people affirm your interpretations, and you affirm theirs, increasing the confidence you both feel in your views. This agreement and mutual affirmation of views is called **consensual validation,** as we saw in chapter 6. Similarities are greatest for those who have had a common cultural background of experience. What is perceived as dangerous, safe, nourishing, or desirable tends to be the same for most members of a society (Natsoulas, 1978).

There are also important *differences* in people's consciousness, however, especially where they have lived in very different habitats and faced different survival tasks. There are also some important variations among people within the same general cultural setting. Since consciousness is a *personal* construction of reality based on a limited selection from the flux of available stimulation, each person attends more to certain features than to others. The uniqueness of an individual's personal consciousness persists over time and across situations, and helps give unity and continuity to a sense of self. It is the center of the *unique personality* that differentiates that person from every other individual in the universe (Buss, 1980).

A personal world view is only one of the possible constructions of reality that an individual makes. In fact, there are times when ordinary consciousness is given up and other forms are constructed. For example, this happens every time a person sleeps and dreams—or has daydreams and fantasies. It can also happen if the normal functioning of the sensory and nervous systems is altered by alcohol, psychoactive drugs, or brain surgery; by sensory deprivation or sensory overexcitement (overload); or by special procedures that occur in hypnosis or some mystical practices. Finally, a unique construction of reality—one that sacrifices consensual validation—is built up in the mind of someone with severe mental disorders. In that person's hallucinations, he or she may respond to voices no one else hears, while in phobias and delusions the individual comes to believe that harmless things and innocent people are threatening and dangerous.

In the next sections, we will briefly review the changing scientific status of the concept of consciousness and the new research on the relationship between consciousness and attention.

"A penny for *my* thoughts?"

The Changing Scientific Status of Consciousness

Scientific psychology started out as the study of consciousness. About a hundred years ago, at Wilhelm Wundt's laboratory in Germany, subjects were reporting their personal mental states using the method of *introspection,* believing that this was the best method for getting at the contents of consciousness. A little later, under the direction of E. B. Titchener, one of Wundt's students, trained observers at Cornell University sipped lemonade and viewed precisely calibrated color patches while describing the sensations and emotions that accompanied these external events. Titchener's interest was not so much in the *contents* of consciousness as in the mind's ways of measuring sensations. At Harvard William James, too, championed the importance of consciousness. He asserted: "Psychology [is] the description and explanation of 'consciousness' as such" (1890, p. 1). Moreover, he regarded the idea that "all people unhesitatingly believe that they feel themselves thinking" to be "the most fundamental of all postulates in Psychology . . . " (1890, p. 5).

Introspection by trained self-observers of laboratory-induced sensations was a sterile approach. It did not do justice to the richness of human thought, emotion, and behavior and, of course, did not provide access to subconscious or unconscious mental processes, such as those illustrated in Karen's case. Moreover, it excluded study of infants, retarded people, and those with mental disorders, since they either could not verbalize their consciousness or could not do so in a trustworthy, acceptable way. As introspection was replaced by more objective research methods, a new psychology arose that also ignored the topic of consciousness.

Objective behaviorism, as advanced by J. B. Watson, dismissed mind along with the then popular method of studying it. In his new view, outlined in *Psychology from the Standpoint of a Behaviorist* (1919), he warned readers that he was purposely doing "violence to the traditional" since his work had "no discussion of consciousness and no reference to such terms as sensation, perception, attention, will, image and the like. . . . I frankly don't know what they mean, nor do I believe anyone else can use them consistently" (p. viii). Skinner and other behaviorists chose consciously to restrict their psychological investigations to external, observable behavior that could be measured. Behaviorism won the early battles against mentalism and directed the attention of researchers away from subjective feelings and introspective reports of thinking to objective experiments—with animal subjects. For many years thereafter, the field of psychology suffered an almost total "loss of consciousness" (see Webb, 1981).

Consciousness returned to psychology gradually, beginning in the 1950s, as the cognitive revolution made inroads into all those areas of study in which research subjects had been treated solely as "behaving organisms." Computers replaced mazes for studying problem solving, comprehension of stories replaced rote memory of nonsense syllables, and researchers again studied mental processes as well as reinforced actions.

In one method used to sample thoughts, an electronic signal generator sends beeps to small earphones at randomly programmed intervals. Subjects wearing the earphones respond to these signals by jotting down the thoughts occurring at the instant the signal began, their activity at the moment, and the time of day. In this way, thought-records can be gathered over a number of days to assess people's thoughts and the cognitive patterns that emerge in their everyday lives (Hurlburt, 1979).

Once cognitively oriented psychologists began to analyze behavior in terms of information-processing models rather than stimulus-response models, then the phenomenon of thinking about one's thoughts—consciousness—was not far behind. The "stream of consciousness" is once again flowing in psychology, thanks to the rise to prominence of this new cognitive orientation as well as to the emergence in the past few decades of more esoteric psychologies. The psychedelic drug scene of the 1960s provided abundant examples of "mind alteration" at work—and at play. A more liberalized view of what is acceptable subject matter for a scientific psychology has also been growing over the last 30 years, as its most reputable researchers have brought into the laboratory investigations of sleep and dreams (Dement, 1976), daydreaming (Singer, 1978), hypnosis (E. Hilgard, 1977), and the dual consciousness of patients with brains surgically split into "two minds" (Gazzaniga, 1985; Sperry, 1968).

Animal Consciousness

Now that most psychologists have accepted the possibility that humans are conscious information processors, ethologists have begun to extend the concept by proposing that animals too have conscious awareness (Griffin, 1984). Their argument centers on the adaptive economy of conscious thinking in animals. By anticipating probable future events, by considering likely effects of one action over another, by observing and communicating with other members of the species, animals avoid wasted effort. They also learn to cope more efficiently with the demands and challenges of their environment by thinking before acting "mindlessly."

Two examples stand out among the many that ethologists advance to support the view of animal consciousness. Chimpanzees have learned to use suitably prepared branches as probes into the openings of termite nests. They "fish" for termites who climb onto the probe (Goodall, 1986). Otters carry stones under their armpits to dislodge the fleshy animal inside shellfish. Sometimes otters use floating beer bottles to hammer open shells; since the bottles float they don't have to be stored under their armpits.

A chimpanzee strips a suitably sized branch of twigs and leaves, transforming it into a tool to capture termites. A sea otter carries a carefully selected stone to use for smashing shells.

"Of all the mysteries of nature, none is greater than that of consciousness. Intimately familiar to all of us, our capacity to contemplate the universe and to apprehend the infinity of space and time, and our knowledge that we can do so, have continued to resist analysis and elude understanding" (Tulving, 1985). How can consciousness be analyzed so that we may have a greater understanding of this mystery whose tell-tale clues we each carry around in the dark recesses of our minds?

Three Kinds of Consciousness

When you read about animal consciousness in the preceding section, didn't you say to yourself, "Yes, but it's different"? A chimpanzee who fashions a tool from a branch to go termite fishing is focused on the immediately perceived present environment. Its behavioral repertoire may be influenced by past learning and specific goals, but the kind of consciousness mediating the animal's actions is very limited. There is no evidence that it has symbolic knowledge of the world in the absence of concrete objects and events in the current situation. An elder chimp does not teach a younger one by sketching models of termite hills and fishing rods from the symbolic representation in its memory.

Three kinds of consciousness have been identified by psychologists, who derived the terms from the Greek *nous* ("of mind"). All are variants of *noesis,* an intellectual or cognitive process; the adjective is *noetic.* The three kinds of consciousness are *anoetic* (nonknowing), *noetic* (knowing), and *autonoetic* (self-knowing). See Hilgard, 1980; Natsoulas, 1981; Tulving, 1985.

Anoetic consciousness is limited temporally and spatially to the current situation. Organisms that possess this most basic kind of consciousness perceptually register, internally represent, and behaviorally respond to aspects of a present situation. Anoetic consciousness is what ethologists refer to when they describe animal consciousness.

Noetic consciousness frees individuals from the constraints of concrete objects and present events. Symbolic knowledge of the world is acted upon in a flexible way, allowing awareness and cognitive manipulation of objects stimuli, events, and relations in their absence.

Autonoetic consciousness is the kind of consciousness that makes people aware of the autobiographical nature of personally experienced events. This self-knowing consciousness is associated with a subjective sense of the past and the future, a sense of the present as a personal continuation of one's own past and a prelude to the future. Autonoetic consciousness is necessary for remembering, anticipating, and for developing a sense of a personal identity. The adaptive value of autonoetic consciousness lies in the heightened *confidence* that it confers on information retrieved from memory. This subjective certainty about the orderliness of the past leads to more decisive present actions and more effective future planning (Lachman & Naus, 1984). Autonoetic consciousness emerges after noetic consciousness, at a later time in children's development.

A fascinating illustration of the *absence* of autonoetic consciousness in an adult is found in the case of patient N.N., who suffered a head injury that damaged the frontal lobes of his cortex.

> *N.N. is conscious, remembers many things about the world, can solve problems in a flexible, symbolic way, has good language skills and general knowledge. Although he has a sense of clock time, he has no sense of personal time perspective, no awareness of his own autobiography over time. He does not know what he did yesterday or what he will do tomorrow. When asked these questions, he reports his mind is blank—like looking for a piece of furniture in an empty room. He lives in a state of "permanent present" without any anxiety over his inability to experience an awareness of his relationship to past and future events. (Tulving, 1984)*

Attention and Awareness

One aspect of consciousness that is now of special interest to researchers is the concept of attention. **Attention** is defined as a state of focused awareness accompanied by central nervous system readiness to respond to stimulation. Attention can be thought of as the bridge over which some parts of the external world—the aspects selectively focused on—are brought into the subjective world of our consciousness so that we may regulate our own behavior (Carver & Scheier, 1981).

Psychological Studies of Attention

What we selectively attend to depends upon a number of external and internal factors. We attend to external stimuli that are intense, novel, changing, unexpected, or stand out as salient or special—a sign with moving parts or a friend's face in a classroom of strangers. Our current physiological condition also can direct our attention, as when hunger makes us notice newspaper ads for food or

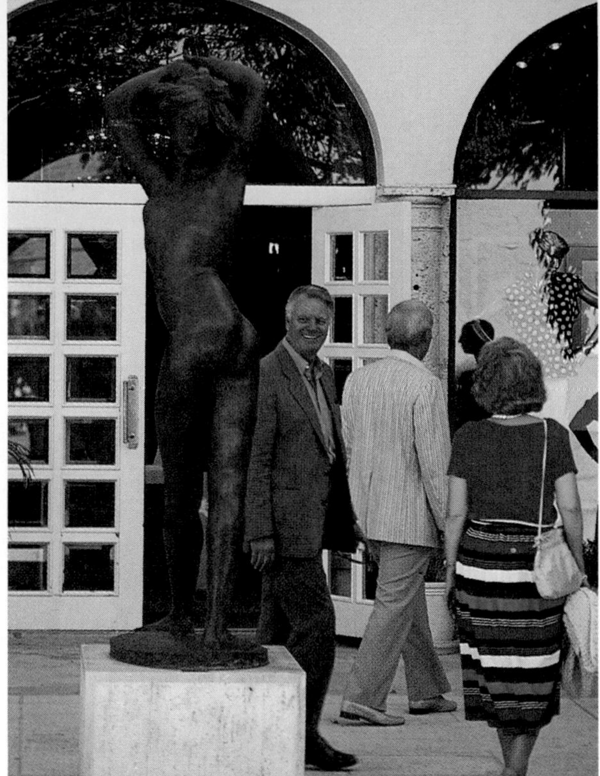

An unusual or unexpected sight is more likely to catch our attention than is one we routinely encounter.

restaurants. Activities we are engaged in can capture our attention, leading us to disregard stimuli that are not "task-relevant." Listening to a charismatic speaker, watching an exciting movie, reading an absorbing novel, and playing a video game are attention-restricting activities. Past experience, special interest, or expertise in a given area carries with it, not just an expanded knowledge base, but a greater sensitivity to particular stimuli, events, and relationships—revealed by Sherlock Holmes' detective work or a birdwatcher's spottings of rare birds that others do not see.

Attention as Essential for Consciousness

Attention has been the focus of research because of its importance for consciousness and, thus, for higher-level mental processing. Of all the things that happen around us of which we *could* be aware, we actually *become* aware—conscious—only of those on which we focus our attention.

Attention is like a spotlight that illuminates certain portions of our surroundings. When we focus our attention on something and become conscious of it, we can begin to process it cognitively—converting sensory information to perceptions and memories or developing ideas through analysis, judgment, reasoning, and imagination. When the spotlight of attention shifts to something else, conscious processing of the earlier material ceases and processing of the new content begins.

When we select something to attend to—because of its striking character or its relevance to some purpose or goal—we inevitably ignore many other possibilities. Only a small portion of the information constantly being taken in by our senses can be attended to. How does the mind deal with this overload of information?

Attention as a Filter for Sensory Input

Credit for reawakening interest in attention as a subject for research goes to English researcher Donald Broadbent. In his book *Perception and Communication* (1958), Broadbent outlined a number of ideas that were novel and exciting to other researchers and provided an empirical basis for investigation of attention.

Broadbent's metaphor for the mind was a communication channel that actively processed and transmitted information. How much information this communication channel could process at any time was limited by the inability of attentional mechanisms to switch between different sources of input.

Imagine listening to a lecture while two students on your left begin to share some gossip and a person on your right starts to tell a joke. What do you hear, notice, and remember? You will probably stay tuned to the lecturer if the material is interesting or important for tomorrow's exam; your neighbors' conversations will be ignored as distracting "noise." If the lecture is boring or irrelevant to your goals, however, and one of the conversations is about your best friend and the other concerns sex, chances are you'll try to attend to what the students are saying. You will *not* be able to listen to all three sources of input simultaneously—or even two; you must selectively attend to only one at a time.

Broadbent and others have simulated the effect experimentally in the laboratory by the technique of **dichotic listening,** in which separate tape-recorded inputs are sent at the same time to a subject using earphones. A different story is presented to each ear and the subject is instructed to listen to one or the other. To increase selective listening, the subject is further told to repeat the story aloud as it comes into the attended ear—that is, to "shadow" it while ignoring the other story.

It is not surprising that subjects do not remember information presented to the unattended ear. What is remarkable is that they do not even notice major changes in that input—for example if the tape is played backward or the language changes from English to German. They do notice a change in pitch—for example, when a speaker's voice switches from male to female (Cherry, 1953). Gross physical features of the unattended message receive perceptual analysis, apparently below the level of consciousness, but the meaning does not get through into consciousness.

Broadbent conceived of attention as a *selective filter* which handled the large amount of sensory information constantly arriving by (a) *blocking out* most unwanted input while (b) *relaying* specific desired information—admitting it to consciousness. Such a filter acted a little like a tuning dial on a radio or TV, which lets us receive certain of the many available messages, but not others. According to Broadbent's theory, the unattended, blocked-out information was sent to a "buffer" where it was held for a short while until either the filter was tuned to it and it got processed or it was lost. (This "buffer" is roughly equivalent to the "sensory memory" of later theories of memory, to be described in chapter 9.)

Broadbent demonstrated this delayed processing of previously blocked material by an ingenious procedure.

> *One set of three digits (say 2–6–1) was presented through earphones to the left ear, and another (say 7–9–5) was presented simultaneously to the right ear. (See* ***Figure 7.1.****) Subjects were asked to report both. They were able to perform this* ***split-span task*** *by recalling all the input to one ear first and then the input to the other ear. Thus they said "261 795" rather than "2–7 6–9 1–5." (Broadbent, 1954)*

Broadbent assumed that the subjects had tuned their selective filter first to the attended ear and then, after responding to that input, had switched the filter to the information being held in the buffer.

According to Broadbent's theory, the limited capacity of attention creates a "bottleneck" in the flow of information through the cognitive system. Filter theory postulates limits on early stages of perception because people can be conscious of only the single channel they are attending to at any one time. Other sensory information is being held briefly, but not processed (Broadbent, 1971).

Attention as a Matter of Degree

Despite the influence of this theoretical approach on consciousness and attention, there were problems it couldn't handle. For example, in dichotic listening tasks, subjects sometimes *did* notice their own names or other *personally relevant material* arriving at their unattended ear. Also, when a story being listened to in one ear and shadowed was suddenly switched to the other ear and replaced by a new story in the first ear, subjects occasionally continued to report a few words from the original story (arriving now in the supposedly unattended ear) if they made more sense than the words in the new story (Treisman, 1960). This meant that there must still have been some analysis for meaning—and hence some attention—in the channel *not* being consciously attended to.

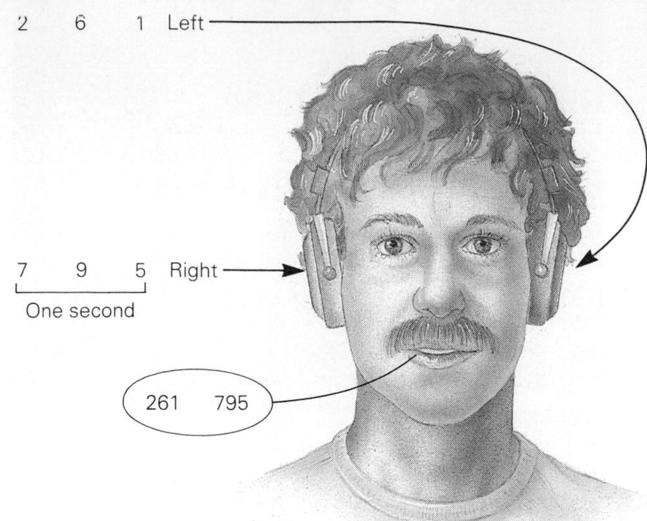

Figure 7.1

Much research has thus converged to support the conclusion that attention is not "all-or-none," as filter theory postulated, but rather a matter of degree. Evidently the supposedly ignored input gets some analysis too, though only partial and not conscious. That which is attended to in consciousness receives more processing over a longer time and, thus, is better remembered in general and in its many details (Norman, 1968).

Attention as a Synthesizer of Input and Knowledge

A second modification in filter theory was necessary to include the finding from many experiments that past learning can influence responding, even without a person's conscious awareness. In one such study, subjects trained to respond physiologically to certain words gave those physiological responses even when the words were presented in the unattended ear and even though the subjects reported not being aware of hearing any of them (Von Wright et al., 1975). Such findings demonstrate that there must be some mechanism below the level of consciousness that monitors unattended input for *meaningful* information—which, in turn, implies that we must be drawing on information already stored in memory.

Ulric Neisser (1967) proposed a theory of attention that included both analysis guided by sensory input and analysis guided by one's already developed world view. According to Neisser's theory, people *constructed* percepts by adding what they already knew to the incoming environmental sensory input. Information that reached consciousness had already been processed in this constructive fashion. Attended new information was synthesized with the already known—whether the latter was consciously attended to or not. In cases where there was either incomplete sensory information or excessive stimulation, people relied more on prior knowledge to predict and construct what the object or event should be.

Attention as a Limited Processing Function

While jogging with a friend, ask your friend to divide 86 by 14 or to tell you how many windows there are in his or her family home. When people do two things at once, attention focused on one task affects performance of the other. In one view, attention is a *processing function* which is a *limited* resource that is used in different ways according to a person's needs, task demands, past history, and skill (Kahneman, 1973).

An ingenious study demonstrated the limited processing capacity of attention.

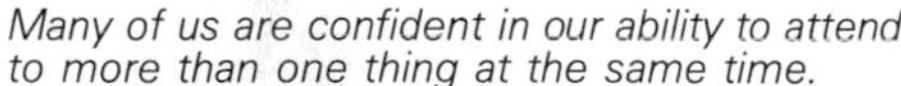

Many of us are confident in our ability to attend to more than one thing at the same time.

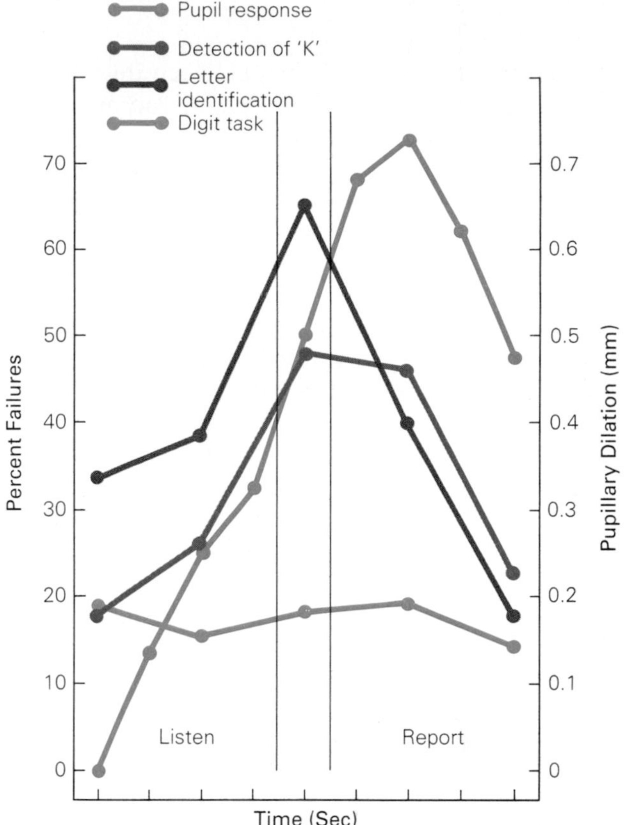

Figure 7.2
The figure shows two measures of perceptual deficit and the pupillary response to a digit-transformation task. Also shown is the probability of success in the transformation task as a function of the time of occurrence of the visual target. (Sources: Kahneman, Beatty & Pollack, 1967; Kahneman, Tursky, Shapiro & Crider, 1969; Kahneman, 1970, with permission)

Subjects were asked to perform two tasks at the same time. Their primary task was to listen to a series of four numbers being presented one digit per second (for example, 4–0–2–7), pause a second, then report aloud a transformed series by adding 1 to each digit (5–1–3–8). The secondary task was a visual one, to identify a single letter briefly flashed before them, reporting it after *reporting the transformed digits. Three dependent variables were used to assess mental effort and the limited capacity for attending to multiple events: (a) size of pupil dilation as a measure of psychological effort produced by attending to the demanding stimulus task of digit transformation; (b) the average percentage of incorrectly reported letters according to the time when they were presented; and (c) the average percentage of errors in the digit task as a function of the time when the visual letter was presented.*

The results shown in **Figure 7.2** *clearly demonstrate that having "something on your mind" interferes with performance on an additional simple task. The capacity for mental effort is shown to be limited and allocated to the primary test. Finally, we see that pupillary response is a useful index of momentary exertion of mental effort. (Kahneman, 1973)*

An analogy can be drawn between this view of attention and a city's power plant. Too much demand for electricity at the same time will cause a brownout, which can be avoided if the available power is allocated flexibly according to anticipated demands. Similarly if there are too many mental processes that demand power, they will not receive it sufficiently unless the supply of attention can be allocated in flexible ways, giving more to difficult tasks, to certain well-learned rules like "Pay attention when someone yells 'Fire!,' " or to conscious decisions.

Another way you make your supply of attention go further is by *routinizing* some of the things you do frequently so that they require little or no attention or mental effort to perform. If you drive a car, recall how much more attention driving took when you were learning than it does now. Bike riding, dancing, and reading are other skills that take little conscious attention once they are mastered.

Could you learn to perform two complex cognitive tasks at once? Apparently so: after a great deal of practice, subjects in one study became able to read and take dictation simultaneously (Spelke et al., 1976). Divided attention is possible when the two concurrent tasks differ sufficiently from each other. Thus speech and music can be processed simultaneously, in parallel, more easily than two messages of the same type (Navon & Gopher, 1979). The ability to perform concurrent tasks under some conditions modifies the view that there is a single, central bottleneck in all information processing caused by the limits imposed by attention.

Mental Processing Without Awareness

Attention is necessary for conscious processing of information; but you can attend to something—in the sense of processing it—at a nonconscious level. For example, driving a car requires constant detection of and adaptation to stimulus conditions that you pay little or no conscious attention to. Also recall our *Opening Case* of Karen's unconscious processing of the surgeon's frightening message. Though our capacity for conscious processing of information is limited, there may be no limit to the amount of nonconscious, "underground" processing that can go on.

Automaticity

The research supporting the filter theory of limited attention emphasizes the complexity of information presented to the senses at any one time and the role of attention in reducing confusion and sensory overload (Broadbent, 1958). People selectively attend to the most important sensory messages, allocating attention to them and ignoring other present, secondary stimuli—exemplified by the handling of multiple messages by air traffic controllers.

Once you learn how to roller skate you don't need to think about how to do it. This routinizing makes your supply of mental energy go further.

However, when the experimental task is simplified so that a subject is *selectively set* to detect which of several possible stimuli to search for, then perceptual processing appears to be independent of attention. Multiple stimuli can be processed simultaneously and rapidly when a simple, familiar target stimulus is searched for among a field of distractor stimuli that are different from the target. When subjects are prepared to search a stimulus array for a particular target—for example a letter among digits, or a red dot among blue triangle distractors—the target figures appear to "pop out" against the background. These "primed" targets are recognized quickly, attract attention, and hold it regardless of the number of distractors in the background. In this simple selective-set paradigm, responding appears to occur *automatically* without consciously directed attention (see Posner, 1982; Schneider & Shiffran, 1977).

Automaticity in information processing is an apparently effortless, involuntary process triggered without a person's supporting intention to engage in it. It does not interfere with other ongoing processes and is not interfered with by other attended activities. Moreover, several such automatic processes can operate in parallel without the limits on attention seen in more complex filtering tasks (see Kahneman & Treisman, 1984). To compare tasks that do and do not require special processing, try the test in **Figure 7.3.**

PURPLE BLUE RED

GREEN YELLOW ORANGE

RED BLACK BLUE

ORANGE GREEN BROWN

BLUE YELLOW PURPLE

Figure 7.3 *The Stroop Task*
1. Time yourself as you read aloud all the words, ignoring the colors in which they are printed.
2. Then time yourself as you read the colors, ignoring what the words say. The first task you probably did quickly and effortlessly, with little or no thought; the second required your full conscious attention because you had to deal with cognitive interference (based on Stroop, 1935; see Posner & Snyder, 1975).

Preattentive Processing in Perception

Imagine exploring a foreign city for the first time, perceiving whole, meaningful objects organized into a coherent framework of houses, stores, people, cars, and trees. Your perception of the visual world seems effortless and automatic. However, this visual process of readily identifying objects and their settings is a later stage in perception that follows an earlier complex operation to which we have no conscious access.

In the earlier stage of *preattentive processing,* features, such as lines, edges, boundaries, and colors, are extracted from patterns of light. Visual processes first decompose stimuli into parts and properties, then recombine them into correct, complex natural objects. Early vision deals with *individual* features of stimuli that form boundaries or segregate figure and ground—and not combinations of features.

When asked to locate boundaries between regions of scenes flashed briefly, subjects report that they "pop out" when there is a difference in simple, single properties of color, shape, or line orientation. As seen in **Figure 7.4A,** a region of upright *T*'s segregates well from a region of tilted *T*'s that differ in only one property but not from a region of reverse *L*'s made of two parts of the *T* (a horizontal and vertical line). Similarly, the boundary of red and blue *V*'s and *O*'s (**Figure 7.4B**) is distinct, whereas the combination of color and shape in **Figure 7.4C** does not form a clear boundary.

The analysis of properties and parts precedes their synthesis into combinations. If attention is diverted or overloaded by concurrent tasks, this feature-synthesis may not occur properly. Errors in synthesis can result in *illusory* combinations of individual features. When this occurs, it reveals that at the preattentive, nonconscious stage of visual processing, independent detection of many individual stimulus features is taking place before they are assembled into whole objects.

> *This effect of illusory combinations is found when three colored letters are flashed briefly (for a fifth of a second) while the subjects' attention is diverted to a second task of reporting a digit to the side of the letters. On a third of the trials, subjects "see" the wrong combination of colors and letters—for example, a red* X*, green* O*, and blue* T*, when the original display was blue* X*, red* O*, and green* T*. They rarely make errors of reporting other colors or letters. Furthermore, when asked to search for dollar signs ($) in an array of* S*'s and line segments (***Figure 7.5A***), they often reported illusory dollar signs when the array contained none (***Figure 7.5B***). They combined the S and the / to form a perceived illusion of a $. Even more interesting was the same illusory $ combination formed when the array was of* S*'s and triangles (***Figure 7.5C***). The visual system detected the lines of the triangles as independent components and combined one of them with the* S *to form the illusory $. (Treisman, 1986)*

Figure 7.4

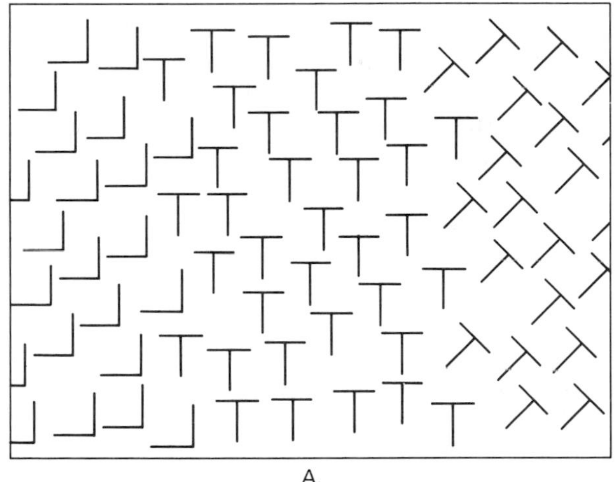

A.

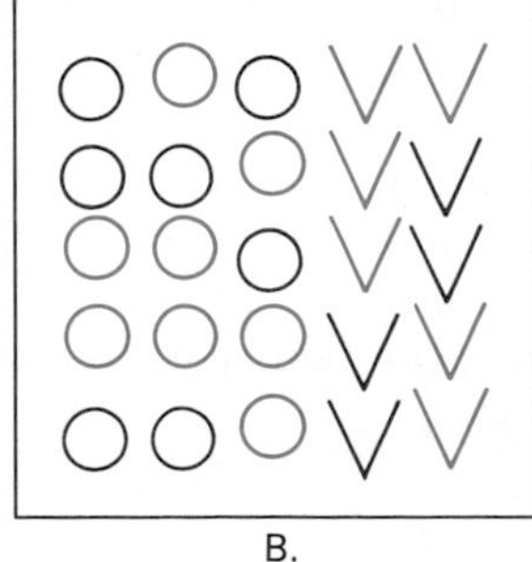

B.

C.

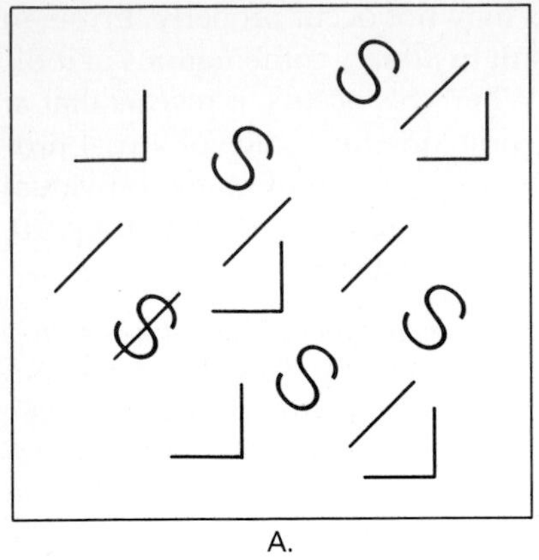

A.

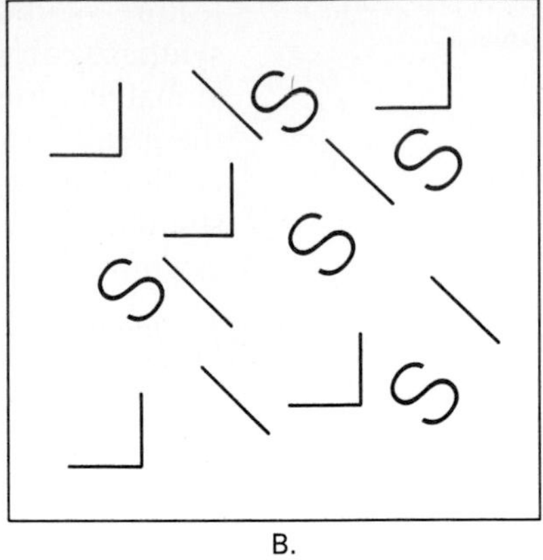

B.

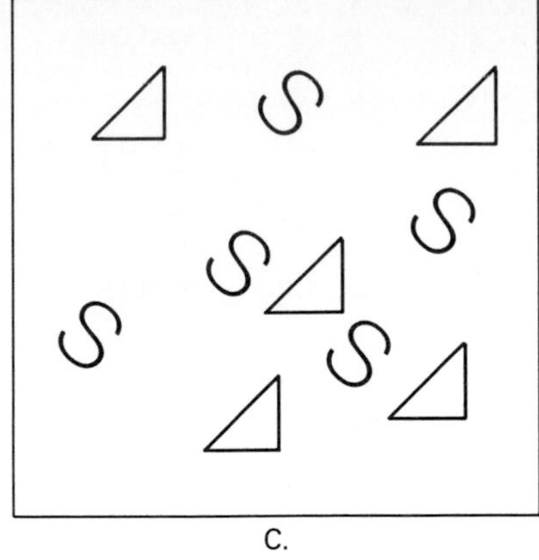

C.

Figure 7.5

New physiological studies of visual processing by single neurons within the visual cortex (of monkeys) also reveal that there are different stages of filtering out irrelevant, unattended stimulus features. Selective attention to a specific stimulus acts as a "visual gate" that filters out irrelevant information simultaneously presented to an unattended location within the receptive field of the same neuron. This filtering occurs at early stages of cortical processing. Thus, paradoxically, more, rather than less, information is processed by single neurons at each successive stage. This neuronal filtering of irrelevant information reduces the array of stimulus features that stimulate our retinas into a more limited set that are recombined to form properties of identifiable objects (Moran & Desimone, 1985).

Mindlessness

Our ability to process information outside of consciousness enables us to deal with far more information than we could handle if it all had to "stand in line" to go through conscious processing one item at a time. On the other hand, mental processing that does not receive our conscious attention can be maladaptive if we react "mindlessly" in a passive, nonquestioning way to situations that require new discriminations and new adaptations.

We expect mindless responses in animals driven by fixed action patterns, like the mother turkey responding to the cheep-cheep sounds (chapter 1). We more sophisticated organisms, however, sometimes behave in similarly mindless ways. For example, the response of *compliance* (doing what someone else wants you to) can be elicited by the single stimulus word *because.*

Students waiting in line to use a library copying machine were asked by a person (the researcher) if she could go ahead of them. She said: "Excuse me, I have five pages. May I use the Xerox machine because I'm in a rush?" Ninety-four percent of the students complied, allowing the researcher to skip ahead. When she made the same request without giving any reason, only 60 percent complied.

Was it the reason *given, or the* because *that elicited the compliance? In a third condition, the request was changed to "because I have to make some copies" [not a reason]. Again, nearly all complied; in 93 percent of those who were essentially told, "do it because of nothing," a compliant response was triggered. The same result occurred when the researcher asked seated subway passengers to give up their seats simply "because." (Langer, 1978)*

Processing information outside of consciousness simplifies our task, but can extract a high price by limiting our awareness of the real present environment and its requirements. In such processing analytic reasoning and objective judgment do not occur. Only in consciousness are we able to mobilize our best and most uniquely human mental resources to work toward particular goals. Perhaps this is why, as Posner and Snyder (1974) have suggested, "Consciousness is reserved for special processing."

Although we tend to believe that we have a running awareness of what is going on in our minds, what we are aware of is only the top of the mind's iceberg. Sometimes we attribute our reactions to a cause that, in fact, was not present. Sometimes we try to explain a conclusion by reasoning backward to a plausible line of thought that could have accounted for it—but actually did not. The errors we make in assuming that these mental processes were conscious have been shown in a recent study.

> *After viewing a documentary film, students rated it on several dimensions, such as how interesting it was and how much it would affect other people who saw it. For one experimental group the projector was out of focus, while a second experimental group had to contend with the distracting noise of a power saw outside. A control group had neither source of distraction. When asked if their ratings were affected by the noise or the poor focus, over 50 percent of the ''noise'' group reported that the noise lowered their ratings, and more than 25 percent of the ''poor focus'' group said that the poor focus did so. Actually, the ratings of all three groups were nearly identical. The distractions reported as being negative influences had no effect on the subjects' ratings.*
>
> *In other conditions, students failed to report (and were assumed to be unaware of) the influence of stimulus factors that* were *shown to have behavioral effects on them, while reporting that stimuli affected their reactions which actually did* not. *(Nisbett & Wilson, 1977, 1979)*

There is little evidence to support our belief in the direct introspective awareness of our complex mental processes. Our illusion of awareness is maintained for several reasons: (a) we confuse what we know with the processes by which we know it; (b) we rely on assumptions of plausible cause-effect relationships instead of true awareness of our "on-line" cognitive processes; and (c) we have inadequate feedback to disconfirm our false beliefs. How might you prove that people are unaware of the way their minds do what they do?

Nonconscious, Subconscious, and Unconscious Processing

We have encountered several examples of the processing of information outside of consciousness that nevertheless influenced behavior, such as the occurrence of blindsight and the studies of field dependence and perceptual defense described in chapter 5. **Nonconscious processes** involve information not represented in either consciousness or memory which nevertheless can influence fundamental bodily or mental activities. Two examples of nonconscious processes are the regulation of blood pressure, in which physiological information is detected and acted on without our awareness, and the basic perception of figure and ground, in which we are unaware of the organizing processes that give us this perception.

One example of this knowledge without awareness comes from studies of patients with a particular type of brain damage that causes a syndrome known as *prosopagnosics.* These patients are unable to recognize visually the faces of persons they previously knew well. Even after they recognize the people through other cues, such as voices, the facial features remain meaningless. However, it can be demonstrated that they do recognize familiar faces at an early stage in the process of recognition.

Looking through a family photo album would be a confusing experience for a person suffering from prosopagnosics.

> *When two patients with prosopagnosia were shown a set of 42 unfamiliar and 8 familiar facial photos, they responded significantly to the familiar faces at an autonomic level measured by their electrical skin conductance—even though they verbally reported no recognition. This autonomic index reveals that primitive recognition without conscious awareness is taking place. (Tranel & Damasio, 1985)*

By contrast, **subconscious processes** involve material not currently in consciousness, but retrievable from memory by special recall procedures. Karen's depression was the result of a subconscious process; once it was brought into her consciousness by hypnotic therapy, she could recognize it and deal with it appropriately.

The term *unconscious* is often used for all processes that are not conscious. In psychoanalytic theory, however, it has a special meaning, referring to processes that are kept out of consciousness to prevent anxiety. Such processes stem from the need to repress unpleasant memories and feelings. Freud described the **unconscious** as "any mental process the existence of which we are obliged to assume was active at a certain time, although [the person was] not aware of it at that time. We infer it from its effects" (1925). For example, unconscious motivation is inferred when a bright student's failures are seen as a way of punishing an overdemanding parent.

Freud assumed that, in such cases, the content of the real ideas or motives is *repressed*—put out of consciousness because it is too upsetting or threatening to deal with continually, but the feelings associated with it remain. One of Freud's contributions was in revealing the extent to which adult behavior is influenced by unconscious processes. His view challenged the comforting picture of humans as totally rational creatures. (These processes will be discussed in later chapters.)

The Duality of Consciousness

When the philosopher Descartes distinguished mind from body, he decided that consciousness had to be located in the tiny pineal gland (see p. 149). It belonged there, he felt, because there was an "undeniable unity" of consciousness, and the pineal gland was the only *single* organ he saw in a brain that consisted mostly of *pairs* of similar parts. The logic was good, but the facts were wrong. We know now that the part of the brain responsible for consciousness is the part most obviously divided into two parts—the two cerebral hemispheres.

Cerebral Dominance

What do you conclude from the following three pieces of evidence? (a) Patients suffering strokes that paralyze the *right* side of their bodies often develop speech disturbances. (b) People with brain damage from an accident or stroke may have difficulty writing, speaking, and understanding others—but only if the brain damage is on the *left* side. (c) Most people's left hemisphere is slightly larger than the right (Galaburda et al., 1978).

Though the two hemispheres of the brain are similar in many ways, both clinical and experimental evidence clearly indicate asymmetry: the two sides of the brain differ in their anatomical, chemical, and electrical properties. This asymmetry can be attributed to the fact that the two sides of the brain have primary responsibility for different functions. This tendency for one cerebral hemisphere to play a more dominant role than the other in controlling particular functions is called **cerebral dominance.** The most notable example of such dominance is that language-related functions are usually controlled by the left side of the brain. This explains why the left hemisphere is usually larger and why damage to it may cause language disorders. It also explains why people suffering paralysis on the right side from a stroke may have speech problems: from the right-side paralysis we know that the damage was to the left side of the brain.

Researchers have now found that the left hemisphere dominates language functions in 95 percent of all right-handers. About 70 percent of left-handers also show left-brain dominance for language. The other 5 percent of right-handers and 15 percent of left-handers have speech controlled by the right hemisphere. For another 15 percent of left-handers, language functions occur in both sides of the brain (this is called *bilateral speech control*). Persons with right-brain dominance in language functions are at higher risk to develop disorders that interfere with language-related functions such as reading. Interestingly, males are more likely than females to be left-handed and also to have more speech-related learning disorders.

Patients with right-hemisphere damage are more likely to have *perceptual* and *attentional* prob-

Brain damage affects opposite sides of the body in different ways.

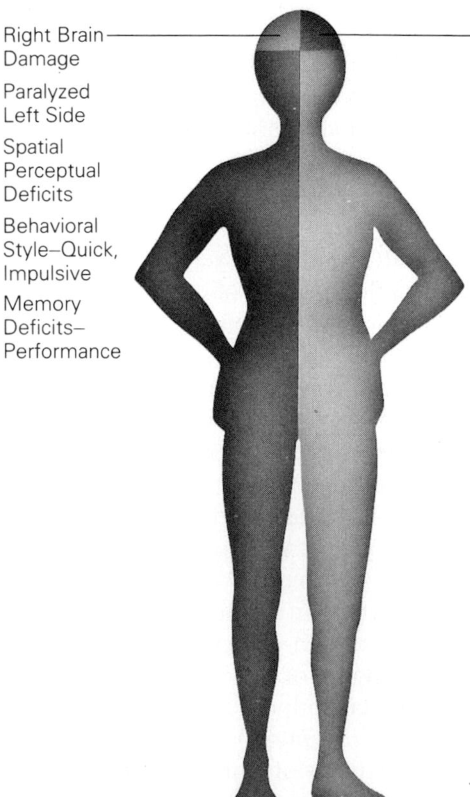

Table 7.1 *Specialization in the Cerebral Hemispheres*

	Left Hemisphere	**Right Hemisphere**
Language and Memory Functions	Controls spontaneous speaking, writing	Can direct repetitive, but not spontaneous, verbal utterances
	Directs formulation of replies to complex commands	Can direct response to simple commands
	Directs recognition of words	Directs recognition of faces
	Controls memory of words and numbers	Controls memory of shapes and music
Perceptual and Cognitive Functions	Orchestrates sequences of movements	Functions in map interpretation
		Functions in mental rotation of images
Emotional Functions	Is involved in feelings of anxiety	Controls emotional responsiveness
	Is responsible for negative emotions in response to unpleasant events	Is responsible for self-generated positive, expansive emotions
Both hemispheres are active in language and memory functions, in perceptual functions, and in emotional functions, but their contributions are different (adapted from Buchsbaum, 1980, and Tucker, 1981).		

(Adapted from F. R. Freeman, Sleep Research: A Critical Review, *1972. Courtesy of Charles C. Thomas, Publisher, Springfield, Illinois)*

lems, possibly including serious difficulties in spatial orientation. For example, they may feel lost in a previously familiar place or be unable to fit geometric shapes together. Patients with right-hemisphere damage in the parietal region may show a syndrome in which they totally ignore the left side of their bodies and left visual fields—eating only what is on the right side of a plate of food, for example.

Much of our knowledge about brain asymmetries has come from observing people who have suffered brain damage on one side or whose cerebral hemispheres could not communicate with each other. Hemispheric differences also exist in normal, healthy subjects. For example, with both men and women and both left-handers and right-handers, the rate of blood flow generally increases in the left hemisphere during verbal task performance and in the right hemisphere during performance of spatial tasks, suggesting greater activity in those parts of the brain for those tasks (Gur et al., 1982).

In general, studies have found the left side of the brain more important in controlling verbal activities and the right side more important in directing visual-spatial activities. One recent study suggests, however, that specialization may be more pronounced in men than it is in women (Inglis & Lawson, 1981).

Another important finding that comes from studies of subjects with normally functioning brains is the degree to which the two hemispheres make different contributions to the same function. For example, as **Table 7.1** shows, both hemispheres contribute to language and memory functions, to perceptual-cognitive functions, and to emotional functions, but their special aptitudes are evidently different.

This generalization is in keeping with the findings of a recent, methodologically sophisticated study. Subjects were given tasks requiring a series of split-second decisions and actions, while measurements were taken of the electrical activity of both hemispheres through brain-wave recordings. Brain-wave activity rapidly shifted back and forth laterally (from one side of the brain to the other), depending on the kind of judgment and response being made at the moment. This shifting lateralization of brain-wave activity was aptly termed "shadows of thought." (Gevins et al., 1983)

Focus on left-hemisphere speech control led to the mistaken belief that cerebral dominance would be found only in humans; but it is found in other species as well. For example, the development of a canary's songs is controlled by the left side of its brain. Also rats handled frequently when young were found to have stored early experiences in the right hemisphere. As adults, they were less aggressive than those not given early handling. This effect was eliminated in animals that had their right hemispheres removed. Continuing research has led to the assertion that "It is now likely that no animal species, no matter how humble, lacks cerebral dominance" (Geschwind, cited in Marks, 1981).

Two Minds in One Brain?

Consider this intriguing question: Would each half of the brain be able to act as a separate conscious mind if it were separated from the other in some way? The chance to investigate this possibility has been provided by a procedure in which surgeons control severe epilepsy by severing the corpus callosum—the bundle of about 200 million association nerve fibers that normally links the two hemispheres (see **Figure 7.6**). The goal of this surgery is to prevent the violent electrical rhythms that accompany epileptic seizures from crossing between the hemispheres (Wilson et al., 1977). The operation is usually successful and a patient's behavior thereafter appears normal.

If the ordinary behavior of split-brain patients appears normal, what gave researchers the idea that the two hemispheres may have different functions? When sensory input from the eyes or ears is registered by the receptors, it automatically goes across to the opposite side of the brain (right eye—left hemisphere). The information is shared by both hemispheres via "cross-talk" through the corpus callosum. When they can coordinate inputs from both eyes, split-brain patients can function without problems. However, when given special tasks that present separate information to each eye or each hand, the effects of the split-brain condition are quite dramatically "not normal."

The first split-brain operations on human patients were performed by William Van Wagener, a neurosurgeon, in the early 1940s (Van Wagener & Herren, 1940). Over a decade later, experimenters cut the corpus callosum in animals and then trained them in visual discrimination tasks with one eye covered. When the eye patch was switched to the other eye, the animals took as long to learn the tasks as they had the first time. The second half of the brain had not learned anything from the experience given to the first half (Myers & Sperry, 1958).

To test the capabilities of the separated hemispheres of epileptic patients, Roger Sperry (1968) and Michael Gazzaniga (1970) devised situations that could allow visual information to be presented separately to each hemisphere (as shown in **Figure 7.7**). The results indicated that the left hemisphere was superior to the right hemisphere in problems involving language or requiring logic and sequential or analytic processing of concepts. The left hemisphere could "talk back" to the researchers while the right hemisphere could not. Communication with the right hemisphere was achieved by confronting it with manual tasks involving identification, matching, or assembly of objects—tasks that did not require the use of words. The right hemisphere turned out to be better than the left at solving problems involving spatial relationships and at recognition of patterns. However it could only add up to 10 and was about at the level of a 2-year-old in the use and comprehension of word combinations.

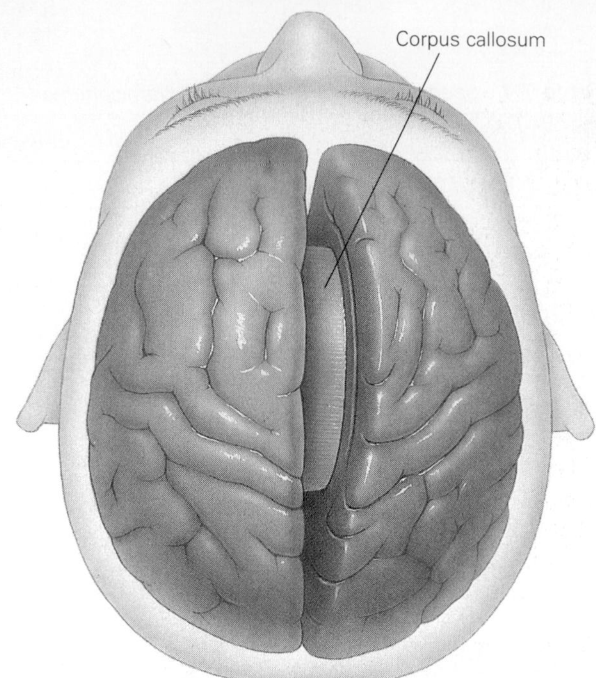

Figure 7.6 *The Corpus Callosum*
The corpus callosum is a large band of about 200 million axons connecting the right and left hemispheres of the cortex. In this diagram the hemispheres have been separated so that the corpus callosum is visible.

The two hemispheres also seemed to have different "styles" for processing the same information. For example, on matching tasks, the left hemisphere seemed to match objects analytically and verbally, by similarity in *function.* The right hemisphere matched things that *looked alike* or *fitted together* to form a *whole pattern.* Thus, when shown pictures of a hat and a knife and fork and asked to match the correct one with a picture of cake on a plate, a split-brain patient would report "You eat cake with a fork and knife"—when the images were presented only to the left hemisphere (via the right eye). When the test stimuli were presented to the right hemisphere, the patient might perceive "hat" going with the "cake" since the items were similar in shape (Levy & Trevarthen, 1976).

The intact brain functions as a whole with a vast, precise communication network integrating virtually all parts and functions. When the hemispheres are disconnected, the result is two separate minds, a split brain with a double consciousness. Each hemisphere can respond independently and simultaneously when stimuli are presented separately to the two sides. When stimuli are presented to only one side, responding will be emotional or analytic, according to which hemisphere gets the task of interpreting the message. Lacking language competence, however, the visual-spatial skills of the disconnected human right hemisphere are limited and vastly inferior to the cognitive skills of a chimpanzee. It is not just language facility that the right hemisphere has failed to develop, but a range of mental processes necessary for comprehension and understanding of both external and internal events.

Consider the following demonstration of the explanation given by the left half-brain to account for the activity of the left hand which was guided by the silent right half-brain.

> *A snow scene was presented to the right hemisphere and a picture of a chicken claw was simultaneously presented to the left hemisphere. The subject selected, from an array of objects, those that "went with" each of the two scenes. With his right hand, the patient pointed to a chicken head; with his left hand he pointed to a shovel. The patient reported that the shovel was needed to clean out the chicken shed (rather than shovel snow). Since the left brain was not privy to what the right brain "saw" because of the brain disconnection, it needed to explain why the left hand was pointing at a shovel when the only picture the left hemisphere was aware of seeing was a chicken claw. The left-brain's cognitive system provided a theory to make sense of the behavior of different parts of its body. (See Gazzaniga, 1985).*

The dominance of the left hemisphere and the role of its language capability in aiding our construction of meaning is conveyed by researcher Michael Gazzaniga:

> *The dominant left hemisphere is committed to the task of interpreting our overt behaviors as well as the more covert emotional responses produced by these separate mental modules of our brain. It constructs theories as to why these behaviors occurred and does so because of that brain system's need to maintain a sense of consistency for all of our behaviors. It is a uniquely human endeavor, and upon it rests not only the mechanism that generates our sense of subjective reality but also a mental capacity to free us from the binding controls of external contingencies. (1985, p. 80)*

Two illustrative case studies of the different functioning of the two "minds" of split brains are presented in the ***Close-up*** on page 236.

Complementary Orientations to the World?

From these and many other studies of hemisphere asymmetries, new views and speculations about human consciousness have emerged (Springer & Deutsch, 1984). Some psychologists have gone beyond the research findings to suggest that the two sides of the brain represent contrasting orientations to the world. In extreme versions of this hypothesis, the left brain is seen as the "masculine," analytic, rational side of human nature; the right brain is seen as the "feminine," sympathetic,

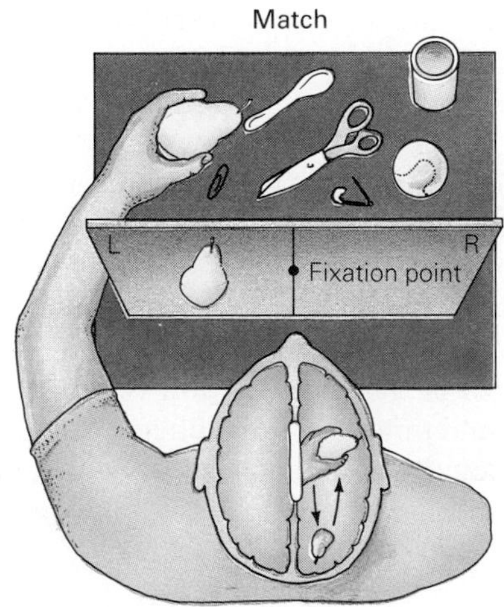

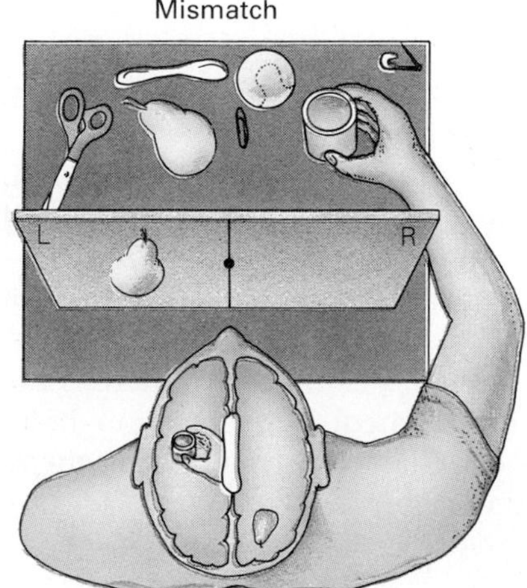

Figure 7.7
Coordination between eye and hand is normal if a split-brain patient uses the left hand to find and match an object that appears in the left visual field (both registered in the right hemisphere). However, when asked to use the right hand to match an object seen in the left visual field, the patient cannot do so because sensory messages from the right hand are going to the left cerebral hemisphere and there is no longer a connection between the two hemispheres. Here the cup is misperceived as matching the pear (Sperry, 1968).

Now You See It, Now You Don't Know That You See It

Mrs. N. G., a California housewife recovered from split-brain surgery, sits in front of a screen that blocks her view of her hands and objects on the table. As she fixates on a point in the center of her visual field, a projector flashes pictures to one or the other eye. Her task is to report verbally what she is shown and then to match that image by touching the appropriate object among the set of those on the table.

A cup is flashed in the right half of her visual field—and thus to her left hemisphere. "Cup," she replies, and she quickly feels through the array with her right hand until she finds a cup. No problem. Next, a spoon is flashed in her left visual field—and thus to her right hemisphere. Mrs. N. G. reports seeing nothing. When asked to pick out the object that was flashed using her left hand (controlled by the right hemisphere), she says it's not possible; but after touching each one she holds up the spoon. "What a lucky guess," she exclaims with surprise. Time after time she picks the correct object although she insists she sees nothing and is totally unaware of the relationship between the image flashed (to the right hemisphere) and the object identified by touch. Often, her left hemisphere comes to the aid of the puzzled right side, constructing stories to help explain the responding of the silent, confused right hemisphere.

A different message sent to her right hemisphere evokes an emotional reaction. When a sexually suggestive picture of a nude is flashed to her right hemisphere, Mrs. N. G. says she sees only a flash of light, but she blushes and giggles. In trying to explain her "uncaused" embarrassment, Mrs. N. G. exclaims, "Oh, doctor, you have some machine!" Again we see evidence of information processing below the level of consciousness, in this case by the language-poor right hemisphere.

Another split-brain patient, Paul is a boy of 15 who has partial representation of language functions in the right hemisphere. Left-hemisphere damage at an early age had probably been compensated for by the "plasticity" of the brain in developing some language ability on the right side. He can answer what his right half-brain sees or hears by spelling out words with letter blocks from a Scrabble game.

For example, the first part of a question, ("Who . . . ") is

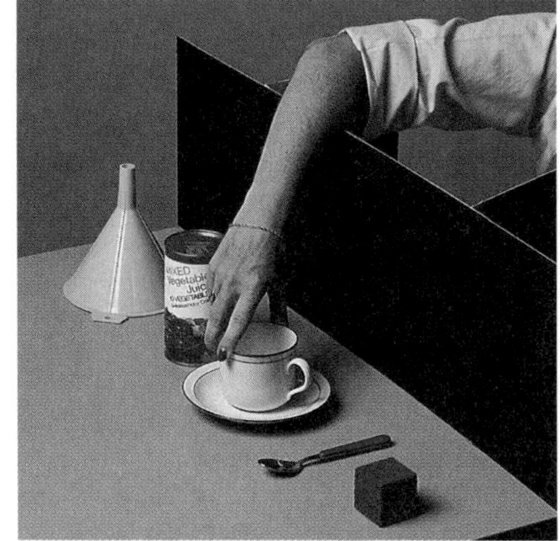

emotional aspect. Recent evidence, however, does not support this interpretation about the way the brain is organized.

It has also been suggested that Western educational systems overemphasize abilities that favor dominance of the left hemisphere—verbal fluency, logical reasoning, and a future orientation, among others. By contrast, in societies influenced by Eastern religious practices, there is likely to be greater development of the intuition, holism, and timelessness characteristic of the right side of the brain (Ornstein, 1972).

Some researchers are developing techniques designed to boost the right hemisphere's role in our mental activities. They attempt to break down reliance on words, names, causal sequences, linear operations, and logical analysis, emphasizing instead organic, nonlinear reasoning to deal with wholes and patterns instead of isolated parts (Buzan, 1976; Edwards, 1979). Systematic evaluation research on the success of these right-hemisphere "enhancers" is needed before these interesting speculations can be accepted as educationally valuable or scientifically valid.

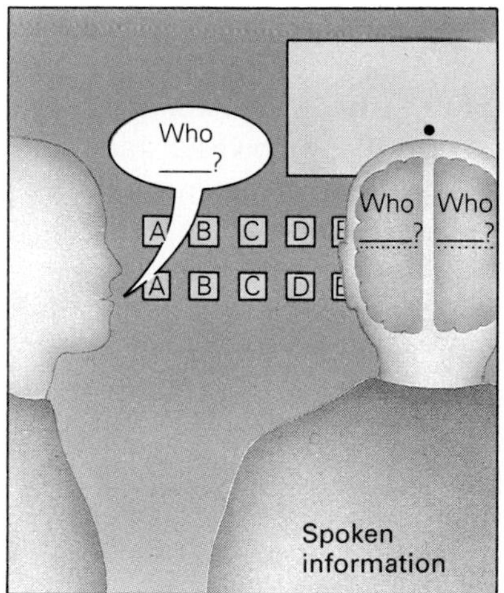

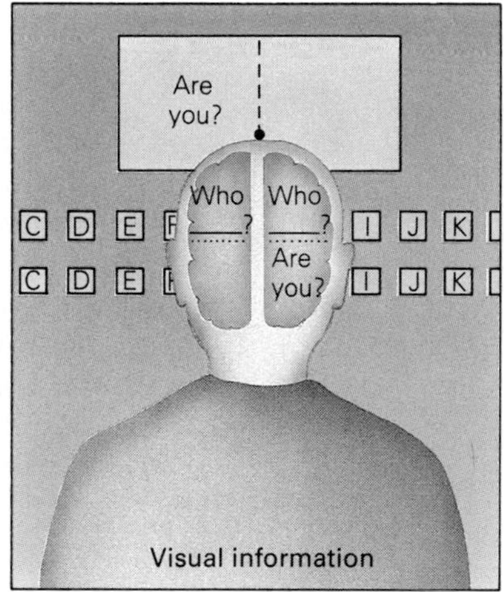

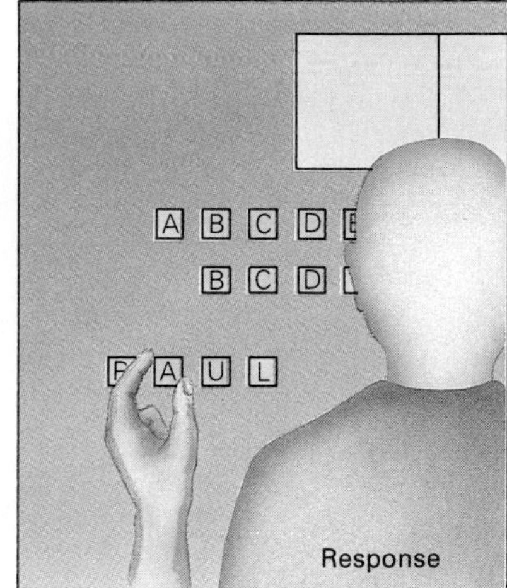

asked orally, thus being picked up by both ears and going to both hemispheres. The end of the question ("are you?") is then flashed in the left visual field, thus going only to the right hemisphere. In response to the input "Who (are you?)," received in this way, Paul arranges the blocks to form his name, "PAUL." He is able to spell his mood ("good"), his hobby ("car"), his favorite person ("Henry Wi Fuzi," for Henry Winkler, TV's Fonzi), tomorrow's day, and questions about his career goals ("automobile race[r]"). The researchers have concluded that Paul's right hemisphere possesses qualities of a conscious state: a sense of self, personal feelings, evaluations, future orientation, and goals.

Interestingly, when the *left* hemisphere is asked what is a desirable job for Paul, it answers, "Oh, be a draftsman." The fact that the two hemispheres do not always agree is seen as further evidence that the right side of the brain possesses conscious properties independent of the left. It seems to have a will of its own. For most of us, however, consciousness and self-awareness appear to be tied to the development of a verbal system, which we then use to represent symbolically what we perceive in both our inner and our outer worlds (Le Doux et al., 1977).

Everyday Changes in Consciousness

Watch children stand on their heads or spin around in order to make themselves dizzy, and ask them why they do it. "So everything looks funny." "It feels weird." "To see things tumble around in my head." Answers like these underscore the assumption that "human beings are born with a drive to experience modes of awareness other than the normal waking one; from very young ages, children experiment with techniques to change consciousness" (Weil, 1977, p. 37).

As they grow older, some people continue these "experiments" by taking drugs, including alcohol and caffeine, that alter their ordinary awareness. Some change their consciousness through prayer, meditation, or hypnosis. We all change our consciousness every time we daydream, have fantasies, or slip from wakefulness into sleep and have nightdreams. Before we examine some of these mental states, we need to consider their general characteristics.

From very young ages, children experiment with ways to change consciousness.

A useful orientation to these realities is provided by Charles Tart, a pioneering researcher in this area.

> *An altered state of consciousness for a given individual is one in which he clearly feels a* qualitative *shift in his pattern of mental functioning; that is, he feels not just a* quantitative *shift (more or less alert, more or less visual imagery, sharper or duller) but also that some quality or qualities of his mental processes are* different. *Mental functions operate that do not operate at all ordinarily, perceptual qualities appear that have no normal counterparts, and so forth. (1969, pp. 1–2)*

The use of the term *altered* has been criticized because it implies that there is one standard, desirable state of consciousness. Most researchers today prefer to speak of *alternate* or *extended* states of consciousness, since these words carry no implication of abnormality or of superiority of the ordinary state. In this section we will look at everyday changes in consciousness that are familiar because they are unavoidable and occur naturally. Then, in the next section, we will examine some more extreme forms of consciousness change that are brought about by external agents or particular physiological conditions.

Daydreaming and Fantasy

How clearly can you imagine each of the following: (a) a full moon coming over the horizon; (b) inheriting a million dollars; (c) what you should have said to the teacher you disliked most in high school? Close your eyes and see.

These "pictures in the mind's eye" are the stuff of daydreams. **Daydreaming** is a mild form of consciousness alteration that involves a shift of attention away from responding to external stimulation toward responding to some internal stimulus. An operational definition of *daydreaming* is "the report of thoughts that involve a shift of attention away from an immediately demanding task" [without, of course, any reference to current external factors] (Singer, 1975, p. 730).

Do you daydream, according to such definitions? You have plenty of company if you do.

> *In one sample of 240 respondents with some college education, ages 18 to 50, 96 percent reported daydreaming daily. Young adults (ages 18 to 29) reported the most daydreaming; there was a significant decline with age. (Singer & McCraven, 1961)*

In general, research by Jerome Singer (1966, 1976) and others shows that daydreaming is a common human activity when people are alone and relaxed. It is reported to occur most often in bed shortly before sleep, and least often upon awakening and during meals. Most people report that they enjoy daydreaming and are not embarrassed by it because they feel it is a normal function.

When we fantasize about what might be "if things were different," we are not necessarily escaping from life, but may be confronting the mysteries of life with wonder and respect. Wishing and planning activities seem to form the basic core of our daydreams. In fact, most daytime dreaming is concerned with practical, immediate concerns, especially future interpersonal behavior, rather than wild speculations. Next in frequency come daydreams dealing with sexual satisfaction, altruistic concerns, unusual good fortune (inheriting money), and likely future events (vacations).

> *In a survey of sexual fantasies, single Canadian women students between the ages of 18 and 47 were asked to check items that applied to them. The top six fantasies checked were having intercourse with a husband or boyfriend (90 percent), being undressed by a man (79 percent), a previous sexual experience (78 percent), intercourse in an exotic place (72 percent), undressing a man (71 percent), oral sex (66 percent). (Pelletier & Herold, 1983)*

Daydreaming is natural for people of all ages. It provides a means of transcending time and space.

Intense imaginative involvement with daydreams comes easily for children and sometimes is a way to deal with difficult home situations, abusive parents, or loneliness. It also occurs for adults too when we "lose ourselves" in a dramatic performance or have an intense sense of the beauty of nature.

Daydreams are rarely as vivid and compelling as nightdreams, but people vary in the extent to which they are able to become imaginatively involved in the realities they create. These individual differences are thought to be enduring personality factors not usually assessed by standard psychological tests (Tellegen & Atkinson, 1974).

Sleeping and Dreaming

We slip daily between states of consciousness as we move from waking to sleeping and then to dreaming. In between being awake and asleep is a drowsy condition which is not sleep, but another alternate state of consciousness.

Although keeping records of dreams has been a popular activity for ages (Calkins, 1893), such dream diaries offer no clues about the transformations of consciousness associated with sleeping. Before psychologists could study sleep, they had to find *external* indicators of sleep that could be observed and measured.

The methodological breakthrough for the study of sleep came with the development of a technology to record brainwave activity in the form of an electroencephalogram (EEG). This provided an objective, ongoing measure of the way brain activity varied when people were awake or asleep. In 1937, Loomis and his associates made the important discovery that brain waves change in form with the onset of sleep and show further systematic changes during the entire sleep period.

The next significant advance in sleep research occurred when it was found that bursts of rapid eye movement (REM) appeared at periodic intervals during sleep (Ascrinsky & Kleitman, 1953). When these rapid eye movements were linked to the occurrence of dreaming, many investigators were excited by this new path into a previously hidden side of human activity (Dement & Kleitman, 1957). Since then our understanding of this nightly alteration of consciousness has been studied in sleep laboratories throughout the world.

The Mystery of Sleep

About a third of your life will be spent sleeping, no matter how much you might wish to extend the active, waking side. Even when you spend totally relaxed, uneventful days on vacation, you still sleep a significant part of the time. It appears that humans have a need to sleep, but why is not known. The wonder of sleep is the universal restriction it forces upon all active creatures to spend so much time doing so little.

One reason you sleep each day can be found in the operation of your "biological clock." Even in an environment where all conditions are held constant (light, temperature, humidity, and noise) humans and animals will go to sleep about once every 24 hours. A regular 24-hour cycle also occurs for body temperature, urine production, secretion of certain hormones, and even your ability to memorize telephone numbers.

Any consistent pattern of cyclical body activities that lasts about 24 hours is called a **circadian rhythm,** or *circadian cycle* (*circadian* means "about a day"). The body's circadian rhythms are generated internally, but the "biological clock" can be set or reset by light and other stimuli. Predictable cycles with peaks and troughs for over a hundred physiological and performance variables have been identified, some with periods longer or shorter than 24 hours. One theory is that our daily cycle of best efficiency in the morning with a let-down in early afternoon is a holdover from the evolution of our species in a tropical climate (Thompson & Harsha, 1984).

Sleep is promoted when large amounts of the hormone *melatonin* are released from the pineal gland (Binkley, 1979). Light inhibits production of melatonin although the pineal gland will release some melatonin even in unchanging light conditions.

Melatonin is not the biological clock, however. Whatever and wherever the biological clock may be, it is based on processes that continue to work despite interference of all kinds. Animals born blind have nearly normal 24-hour circadian rhythms. Nor are these on-off cycles much disturbed by deprivation of food or water, by drugs, by periods of forced activity or inactivity, or even by removal of any of the hormonal organs (Richter, 1965). Human circadian rhythms are sensitive to bright light, however, and can be altered by systematic exposure to bright light in the evening. When the circadian rhythm is experimentally "reset" through exposure to bright indoor light, changes are recorded in body temperature and hormone secretions (Czeisler et al., 1986).

Why Sleep?

How much someone sleeps is not correlated with activity during the day, but with certain personality variables. Individuals who sleep longer than average, when compared to those who sleep less than average, are found to be more nervous and worrisome and to be more artistic, creative, and nonconforming. Short-sleepers tend to be more energetic and extraverted (Hartmann, 1973). Whether sleep influences personality, personality type affects sleep, or a third process causes the two to be related cannot be determined from this correlational study.

The two most general answers to the question of why we need to sleep are *restoration* and *conservation.* Sleep enables the body to engage in restoration of "housekeeping" functions such as digestion and waste product removal. It may also be a period of relative inactivity when neurotransmitters are synthesized to compensate for the quantities used in daily activities or when postsynaptic receptors are returned to their optimal level of sensitivity (Stern & Morgane, 1974). An evolutionary theory of the function of sleep suggests that it is a mechanism that evolved and survived because it enabled animals to conserve energy at times when there was no need to forage for food and mates and no work to be done (Allison & Cicchetti, 1976; Cartwright, 1982; Webb, 1974).

Sleep Stages

Regardless of why we sleep, it is clear that sleep is divided into distinct stages during which different brain activities are taking place. EEGs taken during sleep show two general states of brain activity; **delta sleep,** in which the EEG pattern is slow and orderly, and *desynchronized* or *paradoxical* sleep, in which the EEG pattern resembles the erratic low-voltage pattern of the waking state, although we are very much asleep. Because bursts of *rapid eye movement* occur during such sleep, desynchronized sleep is usually called **REM sleep.** Persons awakened during REM sleep often report dreaming, while those awakened during non-REM sleep are much less likely to do so. The rapid eye movements associated with dreaming are shown in the photograph in **Figure 7.8.**

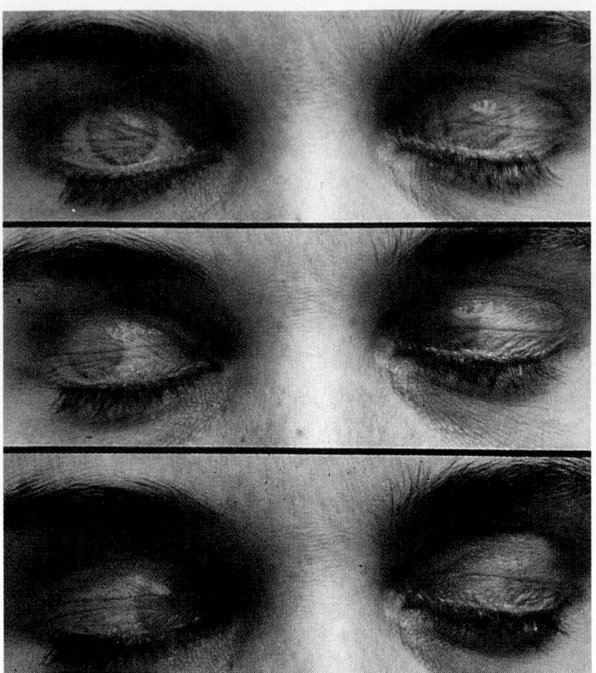

Figure 7.8 REM Sleep
This double-exposure photograph shows the rapid eye movements associated with dreaming.

An adult falling asleep passes through stages 1, 2, 3, and 4 in a cycle lasting approximately 90 minutes and then "emerges" into a period of REM sleep lasting about 10 minutes. A night of sleep usually consists of four to six such cycles. With each subsequent cycle, delta sleep gets shorter and the REM period lengthens. During the last cycle, REM sleep can last for 30 to 60 minutes.

Humans and most other animals exhibit regular sleep-wake cycles, orderly stages of sleep, and some standard ratio of REM to non-REM sleep. For humans, this changes with age. A baby will sleep 16 hours a day with perhaps half of it in REM sleep. By age 1, total sleep time decreases to about 13 hours, of which REM sleep constitutes only 25 to 30 percent. A young adult will sleep 7 to 8 hours with about 20 percent REM sleep; and the elderly sleep about 6 hours with about 15 percent REM sleep. The duration of delta sleep begins to drop at age 30 and by the time a person is 60 to 70 years old, delta sleep virtually disappears. The cyclic nature of the sleep-wake cycle has been associated with activity in specific areas of the brain and with the release of chemicals that influence sleeping and waking (Maugh, 1982). **Figure 7.9** shows these changing sleep patterns.

Deprivation of REM sleep needs to be made up by longer than usual periods of REM sleep during one's next sleep or over several sleep episodes. It may even be that we need to sleep in order to get REM sleep—rather than simply to rest weary bodies and minds. A number of interesting, but not yet fully demonstrated, benefits have been attributed to REM sleep. For example, it is suggested by some that, in infancy, REM sleep is responsible for establishing the pathways between our nerves and muscles that enable us to move our eyes. REM sleep may also establish the functional structures in the brain, like those involving the learning of motor skills. It can play a role in the maintenance of mood and emotion. REM sleep may also be required for storing memories and fitting recent experiences into networks of previous beliefs or memories (see Cartwright, 1978; Dement, 1976).

Jet Lag

When people travel across many time zones in fast jet planes, they may experience "jet lag"—a cluster of symptoms including fatigue, irresistible sleepiness, and unusual sleep-wake schedules. Jet lag occurs because the internal circadian rhythm is out of phase with the normal temporal environment. Your body says it's 2:00 A.M., but local time is noon. Jet lag fatigue is a special problem for flight crews and is implicated in errors made by pilots, as well as in some airplane accidents (Coleman, 1986).

What variables influence jet lag? The *direction* of travel and the number of time zones passed through are most important. Traveling eastbound creates greater jet lag than does westbound flight, since our biological clocks can be extended more readily than shortened (as required on eastbound trips). When healthy volunteer subjects were flown back and forth between Europe and the United States, their peak performance on standard tasks was reached within 2 to 4 days following westbound flights, but required 9 days following eastbound travel!

Figure 7.9 *Patterns of Human Sleep over a Lifetime*
The graph shows changes with age in total amounts of daily sleep, both REM and non-REM, and percentage of REM sleep. Note that the amount of REM sleep decreases considerably over the years, while non-REM diminishes less sharply (adapted from Roffwarg et al., 1966).

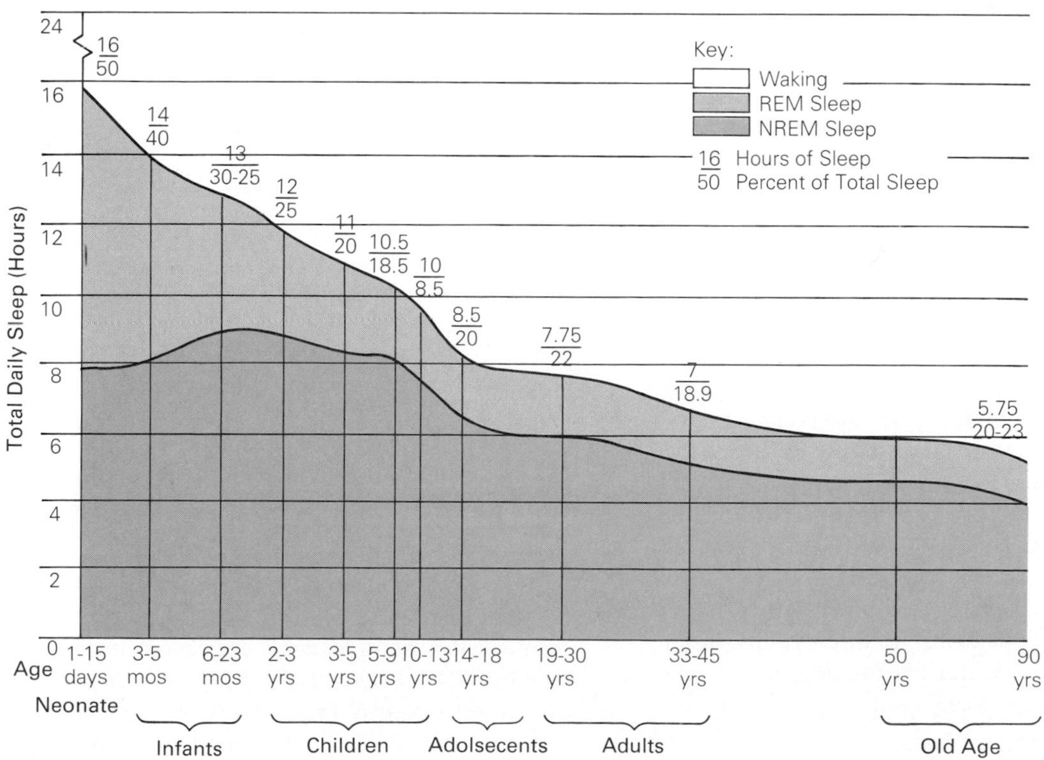

What Causes Dreams?

Dreams offer a royal road to the mind when it is in a state governed by rules and principles quite different from those that apply during waking. (Hobson & McCarley, 1977)

Subjects aroused during REM sleep recall ongoing visual images that form a coherent drama, are vivid, and may be in color with sound. Despite bizarre or fantastic qualities of the plot, the unreal situation is accepted by the sleeper as "natural." Some dreaming also takes place during non-REM periods, but it is of a different quality. Dreaming associated with non-REM states is less likely to contain dramatic story content. It is full of specific thoughts, but has minimal sensory imagery. The percentage of time spent dreaming reported from REM and non-REM awakenings in 10 studies and the definitions of dreaming they used are summarized in **Table 7.2.**

People occasionally report being aware that they are dreaming. The existence of these "lucid dreams" has recently been demonstrated by having subjects signal (by gestures) when they realized that they were dreaming. They were able to signal to the researchers during REM sleep that a lucid dream was taking place, without disturbing their sleep and with memory for the dream. It appears that lucid dreaming is a learnable skill (LaBerge, 1986; LaBerge et al., 1981).

One physiological explanation proposes that dreams are the brain's attempt to form a coherent interpretation of essentially random bursts of cortical activity occurring during REM sleep. The cortex retrieves memories that could be associated with the signals it is receiving from deep within the brain stem. Finding no logical connections in the stimulation, it makes illogical remote associations or fills the gaps with recent memories (Hobson & McCarley, 1977).

According to Freud (1900), however, dreams are much more than the brain's search for a good story to account for its electrical discharges. Freud saw dreams as symbolic expressions of unconscious wishes that had been carefully disguised by an internal "censor." In Freudian terms, what you remember and report of your dreams is only the **manifest content.** The real meaning of a dream is in its **latent** (hidden) **content**—unconscious impulses and wishes that have been denied overt gratification and appear in dreams in disguised forms. The manifest content is the acceptable version of the story; the latent content represents the socially or personally unacceptable version—but the true, "uncut" one. In sleep, the usually vigilant censor is relaxed, and some repressed unconscious material may be expressed.

"The golden arches! The golden arches got me!"

It is evident from Freud's writing in his classic *Interpretation of Dreams* (1900) that *his* mind was on sex. To him, dream symbols were largely sex symbols in varying states of undress.

> *—All elongated objects, such as sticks, tree trunks and umbrellas (the opening of these last being comparable to an erection) may stand for the male organ—as well as all long, sharp weapons, such as knives, daggers and pikes. . . . —Boxes, cases, chests, cupboards and ovens represent the uterus, and also hollow objects, ships, and vessels of all kinds.*
>
> *—Rooms in dreams are usually women; if the various ways in and out of them are represented, this interpretation is scarcely open to doubt. . . . A dream of going through a suite of rooms is a brothel or harem dream. . . . —It is highly probable that all complicated machinery and apparatus occurring in dreams stand for the genitals (and as a rule male ones). . . . Nor is there any doubt that all weapons and tools are used as symbols for the male organ: e.g., ploughs, hammers, rifles, revolvers, daggers, sabres, etc. (pp. 354–56)*

According to Freud, the two main functions of dreams are to guard sleep and to serve as sources of wish fulfillment. They allow uninterrupted sleep by draining off psychic tensions created during the day and allow achievement of the unconscious fulfillment of wishes. (See also "Images of the Night" in *The Best of Science.*)

Dreams are real while they last. Can we say more of Life?

Havelock Ellis

Extended States of Consciousness

It is one thing to have ordinary, waking consciousness undergo daily transformations as we daydream, sleep, or engage in nightdreaming, and quite another matter to go beyond these familiar forms to extended states of consciousness. Examples of these less common "alternate" states of consciousness are seen in hallucinations and in the experiences associated with hypnosis and certain kinds of drugs.

Hallucinations

Hallucinations are vivid perceptions in the absence of objective stimulation and are not to be confused with *illusions,* which are perceptual distortions of real stimuli. The images and sensations experienced in hallucinations are the products of the hallucinator's mind rather than the consequence of external stimuli. However, they are often believed by an individual to be perceptions of reality.

Hallucinations can occur during states of high fever, epilepsy, and migraine headaches. They are also a characteristic of severe mental disorder, in which a patient responds to private mental events as if they were external sensory stimuli and believes in the reality of the voices heard or the figures seen.

Hallucinations have also been associated with heightened arousal states and religious ecstasies. In fact, in some cultures and circumstances, hallucinations are interpreted as mystical insights that confer special status on the visionary. So, in different settings, the same vivid perception of direct contact with spiritual forces may be deprecated as a "hallucination" or honored as a "vision" or "revelation." It is thus important to recognize that evaluation of such mental states depends as much on the judgment of observers as on the content of the perceptual experience itself.

Some visions with religious content clearly represent states induced by mental disturbance, epilepsy, or migraines.

A dramatic example of the blend of religiously inspired visions and physiologically induced visual imagery, or hallucinations, is that of the twelfth-century Catholic nun, Hildegard, of Bingen, Germany. She was "a woman of extraordinarily active and independent mind. She was not only gifted with a thoroughly efficient intellect, but was possessed of great energy and considerable literary power, and her writings cover a wide range, betraying the most varied activities and

Table 7.2 *Dreaming During REM and Non-REM Sleep*

Definition of Dreaming Used in Study	Percentage Recalling REM Dreams	Percentage Recalling Non-REM Dreams
"any item of specific content"	87	74
"visual, auditory, or kinesthetic imagery"	82	54
"a dream recalled in some detail"	69	34
self-definition by each subject	85	24
"specific content of mental experience"	86	23
"detailed dream description"	74	7
"coherent, fairly detailed description"	79	7
"any sensory imagery with . . . progression of the mental activity"	81	7
self-definition by each subject	60	3

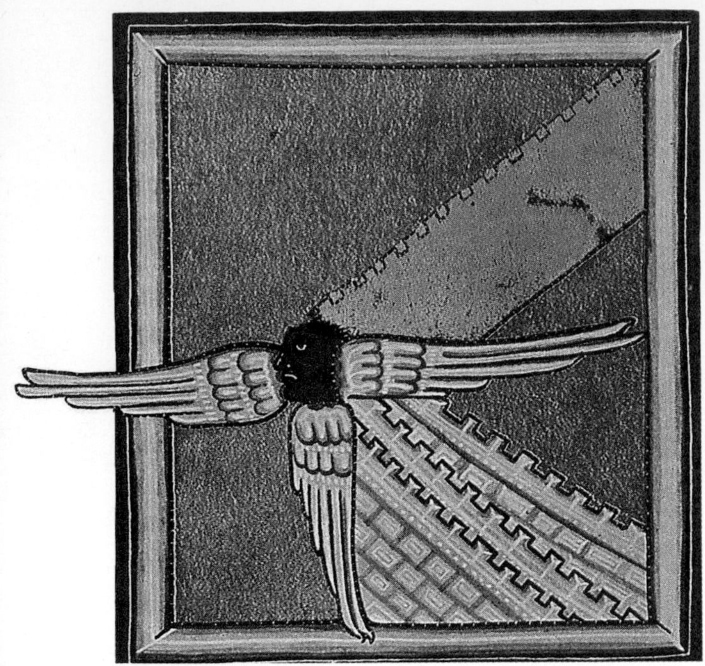

This drawing by the mystic Hildegard of Bingen is typical of a migraine-induced hallucination.

remarkable imaginative faculty'' (Singer, 1958, pp. 199–200). Hildegard wrote mystical essays and was an ecstatic, *believing in intense religious devotion that could lead to a trancelike state. She reported and made detailed drawings of her ''religious visions,'' which, in light of what is now known, resemble descriptions by patients of what they had seen during migraine attacks. (Sacks, 1973)*

Hallucinations may be induced by psychoactive drugs, such as LSD and peyote, as well as by the withdrawal of alcohol in severe cases of alcoholism (delirium tremens, ''the DTs''). For the most part, however, these are not regarded as ''true hallucinations'' since they are direct effects of the drug on the brain rather than part of a new view of reality that a person is creating.

Instead of asking what turns hallucinations on, some psychologists wonder, ''Why do we not hallucinate all the time?'' They believe that the ability to hallucinate is always present in each of us, but normally is inhibited by interaction with sensory input, by our constant reality testing, and by feedback from the environment. When sensory input and feedback are lacking and there is no way to test our ideas against outer reality, there is indeed a tendency to hallucinate. Hallucinations are also fostered by heightened arousal, states of intense need, or inability to suppress threatening thoughts.

Many instances of altered states of consciousness are reported following such ''overstimulating'' experiences as mob riots, religious revival meetings, prolonged dancing (such as is done by ''whirling'' dervishes), extreme fright or panic, trance states during primitive ceremonies of numerous kinds, or moments of extreme emotion, whether the emotion be ecstatic love or unbearable grief. (See also ''The Holy Ghost People'' in *The Best of Science.*)

It also appears that the brain requires some minimal level of external stimulation. Some subjects, when kept in a special environment that minimizes all sensory stimulation, show a tendency to hallucinate. Sensory isolation ''destructures the environment'' and may force subjects to try to restore meaning and stable orientation to a situation. Hallucinations may be a way of reconstructing a reality in accordance with one's personality, past experiences, and the demands of the present experimental setting (Zubeck et al., 1961; see also Suedfeld, 1980, for positive effects of chosen reduced sensory stimulation).

Hypnosis

Hypnosis holds a strange fascination for most people. It seems that mere words spoken by a hypnotist can cause major changes in the behavior of the hypnotic subject. We feel uneasy about this apparent power of one person over another and about the vulnerability of the person so influenced; but is that view of their relationship accurate? What is hypnosis, what are its important features, and what are some of its valid psychological uses?

Hypnosis is a term derived from the name *Hypnos,* the Greek god of sleep. Sleep plays no part in hypnosis, except in a person's *appearance* of being in a deeply relaxed, sleeplike state, in some cases. If a person actually falls asleep, there is no longer any responsiveness to hypnotic suggestions.

There are many different conceptions about hypnosis, along with a variety of definitions. For our purposes, a broad definition of **hypnosis** presents it as an alternate state of awareness induced by a variety of techniques and characterized by the special ability of some people to respond to suggestions with changes in perception, memory, motivation, and sense of self-control (Orne, 1980). More simply, hypnosis is often equated with hypersuggestibility, a state of heightened responsiveness to another person's suggestions—or to one's own during self-hypnosis, also called **autohypnosis.** Not only does a hypnotic subject follow these suggestions, but there is often the feeling that the behavior is emitted as if ''by itself,'' without intention or any conscious effort on the subject's part.

Hypnotic Suggestibility

Most dramatic stage performances of hypnosis give the impression that the power of hypnosis should be credited to the skills of the hypnotist. Perhaps it is something in his or her "hypnotic gaze" that makes the commands so compelling. This is a false conclusion. The real star of the show is the person who is hypnotized—not the hypnotist. The hypnotist is little more than a coach or experienced travel guide who shows the way.

The single most important factor in hypnosis is a participant's ability or "talent" to become hypnotized. **Hypnotizability** represents the degree to which an individual is responsive to standardized suggestions. There are wide individual differences in this susceptibility, varying from a person who is not at all responsive to any suggestion to one who is totally responsive to virtually every suggestion. A highly hypnotizable person may respond to suggestions to change motor reactions (limbs rigid or flexible), to experience hallucinations and amnesia, and to become insensitive to powerful stimuli. Hypnotizing someone is a technique to change the hypnotized person's representation of reality.

The "power" of hypnosis can be traced to the existence of this ability in certain people to respond to suggestion, along with the creation of an appropriate psychological environment. A hypnotizable person can be hypnotized by anyone he or she is willing to respond to, while someone unhypnotizable will not respond to the tactics of the most skilled hypnotist.

Hypnosis begins with **hypnotic induction,** a preliminary set of activities that prepare a participant for this alternate state of awareness. Induction activities involve suggestions to imagine certain experiences or to visualize events and reactions. When practiced repeatedly, the hypnotic induction procedure acts as a learned signal to a subject to experience this special, out-of-the-ordinary state by minimizing distractions, concentrating on suggested stimuli, and believing that a special state of consciousness is about to happen.

The typical induction procedure uses suggestions for deep relaxation, but some people can become hypnotized by the use of an active, alert induction—even by imagining jogging or riding a bicycle. A child in the dentist's chair can be hypnotized while his or her attention is directed to vivid stories or to imagining the exciting adventures of a favorite TV character. Meanwhile the dentist drills and fills cavities with no anesthesia, but the child feels no pain (Banyai & E. Hilgard, 1976).

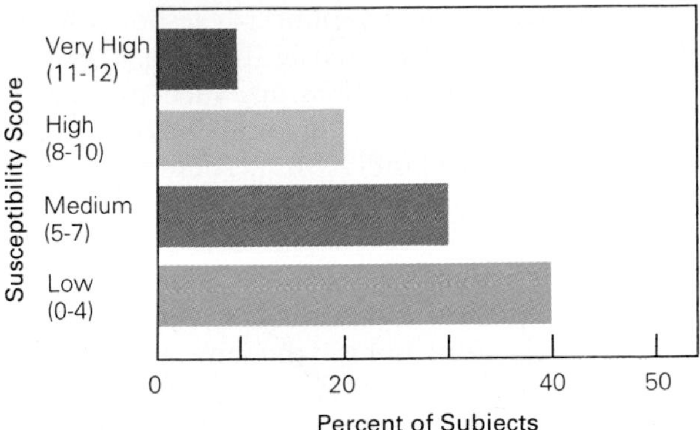

Figure 7.10 *Level of Hypnosis at First Induction*
The graph shows results for 533 subjects hypnotized for the first time. Hypnotizability was measured on the Stanford Hypnotic Susceptibility Scale, which consists of 12 items (based on E. Hilgard, 1965).

The operational definition of *hypnotizability* is the number of items experienced during a standardized induction test. Some "easy" items—such as imagining an arm getting heavier—are passed by most people. More difficult ones—such as hallucinating a buzzing fly or forgetting suggested events—are passed by fewer people. **Figure 7.10** shows the percentage of college-age subjects at various levels of hypnotizability the first time they were given this hypnotic induction test.

This objective measure of hypnotizability is the most important single predictor of a person's responsiveness to a variety of hypnotic phenomena. For example, high scorers are more likely than low scorers to be able to relieve pain by hypnosis (experience hypnotic analgesia) and to respond to hypnotic suggestions to have *positive hallucinations* (see or hear something not objectively present) or *negative hallucinations* (not perceive something that is present).

Hypnotizability is a relatively stable attribute of a given individual. An adult's scores remain about the same when measured over a 10-year period (Morgan et al., 1974). In fact, when 50 men and women were retested 25 years after their first hypnotizability assessment (when they were college students), the results indicated a remarkably high correlation coefficient of .71 (Piccione et al., 1987). Children tend to be more suggestible than adults, with hypnotic responsiveness peaking just before adolescence and declining thereafter. There is some evidence for genetic determinants of hypnotizability, because the scores of identical twins are more similar than are those of fraternal twins (Morgan et al., 1970).

Responsiveness to hypnotic suggestion can be slightly enhanced with intensive practice, as well as by sensory deprivation or drugs such as LSD or mescaline (Diamond, 1974; Sanders & Reyhen, 1969; Sjoberg & Hollister, 1965). These procedures do not transform unsusceptible subjects into highly responsive ones, however.

Although hypnotizability is relatively stable, it is surprising to discover that it is not correlated with any personality trait, nor is it the same as gullibility, conformity, role playing, or reaction to the social demands of the situation (see Fromm & Shor, 1979). It is a unique cognitive ability—a special aspect of the human imagination. It develops early in life along with the sense of being able to become completely absorbed in some experience. A hypnotizable person is one who is capable of deep involvement in the imaginative-feeling areas of experience, such as in reading novels or listening to music. Also associated with hypnotizability is a willingness by individuals to suspend ordinary reality testing temporarily and accept "as if" suggestions as though they were about reality (E. Hilgard, 1970, 1979).

Research efforts to find physiological indicators of the state of hypnosis have not been successful, perhaps because of the many different mental and behavioral events that may be induced under hypnosis. It has been demonstrated, however, that hypnotizability is associated with a preference for greater use of the functions of the right hemisphere of the brain relative to the more analytic left hemisphere (Gur & Gur, 1974).

Altered Personal Reality Under Hypnosis

It is necessary to maintain a scientific skepticism regarding the claims made for hypnosis, especially when the claims are based on individual case reports or research lacking proper control conditions (Barber, 1969). There is also disagreement among researchers regarding the psychological mechanisms involved in hypnosis (see Fromm & Shor, 1979). While some argue for the role of heightened motivation (Barber, 1976) and others for social role playing (Sarbin & Coe, 1972), some investigators advance the hypothesis that hypnosis represents a state of psychological *dissociation* (E. Hilgard, 1977).

Still, there does exist a reliable body of empirical evidence bolstered by expert opinion strongly suggesting that hypnosis can exert a powerful influence on many psychological and bodily functions (Bowers, 1976; Burrows & Dennerstein, 1980; E. Hilgard, 1968, 1973). We will single out only two

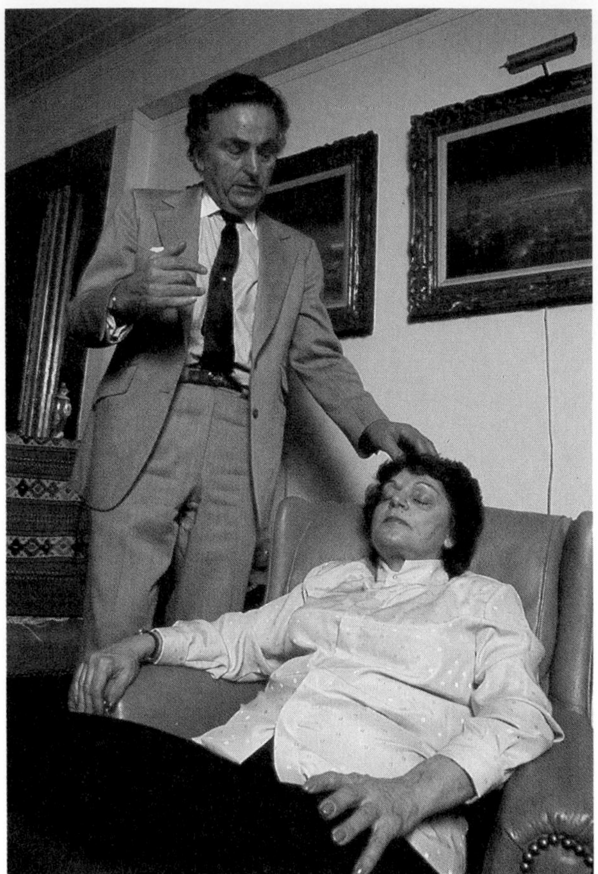

Hypnotic induction is primarily a matter of vivid imagination and openness to the suggestions of the hypnotist.

especially intriguing phenomena that illustrate hypnotic changes in personal reality—"trance logic" and dissociation.

In the following example of "trance logic," an investigator used a procedure known as **age regression,** in which the hypnotized subject was made to believe that he or she was at some particular earlier age.

> *A subject "who spoke only German at age six and who was age regressed to that time answered 'Nein' ['No'] when asked whether he understood English. . . . When this question was rephrased to him 10 times in English, he indicated each time in German that he was unable to comprehend English, explaining in childlike German such details that his parents speak English in order that he not understand. While professing his inability to comprehend English, he continued responding appropriately in German to the hypnotist's complex English questions." (Orne, 1972, p. 427)*

This person, while hypnotized, was showing "trance logic"; he could tolerate paradoxes instead of insisting that his experience make sense by ordinary logic. **Trance logic** is a characteristic feature of some highly hypnotizable subjects, who register information at one level of processing, but deny it at other levels. Information gets in, but then the person acts as if it is not there. It provides yet another example of our ability to process information below the level of consciousness.

Some highly suggestible individuals are especially responsive to stored information that is not directly accessible to their conscious awareness. While they are in the hypnotic trance state, they function at two levels of consciousness—a full, but hypnotic, consciousness of what they are experiencing, as suggested, and a concealed, nonconscious awareness. Such subjects can sometimes reveal this hidden level of their consciousness if they are instructed to engage in "automatic writing," a process in which a person has no conscious awareness of what he or she is writing, yet somehow the pen moves and meaningful words are written. "Automatic talking" can also occur. A person's cognitive system reports on itself without the conscious system becoming aware of what is going on.

Ernest Hilgard has coined the term **hidden observer** to refer to the covert awareness of knowledge that is not acknowledged consciously. This phenomenon was first observed in hypnotic subjects who reported feeling no pain when subjected to a painful stimulus and told they would feel nothing. When they were then told that a hidden part of them knew what was going on in their body and could report it accurately, the subjects processed the pain experience and reported pain as fully as those who had not been hypnotized (E. Hilgard, 1977).

The "double consciousness" revealed by this hidden observer research is shown further in these statements from college student subjects:

> *The hidden observer and the hypnotized part are both* all of me, *but the hidden observer is more aware and reported honestly what was there. The hypnotized part of me just* wasn't aware *of the pain. (Knox et al., 1974, p. 845)*
>
> *In hypnosis I kept my mind and body separate, and my mind was wandering to other places—not aware of the pain in my arm. When the hidden observer was called up, the hypnotized part had to step back for a minute and let the hidden part tell the truth. (Knox et al., 1974, p. 846)*

This **dissociation**—functioning of consciousness at different levels—may also occur in altered states of consciousness induced by religious ecstasy and drugs. These and other hypnotic phenomena not only are interesting in themselves, but point up the subtle operating characteristics and capabilities of a human mind that can function at conscious and nonconscious levels simultaneously. In chapter 15 we will discuss multiple personalities, in which two, or usually more, distinct personalities exist within one individual. Hypnosis is not only the treatment of choice for such cases, but it may also be one of the ways in which the disorder originates. There is evidence to suggest that children employ self-hypnosis as a way of coping with traumatic experiences of abuse and neglect.

Mind Alteration with Drugs

Since ancient times, people have taken drugs that altered their perception of reality. There is archaeological evidence for the uninterrupted use of sophora seed (called mescal bean) for over 10,000 years in the southwestern United States and Mexico. From the ninth millennium B.C. to the nineteenth century A.D., New World peoples smoked sophora to bring about ecstatic hallucinatory visions. Then sophora was replaced by the more benign peyote cactus, which is still used in the sacred rituals of many Indians.

In modern-day use, drugs are less associated with "sacred" communal rituals to reach new plateaus of mystical awareness than with attempts by individuals to feel mellow, cope with stress, tune out the unpleasantness of current realities, or tune in to alternate states of consciousness. This drug-induced alteration in the functioning of mind and in the nature of consciousness was popularized in our era by the 1954 publication of *The Doors of Perception* by Aldous Huxley. Huxley took mescaline as a personal experiment to test the validity of poet William Blake's assertion in *The Marriage of Heaven and Hell* (1793):

> *If the doors of perception were cleansed every thing would appear to man as it is, infinite.*
>
> *For man has closed himself up, till he sees all thro' narrow chinks of his concern.*

The experience for Huxley was one that transcended his perception of ordinary reality, leading to new modes of thought, more mystical than rational. He described the final stage of giving up his ego within the mescaline experience as one where "there is an 'obscure knowledge' that All is in all—that All is actually each. This is as near, I take it, as a finite mind can ever come to 'perceiving everything that is happening everywhere in the universe.'"

We will now focus on the **psychoactive drugs**—those chemicals which affect mental processes and behavior by changing conscious awareness of reality for a while. We will begin by considering what drug dependence is, then we will compare the effects of several kinds of psychoactive drugs, and finally we will see what nondrug factors can increase or decrease their effects.

In few modern societies has there been as extensive use of drugs or as much interest in drugs by such young users as there is in the United States today. Experimenting with drugs, which increased steadily among high-school students during the 1970s, has leveled off and has been declining since, according to annual surveys of 16,000 to 17,000 high-school seniors (Johnston et al., 1982). Nearly two thirds of the current generation of American high-school seniors report having used an illicit drug, however (see **Figure 7.11**). Males are more likely to use drugs than females and to know more users (Brunswick, 1980).

A large-scale 1971 survey of over 8000 secondary-school students in New York State revealed that adolescents were much more likely to use marijuana if their friends did than if their friends did not. Of those who perceived all their friends to be users, 92 percent used marijuana themselves, compared to only 7 percent of those who perceived none of their friends to be users.

*As can be seen in **Figure 7.12**, the influence of best friends overwhelms that of parents. Marijuana use is related in a small way to parental drug use, but it does not make much difference if your parents do not use drugs if your best friend does—chances are that you will too. On the other hand, if your best friend does not use drugs, it does not make much difference if your parents do—chances are you will* not. *(Kandel, 1973)*

Dependence and Addiction

In chapter 4, the effects of drugs in blocking, enhancing, or prolonging activity at the synapses were described. Although a semipermeable membrane called the **blood-brain barrier** surrounds the blood vessels in the central nervous system, generally protecting the brain from harmful substances, many psychoactive drugs can get through this membrane into the brain. Once there, they alter its communication system profoundly, affecting perception, memory, mood, and behavior; but continued use of drugs lessens their effects. This condition is called **tolerance.** As tolerance develops, greater dosages are required to achieve the same effect. Hand in hand with tolerance goes physiological **dependence,** a process in which the body becomes adjusted to and dependent on the substance, in part because of depletion of neurotransmitters by the frequent presence of the drug. The tragic outcome of tolerance and dependence is **addiction,** the state of actually requiring the drug in one's body and suffering painful **withdrawal symptoms** (shakes, sweats, nausea, and in the case of alcohol withdrawal, death) if the drug is not present.

When an individual finds the use of a drug so desirable or pleasurable that a craving develops, with or without addiction, it is known as *psychological dependence.* Psychological dependence can occur with any drug (including caffeine and nicotine). The result of either physiological or psychological dependence is that a person's life-style comes to revolve around drug use so wholly that his or her capacity to function can be restricted or even impaired. In addition, the expense involved in maintaining a drug habit of daily—and increasing—amounts of cocaine, heroin, amphetamines, or

Figure 7.11 *Prevalence and Recency of Drug Use by High-School Seniors, 1982*

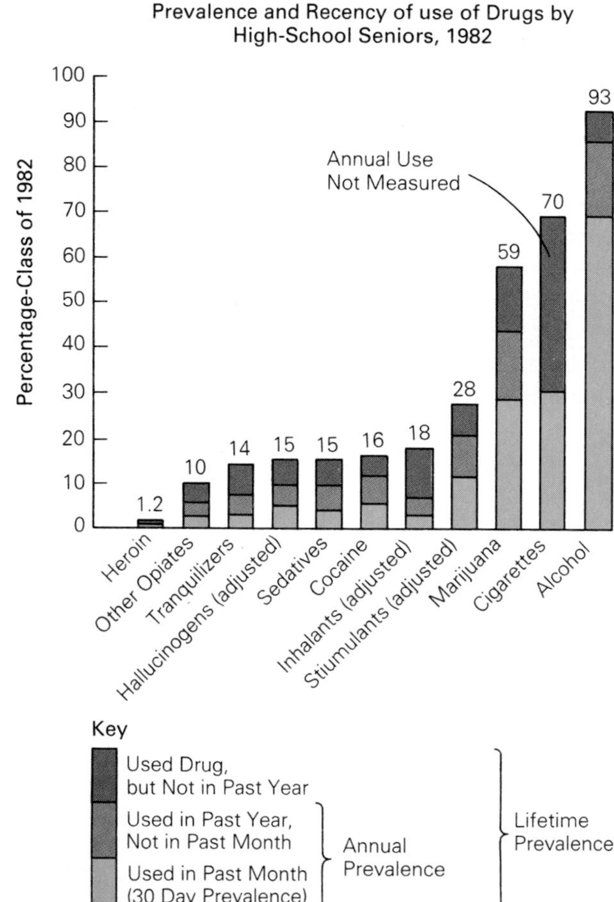

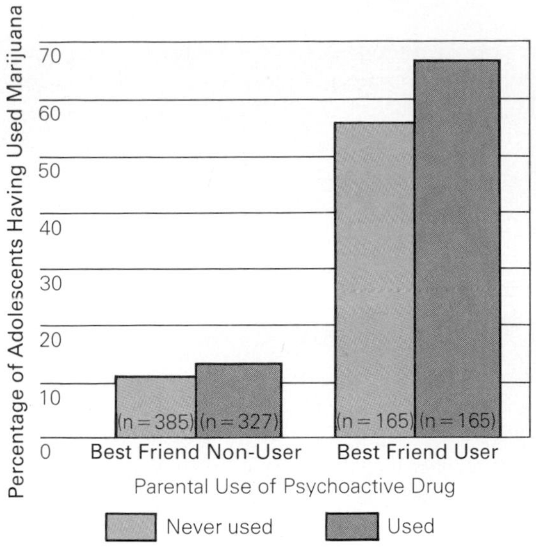

Figure 7.12 *Marijuana Use Among Friends of Users*

other drugs can drive a person to robbery, assault, prostitution, or drug peddling to get money. What started as simple chemical activity of drugs at tiny synapses may turn out to have enormous personal and social consequences.

Kinds of Psychoactive Drugs

Psychoactive drugs have differing effects on the central nervous system. There are three general categories of such drugs: depressants, stimulants, and hallucinogens.

Depressants. Alcohol, opiates, and barbiturates are examples of **depressant drugs.** These drugs tend to depress ("slow down") the mental and physical activity of the body by inhibiting or decreasing the transmission of nerve impulses in the central nervous system.

Alcohol was apparently one of the first psychoactive substances used extensively by our ancestors. Under its influence some people become silly, boisterous, friendly, and talkative; others, abusive and violent; still others, quietly depressed. At small dosages, alcohol can produce relaxation and slightly improve an adult's speed of reaction. However the body can break down alcohol at only approximately one ounce per hour, and greater amounts consumed in a short time period overtax the central nervous system. Driving fatalities and accidents occur six times more often with 0.10 percent alcohol in the bloodstream (resulting from 3 to 4 cocktails or 4 to 6 bottles of beer) than with half that amount. Another way in which alcohol intoxication contributes to accidents is through dilating the pupils, thereby causing night vision problems that drunk drivers are not aware of having. When the level of alcohol in the blood reaches 0.15 percent, there are gross negative effects on thinking, memory, and judgment along with emotional instability and motor incoordination—a very altered consciousness.

Opiates have been used since ancient times for their pain-killing medicinal properties (Beecher, 1972). From the dried sap of the opium poppy's unripe seed capsule come two well-known pain relievers—*codeine* and *morphine,* the latter named after Morpheus, the Greek god of dreams, because of its ability to induce sleep. (It also depresses respiration, lowers blood pressure, and causes sexual impotence.) In the early 1900s a new drug was advertised as a cure for those few who suffered chronic morphine intoxication and as an agent to relieve withdrawal symptoms—*heroin.* As you can guess, it "relieved" the withdrawal symptoms because it provided a similar chemical substance, and heroin proved as addictive as its predecessors.

Heroin, also a derivative of opium, may be liquefied and injected into a vein. There is reported to be a sudden rush of warmth—which the majority of pain-free, nonaddicted individuals who experience it find very unpleasant. In contrast, the addict might describe it as a warm, intense feeling of well-being (euphoria), reportedly "the closest thing to orgasm." A heroin abuser's actual sexual experiences typically involve decreased sexual appetite and performance. There is also subsequent drowsiness, lack of energy, and mental clouding (see Kaplan, 1983).

We are a drug-using culture, and the line between use and abuse is not always an easy one to draw.

Heroin-induced deep sleep is a potential danger to addicts because vital functions can be drastically reduced. The street remedy for overdose is to keep an addict awake and walking so that deep sleep does not become permanent.

Although the estimates of heroin use declined in the late 1970s, heroin has made a comeback in the mid-1980s. Officials of the National Institute on Drug Abuse estimated that, in 1987, there were approximately 500,000 heroin addicts nationwide, with another 400,000 less frequent users. Together they consumed an estimated 6 metric *tons* of heroin.

Barbiturates and other sedatives in low dosages can reduce anxiety, bring about feelings of calm, and reduce muscle tremors. Higher dosages bring about sleep, but reduce the time spent in REM sleep. After the withdrawal of barbiturates given over prolonged periods, there are extended REM periods, but they are punctuated by frightening nightmares. Overdoses of barbiturates lead to loss of all sensations and coma. More deaths are caused by overdoses of barbiturates, taken either accidentally or with suicidal intent, than by any other poison (Kolb, 1973). The combination of alcohol and barbiturates or amphetamines is particularly lethal. The interactive effects of drugs are difficult to predict because many factors are involved. Chronic abuse of drugs may cause organic damage to the brain which results in *toxic psychosis.* This syndrome involves extreme deteriorated perceptual, cognitive, and emotional functioning requiring hospitalization.

Stimulants. Amphetamines, cocaine, and caffeine are examples of **stimulant drugs.** Stimulants increase the transmission of impulses in the central nervous system and tend to "speed up" the mental and physical activity of the body.

Amphetamines, or "speed," have differing effects on mental functioning depending on the dosage and the manner of use. Low dosages can promote feelings of alertness and an increase of abilities, aiding activities that require extended concentration and alertness (Weiss & Laties, 1962). Regular use of oral amphetamines, however—to suppress appetite or to stay awake for very long periods of time—eventually leads to irritability, anxiety, and paranoid fears. When the desirable effects can no longer be maintained with oral doses, individuals may begin to take higher doses intravenously (Goodman & Gilman, 1970).

Regular users of amphetamines are driven to persist and to increase their dosage and frequency of injection by the desire to reexperience the initial rush of pleasurable sensation and remain euphoric, as well as by the desire to avoid the fatigue and depression of the later phase of amphetamine reaction—"coming down" (Kramer, 1969). Amphetamine addicts are likely to become increasingly fearful, hostile, and agitated. The slogan "Speed kills" refers partly to the "death" of the personality, will, and psychological freedom of someone who is dependent upon this drug.

Modern psychopharmacology may have begun with Sigmund Freud's introduction of the drug *cocaine* (Pfefferbaum, 1977). His initial optimism

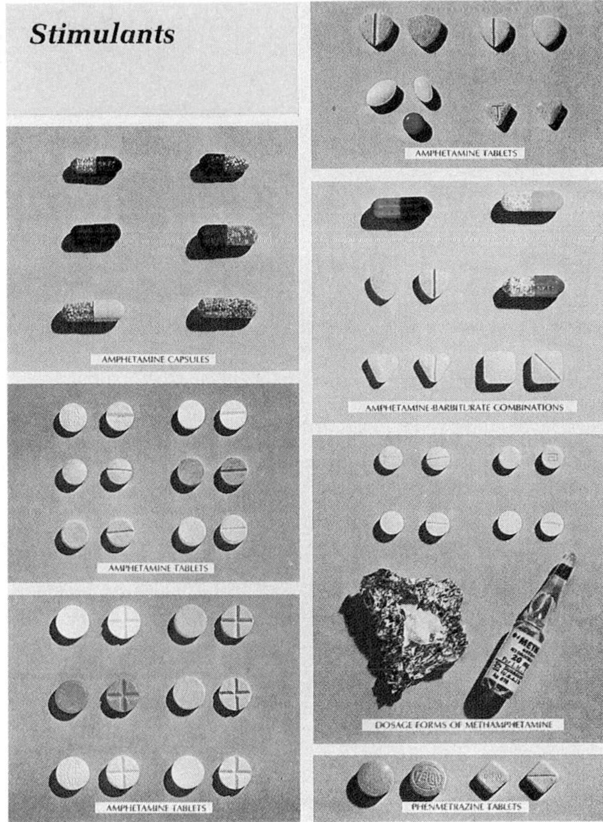

Regular users of amphetamines are driven to increase their dosage and frequency.

that cocaine would relieve psychic distress was based on his personal use of this drug during his own depressions. In 1884 he wrote, "in my last severe depression, I took coca again and a small dose lifted me to the heights in a wonderful fashion" (Jones, 1953, p. 84). However, Freud's initial enthusiasm was soon tempered by the recognition that cocaine could be addicting and could cause a toxic psychosis.

Although the initial effect of cocaine is usually pleasant with small doses, it becomes more unpleasant over time as the dosage increases and a user becomes addicted. As with all stimulants, the general effects of cocaine are to increase blood pressure, respiration rate, and pulse and to decrease appetite. (Amphetamine-based diet pills are sold commercially to control weight by their appetite-reducing action.)

Although cocaine was originally thought to be relatively harmless, there is accumulating evidence that cocaine use contributes to fatal heart damage as well as increased risk of brain damage and psychiatric problems. One survey of 1212 cocaine users who went to the hospital for a variety of reasons found that about 20 percent of them had severe seizures and impaired psychological functioning (reported in Petit, 1987).

Caffeine and *nicotine* are both stimulants. As you may know from experience, two cups of strong coffee or tea administer enough caffeine to have a profound effect on heart, blood, and circulatory functions about 10 minutes later—and to disturb your sleep if taken before retiring.

In higher concentrations than exist in cigarette tobacco, nicotine was the active ingredient used by certain native Indian shamans to attain mystical states or trances. Unlike modern users, however, the Indians believed that nicotine was addictive and chose when to be under its influence.

Hallucinogens. Consciousness is profoundly altered by some drugs that qualify as **hallucinogens,** drugs that are capable of producing states of awareness in which visual, auditory, or other sensory hallucinations occur. Hallucinogens are also called *psychedelic* drugs (from the Greek *psyche* and *delos,* "mind manifesting").

By contrast with the individual use of hallucinogens in our society, use of these drugs in other cultures has often been a collective religious practice, associated with different basic views about reality. For example, among the Jivaro Indians of the Ecuadorian Amazon, sacred rituals relying on drugs are based on the belief that "normal waking life is simply a lie or illusion, while the true forces that determine daily events are supernatural and can only be manipulated with the aid of hallucinogenic drugs" (Harner, 1973, p. 16). In fact, in a survey of 488 societies covering every region of the world, 90 percent were found to engage in one or more institutionalized, culturally patterned forms of consciousness alteration—with or without drugs (Bourguignon, 1973).

Among the designated "true hallucinogens" are *lysergic acid diethylamide* (LSD), *lysergic acid amide* (from morning glory seeds), *psilocybin* (the "magic mushroom"), *diethyltryptamine,* and *mescaline* (from the peyote cactus). Under the influence of hallucinogens bizarre perceptual distortions may occur. Time may seem to contract or expand, one's body image changes in strange ways, sensory stimulation may fuse in *synesthesias* (colors are "heard," and sounds "tasted"), and feelings of ecstasy may commingle with a sense of oneness with the universe (see ***Close-up*** on p. 252).

Close-up Characteristics of Alternate and Extended States of Consciousness

The following are some of the effects hallucinogenic drugs have in common, which are also found in reports of mystical states.

1. *Distortions of perceptual processes, time sense, and body image.* A common characteristic is distortion of many familiar perceptions, including those of the visual and auditory senses, as well as those of time and space. A sense of being separate from one's body, or of having portions of the body feel and/or look very different from usual, is often reported.

2. *Feelings of objectivity and ego-transcendence.* This is the sense that one is viewing the world with greater objectivity, more able to perceive phenomena as if they were independent of oneself and even of all human beings. One seems to be able to divorce oneself from personal needs and desires and see things as they "really" are, in some ultimate, impersonal sense. Sometimes this sense of objectivity is experienced as a loss of control, a feeling of being outside oneself—an experience that may be either positive or negative.

3. *Self-validating sense of truth.* The experience may be seen as more "real" or "true" than the perceptions of ordinary consciousness. Knowledge itself is experienced at an "intuitive" level: one believes one is "seeing" beyond appearances into essential qualities.

4. *Positive emotional quality.* Joy, ecstasy, reverence, peace, and overwhelming love are frequently reported when transcendent experiences are interpreted within a religious or philosophical framework. In the reports of Eastern mystics, the experience is less one of ecstasy than of a deep and profoundly restful peace in which an individual feels in harmony with all things.

5. *Paradoxicality.* Descriptions of alternate states of consciousness tend to seem contradictory and illogical when analyzed on logical, rational grounds. The polarities of life seem to be experienced simultaneously, to reach some resolution, and yet to remain separate.

6. *Ineffability.* Individuals frequently claim an inability to communicate their experiences. The qualities seem so unique that no words seem appropriate. Often, too, the experiences seem to contain so many paradoxical qualities that it makes no sense to describe them.

7. *Unity and fusion.* Distinctions and discontinuities may disappear between self and others; between past, present, and future; between animate and inanimate; between inner and outer reality; and between actual and potential. The separateness of self vanishes, the boundaries dissolve, and there is a fusion of self with what previously was nonself.

Other characteristics sometimes mentioned in various reports are feelings of rejuvenation; sudden, intense emotionality; extreme suggestibility; loss of control; and ideas that assume new significance and meaning (Ludwig, 1966; Nideffer, 1976).

The effects of hallucinogenic drugs may last up to six hours and "flashbacks" may occur later (depending on the presence of certain additives in the hallucinogenic drug). In extreme form, the symptoms may resemble or mimic signs of mental disorders—and produce panic attacks (see chapter 15).

LSD appears to prevent the release of the neurotransmitter serotonin, which is normally released in amounts that vary with an individual's activity level. As activity slows down, less serotonin is released; during sleep hardly any is discharged, and during REM sleep none is released. Under the influence of LSD, however, a nerve cell releases no serotonin even though a drug user is awake, alert, and fully conscious.

> *This may provide an important insight into understanding hallucinations and perhaps, more generally, other altered states of consciousness. In a given behavioral situation, an altered state of consciousness may occur when a key brain mechanism, such as the serotonin system, functions in a manner that is appropriate to a different behavioral situation. (Jacobs & Trulson, 1979, p. 403)*

Despite their mind-altering effects, *marijuana* and *hashish* are actually sedatives. Marijuana is the most popular of all the illicit drugs. It is made from *cannabis sativa,* a hemp plant that was originally used to make rope.

More than in the case of most other drugs, the effects of marijuana depend on social and personal factors. Naive users learn from observing and talking to veteran users. In large quantities, the effects may be more like those of the strong psychedelic drugs, distorting time sense and altering perception. The altered state produced by marijuana is more controllable and generally less intense, although very high doses may cause panic states and failure of judgment and coordination.

While marijuana decreases verbal, analytical reasoning, it has been shown to enhance performance on certain nonanalytical tests of a holistic-visual-spatial nature (Harshman et al., 1976). This finding is in line with earlier experiential reports that marijuana enhances nonverbal perception, depth perception, and the perception of meaning in stimuli that would be seen as meaningless lines or shapes by someone in an ordinary state of consciousness (Tart, 1971). Therefore, from these descriptions, which cerebral hemisphere would seem to be most responsive to the effects of this mind-altering drug?

Psychological and Social Factors in Drug Effects

The *psychoactive chemical agent* is only partly responsible for the changes in consciousness that a drug-taker experiences. Also important are the *amount* taken (the dose), the *manner* in which it is taken (smoked, swallowed, sniffed, or injected), the unique *physiological properties* of the individual (weight and metabolism), the person's *mental set,* (expectations of what the drug experience will be), and the *setting* or *context* of the drug experience (the whole physical, social, and cultural environment in which the drug is taken). The effects produced by a drug may differ from one person to the next, and the effects for the same individual may vary when the same amount of a drug is taken at different times or under different circumstances.

The interaction of psychological variables with chemical factors was shown dramatically in a study of social drinking and behavior.

> *A large group of students volunteered to participate in scientific research by drinking and responding to questionnaires in a social setting. They all knew that only half of them would be receiving alcohol in their "vodka and tonic." However, half of those who actually had vodka were told they* didn't *and half of those who did not were told that they* did.
>
> *After a few drinks, it didn't matter whether their drink actually contained alcohol. Students who* thought *they were getting a "real" vodka and tonic behaved differently from those who* thought *they were drinking straight tonic, regardless of the actual content of their drinks. Those who were falsely led to believe they had alcohol acted as free, uninhibited, and happy, and displayed as much loss of motor control as did the group that had received alcohol and had been told so. Those who reported they felt no difference were all subjects who had been* told *that they had not received an alcoholic drink. Yet half of these subjects had actually had vodka and tonic (Marlatt, 1978). Believing "made it so," regardless of the physical reality.*

One other social psychological correlate of drug taking is an individual's increased affiliation with others in the drug subculture. Once recreational use of drugs becomes an addiction, then more and more of addicts' lives are focused on activities of that drug-taking subculture. As they "tune out" of straight society, intravenous drug addicts are hard to reach for the help and counsel they need. This fact is especially frightening in light of the concern about AIDS. Attempts to inform addicts of the risks of becoming infected with AIDS virus from sharing hypodermic needles—a common practice among IV-drug users—may fall on deaf ears. This is the most likely pathway for the disease to escalate its epidemic fatal consequences in the heterosexual population (for a more detailed discussion of AIDS, see chapter 14).

Consciousness: The Ordinary and the Extraordinary

It has been a long journey from experimental studies of attention as an essential process in ordinary consciousness to the psychedelic creation of an extraordinary reality. Is there an underlying conceptual unity that links together the enormous variety of topics and processes we have gathered under the broad banner of "consciousness"? Put differently, what do we now know about the nature of human consciousness from investigations of such diverse phenomena as split brains, dreaming and hallucinating, psychoactive drugs, and mental processing without conscious awareness? Can we fit these seemingly isolated parts into a coherent framework?

The evolution of the human brain permitted survival of those of our forebears who could cope with a hostile environment even when their sensory and physical abilities were not adequate. They compensated for their relative lack of highly specialized sense receptors, strength, speed, protective coloration, or limited, safe habitat by developing mental skills. Humans became capable of symbolic representation of the outer world and of their own possible actions—enabling them to remember, plan, predict, and anticipate (Craik, 1943). Instead of merely reacting to stimuli in the physical present, the complex human brain offered the option of imagining how what *was* could be transformed into what *might be*.

This was a tremendous new survival tool. Henceforth, the capacity to deal with objective reality in the here-and-now of present time was expanded by the capacity to bring back lessons from the past (memory) and to imagine alternative futures (foresight). A brain that can deal with both immediate *objective* realities and *subjective* realities that are not physically present needs a mechanism to keep track of what is being focused on and whether the source of the stimulation being processed is in external objects and events or in internal thoughts and concepts. Robert Ornstein's (1986) summary of what may be the four basic operating principles of the brain is outlined in **Table 7.3.**

The dramatic advances of homo sapiens beyond all other species may be attributed to the development of a human intelligence and consciousness that was forged in the crucible of competition with the most hostile force in its evolutionary environment—other humans. The origin of the human mind may have evolved as a consequence of the extreme sociability of our ancestors, perhaps originally as group defense against predators and more efficient exploitation of resources. However, close group living then created new demands for cooperative as well as competitive abilities with other humans closely matched in the evolutionary race. Natural selection favored those who could think, plan, and imagine alternative realities that could promote both bonding with kin and victory over adversaries. Those who developed language and tools won the grand prize of survival of the fittest mind—and fortunately, passed it on to us (Lewin, 1987).

If "mind" is the sum of the integrative mental activities that brain processes give rise to, then consciousness is the mind's *active construction of incom-*

Table 7.3 *The Four Basic Operating Principles of the Brain*

1. "What have you done for me lately?"
   (The brain is sensitive to recent information.)
2. "Don't call me unless something new and exciting happens!"
   (The brain focuses on the novel, the unexpected; the "news" get fast access to consciousness.)
3. "Compared to what?"
   (The brain constantly judges by comparison, and judgment of any stimulus depends upon what we are comparing it to.)
4. "Get to the point!"
   (The mental system determines the meaning of any event by its relevance to the person, discarding an enormous amount of information that is not relevant to the person, task at hand, or other situational demands.)

(Based on Ornstein, 1986)

ing information into a coherent, stable, organized pattern of symbols. This construction is a way of making sense of a confusing world, of imposing order on and finding meaning in events that often seem chaotic and nonsensical (see Johnson-Laird, 1983).

Usually the demand to be in touch with ongoing "urgent" events forces our attention to be little more than a shifting searchlight illuminating the task-relevant dimensions of our current experience. However, we are aware that these reality-based constraints on our consciousness limit the range and depth of our experience and do not fulfill our potential. Though there are both constructive and self-defeating ways of doing so, perhaps we all long, at times, to reach beyond the confines of ordinary reality (see Targ & Harary, 1984). The ability to expand our consciousness is the mental equivalent of walking erect when it is easier to crawl and of seeking the uncertainty of freedom when it is safer to accept the security of the familiar.

The New Mind: Multiple Modules

The fundamental notion of human mind has been that of a single entity from which emerges consciousness and a sense of personal identity. That monolithic structure of mind is being revised by many different investigators who are proposing a new view of the mind as a collection of semi-independent entities or modules that are centrally organized but "work on their own" whenever possible. This challenge to the holistic, "imperial" brain conception is occurring in philosophy (Dennett, 1978), artificial intelligence (Hinton & Anderson, 1981), linguistics (Chomsky, 1984), neuroscience (Gazzaniga, 1985), cognitive science (Fodor, 1983), and psychology (Ornstein, 1986).

This new "multimind" is one built around two systems—of modules and central processors. In this view, the mind has many separate modules, each of which analyzes stimulus input of a particular kind or within a particular domain of knowledge and action. It also has central, "executive" processors that are general, domain-neutral systems, which synthesize the messages from the modules to direct coordinated, planned, conscious actions.

The modules are designed for quite limited and specific purposes, to work quickly and relatively automatically without losing time "in thought." The mind in this view "contains a changeable conglomeration of different kinds of 'small minds'—fixed reactions, talents, flexible thinking—and these different entities are temporarily employed—'wheeled into consciousness'—and then usually discarded, returned to their place, after use" (Ornstein, 1986, p. 25). Since these modules are activated automatically and unconsciously to deal with a specific stimulus situation, we do not know which are operating or how to utilize the most appropriate one each time. Nor is it assumed that brain modularity is just a psychological term without a solid foundation. From studies of the behavioral, cognitive, and emotional functioning of patients with split brains and those suffering from brain-lesioned amnesia "it becomes clear that modularity has a real anatomical basis" (Gazzaniga, 1985, p. 128). It is exciting to anticipate how this new view of mind will generate research that will help us better understand all of our minds.

In later chapters we will explore how a variety of cognitive processes operate to enable us to remember, sometimes forget, think, comprehend, solve problems, and make judgments; but first we need to study how we are changed by experience. How do we learn associations between stimulus events, discover the consequences of our actions, and come to predict significant events based on what we already know? These questions about learning will be examined in the next chapter.

Summary

- *Consciousness* is a general term for awareness: it is made up of the whole stream of immediate experience, including the content of awareness and the state of being aware, with some sense of self. It enables us to restrict what we notice, segment the flow of experience, and deliberately use relevant memories. It is our sharpest tool for constructing a representation of reality.
- Psychologists have identified three kinds of consciousness: anoetic (nonknowing), noetic (knowing), and autonoetic (self-knowing). Anoetic consciousness is the type ethologists refer to when they speak of animal consciousness.
- Attention is a focused awareness. Only what is attended to becomes conscious; only in consciousness can higher mental processes be performed. Attention has been thought of as a selective filter, as occurring in degrees rather than all-or-none, as a mechanism that synthesizes input and knowledge, and as a limited resource that can be somewhat extended by learning.

- Preattentive processing of information occurs in the early stages of perceiving. Processing of information outside of consciousness may be nonconscious, subconscious, or unconscious.
- Hemispheric asymmetry is characteristic of all species, though the two cerebral hemispheres are involved in different aspects of many of the same functions. In most humans the left hemisphere has dominance in verbal activity, the right hemisphere in visual-spatial activities.
- When the two cerebral hemispheres are severed, a person with a "split brain" behaves in ways that suggest each hemisphere can function as an independent conscious mind. The right hemisphere is better at solving problems involving spatial relationships and pattern recognition and at matching objects by visual features. The left hemisphere is better at problems involving language, logic, and analysis, and at matching objects by function. It has been speculated that the two hemispheres represent contrasting orientations to the world.
- Everyday changes in consciousness include daydreaming, fantasy, sleep, and nightdreaming. Extended, or alternate, states of consciousness include hallucinations, hypnotic states, and altered consciousness resulting from drugs.
- Sleep occurs in several stages; rapid eye movement (REM) sleep, during which dreaming often occurs, alternates with non-REM sleep in cycles during the night. The sleep-wake cycle is only one of the body's internally generated circadian rhythms.
- Explanations for dreaming range from the hypothesis that dreams are simply the brain's attempt to make sense of random cortical activity to Freud's theory that dreams provide a means for disguised expression of forbidden wishes while guarding an individual's sound sleep.
- Hypnosis is a technique to change a hypnotized person's representation of reality. Individuals differ in hypnotizability—the degree to which they respond to hypnotic suggestions. A hypnotized person may respond to suggestions to change motor reactions, to experience hallucinations or amnesia, or to be insensitive to powerful stimuli; hypnosis can even substitute for anesthesia in surgery.
- Trance logic and dissociation show that a hypnotized person may process information below the level of consciousness, even if the person is unaware of the information on a conscious level.
- Psychoactive drugs are chemicals that affect mental processes and behavior by changing awareness of reality for a time. They act by enhancing, blocking, or prolonging nerve impulse-transmitter activity at synapses.
- Continued use of many drugs leads to tolerance, in which a larger dosage is required to achieve the same effect, and can result in physiological or psychological dependence. With addiction, the body becomes dependent on the drug and withholding it leads to painful withdrawal symptoms.
- Psychoactive drugs include depressants, stimulants, and hallucinogens. With some drugs, such as alcohol and marijuana, the effects may depend as much on psychological variables, such as expectations and social settings, as on the chemical properties of the drug.
- If "mind" is the sum of all the integrative mental activities that brain processes give rise to, then consciousness is the active construction of available information into a coherent pattern that imposes order and meaning on stimulus events.
- A new view of the mind sees it as a collection of semi-independent modules that work on their own but are organized by central processors that synthesize messages from the modules to direct, coordinate, and plan conscious actions.

8

Conditioning and Learning

Have you ever been attacked by a hit-and-run shower? Let's return to the scene of the crime and reconstruct the essential details. You step into a warm, soothing shower to unwind after a long, hard day. The comforting warmth of the water begins to relax you and makes you oblivious to almost everything other than your physical pleasure. Once again, life is sweet. Suddenly, the water pressure drops, and the water becomes scalding hot. Your relaxation is shattered. You scream out in pain, but, just as quickly, the water returns to its previous delightful temperature. You continue your shower, though not quite totally able to regain your former contented state. Soon, the water pressure abruptly drops again. Bam! You again experience the hot flow, accompanied by pain, muscle twitches, and anger.

You do not have to *learn* to react this way. The necessary connections are physiologically built in to your nervous system. After being hit with scalding water several times—always after a drop in water pressure—you begin to react physically and emotionally to the drop in water pressure even *before* the water betrays your confidence. You have begun to anticipate the attack. You have not smarted in vain; you are smarter because the environment has taught you lesson number one: there is an *association between two environmental events* (the drop in water pressure is associated with the following change in water temperature). In addition, because the pressure change is a signal for the temperature change, it now evokes a physical and emotional response similar to the response originally caused by the hot water itself. From now on, you are wise and wary, using the first event as a signal to inform you about the second one.

But that's not all you have learned from this Halloween-like, treat-turned-trick, shower scenario. You have probably also discovered that shrieking in pain, cursing, and jumping up and down produce no relief from the scalding water, whereas getting out of the way does. Therefore, when the water pressure drops,

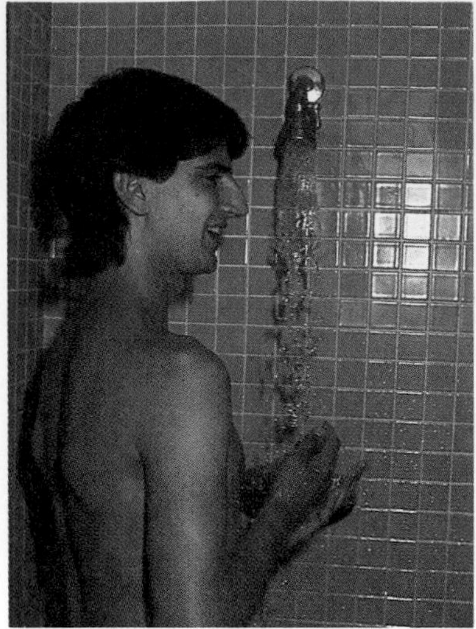

you now move quickly to a safe corner, out of danger. Voilà! Lesson number two: there is an *association between your behavior and its consequences.* You have learned which response, out of all those you were making, is appropriate in order to avoid this unpleasant event.

You might decide to stop showering in places where this plumbing problem exists, or to invent a solution that you make a million dollars from, and become wealthy as well as wiser. In this way, necessity can be the mother of invention—and the father of bathtubs!

This shower scenario illustrates two of the most basic kinds of learning that psychologists study: (a) the learning of associations between two environmental stimuli, and (b) the learning of associations between behavior and its consequences. In this chapter we will see the ways in which these two kinds of associations have been studied. We will also examine a growing body of evidence showing that understanding even these apparently simple kinds of learning is not as simple as it may seem. Although humans and lower forms of animal species all profit from these same basic forms of learning, there are additional learning processes that we can utilize because of the greater complexity of our brains. Finally, we will note how the procedures and paradigms used to study the learning process have become "tools" used to investigate the effects of many different variables on behavior and mental processes, such as drug addiction and memory.

Before getting into the details of the learning process, it is well to step back and appreciate the broader significance of this phenomenon—the "Big Picture." Learning is the parent of adaptability and the sibling of flexibility. Because we can change the way we act, think, and feel through our personal experiences, we are freed from the constraints of a rigidly determined genetic inheritance. We can modify our own nervous system by our learning experiences; nurture can sometimes change nature to a surprising degree. We can also rise above the limits imposed by existing environmental conditions; we can control our environment rather than be controlled by it. The human species has evolved with an enormous capacity to modify both itself and its surroundings. This capacity to profit from experience can make present lives richer and improve the quality of future existence.

It should be apparent, then, why American psychology, at the turn of this century, embraced the learning tradition and continued it forward. It reflected the democratic and capitalistic ideal that people could shape their lives by personal actions (read "hard work") and were not limited by factors such as family background, social class, or religion. However, the optimistic glow that came with this notion that we are what we learn to do—from transactions with the environments in which we function—had a threatening side to it. What happened if people learned the wrong lessons, if they developed habits that hurt rather than helped them? The same person who learned how to use the rules of logic could learn to be superstitious, develop phobias, and adopt irrational beliefs that form the basis of madness. So, at the heart of much that is human nature is the psychology of learning—for better and for worse.

The Study of Learning

Before looking at how psychologists have defined and studied learning, we first need some background about the basic assumptions that guide the questions they ask and the answers they seek. Some of these basic assumptions have come from philosophy, while others have come from a distinctively psychological approach to understanding human nature that emerges from *behavior theory.*

Philosophical Assumptions

Long before psychology existed as a discipline philosophers recognized learning as a source of knowledge and of human action. From their reflections about the reasons we do what we do and the way we learn, two important doctrines have emerged that have been important to psychology: the law of association and the principle of adaptive hedonism.

In brief, the **law of association** holds that we acquire knowledge through associating ideas—mental events that originate in sensory information from the environment. If two experiences occur closely in time or space, a mental association will be formed between them, and this is the way the mind grows. Seventeenth-century philosopher John Locke, among other British philosophers, was a prominent supporter of this view. It followed logically from his claim that our minds, at birth, are unetched slates, and that most of our knowledge and abilities is determined by experience. This emphasis on the role of experience in mental growth, known as **association psychology,** was in opposition to the view of the nineteenth-century German philosopher Immanuel Kant. Kant and his followers stressed the innate powers or faculties of the mind. This rationalistic view, called **faculty psychology,** assumed that the mind had built-in structures for its own development that did not depend on experience.

The **principle of adaptive hedonism,** identified with another British philosopher, Jeremy Bentham, emerged in the eighteenth century as an explanation of the basic source of human motivation. Bentham's principle was that individuals acted in ways that provided pleasure and avoided ways that resulted in pain.

When psychology split off from its philosophical roots to become a laboratory-based science, it took along the doctrines of associationism and adaptive hedonism as basic assumptions. Together they provided a basis for the important roles of idea, or habit, formation and the motivation to take action. The studies of associative learning described in this chapter are based on them, though the focus has been on the way organisms learn associations between stimuli and responses, rather than on the earlier notions of the way people learn associations between ideas. However, as we will see, cognitive psychologists are again pointing out the importance of ideas, such as prediction and information value of events, even in the learning of simple stimulus-response associations.

Behavior Theory

Just as philosophers have sought to explain human nature in terms of these and other assumptions about mind and action, psychologists also have searched for laws of human nature. Most believe that human nature can be studied scientifically and that general causal laws can be discovered through controlled research in the laboratory and in natural field settings. However, one branch of psychology is unique in its assumptions about the way to study human nature and what determines human (and animal) behavior. Experimental psychologists who are behaviorists, and whose work is guided by behavior theory, argue that human nature can be fully understood using only extensions of the methods and principles of natural science, especially physics. Their task is to discover the regularities in human actions that are universal, covering all types of people (and other animal species) in a variety of comparable situations.

Although experience changes people, the change itself follows orderly principles that can be discovered. Identifying these principles will achieve the goal of behavior theory: to predict future action on the basis of past experience. Two special features of behavior theory relevant to this goal are (a) the focus on objective behavior, and (b) the role of the environment in causing behavior.

What is to be explained is behavior, action, and responses, and not ideas, wishes, motives, beliefs, or other internal events that cannot be readily observed and measured. Behaviorist researchers focus solely on overt behavioral events, while ignoring all else that might be going on inside a research subject's body or brain. Furthermore, they look for the causes of this behavior in only one place—the external environment. Behavior theory holds that the determinants of behavior are to be found in environmental events rather than in internal ones. Thus the causes of behavior are seen as residing, not within the actor, but in his or her environment. To know about the determinants of any action, the researchers search only for the environmental events that have been experimentally shown to influence such behavior. What is your reaction to such a set of behavior theory assumptions?

> *It is hard to imagine a view of human nature more opposed to our ordinary conception of ourselves than this one. We have all grown accustomed to thinking of ourselves as the controllers of our own lives. . . . Behavior theory challenges this conception of ourselves. If you want to know why someone did something, do not ask. Analyze the person's immediate environment until you find the reward. If you want to change someone's action, do not reason or persuade. Find the reward and eliminate it. The idea that people are autonomous and possess within them the power and the reasons for making decisions has no place in behavior theory. (Schwartz & Lacey, 1982, pp. 15, 16)*

Although this extreme determinist position has been shown to yield many valuable principles of human nature, we will see that it has not gone unchallenged by other psychologists who insist on keeping a brain, mind, or soul to control the direction of this behavioral machine.

What Is Learning?

We can define **learning** as a process that results in a relatively permanent change in behavior or behavioral potential based on experience. Learning is not observed directly, but is inferred from changes in observable behavior. Let's look more closely at the three critical parts of the definition.

A Change in Behavior or Behavioral Potential

It is obvious that learning has taken place when you "teach an old dog new tricks" or demonstrate a new skill yourself, such as driving a car or earning a high score on a video game. Learning is apparent from improvements in your performance.

Often, however, your performance doesn't show everything that you have learned. The test questions may be too specific, or you may do poorly because of test anxiety. When motivation is either very weak or very strong, performance may not be a good indicator of learning—there's not enough to energize action, it is disruptive because there's too much, or it is of the wrong kind. Sometimes, too, you acquire general knowledge, such as an appreciation of modern art or an understanding of Eastern religions, that may not show up in particular changed actions. In this situation you have learned a *potential* for behavioral change because you have learned attitudes and values that can influence the kind of books you read and the way you spend your leisure time. This change in behavior is more indirect in the way it affects a given type of test performance.

The definition of *learning,* therefore, includes the phrase "or behavioral potential" because learning may have taken place even though it did not show in performance at the time. Learning that does not show up until later—when the circumstances allow, or the right kind and amount of motivation elicit appropriate performance—is called **latent learning.** This is an example of the *learning-performance distinction,* the difference between what

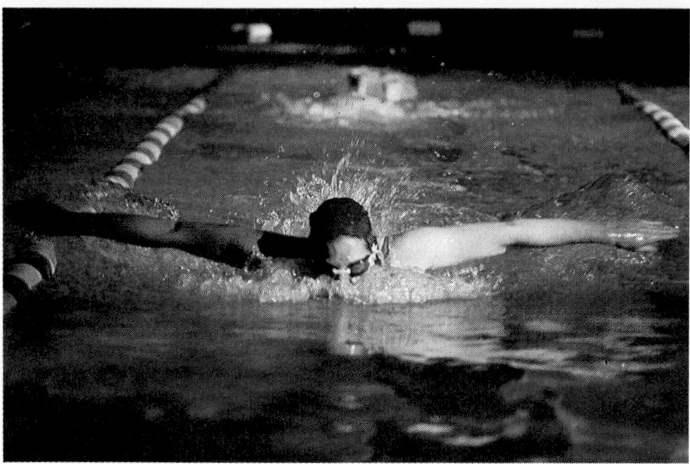

Learning results in a relatively permanent change. Once a person is taught to swim that person will always know how.

is known and what is expressed. If behavior is the primary index of learning, how can we ascertain what infants or animals know when they can't tell us, what mental patients know when they won't tell us, what the shy person knows when he or she is too anxious to tell us, or what a brain-damaged patient knows whose means of expressing it in behavior are destroyed? These are challenges to researchers who must devise special testing procedures to make external, observable, and measurable the silent knowledge and learning hidden within an organism.

A Relatively Permanent Change

To qualify as learned, a change in behavior or behavioral potential must be relatively permanent. Once you learn to swim, you will probably always be able to do so. Some changes in behavior, however, are transitory. Your pupils dilate or contract as the brightness of light changes, and your normally smooth performance in driving may change temporarily because of fatigue or shifting attention. These are changes in behavior that are based on experience, but they do not last; so we cannot say learning has taken place.

On the other hand, some (or much) of your hard-earned learning, especially of ideas, is eventually forgotten or changed by what you learn later—hence the term *relatively permanent* in the definition. Learned changes last longer than the transient ones caused by fatigue, but not necessarily forever.

Based on Experience

Experience means something that happens to us during our lifetime, usually involving interaction with our environment. Experience includes taking in information (and evaluating and transforming it) and making responses that affect the environment, as in practicing the skill of driving a car. Learning can take place only through experience. Psychologists are especially interested in discovering what aspects of behavior can be changed through experience and how such changes come about.

Some lasting changes in behavior require a combination of experience and maturational readiness. As we saw in chapter 3, it is the timetable set by maturation that determines when an infant is ready to crawl, stand, walk, run, and be toilet trained: no amount of training or practice will produce those changed behaviors before a child has matured sufficiently; when a child is mature enough, then new experience can alter behavioral potential and lead to new performance.

Classical Conditioning: Learning Based on Signals

In the *Opening Case* that began our chapter, the first association you learned was between two stimulus events. The drop in water pressure—a harmless, neutral stimulus—acquired importance because it was a reliable signal for the occurrence of the painful stimulus—scalding water. When these stimulus events were paired repeatedly, reactions that, at first, had been aroused only by the hot water began to occur in response to the water pressure change as well.

This kind of associative learning is called **classical conditioning,** which can be defined as a form of learning in which an organism learns a new association between two stimuli—a neutral one and one that already elicits a reflexive response. Following conditioning, the formerly neutral stimulus elicits a new reflexive response, one that is often similar to the original response.

Pavlov's Chance Discovery

Ivan Pavlov (1849–1936), a Russian physiologist, is credited with discovering the principles of classical conditioning. (Thus, classical conditioning is sometimes called *Pavlovian conditioning.*) Pavlov won the 1904 Nobel Prize for his pioneering research on the role of saliva and gastric secretions in digestion. He had devised a technique to study digestive processes in living animals by implanting tubes in their glands and digestive organs that diverted bodily secretions to containers outside their bodies so that the secretions could be analyzed.

Ivan Pavlov (1849–1936) and his staff are shown with the apparatus used in his conditioning experiments. The dog is harnessed to a wooden frame; a tube conducts its saliva to a measuring device that records quantity and rate of salivation.

To start these secretions, Pavlov's assistants put food (meat powder) into the mouths of dogs. After this procedure had been repeated on a number of trials, Pavlov observed a strange phenomenon. The secretions would start *before* the food was put in the dogs' mouths. They would start at the mere sight of the food and, later, at the sight of the assistant who brought the food or even at the sound of the assistant's footsteps. Indeed, any stimulus the dog could perceive that regularly preceded presentation of the food came to evoke the same reaction as the food itself! These observations did not make sense from a purely physiological point of view. Pavlov believed that other principles had to be operating to cause this consistent finding.

It has been said that "chance favors the prepared mind," and Pavlov was ready to realize the significance of these "psychic secretions," as he called them. He ignored the advice of the great physiologist of the time, Sir Charles Sherrington, to abandon such foolish investigations into what seemed to be almost "supernatural" to a medical researcher. Pavlov, at the age of 50, redirected all of his research toward the study of this basic form of learning (see Pavlov, 1928).

The behaviors Pavlov studied were reflexes. **Reflexes** are unlearned responses, such as salivation, pupil contraction, knee jerks, and eye blinking, that are automatically elicited by specific stimuli which have biological relevance for an organism. They temporarily change the organism in some way that promotes biological adaptation to the environment. For example, salivation, the reflex studied by Pavlov, helps digestion of food; eye blinking protects the eye from foreign matter. With conditioning, Pavlov's animals learned to make reflexive responses to new stimuli that had no such original biological relevance for them. (Classical conditioning is also often called *respondent conditioning* because it is these automatic respondent behaviors that are involved initially.)

The Classical Conditioning Paradigm

Paradigm is an important term for you to remember because it is used often in psychology, as well as in other contexts you will come across in your studies. A **paradigm** is a symbolic model or diagram that helps us understand the essential features of a process. It is a way of representing the relationship between basic events. A paradigm provides a structure for defining a set of procedures and analyzing experimental data. It often helps to simplify a complex process.

The classical conditioning paradigm **(Figure 8.1)** reveals the conditions under which organisms come to learn relationships between pairs of stimulus events. In classical conditioning a neutral stimulus, paired one or more times with a biologically significant stimulus, acquires the power to elicit a behavioral response in the absence of the biologically significant stimulus. Initially, there exists a natural relationship between this stimulus and a reflex that it reliably elicits. Because learning has

Figure 8.1 *Classical Conditioning Paradigm*
Originally, the sound of a bell elicits only an orienting response; food elicits salivation. If the food is consistently presented immediately after the bell is rung, the bell will soon come to elicit salivation. Note that the solid arrows in the diagram indicate an unlearned (biologically determined) relationship between a stimulus and a response. The broken arrow symbolizes a learned (experientially determined) relationship.

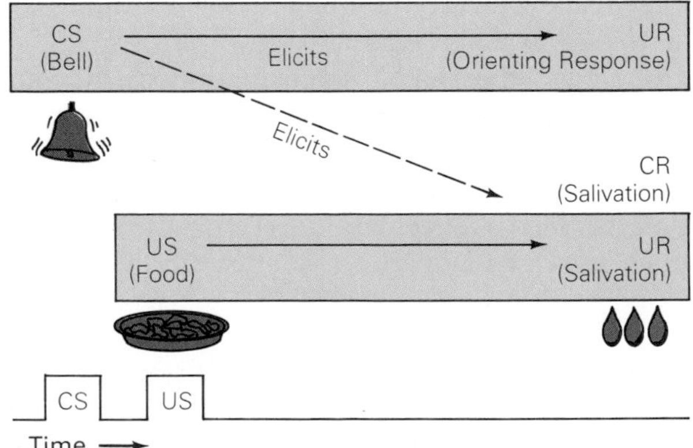

not been necessary for the relationship, such a stimulus (for example, meat powder) is called an **unconditioned stimulus (US)** and the reflex (salivation) is called an **unconditioned response (UR).** Before conditioning, a neutral stimulus, such as a bell, may elicit an **orienting response**—a general response of attention to the source of novel stimulation—but will not elicit the unconditioned response. A dog may prick up its ears, but will not salivate. During conditioning, the neutral stimulus, the bell, and the unconditioned stimulus, the meat powder, are both presented a number of times in close proximity. After repeated pairings, the bell is presented alone; it now elicits salivation. This nonedible object has acquired some of the power to influence behavior that was originally limited to the food. Because learning has taken place, the initially neutral stimulus is now called the **conditioned stimulus (CS)** and the response to the conditioned stimulus alone is called the **conditioned response (CR).** Nature provided the US-UR connection, but conditioning creates the CS-CR connection.

In the classical conditioning paradigm, the organism is a passive recipient of stimuli. The reflexive response occurs involuntarily; it is an automatic reaction elicited by a relevant stimulus. The advantages of this Pavlovian paradigm are (a) association learning processes can be studied under well-controlled laboratory conditions in which the stimuli are controlled and the responses precisely measured, and (b) the results are reproducible by other, independent researchers who follow the same methods. Clearly these are an ideal set of features on which to build a science of conditioning.

"Stimulus, response! Stimulus, response! Don't you ever *think*?"

The Anatomy of Classical Conditioning

In continuing experimentation, many aspects of conditioning have been studied by researchers since Pavlov's time. What conditions are optimal, or not ideal, for learning to occur? This general question has been asked in many different ways and answered in literally thousands of studies. On the basis of the observations of the data from this seemingly simple situation, clues to underlying fundamental principles of learning have been discovered. We will review what is known about these and other aspects of classical conditioning from years of research across many different animal species, stimulus features, and types of responses. The aspects that we will examine next are acquisition, extinction, spontaneous recovery, generalization and discrimination, appetitive versus aversive types of conditioning, second-order conditioning, and conditioned social behavior.

Acquisition

In the acquisition stage of conditioning, as we have seen, repeated pairings of a neutral, to-be-conditioned stimulus with an unconditioned stimulus result in behavioral changes in response to the conditioned stimulus. Each time the two stimulus events are paired is called a **conditioning trial.** From these changes we *infer* the development of associations between the two stimuli.

In studying conditioning, an experimenter may vary several aspects of this basic situation, such as the number of trials an organism gets, the time interval between successive trials, the time interval between the two stimuli, and the intensity or quality of either or both stimuli. Variations in these and other aspects of the situation are the *independent variables* in conditioning studies.

The four major *dependent variables* are (a) the strength of the conditioned response—its *amplitude* (how big it is); (b) how much time it takes before the response is made after the conditioned stimulus appears—its *latency* (how fast it is); (c) how quickly the conditioned response appears and is strengthened—its *rate* of acquisition (how it develops); and (d) how long the response continues to be elicited by the new stimulus in the absence of the unconditioned stimulus—its *persistence,* or *resistance to extinction* (how durable it is).

In conditioning, as in telling a good joke, timing is critical. The conditioned and unconditioned stimuli must be close enough in time—*contiguous,* or *proximal,* enough—to be perceived by the organism as being related. Four patterns of onset and offset of the two stimuli have been studied, as shown in **Figure 8.2.**

The most common type of conditioning is **forward conditioning,** in which the conditioned stimulus comes on *before* the unconditioned stimulus. There are two possible patterns in forward conditioning: **delayed forward conditioning,** in which the conditioned stimulus stays on (is delayed) until the unconditioned stimulus comes on, and **trace forward conditioning,** in which the conditioned stimulus does not stay on, but presumably some form of its memory trace bridges the time gap between its offset and the onset of the unconditioned stimulus. In **simultaneous conditioning** the two stimuli are presented at the same time. Finally, in the case of **backward conditioning,** the conditioned stimulus comes on *after* the unconditioned stimulus.

Figure 8.2 *Four Temporal Patterns in Classical Conditioning*

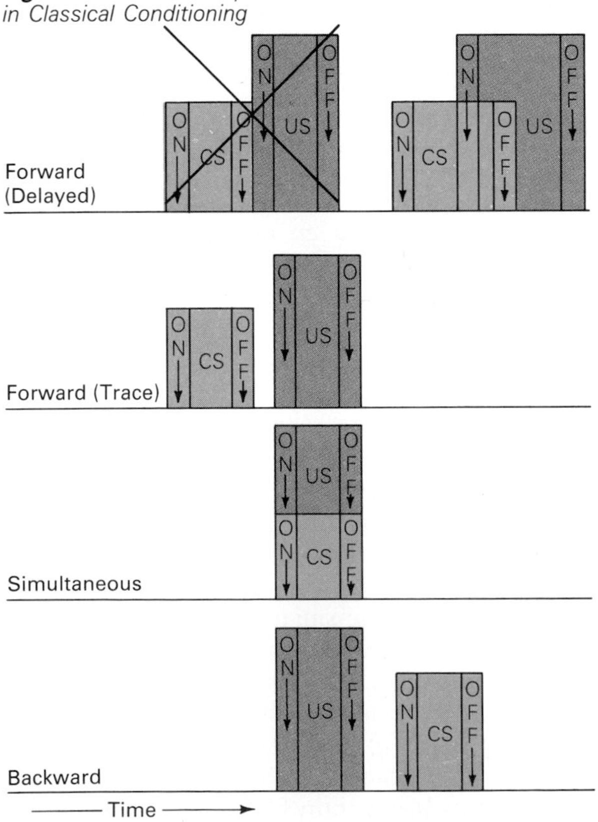

Forward (Delayed)

Forward (Trace)

Simultaneous

Backward

Time

Conditioning is usually better with a short, rather than a long, interval between stimuli and best with forward conditioning procedures. The range of time intervals between stimulus events that will produce the best conditioning varies over different response systems, very brief for some and relatively long for others. For motor and skeletal responses such as eye blinks, a short interval of a second or less is best. For visceral responses such as heart rate and salivation, however, longer intervals of five to fifteen seconds work best. For conditioned fear to develop usually longer intervals of many seconds or even minutes are effective.

Conditioning is generally poor with a simultaneous procedure and worst with a backward procedure. Evidence of backward conditioning may appear after a few pairings, but then disappear with extended training as the animal learns that the conditioned stimulus is followed by a period free of the unconditioned stimulus. In both these cases, conditioning is weak because the conditioned stimulus has *no signal value* regarding the onset of the important unconditioned stimulus.

Conditioning occurs most rapidly when the neutral stimulus, the CS, stands out against the many other neutral stimuli that are also present in the background. Thus, a stimulus will be more readily noticed the more *intense* it is and the more it *contrasts* with the background. Either a strong, novel stimulus in an unfamiliar situation or a strong, familiar stimulus in a novel context leads to good conditioning (Kalat, 1974; Lubow et al., 1976). In general, we might conclude that the feature of the conditioned stimulus that most facilitates conditioning is its *informativeness*—its good record of reliably predicting the unconditioned stimulus (Rescorla, 1972; Rescorla & Wagner, 1972). In real life, as in the conditioning laboratory, the key is to increase the "signal-to-noise ratio" of the CS by making it a stronger signal than all other competing events that are irrelevant noise in the system.

Extinction and Spontaneous Recovery

When an unconditioned stimulus is no longer presented with a conditioned stimulus, a conditioned response to the conditioned stimulus becomes weaker over time and eventually stops occurring. This process is called **extinction.** Returning to our *Opening Case,* if water pressure change stopped

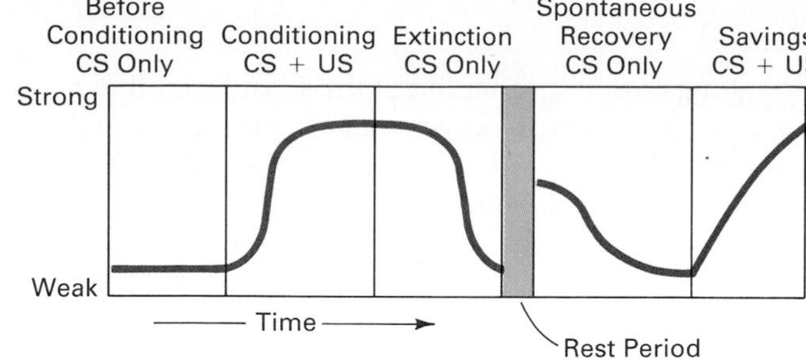

Figure 8.3 *Conditioning and Conditioned Processes*
Response to the conditioned stimulus increases during conditioning trials while it is being paired with the unconditioned stimulus. When the unconditioned stimulus is no longer presented, the response decreases to its original rate. It reappears after a rest period, but then rapidly extinguishes again if not paired with the unconditioned stimulus.

being followed by hotter water, you would eventually stop perceiving the water pressure drop as a signal for scalding sensations and would no longer respond to it.

An extinguished response is out of sight, behaviorally speaking, but not out of mind, cognitively speaking. After a rest period, it will reappear in a weak form when the conditioned stimulus is presented alone again. **Spontaneous recovery** is the name for this reappearance of an apparently extinguished conditioned response without any new pairings of the two stimuli (see **Figure 8.3**). With further acquisition training (further pairings of CS and US), a conditioned response gains strength more rapidly than it did initially. This more rapid "relearning" is an instance of a phenomenon called **savings.** However, it too is quickly weakened with further extinction training (CS and no US); but eliminating a conditioned response completely seems to be harder than acquiring it.

Stimulus Generalization

Once a conditioned response has been acquired to a particular stimulus, similar stimuli may also evoke the response. If conditioning was to a high frequency tone, a lower tone may also elicit the response. A child bitten by a big dog is likely to respond with fear even to small dogs. This automatic extension of conditioned responding to stimuli that have never been paired with the original unconditioned stimulus is called **stimulus generalization.** The more similar the new stimulus is to the conditioned stimulus, the stronger the response will be. When response strength is measured for each of a series of increasingly dissimilar stimuli along a given dimension, as in **Figure 8.4,** a *gradient,* or slope, of generalization is found.

Since important stimuli rarely occur in exactly the same form every time in nature, stimulus generalization builds in a "similarity safety factor" by extending the range of learning beyond the original specific experience. A predator can make a different sound or be seen from a different angle and still be recognized and responded to. In addition, new but comparable events can be recognized as having the same meaning or behavioral significance.

Figure 8.4 *Stimulus Generalization Gradients*
After conditioning to one stimulus, indicated here as a medium green hue, the subject responds almost as strongly to similar hues, as shown in the flat generalization gradient in part A of the figure. When hues of greater difference are presented, the subject responds weakly, leading to a steep generalization gradient, as shown in part B. The experimenter could change the curve in part A to resemble the one in part C by discrimination training, in which the conditioned and unconditioned stimuli continued to be paired while the other stimuli were presented repeatedly alone without the unconditioned stimulus.

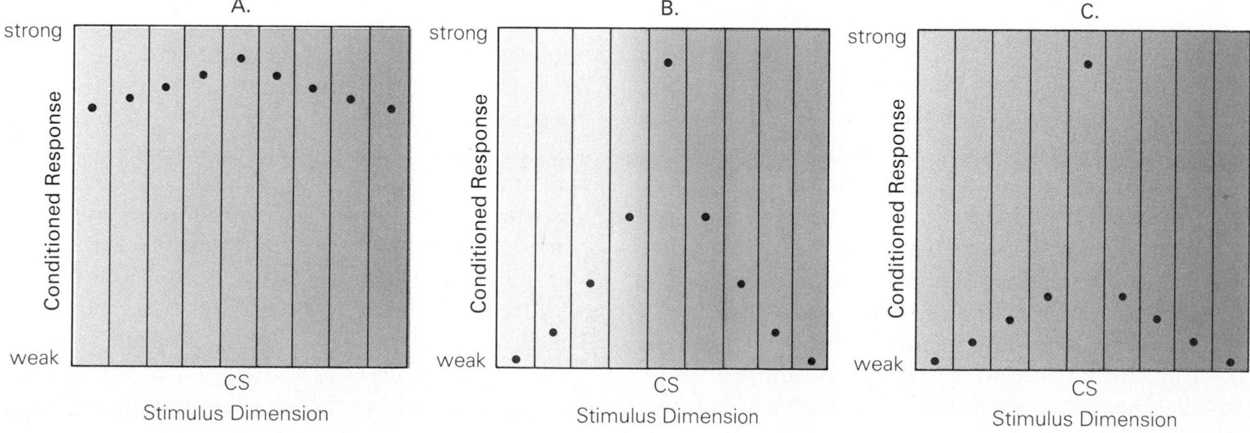

Stimulus Discrimination

Though stimuli similar to the original conditioned stimulus may elicit a similar response, the line must be drawn somewhere. **Stimulus discrimination** is a conditioning process in which an organism learns to respond differently to stimuli that are different from the conditioned stimulus on some dimension (differences in hue or in pitch, for example). An organism's perceptual discrimination between similar stimuli (tones of 1000, 1200, and 1500 cycles per second, for example) is sharpened with training in which only one of them (1200 cps, for example) is associated with the unconditioned stimulus, whereas the others are repeatedly presented without the unconditioned stimulus. This procedure provides an organism with "negative examples," examples of stimuli that should not be treated as similar.

Early in conditioning, stimuli similar to the neutral stimulus being used will elicit a similar response, though not quite as strong. As discrimination training proceeds, the responses to the dissimilar stimuli weaken: an organism learns which events to treat as part of a class that are equivalent signals or predictors of the unconditioned stimulus and which to ignore. For optimum adaptation, the initial perceptual tendency to generalize and respond to all somewhat similar stimuli needs to give way to discrimination between them, with response only to those that are, in fact, followed by an unconditioned stimulus. Ideally, then, conditioning is a process in which discrimination ultimately wins over generalization—but it is a balancing act between these two counteracting tendencies of being overresponsive and too-selective.

It might have occurred to you that these processes can be used to study what an organism can perceive when it can't tell us directly, as with infants or lower animals. Can you see how to apply this paradigm to study the perceptual (or emotional) functioning of a nonverbal subject?

Appetitive and Aversive Conditioning

Pavlov's conditioning with meat powder is an example of **appetitive conditioning**—conditioning in which an unconditioned stimulus is of positive value to an organism. The *Opening Case,* by contrast, involved unpleasant sensations that you needed to escape and avoid the stimulus situation. It was an example of **aversive conditioning**—conditioning in which an unconditioned stimulus is of negative value to an organism, and learning involves specific preparatory responses to a stimulus along with a revaluation of the stimulus and the context in which it occurs. Laboratory studies of aversive conditioning have used unconditioned stimuli like electric shock and puffs of air to the eye that all members of a species find aversive. For example, an electric shock to the leg is an unconditioned stimulus that elicits an unconditioned response of leg withdrawal or muscle flexing. Sounding a bell repeatedly before each electric shock to the leg of a constrained subject will soon condition a muscle twitch in response to the bell alone.

An important discovery from these studies has been that with aversive (also called *noxious*) stimuli, an organism learns not only a specific conditioned muscle response but a generalized fear reaction as well. There is both learning of a specific response to a stimulus and a revaluation of the previously neutral stimulus—as affectively negative. The leg withdrawal is accompanied by reactions of the autonomic nervous system—changes in heart rate, respiration, and electrical resistance of the skin (the *galvanic skin response, GSR*). The muscle response, too, may come to involve more than the limited area stimulated. All these changes become part of an overall conditioned fear response. Furthermore, when strong fear is involved, conditioning may take place after only one pairing of a neutral stimulus with the fear-arousing stimulus. Traumatic events in our lives that may occur only once can condition us to respond with a diffuse set of strong physical, emotional, and cognitive reactions that may not extinguish over years. In many cases learned fear is easy to acquire and difficult to overcome without special training procedures—known as psychotherapy.

A classic early study of conditioned fear in a human being was done by psychologists John Watson and Rosalie Rayner with an infant named Albert. Watson and Rayner (1920) conditioned Albert to fear a white rat he had initially liked by pairing its appearance with an aversive unconditioned stimulus—a loud gong struck just behind the child. The unconditioned startle response and the emotional distress to the noxious noise was the basis of Albert's learning to react with fear to the appearance of the white rat in just seven conditioning trials. This emotional conditioning then was extended to behavioral conditioning when Albert learned to escape from the feared stimulus and was reinforced for doing so by a reduction in his fear. The boy's learned fear then generalized to other furry objects as described in the ***Close-up*** on page 267. In this early period of experimentation with

Close-up Little Albert and the White Rat

When John B. Watson and his colleague Rosalie Rayner set out to induce a conditioned fear in a robust, fearless infant named Albert, to study stimulus generalization, and then remove the conditioned fear, they were unsure of the outcome. They were hoping the experiment would demonstrate the superiority of the behaviorist belief that fears were learnable over the then-popular assumption that human fears were instinctive. Let's look at Watson's laboratory notes to review how it was possible for Albert to be transformed from a child who rarely cried into a "cry baby" fearful even of Santa Claus.

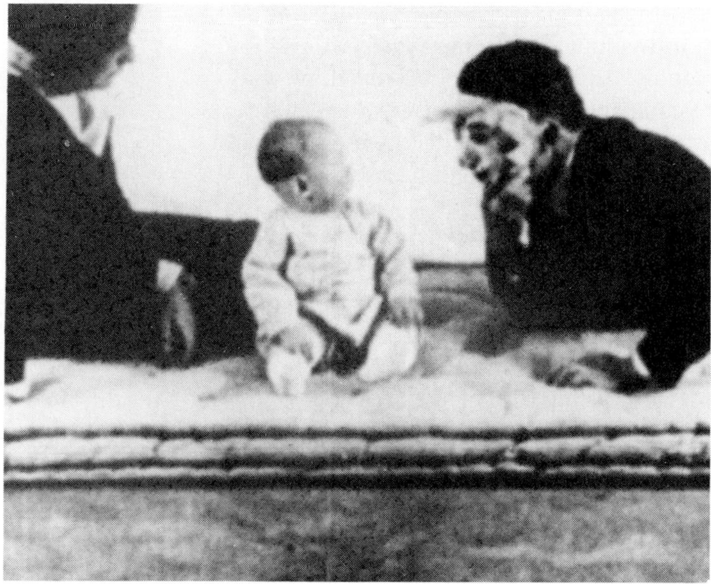

8 months, 26 days old: *Tested for unlearned effects of loud noise (US) of steel bar being struck just behind him. Startle response (UR) was noted; infant jumped violently, fell forward, buried face in mattress, whimpered. Innate US-UR connection recorded.*

9 months old: *Presented Albert with the following animals and objects to play with or observe: a white rat, rabbit, dog, monkey, masks with and without hair, cotton wool, and burning newspapers. No negative response noted to any of these objects.*

11 months, 3 days old: *The white rat, which Albert had played with regularly for weeks, is selected to be the conditioned stimulus. When Albert reached for and touched his rodent playmate, the steel bar was struck. The loud noise startled Albert; he withdrew his hand and became distressed.*

11 months, 10 days old: *Conditioning trials were given in which the white rat (CS) was paired with the loud noise (US). When the rat was next presented alone, it had acquired the power to elicit the strong negative emotional response of fear (CR) of the former friend. Albert began to cry, turned, fell over, and crawled away with all his might.*

11 months, 15 days old: *Tests made for stimulus generalization. The fear response was not elicited by a set of blocks, but it did occur to all furry or hairy objects: a rabbit, dog, fur coat, cotton wool, human hair, and even a Santa Claus mask. Albert had apparently learned a generalized fear of "furriness."*

Whether Albert developed into a Scrooge who hated Christmas with its furry reminders of Santa, we don't know; but we do know that the last phase of the experiment—undoing the learned fear—was never conducted. The experimenters noted that "unfortunately, Albert was taken from the hospital the day the tests were made. Hence, the opportunity of building up an experimental technique by means of which we could remove the conditioned emotional response was denied us" (Watson & Rayner, 1920).

A few years later, an associate of Watson's, Mary Cover Jones (1924), was successful in using conditioning principles to remove conditioned fears in other youngsters (see chapter 16); but her success does not absolve Watson and Rayner from ethical responsibility for having left a child with an unnecessary fear. The record shows that they had known a month earlier that he would be leaving the hospital.

conditioning, the careful attention to possible harmful effects that is characteristic of research with human subjects today unfortunately was sometimes lacking.

We know now that conditioned fear is very resistant to extinction. Even if the overt components of muscle reaction eventually disappear, the reactions of the autonomic nervous system continue, leaving an individual still vulnerable to arousal by the old signals. Conditioned fear reactions may persist for years, even when the original frightening stimulus is never again experienced—as shown in the following demonstration study.

> *During World War II, the signal used to call sailors to battle stations aboard U.S. Navy ships was a gong sounding at the rate of 100 rings a minute. To personnel on board, it was associated with the sounds of guns and bombs; thus it became a conditioned stimulus for strong emotional arousal.*
>
> *Fifteen years after the war, a study was conducted comparing the emotional reactions of hospitalized navy and army veterans to a series of 20 different sound stimuli. Although none of the sounds were current signals for danger, the sound of the old "call to battle stations" still produced strong emotional arousal in the navy veterans who had previously experienced that association. Their response to the former danger signal (as determined by galvanic-skin-response measures) was significantly greater than that of the army veterans. (Edwards & Acker, 1962)*

We all carry around this kind of excess baggage, our learned readiness to respond with fear, joy, or other emotions to old signals (often from our childhood) that are no longer appropriate or valid in our current situation. When we are unaware of their origins, these once reasonable fear reactions are interpreted as "anxiety," and we get additionally upset because we seem to be reacting irrationally—without adequate cause or reason (Dollard & Miller, 1950).

Second-order Conditioning

Following conditioning, the conditioned stimulus has acquired some of the power of the biologically significant unconditioned stimulus, as shown by the fact that it now elicits the response alone. In a sense, it has become a "surrogate" unconditioned stimulus: it can stand in for, and act like, the unconditioned stimulus. Can this conditioned stimulus be used to condition yet another stimulus to produce the same response? It can, for both appetitive and aversive responses. This process of a neutral stimulus becoming a conditioned stimulus solely by its pairing with an established conditioned stimulus is called **second-order conditioning** (also called *higher-order conditioning*).

A child who can approach and play with a dog will probably not have a fear of animals.

> *In Phase One of a study subjects were conditioned to respond to a light (CS_1) paired with food (US). In Phase Two they were exposed to pairing of a sound stimulus (CS_2) with the light (CS_1)—without any presentation of the food. When tested with the sound stimulus alone, they gave the same conditioned response as had previously been elicited by the light (Holland & Rescorla, 1975). Later studies showed such second-order conditioning to be stronger when there was* perceptual similarity *between the two conditioned stimulus events—when both were tones, lights, colors, or patterns. (Rescorla, 1980)*

Second-order conditioning, like original conditioning, is fastest when the new stimulus (CS_2) is a reliable predictor of the original conditioned stimulus (CS_1) and better with a forward conditioning pattern than with a simultaneous or backward one (Leyland & Mackintosh, 1978). With extended trials—during which pairing of the two conditioned stimuli is not accompanied by the unconditioned stimulus—the second-order conditioned response will usually become weaker. Eventually the response to both of the conditioned stimuli will extinguish.

This process vastly extends the domain of classical conditioning, since a biologically powerful stimulus is no longer required for conditioning to take place. Instead, respondent behaviors become potentially controllable by a limitless array of stimuli once they have been associated with other stimulus events whose power is either natural or acquired through learning. This means that conditioning is more than just the development of a behavioral response; it involves associations between stimulus events that become revalued as signals and sources of pleasure and pain. In this sense second-order conditioning is an important process for understanding many types of complex human behaviors, both normal and abnormal.

Though the classical conditioning paradigm was first developed in connection with animals, extensive studies with human subjects have demonstrated its importance in many everyday human reactions. For example, the whirring of a dentist's drill at a given frequency becomes a conditioned stimulus for the pain that the drilling causes. The unconditioned response to that pain is muscle twitching in the mouth area and a general response of tension and anxiety. After a while the sound elicits these reactions (and eventually a dentist's office may come to elicit a generalized fear reaction). However, if the dentist's new drill changes to a very high frequency, then little or no conditioned responding may occur because of a lack of generalization between the two sounds, even though the context is obviously unchanged. Dentists who specialize in working with children often design their environment to create positive associations with the stimuli in the waiting room and office as a means of counteracting or preventing negative associations.

Conditioned Social Behavior

Many of our attitudes have been formed by conditioning processes that take place without our awareness (Staats & Staats, 1958). **Attitudes** are often defined as an individual's learned tendencies to respond to particular target stimuli, such as people, ideas, or things, with a positive or negative evaluation, along with some emotional feelings and also beliefs about them. The targets that become attitudinal stimuli may acquire their power to elicit attitudinal responses by being paired with unconditioned stimuli that elicit emotional or affective responses. Words, symbols, and pictures associated with stimuli that naturally elicit strong positive responses will become conditioned arousers of similarly positive reactions. This principle has not escaped application by advertisers, especially those who promote the sale of "kiddie foods" on Saturday morning TV programs.

In one research study, researchers demonstrated that pairing food words with meaningless trigrams, like *jik* or *daz,* led to more positive attitudes toward the trigrams among college students who were food deprived compared to those who had eaten (Staats et al., 1972). In another study, trigrams were paired with items that were of negative interest to students. The students evaluated these trigrams as unpleasant compared to the pleasant reactions that were elicited by trigrams that had been paired with items of positive interest (Staats et al., 1973). A large body of research shows that social behavior can be studied as response systems that are formed through conditioning, among them attitudes toward people, liking or disliking, aggression, altruism, persuasion, cooperation, and competition (Lott & Lott, 1985; Weiss et al., 1971).

The ability of neutral stimuli to acquire the power to elicit strong responses automatically through conditioning makes us all vulnerable. Although there are some limitations to this process—to be discussed later—the tremendous implications of the ease with which conditioning takes place should not escape you. Virtually any stimulus you can perceive can be associated with almost any response so that you learn to value, desire, or fear the stimulus. (For notable exceptions, see the last section of this chapter on biological constraints.) We learn to use this information about impending events to help us make preparatory responses; we prepare for the future on the basis of our past history of conditioning. The power of classical conditioning to influence the body's immune system is described in the ***Close-up*** on page 270.

Instrumental Conditioning: Learning About Consequences

In classical conditioning, you learn to use one signal to predict something important in your environment. For example, you may learn that a certain look from your lover (CS) signals (enables you to predict) that you are about to be caressed (US) and get positively aroused (UR). You then come to respond with arousal (CR) to that "look of love" even before you feel your lover's actual touch. Score one for the power of classical conditioning! This learning is helpful as far as it goes, but wouldn't you like to learn how to get that look of love to occur in the first place? Just passively learning about signals that already exist or waiting around until they show up is often not ideal.

Learning how to *control* stimulus events, as well as predict them, means learning how to produce the consequences you want and how to minimize the ones you don't. In the *Opening Case,* you learned that jumping into a corner of the shower

Close-up Conditioning the Body's Immune System

Every natural environment is filled with disease-bearing microorganisms, pollutants, and other substances that can damage an organism. To adapt to such environments, the body must protect itself from such assault. It does so through an immune system that develops antibodies capable of counterattack against these invaders.

The immunological system involves both a highly sensitive process for rapid detection of alien substances and a swift response process of releasing highly specific types of antibodies that can contain or destroy specific forms of invaders. Susceptibility to disease becomes greater when the immune system is not functioning adequately.

Until recently, it had been assumed that immunological reactions were automatic, biological processes that occurred without any intervention by the central nervous system. However, it now appears that this vital system is under psychological as well as biological control. This relationship has been demonstrated in studies in which immune responses of animals were suppressed by classical conditioning procedures.

Before we examine the procedure used to show this important finding, it is fascinating to note the curious result that pointed the researchers toward this issue. During a study of conditioned taste aversion, rats were given a distinctively flavored, sweet-tasting solution (CS) followed by a toxic drug (US) that induced illness. The rats quickly learned to avoid or reduce consumption of the sweet solution. However, when the amount of that CS consumed on the single conditioning trial was large, some of the conditioned animals died in extinction trials, when they were presented with the CS but *no* toxic drug (Ader, 1981). What killed them?

It could not have been the toxic drug because its dosage had been too low to be lethal, and it had been given only once during the earlier conditioning. A search for clues turned up the fact that the drug used to produce vomiting, cyclophosphamide, also produces another effect—suppression of the activity of the immune system. Could the sweet CS solution have become a conditioned signal to suppress the immune system as the drug had no doubt done earlier? With the repeated exposure to this CS during extinction training, might the immune system then have been suppressed to the point that the animals became vulnerable to the disease-bearing substances in the laboratory environment?

To test this speculation, Robert Ader and Nathan Cohen (1981) conditioned animals with the same procedure (saccharine solution as the CS, plus toxic drug as the US) and later exposed them to saccharine alone. Three to six days earlier, they had been injected with an alien substance, red blood cells taken from sheep. The animals produced significantly fewer antibodies to combat this assault than did control animals for whom the saccharine solution was not a conditioned stimulus. These results and others from independent investigators support the hypothesis that the learned association *of the conditioned stimulus (saccharine) with the immuno-suppressing drug enabled the conditioned stimulus alone to elicit suppression of the immune system. In this way, conditioning increased the organism's susceptibility to disease.*

The implications of this research are considerable, both for extending our knowledge about how psychological and biological functions interact and for understanding, and perhaps modifying, the process by which organisms resist or become vulnerable to disease.

saved you from the scalding water that you knew was about to come. Similarly, you may learn that when you whisper "sweet nothings" in your sweetheart's ear, the look of love becomes more probable than when you shout, "I know I'm irresistible, so go for it, honey!" Little Albert's efforts to get away from the rat, too, were an attempt to go beyond predicting a bad event to controlling his exposure to it—to reduce a perceived threat—by crawling away.

As a term *instrumental conditioning* is sometimes used interchangeably with *operant conditioning*, contrasting both with respondent or Pavlovian conditioning; but strict usage does not *equate* instrumental conditioning with operant conditioning. Operant conditioning is equated with Skinnerian conditioning, a procedure used by B. F. Skinner who did not believe in any *teleological* assumptions that behavior was instrumental to get a reward. He was an empiricist who asserted only that behavior operated on the environment. If the environment changed as a function of behavior, then the behavior would also change, producing learning.

In **instrumental conditioning** the important relationship that is learned is between a response and its consequences, rather than between stimulus events (as in classical conditioning). Behavior that is *instrumental* to (a means to) changing the environment in some way that is desirable or rewarding is repeated and becomes a learned habit. While classical conditioning rests on the assumption of association, instrumental conditioning rests more on the assumption of adaptive hedonism—we do what avoids pain and gets pleasure.

Through such behaviors an organism actively operates on the environment instead of simply reacting to something the environment does to it, as in the case of respondent behaviors. The effects it achieves—the consequences of the action—then determine the probability that the response will be repeated. Want to change behavior? Do one thing: Change its consequences. In instrumental conditioning the critical environmental stimuli come *after* the response and are obtained by the action of the learner. This contrasts with classical conditioning, in which the learner's behavior has no effect on any environmental consequences, the stimulus is presented before the response, the same sequence of stimuli is presented regardless of the response, and the nature of the unconditioned response determines the form of the conditioned response. In the history of the field of association learning, one difference between these two types of basic learning is in the *content* of the learning. In classical conditioning, a subject learns relationships between stimulus events; in instrumental conditioning a subject learns relationships between its responses and their stimulus, or environmental, consequences. But modern researchers tend to focus on differences in their procedures and methods (the *how* of learning) instead of their content (*what* is learned).

Three American psychologists—Edward L. Thorndike, John B. Watson, and B. F. Skinner—stand out as pioneers in the development of the principles of association between stimuli, responses, and rewards. Let's examine the contributions of each.

Thorndike's Law of Effect

At about the same time that Pavlov was using classical conditioning to induce Russian dogs to salivate to the sound of a bell, Edward L. Thorndike (1898) was watching American cats trying to escape from puzzle boxes in which he had put them (see **Figure 8.5**). He reported his observations and inferences about the kind of learning he believed was taking place in his subjects as follows:

> *When put into the box the cat shows evident signs of discomfort and develops an impulse to escape from confinement. It tries to squeeze through any opening; it claws and bites at the bars or wire; it thrusts its paws out through any opening and claws at everything it reaches; . . . It does not pay very much attention to the food outside (the reward for the hungry cat), but seems simply to strive instinctively to escape from confinement. The vigor with which it struggles is extraordinary. For eight or ten minutes it will claw and bite and squeeze incessantly. . . . Whether the impulse to struggle be due to an instinctive reaction to confinement or to an association, it is likely to succeed in letting the cat out of the box. The cat that is clawing all over the box in [its] impulsive struggle will probably claw the string or loop or button so as to open the door. And gradually all the other nonsuccessful impulses will be* stamped out *and the particular impulse leading to the successful act will be* stamped in *by the resulting pleasure, until, after many trials, the cat will, when put in the box, immediately claw the button or loop in a definite way. (1898, p. 13)*

What did Thorndike's cats learn that was different from the learning of Pavlov's dogs? According to Thorndike's paradigm, learning was an association, not between two stimuli, but between stimuli in the situation and a response that a subject learned to make—a *stimulus-response (S-R) connection.* Thorndike believed that responses repeatedly followed by reward brought "satisfaction," as a result of which they were strengthened, or "stamped in,"

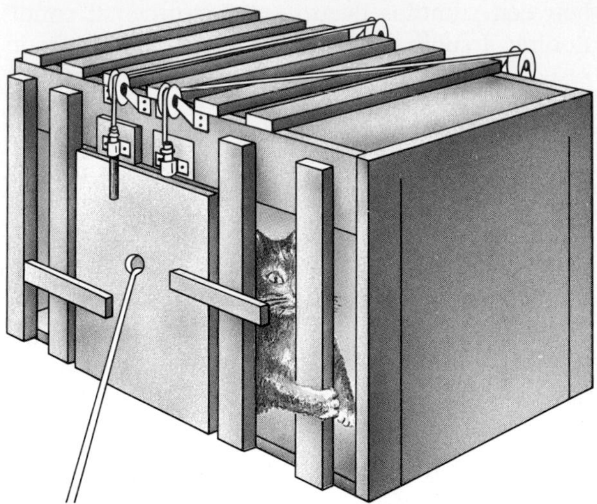

Figure 8.5 *One of Thorndike's Puzzle Boxes*
Thorndike's cats were confined in boxes like this one and food was placed outside of the box. To get out, the animal had to loosen a bolt, bar, or loop in order to release a weight which would then pull the door open. (After Thorndike, 1898)

while nonrewarded responses were weakened, or "stamped out." Thorndike's conditioning paradigm allowed an animal to respond freely, but only one of its responses would have a satisfying consequence. Generally such behaviors are adaptive in aiding survival, but you can probably come up with a list of learned behaviors that feel good in the short run, but are destructive over time—smoking and alcohol abuse are obvious candidates.

According to Thorndike's "connectionist" theory the learning of reinforced S-R connections occurs gradually and automatically in a mechanistic way as the animal experiences the consequences of its actions through blind *trial-and-error.* Gradually, random errors are eliminated as the organism discovers which responses result in satisfaction and which ones do not. The consequences of this satisfaction on behavior are formulated in his law of effect.

The **law of effect** is a basic principle of learning which states that learning is controlled by its consequences. At a general level, it is parallel to the law of natural selection in evolution: from a large pool of possible behaviors some particular ones are selected by events in the environment. Those behaviors that lead to "good" consequences are selected; those that lead to "bad" consequences are not repeated. Another version of this law states that the power of a stimulus to evoke a response is strengthened when the response is followed by a reward and weakened if the response is not followed by a reward. Little Albert learned two different types of response—a conditioned fear response at the sight of the white rat and a learned avoidance response that had the consequence of getting him away from the feared stimulus. Often the two kinds of conditioning occur together. Thorndike believed that the principles he had discovered were also applicable to human learning. His ideas had a major impact on the educational psychology of his time—even though he believed that learning involved trial-and-error without conscious thought. (Some students may facetiously agree that their education consists of the transfer of a professor's notes to their notebooks without the interference of conscious thought by either party.)

A whole generation of researchers used Thorndike's paradigm to study instrumental responses, but used situations in which the responses were more specific, simpler, and more quantifiable than escape from puzzle boxes. The favorite research subjects became rats though many other species were also used. The most popular responses measured were speed of running to the goal box in a runway, number of errors in learning a maze, and number of lever presses in a situation where lever pressing made a reward available or enabled an animal to escape from an aversive stimulus. By the 1950s there were over a thousand research reports a year on factors influencing lever pressing in rats. Why, you ask? The general assumption accepted by these researchers was that elementary processes of learning were "conserved across species," which meant that they were comparable in their basic features from the lowest to the highest level animal species. Complex forms of learning represented combinations and elaborations of these simpler processes. Studying animal learning was easier and

Edward L. Thorndike (1874–1969)

allowed greater control over relevant variables than did human learning. In most cases, the ultimate hope was that this basic research with simpler animals would shed more light on the mysteries of human learning.

Watson's Behaviorist Manifesto

For nearly fifty years American psychology was dominated by a behaviorist tradition expressed in 1913 by John Watson in his article, "Psychology as the Behaviorist Sees It." Watson was influential in advancing the assumptions and methods of behavior theory into many areas of psychological research, most notably into the field of learning. His early work on the way rats learn to solve mazes was a paradigm that others readily adopted; later he adapted Pavlov's conditioned response as the unit of learned habit. For a behaviorist, the only acceptable research method was *objective*, with no place for introspection, or any type of subjective data. Behavior, rather than instinct or inferred internal states, was the thing to be studied; and behavior was viewed with an environmental emphasis—as elicited by environmental stimuli and, in turn, as having consequences in the environment.

The importance Watson attached to conditioning and environmental control of behavior—in contrast to prevailing notions about the importance of inherited traits—led him to boast of its power in terms that would later become labeled as *behavioral engineering.*

> *Give me a dozen healthy infants, well-formed, and my own specified world to bring them up in and I'll guarantee to take any one of them at random and train him to become any type of specialist I might select—doctor, lawyer, artist, merchant-chief, and yes, even beggarman and thief, regardless of his talents, penchants, tendencies, vocations and race of his ancestors. (1926, p. 10)*

You can appreciate how this democratic arrogance was at once welcomed by many psychologists and rejected by others; but it was a controversial and quite persuasive argument for a long period in the history of American psychology (Hilgard, 1986). Watson's ideas were to have a direct influence on a young man who went on to become one of the most famous psychologists of his generation. Burrhus Frederick Skinner began his graduate study in psychology at Harvard in 1928 after reading Watson's textbook, *Behaviorism.* He is still there as Professor Emeritus, having pioneered a new brand of behaviorism.

Skinner's Operant Conditioning: The Experimental Analysis of Behavior

Behaviorist B. F. Skinner embraced Thorndike's view that environmental consequences affected the responses that preceded them; but he rejected any assumptions about "satisfaction," S-R connections being learned, or any interpretation that resorted to inferences about an organism's intentions, purposes, or goals. What an animal wanted was not important; all that mattered, according to Skinner, was what could be observed directly from an experimental analysis of behavior in which predictable relationships between overt actions and environmental conditions were empirically determined. Only in this way could there be a true science of behavior.

> *Skinner called his approach the experimental analysis of behavior, "because a natural datum in a science of behavior is the probability that a given bit of behavior will occur at a given time. An experimental analysis deals with that probability in terms of frequency or rate of responding. . . . The task of an experimental analysis is to discover all the variables of which probability of response is a function." (1966, pp. 213, 214)*

The **experimental analysis of behavior** means discovering, by systematic variation of stimulus conditions, all the ways that various kinds of experience affect the probability of responses. Skinner's analysis is experimental rather than theoretical because he refuses to make inferences about inner states or about any nonobservable bases for the behavioral relationships that he demonstrates in the laboratory. He formulates no theories about what is happening inside an organism. No intervening variables are assumed: inner conditions like "hunger" are defined operationally, in terms of the procedures an experimenter can carry out—for example, "deprivation of food for 24 hours." Approaching food and eating it can be observed and recorded; desire for food or pleasure at receiving it cannot. Therefore, such unobservable variables are never part of Skinner's descriptions. Theorists are guided by the derivations and predictions from their theories. By contrast, empiricists advocate the bottom-up approach of starting with the collection and evaluation of data within the context of an experiment. Skinner represents empirical behaviorism in its most extreme form. He would even reject the descriptive term *instrumental conditioning* to characterize what he was studying, because "instrumental" would imply that an organism had to *do* something to achieve a desired goal.

B. F. Skinner is shown at work building a scale model of a Skinner box, a small cage for housing an animal. The experimenter is in control of the subject's physical environment.

In the *operant conditioning paradigm* spontaneous responses are studied as they change their rate of occurring under different stimulus conditions. An **operant** is any behavior that is *emitted* by an organism and can be characterized in terms of the observable effects it has on the environment. Operant behaviors are not *elicited* by specific stimuli (as are respondents in classical conditioning), since they are already present, repetitive actions. Skinner assumes that responses already in an organism's repertoire are emitted spontaneously—that they are caused by internal conditions and regularly performed by an organism in the absence of specific, eliciting external stimuli. Pigeons peck, rats search for food, babies cry and coo, some people gesture while talking, others stutter or say "like" and "you know" frequently. These emitted behaviors are called *operant behaviors* because they have an effect on the environment (getting food, being picked up or noticed, getting sympathy from others). **Operant conditioning** modifies the probability of different rates of operant responses as a function of their stimulus consequences.

The Operant Conditioning Paradigm

The paradigm for operant conditioning has three parts—behavioral contingencies, reinforcers, and discriminative stimuli. Let's see how these terms help us understand the process of operant conditioning.

Behavioral Contingencies

Investigators can make responses more or less probable by setting up different behavioral contingencies. A **behavioral contingency** is a consistent relationship between a response and the stimulus conditions that follow it. A contingency specifies an "if X, then Y" type of relationship. Contingency between events is a central concept in operant conditioning. Such a relationship can increase or decrease the rate or probability of the response. For example, if a pigeon's disk-pecking response is usually followed by the presentation of grain, then the rate of the pecking response will increase. For a food-deprived pigeon the grain can serve as a reinforcer for any response made contingent upon it. For it to increase *only* the rate of pecking, it must be contingent on the pecking response: it must occur regularly after that response, but not after other responses, such as turning or moving away from the disk. Researchers control behavior by arranging different timing and frequency-of-stimuli patterns and making the reward available only after the desired response.

The approach of Skinner and his students seeks to understand the behavior of organisms in terms of the behavioral contingencies they have experienced in their environment. One of the goals is to show that the complex behaviors learned by organisms can be understood as the product of particular patterns of contingencies. Facts discovered in

For this pigeon there is nothing like an intelligent pecking order.

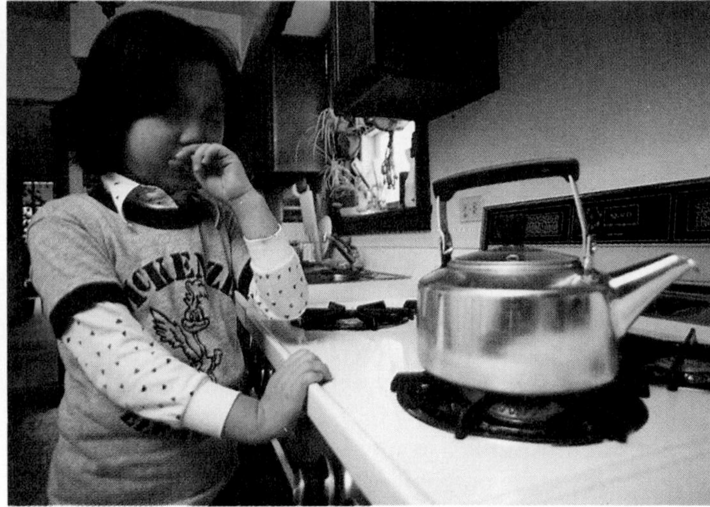

The punishment of the resulting pain suffered when touching a hot flame is likely to decrease the probability that a child will do it again.

the laboratory are used to predict the consequences of particular patterns of responses and stimulus consequences in a wide variety of situations. Indeed, the Skinnerian approach has been applied to many natural settings—programmed learning in schools, behavior modification in therapy, and even the training of porpoises and whales in marine worlds (for the application of behavior principles in everyday life, see Baldwin & Baldwin, 1986).

Reinforcers and Reinforcement

Significant events that can strengthen an organism's responses if they are contingently related are called **reinforcers.** The terms *reinforcer* and *reinforcement* are defined empirically— in terms of their effects on changing the probability of a response. Reinforcers in operant conditioning differ from unconditioned stimuli in classical conditioning because of the variations between the two procedures and not because of any special properties of the stimuli themselves.

A **positive reinforcer** is a stimulus, received after a response, that increases the probability of that response occurring. Receiving a positive reinforcer is called **positive reinforcement.** Getting grain following a pecking response is an example of positive reinforcement—for a pigeon, at least. For us, getting a laugh after telling a joke reinforces the response of joke-telling—making it more probable that the joke will be repeated.

A **negative reinforcer** is a stimulus, *not received* (avoided or terminated) after a response, that increases the probability of that response occurring. The condition of *not* receiving an aversive stimulus is called **negative reinforcement.** Escaping from the scalding water in our *Opening Case* was an instance of negative reinforcement. Both positive and negative reinforcement *increase* the probability or rate of the response that precedes them.

In general, positive reinforcement seems to work better for getting a new response or continuing a present response. Negative reinforcement works better for getting people to avoid some undesirable responses that they have been making frequently. It reinforces—and increases the frequency of—*not* making that response. For example, an automobile seat-belt buzzer serves a negative reinforcing function; its annoying sound is terminated when a driver buckles up.

Suppose you wanted to get rid of an undesirable response, what operant procedure would you use? Extinction training alone can be effective in getting rid of an unwanted response—but only if all reinforcers can really be withheld. This is difficult outside the laboratory, where many aspects of a person's environment may not be under the control of the would-be operant conditioner. In any case, extinction training to eliminate an undesired response is most effective when combined with positive reinforcement to increase the probability of the desired response. Clowning in class to get attention is most likely to stop if the student finds that it doesn't work any more (extinction) and also discovers that other, more socially approved behaviors do bring attention (positive reinforcement).

In experimental research, **extinction** is a procedure in which reinforcement no longer follows the response; the former contingency is not in effect. After repeated responding with no consequences, the behavior returns to the level it was before training, and the conditioned response is said to be *extinguished.*

Punishment is different from negative reinforcement. **Punishment** is the condition of receiving (instead of avoiding or escaping from) an aversive stimulus after a response; the general effect is to *decrease* the probability of that response. Touching a hot stove produces pain that punishes the preceding response; a child is less likely next time to reach out to touch the stove. Responses that are punished immediately tend to get eliminated, while responses that receive delayed punishment are only suppressed. When a formerly punished response no longer produces aversive consequences, it then increases in frequency to prepunishment levels. The complex effects of punishment are examined in the ***Close-up*** on pages 278–79.

Operant researchers assume that any response which persists does so because there is some reinforcement that is continuing. Any behavior, they argue—even irrational or bizarre behavior—can be understood if one can discover what the payoff is. Once acquired, a response may be maintained by reinforcers different from those involved in the original conditioning. For example, symptoms of mental or physical disorders are sometimes maintained, because the person gets attention and sympathy, and is excused from normal responsibilities. These "secondary gains" are the payoffs that continue the irrational and sometimes self-destructive behavior.

Discriminative Stimuli and Stimulus Control

We can learn not only what to do but when to do it. Organisms can learn *when* to make a previously successful response and *when not* to by learning to recognize the advance signals that tell whether a payoff—a reinforcing contingency—will or will not be available if a response is made. These relevant predictor signals that may reinforce future responses are called **discriminative stimuli.**

How do stimuli become discriminative? They do so by being reliable predictors of reinforcement. The most obvious examples are signs in public places that indicate the acceptable behaviors that will be reinforced—"Smoking Permitted," for smokers, and "English Spoken Here" for English-speaking travelers in foreign countries—but any predictable signal can become a discriminative stimulus. If Grandpa always gives the kids who hug and kiss him a shiny silver dollar when he visits, he becomes a predictor stimulus.

But sometimes stimuli warn us that certain behaviors will *not* be followed by reinforcement. Every time your mother had an angry look on her face, you learned that "nothing I do will make a difference." Her facial expression was the discriminative stimulus for not responding.

In Skinner's laboratory an experimenter might have given stimuli different predictive power, for example, by making food available while a green light was present and not available when a red light or no light was present. When a pigeon pecked a disk while the green light was present the pigeon would receive food; however, the same pecking response while the light was red or absent would produce nothing.

The stimulus that signals "reinforcer available"—the green light—is called the *positive discriminative stimulus (S^D).* The "no reinforcer available" signal—a red light or no light—is called the *negative discriminative stimulus (S^Δ,* pronounced "ess delta"). Organisms quickly learn to distinguish between these two conditions, regularly responding to the S^D and withholding response to the S^Δ. A very powerful process takes place when this happens: behavior is said to be under **stimulus control.** By arranging the contingencies in effect and the particular stimuli that signal them, we come to exert this stimulus control over our own behavior as well as the behavior of others. A humorous example from one of the old "Candid Camera" TV shows demonstrates this process of stimulus control. In the episode we see a naïve customer at a restaurant counter whose eating is controlled by a flashing sign; he "learns" to take bites of his sandwich only when the "EAT" light is blinking and to stop when the "DON'T EAT" light flashes. Perhaps you can think of similar examples from your own experience.

The discriminative stimulus is informational: it "sets the stage"—provides the occasion for a response to be made—but does not elicit it. The response is an emitted one, maintained by the payoff; but even though it remains an emitted response, the experimenter, or "behavior modifier," can now control when it will appear simply by presenting or not presenting the discriminative stimulus. Because organisms are alert to discriminative stimuli that

Table 8.1 *Operant Conditioning Paradigm: Five Contingency Patterns*

	Discriminative Stimulus (S^D)	***Emitted Response (R)*** ⟶	***Stimulus Consequence (S)***
1. **Positive Reinforcement:** A response in the presence of an effective signal (S^D) produces the desired consequence. This response increases.	Soft-drink machine	Put coin in slot	Get refreshing drink
2. **Negative Reinforcement:** *escape.* An unpleasant situation is escaped from by an operant response. This escape response increases.	Heat	Fan oneself	Escape from heat
3. **Negative Reinforcement:** *avoidance.* A stimulus signals the organism that an unpleasant event will occur soon. An appropriate response avoids its occurrence. This avoidance response increases.	Sound of seatbelt buzzer	Buckle up	Avoid aversive noise
4. **Extinction Training:** A conditioned operant response is not followed by a reinforcer. It decreases in rate.	None or S^Δ	Clowning behavior	No one notices
5. **Punishment:** A response is followed by an aversive stimulus. The response is eliminated or suppressed.	Attractive match box	Play with matches	Get burned or get caught and spanked

are signposts to reinforcers, they can be taught to make subtle discriminations between many different stimulus events, such as patterns or hues. Selective reinforcement of S^D and not of S^Δ results in controlling the responses of an organism to most of the stimuli that organism is capable of perceiving. In fact, this procedure has been used as a *diagnostic tool* to determine whether an individual is able to perceive the difference between a pair of stimuli, such as similar tones, shapes, or odors, for example.

The concept of the discriminative stimulus completes the three-element paradigm of operant conditioning. This paradigm includes a preceding discriminating stimulus that provides information about the availability of the payoff, an emitted response by an organism contingently related to a stimulus consequence, and the reinforcing consequence of the behavior. **Table 8.1** illustrates five variations in operant conditioning with different contingency patterns.

Properties of Reinforcers

The slogan of operant conditioning might be "all power to the reinforcers." These potent consequences of behavior, which can then change subsequent behavior, have a number of interesting and complex properties. They can start out as weak and become strong, can be learned through experience rather than biologically determined, or can be activities rather than objects; yet, in some situations, even powerful reinforcers, as we shall see, may not be enough to change a dominant behavior pattern.

Reinforcers and punishers are the "power-brokers" of operant conditioning; they change or maintain behavior. When they are an *immediate consequence* of a response, operant conditioning is most likely to occur. Contingent reinforcement strengthens responding; contingent punishment suppresses responding. When reinforcers (and punishers) are given *noncontingently,* their presence has little effect on operant conditioning—for example, when a parent praises your bad work as well as your good efforts, or a teacher is overly critical regardless of the quality of your performance. Such noncontingencies reveal something about the attributes of the loving parent or hostile teacher and little about your performance.

With humans, unlike most other species, operant conditioning can occur even when the behavioral consequences are not immediate. The key is the ability to detect a causal, contingent relationship between a behavior and its later consequence. Indeed, most action *has* only delayed consequences. You typically get feedback on examination performance days after you study and take the test, but if the feedback is positive, the response of studying for the next test is likely to be strengthened. As the time interval between the response and its consequence lengthens appropriate thoughts must fill the gap if conditioning is to occur. You remember the similar contingencies from your past experiences, you anticipate the

Close-up The Psychology and Politics of Punishment

Throughout the ages many voices of authority have been raised in controversy over the benefits or ills of punishment. The Bible warns us, "He that spareth the rod hateth his own son" (Proverbs 13:24); but critics argue that punishment is destructive. Does punishment build character or distort it? What has psychology to say on this question?

To change behavior, either extinction training or punishment may help get rid of an undesired response. Positive reinforcement of a substitute response at the same time will increase the probability that the new response will be repeated; but it is often difficult to follow this procedure because the current reinforcer of the undesired behavior may be obscure or not under the control of the person in authority. Thus many people simply turn to punishment to stop behavior they find objectionable. They do so because punishment stops most behaviors swiftly; also it may help relieve their frustration and give them a sense of control. Instead of a search for elusive reinforcers (or getting to understand an individual well enough to determine what will be reinforcing), they simply increase the intensity of some punishment until the response is suppressed.

Punishment, however, can be counterproductive, causing negative side effects that may be more undesirable than the original behavior it was meant to stop. Punishment may (a) lead to counteraggression against the punisher or the institution; (b) encourage future use of physical abuse on the part of the person who is punished; (c) harm the self-image of the punished person; (d) create so much fear and terror that the undesirable behavior cannot be controlled by the person (as sometimes happens with toilet training); (e) isolate the person from peers who shun him or her as stigmatized by authority; and (f) cause serious physical injury (Bongiovanni, 1977).

Often the punishing agent is agitated and gets "carried away" during the process of administering the punishment. Studies of corporal punishment in schools reveal that it can be brutal and has included beating, paddling, kicking, forced eating of obnoxious substances, and public ridi-

---

consequences, you rehearse a chain of events that ties responding to consequences. In these ways, behavior is more likely to be modified because you recall the behavior-consequence link vividly and frequently (Mahoney, 1974; Schwartz, 1984). This principle should strike you as one that is alien to Skinner's behavioral analysis. It is. It comes from the more recent attempts by "cognitive-behavior modifiers" to add thought processes to analyses of conditioning in humans—an issue we will examine later in this chapter and, at length, in chapter 16 when we consider different types of therapies for behavior problems.

Conditioned Reinforcers

Just as neutral stimuli can become conditioned stimuli in classical conditioning, neutral stimuli paired with reinforcers can become **conditioned reinforcers** for operant responses. When they do, they can come to serve as ends in themselves. In fact, much human behavior is influenced less by biologically significant primary reinforcers than by a wide variety of conditioned reinforcers. Money, grades, praise, smiles of approval, gold stars, and various kinds of status symbols are among the many potent conditioned reinforcers that influence cule. The primary targets of corporal punishment are boys more than girls, minority children more than those of the dominant racial-ethnic group, and, surprisingly, children in grades one to four rather than older children (Hyman et al. 1977).

Psychological research has identified several conditions under which punishment is most likely to eliminate undesired behavior with a minimum of damage (adapted from Azrin & Holz, 1966; Park & Walters, 1967; Walters & Grusec, 1977):

1. Alternative responses. *Availability of at least one alternative response that an individual can make which will not receive the punishing stimulus and which can be positively reinforced.*
2. Response specificity. *Clear explanation of what specific response is being punished and why.*
3. Timing and duration. *Swift, brief punishment immediately after a response occurs; delayed punishment suppresses, but does not eliminate, the response.*
4. Intensity. *For humane reasons, punishment only intense enough to stop the response.*
5. No escape. *No available unauthorized means of escape, avoidance, or distraction.*
6. No mixed messages. *No provision of positive reinforcement, such as displays of sympathy or extra attention, along with the punishment.*
7. Use of conditioned punishers. *Establishment of a physically harmless conditioned stimulus that can stand in for a physical, possibly harmful one (a child spanked in the corner later punished by simply having to sit in the corner).*
8. Use of "penalties." *Withdrawal of a positive stimulus (no TV instead of a spanking for a TV-watcher who hits a younger sibling).*
9. Restricted limits. *Limitation of punishment to the situation in which the undesirable response occurs, not letting it "spill over" to other settings and times.*
10. Limitation to specific responses, not general traits. *Take care never to generalize from the specific undesirable response being punished (cheating on a test, tearing pages from library books) to general traits of the person being punished ("You're stupid," "a born criminal").* Responses *may be undesirable, but* people *should never be made to feel that* they *are undesirable. Indeed, although sticks and stones may break your bones, negative labels may stigmatize forever.*

much of our learning and behavior. The ***Close-up*** on page 282 examines the role of primary and conditioned reinforcers in drug addiction.

When a conditioned reinforcer controls a wide range of responses, it is said to be a *generalized conditioned reinforcer.* Money, for example, can control so much of human behavior because it can "cash in on" so many biologically significant events in our lives. It may become a reinforcer that maintains a high level of responding even when a person hoards it and never exchanges it for "property, pleasures of mind, or flesh." Since virtually any stimulus can become a conditioned reinforcer by being paired with a primary reinforcer, tokens that are inedible can be used as conditioned reinforcers even with animal learners like the chimps in a classic study of the work ethic.

In an early study, chimps were trained to work and learn how to solve problems with edible raisins as their primary reinforcer. Then tokens were delivered along with the raisins. When only the tokens were presented, the chimps continued working for their "money" payoff since they could later deposit their hard-earned coins in a "chimp-o-mat" designed to exchange tokens for the valued raisins. (Cowles, 1937).

Inedible tokens can be used as conditioned reinforcers with animals. In one study chimps deposited tokens in a "chimp-o-mat" and received raisins.

Teachers and experimenters often find tokens and other conditioned reinforcers more effective and easier to use than primary reinforcers because (a) few primary reinforcers are available in the classroom whereas almost any stimulus event that *is* under the control of a teacher can be used for a conditioned reinforcer; (b) conditioned reinforcers can be dispensed rapidly; (c) they are portable; and (d) their reinforcing effect may be more immediate since it depends only on the perception of receiving them and not on biological processing, as in the case of primary reinforcers (eating food).

In some institutions **"token economies"** have been set up based on these principles. Desired behaviors are explicitly defined (grooming or taking medication, for example), and token payoffs are given by the staff when they are performed. These conditioned reinforcers can later be exchanged by the patients for a whole array of rewards and privileges (Ayllon & Azrin, 1965; Holden, 1978). These systems of reinforcement are especially effective in modifying patients' behaviors regarding self-care, upkeep of their environment, and, most importantly, increasing the quality of their positive social interaction.

Preferred Activities as Positive Reinforcers

Positive reinforcers in the laboratory are usually substances—food or water, for example; but not only *things* can be used to reinforce behavior. For example, nursery-school children enjoy running and shouting—much more than sitting still and listening to someone else talk. What would happen if the opportunity to run and shout were made contingent on a period of sitting still first? Would there be an increase in the sitting-still behavior? In a classic study, this was just what happened. Psychologists helped a teacher reprogram the contingencies when her pleas, punishment, and a bit of screaming proved unsuccessful.

> *. . . sitting quietly in a chair and looking at the blackboard would be intermittently followed by the sound of a bell, with the instruction, ''Run and scream.'' The Ss would then leap to their feet and run around screaming. At another signal, they would stop. . . .'' At a later stage, Ss earned tokens for low probability behaviors which could later be used to ''buy'' the opportunity for high-probability activities. With this kind of procedure, control was virtually perfect after a few days. (Homme et al. 1963, p. 55)*

The principle that a more *preferred activity* can be used to reinforce a less preferred one was formulated by David Premack (1965). He found that water-deprived rats learned to increase their running in an exercise wheel when running was followed by an opportunity to drink water, while rats that were not thirsty but exercise-deprived would learn to increase their drinking when that response was followed by a chance to run. This discovery meant that a reinforcer need not be a substance from the environment, but could be a valued activity. The **Premack principle** encourages parents and teachers to use reinforcers valued by an individual child. For a socially outgoing child, playing with friends can reinforce the less pleasant task of getting one's homework done first. For a shy bookworm, reading a new book can be used to reinforce the less preferred activity of playing with other children. Whatever one values can be used to reinforce and, thus, increase the frequency of whatever one does not currently value. Over time there is the possibility that the less-favored activities will come to be valued by having their intrinsic worth discovered.

This principle is enormously useful for self-management. If you wish you could get your studying done, but you have trouble withstanding alluring distractions, try promising yourself a half-hour break to engage in an activity you really want to do—only after you have studied for a given period of time or have read so many pages. If you do this on a regular basis, the sweet delights of the later pleasure will help the medicine of the concentrated study go down in increasing ease—assuming you really do keep the direction of your contingencies straight. A Premack moral: Pleasure before study makes study a pain; pleasure after study makes study a gain.

Shaping and Chaining

When do high standards for performance lead to failure? When an individual is functioning at a much lower level which then never gets reinforced. How can we turn this failure into success? By systematically shaping the desired final response. **Shaping** involves changing behavior in small steps that successively approximate the desired performance. When shaping begins, any element of the target response is reinforced; then, when this element occurs regularly, only responses more like the desired response are reinforced. By carefully combining *differential reinforcement* for the now "correct" response and not for the former response, while gradually raising the criteria for desired performance, an experimenter can shape the desired, higher level action. Following is an example of the use of shaping, with important practical consequences for the individual "being shaped."

> *The patient was a 3-year-old boy who was diagnosed as having childhood schizophrenia. He lacked normal social and verbal behavior, and was given to ungovernable tantrums and self-destructive actions. After having had a cataract operation, he refused to wear the glasses that were essential for the development of normal vision. First the child was trained to expect a bit of candy or fruit at the clicking sound of a toy noisemaker. The sound soon became a conditioned reinforcer. Then training began with empty eyeglass frames. The child was reinforced (with the clicking sound) first for picking them up, then for holding them, then for carrying them around. Slowly, and by successive approximation, he was reinforced for bringing the frames closer to his eyes. After a few weeks, he was putting the empty frames on his head at odd angles, and finally he was wearing them in the proper manner. With further training, the child learned to wear his glasses up to 12 hours a day. (Wolf et al., 1964)*

In everyday life rarely can you get by with making a single response in a situation. Usually you must perform long sequences of actions to complete a behavioral unit. You write essays that consist of many strings of responses, your teacher delivers a lecture that involves many different responses, any sports skill you've mastered is composed of a host of components. To teach a sequence of actions, you could use another technique called chaining. **Chaining** is the operant procedure in which each response in a sequence is followed by a conditioned reinforcer until the final response is

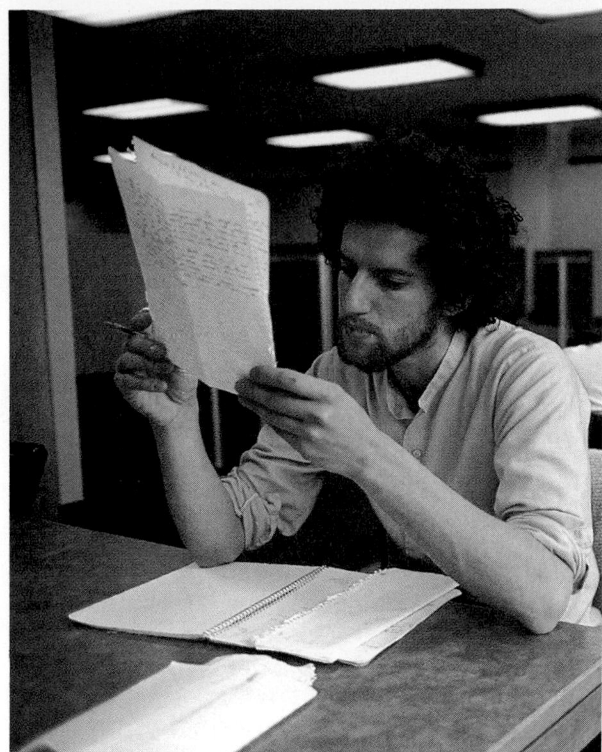

Try the Premack principle: After some time studying, take time to do something you really want to do.

followed by an unconditioned, or primary, reinforcer. You start by teaching the final response, and it is the only one that ever receives *primary* reinforcement. This final response then becomes a conditioned reinforcer for the response that has to occur just before it. In this way, other links are added to the behavior chain one at a time. Each link in the sequence serves as a *discriminative stimulus* to the next response in line and a *conditioned reinforcer* for the response that immediately precedes it. The conditioned reinforcer in a chain is usually a *response-produced stimulus,* a stimulus that is produced by the prior response. When you show enthusiasm while listening to a psychology lecture, that response is a "good news sign" to the teacher and also a conditioned stimulus for the teacher's continuing high level of involvement with the lecture topic.

For parents one of the most valuable lessons to come from operant chaining is its use in helping children to become toilet trained. This achievement is a milestone in the development of a child for many reasons, not the least of which is that it is used by schools as a criterion for readiness to preschool programs and by parents as the sign that the endless chore of changing dirty diapers is finally over. However, toilet training can be a source of tension and frustration for parents and children

Close-up Learning to Be a Drug Addict— and Dying For It

Both classical and operant conditioning appear to be contributing factors in the popularity of drugs that alter mood, arousal, and perception. Several aspects of conditioning influence the effects of these drugs.

An individual trying out a new drug may find that it produces a desired emotional state—perhaps euphoria, excitement, relaxation, or social rewards. These benefits serve as positive reinforcers.

After drugs have been taken for a while, stopping can cause painful withdrawal symptoms. These function as punishment; escaping these aversive consequences provides negative reinforcement.

With repeated drug usage, *tolerance* may develop—decreased responsiveness to a drug. Higher dosage is needed to achieve the same effect—a problem for the drug user and a serious problem in medical treatment of chronic pain. Until recently, this increased tolerance was assumed to be because of physiological changes in the sensitivity of brain receptors (Snyder & Mattysse, 1975); but evidence is accumulating that a *learned* association is at least partly responsible.

Some time ago Pavlov (1927) and, later, his colleague Bykov (1957) pointed out that tolerance to opiates develops when an individual *anticipates* the pharmacological assault of a drug. Perhaps with advance notice—provided by the conditioned stimulus associated with the ritual of injection—the body somehow learns to protect itself by preventing the drug from having its usual effect.

Shephard Siegel (1977) reasoned that if anticipation leads to

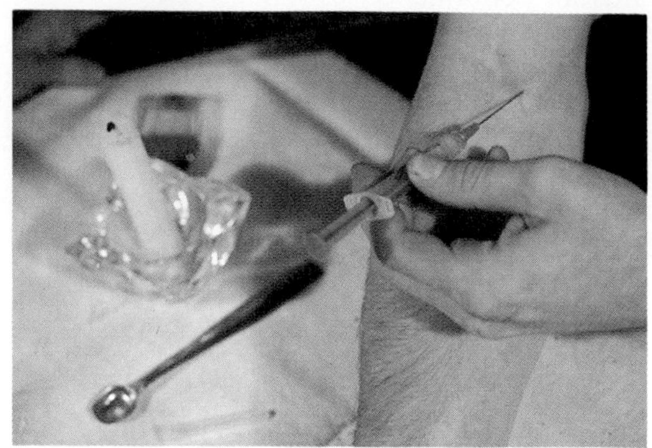

tolerance, then removing the anticipation through extinction training should lower the tolerance—increasing the power of the drug.

In one study, sensitivity of rats to a standard pain stimulus was reduced by morphine. Over six trials, however, tolerance developed and the original dose of morphine had little effect. At that point a randomly chosen half of the subjects, the control group, were given 12 days of rest without exposure to any drug administration. The other half, the experimental group, received 12 days of extinction training during which the drug injection procedure was given but no morphine—only a placebo.

On day 13, when both groups were again given the morphine injections, the control subjects showed the same level of tolerance as before: the morphine still had little effect in reducing their pain. For the experimental group, however, the tolerance had been lowered: once more the morphine reduced their pain. Since tolerance was reduced by the extinction training, Siegel reasoned that the tolerance must have developed originally, at least, in part, from the learning of this association between the biological effect of the drug and the environmental signals from the original procedure.

Is drug tolerance just to a specific drug administration procedure or to the whole stimulus context in which the drug is customarily received? If it is the latter, then overdose and death might result even from a usually nonlethal dose if it were given in a new context.

In another study rats learned, by classical conditioning training, to expect heroin injections (US) in one setting (CS_1), but salt solution injections in a different setting (CS_2). All developed heroin tolerance in the first phase of training. Then, on the test day, all subjects got a larger-than-usual dose of heroin—nearly twice the previous amount. Half of them got it in the setting where heroin was expected; the other half got it in the setting where salt solutions had been given during conditioning.

More than twice as many subjects died when heroin was not expected (salt-solution setting) as when it was expected (usual heroin setting)—82 percent versus 31 percent! They even died more rapidly. The other group had valid expectations and were able to cope with this potentially dangerous situation (in as yet unknown ways). Those that died did not and were not. (Siegel, 1979)

The same thing may happen with human addicts, too. Doses for which they have developed tolerance in a particular setting may be overdoses in a new setting where the stimuli are unfamiliar. This would occur because the new setting does not provide the conditioned cues necessary for eliciting the learned tolerance response to the drug. Without this protective reaction, a drug's effects will be more potent. From these and related studies we have discovered that the context specificity of drug tolerance also holds for alcohol and barbiturates. As a result of tolerance being under stimulus control, it has adaptive significance for an individual; but it is now clear that under some circumstances the same learning can be deadly. Having developed the habit of taking a drug in a dosage that is high enough to be lethal in a context that has been associated with tolerance, a drug abuser may become vulnerable to overdose and death when the same drug, in the same amount, is taken in a different context. Research like that of Siegel's should help convince you of the significant role of "simple" conditioning processes in an organism's attempts to adapt to its environment—and survive.

when it becomes a test of wills rather than a systematically planned program of behavior modification. Psychologists Azrin and Fox (1976) have developed a plan that has proven effective in toilet training children starting about 20 months of age—in less than a day. Their plan shows parents how to combine classical and operant conditioning procedures to achieve their goal. Four types of learning are involved: (a) classical conditioning of sphincter muscle relaxation stimuli (US) with "potty chair" stimuli (CS); (b) operant learning of positive contingencies associated with making the desired response, using shaping and chaining of conditioned reinforcers for the sequence of behaviors involved in "getting to the potty on time"; (c) verbal learning of the sequences of behavior to bridge the gap in time between stimuli and their direct consequences; and (d) social learning in which parents model some of the responses in the sequence, and the child gives self-generated praise each time the pants are dry and clean.

Shaping and chaining are essential parts of every animal trainer's program for teaching complex and unusual behaviors that are not likely to be emitted naturally. Dolphins leaping in tandem over a high wire and back-flipping while tossing a ball around have been trained using both of these operant conditioning techniques.

Biofeedback—Amplifying Weak Contingencies

It was long assumed that involuntary behavior controlled by the autonomic nervous system, such as heart rate or blood pressure, could not come under conscious control. A person had to be able to know that a response was made in order to learn an outcome that was contingent upon it. A weak response or one that was internal (or not overt) was difficult to detect. However operant conditioners have developed an ingenious technique by which subjects can learn to attend to subtle cues

Cindy and Diego have been trained, using operant conditioning techniques, to leap over hurdles at Sea World.

After five years flat on her back in a hospital, Sue Strong learned to increase her blood pressure to the point where she could sit up. She was aided by biofeedback training.

they were not aware of previously. **Biofeedback training** is a procedure that gives people access to response-produced cues allowing them to know that contingent responses have been made. This access comes from using special apparatus that monitors the responses to be changed and informs people through visual or auditory displays about changes in bodily processes such as muscle contractions, brain waves, temperature, and blood pressure. These bodily reactions are amplified and fed back to the subjects in the form of variations in the intensity of signal lights or sounds. This procedure, pioneered by Neal Miller (1978), has helped individuals to gain control over a variety of nonconscious biological processes.

In one especially creative application of biofeedback, children recovering from polio were helped to strengthen their atrophied muscles.

> *Because their muscles were so weak, the children could not notice any effect when they tried to flex them and became discouraged about even trying. To give them reinforcing feedback, a psychologist first recorded the small amount of electrical activity in these weak muscles, then amplified it with a special apparatus, enough that it could light up an electric bulb. When the bulb was put behind a toy clown's face, the face lit up when a child flexed a muscle. This immediate, external feedback was so rewarding that the children gladly did their exercises—and increased their muscle control. (Cited in Stern & Ray, 1977, p. 36)*

Often the most powerful reinforcers in a biofeedback paradigm are not tangible items, like money or candy, but simply the knowledge of success and the personal pride in knowing "I can do it." Applications of the principles of conditioning in helping people modify their own behavior patterns will be presented in greater detail in later chapters.

When Contingencies Fail

Usually positive and negative reinforcement increase a desired response, and punishment or extinction eliminate an undesired response; but, in rare cases, these contingencies do not work as expected. For example there are times when mentally disturbed children repeatedly mutilate their bodies unless physically restrained. Their behavior resists change by any known reinforcement. In such cases it has been found that if punishment is used first to temporarily suppress the self-destructive behavior, the children will begin to respond to positive reinforcers such as ice cream, cookies, M&Ms, and praise. These reinforcers can then be used to shape desired new responses (Lovaas, 1977).

If punishment is clearly related to a prior response, it is said to be *response contingent.* Such punishment, as we have seen, typically suppresses the prior response; but what happens if punishment is not response contingent, if it has no relationship to one's actions? What is the consequence of getting punished no matter what you do? Apparently, this leads to another situation in which reinforcers will not work. The surprising consequences of this effect came to light in an extensive series of important studies by Martin Seligman, Steven Maier, and their colleagues.

> *In the original study, different groups of dogs went through a two-phase experiment. In Phase One, they received painful, unavoidable shocks which some dogs could escape by learning to press a switch (negative reinforcement). The others continued to receive the shock no matter what they did (noncontingent punishment).*
>
> *In Phase Two, the next day, the dogs were put into a different apparatus, in which escape was possible simply by jumping over a small hurdle. A tone (conditioned*

stimulus) signaled that the shocks were about to start. The subjects that had learned to escape in the earlier situation quickly learned the new response, but those that had gotten the noncontingent punishment rarely did so. Instead, they just sat there, crouching, passively getting shocked. This passive, general response of "giving up" following noncontingent, inescapable shocks was termed ***learned helplessness.*** *(Seligman & Maier, 1967)*

The subjects' impaired performance seemed to include three components: deficits in motivation, deficits in emotion, and deficits in cognition. The animals were slow to initiate known actions that could improve the situation (a motivational effect). They were rigid, listless, apparently frightened, and seemed to "give up" (an emotional effect). They were poor learners in new situations where simple new responding would be reinforced (a cognitive deficit). Even when they were shown how to escape by being dragged over to the safe side a few times, they did not learn to do so on their own (Maier & Seligman, 1976).

Parallels have been drawn between the deficits of learned helpless animals and depressed mental patients (Seligman, 1975). We will explore the usefulness of this animal model of human depression in a later chapter. When applied to humans, additional cognitive factors must be considered that influence a person's interpretation of why his or her responding is ineffective. What attributions are made for one's failures? Are they because of one's lack of ability or low effort? Is one's success attributed to such factors or to "luck"? It is also necessary to determine the importance of a sense of control to an individual in order to predict the consequences of losing that control in a noncontingent punishment situation (Abramson et al., 1978).

Patterns of Reinforcement

Sometimes when you raise your hand in class ready with the correct answer, the teacher calls on you—and sometimes not. The best batters in baseball hit .300 for an entire season, which means that their attempts at hitting succeed three times out of ten and, of course, have a negative consequence the other seven times; but on any given day they might get four hits in four at bats—or none. Some slot machine players continue to put coins in the one-armed-bandits even though they get reinforced for doing so only rarely. The obvious point is that behavior is not always followed by reinforcement, or by punishment, and the relationship between behavior and reinforcement may vary according to a variety of patterns. Behavior is affected by different **patterns of reinforcement** that determine the timing and spacing of consequences. Patterns of reinforcement paired with an operant response are called **schedules of reinforcement,** and **schedules of punishment** when associated with patterns of punishment. Since all reinforcers and punishers are part of some schedule, and schedules determine behavior in characteristic ways, they exert powerful influences on what we do, how we do it, and when.

There is a legendary story about the way the first schedule of reinforcement was accidentally discovered by young B. F. Skinner. It seems that one weekend he was secluded in his laboratory with not enough of a food-reward supply for his hard-working pigeons. He economized by giving them pellets after every two responses rather than after each one. From the pigeons' points of view, half the time they responded they got reinforcers, and half the time they did not. Under this condition of partial, or intermittent, reinforcement, the pigeons still acquired the operant response, although more slowly than usual. The surprise came during extinction training. When the reinforcer was omitted entirely, the animals trained under partial reinforcement continued to respond longer and more vigorously than did the pigeons who had gotten payoffs after every response. Half as many experiences of the response-reinforcer contingency had produced a more durable response!

Partial reinforcement effect is the behavioral principle stating that responses acquired under schedules of partial reinforcement are more resistant to extinction than those acquired with continuous reinforcement. This effect has been found repeatedly in research across many different species (Bitterman, 1975). If you want someone to continue to respond in a particular way even when you are not around to provide reinforcement, be sure that you deliver your reinforcers on a partial schedule before you leave.

However, there is one kind of learning in which resistance to extinction is not adaptive—the avoidance responding known as a phobia. A **phobia** is a maladaptive avoidance response that interferes with normal functioning. Although a phobic person knows that the response is an irrational reaction to a harmless stimulus, the fear and avoidance resist extinction. Phobias are common in about 8 percent of the population; they vary in severity and can be directed toward virtually any stimulus a person can imagine as a psychological threat. They are maintained on a partial reinforcement schedule since avoiding or escaping the phobic stimulus—

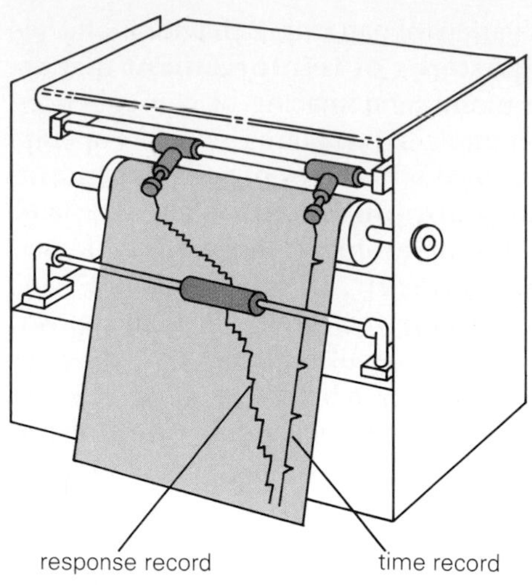

Figure redrawn from "Teaching Machines" by B. F. Skinner. Copyright © 1961 by Scientific American, Inc. All rights reserved.

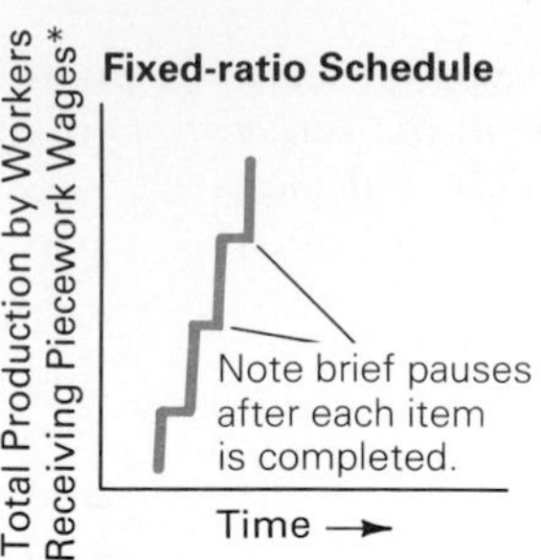

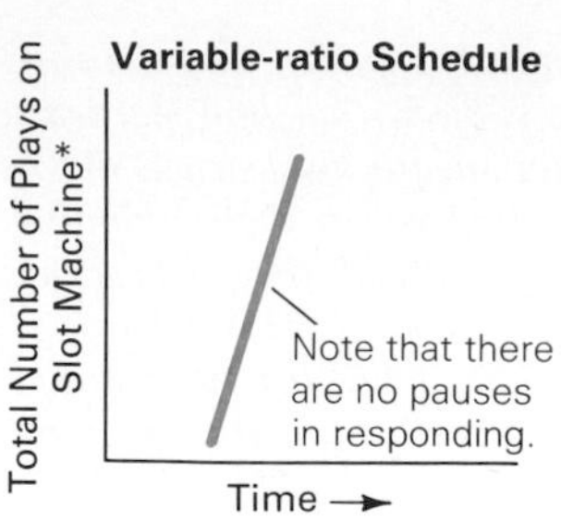

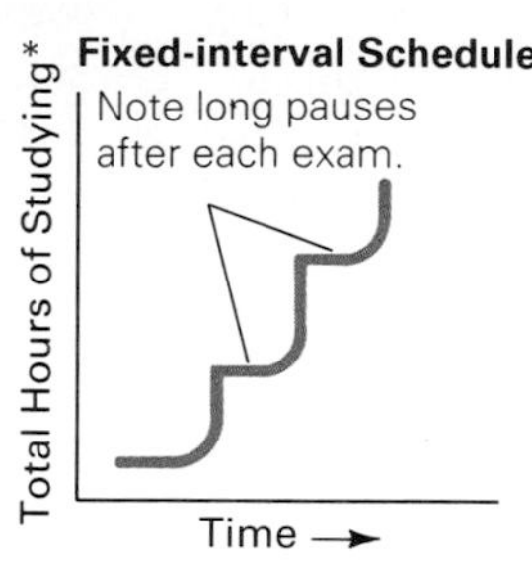

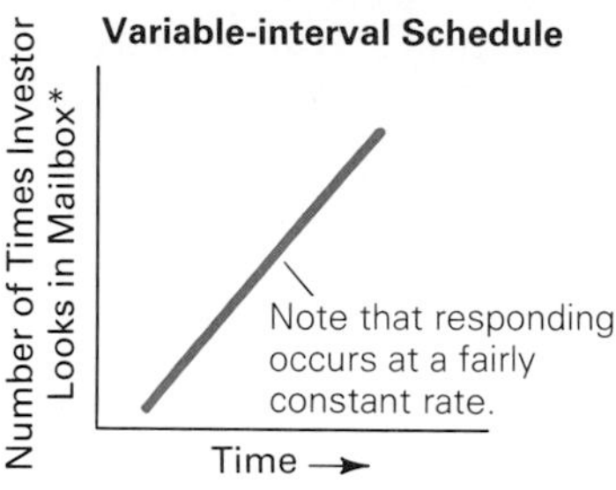

*Cumulative Frequency of Response

Figure 8.6 *Typical Curves for Different Reinforcement Schedules*

Operant responses are recorded on the moving paper of a cumulative recorder (left). The pen moves up each time a response is made; hatch marks indicate when reinforcers are presented. The more responses per time interval, the steeper the line.

Responding is fastest to the ratio schedules, slowest to the variable interval schedule, as shown in these idealized curves (right). The fixed-interval curve shows a "scallop" because the subject stops responding for a time after each reinforcement, then responds rapidly as the time for the next reinforcer approaches. The nearly flat curve shown is obtained by reinforcement of a low rate of responding. These records are characteristic whether the subject is a rat, a pigeon, or a child.

which rarely is encountered—is reinforced by reducing a person's high level of fear.

The discovery of the effectiveness of partial reinforcement led to extensive study of the effects of different reinforcement schedules on human and animal behavior (see **Figure 8.6**). Reinforcers can be given either after a certain number of responses—called a "ratio schedule"—or after a specified interval of time regardless of an organism's rate of response—called an "interval schedule." In each case, there can be either a constant (fixed) pattern of reinforcement or an irregular (variable) one, making four major types of schedules in all. Even when the amount and kind of reinforcement are the same, and deprivation is constant, performance will vary enormously according to the schedule on which reinforcers are given (see Ferster et al., 1975). Let's see the way each schedule affects behavior.

Fixed ratio schedule (FR). In this schedule the reinforcer comes after a fixed number of responses. When it follows one response the schedule is a fixed ratio of one, FR-1. This continuous reinforcement schedule is the most efficient schedule for rapidly acquiring a given response. When the first 24 responses are unreinforced and reinforcement follows only every twenty-fifth response the schedule is a fixed ratio of 25. The rate of responding is high with fixed ratio schedules since a lot of work may be required (sometimes, hundreds of responses) before there is a single payoff. With humans, fixed ratio schedules operate when workers get paid once, only after making or selling a given total number of units, reaching a set quota. The higher the ratio, the more rapid the responding, but the longer the pause after each reinforcement. Stretching the ratio "too thin" by requiring a great many responses before a reinforcement may lead to extinction.

Variable ratio schedule (VR). In this schedule the number of responses required before a reward is delivered varies from one reward period to the next. A VR-10 schedule means that, on the average, reinforcement follows every tenth response; but it might come after only one, or not again until after twenty. Variable-ratio schedules, which keep individuals guessing about the timing of the payoff, generate the highest rate of responding. Gambling behavior is under the control of variable-ratio schedules. The response of dropping coins in slot machines is maintained at a high, steady level by the payoff which comes after an unknown, variable number of coins has been deposited.

Variable ratio schedules resist extinction more than do fixed ratio schedules, especially when the variable ratio is large. A pigeon on a VR-110 schedule will respond with up to 12,000 pecks per hour and will continue responding for hours even with no reinforcement. Gamblers who continue responding with no reinforcement will experience a gradual shift from a VR reinforcement schedule to a VR punishment schedule.

Fixed interval schedule (FI). In this schedule a reward is given for the first response made after a fixed period of time has elapsed. On a FI-10 schedule, the subject, after getting a reinforcer, will have to wait ten seconds before another response is reinforced. Other responses in between, before the time interval is over, are just wasted effort; they do not count toward reinforcement. TV commercials usually are inserted into programs after a fixed period of time, and they have a standard duration. If you hate them, switching channels to escape them is reinforcing, but switching back to your program too soon, say, after 45 seconds when the commercial is on an FI-60 schedule, can be punishing.

FI schedules reveal a typical, but interesting, curve with a "scalloped" form. After each reinforced response, a subject stops relevant responding for a time and does something else. As the time for the next payoff approaches, relevant responding begins again and increases sharply until the reinforcement occurs. Animals on FI schedules learn to discriminate the passage of time between rewards; humans use watches (Church et al., 1976). You can now better appreciate the operant wisdom in the advice: Never buy a product made on Monday by workers paid on Friday.

Variable interval schedule (VI). Life is variable; it doesn't run on fixed schedules—unlike college classes. Many things occur at a given time, with a margin of variation built in (for example, when you figure the average time to commute to school or work). On VI schedules the first response after a variable period of time has elapsed from the last reinforcement gets reinforced. On a VI-10 schedule, reinforcers are delivered for a response that is made ten seconds, *on the average,* after the last reinforced response. Thus there is sometimes a short wait and sometimes a long one between rewards. Nothing can be done to speed them up; responses during these intervals have no consequences. No wonder this schedule generates a low, though stable, rate of response.

Suppose your car-pool driver arrives to pick you up anywhere between 7:45 and 8:15 A.M. If it is cold outside, you will keep running to the window to see if the car is there. Your edgy, window-peeking behavior is under the control of a VI schedule because you are waiting for an unpredictable event. (Recommendation: get an FI driver.)

Extinction under variable interval schedules is gradual and much slower than under fixed interval schedules. Although there is a steady decline in responding without reinforcement, subjects trained with a high variable interval schedule continue to emit responses for a long time. In one such case, a pigeon pecked 18,000 times during the first 4 hours after reinforcement stopped and required 168 hours for extinction (Ferster & Skinner, 1957). This persistence of performance during extinction is one of the most powerful effects of partial reinforcement schedules.

New Developments in Learning Theory

The bulk of research on animal learning has focused on arbitrary responses to stimuli that are conveniently available to a researcher in an artificial laboratory environment. This laboratory approach was adopted purposely by researchers who believed that the laws of learning they uncovered would be powerful general principles of behavior for all organisms and all learning. This strategy is described in the following quote.

> *. . . we arbitrarily choose almost any act from the animal's repertoire and reinforce it with food, water, or whatever else the animal will work to obtain. Although typically we teach a rat to press a bar or a pigeon to peck a key to obtain a pellet of food, we can readily train either to dance around the cage if we so choose. We usually use a light to signal the delivery of a pellet, but we can use a tone or a buzzer or any other stimulus the animal can detect. . . . The same act can be used for any reinforcement. . . . In effect, in any operant situation, the stimulus, the response, and the reinforcement are completely arbitrary and interchangeable. No one of them bears any biological built-in fixed connection to the others. (Teitelbaum, 1966, pp. 566–67)*

The appealing simplicity of such a view has come under attack recently as psychologists have discovered certain constraints on this hoped-for generality of their findings. Some limits are imposed by the biological makeup of the organism and the environmental habitats to which particular species normally must adapt. Other limits are imposed because human learners think, reason, interpret, and attribute meaning and causality to stimulus events and to behavior. The operation of these cognitive processes serves to make conditioning less mechanical and more flexible than originally believed—and makes possible more complex kinds of learning than those envisioned in the simpler paradigms of classical and operant conditioning.

Biological Constraints on Learning

Over generations, organisms that have survived the particular challenges their species faced have passed on their genetic capacities to later members of the species. In order to fit a given ecological niche, each species must develop certain behavioral repertoires that aid survival. For instance, birds living on steep cliffs have to make nests so that their eggs won't roll out; those that make the wrong kind of nests fail to pass on their genes. Some animals develop particular sense modalities (eagles have superior vision and bats have excellent hearing); others develop special response capabilities, such as speed or strength. This, in turn, means that different species may have different capabilities for learning in a given situation. Some stimulus-response pairings may be more difficult to learn than others, depending on their relevance to survival for that species.

A **biological constraint on learning** is any limitation on an organism's capacity to learn that is caused by the inherited sensory, response, or cognitive capabilities of members of a given species. It is important to note that biological constraints challenge two assumptions of traditional learning theory: (a) the universal application of principles of conditioning to all species, across all situations, and (b) the power of behavioral contingencies to result in learning even when a stimulus, response, or reinforcer is arbitrarily designated by an experimenter, trainer, or teacher. This means that the laws of learning are neither universal nor even very general if they must take into account the natural environments of different species and their genetic makeup. In what sense can it be shown that behavior-environment relations are *biased* by an organism's genetically determined character? (See also "The Instinct to Learn" in *The Best of Science.*)

Species-specific Behavior

You have no doubt seen animals performing tricks on television, in the circus, or at zoos or fairs. Some play baseball or ping pong; others drive tiny race cars. For years, two psychologists, Keller and Marion Breland, had used conditioning techniques to train thousands of animals from many different species to perform a remarkable array of these learned behaviors. For some time, they had believed that general principles derived from laboratory research, using virtually any type of response or reward, could be directly applied to the control of animal behavior outside the laboratory—until some of their animals began to "misbehave." For example, a raccoon was conditioned, after great difficulty, to pick up a coin and put it into a toy bank. The problem was that the raccoon would not let go of the coin without holding it a while. Later, when there were two coins to be deposited, the conditioning broke down because the raccoon would not give them up at all. Instead the animal would rub them together, dip them into the bank, and then pull them back out. The behavior seems weird until you learn that raccoons often engage in rubbing and washing behaviors when they remove the outer shells of a favorite food, crayfish. Likewise, when pigs were given the task of putting their hard-earned tokens into a large piggy bank, they instead would drop the coins, root (poke at) them along with their snouts, toss them up in the air, root them again, and so on. Strange beasties? Hardly. Pigs root and shake as part of their inherited food-getting repertoire.

The Brelands' experience convinced them that even when animals have learned to make conditioned responses perfectly, the "learned behavior drifts toward instinctual behavior" over time. They termed this tendency **instinctual drift** (Breland & Breland, 1951, 1961). Animals tended increasingly to "do their own species thing" instead of doing what would get them food in an artificial situation. The examples of animal "misbehavior" are not explainable by operant conditioning principles. They are understandable, however, if we add notions of biological constraints imposed by species-specific repertoires—unlearned behaviors common to all members of a given species. A pig can learn, by experience, that a token is valuable when the token is *paired with* food in a classical conditioning paradigm; but then the token is treated as if it *were* food—and the way a pig treats food is to root it about with its snout. Doing so is incompatible with the operant conditioning task of putting the token in a piggy bank. Thus what we are seeing in these

Even when animals have learned to make conditioned responses perfectly, the "learned behavior will drift toward instinctual behavior" over time.

misbehaviors is the embedding of classical conditioning (with natural, biologically significant S-S relationships) in an operant conditioning procedure designed to teach new contingencies between responses-tokens-food. The intrusion of competing contingencies occurs when an animal deals with the token (CS) the way it normally deals with food (US)—and not simply as a conditioned reinforcer for the preceding operant response.

To demonstrate that operant conditioning principles hold even for pigs, what change might you suggest to the animal trainer? If the token were paired with a water reward for a thirsty pig, it would then not be rooted like food, but deposited in the bank as a valuable commodity—dare we say, a *liquid asset?*

Taste Aversion Learning

Experience teaches us many lessons so that what was true in the past is used to understand the present. If you get sick some time after eating in the school cafeteria, you will likely attribute your reaction to something you ate rather than to the people present or the decor. You are *biased* in forming an association between illness and a small class of likely causes because of past learning experiences. But some biases do not depend on past experience; they are built into an organism by nature, not by nurture.

Taste aversion learning represents a clear instance of a natural bias. For example, studies of taste aversion seem to violate usual principles of conditioning, but make sense when viewed as part of a species' adaptiveness to its natural environment. In this case, a rat eats a food that is poisoned, and many hours later it becomes ill, but survives. After only this one aversive experience and despite the long interval (up to 12 hours) between tasting the food (CS) and the poisoned-based illness (US), the rat learns to avoid the specific flavor of the poisoned food. There is no principle in classical conditioning that can handle these two facts of one-trial learning and such a long interstimulus interval. Interestingly enough, other stimuli present at the same time are not avoided later—only the taste stimuli.

For example, when experimental rats licked a tube containing a flavored solution a light flashed and a sound clicked. Some of them received painful shocks to their feet, others got a dose of poison that produced radiation-induced sickness. Later on when tested for their drinking behavior at the tube with only the light and noise stimuli present, the previously shocked rats licked less of the "bright, noisy water," but the previously poisoned rats drank the same amount as before. However, on the test day when licking the tube produced the flavored solution, the shocked rats licked away, but the once-poisoned rats avoided that flavored water. See ***Figure 8.7.*** *(Garcia & Koelling, 1966)*

Figure 8.7 *Taste Aversion Learning*

Whenever rats licked a tube containing a flavored solution, a light flashed and a click sounded. Rats in one group were shocked; those in another group were fed a poison which made them sick. Later the light and noise stimuli were separated from the flavor stimuli. Licks at the tube produced light and sound, but the rats received plain water rather than the flavored solution. In this condition, the previously poisoned rats drank the same amount as before, but the previously shocked rats consumed less. However, when licking again produced the flavored solution (and no light or sound), the previously poisoned rats licked less, but the previously poisoned rats continued licking as before.

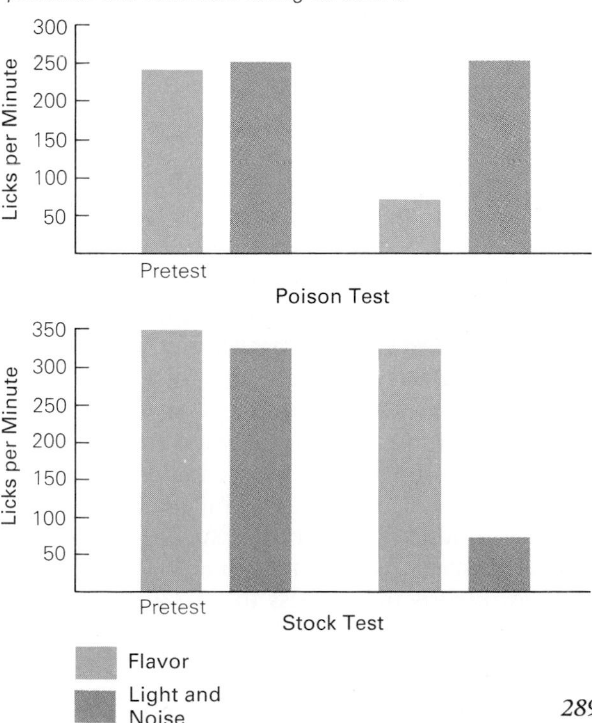

Even without conditioning, many animals show *bait shyness,* an unlearned reluctance to sample new food or food in a strange environment. Of all the stimuli available to them, animals seem to use the sensory cues that are most adaptive in their natural environments. Rats forage for food at night and have relatively poor vision; thus they have developed an ability to learn to avoid poisonous substances by their smells and tastes rather than by their appearances. By contrast, birds that have superior vision rely on it while foraging for food and drink during flight. For example, blue jays are known to reject, on sight, toxic monarch butterflies. These species differences are nicely demonstrated in the following studies.

When rats and bobwhite quail were both given blue salty water that made them ill and later were given a choice between salty water and blue water, the rats avoided the salty water while the quail avoided the blue water. (Wilcoxon et al., 1971)

In another study using rats as subjects, a bright stimulus was a better conditioned stimulus for danger than a dim or dark one, perhaps because darkness is associated with safety for rats in the wild. (Welker & Wheatley, 1977)

Conditioning, then, depends not only on the pairing of any stimuli and responses, as was long thought, but also, in part, on the way an organism is genetically predisposed toward the particular features of the stimuli and responses to be associated (see Barker et al., 1978). What any organism can and cannot readily learn in a given setting is as much a product of its evolutionary history as it is the arrangement of optimal stimulus pairings and behavioral contingencies. The study of organisms' behavior in their natural habitat and the characteristic ways their learning is biologically based is the task of **ethologists,** who discover what organisms do in using their genetic endowments to adapt to environmental challenges.

Paradoxically, acknowledging these biological effects on conditioning is leading us to a richer, more comprehensive view of the learning process. It also leads some psychologists to argue for a new definition of learning that takes account of: (a) forgetting (learning is not necessarily permanent); (b) changes in stimulus effectiveness (learning is not always a change in behavior); and (c) one-trial learning (learning does not always demand practice). Toward this end a proposed alternative definition of learning that focuses on the process and not the products of learning, such as habits or skills, is given by Sheldon Lachman (1983). In his view *learning* is the process that results in a relatively stable modification in stimulus-response relations as a consequence of an organism's interaction with the environment by means of its senses. Think about whether and how this definition improves the original definition.

The psychology of learning has also become more interesting and comprehensive by recognizing the role of cognitive variables, a few of which we shall consider next. A full analysis of cognitive factors will be given in chapters 9 and 10.

Cognitive Influences on Learning

Despite Skinner's insistence on building a psychology of learning based solely on observable events, cognitive—thought—processes are significant in many kinds of learning—in animals as well as humans. Some of these processes that enrich the learning tradition are those that point up the importance of the informational value of stimuli to the organism and the learner's expectations, as shown in studies of blocking and sensory preconditioning (see Rescorla, 1980). Others involve learning not by reinforcing the learner's direct actions but rather learning by passively observing models and by rules.

Blocking

In natural situations where learning enables organisms to adapt to changes in their environment, stimuli come in clusters and not in neat, simple units as in traditional laboratory experiments. It becomes essential to detect which stimuli are relevant for signaling rewards and dangers and which are not. Organisms use as their guideposts the stimuli that are most *informative.* What makes a stimulus informative? First, a stimulus that is more intense or more salient (noticeable) will *overshadow* one that is also a predictive signal (Mackintosh, 1975). Second, from past experience an individual learns which of a set of competing stimuli are *redundant*—carry no additional information—and which are not redundant, but information rich. This second kind of overshadowing resulting from prior experience is called **blocking,** and it reflects the significance of informativeness in conditioning.

In a typical study of blocking, a conditioned response is established by pairing a tone with an unconditioned stimulus—a shock—in Phase One. In Phase Two, a *compound* stimulus—tone plus light—is paired repeatedly with the shock. According to traditional conditioning theory, the light should now also become a conditioned stimulus, but this does not happen. The ability of the new stimulus to

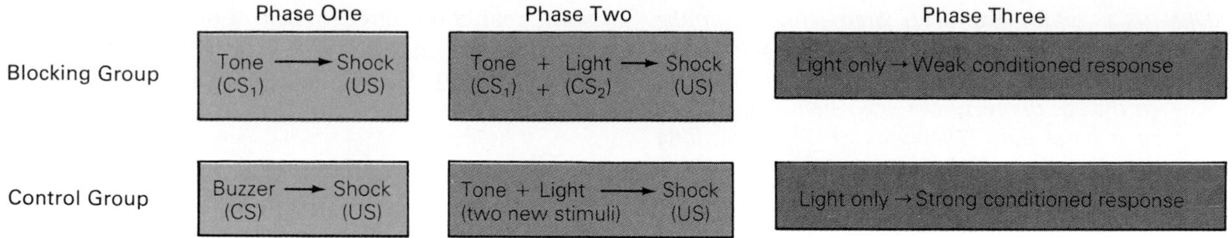

Figure 8.8 *The Blocking Paradigm*
In Phase One, subjects of both groups learn a conditioned response—one to a tone and other to a buzzer. In Phase Two, both groups are presented with tone plus light, followed by shock. The light provides no new information to the blocking group subjects and is ignored, but the control group subjects learn a new conditioned response to tone-plus-light. *In Phase Three, when the light is presented alone, the blocking-group subjects respond only weakly, showing that no association between light and shock was formed in Phase Two. The control group subjects, however, respond strongly, demonstrating the existence of the conditioned association.*

signal the unconditioned stimulus is not learned when it is presented in a compound with a stimulus that is already effective as a signal (Kamin, 1969). There is no conditioning to the light, because it provides no additional information beyond that already given by the tone (see **Figure 8.8**).

This cognitive explanation postulates intervening processes of assessing the informational value of a stimulus, assessments which then influence learning. Leon Kamin argues that conditioning occurs only when the powerful stimulus comes as a *surprise* to an organism. In this view, when an organism is surprised by a powerful stimulus, it scans its memory for a recent stimulus event that might be associated with it. If it finds such a stimulus, conditioning takes place. However once a conditioned stimulus is acting as a signal, another stimulus added to it will not motivate a memory search later because the unconditioned stimulus (for example, the shock in the previous example) has not been a surprise; so further conditioning will not occur. With humans the equivalent process is actively seeking events that might be the cause of a significant effect—often in order to attribute blame or credit to them, depending on the value of their effect to the person.

Are you somewhat puzzled at this point? What's the difference between blocking and second-order conditioning (which we discussed on page 268)? They seem similar, but have exactly the opposite results. Not so. The difference is in a key, though subtle, distinction: in second-order conditioning, the CS_2 is a *signal* for the CS_1 (which had been previously paired with the US), while, in blocking, both conditioned stimuli occur together as a pair. Thus one of them is redundant—it carries no extra news about the coming event of US. In some cases the two processes may co-occur, but we still see blocking in spite of whatever second-order conditioning may result.

A second puzzlement may present itself here, too. Earlier you were told that predictability of events was important, but now you are being told that surprise is also an important element. This apparent contradiction, which you no doubt already detected, is resolved when you realize the way in which each is important. The power of surprise promotes the initial learning about an important signal and its relation to a coming event of importance. This learned recognition of the signal then makes possible prediction of the event before it happens—a very useful ability. What the blocking studies show is that once an individual expects the unconditioned stimulus on the basis of one dependable signal, the individual does not bother to learn about other stimuli that are also consistently present, presumably because their information is redundant. This is an economical use of an organism's cognitive capacity. The power of any particular stimulus to become a signal depends on the presence of other stimuli that could serve as signals (Rudy & Wagner, 1975).

Sensory Preconditioning

Another case where experimental findings seem to require a cognitive interpretation is one in which learning occurs in places it would not be expected.

In a demonstration of this phenomenon, two neutral stimuli—such as a tone and a light—are paired in Phase One and elicit no overt response. No surprise so far: they have nothing of significance to predict. Then, in Phase Two, the tone (CS_1) is paired with a powerful unconditioned stimulus, such as shock, and a conditioned response develops. Finally in Phase Three, the *light (CS_2), which has never been paired with the shock, is presented alone. Voilà! It, too, elicits the conditioned response! CS_2 has become a predictive signal for US even though the two have never been paired—not even on a blind date (Thompson, 1972). Something must have been learned during Phase One, but what?*

In **sensory preconditioning** an association is learned between the *sensory qualities* of two paired stimuli prior to any pairing with an unconditioned stimulus. However, it is "behaviorally silent," a latent learning that does not show up till later (Dickinson, 1980). This behaviorally silent association is revealed by the revaluation of the light. At first glance, sensory preconditioning seems similar to second-order conditioning; but there is one big difference: the reversal of Phases One and Two. In second-order conditioning, a second neutral stimulus (CS_2) becomes a signal for an already conditioned stimulus (CS_1), thereby acquiring the power to elicit the conditioned response. The preconditioning effect is weaker, but still reveals that sensory stimuli are being associated with each other even prior to the role of either one as a predictor of significant events like food or shock. **Figure 8.9** compares the three phenomena of blocking, sensory preconditioning, and second-order conditioning. We learn from studying these processes that *information* is a major determinant of conditioning through the predictive value it confers on stimuli. The more informative a stimulus is in predicting reinforcement or punishment, the more power it will have as a conditioned reinforcer ("I've got some real good news for you") or as a conditioned punisher ("I hate to be the bearer of bad tidings, but disaster is on the way and to make matters worse . . . .").

Observational Learning

If important stimuli carry information for us, then we had better be able to do two things: pay attention to them and decode their information. Observational responses can be made through any sense modality, not just vision, and are reinforced by the information obtained. When are you most likely to make observing rather than action responses? Unless you enjoy risk-taking, chances are that you "look before you leap" into new situations and at times of uncertainty. Recognizing the right cues enables you to behave with the "right stuff," avoiding embarrassment and achieving your objective at your first formal dance, on your first day in a seminar, or when you are playing fast sports.

Much social learning occurs in situations where learning would not be predicted by conditioning theory, because a learner has made no active response and has received no tangible reinforcer. The individual has simply watched another person doing something that was reinforced or punished—and later did exactly the same thing or refrained from doing so. **Observational learning** is the type of learning that occurs when one person uses the observations of another person's actions and their consequences to later guide his or her actions. It is learning to do new things by observing how

Figure 8.9 *Comparison of Blocking, Second-Order Conditioning, and Sensory Preconditioning*
The effect of pairing two neutral stimuli, such as a light and a tone, depends on what precedes, accompanies, and follows this pairing: (1) pairing two stimuli with shock after *conditioning one stimulus to shock → **blocking** of the other; (2) pairing two stimuli without shock* after *conditioning one stimulus to shock → **second-order conditioning;** (3) pairing two stimuli without shock* before *conditioning one stimulus with shock → **sensory preconditioning** to the second stimulus.*

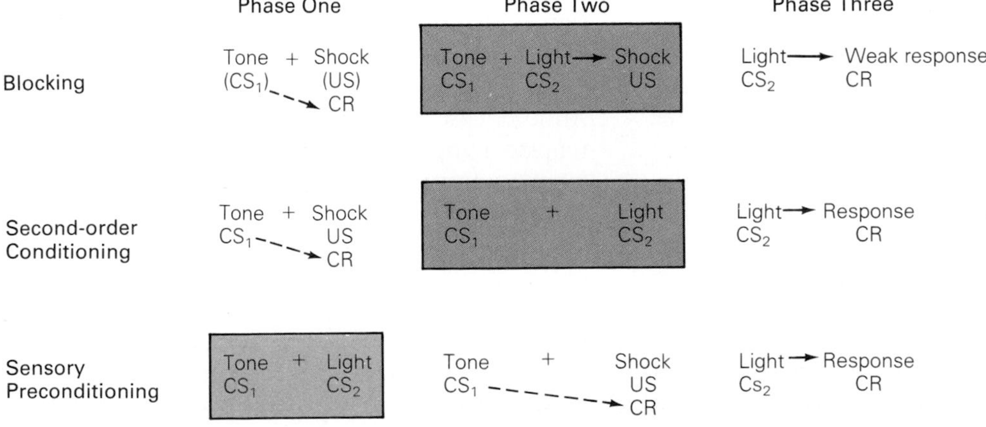

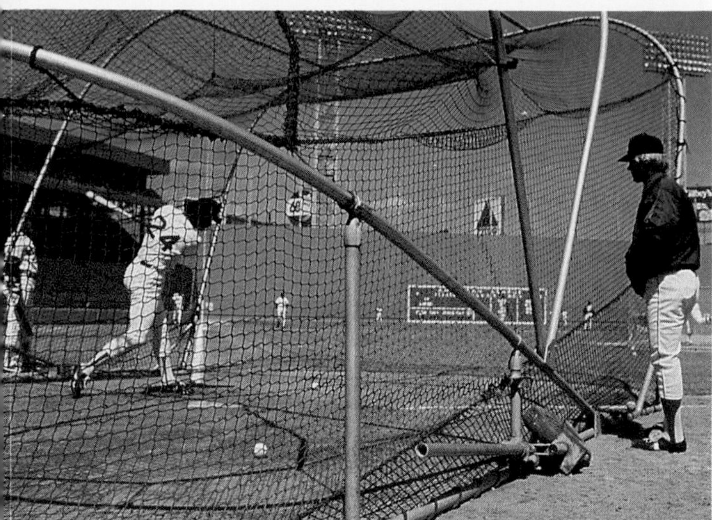

By watching batting practice, ballplayers can use their observations to improve their own performances.

particular models do them and then imitating the behavior of those models.

The classic demonstration of this kind of observational learning occurred in the laboratory of Albert Bandura. After watching adult models punching, hitting, and kicking a large plastic ''BoBo'' doll, the children in the experiment later showed a greater frequency of the same behaviors than did children in control conditions who had not observed the aggressive models. (Bandura et al., 1963)

Subsequent studies showed that children imitated such behaviors just from watching film sequences of models, even cartoon characters. As you might expect, given these findings, and the great amount of time most of us spend watching TV, much psychological research has been directed at assessing the behavioral impact that TV's modeled behavior has on viewers (see Huston, 1985; Milavsky et al., 1982; Williams, 1986).

There is little question now that we learn much through observation of models, both prosocial (helping) and antisocial (hurting) behaviors; but what variables are important in determining which models will be most likely to influence us? Although this is a complex issue to resolve, methodologically isolating the impact of observational learning from all other possible causal events, the following general conclusions appear warranted (see Baldwin & Baldwin, 1986; Bandura, 1977a). A model's observed behavior will be most influential when: (a) it is seen as having reinforcing consequences; (b) the model is perceived positively, of high status, liked, respected; (c) there are perceived similarities between features and traits of the model and the observer; (d) the observer is reinforced for paying attention to the model's behavior (a sleeping student gathers moss, but none of the lecturer's information); (e) the model's behavior is visible and salient—stands out as a clear figure against the background of competing models; and (f) it is within the observer's range of competence to enact the behavior. Having acquired the knowledge, it is more likely to be performed under circumstances where the context cues (S^D or S^Δ) are perceived as comparable to those in the original learning situation, reinforcement for imitation seems probable, and the observer is motivated to achieve an objective or desired goal for which the learned behavior becomes a means.

The capacity to learn from watching, as well as from doing, is extremely useful. It enables us to acquire large, integrated patterns of behavior without going through the tedious process of gradually eliminating wrong responses and building up the right ones through trial-and-error. It enables us to profit from the mistakes and successes of others. How to recognize snakes, mushrooms, or ivy that are poisonous or how to protect our eyes during a solar eclipse are examples of lessons better learned through observation than personal experience.

Mass Media Models May Make You Break Bones

Because of the high level of violence in American society, there is concern over the possible contributing role of televised violence. Does exposure to acts of violence—murder, rape, assault, robbery, terrorism, and suicide—increase the probability that viewers will imitate them? The conclusion from psychological research is—yes, it does for some people (Milavsky et al., 1982; National Institutes of Mental Health Report, 1982). The two major effects found in controlled laboratory studies on viewing filmed violence are a reduction in emotional arousal and distress at viewing violence, called "psychic numbing," and an increase in the likelihood of engaging in aggressive behavior (Murray & Kippax, 1979).

In the natural environment outside the laboratory the same effects of violence modeling also occur. When heavy-weight prize fights are given a great amount of media coverage homicides increase by 12 percent and are directed at the type of person who *lost* the fight—for example, against whites if a white boxer were defeated and against blacks if a black boxer were defeated. However homicides decrease in number following media coverage of highly publicized executions, according to data collected for more than 60 years in England. Perhaps most startling is the link between publicized suicides and the subsequent rise in suicides in the general population—as well as the increase of about 9 percent in deaths from single-vehicle "accidents" (Phillips, 1974). Within two months after a front-page suicide story, 58 more people than usual had committed suicide. In these cases the age and often sex of the driver matches that of the public figure who committed suicide (Phillips, 1983, 1985). Within a week of six teenagers committing suicide in a "suicide pact" in New Jersey and also in suburban Chicago, four separate teenage "imitation" suicides were reported. All killed themselves by the same method—carbon monoxide intoxication from inhaling auto exhaust in closed garages. Police found newspaper clippings of the earlier suicides under the mattress of one of the young suicide imitators ("More Apparent Teen Suicides," 1987).

Going beyond statistics to the lives and deaths of real people, we realize the tragic consequences possible when some of us mislearn a media message. Four Malaysian children, wearing Superman T-shirts, plunged to their deaths, apparently believing that they could fly like their TV hero (Reuters, 1982). In another incident, a 12-year-old boy sexually assaulted a 10-year-old girl on a pool table while other children watched, in a reenactment of a barroom rape described in a trial shown on TV (Associated Press, 1984). And recently, a number of Japanese female teenagers committed suicide by jumping out of buildings to their deaths—imitating the suicide of a female teenage rock star ("Five More Teenagers," 1986).

Rule Learning

"Smoking may be dangerous to your health. Do not smoke." "To reduce the risk of AIDS, practice safe sex." These are just two of a host of rules in our lives that attempt to influence our behavior. Information from watching models may help us to learn many things faster or better, but verbal instructions can serve as rules that guide our actions in a wider variety of situations, especially those we have never personally observed. **Rules** are behavioral guidelines for the way to act in certain situations, verbally encoded as instructions, suggestions, commands, hints, and other forms such as proverbs, morality tales, and of course the rules of etiquette. **Rule learning** involves recognizing the behavioral implications of rules, the contexts in which they are relevant, and the perception of reinforcing contingencies for obeying or violating them. It is through rules that a society passes along its accumulated wisdom—and prejudices—to future generations to help its new members cope better and behave "appropriately" to gain rewards and avoid punishment. The most powerful rules, however, are those that are internalized as "my own rules," self-instructions on what *you* can and can't do, where, when, and how. Attempts to change negative behavior patterns of ineffective, unassertive, shy, or neurotic individuals often involve teaching them to modify the pattern of self-limiting rules they impose on themselves (Martin & Pear, 1983).

What Is Learned in Conditioning?

In experimental studies of conditioning, a psychologist is interested in what factors affect learning and performance. The learning organism, typically, has no interest in the measurements the psychologist is making, but copes the best it can with what may be a very artificial and constraining environment. It meets its needs by using a variety of resources and skills, including its ability to learn associations between stimuli and associations between responses and their consequences. It also seems to learn much more.

Until recently, it was assumed that an individual played a passive role in conditioning, with associations formed and strengthened automatically by the reinforced pairing of stimulus events and behavior manipulated predictably by environmental events. What was learned was assumed to be fixed associations and specific responses. However evidence has been accumulating that what is learned is neither so automatic nor so specific. The examples of blocking and sensory preconditioning cited in the previous section, as well as the findings on observational learning, are indications that something important is happening in the mind of the learner between stimulus input and behavioral output.

Actions—and Information

Earlier in the chapter a distinction was made between the covert process of learning and the overt performance that reveals it. We have also seen several cases in which behavior did not accurately reflect what the learners "knew." Organisms seem able to express or withhold what they know on different occasions and even to weigh likely payoffs against likely costs. They show a flexibility and appropriateness of responding that would not be possible if they had learned only specific responses and had only fixed associations with which to work.

The importance of cognitive processes in stimulus-response learning was demonstrated many years ago by psychologist Edward Tolman. He accepted the behaviorists' idea that psychologists must study observable behavior, but he created many situations in which mechanical, one-to-one associations between specific stimuli and responses could not explain the behavior that was observed. Rather, Tolman (1948) claimed that what was being learned had to be something more like a **cognitive map,** an inner representation of the learning situation as a whole, and an *expectancy* about what the results of different actions would be, rather than merely a specific path that had led to goals in the past.

To show that animals, like humans, are capable of learning more than just a fixed response stamped in by being reinforced, Tolman and his students performed a series of studies on "place learning." They were able to demonstrate that when an original goal-path is blocked, an animal will take the shortest detour around the barrier even though that particular response was never previously reinforced (Tolman & Honzig, 1930). **Figure 8.10** shows the arrangement of one of these mazes. Rats seem to be reading their cognitive maps rather than blindly following habits previously elicited by particular stimuli in the setting.

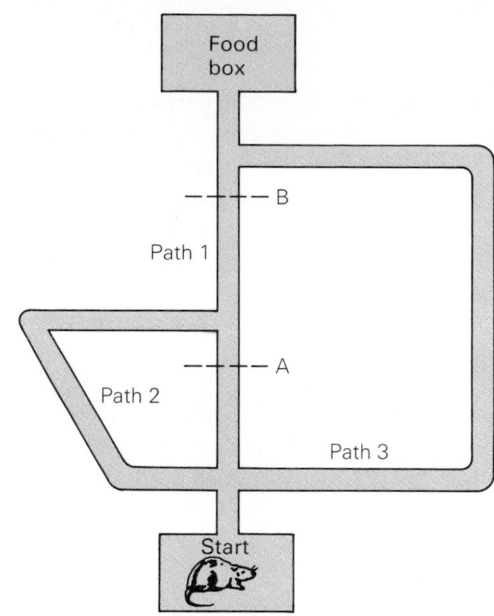

Figure 8.10

Example of a maze used to study place learning with rats. Subjects preferred Path 1 when it was open. With a block at A, they preferred Path 2. When a block was placed at B, the rats usually chose the longer Path 3, normally the least preferred one, as though they had a cognitive map and realized that Path 2 would be closed too. (Adapted from Tolman & Honzik, 1930)

Recent experiments on cognitive maps in rats, chimpanzees, and humans have confirmed Tolman's earlier findings (Menzel, 1978; Moar, 1980; Olton, 1979). Organisms learn the general layout of their environment by exploration, even if they are not reinforced for learning particular paths. In fact, when foraging animals have found food in one spot, they are more likely to seek it elsewhere and *not* return to the same place for a while.

These findings, taken together, show that conditioning is neither blind nor simple. Besides the formation of an association between particular stimuli or between a response and a reinforcer, conditioning seems to include also the learning of expectancies, predictions, and evaluations of information—cognitive factors—and also learning about other complex aspects of the total *behavioral context* (see Balsam & Tomie, 1985).

Associations—and Generalizations

Learning rules from observing models and learning to be helpless after inescapable shock are but two examples in which general reaction strategies, as well as specific stimulus associations and stimulus-response pairings, were learned. In the observational learning studies, children learned particular behaviors, general rules, and the way to recognize the usefulness of their rules so that they could apply them in situations with new elements. (This last principle is especially true of learning grammatical rules for one's native language.) The helpless dogs learned to be passive and accept noncontingent shocks, and also learned a generalized inhibition against taking action in new situations. As we learn particular responses, we are also making generalizations—about comparable stimulus situations, about our capability to meet life's requirements, and about our expectations of the other actors in the situation. We interpret, compare, contrast, give meaning to, and integrate the environmental challenges we meet and our responses to them; and we create symbols that go beyond anything we have experienced. From our encounters with the environment we learn particular associations—but build upon them to develop a broad foundation of knowledge.

Rote Responses—and Insight

Based on his experiments with cats, Thorndike believed that all learning depended on blind trial-and-error. His conclusion supported educational practices of the time, which emphasized rote practice and were not concerned with what learners might be perceiving and understanding. A young German psychologist, Wolfgang Köhler, waiting out World War I on Tenerife Island off the coast of Africa, challenged this blind trial-and-error, associationist view of learning. He pointed out that, although the cats could only have escaped by the means they used, many puzzles in real life have meaningful internal relationships providing clues to the responses that are appropriate. Sometimes these puzzles require putting known facts together in new ways; sometimes they enable one to formulate hypotheses to test, or work out new theories that make sense of partial knowledge.

> *Since chimpanzees were available on the island, Köhler used them as subjects in a new line of research on insightful problem solving. He put them in enclosed areas where tasty morsels were in sight but out of reach—suspended high up or placed a few feet outside the enclosure—and watched what happened. Typically, his subjects would try unsuccessfully to reach the food directly and then would stop and survey the situation. After a period, often suddenly, they would try a new approach based on a novel way of using the objects at hand. They would drag a box under the fruit and climb onto it to reach the prize; later, when the fruit was hung higher, they reached it by piling boxes on top of each other. They would get the food placed outside the enclosure by raking it in with a stick or—later—by using the short, accessible stick to rake in a longer stick that could do the job or even by fitting two sticks together. (Köhler, 1925)*

Köhler concluded that whether an organism will solve a problem by gradual, blind trial-and-error or by **insight**—a sudden understanding of the relationships of elements in the situation for the solution to a particular goal—will depend on: (a) whether there are internal relationships in the problem that can be discovered, and (b) whether they are within the cognitive capacity of the organism. Even if the latch in Thorndike's puzzle boxes had not been out of sight, the cats might not have had the ability to understand its mechanism by looking at it. Other research on problem solving will be presented in chapter 11.

Conditioning in the laboratory provides little opportunity for subjects to make much use of the full range of their higher cognitive processes; but, even there, the subject is clearly an active processor of information, scanning its environment for significant events, storing in memory many features encountered in its experience, integrating and organizing this stored information in useful ways, and drawing on appropriate parts of it to decide on the best response in the current situation. In this cognitive view, changes in behavior are viewed as manifestations of cognitive processes.

In the past two decades there has been a significant shift among psychologists toward this cognitive approach to learning. In subsequent chapters, we will see how it has guided our study of memory and thinking. At the same time there has been an increased recognition of the significance of evolutionary and neurological processes in learning (see Garcia & Garcia y Robertson, 1985; McGaugh et al., 1985; Thompson, 1986). Despite such widening of focus, there is still much research going on in the associationist tradition, many learning theory applications in the environment of everyday society (called LTE), and considerable use of the behavioral paradigm for studying many processes in addition to learning. Of the utility of learning theory in our lives, a recent review concludes:

> *It is clear that illustrations of the application of LTE in almost all aspects of American society abound. There are now a growing number of fields that by their use of the* behavioral *label (for example, behavioral medicine, behavioral pediatrics, behavioral geriatrics, behavioral ecology, and behavioral community psychology) indicate their LTE allegiance. LTE has been applied in homes, sports arenas, businesses, supermarkets, industries of every type, transit systems, television, all levels of school systems, and, of course, various mental health settings. (Krasner, 1985)*

An initially baffled pigeon uses a box to finally get to an out-of-reach banana.

Conditioning Procedures as Tools for Research and Application

The final point to be made in this chapter is to note how the conditioning paradigm and methodology have become standard tools used routinely by many different kinds of researchers to investigate a broad range of topics. The following summarizes the uses of these two tools as:

1. tools for studying the learning capacities of a species by defining the variables and conditions that favor or disfavor learning, and using these data to infer what a particular type of organism is capable of learning;
2. tools for studying the memory capacities of a species by assessing performance on recognition tasks and other behavioral tests;
3. tools for determining the sensory and perceptual capacities of a species through discrimination learning tasks;
4. tools for getting animals, infants, and people without language to tell us what they know when such knowledge is otherwise "behaviorally silent," through the use of sensory preconditioning tasks and studies of habituation and dishabituation; and
5. tools being developed by neuroscientists for uncovering the relationships between brain structure, brain function, and the facts of behavior.

Some of these methodological contributions of behavior analysis have been described in previous chapters; the others will be explained in detail in coming chapters.

Summary

- Psychologists define learning as a relatively permanent change in behavior or behavioral potential based on experience. When psychology split off from philosophy, two assumptions it took along were that learning occurs through the association of ideas (law of association) and that all organisms are motivated to seek pleasure and avoid pain (principle of adaptive hedonism).
- Two procedures for investigating learning widely adopted by psychologists are classical conditioning and instrumental conditioning. They provide means of experimentally studying associative learning.
- Classical conditioning, developed by Pavlov, is a procedure to study the way organisms learn about relationships between events in their environment. In the classical conditioning paradigm, a biologically significant stimulus, called an unconditioned stimulus (US), elicits a reflex, called an unconditioned response (UR). A neutral stimulus that is then paired repeatedly with the unconditioned stimulus becomes a conditioned stimulus (CS), a stimulus capable of eliciting a similar response. This response, elicited by a conditioned stimulus, is called a conditioned response (CR).
- If, after training, the unconditioned stimulus is no longer presented with the conditioned stimulus, the conditioned response disappears. This is called extinction. After a rest period, however, conditioned responding partially returns when the conditioned stimulus is presented alone again. This is called spontaneous recovery.
- Stimuli similar to the conditioned stimulus also elicit a conditioned response (stimulus generalization). If, however, they are not followed by the unconditioned stimulus, stimulus discrimination occurs: the organism stops responding to the irrelevant stimuli and responds only to those associated with reinforcement.
- Instrumental conditioning procedures, developed by Thorndike, involve arranging relationships between a stimulus situation and responses to it that get reinforced. In this S-R approach, learning is instrumental to getting desired outcomes and the successful response is repeated.
- The operant conditioning paradigm, developed by Skinner, is an arrangement to study the effects of various reinforcement contingencies on emitted behaviors. Emitted behaviors are also called operants because they operate on—change—the environment. Partial, or intermittent, reinforcement leads to greater resistance to extinction when reinforcement is withheld.
- Both positive and negative reinforcement increase the rate of responding, Negative reinforcement is the condition of not receiving (or escaping) an aversive stimulus. Extinction and punishment decrease the rate of responding. In extinction training, reinforcement is withheld and response rate declines. Punishment involves receiving an aversive stimulus after a response; it may eliminate or temporarily suppress the response. The effects of punishment on learning and performance in humans are complex and depend on many variables.

- Discriminative stimuli inform subjects when a particular reinforcement contingency is in effect. Responding is said to be under stimulus control when the response is made in the presence of a particular stimulus but not in its absence. The discriminative stimulus does not elicit the response but simply signals that reinforcement will be available if the response is made.
- Primary reinforcers are biologically important stimuli that function as reinforcers without learning. Conditioned reinforcers are learned; for humans they include money, praise, and symbols of status.
- New complex responses may be learned by shaping or chaining procedures. A desired response may be shaped through successive reinforcement of closer approximations of the desired response. A chain of responses may be taught by making completion of each link a conditioned reinforcer for the response that comes before it and a discriminative stimulus for the next one in the chain.
- Biofeedback training is a procedure in which an individual is given information about subtle changes in body functions through amplified visual or auditory signals and learns to control these inner changes.
- Behavior is affected by patterns of reinforcement that may be fixed or vary in ratio or interval. On ratio schedules reinforcers are given after a certain number of responses, which may be constant (fixed) or irregular (variable). On interval schedules reinforcers are given after a specified interval of time, which may also be fixed or variable.
- Several kinds of research evidence that did not fit predictions of traditional conditioning theory have led to a broader understanding of the conditioning process by revealing biological biases. The species-specific repertoires of different organisms, adaptive in their natural environments, make some response-reinforcement connections easier to learn than others; they may also prevent conditioning from occurring in artificial settings.
- Cognitive influences on learning are shown in demonstrations of blocking and sensory preconditioning. Such influences are also apparent in subjects' ability for vicarious learning by observing models even though they make no response and receive no reinforcement themselves. Rule learning is another type of cognitive influence on learning. The most powerful rules are those internalized as one's own rules.
- Current research on conditioning and learning reveals that organisms can do much more than learn specific responses and associations between concrete events. They can learn abstract, symbolic associations, general response patterns, rules, and an understanding of the meanings of relationships between stimuli and responses.
- Conditioning procedures have many applications outside of learning theory. Conditioning tools are currently being used in studies of memory, sensation, perception, language, and brain structure and function.

9

Remembering and Forgetting

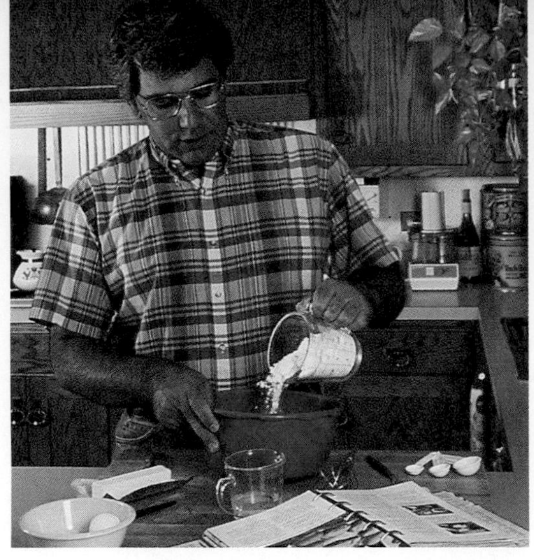

Nick A. is like most of us who tie a string around a finger, tack up a reminder on the door, or set our digital watch alarm when we need to remember something important. So it was not surprising to see Nick clutching the note he had scribbled earlier in case he forgot the question he wanted to ask his doctor; however, its message was rather surprising: "Ask Dr. S. if my memory is getting better." Nick suffers from a rare form of amnesia that makes him forget many events right after they happen.

Nick's partial amnesia is the result of a freak accident that occurred in 1960, when he was 22. A friend playfully thrust a miniature fencing foil toward him; it entered his nostril and severed a small area on the left side of his brain. Brain scans revealed no further damage.

Although Nick has good recall for events before 1960, he has been unable to establish new memories readily for events since that time. Because of this, he is not only isolated from much of his past (that from 1960 on), but he is also alienated from many events in the present. He cannot remember his dreams, or even if he has had any. Although he is friendly and polite, and others seem to enjoy his company, he has no close friends. Typically, he recognizes someone he has met, but he cannot recall the person's name. He has stopped making dates because he forgets the appointed day, time, and place.

The simple, routine activities that we all take for granted pose serious, often insurmountable problems for Nick. After he reads a few paragraphs, he finds that the first sentences begin to slip from memory. Unless he looks away during television commercials and actively thinks about what he was just watching, he cannot remember the plot of the show. A phone call is enough to distract him from any ongoing activity, after which he usually starts something new. Cooking is a major challenge: "If I have two things on the stove, I can't remember how long each one is supposed to cook, or how long they've been on." Nick reports that, as a consequence, he ends up eating "a lot of cereal."

Nick's memory disorder raises many provocative questions about the way memories are formed and experiences forgotten. Because Nick's case is a unique "natural experiment," psychologists and psychiatrists have been studying his behavior and his brain for some time. Their efforts are twofold: to help Nick overcome his problem and to discover more about the phenomena of human memory (Kaushall et al., 1981; Squire, 1986).

Since the accident, Nick has taken numerous psychological and medical tests in an effort to determine the extent of his injury. He scores "above average" in intelligence and "normal" on perceptual ability, language, and motor functions; however, he performs very poorly on memory tests in which he must associate words that are presented together repeatedly. His memory impairment is most severe for verbal material.

One thing Nick remembers quite well is that he has a memory problem, yet he maintains a positive outlook and reveals a healthy, normal personality. His ability to function reasonably well and to remain optimistic despite his severe memory loss may be because he has learned memory strategies that help him connect his past with the present. The primary way that Nick maintains a sense of his own past is by collecting things—mementos of trips, places, hobbies. These concrete, physical objects give him cues: having them in front of him, he can then "read" them in somewhat the way the rest of us "read" our stored memories.

Curiously, Nick's inability to recall recent events does not extend to remembering how to do things. For instance, he can remember how to mix, stir, and bake the ingredients in a recipe—but forgets what those ingredients are supposed to be. So he still has the capacity to store *procedural knowledge* (to remember *how*), but he has lost the ability to store facts about his environment—*declarative knowledge* (to remember *what*). Using his capacity to acquire new information when it is related to procedures or motor skills, he has worked out routines and stock stories to give the appearance of "remembering."

Nick's case is a fascinating one. Through it we recognize the powerful influence that an "ordinary" process like remembering has on our lives. Anything that interferes with the way our memory normally works not only changes how we think and behave, but also may alter our emotions and even change our personalities. Try to imagine what it would be like if suddenly you had no memory for your past, no memory of people you have known or things that have happened to you. Without such "anchors," what would happen to your sense of who you are?

The failure of memory for a prolonged period is called *amnesia.* Research on amnesiacs like Nick is just one way psychologists are trying to understand the complex mechanisms of memory. More often researchers study the way people with normal, intact memories go about storing the enormous amount of information that they acquire, the way they get it out of their memory when they need it, and also the way they sometimes cannot find what they have stored away.

When someone cannot remember a past event, is the memory truly lost or is it simply not accessible? The failure to retrieve information about an experienced past event may be the result of psychological factors or physical ones. Recently, when President Reagan said he did not remember conversations with his White House staff regarding arms deals with Iran and monies for the Contras in Nicaragua, questions arose about the President's memory. One elderly doctor wrote that the problem may have been a natural consequence of old age. "In the elderly, recent memory begins to fail. His staff may brief him immediately before a press conference, but in a few minutes he could honestly forget almost everything that had been prepared. "At my age [74] I can go into the next room to get something, only to find when I get there that I have forgotten my original purpose" (quoted in Reston, *New York Times,* 1986, December 24).

Whatever the cause of the President's inability to remember vital information, his memory failure raises questions about what memory is and the role it plays in our lives. What good would all your learning be were it not for a brain that could store its lessons and a mental system that could call them up upon demand—say, on a multiple-choice examination? It is estimated that the average human mind can store 100 trillion bits of information, yet forget the car keys or forget to call home.

In this chapter you will learn why the study of memory is intriguing to many psychologists and neurobiologists. It has become a pathway to studying both the functions of the mind and the processes of the brain. You will also discover how information gets into and out of your several memory systems—with or without distortion.

What Is Memory?

Memory is the mental capacity to store, and later recall or recognize, events that were previously experienced. The term *memory* also refers to what is retained—the total body of remembered experience, as well as a specific experience that is recalled. The term *remembering* is used to mean either retaining experiences or recalling them.

Most cognitive psychologists define *memory* as a perceptually active mental system that receives, encodes, modifies, and retrieves information. This view focuses on the part of a responsive organism neglected by the behaviorist focus on stimulus input and response output—what happens *between* these two processes. The associations formed between stimulus events and responses are themselves units of memory. An organism without a capacity for memory is not able to profit from experience or training, to use associations to predict what *will* be on the basis of what *was.*

It quickly becomes apparent that memory is not like a photo album or documentary film, because memories are rarely exact copies of earlier experiences. In addition to remembering previously experienced stimulus events, we remember "secondhand" descriptions of events. We may even confidently remember actually "being there," but such confidence is often misplaced in a false memory.

After fifty years, the memories are not exact, but they are certainly worth remembering.

What we remember is influenced by many factors, some operating at the time of the original event, others operating during storage, and still others operating at the time of recall. Even vivid memories may be distortions of what "really" happened in the past. They can be constructions or collages that blend past reality with expectation, fantasy, and social desirability. Memories can be affected by physical health, attention, emotion, prejudice, and many other conditions, as we shall see.

The collection of all your memories is the library of your personal history. Your memories form a living record of what you have heard, read, and experienced over the period of your life so far, but they are much more. As you saw in Nick's case, memories help you define yourself, connect your present thoughts and actions to the roots of your past, and prepare for a meaningful future.

The main approach of this chapter is an information-processing view of memory. It outlines three types of mental processes that transform stimuli into remembered bits of information. It also proposes three different memory systems. Later, some of the new insights coming from neurobiologists who are charting the brain's hardware and the chemistry of memory will be presented.

An Information-processing View

In earlier times, many psychologists were content to analyze behavior solely in terms of its relationship to stimulus inputs. It mattered little what activities were occurring in the "black box" of the mind into which stimuli went and out of which responses came. Today psychologists studying remembering and other mental processes view the mind as an information-processing system. They find it helpful to talk about mental processes in the precise language of computer programming and functioning because they can break down the complex process of remembering into simpler subprocesses or stages.

Using this analogy, psychologists suggest that units of information are stored in our brains as memories in much the same way that bits of information are stored in a computer's "data bank." They recognize that the human mind operates in more complex and subtle ways than any current computer, however. A digital computer processes one thing at a time using transistors that respond to only two signals, 1 (on) and 0 (off), whereas a brain uses graded and changing signals, and processes many different kinds of information at the same time. A computer that processes one piece of information at a time is called a *serial processor.* A human has the ability to process different types of information at the same time, a process known as **parallel processing.** (Computer engineers are currently working to develop reliable parallel-processing computers.)

A human and a computer also differ in the stability of their memories; a computer does not spontaneously add to or modify its stored memories. The trillions of variable-strength synapses in the brain permit processing far more complex than that provided by any computer so far (Sinclair, 1983). On the other hand, the brain's memory units are not as stable and unchanging as those of computer memory. The very act of recalling information changes it in some way. Nonetheless, borrowing from computer science has been enormously useful in helping researchers to formulate hypotheses about remembering and forgetting that can be tested experimentally on humans.

Encoding, Storage, and Retrieval

Being able to recall an experience at some later time requires the operation of three mental processes: encoding, storage, and retrieval. **Encoding** is the translation of incoming stimulus energy into a unique neural code that your brain can process. **Storage** is the retention of encoded material over time. **Retrieval** is the recovery of the stored information at a later time. In computer terminology, encoding, storage, and retrieval are processes that put information into a memory system, hold it there, and later get access to that stored information.

Encoding requires that you first attend to (notice) some selected stimulus event from the huge array nearly always available to you (though, as we saw in chapter 7, some preattentive processing occurs at nonconscious levels). Then you must identify the distinctive features of that experienced event. Both "bottom-up" and "top-down" processing will be involved here (see pp. 209–211).

Is the event a sound, a visual image, or a smell? If a sound, is it loud, soft, or harsh? Does it fit into some pattern with other sounds to form a name, a melody, or a cry for help? Is it a sound you have heard before? During encoding you try to tag an experience with a variety of labels; some are specific and unique—"it's Adam Paisley,"—while others put the event into a general category or class—"it's a young student." This encoding process is usually so automatic and rapid that you are unaware you are doing it.

Further encoding processes relate the new input to other things you already know or to goals or purposes for which it might later prove relevant. Retention will be better the more "links" you can establish between this new item and what you already know. Some researchers believe that you remember relationships between single memories (of actors, actions, and consequences, for example) by forming *networks* of ideas that link together what you know. Memories with connections to other information are much more usable than isolated memory units.

Storage retains encoded information over time. Many psychologists believe that stored information is held forever in memory. Not all information is retained; some of it is lost. Encoded information tends to be lost when it cannot be stored in terms of already stored information; however, the more often some bit of information is rehearsed or "practiced," the more likely it is to be retained. Researchers are just now uncovering the neurophysiological changes in certain synapses and other biochemical processes that are associated with information storage.

Minds, like libraries, must rely upon proper encoding and systematic storage to be useful. When you read "for fun," you make no special effort to organize the ideas for later retrieval. If you used that same process with information units in this text, making no effort to organize what you take in, you would be in trouble when test time came. Good encoding and storage organize information so that it will be easy to find when needed, thus anticipating the third process, retrieval.

Retrieval is the payoff for all your earlier effort. When it works, it enables you to gain access—sometimes in a split second—to information you stored earlier. Can you remember what comes before storage: decoding or encoding? The answer is simple to retrieve now, but will you still be able to retrieve *encoding* as swiftly and with as much confidence when you are tested on this chapter's contents days or weeks from now? Discovering *how* you are able to retrieve one specific bit of information from your memory storehouse filled with so much information is a challenge facing psychologists who want to know how memory works and how it can be improved.

We saw in chapter 6 that perceptual processes can alter sensory information and that past memories can sometimes distort perception. In this chapter we will see that there is a continuing interplay between what we perceive and what we remember. This interaction among encoding, storage, and retrieval is complex, and disturbances that occur during any one of them will affect what is remembered. The whole process is further complicated by the fact that encoding, storage, and retrieval processes take place in each of three basic memory systems.

For firsthand experience of some of the factors we will be discussing, answer the following questions. tions.

1. *What is your social security number? What is your best friend's?*
2. *What was your first-grade teacher's name and eye color? What is the name and eye color of your current psychology instructor?*
3. *Name the title, edition, and author of this textbook.*
4. *Can you form an image of this page when you close your eyes?*
5. *When did you first experience the emotion of guilt? When was the last time you told your parents that you loved them?*
6. *Do you know the difference between iconic and echoic sensory information storage?*
7. *What is the significance of "Rosebud" to Citizen Kane? and "Watergate" to Richard Nixon?*
8. *(Don't look back!) Citizen who?*
9. *Can you recall a complete dream you've had in the past week?*
10. *Were you a bit irritated the last time you had to answer a silly test such as this (so why did you do it)?*

Was your recall quick and certain on some items, incomplete and vague on others? Were there some answers you didn't remember, but you thought you might have known them once? Were there some events you had experienced, but didn't remember, because you didn't see them as significant at the time? Was your memory for negative emotional experiences similar to your ability to recall dates and places? Would questions phrased differently have helped you remember better? This experience of getting to know your own memory and retrieval mechanisms should help make concrete some of our more abstract discussions of the memory types and processes that follow.

Three Memory Systems

Although there is much that psychologists do not know about memory, they are fairly well agreed that there are three memory systems within the overall system of remembering and recalling information: sensory memory, short-term memory, and long-term memory. **Sensory memory** preserves fleeting impressions of sensory stimuli—sights, sounds, smells, and textures—for only a second or two. **Short-term memory** includes recollections of what we have recently perceived; such limited information lasts only up to 20 seconds unless special attention is paid to it or it is reinstated by rehearsal. **Long-term memory** preserves information for retrieval at any later time—up to an entire lifetime. Information in long-term memory constitutes our knowledge about the world.

For examples of these three kinds of memories, imagine that as you are passing a movie theater, you notice a distinctive odor and hear loud sounds from inside (fleeting *sensory memories*). When you get home you decide to check the time of the next show, so you look up the theater's number and then dial the seven digits. Your *short-term memory* holds these digits for the brief period between looking up the number and dialing it; however, you will probably have to look up the number again if the line is busy because your memory of the number will fade very soon unless you work at remembering it. Once you are given the show times, you will have to rely on your *long-term memory* to get you to the theater on time. (It was your long-term memory that you relied on for most of the items on the memory test.)

These three memory systems are also thought of as stages in the sequence of processing information. They differ, not only in how much information they can hold and how long they can hold it, but also in the way they process it. Memories that get into long-term storage have passed through the sensory and short-term stages first. In each stage, the information has been processed in ways that made it eligible for the next stage. Sense impressions become ideas or images; these, in turn, are organized into patterns that fit into existing networks in long-term memory.

It is important to keep in mind that memory is not a *thing*, but a *process*. This is why *remembering* is perhaps a better term to use than *memory*. The three systems or stages of remembering are conceptual models of the way psychologists believe that we process incoming information, retaining and later using it when needed. It is not known whether they involve physically separate brain areas. They seem to be functionally distinct subsystems within the overall system of remembering and recalling information. By finding out how information is processed in each subsystem, our hope is to understand why some conditions help us remember experiences, even "trivial" ones, while other conditions lead to the forgetting of even important experiences. **Figure 9.1** shows the hypothesized flow of information into and among these subsystems.

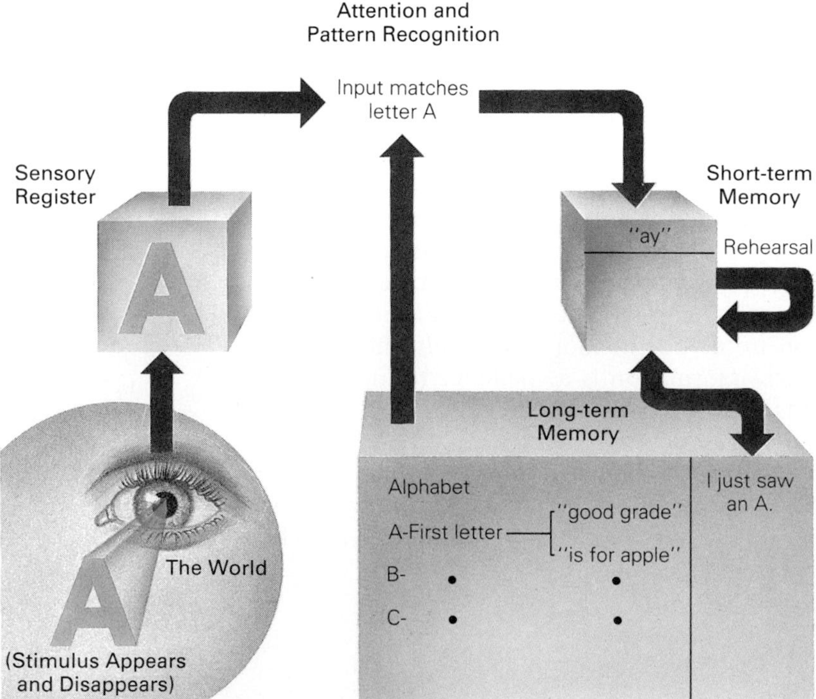

Figure 9.1 *A Model of the Human Memory System*

From Human Memory: Structures and Processes, *Second Edition by Roberta Klatsky. Copyright © 1975, 1980 by W. H. Freeman and Company. Reprinted by permission.*

A trader at the Board of Trade must be able to use short-term memory, long-term memory, and sensory memory to conclude a successful transaction.

Sensory Memory

A sensory memory—also called a **sensory register**—is an impression from any of the senses. It is the first-stage component of most information-processing models of human memory. It is assumed that a register for each sense holds appropriate incoming stimulus information for a brief interval and does so in a form that faithfully reproduces the original stimulus. This storage represents a primitive type of memory that occurs *after* sensation, but *before* a stimulus is assigned to some category ("a bird") during the process of *pattern recognition.* The form in which a sensory memory is held is called *precategorical* since it takes place prior to the process of categorization (Crowder & Morton, 1969).

We know more about visual and auditory memories than the others. A visual memory is called an **icon** and lasts about half a second. An auditory memory is called an **echo** and lasts several seconds (Neisser, 1967). You can easily demonstrate the difference for yourself. When you turn off a radio, the sounds of the music tend to "echo" in your head for a while after the sound is gone, but if you pull down a window shade, the scene outside is gone almost at once.

Why should a memory system depend on the presence of icons and echos? What would happen if they did not occur? Without them, we could "see" and "hear" stimuli only while they were physically present, not long enough for recognition to take place. Sensory registers are essential to hold input long enough to be recognized and passed on for further processing.

Encoding for Sensory Memory

To get into the sensory register, the physical stimuli that impinge on your sensory receptors must be encoded into the biochemical processes that give rise to sensations and perceptions. Even at this stage there is selectivity, as we have seen in earlier chapters. Stimuli of vital importance to organisms take priority over others that aren't as important—for example, soldiers in battle who are focusing on detecting enemy gunners may be unaware of pain information from their wounds. Through **sensory gating,** directed by processes in the brain, information in one sensory channel is boosted while information in another is suppressed or disregarded.

Storage: How Much and How Long?

Though fleeting, your sensory storage capacity is large—more than all your senses can process at one time. At first, researchers underestimated the amount that could actually be stored during this brief interval because of the reporting procedure they used. They asked subjects to look at a visual display (such as the one that follows) for a fraction of a second and then to recall as many letters as they could. With this method, called a **whole-report procedure,** subjects could report only about 4 items; but was that the limit of their immediate memory span?

D J B
X H G
C L Y

George Sperling was a young researcher who suspected that the number of items recalled might not be an accurate indication of the number that actually had gotten into the sensory memory. He devised an ingenious method—called the **partial-report procedure**—to test his hypothesis.

Sperling flashed the same arrays of consonants for the same amount of time (one twentieth of a second), but now asked his subjects to report only one row rather than the whole pattern. A signal of a high, medium, or low tone was sounded immediately after *the presentation to indicate which row from the entire set the subjects were to report. He found that, regardless of which row he asked for, the subjects' recall was nearly* perfect. *Sperling took this to indicate that all the items must have gotten into the sensory memory. When three rows of 4 items were flashed to other subjects, the subjects were 76 percent accurate in their reports—indicating again, that there were 9 items available for immediate recall. (Sperling, 1960, 1963)*

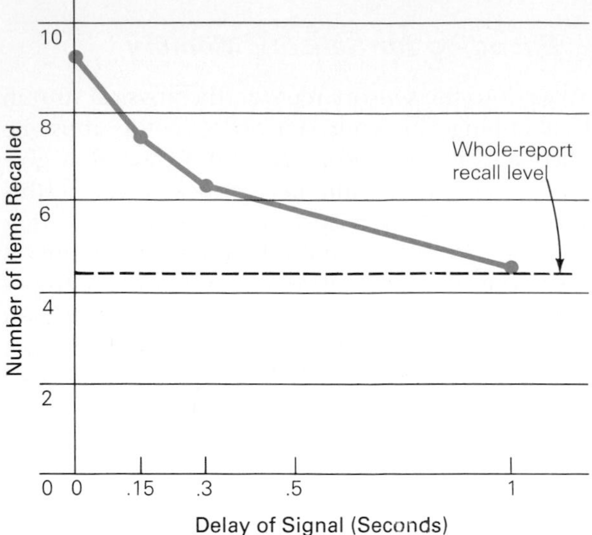

Figure 9.2 *Recall by the Partial-Report Method*
The dots in the solid line show the average number of items recalled (for 4 subjects) by the partial-report method immediately following presentation and at three later times up to one second. For comparison, the number of items recalled from the 12 letters available by the whole-report method is shown by the dotted line. (Adapted from Sperling, 1960)

What happens if the identification signal is not immediate but slightly delayed? **Figure 9.2** shows that, as the delay interval increases from zero to one second, the number of items reported declines steadily. Sperling's experiments demonstrate that immediate visual storage is quite accurate, but that the image or trace of the stimulus *decays* very rapidly.

Using Sperling's procedure, other researchers have shown that in auditory memory, too, more information is available than people can typically report (Darwin et al., 1972). Echoic memories may be necessary to process many aspects of speech, such as intonation and emphasis.

Would we be better off if sensory memories lingered longer so that we would have more time to process them? Not really, because new information is constantly coming in, and it, too, must be processed. Old information must last just long enough to give a sense of continuity, but not long enough to interfere with new sensory impressions. As we read, the part we just attended to must be processed along the system and drop out of sensory memory quickly so that our sensory systems can register new information.

In addition to the rapid decay of stimulus traces, there is another way by which sensory registers get cleared of "old inputs." New inputs that are similar can erase iconic and echoic representations.

In one study two rows of letters were flashed briefly and 100 milliseconds later a circle was flashed where one of the letters had been. Normally, all the letters would have been seen 100 milliseconds after presentation, but, instead of seeing all the letters with a circle around one of them, the subjects saw the two rows with the circle in place *of that letter (Averbach & Coriell, 1961).* ***Figure 9.3*** *shows this sequence of events.*

This phenomenon is known as **backward masking.** A stimulus following another of a similar kind erases or masks the preceding one, evidently because it interferes with the ongoing perceiving process. At this first stage of information processing there is a race against the clock to complete pattern recognition and other coding before the sensory memory fades away. Most sensory inputs lose that race and fail to make it to either short-term memory or long-term memory.

Processing for Transfer to Short-term Memory

Though sensory gating has kept some stimulus input from being translated into sensations and perceptions, you still receive far more sensory information than you can remember—or can use if you did. Actually, only a tiny fraction of what you sense stays with you permanently, as you may have discovered in frustration when you tried to remember everything you saw and heard on a trip. What processes must take place before the sensory memories fade to get into short-term memory—and thus have a chance of being remembered?

The first requirement is that they be attended to. Of the vast range of sense impressions you experience and retain briefly in your sensory memory, only those that capture your attention become eli-

Figure 9.3 *Sequence of Events in Backward Masking*

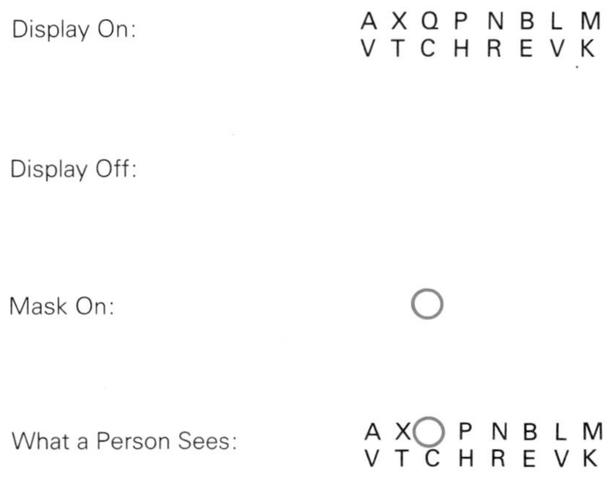

Display On: A X Q P N B L M
V T C H R E V K

Display Off:

Mask On: ○

What a Person Sees: A X ○ P N B L M
V T C H R E V K

gible for more lasting memory (remember our discussion of attention in chapter 7?).

Selective attention—being aware of only part of the available sensory input—is a familiar experience for all of us. At a party we can participate intelligently in only one conversation at a time; we manage to "tune out" the others going on around us. In a student dorm a half dozen stereos may be blasting away at once, and, although all are detected by the receptors in our ears, we can hear the stereo we want to hear. Then, if we get engaged in an animated conversation, we can selectively attend to what is being said and push the music to the background of our attentional focus, though it is as loud as ever. Through selective attention we can choose which inputs to focus upon. Stimuli that are not attended to are lost. Only those inputs which somehow command attention become candidates for the further processing required for later remembering.

Information in sensory stores becomes eligible for longer storage when pattern recognition occurs. As we saw in earlier chapters, the global process of taking in sensory input actually includes three parts: transformation of stimulus energy into sensory data (sensation), organization of data from individual receptors into groupings (perception), and "top-down" processes in which long-term memories help give meaning to the new information (classification). This third perceptual stage includes pattern recognition and incorporates influences from expectations or personal needs.

What kinds of information have the best chance of receiving attention and getting into short-term memory? In general, familiar, rather than completely unfamiliar, information will make it into this stage of processing. *Eetpnvma* will not be processed, but *pavement* will be, even though both "words" have the same letters. Similarly, it is harder to remember music with tonal scales very different from the familiar ones used in Western music. A limitation to this principle is that "familiarity may breed contempt"—when something is repeated so often that it becomes boring, it is habituated to and "tuned out."

Some types of novel stimuli, however, are better remembered than familiar ones. We remember a vivid, bizarre variation within a known, established structure: a purple dog, a two-headed cow, a story with a "surprise" ending. Also, since we are subjective human information processors, we will more likely notice and recall anything of personal significance to us.

The representation of information in some encoded form in storage is called a *memory code.* When there is no memory code already in long-term memory that matches or relates to a stimulus, encoding for short-term memory is harder, takes longer, and is less likely to happen at all. This is why it is easier to remember new information if you can relate it to something you already know. It may also be one reason why you probably have so few memories of your earliest years: you had very few memories already stored that could help you in encoding new experiences.

Short-term Memory

A stimulus that has been recognized is likely to be transferred to *short-term memory,* an intermediate memory process between the fleeting events of sensory memory and the more permanent storage of long-term memory. A number of interesting characteristics distinguish this memory-processing phase from the other two stages.

Short-term memory has a very limited capacity. Much *less* information is stored in this stage than in either of the other two stages. It also has a short duration of retention: what is stored is lost after about 20 seconds *unless* it is held in consciousness. But short-term memory is the only memory stage in which conscious processing of material takes place, and material held in it survives as long as it is held in conscious attention—far beyond the 20-second limit possible without attention. This is why short-term memory is also called *working memory:* material transferred to it from either sensory or long-term memory (both of them nonconscious) can be worked over, organized, and thought about.

Working memory is part of our psychological present. It is what sets a context for new events and links separate episodes together into a continuing story. It is short-term memory that enables us to maintain and continually update our representation of a changing situation and to keep track of the topics under discussion during a conversation.

Short-term memory gives a context for both comprehension and new perceptions. For example, suppose a waiter moves by your table carrying a tray of used dishes while you are deeply engaged in conversation with your date. A minute or so later, there is a crashing noise. You know it is not a falling tree or a car crash; you interpret it immediately as most probably the crashing of dishes from that waiter's tray. In this situation short-term memory is using information from a recent event and from long-term memory about the sounds of different events to help you interpret a new perception (Baddeley & Hitch, 1974).

Encoding in Short-term Memory

Information enters short-term memory as organized images and patterns that are usually recognized as familiar and meaningful. Verbal patterns that enter short-term memory usually seem to be held there in *acoustic* form—according to the way they sound—even when they come through an individual's eyes rather than ears. We know this from research in which subjects were asked to recall lists of letters immediately after seeing them. Errors of recall tended to be confusions of letters that *sounded* alike, rather than letters that looked alike. For example, the letter *D* was confused with similar sounding *T* rather than with more similar looking *O* (Conrad, 1964).

You may be wondering how deaf people can manage if short-term memory uses acoustic encoding. Apparently the deaf use two alternatives to the acoustic coding most others use. They rely on *visual encoding* (identifying letters, words, and sign-language symbols) and, to a lesser extent, on *semantic encoding* (identifying the categories or classes to which visually observed events belong). This we deduce because the errors they make result from confusing items that are similar in appearance or in meaning instead of in sound (Bellugi et al., 1975; Frumkin & Anisfeld, 1977). Even though hearing persons generally rely on acoustic encoding in short-term memory, there is evidence that they, too, sometimes rely on visual and semantic encoding (Conrad, 1972).

Storage in Short-term Memory

The limited, brief storage capacity for short-term memory is called the **immediate memory span.** When the to-be-remembered items are unrelated, the capacity of short-term memory seems to be between five and nine "chunks" of information—about seven (plus or minus two) familiar things: letters, words, numbers, or almost any kind of meaningful item. When you try to force more than 7 ± 2 items into short-term memory, earlier items are lost at the expense of more recent ones. This "bumping out" process is like laying out seven foot-long bricks on a seven-foot table. When an eighth brick is pushed in at one end, the brick at the opposite end is pushed off. (We will learn in the next section that there are special ways of stacking the bricks to get more of them on the table at the same time.) For an account of George Miller's (1956) discovery of this "magical number seven," see the ***Close-up*** on page 309.

Even these seven items are not guaranteed to last for the 20 seconds that we could hold them, however. If we focus our attention on processing just a few of them, the other ones may slip away.

Processing in Short-term Memory

There are two important ways to increase the limited capacity of short-term storage so that more of the information there can be put into long-term memory. These are *chunking* and *rehearsal.* You already use them and now you'll discover why they help you.

Chunking

A **chunk** is a meaningful unit of information. A chunk can be a single letter or number, a group of letters, or other items, even a group of words or a sentence. For example, the sequence 1, 9, 8, 4 consists of four digits, which could be four chunks—about half of what your short-term memory can hold; but 1984 is only one chunk if you see the digits as a year or the title of George Orwell's book—leaving you much more capacity for other chunks of information. **Chunking** is the process of taking single items and recoding them by grouping them on the basis of similarity or some other organizing principle, or combining them into larger patterns based on information stored in long-term memory.

A good listener uses the process of chunking while listening to a lecture.

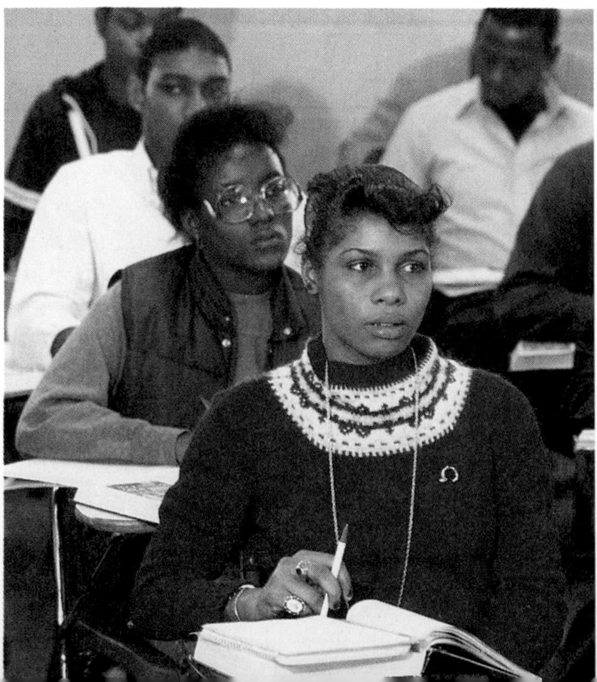

Close-up The Magical Number Seven

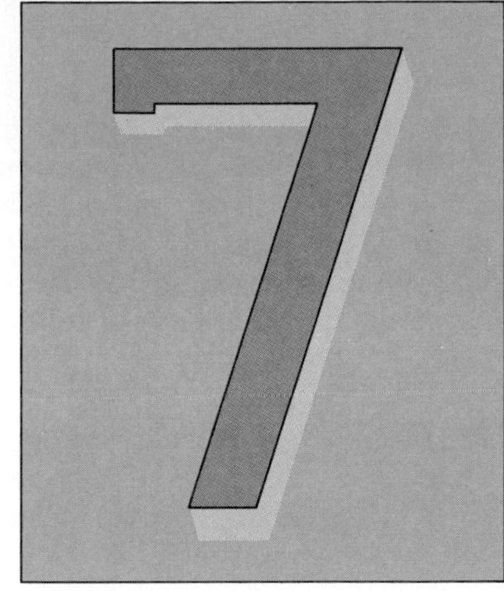

I have been persecuted by an integer. For seven years this number has followed me around, has entered in my most private data, and has assaulted me from the pages of our most public journals. . . . There is . . . a design behind it, some pattern governing its appearances. (Miller, 1956, p. 81)

So wrote psychologist George Miller about his persecution by the "magical number seven." Recall the power and glory of that special number:

The seven *days of creation.*
The seven *ages of man.*
The seven *deadly sins.*
The seven *levels of hell.*
The seven *digits in phone numbers.*
The seven *wonders of the world.*

The power of the number seven in human thinking knows no cultural bounds. When African tribal historians, for example, tell stories of their ancestors, they may be able to recite by heart 12,000-word tales, such as *The Mwindo Epic,* but they usually go back only seven generations. Anthropologists have noted that, after tracing back their roots for seven generations, these oral historians usually say that the Primal Ancestor then "came from heaven" (D'Azevedo, 1962).

The special relevance of "seven" for our purposes is that human memory seems bound by that number. Read this list of random numbers once, cover them over, and write down as many as you can in the order they appear.

8 1 7 3 6 4 9 4 2 8 5

Number Correct ____

Now read this list of random letters and perform the same memory test.

J M R S O F L P T Z B

Number Correct ____

If your short-term memory is like that of most others, you probably recalled about *seven* numbers and *seven* letters. Some people will recall five units, some as many as nine—that is, seven plus or minus two (7 ± 2). You will discover the same principle operating with recall of lists of random words or names (*seven* again!).

Miller's conclusion has been supported by much research validating the rule that the average capacity of short-term memory is about seven units of unrelated information; but units can vary in size, and some—like words made up of letters—actually contain several related parts. Realizing that a new concept was needed to describe the units of short-term memory, Miller dubbed them *chunks.*

Chunks vary in both size and complexity, and your chunks may differ from mine. Chunks are the personal currency of our memory banks. When memorizing numbers, you may store pairs of digits (35-46-21) while I may store triplets (354-621). Looking at a picture, I may chunk by location (grass with ball at bottom; tree with bird at top), while you may chunk by color (blue ball and blue bird; green grass and green tree). "A chunk is a mental refashioning of reality that each mind comes up with for itself" (Kanigel, 1981, p. 34).

Regardless of what is stored in any of your chunks or mine, there are only about *seven* chunks in action at any given time. How many? ____ !

How many chunks do you find in this sequence of 20 numbers: 19411914186518121776? You can answer "20" if you see them as unrelated digits, but "5" if you group them as dates of major wars in American history. If you see them as the latter, it becomes easy for you to recall all the digits in proper sequence after one quick glance, whereas it would be impossible for you to remember them all from a short exposure if you saw them as 20 unrelated items. Your memory span can always be greatly increased if you can discover how to organize information into chunks.

You can also structure incoming information according to its personal meaning to you (linking it to the ages of friends and relatives, for example); or you can match new stimuli with various codes that have been stored in your long-term memory. Thus your memory for the sequence ERATVCIAFBIGMGEUSA will be better if you chunk it as ERA-TV-CIA-FBI-GM-GE-USA (Bower, 1972).

Even if you do not have appropriate rules, meanings, or codes to apply from your long-term memory, you still can use chunking. You can simply *group* the items in a rhythmical pattern or temporal group (181 pause, 379 pause, 256 pause, 460 pause . . . rather than 181379256460).

Rehearsal

The usefulness of repeating the digits of a telephone number to keep them in mind has already been mentioned. This is called **maintenance rehearsal.** The fate of unrehearsed information was demonstrated in an ingenious experiment.

> *Subjects heard three consonants, such as FCV, read aloud and had to recall them when given a signal after a variable interval of time, ranging from 3 to 18 seconds. To prevent rehearsal, a* distractor task *was put between the stimulus input and the recall signal. (The subjects were given a 3-digit number and told to count backward from it by threes until the recall signal was presented.) Many different consonant sets were given and several short delays were used over a series of trials with a number of subjects.*
>
> *As shown in* **Figure 9.4,** *recall deteriorated increasingly as the retention interval increased. After even 3 seconds there was considerable memory loss, and, by 18 seconds, loss was nearly total. In the absence of an opportunity to rehearse the information, short-term recall was impaired with the passage of time. (Peterson & Peterson, 1959)*

In addition, there was probably interference from the competing information of the distractor task. Interference as a cause of forgetting will be discussed later in this chapter.

Rehearsal keeps information in working memory and prevents competing inputs from pushing it out; but even information that is rehearsed verbatim does not necessarily get transferred to long-term memory. To make sure, you need to engage in **elaborative rehearsal,** a process in which the information is analyzed and related to already stored knowledge. This happens when you note that the telephone number 358-9211 can also be thought of as 3 + 5 = 8 and 9 + 2 = 11. This elaboration depends upon your having addition rules and summations stored in and transferred from long-term memory. If you do, it helps give pattern and meaning to the otherwise unrelated and meaningless items. Similarly, once you have learned the rules of syntax—how words can be arranged to form acceptable sentences—you group the words in English sentences into chunks. We will have more to say about elaborative rehearsal later when we discuss encoding for long-term memory.

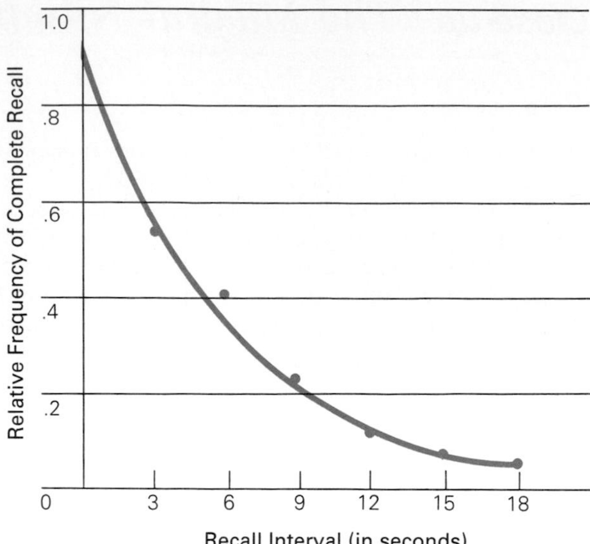

Figure 9.4 *Short-term Recall Without Rehearsal*
When the interval between stimulus presentation and recall test was filled with a brief distracting task, the longer the interval, the poorer the recall. (Adapted from Peterson & Peterson, 1959)

The limited capacity of short-term memory is one of the fundamental and stable features of the human memory system; yet we hear of "memory experts"—people who can remember long strings of numbers after a single presentation or multiply large numbers in their heads in a few seconds. Apparently part of their secret is in learning to shift information back and forth between short-term and long-term memory. To see how this skill might be developed, cognitive psychologist William Chase worked with a student, identified as S.F.

> *At the beginning, S.F. could repeat only the standard seven numbers in proper sequence, but after two and a half years of practice (an hour a day, two to five days a week), he could recall up to 80 digits or reproduce perfectly a matrix of 50 numbers—and do so more quickly than lifelong memory experts.*
>
> *S.F. was neither coached nor given special training. He merely put in hundreds of hours' practice listening to random digits being read one per second and then recalling them in order. When he reported them correctly, another digit was added on the next trial; if he was incorrect, one digit was dropped on the next trial. After each trial S.F. gave a verbal report (a protocol) of his thought process.*
>
> *S.F.'s protocols provided the key to his mental wizardry. Because he was a long-distance runner, S.F. noticed that many of the random numbers could be grouped into running times for different distances. For instance, he would recode the sequence, "3, 4, 9, 2, 5, 6, 1, 4, 9, 3, 5," as "three forty-nine point two, near*

record mile; fifty-six point fourteen, 10-mile time; nine thirty-five, slow 2 miles.'' Later S.F. also used ages, years of special events, and special numerical patterns to chunk the random digits. In this way he was able to use his long-term memory to convert long strings of random input into a smaller number of manageable and meaningful chunks. However S.F.'s memory for letters was still only 7 ± 2 because he had not developed any chunking strategies to recall alphabet strings. (Chase & Ericsson, 1981; Ericsson & Chase, 1982)

Retrieval from Short-term Memory

You now know something about how to get 7 ± 2 chunks of information into your short-term memory, but how do you get them out? This is the problem of *retrieval.*

Retrieval from short-term memory has been studied experimentally by Saul Sternberg (1966, 1969). Although the task he used was quite simple, the results revealed in detail how items seem to be retrieved from short-term memory.

On each of many trials, subjects were given a memory set consisting of from one to six items—for instance, the digits 5, 2, 9, 4, 6. From trial to trial the list would vary in the digits shown and in length. After presenting each set, Sternberg immediately presented a single test ''probe''—say, 6; the subjects had to determine whether the probe had been a part of the memory set. Since the size of the set was less than the capacity of short-term memory (7 ± 2), subjects could easily perform the task without error.

The dependent variable was not accuracy, but speed of recognition. *How quickly could subjects press a ''yes'' button to indicate that they had seen the test item in the memory set or a ''no'' button to indicate they had not seen it? Reaction time was used to find out the mental activities that were occurring when short-term memory was being searched. Three components of the retrieval process were assumed to make up this reaction time: (a) the subject perceived and encoded the test stimulus—''it's a six''; (b) the test stimulus was then matched against the items in the stored memory set (5,2,9,4,6); and (c) a recognition response was made by pressing the ''yes'' button, in this case, or the ''no'' button had the set been 5,2,9,4,7.*

Sternberg believed that short-term memory might be scanned using any of three possible search strategies (see **Figure 9.5**):

1. In *parallel processing scanning* the entire stored set would be treated as a composite, and separate digits would be examined simultaneously, all "in parallel." If this were what occurred, it would take no longer to search big sets than short ones, and reaction time would be the same.

Figure 9.5 *Retrieval from Short-term Memory*
Reaction time for retrieval from short-term memory increases with the length of the memory set and is the same for "no" and "yes" responses, as predicted for serial exhaustive processing. (Adapted from Sternberg, 1966)
Note: The same line is predicted for both no (red) and yes (blue) in a and c. They are drawn apart for clarity.

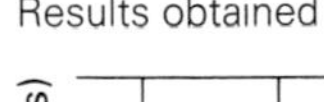

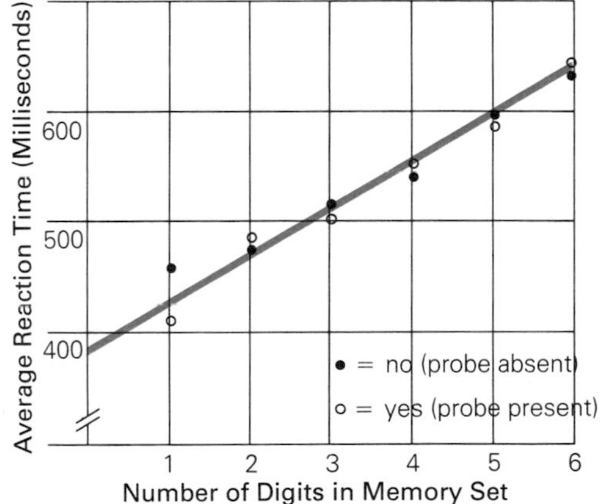

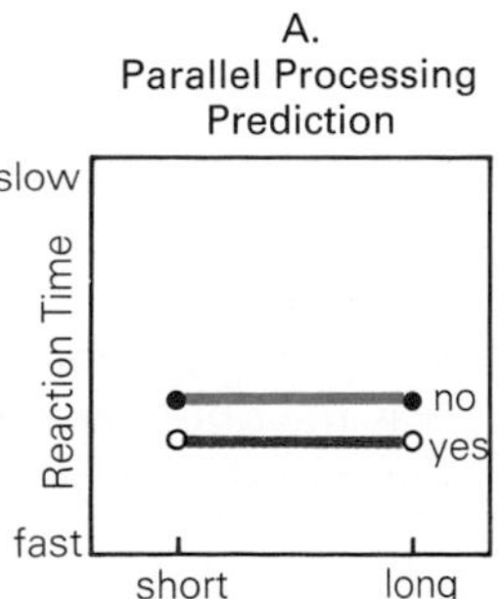

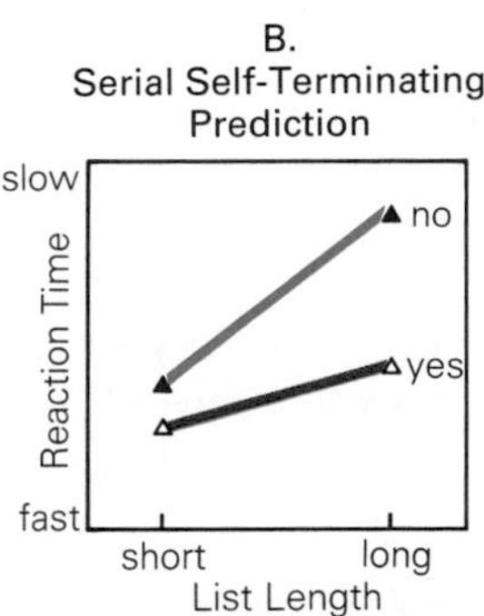

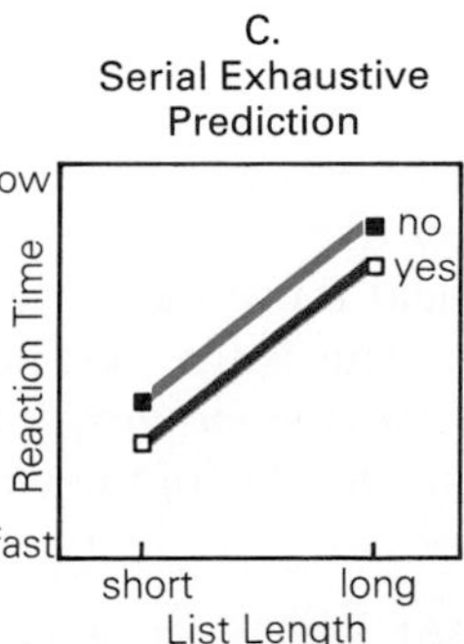

2. In *serial self-terminating scanning* each digit would be examined in turn until the test probe digit was found; then the search would be terminated. With this process longer lists would require more search time than shorter ones. In addition, it would take more time for a "no" than for a "yes" because the subject would stop searching as soon as a match ("yes") was found, but would have to scan all the digits in the set before deciding "no."
3. In *serial exhaustive scanning* the digits in the stored memory set would be scanned separately and the entire set would be examined before a "yes" or a "no" response was made. In this case, longer lists would have a slower reaction time, but "yes" and "no" responses would take equal time.

The results fit the memory scanning prediction of a serial exhaustive search. It took more time to recognize test stimuli from longer memory sets, but it took the same time to give a "yes" as a "no" response. Sternberg figured that it took about 400 milliseconds to encode the test stimulus and then about 35 milliseconds more to compare it to each item in the memory set. In a single second, a person could make about 30 such comparisons. With such fast scanning, that person could afford the security of doing an exhaustive search before deciding what he or she really remembered.

Although other researchers have offered a different interpretation (Townsend, 1972; Wingfield, 1973), Sternberg's work has been very influential in helping our understanding of retrieval from short-term memory. It not only shows how items were retrieved from short-term memory but also how effectively reaction time can be used as a dependent measure to test theories about mental processes. Reaction time is used very frequently as the dependent variable in studies of other cognitive processes, as we shall see in chapter 10.

Long-term Memory

A 95-year-old woman describes a family event that happened when she was 5 years old. She may even recall the expression on her mother's face, a twisted gold ribbon on a package, and the way she felt. Somehow, despite all the activities and thoughts of the 90 intervening years, her brain has held those memories.

This is the miracle of our third memory system, *long-term memory.* It constitutes each person's total knowledge of the world and of the self. Long-term memory is the storehouse of all the experienced events, information, emotions, skills, words, categories, rules and judgments—and more—that have been transferred into it from sensory and short-term memories; but this memory system enables you to do much more even than just retain a record of past events or thoughts. Material in long-term memory helps you deal with and store new information by "top-down" processing, as you have seen. It also makes it possible for you to solve new problems, reason, keep future appointments, and apply a variety of rules to manipulate abstract symbols—to think and even to create something you have never experienced.

Given the amount of information stored in long-term memory, it is a marvel that it is so accessible. You can often get the exact information you want in a split second: Who discovered classical conditioning? Name a play by Shakespeare. What was your happiest birthday? How often should you brush your teeth? The answers to these questions probably came effortlessly because of several special features of long-term memory: (a) words and concepts have been put into it (encoded) by their *meaning,* which has given them links to many other stored items; (b) the knowledge in your long-term memory is filed in a well-organized, orderly fashion (storage); and (c) many alternative cues are stored to help you extract exactly what you want from all that is there (retrieval).

Encoding for Long-term Memory

We have seen that short-term memory is a little like an office in-basket. Items are stored sequentially in a temporal order according to their arrival. Long-term memory, by contrast, is more like a set of file cabinets or a library. Items are stored according to their meanings with perhaps many meanings for one item (corresponding to title, author, and subject in a card catalog) and numerous cross-references to related material. Thus, in many cases, there are a variety of possible ways to retrieve a particular item.

Meaningful Organization

The importance of meaningful organization as the key to long-term storage is demonstrated by your remembering the gist or sense of an idea rather than the actual sentence you heard. For example, if you hear the sentence, "Mary picked up the book," and later hear, "The book was picked up by Mary," you are likely to report that the second sentence was the one you heard earlier, because the meaning was the same though the form was different.

Participants in a knowledge bowl need to draw on their long-term memories to answer the varied questions that are asked.

Research has shown that information about the *meaning* (or gist) of sentences is more likely to be stored than the exact structure of the sentences (Bransford & Franks, 1971). Moreover, if you do not understand the meaning of a sentence or paragraph, you will be unable to organize it into a "memorable" unit of information. Even descriptions of common events can't be properly understood and remembered without sufficient organizational cues provided by the context or the title. To demonstrate this principle, read the following passage and then write out as much as you can recall. After doing so, read the title for the passage, which was "misplaced" on the next page. You might test your friends' recall for the passage with and without the title (Bransford & Johnson, 1972, 1973).

The procedure is actually quite simple. First you arrange items into different groups. (Of course one pile may be sufficient depending on the amount there is to do.) If you have to go somewhere else because of lack of facilities you'd better do so; otherwise, you are pretty well set. It is important not to overdo things. That is, it is better to do too few things at once than too many. In the short run this may not seem important, but complications can easily arise. A mistake can be expensive as well. At first, the whole procedure will seem complicated. Soon, however, it will become just another facet of life. It is difficult to foresee any end to the necessity for this task in the immediate future, but then, one never can tell. After the procedure is completed one arranges the materials into different groups again. Then they can be put into their appropriate places. Eventually they will be used once more and the whole cycle will have to be repeated; however, that is part of life.

Chunking and elaborative rehearsal are helpful in preparing material for long-term storage because they organize it and make it more meaningful. When you are not limited to the 20 seconds of short-term memory, but can study material in front of you that you want to remember, there are several other things you can do to organize the material and give it meaning.

For example, you may "make sense" of new information by putting it in a category you already have, transforming it into something familiar, or organizing it in some other way that is meaningful to you. Suppose, for example, you are asked to learn the following list of words for later recall and are told that you may recall them in any order. (This task is called *free recall.*)

house	yellow
tree	green
bird	nest
dog	tiger
grass	tent
purple	shoe
horse	

How might you begin? You could first note that the list has 13 items and then see how many fit into different categories: animals—4; living places—4, if you include *tree;* colors—3; and so on. Or you could encode this input by grouping pairs together: tree—house; bird—nest; green—grass; horse—shoe; and yellow—tiger.

According to researchers older children (sixth-graders) recall such lists better than younger ones, because they are more likely to organize the items in pairs or group them by category. Most third-graders use only maintenance rehearsal—simply repeating the items. By teaching the younger children how to look for ways to organize the items, their recall becomes as good as that of the older children (Ornstein & Naus, 1978).

The same material can usually be meaningfully organized in more than one way. Sometimes you encode by noticing the structure already in the material, such as the different levels of headings in this chapter. Other times you impose your own organization by outlining the main points and subpoints or by fitting new items into a structure of knowledge you already have. You may "boil down" several paragraphs into two main ideas with an example for each. You may make new distinctions for an old concept you already have stored, such as you have now done with the three stages of *memory* in an overall system; or you may add meaning or organization to new material by using personal experiences, references, or physically present reminders like a string around your finger or the mementos Nick used to help him remember.

Use of Mnemonics

To help yourself remember, you can also draw on special strategies or devices called **mnemonics** (from the Greek word meaning "to remember"), which are ways of associating new information to be remembered with something familiar, previously encoded, and easily recalled. Among the mnemonics are natural language mediators, the method of loci, and visual imagery.

Natural language mediators are word meanings or spelling patterns already stored in long-term memory that can be associated with new information. For example, you might encode the paired nonsense syllables *pab-lom* by associating them with *pablum;* or you might encode the word pair *girl-stage* as "The girl danced on the stage." You might remember more complex material or a list of words by making up a story to connect the parts. Associations that use rhyming can also help you remember. Even though the encoded item is then longer than the original one, your recall is better because you remember those mediators easily, and they, in turn, lead you to the material you are looking for (Montague et al., 1966).

Another common mnemonic strategy is the *method of loci* (*locus* means "place"). To remember a list of people you are meeting, you might mentally put each one sequentially in a separate room in your house; to remember the names, you mentally go through your house and find the name associated with each spot.

You might remember a list of words like *mouse, car,* and *melon,* by associating them with the things you would see while walking around your living room. You might associate *mouse* with the *door,* possibly picturing the mouse opening the door for you. If a *couch* is next to the door, you might imagine a *car* resting on it, with its hazard lights blinking. (See **Figure 9.6.**)

Visual imagery is one of the most effective forms of encoding, perhaps because it gives you codes for both verbal and visual memories simultaneously (Paivio, 1968). You remember words by associating them with visual images—the more vivid and distinctive the better. For example, if you wanted to remember the pair *cat-bicycle,* you might use an image of "a cat riding on a bicycle to deliver pizzas" (Bower, 1972). To test your own visual imagery, try the task in **Figure 9.7.**

The title of the passage is "Procedure for Washing Clothes."

Figure 9.6
The method of loci is a means of remembering the order of a list of names or objects by associating them with some sequence of places with which we are familiar.

Other mnemonic devices use organizational schemes or strategies that rely on word or sound associations or that put the items into a pattern that is easy to remember. For example, a mnemonic to remember the colors of the spectrum converts to a person's name, *Roy G. Biv* (red, orange, yellow, green, blue, indigo, violet). Similarly, the familiar "*E*very *g*ood *b*oy *d*oes *f*ine" is a mnemonic for remembering the musical notes on the treble clef: *E, G, B, D, F.*

You may have wondered how waiters and waitresses can remember many different orders when they do not write them down. Even after a delay of many minutes, they usually manage to set the right glass or plate in front of the right customer.

> *In a recent study of this phenomenon, 40 waitresses and 40 control subjects (college students) had to remember 7, 11, or 15 drink orders and later place them in front of customers (actually dolls seated around tables).*
>
> *When only 7 orders were taken, there was no difference between the two groups; but with 11 or 15 orders, the waitresses were significantly more accurate. In fact, some were 100 percent accurate with 15 orders. The waitresses reported that they worked to develop their memories by using mnemonic techniques that helped them associate each order visually with a particular face or specific location: "bourbon and soda poured over big eared brute first out of the chute" (first on her left). Interestingly, most of the waitresses reported that their memories were best on the busiest evenings. The investigator noted that motivation for performing their tasks well would be high since customer satisfaction and tips are strongly influenced by waitress accuracy. (Bennett, 1983)*

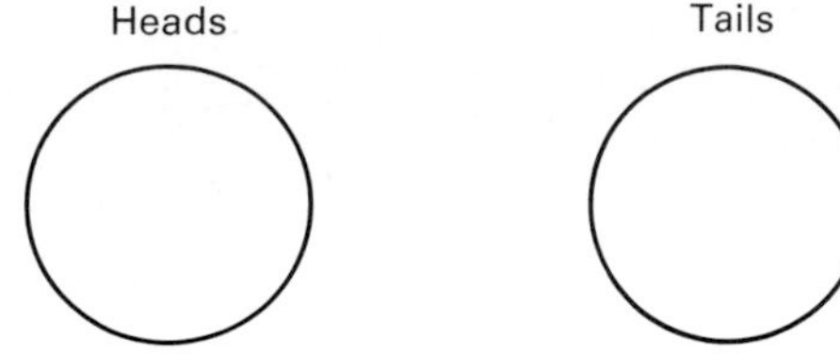

Figure 9.7
How well do you know a penny? See if you can draw what both sides look like. For the answer, check your loose change.

Encoding Specificity

Your method of organizing material in the encoding stage directly affects not only how it is stored but, equally important, what cues will work when you want to retrieve it. The close relationship among encoding, storage, and retrieval is called the **encoding specificity principle.** The better the match between your organization for encoding and the cues you are likely to be given later, the better your recall will be. For example, if you memorize the word *jam* in the context of traffic *jam,* you will have trouble recognizing it when its context is changed to strawberry *jam.* This means that it will be worth your while to study new material in a way that will make it easier to retrieve later. If you expect essay questions, during encoding you should look for and try to remember general information about abstract relationships, implications, and conceptual analysis, because that is probably what you will be asked to retrieve. If you expect multiple-choice questions, you should pay more attention to specific, concrete, right-or-wrong factual details, comparisons, and distinctions.

The encoding specificity principle also means that when you are learning new material, you will be encoding details about the circumstances around you at the time—the context of the encoding. This learning can provide additional retrieval cues *if* you are in similar circumstances when you try to retrieve the material you have studied. The power of such *context dependence* was demonstrated by the finding that divers who learned material underwater remembered it better when tested underwater, even when the material had nothing to do with water or diving (Baddeley, 1982). Context dependence is one reason why studying in a noisy environment may not help your retrieval when you will be tested in a quiet room.

State dependence is important too: retrieval will be better if there is no big change in your physical or psychological state between the time of learning and the time of retrieval. If you learned something when you were happy, it will be harder to remember it if you are sad than if you can reinstate the happy mood.

Storage in Long-term Memory

Stored in your long-term memory is not only outside sensory diverse information, but also internally generated information such as creative thoughts, opinions, and values. How are all these kinds of information represented in storage? Three varieties of memory are distinguished by the kinds of information for which they are each specialized: procedural, semantic, and episodic.

Procedural Memory

Do you remember how selective Nick's amnesia was? After his accident, he could store *procedural knowledge*—ways to do things like brush his teeth or cook—but not some kinds of *declarative knowledge*—facts about events since his accident, how they were related, and what they meant. Cases like Nick's have led to the conclusion that procedural ("skill") knowledge and declarative ("fact") knowledge must somehow be stored differently.

Procedural memory is the way we remember how things get done and how perceptual, cognitive, and motor skills are acquired, retained, and utilized (Anderson, 1982; Tulving, 1983). Skill memories are memories of *actions* and are acquired by practice and observation of models (Bandura, 1986). Skills, such as bicycle riding or tying one's shoelaces, are difficult to learn, but even harder to forget. Skill memories are only consciously recalled during early phases of performance. Experts perform their skilled tasks without conscious recall of the appropriate skill memories. In fact, trying to do so often is distracting and makes their performance worse. (Try to describe how to tie a shoelace or how to swim. Describing such a task is more difficult than just doing it.) Fact memories, by contrast, are memories of explicit *information;* they are recalled with conscious effort.

Procedural memory is thought to be a capacity of subcortical areas in the evolutionally old brain, with the declarative memory system more recently evolved and built upon the primitive base (see pp. 127–128). This difference may account for the reason that both human and animal babies develop skill memories earlier than fact memories.

Young monkeys were tested at different ages on both a skill acquisition task and a simple memory association task. At three months of age they were as proficient as adults on the skill task, but could not do the other task until they were six months old and did not develop adult proficiency at it until they were almost two years old. (Mishkin, 1982)

It looks as though we were workers who got things done before we became intellectuals who think about the dignity of labor.

Within memory for declarative knowledge there are two different types—semantic and episodic. This distinction was first proposed by Canadian psychologist Endel Tulving (1972).

Semantic Memory

Semantic memory is concerned with the symbolically represented knowledge that individuals possess about their world. It is the generic, categorical memory that stores the basic *meaning* of words and concepts without reference to their time and place in experience. It is more like an encyclopedia than an autobiography. The meaningful relationships in your semantic memory are organized around abstract and conceptual information. Your semantic memory includes "generic" facts (true for other people and independent of personal experience) about grammar, musical composition, or scientific principles, for examples. The formula $E = MC_2$ is stored in semantic memory. Nick's semantic memory for things learned before his accident was apparently unaffected by his accident and he can remember those things well.

Episodic Memory

This third variety of long-term memory storage is concerned with the remembering of events that have been personally experienced. **Episodic memory** stores autobiographical information—an individual's own perceptual experiences along with some *temporal* coding (or "time tags") to identify when the event occurred and some coding for its *context*. Memories of a happiest birthday or of a first love affair are part of a personal history and are stored in episodic memory. Nick suffered from impaired episodic memory for events after his accident.

Successful recall of much of the factual information you have learned in college also involves episodic memory; many events, formulas, and concepts are stored, in part, according to a variety of personally relevant context features. For example, in trying to answer a particular test question you remember which course the material probably came from, whether you heard it during the lecture

or read it in the text, whether you discussed it in a study group, and whether you put it in your notes. You may even have a mental image of the relevant graph or figure.

Ironically, every time you take anything *out* of your episodic memory storage, you also increase what is *in* there. You do so because you then remember and store your act of recalling it (when and where did you reply "Pavlov" and "Hamlet"?). Such additions often make what is there less accessible.

Until quite recently, most research on long-term memory was concerned with only episodic memory for lists of nonsense syllables or pairs of unrelated stimuli. This research was based on the assumption that there was only one kind of remembering. By studying it in as "pure" a form as possible, uncontaminated by meanings in the stimulus materials, researchers hoped to find basic principles that could then be used to help understand more complex examples of remembering. (See the ***Close-up*** on p. 317.) The study of the memory of *meaningful* material was neglected until the 1950s when theorists began to use computers to simulate psychological processes in memory, language understanding, and comprehension of

Close-up Ebbinghaus and His Nonsense Syllables

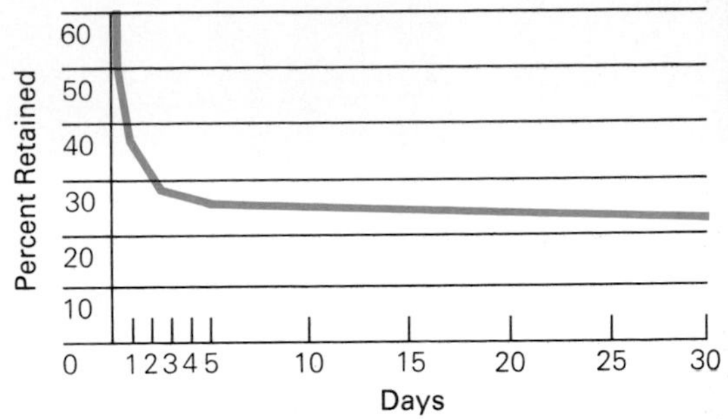

The first significant study providing a truly quantitative measure of memory was published in 1885 by the German psychologist Hermann Ebbinghaus. Ebbinghaus used "nonsense syllables"—meaningless three-letter units consisting of a vowel between two consonants, such as CEG or DAX. He used nonsense syllables, rather than meaningful three-letter words, because he hoped to obtain a "pure" measure of memory, one uncontaminated by previous learning or associations that the person might bring to the experimental memory task.

Not only was Ebbinghaus the researcher; he was also his *own subject.* The task he used was called *serial learning,* and the method he used was rote learning. A list of nonsense syllables was presented one at a time and then repeated, in the same order, until he could recite all items in the correct order—the *criterion performance.*

Later, he would test himself to see how much he remembered. During the retention interval, he distracted himself from rehearsing the original list by learning other lists. Then, instead of trying to recall all the items on the original list, Ebbinghaus measured his memory by seeing how many trials it took him to *relearn* the original list. If he took fewer trials, it meant that he had *saved* information from his earlier learning.

For example, if Ebbinghaus took 12 trials to learn a list and 9 trials to relearn it several days later, his savings score for that elapsed time would be 25 percent (12 − 9 trials = 3 trials saved; 3 divided by 12 = 25 percent). This *savings method* for measuring retention is a very sensitive one, often showing evidence of some memory even when no items can be recalled at the start of the second learning period.

Using the savings method, Ebbinghaus examined how much memory was lost after different time intervals. The curve he obtained is shown above. As you can see, he found a rapid initial loss, followed by a gradually slower decline. Ebbinghaus' curve is typical of results from experiments on rote memory of meaningless material.

Why did Ebbinghaus' memories fade so quickly? You might think that it was just because of the passage of time, but most of what we learn is remembered far longer than Ebbinghaus' forgetting curve implies. It turns out that there are several reasons why Ebbinghaus forgot faster than usual.

One reason is that the materials he used—nonsense syllables—could not be tied to information already stored in his memory, nor could they easily be chunked or rehearsed elaboratively. How can you image a CEG or a DAX when there are no such things? A second reason in *interference.* Because he learned so many lists of similar items, they began to get confused in his memory. If he had learned only one list, he probably would have remembered it a great deal longer.

Following Ebbinghaus' lead, the standard method of studying human verbal learning for many decades was to have subjects learn nonsense syllables. Besides avoiding the "complicating influence of meaning," such studies were in keeping with the interest in recording overt responses rather than investigating mental processes. Not until the focus changed to the way information is processed did the study of memory shift to meaningful material.

---

material read. Since then, this type of study has become a major branch of memory research.

Figure 9.8 is a summary of the memory "triads" discussed thus far. Let us now add one more "set of three" relating the three kinds of memory content to the varieties of consciousness described in chapter 7.

Memory and Consciousness

It is possible to relate each of the kinds of memory content to a type of consciousness (Tulving, 1985). Episodic memory is associated with *autonoetic* (self-knowing) *consciousness.* It gives our memory its uniquely subjective flavor as we recall personally

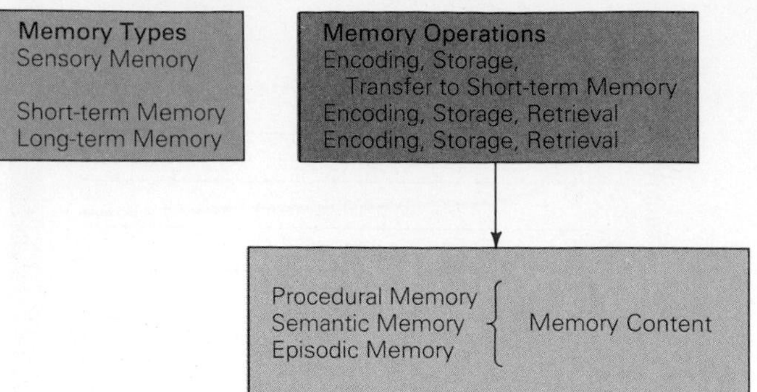

Figure 9.8 *A Summary of the "Sets of Three" Aspects of Memory*

tagged events. This autobiographical, ego-centered consciousness sets remembering apart from all other kinds of awareness, such as thinking or perceiving.

Semantic memory is associated with *noetic* (knowing) *consciousness.* When symbolic information is entered into and retrieved from semantic memory, those processes are accompanied by noetic consciousness. Our awareness of objects, events, and relationships—in their absence—is made possible with this kind of consciousness.

Finally, procedural memory and *anoetic* (nonknowing) *consciousness* are associated since they are concrete, specific, situation-bound aspects of memory and awareness.

How Is Information Represented in Memory?

We know that information in long-term memory is stored in organized patterns, with networks of meaningfully related concepts and multiple connections for many—perhaps all—chunks of knowledge. From the functional differences among procedural, semantic, and episodic memories we guess that there is probably some difference in the ways or places they are stored. Also one memory ability can be lost and another retained. We know that somehow there must also be representations of past sensory experiences (sights, sounds, and smells, for example), emotional experiences, experiences of movement (as in skill learning), and even episodes of interpersonal experiences—representations not only stored, but stored with interconnections (Forgas, 1982). We really know very little about the way all the forms of experience that we remember are actually represented in long-term memory.

Researchers who study the comprehension and memory of verbal material have hypothesized that the memory code is verbal—that people store representations of ideas in some type of linguistic code (see Clark & Clark, 1977). They use the term *proposition* to refer to the meaning unit in such a representation. A **proposition** is an abstract unit of meaning, an idea that expresses a relationship between concepts, objects, or events. It is the smallest unit of knowledge that makes an assertion (containing a subject and a predicate) which can be judged to be true or false. "People drink water." "Grandparents spoil grandchildren." These are simple examples of propositions.

Propositions are assumed to be represented in our minds in some *non*linguistic form, however. The same propositions (deep structure) can be expressed in different sentences (surface structures). For example, the meaning conveyed by the sentence "They drank water" is also conveyed by the sentences "They imbibed H_2O" and "Water was drunk by them."

"Don loves Joan who is pretty and lives in New York" is a sentence with three meaning units and, hence, three propositions: Don loves Joan; Joan lives in New York; Joan is pretty. Propositions are seen as "meaning atoms," the smallest abstract units of knowledge.

According to some theorists, networks of such propositions form the structural building blocks of long-term memory. These semantic (meaning) networks enable us to locate stored information and alter or add to it (Anderson, 1976). **Figure 9.9** is a representation of the semantic network for the "Don loves Joan" sentence.

Evidence for the importance of propositions in our thought processes is found because it takes longer to understand the meaning of sentences containing more propositions even when the number of words in the sentences is the same (Kintsch, 1974). Researchers have also shown that when subjects are asked to remember a set of interrelated sentences, the more propositions there are related to a given concept, the longer it takes to recall any one of those propositions (Anderson & Bower, 1973).

Other investigators believe that people use visual codes in addition to verbal ones for storing memories. This view of two forms of memory storage—in both verbal and visual codes—is called the **dual-code model of memory** (Begg & Paivio, 1969; Paivio, 1983). According to this view, sensory information and concrete sentences are more likely to be stored as images, while abstract sentences are verbally coded. In one version of this dual-code theory, images reside in a "visual buffer"—a spatial medium—where they can be worked on and transformed in various ways (for example, rotated or scanned) by other cognitive processes (Kosslyn, 1983). In this model of memory, verbal codes cannot act as indexes or reference pegs for visual codes.

Heated debate has surrounded the selection of the type of memory codes to be used to represent different kinds of information. Some researchers argue for a single code represented in propositional networks (Anderson, 1978). Other researchers question the efficiency of a memory system that uses the same code for all of the varied types of informational input (Kosslyn, 1983). Some point to the use of different types of codes to accurately represent different types of information (Day, 1986). Thus, propositional networks are suggested for encoding test information (Anderson & Bower, 1973); mental images are more appropriate for maps (B. Tversky, 1981), and for mentally rotating complex figures (Cooper & Shepard, 1973). It seems that the answer to the debate is that both propositions and images represent information, only at different times for differing processing demands.

Eidetic Imagery

Evidence that literal images may be stored in memory is seen in the phenomenon of apparent "photographic memory," known technically as **eidetic imagery.** Research subjects who claim to have eidetic imagery report "seeing" a whole stimulus picture in front of their closed eyes as if they were experiencing it directly rather than scanning memory for traces of it. This skill is rare, found only in about 5 percent of the children studied (Gray & Gummerman, 1975).

Instead of asking subjects to describe pictures they have been shown, researchers have developed a more demanding test for eidetic imagery. Two pictures are shown in succession, each meaningless by itself, but together forming a meaningful composite. This superimposition method forces the subjects to hold the two images in visual memory in enough detail so that the images will fuse to form a single picture that is not predictable from either part alone. Using this method, those who qualify as true "eidetikers" are rare, especially as the pictures become complex (Gummerman et al., 1972; Leask et al., 1969).

One unusual case exists in the literature of a woman, Elizabeth, who appeared to have an amazing degree of eidetic imagery. She passed all the tests the researchers developed to challenge the existence of her "photographic memory." In the most stringent test, Elizabeth saw a special complex pattern of a million dots with one eye, then later (up to several hours) looked at another seemingly random dot array. She was able to fuse the earlier image with the currently perceived one to form a 3-D picture. Normally this can be accomplished only by looking at the two images at the same time with special 3-D glasses. Elizabeth must have had the ability to retain the first image in long-term memory and retrieve it on demand. There may be other people with her remarkable type of memory who have not yet been studied, but even this one rare case forces us to acknowledge the possibility of vivid visual memory storage. (Stromeyer & Psotka, 1970)

New evidence for eidetic imagery comes, not from rare exceptional humans, but from ordinary honey bees! For most animals remembering the cues that identify a desirable food source is of great

Figure 9.9 A Propositional Network Representation

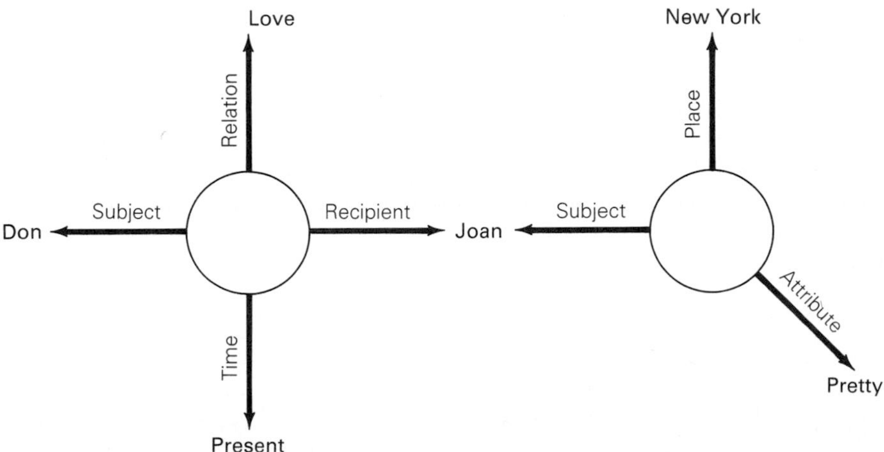

significance; learning specific food cues is essential for survival. Honey bees store information about their food sources in constellations of associated features. If a single feature of a food source is changed (say, a flower's odor), the bees must forget everything else they know about the flower in order to relearn its shape, color, and other features, even though these features have not changed (Gould & Marler, 1984).

In a well-controlled study honey bees were given a sweet sucrose reward to respond differently to complex colored patterns. The results revealed that bees remember shapes "photographically." They are able to store complex patterns, not as isolated features, but as low-resolution eidetic images of the total pattern of colored shapes. The data suggest that bees were remembering the spatial relationship of elements in each pattern (Gould, 1985).

Much remains to be learned about the structures and networks involved in memory storage, and we will consider further evidence in the next chapter. It is clear, however, that the computer models of memory proposed so far are much simpler than the rich reality of personal memory.

Retrieval from Long-term Memory

Some researchers believe that information is never lost from long-term memory. They argue that all information encoded in long-term memory is stored there permanently. Retrieval failures only occur when the appropriate retrieval location or pathway for a given memory is forgotten (Linton, 1975). A great deal of research has focused on the retrieval process and on the cues that are most effective for locating specific memories among the massive number being held in long-term storage.

The stimuli available to us as we search for a memory are called **retrieval cues.** They may be externally provided, as items on a quiz (What memory principles do you associate with the research of Sternberg and Sperling?) or internally generated (Where have I met her before?). In the same way that the correct call number will get us the library book we want, a suitable key—retrieval cue—will unlock the particular stored memory we are after. Luckily, more than one key often works.

Aids to Retrieval

The importance of encoding specificity has already been mentioned. Remembered material is much more accessible if it has been encoded in accordance with the retrieval cues that you have to work with. As we have seen, cues can be provided both by the content of a test question and by the context during encoding. If these are the same during your memory search as during your earlier learning, you will have better access to what you learned.

Since organization helps you put information into storage, it is not surprising that cues based on *organization* can also help you get out what you know.

In one study, subjects were given a list of words to memorize for free recall. The words were arranged by categories, with each category label preceding the words. The category labels were not mentioned; instructions were simply to memorize the words. During the recall test, half the subjects were given the category labels as retrieval cues, while the other subjects were asked only to recall as many items as they could. Recall was much better for the subjects given the category labels as retrieval cues.

In the second recall test, however, where both groups were given the category retrieval cues, they remembered equally well. The information had evidently been available in the long-term memory store of all the subjects, but was just not as accessible without the retrieval cues to help locate the items. (Tulving & Pearlstone, 1966)

Other research has shown that recall is aided whether the organization is imposed by the experimenter or generated by the subject (Mandler, 1972).

Even with good cues, not all stored content is equally accessible, as you know only too well. In the case of familiar, well-learned information, more aspects of it have been stored and connections with many different parts of the memory network have been established, so a number of cues can give you access to it, and you can get to a lot of information quickly be accessing any part of the network. On the other hand, in trying to find the one key that will unlock a less familiar memory, you may have to use special search strategies. (See the ***Close-up*** on p. 321.)

If you are asked whether a particular statement is true, you can answer most quickly if it involves a concept familiar to you. You also have more confidence in your answer. By contrast, where you must check less well-established memories, your retrieval processes will be slower, more conscious and intentional, and more uncertain, because there are fewer possible routes to the material.

Methods of Retrieval

You might assume that you either know something or you don't, so any method of testing what you know would give the same results. Not so. The two most used methods—recall and recognition—give quite different results.

Close-up Don't Tell Me—It's on the Tip of My Tongue

1. *What is the waxy substance derived from sperm whales that is often used in perfumes?*
2. *What are the small boats used in the harbors and rivers of China and Japan?*
3. *What is the patronage bestowed on a person based on a family relationship rather than on merit?*

When these questions were asked of a large number of college students, there was one of three reactions: immediate recall of the correct word, failure to identify the word from the definition, or awareness of knowing the right word, but not being able to recall it. This last reaction is a common phenomenon we all experience when a memory we are searching for is "on the tip of the tongue"—the TOT phenomenon (Brown & McNeil, 1966).

If these TOT words are really known and stored in memory, but are not available in a person's active-recall vocabulary, then it should be possible to demonstrate that many of their characteristics can be retrieved through questioning. When asked to write down all the words they were thinking of as possible answers, subjects gave some words that were similar in meaning to the elusive TOT words, but more often they answered with words similar in sound. For the second question, they tended to answer *Siam, Cheyenne, Sarong,* or *Saipan* more frequently than *junk* or *barge*. They were also able to recall other details of the target word, such as its number of syllables and first letter.

You might want to demonstrate this phenomenon for yourself using your roommate or friends as subjects to see what they say while searching for *ambergris, sampan, nepotism,* and other words that might fall into the TOT category. From such research we learn that retrieval from memory storage is a complex process, rather than an all-or-none experience; and from our search experiences in such cases, we learn that our storage must include many aspects of words, including sound, shape, and context, as well as meaning.

Recall means reproducing the information to which you were previously exposed. A recall question might be, "What are the three memory systems?" **Recognition** means realizing that a certain stimulus event is one you have seen or heard before. A recognition question might be, "Which is the term for a visual sensory memory: (a) echo; (b) engram; (c) icon; (d) abstract code?" By giving different retrieval cues to work with, these two methods call for different mental processes.

In trying to identify a criminal, the police would be using the recall method if they asked a victim to describe, from memory, the person's distinguishing features: "Did you notice anything unusual about the attacker?" They could use the recognition method in one of two ways. A victim could be shown photos, one at a time, from a file of criminal suspects, or the victim could identify a suspect in a police line-up.

Both recall and recognition require a search using the cues given. Recall questions usually give fewer cues and less specific ones than recognition questions; but, even when both lead to a successful search, the next stage is different. For recognition, you need simply to match a remembered stimulus against a present perception; both are in your

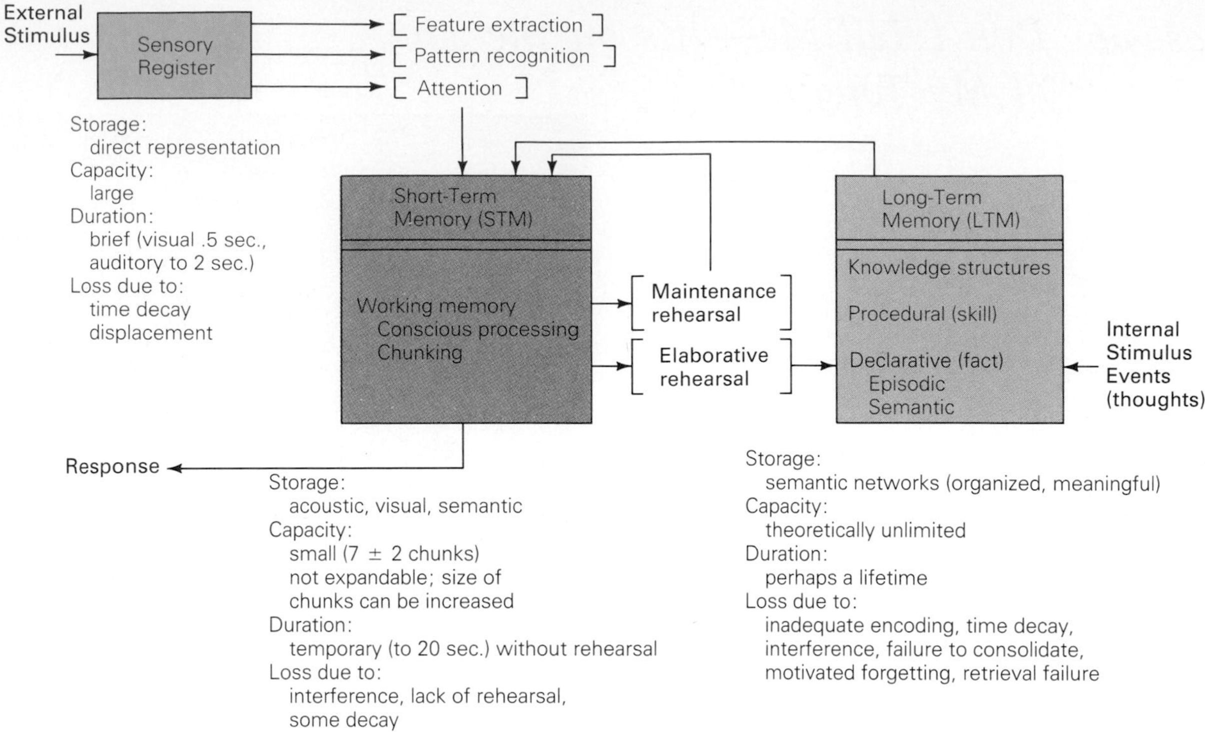

Figure 9.10 *A Flowchart of Hypothesized Memory System*

consciousness. For recall, you must reconstruct from memory something that is not in the present environment and then describe it well enough so that an observer can be sure, from your words or drawings, that it really is in your mind.

It is hardly surprising, therefore, that you can usually recognize far more than you can recall. It also explains why students find true-false or multiple-choice tests (recognition) easier than fill-in-the-blank tests (recall) and why recognition tests usually lead to better test performance—though not necessarily higher grades. But a qualification is in order. A crucial factor in the superiority of recognition tests is the nature of the alternatives. As the incorrect alternatives become more similar to the correct one, then recognition becomes difficult and recall is better.

Two Memories Versus Multiple Levels

The presentation so far has been based on a theory of qualitatively different systems for short- and long-term memory. Known as the **duplex theory of memory,** it postulates a flow of information from temporary sensory memory (Atkinson & Shiffrin, 1968). Its main features are summarized in **Figure 9.10.** Duplex theory focuses primarily on the differences between short-term memory and long-term memory.

Although the duplex theory is now widely accepted, it has been challenged in recent years. Critics believe that there may be a single system of memory in which the only differentiation is in levels of processing: deeper processing results in better and longer memory, because more analysis, interpretation, comparison, and elaboration take place. This view is called the **levels of processing theory** (Cermak & Craik, 1979; Craik & Lockhart, 1972).

Consider three levels at which the word *memory* can be processed: (a) *physical,* in terms of its appearance, the size and shape of the letters; (b) *acoustic,* involving the sound combinations that distinguish it from similar sounds (such as "memo"); and (c) *semantic,* according to its meaning (memory as a mental capacity or product of remembering). Levels-of-processing theorists claim that these processes differ in "depth." It takes least "mental work" to process input at a physical (visual) level, more at an acoustic level, and still more at a semantic level. Moreover, within any of these three types of processing, there can also be variations in level. It should now require "deeper" processing for you to complete the sentence "Memory means . . . ." than it did before you started this chapter, because the word is now linked to many new concepts and associations beyond just "what people remember."

One way in which level of processing is shown to influence memory comes from research in which subjects work on tasks requiring either low-level processing or deep processing. Those subjects who read sentences and rated their pleasantness recalled more total words from the sentences (deep processing) than did subjects who read the same sentences, but focused on counting the number of *e*'s in them (shallow processing) (Jenkins, 1978).

This levels-of-processing view is important because of the emphasis it places on the varying depths at which information can be processed; however, it is unlikely to replace the duplex theory. A major problem with the levels-of-processing theory is that it is often difficult to determine in advance which tasks will require deep processing and which ones shallow levels of processing. Moreover, the notion of separate memory structures is bolstered by several lines of evidence, including studies of amnesia, brain responses, and serial position effects. Let's briefly review this evidence.

Nick's case of amnesia reveals a person who retains long-term memory for events *prior* to his brain injury and a short-term memory for events currently taking place, but no ability to transfer new information from short-term to long-term memory. Other amnesiacs have shown more impairment of long-term than short-term memory, suggesting that there are two memory systems (Milner, 1966; Wingfield & Byrnes, 1981).

A second source of support for a separate short-term memory system comes from a physiological study of brain responses during a test of recall. A unique brain wave form (a particular *evoked potential*) was found to be related to recall in a standard task that measured memory for very recent events, within the short-term memory period. The researchers interpreted this as evidence for a memory storage system that holds incoming information for a short time (Chapman et al., 1978). We will also see in a later section that different biochemical processes seem to operate in temporary versus permanent storage of memory.

The third type of evidence supporting a dual memory system comes from studies of the *serial position effect* in episodic memory. When trying to remember a list of unrelated items, we recall best those at the beginning and end of the list, as shown in **Figure 9.11.** The free recall results are obtained when a subject is free to recall, in any order, the items presented for memorization. Presumably, all items would have been processed at the same level in this case. The difference in retention could be explained, however, by two memory systems. At testing time, the items at the beginning of the list would be safely in long-term storage and those at the end would still be in short-term memory; however, those in the middle would have neither advantage, and remembering them would be further hampered by interference from items before and after.

This interpretation is bolstered when subjects are given a distracting task after exposure to the list but before the testing. The items in the last part of the list are recalled as poorly as those in the middle of the list, whereas early items are remembered as well as ever (Glanzer & Cunitz, 1966; Postman & Phillips, 1965).

This poorer memory for the middle position of any series—the **serial position effect**—is a general phenomenon that holds for different types of materials and different modes of presentation (Roediger & Crowder, 1976). For instance, in learning the alphabet, children make most errors on the middle letters (I to M). Most spelling errors also occur for letters in the middle of words. College students fail more exam items on material from the middle of a lecture than on material from

Figure 9.11

The effects of a distracting task (of 0, 10, or 30 seconds) between the presentation of the list and the request for recall. The major effect is on short term memory-related recency effect. (After Glanzer & Cunitz, 1966.)

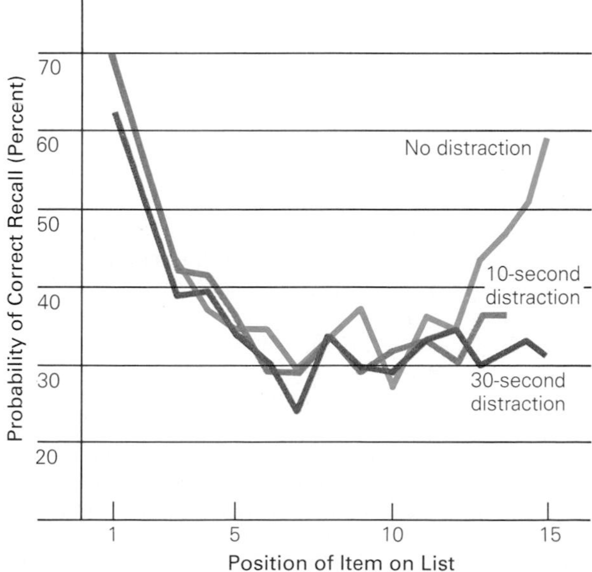

the start or end of the lecture (Holen & Oaster, 1976; Jensen, 1962). So now you know what to devote some extra time and effort to—hit that middle! (You might also take note that this chapter is in the middle of the book.)

Remembering as a Constructive Process

So far we have been talking as if we simply store and remember varying amounts of the information we receive, but sometimes what we "remember" is either more than what we actually experienced or different from it in important ways. From laboratory studies about the way people process and remember meaningful material, psychologists have been forced to accept a new conception of remembering as a continuation of the active, *constructive* process of perception. According to this view, as we organize material to make it meaningful, we frequently add details to make it more complete or change it to make it fit better with other, already existing information in our personal memory store.

Adding new information to what we take in is a constructive process that happens when the given information seems incomplete and we proceed to fill in the rest to make a "good figure," as we saw in our perception study of incomplete visual figures. In remembering, this process may involve putting material into a context that makes sense to us or making inferences about events preceding an experienced action, unstated motives of the actors, or expected outcomes. For example, we see two friends parting and hear one say " . . . between 8 and 8:30." We may "remember" hearing them planning their next meeting, though the time may have been related to something else entirely.

Changing information to make it conform to knowledge already in memory is a *distortion process.* When a new idea or experience is incompatible with our values, beliefs, or strongly felt emotions, it may be altered to be more consistent with our world view or self-concept. See **Figure 9.12** for the stimulus picture used in a classic study.

> *Subjects were shown this picture briefly and asked to describe it to another person who had not seen it; that person, in turn, would communicate the information to someone else, and so on. Before long, the razor, which was in the white man's hand in the original scene, was being held by the black man in a number of the "remembered" scenarios. (Allport & Postman, 1947)*

Distortion can occur either at the encoding stage when the material is first processed or later at the retrieval stage, and perhaps even in between, during storage, as apparent inconsistencies and contradictions are dealt with. Usually we are quite unaware of such changes and confidently believe that our "memory" is an accurate record of what took place—surely not just a rumor transmission funnel (Spiro, 1977).

Schemas

The study of constructive processes is one of the most exciting new directions in memory research. Its focus is on the way people organize, interpret, and retain meaningful input. Its most general principle is the following: *How and what you remember is determined by who you are and what you already know.*

Much of what we know seems to be stored as **schemas** (the singular is **schemata**), general conceptual frameworks or clusters of knowledge and preconceptions regarding certain objects, people, and situations and the way they are related. Schemas are "knowledge packages" that provide expectations about the attributes we will find in future examples of various concepts and categories. For example, the term *registration day* probably conjures up a scene of noise, hassle, long lines, delay, and frustration. These features are all part of a student's schema for this term; to a political candidate, *registration day* will evoke quite a different schema.

Many of our constructions and distortions in remembering new information are the result of in-

Figure 9.12
Subjects were shown this picture in which the taller, better-dressed man is black and the man holding a razor is white. The scene became distorted as the subjects described it to others, indicating that previously held beliefs can alter the processes of encoding and retrieval.

terpreting it in the light of expectations we have from existing schemas. Cues in the present input steer us to a particular schema and we proceed to fill in the rest of the picture from schema-relevant information.

The importance of schemas in helping us organize and make sense of details—and remember them—has been shown in many studies (see Alba & Hasher, 1983).

In one study, a story read to the subjects included the following sentences: "Now three sturdy sisters sought proof. Forging along, sometimes through calm vastness, yet more often over turbulent peaks and valleys, days became weeks as many doubters spread fearful rumors about the edge. . . ."

Some subjects were given no title for this story, while others were told it was "Columbus Discovering America." The latter group recalled much more of the story, evidently because the title brought to mind a well-known schema (remember the Pinta, Nina, *and* Santa Maria?*) that provided a meaningful context for the ambiguously presented information. (Dooling & Lachman, 1971)*

In another study, some subjects read a story titled, "Watching a Peace March from the Fortieth Floor," while other subjects read the same story under the title, "A Space Trip to an Inhabited Planet." While most of the story was ambiguous enough to fit either title, one sentence fit only the space-trip title: "The landing was gentle, and luckily the atmosphere was such that no special suits had to be worn."

While more than half of those who were given the space-trip title remembered this sentence, only a few remembered it from the "peace-march" story. The titles seemed to have activated different schemas. For one schema the critical sentence fit, was interpreted as relevant, and was remembered; for the other it had no meaning and was lost or not retrievable. (Bransford & Johnson, 1972)

We also have people-related schemas that can influence what we perceive and remember about people who are described to us (Cantor & Mischel, 1979b). For example, most of us have schemas for Republicans, cult leaders, environmentalists, and used-car salesmen. If a person we do not know is described as being a member of one of these categories, our schemas lead us to assume the presence of particular personality characteristics and to have an emotional reaction favoring or disapproving the person. On the other hand, when we hear several details about someone we do not know, we remember more of the details if we can relate them to an appropriate organizing schema.

Subjects were presented with a list of behaviors (ate lunch in the park, rented an apartment near work). Some of the subjects were told that this was a memory experiment and that they should try to remember as much of the information as possible. Other subjects were told that this was an experiment about the way people form impressions of others and that they should form an impression (or schema) of the person who had supposedly engaged in these behaviors.

After a short delay, all subjects were asked to recall as many of the behaviors as possible. The subjects who had processed the information in terms of a schema about a certain kind of person (thus, in "more depth") remembered more than did those who tried to remember the same information as unrelated items on a list. (Hamilton et al., 1980)

When we try to recall information that is not consistent with a schema we have formed about certain individuals, our memory may distort the input to make it more schema-consistent. For example, if we are told that a couple are having a lot of disagreement during their courtship, but later are told that they are happily married, we are likely to forget about the earlier disagreement or else to be suspicious of their "happy" marriage. Either distortion permits a memory consistent with our schema. Where the same early information about disagreement is followed by a report of an *unhappy* outcome, we tend to remember the disagreement quite accurately (Spiro, 1977).

The same process is probably at work when people have difficulty learning and fairly representing an opponent's point of view. In political (and other) arguments both sides tend to remember the opposing viewpoint as oversimplified, less rational, and more extreme than their own, thereby achieving a more comfortable overall perspective of the problem and their relation to it.

Although the study of constructive processes in memory represents the "new look" in memory research, it was actually begun over 50 years ago by British psychologist Sir Frederic Bartlett and described in his classic book *Remembering* (1932). Bartlett's focus was on the kinds of construction that take place. His method was to observe the way British undergraduates transmitted and remembered simple stories whose unfamiliar themes and wording were taken from another culture. His most famous story was "The War of the Ghosts," an American Indian tale.

Bartlett used two procedures to study the way his subjects transformed this alien story into a coherent narrative that made sense to them.

In political debates both sides tend to remember the opposing viewpoint as less rational and more extreme than their own, seeing their relationship to the problem as more reasonable.

> *In* serial reproduction, *one person would read the story and tell it from memory to a second person, who communicated it to a third, and so on. In* repeated reproduction, *the same person would read the story and retell it from memory over a number of repeated sessions (up to years apart). In both cases memory was very inaccurate—the "recalled" story that came out was often quite different from the story that went in.*
>
> *He found that constructive processes were intervening between input and output.*

The original stories had evidently been unclear to the subjects because of a lack of cultural understanding. To get the stories to make more sense, the subjects unknowingly changed details to fit their own schemas. What came out of this process were coherent stories that were briefer, more clearly focused, and more understandable to the individuals—but not exactly what originally went into their memory systems.

The distortions Bartlett found usually involved three kinds of constructive processes: (a) *leveling*—simplifying the story; (b) *sharpening*—highlighting and overemphasizing certain details; and (c) *assimilation*—changing the details to fit the subject's own background or knowledge better.

Eyewitness Testimony

Juries tend to give much weight to the testimony of witnesses who are "at the scene" and report on what they see "with their own eyes"; but if memory is reconstructed to fit our schemas, how far should the memory of such witnesses be trusted?

The ease with which we can be misled into "remembering" false information has been amply demonstrated in the laboratory research of Elizabeth Loftus (1979, 1984) and her colleagues. Bright college students with good memories have been misled into "recalling" that a *yield* sign was a *stop* sign, that a nonexistent barn was at the scene, that a green stoplight was red—and more.

The basic research design used in these studies typically involved two groups of people, both of whom view the same stimulus materials on film or slides. Members of the experimental group later received information designed to "contaminate" their memories, indirect suggestions that certain events were present or certain actions occurred. For example, they may hear another "witness" report something about a man's mustache when, in fact, the man had no mustache.

Evidence for the malleability of memory comes from comparing recall of the original materials by the experimental subjects with recall by the control subjects, who have been given no subsequent information. Although many subjects resist being misled, a significant proportion integrate the new information into their memory representation and report the nonexistent mustache or other misinformation as part of what they saw.

Sometimes words used in the questioning suggest a particular interpretation. These words then function as *misleading* retrieval cues. Such findings help explain the success of skillful lawyers in getting the responses they want from witnesses.

This line of research has practical, applied value and also contributes to basic knowledge (see ***Close-up*** on p. 328–329). Memory researchers are using this research paradigm to discover *how* memories are changed by subsequent information. Are they lost, suppressed, or blended? Researchers are also testing variables that extend or limit the general conclusion that "misleading mentions may make memories mucky" (see Bekerian & Bowers, 1983; McCloskey & Egeth, 1983).

Our capacity for constructive memory not only increases the problem of getting accurate eyewitness testimony, but can shield us from some truths we do not want to accept. To the extent that it does so, we carry around a false picture of some aspects of reality. It makes bigots more bigoted because corrective information gets distorted, and it makes all of us more likely to disregard new details in familiar contexts, where we remember what we expected.

Despite its faults, constructive memory is an enormously positive aspect of creative minds-at-work. More often than not, it helps us to make sense of our uncertain world by providing the right context in which to understand, interpret, remember, and act on minimal or fragmentary evidence. Without it, our memories would be little more than transcription services that would lose much of the significance of what transpired.

Why Do We Forget?

We all remember an enormous amount of material over long periods of time. College students can accurately recall many documented details surrounding the birth of a sibling 16 years earlier when they were only three or four years old (Sheingold & Tenney, 1982). Conductor Arturo Toscanini, even at an advanced age, is reported to have known "by heart every note of every instrument of about 250 symphonic works and the words and music of about 100 operas"—plus many scores for other forms of music (Marek, 1975).

Knowledge in semantic memory is remembered even better than knowledge in episodic memory, regardless of the time interval since you experienced it. You will remember many basic things about psychology even if you forget your instructor's name and the details of taking the course. In semantic memory, you will retain generalizations longer than details. For long-term retention, as for efficient encoding and retrieval, meaningful organization seems to be the key.

Yet even well-learned material may be unretrievable over time. Why? In this section, we will explore several different perspectives on forgetting. Each one gives an explanation for what has happened to stored information when we cannot remember it:

1. *Decay*—stored information is lost over time, like the colors of a picture bleached by the sun.
2. *Interference*—it is blocked by similar inputs, as when multiple exposures of a negative interfere with the clarity of the original image.
3. *Retrieval Failure*—it cannot be located, as when you can't find your car in a huge parking lot without knowing the appropriate section number.
4. *Motivated Forgetting*—it is being hidden from consciousness for some personal reason, as when you forget the name of someone you don't like.

Let's look at each of these explanations in more detail.

Decay of Memory Traces

According to the first explanation, the primary problem is one of gradual storage loss. You remember what you wore yesterday better than you remember what you wore last Wednesday; you remember the details of today's lecture better than yesterday's.

Many memories are lost or become "dim" or incomplete over time. On the other hand, to prove that decay is to blame for forgetting, we would have to prove that (a) no mental activity had occurred between original learning and the recall test that could have changed or interfered with the memories, and (b) the memories were, in fact, gone from the brain and not merely inaccessible for some reason. Although it seems plausible that decay is partly responsible for the inability to remember things learned long ago, the only thing we can say with certainty is that decay is an important factor in sensory memory and in short-term memory when all maintenance rehearsal is prevented.

Some memories do not seem to become weaker. Recall that learned motor skills are retained for many years even with no practice. Once you learn to swim, you never forget how. In addition, trivia and irrelevant information, such as song titles and commercial jingles, seem to persist in memory.

Close-up Eyewitness Testimony on Trial: One Issue in Psychology and Law

The same event is not perceived in the same way by different observers. That was the basic message of Munsterberg's story about the two reporters who listened to his speech (see chapter 2, p. 28). This kind of discrepancy led Munsterberg to conclude, in his 1908 book entitled *On the Witness Stand,* that eyewitnesses to a crime cannot be relied on to provide accurate evidence. Such a conclusion is at odds with the American judicial system, which assumes that eyewitness testimony is one of the most accurate and influential forms of evidence that can be presented in court. Which conclusion is right?

Despite Munsterberg's provocative arguments, it was not until the 1970s that systematic research was done on the issue of eyewitness testimony. The results of this research support Munsterberg's position—namely, eyewitness testimony is often untrustworthy. Many factors operate to influence and distort a witness' perception and memory. For example, the way in which a witness is questioned about an event can affect his or her recall.

In one study, people were shown a film of an automobile accident and were asked to estimate the speed of the cars involved; however, some people were asked, "How fast were the cars going when they smashed into each other?" while others were asked, "How fast were the cars going when they contacted each other?" When "smash" was used in the question, the eyewitnesses reported that the cars had been going over 40 mph. Those same cars were reported to be going 30 mph by eyewitnesses who had been asked the "contact" question. About a week later, all the eyewitnesses were asked to remember the car accident they had seen—"Did you see any broken glass?" (In fact, no broken glass had appeared in the film.) Of the eyewitnesses who had been asked the "smash" question the week before, about a third reported that yes, there had been broken glass, while only 14 percent of the "contact" eyewitnesses said they had seen it. Clearly, the type of verb used in the original question altered people's memory of what they had witnessed. Moreover, these witnesses had "filled in the gaps" with plausible details that fit the general context suggested by the verb. (Loftus, 1979)

The issue that is involved is of central importance to both psychologists and professionals working in the legal system. The process by which a person perceives an event, encodes that information, and recalls it at a later time is at the heart of psychological interest in learning and memory. From the legal perspective, the limitations of that process, and the perceptual and cognitive biases that may be involved, could have profound implications for the use of eyewitness testimony in courtroom trials.

This mutual interest in eyewitness testimony is just one example of the rapidly growing field of *psychology and law* (Tapp, 1976). Many psychologists have turned to the law as a source of

Interference

We never learn anything in a vacuum; we are always having other experiences before and after we learn new material. Both our learning and our retention of new material are affected by interference from these other experiences. When the vocabulary list you learned yesterday interferes with your learning of today's list, the phenomenon is called **proactive interference** (forward acting, earlier disrupts later). When studying today's list interferes with your memory for yesterday's list, the phenomenon is called **retroactive interference** (backward acting, later disrupts earlier).

The greater the similarity between two sets of material to be learned, the greater the interference between them. Two vocabulary lists in the same foreign language would interfere with each other more than would a vocabulary list and a set of chemical formulas. Meaningless material is more vulnerable to interference than meaningful material, and the more difficult the distracting task, the more it will interfere with memory of material learned earlier.

ideas for research or have begun to study various aspects of the legal system. Psychological research, on the other hand, has been increasingly accepted and used by the law. Research may be cited in judicial decisions (such as the Supreme Court decision on school desegregation), or psychologists may appear in court as expert witnesses on some particular topic. For example, psychologists have testified in many court cases about the unreliability of eyewitness identification, and this testimony has then been used to discredit the evidence presented by a particular eyewitness. Such expert testimony is controversial, however, with some critics arguing that the general findings of research studies are not always applicable to the specific facts of any one case (Koněcni & Ebbesen, 1986).

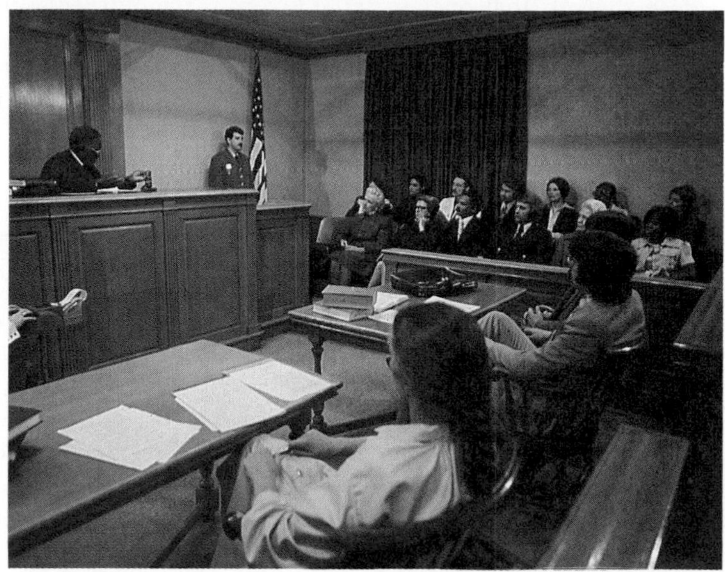

Most of the work in psychology and law has focused on the criminal justice system. The jury has been a predominant topic of study. Research has investigated how jury verdicts are affected by jury size (12 versus 6 members) and by the constraint of reaching a unanimous decision (Saks, 1977). Other studies have investigated the impact of jury selection procedures—for example, the process of "death qualification" (only selecting jurors who state that they can vote for the death penalty, if warranted) makes it more likely that a jury will be biased in favor of the prosecution and a verdict of "guilty" (Fitzgerald & Ellsworth, 1984; Haney, 1984).

In addition to juries, the decisions made by judges have also been studied by psychologists. The results show that judges use very simple strategies for making decisions (such as setting bail solely on the basis of the district attorney's recommendation), even though they report that their decision-making process is very complex and takes many factors into account (Koněcni & Ebbesen, 1984). Research on these and many other legal issues not only contributes to our understanding of human behavior, but has the potential to stimulate improvements in our system of justice.

Ebbinghaus, after learning dozens of lists of nonsense syllables, found himself forgetting about 65 percent of the new ones he was learning. Fifty years later, students at Northwestern University who learned Ebbinghaus' lists had the same experience. At first, they remembered much more. Then, after many trials with many lists, what they had learned earlier interfered proactively with their recall of current lists (Underwood, 1948, 1949).

The most obvious prediction from interference theory is that information undisturbed by new material will be recalled best. A classic study by Jenkins and Dallenbach (1924) provided support for this hypothesis. Subjects who went to sleep immediately after learning new material recalled it better the next morning than those who spent the same number of waking hours in their usual activities. Try this study for yourself by reading the same amount of this text just before going to sleep as you do in the morning. Then test your retention of the material using the relevant self-tests from the *Working with Psychology* Study Guide. The lack of retroactive interference should result in superior performance after the learn-sleep-recall sequence.

Short-term memory seems most vulnerable to interference. Evidence from the studies of serial position effect, suggests that once material is consolidated in long-term memory, it is less subject to interference from later material.

Retrieval Failure

Often an apparent memory loss turns out to be only a failure of retrieval. A question worded a little differently will guide us to the information; or a question requiring only recognition will reveal knowledge that we could not get access to and reproduce by recall. Underwood's students who were having trouble recalling Ebbinghaus' lists often remembered better when retrieval cues were given. Some individuals can recall details under hypnosis for which they have no conscious memory; this is especially true of those with multiple personalities (to be discussed in chapter 15).

However, it should be noted that there is no evidence that hypnosis can refresh recall of meaningless material nor recognition of any type of material. "Pseudomemories" may result when accurate information is combined with fantasies and possibly suggested thoughts given during hypnosis. This conclusion was reached by a panel of experts organized by the American Medical Association to evaluate the scientific evidence for the effects of hypnosis on memory (see Council on Scientific Affairs, 1985). In cases of psychologically caused amnesia, the "forgotten" material is retained but blocked from retrieval, as can be shown when it is later uncovered in psychotherapy.

In fact, research is even suggesting that some inability to remember events during infancy may be because of retrieval failure.

> *Three-month old babies learned to activate a mobile by kicking a foot to which a ribbon leading to the mobile was tied. After eight days of no experience with the mobile, a test of retention showed no sign of memory for the previous learned response.*
>
> *The experimenters then repeated the procedure, but they showed the infants the moving mobile the day before the test of retention. When the test was given, the learned response appeared as strong as ever, even when the test was as much as four weeks after the learning. The memory must have been present in the first part of the study, but must simply not have been retrieved. The researchers hypothesized that much infant learning is kept alive by natural reinstatement of the retrieval cues in a child's ordinary environment. If this is true, it would provide a mechanism by which an infant's early experiences could continue to influence subsequent learning and behavior over an extended period. (Rovee-Collier et al., 1980)*

Even the best retrieval cues will not help if we did not store the material properly, just as a book not listed in the card catalog will not be retrievable in the library even if it is on a shelf—somewhere. In any case, it seems clear that much of our failure to remember reflects poor encoding or inadequate retrieval cues rather than loss of the memory. Failure to call up a memory is never proof positive that the memory is not there.

Motivated Forgetting

Sometimes we forget because we do not want to remember. We may push certain memories out of conscious awareness because they are too frightening, too painful, or too personally degrading. Rape victims, for example, sometimes cannot remember the details of their attack.

It was Sigmund Freud (1923) who first saw memory and forgetting as dynamic processes that enable us to maintain a sense of self-integrity. We all "forget" some ideas we do not want to recognize as part of us, appointments we do not want to keep, names of people we do not like, and past events that threaten our basic sense of self or security. Freud gave the label *repression* to the mental process by which a person supposedly protects himself or herself from remembering unacceptable or painful information by pushing it out of consiousness. In chapter 6 we reviewed experimental evidence for perceptual defense, in which painful or unpleasant information may be blocked out and, hence, neither perceived nor remembered.

Our motivational needs not only prevent retrieval of certain memories, but can change the tone and content of memories that we do retrieve.

> *Research on childhood memories recalled by adults found that the most common emotion associated with the original experiences was* joy *(about 30 percent of the total). Next came* fear *(about 15 percent) followed by pleasure, anger, grief, and excitement. In general, unpleasant events were more often forgotten than pleasant events. (Waldvogel, 1948)*

> *Another study of early recollections revealed that many memories judged as traumatic by the researchers were selectively recoded as neutral or even pleasant by the subjects during recall. Evidently we can reconstruct our early childhood so that we remember the "good old days" not the way they were, but the way they "should have been" (Kihlstrom & Harackiewicz, 1982). Our parents are also likely to remember our childhoods as more pleasant and less difficult than they really were (Robbins, 1963). (Try testing this idea with their recall of events you rate as positive or negative.)*

The Neurobiology of Memory

Psychologists study memory as a whole behavior, using theoretical models of an information-processing organism that forms and holds learned experiences. We have seen that they test their theories with behavioral data from a variety of laboratory experiments. Neuroscientists are also in pursuit of the keys to unlock the mysteries of memory. Their general strategy for understanding the mechanisms of memory involves studying how experience modifies the nervous system. Three tactics that emerge from this molecular level of analysis are (a) studying the anatomy of memory—*where* the brain forms and stores memories; (b) analyzing the changes in synapses and neurons that are assumed to underlie memory; and (c) discovering the physiological systems that regulate or modulate memory storage after an experience. Let's examine some of the evidence being uncovered from the neuroscientists' "inside-out" look at memory.

The Anatomy of Memory

In addition to the coding of genetic information in the DNA of every cell nucleus, nature has developed a second kind of information coding. Acquired information from a lifetime of experience is encoded in the neurons of the brain. The general term for this coding of acquired information in the brain is the **engram** or **memory trace.** The sum of a person's store of engrams is the *biological substrate* of human memory and the foundation upon which each human being's uniqueness rests.

Where in the vast galaxy of the brain are these memory traces to be found? Are they *localized* in particular brain regions or *distributed* throughout many different areas? The "search for the engram" was begun many years ago by physiological psychologist Karl Lashley (1929, 1950). His procedure was to train rats to learn mazes, remove portions of their cerebral cortex, then retest their memories for the mazes. He found that memory impairment from brain lesioning was proportional to the *amount* of tissue removed, worse as more of the cortex was damaged. However memory was not affected by the *location* from which the tissue was removed. Lashley gave up in disappointment, concluding prematurely that the elusive engram did not exist in any localized regions of the brain, but was widely distributed throughout the entire brain.

We now know that Lashley was partly correct—and partly wrong. Memory for complex sets of information is distributed across many neural systems; maze learning, which involves spatial, visual, and olfactory signals, is complex. However, memory for each specific type of sensory information and discrete types of knowledge are separately processed and localized in limited regions of the brain. Modern neuroscientists are now able to trace the neural circuitry that is necessary and sufficient for a particular type of learning—and its remembrance. The four brain structures involved in memory are the hippocampus, the cerebellum, the amygdala, and the cerebral cortex (see **Figure 9.13**).

To investigate the anatomy of memory, neuropsychologist Richard Thompson has used Pavlovian eyelid conditioning in rabbits as a "model system" for relating an organism's adaptive behavioral responding to known brain circuits. The cerebellum is found to play an essential role in both the learning and memory of specific conditioned responses to aversive events. A lesion of only one cubic millimeter of cell tissue in the cerebellum of a rabbit causes permanent loss of a conditioned eyeblink to a tone that signals an air puff to one eye. The memory deficit is highly specific only to that learned association. The animal can still respond to the air puff, hear the tone, and learn the conditioned response in the other eye, but it cannot relearn the response in the first eye.

The entire circuitry for learning and storing this simple conditioned response has been traced to specific nuclei in and around the cerebellum. In

Figure 9.13

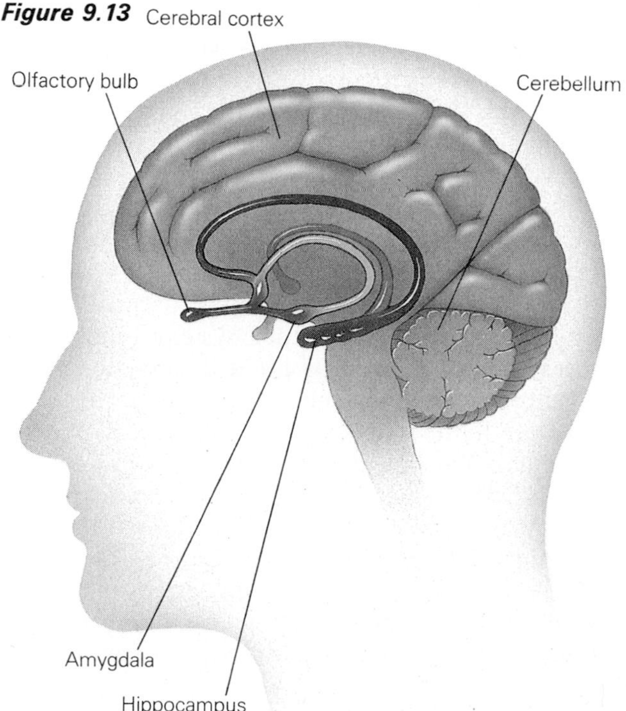

more complex conditioning, as when the subject learns to remember that there is a delay between the tone and the air puff, circuits in the hippocampus also become involved (McCormick & Thompson, 1984).

The hippocampus and amygdala are currently believed to be involved in encoding while the cerebral cortex is the likely candidate for the storage center of long-term memory (McGaugh et al., 1985). Studies of human patients with amnesia have identified the important role of the hippocampus in encoding new fact memories. Comparable memory deficits are found in monkeys with lesions in the hippocampus and amygdala (Mishkin et al., 1984).

Some researchers are studying memory in cortical networks by stimulating or blocking smell memory which is very important in rodents. The olfactory system is unique among the senses because it has fairly direct connections to the hippocampus, amygdala, and the thalamus. That may account for the power of certain odors to evoke strong childhood memories in humans. Remarkable parallels occur in the smell memory of rats and humans. Lesions that separate the olfactory system and the hippocampus in rats produce forgetting for learned odors that are similar in kind to the amnesia experienced by humans, like Nick, who have damage to their temporal lobes and hippocampus (Lynch, 1986).

Other research supports the conception of the brain's organization of memory functions around two different systems for information storage. The distinction we encountered earlier between procedural (skill) and declarative (fact) knowledge is supported by a variety of experiments with amnesic patients, patients with temporarily impaired memories as a result of electroconvulsive shock therapy (for a mental disorder), and brain-lesioned monkeys (see Squire, 1986; Thompson, 1986).

Skill learning appears more primitive than fact learning in the evolution of learning systems. It may involve a collection of special purpose abilities that are stored in structures evolutionally even more primitive than the limbic system. These structures are *not* affected by brain damage to higher level brain centers. While fact learning seems to be centered in the hippocampus and amygdala (limbic system structures), skill learning may be located in the basal ganglia striatum. Emotional memories appear to be stored in the amygdala while spatial memories are centered in the hippocampus.

The hippocampus is also implicated in another vital aspect of memory we have not yet mentioned—how preexisting stored information and new information are connected. Memory is not fixed at the time of learning, but is gradually transformed into a durable long-term memory code by the dynamic process known as **consolidation** (Hebb, 1949; McGaugh & Herz, 1972). This stabilizing or consolidating of memories can proceed for as long as several years in humans and for weeks in lower animals.

The idea that memory changes or consolidates after learning is demonstrated by studies of induced **retrograde amnesia.** In this type of amnesia, memory for events experienced prior to the event that precipitated the amnesia is lost. By contrast, in **anterograde amnesia,** there is a loss of ability to form memories for newly presented facts. Nick, in the *Opening Case,* suffers from anterograde amnesia.

In research with both rodents and humans, treatments given *after* initial learning disrupt memory—but this amnesia decreases over time. Drugs, hormones, and electroconvulsive shocks given after learning influence the strength of memory for the most recent experience; but, over time, as consolidation occurs, the memory strength becomes normalized.

> *Psychiatric patients with prescribed electroconvulsive therapy (ECT) were tested for their memory of TV programs, each of which appeared only once during the past 16 years. Before receiving the first ECT treatment, they remembered best programs that had appeared recently and less well those that were more remote in time. When tested one hour after their fifth ECT treatment (when verbal IQ was intact), memory was* worst *for recent programs broadcast within the past two years, while memory for older programs was normal (see* ***Figure 9.14****). (Squire & Slater, 1975)*

Cellular Mechanisms of Memory

It is now generally accepted by neuroscientists that human memory involves changes in the physiology and/or structure of synaptic membranes (see Lynch, 1986). Neural impulses, signaling specific experiences, modify subgroups of the many billions of synapses in the cortex. In this view, the chemistry of memory must be able irreversibly to modify the structure of a small group of synaptic contacts on a single cell—without affecting neighboring units.

Researchers have reached this conclusion by using high frequency stimulation of inputs to the hippocampus. This stimulation *increased* memory strength for new learning which persisted for 32 months. This technique, called *long-term potentiation,* was found to cause changes in the shape of synapses, to lead to the formation of new synaptic

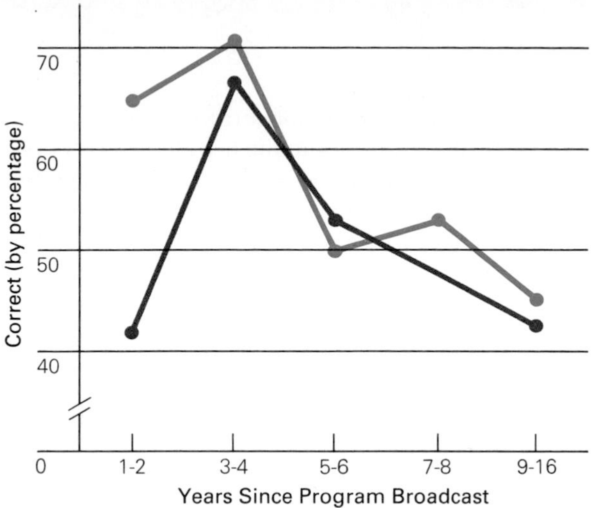

Figure 9.14 *The Effects of Electroconvulsive Shock on Memory*

The red line indicates patients' memory before receiving ECT. They remember best the programs televised recently. After the fifth ECT treatment, their memories were worst for the recent programs (blue line). Apparently administration of ECT leads to retrograde amnesia.

contacts on nerve cells, and to increase the number of receptors for the neurotransmitter glutamate used by the hippocampus (see McGaugh et al., 1985).

This long-lasting potentiation effect alters cortical synapses through a *chemical* process triggered by neural impulses (or the experimental high frequency stimulation). The chemical process then appears to involve the sudden increase in *calcium* within neurons. Calcium activates a special kind of enzyme called *calpain,* which causes the breakdown of parts of the cell membrane. The result is the formation of new receptors on the membrane and changes in the synaptic contacts. Calpain's effects are permanent and irreversible, thus making it ideal for producing long-lasting changes in cellular chemistry and anatomy that may be the basis of human memory. (See also "Our Dual Memory" and "The Way We Act" in *The Best of Science.*)

Hormones and Memory Storage

We have seen that, following a learning experience, memory can be *impaired* by a variety of treatments that produce retrograde amnesia, but memory can also be *enhanced* by certain post-training treatments. Mildly stimulating conditions of the kind used in animal learning studies elicit stress-related hormones, such as epinephrine, corticosteroids, and vasopressin. These hormones are reported to influence memory storage (McGaugh, 1983).

Retention of recently learned information is enhanced if animals are given low doses of epinephrine shortly *after* training. High doses impair memory and delayed administration of the hormone has no effect on memory. When the natural release of such hormones is blocked by surgically removing the adrenal gland, then memory for recent experience is impaired; but when these animals are given injections of epinephrine after training, their memory impairment is lessened. This and other research is leading researchers to believe that hormones modulate memory storage (Gold, 1984).

Why should hormones secreted during states of mild arousal affect memory storage? One answer is that they provide to the brain added information that recent events are important and worth remembering. They then direct the brain to store the new memories. In this sense hormones may regulate or modulate memory storage. However, epinephrine is a hormone that does *not* pass across the blood-brain barrier to the brain cells. How can it then regulate memory? It does so indirectly. It now appears that, when aroused, humans and animals release epinephrine, which, in turn, stimulates an increase in plasma glucose levels. Glucose does get into brain cells and it enhances memory directly. Glucose is a harmless drug, one that can be added to lemonade and taken as a drink to "refresh memory" (Gold, 1987).

Integrating the Biology and the Psychology of Memory

Understanding the human mind is the central goal of much psychological research. The learning and memory of experiences fills our minds with thoughts or cognitions that give meaning to our existence and purpose to our actions. There can be no mind without memory and no sense of human consciousness without mind. The psychological study of memory in the laboratory and in real life has revealed new insights into the multiplicity of systems and operations involved in processing information into memory codes. Theoretical speculations by cognitive psychologists about the dual coding of short-term and long-term memory and distinctions among procedural, semantic, and episodic memory have now been validated by researchers from neurobiology and neuropsychology.

These investigators study the brain as the biological substrate of the mind and memory as "the essential brain substrate for all higher mental processes" (Thompson, 1984, p. 5). Despite differences in the way each of these disciplines approaches the study of memory, there is a new level of cooperation and integration between them.

The ultimate goal is to be able to move across levels of analysis, from formal descriptions of cognition to underlying brain systems and finally to the neurons and cellular events within these systems. The problem of memory needs to be studied at all these levels, and should draw jointly on the disciplines of cognitive psychology, neuropsychology, and neurobiology. (Squire, 1986, p. 1618)

A memory may be vulnerable to distortion and loss over time, and we could all improve the ways we commit information to memory; but to psychologists, memory is the "Queen of the Cognitive Sciences," and to poets, the very center of one's being.

I have a room whereinto no one enters
Save I myself alone:
There sits a blessed memory on a throne,
There my life centres; . . .

Christina Rossetti, "Memory"

Summary

- Remembering is studied by cognitive psychologists as a way of processing information. It is seen as a three-stage process in which information that arrives through our senses is encoded, stored, and later retrieved. Three separate memory systems have been proposed: sensory, short-term, and long-term.
- In encoding for sensory memory, stimulus energy is changed to a neural code. Sensory memory has a large capacity but a very short duration. Attention and pattern recognition help sensory information to get into short-term memory.
- Short-term memory has a limited capacity (7 ± 2 items) and lasts only briefly without rehearsal. It is part of our psychological present and is also called *working memory.* Material may be transferred to it from either sensory or long-term memory; information can be consciously processed only in short-term memory.
- Information entering short-term memory from sensory memory is usually encoded acoustically. Its capacity can be increased by chunking of unrelated items into meaningful groups. Maintenance rehearsal extends the duration of material in short-term memory indefinitely; elaborative rehearsal prepares it for long-term storage.
- Long-term memory constitutes a person's total knowledge of the world and of the self; it is nearly unlimited in capacity. Meaningful organization is the key to encoding for long-term memory: the more familiar the material and the better the organization, the better the retention.
- The more specifically material is encoded in terms of expected retrieval cues, the more efficient later retrieval will be. Similarity in context between learning and retrieval also aids retrieval.
- Three kinds of memory content are procedural, semantic, and episodic memory. Procedural memory is memory for skills—how things get done. Semantic memory is memory for the basic meaning of words and concepts. Episodic memory is concerned with memory of events that have been personally experienced; it stores autobiographical information.
- Investigators disagree about the number of memory codes—whether only verbal, both verbal and visual, or some other combination or relationship.
- There is also disagreement about whether there are actually three different memory systems (sensory, short-term, and long-term) or whether we simply process memories at different levels (that is, use varying depths of processing).
- Remembering is a constructive process and not simply a recording one. We remember what we want to and what we are prepared to remember. Schemas play a major role in constructive memory processes. Schemas are cognitive clusters built up from earlier experience that provide expectations and a context for interpreting new information and, thus, influence what is remembered. Information or misinformation provided during retrieval can bias our recall without our realizing it.
- Explanations for forgetting include decay, interference, retrieval failure, and motivated forgetting. Each one is shown to play a role in some specific instances of forgetting.
- Study of the neurobiology of memory is concentrated in three areas: identification of brain structures involved in the formation and storage of memories, analysis of the synaptic and neuronal changes assumed to underlie memory, and discovery of the physiological systems that regulate or modify memory storage.
- Four brain structures involved in memory are the hippocampus, the amygdala, the cerebellum, and the cerebral cortex. It appears that memory may involve lasting changes in the membranes of synaptic cells at some synapses. Memory can be impaired or enhanced through a variety of treatments (such as administration of drugs and electrical stimulation). Hormones such as epinephrine may play a role in regulating memory.

10

Thinking and Communicating

Allow me to introduce you to "Clever Hans," a remarkable horse who performed intellectual feats in Germany around the turn of the century. He became a legend in his time, because it appeared that he could read German, spell, comprehend complex questions, count, do mathematical operations—and that he possessed a remarkable memory.

Skeptical? So were the members of a scientific investigating commission who carefully checked out the claims of Hans' trainer, Mr. von Osten, and those of many witnesses. They concluded, however, that Hans was indeed clever-as-claimed, a "horse of a different color" who could think and reason about as well as most humans.

An animal who can perform higher mental processes assumed to be limited to humans challenges basic conceptions about the evolution of human intelligence. Let us maintain our scientific skepticism a little longer while reviewing some of the observations reported by that Berlin Commission.

. . . The stately animal, a Russian trotting horse, stood like a docile pupil, managed not by the means of a whip, but by gentle encouragement and frequent reward of bread or carrots. He would answer correctly nearly all of the questions which were put to him in German. If he understood a question, he immediately indicated this by a nod of the head; if he failed to grasp its import, he communicated the fact by a shake of the head. We were told that the questioner had to confine himself to a certain vocabulary, but this was comparatively rich and the horse widened its scope daily without special instruction, but by simple contact with his environment. . . .

Our intelligent horse was unable to speak, to be sure. His chief mode of expression was tapping with his right forefoot. A good deal was also expressed by means of movements of the head. Thus, yes *was expressed by a nod,* no *by a deliberate movement from side to side, and* upward, downward, right, left, *were indicated by turning the head in these directions. . . .*

Let us turn now to some of his specific accomplishments. He had, apparently, completely mastered the cardinal numbers from 1 to 100 and the ordinals to 10, at least. Upon request he would count objects of all sorts, the persons present, even to distinctions of sex. Then hats, umbrellas, and eyeglasses. . . . Small numbers were given with a slow tapping of the right foot. With larger numbers he would increase his speed and would often tap very rapidly right from the start. . . . (Pfungst, 1911, pp. 18-24)

Clever Hans was tapping his way to stardom, until one day someone noticed that he could not solve any of the problems posed to him when his trainer stood *behind* him. There were two other circumstances under which Hans had trouble: when the person asking a question did not know the answer or when blinders covered Hans' eyes.

What was happening? Can *you* shut your eyes and figure it out? Then you are able to think in ways that Hans could not.

The key to the puzzle is the evidence that not only did Hans have to see the person who gave him the problem but that the person had to know the answer. It turned out that Hans had learned to respond to subtle visual cues unintentionally displayed by the questioners. The questioners expected the horse to think and reason, and communicated their expectations nonverbally, without realizing it or intending to cheat. Hans surely was skilled at detecting these cues—and learned when to start tapping and when to stop, when to indicate yes and when to indicate no. He could always make the association between the action and the carrot reward; but however good his horse sense, Hans never had "people sense." He could tap all right, but he never really understood the lyrics. (For a more detailed discussion account of the Clever Hans phenomenon see Sebeok & Rosenthal, 1981; Fernald, 1984.)

In order to figure out why Hans was not solving problems by exercising reason, you have to exercise yours. In doing so, you affirm the greatest achievement of the human species—the ability to think and communicate abstract and complex thoughts.

In this chapter we continue our quest to understand the nature of the human mind. We have arrived at this important place in our journey via earlier paths that led us to consider several aspects of this general topic—consciousness, learning, and memory. Now we are better prepared to understand how humans think, reason, and solve problems, and how they use language to communicate what they know, value, and feel.

There is more to be gained from studying how the mind functions than just the satisfaction of scientific curiosity. Nobel Prize-winning psychologist-computer scientist Herbert Simon underscored the pragmatic side of studying the way the mind manipulates mental and muscular matters in a lecture to members of the U.S. Congress.

> *To what does the understanding of the nature of the mind lead? Presumably it can lead to all kinds of advances in our ability to use the central human resource, the resource that makes us truly human and able to do the things that other creatures in this world cannot do. If we ask what good it can do to understand the mind better, we need to look in the direction of improving management, the process of learning, the decision making and problem solving that takes place in organizations, . . . and in Congress. [T]he human mind really is our biggest . . . economic resource. Human muscles are nice to have around, but they are not so important anymore since we have had steam engines and other sorts of power. The human mind is the resource that human beings apply to the world of work; it is therefore required for productivity increases in the post-industrial world. (1985, pp. 2, 9)*

Studying Thinking

Seventeenth-century philosopher René Descartes' classic statement, "Cogito, ergo sum" ("I think, therefore I am"), was a recognition that a sense of personal identity depends on an awareness of one's own thought processes. It is thinking that turns violations of moral codes into "guilt," inappropriate or stupid deeds into "shame," and accomplishments into "pride."

Only humans have the capacity to think about what was, is, will be, might be, and should be. Thinking provides the context for our perception, the purposes for our learning, and the meaning for our memories. Thinking interprets our existence. Humans are not only information processors, but also information interpreters, ambiguity resolvers, event predictors. It is our thoughts in the inner universe of the mind that enable us to form an abstract working model of the outside world and then to use it to improve some aspect of that world (see Hunt, 1982).

Cognition and the Cognitive Approach

The study of thinking is the study of all the "higher mental processes." **Cognition** is a general term for all forms of knowing. These include attending, remembering, reasoning, imagining, anticipating, planning, deciding, problem solving, and communicating ideas. Cognition includes *processes* that mentally represent the world around us, such as classifying and interpreting; *processes* that we generate internally, as in dreams and fantasies; and the *content* of these processes, such as concepts, facts, and memories. The study of mental processes and structures is **cognitive psychology.** Cognitive

psychologists investigate the ways people take in, transform, and manipulate information.

Besides the mental activities normally associated with thinking, such as solving physics problems and making business judgments, psychologists who study cognition are also interested in many mental processes you may not have associated with *thinking*. Examples are the development of motor skills and the perceptual-cognitive process of pattern recognition by which you can tell that a blob of light waves is, in fact, your mother (our earlier concern in chapters 5 and 6).

As we have seen, modern psychology has been shifting from its earlier emphasis on outer behavior and its external determinants to a concern for understanding the inner, private information processing that goes on out of sight, but gives observed behavior its direction, meaning, and coherence. What early psychologists used to consider an inaccessible "black box" has become the primary focus of cognitive psychology, with new tools and strategies to open and explore its content and organization. The shift in focus began in the late 1950s with the convergence of an unlikely threesome of new research approaches involving computers, children, and communication.

1. Researchers Herbert Simon and Allen Newell used computers to simulate human problem solving, providing new ways of studying mental processes (Newell, Shaw, & Simon's "Elements of a Theory of Human Problem Solving," 1958). Simon is reputed to have told his 1955 class at Carnegie Institute of Technology that over the Christmas break, he and Newell "invented a thinking machine." It was a computer able to work out a proof of a theorem in mathematics. If computers could process symbols in this reasoning exercise, then human minds could be studied as symbol-processing devices.
2. Psychologist Jean Piaget was pioneering a successful way to infer children's mental processes in understanding physical realities from observing the way they solved tasks and described events (Piaget's *The Construction of Reality in the Child,* 1954).
3. Linguistic researcher Noam Chomsky's studies of language showed that expression of ideas through language was not merely reinforced verbal behavior, but part of a unique cognitive system for comprehension and production of symbols (Chomsky's *Syntactic Structures,* 1957).

These three new approaches to thought, coming at approximately the same time, boosted the scientific legitimacy of research on higher mental processes. Since then, the cognitive approach has gradually achieved a central position not only in the study of thinking, but in many other areas of contemporary psychology as well (Mayer, 1981). Cognitive theory has become the guiding viewpoint in the psychology of the 1980s. We have already noted its importance in research on consciousness, learning, and memory, and will see further evidence of the influence of cognitive processes in our study of stress, personality, therapy, and social psychology.

Jean Piaget

Noam Chomsky

An exciting interdisciplinary field, **cognitive science,** has developed as a broad approach to studying the systems and processes that manipulate information. Cognitive science draws on the overlapping disciplines of cognitive psychology, linguistics, computer science, psychobiology, anthropology, philosophy, and artificial intelligence. Cognitive science is said to have as its ultimate goal solving the classic problems of Western thought—identifying the nature of knowledge and the way it is represented in the mind (Gardner, 1985). Central to this quest is the use of the computer to study human thinking; doing so links basic and applied research across several disciplines. Currently even the wide boundaries of cognitive science are being extended in many directions. There is a new union of cognitive psychology and neuropsychology, wedding mind to brain and behavior (Farah, 1984). There is also the cognitive-literary analysis of the way the human mind constructs and understands good stories, drama, myths, and rituals—acts of imagination that give meaning to human existence (Bruner, 1986).

In this chapter we will consider only a handful of the many interesting subareas of the widely diverse field of cognitive science. We will begin with an analysis of the ways in which researchers try to measure the inner, private processes involved in cognitive functioning. Then we will outline some of the classic models of information processing that try to account for the way we think, comprehend, and reason. Finally, in the last part of the chapter, we will examine some of the topics in cognitive psychology that are currently generating much basic research, application, and debate—decision making, problem solving, expert systems, and the creative use of language. (See also "Mindworks" in *The Best of Science.*)

For an example of the method of introspection, consider your thoughts as you answer the following questions as quickly as possible. (The answers are in the footnote on page 340.)

a. *What animal's name begins with I?*
b. *What series of letters comes after BCZYMCDYXN? (Hint: the first subset ends at M.)*

How did you find an answer for the first question? the second question? Could you follow your thoughts in both cases? If they were different, why?

Measuring the Unobservable

If your thinking is an internal, private process that only you can experience, how can it ever be studied scientifically? Several general approaches and many specific methods have been tried. In this section we will review briefly some of the most important: refining the method of introspection, observing a subject's behavior, measuring reaction time, analyzing errors, recording eye and muscle movements, and measuring brain wave patterns.

Introspection and Think-aloud Protocols

Introspection, as we saw in chapter 1, was developed by pioneering psychologist Wilhelm Wundt in the late 1800s. It involved training people to analyze the contents of their own consciousness into component parts, such as sensations, images, and feelings. It yielded catalogs of these "elements" of consciousness, but no clues about actual sequences of mental processes in life situations. When the introspections of two people differed in the same situation, there was no empirical way to resolve the discrepancy.

A more serious problem with introspection becomes apparent when we realize that many, or most, of our mental processes are not even available for *our own* conscious inspection. As we saw in chapter 7, an enormous amount of routine information processing occurs swiftly, almost automatically, *out of conscious awareness.* In the five seconds or so that it took you to read that last sentence, you identified the letters and words, retrieved the stored meaning of each of them, and (I hope!) comprehended the meaning of the sentence. You even began to store that unit of information under different retrieval labels for ready access should it appear on a test. Do you know *how* you did *what* you just did so efficiently?

Introspection can be used to supplement other methods, but it can never be a general technique for studying cognition. For that, we need a net broad enough to catch all the essentials of the events we are studying, and we must satisfy the basic requirement of any science—objective, repeatable measurements.

Recently, however, researchers have found a way to use introspection as an exploratory procedure to help map more precise research. During the process of working on a task, experimental subjects orally describe what they are doing and why. Their reports, called **think-aloud protocols,** can be used by researchers to infer the mental strategies employed to do the task and the ways knowledge was represented by the subject.

An example of the use of think-aloud protocols was cited in chapter 9 in the report of a subject's ability to remember 80 digits. Another example, an investigation of the way people plan everyday shopping trips, follows.

> *Subjects were presented with a map of the city identifying several stores and businesses. They were given several items to purchase and required to plan a day's shopping trip, thinking aloud while they planned.*
>
> *From the protocols, the researchers discovered that planning is not a logical, organized, hierarchical process. Instead, it is an opportunistic process: a person follows many trains of thought simultaneously, jumping back and forth while discovering information that is relevant to one line of thought or another. (Hayes-Roth & Hayes-Roth, 1979)*

This jumping around is in sharp contrast to the models of planning that are built into robots or computerized decision aids in business. Those models set up planning in a very systematic manner with main points and subpoints recognized and treated in a logical fashion. Because the think-aloud protocols show how people *actually* proceed instead of how a purely logical approach assumes they *ought* to behave, such protocols have been collected in a wide variety of studies. They have proven to be particularly useful in studies of the cognitive processes involved in problem solving.

To experience the think-aloud protocol method, solve this problem, describing aloud each of the steps you take.

$$\begin{array}{r} 946 \\ \underline{-357} \end{array}$$

Now ask someone over 50 to explain the steps in this subtraction problem. You will probably hear something "strange" like, "You borrow 1 from the 4 and use it with the 6 to make 16. (16 − 7 is 9.) Then you pay back 1 to the 5, making it 6, and borrow another 1 from the 9 to put with the 4 to make 14 (14 − 6 is 8.) You pay it back to the 3, making it 4, and subtract 4 from 9 to get 5. Answer 589."

That's the way your author and other people of his generation learned it. Younger people learned the simpler method of just borrowing across the top and leaving the bottom numbers alone.

Behavioral Observation

A basic task of much psychological research is to infer internal states and processes from observations of external behavior. If the context in which the behavior occurred is known, it is possible to theorize about the affective, motivational, or cognitive determinants of that behavior. Crying at a funeral is evidence of grief, while crying at winning a prize is evidence of great joy. Anxiety is revealed by certain patterns of "body language," while concentration on a task is inferred from visual focus on a target and a very tense posture.

In one case, for example, an experimenter was interested in finding out the age at which babies began to supplement simple perceiving with mental representations of external objects that were not present. This is the concept of *object permanence*—when "out of sight" does not mean "out of reality" and thus should not be "out of mind" (see chapter 3).

> *Eighty babies, ranging in age from about three to nine months, were observed while watching an electric train move around a circular track. The train entered a tunnel, was out of sight for a few moments, then exited and continued its circular path. The first appearance of the moving train stopped the babies' previous, random behavior, whatever their ages; they seemed "frozen" in their intense observation of it. Most of them then tracked it steadily until it went out of sight into the tunnel. They continued to look at the tunnel entrance ("like cats at a mouse hole"), however, instead of at the exit at the other end.*
>
> *Over the course of a few successive runs, the older babies (especially those seven months and older) began to look more toward the exit as soon as the train vanished from view (as can be seen in the photo). From their shift in focus without any change in the stimulus, the experimenter inferred that a new mental process was taking place. The babies seemed to be using stored experiences to anticipate a not-yet-present event. (Nelson, 1971, 1974)*

> *In a more recent study, researchers played a peekaboo game with 7-month-old infants. The children smiled less and raised their eyebrows more when the adult who appeared from behind a screen was different from the one they had watched going behind it. This behavioral finding suggests that the children had a mental representation of the first adult and, thus, were experiencing surprise when the adult's appearance was different. (Parrott & Gleitman, 1984)*

Measuring Reaction Time

The elapsed time between the presentation of some stimulus or signal and a subject's response to it is known as **reaction time.** In the preceding chapter you saw how Sternberg (1969) used measurement of reaction time to infer that retrieval from short-term memory involved a serial exhaustive search of all items in a remembered list.

The reaction-time technique is also being used to assess the steps in understanding the meaning of words that we read.

> *In one situation, a subject who was seated before a video screen saw pairs of words appear and had to decide as quickly as possible if they belonged to the same semantic (meaning) category. One button was pressed if they were judged "same," another if "different." Reaction time measurement began with the second word in the sequence and ended with the subject's response. In this sequential presentation, for example, when the pair* cow–tiger *appeared, the subject responded "same," requiring about three fourths of a second to do so.*
>
> *After several pairs were responded to, the word* banana *appeared alone on the screen, followed less than a second later by* apple. *The subject's response—"same"—required a fifth of a second* less *than before, when the word pairs were presented together. (Hunt, 1982)*

Answers to the questions on page 339 are (a) there aren't many animals whose names begin with *I*—two are ibis and impala; and (b) the next series of letters would be DEXWO.

From this finding, the researcher concluded that one of the mental processes included in a subject's reaction time was looking up the meaning of each word in the "word dictionary" stored in long-term memory. When the first word of the pair was flashed early, its meaning must have been already retrieved before the second appeared, thus shortening the time required to decide if the words were similar. (For some background on the discovery and use of reaction time, see the ***Close-up*** on p. 342.)

Analyzing Errors

When we come to a wrong conclusion, make an illogical inference, or remember something incorrectly, it is assumed that our errors probably are not random, but reflect systematic properties of the thought processes involved. Analysis of thought errors can give us clues about these properties. This was the technique, mentioned in the previous chapter, that revealed people's tendency to store the *sounds* of visually presented letters in short-term memory rather than their images. Therefore, when trying to recall a short list of letters displayed on a computer screen, the subjects tended to make errors that confused letters which *sounded* alike, such as *F* and *S*, rather than those that *looked* alike, such as *F* and *E* (Conrad, 1964).

Sigmund Freud (1904/1914) pioneered the analysis of speech errors—slips of the tongue—to detect latent sexual or hostile impulses. (For example, a competitor pretending to like you might say, "I'm pleased to *beat* you" instead of "I'm pleased to *meet* you.")

Freud's focus on the *motivational* basis for verbal errors is being extended by current researchers who are looking for their *cognitive* basis. These researchers hope to discover some principles of mental functioning. They believe that some slips arise merely from lapses of attention to the specifics of what is being said; others reveal a mental competition between similar verbal choices. People often say, "I'd be *interesting* in . . ." instead of the correct "I'd be *interested* in . . . ." The sentence structure allows the two suffixes-*ing* and *-ed* to be exchanged if the person's attention is not focused.

A *spoonerism* is the exchange of the initial phonetic elements of two (or more) words in a phrase or sentence. The term derives its name from Reverend W. A. Spooner of Oxford University who made many such remarkable exchanges. In tongue-lashing a student for not studying and wasting the term, Rev. Spooner said, "You have tasted the whole worm!" Spoonerisms show that whole phrases and sentences are planned in advance of being uttered. In this, and other instances, cognitive psychologists are studying mental processing of information by putting verbal errors under their analytic microscopes (Norman, 1981, 1983).

Another view about the way these verbal errors arise—and what studying them reveals—is found in *spreading activation theory.* According to this theory, a person's mental dictionary is organized into a network so that each word is interconnected with many others that are similar in meaning, sound, or grammar. As the person prepares to speak, relevant parts of the network become activated, causing a

Close-up Taking Time to Think

The relationship between reaction time and thought can best be appreciated if we examine it from a historical perspective. Reaction time studies fall roughly into four chronological periods:

1. *In 1796 an assistant to the Astronomer Royal was fired from his post at the Greenwich Observatory because he consistently recorded the transit of a star about one second later than the Astronomer Royal himself. Not much scientific note was taken of this discrepancy until 1819, when the German astronomer Friedrick Bessel became interested in such "errors" of observation. He carefully compared his own reports of stellar transits with those of other astronomers and found consistent differences. Bessel expressed these differences in the form of an equation. For example, the difference between the reports of Walbeck, another astronomer, and himself was*

   W (Walbeck) − B (Bessel) = 1.041 sec.

   This phenomenon of consistent discrepancies in observation was called the **personal equation.** *The concept was one of the first instances of the systematic study of* individual differences *in behavior, a precursor of the personality traits concept as an explanation for differences in reaction to the same situation.*
2. *Before 1850, scientists believed that impulses were conducted instantaneously along the nerves. However, in that year, Helmholtz demonstrated (a) that nerve conduction took time, and (b) that the time it took could be measured, as we saw in chapter 4. Helmholtz administered a weak electric shock first to a man's toe and later to his thigh. The difference between the man's reaction times to these two stimuli was the measure of the speed of conduction in the sensory nerves. These experiments were the first true studies of reaction time ever to be done.*
3. *After Helmholtz had shown that there is an interval of time between a physical stimulus and a person's physiological response to it, scientists began to think that this might be a good measure of a person's mental processes. From the 1850s to about the 1930s, reaction time was studied under a variety of conditions, using different versions of a measuring device called the* chronoscope.

   It was found that simple reaction time, *the single response to a single stimulus, is shorter than* discrimination reaction time, *in which different stimuli are presented and the subject responds only to a designated one. The longest time is taken by* choice reaction time, *in which there are several different stimuli and a different response must be made for each of them.*
4. *Adopting the principle that complex mental processes take more time than simple ones, present-day researchers are using reaction time in a number of research designs to infer the occurrence of various cognitive processes (as described in this chapter).*

"vibration" of the web that spreads to closely related words. The word with the highest total activation is then selected. Problems arise when competing choices have about equal activation levels (see Hillis, 1985).

Slips of the tongue also provide evidence of the way the human mind represents language structures. For example, an English-language speaker might exchange initial consonants ("tips of the slung" for "slips of the tongue"), but never would say "stip the of tlung," which would violate several grammatical rules (Fromkin, 1980). Thus verbal errors of this type are never considered to be random; they provide clues to the structure and function of the mind.

Recording Eye and Muscle Movements

Much of our thinking depends on gathering information from the environment. One of the primary ways we do this is through our eyes. Monitoring the way people move their eyes—what they look at in a picture and for how long—can provide a rich source of data about their ongoing thought processes. A record of a reader's fixations also provides considerable insight into the cognitive processes that occur in comprehension of the content.

One study used these two similar sets of sentences:

I

It was dark and stormy the night the millionaire was murdered.
The killer left no clues for the police to follow.

II

It was dark and stormy the night the millionaire died.
The killer left no clues for the police to follow.

Researchers asked each subject to read either the first or second sentence pair and measured the time he or she took to read it. They found that the second pair took about a half second longer to read than the first, generally because the reader had to make an inference. Since the cause of death was not mentioned in the first sentence, the reader had to connect "the killer" in the second sentence to the death in the first sentence by inferring "murder." No such inference was required in the first pair since the word murder *implied that there was a killer involved.*

In addition to this reaction-time analysis, the researchers used a special apparatus to examine each subject's eye movements while reading the sentences. They found that most of the extra time spent on the second pair was taken up in longer eye fixations on the word killer *and also on the word* died. *These eye-movement patterns supported the hypothesis that an inference was being made about the meaning of the word* killer *during the reading of the second pair of sentences, but not the first. The subjects' eye movements provided a "window" into the private thoughts of a mind-at-work. (Just & Carpenter, 1981)*

Mental processes are often accompanied by small movements of appropriate muscles. For example, if you are thinking about "pounding with a hammer," there may be electrical activity in your arm muscles (*electromyograms,* or *EMG*) that can provide a measure of the invisible thinking. If you imagine "telling someone off," there may be patterns of muscle activity around mouth and throat, similar to the overt responses that would actually express the thought, "Who do you think you are?" (see Lang, 1979).

Reading the Mind in Brain Waves

As we saw in chapter 4, stimuli elicit electrical waves in the brain that can be measured at the scalp. A brain wave evoked by stimulus events is called an **evoked potential,** or an *event-related potential (ERP),* to distinguish it from the spontaneous electrical activity that is going on all the time in the living brain. It appears that such a brain wave first reflects properties of the stimulus, such as its intensity, but then begins to reflect cognitive processes, such as the person's evaluation of the stimulus. For example, the evoked potential is larger for the last word in the sentence "He took a sip from the *computer*" because it is more unusual and unexpected than the word *glass* might be. (Donchin, 1975; Woods et al., 1980).

One component of *ERP*s is a brain response that is used to measure attention and detection of low probability events. It is also used as an index of the mental workload involved in certain tasks—like those performed by air traffic controllers. It is called the *P300* component because it is a positive waveform that peaks 300 milliseconds after a stimulus event (Donchin, 1985).

The mind is also being "read" in the brain waves in other ways. Electroencephalograms (EEGs), described in chapter 4, are used to probe the relationship between the functioning of the two cerebral hemispheres in mental tasks. For example, it has been found that tasks with attentional demands are reflected in EEG *alpha waves* (middle frequencies of 8 to 15 herz), while cognitive and emotional tasks are reflected in higher frequency *beta waves* (16 to 24 Hz). Moreover, alpha wave activity is sensitive to the *type* of attentional task. It is *greater* for tasks such as mental arithmetic that require a focus on internal processes than for tasks that focus on monitoring environmental stimuli (Ray & Cole, 1985).

There are two other applications that use the electrical activity of the brain to index mental processes. In the first research program, it is found that each of the cerebral hemispheres picks up different emotional reactions. The left frontal region is more involved with positive affects, while the right frontal region processes negative affects. People who are *repressors* maintain a coping style in which their verbal reports of feeling "good" or "calm" are contradicted by autonomic arousal responses associated with stress. Repressors may maintain this cognitive-affective dissociation through deficits in transferring affective information from their right hemisphere to their left (verbal) hemisphere (Davidson, 1983).

The other research program uses recordings from a great many electrodes placed on the scalp to measure the rapidly changing patterns of brain electrical activity that occur *prior* to a subject's overt response to a cue. The human brain seems to "program" different regions or subsystems in anticipation of the need to process certain types of information and take certain kinds of action. Analyses of the brain wave patterns of these *preparatory sets* enable researchers to predict whether a response will be accurate or inaccurate. Performance is likely to be inaccurate when these preparatory sets are incomplete or incorrect—when the mind is not properly prepared to direct the correct response (Gevins et al., 1987).

Mental processes are no longer as inaccessible to the scientist as they were when introspection was the only method available for studying mental activity. They can be better explained by precisely measuring the way the mind processes information so that a researcher can really understand what is happening inside that formerly mysterious "black box" called the mind.

Mental Structures for Thinking

In the last chapter we saw that remembering starts when "top-down" processing uses stored information to help us make sense of perceptual information coming from the outside world. It is as though we match our inner structures against the sensory input, enabling us to identify it as new or familiar, dangerous or desired, useful or irrelevant. This process of pattern recognition, however rudimentary, helps new input get past the sensory register into short-term memory. Once there, further organizing processes may help us store it more permanently in long-term memory. Pattern recognition and the later organizational processing, in turn, are the first stages of our "higher mental processes"—the beginnings of what we call *thinking*. They go beyond the information supplied by the sensory input by using stored knowledge to interpret it (see Bruner, 1973).

As already indicated, our major task in storing information is to build an abstract working model of the outside world to use in our encounters with it. Some of the mental structures we seem to use in doing this, such as schemas, propositions, and abstract codes, were mentioned in the last chapter. Others include concepts, scripts, and cognitive maps. Actually, understanding of the forms of representation that we use remains fragmentary, often reflecting the hypotheses and research of particular psychologists who have started with different questions and definitions and used different methodologies. Thus schemas are associated with Bartlett, cognitive maps with Tolman, and so on.

There is ongoing controversy among investigators about a number of basic issues in cognitive psychology. Eventually better data will decide these issues. In this section we will look more closely at the mental structures currently being investigated in research on thinking.

Concepts

Imagine a world in which every object and every event looked new to you, unrelated to anything that had happened before. Getting burned yesterday would have taught you nothing about the way to respond to a hot object today. In such a world of perpetual novelty, with no way to classify information, you could not build on your experience one day for more effective behavior the next. Fortunately, you have the capacity to respond to stimuli not as unique, unrelated sensory events, but as instances of categories that you have formed through your experiences. This ability to categorize individual experiences—to take the same action toward them or give them the same label—is regarded as one of the most basic abilities of living organisms (Mervis & Rosch, 1981). Recall from chapter 3 that, from the start, infants are able to categorize objects in their environment—an apparently innate cognitive ability.

The categories we form are called **concepts.** They are mental representations of *kinds* of things. Concepts may represent kinds of *objects,* such as balls; kinds of *events,* such as walking or talking; or kinds of *living organisms,* such as people or horses. Concepts can also represent kinds of *properties* such as red or large; *abstractions,* such as truth or love; or even *relations,* such as smarter than, which tells us about a relative difference between two organisms, but does not tell us about either of the individuals being compared (see E. Smith & Medin, 1981).

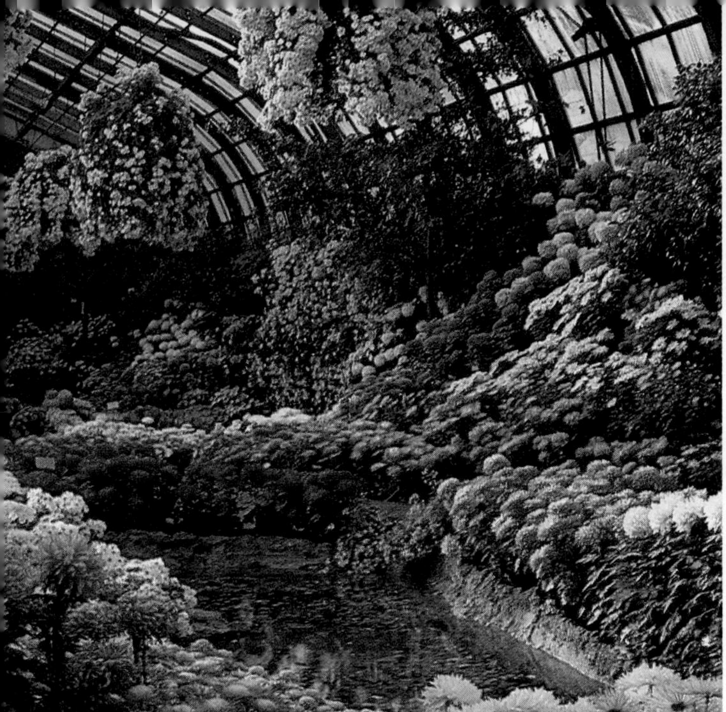

A concept is a mental event that represents a category or class of objects. The concept of flower *encompasses many different flowers.*

Critical Features or Prototypes?

What do we store when we store a concept in memory? Do we store a definition, including the characteristics that a stimulus must have to be recognized as an instance of that concept? Do we store a cluster of characteristics that *tend* to be found, with more typical examples of the concept having more of the characteristics?

The **critical features** approach suggests that we store definitions, or lists of critical features—attributes that are necessary and sufficient conditions for a concept to be included in a category. The rule is that a concept is a member of the category if, and only if, it has every feature on the list. An alternative approach is *prototype theory,* which suggests that categories are structured around an *ideal* or *most representative instance.* The most representative example of a category is called a **prototype** (Rosch, 1973). According to the prototype approach, a concept is classified as a member of a category if it is more similar to the prototype of that category than it is to the prototype of any other category. Prototype theories assume that a prototype is stored along with some *allowable variation.* Thus, although a stimulus might not fit precisely within the limits of a stored category, it would not be misclassified as long as its variation from the prototype was within the range of acceptance.

Since pattern recognition combines "top-down" and "bottom-up" processes in which new perceptual information is being matched against stored concepts, we run into a dilemma when we try to understand how we formed those concepts in the first place. Though the question has not been resolved, it may be that the bases are somewhat different for different kinds of concepts. For example, concepts in science are often based on definitions of critical features: "Mammals are vertebrates that nurse their young." The boundaries between categories are clear and a list of critical features seems to work.

But what about the concept *bird?* The dictionary defines this concept as "a warm-blooded vertebrate with feathers and wings." If you were asked to build a cage for a bird, you would probably visualize a robin-sized bird and construct a cage that would be far too small for an ostrich or a penguin—both of which are also birds. Your concept of *bird* seems to include something about *typicality*—the most typical member of the class—which goes beyond the list of features that qualifies creatures for birdhood.

Or consider the concept *game.* There is no single property that card games, video games, football games, Olympic games, and cooperative games all have in common. Nevertheless we regard them all as instances of our concept *game.* They share a "family resemblance" much as the members of a family do, where different children show somewhat different combinations of traits but can be recognized by outsiders as belonging to the same family.

Many—perhaps most—of our concepts in everyday life are like this. We can identify clusters of properties that are shared by different instances of a concept, but there may be no one property that *all* instances show. We consider some instances as more representative of a concept—more typical of our mental prototype—than others.

Research studies have determined that typical instances can be more quickly verified as members of a category than unusual ones. Reaction time to determine whether a robin is a bird is quicker than reaction time to determine whether an ostrich is a bird, because robins are more typical birds than are ostriches (Kintsch, 1981; Rosch et al., 1976).

Typicality, or representativeness, has practical implications too. Suppose you were given the job of designing direction signs for a zoo. If you put up a sign with a picture of a penguin, people would expect a penguin display. For the general bird house, you would do better to use a picture of a more typical bird.

Hierarchies and Basic Levels

Concepts are often organized in hierarchies. You have the broad category of *bird,* as well as several subcategories like robins, ducks, ostriches, and so forth. Your *bird* category, in turn, is a subcategory of a still larger category, *animals,* which is a subcategory of *living things.* These concepts and categories are arranged in a *hierarchy* of levels, from the most general and abstract at the top, to the most specific and concrete at the bottom. They are also linked to many other concepts; some birds are edible, some are endangered, and so forth.

There seems to be an *optimal* level in such hierarchies for people to categorize and think about objects. That level—called the **basic level**—is the one that can be retrieved from memory most quickly and used most efficiently. For example, think about the chair at your desk. It belongs to three obvious levels in a conceptual hierarchy: *furniture, chair,* and *desk chair.* For most purposes, it would be optimal to think of it as a *chair.* The lower level category, *desk chair,* would provide more detail than you generally need, whereas the higher level category, *furniture,* would not be precise enough. In spontaneously identifying objects, you would call it a "chair" rather than either a "piece of furniture" or a "desk chair." If you were shown a picture of it, your reaction time would be faster if you were asked to verify (yes or no) that it was a chair than if you were asked to verify that it was a piece of furniture (see Rosch, 1978). It is now believed that dependence on basic levels of concepts is a fundamental aspect of thought.

Schemas and Scripts

You are already familiar with the important concept of **schema** as a general cluster of stored knowledge that helps determine what we perceive and remember. Now we are ready to refocus on schemas as structures for *thinking.*

As we have seen, schemas include preconceptions and expectations about what attributes are typical for particular concepts or categories. New information, which is often incomplete or ambiguous, makes more sense when we can relate it to knowledge in our stored schemas. Going one step further, once we have assigned it to a particular schema, we then think about it and deal with it as if all the expected characteristics are present, whether or not they actually are.

For example, take the statement, "Tanya was upset to discover, upon opening the basket, that she'd forgotten the salt." Salt implies a picnic basket, which also suggests food on which salt might be put, such as hardboiled eggs and vegetables. You automatically know what else might be there, and, equally important, what definitely is not: everything in the world larger than a picnic basket and all that would be inappropriate to take on a picnic—like a boa constrictor or your bronze-plated baby shoes. This body of information has been organized around your "picnic-basket schema." By relating the statement about Tanya to this preestablished schema, you understand the situation better, because you can "read in" much more about what is happening than is contained in the statement itself.

According to researchers Rumelhart and Norman (1975), schemas are the primary units of meaning in the human information-processing system. In their view, the mind is a network of interrelated schemas, in which parts of schemas are themselves schemas. Schemas are clusters of knowledge and expectations and always have to do with general categories. Propositions, on the other hand, are assertions and can relate specific *or* general items. We often derive specific propositions from our various schemas.

Comprehension of new information seems to occur through (a) integrating consistent new input into what we already know, and/or (b) overcoming the discrepancy between new input and stored schema by changing a knowledge structure or by changing or ignoring the input.

What do these sentences mean to you?

1. The notes were sour because the seam was split.
2. The haystack was important because the cloth ripped.

In isolation, these sentences make little sense. In the first one, it is not clear what notes are being referred to, what the seam is, or how the two relate to each other to make the notes sour. In the second, there seems no relation between haystack and cloth. However, if you are given the words *bagpipes* and *parachute,* the sentences suddenly become understandable. The notes were sour because the seam in the bag of the bagpipes was split. If you were coming down in a torn parachute, the haystack could save your life. The sentences were not comprehensible until you could somehow integrate them into what you already knew. You needed cues to find the appropriate schemas to fit them into, but these cues were all you needed if you already knew what *bagpipes* and *parachutes* were.

You can apply this information to the optimal way to read a chapter in this textbook. Before you begin to read a chapter carefully, skim over it, noting the headings, subheadings, and the terms in **boldface type.** Also skim over the introduction to the chapter and the conclusion. Skimming enables you to become generally familiar with the information in the chapter. The cues provided in the headings, brief overview thematic sentences, and boldfaced terms are pedagogical aids that mentally prepare you to comprehend the upcoming information.

Comprehending, like perceiving and remembering, is a constructive and reconstructive process in which we draw on our existing mental structures to make the most sense we can out of new information. Once we interpret information as belonging to a particular schema, we may unwittingly change the information in our internal representation of it.

To see how this can occur, read the following passage.

Chief resident Jones adjusted his face mask while anxiously surveying a pale figure secured to the long gleaming table before him. One swift stroke of his small, sharp instrument and a thin red line appeared. Then the eager young assistant carefully extended the opening as another aide pushed aside glistening surface fat so that the vital parts were laid bare. Everyone stared in horror at the ugly growth too large for removal. He now knew it was pointless to continue. (Stop. Without looking back do the following exercise.)

Check off the words below that appeared in the story of resident Jones.

_____ patient	_____ scalpel	_____ blood
_____ tumor	_____ cancer	_____ nurse
_____ disease	_____ surgery	

Most of the subjects that read this passage identified the words *patient, scalpel,* and *tumor* as having been in the story. None of them was! Interpreting the story as a medical one made it more understandable, but also resulted in inaccurate recall (Lachman et al., 1979). Once they had related the story to their schema for hospital surgery, the subjects "remembered" labels from their schema that were not in what they had read. In this case drawing on a schema not only gave them an existing mental structure to tie the new material to, but led them to change the information to make it more consistent with their expectations.

A **script** is a cluster of knowledge about *sequences* of interrelated, specific events and actions expected to occur in a certain way in particular settings. A script is to procedural knowledge what a schema is to declarative knowledge. Each person has a script for going to a restaurant, using the library, listening to a lecture, and visiting a sick friend. Like a script in a play, a mental script outlines the "proper" sequence in which actions and reactions are expected to happen in given settings. When all people in a given setting follow similar scripts, they all feel comfortable because they have comprehended the "meaning" of that situation in the same way and have the same expectations for each other (Schank & Abelson, 1977). When all people do not follow similar scripts, however, they are made uncomfortable by this script "violation" and may have difficulty understanding why the scene was "misplayed."

Bob arrived promptly at 8 P.M. for his first date with Carol. She invited him to meet her parents. He asked them if he could have her hand in marriage. They went to the church square dance. Afterwards they had a pizza and talked about their career plans after graduation.

You don't have to be brilliant to recognize what part does not fit in this "first-date" script. There are situations like this, however, where misunderstandings, hurt feelings, or anger are caused because we are using a script different from someone else. And sometimes we find ourselves in situations so different from our past experience that we have no script for them and must deal with them "fresh." Did you have any "unscripted" experiences when you first came to college? How did you feel while you were engaged in them? How did you try to understand them and decide what you should do?

Some scripts, such as being quiet in libraries, are controlled by the aspects of a situation; these are *situation-driven scripts.* Others are controlled by particular roles we are expected to play in society—for example, parent, teacher, or counselor. These can be thought of as *role-driven scripts.* Still other scripts are learned for informal situations where there is no traditional role to fulfill; they are *person-driven scripts.* They represent ways we have programmed ourselves to try to act consistently in different situations regardless of the different roles we are playing. They might be "honesty" scripts, "generosity" scripts, or "helpfulness" scripts, depending on our concept of ourselves. Person-driven scripts can be thought of as expressions of our personal style.

We have trouble comprehending inconsistencies and parts that do not fit scripted patterns. When we encounter new information that either does not readily fit into our mental structures or contradicts them, we are uncomfortable. One way to reduce the discrepancy is by enlarging and changing our mental structures in appropriate ways to make a broader understanding possible. This process of accommodation is one that begins in infancy and continues as long as we increase our knowledge and competence in any field. It is what is happening as a child develops the concept of *conservation,* as a novice becomes an expert. It is the way the mind matures by being open to new possibilities that challenge old actualities.

However, when new ideas are so different that the discrepancy between new and known cannot be overcome, they may simply be rejected and ridiculed as "nonsense" instead of being taken seriously, examined, and responded to in their own terms. This is what often happens when new ideas challenge traditional ways of thinking. The thinkers who propose them—whether in politics or in science—are likely to be labeled "foolish," "crazy," or "dangerous." Many "revolutionary" thinkers have met with initial rejection: Jesus (love thine enemy); Copernicus (the earth goes around the sun); Freud (unconscious processes have influence on behavior); and Picasso (reality can be represented in symbolic art forms).

When scientist Louis Pasteur said, "Chance favors the prepared mind," he meant a mind not only filled with relevant knowledge, but also one that is tolerant of novelty and ambiguity. It is the exceptional case, however, that forces us to change our trusty old concepts, categories, and theories to more accurate and adaptive ones. Typically, we do so only after stubbornly hanging onto the old as long as possible. A scientific theory that is wrong is like a prejudiced ethnic or racial stereotype that resists change despite a great deal of information supporting its falsity (see Conant's *On Understanding Science,* 1958, and Kuhn's *The Structure of Scientific Revolution,* 1970).

Visual Images, Cognitive Maps, and Computational Theories

Do you think only in words or do you sometimes think in pictures and spatial relationships? Although you may not actually store visual memories in visual form (see chapter 9), you clearly are able to use imagery in your thinking.

Visual Images

Visual mental imagery is a "re-seeing" of information previously perceived and stored in memory. It takes place in the absence of appropriate immediate sensory input.

History is full of examples of famous discoveries made on the basis of mental imagery. For example, the discoverer of the chemical structure of benzene, F. A. Kekulé, often worked with mental images of dancing atoms that fastened themselves into chains of molecules. His discovery of the benzene ring occurred in a dream in which a snakelike chain molecule suddenly grabbed its own tail, thus forming a ring—a new hypothesis about molecular structure. Albert Einstein claimed to have thought entirely in terms of visual images, translating his findings into mathematical symbols and words only after the work of visually based discovery was finished. Michael Faraday, who discovered many properties of magnetism, knew little mathematics, but worked by placing the supposed properties of magnetic fields in a visual image of relationships. (These and other historical examples have been chronicled by Roger Shepard, 1978.)

Many psychologists regard visual thought as a mode of thought different from verbal thought (Kosslyn, 1983; Paivio, 1983). Evidence of the psychological reality of mental images is provided in the following study showing their behavioral consequences.

Each student was shown examples of the letter R *and its mirror image that had been rotated various amounts from 0 to 180 degrees (see* **Figure 10.1***). As the figure appeared, the student was to identify it as the normal* R *or the mirror image. The time it took to make that deci-*

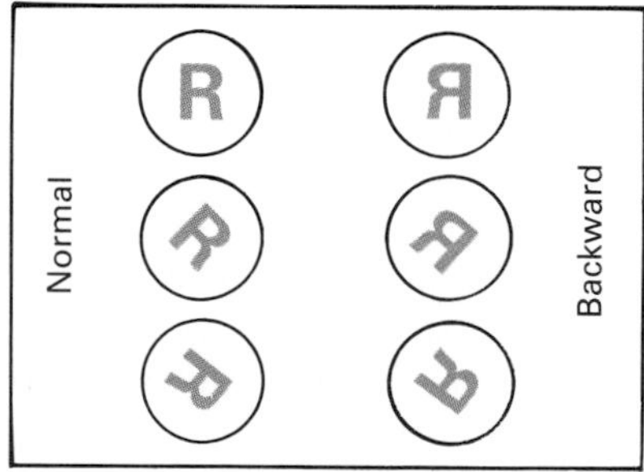

Figure 10.1
Subjects presented with these figures in random order were to say as quickly as possible whether each figure was a normal R or a mirror image. The more the figure was rotated from upright, the longer the reaction time. (After Shepard & Cooper, 1982)

sion was longer the more the figure had been rotated. This finding indicated that a subject was imaging the figure in his or her "mind's eye" and rotating the image into an upright position, before deciding whether the figure was an R *or a mirror image. Such results support the idea that* thinking *processes using visual imagery are similar to the processes involved in visually* perceiving *real-world objects. (see Shepard & Cooper, 1982)*

It also appears that people scan their mental images of objects in much the same way they scan the actual perceived objects.

In one study, subjects first memorized pictures of a complex object such as a motorboat (see ***Figure 10.2****). Then they were asked to recall their visual image of the boat and focus on one spot—for example, the motor. When asked if the picture contained another object—a windshield or an anchor, for example (both were present)—it took longer to "see" the anchor at the other end of the boat than the windshield, which was only half as far away from the motor. The researcher regarded the reaction-time difference as evidence of the times it took the subjects to scan the two physical distances in their mental images. (Kosslyn, 1980)*

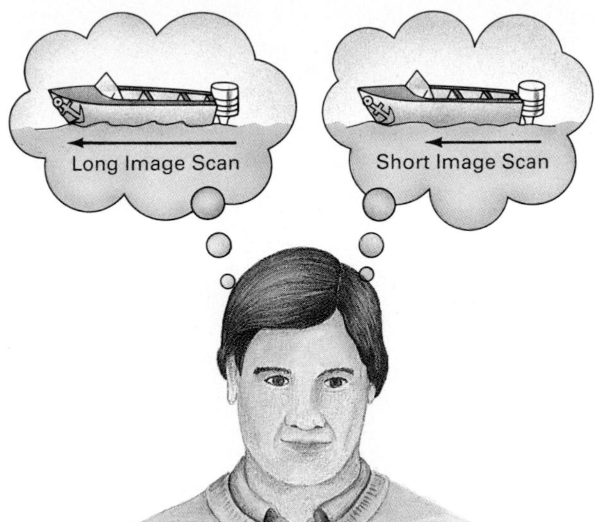

Figure 10.2
Subjects studied a picture of a boat and then were asked to look at the motor in their image of it. While doing so, they were asked whether the boat had (a) a windshield, or (b) an anchor. Their faster response to the closer windshield than to the more physically distant anchor was taken as evidence that they were scanning their visual images. (After Kosslyn, 1980)

Many problems cannot be solved by visual imagery, however, as you will discover by trying to solve the following (Adams, 1979).

Take a large piece of typing paper. Fold it in half (now you have two layers), fold it in half again (now you have four layers), and continue folding it over 50 times. (It is true that it is impossible to fold an actual piece of paper 50 times, but, for the sake of this problem, imagine that you can.) About how thick is the 50-times folded paper? Mark your estimate:

The actual answer is about 50 million miles, about half the distance between the earth and the sun [2^{50} x .028, the thickness of this paper]. Your estimate was probably way off. Why? If you are like most people, you visualized the piece of paper, imagined folding it over once, then twice, and then extrapolated the result to 50 folds. What happened was that you tried to solve the problem using *only* this familiar visual imagery. However, the effect of folding the paper 50 times, doubling the thickness each time, was so large that the problem had to be translated into mathematical symbols to be solved.

Visual thought adds complexity and richness to our thinking, however, as do the less studied forms of thought using our other senses of sound, taste, smell, and touch. It can also be very useful to solve types of problems in which relationships can be grasped more clearly in diagram form than in words, as in the case of flowcharts or structural models showing the relationships among processes.

Cognitive Maps

Visual thought is useful in spatial or geographical relationships. A mental representation of physical space is called a **cognitive map.** E. C. Tolman's pioneering hypothesis about cognitive maps in learning was mentioned in chapter 8. To explore some of your cognitive maps, try answering the following questions.

1. What is the most direct route from your psychology classroom to the bookstore? To your residence?
2. Which is farther north: Seattle or Montreal?
3. Which is farthest west: the entrance to the Panama Canal from the Atlantic Ocean (Caribbean side) or the Pacific Ocean (Gulf of Panama side)?

To find the answers to these questions, you must use a mental representation of the spatial environment as you have personally experienced it, remember it from a map you have seen, or reconstruct it from separate bits of information that you

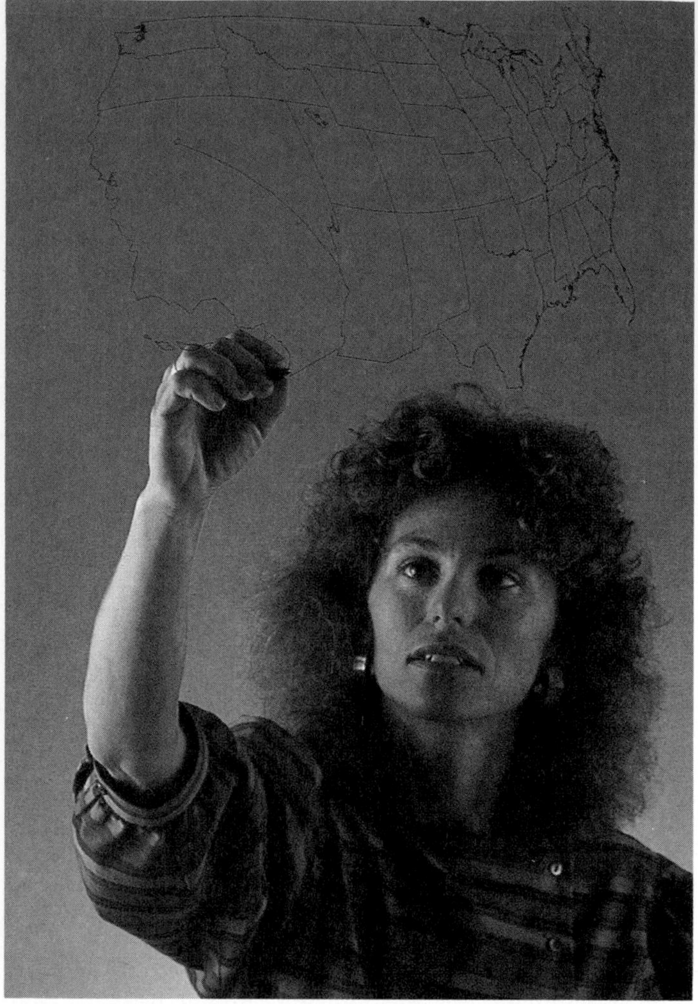

Studying cognitive maps sheds light on decisions people make about their surroundings that might otherwise be hard to understand. For example, this "Californian Perspective Map" is a somewhat inflated view of the United States.

possess. Your cognitive maps help you effectively move about to get where you want to go. They also enable you to give directions to someone else. By using cognitive maps you can get to the bathroom at home with your eyes closed or to school even when your usual route is blocked (see Hart & Moore, 1973; Thorndyke & Hayes-Roth, 1978).

Although everybody seems to develop cognitive maps to help navigate through the complex environments in which they live, they can sometimes be led astray. Did you know that Seattle is farther north than Montreal? Most people miss this one because they think of Canada as north of the United States and don't realize how far south the border drops around the Great Lakes.

Did you realize that the Atlantic Ocean is actually more *westerly* than the Pacific Ocean at the Panama Canal entrances? Most people are surprised at such information because their mental maps of Central America distort the sharp eastward curve of both coastlines to make them more vertical (B. Tversky, 1981). Similarly, on the mental maps of Parisians, the Seine River curves only gently through Paris instead of curving more sharply as it actually does. Thus some places that are on the Right Bank of the Seine are misjudged as being on the Left Bank by Parisians "who should know better" (Milgram & Jodelet, 1976). In addition, because nearby geography is so much more familiar to most of us than distant places, our cognitive maps of places far away become increasingly foreshortened.

Computational Theories

Support for notions about visual mental imagery has come recently from a new approach in cognitive science called *computational neuropsychology*. In this approach, cognitive methodologies that study information processing are integrated with methodologies in the brain sciences that study the way the brain carries out specific functions. The two areas are combined around *computational theories* that attempt to specify, in precise computer language, the computations performed by a sensory or brain system in order to process certain information.

The components of a given type of information are programmed into a computer to generate explicit predictions. These predictions, based on a computer simulation model that mimics information processing in the human brain, are then tested with human subjects in behavioral experiments. A computational theory specifies what must be computed, what problems must be solved, and the goals of the computation—given the nature of the input and the known limitations on the solution (Marr, 1982).

Since visual mental imagery is assumed to share basic mechanisms with visual perception, theories of computation are now being extended to some of the basic problems solved by the primate visual system. It is obvious that human beings have solved problems such as segregating figure from ground or recognizing the same objects that occur in various positions in the visual field. Computational theories attempt to define the processing mechanisms necessary to achieve the solutions already developed by our brains and visual systems.

Some of this knowledge of visual processing components is being extended to formulate a computational theory about the way mental images are generated. Computer simulation models of mental imagery suggest that it is not a unitary phenomenon, but one that consists of many separate modules, each of which performs a distinct function. Thus, while one module activates visual memories, others inspect parts of imagined patterns, evaluate shapes, make comparisons, and respond (Kosslyn, 1985). Recall from chapter 7 that many investigators of consciousness have independently come to the same conclusion that the mind functions as a system of integrated modules.

In a research study, a split-brain patient performed a task in which lower-case letters were flashed to each hemisphere. He had to decide whether the corresponding version of the upper-case letter had any curved lines (a–A; b–B). When the cue letter was projected to the right hemisphere, he could not do this simple task. He could, however, when the cue was projected to the left hemisphere. A series of control experiments indicated that the right hemisphere deficit was caused by difficulty generating a visual image of the upper-case letter on the basis of visual memory of the lower-case letter.

Research with another split-brain patient showed that the right hemisphere had difficulty generating images with *multiple* parts, suggesting that the problem was with the computation that retrieves stored descriptions of relations between parts and arranges (or puts) them in the correct positions in an image. The basis for this deficit is shown to be unrelated to difficulties in encoding, storing, or remembering visual details, nor is it a module used in language, drawing, or visual perception. It seems to be exclusively a mental imagery brain function (Kosslyn et al., 1985). This new approach holds promise to bridge the conceptual barriers between cognitive scientists and neuroscientists as they seek to understand mind-brain functioning. (See also the new "connectionist" approach by cognitive psychologists that uses a brain metaphor instead of a computer metaphor to build a model of the human mind. This can be found in Rumelhart & McClelland, 1986.)

Making Inferences, Judgments, and Decisions

We live in a world of *uncertainty*, yet we are constantly making personal, economic, and political decisions that have enormous impacts on our lives. Are there accepted guidelines or models for the way to make "good decisions," while avoiding "bad" ones? When scientists, physicians, lawyers, politicians, stockbrokers, or your parents make their important decisions, what procedures do they follow to get the most acceptable outcomes? In this section we will learn that most decision making is subjective, often error-prone, and, to a surprising extent, irrational. However, by recognizing the underlying cognitive mechanisms that guide our choices, we can improve our decision making.

The complex cognitive processes involved in decision making share much with those that we use in making inferences and judgments. **Decision making** is the process of choosing between alternatives, selecting and rejecting among available options. **Inference** is the reasoning process of drawing a conclusion on the basis of a sample of evidence or on the basis of prior beliefs and theories. **Judgment** is the process by which we form opinions, reach conclusions, and make critical evaluations of events and people based on available material. It is also the product or the conclusion of that mental activity.

For example, you meet someone at a party, and, after a brief discussion and a dance together, you *infer* that this person is similar to you in some important ways. You *judge* the person to be intelligent, interesting, honest, and sincere. You *decide* to spend most of your party time with that person and to arrange for a date next weekend. Behind this apparently ordinary, routine social process lies a host of cognitive strategies, procedures, and phenomena, many of which you are not aware of as they smoothly operate to influence what you think and how you act. Most of the time they work for you, but, as we will see, under some circumstances your mind becomes your own worst consultant. It does so by making erroneous inferences from the evidence, by generating faulty, nonrational judgments, and by misdirecting decisions away from the objectively ideal alternative. Awareness of these mental traps is the first step in avoiding them—on the way to becoming more perceptive and accurate in making the inferences and judgments which guide important decisions in life.

Making Sense of the World

Humans make sense of their world in various ways. They apply old knowledge, organized through experience, to understand and make familiar new events. They process new information that either changes their prior beliefs and knowledge, or is interpreted in the light of their preexisting theories. They utilize certain cognitive strategies and procedures that are basic to making inferences and judgments. Ordinarily these mental activities serve them well; however, there are circumstances in which they misapply what they know and believe to new data. They misprocess new information because they insist on forcing it into compartments of an established theory, and they misuse rules of thought that make them overconfident when they should be wary.

Cognitive researchers have typically characterized the human information processor as fallible, as susceptible to a great many types of errors in thinking. People are viewed as "cognitive misers" who avoid mental effort whenever sustained attention, comprehension, or analysis is required (Taylor, 1980). They are seen as users of *mental shortcuts* that enable them to make up their minds quickly, easily, and with maximum confidence (Kahneman et al., 1982). They are regarded as too ready to be led astray by their theories about what *ought* to be rather than influenced by data about what really *is* (Nisbett & Ross, 1980).

This "human folly" should not so much be interpreted as a defect in humanity or even human intelligence as much as it should make us aware that humans can sometimes be misled by the very same cognitive processes that work remarkably effectively for most people, most of the time, across many situations. In the same sense that the process of learning which enables us to profit from experience can also cause us to "mislearn" phobias and superstitions, the processes of inference and judgment can have negative costs as well as benefits.

For example, it is cognitively efficient to identify a few significant, stable characteristics around which to organize our initial reactions of others, but we may form stereotypes based on minimal, faulty, or false information. These stereotypes then strongly influence the way we behave toward these people, and, in turn, the way they behave toward us. For example, if you are told that someone you are about to meet is schizophrenic, you are likely to form an emotional impression that is different from what it would have been had you not been given the label—even though the person's behavior was identical (Fiske & Pavelchak, 1986).

Why does such knowledge persist over time and not change in the face of new situations and contradictory data? And what are the sources of irrationality that exert a distorting influence on the way we interpret the evidence of our senses, the memories we retrieve, and the decisions we make?

Perseverance of False Beliefs

Recall from chapter 3 Piaget's view of a child's cognitive development as the interweaving of the twin processes of assimilation and accommodation. A child interprets the new by assimilating it into known categories, while changing old mental structures by accommodating them to new information. So too, the adult mind must decide again and again when new data supports (or can be stretched to fit) old theories and when old theories must be changed because new data just doesn't fit. The proper balance between the processes of accommodation and assimilation enables us to make optimal use of past knowledge, experience, and personal theories without forfeiting the opportunity to learn something new about the world around us and about ourselves.

We generally continue to persevere in beliefs, theories, and ways of doing things because we *assimilate* data or new experiences in a biased fashion (Ross & Lepper, 1980). Any data that might be congruent with our beliefs are accepted without real evaluation "at face value" as confirmatory. Data that are incongruent and might challenge our theories are ignored, reinterpreted, or explained away so that they cannot disconfirm what we already believe, and ambiguous data are resolved in terms of existing beliefs. Thus, once strong beliefs or theories are formed, mixed data or even *random data* pose little threat. In fact, such "bad" data may allow the theories to survive and even become stronger through the way they are misused.

Two other ways in which our beliefs are maintained and can lead to faulty inferences and judgments in addition to biased assimilation are through selective exposure and self-fulfilling prophesies. By *selective exposure* to some, but not other, sources of information, we attend to, notice, and process only data that support our beliefs while avoiding data that disconfirm our theories. We seek out others who share our points of view. We talk to people, gather information, and expose ourselves to information in the mass media that tends to agree with what we want to believe (Festinger, 1957; Olson & Zanna, 1979). Expectations from our personal theories can also serve as *self-fulfilling prophesies* about future events and relationships, expectations that become true because we create the circumstances that generate the evidence to prove them so (Snyder, 1984).

Sources of Irrationality

How have social scientists explained the apparent lapses into irrationality of the rational human mind? Three sources have been identified: the mob, the passions, and the biases.

The Greek philosopher Plato, and later, the sociologist LeBon (1895/1960), described the reason of the individual as undermined when faced with "vulgar" influences of the masses. The person under the influence of the crowd ceases to think logically and succumbs to the social disorder inherent in the "mob psychology."

A different view emerges from the distinction between human reason and animal appetites or passions. When driven by animal needs that demand immediate gratification, people cease to be rational. Society's task, often accomplished with the help of religion and education, is to suppress those animal urges by replacing them with more lofty principles and rules of conduct. Freudian theory is in this tradition, arguing as it does for the power of sexual and aggressive instincts and the unconscious motivational influences on perception and thought. Rationality is thus seen as opposed by emotionality and the self-centered focus on satisfying one's primitive needs.

The third source of irrationality comes from the modern view represented by cognitive and social psychologists. In this perspective, the place to look for the origins of irrationality is within the very processes of intellect itself. Let's examine this source of "ordinary" irrationality in more detail.

Cognitive Biases

Fundamental to the way humans make inferences, judgments, and decisions are mental strategies that are biased. These **cognitive biases** are systematic ways of thinking that are responsible for errors in drawing inferences from evidence, making judgments from inferences, and making decisions from judgments. They are not wrong or irrational in themselves, but are aspects of normal mental strategies and procedures for processing information that generally work for the person and the species. However, they lead to irrational modes of thinking when people fail to *discriminate* between appropriate and inappropriate conditions for their use. It is the failure to recognize that a way of thinking or a cognitive strategy which has worked in the past or in a given condition is inappropriate for the present situation. Because we wheel out these cognitive biases automatically, and, paradoxically, without much thought, we rely on familiar rules and shortcut methods when newer sources of information and inference would yield better, more useful, or more precise evidence.

For example, one's personal experience teaches a lot of useful lessons and obviously aids in making sense of the world. Under many circumstances, however, the conclusions based on personal intuition are shown to be inferior to those based on statistical evidence compiled objectively from many such similar cases (Meehl, 1954). Nevertheless, we tend to maintain the myth of the validity of our intuition and personal sensitivity, and ignore or discard better objective evidence that is less susceptible to subjective error.

When people were asked to compare themselves in terms of their driving safety to others they knew, they typically (the median response) judged themselves to be better than 85 percent of the other people. These subjects were confident that they were safer drivers than the majority—which of course, they all couldn't be—statistically speaking (Slovic, 1984).

Researchers have identified many different biases that can exert negative influences on information processing (see ***Close-up*** on p. 354). For example, we tend to perceive random events as nonrandom, correlated events as causally related, and people as more likely causal agents than situational variables.

Heuristics are mental shortcuts useful to reduce the range of possible answers to a question or solutions to a problem by applying a "rule-of-thumb" strategy. A heuristic for psychology multiple-choice tests might be that, when in doubt about the right alternative, select the longest one, since psychological truths tend to be qualified and not simple. How can a heuristic that helps in such ways come to hurt in others? Two biases illustrating the way a cognitive strategy sometimes can backfire and yield inferential errors are the *availability heuristic* and the *representativeness heuristic* (see Tversky & Kahneman, 1973, 1980).

Availability Heuristic

Question: How do the number of deaths from tornadoes annually in the United States compare with those from asthma, and how do accidental deaths compare with deaths from disease? When asked to estimate the frequency of deaths from all causes, subjects overestimated those that were rare, but dramatic and sensational, and underestimated those that were more frequent, that occurred one at a time in private, ordinary circumstances (Slovic, 1984). Asthma causes about 20 times more deaths than tornadoes, and diseases kill 16 times as many people as do accidents. Nonetheless, the subjects judged accidents and disease to be equally lethal, and tornadoes to be three times more deadly than asthma. Why do you suppose they were so far off?

The **availability heuristic** is a cognitive bias that operates when estimating the probability of

Close-up Anchors Aweigh!

Try this interesting experiment with a group of friends or family members. First, divide your "subjects" arbitrarily into two groups. Then, once they are separated from each other, give members of the first group five seconds to estimate the mathematical product $1 \times 2 \times 3 \times 4 \times 5 \times 6 \times 7 \times 8$ and give members of the second group the same amount of time to estimate $8 \times 7 \times 6 \times 5 \times 4 \times 3 \times 2 \times 1$. After you have collected everyone's estimates, compute the median estimate for each group—that is, the number above and below which half of the estimates fall.

If your results are similar to those found by Amos Tversky and Daniel Kahneman, who published this experiment in 1973, you will notice that members of the first group tended to provide lower estimates than members of the second group. In the original experiment, the researchers reported a median estimate of 512 for members of the first group and 2250 for members of the second group (neither of which, incidentally, bore any resemblance to the correct answer of 40,320!). These findings were explained in terms of an *anchoring bias,* or the *insufficient adjustment* up or down from an original starting value. Because members of the first group began to evaluate the product with $1 \times 2 \times 3$ . . . , their estimates were anchored to low numbers. In contrast, members of the second group began with $8 \times 7 \times 6$ . . . and were therefore anchored to relatively high numbers.

Since 1973, researchers have demonstrated the influence of anchoring on estimates as diverse as the percentage of working mothers with children under five, the proportion of Iranians who are Islamic, the ratio of chemistry professors who are women, and even the share of soap operas carried by NBC (Quattrone et al., 1984). Nor is anchoring restricted to impersonal, numerical domains. For example, randomly assigned anchors can affect opinions about the SALT-II treaty (Quattrone et al., 1984), and anchors can change people's estimates of their personal efficacy, estimates which, in turn, affect how persistent they are in performing various tasks (Cervone & Peake, 1986).

Surprisingly, the effects of anchoring do not disappear with outrageously extreme anchors. In one experiment, subjects were asked whether the number of Beatles records that had made the top ten fell above or below 100,025, whether the average price of a college textbook was more or less than $7128.53, and whether the average temperature in San Francisco was greater or less than 558 degrees Fahrenheit. After the subjects responded, the researchers asked them to estimate the precise number of top-ten Beatles hits, the average price of a textbook, and the average temperature in San Francisco. What these researchers found was that, instead of disregarding the unreasonably high anchor values, subjects were affected as much as when more plausible anchors were provided in the opening round of questions (Quattrone et al., 1984). The influence of anchoring grows with the *discrepancy* between the anchor and the "preanchor estimate" (the average estimate subjects make without explicit anchors), until the effect reaches a leveling-off plateau. If true, these findings are rich with implications for marketing, negotiation, survey research, and a number of other fields.

In a recent study of more than 1000 students, anchoring greatly influenced estimates of both the likelihood of nuclear war and the effectiveness of strategic defenses (Plous, 1986). Students who were initially asked whether the probability of nuclear war was greater or less than 1 percent subsequently set the odds at 10 percent, whereas respondents who were first asked whether the probability of nuclear war was greater or less than 90 percent gave estimates averaging 26 percent. Similarly, students who were provided with a low anchor in a survey about strategic defenses estimated that, under the best of conditions, nearly one fourth (24 percent) of Soviet missiles would penetrate strategic defenses, while students who were provided with a high anchor estimated that the majority (57 percent) of all missiles would reach their targets.

These results raise intriguing questions for future research: Do budgets from one year anchor appropriations for the next? Do initial arms control positions unwittingly anchor later ones? Do current nuclear weapons deployments anchor beliefs about what constitutes a minimal nuclear force adequate for deterrence? By understanding the way people make such estimates and what influences their decision, political policy can be better informed by the psychology of anchoring.

some future event or the frequency of some past event. It leads to judging as more frequent or probable those events that are more readily available in memory, more easily and quickly retrieved. The mental cues of ease of recalling, noticing, or imagining are usually good cues for making frequency and probability judgments. They lead us off the track, however, when they give rare events that are dramatized and sensationalized more power to become miscues by making them more memorable than a large number of more representative instances, statistical averages, and abstract or mundane sources of evidence.

Joseph Stalin is reputed to have said, "A single death of a Russian soldier is a tragedy; a million deaths is a statistic." Journalists exploit this error of emphasis when they present national trends or social movements in terms of a few individual character sketches.

We tend to overvalue available information that is concrete and vividly presented, such as an uncle's complaint about the lemon of a car he got stuck with, and to undervalue the abstract statistics, base rates, or annual repair records of that particular make of car which show it is, in general, very reliable and needing few repairs. This explains why a study showed that a *New Yorker* article profiling the problems of a single, supposedly "typical," welfare case had more impact in changing readers' attitudes toward welfare than did a presentation of essentially the same relevant data in summary form (Hamill et al., 1980). Research on the power of the vivid case study has led to the conclusion that the lay person is an "intuitive psychologist [who] is, perhaps, as often misled by overreliance upon his senses as he is dogged by adherence to prior theories" (Ross, 1978).

Representativeness Heuristic

Another judgmental heuristic that simplifies the complex task of social judgment under conditions of uncertainty is the **representativeness heuristic.** It is used whenever we presume a connection between belonging to a particular category and having the characteristics considered typical of the members of that category. We ask what the likelihood is that this specific instance is representative of the general category to which it is assumed to belong. Given a specific unknown instance, *X*, we search our memories to discover what *X* is like, where we have seen it before, what it resembles, what else is like it or shares its apparent features. This process should remind you of prototype theory discussed earlier (p. 345). The representativeness heuristic goes wrong when our judgment of the most typical instance is not valid or the stimulus person's behavior is determined, not by his or her membership in a class, but by the specific situation in which the judge's observations are made.

For an example of your use of the representativeness heuristic, use the following information to answer the question:

The author has a friend who is a college professor. He is an excellent gardener, reads poetry, is shy, and is slight of build. Would you judge that he is probably in (a) Japanese studies, or (b) psychology?

If you decided that the author's friend was in Japanese studies, you were matching the description with your stereotypes of representative people in the two fields. You probably did not take into consideration the much larger number of professors who teach psychology and, thus, the statistical probability that the friend is a psychologist. Neither did you consider the probability that, as a psychologist, the author would be likely to have more friends in his own area of study (Nisbett & Ross, 1980). Actually, the friend just described is a psychology professor.

In one study, subjects were presented with a series of personality descriptions, supposedly drawn at random from a list of 100 engineers and lawyers. They were to assign each description to one category or the other. Though they were told the proportion of the two groups, this information about statistical probability was disregarded. A given type of description was likely to be assigned to the "engineer" category if it was representative of a subject's schema about engineers even if the subjects were told the engineers comprised 30 percent of the group in one condition or 70 percent in the other condition. The subjects relied only on representativeness in making their judgments and ignored the relevant probability data. (Kahneman & Tversky, 1973)

If I were to tell you I was going to a baby shower, you might assume it was being given for a woman. You would be wrong!

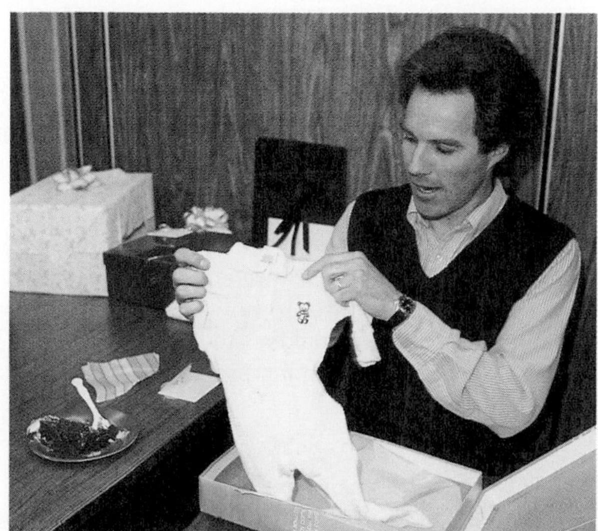

Thus we often err by ignoring or underutilizing *base rate information* that is more reliable than representativeness information.

Availability and representativeness are just two of the many heuristics that we tend to use in making judgments about the world every day. The biased judgments resulting from these and other rules of thumb can systematically distort our views of reality and remain compelling even when we know the true state of affairs. We store many complexity-reducing rules of thumb, because they allow us to make quick, acceptable judgments almost all of the time. Often they are the best we can do, given the constraints and uncertainties of the situation, and they serve us well by guiding us down a simple, straight-and-narrow path. Problems arise, however, when the path in the real world is neither straight nor narrow. Other problems arise when these mechanisms are overapplied or misapplied (see Kahneman et al., 1982; Nisbett & Ross, 1980).

The Psychology of Decision Making

Classic economic theory, which is based on a "rational mind-in-the-marketplace" model, starts with the assumption that people seek to maximize gain, minimize loss, and allocate their resources efficiently. It is a *normative model* of the way reasonable people *ought* to behave. It also assumes that people have enough reliable information about the events in question and that they understand the laws of probability necessary to make the ideal, rational choice. A *descriptive analysis* of actual human choice and decision making by cognitive psychologists shows that the assumptions of economic theory are usually wrong (Simon, 1955; Tversky & Kahneman, 1986). People make many decisions under conditions of uncertainty, do not use probability information as statisticians would, and are subject to cognitive biases that expose the fallacy of the rational decision-maker model.

Many demonstrations have shown that normative rules for the way people should behave are often violated in actual practice. Two criticisms of the economic perspective on decision making come from (a) analysis of alternative descriptions of the same decision problem that result in different choices—by both laypeople and professionals, and (b) from analysis of risk preferences. These two types of criticisms illustrate how easy it is to lead reasonable decision makers to make irrational choices. Other nonrational psychological factors that influence decision making include wishful thinking and misinterpretation of utility and probability information.

Decision Frames

In decision making, preferences between options should be independent of the way a problem is presented. This *invariance principle* is an essential aspect of normative models of choice. However, people's decisions *are* influenced by the way in which a decision problem is framed or presented to them, even when all the important decision criteria are held constant.

Respondents were given statistical information about the outcomes of radiation and surgery treatments for lung cancer. For some subjects the data were framed in terms of mortality rates. For others, the identical data were presented in terms of survival rates. The task of the subjects was to indicate their preferred treatment on the basis of this information. First read the survival frame for the problem and give your choice of treatment; then see if you feel like changing it after reading the second frame.

Survival Frame

Surgery: *Of 100 people having surgery, 90 live through the postoperative period, 68 are alive at the end of the first year, and 34 are alive at the end of five years.*

Radiation Therapy: *Of 100 people having radiation therapy, all live through the treatment, 77 are alive at the end of one year, and 22 are alive at the end of five years.*

Decision: ____________________

Mortality Frame

Surgery: *Of 100 people having surgery, 10 die during surgery or the postoperative period, 32 die by the end of one year, and 66 die by the end of five years.*

Radiation Therapy: *Of 100 people having radiation therapy, none die during treatment, 23 die by the end of one year, and 78 die by the end of five years.*

Decision: ____________________

The results indicated that the framing differences had a marked effect on the choice of treatment. Radiation therapy was chosen by only 18 percent of the subjects given the survival frame, but by 44 percent of those given the mortality frame—although the data presented are identical in each frame. This framing effect held equally for a group of clinic patients, statistically sophisticated business students, and for experienced physicians. (McNeil et al., 1982)

Thus the way a decision problem is framed can influence the way it is perceived and misdirect the choice of options.

Risk Strategies

People have attitudes toward risks that they bring into most decision situations and those attitudes influence whether they will choose options that are risk aversive or risk seeking regardless of the actual expected utility of their choices. Consider the following examples:

(a) You have an 85 percent chance to win $100.
(b) You have a sure gain of $80.
Which do you choose?
(c) You have an 85 percent chance to lose $100.
(d) You have a sure loss of $80.
Which do you choose?

Most people choose *b* over *a*, a risk-*aversive* preference for a sure gain over a probable large gain. They also choose *c* over *d*, a risk-*seeking* strategy, preferring a gamble over a sure loss (Tversky & Kahneman, 1986).

The perception of potential risks is also influenced by other psychological factors—whether the risks are perceived as controllable, voluntarily exposed to, possibly catastrophic, shared by others, delayed in time, or unfamiliar. Experts who assess the degree of risk from various hazards, such as asbestos, terrorism, nuclear power, medical X-rays, or motor vehicles stick close to the actuarial statistics of the known estimates of deaths and injuries from each type of risk. Those statistical outcomes define the severity of a risk to "risk experts." However, when knowledgeable subjects (members of the League of Women Voters) judged risk potentials of 30 possible hazards, they ranked nuclear power as the most risky and X-rays among the least risky. Experts made opposite predictions, based on statistical evidence: X-rays were highly risky relative to the low risk of nuclear power.

People judge risks to be greater if they are "dreaded," unfamiliar, and potentially catastrophic than if they are known, familiar, and have delayed effects. Experts do not make these psychological differentiations (Slovic, 1984). This difference in risk perception creates problems when experts in government or business want to communicate to the public that some action is necessary in order to avoid a serious risk. The statistical evidence is not psychologically compelling to the public, and the experts ignore the psychological reality of the nonstatistical risk estimate (see Vaughan, 1986).

Nonrational Influences

Sometimes we make faulty decisions even when adequate facts are available. That is because we can be influenced by nonrational psychological factors like wishful thinking or misinterpretation of utility and/or probability information. In other cases, especially where we have incomplete information, we make faulty decisions because we rely on rules of thumb that give us quick answers—but oversimplified views.

If we want something very much (high utility), we may underestimate the likelihood of negative outcomes and overestimate the likelihood of positive ones. *Greed* typically gets us in trouble by activating this cognitive process. This misjudgment of the probabilities seems to occur in many cases where teenagers become pregnant. Their decision not to use contraception is based, in part, on an underestimate of the risk despite what they "know"(Luker, 1975).

Groups can make the same kind of mistakes, even at the highest levels of political decision making. The disastrous "Bay of Pigs" invasion of Cuba in 1960 was approved by President Kennedy after Cabinet meetings in which contrary information was minimized or suppressed by those who were eager to undertake the invasion (Janis, 1982).

Negotiators who bargain with each other in the industrial relations field sometimes fail to reach mutually beneficial agreements, even when a "zone of agreement" exists that should rationally lead to a settlement (Raiffa, 1982). New views of negotiation recast it as a judgmental process in which even expert negotiators use inappropriate decisional heuristics, misuse the ambiguous feedback available, and fail to take the perspective of the other side. The success of negotiators may be improved by recognizing the influence of the decision makers' cognitive processes and training them to eliminate their decisional biases and personal attitudes toward risk and perspective taking (Neale & Bazerman, 1985).

Other nonrational factors include (a) simplifying complex situations by not considering all the alternatives or all the relevant facts; (b) letting either optimism or negative preconceptions blind us to certain facts; and (c) making decisions under stress, which may disrupt both our search for relevant facts and our reasoning about them. We cannot avoid making decisions every day of our lives, but we can avoid some of the pitfalls of making bad decisions by becoming better information processors. We can improve our decision making by being alert to the biasing effects of beliefs and theories, of oversensitivity to vivid cases, of failure to take into account base rate information, of misuse of heuristics, and of decision frames and personal attitudes toward risk.

Solving Problems

What goes on four legs in the morning, on two legs at noon, and on three legs in the twilight?

In Greek mythology, this was the riddle posed by the Sphinx, an evil creature who held the people of ancient Thebes in tyranny until someone could solve it. Oedipus solved the riddle and delivered his people from bondage. To break the code, he had to translate two key elements that were being used in a special way. *Morning, noon,* and *twilight* were meant to represent different periods in a human lifetime, not times of one day. The "legs" were hands and knees for a crawling baby, legs later on, and two legs and a cane in old age. The solution to the riddle was *man* (used generically).

Many problems are discrepancies between what you know and what you need to know. When you solve a problem, you reduce that discrepancy by finding a way to get the missing information. To get into the spirit of problem solving yourself, try the problems in **Figure 10.3.** See **Figure 10.4** on page 360 for the answers.

In information-processing terms, a problem has three parts: (a) an *initial state*—the incomplete information you start with, perhaps corresponding to some unsatisfactory set of conditions in the world; (b) a *goal state*—the set of information or state of the world you hope to achieve; and (c) a set of *operations*—the steps you must take to move from an initial state to a goal state (Newell & Simon, 1972). Together, these three parts define the *problem space.* You can think of solving a problem in the same way you think of searching for—and finding—a path through a maze (the problem space) that gets you from where you are (the initial state) to where you want to be (the goal state) by a series of turns (the allowable operations) leading from each place in the maze to the next.

Figure 10.3 *Can You Solve It?*

A. Can you connect all the dots in the pattern by drawing four straight, connected lines without lifting your pen from the paper?

B. A prankster has put 3 ping pong balls into a 6-foot long pipe that is standing vertically in the corner of the physics lab, fastened to the floor. How would you get the ping pong balls out?

C. The checkerboard shown has had 2 corner pieces cut out, leaving 62 squares. You have 31 dominoes, each of which covers exactly 2 checkerboard squares. Can you use them to cover the whole checkerboard? (From How to Solve Problems: Elements of a Theory of Problems and Problem Solving *by Wayne A. Wickelgren. Copyright © 1974 by W. H. Freeman and Company. Reprinted by permission.)*

D. You are in the situation depicted and given the task of tying 2 strings together. If you hold one, the other is out of reach. Can you do it?

E. You are given the objects shown. The task is to mount a lighted candle on the door. Can you do it?

F. You are given 3 "water-jar" problems. Using only the 3 containers (water supply is unlimited), can you obtain the exact amount specified in each case? (After Luchins, 1942)

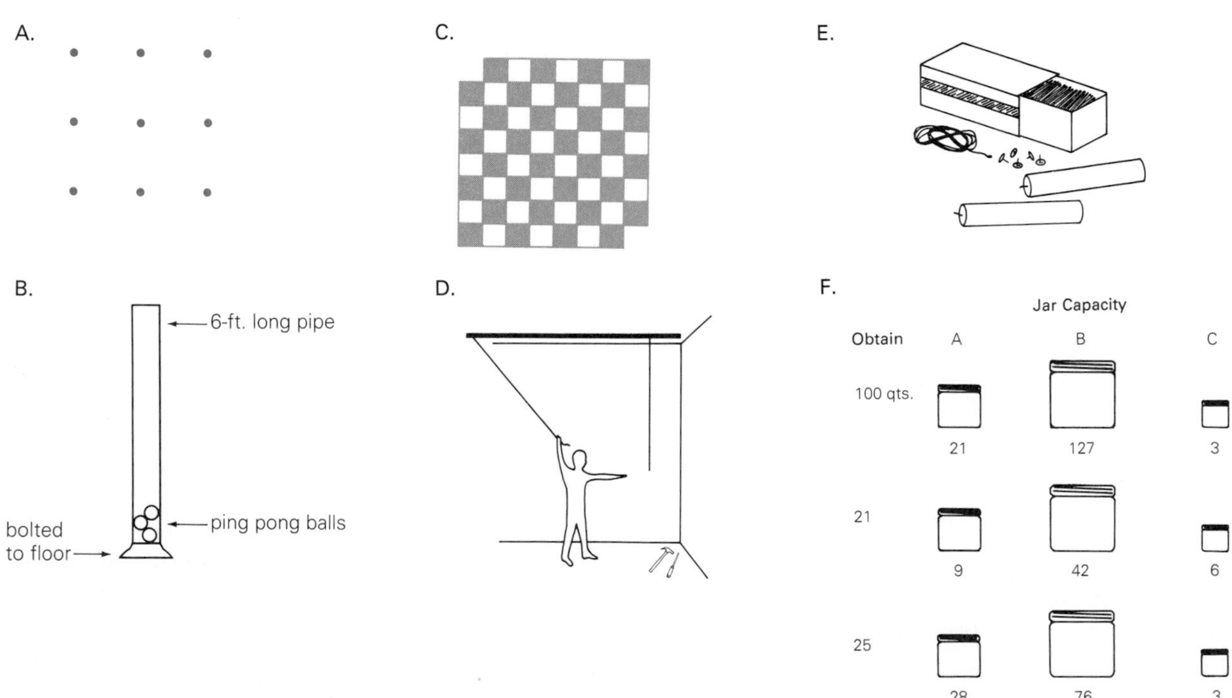

Well-defined and Ill-defined Problems

There is an important distinction between well-defined and ill-defined problems (Simon, 1973). A *well-defined* problem is like an algebra problem, in which the initial state, the goal state, and the operations are all clearly specified. The task is simply to discover how to use allowable known operations to get the answer. By contrast, an *ill-defined* problem is one in which the initial state, the goal state, and/or the operations may be unclear and vaguely specified. In some cases there may not even be a single correct solution. Designing a home, writing a novel, and curing cancer are examples of ill-defined problems. In such cases, the problem solver's major task is first to define exactly what the problem is—to make explicit a beginning, an ideal solution, and the possible means to achieve it. Once that is done, the task becomes a well-defined problem which can be solved by finding a sequence of operations that will, in fact, achieve an acceptable solution.

As we know more, have more abilities, and understand better how to solve problems, problems that may still be ill-defined for others become more well-defined for us. The "I can't" lament of the three-year-old child facing the problem of carrying four liquid-filled glasses becomes the older child's confident solution: "Of course I can do it; it's a cinch! I'll use a tray."

Understanding the Problem

Setting up an *internal representation* of the problem space—specifying all the elements in it—is not automatic. Often it means finding the appropriate schema from analogous previous tasks or situations—but not being restricted by them when the new problem calls for something beyond the existing schemas.

If you solved the problems on page 358, you found out that all of them show the importance of an accurate internal representation of the problem space. To connect the nine dots, you had to realize that nothing in the instructions limited you to the area of the dots themselves. To get the ping pong balls out of the pipe, you had to fill the pipe with water so that the balls would float to the top. In the checkerboard problem, if you reasoned that any domino must cover both a white and a black space, you knew at once that with two white squares missing, you could not cover the rest with 31 dominoes. To connect the two strings, you needed to see one of the tools as a weight rather than as an instrument. By tying one of them to the end of one string and setting it swinging, you could have grasped the other string and caught the tool as it swung close to you. To mount the candle on the door, you had to see the match box as a platform instead of a container, tack it to the door, and fasten the candle to it (if you had dripped some wax on it from the lighted candle, the bottom of the candle would have stuck to it as the wax hardened).

The last two problems show a phenomenon called *functional fixedness* (Duncker, 1945; Maier, 1931). **Functional fixedness** adversely affects problem solving and creativity by inhibiting the perception of a new function for an object that was previously associated with some other purpose. You put your conceptual "blinders" on and use only your familiar schemas—showing, again, the power of schemas to guide—or misguide—perception of reality.

Another kind of mental rigidity may have hampered your solution of the third water-jar problem. If you had discovered in the first two problems that jar B minus jar A minus twice jar C gave you the answer, you probably tried the same formula for the third problem—and found it didn't work. Actually, a much simpler formula of simply filling jar A and pouring off enough to fill jar C would have left you with the right amount. If you were using the other formula, you probably did not notice this simpler possibility. Your previous success with the other formula would have given you a **mental set** (*Einstellung* in German)—in this case a readiness to respond to new water-jar problems using the same procedure (Luchins, 1942).

Another restrictive mental set is seen in the tendency to take the "safe course" and stick with the "tried and true" instead of trying to see things with fresh eyes and find better ways of doing things. Sometimes this is simply habit, but sometimes it is motivated by fears of making a mistake or being criticized. Using the knowledge available to them, children are sometimes more creative problem solvers than adults, because they are not constrained by existing mental sets or schemas and have not yet been socialized away from fantasy toward logical, linear forms of thought. (See Adams, 1979, and de Bono, 1970, for a more detailed discussion of how you can learn to be a more creative problem solver.)

Another approach to improving problem solving contrasts *descriptive* thinking—how computers and people solve problems—with *prescriptive* thinking—how we *ought* to solve problems (Levine, 1987). People need to be taught ways to avoid reasoning fallacies, to be sensitive to preceptual sets and biases, and to follow prescriptive principles for solving problems. Although some of these principles seem obvious, they are not routinely employed; when they are they can improve problem-solving success. Some prescriptive principles are the following:

a. Formulate a plan. Make it sufficiently concrete to be action-oriented and sufficiently abstract to generalize beyond specific, limited applications.
b. Work in an organized way.
c. Work, at first, with simpler versions of complex problems.
d. Rehearse mentally doing the right thing. This visual imagery can especially aid in learning motor habits.
e. "Intimately engage" the problem, with zest and enthusiasm to "give it time" and energy rather than quitting before ever trying. Try to overcome "dispositional" fallacies, such as "I'm not good at numbers," "women can't work with machines," and "men aren't good at interpersonal problems."

Finding the Best Search Strategy: Algorithms or Heuristics?

After the problem space is known, the problem is well defined—but not yet solved! Solving the problem still requires using the operations to get from the initial state to the goal state. Using the problem-as-a-maze analogy, you must still decide on a strategy for "searching" through the maze for the right path.

One search strategy is an **algorithm,** a methodical, step-by-step procedure for solving problems which guarantees that eventually a solution will be found. For example, to solve the problem of making a word out of the letters *otrhs,* there would be 120 possible combinations that you could try on the way to the solution: *short.* For an eight-letter group such as *teralbay,* there would be 40,320 possible combinations (8 x 7 x 6 x 5 x 4 x 3 x 2 x 1). A search of all the combinations would be long and tedious—but it would have the virtue of finding the solution.

Luckily, there is an alternative that most of us use to solve a great many problems every day. In problem solving, just as in making judgments, we can use *heuristics,* informal rules of thumb that provide shortcuts. These are general strategies that have often worked in such situations in the past and may work in the present case. For example, in the word jumble *teralbay* a heuristic might be "Look for short words that could be made from some of the letters and then see if the other letters fit around them." Using such a strategy, you might generate the string *ably (tearably?),* or *able (raytable?),* or *tray (latraybe?).* By using this search strategy, you would probably not need to try more than a few of the possibilities before you came up with the solution: *betrayal* (Glass et al., 1979).

Figure 10.4 *Solutions to the Problems*

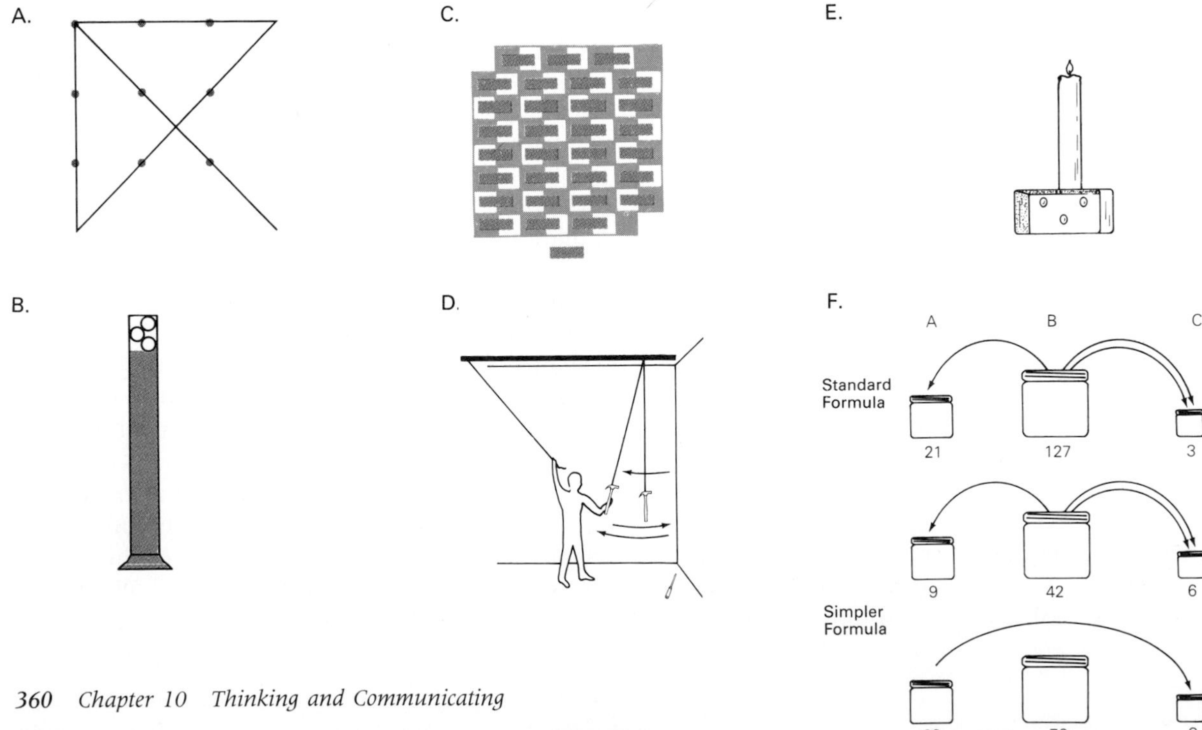

Using a heuristic does *not* guarantee that a solution will be found eventually; using an algorithm, tedious though it might be, does. Heuristics do work often enough, however, that we use them and gradually learn which ones to depend on in which situations. One way experience teaches us to be better problem solvers is by teaching us when and how to use heuristics appropriately.

Improving Cognitive Skills

When Charles Berlitz was a child, each member of his family spoke to him in a different language. By the time he was three years old, he spoke 4 languages; now, as an adult and founder of the Berlitz Schools for foreign languages, he speaks more than 24. His expertise, however, hardly compares to the language prowess of his grandfather, who spoke 58 languages!

If you have been struggling to acquire only one or two foreign languages, it is hard to imagine how anyone could become so skilled. Yet you have many cognitive skills—perhaps in reading, mathematics, or computer programming—that *you* take for granted but that may seem remarkable to others who are novices in those domains. Investigating cognitive skills is a new focus in psychology. In this section we will look at two of the ways they are being studied: (a) through direct observation of skill learning; (b) through investigation of expertise, by comparing experts with novices.

Acquiring and Perfecting Skills

When a person has reached the point of quick, error-free, effortless performance at a task, that person is said to be *skilled.* Skills, in general, have five defining characteristics (Adams, 1987; Pear, 1927).

a. Skills represent a wide domain of complex behaviors, including such activities as proofreading, juggling, bicycling, typing, and using language.
b. Skills are *learned* integrations of well-adjusted performances, distinguished from capacity or ability.
c. Skills always involve a specific quality or quantity of goal attainment: how well, how fast, or how much performance is sought and desired.
d. Skills are improved with practice.
e. Skills involve combinations of perceptual, cognitive, and motor processes in different degrees.

Research on cognitive and motor skills indicates that people progress through a distinct series of phases, or stages—*if* they practice sufficiently and receive adequate feedback.

Steps in Learning a Skill

Investigators have identified three stages in skill learning, whether the skill is a motor or a cognitive one: (a) the knowledge stage, (b) the associational, active practice stage, and (c) the autonomous, or automatic, stage (Fitts & Posner, 1967). In the first stage you learn the facts of the task, including the sequence of steps to be taken. You build a mental structure of what must be done. For example, you memorize the location of the gear shift or the names and moves of each chess piece.

In the second stage, you begin to use this knowledge. Your declarative knowledge is changed into procedural knowledge as you go through the motions you have learned about. Errors of understanding are eliminated, associations among the parts of the sequence are built and strengthened, and separate elements become parts of larger units, as in the chunking we talked about in chapter 9.

In the third stage you learn to produce the responses automatically, with little or no thought. As it becomes automatic, any skill requires less attention, is available on call, and does not interfere with other skills. Verbal mediation becomes unnecessary and the ability to verbalize what you are doing may even be lost. Eventually the skill becomes truly "mindless." For example, you drive, dance, read complex prose, carry on complex conversations, and much more without explicitly thinking about how you are doing so or what rules you are using so effectively. Once this happens, you can concentrate on higher level features of an activity, such as strategy, style, or interpretation.

Practice and Feedback

The key ingredient that changes your first, slow, awkward, effortful attempts into smooth proficiency is practice. The effect of practice on improving skills is one of the most reliable effects found by psychologists—assuming that there is prompt, accurate, specific feedback to help you identify and eliminate errors.

In the early stages of learning a skill, performance improves rapidly. Later, improvement continues, but usually at a slower and slower pace: it takes increasing amounts of practice to make comparable advances. Discovered long ago for motor skills, the same generalization has been found to apply to cognitive skills (Anderson, 1980). This relationship between practice and improvement, with less and less improvement for the same amounts of practice, is called a *power function*. Equal amounts of improvement for equal amounts of practice is a *linear function*. The amazing thing is that no matter how good you are, more practice can always make you better still (see **Figure 10.5**).

Feedback serves three distinguishable functions: (a) it provides *information* both about the results of a response and about its characteristics (temporal, spatial, directional, level of intensity, and so on); (b) it provides positive or negative *reinforcement*, depending on the adequacy of the response; and (c) it provides *motivation* to continue a task by helping to make the world and one's behavior predictable and potentially controllable.

In order for sensory feedback to act as an *informative signal* to guide physical actions so they will result in desired consequences, several conditions must be met. The feedback must be strong and clear enough to be detected and responded to immediately, while noise in the form of external and internal distractions needs to be minimized. Complex or weak feedback can be changed into a more usable form by being amplified or slowed down and separated into components. For example, if you watch a videotaped, slow-motion recording of a behavioral sequence such as a golf swing or tennis backhand, you can become aware of just what you are doing in each part of the sequence.

Figure 10.5 Continuing Improvement with Practice
This curve records the continuing improvement in memorizing strings of digits shown by S. F., the student described in chapter 9 (p. 400). Digit span was defined as the length of sequence that he remembered correctly half of the time. Each day represented about an hour of practice. Starting with a digit span of about 7, S. F. was still improving when he had reached a digit span of 79. With continued practice, we would expect the curve to begin to level off, to resemble a power function. Note that this student was able to repeat the digit strings in the exact order he heard them because he could use his knowledge of running (e.g., track times, etc.) to chunk the information. However, his ability to remember letter strings remained at only about 7 letters—the capacity for short-term memory. (From Ericsson et al., 1980, p. 1181)

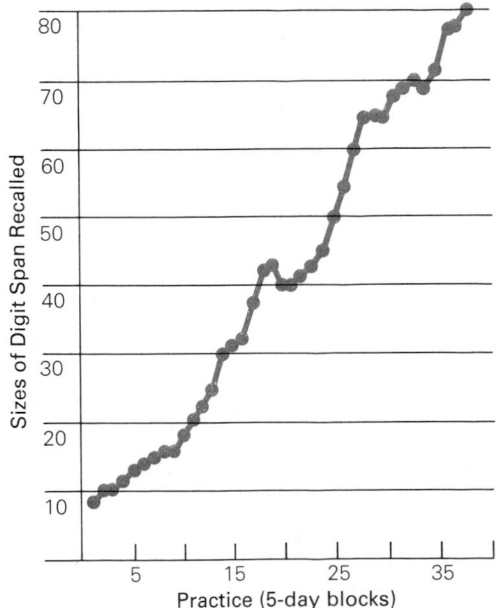

Greatest use of feedback information also requires a clear image of the ideal, or goal, performance you are working toward, so that the *differences* you detect between current performance and desired performance can be very precise. Practice can then be directed toward the *criterion* of no difference at all between ideal and actual performance.

For many kinds of cognitive and social skills, such as thinking, writing, conversation, or dating, feedback comes in the form of social evaluation of performance quality. Such feedback is often delayed, inconsistent, unreliable, or even unavailable unless requested. Often it is difficult to ask for such feedback, especially for children, the shy, or an uncertain person in a new situation (see Hollin and Trower, 1986, for applications of social skills training). In addition, the setting may be a public one, as in large high-school or college classes where public feedback is threatening. If appropriate feedback is essential for developing adequate performance skills, then it is a performer's responsibility to find a means of getting it. For some tips on developing cognitive skills, see **Table 10.1.**

Becoming an Expert

How does an expert research scientist, physician, chess master, or chef differ from a novice? Simply put, the expert knows more.

Interestingly, many experts can *show* you what they do, but cannot *tell* you how they do it. Their performances have become so automatic that they have difficulty becoming aware again of the steps in the process. (Try verbalizing to a child how you tie your shoelaces, ride a bike, or understand a joke.) Even experts in highly technical professions, such as cardiologists who can make accurate diagnoses based on only a few bits of case history, probably cannot tell you how they know.

In this section we'll examine some of the ways in which experts differ from novices. Although experts may not be able to communicate their skills to you, you can understand the process by comparing how the experts and novices go about solving the same cognitive tasks. Experts differ from novices in their metacognitive knowledge—their knowledge of what they know. Finally, computer programs that act as "expert systems" are being

Table 10.1 *Tips for Developing Cognitive Skills*

Principles for developing cognitive skills can be summarized as follows (Anderson, 1981, 1982):

1. *Space your practice.* In learning a new skill, regularly practice a short time each day, trying to complete a unit of study or one action pattern. One early study found that four hours a day of practice on Morse code netted as good results as seven hours a day (Bray, 1948).
2. *Master the subskills.* Many skills have component parts. Develop these to the point where they are automatic so you don't have to attend to them. Then start focusing on the higher level, overall skill.
3. *Internalize an ideal model.* Observe the correct performance of an expert role model so you can get a good picture of what you are trying to achieve. Then monitor your own performance, noting explicitly how it compares with that of your model. This is what happens when children learn to play the violin by the Suzuki method: they listen to the music, become familiar with the way it should sound, and then try to match their own performances to that model.
4. *Seek immediate feedback and use it immediately.* Get knowledge as quickly as you can about the quality of your performance—if possible while the feeling of your action is still in your working memory. Then try to use the feedback while *it* is still in your working memory. Skill at video games can be acquired quickly because of the immediate electronic feedback and opportunity to use it to alter responding.

used to investigate the way human experts solve problems. In the last part of this section we will consider the question of whether thinking and problem-solving skills can be taught.

Novices and Experts

The most obvious difference between novices and experts is in the extensive knowledge about a narrow class of issues and problems that experts have built up through practice with feedback. Their expanded knowledge structures include: (a) efficient systems of rules, schemas, and scripts; (b) heuristic shortcuts for searching through a large amount of information and stored knowledge for a limited number of relevant possibilities; (c) a capacity for both "top-down" and "bottom-up" processing at or close to the same time; (d) the storage of a great deal of factual and procedural information as well as an overall perspective; and (e) the ability to bring general or commonsense knowledge to bear on technical or special domains of knowledge.

Cognitive psychologists have long been interested in the complex game of chess as a focus for understanding specialized information-processing skills (Binet, 1894; Chase & Simon, 1973). Chess masters and novices have been found to be similar on many dimensions—intelligence, memory, and the number of moves they consider before selecting the move to make. They differ in their abilities to recognize and remember possible patterns—their abilities to chunk information. They also differ greatly in the amount of practice time they have devoted to chess. Masters are found to have put in over 10,000 more hours of practice time than chess players who are merely good.

When chess masters were asked to examine a pattern of pieces on a board for five seconds, then reproduce it from memory, they could do so for patterns of about 20 pieces. Novice chess players could reconstruct patterns of only 5 pieces—which you will remember as near the average amount stored in short-term memory. However, this difference held true only when the pieces were arranged in "legal" patterns—patterns that could occur in a chess game. When the pieces were in random "nonlegal" patterns, chess masters could reproduce only about 5 pieces—the same as the novices. (de Groot, 1965)

This finding evidently reflects the fact that chess masters, after years of experience, have developed complex, comprehensive knowledge structures about legal chessboard configurations which have been stored as chunks. It has been estimated that a chess master knows about 50,000 of these patterns (Simon & Gilmartin, 1973).

Chess experts seem to have developed greater skill at relating visual information from the external world to patterns of positions stored in long-term memory networks (Chase & Simon, 1973).

Novices and a chess master were briefly shown chess pieces in various positions. As the number of spaces between the two pieces increased from one to four, it took novices longer to determine whether one designated piece could capture another. By contrast, the reaction times of the chess master were the same regardless of the distance; his visual imagery did not seem to involve distance coding. (Milojkovic, 1982)

Studies of the way people solve problems in physics and geometry reveal other ways in which experts and novices differ.

When asked to sort physics problems into categories according to their similarities, novices and experts differed in the way they represented problems internally. Novices relied more on the surface information given in the description of the problem; experts classified the information according to their knowledge of physical laws and common principles. The experts saw underlying structures from previous analysis of many problems in that field. (Chi et al., 1981)

These and other differences between experts and novices suggest that there is a good deal more to expertise than simple accumulation of facts. Research strongly supports the view that an expert's advantage comes from "his or her memory-storage structure—how richly the facts and procedures and relationships relevant to a domain are represented in one's mind. The expert has condensed or chunked many large blocks of basic information in a meaningful way so that he or she can quickly and successfully search for well-organized, well-encoded memories" (Farr, 1984).

Metacognitive Knowledge

Another way in which experts differ from novices is in their *metacognitive knowledge*. **Metacognitive knowledge** is the awareness of what you know and of how well you are comprehending current information. Metacognitive processes enable you to monitor your own mental activities—what you are learning and understanding in a given situation. They enable you to analyze what you need to know, predict the outcome of different strategies (and check the results later), and evaluate your progress. You use your metacognitive knowledge when you organize your studying differently for a multiple-choice exam than for an essay exam, or when you decide which options to take on an essay exam and how much time to devote to each part, according to the points it is worth.

In dealing with a task, your metacognitive knowledge search leads you to (a) evaluate your own skills and your physical and mental state, as well as those of the other persons involved; (b) search your stored knowledge for various possible strategies and evaluate them; (c) decide how much knowledge you have and how much you still need; and (d) assess how much attention to pay to incoming information. These four variables of person, task knowledge, strategy, and sensitivity may act separately to influence your decisions; more often they *interact* (Brown & De Loache, 1978).

John Flavell (1979, 1981) has been the pioneering theorist and researcher in this area. He believes that a better understanding of the way metacognitive knowledge develops and is used or misused will help greatly in teaching children and adults to gather information and evaluate the strategies they are using.

Some kinds of metacognitive knowledge concern self-knowledge. Other kinds are about the nature of different tasks, different situations, different types of people, and different possible strategies. This knowledge is translated into appropriate action when supplemented by: (a) an awareness of reasonable cognitive *goals* for the contemplated action, (b) an adoption of workable *strategies* to go from knowledge to goal attainment, and (c) utilization of *self-monitoring* during an activity to know one is on the right track.

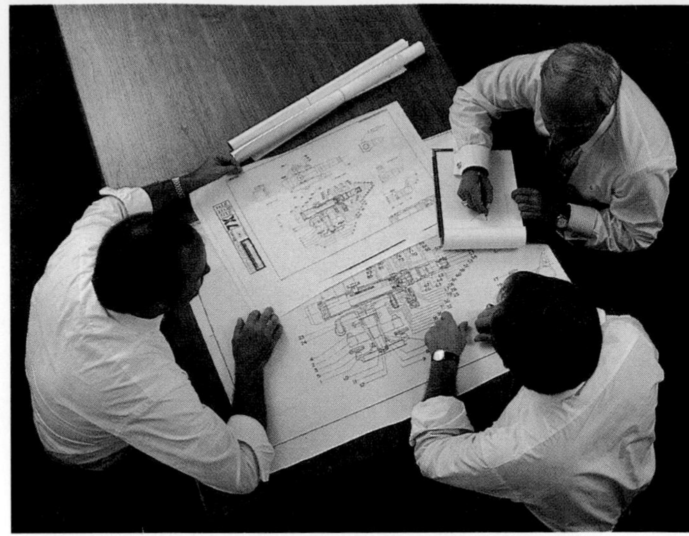

Designing a building is an example of an ill-defined problem. The architects must determine the function, location, and number of people the building will serve, and then draw plans.

The implications of research on metacognitive processes are profound. To become proficient, you need to go beyond learning specific knowledge and skills. You must become aware—and maintain a running awareness—of what you know and can do, where you are in a sequence, when procedures should be modified to meet the special requirements of the problem, and so on. These are all aspects of metacognitive knowledge. Children should be encouraged early to start dealing with problems by analyzing what they already know about such problems, where they are deficient, and what successful solutions might look like. Then they need to be taught to keep monitoring their progress or lack of it, detecting confusion in themselves or in information sources, while being aware of when they need additional information or resources. Novices become experts—and learners become their own teachers—when they take charge of their own search for knowledge (Scardamalia & Bereiter, 1985).

Expert Artificial Intelligence

Another way to study expertise is by developing computer programs that can make the kinds of judgments human experts make. Such "computer thought" is called **artificial intelligence (AI).**

The basic method used to study the complex cognitive activity of humans is that of *simulation modeling*. Computer programs originally attempted to simulate or mimic the mental processes of persons performing particular activities, such as forming concepts or making decisions. Herbert Simon won a Nobel Prize in 1978 for his work on decision making under conditions of uncertainty.

To program a computer to find "intelligent" solutions to intellectual problems, two basic ingredients are built in: a *knowledge base* and a *method of search*, consisting of certain heuristics, the rules of thumb we discussed earlier. Factual knowledge is stored as a network of propositions; rules of thumb are stored in the form of "if-then" instructions: *If* this condition occurs, *then* do that. A program specifies efficient ways to search through the information stored in a computer's memory of data, facts, and associations in a sequence of steps that narrows all possible combinations and permutations into manageable proportions.

The range of problems that researchers in artificial intelligence are working on includes problems related to speech recognition, language understanding, image analysis, robotics (apparatus programmed to carry out motor functions), and consultation systems. When AI computer programs are designed to serve as consultants for decision making, they are called "expert systems." Each one addresses a specific problem area, such as diagnosis of internal medical symptoms or geological exploration.

The most successful expert systems are classification programs. They are used in a limited, well-defined context to weigh and balance all the evidence in a given case and then to decide how it should be categorized.

The first step in constructing an expert system is to make overt and explicit the relevant knowledge that human specialists possess. It is very difficult to identify and then encode all this semiorganized, and sometimes subconscious, information. Often experts have difficulty expressing what they know, and programmers have difficulty faithfully capturing both major and subtle aspects of an expert's knowledge.

Expert systems face many other "cognitive pitfalls" even after a specialist's knowledge base is well represented. How should the system reason and make inferences—from goals backward to data or from data forward to conclusions? How can it recognize the limits of its knowledge and make "best guesses" in situations of uncertainty?

Three additional issues of concern to AI researchers are (a) how to integrate different domains of knowledge; (b) how to get the expert system to learn from experience; and (c) how to build some common sense into it. For example, while a program like *Internist-1* may know a great deal about internal medicine, it has no stored information about anatomy, physiology, or the time course of disease processes. A still unanswered question is how much information *outside* of a specific domain of knowledge is essential for accurate decision making *in* that domain.

A present challenge is to enable expert systems to discover new rules and refine old ones. Surprisingly, the thing that expert systems and all applications of AI lack most is "common sense." For example, a computer's conclusion, based on integrating all data on a patient, might include "suffering menstrual distress"—even for a male patient.

> *What makes common sense reasoning so difficult is that you need to know so many facts about the world. How many facts? A million? . . . (Feigenbaum, quoted in Waldrop, 1984, p. 804)*

Despite these problems, expert systems are fast losing their novice status. *Internist-1* made the correct diagnosis in 25 cases that represented 43 different categories taken from a medical research journal. This score of 58 percent correct compares favorably with the 65 percent score obtained by the physicians who were caring for the patients, but was not as high as the score of 81 percent correct in diagnoses made by expert clinicians.

Prospector is a mineral exploration consultation system that has made assessments which repeatedly agreed closely with those of expert geologists. *Mycin* is an expert system developed to aid physicians in the selection of antibiotics for patients with severe infections. In one evaluation of its recommendation decisions, expert evaluators preferred them to or found them as good as those made by five infectious disease experts who recommended therapy for the same patients. It is important to add that the evaluators made "blind" evaluations of the recommendations, not knowing who or what had made them (see Duda & Shortliffe, 1983).

The goal of expert systems is not to duplicate intelligent human behavior in all its aspects, but to go beyond what is presently known or known incompletely. By discovering new ways to encode knowledge and use it more powerfully, these systems can help solve human problems across many different domains. In the process of doing this, AI expert systems may also help us understand how to make human experts even better at what *they* do best and maybe even find some new shortcuts that the rest of us can use. (For more details on this area of application of cognitive psychology, see Feigenbaum & McCorduck, 1983; Gevarter, 1982; Shortliffe, 1983.)

Teaching Thinking Skills

For centuries educators, parents, and government agencies have advanced the goal of teaching students thinking and problem-solving skills. A recent report charged that such skills are not adequately developed in today's students (National Assessment of Educational Progress, 1983). The traditional approach has been to develop "mental discipline" in students by *subjecting* them to the rigors of learning difficult subjects such as Latin and mathematics (see Mann, 1979). There is no empirical evidence that general training in those areas carries over to unrelated areas of thinking via "strengthening mental muscles."

However, a variety of new evidence shows that reasoning, problem-solving, and thinking skills can be improved through the application of principles and methods of cognitive psychology. By understanding how the mind goes about solving problems and what goes into various intellectual performances, cognitive scientists can design more effective "mind training" strategies (Sternberg, 1986a). For example, verbal skill learning is seen to involve the teachable components of *encoding* the relevant information, *combining* parts of this encoded material in a meaningful way, and making selective *comparisons* that relate the new to the already known.

Two broad research approaches to discover how to teach thinking skills focus on the role of "domain-specific" knowledge and general strategic knowledge. From the first, we learn how people become experts in a specific area of knowledge or skill; how they perceive relevant information, represent it, and call it up on demand. From the second, we learn how people use "domain-free" general strategies and metacognitive knowledge to transfer their proficiency in one area to a variety of contexts. Both of these approaches must be integrated in teaching thinking skills (Bransford et al., 1986).

Training in the way to use highly general *rule systems,* such as rules for making probability estimates or rules for determining the truth of a hypothesis, has been shown to improve reasoning about all kinds of everyday problems. While training in formal logic has *no* effect on enhancing general reasoning, training in *pragmatic reasoning schema* does. The rules are abstract, but they deal with particular types of relations that occur frequently in the real world. Thus they have practical value in a learner's experience (Nisbett el al., 1987).

A team of cognitive scientists developed an experimental course for junior-high-school students (Herrnstein et al., 1986). The course was designed to teach general skills relevant to learning and intellectual performance independent of specific subject matter. Students were trained to use the cognitive skills of observation and classification, verbal and spatial reasoning, critical use of language, problem-solving strategies and tactics, inventive thinking, and decision-making procedures.

Over 400 Venezuelan seventh graders received 56 cognitive skills lessons taught by their trained teachers over one year. Their performances on a battery of general mental abilities tests was measured before and after the experimental course and compared to that of a matched control group. On all four of these outcome tests the experimental group demonstrated sizable gains over their pretest scores and especially over the performance of the control group. ***Figure 10.6*** *shows the substantially greater gains of the students given the cognitive skills training over those given the traditional curriculum. The 200 + percentage gain on the Target Abilities Test (TATs) most directly assessed the skills and process, but not the content, employed in the lessons.*

Figure 10.6 Gains of Students Given Cognitive Skills Training

The three standardized tests used to measure the gains of the students given the cognitive skills training included the Otis-Lennon School Ability Test (Olsat), the Cattell Culture Fair Intelligence Test (Cattell), and a group of General Abilities Tests (GATs). The Target Abilities Tests (TATs) were tests designed by the researchers who conducted the study. (From Herrnstein et al., 1986)

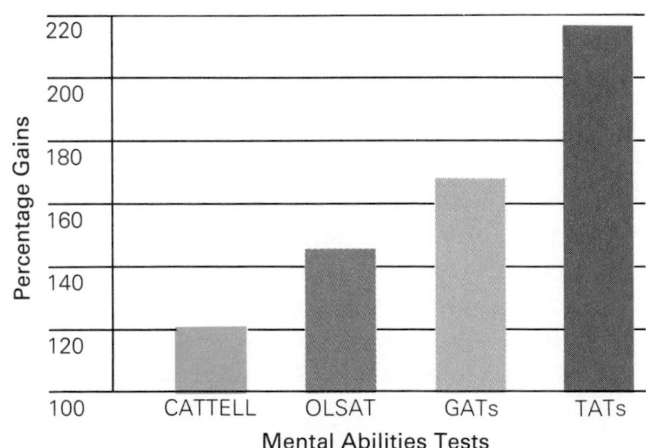

Whether this beneficial effect of teaching thinking skills will be enduring awaits evaluative research on the long-term effects. The potential and the promise for improving this fundamental aspect of education are certainly evident.

Communicating Thoughts

Imagine yourself among a group of people who are speaking a language foreign to you. They share their thoughts, plan actions, and express feelings; their use of language helps bind them into a social community—and isolates you. You cannot comprehend what is being communicated, nor can you tell them what's on your mind. Without the ability to express your thoughts in words, you feel both ignorant and childlike. You can use some universally understood gestures like pointing to objects or shaking your head, but that doesn't get you very far. You need language to communicate abstract concepts (such as "yesterday" or "democracy"), to express what things mean to you, or to tell how you perceive relationships.

The acquisition of language by a child during the first years of life is considered by many to be the single greatest achievement of human intelligence. Ten linguistic experts working full time for 10 years could not program a computer to use the English language as well as the average young child does (Moskowitz, 1978).

We looked at children's development of language in chapter 3. In this section we are interested in some of the ways in which thoughts can be transmitted to other people, the relation between language and thought, the criteria for language, and whether only humans can use language.

Verbal and Nonverbal Communication

The central process in communication is converting private thoughts and feelings into symbols, signs, or words that others can recognize and convert back into ideas and feelings. Four communication systems carry our messages: natural language, artificial languages, visual communication, and nonverbal communication.

Natural language is an extremely complex cognitive skill and system for transmitting specific meanings through words, which can be spoken, written, signed, or sung. *Artificial languages* include musical notation, math equations, and some computer programs that communicate specialized information concisely and with little ambiguity by using agreed-upon systems of symbols, signs, and formulas. Pictures and diagrams are means of *visual communication* that are used to convey ideas or feelings or both. *Nonverbal communication* includes body movements (postures, gestures, smiling, eye contact, and use of physical space) as well as nonlinguistic characteristics of speech, such as voice tone, hesitation, and volume. Nonverbal acts are not randomly committed; they occur at certain times during the social process of interacting with a partner or a group. Researchers are studying how the multiple channels of nonverbal behavior, often generated spontaneously by a sender, are integrated by a receiver to signal such messages as warmth, sympathy, threat, deception, or status (Siegman & Feldstein, 1985).

Although natural language makes possible more precise cognitive communication, nonverbal elements account for a significant portion of the total message being conveyed when two people are interacting with each other (Mehrabian, 1971). For example, gaze and eye contact are correlated only weakly with verbal behavior, because people are not aware of their gazing behavior during an interaction. Nevertheless, this one channel of nonverbal behavior provides information about liking and attraction, attentiveness, competence, credibility, dominance, and mental health. Gaze and other nonverbal behaviors also regulate turn-taking in a conversation, usually when a speaker is starting and stopping an utterance and ready to become a listener (Kleinke, 1986).

The Relation Between Language and Thought: Psycholinguistics

Controversies about the relationship between language and thought have raged for many years. Both are vital to the human enterprise, but there have been difficulties in gathering evidence to support or refute the claims of one view or another. We will briefly review some of the principal views concerning the way language and thought are related.

Previous Theories

Nearly 2000 years ago, Aristotle championed the view now held by most cognitive psychologists—that the processes and structures of thought determine the structure of language. In this analysis, language is seen as a tool of thought, shaped to fit the requirements of the cognitive and communicative processes it serves. Language is one way people encode events and experiences that are important to remember.

By the time psychologists began to study language, the idea that thought could have primacy over language was heresy. Thoughts could be allowed into a scientific view of human behavior only if they could be defined as overt responses of some kind. Behaviorist John B. Watson (1930) defined them as subvocal speech, a kind of "silent talk," asserting that thinking could not take place without movements of the vocal apparatus. He noted that people who use sign language to communicate have been observed to make signs during their sleep. By analogy, it seemed logical to expect that people who speak using their vocal cords would have to use the same muscles when they think.

In this case, a critical test of Watson's position was possible. It was conducted by a team of researchers, the senior member of which served as the experimental subject. He allowed himself to be temporarily paralyzed by a curare-like drug that prevented him from making any muscular movements at all (his breathing required a respirator). He found that he could indeed still think, even though he could not move a muscle in his voice box (S. Smith et al., 1947). So Watson was wrong—thought does not require any motor activity.

If thought is not the same thing as subvocal language, then perhaps it is determined and shaped by the language that people use. This view, put forth by linguist B. L. Whorf (1956) was called *linguistic determinism.* Whorf argued that the languages developed by different cultural groups structure and determine their world views in different ways. He cited as evidence the fact that Eskimos have many different words for *snow* while groups for whom snow is not so important have only one or a few. Some rice-eating cultural groups have nearly a hundred names for different kinds of rice, and there are thousands of words for *camel* in Arabic.

Although interesting, these examples are not unequivocal support for Whorf's hypothesis. Perhaps it is the other way around. Perhaps cultural needs first alter the way people think about their environment, in turn requiring a more precise vocabulary. Maybe it is the concepts that are important for which people then develop more terms and terms of greater precision; this could explain the differences from one culture to another.

There are many sources of support for a belief in the primacy of thought over language. Language is a relatively late invention on the evolutionary timetable, certainly coming long after prehistoric peoples were using thought to solve problems and even making cave drawings to represent what they believed was significant in their lives. Also, in declarative sentences there is a preferred word order the world over in the use of subjects, verbs, and objects. In 80 percent of the world's languages, the subject comes first and the object is last. This consistency in languages is assumed to reflect a basic property of human thought (Ultan, 1969).

Language Knowledge

Following Watson's lead, psychologists continued to treat language as a performance—as conditionable behavior (Skinner, 1957). By the 1950s, however, linguists, led by Noam Chomsky (1957, 1975), were arguing forcefully that behaviorists missed the unique features of language by focusing on recurring aspects of small speech units such as words. For Chomsky, language could be understood only as a complex, abstract system governed by rules and built upon an *innate* capacity for language and linguistic competence. To him, the study of language should not be about what people *do* in learning words, but about what they *know* about language structure, as evidenced by their competence in constructing meaningful sentences.

Although humans learn some aspects of language use, children come "prepared" to acquire languages quickly and more effortlessly than any other complex skill. Without any training, children demonstrate in their language that certain rules for proper grammatical use are somehow "built in" ahead of time. There are specific linguistic constraints on what parts of speech are permissible to move to new positions in a sentence. Chomsky (1986) describes these constraints as part of the "deep structure" of language that is innate to the species and found universally across different language communities. An evolutionary perspective on language development suggests that human culture begins with the emergence of language (Waldron, 1985). The ability to use spoken and written language makes possible the unique achievements of human culture, among them moral codes, religion, history, literature, and advanced technology.

Joining the linguists in their challenge to the behavioristic psychologists' view of language was an emerging band of psychologists who were becoming interested in studying information processing. These psychologists demonstrated the psychological reality of syntax and other covert features of language through studies such as the following.

Subjects memorized strings of pseudowords that meant nothing, ordinarily had zero frequency of appearing together, and were without any pattern of regularity.

In the first condition, the string was simply a list of nonsense words, such as: haky deeb um flut recile pav tolfent dison. *In the second condition, articles* (the, a) *and suffixes* (-s,-est,-ed,-ly) *were randomly added to these nonsense words:* haky deebs the um flutest reciled pav a tolfently dison. *In a third condition, capital letters and periods were added, and the nonsense strings were constructed to resemble sentences:* A haky deebs reciled the dison tolfently um flutest pav.

Although the word strings in the first condition were the shortest, they were the hardest to recall. Next hardest to recall were the words in the second condition. Best remembered were the word strings in the third condition. (Epstein, 1961)

This result could be explained only by the differences in grammatical information in the three word strings.

A large body of research has provided other behavioral data supporting the view that people possess and act upon complex linguistic knowledge (for example, G. Miller, 1962). In recent years, however, cognitive psychologists have diverged from their earlier allegiance to the strictly linguistic views of language. In the first place, they feel linguists have underrated the importance of semantic (meaning) factors. Many of the experimental findings have shown the operation of *nonlinguistic* factors, such as context, expectations, general knowledge, or focus of attention. Also, it was found that details of the syntactic structure or other grammatical features were forgotten much sooner than the semantic content. For example, given the sentence, "The ball that Bruce threw went to Joanne," subjects would remember the meaning—that Bruce threw the ball to Joanne—better than the grammatical structure. The interpreted, *deep* structure of sentences was thus shown to be partially independent of the literal, *surface* structure, indicating the importance of meaning (Slobin, 1979).

Cognitive psychologists have also rejected the linguists' notion of language and thought as independent systems, arguing for many interdependencies between language and thought. Much current research, in fact, is aimed at showing the convergence and interrelationships between concepts related to language and concepts related to long-term memory and comprehension (Clark & Clark, 1977).

Researchers are also studying the contrasts between speech and written language. They want to discover why speech is learned readily, while reading and writing—though always based on spoken language—involve a great deal of effort. Cross-cultural studies comparing language systems that use pictorial characters, such as Chinese and Japanese *logographs,* with Western alphabetic script

Figure 10.7
When a lesser number is written in a larger size than a greater number, the incongruence between the number and its size causes a subject to take longer to decide which number is greater. However, the amount of the effect, or interference, varies according to the way the numbers are written. Using Arabic numerals and Chinese logographs causes more interference than using English or Spanish words.

enable psycholinguists to study the way different visual and cognitive processing strategies are developed to meet the demands imposed by these different writing systems (Tzeng & Wang, 1983). For example, in a silent variation of the Stroop interference test (described in chapter 7, p. 229), subjects had the simple task of pressing a button to choose which of a pair of projected numbers, 6 or 9, was larger. When the smaller number was written physically larger than the greater number, reaction times were longer than when they were the same size. This interference effect disappeared when the Arabic numerals were replaced with English or Spanish words for the numbers, but the same interference appeared with Chinese logographs for the numbers (see **Figure 10.7**). This is an instance of cognitive-perceptual interaction in information processing.

Criteria for "True" Language

Many animal species have communication systems. Dolphins whistle, birds call, bees dance, dogs bark. Do these qualify as "true" language? What are the criteria by which a communication system can be evaluated as a language system?

Although the thousands of modern human languages differ in many ways, they all share the following basic characteristics (taken from a longer list by Hockett, 1960):

1. *Specialization.* The chief purpose of a language is to communicate information to others. Other behaviors may also communicate a message without that being their primary purpose. For example, a panting dog communicates that it is hot, but the panting is a physiological mechanism designed to relieve the animal's discomfort. It is not done for the purpose of sending its master a message. The dog would still pant in the master's absence.

2. *Arbitrariness.* The combination of sounds selected to refer to something is arbitrary: there is no direct connection between the thing identified and the features of the word chosen to identify it. The color we call *green* is *vert* in French and *z'old* in Hungarian. Once a word is selected to stand for something, however, then all speakers of the language must agree to use it in the same way.
3. *Displacement.* Unlike the warning cries of animals sensing danger, language may be generated in the absence of any immediate controlling stimuli. Similarly, we use language to talk about things not in the "here and now"—about the past, the future, and even imagined realities.
4. *Productivity and Novelty.* Language makes possible a virtually infinite number of utterances. Speakers of a language can produce novel phrases and sentences that they have never heard before.
5. *Iteration and Recursion. Iteration* is the addition of words and phrases to sentences; *recursion* is the embedding of one language structure within another of the same kind. Both of these processes allow for infinite variability. Following are examples of iteration:

   Iteration extends the meaning.

   Iteration extends the meaning and adds complexity.

   Iteration extends the meaning and adds complexity and is a feature found only in human communication systems.

   Both iteration and recursion are used in the popular children's story *The House That Jack Built.*

Is Language Uniquely Human?

It is obvious that only human language meets all five of these criteria for language, but does that mean that no other species has the *ability* to use language to express thoughts? Would it be possible to train members of another species, such as chimpanzees, to use a symbolic language system? Several researchers have been engaged in just such a venture for a number of years. Although this research requires an enormous investment of time, patience, and ingenuity, the effort has not deterred psychologists from attempting to teach apes to use language.

Early attempts at getting apes to use spoken language met with little success (Hayes, 1951; Kellogg & Kellogg, 1933). Did these failures mean that apes could not handle the rules of a language or only that the subjects did not have the vocal apparatus necessary for producing speech?

In the late 1960s, a different approach was tried that did not depend on an animal's vocal apparatus. Some investigators were able to teach apes, mostly chimps, to communicate using American Sign Language for the deaf (Fouts & Rigby, 1977; Gardner & Gardner, 1972). Others taught chimps to use plastic symbols as words, to combine them to communicate thoughts, and even to type messages on a keyboard console where each key represented one of their symbol words (Premack, 1976; Rumbaugh, 1977). These animals learned to use hundreds of different signs or symbols, to combine them to form larger units, and to generalize a sign or symbol (for example, from "more tickling" to "more banana"). In addition, they used their words as we do—as symbols representing objects in order to convey information to another individual.

The research results seemed to prove that these animals were capable of true language until observation of a young chimp, named Nim Chimpsky (in honor of Noam Chomsky) suggested that it really wasn't so. Close videotape analysis of Nim's sign combinations led to the conclusion that Nim was merely producing a string of signs and not true sentences. Nim's utterances seemed to be largely imitations of his trainer's signs, along with signs that would elicit a quick response (and a tasty reward). What was lacking was the essential characteristic of human language—*the spontaneous combination of words to form novel phrases or sentences that are understandable by others.* After years of intense training, neither Nim nor any of the other apes had been able to increase the length and complexity of the phrases they produced. The crux of the argument is that chimps did not learn to use word signs *creatively* to form new combinations of signs in a grammatically competent way and they could not identify their internal states (Terrace, 1979, 1985).

Other researchers are challenging these negative conclusions, however. Some claim that, even if language training does not lead chimps to use language spontaneously, it does enhance their ability to perform certain abstract reasoning tasks (Premack, 1983). Several other sources of recent evidence suggest that primates may be closer to humans in their ability to use language than many scientists have thought. In the wild, vervet monkeys use vocalizations that discriminate among aspects of their environment. When these alarm calls were tape recorded in Africa and played back to captive monkeys, each call elicited an appropriate response from the monkeys. They ran up a tree when the leopard warning call was heard;

Washoe is signing the word brush.

searched the sky in response to the eagle call; and looked down when there was a snake call (Cheney & Seyfarth, 1985).

Washoe, the first chimp to use sign language, has recently gone from being student to teacher. When a ten-month-old chimp, Loulis, was placed in the care of Washoe, she began to teach her pupil how to sign—without any human training. According to Roger Fouts, one of the pioneering psychologists in teaching chimps to sign, "Washoe adopted Loulis and, within eight days, spontaneously began teaching him simple signs. Washoe would demonstrate the signs for Loulis, and occasionally we saw her take the young chimp's hands and mold them into the proper sign, much as the Gardners [R. Allen and Beatrice, Washoe's teachers] had done with her" (Fouts, quoted in Maugh, 1985, p. 20; see also Fouts et al., 1984). Loulis at the age of 6 can use nearly 70 signs in their proper context. Observing this feat led ethologist Jane Goodall (who had studied chimps in their native habitats for three decades) to conclude, "I have no hesitation in saying that chimpanzees can learn to use signs in a meaningful way to communicate to humans and to each other" (speech at the San Francisco Commonwealth Club, April 15, 1987). The notion of true language as being "for humans only" is also being challenged by research with gorillas.

> *For over a decade two gorillas, Koko and Michael, have been studied and coached in sign language by Francine Patterson (1986). Koko signs to herself and her dolls when she is alone, combines signs into new patterns, and uses language to express complex concepts, as when she refers to herself and signs "fine animal gorilla." The pair of gorillas also use sign language with each other. Patterson recently reported that Koko does more than use signs as a means of expressing demands for incentives. She used question signs, for example, when first seeing a woman wearing hair curlers. Koko also can respond to complex questions with complex answers at more than one level of meaning. For example, when asked, "What can you think of that's hard?" Koko responded, "Rock . . . work." So perhaps there is a continuum of communicative behavior between humans and their closest biological relatives in the animal kingdom. (Patterson et al., 1987)*

The dispute over various species' capacity for language is not resolved, but it is interesting to note in concluding this chapter that the "Clever Hans" phenomenon with which we began our study of thought processes has been at work once again. Like Hans, Nim Chimpsky was discovered to have been responding to unintended prompting by the trainers who were reinforcing his use of symbols. Maybe higher levels of thinking and language are uniquely human attributes, but we humans may still be fooled by a horse that taps in German or a chimp that signs for his supper.

Summary

- *Cognition* is a general term for all forms of knowing including attending, remembering, reasoning, imagining, anticipating, planning, deciding, solving problems, and communicating ideas. Cognitive psychology is the study of these higher mental processes and of the mental structures that make them possible. Cognitive science is an interdisciplinary approach that attempts to discover the nature of knowledge and the way it is represented in the mind.
- Though thinking cannot be observed, it can be inferred from observation of several kinds of processes, such as reports of introspection, think-aloud protocols, adaptive behavior, reaction time, errors, eye and muscle movements, and brain waves.
- The basic mental structures for thinking are concepts, which are mental representations of *kinds* of things. Our ability to form concepts enables us to react to new events as members of categories. We organize concepts in networks and hierarchies in our mental structures but depend on basic levels in thinking and in recognizing stimuli.
- Most complex thought is believed to be based on schemas and scripts, knowledge clusters about factual and procedural information, respectively. Schemas and scripts include expectations and thus influence perception, thought, and memory.

- Comprehending new information is a process comparable to the interweaving of assimilation and accommodation in childhood: what is familiar is added to existing structures and what is unfamiliar or does not fit forces changes in the structures or is distorted or ignored.
- Visual images and cognitive maps are mental structures used in thinking in which spatial relationships are important. Computational theories attempt to specify the processing mechanisms involved in generating mental images.
- Decision making is the process of selecting among available options. Inference is the reasoning process of drawing conclusions. Judgment is the process of forming opinions, reaching conclusions, and making evaluations, as well as the product of those mental activities. These interrelated cognitive processes are central to the daily activities of the lay person, scientist, and professional planner.
- Most of the cognitive processes underlying decision making work well and effectively, but sometimes these same processes exert a negative, distorting influence. Old beliefs tend to be preserved because we assimilate new information in terms of what we already believe. The mob, the passions, and cognitive biases contribute to irrationality and faulty decision making.
- Cognitive biases are systematic ways of thinking that are responsible for errors in decision making. Heuristics are mental shortcuts useful for reducing the range of possible answers, but they can be applied inappropriately. Two heuristics frequently employed in decision making are the availability heuristic and the representativeness heuristic, which are decisional biases we use without awareness of their consequences.
- Analyzing people's decision making shows that they are influenced by the way a problem or question is framed, by the psychological perception of risk, and by such nonrational psychological factors as wishful thinking, oversimplification, or misinterpretation of utility or probability information.
- In solving problems we must define the initial state, the goal state, and the operations that can get us from the first to the second—a difficult task in ill-defined problems. Functional fixedness and other mental sets can hamper creative problem solving. Algorithms ensure an eventual solution if there is one, but are impractical in many cases. Heuristics can often reach a solution faster if the correct ones are selected.
- In skill development, declarative knowledge is gained, converted into procedural knowledge, and eventually made automatic. Both practice and adequate feedback are essential.
- Experts, compared with novices, have more specific and general knowledge, have greater facility in using appropriate rules and strategies, and represent problems internally according to common principles rather than surface structure. Most of this simply comes from greater practice. Experts also have greater metacognitive knowledge than novices about their domain of information.
- Expertise is being studied via artificial intelligence—computer programs that attempt to make the kinds of judgments human experts make. Current research in artificial intelligence is focused on the way to supplement specialized knowledge with essential general knowledge, the way to build in the ability to learn from experience, and the way to build some common sense into expert systems.
- Evidence indicates that it is possible to teach ways of improving reasoning, problem solving, and thinking skills. Teaching thinking skills involves integration of domain-specific knowledge and general, strategic "domain-free" knowledge.
- Humans communicate ideas through natural language, artificial languages, visual communication, and nonverbal means such as gestures. Nonverbal elements carry a large part of the message conveyed in social interaction.
- Theories of the relation between thought and language have included a number of opposing claims: that language depends on thought, that thought depends on language, and that they are closely interrelated, with innate linguistic predispositions providing structural constraints, but experience providing meaning and other nonlinguistic features. Cognitive psychologists are demonstrating close interrelationships between language and other cognitive processes.
- Criteria for "true language" include use of speech symbols specifically for communication, an arbitrary relationship between objects and the symbols for them, use of the symbols independently of the stimulus situation, capacity for originality and a virtually infinite number of utterances, and iteration and recursion in sentence structure.
- Chimpanzees and gorillas lack the vocal apparatus necessary for spoken language, but can learn to use both tangible symbols and sign-language symbols for communication. Whether they can employ these symbols in true language is still a matter of debate.

11

Motivation and Emotion

It was soon after Keith's seventeenth summer when he began to change. He had been second-string on the football team because he was "too easygoing." His girlfriend liked Keith's gentle manner, but was, at times, distressed because he was so slow getting turned on to her charms. That was before the changes began.

During team practice one day, Keith smashed through the blockers on an end run and nailed the halfback for a big loss—in fact, tackled him so hard that he broke his leg. A fight started when the burly center for the White Shirts cursed Keith for playing dirty. Keith knocked him out with a solid right hook. "Hey, what's gotten into Keith?" everyone was wondering. "Who cares?" was the coach's reaction. "The man is varsity material; he's got what it takes—he's all man!"

Off the playing field, Keith's life was changing in similarly dramatic ways. His girlfriend now called him "Tiger." Before, he could take sex or leave it; now it was an all-consuming passion. His appetite for food became enormous too. Keith seemed to be always hungry, eating, gaining weight, and growing steadily bigger.

He was encouraged to join the army, to fight in the Vietnam War instead of in the town's bars. Once there, he became a legend of sorts. He volunteered to drive a high-explosive truck when no one else would. He was fearless during enemy raids when everyone was justifiably afraid. Keith never felt particularly brave; he just didn't understand why the others were "so chicken."

In a society where the masculine traits of aggressiveness, sexuality, and fearless bravery are prized, big, bad Keith was a perfect "10"; but something was wrong! Keith was having terrible headaches, which were coming on more frequently and more intensely.

Back home for his dad's funeral, Keith noticed a strange thing. He had really loved his father, but he was unable to experience the death emotionally. He felt only a cold emotion, "as if" he were sad. The same was true in his relations with his girlfriend; his emotions lacked any feeling tone. They seemed to be flat, without highs or lows, but why? Why the sudden growth spurt, the raging appetite for food and sex, the aggressiveness, the loss of emotions? And why those blinding headaches?

Matters came to a head literally when Keith fainted from his headache pain. Fortunately the examining doctor recognized the unusual symptoms associated with the headaches—Keith had developed a brain tumor on his pituitary gland. He was suffering from a condition known as *acromegaly.* Over the past four years, since that seventeenth summer, as the tumor grew, so did the pressure on the pituitary, and so did Keith. Keith may have been a "superman" but he was not "his own man" at all. This big guy was at the mercy of a silent secretion coming from a tiny gland the size of a pea!

You will recall that the pituitary gland secretes a variety of chemicals, some of which control several of the endocrine glands, among them the adrenal glands (stress reactions of fight or flight), the testes (sexual behavior), and the thyroid (energy level). The pituitary also secretes a growth hormone. Together, these chemical reactions programmed Keith's desires, activities, and changes in body and mood. A variation in arousal is essential for experiencing appropriate emotional reactions, but he was too high, too "on" all the time to respond differently to making love or war, to the death of a parent or the attraction of a girlfriend.

The tumor was frozen surgically. As the headaches stopped, so did all of the other extreme effects of that powerful pituitary gland. Keith's appetite for food, sex, and aggression diminished. He became mild-mannered Clark Kent again—permanently.

Then Keith had to adjust to a new problem. He had lost his motivation to engage in any of the "masculine" activities that had become part of his life-style over the past four years. He was helped back to normal functioning by a combination of hormone therapy and supportive counseling. He was able to understand how he had become a victim of biological mechanisms that took away his personal control and distorted his motivation and emotional state. Keith has gone on to lead a healthy, well-adjusted life—happy to be an ordinary mortal, like most of the rest of us.*

*An actual case account of a former student of the author (with name changed).

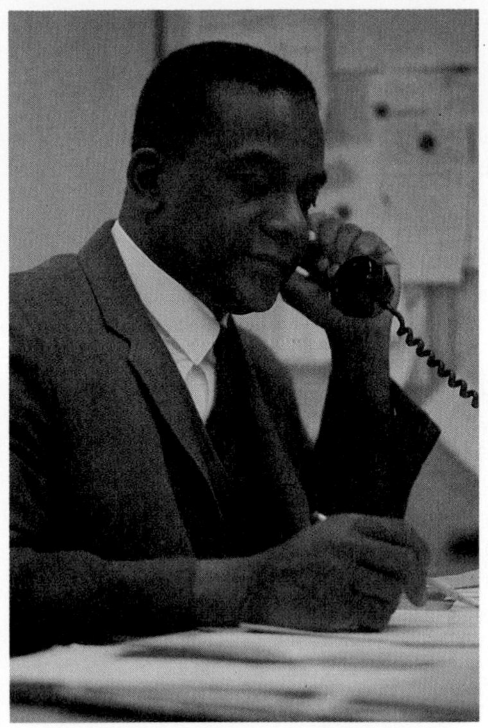

In the previous example we see how internal physical forces can cause behavior changes; in the next example we show how emotional and attitudinal factors can alter behavior patterns.

Charles T. loved his work. He had started on the assembly line in a TV factory and, over the next 20 years, had worked hard and well, moving steadily upward to become supervisor and, finally, chief personnel officer. He was entrusted with important decisions and became a valued troubleshooter. Charlie's executive status brought him special privileges, and the respect of his coworkers. "Mr. T." was a good boss and a fine man. He deserved all he got.

But one day he lost it all! His company went out of business, a victim of more efficient foreign competition. Sad, but not too bad, because Mr. T. was given the highest recommendation by the company's senior executives attesting to his intelligence, ability, and total company loyalty, and he was only 46 years old at the time.

Armed with these glowing letters and an impressive résumé Mr. T. began searching for the ideal replacement job. Interviewers were clearly impressed by the way he handled himself, but none called back. He was either "overqualified" or lacked experience for jobs requiring new high-technology skills. As his savings dwindled, Mr. T.'s usually cheerful disposition changed. He was irritable for the first time anyone in his family could remember—and depressed. He moved to Florida where many of his family lived and the cost of living was lower. Still no work.

One honest personnel officer finally told him why: "It's got nothing to do with your education, experience, references, whatever, Mr. T. The company doesn't want to hire older men, that's all."

Charlie was too old! He would show them, prove they were wrong, if only they'd give him a chance. They didn't. He grew resentful and bitter toward "them," and toward others less deserving who had jobs.

His once vibrant personality seemed to slowly drain out of him. He gave up looking for work. He had organized his life around his job. He had lived to work; but "when they take away your job, they. . . ." Charles T. was only 51 when he died of "natural causes" (Buczek, 1979).

The stories of Keith and Charlie introduce us to the complexity and range of human motivation and emotion. Keith's case forces us to acknowledge the role of physiological processes in regulating—and sometimes disrupting—our behavior. In Charlie's case we see the power of psychological and social processes influencing our actions, feelings, and even life itself. The mind turned on the body in Charlie's case, while the body turned on the mind for Keith.

Why do we do what we do? What are the determinants of our actions? What internal and external forces stimulate passive organisms to become *actors?* These are the broad questions we try to answer in studying motivation.

After we consider different answers that psychologists have given to these questions—in the form of theories of motivation—we will examine, in some detail, three significant kinds of motivation: hunger, a primarily biologically based source of motivation; sex, which in humans mixes biology with psychology; and motivation for work and achievement, which clearly has a psychosocial basis. Unfortunately, it is not possible to include many other kinds of motivation that play significant roles in our lives, such as thirst, affiliation, and religion, to name but a few.

The final section of the chapter will focus on human emotion. In it we will examine the motivational significance of emotion in adapting to situational demands. Of special interest will be the many faces of emotion—how we express universal emotions and recognize them in others.

Understanding Motivation

Motivation is the general term for the process of starting, directing, and maintaining physical and psychological activities. It is a broad concept that embraces all the internal mechanisms involved in (a) *preferences* for one activity over another, (b) *vigor* of responses, and (c) *persistence* of organized patterns of action toward relevant goals.

The word *motivation* comes from the Latin *movere*—"to move." Action is a fundamental property of living systems. Evolution favors organisms that can act to move toward and obtain what they need for survival and move away from or oppose what threatens them. Psychologists who study learning in lower animals are interested in the specific sources of motivation that lead to the discrete responses that are changed through learning. Other psychologists want to understand how broad motivational currents can shape a person's whole lifestyle.

No one has ever "seen" motivation, just as no one has ever "seen" learning. All we see are changes in behavior. To explain these observed changes, we make *inferences* about underlying psychological and physiological variables—"educated hunches" that are formalized in the concept of motivation. Among the words most commonly associated with motivation are *goals, needs, wants, intentions,* and *purposes;* all of which relate to factors that cause us to act. Two motivational terms that are frequently used by researchers in this area are *drive* and *motive.* Psychologists usually use the label **drive** to mean motivation for action that is assumed to be primarily biologically instigated, as in hunger. They often use **motive** to refer to psychologically and socially instigated motivation, which is generally assumed to be, at least in part, learned. A motive can be either conscious or nonconscious (in the ways we distinguished between them in chapter 7).

Psychologists vary in their usage of motivational concepts, however. Some, for example, prefer to use the term *need* only in connection with biological demands (the body's need for water). Others think *need* is appropriate in discussing psychological requirements also (the need for achievement).

Another important difference which generates heated arguments among psychologists is whether motivation is *teleological*—leading to purposeful action—or is just a general energizer of behavior without any implication that the organism is "striving toward a desired state." One support for the teleological view comes from those who accept the doctrine of *hedonism,* which states that organisms are motivated to seek pleasure and avoid pain. In chapter 8 we saw that some psychologists study learning as the behavioral process that is started and maintained by such hedonistic forces within an organism. While radical behaviorists, such as Skinner, reject all motivational concepts, other learning theorists, such as Clark Hull and Neal Miller, propose a strong necessary link between motivation and learning. They argue that an unmotivated organism is passive, does not act, does not explore its environment, and, therefore, does not learn about the consequences of its responding. They propose that responses that are followed by reinforcers (such as food) are learned, because they reduce the motivation (hunger) presumed to have been responsible for an animal's responding in the first place.

Why Use Motivational Concepts?

Despite the arguments of extreme behaviorists, other psychologists—and people generally—have found motivation a useful concept for several reasons. It helps to account for variability of behavior, to relate biological processes to behavior, to make observable behavior more intelligible, to assign personal responsibility for actions, and to explain perseverance of behavior despite adversity.

To Account for Behavioral Variability

Why might you do well on a task one day and poorly on the same task another day? Differing motivations could be one explanation. Likewise, when one child does very well at a competitive task and another child with roughly the same ability and knowledge does very poorly, motivational differences seem a useful starting point in looking for explanations. Motivational explanations are used when the variations in people's performance in a constant situation *cannot* be traced to differences in practice, reinforcement history, ability, skill, factors in the situation, or chance. More generally, then, if behavior never varied there would be no need for motivational concepts—or for psychology!

To Relate Biology to Behavior

The concept of motivation reminds us that we, like Keith, are biological organisms. Besides reacting to external stimuli, we engage in behaviors that promote our survival and well-being, such as eating, sleeping, and keeping warm. Though we react to situational stimulation in engaging in these behaviors, the external stimuli do not seem adequate to account for their universal occurrence in the species or the guidance of individual behaviors by internal physiological processes.

The concept of motivation as an inner drive that determines behavior was introduced into psychology by Robert Woodworth (1918). He defined *drive* in biological terms as energy released from an organism's store. This energy was nonspecific, blind as to direction. It was called forth by initiating stimuli and made available for goal-directed activities. Other mechanisms, such as perceptual and learning processes, were thought to guide it in appropriate directions. According to Woodworth, drive is like the fuel in a vehicle, providing the energy of movement; other mechanisms determine when and where the vehicle goes, as well as the quality of the ride.

To Infer Private States from Public Acts

'Tis e'er the wont of simple folk to prize the deed and o'erlook the motive, and of learned folk to discount the deed and lay open the soul of the doer.

John Barth, The Sot Weed Factor

This novelist's words suggest two ways of responding to someone's behavior. We can take it at face value, or we can see it as a symptom of an underlying emotional or motivational state. To the greeting "Good morning," do you respond "Good morning to you" or do you look for signs of what the person is really thinking or secretly feeling? Sigmund Freud's belief that all behavior has underlying, often unconscious, causes, coupled with his idea that sex and aggression instigate much of our behavior, has had a profound effect on psychologists' study of motivation as well as on popular views. Researchers in cognitive and social psychology are currently investigating the inferences that we make about inner determinants of outer behavior—and what makes them accurate or false.

To Assign Responsibility for Actions

The concept of personal responsibility is basic in law, religion, and ethics; personal responsibility, in turn, presupposes inner motivation and ability to control one's actions. People are judged less responsible for their actions when (a) they did not intend for the consequence to occur; (b) external forces were powerful enough to determine the behavior; or (c) the act was not under voluntary control because of the influence of drugs, alcohol, or intense emotion. Although these factors may be hard to sort out in a particular case, the concept of personal responsibility dissolves without the concept of consciously directed motivation.

To Explain Perseverance Despite Adversity

Motivational constructs also help us to understand the way organisms can continue to perform consistently despite marked variations in stimulus conditions. That is the motto of the Postal Service: "Neither wind, nor rain, nor dark of night can stay these couriers from the swift completion of their appointed rounds." Motivation gets you to work or class on time even when you're exhausted, and it helps you persist even when you are losing. One of the most dramatic examples of this occurred at the 1984 Olympic Games when an athlete refused to quit—even after her body did.

Gabriella Andersen-Schiess staggered to the marathon finish, nearly fell, and was assisted from the track by medics.

Using Motivational Concepts in Research

Because motivation is an invisible, intervening variable, it is a slippery concept—and if we are not careful, a *circular one*. For example, we cannot say, "He ate because he was hungry," and then cite as evidence, "He must have been hungry because he ate." To be scientifically useful, the concept of motivation must be tied both to external behavioral indicators (dependent variables) that can be measured and to observable operations that a researcher can perform (independent variables). Only then can we start to look for consistent effects of motivation or for relationships between changes in stimulus conditions, assumed changes in the intervening variable of motivation, and changes in behavioral consequences.

Instead of trying to link each aspect of the behavior we see to particular preceding stimulus input, we postulate an overall *intervening variable* like hunger or sex or achievement, as shown in **Figure 11.1.** A psychologist, like a detective, must use the available evidence from the stimulus conditions and the observable behavior to identify this basic internal variable—to establish the motive for the deed.

Behavioral Indicators of Motivation

Among the many behaviors that have been taken as indicators of motivation and used to measure its strength are (a) activity level, (b) rate of learning (with practice held constant), (c) final level of performance reached, (d) resistance of a response to extinction, (e) interference with ongoing activities, (f) preference for a particular goal or activity, and (g) consummatory behavior (for example, amount eaten or speed of eating). These are all *index variables:* they indicate the presence of motivation and something about its strength. Any one of them can be used in an *operational definition* of motivation because they all are external events that can be observed and objectively measured; thus the concept is defined by the operations used to measure it. (For an example of persistence in overcoming barriers to reach a goal as an indicator of strength of motivation, see the ***Close-up*** on p. 380.)

With humans, motivation can be measured in additional ways. Researchers may ask participants to fill out questionnaires evaluating their own needs, desires, and anxieties, and use the scores as indicators of strength of motivation. These scores can then be correlated with other behavioral measures.

> *In one study using this approach, students' levels of anxiety were first measured on a standardized questionnaire and then all subjects experienced a conditioning situation. The unconditioned stimulus (US) was the aversive stimulus of a blast of air to the eye, eliciting an eye blink, and the conditioned stimulus (CS) was a tone or light paired with the blast of air.*
>
> *Subjects who were high in anxiety (drive), as measured by the questionnaire, acquired the conditioned eyelid response faster than those whose anxiety was low (see* ***Figure 11.2****). The investigator reasoned that high anxiety increased the intensity and, hence, the aversive motivational value of the unconditioned stimulus, leading the high-anxiety subjects to respond more strongly than the low-anxiety subjects. (Taylor, 1951)*

Figure 11.1 *Motivation as an Intervening Variable*

Since motivation is an intervening variable, only certain kinds of stimulus input and response output can be observed. Any particular motivation, such as hunger, is assumed to be the result of a number of primary and acquired variables, such as those listed, and may lead to one or more of the kinds of response output shown. The function of the intervening variable is to link the input conditions to the output consequences.

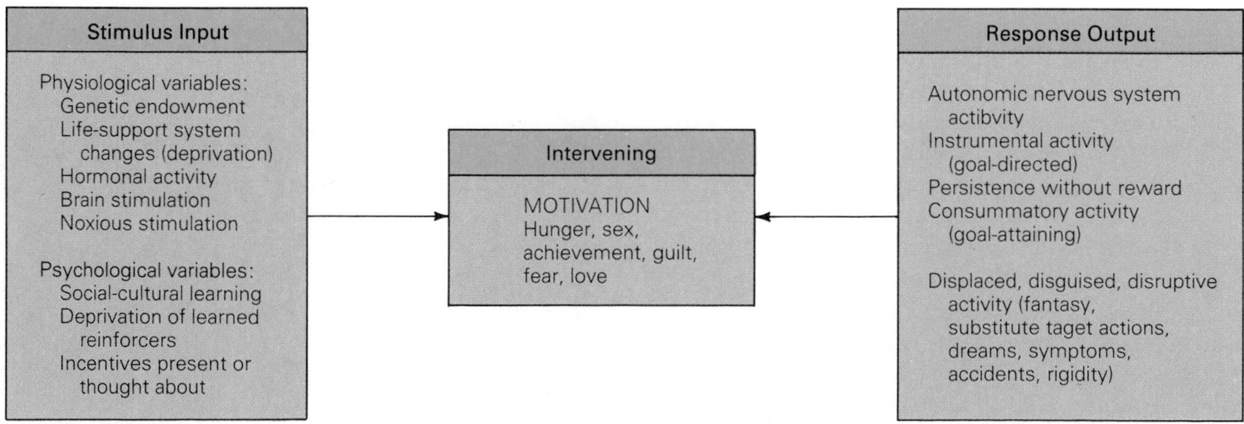

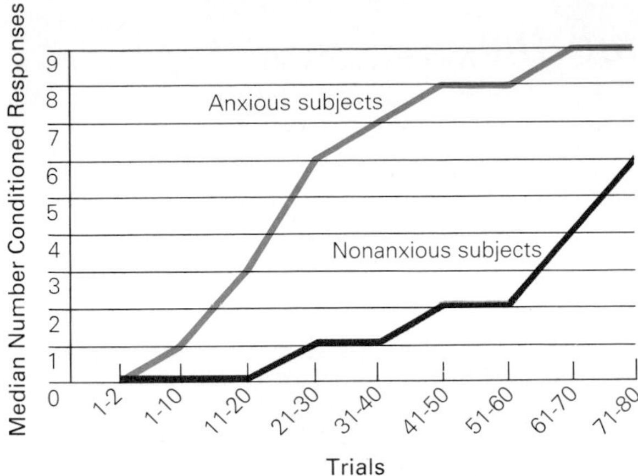

Figure 11.2 *Effect of Anxiety on Conditioning*
With successive blocks of trials, more anxious than nonanxious subjects showed conditioned responses. (Adapted from Taylor, 1951)

Manipulating Drives and Motives

The cited study, relating existing individual differences in anxiety level (from self-reports) to speed of conditioning, was a *correlational study.* Often researchers studying motivation want to see how changes in motivation will change behavior. This means using an *experimental design,* in which motivational conditions are manipulated to induce the motivational state or make it stronger or weaker. The two general classes of procedures used to induce or change drive states are *deprivation* and *stimulation.*

Deprivation for animal subjects may involve denial of food, water, or specific substances like calcium or thiamine. Deprivation for human subjects may involve withholding desired psychological conditions—perhaps the presence of other people. Social deprivation is assumed to be an aversive state that will motivate people to do something to end it. This is one justification given for solitary confinement in prison as an extreme form of punishment.

Stimulation to trigger motives may involve giving aversive stimuli such as shocks, noise, heat, or cold, which lead to responses of avoidance or escape. Stimuli leading to affectively positive states may be investigated—for example, the general stimulation that arouses the sex drive, or the self-stimulation of pleasure centers by electrical current through implanted electrodes (described in chapter 4).

Barriers, unsolvable tasks, and competition are other stimulus conditions that researchers have used in studies of motivation to induce drives. Finally, motives may be aroused by the presentation of *incentives*—opportunities to gain something that is desired. For example, the purpose of showing prizes to contestants prior to some performance is to motivate the competitors. This is called *incentive motivation.* Similarly, the presence of a novel environment may induce motivation to explore. It is believed that the external stimulus interacts with an internal predisposition toward certain actions that would not, by itself, lead to action. Across many species, exploration and curiosity have been shown to be among the most powerful motives (Butler & Harlow, 1954; Fowler, 1965).

Theoretical Perspectives

It will not surprise you to learn that there have been many attempts to explain motivation. These attempts differ in their explanations of the way motivation originates, what processes occur, what role the environment plays, and the extent to which people's motives are aspects of their unique personalities or simply characteristic of the species. We will look briefly at four theories of human motivation: instinct theory, drive theory, a theory of deficiency and growth motivation, and the theory that cognitions can be motivating.

Instincts as Motivations

One of the earliest views on what motivates behavior centers on the notion of instincts. According to instinct theory, organisms are born with certain preprogrammed tendencies that are essential for the survival of their species. Some instinct theorists have seen this biological force as *mechanistic,* motivating behavior without purpose and beyond individual control, much like a complex reflex. Others have adopted a conception of instincts that allows an organism choice in deciding upon different courses of action. (See also "The Instinct to Learn" in *The Best of Science.*)

Animal Instincts

All over the world, animals engage in regular cycles of activity that enable their species to survive. Salmon swim thousands of miles back to the exact stream where they were spawned, leaping up waterfalls until they come to the right spot, where the surviving males and females engage in ritualized courtship and mating. Fertilized eggs are deposited, the parents die, and, in time, their young swim downstream to live in the ocean until, a few years later, it is time for them to come back to complete

Close-up For You, Baby, I'd Climb the Highest Mountain . . . .

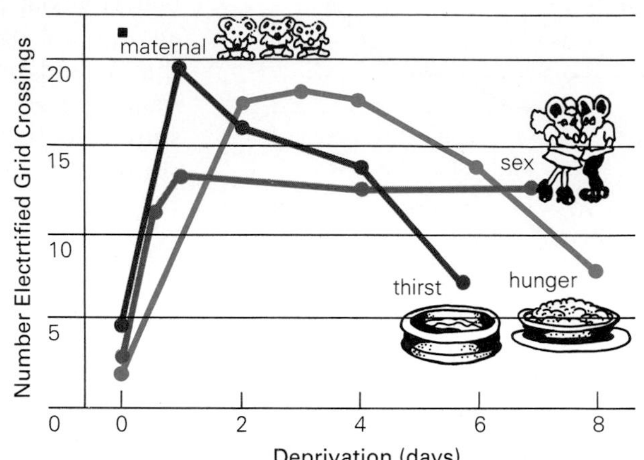

To assess the relative strengths of various drives, a group of psychologists at Columbia University in the late 1920s devised an *obstruction box* in which an electrified grid separated a motivated rat from something which it was assumed to want. The strengths of a variety of drives (induced by deprivation) were pitted against a constant level of shock that the animal had to endure in order to reach food, water, a sexually responsive mate, or its own offspring. The behavioral index of drive strength was the number of times the animal would cross the "hot" grid in a given period of time. (It could also have been the highest level of shock intensity that would be tolerated to reach the goal.) Typical of the data obtained with this method are the patterns reported in the figure.

The motivating effects of thirst (and hunger) were greatest after a short period of deprivation. Motivation declined when water or food deprivation became extreme. This is a pattern found with many kinds of motivation; it is called an *inverted-U function.* As motivation increases, the curve of performance first rises and later declines.

This curve was not found in two cases, however. With a little sex as a reward, sex-deprived rats kept running at a constant rate (after the first few hours). Mother rats endured the most suffering, running most often across the "hot" grid. This was interpreted as evidence for the existence of a powerful "maternal drive" in some animals.

You may be interested in another, incidental finding of these studies. Even without deprivation of any kind, the animals still crossed the grid a few times. Furthermore, even when there was nothing on the other side—except a chance to explore the novel environment—they crossed the barrier. In other research, when rats deprived of food or water were placed in a novel environment with plenty of opportunities to eat or drink, they explored instead. Only later did they begin to satisfy their hunger and thirst (Zimbardo & Montgomery, 1957). This behavior appears to be evidence of an exploratory drive that operates outside the constraints of homeostatic mechanisms.

their part in this continuing drama. Female green turtles living off the Brazilian coast regularly migrate 1400 miles to lay their eggs on a beach on Ascension Island where they were hatched, a target only five miles wide that they somehow locate in the open ocean.

Similarly remarkable activities can be reported for most species of animals. Bears hibernate, bees communicate the location of food to other bees, army ants go on hunting expeditions, birds build nests, spiders spin webs—exactly as their parents and ancestors did before them.

These are all examples of **instincts,** unlearned behavior patterns that appear in the same form at a certain point in its development in every member of a species. Instinctive behaviors are also found in response to specific types of stimulation. Often they are elicited by combinations of internal secretions, such as hormones, and external stimulation, such as odor cues called *pheromones,* to be discussed later. Environmental cues that reliably evoke a specific response pattern in the members of a particular species are called **releasers.** (Do you remember the releaser that changed Tina's behavior toward her turkey chicks described in chapter 1?) When an organism is at a given stage in its development, a behavior that is truly instinctive will appear "full blown" the first time that adequate stimuli are present. It will be performed adequately the first time, despite lack of previous opportunity to learn or practice it. Once released, it no longer depends on the external cue, but is completed automatically.

Originally, instinct theorists were content to describe instincts in terms of mysterious inner forces that impelled certain activities to emerge. Today, instincts in animals are more often studied as **fixed action patterns** by ethologists (discussed in chapter 1). **Ethology** is the observational study of animal behavior patterns that occur in animals' interactions with their natural environment (rather than in artificial laboratory settings). Ethologists study eliciting stimuli, environmental conditions, developmental stages, and specific response sequences in different animal species.

Human Instincts

Early Christian theologians assumed that only animals were guided by instinct. They believed that God had given humans reason, free will, and, thus, responsibility for their actions which gave them a chance to earn their way into heaven. Then, in 1859, Charles Darwin presented evidence of a continuity of species from lower animals to humans, and ideas in psychology as well as in other fields began to change. William James, writing in 1890, stated his belief that humans rely on even more instincts than lower animals do to guide their behavior. Besides the biological instincts they share with animals, he described a host of human social instincts, such as sympathy, modesty, sociability, and love. For James, both human and animal instincts were purposive.

A bee instinctively lets other bees know where food is.

This view of instincts was extended by psychologist William McDougall. In 1908 he wrote: "The human mind has certain innate or inherited tendencies which are the essential springs or motive powers of all thought and action, whether individual or collective, and are the bases from which the character and will of individuals and of nations are gradually developed . . . ." (p. 20). McDougall defined *instincts* as inherited dispositions that had three components: an *energizing* aspect, an *action* aspect, and *goal directedness.*

Sigmund Freud (1915) had a somewhat different view of instinct. Contrary to James and McDougall, Freud thought instincts had neither conscious purpose nor predetermined direction, and that many means of satisfying them could be learned. He believed that instinctive urges exist to satisfy bodily needs, and that they create a tension, or *psychic energy.* This tension drives us toward activities or objects that will bring satisfaction through reduction of the tension. Although Freud assumed that instincts operated largely below the level of consciousness, he also knew that they affected our conscious thoughts and feelings as well as our actions in many ways, and frequently they put us in conflict with society's demands. We were then motivated to reduce the tension caused by such conflicts.

The most fundamental aspect of human nature, according to Freud, was the conflict between the primal instincts of life and death. The *life instinct* (or *Eros*) functioned to maintain life and to lead an individual to reproduce sexually. The *death instinct* (or *Thanatos*) was the negative force of nature that kept even the noblest of creatures mortal through illness, aging, and finally death. In this view, all self-destructive behaviors were motivated by the death instinct turned inward, while aggression and vandalism resulted when it turned outward.

By the 1920s, lists of over 10,000 human instincts were being compiled by psychologists (Bernard, 1924). Humans were soon seen as better than animals, because they had more instincts *plus* the power to reason.

Challenges to Instinct Theory

At this same time, however, the notion of instincts as universal explanations for human behavior was beginning to stagger under the weight of critical attacks. Researchers were pointing out that instincts were not really explanations at all, not really universal, and not useful, because they overemphasized fixed, inborn mechanisms whereas much behavior was clearly modifiable by learning. It became apparent that instincts were being postulated to explain every action. Even spitting, frowning, and studying psychology were supposedly motivated by instincts; but such explanations were *circular:* they did not really "explain," but only "named." Instead of postulating processes, mechanisms, or structures to account for observed behavior, instinct theorists merely provided convenient labels. Thus the "aggression instinct" was used to explain why people behaved aggressively, and aggressive behavior was taken as evidence for an instinct to aggress (see Beach, 1955).

Meanwhile cross-cultural anthropologists like Ruth Benedict (1959) and Margaret Mead (1939) had found enormous behavioral differences in different cultures. Behavior patterns that had been assumed to be universal expressions of "human nature" were now seen to be variable, reflecting specific cultural experiences and learned values.

Most damaging to the early instinct notions, however, were the empirical demonstrations by the behaviorists that important behaviors were learned rather than inborn. Beginning with Watson, experimenters demonstrated environmental determinants of actions and even of emotions, as we saw in chapter 8 in the learned fear of little Albert. Freud's instinct doctrine fared better than McDougall's, because it was part of his psychoanalytic theory, which included a basic conception of human nature; it also provided a therapeutic approach to mental disorders. For research psychologists, vague notions of inborn instincts were replaced by precise analyses of the environmental determinants of behavior. There is a general recognition today that the complexity that is the human-organism-in-action is usually influenced by the *interaction* of internal and external factors—by both what we are as biological organisms and what we can become through learning. The mechanism thought to be responsible for translating motivation into learning and learning back into motivated behavior was first described in *drive theory.*

Drive Theory and Learning

As you are watching television, you go to the refrigerator, get a cold drink, consume it, and feel better. According to drive theory, your drive—your motivation to find and consume a drink—is based on an internal biological need—namely thirst. You go to the refrigerator and get something to drink, instead of taking out a book to read, because the refrigerator sequence has been reinforced previously by reduction of your thirst. In addition, because you have repetitively associated the sight of the refrigerator with thirst, merely seeing it can now motivate you to open it and search for a cool drink even when you are not thirsty. Similarly, the sight of soft drinks or beer on TV commercials can induce a drive to get something to drink even if you aren't thirsty.

This example outlines the main features of a theory of drive as proposed by Clark Hull (1943). Hull viewed motivation as necessary for learning to occur, and learning as essential for successful adaptation to the environment. Like Freud, Hull emphasized the role of *tension* in motivation and of *tension reduction* as a reinforcer; but unlike his psychoanalytic colleague, Hull believed that most human behavior was motivated less by innate forces (instinctual urges) and more by learned drives resulting from experience.

The main elements of this drive theory approach, which were shared by many other behaviorists in the 1940s and 1950s, can be outlined as follows:

1. A biological need triggers a strong drive (D).
2. This nonspecific drive state energizes random activity.
3. When one of the random actions leads to a goal that reduces drive tension, an organism stops being active.
4. The reinforcement (tension reduction) strengthens the association between the goal stimulus (S) and the successful response (R).

Using our previous example, having your thirst quenched after consuming a cold drink strengthens your association between the cold drink and the actions that produced it. In this way, over time, a learned *habit,* a learned association between stimulus and response $({}_sH_r)$, develops.

Drives can be induced by any intense internal stimulation (such as hunger or thirst) or by strong external stimuli (such as electric shock or noise). **Primary drives** are induced by internal biological needs and do not depend on learning; but just as neutral stimuli paired with reinforcers can acquire reinforcing power, so neutral stimuli paired with strong drives can acquire motivating power. The desire to possess money, for example, is a powerful acquired motivator for most of us. Drives acquired through conditioning are called **acquired drives** (also *secondary drives*). It was assumed by drive theorists that most psychological motives, such as seeking parental approval or desiring affiliation with other people, were secondary drives, acquired through learned association with some primary drive. (See also "The Delicate Sex" in *The Best of Science.*)

Fear as an Acquired Drive

Drive theorists studied fear not just as an emotional reaction to danger, but as a powerful, acquired motivational state. In fact, they used it as a model to explain the supposed development and functioning of all psychological motives.

> *In the classic demonstration of fear as a learned drive, rats were shocked in one side of a two-compartment apparatus; but they could escape the painful shock by jumping through the door between them to the other, safe side, and they soon learned to do so. Later, when the door was locked and they were put into the original compartment, but* not *shocked, they still learned to escape to the other side by turning a wheel that opened the door (and later by pressing a lever that did so). The experimenter reasoned that* learned fear *was elicited by the external cues of the apparatus (the color or brightness of each compartment), and this fear motivated the animals to escape just as the shock itself had done. He also assumed that this learned fear provided the motivation necessary for learning the new responses. (N. Miller, 1948)*

Learned fear is an important acquired motivator, because fear can so easily become associated with any situation in which pain or distress has been experienced and is very hard to extinguish. Learned fear is regarded as a drive, because it energizes a wide variety of responses and leads to the learning of new behaviors that are reinforced through fear reduction. In some cases moderate levels of learned fear can motivate responses in humans that help them adjust to and prepare better for realistic impending threats, such as surgery (Janis, 1958; Leventhal, 1970). However, extreme fear without a rational basis is found in the many *phobias* that can severely limit a person's activities (to be discussed in chapter 15).

Incentives and Optimal Arousal

Two additions to drive theory came from research which showed (a) that organisms can become energized by external stimuli rather than only by inner conditions, and (b) that humans often act to *increase* tension rather than only to reduce it.

External stimuli often attract or repel us regardless of our inner state. The sight of a refrigerator, beverage ad on TV, or beautiful person, or the smell of certain foods, such as hot pizza, can arouse us to take appropriate actions even when we are not impelled from within by thirst, sex, or hunger drives. External stimuli such as these, which serve as anticipated rewards, are called **incentives.**

Incentives refer to the activating and energizing effect on behavior that occurs before a goal is reached; they characterize the reinforcement received because of apparent *anticipation* of goals or rewards. Incentives provide a way to classify reinforcement as a motivational variable that affects only the acquisition of a response. Learning theorists use the term *incentive motivation* to ensure that the motivating function of incentives is not missed.

Ever hear, "I'll really love you, if you do it for me"? When you are given an *inducement* to respond, and that inducement is perceived as satisfying some need, you have an external incentive to perform. Weight-reduction clubs use incentives in the form of supplemental rewards—prizes, certificates, public recognition of weekly successful weight loss—prior to reaching the primary goal of significant, permanent weight reduction.

It seems clear that external cues that have been associated with reduction of a drive in the past (like refrigerators and cold drinks) can motivate behavior even when no drive exists. Research has demonstrated that even stimuli that have no biological utility can serve as incentives—for animals as well as humans. For example, saccharine, which does not satisfy hunger or have any biological value, will reinforce learning and performance for many organisms because of its sweet flavor (Sheffield, 1966; Sheffield & Roby, 1950).

Accordingly, in successors to Hulls' drive theory, motivational arousal is seen as involving a relationship between environmental incentives that "pull" behavior and the inner psychological and physiological conditions that "push" behavior (Logan, 1960). More recent investigations have even revealed that "preparatory" responses (including secretion of saliva, gastric juices, pancreatic enzymes, and insulin) are induced by the sensory qualities of food (its sight, smell, taste). The intensity of these responses is directly related to a food's perceived palatability—its incentive value, not its biological value (Powley, 1977).

According to drive theory, all activity is directed toward tension reduction. Such a theory has no explanation for the tension-arousing activities that people often choose (watching horror movies, going on roller-coaster rides, engaging in a protest hunger strike). People also explore new environments, work on crossword puzzles "for their own sake," search for knowledge, and "stir up trouble."

From these and other observations, a theory of *optimal arousal* was developed; it states that performance depends on both a preferred level of arousal and the complexity of the task (Berlyne, 1960, 1967; Hebb, 1955). There seems to be a general preference for moderately stimulating environments, neither too low (sensory deprivation) nor too high (aversive sensory overload).

There are individual differences in preferences for complex versus simple stimuli (Dorfman, 1965). You have probably noticed such differences in your friends' preferences for types of music, art, or leisure activities—and considered them just differences in "taste." There is some optimal level of arousal for each organism: when below it, stimulation is sought; when above it, stimulation is avoided.

Another factor enters in too. With experience, most events become less stimulating, thus motivating us to regain the original thrill by seeking more exciting ones (Zuckerman, 1979). As experience makes us "jaded," what used to arouse us may leave us indifferent or bored. To escape from boredom then becomes a new source of motivation.

> *Ennui has made more gamblers than avarice, more drunkards than thirst, and perhaps as many suicides as despair.*
>
> *C. C. Colton,* Lacon *(1820)*

Deficiency Versus Growth Motivation

A theory of human motivation that explains both tension-reducing and tension-increasing actions is that of humanist psychologist, Abraham Maslow (1970), mentioned in chapter 1. Maslow contrasted **deficiency motivation,** in which individuals seek to restore their physical or psychological equilibrium, and **growth motivation,** in which individuals seek to go beyond what they have done and been in the past. Growth-motivated people may welcome uncertainty, an increase in tension, and even pain if they see it as a route toward greater fulfillment of their potential and as a way to achieve their goals. Thus, for example, a martyr or revolutionary who voluntarily suffers for a religious or political cause may accept pain or humiliation as necessary in the attempt to change prevailing attitudes and institutions. Such a person suffers to achieve meaningful goals that fit with personal values.

Maslow's theory holds that we all have a **needs hierarchy,** as shown in **Figure 11.3,** in which our inborn needs are arranged in a sequence of stages from most "primitive" to most "human." At the bottom of this hierarchy are the basic *biological needs,* such as hunger and thirst. When they are pressing, other needs are put on "hold" and are unlikely to influence our actions; but when they are reasonably well satisfied, then the needs on the next level—*safety needs*—motivate us. When we are no longer concerned about danger, we become motivated by *attachment needs*—needs to belong, to affiliate with others, to love and be loved. If we are

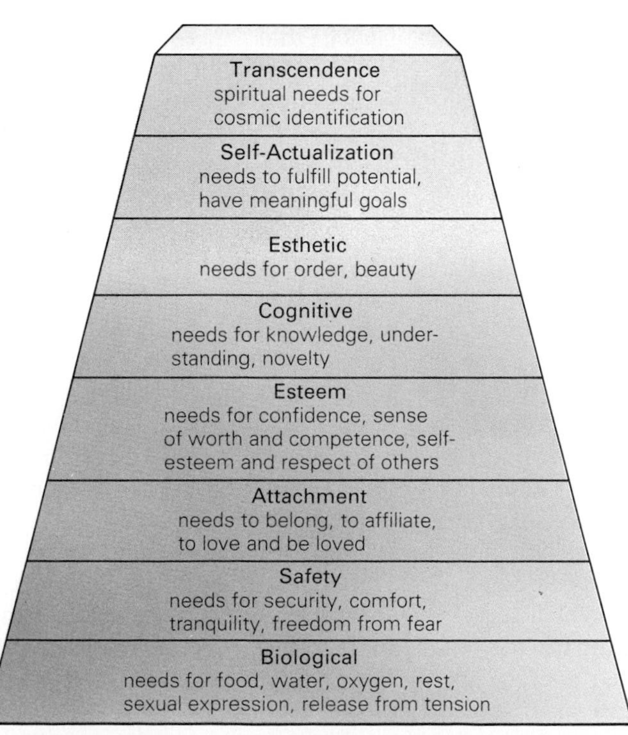

Figure 11.3 *Maslow's Hierarchy of Needs*

According to Maslow, needs at the lower levels of the hierarchy dominate an individual's motivation as long as they are unsatisfied. Once these are adequately satisfied, however, the higher needs occupy the individual's attention and effort. (After Maslow, 1970)

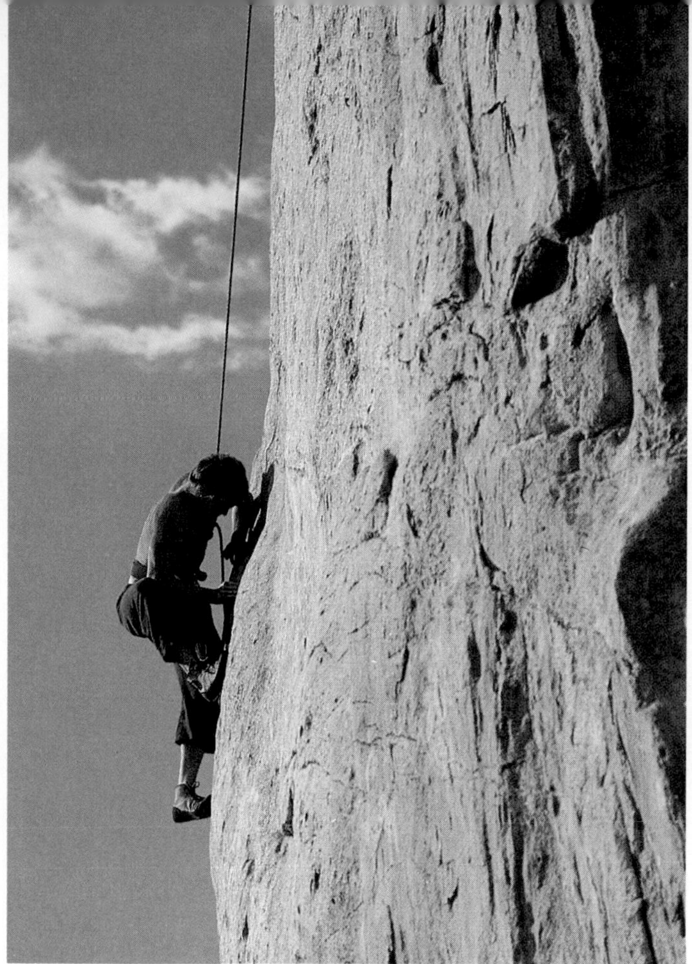

A person who climbs mountains is looking beyond basic needs to fully develop his or her potential.

well fed, safe, and feeling a sense of social belonging, we move up to *esteem needs.* These include the need to like oneself, to see oneself as competent and effective, and to be held in esteem by others.

At each level, Maslow argues, the need is inborn, not learned, although the way it is elicited and expressed is affected by the values learned in one's family and culture. Pathology may result when needs at any level are frustrated. Frustrated love needs, for example, can lead to hostility and perversions of sexuality.

As we move to the top of the hierarchy, we find a person who is nourished, safe, loved and loving, secure in a sense of a worthwhile self. Some people go beyond these basic human needs in the quest for fullest development of their potentials, or **self-actualization.** A self-actualizing person is self-aware, self-accepting, socially responsive, creative, spontaneous, and open to novelty and challenge, among other positive attributes.

Maslow's hierarchy goes several steps further to include *needs for transcendence.* Such needs may lead to higher states of consciousness and a more "cosmic" vision of one's part in the universe. You probably recognize a similarity between this highest level of human striving and Kohlberg's top stage of moral development (see chapter 3).

Maslow's theory has had more influence on therapy and education than on psychological research. For Maslow, as for his fellow humanistic psychologist, Carl Rogers (1959), the central motivational force for humans is the innate need to grow and actualize one's highest potentialities. Other psychologists have suggested that self-actualization motivation is essentially motivation to be open to new experiences, ideas, and feelings, to explore both the external and mental environments, and thus is a form of curiosity or stimulus motivation (Butler & Rice, 1963). Anxiety and guilt inhibit this motivation. In any case, becoming free from deficiency motivation allows a person to become more competent and fulfilled.

Such an "upbeat" approach was welcomed by many psychologists who had grown up on the earlier diet of negative motivational views, filled as they were with instincts, tension-reduction, unconscious urges, and other less than noble forces. "Accentuating the positive" in man and woman fit a new therapeutic conception of helping normal people toward greater potential, rather than just making disturbed people less so. Therapy to release and optimize each individual's human potential grew out of this motivational approach (an issue to be discussed in chapter 16).

Some psychologists have resisted this theory of the inherent goodness of individuals. They criticize this approach because (a) it lacks adequate experimental confirmation; (b) its concepts are vague, fuzzy, and not operationally defined; (c) the world is filled with too much violence, evil, and destructive behavior patterns for this goodness model to account for; and (d) environmental forces clearly exert strong influences on individual behavior, even overcoming the best intentions of "innately" good people (as we shall see in our later discussion in chapter 18).

Cognitions, Expectations, and Attributions

Consider the Wizard of Oz *as a psychological study of motivation. Dorothy and her three friends work hard to get to the Emerald City, overcoming barriers, persisting against all adversaries. They do so because they expect the Wizard to give them what they are missing; but the wise Wiz makes them aware that they, not he, always had the power to change their deficiencies to fulfilled wishes. For Dorothy, "home"' can be a sense of security, of feeling comfortable with people she loves, wherever her heart is. The courage the Lion wants, the intelligence the Scarecrow longs for, and the emotions the Tin Man dreams of are shown to be attributes they already possess if only they will think about them differently—not as things inside of them, but as positive ways they are already relating to others. After all, did they not demonstrate those qualities on the journey to Oz—motivated itself by little more than an* expectation, *an idea about the future likelihood of getting something they wanted? The Wizard of Oz was clearly a cognitive psychologist.*

Cognitive approaches are currently being used by many psychologists to account for what motivates a variety of personal and social behaviors. They all share the Wizard's point of view, the concept that significant human motivation comes not from objective realities, but from our interpretation of them. The reinforcing effect of a reward is lost if we don't believe our actions obtained it. What we do now is often controlled by what we *think* caused our past successes and failures, what we *believe* is possible for us to do, and what we *anticipate* the outcome of an action will be. Cognitive approaches to motivation put higher mental processes like these—rather than the arousal energy of drives, other biological mechanisms, or stimulus features—in charge of the acting self.

The importance of expectations in motivating behavior was developed in Julian Rotter's *social-learning theory* (1954) and extended in ways we shall see later in this chapter when we study achievement and work motivation. For Rotter, the probability that a person will engage in behavior X (studying for an exam instead of partying) is determined by his or her *expectation* of attaining a goal (getting a good grade) that follows that activity and the *personal value* of that goal to that person. This view about a future happening is based on a person's past reinforcement history which, in turn, has helped develop a locus of control orientation. A **locus of control orientation** is a belief that the outcomes of our actions are contingent on what *we* do *(internal control orientation)* or on events outside our personal control *(external control orientation).*

A similar concept has been developed by Fritz Heider (1958) who postulates that the outcome of our behavior (a poor grade, for example) can be attributed to *dispositional* forces, such as lack of effort or insufficient intelligence, or to *situational* forces, such as an unfair test or a biased teacher. These attributions influence the way we will behave; we are likely to try harder next time if we see our poor grade as a result of our lack of effort, but may give up if we see it resulting from injustice or lack of ability (Dweck, 1975).

These ideas have been developed in attribution theory, which will be further discussed later in this chapter and in chapter 17. Now let's take a close look at a sampling of three very different motives that influence our lives—hunger, sex, and work and achievement motivation.

Hunger and Eating

The primary drives, such as hunger and thirst, represent nature's way of keeping its long-running show on the road even when there isn't time for everyone to learn how to play the part. In chapter 4 we saw that the body has many homeostatic mechanisms for maintaining optimal internal conditions. Hunger motivation is one aspect of that general process, and mental and behavioral processes as well as physiological ones are required to maintain the balance. Automatic mechanisms cannot do the job, because in order to survive, we must periodically seek out and consume plants and animals. To maintain health, we need to ingest regularly at least 22 different amino acids, a dozen vitamins, some minerals, and sufficient calories to meet our energy needs. The physiological and behavioral processes organized around hunger turn out to be enormously complex both for our species and across the range of different species.

The Search for Feeding Regulators

To regulate its food intake effectively, an organism must be able to (a) detect its internal food need; (b) initiate and organize eating behavior; (c) monitor the quantity and quality of the food eaten; and then (d) detect "enough" and stop eating. Researchers have tried to understand these processes by relating them either to peripheral mechanisms in different parts of the body, such as stomach contractions, or to central brain mechanisms, such as the functioning of the hypothalamus. Although hunger is probably the most studied drive, our understanding of it is still incomplete.

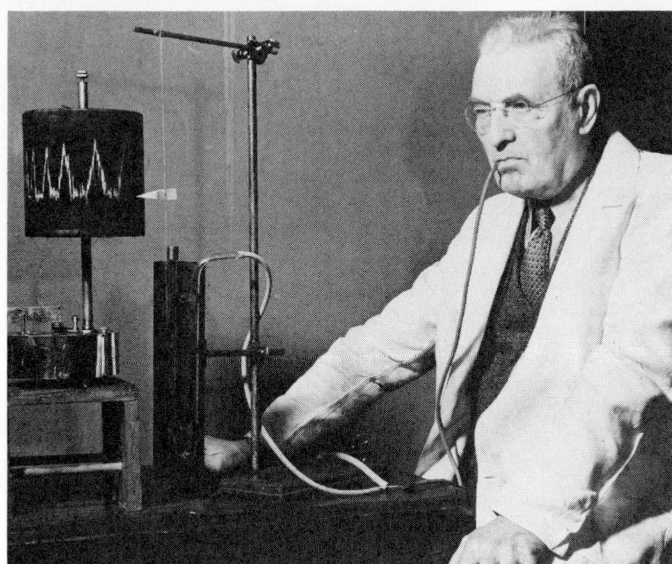

Shown is a stomach-balloon apparatus like the one used by Cannon and Washburn. This apparatus records stomach activity.

Hunger Pangs as the Basis for Hunger

When you feel hungry where do those sensations come from? Does your stomach rumble and send out distress signals—pangs and cramps? A pioneering physiologist, Walter Cannon (1934), believed that these localized sensations of hunger from gastric activity were *the* basis for hunger. His basic view was that an empty stomach created disagreeable stimulation, "cramps," which triggered activity directed toward filling the stomach and turning off these disagreeable stimuli.

Cannon tested his hypothesis in an interesting experiment with a faithful student, A. L. Washburn.

> *The student trained himself to swallow an uninflated balloon attached to a rubber tube. The other end of the tube was attached to a recording device that would move with changes in air pressure. Cannon then inflated the balloon in Washburn's stomach; as his stomach contracted, air would be expelled from the balloon and deflect a recording pen (see photo).*
>
> *When the student reported hunger pangs, the stomach was also severely contracted, the balloon deflated, and a record made of this internal change. Cannon thought he had proved that stomach cramps were, therefore, responsible for feelings of hunger. (Cannon & Washburn, 1912)*

Cannon had only established a *correlation,* not a *causal* connection. Although hunger pangs accompanied stomach contractions, maybe something else was causing both of those responses. (Remember our discussion in chapter 2 about the dangers of misinterpreting correlations as causal relationships?)

Later research showed that stomach contractions are not even a necessary condition for hunger. Injections of sugar directly into the blood will stop the stomach contractions, but not the hunger, of an animal with an empty stomach. Human patients with their stomachs entirely removed still experience hunger pangs (Janowitz & Grossman, 1950), and rats with surgically removed stomachs still learn mazes when rewarded by food (Penick et al., 1963). So although those sensations, originating in the stomach, may play a role in our usual feelings of being hungry, they do not explain how the body detects its need for food.

Hypothalamic Control of Feeding: The Dual Hypothalamic Theory of Hunger

The hypothalamus is generally acknowledged to be the master control center for all homeostatic processes. Two parts of the hypothalamus were identified some years ago as possible control centers for feeding. Stimulation in the *lateral hypothalamus* excited feeding; stimulation in the *ventromedial hypothalamus* inhibited feeding. Not only did chemical or electrical stimulation to the "feeding center" excite feeding, but destruction of it caused the opposite effect: animals would not eat even if they had been deprived of food for a long time. Similarly with the "satiety center": stimulation of it caused animals to stop eating, whatever their need for food, while destruction of it led to gross overeating. These findings led to the **dual hypothalamic theory of hunger,** a theory showing that these two brain centers control the start and stopping of feeding (Grossman, 1979; Stellar, 1954).

Although this view was appealingly simple, it was challenged by the finding that nerve tracts passing through the hypothalamus from other brain centers are also playing a role. When these tracts are destroyed by damage to the hypothalamus, there are deficits in sensory and arousal functions related to eating behavior (Almli, 1978). A broader picture is still needed.

A Multiple-system Approach

The current view is that the brain works in association with other systems, both biological and psychological, to gather information about an organism's energy requirements, nutritional state, acquired hungers, and food preferences, as well as social-cultural demands. It sends signals to neural, hormonal, organ, and muscle systems to initiate food seeking, eating, or inhibitory responses.

Table 11.1 *Factors in the Control of Feeding*

Mechanisms Controlling Eating (integrated by lateral hypothalamus)	Mechanisms Controlling Not Eating (integrated by ventromedial hypothalamus)*
Factors of Biological Origin Nutritional deficiencies Low levels of blood glucose (sugar) High levels of fatty acids in the blood —both stimulate lateral hypothalamus Set point (level) of stored fats —when below critical set point, food seeking initiated ***Factors of Psychological Origin*** Specific hunger —learned preference for diets containing substances (salt, calcium, etc.) they lack Stress-induced eating Socially stimulated eating —family and cultural eating rituals, symbolically significant food ***Factors of Mixed Origin*** Sensory cues —sensory input to central nervous system elicits reflexes activating autonomic nervous system, preparing for digestion, metabolism, storage —palatability of food *maintains* eating by eliciting reflexes in brain that stimulate the lateral hypothalamus Anticipatory activities —eating that prevents depletion	***Factors of Biological Origin*** Metabolic signals High levels of blood glucose Low levels of fatty acids Peripheral signals Full stomach, monitored by pressure detectors, stimulates ventromedial hypothalamus Taste cues from unpalatable foods induce rejection reflex Set point signals Level of stored body fat reaches critical set point of satiety, stimulating ventromedial hypothalamus ***Factors of Psychological Origin*** Fear Conditioned food aversions Conditioned satiety Cultural pressures toward slimness, dieting Mental disorders, such as anorexia *Includes short-term (stop eating) controls and long-term (suppression between meals) controls

Table 11.1 summarizes the factors now believed to be involved in the complex regulation of hunger detection, feeding, and satiation. In general, the biological systems involved are responsive to an organism's energy needs and nutritional state. The psychological systems account for acquired food preferences and are responsive to social, emotional, and environmental stimuli that make both eating, in general, and specific foods, in particular, either desirable or aversive. We can only touch briefly on the features of each kind of factor.

To Eat . . .

Sugar and fat are the energy sources for metabolism. Evidently the two basic signals that initiate eating come from receptors that monitor the levels of sugar and fat in the blood.

According to the *glucostatic* theory of hunger (Mayer, 1955), when blood glucose is low or unavailable for metabolism, signals from liver cell receptors are sent to the lateral hypothalamus. The pancreas is then stimulated to release hormones that convert available glycogen in the liver into glucose, and an organism is motivated to seek and eat food. **Figure 11.4** shows the immediate effect of the unavailability of glucose on increase in reported hunger in healthy adults (Thompson & Campbell, 1977). (See also "Do Diets Really Work?" in *The Best of Science.)*

In addition, during food deprivation, fat stored in body cells is released into the blood as a temporary energy source in the form of *free fatty acids.* According to the *lipostatic* theory of hunger, receptors that detect free fatty acid levels signal the lateral hypothalamus, which then stimulates the pituitary gland to release certain hormones and also stimulates the central nervous system to initiate eating responses (Kennedy, 1953).

With free access to food, adult animals and humans will maintain a stable body weight over their lifetime at a level consistent for them. An internal biological "scale" weighs the fat in the body and keeps the central nervous system informed. Whenever fats stored in specialized fat cells fall below a certain level, termed the *critical set point,* "eat signals," are sent out (Keesey & Powley, 1975). This internal set point exerts a major influence on the amount you eat and the weight you are.

People programmed to be obese have more fat cells than people of normal weight, as a result of either genetic factors or overfeeding at critical periods in infancy. Beyond infancy, dieting or overeating changes the *size* of the fat cells, but not their *number*. The number of fat cells a person has remains constant throughout life. This means that someone with a large number of fat cells who diets will lose weight and may become skinny, but will still have the same critical set point and so will be a hungry, "latent fat" person (Nisbett, 1972).

Eating behaviors are also motivated by a variety of psychological influences. We all develop *specific hungers*, acquired through pairing of hunger with particular environmental stimuli. In addition, we develop specific hungers for essential substances such as calcium, salt, or vitamins if these substances are lacking in our diet. These hungers motivate selective eating. Animals avoid diets that have deficiencies, search for better ones, and develop a preference for diets that have been associated with recovery from deficiency-caused illnesses (Rozin & Kalat, 1971). Stressful stimulation also leads to overeating in both human and animal subjects (Antelman et al., 1976; Schachter et al., 1968).

My mother would respond to protests of "No more food, please! I'm not hungry!" with the rejoinder, "Anyone can eat when he's *hungry*—animals can do that. Eating my food when you're not hungry shows that you love me." Humans may eat (or fast) for the symbolic value of food as well as its nutritional value. Social and cultural factors determine when, how much, how fast, and what we eat.

Figure 11.4 *Glucose Level and Felt Hunger*
Hunger ratings increase in well-fed males soon after an injection of the drug 2DG, which inhibits glucose in the blood. As food deprivation time gets longer, the control group (given saline injection) gradually begins to report more feelings of hunger, though not ever as high as the glucose-inhibited group. Eating lunch rapidly reduces hunger in both groups, though not as much in the glucose-inhibited group. Hormone release, metabolism, and several other processes are also affected by the glucose injections. (Adapted from Thompson & Campbell, 1977)

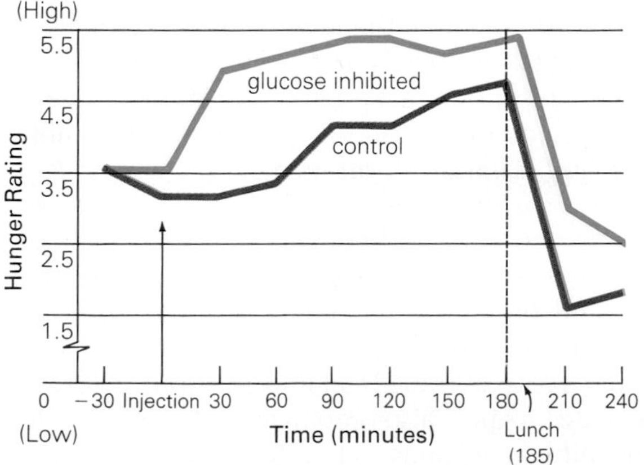

Both biological and psychological factors influence our responses to the smell, taste, and appearance of foods. As we noted earlier, sensory input to the central nervous system elicits reflexes in the brain which activate the autonomic nervous system to secrete saliva, gastric juices, certain enzymes, and insulin—preparation for the digestion, metabolism, and storage of food (Powley, 1977). The body is thus ready to "put away" a meal properly after only one bite, one look, or one sniff. As signals of palatability, sensory cues have more influence on maintaining eating once begun than on initiating eating (Snowden, 1969).

Besides eating to *satisfy* hunger, we eat to *prevent* it. Observations of free-ranging animals in their native habitat suggest that they do what you probably do—eat *before* hunger sets in. Predators invest enormous energy in hunting for prey before hunger weakens them. Similarly, many species gather, store, and hoard food—"for later." Consider the motivations that go into the production, storage, and distribution of food in human societies. This eating *prevents depletion* instead of making up for a deficiency already present (Collier et al., 1972).

. . . or Not to Eat

Many of the mechanisms that stop eating are similar to those that start it, but they work through the ventromedial hypothalamus and rely on an opposite set of cues. We must also distinguish between *short-term inhibitors* (which terminate ongoing feeding) and *long-term inhibitors* (which suppress eating activities between meals).

High glucose levels and low free fatty acids in the blood are signals that the set point has been reached; but even before this nutritional information is processed by the brain, several peripheral cues are signaling "stop." Pressure detectors in the stomach signal distension, while unpleasant taste cues can induce a *rejection reflex* (including vomiting).

Like eating, inhibition of eating is influenced by a host of emotional and learned psychological processes, some occurring during a meal, some between meals. Humans and animals do not eat when fearful. Animals do not eat much of a new food; they'll sample a bit, then wait for several hours before eating more—if no illness has developed. This protective "bait-shyness" reaction keeps animals preferring "tried and true" diets and not trying new potentially harmful foods—unlike most of us.

Satiety, like hunger, can be conditioned if it is regularly paired with stimuli that usually occur at the end of a meal, such as someone's turning on the TV; and, just as some cultural influences encourage eating as an important social ritual, others discourage it. Ultra-thin fashion models are portrayed as the ideal for women in our society, an ideal that becomes distorted in the self-destructive eating syndromes of young women who develop *anorexia* or *bulimia*. These serious disorders, which are being seen increasingly among college students, will be discussed in chapter 15.

On the other hand, we should note that when obese people diet and reach their new reduced weight, their body chemistry is severely affected. It becomes "deranged." Fat cells shrink, menstruation may stop, thyroid hormone levels and white blood cell counts are low, as is blood pressure and pulse rate. These formerly obese individuals complain of intolerance to the cold, and they are obsessed with thoughts about food. Their bodies are programmed to be fat and rebel against extreme interventions that try to make them slim. Sadly, it tends to be the rule that weight loss from dieting programs is short-term; gradually the body's own weight regulators take over and restore its weight "equilibrium" (Kolata, 1985). This is a case where it is not "mind over matter," but biology asserting itself over psychology.

Sex and Sexuality

While eating is essential to individual survival, sex is not. Some animals and humans remain celibate for a lifetime without apparent detriment to their daily functioning. However, survival of the species does depend on sex. The issue for evolutionary design was how to encourage animals to engage in the "altruistic" act of helping the species make it. This was not an easy problem, since the sexual act requires great energy consumption and subjects an individual to considerable stress. Nature's answer was to make sexual stimulation intensely pleasurable—a positive side effect of its more limited evolutionary purpose. A climactic orgasm serves as the ultimate reinforcer for all the time, effort, and work that go into the process of mating sperm with ova. So effective is this design that it has resulted in "altruism" above and beyond the call of nature.

There are a number of ways in which the sexual drive is unique:

- It is not essential to individual survival, but only to species survival.
- Its arousal may be independent of deprivation.
- Arousal is as actively sought as reduction of tension.
- It will motivate an unusually wide variety of behaviors and psychological processes.
- It can be aroused by almost any conceivable stimulus—from genital touch, to fleeting fantasy, to conditioned fetish.
- Any stimulus associated with sexual arousal can become an acquired motivator, while any stimulus associated with sexual release can become a conditioned reinforcer.

Much of what is known about the physiology of sexual arousal and behavior comes from research on lower animals. In part, this is because of the long-standing taboo against a scientific study of sex in humans. Though Freud called attention to the importance of sexual motivation, research psychologists did not follow up on his ideas, partly because sex did not fit well into the then-prevalent tension-reduction theory of motivation, according to which the motivated organism seeks to recover equilibrium—certainly not to increase tension! Fear and anxiety fit the model better and so received more research attention (Brown, 1961). We will first consider some of what is known about the sex drive in animals and then turn our attention to human sexuality.

Sexual Arousal

In species other than humans, sexual arousal is determined primarily by physiological processes. An animal becomes receptive to mating largely in response to the flow of hormones controlled by the pituitary gland and secreted from the *gonads*, the sex organs. In males these hormones are *androgens*, and they are continuously present in sufficient supply so that males are hormonally ready for mating at almost any time; but in the female of many species, the sex hormone, *estrogen*, is released according to regular time cycles of days or months or according to seasonal changes. Thus, the female is not always hormonally receptive to mating.

These hormones act on both the brain and genital tissue and often lead to a pattern of predictable, *stereotyped behavior* for all members of a species. If you've seen one pair of rats in their mating sequence, you've seen them all. The male rat chases the receptive female, she stops suddenly, raises her rear, and he enters her briefly, thrusts, and pulls out. She runs away, and the chase continues with ten to twenty of these brief intromissions before he ejaculates. Apes also copulate only briefly, for about fifteen seconds, while for sables copulation lasts as long as eight hours. Predators, such as lions, can afford to indulge in long, slow copulatory rituals. Their prey, such as antelope, copulate for only a few seconds, often on the run (Ford & Beach, 1951).

Even in animals, sexual arousal is not determined only by inner states and hormonal influences. Peripheral stimuli can sensitize or activate innate response patterns. In many species the sight and sound of ritualized display patterns by potential partners is a *necessary* condition for sexual response. Touch, taste, and smell can also serve as stimulants for sexual arousal. Some species, for example, secrete chemical signals, called *pheromones,* that attract suitors, sometimes from great distances. In many species, pheromones are emitted by the female when her fertility is optimal (and hormone level and sexual interest peak). These secretions are unconditioned stimuli for arousal and attraction in the male of the species. When captive male rhesus monkeys smell the odor of a sexually receptive female in an adjacent cage, they respond with a variety of sex-related physiological changes, including an increase in the size of their testes. In humans, though, reactions to sex-related odors are quite variable, determined more by *who* is giving off the smell than by any unlearned, irresistible, olfactory properties of the chemical communication (see Hopson, 1979). Recall the discussion of pheromones in humans in chapter 5.

The courtship ritual is extended in species in which the male remains with the female to protect or raise the young. Albatrosses may bow, preen, or clatter their bills for days before breeding.

Human Sexuality

In humans, sexuality is far more dependent on psychological factors, and, hence, more variable than is the case with other species. **Human sexuality** is described as including "the physical characteristics and capacities for specific sex behaviors, together with psychosexual learning, values, norms, and attitudes about these behaviors" (Chilman, 1979, p. 3). **Sexual arousal** in humans is the motivational state of excitement and tension brought about by physiological and cognitive reactions to erotic stimuli. *Erotic stimuli,* which may be physical or psychological, give rise to sexual excitement or feelings of passion. Sexual arousal induced by erotic stimuli is reduced by sexual activities that are satisfying, especially by achieving orgasm.

Scientific investigation of normal human sexual behavior was given the first important impetus by the work of Alfred Kinsey and his colleagues beginning in the 1940s (1948, 1953). They interviewed some 17,000 Americans about their sexual behavior and revealed—to a generally shocked American public—the extent to which certain behaviors, previously considered rare and even "abnormal," were actually quite widespread—or at least reported to be. However it was William Masters and Virginia Johnson (1966, 1970, 1979) who broke down the traditional taboo. They legitimized the study of human sexuality by directly observing and recording under laboratory conditions the physiological patterns involved in ongoing human sexual performance, studying not what people said but what they actually did.

The Sexual Response Cycle

In order to study the human response to sexual stimulation directly, Masters and Johnson conducted controlled laboratory observations of thousands of males and females during tens of thousands of sexual response cycles of intercourse and masturbation. Their pioneering research on sexual arousal dispelled a number of myths and provided a useful model of the phases of human sexual response. Masters and Johnson studied arousal and response only. They did *not* study the psychologically significant initial phase of sexual responding—that of *sexual desire,* the motivation to seek out or be available for sexual experience.

Masters and Johnson found that (a) men and women have similar sexual responses regardless of the source of arousal; (b) penis size is generally unrelated to any aspect of sexual performance; (c) although the sequence of phases of the sexual response cycle are similar in the two sexes, women are more variable, tending to respond more slowly, but often remaining aroused longer; and (d) most women are able to have multiple orgasms, while men rarely do in a comparable time period. Masters and Johnson found four phases in the human sexual response cycle: excitement, plateau, orgasm, and resolution (see **Figure 11.5**).

In the *excitement phase* (lasting from a few minutes to more than an hour) there are *vascular* (blood vessel) changes in the pelvic region. The penis becomes erect and the clitoris swells; blood and other fluids become congested in the testicles and vagina. Women may experience a "sex flush," a reddening of the body.

During the *plateau phase,* a maximum (though varying) level of arousal is reached. There is rapidly increased heartbeat, respiration, and blood pressure, increased glandular secretions, and both voluntary and involuntary muscle tension throughout the body. Vaginal lubrication increases and the breasts swell.

During the *orgasm phase,* both partners experience a very intense, very pleasurable sense of release from the sexual tension that has been building up. Orgasm is characterized by rhythmic contractions that occur approximately every eight-tenths of a second in the genital areas. Respiration and blood pressure reach very high levels in both men and women, and heart rate may double. In men, throbbing contractions lead to ejaculation, an "explosion" of semen. In women, orgasm may be achieved from effective stimulation of either the clitoris or the vaginal wall.

During the *resolution phase,* the body gradually returns to its normal preexcitement state, with both blood pressure and heartbeat slowing down. After one orgasm, most men enter a refractory period, lasting anywhere from a few minutes to several hours, during which no further orgasm is possible. Women, however, are capable of multiple orgasms in fairly rapid succession if their sexual arousal is maintained.

Figure 11.5 *Phases of Human Sexual Response*

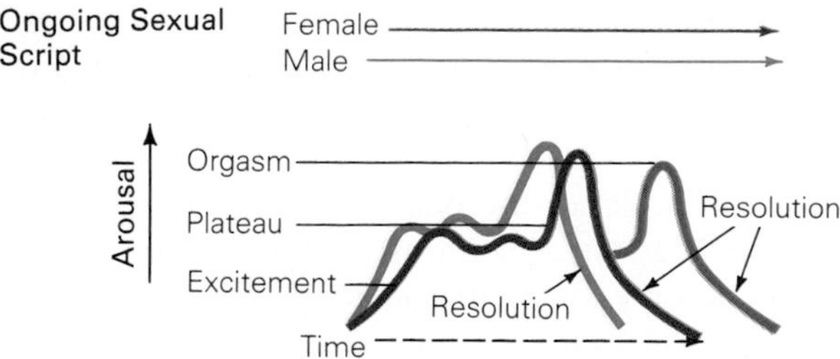

Touch, Imagination, and Association

Although Masters and Johnson's research focused on the *physiology* of sexual responding, perhaps their most important discovery was the central significance of *psychological* processes in both arousal and satisfaction. They demonstrated conclusively that problems in sexual response often have psychological, rather than physiological, origins and can be changed through therapy. Of particular concern are the inability to complete the response cycle and achieve gratification, called *impotence* in men and *frigidity* in women. Often the basis of the problem is a preoccupation with personal problems, fear of the consequences of sexual activity, or anxiety about a partner's evaluation of one's performance. However, poor nutrition, fatigue, stress, and excessive use of alcohol or drugs can also diminish sexual drive and performance—yet not be recognized as "downers."

Hormonal activity, so important in regulating sexual behavior among female mammals in other animal species, has no known effect on sexual receptiveness or gratification in women. In males, the sex hormone testosterone (one of the androgens) is necessary for sexual arousal and performance. Testosterone levels become high enough only after puberty. Sexual stimulation and orgasm raise the level of this hormone, but so do hostile or anxious mood states. Perhaps this similar reaction contributes to the association of sex with aggression reported by many men. Testosterone levels may also affect sexual drive in females, with sexual interest often peaking before and after menstruation. Low estrogen levels can interfere with sexual satisfaction by causing vaginal dryness.

The sequence of sexual activities that may culminate in orgasm can be started by only one unconditioned stimulus, but an endless variety of conditioned stimuli. The unconditioned stimulus is *touch.* Touch in the form of genital caresses is a universal aspect of sexual foreplay in cultures throughout the world (Ford & Beach, 1951); but virtually any stimuli that become associated with genital touch and orgasm can become acquired motivators. This is true whether the stimuli are in the external environment or in one's memory or fantasy. Even the picture of a shoe can come to lead to sexual arousal in this way (Rachman, 1966). A nonsexual object that becomes capable of producing sexual arousal through conditioning is called a **fetish.** A fetish may become a psychological problem when it is *necessary* for arousal and/or objectionable to other people.

It has been suggested that sensations and fantasy during masturbation provide the primal setting for associating virtually any stimulus with pleasurable arousal (Storms, 1980, 1981). Inanimate objects, textures, sounds, visual images, odors—any tangible or imagined stimulus event—can come to elicit arousal through conditioned association. In this way, some people learn to become aroused *only* by those conditioned stimuli, such as the sight of high-heel shoes, young children, or even painful stimuli. Some of us learn culturally acceptable sexual orientations in this way, while others learn sexual deviations (to be discussed in chapter 15).

In humans, sexuality can be less concerned with meeting physiological need than with satisfying cognitive desire. For most humans the goal of sexual activity is "the attainment of a cognitive state: the conscious perception of sexual satisfaction. This state depends on a combination of experiences originating in the experiencer's body and in that of the sexual partner" (Davidson, 1980, p. 227). Interpretations of experiences, the meaning of specific sexual events, sexual beliefs and values, and imagination and expectation all play a part in human sexual behavior and satisfaction (see Byrne, 1981). Even the subjective experience of orgasm, which has been compared by some to a profound altered state of consciousness (Davidson, 1980), usually depends not only on physical stimulation, but also on interpersonal factors, such as being in a close, trusting relationship.

Sex is more than just a set of learned techniques, a performance of bodies in space, a giving or receiving of pleasurable physiological sensations. We need, as a very first step, to accept our own body and the responsibility for someone else's. We must want to give and be open to receive. We need to be willing to learn over time how best to give our gift and accept the gift of another.

It is not enough to know what to do physically. For many, the most satisfactory sex takes place within a loving, caring relationship. For sex to reach its potential as a fulfilling human experience, we need to develop attitudes of trust and sharing. Sex strips us literally and figuratively of our protective garments. It lays bare our vulnerability. That is why sex can at the same time be so frightening if misused with power and hostility, and so glorious if filled with assurances of mutual satisfaction, respect for the needs of one's partner, and love of his or her unique qualities.

Sexual Scripts

Generalized sexual arousal can be channeled into different specific behaviors, depending on how the individual has learned to respond and think about sexual matters. **Sexual scripts** are socially learned programs of sexual responsiveness that include prescriptions, usually unspoken, of what to do, when, where, how, with whom or with what, and why (Gagnon, 1977). Different aspects of these scripts are assembled through social interaction over one's lifetime. The attitudes and values embodied in one's sexual script define one's general orientation to sexuality.

Scripts combine social norms, individual expectations, and preferred sequences of behavior from past learning. Your sexual scripts include not only scenarios of what you think is appropriate on your part, but also your expectations for a sexual partner. Differing scripts can create problems of adjustment between partners when they are not discussed or synchronized.

For example, there is evidence that touch has different meanings for men and women.

"Now, tell me. What's it like being a sex symbol?"

Researchers questioned 40 male and 40 female undergraduates about the meaning they attach to touch, when applied to different parts of the anatomy by a friend. Quite different meanings were found between the sexes. For females, the more a touch was associated with sexual desire, the less it was considered to imply warmth, pleasantness, or friendliness. When a close male friend touches a woman in an area of her body that communicates sexual desire to her, then that is its only meaning to her. For males, the same touch is interpreted as having a cluster of meanings: pleasantness, warmth, love, and sexual desire. Misunderstandings can arise when one person's "friendly touch" is perceived by the other as a "sexual advance." (Nguyen et al., 1975)

Sexual scripts include similar "stage directions" for most sexual actors within a given culture, socioeconomic class, gender, and educational level. However, there are unique features in each individual's personal script, learned through his or her own history of sexual experience and thought. Because erotic stimuli can be intensely pleasurable, while also often strongly prohibited by society and religion, we learn many different ways of responding to the variety of erotic stimuli we experience in this society. Here's where we really see the power of conditioned associations. Because any stimulus that has been associated with sexual arousal can become a potent elicitor of arousal later, there are enormous variations in the forms our human sexuality takes.

Even the apparent biologically based differences between men and women in the physiological pattern of sexual response, as catalogued by Masters and Johnson, may be influenced by social learning. Females are socialized not to acknowledge their sexuality, to act as passive sexual partners, to appear alluring, yet sexually innocent, and to be responsible if "anything goes wrong." Males, by contrast, are socialized to think of sexual intercourse as validation of their masculine identity, as a performance to be evaluated, and as the prelude to orgasm. As such socialization practices change with new views about gender roles, differences between male and female sexual responsiveness diminish (P. Schwartz & Strom, 1978).

Social-class differences probably exert a more significant influence on sexual behavior than do gender differences within the same social class. Less educated women expect less from their mates in terms of frequency of intercourse and variety of sexual practices (Bell, 1974). If their husbands begin to demand more "exotic" sexual practices they are more likely to feel guilty about "giving in" and to feel that their status as "good girls" is being endangered. Blue-collar couples seem to have more problems involving sexuality than do more affluent, better educated couples, although many couples in both groups report problems with sexual adjustment (Rubin, 1976).

Regardless of whether sex is a source of problems or pleasures, it remains an inescapable source of motivation in many aspects of our daily lives. Plots of novels, plays, films, and soap operas revolve around sexual themes. Prostitution, pornography, the sale of birth-control products, and sexual advertising are major industries in many countries. That is why a study of introductory psychology students discovered that, in about 20 percent of the time that they were supposedly listening to the instructor, they were having sexual thoughts unrelated to the teacher's topic (Cameron et al., 1968). However, a recent survey shows that the Protestant work ethic is hard at work in America. A survey of nearly 2500 adults indicated that many women thought more about money than about sex, and, for men, sex barely edged out money. When it comes to enjoyment, however, men *reported* enjoying sex much more than money, while the two were about equally enjoyable for women (see **Figure 11.6**). OK, now it's time to get back to work if you want to get ahead in life.

Achievement Motivation

Not all societies value achievement to the extent that Americans do. There does not seem to be any universal motive to achieve; yet, for many people, the need to achieve clearly energizes and directs behavior. It also influences their perceptions of many situations and their interpretations of their own and others' behavior. For the past 30 years David McClelland and other psychologists have been investigating the conditions under which people develop a motive to achieve, and its impact on behavior.

The Need for Achievement

As early as 1938, Henry Murray had postulated a "need to achieve" which varied in strength in different people and influenced their tendency to approach success and evaluate their own performances. McClelland and his colleagues (1953) devised a way to measure the strength of this need and then looked for relationships between strength

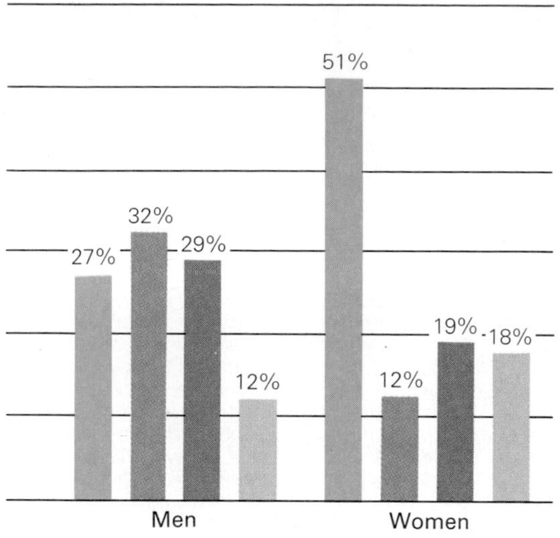

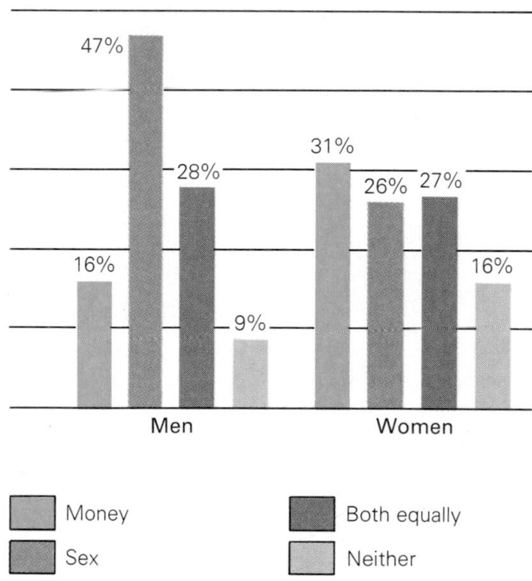

(Based on a 1985 sample conducted by Lieberman Research Inc.)

Figure 11.6 *What Americans Think About Money and Sex*

of achievement motivation in different societies, conditions that had fostered it, and its results in the work world.

To measure the strength of the need for achievement, McClelland used his subjects' fantasies. Subjects were shown pictures and asked to make up stories about them—saying what was happening in the picture and what the probable outcome would be. Presumably, what they projected into the scene reflected their own values, interests, and motives. As McClelland put it, "If you want to find out what's on a person's mind, don't ask him, because he can't always tell you accurately. Study his fantasies and dreams. If you do this over a period of time, you will discover the themes to which his mind returns again and again. And these themes can be used to explain his actions . . . ." (1971, p. 5). Clinical use of such projective pictures with people experiencing emotional problems will be described in chapter 13.

From subjects' responses to a series of pictures like these, McClelland worked out measures of several human needs—needs for power, for affiliation, and for achievement. The *need for achievement* was designated as *n Ach*. For example, one picture used was of a boy holding a violin. **Figure 11.7** gives hypothetical stories that subjects with high need for achievement and low need for achievement might have told. A great many studies in both laboratory and real-life settings have validated the usefulness of this measure. For example, persistence in working on an impossible task was greater for those with high *n Ach* when the task was announced as difficult rather than easy. Low *n Ach* subjects gave up sooner when they were led to believe the task was difficult, but they persisted for the supposedly easy (actually impossible) task. In other research, high-scoring *n Ach* people were found to be more upwardly mobile than those with low scores; and sons who had high *n Ach* scores were more likely to advance above their father's occupational status than sons with low *n Ach* measures (see McClelland et al., 1976).

Even the economic growth of a society can be related to its encouragement of achievement motivation (often at the expense of social-emotional-community concerns). McClelland (1955, 1961) found that, in general, Protestant countries (in which achievement and independence tend to be twin virtues) were more economically advanced than Catholic countries. He found that men in these "achieving societies" were more often trained to be self-supporting earlier in life, thus to value autonomy as a success-seeking style.

Cultures socialize children to accept their preferred patterns of living through folk tales, school books, and formal education, among other "training devices." As mentioned in chapter 2, an archival study found that the amount of achievement imagery in children's books read in one era was significantly correlated with several measures of economic achievement in the society of a few decades later. Among the measures used were the number of patents issued and the amount of electric power produced (De Charms & Moeller, 1962).

Figure 11.7
Story Showing High n Ach
The boy has just finished his violin lesson. He's happy at the progress he is making and is beginning to believe that all his sacrifices will be worth it. To become a concert violinist he will have to forego playing with his buddies, cut out a lot of dates and partying, and practice everyday, 'no matter what.' Although he knows he could make more money by going into his father's business, the image of being a great violinist, of giving people joy with his music, counts more. He renews his personal commitment to do all it takes to make it—to give it his "best shot."

Story Showing Low n Ach
The boy is holding his brother's violin wishing he could play it, but knowing that it isn't worth all the time and energy and money for lessons. He feels sorry for his brother who has to give up all the fun things in life to practice, practice, practice. It would be great to wake up one day and presto you're a top-notch musician, but it doesn't happen that way. The reality is boring practice, a no-fun youth, and a big possibility of not being anything more than just another guy who can play some musical instrument in a small-town band.

Attributions About Outcomes

People's motivation for achievement is further complicated by their attributions (interpretations) regarding the reasons things turn out the way they do. Earlier (p. 386) the importance of a *locus of control orientation* was mentioned—our interpretation that the outcomes of our actions are the result of what *we* do (internal control orientation) or the result of *factors in the environment* (external control orientation). Another basic interpretation that we tend to make concerns *stability*—whether a situation is consistent over time or is variable. Four possible interpretations about the causes of outcomes follow from the combinations of these two dimensions, as shown in **Figure 11.8.** For example, students may believe that a grade they get is primarily the result of internal factors, such as ability (a stable personality characteristic) or effort (a changing personality characteristic). Or they may see it as caused primarily by external factors, such as the difficulty of the task (a stable situational problem) or luck (an unstable external feature).

Interpretations regarding the causes for a success or a failure also determine what emotion one feels about it.

Students were given short stories of successes and failures with a cause described for each one, and then were asked to report how strongly the character in the story would have experienced each of a list of emotional reactions. As expected, success was associated with "happy" and "satisfied" and failure with "upset" and "uncheerful." Other emotions were specific to a person's beliefs about the reason the success or failure occurred, as shown in **Table 11.2.** *(Weiner et al., 1978)*

Figure 11.8 *Attributions Regarding Causes for Behavioral Outcomes*

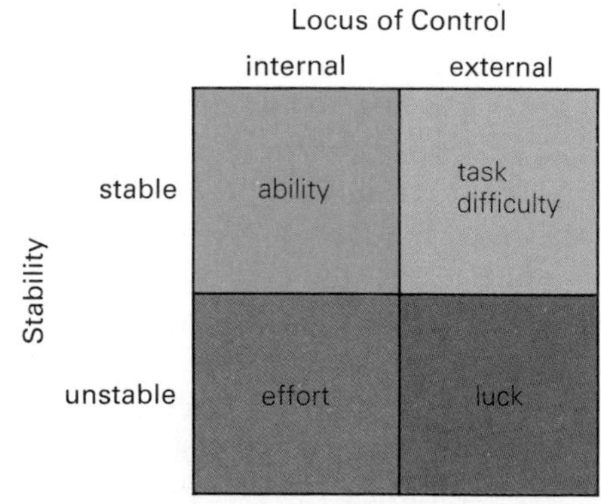

Table 11.2 *Emotional Reactions with Different Interpretations for Success and Failure*

When Success Is Attributed To:	**It Leads To:**
Ability	Confidence (competence)
Unstable effort	Activation, augmentation
Stable effort	Relaxation
Own personality	Self-enhancement
Other's effort, personality	Gratitude
Luck	Surprise
When Failure Is Attributed To:	**It Leads To:**
Ability	Incompetence
Effort (stable or unstable)	Guilt (shame)
Personality; intrinsic motivation	Resignation
Other's efforts, motivation, personality	Aggression
Luck	Surprise

(Adapted from Weiner, 1980)

A person's explanation for success or failure also determines the amount of effort likely to be put in next time. For example, suppose Joan attributed her successes to skill and effort, and her failures to bad luck, unfair tests, or external sources of discrimination. How would you expect her willingness to take risks to differ from that of Don who attributed his successes to luck, easy tests, and the hard work of teachers or coaches, and his failures to his personal qualities? Joan has "nothing to lose" by always taking a chance, while Don has "little to gain" by ever taking risks or even putting out effort.

Beliefs about *why* we have succeeded or failed, then, are important because they lead to (a) different interpretations of our past performance and general worth; (b) different emotions, goals, and effort in the present situation; and (c) different motivation in the future—in turn, making future successes more likely or less so. When we attribute a failure to our low ability and a difficult task, we are likely to give up sooner, select simpler tasks, and lower our goals; but if we attribute our failure to bad luck or lack of effort, then we are likely to have higher motivation to try again for success (Fontaine, 1974; Rosenbaum, 1972; Valle & Frieze, 1976).

Changing students' explanations of their past failures can improve their level of performance. When schoolchildren were trained to attribute past failure to lack of effort rather than to lack of skill, they increased their effort on subsequent tasks—and had more success (Dweck, 1975).

When people acquire an internal control orientation that leads them to set goals and develop generally successful means of attaining them, they develop a sense of personal **self-efficacy.** This is a feeling that they have control over what happens to them. Perceived self-efficacy, in turn, influences an individual's thought patterns, performance, and emotional arousal: with higher perceived self-efficacy, performance is better and emotional arousal less. One's perception of self-efficacy also influences one's choice of coping patterns in response to stress as well as one's level of physiological arousal. By contrast, a feeling of *self-inefficacy* can lead to apathy, despondency, a sense of futility and a feeling that one is a victim of external forces (Bandura, 1977b, 1982b).

Attributional Style

The way we explain the events in our lives—from winning at cards to being turned down for a date—can become lifelong attributional styles that affect the way we view ourselves (see Trotter, 1987). Pessimists attribute problems to stable-internal-global factors. "I've always had this problem; it's never going to get better; it will ruin my career." Optimists tend instead toward an attributional style that deals with "problems" by perceiving them as unstable-external and specific. "Sometimes my mate gets into terrible moods and that causes temporary glitches in our relationship." However, when things go well, the optimist rushes in to take the stable-internal-global credit. "It's just part of my nature to always be a winner."

When the garden-variety, ordinary pessimist overuses an attributional style that is self-blaming and all-encompassing, it becomes unhealthy. It is one of the contributing factors to the development and maintenance of serious depressive disorders (to be discussed in chapter 15).

Intrinsic and Extrinsic Motivation

Motivation to engage in an activity for its own sake is called **intrinsic motivation.** Things that we do because we simply enjoy doing them—like playing video games, singing in the shower, or keeping a secret diary—are intrinsically motivated. Work, too, can be intrinsically motivated when an individual is deeply interested in the job to be done. It is intrinsic motivation that keeps one working late into the night just for the sake of solving a problem or doing the best possible job—even if no one else knows it.

Extrinsic motivation is motivation to engage in an activity for some outside consequence rather than for its own sake. Gold stars, grades, and penalties for failure or misbehavior are testament to the belief that schoolchildren are extrinsically motivated and must be given external consequences if they are to learn. In extrinsic motivation, behavior is instrumental to obtaining something else, while in intrinsic motivation, behavior is carried out without a purpose beyond the immediate rewards of "doing it," consuming it for its pleasure. Taking vitamins is extrinsically motivated; eating cream puffs is intrinsically motivated.

What do you suppose would happen if there were also extrinsic rewards for behavior that children were engaging in out of intrinsic motivation? A classroom study gave a clear answer.

> *Preschoolers were first observed during free play periods in their classrooms, where they could choose among many available activities without any imposed constraints. The amount of time they spent on drawing activities was recorded. Next, in a different setting within the school, children were asked to engage in a drawing activity. They were randomly assigned to one of three conditions. (1)* Expected reward—*children were shown tangible rewards they would receive for engaging in the activity of drawing. (2)* Unexpected reward control—*children were asked to draw, but with no mention of any reward. However, after they drew their pictures, they got the same reward as those in the first group. They were a control group to show that it is not just getting the reward, but the perceived contingency between activity and reward that is crucial. (3)* No reward control—*children neither expected nor received a reward for engaging in the activity.*
>
> *Two weeks later unobtrusive observations were made in these children's classrooms of the amount of free time spent in drawing activity—when they were "on their own." The results were strong and direct. Those in the expected reward condition were spending* less *time on the target activity than were those in either of the other groups. In addition, they were less interested in the task than they had been during the initial observation period. Those in the other two conditions continued to show a high level of interest in the drawing task (Lepper et al., 1973).* Moral: a reward one day can take the former joy out of play.

Evidently, extrinsic rewards in this case were superfluous. More important, they were actually detrimental. With a reward, the task itself is not enjoyed as much, and when the extrinsic rewards are withdrawn, it is less likely that the activity will be engaged in again (Lepper, 1981; Lepper & Greene, 1978).

This *hidden* cost of rewards seems to be greatest where the rewards are (a) made obvious and given for activities with high intrinsic interest; and (b) provided for open-ended activities like problem solving and creative tasks, in which the performance plan is not well defined in advance. On the other hand, rewards may improve performance and not destroy intrinsic motivation when they are perceived as (a) conveying information about one's competence and progress, and not as a means of control, and (b) given for well-learned activities that are part of a routine (Deci, 1975).

Motivation and Future Time Perspective

Which of the following statements is most characteristic of you—*a* or *b, c* or *d?*

a. I am able to resist temptations when I know there is work to be done.
b. I do things impulsively, making decisions on the spur of the moment.
c. When I want to achieve something, I set subgoals and consider specific means for reaching these goals.
d. I try to live one day at a time.

If you endorsed *a* and *c,* you are more likely to be a future-oriented person than if you agreed with *b* and *d,* which are more typical of present-oriented people (Gonzalez & Zimbardo, 1985). What difference does it make if you are future- or present-oriented?

One aspect of *psychological time,* as contrasted with clock time, is **time perspective,** the way we partition the flow of perceived events and experiences into the frames of past, present, and future. Depending on the way we are socialized by our culture, family, peers, and religious and educational agencies, our time perspective can become biased. This means that there is a greater focus on one of these time frames and lesser, or no, empha-

SCHOOL STARTS NEXT WEEK..I HOPE I GET BETTER GRADES THIS YEAR

I HOPE I'LL BE THE PRETTIEST AND SMARTEST GIRL IN THE WHOLE CLASS..

"HOPE IS A GOOD BREAKFAST, BUT IT IS A BAD SUPPER"

WHEN WE GO TO COLLEGE, MARCIE, I'M NOT GOING TO ROOM WITH YOU..

sis on the others. A person's time perspective is a global cognitive structure that influences a wide range of psychological processes, from attention and perception to decisions and actions. This subtly learned, pervasive cognitive tendency to have one or another time frame influence our thoughts, feelings, and actions is a fundamental mechanism in human achievement and work motivation that is not often appreciated.

While a present-oriented individual either lives hedonistically "for the moment," or fatalistically avoids worrying about a future that is presumed to be determined, the future-oriented person delays gratification, plans, sets goals, "saves for a rainy day," endures boring lectures for an anticipated desired good grade, and makes "to do" lists, which are followed. In a setting that supports a future time perspective, such as college, the present-oriented student is "at risk" for incompletes, lower grades, and failures. However, in a setting that supports a present time perspective, such as parties, the future-oriented student will seem like a "nerd," less able to enjoy the social and emotional pleasures of peers for "its own sake."

In our *Opening Case,* when Charles T.'s job was terminated, his future was suddenly deleted as well. With no picture of a future, helpless resignation and eventually stress-related death took over. It is apparent that human motivational theories need to take account of the temporal perspective of individuals and societies if they are to capture some of the subtle richness of human dynamics (see Gorman & Wessman, 1977). What may appear to be a lack of motivation or lack of cognitive planning ability may be better explained in terms of differences in people's time perspective.

Most theories of motivation focus on *current* stimuli and conditions that arouse and direct behavioral responses in the present; but they do not explain why you might persist in working hard even on a tedious class assignment, or tolerate unpleasant interactions for a good letter of recommendation you anticipate needing when you get to your senior year. A major contribution of the research on motivation for achievement and work is its highlighting of the importance of a future orientation for the understanding of all human motivation. Many of the things we all do are for their future significance, not their present hedonistic value (De Charms & Muir, 1978).

One of the few psychologists studying the relationship between time perspective and motivation is Belgian psychologist Joseph Nuttin. He argues forcefully for an expanded scientific interest in investigating the effects of psychological time on human affairs:

> *Although ignored in many psychological textbooks, the future is an essential component of a person's behavior and his behavioral world. The ability to construct far-distant personal goals and to work toward their realization is an important characteristic of human beings. It is implied in the achievement of major projects where long-term instrumental steps are required and where the regulating impact of a goal is necessary from the very beginning of the enterprise. It seems plausible to admit that the psychological inability of some people to achieve long-term projects is related to a lack of future time perspective. (Nuttin, 1985, p. 10)*

A future orientation toward achievement can intensify one's present tendency to put forth effort, but it does much more than that. A future orientation provides a path in which the stream of human action flows. It transforms a job into a career, an actor's lines into a plot. Human action is not a static sequence of specific behavioral acts bound by eliciting stimuli. Rather, it is a continuing series of episodes perceived by the actor as extending into the future. We want to know that to get to Oz we must "follow the yellow brick road," not just that we should "turn left at the scarecrow, then right . . . ." To understand human motivation, we need to understand what causes changes in the entire stream of action, not just what causes specific behaviors to start and stop (Atkinson & Birch, 1970).

Work Motivation

When a strike of public transportation workers in New York City threatened to paralyze that great work center of millions of people, most of the workers, undaunted by the inconvenience, managed to get to their jobs. Even starting from miles away, they walked, jogged, biked, roller skated, and used any form of locomotion they could devise.

But why? The motivation to work energized their behavior, directed it, and led them to invent new solutions. This is one of the most potent and complex human motives, and there have been many attempts to explain it. Some answers have come from employers and some from *organizational psychologists* who study work motivation and the psychology of the work place (see the ***Close-up*** on p. 401).

Views of Human Nature at Work

Theories of work motivation are based on different views of human nature. If you were to ask two managers why people work, you might very well hear two quite different responses, reflecting divergent assumptions about what makes people tick. Many business organizations base their policies on one of two distinct views about human nature; these two views have been labeled, arbitrarily, as *Theory X* and *Theory Y* (McGregor, 1960).

Theory X

Theory X, the classical theory, is based on beliefs that people are lazy, ignorant, selfish, prone to error and motivated exclusively by money. Workers are considered dispensable "cogs" in the organizational machinery. By extension, therefore, jobs should be designed as simply as possible, minimizing both intellectual qualifications and necessary training time. Furthermore, workers need constant supervision and extrinsic incentives to work.

The most notable proponent of Theory X was Frederick W. Taylor (1856–1915) who developed a set of principles to design work and manage workers in the most efficient way. Engineers and business executives had been bothered by the fact that an efficient technology did not always increase productivity, because people were "gumming up the works." Work and workers, therefore, were approached as engineering problems, and the solutions were to simplify, specialize, and routinize jobs, reducing worker involvement and responsibility. Time and motion studies were used to analyze specific jobs, isolating the components or movements involved in successful performance of the task, so that the jobs could be designed more efficiently (Taylor, 1911). The classical Theory X views of human nature were prevalent during the early 1900s, when large numbers of people entered the work force, primarily in factory and assembly-line jobs.

These views changed in the late 1920s and early 1930s, challenging the very principles of "Taylorism." The impetus for change resulted from the famous (and "thorny") Hawthorne studies described in chapter 2. Recall that researchers at the Hawthorne plant of the Western Electric Company studied the relationship between physical conditions of work and worker productivity. The results were sometimes baffling—when workers showed increased levels of productivity whether the room illumination was increased, decreased, or not changed.

Although the Hawthorne studies were flawed methodologically, they had a profound impact on theories of work motivation and human nature. Work places were acknowledged to be complex social settings where worker productivity was influenced by factors other than monetary incentives and illumination. Workers responded to their social environment as well as to their physical environment, and, thus, workers' human needs and social relationships were of central importance. For the first time, work itself was viewed as a potential motivator, offering avenues for achievement, personal growth, and sense of meaningfulness.

Theory Y

Given the realization that work was inherently social and that people worked for more than money, the underlying assumptions about human nature had to be changed. This new view of human nature at work, known as Theory Y, came to fruition in the 1960s. According to **Theory Y,** people are basically creative, responsible, and intrinsically motivated to do good work to the extent that the work is challenging (McGregor, 1960). Instead of being restricted, workers should have their freedom expanded so that they have the opportunity to be creative and achieve their full potential. The goal of making work more efficient was replaced by an emphasis on creating a work force with high morale.

A somewhat similar theory is *Theory V,* which asserts that the level of a worker's motivation depends on the extent to which effort on the job contributes to the attainment of his or her personal values, whatever they are. Ambitious people are

Close-up Organizational Psychologists Are Motivated by More Than Just Work Motivation!

Organizational psychologists have made many contributions to the study of people at work. At first, their primary role was that of "efficiency experts." Their focus on employee efficiency and productivity was often in response to such real-world concerns as absenteeism, turnover, low productivity levels, and associated lackluster profits. Psychologists were asked to select and train employees, and to design jobs so that they could be performed most efficiently. The emphasis was often on workers' shortcomings, and proposed solutions included hiring the "right person for the job" and restructuring jobs in order to motivate workers and to minimize the possibility of human error.

Nowadays, organizational psychologists continue to address practical concerns of the business community; however, the scope of their contribution has expanded considerably. The previous emphasis on increasing productivity and profits has been complemented by a concern for enhancing individual well-being, because this is believed to influence organizational effectiveness. Recognizing that work settings are complex social systems, organizational psychologists study various aspects of human relations, such as communication among employees, socialization or enculturation of workers, leadership, attitudes and commitment toward a job and/or an organization, job satisfaction, stress and burnout (see chapter 14), and overall quality of life at work. As consultants to businesses, organizational psychologists may assist in recruitment, selection, and training of employees. In some cases, they may recommend against searching for an "ideal" job candidate and suggest instead that efforts be directed toward job redesign, or "tailoring a job to the *person.*" Finally, new theories of management, organizational design, decision making, development, and change are emerging, providing breadth and scholarly foundation for practical applications offered to businesses and organizations.

The explosion of research interest and activity has been due in part to the development of "O.B.," or the field of *Organizational Behavior.* O.B. is a relatively new field comprised of psychologists, engineers, management scientists, and other behavioral and social scientists devoted to understanding human behavior in organizational settings. Bringing together concepts, theories, and models from their individual specializations, this rich, interdisciplinary group of researchers shares a commitment to a systematic, science-oriented approach to the study of individual, group, and organizational processes. In addition, it recognizes that knowledge about organizational behavior must be suited for business executives or managers in organizations, leading to practical applications of research findings.

Psychologists bring to the study of organizational behavior the belief that behavior is goal-directed and that it is determined by multiple factors, including dispositional, situational, and interpersonal influences. They assume that people share many human qualities and yet show

individual differences and variability in their beliefs and behaviors. Most importantly, however, organizational psychologists emphasize the significance of people's personal interpretations of the world and the impact of such interpretations on human behavior. For example, the same smile and handshake may be warmly received by one worker, while they may raise doubt and suspicion in the mind of another. Organizational psychology offers a wealth of information about the way people understand and perceive the world and the factors that influence their interpretations and subsequent behaviors. Knowledge about human behavior, together with a commitment to controlled observation and experimentation, provides organizational psychologists with the necessary tools to make meaningful contributions to our understanding of people at work and to the enhancement of both organizational effectiveness and individual well-being.

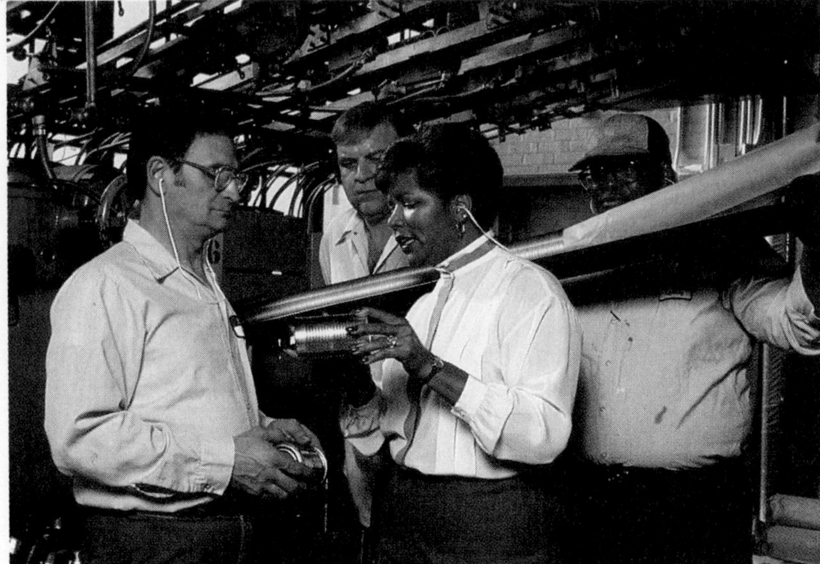

The QC team at the Campbell Soup plant in Camden, New Jersey, is an example of a Theory Z work group. Participation in this group has had a strong impact on decision-making opportunities, group communication opportunities, and opportunities to develop skills needed for advancement.

those who have personal values that work can serve (Locke, 1982). According to still another theory, *Theory Z,* worker motivation, morale, and loyalty are highest when worker values and organization goals are meshed. Company policies that may do this include guaranteed lifetime employment, informal systems of social control, decision by group participation and consensus, emphasis on individual responsibility, and job rotation permitting workers to become generalists (Ouchi, 1981). Such policies have traditionally been characteristic of Japanese companies and are now being incorporated into some of the most successful American businesses in their "search for excellence" (Peters & Waterman, 1983).

Theories of Work Motivation

Organizational psychologists have proposed many theories of work motivation; however, these theories can be categorized in terms of three basic approaches. *Need theories* focus on what energizes individual workers. *Cognitive theories* describe the way motivation occurs. Finally, *job-design* and *goal-setting* offer practical applications for enhancing worker motivation.

Need Theories

Need theories are based on Maslow's theoretical approach, which was described earlier in this chapter (p. 384-85). One of these, known as **ERG theory,** specifies only three sets of needs—*E*xistence needs, *R*elatedness needs, and *G*rowth needs (Alderfer, 1972). Existence needs (which are similar to Maslow's physiological and safety needs) include the need for food, shelter, pay, and safe working conditions. Relatedness needs are social in nature, emphasizing the need for clear and available interpersonal communication. Growth needs encourage development of one's true potential and correspond to Maslow's self-actualization and esteem needs. In contrast to Maslow, ERG theory assumes that higher-level needs can become activated *before* lower-level needs are completely satisfied. Research is generally more supportive of ERG theory than of Maslow's need hierarchy (Betz, 1982; Wahba & Bridwell, 1976).

Cognitive Theories

Cognitive theories of work motivation, such as *equity theory* and *expectancy theory,* go beyond the individual need level to include social and organizational factors. These theories attempt to explain and predict how people will respond under different working conditions. They assume that workers engage in certain cognitive activities, such as assessing fairness via social comparison processes, or estimating expected rewards associated with performance.

Equity theory proposes that workers are motivated to maintain fair or equitable relationships with other relevant persons (Adams, 1965). Workers take note of their inputs (investments or contributions they make to their jobs) and their outcomes (what they receive from their jobs), and then they compare these with the inputs and outcomes of other workers. When the ratio of outcomes to inputs for Worker A is equal to the ratio for Worker B (Outcome A/Input A = Outcome B/Input B), then Worker A will feel satisfied; however, dissatisfaction will result when these ratios are *not* equal. When Worker A's ratio is less than that of other workers (perceived underpayment), he or she will feel angry; but when Worker A's ratio is greater than others (perceived overpayment), he or she will feel guilty.

Since inequity is unpleasant, workers will be motivated to restore equity by changing the relevant inputs and outcomes. These changes could be *behavioral* (for example, reducing input by working less, increasing outcome by asking for a raise), or they could be *psychological* (for example, reinterpreting the value of the inputs—"my work isn't really that good").

Research has supported the predictions of equity theory, particularly with regard to perceived underpayment. (Carrel & Dittrich, 1978). One study showed that underpaid clerical workers were less productive, and overpaid workers more productive, than equitably paid workers (Pritchard et al., 1972). Similarly, college students who were given additional responsibilities plus a high-status job title maintained high levels of performance, whereas students who were given additional responsibilities but no title (underpayment inequity) dramatically reduced their performance, presumably in order to restore equity (Greenberg & Ornstein, 1983).

Expectancy theory proposes that workers are motivated when they expect that their effort and performance on the job will result in desired outcomes (Porter & Lawler, 1968; Vroom, 1964). In other words, people will engage in work they find attractive (leads to favorable consequences) and achievable. Expectancy theory emphasizes three components. *Instrumentality* refers to the perception that one's performance will be rewarded. *Valence* refers to the perceived attractiveness of particular outcomes. *Expectancy* refers to the perceived likelihood that a worker's efforts will result in successful performance. According to expectancy theory, workers rationally and logically assess the probabilities of these three components and combine them in a multiplicative manner, rather than merely summing them additively. Highest levels of motivation, therefore, result when all three components have high probabilities, whereas lowest levels result when any single component is zero.

One of the strengths of expectancy theory is that it distinguishes between motivation and performance, indicating that factors such as skill, ability, and job opportunities can influence performance, in addition to motivation. In other words, poor performance does not necessarily result from low motivation. Research has been supportive of expectancy theory, demonstrating proposed relationships between expectancy, instrumentality, and motivation (Garland, 1984; Mitchell, 1974). However, the theory is not always easy to test. Furthermore, it is not clear that people actually compute subjective probabilities and use these estimates to make decisions in the rational manner prescribed by the theory, as we noted in chapter 10 (Kahneman et al., 1982; Nisbett & Ross, 1981).

Job Design and Goal-setting

Rarely have organizational psychologists proposed theories of work motivation without considering their application to managers and workers in organizations. *Job design* and *goal-setting* are two examples of theory, research, and practice aimed at enhancing work motivation.

Goal-setting refers to the intention to work toward an explicit goal. It is a primary motivating force in work behavior and task effort because goals direct and focus attention, mobilize effort, increase persistence, and encourage a person to work out appropriate strategies (Latham & Yukl, 1975; Steers & Porter, 1974). Specific, challenging goals lead to higher performance than either easy goals, no goals, or the vague goal of "do your best."

For a goal to be an effective motivator, the following conditions must be met: (a) it must be specific and challenging to the worker; (b) the worker must have adequate ability to achieve it; (c) feedback must be available about progress toward the goal; (d) tangible rewards must accompany goal (and subgoal) attainment; (e) the management must be supportive of worker needs and problems; and, perhaps most important, (f) the worker must *accept* the goal as a personal intention (Locke et al., 1981). Even in an organization where management sets group goals, a worker can still set his or her own personal goals and standards. For example, "happy workaholics" are people whose hard work becomes a vital extension of their personal identity (Machlowitz, 1980).

The goal of **job design** is to identify the characteristics of work that make it enjoyable and motivating and then to use this knowledge in designing (or redesigning) jobs. In studying job design as a motivator, organizational psychologists emphasize the potential intrinsic value of work.

Job enlargement, in which a number of similar tasks are combined, was one of the first attempts to make work more intrinsically interesting to workers. Unfortunately, the attempt was not very successful. A combination of tasks at the *same* level of scope and responsibility (horizontal loading) simply resulted in a bigger, uninteresting job. On the other hand, *job enrichment,* in which the tasks that are combined are of *different* scope and responsibility (vertical loading), has achieved the intended goal.

> *Job enrichment programs have been introduced in many organizations, most notably (and successfully) in assembly plants of Volvo, the Swedish automobile producer. Because of low productivity and high absenteeism and turnover, Volvo decided to experiment. In the late 1960s, the president proposed to build an assembly plant with no assembly line. Instead, groups of about 15 workers were responsible for a fairly complex task, such as installing the interior of an automobile. Members of each group decided who would work on what aspect of the larger job, and the work group as a whole was responsible for any errors. The experiment has been a success for Volvo. Worker attitudes are favorable, and absenteeism and turnover are lower than at assembly-line plants. (Dowling, 1973; Walton, 1977)*

Evidence supporting job enrichment as a method of job design is limited, in large part because of the difficulty in implementing such programs. Most reports describe isolated examples of its success; anecdotes about its failures are cited as well. According to one American auto worker who spent one month at an "enriched" Saab plant in Sweden, "If I've got to bust my a__ to be meaningful, forget it; I'd rather be monotonous" (Goldman, 1976). Not all workers want enriched jobs, especially when it requires more work and no increase in salary or job status.

In a more recent approach, a *job characteristics model* has attempted to specify what makes one job more intrinsically interesting than another (Hackman & Oldham, 1980). Five core job characteristics are believed to affect worker motivation: (a) skill variety, (b) task identity, (c) task significance, (d) autonomy, and (e) job feedback. In general, jobs that are most intrinsically interesting are those that involve lots of different skills and activities, all of which fit together to form a complete "whole" that has a meaningful impact on other people. In addition, high levels of individual autonomy and clear feedback about the quality of work enhance intrinsic motivation. These core characteristics are related to associated psychological states, such as the perceived meaningfulness of one's job and the personal responsibility one feels for the fruits of one's labor. These states reflect one's sense of self and influence one's performance at work, in part through generating a set of positive emotions about one's work.

Human Emotions

Keith's "superhuman" motivation in our *Opening Case* (as expressed in his hunger, sexuality, and aggression) was created by a tumor, which triggered an excessive discharge of hormones into his body. It also functioned to make Keith "subhuman" because it took away the feeling side of his motivation. He lost the ability to experience the human emotions of joy and sadness, pride and fear, love and grief. Since his constant level of high arousal did not change in response to changes in external events and activities, he had no way to correlate his internal feelings with the various happenings in his life. His experience highlights the extent to which we normally depend on our emotions to measure the impact that life events are having upon us.

Emotion and *motivation* have the same Latin origin referring to movement or activity. While the *motivated person* usually moves physically toward some goal or away from some aversive situation, the *emotional person* is "moved internally" by psychologically significant situations. This "moving experience" of emotion involves both physiological reactions and "stirred-up feelings" as well.

Aristotle was the first to distinguish between the *physiological* component of emotion, which he referred to as its "matter," and the *psychological* component, its "form" or "idea." Seventeenth- and eighteenth-century philosophers generally thought that the emotions were instinctive and nonrational, meant to be curbed by the proper exercise of human reason and intellect. Many common expressions still reflect this view: "I got so mad that I couldn't think straight, so I shot him"; or "In the heat of passion, I didn't realize what I was doing, and now I'm pregnant." Some psychologists have described emotion as an inner disturbance or disorientation resulting from suddenly being overwhelmed by an especially significant personal experience (Young, 1961).

Despite differences in definition and emphasis, there is a general consensus among contemporary psychologists that an **emotion** is a complex pattern of changes including physiological arousal, feelings, cognitive processes, and behavioral reactions made in response to a situation perceived by an individual to be personally significant in some way (Kleinginna & Kleinginna, 1981). The physiological arousal includes neural, hormonal, visceral, and muscular changes. The feelings include both a general affective state (good-bad, positive-negative) and a specific feeling tone, such as joy or disgust. The cognitive processes include a person's interpretations, memories, and expectations. The overt behavioral reactions are both expressive (crying, smiling) and instrumental (screaming for help). Psychologists with different theoretical orientations tend to focus on one or another of these different aspects of human emotions. Having defined the domain of emotions, we now want to know the functions that emotions serve, and the way the emotional process colors our existence.

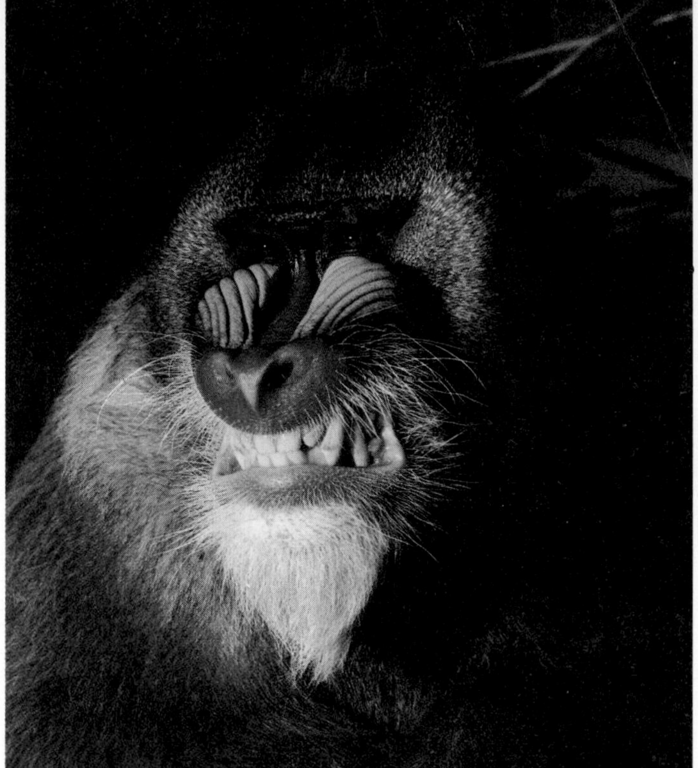

This mandrill monkey is displaying aggression. Notice the bared teeth and clenched jaws.

Why Are We Emotional?

Who is someone you know who is never emotional in any situation? Spock, the Vulcan, in the *Star Trek* movies, is the model of a creature more highly evolved than humans. His superior, logical mind is never sullied by primitive emotions that bother the rest of Captain Kirk's crew. You might also think of a "cold-blooded" murderer who kills without remorse or any normal human emotion. These fictional and real instances are obvious exceptions to the principle that emotions are a basic part of human existence, but what good are they? Why do we have emotions?

"No good," was the answer that a number of theorists came up with in the late 1920s (Angier, 1927; Howard, 1928). These psychologists proposed *conflict theories* of emotion, which stated that emotion was a physiological disturbance produced *only* when an organism couldn't cope with the environment. And once aroused, emotions further interfered with one's ability to use effective coping strategies. The claim that emotions served no useful function was echoed by one of these conflict theorists: "Fear occurs only when flight is impossible. Anger is displayed only when one cannot strike his enemy. The uselessness, or even harmfulness of emotion, is known to everyone. . . . Sorrow, joy, anger, by enfeebling attention or judgment, often make us commit regrettable acts" (Clapardere, 1928, pp. 126–27). These conflict theories all folded under the weight of critical analysis which made obvious their weakness in accounting for joy in terms of conflict, or the usually adaptive functions of emotions under levels of arousal that were not extreme. Fearful people flee, angry people attack, happy people smile and attract others to them (Arnold, 1970; Leeper, 1948).

"For survival," was Charles Darwin's (1872/1965) answer to the question of what function emotions serve. Certain situations evoke emotions and associated behaviors, as when an organism prepares to fight after being made angry by a threatened takeover of its territory. Darwin held that it was adaptive for organisms to prepare to fight under such circumstances, to increase general muscle tone of the body, clench fists, bare teeth, ready weapons, and so forth. By learning and natural selection, over time, these preparatory reactions have become part of the emotional *expression* of anger. Darwin believed that the bodily changes which comprise any emotion are weak preparatory forms of behaviors that originally had adaptive value under circumstances that evoked the emotion in the past. Thus for Darwin, emotional expressions were *innate,* not learned from experience—the evolutionary remnants of previous adaptive behaviors.

As we ascend the scale from simple organisms to humans we observe both increasing differentiation of the facial muscles used to express emotion and an increasing diversity of emotional behavior. Humans have not evolved *away from* nonrational, primitive emotions as we evolved our superior brains. We seemed to have evolved *toward* a combination of intellect and emotion (Scherer, 1984). Why are we the smartest and, at the same time, the most emotional of all living creatures?

Motivational Functions of Emotion

Most contemporary theories of emotion share the Darwinian core, assuming that emotions evolved to prepare and *motivate* an organism to *cope adaptively* with the demands of its environment (as seen in Ekman, 1984; Izard, 1971; Lazarus, 1986; Leventhal, 1984; Mandler, 1975; Plutchik, 1980; and Tomkins, 1962). While intense or chronic emotional arousal can be debilitating, under most ordinary circumstances emotions play important, beneficial roles in our lives.

One of the primary functions of emotions is to increase our *behavioral flexibility* in responding to environmental stimulation. Instead of reacting to a given stimulus situation instinctively, we are freed from rigid, fixed-action patterns because our emotions combine an account of the *context* of the stimulus and also our current needs, desires, and expectations. For example, watching a friend driving a motorcycle may evoke many different emotions, each with a motivational force to take some directed action. Joy and interest in sharing this exciting adventure encourage you to hop on behind her; fear at the potential danger of her reckless driving style makes you warn her; anger at her ignoring your advice motivates you to threaten her; and envy at her apparent freedom gets you to buy one for yourself. The subjective feeling of emotion thus includes a distinctly felt motivational component, a tendency toward or away from some type of action. Accompanying emotions there are also bodily changes which prepare us physically to respond to a situation in ways that are, or, at one time, were, usually adaptive. Other social functions of emotions as nonverbal communication will be discussed later when we examine the role of the face in emotional expression.

Nature Versus Nurture of Emotions

Again, the consensus of current researchers in this field supports Darwin's position of the innate nature of emotions. We may learn when to show and when to hide a given emotion depending on the circumstances, but expression of the emotion is built into the organism. All infants show similar emotional expressions at birth or soon after. Other research shows that people from different cultures can recognize a set of "universal" emotional facial expressions displayed in photos of actors from other cultures. One proposal for which set of emotions is inborn is that of Robert Plutchik (1980). As can be seen in **Figure 11.9,** there are eight basic inborn emotions, made up of four pairs of opposites: joy and sadness, fear and anger, surprise and anticipation, and acceptance and disgust. All other emotions are assumed to be variations, derivatives, or *blends* of these basic eight. For example, love is a combination of joy and acceptance; awe of fear and surprise. Each primary emotion is associated with an adaptive response. Disgust is considered an evolutionary outgrowth of rejecting distasteful foods from the mouth, while joy is associated with reproductive activities.

Recent analyses have taken the position that both innate and learned factors are involved in emotion. As we saw in earlier chapters with the ability to think and to use language, a child's emotional development seems to follow a genetically set timetable—if appropriate stimulation is available. Some of the developments in emotional response may be linked to specific anatomical changes in the brain (Konner, 1977). For example, smiling emerges in infants of all cultures when the

Figure 11.9 *Dimensions of Emotion*

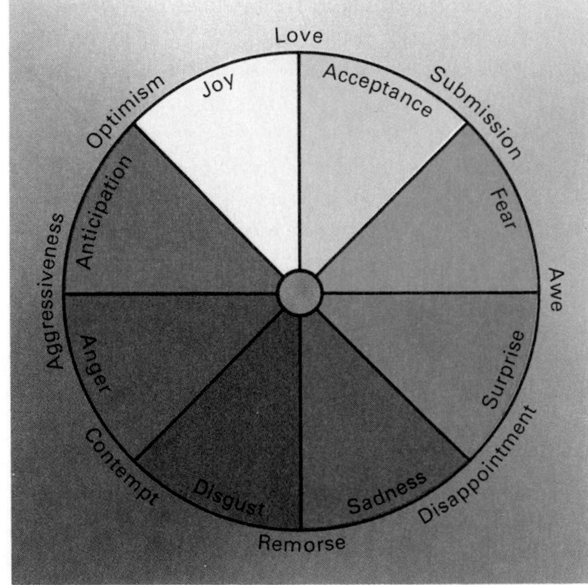

From "A Language for the Emotions" by Robert Plutchik, reprinted by permission from Psychology Today, February 1980. Copyright © 1980 American Psychology Association.

necessary nerve pathways acquire their myelin sheaths, one or two months after birth. Similarly, a fairly universal occurrence in infants of fear of separation from their parents and "stranger anxiety" coincides with the development of neural tracts within the limbic system around the eighth month of life.

According to one *development* account of emotion, an infant, at birth, is capable of feeling only a generalized positive state, a generalized negative state, and the emotions of interest and sadness (Izard, 1982). A few months later, joy and anger develop. By the time the infant is nine months old, shame and fear appear—emotions requiring a degree of self-awareness that a younger child is believed not to have. Emotional responses may continue to change throughout life, reflecting changes in both physiological and cognitive processes (Mandler, 1984). Many complex emotions involve the ability to empathize with someone else's feelings, an ability that young children must learn from social experience; and, as memory and expectation develop, emotions can be triggered by thoughts as well as by a wider range of sensory stimuli (see Bower, 1981). Imagine you have just won a grand prize of $5 million, a Ferrari, and a date with your favorite movie star, and . . . smiling?

Stirring Up the Emotional Stew

With physiological processes, feelings, cognitions, and behavioral reactions all parts of an emotion, what is the chain of events in an emotional response? Emotion researchers need to synthesize three aspects of the total emotion sequence: the antecedents of internal and external stimuli that precede feelings; the physiological changes associated with those feelings; and the thoughts and reactions that accompany those physiological changes.

Innate Stimulus Elicitors

Those who believed emotions were innate thought there must be "adequate stimuli" that would elicit each type of emotional reaction; but research did not bear them out. If each of the emotions is initiated by its own stimuli, then it should be possible, when we see a person expressing an emotion, to identify the emotion and infer the kind of stimulus needed to arouse it. The problem is that similar-appearing emotions occur in widely varying situations, and observers cannot identify the emotion being experienced unless they know what situation the subject is facing (see Woodworth & Schlossberg, 1954).

A different mechanism for producing arousal proposes that there are *innate releasers,* such as loud noises or tissue damage, that arouse emotions. The most important of these releasers—and the primary source of arousal for all emotion—is the interruption of ongoing plans and the occurrence of any unexpected event, according to Mandler (1984). A secondary source of arousal is the activation in memory of a previously arousing experience; but this conflict view of emotional arousal neglects the positive emotions we feel when in the presence of loved ones or the joy of receiving an expected prize for an effortful task. The concept of innate stimulus elicitors offers no explanation for most of the positive or low intensity emotions we experience, such as contentment or boredom.

Physiological Processes

Physiological systems provide the machinery of response to internal and external stimuli by sending signals that activate or inhibit emotional responding. These reactions begin with the arousal of the brain as a whole by the *reticular activating system,* through which incoming sensory messages pass on their way to the brain (Lindsley, 1951; Zanchetti, 1967). As we saw in chapter 4, this system functions as a nonspecific, general alarm system for the rest of the brain.

The influence of *hormones* on emotion has been shown in several kinds of studies. Hormone levels in the blood and urine rise during emotional states, whereas changes in emotional responding occur when hormones are administered and in diseases affecting the endocrine glands. Much research has also shown that perception of emotional stimuli is accompanied by release of hormones such as epinephrine and norepinephrine. *Steroid hormones* act on many different kinds of body tissue, including nerve cells. These normally occurring steroids can affect the receptors on the membrane surfaces of nerve cells, causing them to change their excitability rapidly and directly. They can produce euphoria in short-term low doses, but depression in long-term high doses (Majewska et al., 1986). Many of the mood changes associated with stress, pregnancy, and the menstrual cycle may be related to the effects that steroid hormones have on brain cells.

The *autonomic nervous system* also prepares the body for emotional responding by action of both its divisions; the balance between them depends on the quality and intensity of the arousing stimulation. With mild, unpleasant stimulation, the *sympathetic* division is more active; with mild, pleasant stimulation, the *parasympathetic* division is more active. With more intense stimulation of either kind, both divisions are increasingly involved.

Integration of both the hormonal and the neural aspects of arousal is controlled by the *hypothalamus* and the *limbic system,* old-brain control systems for emotions and for patterns of attack, defense, and flight (see chapter 4). Either lesioning or stimulation in various parts of the limbic system produces dramatic changes in emotional responding. Tame animals may become killers; usual prey and predators may become peaceful companions. Finally, in all complex emotions, the *neocortex* is involved through its internal neural networks and its connections with other parts of the body. The neocortex provides the associations, memories, and meanings that integrate psychological experience and biological response.

Organic or Mental: Which Comes First?

Theories of emotion fall into two camps depending on whether they place greater emphasis on organic, bodily processes or mental, cognitive processes (Fraisse, 1968). This distinction also comes under another heading, that of *peripheral* versus *central* theories of emotion. The peripheralists are concerned with peripheral or visceral reactions, especially those of the autonomic nervous system (ANS), while the centralists focus their concern on the activities of the central nervous system (CNS), especially the role of the brain in emotion.

Those in the organic, or peripheralist, tradition have argued that the *precursors* of emotion are physiological events. To the contrary, assert those in the mental, or centralist, tradition. They argue that, in the causal chain of any emotion, thoughts and psychological processes are primary; bodily reactions are influenced by, and follow from, these psychic events. William James' theory of emotion is in the organic tradition; Richard Lazarus is a modern proponent of the mental tradition; Stanley Schachter has tried to combine the two factors as both being necessary, but neither by itself being sufficient to cause an emotion.

James-Lange Peripheral Theory of Emotion

William James offered an explanation for the subjective feeling component of emotion by reversing the commonsense sequence of emotion and behavioral reaction. Do you cry because you are sad, or as James believed, are you sad because you perceive yourself crying? He argued that certain instinctive reactions, such as trembling when threatened, are accompanied by visceral, "gut" arousal. Different instinctive responses would then send different sensory and kinesthetic (motor) feedback to the brain—which, in turn, would flood a person's consciousness and create the feeling of a specific emotion. As James put it, " . . . we feel sorry because we cry, angry because we strike, afraid because we tremble" (James, 1884). Although contrary to common sense, this view was taken seriously by many psychologists and became known as the **James-Lange theory** of emotion (Carl Lange was a Danish scientist who presented similar ideas the same year as James). An outline of the proposed sequence of emotion generation in this theory is shown in **Figure 11.10.** A stimulus event occurs that triggers physical reactions which are noticed and then are interpreted to give the emotion its subjective aspect. James said, "My thesis is . . . that the bodily changes follow directly the *perception* of the exciting fact, and that our feeling of the same changes as they occur *is* the emotion" (1890, p. 449).

The James-Lange theory was seriously challenged by physiologist Walter Cannon (1927, 1929) and others who used several lines of experimental evidence and logical analysis. These researchers noted that animals continued to respond emotionally even after their viscera were separated surgically from the central nervous system. Therefore, they reasoned, emotions could not necessarily only follow prior physiological arousal if they occur in the absence of viscera. Secondly, the same visceral reactions are found to occur in very different situations; palpitations of the heart accompany aerobic exercise, love making, or running away from danger—but clearly do not lead to the same emotions. So something more is required than merely perceiving how one is responding. Third, though rage and grief have different physiological components, many emotions cannot be distinguished physiologically; therefore, a person cannot experience different emotions simply by "reading" visceral reactions that are not well differentiated. Fourth, ANS responses are typically slow; their onset of about two seconds would mean that emotions would also have to be slow in their onset; therefore, rapidly elicited emotions can't be accounted for by the slowpoke ANS that was so critical to the James-Lange visceral theory.

A modern version of the theory of emotion as produced by behavioral responses is called the *facial feedback hypothesis:* smile and you will feel happy; frown and you will feel upset (Izard, 1971; Tomkins, 1962). A recent study did find several different emotions associated with particular patterns

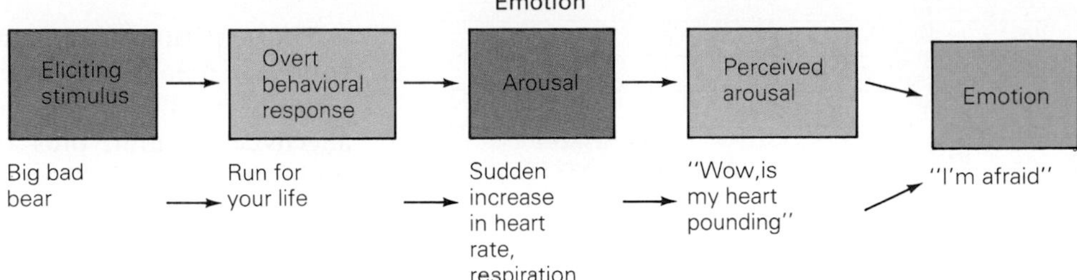

Figure 11.10 *Emotion Generation According to the James-Lange Theory*

of facial muscle movement (G. Schwartz et al., 1980). Many researchers hypothesize that the connections between facial muscle emotional expressions, the motor cortex, and the hypothalamus are "hardwired," while interpretation of emotional experience depends on learning. (We will analyze the role of the face in emotion in the next section.)

Cognitive Appraisal and Meaning Analysis

Most theories of emotion reserve a place of prominence for cognitive processes as the centerpiece that makes possible optimally adaptive emotional responding (Lazarus, 1987; Roseman, 1984; Smith & Ellsworth, 1985). Sensory experiences lead to emotion only when the stimuli are appraised by the individual as having personal significance. The constantly changing relationship between person and environment becomes a source of emotion when "central life agendas," such as survival, values, and goals, are engaged—but only as stimuli are recognized as being related to these values and goals. The particular emotion that is felt depends on the way a situation is interpreted by the individual and the meaning attributed to it.

In the words of Richard Lazarus, a leading proponent of this cognitive appraisal view, " . . . emotional experience cannot be understood solely in terms of what happens in the person or in the brain, but grows out of ongoing transactions with the environment that are evaluated" (1984, p. 124). The interplay of environmental factors, cognitive appraisal, and emotional experience is well illustrated in a situation familiar to every college student—taking examinations. A recent study collected information about student reactions before they took their college midterm in an introductory psychology course, and again after they received their grades.

> *At both measurement times 50 students completed questionnaires assessing their appraisals of the current situation and their emotional states. Appraisals were made on a number of dimensions such as pleasantness, effort required, responsibility, control, and perceived obstacles. Emotions were measured on rating scales for 25 emotional adjectives, among them fear, happiness, disgust, and challenge. Before the exam both appraisals and emotions were homogeneous across all students. After the students found out their grades, appraisals and emotions were varied, according to how well or poorly the students had done. Before the exam students were highly attentive to the situation, anticipated expending much effort, and were optimistic. Their primary emotions were hope and challenge, mixed often with some fear. Afterwards those who did well rated the situation as fair and pleasant, and had strong feelings of happiness combined with hope and challenge. Those who did poorly interpreted the "same situation" as unpleasant and unfair, reported feeling angry, which was combined with fear, guilt, or apathy in different students. Most emotions could by* predicted *from knowing the characteristic appraisals given by the subjects at both times. Some of the pairings were anger-unfairness; fear-unpleasantness; happiness-pleasantness; hope/challenge-anticipated effort. Finally, students who felt apathy appraised the situation as one in which they were neither responsible nor in control of the outcome; instead the outcomes were attributed to "other agencies"—teacher and graders. (Smith & Ellsworth, 1987)*

Situations with different meanings for an individual seem to induce different biochemical responses. For example, human tears flow in sadness, happiness, anger, and sympathy, as well as in response to an irritating stimulus. However, tears expressing sadness contain a greater concentration of protein than is found in tears shed in response to raw onions (Frey & Langseth, 1986). For a comparison of sex differences in crying, see **Figure 11.11.**

Do cognitions precede and *elicit* emotions, or are they used to define emotions *after* they have been elicited? This question is still being as hotly debated now as it was decades ago.

The Two-Factor Theory of Emotion

According to Stanley Schachter (1971), the experience of emotion is the joint effect of physiological arousal and cognitive appraisal, with both parts necessary for an emotion to occur. The arousal is assumed to be general, undifferentiated, and first in

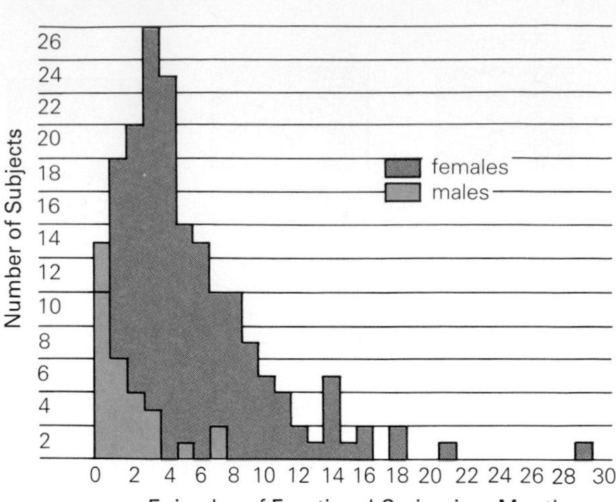

Figure 11.11 *Episodes of Emotional Crying*
In the first formal investigation of adult crying behavior, 45 male and 286 female subjects judged to be psychiatrically normal kept records of their emotional crying behavior during a month. Duration of episodes for both groups was about 6 minutes, and the most frequent stimuli for crying for both involved interpersonal relations and media presentations. A high proportion of both groups said they felt better after crying. (Frey et al., 1983)

the emotion sequence. The cognition serves to determine how this ambiguous inner state will be labeled. This position has become known as the **two-factor theory of emotion** (Mandler, 1984; Schachter & Singer, 1962). Organic, visceral factors *interact* with mental factors to produce an emotion. Thus when there is sympathetic arousal *without* a known, specified source, a person will search the environment for cognitions that can be used to label the arousal and give it emotional meaning.

> *In an ingeniously designed experiment, physiological arousal was manipulated for experimental subjects by disguised injections of epinephrine (arousing); control subjects received a placebo (nonarousing). The experimental subjects' cognitions about the cause of their arousal were manipulated by giving them either accurate information or misinformation about the connection between the arousal they felt and the earlier injection. The subjects then were given different social cues by having them spend a waiting period with another student (a confederate of the experimenter) who behaved emotionally in a euphoric manner. Others spent time with a confederate who behaved in an angry manner. The researchers reported that experimental subjects who did not have an appropriate explanation for their arousal felt happy if they had been with the euphoric confederate, angry if they had seen him act in an angry manner. Presumably, perception of the confederate's mood provided a relevant cognition for labeling their own unexplained arousal. This pattern of reported emotions was not found for control groups, who either were not aroused or already had an appropriate explanation for their arousal. (Schachter & Singer, 1962)*

The experimenters' explanation was that the emotions reported by the experimental subjects were the result of physiological arousal that was affectively neutral, plus cognitive appraisal that transformed it into anger or happiness. They reasoned that, in most cases, we attribute our arousal to some obvious stimulus situation, as when we laugh at a good joke. However, when we experience arousal without a known source, as in this case, we use cues from the immediate environment to interpret and label arousal according to whatever emotion is appropriate to the social setting.

This research was important in drawing attention to the role of cognitive interpretations in emotional experience and in showing that independent components of emotion could be manipulated and studied in a laboratory setting. Better designed research has since challenged the two-component theory, however (see Marshall & Zimbardo, 1979; Maslach, 1979; Reisenzein, 1983). It is not now believed that emotions necessarily follow from labeling unexplained arousal or even that physical arousal is a necessary condition for all emotional experience. Moreover, research has shown that some emotional experiences are accompanied by differentiated physiological arousal; between pleasant and unpleasant emotions (Winton et al., 1984); sadness and mirth (Averill, 1969); and sadness and fear (Tourangeau & Ellsworth, 1979).

On the other hand, there has been evidence to support Schachter's notion that emotions can be readily *misattributed* to arousal states that are actually unrelated. If you are unaware of the true source of the arousal you are experiencing, it is possible to identify another candidate as the cause, and then come to believe and act as if it were the actual cause.

> *In one study, male subjects who had just finished jogging were more attracted to a female (a confederate of the experimenter) than subjects who were not physically aroused. Similarly, subjects who had listened to an emotionally arousing tape recording were more attracted to the female confederate than those who heard an unarousing tape. The attraction occurred whether the tape involved positive arousal (a comedy routine) or negative arousal (a grisly description of a mob killing). (White et al., 1981)*

Apparently, physiological arousal caused by an exciting event or even just by physical exercise can be interpreted as sexual attraction or love depending on the social cues present at the time. **Figure 11.12** shows two possible sequences of emotion generation, depending on whether there are recognized emotional eliciting stimuli in the environment or not.

Emotion generation in everyday life

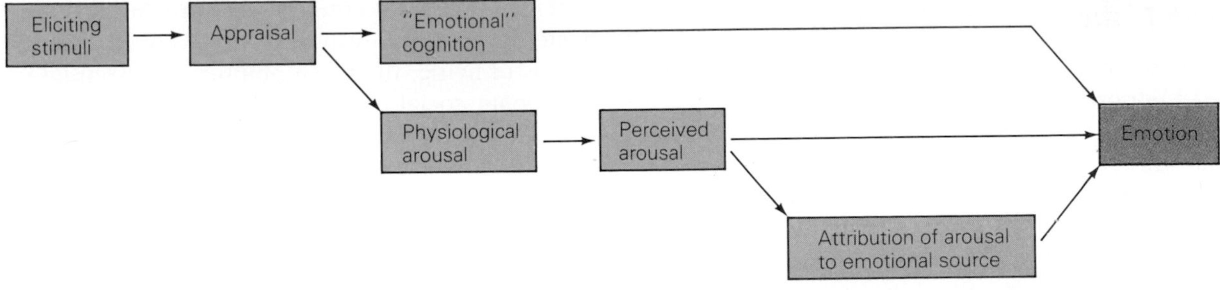

Emotion generation in the case of unexplained arousal

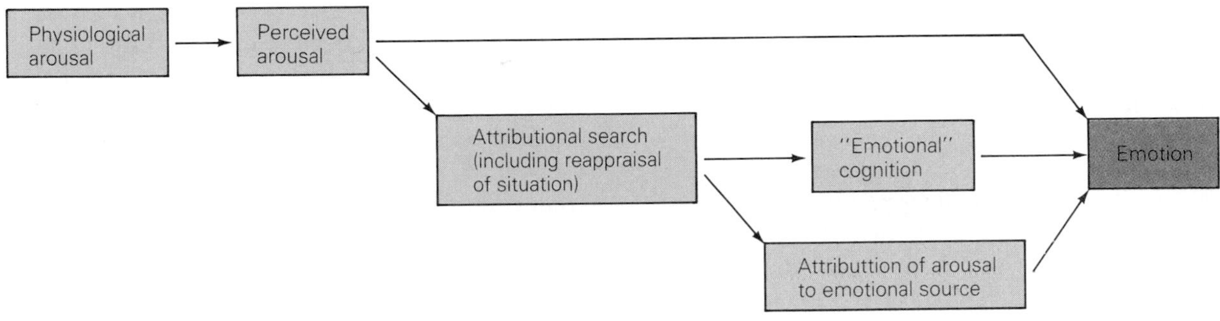

Figure 11.12 *Possible Sequences in Emotion Generation*

Emotion Without Awareness

The cognitive revolution is credited with replacing behaviorism's actor with a thinker, one whose head is filled with "cold cognitions." According to this view, liking or disliking comes only after we have analyzed the situation cognitively. Feelings and preferences follow cognitions and inferences.

An alternate view is that feelings and preferences are not necessarily derived from thoughts, but may be immediate reactions to stimuli, independent of cognitive analysis. We like this person and distrust that one, find her beautiful and him pretentious, enjoy chocolate and hate liver, are attracted to smiling faces and repulsed by frowns. These "gut reactions" give our experiences an immediate feeling tone that is part of their overall meaning and can be independent of our reasoning about them.

One of the first psychologists to emphasize the pervasive role of immediate, unlearned affective reactions was Sylvan Tomkins (1962, 1981). He points out that infants respond with fear to loud sounds or difficulties in breathing with no need for cognitive appraisal or prior learning. They seem "prewired" to respond to certain stimuli, with an emotional response general enough to fit a wide range of circumstances. As adults, humans are excited by sex—and also by solving difficult problems. Tomkins, in fact, sees emotions as the primary motivating forces for human actions: they amplify our innate needs and acquired motives by providing a sense of urgency. It is emotions that endow any activity with a sense of importance and transform indifference to desire. In this view, without emotion, nothing matters; with emotion, anything can matter.

Don't you have to discriminate, recognize, and interpret what a stimulus *is* before you can feel anything about it? Not according to research by Robert Zajonc (pronounced "Zy-onts").

> *In an extensive series of experiments, subjects were presented with a variety of stimuli such as foreign words, Japanese characters, sets of numbers, and strange faces. The stimuli were exposed on a tachistoscope, which flashed them briefly at exposure times below those necessary to recognize what they were. Subjects were still able to express a* preference *toward them without knowing why they liked some more than others.* Mere repeated exposure *to given stimuli increased their attractiveness: those stimuli which were repeated most often produced the strongest liking; yet this increased liking was shown to occur independently of recognition. (Zajonc, 1980)*

This line of research forces us to consider the extent to which our reactions, including simple emotional preferences, are influenced by nonvoluntary appraisals that are consciously inaccessible (Lazarus, 1984; Zajonc, 1984).

The Many Faces of Emotion

"Let's face it," what would you be without your face? Suppose your face were masked, bandaged, changed dramatically by plastic surgery, or rendered immobile by drugs or a stroke that afflicted the facial muscles. Thinking about what your face does for you reveals some of its significant social-emotional functions. First, a face enables us to recognize the unique identity of its possessor. It is the criterion we use to judge attractiveness, and those who are perceived as more attractive get more social rewards across many different situations (Hatfield & Sprecher, 1986). We "read" what others are feeling through the internal states they display in their facial expressions. But the face is more than merely a *read-out* display instrument. The human face is also a *read-in* emotion-activating instrument and a *read-across* social instrument. One's facial expressions can influence the personal experience of emotion—putting on a happy face can feed back to make us feel happier. The face also influences others in social settings by stimulating similar emotional reactions in them as they mimic facial expressions and then feel corresponding emotions. The "faceless mob," the masked terrorist, and the official wearing silver-reflecting eyeglasses are upsetting to us; in part, we are cut off from establishing any human connection with them because we don't have access to their faces.

If the function of emotion is to prepare and motivate a person to respond adaptively to the demands of living, then two abilities are essential to coordinate social behavior. We must be able to communicate effectively our emotional feelings to others and to determine the way others are feeling. If, for instance, we can efficiently signal to someone else that we are angry at him or her and therefore are likely to become aggressive, we can often get the person to stop doing whatever is annoying us—without resorting to overt aggression. Alternatively, if we can communicate to others that we feel sad and helpless, we increase our chances of getting the help that we need to make it through difficult situations we might not otherwise be able to handle.

It appears that one of the most effective modes of emotional communication is through emotional facial expression. *Ethologists* have provided evidence that nonhuman primates use facial expressions to establish and maintain dominance hierarchies, and psychologists have shown that facial expression is an important channel of communication for humans in a variety of social situations. For example, some new psychological research, which parallels that of the ethologists, suggests that the facial expressions displayed by political leaders in the United States help shape citizens' attitudes toward those leaders (see ***Close-up:*** *The Politics of Facial Expression* on p. 414).

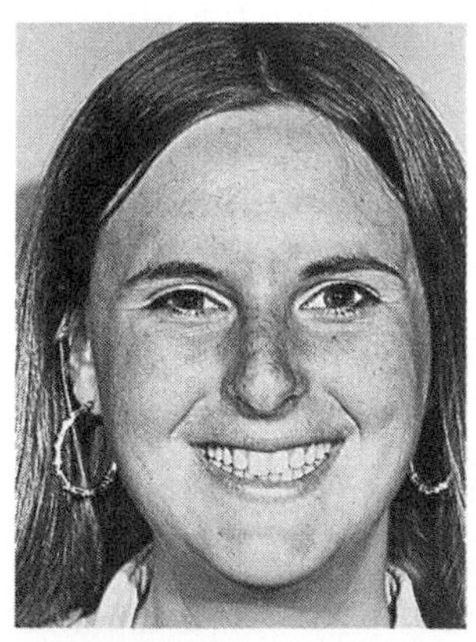
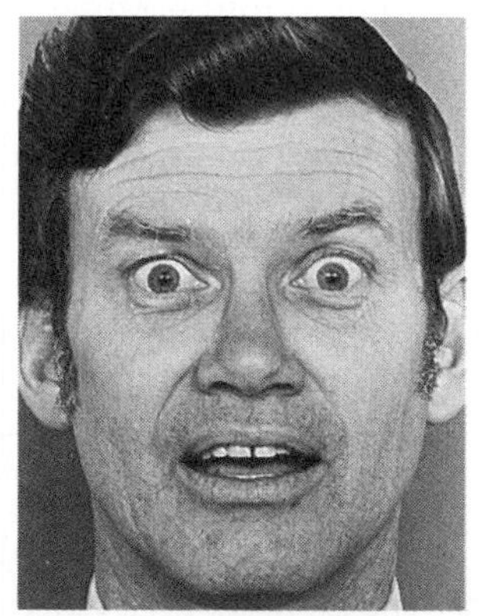
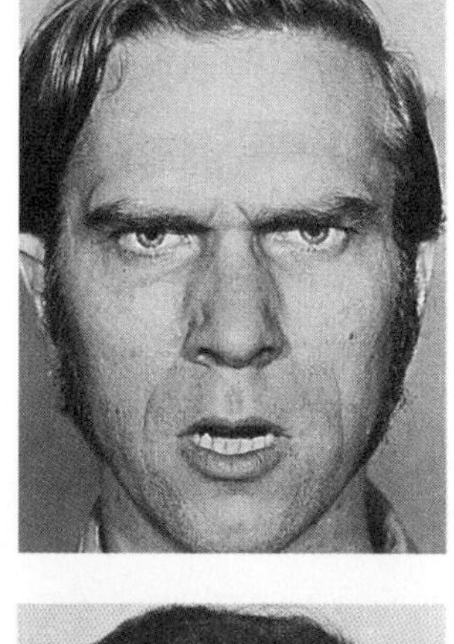
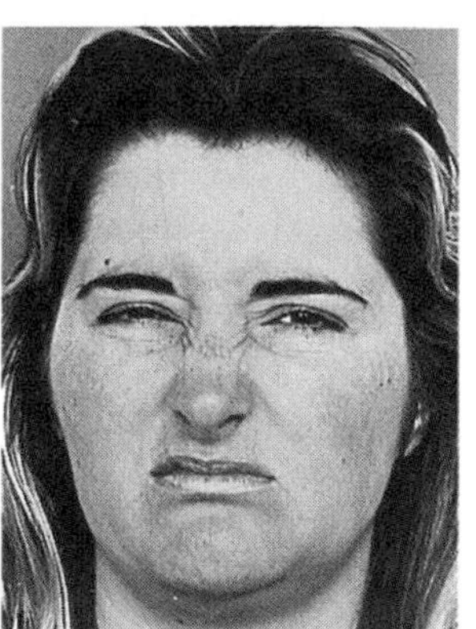
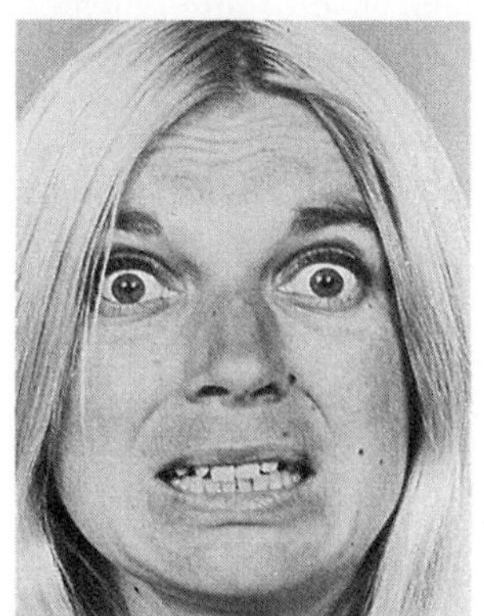
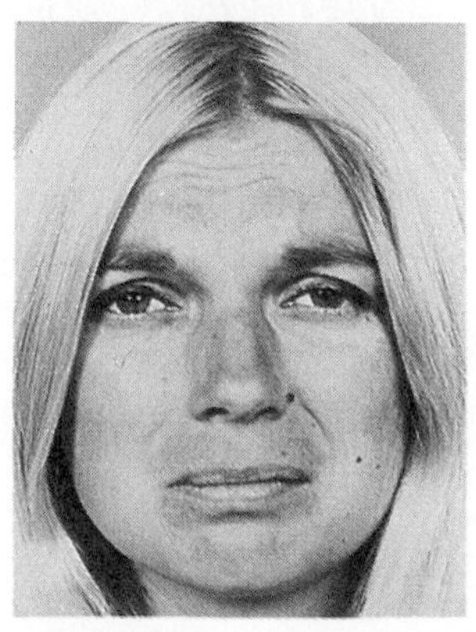

Can you tell from these people's faces what emotions they are probably experiencing?

Other innovative research on the development of emotional responsiveness in infants reveals that babies often look to their mothers' faces to help them interpret and respond to ambiguous situations. When an infant is in a *context of uncertainty*, emotional information provided by the mother's facial display is sought out by the baby and serves as a useful signal to guide the child's approach and avoidance behavior. This process of searching for emotional information as a behavioral regulator is termed **social referencing** (Klinnert et al., 1983). The effects of maternal emotional signaling on the reactions of year-old infants is clearly shown in a study that puts the child at the edge of a "visual cliff."

Mothers were trained to signal a particular emotion by changing only their facial muscle movements. When their child looked at them, they displayed one of the following emotions: fear, anger, sadness, interest, or joy. The dependent variable was whether the child approached and crossed the visual cliff or retreated from its apparent edge to a position of greater safety. The combined results from two studies with 69 mothers and infants are shown in ***Table 11.3.***

A mother's display of negative emotion "freezes" the child's approach and curiosity, leading most infants to retreat. (Perhaps this is the origin of the proverb "only fools rush in where angels—and mothers—fear to tread.) On the other hand, a mother's show of interest and joy are "go explore" signals that define the situation as safe. Sadness, though negative, carries no information relevant for approach and avoidance decisions, and thus has a weak effect on this behavior.

When the visual cliff illusion was changed so the child saw two shallow sides separated by a center strip, the situation was no longer ambiguous. What did they do then? They did not bother to reference the mother, and when they did and she displayed fear, they ignored her and crossed anyway! (Sorce et al., 1985)

Table 11.3 *Social Referencing: Percentage of Infants Crossing the Visual Cliff as Mother Displays a Given Emotion*

Emotion	Percentage Crossing the Visual Cliff
Fear	0
Anger	11
Sadness	33
Interest	73
Joy	74

(Sorce et al., 1985)

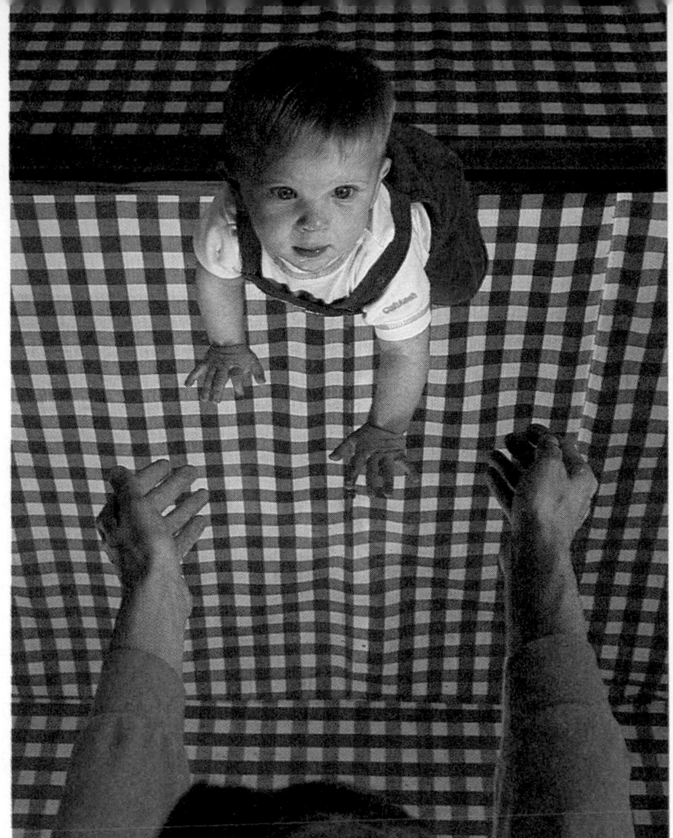

A trusting infant is coaxed across the optical illusion of an abyss. At the age of about one year, however, even though the baby will never fall, he or she will become wary.

Expressive Universals

It seems that facial expression is such a basic and important channel of communication that all people speak the same facial "language." You probably had little difficulty identifying which of the photographs on the previous page depicted happiness, and which depicted sadness, and so on. A number of theorists, beginning with Darwin, have proposed that these facial expressions are innate components of our evolutionary heritage, and, therefore, the same set of emotional expressions is universal to the human species. Today there is considerable evidence indicating that at least six expressions are recognized and produced worldwide, for the emotions of happiness, sadness, anger, fear, surprise, and disgust. Contempt has recently been added to bring the total to seven "universal" emotions (Ekman & Friesen, 1986).

This evidence comes from a number of cross-cultural studies in which people from a variety of cultures were asked to identify the emotions associated with a variety of expressions in standardized photographs (Ekman, 1972; Ekman et al., 1969; Izard, 1971). These studies have found that people all over the world are accurate in their ability to

Close-up *The Politics of Facial Expressions*

The importance of emotional facial expression in communicating our feelings and in coordinating social behavior may not be limited to direct interactions with the people around us in our day-to-day lives. Instead, there is mounting evidence that, through television exposure, the facial expressions displayed by politicians and newscasters may exert subtle, but important, influences in shaping voters' attitudes toward political leaders.

A research team of psychologists and political scientists conducted a series of studies investigating the effects of televised facial displays on viewer attitudes (Lanzetta et al., 1985). They found that the facial expressions that viewers saw politicians display during TV newscasts influenced their attitudes toward the politicians. This was most clear when the politicians were relatively unknown to the viewers and also when the viewers did not already have strong prior attitudes toward them.

In one study, three groups of college students were shown the same set of 20 news clips, taken from network broadcasts about President Reagan. Student attitudes toward Reagan both before and after viewing the clips were measured. In each clip a brief film of Reagan was shown in the background while the newscaster described the story. Ten of these news clips were identical for all three groups. However, the experimenters edited the remaining 10 clips so that each group saw President Reagan display a different type of expression. In the happy condition subjects saw Reagan display expressions of "happiness/reassurance," those in the neutral condition saw him display neutral expressions, and in the anger condition subjects saw Reagan display expressions of "anger/threat." These differences in emotional expression had no effect on the attitudes of those who had been either strongly for or against Reagan before the experiment. However, for those whose attitudes were relatively neutral to begin with, the President's facial displays of emotion changed their attitudes in predictable ways—particularly so for male students. Among those students with previously neutral attitudes, when they saw Reagan display happy/reassuring expressions, they subsequently reported more positive attitudes toward him, while those who saw Reagan display either neutral or angry/threatening expressions became more negative toward him.

In a second study the same researchers examined the neutral and happy expressions produced by all nine of the declared candidates in the 1984 presidential election. Since the study was conducted in January 1984, before any of the primaries, the subjects were not familiar with many of the candidates (such as Reuben Askew, Ernest Hollings, Alan Cranston, or Gary Hart), but were very familiar with others who had already gained national visibility: Walter Mondale, Jesse Jackson, and Ronald Reagan. One finding was that, at least in the news clips the researchers examined, the smiles of the candidates varied greatly in their display of expression. Both Reagan and Hart were rated by student judges as being extremely expressive, while Hollings, Cranston, and Mondale were judged as being rather unexpressive. The researchers also found that the expressivity of the unknown candidates had important effects on the viewers' attitudes toward them. In general, viewing the facial displays for a particular unknown candidate tended to polarize the viewers' attitudes toward the candidate along party lines. Democrats generally became more positive and Republicans more negative toward the candidates after seeing the news

identify the expressions associated with the seven listed emotions. Children after age 5 can also detect the emotion depicted in stimulus displays about as accurately as college students. In fact, in one study researchers tested the members of a preliterate culture in New Guinea (the Fore culture), who had almost no exposure to Westerners or to Western culture prior to this experiment (Ekman & Friesen, 1971). They found that, although the Fore people had difficulty distinguishing between expressions of fear and surprise, they could identify the other emotional expressions quite well in these photos of Caucasian faces.

The same investigators asked other members of this culture (who had not participated in the first study) to model the expressions that they used to

clips. This divergent pattern might have been because of the effect that viewing the clips had on reminding viewers of their political allegiance.

Curiously, this polarization was weakest for Senator Hart, the most expressive of the unknown candidates. Instead, more people reported stronger positive attitudes toward Hart after viewing his film clips than they had reported toward any of the other unknowns. The researchers suggest that Hart's expressive skills may have contributed to his ability to become a major contender during the early part of the 1984 campaign. Similarly, they suggest that Reagan's superb expressive skills, developed during his acting career, may have contributed to his extreme popularity as President. Indeed, his expressive style continued to serve him well later on as he eluded much of the stigma associated with the Iran-Contra scandal that rocked his administration.

Following up on this research, a second group of investigators have found that the facial expressions displayed by newscasters while talking on TV about politicians also seem to influence our attitudes and even our vote for them (Mullin et al., 1986). First, the newscasts of all three major networks were examined from the last eight days of the election campaign. The researchers were looking for evidence of expressive biases on the part of any of the anchormen (Peter Jennings on ABC; Dan Rather on CBS; and Tom Brokaw on NBC) while they were reporting on Ronald Reagan and his Democratic opponent, Walter Mondale. There was no evidence of bias for either Dan Rather or Tom Brokaw, who wore equally pleasant expressions when talking about either Reagan or Mondale. However, Peter Jennings of ABC did display a strong positive expressive bias toward Ronald Reagan. His facial expressions were noticeably more pleasant when he talked about Reagan than when he talked about either Mondale or other news topics. The effect of the "Jennings' smile" was assessed several months after the election when the investigators conducted a small survey in several parts of the country. They asked randomly chosen voters which network they usually watched for news, and who they had voted for in the election. They found that people who regularly watched the news on ABC were even more likely to have voted for Reagan than were the regular viewers of either NBC or CBS. Although there are many possible explanations for this finding, the investigators think that the most likely one is that Peter Jennings' facial bias influenced the voters' attitudes and votes. They dismiss the alternative explanation that pro-Reagan voters selectively chose to watch ABC news because of a general pro-Reagan bias on that network. A separate study of the informational content of the news on all three networks indicates that the stories run by ABC were less pro-Reagan than those run on either CBS or NBC (Clancey & Robinson, 1985; Robinson, 1985).

This line of research represents the start of inquiries into the importance of emotional facial expressions in our everyday social life. Taken together, this body of data indicates that such facial expressions are an important source of social information which influences our behaviors and attitudes in important ways—often hitting us below the belt of conscious awareness.

communicate each of the first six emotions noted before. When American college students viewed videotapes of these, they were able to identify accurately most of the emotions—with two exceptions. Not surprisingly the Americans had difficulty distinguishing between the Fore poses of fear and surprise, the same emotions that the Fore had confused in the Western poses.

The photos you were asked to identify on page 412 represent clear examples of each of the seven universally recognized facial expressions. **Table 11.4** indicates the muscle movements that many theorists and researchers agree are important in the expressions of the seven emotions. We should hasten to note that these are not necessarily the only components of these expressions. Instead, they are

Table 11.4 *Important Components of Universally Recognized Facial Expressions*

	Raised Eyebrows	Lowered Eyebrows (Eyebrow Frown)	Upper Eyelid	Lower Eyelid	Corners of Mouth	Open Mouth	Raised Upper Lip	Lip Corner Raised, Tightened on one side
Happiness				tensed	raised			
Surprise	X		raised			X		
Anger		X	raised	tensed				
Disgust				tensed			X	
Fear	X	X	raised			X		
Sadness	X	X			lowered			
Contempt								X

the ones for which there is general agreement. Thus, for example, the expression of happiness consists of raised mouth corners (a smile) and tightened lower eyelids; the expression of surprise consists of raised eyebrows, raised upper eyelids to widen the eyes, and an open mouth; and the expression of fear is very much like the expression of surprise, except that, in addition to being raised, the eyebrows are pulled together and lowered back down slightly into an eyebrow frown (the similarity between the surprise and fear expressions might explain why the Fore had such trouble discriminating between these two expressions.

One thing to notice about these expressions is that, in general, the emotions are communicated through the entire *pattern of muscle activity* on the face, rather than by the presence or absence of any single muscle movement. Thus, anger is communicated by the combination of lowered eyebrows, raised upper eyelids, and tensed lower eyelids, and no single one of these movements can be used in isolation to identify the expression as one of anger. For instance, the lowered eyebrows, which are probably the most salient feature of the angry expression, are also present in the expressions of fear and sadness (see Smith, 1986).

Facial Lying

Although emotional facial expression is an important channel of communication that provides much information about the way a person is interpreting and responding to his or her circumstances, it is important to realize that facial expressions are not infallible sources of information. Whenever we experience a particular emotion there appears to be a strong tendency to express the emotion facially. However, we have considerable ability to inhibit or alter our spontaneous expressions. Often we may not want to show others the way we are feeling, and, in such cases, we can usually inhibit the spontaneous expression and pose a different one to "mask" our true feelings. It appears that we often control our emotional expressions in order to obey personal or cultural **display rules** that state the *conditions* under which it is socially *appropriate* to display certain emotions (Averill, 1976; Ekman, 1972). Display rules help regulate the where, when, what kind, how long, and how strong of our emotional displays.

These display rules vary greatly from culture to culture. Differences in display rules across cultures explain why it sometimes appears that members of different cultures use different facial expressions to communicate the same emotions or react differently to what seems to be the same eliciting circumstances, such as winning, losing, grieving, or receiving gifts. Although the *objective* circumstances that elicit a given emotion vary across cultures and between individuals within a culture, the *subjective meanings* or interpretations derived from those circumstances are the common, universal elicitors of the emotion. One prevalent (and sexist) display rule in our culture is that "big boys don't cry." It is generally considered inappropriate in our culture for males past a certain (young) age to openly display feelings of sadness, but it is often expected for females of any age to do so.

Because of our ability to exert considerable (but not absolute) voluntary control over our facial expressions, it is often the case that our face will not express our "true feelings." This fact does not necessarily reduce the usefulness of facial expression as a channel of communication. In fact, the ability to control our expressions may endow facial activity with the flexibility it needs to facilitate complex social behavior—for instance, to hide our "true" angry feelings while our seemingly friendly face tells a "little white lie" (see Ekman, 1985).

Facial Efference

We have seen how Darwin's approach stressed the adaptive value of emotions and led to the generally accepted view that facial expressions *follow* the internal experience of emotions. These expressions furnish feedback about what was just being felt. A different view emphasizes *anatomy* over adaptiveness of emotions. It proposes that facial expressions are not the last link in the emotional process, but rather the *first* link in a chain of biological reactions that result in an emotional experience. Changes in the 80 muscles laced across the face alter the blood flow to the brain (the critical vascular change), thereby affecting brain temperature and the release of neurotransmitters. Depending on the inhibition or facilitation of certain kinds of brain transmitters, different emotions will be aroused. According to this vascular theory of *emotional efference,* emotional facial movements serve a physiological function of restoring equilibrium of the vascular system of the brain by adding or draining blood from it. (This theory was first advanced by a turn-of-the-century physician, Israel Waynbaum, and recently updated by psychologist Robert Zajonc, 1985a, 1985b). Whether this view supplements the evolutionary one of the adaptive, communicative side of expression awaits more empirical data (see criticisms by Fridlund & Gilbert, 1985; Izard, 1985).

Although our faces certainly contribute to making us identifiably different from one another, what are the less obvious and "cheeky" ways in which individuals establish their uniqueness and put a distinctive stamp on their behavior? Personality does it, as we will see in the next two chapters.

Summary

- Motivation is a general term for the process of initiating, directing, and sustaining physical or psychological activities. It includes mechanisms involved in preferences, vigor of responses, and persistence of organized patterns of action toward relevant goals.
- Motivation is an intervening variable. It can be induced by physiological and/or psychological variables and may lead to physiological responses as well as conscious and nonconscious psychological ones.
- The strength of motivation is measured using index variables such as activity level, rate and amount of learning, resistance of a response to extinction, preferences, and consummatory behavior. Motivation has been manipulated in research by deprivation and by stimulation.
- According to instinct theory, motivation is mechanistic and inborn. Instinct theory as an explanation for human behavior was popular for a time, but provided circular explanations and was replaced by behaviorism's emphasis on learning and environmental determinants of behavior. Contemporary psychologists view instincts as fixed action patterns, triggered by specific releaser stimuli without prior learning.
- Drive theory related motivation to learning. According to drive theory, the tension of primary or secondary drives leads to action, including new responses. Successful responses, reinforced by tension reduction, are learned and retained. Learning is seen as requiring motivation, and tension reduction as explaining learning of new habits.
- Contrary to the assumptions of drive theory, organisms choose many activities that increase tension rather than reduce it, apparently preferring some optimal level of arousal rather than none at all.
- Humanistic approaches to motivation postulate a hierarchy of innate human needs. Only as lower biological needs are met will an individual be motivated by higher psychological ones. In deficiency motivation, people seek to restore equilibrium; in growth motivation, they seek to go beyond present accomplishments to greater fulfillment of their potential—to become self-actualized.
- Cognitive theorists are demonstrating the importance of our interpretations on motivation. What we believe about ourselves and the situation and expect the outcome of our action to be is as important as the external stimulus-based reality in determining the direction and strength of our motivation.
- According to the dual hypothalamic theory of hunger, starting and stopping eating are both controlled by centers in the hypothalamus. Although understanding is still incomplete, it is now recognized that many physical and psychological processes, both innate and learned, play a role in eating and its inhibition. Food intake and body weight are regulated according to a "set point," measured by the fat stored in specialized fat cells.
- Sexual activity in lower animals is controlled hormonally and follows stereotyped, genetically determined patterns consistent for each species but widely variable among species.

- In humans, sexual arousal, sexual behavior, and sexual satisfaction are quite variable and subject to learning. Though only touch is an unconditioned stimulus for sexual arousal, anything associated with sexual arousal through experience can become a conditioned stimulus for arousal. Most human sexual problems are the result of psychological, rather than physiological, factors.
- We learn "sexual scripts" that guide our sexual behavior and our expectations of others. Discrepancies in partners' sexual scripts can lead to misunderstanding and frustration.
- Achievement motivation is learned; for many people, the need to achieve energizes and directs behavior. The need for achievement has been studied through people's fantasies in response to ambiguous pictures.
- Whether they are responsible for outcomes and whether that condition is a stable one influence people's attributions of their successes or failures, their emotional reactions, and their subsequent motivation. With a perception of self-efficacy, performance and coping patterns are more effective.
- Rewards given for activities we enjoy may lessen our intrinsic interest and motivation for that activity when the extrinsic rewards are no longer available.
- Motivation is also affected by a person's time perspective, the extent to which there is a learned cognitive bias toward being future-oriented instead of present- or past-oriented.
- Two views of human nature that are the basis for theories of work motivation are Theory X and Theory Y. According to Theory X, people are motivated to work solely by money; Theory Y states that people are motivated by work that is challenging. Organizational psychologists have proposed theories of work motivation based on need, cognitive approaches, and goal-setting and job design.
- An emotion is a complex pattern of changes including physiological arousal, feelings, cognitive processes, and behavioral reactions made in response to a situation perceived as personally significant.
- Conflict theorists argued that emotions served no purpose; Darwin and contemporary theorists believe that emotions are necessary for survival because they motivate organisms to cope adaptively with the environment.
- The chain of events involved in an emotional response include the stimuli that arouse emotions, the physiological reactions to external and internal stimuli, and the thoughts or cognitions that accompany these reactions.
- Theories of emotion have included: (a) the James-Lange theory, that behavioral reactions precede the other aspects of emotional response; (b) Lazarus' theory that cognitive appraisal of a situation comes first, determining whether we will feel emotion and if so, which one; (c) the two-factor theory, that emotion results when unexplained physiological arousal is given meaning because of cues in the current social situation; (d) the theory that affective preferences and feelings may precede cognitive appraisal or even recognition of a stimulus.
- Seven universal emotional facial expressions are happiness, sadness, anger, fear, surprise, disgust, and contempt. Emotional facial expression allows us to communicate emotional feelings to others; others can use this information as an indicator of the way to act in uncertain or ambiguous situations. We also have the ability to alter our expressions of emotion. Socially based display rules specify the conditions under which it is appropriate to display certain emotions.

12

Understanding Human Personality

Dear Dad,

Please accept my apologies for not writing earlier as promised, but I have spent this first week at college trying to undo the mismatch of the century. I cannot imagine that there was any intelligent rationale for a roommate assignment that stuck me with a 1960's flower child—who, at this very moment, is deafening me with his electronic guitar rock "music" (if you'll pardon my liberal use of that once revered term). None of my cogent arguments were able to sway the bureaucratic mentalities that run the housing office to separate us. Can you imagine—he has dyed blond-black hair down to his shoulders, triple earrings in one ear, and jeans with more holes than Swiss cheese? "The Weird One" certainly stands out in the freshman dorm, which, fortunately, is fairly conservative in dress and politics. He hasn't brought a single book; he put his desk out in the hall to make room for his hi-fi equipment; he doesn't take any notes in our Western Civ class, and he has already had a party for our entire floor. I'm amazed that he somehow managed to get an A on the first quiz; he certainly doesn't follow your advice to resist temptations when there is work to be done. *I* agree with you when you say that gratification delayed is gratification enjoyed when the time is ripe.

Sorry to complain, but I just do not see how I will endure this impossible situation for a whole term, let alone the year. Write soon.

With affection,

Timothy

Timothy

Hi there, parental unit 1. Good to hear from you. Bad connection? Nah, I've got a cold. Of course it's me, Adam, your son; you want maybe Burt Reynolds or one of those other studs you drool over when parental unit 2 isn't looking? Did I promise to call last week? Wow, sorry, blew it off because of the heavy stuff coming down in this dorm room 101—great coincidence with Orwell's ultimate torture chamber in *1984,* is it not? Now feature this, I got sentenced to one year of hard-headed labor with a top gun from an Eastern military school. The dude is so straight he's got a laser beam where his spine should be. He says "sir" more often than an English butler working for Prince Charlie. It's been one week, 148 hours, on the rack of Timmy's predictable prattle. How could they have let anyone so loyal to the cause of consistency out from his job as mass executioner for the Republican National Youth for Hitler? No, honestly, ma, he is too much to bear without breaking up constantly. I push his buttons the wrong way because I work hard to be different and work soft in class and seem to be able to handle it. But what really gets Timmy is that he's so predictable I can already finish most of his sentences. My goal is to be able to finish them all by the end of the term. Can you believe he really says, in a pensive tone, "Yes, sir, there's more than . . ." and I join the chorus, "one way to skin a cat." He gets angry and says "Damn Adam," and I get nauseous thinking about all the ways Timmy might come up with for skinning cats. Gotta go, practice time. What's that? Why were we put together? Simple, on our applications we were the only two in the entire dorm who

admitted to smoking, so they isolated us from the nonsmokers. Timmy, of course, smokes only cigarettes, but I'm sure he'll give in to peer pressure to clean up his act. I remain steadfast in the pursuit of higher pleasure in this all-too-serious institution of higher learning. Stay cool, huh. Love ya. Call Sunday, but not before noon, okay?

From these brief glimpses of this "odd couple" what impressions have you drawn about each of the students? How would you summarize what is distinctive about each one? On what dimensions of personality do Adam and Tim seem to differ most? Is it possible for you to visualize the way they look and sound? What does each do to maintain his self-image? Do you imagine that it would be possible to predict the way one or the other might behave in some future situation? Can you think of situations where it might be more difficult to predict their behavior with confidence? Which one do you like most, are more similar to in important ways? Or are you uniquely different from both of them . . . and all others?

Personality psychologists ask these kinds of questions about the distinctiveness, uniqueness, and consistency of personality across situations. They, like you, are curious to discover what there is about individuals that makes them distinctive from others in the same situation. It is not just that people look different or respond differently to a given stimulus; there also seems to be a subjective, private aspect that gives coherence and order to their behavior. Taken together, these special features, unique aspects, and orderly and consistent properties of individuals are what we usually mean by *personality*.

If psychologists studied *you*, how might their portrait of your personality be similar to and different from their portrait of your roommate or best friend? Most of us like to think of ourselves as unique, but if so, how so?

Up to this point in our psychological journey we have seen how scientific investigations focus on specific processes that are similar in all of us, such as nerve signal transmission, perception, conditioning, and decision making. We have also been aware that the goal in much of this research is to discover general laws of behavior that explain why different individuals in the same stimulus situation react alike.

In this chapter a different perspective on psychology is presented, one that studies the whole person as the sum of those separate processes of feelings, thoughts, and actions. We will begin by examining the major issues and strategies in the psychological study of personality. Then we will survey the major theories of personality, each of which attempts to provide the "best" or "right" approach to understanding human nature.

Interest in personality is obviously not limited to psychologists. Philosophers, theologians, dramatists, and novelists have long sought to understand how personality and character are formed, maintained, or transformed. The special province of the psychologist, however, is the *measurement* of personality. Only a few years after Wundt established his psychological laboratory the English scientist Francis Galton began the first scientific study of the way individuals differ. Galton staked out the claim for personality measurement when he wrote: "The character which shapes our conduct is a definite and durable 'something,' and therefore . . . it is reasonable to attempt to measure it" (1884, p. 179). The next chapter deals with assessment of individuals, especially their intelligence and personality.

Studying Personality

In popular usage, the word *personality* is something akin to *attractiveness, charm,* or *charisma.* "She may not be pretty, but she has a nice personality." "Be careful, he has a very forceful personality." Personality is a quality movie stars and those politicians we like have a lot of, while the rest of us must make do with less.

Even as a child, you had probably developed and put to use your own system of appraising personality. You tried to determine who in your class would be friend or foe; you worked out techniques for dealing with your parents or particular teachers, and you tried to understand your own strengths and weaknesses. Your judgments were, in fact, primitive personality assessments. They were based largely on intuition and limited observations; such naive judgments can often be accurate; they may also be open to many sources of error.

By now you have become a full-fledged personality theorist. Whether you are aware of it, you have a set of ideas about your own personality and about the personalities of others with whom you interact. Like the rest of us, you carry around an "implicit personality theory" that helps you explain and predict people's behavior, and maybe even control your own at times. We will see shortly how your "naive" theory differs from the formal theories of professional psychologists. As we present different theories, be sensitive to the points of agreement and disagreement between your implicit theory and those of formal personality theorists.

Children develop their own styles of assessing the personalities of others.

The field of **personality psychology** puts the "person" back into psychology by attempting to integrate all aspects of an individual's functioning. This requires building upon the accumulated knowledge of all the areas of psychology we have studied so far plus that of social psychology, which includes interpersonal and group processes. Personality psychology also goes beyond an interest in the normally functioning individual. It provides the research and theoretical foundation for understanding personal problems and pathologies of body, mind, and behavior (chapters 14 and 15), as well as a basis for therapeutic approaches to change personality (chapter 16).

Psychologists give a variety of definitions for personality, but common to all of them are concepts of *uniqueness* and *characteristic behavior.* Simply put, **personality** is what characterizes an individual. It includes the *unique psychological qualities of an individual that influence a variety of characteristic behavior patterns* (both overt and covert) *across different situations* and *over time* (see, too, **Table 12.1** for additional terms used in personality descriptions). Although it is not clear just how consistent individuals *really* are, most personality theorists continue to expect considerable consistency. What makes people behave in characteristic ways as unique individuals is looked on as *the* issue to be studied.

Yet this does not mean that psychologists working in personality are not interested in finding general laws. As in other areas of psychology, many personality theorists believe that there are principles that can be applied to all human beings, but think it is vital for theorists to account for *differences* among people too. As we will see, many theories have been developed that attempt to accomplish this dual aim.

Strategies for Studying Personality

Just what *does* characterize an individual? Without really thinking about it, we are able to recognize our friends, even if we have not seen them for some time. If we know people well enough, we are even able to recognize them from someone else's account of their behavior. ("Oh, that must have been Jim. He always does things like that.") How are we able to do it? One key would seem to lie in *consistency.* We are able to recognize individuals, and to characterize them to others, by the ways they are consistent—across different situations and over time. Even if they are consistently unpredictable, that is something we can say about them that distinguishes them from those who fit the predictable mold—like Timmy in our *Opening Case.* A second important component of an individual's personality is *distinctiveness,* the unique combination of traits, beliefs, and experience that makes each person different from others.

But the matter is more complex. Try the following test. Think about two people who are important in your life—one you like and one you do not like. Is either one primarily "good" (strong, kind, understanding) or primarily "bad" (weak, cruel, inconsiderate)? Or does it *depend on the situation?* Now apply those questions to yourself.

Most often, this simple demonstration shows that we see other people we know well as consistently good or bad regardless of the situation, while we see ourselves as more influenced by circumstances and, thus, more variable. This paradox highlights our tendency to attribute consistency to the behavior of others, formulating consistent patterns of responses and traits when we characterize them.

This tendency to perceive consistency in other people is an extension of a more general tendency to perceive consistency in all events, part of a general process of organizing our world to make it coherent, orderly, and more readily predictable. Thus we must question whether the consistency we perceive in people, around which personality trait theories are organized, actually exists in the people we observe or only in our minds.

Over the years, personality theorists have differed markedly in the ways they have described and accounted for this consistency. In fact, as we shall see, many researchers today are finding that the notion of consistency in personality across different situations and over time may not be as simple as had been thought. When we study human behavior we observe *both* personal consistency and variability because of situational influences. Theories and research must indicate when and how past life circumstances influence the personal characteristics people bring to those situations, as well as how personality affects reactions to those situations, and how present situational variables influence individual differences in reactions.

Some psychologists who use the *case study method* to identify a person's unique characteristics follow an **idiographic approach.** In this approach, each trait is viewed as unique in each personality because it functions differently, depending on the overall pattern of traits. For example, if Jeremy is discriminating, bold, and demanding, while John is discriminating, careful, and sensitive, then

Table 12.1 *Terms Used in Personality Descriptions*

Term	Definition	Example
Temperament	Biologically-based characteristic manner of reacting, evident at or soon after birth, notably in emotionality and activity level.	Some newborns are excitable and active; others in the same nursery (or from different cultures) show a calm and passive temperament.
Trait	A constant, persistent, and specific way of behaving that can be measured along a continuum and is used both to characterize individuals and to predict their future behavior.	A person who donates to charity, gives money to friends in need, and gives up time for a worthy cause could be said to be high on the trait of "generosity."
Type	A distinct category to which people showing a particular pattern of traits can be assigned.	"Type-A" people are prone to coronary problems because of their characteristic way of dealing with life challenges.
Disposition	A tendency or set, within an individual, to react to a given situation in a characteristic way; synonymous with *trait* in discussions of dispositional vs. situational explanations of behavior.	A person who is ready with a smile, kind word, or sympathetic ear is said to have a "friendly disposition."
Character	Nearly the same as *personality* when used to refer to the individual's total pattern of regularly occurring behavior. When used in evaluation of the *quality* of someone's personality, implies judgment of the person's morals and values along with other attributes.	Letters of recommendation usually refer to the person's trustworthy or emotionally stable character.
Character Types	Used in some theories to designate identifiable, adult patterns of behavior organized around certain themes and formed early in life.	Freud's oral and anal character types.
State	A subjective, consciously perceived set of feelings of a certain kind, accompanied by autonomic nervous system arousal, or by cognitive processes. A state is more transitory than a trait.	Not being prepared for an exam will induce a state of worrying; always being upset at exams is a sign of the trait of test anxiety.
Mood	An extended emotional state that may dominate one's outlook and appearance for a period of time.	Success brings on euphoria, failure puts us in a depressed or irritable mood.
Habit	A learned mode of behaving that is relatively fixed and reliably occurs in certain situations.	A prize-fighter may have the *habit* of making the sign of the cross before each round.
Attitude	A learned tendency to evaluate classes of objects or people favorably or unfavorably based on one's beliefs and feelings.	Authoritarian people often hold prejudiced attitudes toward minority groups.
Values	Something the individual learns to believe is important, worthwhile to have; a value can be a principle to live by or something to achieve or maintain.	For authoritarian personality types, order and power are important values.

(Based on Corsini, 1977)

"being discriminating" would be quite a different trait in the two personalities. When traits are averaged across people to get group scores or correlations, this uniqueness is lost.

The contrasting **nomothetic approach** assumes that there is an underlying basic structure to personality provided by universal trait dimensions common to everyone. In this view, individuals differ only *in the degree* to which they possess personality traits. Researchers using a nomothetic approach try to establish universal, lawful relationships among different aspects of personality functioning, such as traits, by means of the *correlational method.*

Theories About Personality

Theories of personality are hypothetical statements about the structure and functioning of individual personalities. They help us achieve two of the major goals of psychology: (a) *understanding* different aspects of personality—its origins, correlates, and consequences, and (b) *predicting* behavior based on knowing something about personality. Different theories make different predictions about the way people will behave under certain conditions.

Before we examine a number of major theoretical approaches, it is well to ask why we need so many different (often competing) theories. The answer is like the one given in chapter 1 for the variety of alternate general conceptual models. Different theorists approach the complexity of human nature and the functioning of mind and behavior from different starting points, using different levels of analysis, while seeing some variables and processes as more important than other investigators believe them to be. Some deal with specific traits and behaviors, while others deal with more general dispositions. Some are more concerned with what a person *is,* while others place more emphasis on how he or she has changed or may develop in the future. Some theories developed from observing people with psychological problems, while others were based on observations of normal people in normal circumstances. Thus, each theory approaches the subject from a different orientation. Each can teach us something about personality, and together they can teach us even more about human nature.

The many current theoretical approaches to understanding personality can be grouped into five categories: type and trait theories, psychodynamic theories, humanistic theories, learning theories, and cognitive theories.

Type and Trait Theories

Labeling and classifying the many personality characteristics we observe can help us organize the diversity of human behavior. However, simplicity in the task is not guaranteed! One dictionary search found 18,000 adjectives in the English language to describe personality traits.

Two of the oldest approaches to describing personality involve describing people as belonging to a limited number of types or possessing particular traits that all people are assumed to have in varying degrees. Let's examine what each conception contributes to our understanding of personality.

Categorizing by Types

Do you ever classify the people in your life according to their college class, academic major, sex, race, or fraternity or sorority affiliation? Some personality theorists group people according to their personality types, which are distinct patterns of personality characteristics. In a typological approach, people are assigned to categories on the basis of particular similarities. These categories do not overlap: if a person is assigned to one category—say, according to a type of physique, occupation, or sex—he or she is not in any other categories within that type. That is, personality types are all-or-none phenomena and not a matter of degree.

Most personality typologies are designed to specify a relationship between a simple, highly visible or easily determined characteristic and some behaviors that can be expected: if fat, then jolly; if an engineer, then conservative; if female, then sympathetic; and so it goes. You can appreciate why such systems have traditionally had much popular appeal.

One of the earliest type theories was proposed in the fifth century B.C. by Hippocrates. He theorized that the body contained four basic fluids or *humors,* each associated with a particular *temperament.* Each individual's personality depended on which one of these humors was predominant. Hippocrates' pairing of body humors with personality temperaments was the following:

- Blood—Sanguine temperament, cheerful and active
- Phlegm—Phlegmatic temperament, apathetic and sluggish
- Black bile—melancholy temperament, sad and brooding
- Yellow bile—choleric temperament, irritable and excitable

An interesting, popular type theory of personality was one advanced by an American physician, William Sheldon (1942), who related physique to temperament. He assigned people to categories based on their **somatotypes,** or body builds: **endomorphic** (fat, soft, round), **mesomorphic** (muscular, rectangular, strong), or **ectomorphic** (thin, long, fragile). The typology specified relationships between the physiques (or bodily constitutional types) and particular personality traits, activities, and preferences.

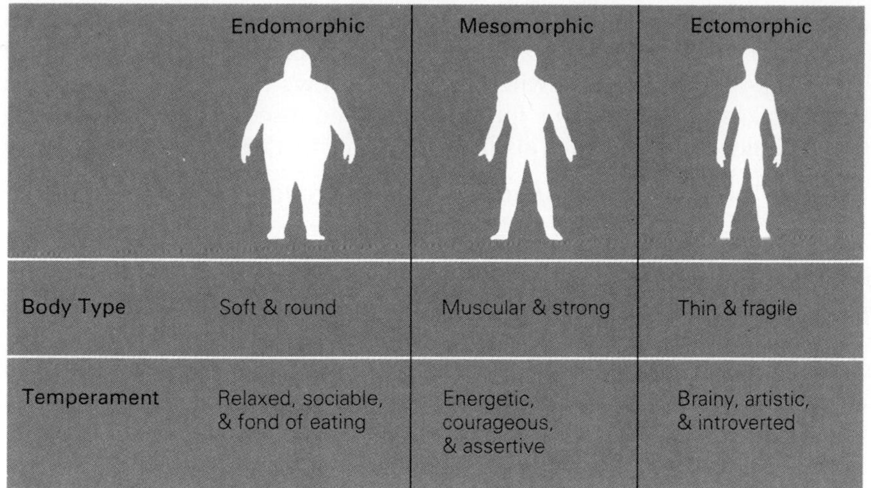

Endomorphic
Mesomorphic
Ectomorphic
Body Type
Soft & round
Muscular & strong
Thin & fragile
Temperament
Relaxed, sociable, & fond of eating
Energetic, courageous, & assertive
Brainy, artistic, & introverted

Figure 12.1 *Sheldon's Somatotype Theory*
Sheldon's (1942) theory of personality and body types is intriguing, if unsubstantiated.

What would you expect people with these body builds to be like? You might guess that endomorphs would be relaxed, fond of eating, sociable, and gut-oriented. Mesomorphs would be physical people, filled with energy, courage, and assertive tendencies. Ectomorphs would be brainy, artistic, and introverted; they would think about life rather than consuming it or acting upon it (see **Figure 12.1**).

Though appealing in its simplicity, Sheldon's typology has proven to be of little value in predicting an individual's behavior from his or her somatotype—once the stereotypes that bias most people's expectations are eliminated (Tyler, 1965). In addition, people come in many different shapes, and they cannot be assigned readily to one of Sheldon's pure somatotypes.

An updated version of typing people according to their biology can be seen in the use of *blood-typing* to reveal personality. By correlating responses to self-report questionnaires and surveys with blood types (O, A, B, and AB), Japanese researcher Toshitaka Nomi claims there are strong links between the type of blood you have and the type of person you are. From data on a large Japanese sample, Nomi has categorized people according to the following types:

Type A (40 percent): industrious, peace-loving, detail-oriented, and image conscious

Type B (30 percent): creative and individualistic

Type O (30 percent): aggressive and realistic

Type AB (10 percent): moody and two-faced

A better supported type approach attempts to reduce the complexity of personality to a few major categories. H. J. Eysenck (1970, 1975) suggested that the two major dimensions of personality are *introversion-extraversion* and *stability-instability* (or *''neuroticism''*). Extraverts are sociable, outgoing, active, impulsive, ''tough-minded'' people. Introverts are their psychological opposites–''tender-minded,'' withdrawn, passive, cautious, and reflective.

Eysenck's theory is based on a large amount of personality test data. Although the data show that people have many traits, the traits cluster into four categories that represent the smallest number of basic personality types according to this view. While most people fall at intermediate points within each of the four quadrants of Eysenck's personality circle (shown in **Figure 12.2**), it is the extremes that distinguish the types. When a person is high on extraversion and also on instability points,

Figure 12.2 *The Four Quadrants of Eysenck's Personality Circle*

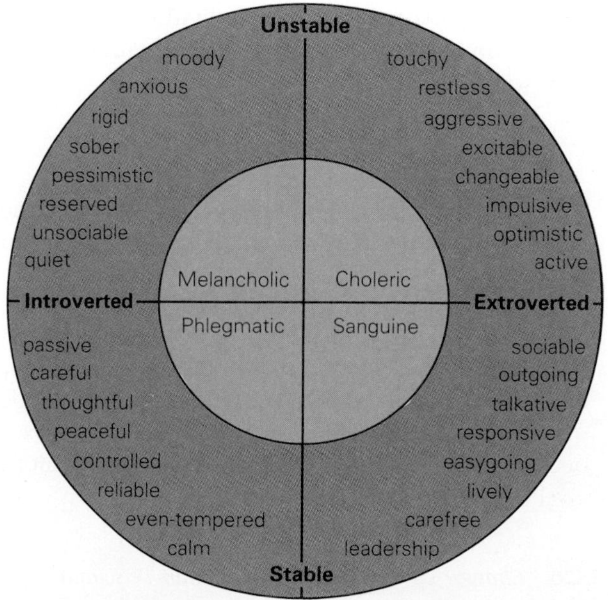

criminality is a possible life-style. Individuals diagnosed as *neurotic,* on the other hand, are people who combine introversion with instability.

Eysenck has used standard behavioral tests to study the way extraverts, as a group, differ from introverts. One finding shows introverts as having lower thresholds for pain than extraverts. Introverts also learn faster than extraverts when unconditioned stimuli are weak or reinforcement is partial rather than continuous; associations learned in the presence of stimuli that create low levels of arousal are better recalled immediately than those learned when arousal is high. In contrast extraverts perform better when they are more aroused and also seem to need more external arousal to maintain their performance than do the self-stimulating introverts (Howarth & Eysenck, 1968).

As brain researchers and psychiatrists begin to study the possible physiological bases for some major personality differences, they are uncovering some intriguing links. It appears from one current study that extraverts have higher levels of the brain chemical *dopamine* than more introverted people (King et al., 1986).

Animal studies had already suggested that dopamine in certain areas of the brain may help to regulate reward-seeking behavior, such as excitement that accompanies food-seeking in hungry animals (see King, 1986). The researchers hypothesized—and found—high levels of dopamine activity in similar brain regions of human extraverts since extraverts are more energetic and excitable than introverts. Whether the level of dopamine is higher and "causes" extraverted behavior or is higher as a consequence of the more energetic behavior of extraverts is not known from this correlational study of the neurochemistry of temperament. The role of genetic factors in the development of different temperments is also being studied as significant in human personality and in individual differences within animal species (Buss and Plumin, 1984; Goldsmith, 1983).

Describing with Traits

Psychologists who identify people as types assume that there are separate, *discontinuous* categories into which people fall. By contrast, psychologists who describe people in terms of traits typically assume the existence of underlying, continuous dimensions, such as intelligence or generosity, that everyone has to some degree. Traits are assumed to be qualities or attributes which influence behavior because they act as "generalized action tendencies." Knowing someone's traits ought to enable us to explain and perhaps predict better what he or she will do. Sometimes we can, but sometimes we can't for reasons to be discussed in this section. (See also "The Delicate Sex" in *The Best of Science.*)

Allport's Trait Approach

Gordon Allport (1937, 1961, 1966) viewed traits as the building blocks of personality and the source of individual uniqueness. They produced consistencies in behavior because they were *enduring* attributes of the person and were *general* or broad in their scope. That is, they connected and unified a person's reactions to a variety of stimuli (**Figure 12.3**).

Allport identified three kinds of traits. **Cardinal traits** were traits around which a person organized his or her life. For some it might involve power or achievement; for others, self-sacrifice for the good of others. Not all people developed cardinal traits, however. **Central traits** were traits we think of as major characteristics of a person, such as honesty or conscientiousness. **Secondary traits** were less important characteristics that were not central to our understanding of an individual's personality, such as particular attitudes, preferences, and style of behavior.

According to Allport, these three kinds of traits formed the structure of the personality—which, in turn, determined an individual's behavior. Allport saw *personality structures,* rather than environmental conditions, as the critical determiners of individual behavior. "The same fire that melts the butter hardens the egg," he said, as a way of showing that the same stimuli could have different effects on different individuals. Although he recognized *common* traits that were shared by individuals in a given culture, Allport was most interested in discovering

Figure 12.3
Traits may act as intervening variables, relating sets of stimuli and responses that might seem, at first glance, to have little to do with each other.

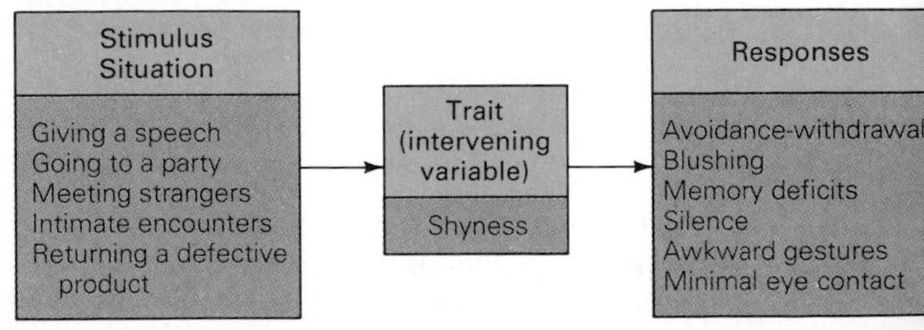

the *unique traits* that made each person a singular entity. He argued for this view by stating that

> *we must acknowledge the roughness and inadequacy of our universal dimensions. Thereby shall we enhance our own ability to understand, predict and control. By learning to handle the individuality of motives and the uniqueness of personality, we shall become better scientists, not worse. (Allport, 1960, p. 148)*

Allport was the most influential of the idiographic trait theorists. He is identified as an idiographic trait theorist because he believed that each person has some unique, idiosyncratic traits as well as a unique combination of traits.

An example of how Allport's trait approach is applied to understanding the personality of an individual follows.

> *Jenny was a mother whose life was "beset by frustration and defeat." She described much of her life in 301 letters she sent to a young couple over an 11-year period, starting when she was 58 years old and ending with her death. (The husband of the couple had been the college roommate of Jenny's son.) Each letter was read in sequence by 36 judges who assigned 198 descriptive adjectives as illustrative of Jenny's personality. These adjectives were then reduced to a set of eight cardinal traits—such as aggressive, sentimental, possessive—by combining all adjectives that were similar. A second evaluation, based on statistical data, was done as a comparison against the impressionistic data of the judges. In this evaluation, key words in Jenny's letters were scored for the frequency with which they were paired with certain other words to form distinctive units of meaning. When these word pairs were statistically analyzed (by factor analysis), seven traits were found to characterize Jenny's personality—as expressed in her letters.*
>
> *The descriptive and statistical data revealed a high degree of similarity and represented an instance in which a personality was* reconstructed *from available information when other kinds of data (from observations or personality tests) could not have been collected about the person. (Allport, 1965, 1966)*

Allport championed this idiographic research as the means to preserve a sense of the wholeness and uniqueness of each individual's personality. His approach required intensive study of single individuals in a variety of their life contexts over time.

Modern Trait Approaches.

For decades personality researchers have been trying to develop a comprehensive description and classification of personality traits. The four goals of this research effort are (a) to provide a *common* language for researchers with different theoretical orientations; (b) to have a common basis for comparing and evaluating the many personality theories; (c) to establish a framework for assessing the validity of personality scales (to be discussed in the next chapter); and (d) to guide the improved assessment of individual clients (McCrae et al., 1986).

Many traits have been generated by analyzing natural language descriptions of personality in the dictionary, as well as from trait names used by various personality theorists. They have been put into self-report scales or personality inventories in the form of questions that are then statistically analyzed to reveal a set of underlying common factors. When a number of different approaches for measuring traits was compared, five factors emerged as adequate for a taxonomy of personality (McCrae & Costa, 1987).

- *Neuroticism:* anxious, irritable, guilt-prone
- *Extraversion:* talkative, gregarious, socially poised
- *Openness to experience:* values intellectual matters, rebellious, nonconforming, unusual thought processes
- *Agreeableness:* sympathetic, warm, arouses liking
- *Conscientiousness:* behaves ethically, dependable, productive

Criticisms of Type and Trait Theories

Type and trait theories have been criticized for not being "real theories" because they do not *explain* how behavior is caused, but merely identify and describe characteristics that are supposedly *correlated* with behavior. Furthermore, these theories offer no conception of the *development* of personality. Emphasis is on its *structure* and its elements as they currently exist, with no corresponding concern for its origins or the dynamic relationships among the traits that together are assumed to form the whole personality.

We have seen that both kinds of theories represent a purely *dispositional* approach to the study of personality. As such, they rely heavily on self-reports of subjects from personality inventories and ignore the influences of situational variables. The subjective description of a person responding to test questions is assumed to be a direct measure of his or her traits, which, in turn, are seen as the basic components of personality. According to some critics (Tryon, 1979), there is a fallacy in making these test-trait-personality links. All we really can say scientifically is that the tests assess *performance* in a highly artificial situation, which may be influenced by aspects of the test situation and the person's response biases (for example, to give socially desirable answers).

If a test-trait score is assumed to be an index of an underlying personality dimension, then it should predict that a personality disposition will be manifest in *patterns of consistency in behavior across situations.* At least it has to predict how someone behaves in a given situation. The introvert, the generous woman, or the hostile man, as identified by test-trait scores, ought also to be similarly identifiable by their actions in certain settings. However, if only the personality test score is known, it is usually *not* possible to predict what someone will do in a given situation. To make matters worse, the correlations between scores on one personality test and those on other tests are low (Mischel, 1968; Rotter, 1954). Using personality traits as predictors, it does not appear possible to predict the behavior of even most of the people most of the time—much less the behavior of a particular individual.

Are People Really Consistent?

The failure of the nomothetic trait-based approach to predict relevant behavior in different situations has led in recent years to a basic challenge of the whole notion that personality-relevant behaviors are consistent. This challenge is based on a body of evidence such as the following:

> *Hartshorne and May, in their classic* Studies in the Nature of Character *(1928, 1929), found little consistency among different measures of moral character, such as honesty and self-control, in a sample of over 10,000 schoolchildren. It was not possible to predict whether a child who cheated in class would cheat on take-home examinations or would lie or steal money. "Honesty" was therefore, declared to be composed of* situation-specific habits *rather than being a general trait.*
>
> *"Punctuality" seems a good candidate for general trait status. Getting to class on time, keeping appointments promptly, not being late for the start of movies or church services ought to be components of a general personality trait of punctuality. Not so, according to the results of a study of over 300 college students (Dudycha, 1936). More than 15,000 observations were made of students' time of arrival to various college-related events. Punctuality in one situation was virtually* unrelated *to being on time in other situations.*
>
> *In a third extensive study of consistency—of introversion and extraversion—counselors were trained to keep records on 51 boys. For three weeks they noted occurrences of behaviors related to nine personality traits (such as independence and gregariousness) in over 30 situations (cookouts, sports, and so forth). When the scores on any two behavioral items designed to measure the same trait were compared, the average correlation was very weak. (Newcomb, 1929)*

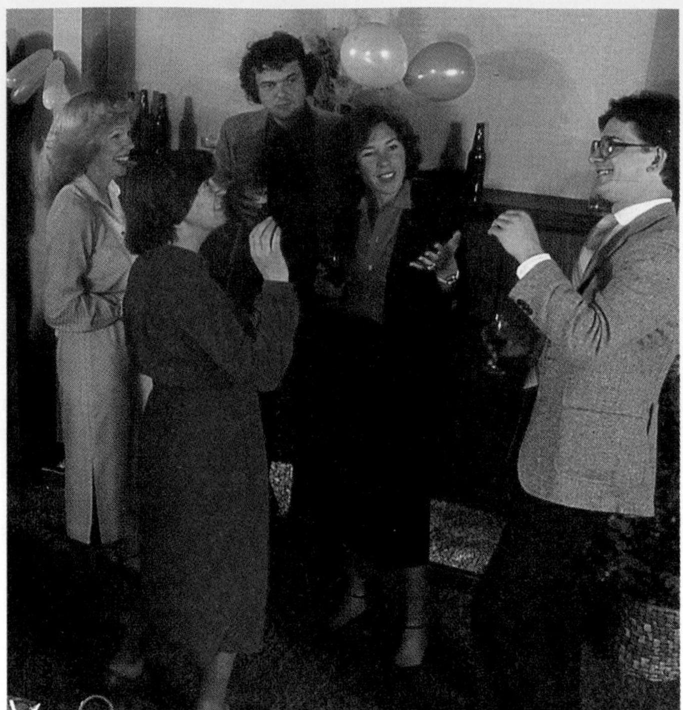

People at a cocktail party exhibit talkative, gregarious behavior. Are they extroverts?

The Consistency Paradox

In our study of perception in chapter 6, we saw that the attempt to impose stability and constancy on the variability of our experience is the hallmark of human perception. Could it be that our tendency to perceive consistency in personality is an extension of this general process of organizing our world to make it coherent, orderly, and more readily predictable? It seems to be "common sense" that people can be characterized according to dominant traits that they exhibit across different situations. We all know "gregarious" people, "shy" people, and "honest" people. There is also considerable agreement about the labels most appropriate for particular individuals.

> *Subjects rated themselves on a list of trait descriptions and were also rated by their spouses. The two sets of ratings matched fairly closely: if a subject saw him- or herself as possessing a certain trait, the spouse usually did too. (McCrae, 1982)*

From such evidence, we might assume that the reason we *see* certain people as consistent is simply that they do, in fact, have traits that *are* consistent. Not so; in general, efforts to predict people's behavior in given situations, from trait scores or from behavior in another situation, have *not* been successful. Following are some of the reasons why we (and some personality theorists) might "perceive" more consistency than actually occurs (adapted from Bem & Allen, 1974).

1. Each of us carries around an "implicit personality theory" which we use to connect the behaviors we see with the traits we infer and to predict other behaviors that we *don't* see. Our theories encourage us to fill in the gaps with what we think is probably there—what *ought* to be there according to our theory. In addition, there is *some* consistency (such as in intellectual ability or cognitive style), and this leads us to overgeneralize to other areas of personality (such as aggression or moral behavior) where consistency may not really be present.
2. We *underestimate* subtle forces in situations that may influence behavior. In doing so, we incorrectly attribute the causes of others' behavior to internal factors we overestimate as enduring, stable causes of their acts. We fail to account sufficiently for external pressures toward conformity or social desirability, for example.
3. Often others will behave the way they think we want them to, thus exaggerating their apparent consistency in our eyes. They may act quite differently in the presence of other observers—but we don't see that difference.
4. Most of us are free to choose the situations we enter, and we enter those we expect to feel comfortable in and able to handle. Those situations tend to be familiar ones, where the opportunities for new stimulation, conflict, or challenge are limited. In those situations our behavior tends to be restricted and, thus, does indeed tend to be consistent. It is no wonder that we act consistently in situations we have chosen for the sake of their constancy. When researchers put subjects in novel situations, they do strange, personality-inconsistent things that they report are "not the real me." We will examine such studies in chapters 17 and 18, the social psychology chapters.
5. Our judgments of others often come, not from what we *observe* them doing, but from what they *tell* us they do. Such self-reports are often biased and not accurate evidence of their behavior.
6. Our first impressions bias us strongly. Thereafter, we tend to interpret what we see as fitting in with and confirming our original view, which we assume was accurate. Once established, a belief needs little evidence to support it—but much to refute it—and prop up an illusion of consistency.
7. We tend to see consistency where it is not, because we have come to equate consistency with goodness, reliability, and stability. As Mark Twain put it: "There are those who would misteach us that to stick in a rut is consistency—and a virtue, and that to climb out of the rut is inconsistency—and a vice" ("Consistency," 1923).

Attack on Trait Theory

Columbia University psychologist Walter Mischel (1968) is one of the strongest critics of the concept of general personality traits. He surveyed a large body of literature on trait consistency across situations and was forced to conclude that the evidence for consistency was modest at best. Low correlations of .30 were often the most typically weak associations found between any predictor trait and a predicted dependent variable. These low relationships mean that knowing a person's trait score provides little help in predicting his or her behavior. Even when *behavior* is related to that trait in one situation, it offers little predictive value for behavior in other situations.

Mischel holds that *behavioral-situational specificity* is much more typical. Behavior is specific to the demands of each situation. You have probably had the experience of being very conscientious in one course for one teacher and just not caring in another course. Mischel would say that your apparent "inconsistency" was because of your ability to see the two situations presenting different demands (Mischel, 1976).

Yet Mischel has not totally abandoned the concept of consistency in personality. He says, "No one seriously doubts that lives have coherence and that we perceive ourselves and others as relatively stable individuals who have substantial identity and continuity over time" (Mischel & Mischel, 1977, p. 335). Mischel argues that personality is better understood as having *temporal stability* (not changing over time) than as showing *cross-situational consistency* (consistency from one situation to another).

Even Allport believed that the low correlations found between traits and behavior proved only that people "are not consistent *in the same way,* not that they are inconsistent with *themselves*" (1937, p. 250). They may seem to behave inconsistently because the researcher's arbitrarily imposed general trait dimension is not relevant for them. For example, you may tell a lie to avoid hurting a friend's feelings or cheat by giving test answers to someone in danger of flunking out. You may value honesty, but not interpret either of these acts as "dishonesty."

Counterattacks to Bolster Trait Theories

Some researchers have attempted to merge the idiographic and nomothetic trait approaches to counter Mischel's argument against consistency of traits across situations. For example, Daryl Bem has proposed using idiographic assessment methods within a nomothetic research paradigm. He advocates using people only who define *themselves* as consistent on a particular general trait dimension and then looking at actual behaviors that are assumed to be related to that personality construct.

> *College student subjects were classified according to their responses to two questions: (a) How friendly are you? (on a seven-point scale) and (b) How much do you* vary *in friendliness from one situation to another? If their self-ratings of variability were above the average for students of their own sex with the same self-rating of friendliness, they were designated* high in variability *(not consistent). If their ratings were below the average, they were called* low in variability *(consistent). Independent assessments of friendliness were obtained from each subject's father and mother, from a friend, and from behavioral observations of the subjects in a group discussion and with a solitary stranger.*
>
> *The subjects* self-reported variability *did relate highly to their consistency in friendliness across situations. Those who perceived themselves as* low in variability *(either generally friendly or generally not friendly)* did *show consistency across the different ratings and test situations. For the* high variability *subjects, on the other hand, the correlations between self-reported friendliness and the other measures of friendliness were low. (Bem & Allen, 1974)*

Some trait theorists have welcomed the criticism by Mischel and other "situationists" because it has forced them to explore the *interactions* between dispositional variables and situational variables, thereby leading to a richer portrait of personality (Endler, 1983; Magnusson & Endler, 1977). They have tried to unravel and interpret these interactions between people and situations by assessing the functional relationship between such interactions and individual differences in perceiving situations. These systematic differences in the way individuals perceive, define, and structure the situations they face are known as *construal styles* (Golding, 1977).

Others have contended that the resolution of the consistency paradox is to be found in better behavioral criteria and measurement procedures, and in taking more measures over a larger number of situations (Epstein, 1979). However it may be most correct to say that we can predict behavior from personality, but that we need to specify the circumstances under which behavior is person-guided, rather than situation-guided (Mischel, 1984).

Regardless of the way this controversy is resolved, we should not lose sight of a basic property of trait theories. They provide a *static* view of personality as a set of more or less enduring qualities. The emphasis is on an accurate description of a person's present personality without concern for the way it might develop or the way undesirable traits might be changed by therapy. The opposite of *static* is *dynamic;* a dynamic theory of personality emphasizes change, development, conflicting forces, and continual challenge of the environment. Let's see such a theory in action.

Psychodynamic Theories

By the end of the nineteenth century, Charles Darwin had made the world aware of the common bonds that link human beings and animals. As we saw in chapter 11, psychologists were quick to borrow Darwin's concept of "instinct" and transform it from its original use in accounting for stereotyped patterns of animal behavior to a concept representing the force underlying virtually all human actions. If a person went around hitting other people, that person might have an inborn "instinct of pugnacity." If someone was miserly, he or she might have a "hoarding instinct." If psychologists had a new kind of behavior they wanted to explain, they had only to postulate a new instinct; but identifying something is not the same as explaining it. Psychologists had a new term—*instinct*—but not a better understanding of the psychological processes it was meant to describe. Clearly a more fruitful approach was needed. For many, this was provided by the work of Sigmund Freud.* He gave new meaning to the concept of human instinct, and in doing so, he revolutionized the very concept of human personality, as Darwin had done for the concept of human evolution. To Ernest Jones, Freud's biographer, Freud was "the Darwin of the mind" (1953).

Freudian Psychoanalysis

Freud's theory of personality is a "grand theory" that boldly attempts to explain the origins and course of personality development, the nature of mind, the abnormal aspects of personality, and the

*Freud's ideas about the origins, development, and expression of both normal and abnormal personality are complex, numerous, and subtle. You have already met some of them in earlier chapters and can supplement the bare structure to be sketched with your own reading of Freud's *Psychopathology of Everyday Life* (1904/1914), *Introductory Lectures of Psychoanalysis* (1923), and also Munroe's *Schools of Psychoanalytic Thought* (1955).

way personality can be changed by therapy. We will focus only on normal personality; Freud's other views will be treated at length in chapters 15 and 16.

At the core of personality, according to psychoanalytic theory, are events within a person's mind, *intrapsychic events* that motivate behavior or are intentions to act. Often we are aware of these motivations (when we study hard in order to achieve success). However some motivation also operates at an *unconscious* level (when we do not study and fail a test that is important—to our demanding parents).

The *psychodynamic* nature of this approach comes from its emphasis on these inner wellsprings of behavior. For Freud, all behavior was motivated; every human action had a purpose and a cause that could be discovered by psychoanalyzing a person's thought associations, dreams, errors, and other behavioral clues. There is no room for chance events in psychoanalytic theory; all acts are determined by motives. The wish is parent to the deed; our actions emerge from what we really desire—even when they surprise us. Prominent among our desires, according to Freud, are sexual and aggressive wishes. Through both conscious and unconscious processes, these wishes affect our thoughts and behaviors.

The primary data for Freud's hypotheses about personality came from clinical observations and in-depth case studies of individual patients in therapy. Although this ideographic approach yields a rich harvest of ideas from which to formulate a complex theory, the theoretical ground is too soft for the heavy methodological equipment necessary to test a hypothesis scientifically. We shall return to the problem of validating Freud's ideas after we consider some of his fundamental concepts, his original ideas on the way personality is structured, and the roles of repression and psychological defenses.

Fundamental Concepts

Four concepts form the core of the psychodynamic approach: psychic determinism, early experience, drives and instincts, and unconscious processes. Together they provide a conceptually rich perspective on the development and functioning of personality.

Psychic determinism. In the late 1800s, cases of *hysteria* were recorded in Europe for which no adequate physical explanation could be found. Those afflicted (mostly women) would experience impairments in bodily functioning—paralysis or blindness, for example—and yet they would have intact nervous systems and no obvious organic damage to their muscles or eyes. Freud, a neurologist, studied and attempted to treat the bizarre symptoms of this disorder.

Along with his colleague, Joseph Breuer, Freud observed that the particular physical symptom often seemed related to a prior forgotten event in a patient's life. For instance, under hypnosis, a "blind" patient might recall witnessing her parents having intercourse when she was a small child. As an adult, her anticipation of her first sexual encounter might then have aroused powerful feelings associated with this earlier, disturbing episode. Her "blindness" might represent an attempt on her part to undo seeing the original event and perhaps also to deny sexual feelings in herself. Her symptom would also have a secondary function (*secondary gain*). By making her helpless and dependent, it would bring her attention, comfort, and sympathy from others—social reinforcement.

Freud thus believed that *symptoms,* rather than being arbitrary, were related in a meaningful way to (and determined by) significant life events. He saw clinical observation and rational analysis as the keys that could unlock the secrets of both pathological and normal personality.

Early experience. Freud assumed a *continuity* of personality development from "womb to tomb," with all a person's past experiences contributing to the personality he or she showed presently; but Freud believed that it was in infancy and early childhood that experience had its most profound impact on personality formation. This was especially true of the early stages of psychosexual development, which we discussed in chapter 3 (see pp. 89–90); but as we saw, Freud's theories were based on his adult patients' recollections and descriptions of their childhood experiences—*not* on direct observations of children. Nonetheless, his emphasis on early experience did much to make the scientific study of infant and child behavior respectable and fashionable.

Drives and instincts. His medical training as a neurologist led Freud to postulate a common biological basis for the mental abnormalities he observed in his patients. The source of motivation for human actions was ascribed to *psychic energy* found within each individual. How this energy was exchanged, transformed, and expressed was a central concern of psychoanalysis. Each of us was assumed to have inborn instincts or drives that were tension systems created by the organs of the body. These energy sources, when activated, could be expressed in many different ways. Although they were often referred to as instinctual urges, Freud's German term *Triebe* is closer to the concept of *drive* than to instinct (which is an inherited tendency to act in a characteristic way). One of Freud's contributions was in showing the way the same drive, say that of sex, could be expressed directly through intercourse or masturbation, as well as indirectly through "dirty" jokes or creative art.

Freud originally postulated two basic drives. One he saw as involved with the *ego,* or *self-preservation* (hunger, thirst, and other physical needs of existence). The other he called **Eros;** it is related to *sexual urges* and involves preservation of the species.

Freud was more interested in the sexual urges, although some of his followers have given the ego drive an important place in personality, as we will see. Freud greatly expanded the notion of human sexual desires to include, not only the urge for sexual union, but also all other attempts to seek pleasure or to make physical contact with others. He used the term **libido** to describe the source of energy for sexual urges; he saw it as a psychic energy that drives us toward sensual pleasures of all types. Sexual urges demand immediate satisfaction, whether through direct actions or through such indirect means as fantasies and dreams.

According to Freud, this broadly defined sexual drive does not arrive at puberty, but is already operating in infants. It is evident, he argued, in the pleasure infants derive from physical stimulation of the genitals and other sensitive, or *erogenous,* areas, such as the mouth and the anus. *Infantile sexuality* was a radical concept in Victorian times, when even adult sexuality was not mentioned in proper society.

Freud postulated the radical concept that sexual drives operate in infants.

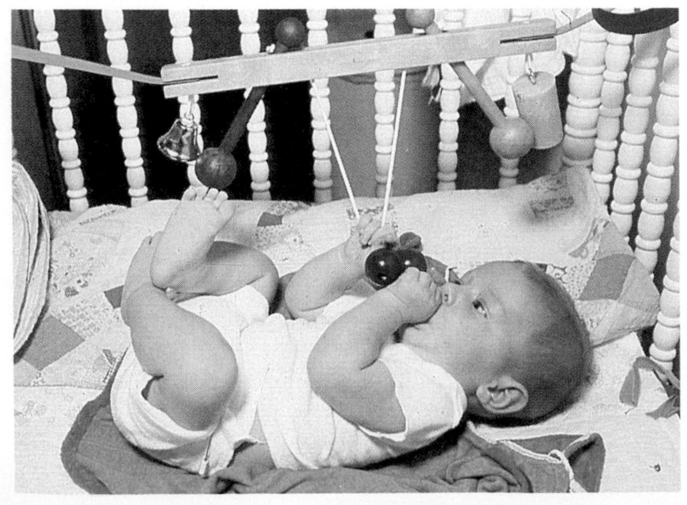

Clinical observation of patients who had suffered traumatic experiences during World War I led Freud to add the concept of **Thanatos** (the death instinct) to his theory. These patients continued to relive their wartime traumas in nightmares and hallucinations, phenomena that could not be assimilated into self-preservation or sexual drive theory. Freud postulated that Thanatos drove people toward aggressive and destructive behaviors. He suggested that this primitive urge was part of the tendency for all living things to follow the law of entropy and return to an inorganic state.

In his dual theory of drives, Freud believed that both the sexual and aggressive drives were sources of motivation for virtually all behavior. We will discover (in chapter 18) that pornography depicting a hostile view of women stimulates both aggressive and sexual fantasies in males as well as overt aggression (Donnerstein, 1983; Malamuth and Briere, 1986).

Unconscious processes. Though public reaction was strong against the loss of innocence in the notion of infantile sexuality, it was even stronger in opposition to another of Freud's novel ideas—the unconscious. Other writers had pointed to such a process, but Freud put the concept of the unconscious determinants of human thought, feeling, and action on a very special pedestal. Behavior can be motivated by drives of which we are not aware. We may act without knowing why, or without direct access to the true cause of our actions. There is a *manifest* content to our behavior—what we say, do, and perceive—of which we are fully aware; but there is also a *latent* content that is concealed from us by unconscious processes. The *meaning* of neurotic (anxiety-based) symptoms, as well as of dreams and slips of the pen and tongue, are to be found at the unconscious level of thinking and information processing.

Consider the *Freudian slip.* According to Freud, impulses within us that we find unacceptable still strive for expression, even if inhibited, suppressed, or repressed. For example, "forgetting" a dentist appointment or being consistently late for dates with a particular person are not accidental, but may be an instance of this striving to express the way we *really* feel. A host's greeting unwanted guests with "I'm so sorry—oh, I mean glad you could come," may reveal his true feelings. When a faculty member at Oxford University rose to ask the invited guests to raise their glasses in a toast to their "dear queen," was he really expressing something quite different when it came out as "Let us toast our queer dean"?

According to Freud, such "errors" are meaningful, the meaning being in the *unconscious intention.* They can be explained in terms of the final result produced, even though some other meaning was expected by the hearer or apparently intended by the speaker. New experimental research is providing validation for the theory that hidden thoughts compete with intended verbal statements to create *Freudian slips* (Motley, 1987).

> *Two groups of men saw word pairs such as "shamdock" or "past-fashion" flashed on a screen at one-second intervals. The pairs were read silently unless a buzzer signaled reading aloud the pair on the screen. In the fear condition, the subjects anticipated receiving an electric shock, while in the sexual arousal condition, the task was performed in the presence of a provocative female experimenter. The word lists contained an equal number of words that could result in slips related to shocks or sexy women.*
>
> *The kinds of errors made by the men randomly assigned to the two conditions were quite different. Those expecting to be shocked were more likely to say "damn shock" for "sham dock" and "cursed wattage" for "worst cottage." When in the presence of the sexy female, more men read "past fashion" as "fast passion" and "brood nests" as "nude breasts."*

Most slips of the tongue appear to be the result of mental competition between two or more words, some from hidden thoughts, others from simple linguistic alternatives not unconsciously motivated ("chee canes" instead of "key chains").

The concept of unconscious motivation adds a new dimension to personality by allowing for greater complexity of mental functioning than does a rational model. It is an elusive quality, not readily captured in an objective personality test. The notion of an unconscious mind threatens those who want to believe they are in full command of their ship of mental state as it travels along.

The Structure of Personality

Freud accounted for personality differences by attributing them to the different ways in which people dealt with their fundamental drives. To explain these differences, he pictured a continuing battle between two parts of the personality, the id and the superego, moderated by a third aspect of the self, the ego.

The **id** is conceived as the primitive, unconscious part of the personality, the storehouse of the fundamental drives. It operates irrationally, acting on impulse and pushing for expression and immediate gratification "no matter what," without considering whether what is desired is realistically possible, socially desirable, or morally acceptable. The id is governed by the *pleasure principle,* the unregulated search for gratification, especially sexual, physical, and emotional pleasure.

The ego, governed by reality, substitutes a desire to sky-dive, which is reasonable, for the unrealistic wish to fly from a cliff.

The **superego** is the storehouse of an individual's values, including moral attitudes learned from society. The superego corresponds roughly to the conscience; it develops as a child *internalizes* the prohibitions of parents and other adults against socially undesirable actions. It is the inner voice of "oughts" and "should nots." The superego also includes the **ego ideal,** an individual's view of the kind of person he or she should strive to become. Thus the superego, society's representative in an individual, is often in conflict with the id, survival's representative. The id wants to do what feels good, while the superego, operating on the *morality principle,* insists on doing what is "right."

The **ego** is the reality-based aspect of the self that arbitrates the conflict between id impulses and superego demands. The ego represents an individual's personal view of physical and social reality, his or her conscious beliefs about what will lead to what and which things are possible. Part of the ego's job is to choose actions that will gratify id impulses without having undesirable consequences. The ego is governed by the *reality principle,* which puts reasonable choices before pleasurable demands. Thus, the ego would block an impulse to "fly" from the edge of a cliff by substituting sky diving or a roller coaster ride.

When the id and the superego are in conflict, the ego arranges a compromise that at least partially satisfies both. As id and superego pressures intensify, it becomes more difficult for the ego to work out optimal compromises.

Repression and Ego Defense

Sometimes the compromise involves "putting a lid on the id." Extreme desires of the id may have to be *repressed.* **Repression** is an important, uniquely Freudian concept that provides a psychological means through which strong conflicts created by id impulses are taken out of conscious awareness—pushed into the privacy of the unconscious—and their public expression controlled. Repression is the most basic of the **ego defense mechanisms,** which are mental strategies the ego uses to defend itself against the conflicts experienced in the normal course of life.

These mechanisms are vital to an individual's psychological adaptation to conflicting demands from id, superego, and external reality. They are mental tactics and strategies that enable a person to maintain a generally favorable self-image (as outlined in Table 12.2). For example, if a child has strong feelings of hatred toward a parent—which, if acted out, would be dangerous—repression may take over. The hostile impulse is no longer consciously pressing for satisfaction or even recognized as existing; though not seen or heard, however, it is not gone. It continues to play a role in personality functioning.

One of the more interesting aspects of repression is its effect on cognition and affect. A person may no longer be consciously aware of the ideas that have been repressed but may continue to experience feelings associated with the repressed material. This "unexplained arousal" or "affect without appropriate cognitions" may find expression in a variety of disguised forms. For example, repressed hostility toward a parent might be expressed as general rebellion against authority; repressed sexual urges might account for someone's joining an antismut campaign to stamp out pornography—while being "forced" to carefully examine the offending material. A person may find some inaccu-

Table 12.2 *Summary Chart of Ego Defense Mechanisms*

Compensation	Covering up weakness by emphasizing desirable traits or making up for frustration in one area by gratification in another
Denial of Reality	Protecting self from unpleasant reality by refusal to perceive it
Displacement	Discharging pent-up feelings, usually of hostility, on objects less dangerous than those which initially aroused the emotion
Emotional Insulation	Withdrawing into passivity to protect self from being emotionally hurt
Fantasy	Gratifying frustrated desires in imaginary achievements ("daydreaming" is a common form)
Identification	Increasing feelings of worth by identifying self with another person or institution, often of illustrious standing
Introjection	Incorporating external values and standards into ego structure so individual is not at the mercy of them as external threats
Isolation	Cutting off emotional charge from hurtful situations or separating incompatible attitudes into logic-tight compartments (holding conflicting attitudes which are never thought of simultaneously or in relation to each other); also called *compartmentalization*
Projection	Placing blame for one's difficulties upon others, or attributing one's own "forbidden" desires to others
Rationalization	Attempting to prove that one's behavior is "rational" and justifiable and thus worthy of the approval of self and others
Reaction Formation	Preventing dangerous desires from being expressed by endorsing opposing attitudes and types of behavior and using them as "barriers"
Regression	Retreating to earlier developmental levels involving more childish responses and usually a lower level of aspiration
Repression	Pushing painful or dangerous thoughts out of consciousness, keeping them unconscious; this is considered to be *the most basic of the defense mechanisms*
Sublimation	Gratifying or working off frustrated sexual desires in substitutive nonsexual activities socially accepted by one's culture
Undoing	Atoning for, and thus counteracting unacceptable desires or acts

rate explanation for the feelings and behavior or, lacking any rational explanation, acknowledge his or her "irrationality"—leading to further distress.

For Freud, **anxiety** is an intense emotional response caused by the preconscious recognition that a repressed conflict is about to emerge into consciousness. That is, anxiety is a danger signal: Repression is not working! Red alert! More defenses needed! This is the time for a second line of defense, one or more additional ego-defense mechanisms that will relieve the anxiety. For example, a mother who does not like her son and does not want to care for him might use "reaction formation" and transform her unacceptable impulse into its opposite: "I don't hate my child" becomes "I love my child. See how I smother the dear little thing with love?" She might use "projection" as an ego defense, seeing other people wanting to limit her freedom, posing a threat to her child's life, or not being concerned enough about the proper care of their children. Through "displacement," the rejecting mother might redirect hostile impulses away from her child by throwing away the child's toys after tripping over them.

> *From a psychoanalytic point of view, ego mechanisms of defense are mental processes that attempt to resolve conflicts among drive states, attacks, and external reality . . . they moderate levels of emotion produced by stress, they help keep awareness of certain drives at a minimal level, they provide time to help an individual deal with life traumas, and they help deal with unresolvable loss. (Plutchik et al., 1979, p. 229)*

But useful as they are, they are self-deceptive and can get us into trouble.

According to Freudian theory, all people have some urges that are unacceptable and use these defense mechanisms to some extent. Overuse of them, however, constitutes *neurosis.* People who are neurotic spend so much of their psychic energy deflecting, disguising, and rechanneling unacceptable urges to lessen their anxiety that they have little energy left over for productive living or satisfying relationships.

It is important to remember that sexuality and aggression were considered by Freud to be central aspects of *normal* personality development. The pleasure derived from destroying someone's sand castle with one swift kick, or defacing a building with graffiti, or smashing an automobile is readily observable in normal children and adults. Nonetheless, Freud was rather pessimistic about the chances for escaping neurotic disorders. Perhaps because he grew up in the Victorian era, Freud believed that any society must teach its children that most expression of their basic drives is bad. Hence nearly everyone will have to be defending against such impulses nearly all the time. In chapters 15 and 16 we will take a closer look at the way a psychoanalytic perspective is used to explain and treat mental disorders.

Criticisms of Freudian Theory

Critics of Freudian theory and its application to both normal personality and the treatment of neurosis through psychoanalysis have raised a number of objections. One criticism is that many psychoanalytic concepts are vague and not operationally defined; thus much of the theory is difficult to evaluate scientifically. It has been hard to make predictions that can be tested in controlled experiments. Because some of its central hypotheses cannot be *disproved* even *in principle,* its general theoretical status remains questionable. How can the concepts of libido, fixation, or repression be studied in any direct fashion? How is it possible to predict whether an overly anxious person will use projection, denial, or reaction formation to defend a threatened ego?

Another criticism of psychoanalytic theory is that it is good history, but bad science. It does not reliably predict what will occur; it is applied *retrospectively* after events have occurred. Using psychoanalytic theory to understand personality typically involves *historical reconstruction* of the kind made famous by detective Sherlock Holmes—not scientific construction of probable actions and predictable outcomes. In addition, its overemphasis on historical origins of current behavior directs attention away from current stimuli that may be inducing and maintaining the behavior. The theory neglects a person's expectations, goals, and future-based ideas.

Research that has attempted to isolate predictor variables derived from the theory is beset by problems of validity of the dependent measures of psychoanalytic constructs (Silverman, 1976). For example, one researcher predicted that women would hoard more pencils than men, because pencils are phallic symbols and women allegedly have penis envy. He did, in fact, find more hoarding among female subjects (Johnson, 1966); but perhaps females hoard more pencils because they are more likely than men to be asked if they have a pencil that can be borrowed (Who would you be more likely to ask?) or because they carry handbags. Maybe women also "hoard" more things, in general, than do men.

Freud's theory developed from speculation based on clinical experience with people suffering from anxiety disorders and other problems of adjustment—people in whom something had gone wrong. Thus, another criticism is that this theory has little to say about *healthy* life-styles, which are not primarily defensive or defective. The theory offers the pessimistic view that human nature developed out of conflicts, traumas, fixations, and anxieties. As such, it does not fully acknowledge the positive side of our existence or offer any information about healthy personalities striving for happiness and realization of their full potential.

Other criticisms of Freudian theory are (a) it is a *developmental* theory that never included observations or studies of children; (b) it relies on adult memories of childhood events, but fails to discount adequately for memory distortions and ordinary forgetting; (c) it denies the reality of a patient's perception in favor of the fantasy of his or her interpretation of fantasy, thus minimizing an offense like child abuse by explaining it in terms of the child's desire for sexual contact with parents; (d) its bias toward sexual and aggressive themes results in their being sought out in dreams and free associations by psychoanalytic interviewers, while alternatives are less likely to be considered; and (e) its clearly *androcentric* bias that uses a male model as the norm (penis envy, castration anxiety, father figure) and gives females a secondary status.

We have devoted so much space to Freudian theory and criticism because Freud's ideas have had a greater impact on psychology and on society than those of any other psychologist. Despite the criticisms leveled against them, a recent critical evaluation of Freud's ideas has validated many of his theories about the development of aspects of personality and psychopathology (Fisher & Greenberg, 1985). What Picasso did for art, Freud did for the human mind, changing forever the way we think about its possibilities and variations.

Post-Freudian Theories

Many of those who came after Freud kept his basic representation of personality as a battleground on which unconscious primal urges fought it out with social values. Many of Freud's intellectual descendants were also dissidents who made some major changes in the psychoanalytic view of personality. In general, these post-Freudians have: (a) put greater emphasis on ego functions (such as ego defenses, development of the self, thinking, and mastery); (b) seen social variables (culture, family, and peers) playing a greater role in shaping personality; (c) put less emphasis on the importance of general sexual urges, or libidinal energy; and (d) viewed personality development extending beyond childhood to the entire life span.

In chapter 3 we outlined the developmental theories of the neo-Freudian Erik Erikson. Two others, Harry Stack Sullivan and Margaret Mahler, will be discussed in chapter 16.

Erich Fromm (1947) and Karen Horney (1939) were other followers who attempted to balance Freud's biological emphasis with more attention to social influence. But Freud's two most celebrated followers were Alfred Adler and Carl Jung, who operated on Freudian theory, not with theoretical scalpels, but with conceptual swords.

Adler (1929) accepted the notion that personality was directed by unrecognized wishes: "Man knows more than he understands"; but he rejected the significance of Eros and the pleasure principle. Adler believed that we all experience feelings of *inferiority* as helpless, dependent, small children and that our lives become dominated by the search for ways to overcome those feelings—*compensating* to achieve feelings of adequacy or, more often, *overcompensating* in an attempt to become superior. Personality is structured around this underlying striving; the life-styles people develop are based on particular ways of overcoming their basic, pervasive feelings of inferiority. Personality conflict arises from incompatibility between external environmental pressures and internal strivings for adequacy rather than from competing urges within the person.

Carl Jung (1959) expanded the conception of the unconscious. For him, the unconscious was not limited to an individual's unique life experiences, but was filled with fundamental psychological truths shared by the whole human race. The concept of **collective unconscious** predisposes us all to react to certain stimuli in the same way. It is responsible for our intuitive understanding of primitive myths, art forms, and symbols—which are the universal archetypes of existence. An **archetype** is a primitive symbolic representation of a particular experience or object. Each one is associated with an instinctive tendency to feel and think about that object or experience in a special way. Jung postulated many archetypes from history and mythology: the sun god, the hero, the earth mother. *Animus* was the male archetype that women experienced, while *anima* was the female archetype that men experienced. In reacting to someone of the opposite sex, then, we react to both

In the Balinese dance Barong, a dancer wears a mask of Rangda, a malign female spirit. Rangda is anima.

their own particular characteristics and their male or female archetype. The archetype of the self is the *mandala* or magic circle; it symbolizes striving for unity and wholeness (see Jung, 1973).

The healthy, integrated personality was seen by Jung as balancing opposing forces, such as masculine aggressiveness and feminine sensitivity, *within* the individual. This view of personality as a constellation of competing internal forces in dynamic balance was called *analytic psychology*.

Jung, chosen by Freud as the "crown-prince" of the psychoanalytic movement, led a palace revolt by rejecting the primary importance of libido, so central to Freudian sexual theory. To the basic urges of sex and aggression Jung added two equally powerful unconscious instincts, the *need to create* and the *need to self-actualize*. Jung's views became central to the emergence of humanistic psychology in America. Carl Jung's contribution to the study of human nature could be poetically summarized in the following way:

> *He looked at his own Soul with a Telescope. What seemed all irregular, he saw and showed to be beautiful Constellations; and he added to the Consciousness hidden worlds within worlds.*
>
> *Samuel Taylor Coleridge, Notebooks*

Humanistic Theories

Humanistic approaches to understanding personality are characterized by a concern for the integrity of an individual's personal, conscious experience and growth potential. Humanistic personality theorists, such as Carl Rogers and Abraham Maslow, have stressed a basic drive toward self-actualization as the organizer of all the diverse forces whose interplay continually creates what a person is.

In this view, the motivation for behavior comes from a person's unique biological and learned tendencies to develop and change in positive directions toward the goal of self-actualization. This innate striving toward self-fulfillment and the realization of one's unique potential is a constructive, guiding force that moves each person toward generally positive behaviors and the enhancement of the self.

Humanistic theories have been described as being holistic, dispositional, phenomenological, and existential; and they are definitely optimistic about human nature. They are **holistic** because they explain people's separate acts always in terms of their entire personalities. People are seen *not* as a collection of discrete traits, like different beans in a jar, but as balloons filled with a mixture of helium and other light gases. They will soar naturally if let free and not held back by environmental constraints.

Humanistic theories are **dispositional** because they focus on the innate qualities within a person that exert a major influence over the direction behavior will take. Situational inputs are more often seen as constraints and barriers, like the strings that tie down the balloons. Once freed from negative situational conditions, the actualizing tendency should actively guide people to choose life-enhancing situations. It should be emphasized that humanistic theories are *not* dispositional in the same way as trait theories—which focus on enduring, stable characteristics—nor like the psychoanalytic view of childhood experiences that develop into restricting lifelong patterns. Humanistic dispositions fill the personality with a unitary tendency to become actualized so that it will find its natural expression in a healthy personality.

These theories are **phenomenological** because they emphasize an individual's frame of reference, the person's *subjective* view of reality—not the objective perspective of an observer. This view is also one of the "here and now," the present as perceived by the person. Past influences are important only to the extent that they have brought the person to the present situation.

Finally, humanistic theories have been described by theorists such as Rollo May (1975) as having an **existential** perspective. They focus on a person's conscious, higher mental processes that interpret current experiences and enable the person to meet or be overwhelmed by the everyday challenges of existence. These theories are unique in their emphasis on freedom, which separates them from the behaviorists and psychoanalysts whose conceptual frames are markedly deterministic.

In this section we will briefly mention some of the special features of Carl Rogers' personality view and also the theory of self. Maslow's ideas have been outlined earlier in our study of human motivation (chapter 11).

A Person-centered Approach

For Carl Rogers (1947, 1951, 1977), therapy is "client-centered" and personality theory is "person-centered." It is an individual's private world—his or her *phenomenal field*—that must be understood. Rogers' advice was to listen to what people said about themselves, to attend to their concepts and to the significance they attach to their experiences.

As we have noted, at the core of this theoretical approach is the concept of **self-actualization,** a constant striving to realize one's inherent potential, to fully develop one's capacities and talents. Experiences are evaluated positively and sought after when they are perceived to maintain or enhance the self. Those experiences which oppose the positive growth of the person are evaluated negatively and avoided.

Unfortunately, this drive at times comes into conflict with the need for approval or *conditional positive regard* from both the self and others. If important people in a child's environment express dismay at some things the child does without making it clear that their criticism applies to the *behavior* rather than to the *child,* he or she may begin to do only things that are "acceptable" to others.

It should be apparent why such an "upbeat" view of personality was a welcome treat for many psychologists who had been brought up on a diet of bitter-tasting Freudian medicine and its less wholesome—even if more tempting—morsels.

This blind skier is definitely striving to develop a sense of his own identity, an important concept in Carl Roger's person-centered approach.

Criticisms of Humanistic Theories

It is difficult to criticize theories that are on the side of the angels. Who could possibly object to the importance of the self-concept, to fulfilling one's human potential or to motives for growth? Behaviorists do. They criticize humanistic concepts for being fuzzy, without clear definitions. What exactly is self-actualization? Is it an inborn tendency or is it created by the cultural context? Humanistic theories also have difficulty accounting for the particular characteristics of individuals. They seem to be theories about human nature, about qualities we all share, more than theories about differences among people.

Behaviorists also claim that the general level at which such theories are formulated minimizes their research value. (An extensive bibliography of research using humanistic concepts [Roberts, 1973] suggests otherwise.) They go on to note that, in emphasizing the role of the self as a source of experience and action, humanistic psychologists neglect the important environmental variables that also influence behavior.

Psychoanalytic theorists criticize the emphasis of humanistic theorists on present conscious experience. They argue that the power of the unconscious is not recognized in this approach. People who have unconscious conflicts and use defensive strategies for dealing with their conflicts cannot accurately describe themselves by simply looking at conscious processes.

Other criticisms of this general theory of personality are that it (a) ignores a person's unique history and influences from the past, as well as the developmental aspects of personality; (b) oversimplifies the complexity of personality by reducing it to the simplistic "given" of a self-actualizing tendency; (c) fails to predict how a specific individual will respond in a given situation; (d) makes the self a "take charge" little *homunculus,* a tiny mind with a personality that is not accountable to skeptical researchers. As some critics conclude, "In the last analysis, explaining personality on the basis of hypothesized self-tendencies is reassuring double-talk, not explanation" (Liebert & Spiegler, 1982, p. 411). "And in the opposite corner, we have learning theory approaches weighing in heavy and tough. . . ."

Learning Theories

In the heyday of football at the United States Military Academy at West Point, "Doc" Blanchard made yardage running straight ahead inside the opposing line, while Glenn Davis did so running around the end, on the outside. Their nicknames of "Mr. Inside" and "Mr. Outside" also seem to be apt characterizations of two of psychology's leading ball carriers, Carl Rogers and B. F. Skinner. Rogers, "Mr. Inside," focused his attention on what is going on inside a person; Skinner is the "Mr. Outside" of psychology, focusing his attention on the environment. Learning theorists, like Neal Miller, have tried to reconcile these views by showing how behavior is internally generated and externally influenced by reinforcing contingencies.

A Strict Behaviorist Approach

You will recall from our discussions in the learning chapter (chapter 8) that the crux of a behavioristic approach is its focus on environmental contingencies (reinforcing circumstances) that control behavior. A strict behavioristic approach ignores what is "in" the person and denies that the "inside approach" has any psychological validity. From this perspective, behavior and personality are shaped primarily by the outside environment. Personality, then, is seen as the sum of overt and covert responses that are reliably elicited as consequences of an individual's reinforcement history. People are different because they have had different histories of reinforcement. When people seem to be acting differently in the same situation, behaviorists believe they are actually responding to slightly different stimuli or their behavior is on different reinforcement schedules—not because of their different personalities.

For an operant psychologist, like Skinner, personality is studied as the set of a person's responses to the external environment. If you want to understand why a particular person does a particular thing, look to the situation—not to traits, states, dispositions, or similar "mental way stations." In support of this view, Skinner has argued that

> *the practice of looking inside the organism for an explanation of behavior has tended to obscure the variables which are immediately available for a scientific analysis. These variables lie outside the organism, in its immediate environment and in its environmental history. (1953, p. 31)*

Behaviorists are interested not in the *consistencies in behavior*—which led other theorists to propose enduring traits, instincts, or self-concepts—but in the *changes in behavior* as environmental conditions change. Their aim is to identify the external variables that change responding. No mental states and no inferred dispositions are allowed—or needed—in their explanations of behavior.

Can you see why learning-behavioral approaches to personality are good for developing treatments to change personality—to reduce undesirable behaviors and to increase desirable ones? Can you also see why they do not provide a very satisfying view of the way the environmental inputs and response outputs are organized and meaningfully integrated in a unique way by personality constructs? (See the ***Close-up*** on p. 440 for more of the important dimensions on which environments differ.)

Reconciling the Analytic and Behavioral Approaches

Is there a way to integrate some of the ideas in Freud's rich psychoanalytic theory with those in the more formal views based on learning principles? John Dollard and Neal Miller (1950) did so, using the behaviorist formulation of Clark Hull (1952) rather than Skinner's, because Hull allowed for concepts such as drive, inhibition, and habit, concepts that Skinner had excluded.

Common to both Freudian and Hullian theory was the key role attributed to the motivating force of tension and the reinforcing (pleasurable) consequences of **tension reduction.** Both theorists conceived of an organism acting in order to reduce "tension" produced by unsatisfied drives. Behavior that successfully reduces such tensions is repeated, eventually becoming a learned habit, reinforced by repeated tension reduction. Another common

Close-up The "Personality" of Situations

What do we mean by a "situation"? What are the important features of settings that cause people's behavior to change from one setting to another?

Many psychologists have studied this question by setting up laboratory experiments in which they manipulated particular conditions. Recently, some psychologists have approached the question from a different angle. They have tried to learn about the important features of real-life settings.

Rudolf Moos (1979) has been particularly influential in this kind of research on the ecology of behavior settings. In a series of studies conducted over a 15-year period, he has examined 10 different kinds of real-life social settings, ranging from psychiatric treatment facilities to military basic training settings. The focus of the research has been twofold:

1. *to examine the differences among various examples of the same type of setting—such as differences among inpatient wards; and*
2. *to examine the differences and similarities among different types of settings—for example, to discover the characteristics needed to describe the "personalities" of treatment facilities as compared with the "personalities" of military training centers.*

In all settings, he has found three basic domains to be important for describing the "personality" of the setting. These are (a) the interpersonal relationship qualities; (b) the personal growth opportunities; and (c) the emphasis on system maintenance or change.

One setting which has been the focus of research by Moos is college student living groups. In that research, the University Residence Environment Scale (URES) was developed to measure each of the three basic domains. Using this scale, Moos has studied over 10,000 students and residence staff, representing 229 living groups at 25 colleges and universities in 12 states. He has included diverse kinds of residence halls, such as student cooperatives, fraternities, freshman single-sex dorms, coed houses, and special graduate student housing.

Moos found that clear profiles emerged for different kinds of living groups. For example, women's living groups seemed to place special emphasis on emotional support and a formal, organized structure, whereas men's groups emphasized competition and a nonconformist stance. Mixed-sex groups combined many qualities of each. They emphasized emotional support (like the women's groups) but also independence and competition (like the men's groups).

When Moos compared the changes that occurred during an academic year in women who lived in coed dorms and women living in single-sex dorms, he found that those in coed dorms were more likely to have lowered their career goals and increased their social activities. By contrast, women who had lived in women's dorms showed an increase in leadership and assertiveness, and higher career goals.

Moos contends that these changes were the result of the different "personalities" of the living settings. Since coed groups emphasized community and nonacademic personal development, it was not surprising to find coed students more likely to pursue personal goals not related to a strong academic commitment.

While the data are quite consistent with his explanations, they do not provide conclusive evidence that the setting actually had a major role in bringing about these changes. After all, students typically have considerable power to select their living environments. Students who choose to live in coed dorms may be different from those who choose to live in single-sex groups. The setting, then, can be just a reflection of the student's prior attitudes, not a cause of them.

Thus, the question of what is cause and what is effect is hard to answer. Nonetheless, Moos's research is an interesting example of an attempt to look at the impact of natural settings. His results suggest that:

1. *The dimensions of relationship, personal growth, and system maintenance or change are relevant in living settings of student groups, as they are in other social settings he has studied.*
2. *Different kinds of living groups do seem to have "personalities," which can be described by the pattern of scores on the URES obtained by individuals living in them.*
3. *Changes that occur during an academic year in a student's attitudes and behavior seem to be in the directions emphasized by that student's living group.*

ground is the emphasis of both theories on the importance of early learning in determining what an organism does later in life. Although the two theoretical systems use very different words to describe their conclusions, they come out with models of the human organism that have important parallels.

The central focus in Dollard and Miller's (1950) formulations is on the process of learning, or habit formation. They discuss four significant features of this process: drive, cue, response, and reinforcement (reward). *Drives* get an organism into action, *cues* suggest what behavior is appropriate (will lead to drive reduction), *response* is the behavior itself, and *reinforcement* strengthens the connection between cues and response by reducing the tension of drives.

A different way to reconcile a strict operant theory of behavior with personality approaches that stress aspects of the self is to add coverants to operants. A **coverant** is an "operant of the mind," a covert operant response that is influenced by the consequences it produces (Homme, 1965). Self-statements are thoughts we express to ourselves that are coverants. They may influence operants; the thought "he makes me angry" influences my aggressive action toward him. They may be influenced by operants; studying hard increases the probability you will think "I'm learning a lot and I enjoy this course." They can influence other coverants; one thought leads to another, as when you think "What a jerk I was for believing him" and other statements follow with greater probability—"I'm really gullible," "You can't trust men."

By adding a concern for these inner processes, learning theorists have widened the scope of the behavioristic view of human nature. Although modern behavioral approaches still place most of the emphasis on the situational determinants of behavior, they acknowledge that thoughts and feelings, beliefs and anxieties exert powerful influences on our actions.

Criticisms of Learning Theories

Critics hold that some behavioristic approaches to personality have thrown out the baby's vibrant personality and kept the cold bath water. In placing such emphasis on environment, they have lost contact with the person. Is it stimulus variables or living people that personality is all about, they ask? If one insists that personality is built upon the learned repetition of previously reinforced responding, where is the origin of all *new* behavior—creative achievements, innovative ideas, inventions, and works of art? Other criticisms reject views of behavior that seem to deny choice and the freedom to reject and rise above one's past history of reinforcement. In addition, critics argue, much of the learning observed by behaviorists is performance that is reinforced because an organism is in a state of deficiency motivation (hungry and thirsty) and other kinds of action and reinforcements are not available. The full realization of human potential comes, not from acting out of such appetitive motives, but from people's aspirations toward joy, immortality, altruism, and love—motives that put us above "lower animals" and on the side of angels.

Some of these criticisms, leveled primarily against the radical behaviorism of Skinnerian psychology, lose their force when confronted by new, broader social-learning theories. Increasingly, learning approaches are including cognitive processes along with behavioral ones, returning a mind to the body and perhaps even adding a unique personality "for good measure."

Cognitive Theories

Those who have proposed cognitive theories of personality point out that there are important individual differences in the way people think about and define any external situation. Cognitive theories stress the processes through which people turn their sensations and perceptions into organized impressions of reality. Like humanistic theories, they emphasize that individuals participate in creating their own personalities. People actively *choose* their own environments to a great extent; so even if the environment has an important impact on us, we are not just passive reactors. We weigh alternatives and select the settings in which we act and are acted upon.

The relationship between situational variables (social and environmental stimuli) and cognitive variables in regulating behavior is found in a number of personality theories. In this final section of our presentation of conceptual approaches to the study of human personality we will review the contributions of personal construct theory of George Kelly, examine the cognitive social-learning theories of Walter Mischel and Albert Bandura, and conclude with contemporary viewpoints from self theory.

Personal Construct Theory

George Kelly (1955) developed a theory of personality that places primary emphasis on each person's active, cognitive construction of his or her world. He argued strongly that no one is ever a victim of either past history or the present environment. Although events cannot be changed, all events are open to *alternative interpretations,* Kelly argued. People can always reconstruct their past or define their present difficulties in different ways.

Kelly used science as a metaphor for this process. Scientists develop theories to *understand* the natural world and to *make predictions* about what will occur in the future under particular conditions. The test of a scientific theory is its utility—how well it explains and predicts. If a theory isn't working well, or if it is extended outside the set of events where it does work well, then a new, more useful theory can and should be developed.

Kelly argued that *all* people function like scientists. We want to be able to predict and explain the world around us, especially our interpersonal world. The theories we use are called "personal constructs." Kelly defined a **personal construct** as a person's belief about the way two things are alike and the way they are different from a third. For example, I might say that my uncle and my brother are alike because they are highly competitive, but my sister is different from them because she likes to "take a back seat" to others. In this case, I seem to be using a construct of "competitiveness versus giving in to others" to organize my perceptions of people around me. Other personal constructs might be based on attractiveness or on the way others can be exploited for one's personal gain.

Personal constructs are not just labels that an outsider applies after seeing what a person does, according to Kelly. They guide what we see when we look at the world and influence how we respond to it. Each person's belief system—set of personal constructs, in Kelly's terms—determines the way he or she will think, feel, act, and define new situations. In other words, for Kelly, each person's total system of personal constructs is that individual's "personality."

Construct systems are completely idiographic in Kelly's view: each person has a unique set of constructs. People differ in the content of their constructs, the number available, and the ways they are related. In order to understand other people, we have to try to see the world as they see it, through their construct system rather than through our own.

Little direct research has come from Kelly's theory, largely because it places so much emphasis on the uniqueness of each person's personality. This approach has had more impact on clinicians, who can approach each case as an individual story, than on personality researchers, who are searching for general principles.

Cognitive Social-learning Theory: Bandura

Through his theoretical writing and extensive research with children and adults Albert Bandura (1986) of Stanford University has been an eloquent champion of a social-learning approach to understanding personality, an approach that combines principles of learning with an emphasis on human interactions in social settings. From a social-learning perspective, human beings are neither driven by inner forces nor helpless pawns of environmental influence.

A social-learning approach stresses the uniquely human cognitive processes that are involved in acquiring and maintaining patterns of behavior and, thus, personality. Because we can manipulate symbols and think about external events, we can foresee the possible consequences of our actions without having to actually experience them. Often we learn *vicariously* through observation of other people, in addition to learning from our own experience. We can evaluate our own behavior (according to personal standards) and provide ourselves with reinforcements (such as self-approval or self-reproach). Thus we are capable of self-regulation, able to control our own actions, rather than being automatically controlled by external forces.

Social-learning theory rejects the environmental determinism of a strict behavioristic perspective. Instead, it points to a complex interaction of individual factors, behavior, and environmental stimuli. Each can influence or change the others, and the direction of change is rarely one-way; instead, it is *reciprocal.* Your behavior can be influenced by your attitudes, beliefs, or prior history of reinforcement, as well as by available stimuli in the environment. What you do can have an effect on the environment, and important aspects of your personality can be affected by the environment or by feedback from your behavior. In this important concept of social-learning theory called **reciprocal determinism** (Bandura, 1981a), all the components are necessary if you want to completely understand human behavior, personality, and social ecology.

Observational Learning

Perhaps the most important contribution of Bandura's theory is its focus on **observational learning** as the process by which one person observes the behavior of another person and changes merely by being exposed to that model's behavior. Through observational learning, children and adults acquire an enormous range of information about their social environment—what is appropriate and gets rewarded, and what gets punished or ignored. In chapter 8, this approach was presented as a challenge to traditional behavioristic theory because an individual does not have *to act* in order to learn. Skills, attitudes, and beliefs may be acquired simply by watching what others do and the consequences that follow. This means that a child can develop a gender identity and sex role by observing how men and women behave in their culture and how the culture responds differently to them (S. Bem, 1984). Children may also learn "personality traits" of altruism (Straub, 1974) or the ability to delay gratification through observation of models, whether "live" and physically present, or presented indirectly in "symbolic" form through books, movies, or TV. The effects of these models on children's willingness to delay gratification was demonstrated in an experiment with fourth- and fifth-graders.

> *Children's preferences for a high or low delay of reward were first assessed by giving them a series of 14 choices between small immediate rewards and larger delayed ones. The researchers wanted to show that exposure to a person who modeled behavior* opposite *to the children's initial preference would modify their delay or immediate reward-seeking behavior. Children who initially found it difficult to delay were shown an adult model who consistently chose the postponed reward, while those who initially showed a high-delay preference saw an adult model who chose the immediate reward. The models also discussed their general philosophy toward aspects of life relevant to attitudes about delay of reward. Subjects were randomly assigned to one of three conditions: a live model, a symbolic model (information presented in written form), or no model present. They were then given a second test of their preferences in the absence of any model and a third test a month later to see if any immediate effects had generalized. The results indicated that modeling clearly altered delay preferences, that this effect remained over time, and that either type of model was equally effective in getting children to delay when they previously had not. However, live modeling was more effective than symbolic modeling in changing a "delayer" into an "impulsive hedonist" who opted for the bird in the hand and left the two in the bush for those who preferred to delay. (Bandura & Mischel, 1965)*

Undaunted by arthritis, Marian Green learned how to cope with her disorder through a course developed at Stanford University.

Self-efficacy

Bandura has recently (1986) elaborated the concept of self-efficacy as a central part of social learning theory. As described briefly in chapter 11, **self-efficacy** is a belief that one can perform adequately in a particular situation. A person's sense of capability influences his or her perception, motivation, and performance in many ways. We don't even try to do things or take chances when we expect to be ineffectual. We avoid people and situations when we don't feel adequate to the performance they require. Even when we do, in fact, *have* the ability—and the desire—we may not take the required action or persist to complete the task successfully, if we *think* we lack what it takes.

Self-efficacy, as a sense of personal mastery, is not the same as an overall sense of self-confidence. Bandura believes that perceptions of one's abilities are best thought of as a host of *specific* evaluations. This view cautions that we should be careful to avoid oversimplifying people's complex self-knowledge and self-evaluations into a simplistic single label like "self-esteem." However, a sense of self-efficacy can affect behavior in situations which differ from those in which it was generated, since, once established, positive expectations about one's efficacy can generalize to new situations (Bandura, 1977b).

Beyond our actual accomplishments, other sources of efficacy judgments include: (a) our observations of the performance of others; (b) social and self-persuasion (others may convince us that we can do something, or we may convince ourselves); and (c) monitoring our emotional states as we think about or approach a task. For example, anxiety suggests low expectations of efficacy; excitement suggests expectations of success.

Besides influencing our choices of activities, tasks, situations, and companions, our self-efficacy judgments also influence how much effort we expend and how long we "hang in" when faced with difficulty. How vigorously and persistently a student pursues academic tasks depends more on his or her sense of self-efficacy than on actual ability. Expectations of success or failure can change in light of feedback from performance, but they are more likely to create the *predicted* feedback and, thus, to become self-fulfilling prophecies.

Expectations of failure—and a decision to stop trying—may, of course, be based on a perception of a situation as unresponsive, punishing, or unsupportive, rather than on a perception of one's own inadequacy. Such expectations are called *outcome based* rather than *efficacy based* expectations. The person who believes that responding is useless because of low self-efficacy needs to develop competencies that will boost self-perception of efficacy. On the other hand, where a tendency to give up is based on outcome expectancies, then the environment, and not the person, may need to be changed so that reinforcements will, in fact, follow competent responding.

Can the sense of teachers' self-efficacy affect student achievement? The results of a classroom field study strongly support the association between these personality and performance variables.

> *Forty-eight teachers in four high schools with large numbers of "culturally deprived" students participated in this study. The researchers measured the teachers' sense of teaching efficacy on self-report scales, made classroom observations of "climate and atmosphere," and assessed student achievement on standardized tests. Correlations between these (and a number of other measures) reveals that teachers with a greater sense of self-efficacy tend to maintain a positive emotional climate in their classes, while avoiding harsh modes of behavior control that tend to characterize low-efficacy teachers. In addition, student achievement on the mathematics test was significantly correlated with the teachers' self-efficacy; students scored higher as teacher self-efficacy was higher. However, this effect was situation specific to the teaching of mathematics. It did not hold for reading achievement test performance—perhaps because the "basic skills language class" the teachers taught did not teach reading. (Ashton & Webb, 1986)*

Cognitive Social-Learning Theory: Mischel

Mischel has already been mentioned as one of those who questioned the utility of traits as a way to describe personality. As an alternative, Mischel proposes a cognitive theory of personality which also draws heavily on principles from social-learning theory.

Like other social-learning theorists, Mischel places a great deal of emphasis on the influence of environmental variables on behavior. In his view, much of what we do and many of our beliefs and values are *not* best thought of as emerging properties of the self. Rather, he sees them as responses developed, maintained, or changed by our observation of influential models and by specific stimulus-response pairings in our own experience.

Dimensions of Individual Difference

Mischel also emphasizes the active role of a person in cognitively organizing his or her interactions with the environment (Mischel & Peake, 1982). (It is interesting to note that Kelly was Mischel's graduate advisor.) How you respond to a specific environmental input, according to Mischel, depends on any or all of the following variables or processes:

- *Competencies*—what you know, what you can do, and your ability to generate certain cognitive and behavioral outcomes
- *Encoding strategies*—the way you process incoming information, selectively attending, categorizing, and making associations to it
- *Expectancies*—your anticipation of likely outcomes for given actions in particular situations
- *Personal values*—the importance you attach to stimuli, events, people, and activities
- *Self-regulatory systems and plans*—the rules you have developed for guiding your performance, setting goals, and evaluating your effectiveness

What determines the nature of these variables for an individual? According to Mischel, they result from an individual's observations and interactions with other people and with inanimate aspects of the physical environment. When people respond differently to the same environmental input, it is because of differences in these person variables (Mischel, 1973).

Person Versus Environment

Mischel emphasizes the *adaptive flexibility* of human behavior. Although the person variables previously listed are a continuing influence on our behavior, we also are able to adapt and change in response to

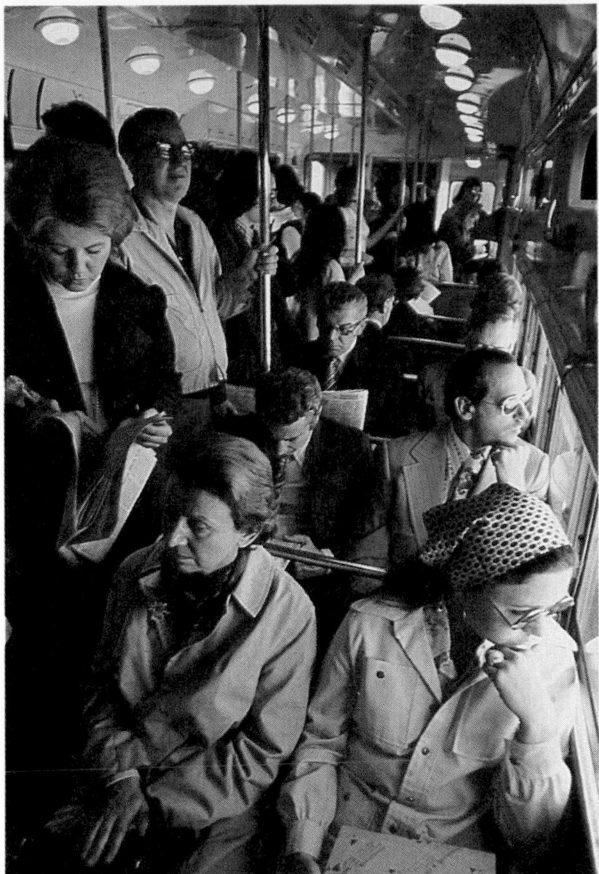

The situational cues on a bus are strong and clear. People do not generally interact.

the new demands of our environment. Mischel hypothesizes that, in general, person variables will have their greatest impact on behavior when cues in the situation are weak or ambiguous. When situations are strong and clear, there will be less individual variation in response. For example, in a dentist's waiting room, most of us tend to behave pretty much the same in response to the strong situational demands. At the beach, however, where many behaviors are appropriate, person variables will lead to large differences in behavior. A good deal of evidence in support of this view has been reported (Mischel, 1979; Monson et al., 1982).

Self Theory

Just as Bandura's cognitive-social approach has its roots in the learning theory tradition, self theory, though clearly cognitive, has come out of the humanistic tradition. For humanistic psychologists the **self** is the irreducible unit out of which the coherence and stability of the personality emerge. The notion of a self is hardly new. "Know thyself" is an inscription carved on the shrine of the Delphic oracle in ancient Greece.

Within early psychology, the concern for analysis of the self found its strongest advocate in William James (1890). James identified three components of self-experience: the *material me* (the bodily self, along with physical objects one is surrounded by); the *social me* (one's awareness of his or her reputation in the eyes of others); and the *spiritual me* (the self that monitors private thoughts and feelings).

In Carl Rogers' view the self or *self-concept* emerges as part of the actualizing tendency's process of enabling a child to *differentiate* between all that is within or part of him or her and all that is external. The *self* becomes a consistent, whole set of organized perceptions of the characteristics of "I" or "me" along with the relationships of that "I/me" to other people, and other aspects of life. Self-concept includes both what people perceive themselves to be and what they would like to be ideally. *Consistency* in personality, according to Rogers, is between this *actual* and *ideal self* rather than between parts of personality, traits and actions, or past and present aspects of functioning.

Self-concept

There is a growing recognition among psychologists about the importance of self-concept and the development of a person's sense of self for a full understanding of human personality (Gordon & Gergen, 1968; Walsh & Vaughan, 1980; Wylie, 1974). A sense of **identity** includes the perception of one's self as distinct from other people and of other things as related to one's self or alien to one's self. It is central to our sense of a unique personality. A person's **self-esteem,** as a generalized evaluative attitude toward the self, influences both moods and behavior. Interestingly, the belief in the impact of self-esteem on performance across many situations has led to a congressional appropriation in California (1987) to establish a Self-Esteem Commission. Its task is to discover ways in which self-esteem can be enhanced to benefit both individuals and society.

Early psychological work on the self tried to relate global, complex behavior, such as delinquency or marital conflict, to single aspects of the overall self-concept, such as self-esteem. However, emerging perspectives on self theory are more dynamic and anchored in both cognitive information-processing approaches and social psychological foundations (Salovey & Rodin, 1985). In this new view the **self-concept** is a dynamic mental structure that interprets and mediates many *intra*personal processes (motivation, affect, information processing) and *inter*personal processes (social perception, social choices).

The self-concept is thought to be an internal regulator of thoughts, feelings, and actions. For different psychologists, self-concept is a multifaceted phenomenon made up of a vast set of schemas, prototypes, goals, or personal theories (see Yardley & Honess, 1987). As schema, it has a dual nature: the self as object or structure known (the contents of mind related to self-relevant thoughts) and the self as agent of knowing (the process of discovering information about the self).

Five features of this new view of the self-concept are that it: (a) mediates and regulates ongoing behavior; (b) is dynamic in being active, forceful, and capable of change; (c) interprets and organizes actions and experiences of personal relevance; (d) has motivational impact on behavior by providing incentives, plans, rules, and scripts; and (e) adjusts in response to feedback and challenge from the environment (Markus & Wurf, 1987).

Social Aspects of the Self-concept

Although the concept of self has to do with individuals, full development of the self enables an individual to relate effectively to other people. Social psychologists have long acknowledged the powerful role that self-concept plays in social situations. Erving Goffman's classic study of *The Presentation of Self in Everyday Life* (1959) focused researchers' attention on the strategies and tactics people use to "manage the impressions" they create on others (see Jones & Pittman, 1982).

Once a person has formed a self-concept, as did Adam and Timmy, the students in our *Opening Case,* then he or she engages in activities of *self-verification* and *self-enhancement* (Swann, 1985). Children forge a coherent concept of self from information of three kinds: (a) observing how others act toward them; (b) observing how they act and noting the causal inferences from those self-perceptions; and (c) noticing how they compare with others in their opinions, abilities, and emotions. These self-concepts then direct cognitive and behavioral processes designed to construct *social reality* that verifies and maintains their self-concept. How is it done? Self-verification involves ensuring that others see you the way you see yourself; but it may be a risky task to hope passively that others will come to evaluate you as you do yourself.

A more active form of "strategic self-presentation" leads to behavioral tactics that increase the probability of agreement between your self view and the view others have of you. One way to do so is by means of *behavioral confirmation* (Snyder, 1984). This is a process in which beliefs about the self control one's behavior (source) in the presence of others (target). These target people are then more likely to react according to the behavioral context established and confirm the original belief about what kind of person the source "really is." In this way, "beliefs create reality." People who are extraverted solicit extraverted behaviors in others (Fong & Markus, 1982); those who are anxious interact with others in ways that cause them to behave anxiously (Riggs & Cantor, 1981), while those who are feeling depressed provoke depressed, hostile feelings in others with whom they converse (Strack & Coyne, 1983).

Sometimes when we have doubts about important self qualities, we may engage in activities designed to sustain a positive image by conveniently excusing anticipated negative evaluations. This process of "self-handicapping" externalizes potential failures (explains them away), while internalizing success (taking credit for it). See the ***Close-up*** on pages 448–49 for more on this new area of investigation into the self.

Criticisms of Cognitive Theories

One set of criticisms leveled against cognitive theories is that they generally overlook emotion as an important component of personality. The variables emphasized (constructs, encoding strategies, and the like) are rational, information-processing variables. Emotions are reduced to the status of byproducts of thoughts and behavior rather than having independent importance. For those who feel that emotions are more central to the functioning of human personality, this is a serious flaw. Several new lines of research have demonstrated that emotions have an important effect on cognitive processes such as memory, reaction time, and decision making (Bower, 1981; Zajonc, 1980). Feelings may themselves be important determinants of cognitive content and structure, rather than just "cognitive coatings." These approaches are also attacked for not fully recognizing the impact of unconscious sources of motivation on behavior and affect.

A second set of criticisms focuses on the vagueness of explanations about the way personal constructs and competencies are created. They have little to say about the developmental origins of adult personality, tending to be ahistorical in their focus on the individual's perception of the current behavior setting. This is particularly true of Kelly's theory—much less true of Mischel's and Bandura's. Although it is central to Kelly's view that people are free to change their constructs, it is unclear from his theory how constructs develop and what is needed for them to change. Moreover, an important theme in Kelly's personal construct theory is the prediction of future events, but the theory deals less with how someone anticipates his or her own behavior than it does with the way that person anticipates other people's behavior.

Critics of self theory approaches argue against the limitless boundaries: "Where does the self end and the gutter begin?" The global, macro level of the variables that are included as aspects of the self and the fuzziness of ways to operationalize concepts like self-actualization have also been targets of critical review.

Despite these criticisms, cognitive personality theories have made major contributions to current thinking. For example, Kelly's theory has influenced a large number of cognitive therapists. Mischel's theoretical views have also had a great deal of influence on views about *when* person variables can be expected to be important and *when* situation variables probably will be. This may be a more useful perspective than controversy about *whether* person variables overall are more or less important than situational variables.

Comparing Theories

A unified theory of personality that a majority of psychologists can endorse does not exist. Perhaps in the future such a theory may emerge, or maybe there will always be diverse theories, since different approaches start with different premises and explore different perspectives.

Several differences in basic assumptions have come up repeatedly as we have surveyed the various theories. It may be helpful to list the most important of these and to compare the emphasis given to them by the different approaches.

1. **Heredity versus environment**—nature or nurture, the importance of genetic and biological factors as compared with influences from the environment. Trait theories have been split on this issue; Freudian theory depends heavily on heredity; humanistic, learning, and cognitive theories all emphasize either environment as a determinant of behavior or interaction with the environment as a source of personality development and differences.
2. **Learning processes versus innate laws of behavior**—emphasis on *modifiability* versus a view of personality development following an internal timetable. Again, trait theories have been divided. Freudian theory has favored the inner determinant view—a pessimistic one—while an optimistic brand of innate striving is postulated by humanists.
3. **Emphasis on past, present,** or **future**—trait theories emphasize past causes, whether innate or learned; Freudian theory emphasizes past events in early childhood; and learning theories emphasize past reinforcements and present contingencies. Humanistic theories tend to emphasize present phenomenal reality or future goals. Cognitive theories emphasize past and present (and the future if goal-setting is involved).
4. **Consciousness versus unconsciousness**—Freudian theory emphasizes unconscious processes; humanistic and cognitive theories emphasize conscious processes. Trait theories and learning theories, which are less concerned with mental processes, pay little attention to either consciousness or unconsciousness.
5. **Inner disposition versus outer situation**—Learning theories emphasize situational factors; the others emphasize either dispositional factors or an interaction and joint contribution.

So each group of theories makes different contributions to our human "vehicle." Trait theories provide a catalog that describes the parts and structures. Psychodynamic theories add a powerful engine and the fuel to get the vehicle moving. Learning theories supply the steering wheel, directional signals, and other regulation equipment. Humanistic theories put a person in the driver's seat—a man or a woman who wants to travel to a unique place and enjoy the trip as much as the arrival at a destination. Cognitive theories add reminders to the driver that the way the trip is planned, organized, and remembered will differ according to the mental map he or she chooses for the journey.

Personality theories are, in part, attempts to explain how and why people differ. Another important activity for psychologists has been the *measurement* of differences among people. Different theories have different implications about *what* should be measured, *how* it should be measured, and *when* the information obtained justifies a decision to intervene in someone's life—to hire, fire, admit, reject, or treat the person being assessed. In the next chapter we take an in-depth look at the techniques and results of psychological assessment.

Close-up Self-Handicapping: For Better . . . or for Worse?

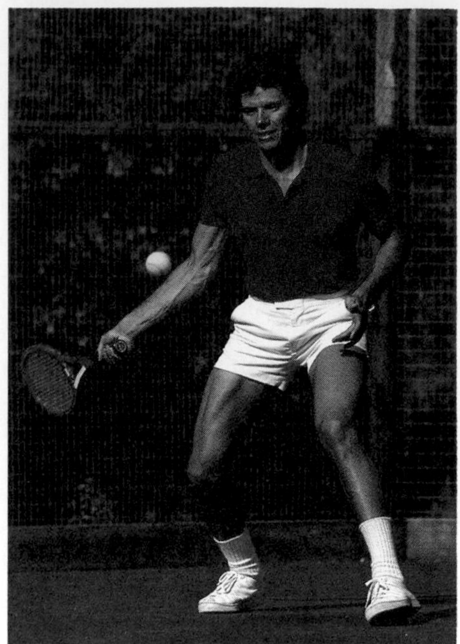

A basic assumption about self-concept is that people seek to define themselves clearly, searching for a coherent identity and self-definition. Adolescence and middle adulthood are times of intensive search, spurred by questioning and change. Much of social psychology, to be introduced in forthcoming chapters, has been based on the idea that people seek accurate information about their environment and their own place in it (for example, Festinger, 1954; Heider, 1958; H. Kelley, 1971).

Surprisingly, some of the most interesting contemporary research on the self has found that people often do just the opposite. For example, individuals who suffer from anxious uncertainty and self-doubts can only sustain their sense of personal efficacy by avoiding a clear test of their competence; ironically, the benefits of avoiding a test of one's competence simply outweigh the benefits of a clear and precise self-evaluation. The phenomenon called *self-handicapping* is an illustration.

In self-handicapping, the goal of the self-doubter is to minimize ability (or lack of ability, really) as a plausible explanation for poor performance (Jones & Berglas, 1978). We live in a world where a great deal of what we do is evaluated, both by ourselves and by others, with an eye toward assessing the level of ability underlying performance (Darley & Goethals, 1980). Performance on the tennis court, in the classroom, in the concert hall, and across a table for two is scrutinized closely to determine athletic, intellectual, artistic, or social competence; but what if the person under scrutiny has a handicap—a broken tennis racket, a bad headcold, a sleepless night, or an unresponsive date? Then failure can't be taken as a reflection of one's "self," can it? The self-handicapper uses this logic to advantage, placing a barrier to successful performance on the road to performance.

In the original experiment on self-handicapping (Berglas & Jones, 1978), subjects who had previously succeeded at a task, but did not expect that success to recur on a repetition of the task, took the opportunity to protect themselves—their "selves"—by ingesting a performance-debilitating drug instead of a performance-facilitating drug (both of which were presumably under study by the psychologists). By taking the drug the subjects were able to manipulate the situation so that

Summary

- Personality is what characterizes an individual—what is characteristic and unique about a person across different situations and over time. Personality theorists study the whole person as the sum of the separate processes of feelings, thoughts, and actions.
- The focus of the idiographic approach is the organization of the unique person; that of the nomothetic approach is the uniformities across people, as well as the ways they vary on the same set of dimensions. Descriptions of consistency and even opinions of how much consistency there is have varied widely.
- Some theorists, such as Sheldon and Eysenck, categorize people by all-or-none types, assumed to be related to particular characteristic behaviors. Others view traits as the building blocks of personality. Allport, an idiographic theorist, differentiated cardinal, central, and secondary traits.

their impending failure, if it occurred, would be seen as plausibly attributable to the debilitating drug. In this way the subjects could at least sustain the illusion that their first performance might be because of their true abilities. Also they could avoid the frightening possibility that their upcoming performance, likely a failure, would completely undermine their sense of personal efficacy.

The only subjects who self-handicapped in this way were those who had self-doubt about their original success. Half the subjects had taken an initial test comprised of 16 solvable and 4 unsolvable problem items: the other half had taken an initial test made up of 4 solvable and 16 unsolvable problems. In both instances, the experimenter exclaimed, "You have done extremely well, in fact better than nearly all the participants who have taken this test thus far." Those who had taken the test comprised mostly of unsolvable problems, problems they later reported seeming almost impossible, were confronted with a success they couldn't imagine they had really achieved—or at least couldn't imagine how they had achieved it! (Actually, of course, they had not succeeded.) To protect their fragile sense of competence, of self-esteem and feelings of efficacy, they self-handicapped. The performance-debilitating drug protected them from failure and also protected their belief that their first success might be claimed as their own.

Self-handicapping, in short, is a "response to an anticipated loss in self-esteem" (C. R. Snyder & Smith, 1982, p. 107); a phenomenon placed squarely under the time-honored umbrella of the motive to protect or sustain self-esteem. A self-handicapping individual must have a precarious and fragile, but not entirely negative, self-concept. A "perpetual loser" who, after a long and scarring history of inadequacy, has little or no self-esteem is not a prime candidate for self-handicapping; the very basis of the self-handicapping strategy must be "that the strategist has something to protect" (Jones & Berglas, 1978, p. 205).

If you are guessing that a wide variety of behaviors can reflect self-handicapping tendencies, you're on the right track. A review of the three dozen studies on the topic since 1978 discussed cases of procrastination, laziness, drug and alcohol abuse, moodiness, trying the impossible, and many other illustrations of self-handicapping in everyday life. While self-handicapping is surely not as common as the seeking of self-understanding (most of the time most people live up to the recommendation of the oracle of Delphi), it seems clear that people also frequently prefer ambiguity, rather than clarity, about their attributes—especially when the clarity may prove unflattering (Arkin & Baumgardner, 1985).

- Traits, as measured by personality tests, are poor predictors of specific instances of behavior. Correlations between different behaviors assumed to reflect the same traits are low, though there is more temporal stability than cross-situational stability in behavior.
- In his psychodynamic theory, Freud accepted Darwin's emphasis on instinctive biological energies as basic motivators and further proposed unconscious motivation as the key to behavior. Basic concepts of Freudian theory include psychic determinism in both behavior and some forms of illness; early experiences as key determinants of lifelong personality; psychic energy from basic drives as giving power and direction to behavior; and powerful unconscious processes determining behavior, feelings, dreams, and even slips of the tongue.
- Freud saw personality composed of the id (guided by the pleasure principle), the superego (guided by learned social and moral restrictions), and the reconciling ego (guided by the reality principle). Unacceptable feelings and wishes were repressed; an individual developed various ego-defense mechanisms to lessen anxiety and bolster self-esteem.

- Freudian concepts are vague, not operationally defined, and difficult or impossible to test scientifically; they are applied retrospectively and do not predict a person's behavior or take into account his or her goals and ideas. Also, they are based on clinical experience with disturbed individuals and have little to say about healthy life-styles.
- Post-Freudians have put greater emphasis on ego functioning and social variables and less on sexual urges. They see personality development as a lifelong process. Adler thought each person developed a consistent life-style aimed at compensating or overcompensating for feelings of inferiority. Jung emphasized the notion of a collective unconscious, including archetypes (symbols of universal significance); he saw the needs to create and self-actualize as powerful unconscious instincts in all people.
- The focus of humanistic theories is on the growth potential of the individual. These theories are holistic, dispositional, phenomenological, existential, and optimistic. At the core of Rogers person-centered personality theory is the concept of self-actualization, a constant striving to realize one's potential and to develop one's talents. To understand the individual, one must understand his or her private world.
- Humanistic theories are criticized for vagueness and oversimplification; for having little to say about individual differences; for neglect of environmental variables, unconscious influences, and an individual's past; and for inability to make predictions.
- Strict behaviorists see personality as the sum of overt and covert responses that are reliably elicited as a consequence of an individual's reinforcement history. Different histories of reinforcement account for individual differences. Their interest is not in people's behavior being consistent, but in how behavior changes when stimulus conditions change.
- Learning theories have been criticized for disregarding important characteristics of human organisms, for overemphasis on environmental determinants, and for being based on research with subjects in a state of deficiency motivation. Increasingly, however, approaches based on learning are taking into account cognitive processes as well as behavioral ones.
- Cognitive theorists emphasize individual differences in perception and interpretation, and an individual's creation of his or her own environment. According to Kelly's theory of personal constructs, all people, like scientists, construct the best picture they can of reality; personality is a person's total system of such constructs.
- Bandura's cognitive social-learning theory combines principles of learning with an emphasis on social interactions. Important concepts are reciprocal determinism, observational learning, and self-efficacy as critical to the analysis of person-behavior-situation interactions.
- Mischel stresses a person's active role in cognitively organizing interactions with the environment in the light of his or her competencies, ways of processing information, expectancies, values, and self-imposed rules and plans. He sees person variables having the greatest influence in weak or ambiguous situations, and situations having greatest impact when they are strong and clear.
- Self theory, a cognitive theory which developed from the humanistic tradition, focuses on the importance of the self-concept for a full understanding of human personality. The self-concept is a dynamic mental structure that motivates, interprets, organizes, mediates, and regulates intrapersonal and interpersonal behaviors and processes. Once formed, the self-concept is maintained through processes of self-verification, self-enhancement, and behavioral confirmation.
- Cognitive theories are criticized for overemphasizing rational variables and neglecting emotion and unconscious processes, as well as for vagueness about the way personal constructs and competencies develop.
- The different theories vary their assumptions about nature versus nurture; the modifiability of behavior; emphasis on past, present, or future; conscious versus unconscious; and the importance of inner dispositions versus outer situations in producing consistency in behavior.

13

Assessing Individual Differences

Little Maria loved her kindergarten class. There were such delightful things to do and nice friends to play with that she often wished she could live in that clean, colorful schoolroom. When most of her friends moved up to first grade, however, Maria and a few others were sent to a class for children who were "different." She couldn't be with her friends in the regular first grade because she had been assigned to the class for "retarded children."

That made her sad, and she was even more confused and upset later when former classmates began calling her things like "dummy" and "retard." Soon she realized that she must indeed be different from them, because a lot of the children in her new class were handicapped or couldn't talk right. There weren't the same kinds of games to play, and everything seemed to take so long, to go so slowly.

Maria began to daydream to escape the boredom that was taking the joy out of her young life, so sometimes she was not prepared to hear the teacher's questions. She thought that the teacher, too, must think she was a "dummy." She couldn't even enjoy the coloring book that her teacher gave her, because the pictures were not printed clearly. The lines and letters were so fuzzy that she made silly mistakes when she had to read the numbers and words.

The following year, Maria was reassigned to the remedial class and might have gone through her entire public school education there were it not for some special tests she took: not mental tests of what she knew and could do, but sensory tests of her vision and hearing. The test results clearly showed that Maria's academic problems were traceable, at least in part, to an undetected visual impairment—poor close vision. In addition, she was somewhat hard of hearing.

The tester from this sensory assessment program arranged to have Maria's intelligence assessed using individually administered tests. She performed well above average! Maria had been misdiagnosed as "retarded" by her teachers because

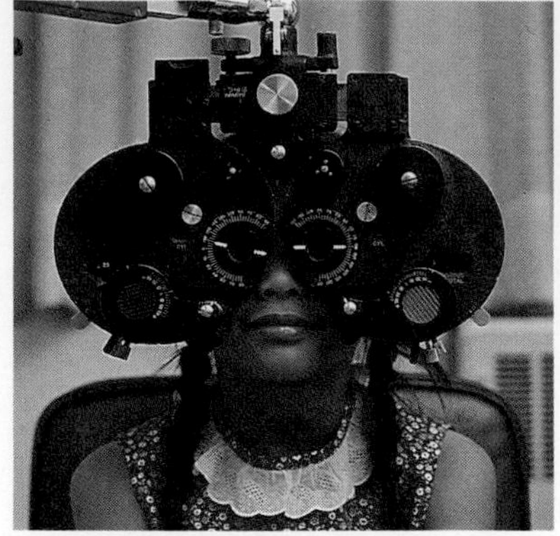

her sensory impairments led to the false impressions that she did not *understand* what she saw and heard.

On the basis of the new test data, Maria was given eyeglasses and eye muscle exercises to improve her vision. She was also seated in the front of the class, where she could hear the teacher better. Most important to her, she was transferred to a regular class, to be with some of her former good friends. She forgave them for the name-calling because they had made the same mistake that the teachers and even she had made. Maria went on to perform well academically and to enjoy school as a special place where people are concerned about helping others.

The special sensory testing program described in the vignette is called P.A.T.H.S. (Paramedical Approaches to Health Services) and is run by New York City Community School District 11; the original screening and help in arranging further testing is carried out by paramedical health interns. Similar programs in other cities help many children by assessing their ability to perform academically. They help correct mistaken judgments based on a teacher's limited—or in some cases, too readily prejudicial—observations. Those judgments may be confounded by undetected problems of a nonintellectual nature—in Maria's case, sensory problems; for other children, motivational or attentional problems. An untold number of children, like Maria, have been helped by such assessment procedures.

Psychological assessment of the attributes of individuals—measurement of intelligence, personality, creativity, and more—is a major contribution that psychology has made to society. It takes place in many educational and vocational settings. When a person's aptitudes, interests, attitudes, and personality are all taken into account, the chances of improving the "fit" of person to school or job are greatly increased.

The use of objective assessment procedures to estimate a person's abilities and skills removes the arbitrary, subjective, and unconsciously biased evaluations of authorities such as employers and admissions officers. Assessment also helps clinical psychologists detect problems in functioning that may require special counseling or treatment. Finally, assessment techniques can give researchers a way to see if individuals have the characteristics predicted by their theories and to select as subjects individuals who have the particular characteristics most relevant for their research.

There is much controversy about the use and misuse of test results and about some of the assumptions on which assessment is based. In this chapter we will examine what psychological assessment does, how it does it, and what problems it can help correct—and create.

What Is Assessment?

Psychological assessment is the use of specified testing procedures to evaluate the abilities, behaviors, and personal qualities of people. Assessment contributes to better understanding of a person so that more informed decisions can be made about current problems or future choices in a person's life (Maloney & Ward, 1976). It is often referred to as the measurement of *individual differences,* since the majority of assessment procedures describe individuals by specifying how they are different from or similar to other people—how many more test questions they can answer than other people their age, whether they seem more hypnotizable, or paranoid, whether their performance is similar to that of a computer scientist or a creative artist.

History of Assessment

The development of formal tests and procedures for assessment is a relatively new enterprise in psychology. It is surprising to discover that long before Western psychology began devising tests to see how people "measured up," assessment techniques were commonplace in ancient China. In fact, China employed a sophisticated program of civil service testing over 4000 years ago, when officials were required to demonstrate their competence every third year at an oral examination. Two thousand years later, during the Han Dynasty, written civil service tests were used to assess competence in the areas of law, the military, agriculture, and geography. During the Ming Dynasty (1368–1644 A.D.), public officials were chosen on the basis of their performance at three stages of an objective selection procedure. Examinations were first given at the local level. The 4 percent who passed these tests had to endure nine days and nights of essay examinations on the classics. The 5 percent who passed the essay exams were allowed to complete a final set of tests conducted at the nation's capital.

China's selection procedures were observed and described by British diplomats and missionaries in the early 1800s. Modified versions of China's system were soon adopted by the British, and later by the Americans, for the selection of civil service personnel (Wiggins, 1973). While these early assessment techniques were used for job placement only, they now are used for many different purposes and take place in a multitude of settings. Tests to see how people do in school, how well they may do later, what their strengths and weaknesses are, and how well they will function in different settings are varieties of aptitude and ability assessment.

Purposes of Assessment

The purposes of formal assessment are not really very different from most people's informal goals in "sizing up" others. Your parents probably wondered if you "had it in you" to "make it in college." If they had predicted incorrectly it would have been financially and emotionally costly. The *error* in such predictions, of course, can go in either of two directions: it is possible to predict failure (and withhold a college education) when a student will be effective, or to estimate success (and support a college education) when the student is actually ineffective and flunks out. Similarly, of course, there are two kinds of accurate predictions: those in which success is predicted and achieved, and those in which failure is predicted and observed.

In many areas of our lives we also want to predict the future behavior of someone under largely unknown or uncertain circumstances. Your choice of a person to live with you as roommate, or later as spouse and perhaps as parent of your children, involves an important assessment prediction. So does choosing a career for yourself. While you are acting as assessor, you are also being assessed by others—potential dates, mates, employers, judges, and superior officers who are sizing up your qualifications.

Scientific psychology attempts to formalize the procedures by which predictions about individual behavior can be made with a minimum of error and a maximum of accuracy. Assessment begins with the measurement of a limited number of individual personality attributes and samples of behavior. From this narrow body of information about a person in a testing situation(s), predictions are made about his or her likely reactions at some future time in some other situation (not identical to the test situation).

Psychologists use assessment techniques to make sense of the incredible range of individual differences. They want to understand how different traits go together to form a unique personality. They are curious to discover ways of describing the diversity of individual behavior. By testing, classifying, and categorizing individuals who share similar traits, psychologists can correlate behavioral differences with personality types. Part of such research is designed to test empirically the predictive value of different theories of personality looked at in the previous chapter.

Another aspect of the scientific concern for assessment has to do with learning about the way people develop. At what ages do children develop which skills, attitudes, and ways of dealing with the world? How important are sex, race, intelligence, and other human characteristics in predicting specific behavioral outcomes? A personality psychologist is interested in general answers to these and similar questions about relationships between the average behavioral tendency of people with certain characteristics. While a clinical psychologist's goal is to make predictions about an individual client, a research psychologist's goal is to discover consistencies and regularities in personality that translate to behavior in general. In all such testing, the goal is to find out more information that will further the development of psychology as a theoretical and applied science.

When assessment is used for an applied purpose (in contrast to a theoretical one), the process begins with a *referral.* When certain questions arise about the behavioral or mental functioning of a particular individual, he or she is referred to a psychologist who is trained to make an assessment that might provide some answers. A judge may want to know if an admitted murderer is capable of understanding the consequences of his actions so that responsibility can be assigned to him. A teacher may want to know why a child, like little Maria, has learning difficulties or shows behavior problems. Parents are often eager to know how intelligent their children really are, regardless of class grades. A clinical psychologist will ask about a patient's status prior to treatment and will want to know about changes during or after treatment, in order to guide therapeutic strategies (Korchin, 1976).

The kinds of questions asked influence the kinds of assessment that will be undertaken and the way the assessment conclusions will be phrased and interpreted. The clinicians involved in the assessment, depending on their theoretical orientations, may each focus on something different and get different views of the same person or assessment data. "There is a psychoanalytic reality, a social-learning reality, an existential reality, and so on. The purpose of assessment is not to discover the true essence of the client but to describe that client in a useful way—a way that will lead to the solution of a problem" (Phares, 1984, p. 174).

Methods of Assessment

While there are clearly parallels between the informal assessment of ourselves and other people that we all do, and the more formal assessment carried out by professionals, there are important differences, too. As already noted, the methods of assessment used by psychologists are developed in more systematic ways; they are used in a more organized manner for more carefully specified purposes. Indeed, that is what we mean when we call the everyday assessments *informal* and call those carried out in professional settings *formal.*

We will first consider some of the characteristics that make professional assessments "formal." After discussing these requirements, we will examine some of the information sources psychologists use to make assessments. Note that some of their techniques are derived from the kinds of different *theoretical* perspectives outlined in the previous chapter. However, there are also assessment techniques based on an *empirical,* rather than a theoretical, foundation. That is, their construction was not guided by any theory of personality or intelligence or psychopathology. Instead, tests were developed on which different types of people responded differently, so that they (and others) could be categorized on the basis of those performance differences.

Basic Features of Formal Assessment

To be useful for classifying individuals or selecting those with particular qualities, an assessment procedure should meet three requirements. The assessment instrument, or test, should be (a) *reliable,* (b) *valid,* and, for most purposes, (c) *standardized.* If a test fails to meet these requirements, then we cannot be sure that a person's score really indicates what it is supposed to or that an assessment conclusion will be trustworthy.

Reliability

A test is *reliable* if it measures something consistently. **Reliability** is the extent to which an assessment instrument can be trusted to give consistent scores—either on retests or when different raters judge the same performance. If your bathroom scale gives you a different reading each time you step on it—sometimes higher, other times lower (even though you haven't eaten or changed your clothing and little time has passed between "testings")—then your scale is not doing its job. We would call it *unreliable* because we could not count on it to give consistent results.

One straightforward way to find out if tests are reliable is to calculate their **test-retest reliability.** This is a measure of the correlation between the scores of the same people on the same test given on two different occasions. A perfectly reliable test will yield a correlation coefficient of +1.00. This means that the same exact pattern of scores emerges both times; the same people that got the highest and lowest scores the first time do so again. A totally unreliable test results in a .00 correlation coefficient. That means there is no relationship between the first set of scores and the second set; someone who got the top score initially might get any score, even the lowest, the second time.

There are two other ways of assessing reliability. One is to administer alternate, *equivalent forms* of a test instead of giving exactly the same test twice. Doing so reduces effects of direct practice, memory, or the desire of an individual to appear consistent. The other is to measure the *internal consistency* of responses on a single test. For example, we can compare a person's score on the odd-numbered items of a test to that on the even-numbered items. A reliable test yields the same score for each of its halves; it is then said to have high internal consistency on this measure of *split-half reliability.*

Correlation coefficients of reliability above .70 are found for the best psychological tests. By comparison, achievement tests constructed by classroom teachers generally range in reliability from as low as .30 up to only about .60. These correlations are for objective, true-false, and multiple-choice tests; you already know about the greater unreliability of essay-test scores from personal experience.

Although a reliable test tends to give the same test scores when repeated, obtaining different test scores does not necessarily mean that a test is unreliable. Sometimes the variable being measured actually changes. For example, if you took a test on theories of personality before and after reading chapter 12, you would (I hope!) do better the second time—because you would actually know more. In addition, many variables other than the one of primary interest may affect test scores. You may score differently on two different occasions because of changes in your mood, how tired you are, how hard you are trying, and so forth. If a test is designed to measure mood, fatigue, or motivation, then this change is just what we want; if not, then these variables will alter the desired test performance, to give a false picture of your ability.

Validity

If a test is reliable, we know it is doing a good job of measuring something. Of course, we also want to know what that "something" is. The **validity** of a test is the degree to which it measures what an assessor intends it to measure. A valid test of intelligence gives a measure of a person's intelligence and predicts performance in situations where intelligence is important. Scores on a valid intelligence test are not affected by how experienced a person is at taking tests. Scores on a valid measure of creativity reflect actual creativity, not merely drawing ability, deviance, or a joyful mood.

To assess the **criterion validity** of a test, we compare a person's score on that test to his or her score on some other standard, a *criterion,* theoretically associated with what was measured by the first test. Ideally, scores on the criterion directly reflect a personal characteristic or behavior theoretically related to, but not the same as, that assessed by the original test. For example, if a high-school test is designed to predict academic success in college, then college grades are an appropriate criterion. If the correlation of test scores with subsequent college grades is high, then the test is a valid predictor.

For many personal qualities of interest to psychologists, no ideal criterion exists. No single behavior or objective measure of performance can tell us how anxious, depressed, or aggressive a person is. Psychologists have theories about these more abstract variables, or *constructs*—ideas about what affects them, how they show up in behavior, and how they relate to other variables. **Construct validity** is the degree to which scores on a test based on a defined variable—the construct—correlate positively with scores of other tests, judges' ratings, behavioral measures, or experimental results already considered valid indicators of the characteristic being measured (Cronbach & Meehl, 1955). A new test of a construct such as "aggression" should correlate positively with existing tests of "aggression" that also assess that construct. For example, suppose you designed a test to measure aggressive tendencies in children. To assess its construct validity you might compare scores on the test to measures of how often the children fight with others, how many hostile comments they make, and how aggressive their teachers think they are.

Often problems of validity arise not because a test is defective, but because the *criterion* is poorly conceptualized or not well measured. If a criterion is not well-chosen and does not itself adequately represent that important "something" the psychologist is trying to test, then checking test scores against it can tell us little about how well the new test is serving its intended purpose.

An example of a reliable test that is not valid for some specific purposes is a medical school admissions oral interview administered by a team of faculty. What criterion shall we use to judge the validity of the score a candidate earns on this type of interpersonal-evaluative stress analysis? Is the score likely to be related to an ability to handle the stresses a medical student experiences taking course examinations? Is it related to a physician's ability to make medical decisions under the stress of uncertain information? Both criteria are important, but at different stages of one's medical training. If a stress interview predicts *only* how well a student will cope with classroom stress and *not* how well he or she will handle "on-the-job stress" as a new doctor, is it doing what it was intended to? Is an interview valid if it leads to the rejection of students who are shy in socially threatening situations but who would still make good physicians? To determine the validity of any test, we must first know what it is supposed to be measuring and then decide what observations will best reveal that characteristic. It is essential to ask not only whether a test is valid but to ask "valid for what purpose." (For another example of a test with moderate reliability and poor validity, see the ***Close-up*** on pp. 458–59.)

The bathroom scale, mentioned earlier, is unreliable and also not valid because it cannot be used to measure your weight accurately. It changed when you didn't and was constant when you lost weight. Usually if a test is not reliable, it is also not valid, but, under some circumstances, a generally unreliable test may be valid for predicting behavior in specific situations. This might occur when the construct being measured is complex and open to multiple interpretations, such as "self-actualized," "honest," or "generous." A specific criterion behavior may still distinguish between those who score high or low on the measure at a given time.

When the content of test items appears to test makers to tap attributes of interest, the test is said to have **face validity.** A test with obvious face validity may be faked by respondents who want to influence the decision based on the test results. One interesting instance of the phenomenon was reported among institutionalized mental patients who did *not* want to be released from their familiar, structured environment.

> *These long-term schizophrenic patients were interviewed by the staff about how disturbed they were. When they were given an interview to assess if they were well enough to be on an open ward, these patients gave generally* positive *self-references. However, when the purpose of the interview was to assess their suitability for* discharge, *then these patients gave more negative self-references. Psychiatrists who rated the interview data, without awareness of this experimental variation in the purpose of the interview, judged those who gave more negative self-references as more severely disturbed—and recommended against their being discharged. (Braginsky & Braginsky, 1967)*
>
> *In a companion study, newcomers motivated to leave a mental hospital answered true to personality test items when they were led to believe that true was a sign of insight and avoided answering true when they believed it was an indication of their sickness. The old-timers did exactly the opposite. They attempted to fake their answers to the personality test by answering true more often when it was believed to be a sign of their sickness. (Braginsky et al., 1969)*

Standardization and Norms

To be most useful, a measuring device should be standardized. **Standardization**, the administration of a device to all persons in the same way under the same conditions, is a method that can establish **norms,** or statistical standards, so that an individual's score can be compared with those of others in a defined group.

Suppose you get a score of 18 on a test designed to reveal how depressed you are. What does that mean? Are you a little depressed, not at all depressed, about average, or what? You can find out be checking the test norms to see what the usual range of scores is and what the average is for students of your age and sex. You probably encountered test norms when you got your scores on aptitude tests (such as the SAT). The norms let you know how your scores compared to those of other students and helped you know how well you had done relative to that normative population.

Group norms are most useful for interpreting individual scores when the standardization group shares important qualities with those individuals (such as age, social class, and experience). When this is the case, the group norms provide a useful yardstick against which an individual's score can be interpreted. So whenever you are given the results of any psychological test, the first question you should ask is, "Compared to what?" What norms were used to interpret *relative* performance?

For norms to be meaningfully used to compare test performances, it is essential that everyone take the "same test." That sounds obvious, but it may not always occur in practice. Some people may be allowed more time than others, given clearer or more detailed instructions, permitted to ask questions, or motivated to perform better by a tester's suggestions. For example, before administering a scale to assess children's degree of test anxiety, one teacher told her class, "We're going to have some fun with this new kind of question game this nice man will play with you." A teacher in another classroom prepared her class for the "same" assessment by cautioning, "This psychologist from Yale University is going to give you a test to see what you are thinking; I hope you will do well and show how good our class is!" Did the children's performance scores reflect only what the test was intended to measure?

Could you directly compare the scores of the children in these two classes on this "same test"? The answer is no, because the way in which the test was administered was not standardized. When procedures do not include explicit instructions about the way to administer the test or the way to score the results, it is difficult to interpret what a given test score means or how it relates to any comparison group. We will see in a later section of this chapter that serious interpretative problems arise when a test has been "normed" for one population, such as males or middle-class whites, and those norms are used to evaluate the test scores of other populations, women or lower-class blacks, for example.

Sources of Information

Psychological assessment methods can be organized according to four techniques used to gather information about a person: interviews, life history and archival data, tests, and situational observations. They can also be classified according to the person who is supplying the information: the one being assessed or other people. If the person being assessed is providing the information, the methods are called *self-report measures;* if others are supplying the data, the methods are called *judges' ratings.*

Four Assessment Techniques

If you want a direct approach to learn about someone, ask him or her questions about values, beliefs, attitudes, behavior, and so forth in the form of an *interview.* Interviews may be unfocused, not structured, and the questions asked may only indirectly get at the information an interviewer wishes to elicit from a person. They may go the other extreme, however, and be highly structured; the questions may directly relate to the nature of the information being sought. In addition to interviewing the person in question, it is, of course, possible to interview others who are able to give information about him or her—friends, parents, or coworkers, for example.

A psychologist may administer a battery of tests to determine if there is an emotional problem.

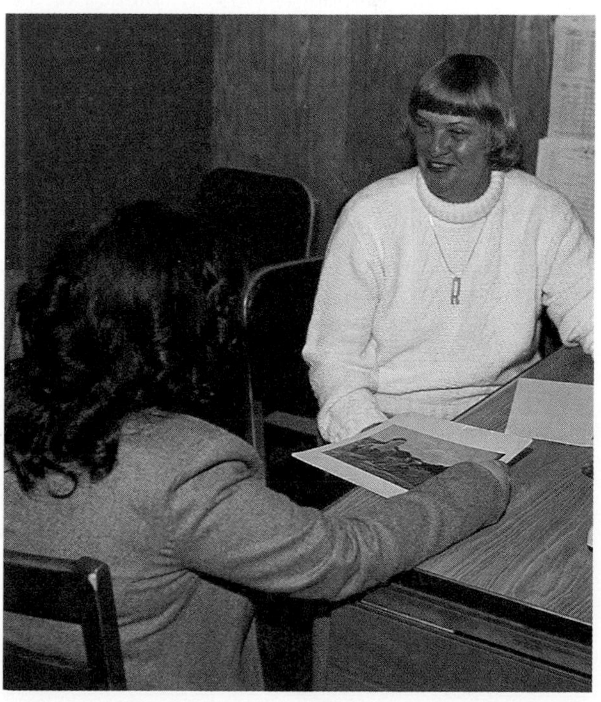

Close-up *On Trial: Lie Detection by Polygraph*

People lie. They often deceive others, distorting the truth while claiming to be truthful. We also know that people accuse of lying others who, in fact, are honest when they claim to be telling the truth. How can we tell the difference? Why is it important to do so, and what are the consequences of erring in making the decision that someone is or is not lying?

Adolf Hitler convinced British emissary Neville Chamberlain that he had no intentions of starting a war—just before World War II. The political careers of Senator Edward Kennedy and Presidents Richard Nixon and Ronald Reagan were tainted by public doubts of their truthfulness in attempting to cover up suspected illegal actions. Recently, spy ring leader Anthony Walker, Jr., was found guilty of having deceived the Navy for nearly 20 years while he passed top secrets to the Soviets. Walker had received "top clearance" to handle classified material, but somehow was able to "beat the system" at its own intelligence game. Gary Dotson was sentenced to prison for the rape of Cathy Webb; despite his claim of innocence, Webb's courtroom testimony persuaded the jury and judge of Dotson's guilt. Several years later, she recanted, saying that she had lied about the rape, that Dotson had told the truth. If so, how can the judge believe a confessed liar when she is allegedly telling the truth?

Lie detection theory. In earlier times, tests of lie detection were based on the assumption that emotionality is associated with lying: a liar's nervousness will be revealed in bodily reactions that change under stress. Thus, the Bedouins of Arabia made conflicting witnesses lick hot irons—the liar was the one whose tongue stuck to the iron. The Chinese are reputed to have had suspects chew rice powder and then spit it out—the guilty party's rice was dry. During the Inquisition, suspected witches swallowed a slice of bread and cheese—the deceptive person was the one whose bread stuck in the throat. These tests share the belief that saliva will dry up when a person who is lying is frightened of being caught. Although less dramatic, modern tests of lying use the same theory about the relationship between lying, emotions, and physiology (Kleinmuntz & Szucko, 1984).

Modern lie detection theory assumes that if lying is deliberate and purposeful, a person aware of his or her attempted deception will become emotionally aroused as the sympathetic branch of the autonomic nervous system is activated. These changes in the autonomic nervous system can be tracked by attaching to the subject electrodes or sensors that detect a wide range of bodily functions such as breathing, heart rate, skin temperature, and GSR (galvanic skin response). Printouts of these changes are used as an index of emotionality. The graphed results of these channels of physiological information is what the *polygraph* is designed for.

Polygraph uses. More than a million polygraph tests are given annually by private agencies, businesses, police departments, and federal agencies, including the military and the CIA (Lykken, 1981). In many states polygraph evidence is admissible as evidence in civil and criminal trials. A fifth of the nation's major corporations and about half of the fast-food companies, such as McDonald's, use preemployment polygraph tests to screen prospective employees, attempting to identify those who can be expected to carry out their jobs honestly and faithfully. The Chief of Naval Intelligence told a Senate subcommittee on investigations that it is Navy policy to use this test for national security purposes. "The polygraph is a valuable and effective tool for specific personnel security purposes . . . particularly useful in assessing candidates for access to our most sensitive information" (Rear Admiral John Butts quoted in Squires, 1985, p. 9). It is reasonable to assume that the general public also believes in the validity of the polygraph test for lie detection.

Polygraph testing. If you were to undergo a polygraph test, to what procedures would you be subjected? First there would be an initial structured interview designed to get biographical data, to evaluate your attitudes toward dishonesty, and to judge your views toward the test situation. The interviewer would also be trying to get leads to use during the next phase when you were hooked up to the electrodes that measure a half dozen or so of your physiological reactions. You would be asked a series of questions to be answered yes or no, and the answers would be reviewed prior to the actual testing. Three types of

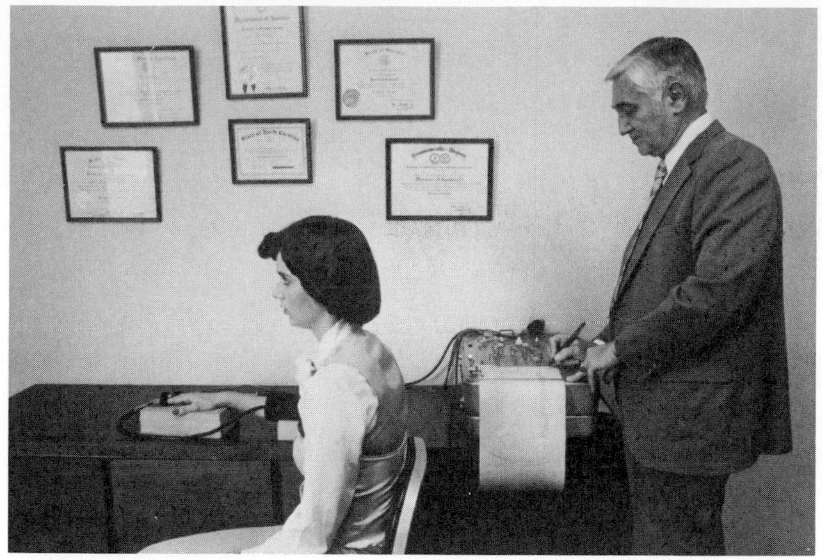

questions are asked: (a) case-irrelevant, about established biographical data; (b) case-relevant, about the specific issues being investigated; and (c) control questions that encourage lying or mild emotional arousal. Answers to these control questions are used to compare your reactions to the predicted greater arousal when lying to relevant questions.

The tester then evaluates your polygraph record using intuition to detect signs of greater autonomic disturbance to relevant questions, predicted if you are lying or the opposite if you are being truthful. In some cases this "clinical" interpretation is replaced by statistical analysis based solely on an objective evaluation of the numerical scores assigned to each difference in autonomic functioning. Statistical evaluation has been shown to be superior to the clinical evaluation—but neither technique meets acceptable standards of validity.

Polygraph misuses. Despite the fact that polygraph testing has become standard operating procedure in many areas of society, is itself a big business for polygraph experts, and has been written about in thousands of books and articles, the best recent evidence clearly indicates that the polygraph test is *not valid* for systematically detecting those who are truthful. It is a psychological test with moderately high reliability and poor validity (Barland & Raskin, 1976; Horvath, 1977; Kleinmuntz & Szucko, 1984; Lykken, 1979, 1981, 1984).

Validity is assessed in laboratory studies where subjects are instructed to lie or tell the truth during polygraph testing, and in field studies where polygraph charts of those previously found to be innocent or confessed to a suspected crime are evaluated by polygraph experts. Using signal detection analysis (recall chapter 5), researchers found a *high false alarm rate,* or *false positives,* of truthful subjects classified as liars by the polygraphers. The best "experts" call innocent people guilty about 20 percent of the time, while some studies have found over 50 percent of truthful subjects misclassified as deceptive. Organizations are willing to tolerate these false positive errors in order to catch a few risky job candidates or dishonest employees, because only the victim suffers. Then, of course, there are the Anthony Walker, Jr.-type *false negative errors* in which liars pass polygraph tests with "flying colors."

Although a polygraph test reliably detects changes in human involuntary responses associated with emotions, there is no known direct relationship between deception and emotionality. Measureable physiological changes can be produced by a great many situational and dispositional variables which have nothing to do with lying. "The polygraphic pens do no special dance when we are lying" concluded one reviewer of the evidence (Lykken, 1981).

Conclusion. At a 1987 congressional hearing on the use of polygraph technology, psychologist Edward Katkin presented the conclusion on behalf of the American Psychological Association that "other than anecdotal data, we have no basis to assume such tests to be valid" (APA News Brief, 1987, March 11). This does not mean that lying cannot sometimes be detected by physiological changes or that liars cannot be betrayed by changes in voice, facial expressions, word usage, or body movement, as shown in research by Paul Ekman (1985). No test can do so with sufficient precision to protect the innocent from false accusation and the associated negative consequences nor unmask the talented, trained, or pathological liars among us. Polygraph results are not only fallible, they are also fakable. The practical application of this information is never to submit to a polygraph test if you know you are innocent, but take a chance on the invalidity of the test to misclassify you if you are guilty.

A skillful interviewer is trained to be effective in five aspects of a *diagnostic interview* (one used to assign an individual to some ordered, organized categories). An interviewer must be able to: put the respondent at ease, know how to elicit the desired information, maintain control of the direction and pace of the interview, establish and maintain feelings of rapport, and, finally, bring the interview to a satisfactory conclusion. "Diagnostic interviewing has always been the clinician's personal, subjective effort to gain information and understanding and it remains the most important tool in clinical assessment and diagnosis" according to a recent—but disputed—appraisal of this form of assessment (Weins & Matarazzo, 1983, p. 327).

Interview data may be supplemented with secondary *life history* sources of information about a person, taken from different types of available records. These may include school or military performances, written productions, medical data, photographs, or videotapes, especially those of different time periods and in relation to other people.

Psychological testing is the major method usually associated in most student's minds with assessment. Indeed the construction and use of tests, scales, and inventories to measure virtually all aspects of human functioning, such as intelligence, personality, and creativity, is a substantial activity for many psychologists.

We will see later in this chapter that tests may vary on a number of dimensions—general or specific, objective or subjective, verbal or nonverbal (performance), and others. A major virtue of tests over interviews is their *quantitative* characterizations of an individual along with the normative comparisons with others. We will also see that some psychological tests are based on, or derived from, particular personality theories that specify what is important to measure.

Situational observations can be used to assess behavior in real-life settings. An observer, rater, or judge observes an individual's behavioral patterns in one or more situations, such as work or leisure, at home or in school. The goal is to discover the determinants and consequences of various responses and habits of the individual. This general approach comes out of the tradition of experimental psychology, social-learning theories of personality, and behavior modification therapies. Direct observation as an assessment technique has, until recently, taken a back seat to the preferred use of tests, which were more economical, less effortful, and provided normative data. However, situational observation is increasing in use across many areas of psychology and other social sciences. It is based on empirical investigations of what people say and do in a given context and what influences that behavior. Although assessing samples of individual behavior is less efficient than mass paper-and-pencil test inventories, many psychologists argue for the greater validity and usefulness of behavioral assessment (Ciminero et al., 1977; Haynes, 1983).

Self-reports

Self-report methods, also called *self-inventories,* require respondents to answer questions or give information about themselves. They may be asked to tell what they like or dislike, whether they agree with certain statements, or how they feel in certain situations. For example, respondents might indicate which of the following they agree with more: "I live one day at a time, never planning far ahead," or "I enjoy setting goals and planning how to reach them as much as engaging in the activities themselves." Such measures are valuable because they tap an individual's personal experience and feelings. They are convenient to give because trained interviewers are not needed, and they are generally easy to score.

The chief disadvantage of self-report measures is that people do not always give accurate responses on these inventories. We are not always in touch with our own feelings, we cannot remember all we have done or thought, and we may even intentionally lie to make ourselves look better. Despite this disadvantage, self-report measures are often very useful. This is especially true for those on which steps have been taken to spot response inaccuracies.

Judges' Ratings

In psychological assessment, a judge's rating involves a systematic evaluation of some aspect of a person's behavior by another person, which, in itself, moves it into the observable, and, therefore, more readily objective, realm. For example, your teachers may be asked to rate your school performance and your interactions with peers ("Does Charlie work and play well with others?"); your parents may rate your cooperativeness as a young child; and your friends may give their impressions of your personality.

A number of well-known assessment techniques involve ratings made by judges who do not know you personally. Often they are psychologists, counselors, or trained interviewers who interact with you in a structured way, asking you to answer specific interview questions or to respond to specific test stimuli. Their interaction with you may be relatively unstructured and casual, or they may simply observe you without any interaction—either concealed or with your awareness. Afterwards, they may evaluate your responses on various dimensions. In some cases, they may base their evaluations on detailed guidelines provided by the developers of the assessment instrument. Sometimes the guidelines are less precise, allowing spontaneous reactions and informal impressions to play a greater role.

Can you think of any drawbacks that may result from the use of ratings by interviewers or other judges? Some were covered briefly in our discussion of research foundations in chapter 2 (see especially pp. 31-33). An important one to point up is that the ratings made of another person may tell more about the *judge*, or about the judge's relationship with the person, than about the true characteristics of the person being rated. For example, if you like someone, you may tend to judge him or her favorably on nearly every dimension, overlooking faults. This type of *rating bias* is referred to as a **halo effect.** If a rater thinks most people in a certain category (blacks, Jews, Italians, women) have certain qualities, then that rater may "see" those qualities in any individual who happens to be in that category. This type of bias is called a **stereotype effect.** These unwanted biases in ratings can be lessened if the rules for making ratings are clearly specified ("If he does X, then give him a 10"); and yet, even trained observers can fall prey to bias.

Ratings are most reliable when they are of specific behaviors ("makes eye contact and smiles"); they become less reliable when the rating categories are general or vague ("is open to new experiences" or "is a sensitive person"). Focused behavior ratings allow less room for personal, and potentially biased, impressions. In addition, bias can be reduced by using more than one rater, which makes it possible to calculate the *interrater reliability*. That is, if two different raters independently make very similar judgments of the same individual, then we can feel more confident that the judgments accurately reflect that individual's characteristics and not one judge's biases.

Judges' ratings based on samples of behavior that they observe directly and score on objective checklists are being used more and more to assess problem behaviors. Trained observers may visit a child's home, school, or play setting to try to record unobtrusively what the child is doing at selected fixed intervals, say every 30 seconds, or in response to a randomly generated signal. In this way, a *baseline rate* (an initial measure of frequency) of the problem behavior can be determined for temper tantrums, inattention, or social isolation, for example. Then, during and after a treatment program, the frequency of the behavior can also be measured and compared to the baseline measure to see if the treatment is having the desired effect. In this way better programs for treatment and for prevention of behavior problems are being designed (Haynes & Wilson, 1979).

Assessing Intelligence

Intelligence is the capacity to profit from experience and to go beyond the given to the possible. It is in our intellectual development that we humans have been able to transcend our physical frailties and gain dominance over more powerful or numerous animals. No wonder, then, that intelligence is our most highly prized possession; but what is intelligence? What are its origins? How can it be assessed? What are its advantages?

The first major assessment endeavor by psychologists was an attempt to measure intelligence. The history of this endeavor illustrates some of the steps in the design of instruments for assessment, as well as some of the problems that may be encountered. The complexity of the task is reflected in the fact that, while intelligence testing has been with us for many years, some of the problems remain unsolved, and hot debate still rages about the meaning, measurement, and personal-societal implications of intelligence.

Is intelligence basically a single dimension on which people can be assessed in terms of how "smart" or "dumb" they are? Or should it be conceptualized not as a unitary attribute like a person's height, but as a collection of mental competencies analogous to athletic ability? In this section we will consider alternative views about the way to define and understand what intelligence is.

The way we think about intelligence and mental functioning influences the way we try to assess it. Can the complexity and richness of human intelligence be quantified and reduced to a single score? Some psychologists believe so, while others argue that "assessment should depend on a picture, not a number"—a picture of the way the different components of a person's intelligence interrelate (Hunt, 1984; Sternberg, 1982).

Even if we can measure intelligence and agree on a definition of it, what difference does it make to a person or a society? What practical consequences follow from assessing someone's intelligence, from discovering individual differences in intellectual functioning? In this section we want to inquire not only whether intelligence tests are valid, but for what purpose and for what people.

Many investigators believe that assessment of intellectual abilities is one of psychology's most significant contributions to society. In opposition are those who maintain that it has been, and continues to be, a systematic attempt by elitists to "measure" people so that the desirable ones can be put into the right slots and the other ones can be rejected (Gould, 1981). Let's examine some of the evidence for such claims.

Historical Context

A brief look at the history of intelligence testing will reveal how practical social and political concerns, measurement issues, and theory were entwined in the development of means to measure intellectual differences among children and among adults. The initial impetus to discover a way to do so came from Europe, specifically France, where the educational objective was to identify children who were unable to learn in school. Soon, however, intelligence testing became an "All-American" enterprise. At the beginning of the twentieth century, the United States was a nation in turmoil. The economic, social, and political order of the country was rapidly changing, and the vast impact of millions of new immigrants contributed to the confusion. At that time, "intelligence test results were used not only to differentiate [among] children experiencing academic problems, but also as a measuring stick to organize an entire society" (Hale, 1983, p. 373).

Binet's First Intelligence Test

The year 1905 marked the first published account of a workable intelligence test. Alfred Binet had responded to the call of the French Minister of Public Instruction who wanted to find a way to best teach mentally retarded children in the public schools. Binet and his colleague, Theophile Simon, believed that, before a program of instruction could be planned, it was necessary to develop a way to measure the intelligence of the children they would be teaching.

Binet attempted to devise a test of intellectual performance that could be used as an objective way to classify and separate retarded from normal schoolchildren (Sattler, 1982). He hoped that such a test would have the virtue of reducing reliance on the more subjective, perhaps biased, evaluations of teachers.

Before seeing how Binet developed his first test, it is important to note four general features of his approach. First, he believed that these test scores were nothing more than a practical estimate of current performance differences, not a measure of innate intelligence. Second, he wanted these practical estimates to be used to identify children who needed special help in school because of learning disabilities. Third. since he emphasized the role of training and opportunity in influencing intelligence, Binet sought to identify areas of performance in which such children's abilities might be improved with special education. Finally, he began by using an empirical method of test construction rather than basing his test on a theoretical conception of what intelligence was.

Unlike Dr. Itard, who attempted to train the wild, retarded boy of Aveyron (see chapter 3), Binet believed that it was first necessary to measure a child's intellectual ability before planning an instructional program. The key to his testing approach was *quantification* of intelligence test performance. Children at a given chronological age were given a number of problems or test items. These problems were chosen so that they could be scored objectively, were varied in nature, were not much influenced by differences in children's environments, and called for judgment and reasoning rather than mere rote memory (Binet, 1911).

Children of various ages were tested, and the average score obtained by normal children at each age was obtained. Then, an individual child's performance was compared to the average for other children of his or her age. Test results were expressed in terms of the average age at which normal children achieved a particular score. This measure was called the **mental age (MA).** When a child's scores on various items of the test added up to the average score of a group of 5-year-olds, the child was said to have a *mental age* of 5, regardless of his or her actual **chronological age (CA).** *Retardation* was then defined operationally by Binet as being two mental-age years behind chronological age.

As more children were tested longitudinally, it was found that those assessed as "retarded" at one age fell further behind the mental age of their birth cohorts as they grew older. A child of 5 who performed at only the level of 3-year-olds might, at the age of 10, be comparable to 6-year-olds. Although the *ratio* of mental age to chronological age would be constant (3/5 and 6/10), the total number of mental-age years of retardation would have increased from two to four.

Mental Measurement in America

Nowhere did Binet's successful development of an intelligence test have a greater impact than in the United States. A unique combination of historical events and social-political forces made the United States fertile ground for a virtual explosion of interest in assessing mental ability. Since that time the interest of psychologists in intellectual assessment has flourished into a mental measurement industry.

Among the contributing factors that made assessment of intelligence so important were (a) the enormous immigration of millions of people from Europe and Asia; (b) the emergence of a vast public school system and a philosophy of education to teach cultural values to these newcomers so they might rise above their lowly "station in life" through personal merit; and (c) the national emergency created by World War I that necessitated the formation of an efficient military in a short time (see Fass, 1980; Marks, 1976–77). Assessment was seen as a way to put order into a chaotic society and an inexpensive, democratic means to separate those who could benefit from education or military leadership training from those who were not competent.

In 1917 when the United States declared war on Germany it was necessary to establish quickly a military force led by competent leaders. Drafting many immigrants who were not literate created a problem of determining who had the ability to learn quickly and benefit from special leadership training. The solution was to use tests that did not rely on verbal performance. Over 1.7 million recruits were evaluated with newly devised nonverbal, group-administered tests of mental ability. Incidentally, a group of famous psychologists designed these tests in only one month's time; they included Lewis Terman, Edward Thorndike, and Robert Yerkes (Marks, 1976-1977). Two consequences of this large-scale testing program were (a) growing acceptance by the American public of the idea that intelligence tests could be used to differentiate people in terms of their leadership ability and other socially important characteristics, and (b) new attention, in the army report, given to alleged intellectual differences because of race and country of origin (Yerkes, 1921).

The first effect encouraged the widespread application of assessment methods in industry, the military, and schools. The second had the unfortunate result of providing statistical justification for prevailing prejudices against blacks and immigrants from southern Europe. The data could have been used to show that environmental disadvantages limit people's chances of fully developing their intellectual abilities. Instead, the poorly collected data were used to support arguments about the inherited superiority of Anglo-Saxons and the intellectual inferiority of those alien "others." We shall return to this sore point regarding misuse of assessment techniques.

IQ Tests

Lewis Terman of Stanford University had been a public school administrator. Feeling that Binet's method for assessing intelligence was important, he adapted the questions for American schoolchildren, standardized administration of the test, and developed age-level norms by giving the test to thousands of children. In 1916 he published the Stanford Revision of the Binet Tests, commonly referred to as the **Stanford-Binet Intelligence Test** (Terman, 1916).

A psychologist administers an intelligence test to a 4-year-old child. The performance part of this test includes a block design task, an object completion task, and a shape identification task.

With his new test, Terman provided a base for the concept of the **intelligence quotient,** or **IQ** (Stern, 1914). This was the ratio of mental age to chronological age (multiplied by 100 to eliminate decimals):

$$IQ = \frac{MA}{CA} \times 100$$

A child with a CA of 8 years whose test scores equaled those of 10-year-olds had an IQ of 125 ($\frac{10}{8} \times 100$), while a child of that age who performed at the level of 6-year-olds had an IQ of 75 ($\frac{6}{8} \times 100$). Individuals who performed at the mental age equivalent to their chronological age had IQs of 100, which was considered to be the average or "normal" IQ.

The new Stanford-Binet test soon became a standard instrument in clinical psychology, psychiatry, and educational counseling. At the same time, Terman's adoption of IQ contributed to the development of a new conceptualization of the purpose and meaning of intelligence testing. Terman believed that intelligence was an inner quality, that it had a large hereditary component, and that IQ tests could measure this inner quality throughout the range of abilities that make up intelligence. The implicit message was that IQ characterized something essential and unchanging about human intelligence.

In line with these changes in the concept of intelligence, the next revision of the test (a) extended the upper limits of the scale to differentiate among adults of superior intelligence; and (b) extended the downward limits to assess the intelligence of children as young as two years (Terman & Merrill, 1937). Parallel test forms of high reliability were also designed so that people could be retested without having memory and practice effects influence their scores. Another revision of the Stanford-Binet intelligence test was made in 1960 to take into account vocabulary changes in society over time (Terman & Merrill, 1960). For example, the word *Mars,* which was difficult for children in 1916 (equal in difficulty to *conscientious*), had, by 1937, become as familiar as *skill,* and by 1961 was as easy as the everyday word *eyelash.* In 1972–73, there was a further revision, and the test norms were revamped to take into account the overall increase in test scores for the population; the norms were shifted up about one-half year per age level (Terman & Merrill, 1972).

IQ scores on this test are no longer derived by dividing chronological age into mental age. If you took the Stanford-Binet test now, you would receive 2 points for each of 6 questions you answered, within each mental age grouping (12 points per year). Then the tester would add up your points and check a table to compare your score with the average for your age. An IQ of 100 would indicate that 50 percent of those your age earned lower scores. Scores between 90 and 110 are labeled "normal," above 120 "superior," and below 70 as evidence of "mental retardation" (see **Figure 13.1**).

It is important to remember that IQ scores, by themselves, do not tell how much children know or what they can do. A high-school student with an IQ of 100 would have knowledge and skills that a fourth-grader with a higher IQ of 120 would not have. In addition, people labeled "retarded" on the basis of their IQ scores vary considerably in what they are able to do and how much they can learn

Figure 13.1
Shown is the distribution of IQ scores expected among a large sample of individuals. (From Matarazzo, 1972, p. 124)

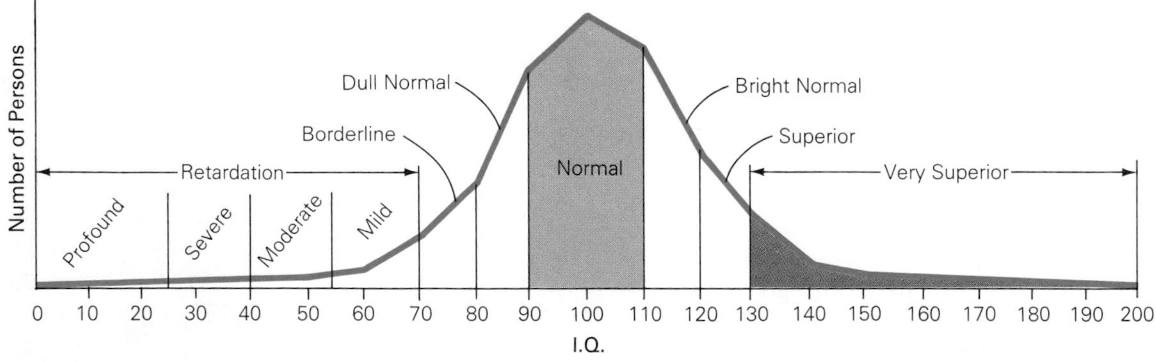

through instruction. It is also well to recall the plight of little Maria from our *Opening Case;* there are many reasons why people's intelligence test scores can be lower than their actual ability. Even the latest version of the Standford-Binet is based largely on the use of words or ability to think and communicate using written English. Children who have language impairments or come from non-English-speaking homes would not get a fair estimate of their intellectual ability.

David Wechsler, working at Bellevue Hospital in New York, provided a remedy for this problem of language dependence in the form of new intelligence tests that combined verbal subtests with performance subtests. Thus, in addition to an overall IQ score, separate estimates of verbal IQ and nonverbal IQ became possible.

The *verbal* sections of these instruments include tests of general information, comprehension, vocabulary, arithmetic, and digit span (repeating a series of digits after the examiner). The *performance* sections, which involve manipulation of materials with little or no verbal content, also have several parts. In the block design test, for example, a subject tries to reproduce designs shown on cards by fitting together blocks with colored sides. In the picture arrangement test, the task is to arrange a series of pictures in the correct sequence so that a meaningful story is depicted. Other performance tests involve mazes, picture completion, and object assembly.

Today, for children from 2 through 15 years of age the assessment of intelligence on individually administered tests is made by the *Wechsler Intelligence Scale for Children-Revised,* or *WISC-R* (1974). For those ages 16 and older there is the *Wechsler Adult Intelligence Scale-Revised,* or *WAIS-R* (1981).

In addition to the individually given Stanford-Binet and Wechsler scales, many other tests have been developed that are given to groups, more easily scored, and more economical. More than a million Americans a year take some form of standard intelligence test. A proponent of such testing, Julian Stanley, argues for their value, especially that of the Stanford-Binet:

> *Though "IQ tests" are much maligned, especially because results from them can be misused greatly, the* Stanford-Binet Intelligence Scale *remains a psychometric marvel. No other instrument spans so well almost the entire range of mental ability from slow-learning preschoolers to brilliant adults. No other one mental test can provide the well-trained school or clinical psychologist with as valid a single IQ. (1976, p. 668)*

One of the test adults can take is the WAIS-R.

What Is Intelligence?

In the area of intellectual assessment, psychologists have put the tests before the definition of what they are testing. There has been little agreement about the concept of intelligence or how to define it. Early attempts sought to link intelligence to a person's *social worth* by associating low intelligence with criminality and poverty (in the infamous studies by Goddard of the Kallikak Family in 1914, and Dugdale's case study of the Jukes family in 1912). No longer, however, is intelligence linked to an individual's moral behavior.

An operational definition states "intelligence is what intelligence tests measure," while a somewhat less empirically based definition says it is "how well you do on an intelligence test." Today, however, at least some agreement has been reached. Both scientists and the general public see two kinds of abilities as central to intelligence—*verbal abilities* and *problem-solving abilities* (R. Sternberg et al., 1981). Verbal abilities include verbal fluency, reading comprehension, conversational facility, and vocabulary. Problem-solving abilities include getting to the heart of a problem, approaching a problem in an optimal way, and making a good decision—those intellectual functions we discussed in chapter 10.

We might say that underlying most conceptions about intelligence are three general classes of skills or abilities: (a) adapting to new situations and changing task demands, (b) learning or profiting optimally from experience or training, and (c) thinking abstractly using symbols and concepts (Phares, 1984).

It is also well for us to distinguish three concepts that are often measured by subtests of various intelligence tests and contribute to our general view of someone's intelligence.

> Ability *is the currently available power to perform something, and* aptitude *is the potential for performance after training. Both concepts have similarities with* achievement, *which is a measure of successful performance in the past. (Sundberg, 1977, p. 228)*

Many theories of intelligence have emerged from the theoretical models we have been considering throughout our journey, such as neurological-biological, learning, and developmental theories. **Psychometrics** is the field of psychology that specializes in mental testing in any of its facets, including personality assessment, intelligence evaluation, and aptitude measurement. Earlier when we studied laws of sensation (chapter 5), we encountered the psychometric attempt to relate values of physical, sensory stimuli to the psychological reactions they elicited. *Psychometric* theories of intelligence are based on inferences derived from special statistical analyses (called *factor analysis*) of intelligence test measurements. In some of these approaches general intelligence is identified as a general, central *''g-factor''* and many specific *''s-factors.''* The psychometric approaches to understanding intelligence that are of most current interest to psychologists are those of Raymond Cattell (1971) and J. P. Guilford (1967).

Guilford's Structure of Intellect

Guilford classifies intellectual factors according to *content* (kind of information), *product* (form), and *operation* involved. There are four kinds of content—figural, symbolic, semantic, and behavioral; six kinds of products—units, classes, relations, systems, transformations, and implications; and five kinds of operations—evaluation, convergent production, divergent production, memory, and cognition.

The different intellectual abilities represent different combinations of contents, products, and operations. That is, any of the four types of content may take the form of any of the six products (4 × 6 = 24). On these 24 resulting kinds of information, any of the five types of operations may be performed (24 × 5 = 120). Thus we have a total of 120 possible intellectual abilities. An example of one such ability is ''verbal comprehension,'' which, under this system, is classified as *cognition of units* with *semantic* content (see **Figure 13.2**).

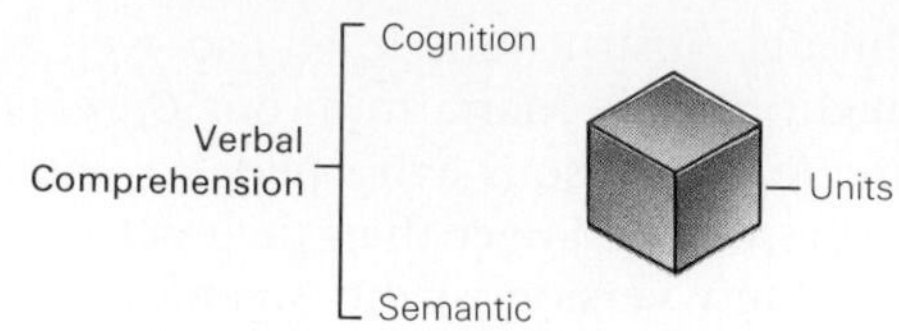

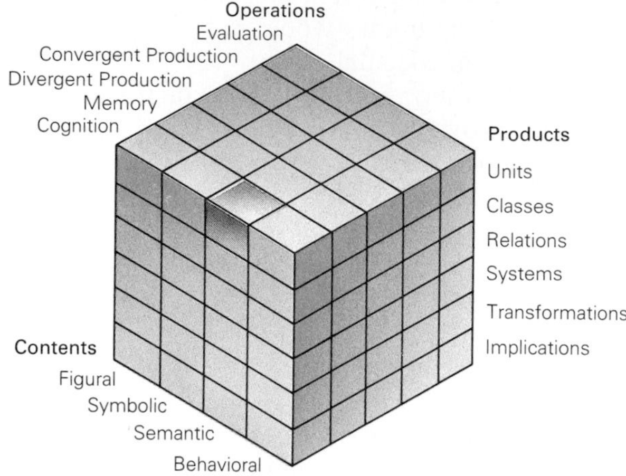

Figure 13.2 *The Structure of Intellect*

This theoretical model is analogous to a chemist's periodic table of elements. By means of such a systematic framework, intellectual factors, like chemical elements, may be postulated before they are discovered. In 1961, when Guilford proposed his model, nearly 40 intellectual abilities had been identified. Since that time, researchers have accounted for close to a hundred abilities (Guilford, 1973).

Cognitive Science Approaches

Although the concept of IQ has come to be equated by the public with how smart a person ''really is,'' and by some psychologists with a unitary trait of mind, Alfred Binet held a quite different view.

> *. . . intelligence is before all a process of knowing that is directed toward the external world, that works to reconstruct it in its entirety, by means of the little fragments that are given to us . . . comprehension, inventiveness, direction, and criticism: intelligence is contained in these four words. (Binet, 1911, pp. 117–188)*

Three current approaches to understanding and assessing intelligence share aspects of Binet's early view. They focus on cognitive skills that have value to the thinking-acting person, and on multiple intelligences. They offer provocative challenges to traditional psychometric notions of intelligence.

One of Gardner's seven intelligences is bodily-kinesthetic ability, shown in the picture by the grace and coordination of the dancers.

Hunt's problem-solving intelligence. Earl Hunt (1983) a proponent of this new view, argues that the way to appreciate intelligence begins not by making a better IQ test, but with a theory of *cognitive processes* based on identification of important aspects of the mental performance. Three classes of cognitive performance identified as central to intellectual functioning are (a) a person's choice about the way to internally (mentally) represent a problem; (b) his or her strategies for manipulating mental representations; and (c) the abilities necessary to execute whatever basic information-processing steps a strategy requires.

In this view, experimental researchers and cognitive theorists are invited to do something they have largely avoided: study *individual differences,* instead of only the averaged reactions of many people to the same experimental stimuli. Based on theoretical guidelines, tasks would be designed to tap individual differences in the way problems are represented (using images or verbalization, for example), the way material is encoded, the way information is transferred in one's working memory, and other aspects of information processing.

By studying intelligence in terms of the various mental activities we use to solve the problems and challenges posed by our environment and culture, several important consequences result. This approach encourages us to see the flexibility and adaptiveness of human thinking. It also encourages a different view of classification and selection. Rather than discriminating between those who *have* a given IQ (and get accepted) and those who are below that level (and get rejected) this view supports *diagnostic assessment* based on the way to make the best use of each person's cognitive abilities and skills (Hunt, 1984).

Gardner's seven intelligences. Another new and different theory of intelligence has been proposed by Howard Gardner (1983). He identifies intelligence in terms of seven ways to view the world, each of which is equally important. The value of any of them is culturally determined, according to what is needed, useful, and prized by a given society. The seven intelligences are the following:

1. linguistic ability;
2. logical-mathematical ability;
3. spatial ability—navigating in space, forming, transforming, and using mental images;
4. musical ability—perceiving and creating pitch patterns;
5. bodily-kinesthetic ability—skills of motor movement, coordination;
6. interpersonal ability—understanding others; and
7. intrapersonal ability—understanding one's self, developing a sense of identity.

Gardner argues that Western society promotes the first two intelligences; other societies promote different ones. For example, in the Caroline Island of Micronesia, sailors must navigate without maps among hundreds of islands using only their spatial intelligence and bodily-kinesthetic intelligence. Such abilities count more in that society than do those you call upon to write a term paper. In Bali, where artistic performance is part of everyday life, musical intelligence and bodily talents involved in coordination of fine dance steps are more highly valued. Interpersonal intelligence can be seen as central in societies where collective action and communal life are more important than in individualistic societies.

To assess these kinds of intelligence demands more than one paper-and-pencil test and simple quantified measures. Gardner's tests of intelligence require the person taking the test to be observed and assessed in a variety of life situations as well as in the artificial samples of life depicted on traditional intelligence tests.

Steinberg's intelligence triad. A third contemporary approach to the question of "what is intelligence?" is that of Robert Sternberg (1985, 1986b). His theory rejects the traditional psychometric approach of analyzing intelligence in terms of the *structure* of intellect or inferences based on intelligence test factors. Instead, Sternberg's theory attempts to understand the cognitive *processes* the human mind uses to solve problems and to expand the concept of IQ to include creativity and the ability to effectively manipulate the environment. Three types of intelligence can be distinguished: componential, experiential, and contextual.

The fundamental aspect of traditional intelligence tests is measuring the way people process a standardized set of information. A *componential* analysis of intelligence focuses on the mental processes involved in solving the kinds of problems given on IQ tests. Componential analysis is concerned with the components of mental functioning involved in cognitive tasks that underlie learning, acquisition of vocabulary, knowledge, insight, and analogies. In addition, the componential analysis of intelligence studies the metacognitive tasks of planning strategies, monitoring progress, and allocating internal and external resources to problem solving.

The *experiential* aspect of intelligence focuses on the way a person's inner, mental world and the outer, external world are related. How does intelligence affect the experiences one has or creates? How is intelligence modified by interactions with the social and physical environment? This view adds creativity to the overall conception of intelligence. A creatively intelligent person may not do particularly well on standard tests, but is able to combine quite different experiences in uniquely original ways. Steven Jobs, the founder of Apple Computer company, is a college dropout with this kind of creative intelligence—intelligence that made him a multimillionaire.

The third kind of intellectual functioning is the *contextual*. This aspect of intelligence deals with the way people effectively shape their environments, adapt to different contexts, and make the most of their available resources. Contextual intelligence is "street smarts"; it is the effective management of self and the practical management of the business of everyday life. Lee Iacocca, the president of Chrysler Corporation, exemplifies the power of contextual intelligence in the world of business.

IQ test scores and college grades get at only componential intelligence. Success in creative careers is better understood in terms of aspects of experiential intelligence. Effectiveness in business and in coping with the everyday tasks of life beyond those measured by traditional IQ tests is seen in contextual aspects of intelligence. Thus, children who score low enough on IQ tests to be labeled "mentally retarded" may still become successfully functioning adults if they use their contextual intelligence.

A 40-year follow-up of 160 men and women who were evaluated as mentally retarded in IQ tests given to them in grade school revealed how effective contextual intelligence can be. Those in a stable, supportive environment were able to compensate for the shortage of IQ points. The majority led satisfying lives, had found jobs, remained employed, and viewed their future with optimism. Their poorer componential intelligence did have costs in terms of getting paid less for less intellectually demanding jobs. (R. Ross et al., 1986)

The Use and Misuse of IQ

"What are IQ test scores good for? What is their predictive utility?" The answer is not as simple as one might expect. Making it even more complicated are emotionally colored claims from various groups. These include claims that IQ is a relatively fixed, inherited trait; that it can be used as an index of the genetic inferiority of certain groups; and that the tests are biased.

We will first outline what is currently known about the validity, stability, and usefulness of IQ test scores. Then we will open the issue of the heritability of IQs, and finally we will review some of the concerns and evidence about misuse of IQ scores because of bias.

Predicting School Success and Job Status

IQ scores are valid for two types of prediction: academic success and the status of one's occupation. Grades in school are significantly correlated with intelligence test scores (Tyler, 1965; Wing & Wallach, 1971). This could simply mean that intelligence tests tap the same kind of performance that teachers require and to which they assign grades. It is also apparent that getting good grades is more than just having a big *g*-factor. To having "smarts," one must add motivation, positive parents' attitudes, and teacher's expectations—to name a few of the variables that contribute in unknown ways to school success or failure.

IQ also predicts the kind of job one will obtain. Occupational status is positively correlated with level of IQ, whether *status* is defined as income or prestige (Brody & Brody, 1976). Two limits on this relationship exist, however: (a) educational success may be the intervening state that determines the quality of the job one gets, so that IQ may really predict job status only indirectly through its correlation with academic achievement, and (b) once in the profession, intelligence score differences do *not* discriminate among those who are eminent and those who are less successful (Matarazzo, 1972). Once on the job, nonintellectual factors such as investment of energy, social skills, and work habits, play a greater role in one's success. In a longitudinal study that compared early IQ with later adult success, the best predictor of a person's educational and occupational status as an adult was not childhood IQ, but the educational level of his or her father (McCall, 1977).

The predictive utility of IQ for even academic achievement can be affected by complex interactions with many factors. IQ scores will change over time with certain environmental changes, such as special education programs, change from a hostile or impoverished environment to a stimulating one, and increasing familiarization with mainstream cultural standards (Morris & Clarizio, 1977). IQ scores are also less stable the longer the time interval between testings. While there is relatively high reliability of IQ scores on repeated testing for *older* children as a group, IQ can still change substantially in individual cases. Inconstancies in IQ scores remind us that intelligence is not an inflexible entity but one continually influenced by many variables.

Heredity Versus Environment

Is intelligence inherited, dependent on genes and biological background, as some claim, or is it developed as people learn how to adapt to the demands of their environment and specific cultural experiences, as others insist? This heated controversy is still being debated among psychologists on both scientific and political grounds (see Cattell, 1982; Jensen, 1973; Kamin, 1974; Leowontin et al., 1984; Scarr, 1981).

Henry Goddard studied the genetic transfer of mental deficiency and worked on the training of handicapped and gifted children.

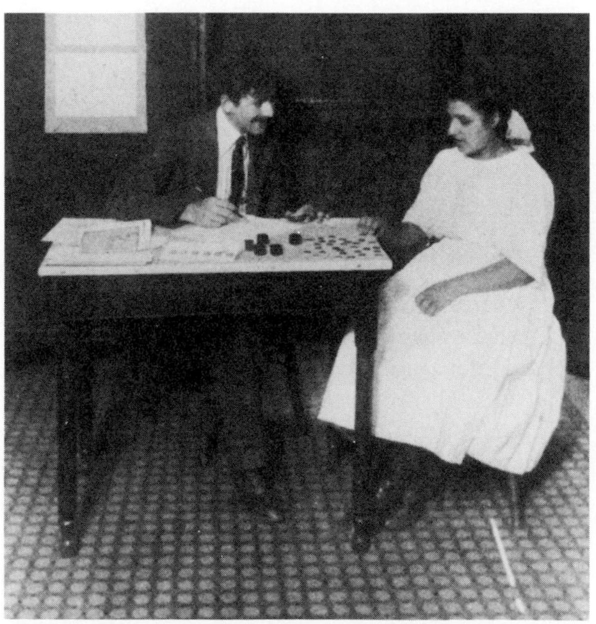

The debate also goes beyond the realm of psychological theories to have very practical consequences in everyday life. In the early 1900s psychologist H. H. Goddard endorsed the IQ scale as a fixed measure of the mind. He advocated mental testing of all immigrants and the selective exclusion of those who were "mentally defective." Vast numbers of Jewish, Italian, and Russian immigrants were classified as "morons" on the basis of IQ tests—with middle-class American norms.

Recently the debate was fueled when Japanese Prime Minister Nakasone alleged a genetic basis for the superior academic performance of Japanese schoolchildren compared to their American counterparts. He claimed the genetic purity of Japanese society and the heterogeneity of genetic stock in the United States as the source of academic performance differences between the two nations. In specifically citing the lower IQ scores of black Americans, the Japanese official revived a racial superiority notion of IQ that had been maintained by William Shockley, Nobel prizewinner in physics. This racist viewpoint alleges that the lower IQ test scores of blacks and Hispanics in the United States is "hereditary and racially genetic in origin, and thus not remedial to a major degree by practical improvements in environment" (Shockley, 1986, p. 67). Thus the argument over the sources of variability in intelligence are more than academic since social, educational, business, and political actions may follow from the assessment of someone's or some group's inherent, fixed mental inferiority.

Many early investigators approached the study of intelligence with a firm conviction that it was an innate, nonmodifiable potential, and thus an objective measure of the person. Around the 1930s the social climate began to change toward greater emphasis of environmental influences on behavior and intellectual performance. In this view it was not the bad seed, but the bad soil that created a poor intellectual crop.

Today the most reasonable view is that of the *interaction* of heredity and environment in determining intelligence. Genes may set the intellectual limits for a *given* person behaving in a *given* environment, but even those limits can be changed by changing the environment in major ways (see Eysenck & Kamin, 1981; Gottesman, 1963). As we saw in chapter 3, an interactive view suggests that there is a continuing interweaving between the two influences, with each factor's contribution at a given time helping determine what the other can achieve.

Prime Minister Nakasone ignored the major impact on test performance of cultural factors such as discipline, expectations, regimented conformity, and higher average socioeconomic class in homogeneous Japanese society. In pluralistic American culture, it is impossible to determine how much of a variation in intellectual performance on a standard test can be assigned entirely to hereditary factors and what proportion is attributable to environmental influences.

Studies have found that the average IQ score of blacks in the United States is about 10 to 15 points below that of whites (Loehlin et al., 1975), but there is much overlapping of scores, and the differences *within* each group are much greater than the differences *between* them. Moreover, many other variables are confounded with race, each of which can influence IQ scores (see **Figure 13.3**). For example, in a large-scale, longitudinal study of more than 26,000 children, the best predictors of a child's IQ at age 4, for both black and white children, were the family's socioeconomic status and the level of mother's education (Broman et al., 1975).

Poverty can lower IQ indirectly through its correlation with family size. Poor people tend to have larger families, with children closer in age, than do richer people. It has been found that IQs are lower in children from large families, especially among those who are later born and close in age to their siblings. Psychologist Robert Zajonc (1976) believes this negative correlation of intelligence and birth order is traceable to the less stimulating intellectual environment of such children. The ideal situation for optimal IQ, he has found, is to be the eldest child in a small family with a wide age gap between siblings.

Figure 13.3
This chart shows evidence for the contribution of heredity and environment to IQ scores. We see similar IQs for fathers and sons (influence of heredity), but the IQs of both fathers and sons are also related to social class level (influence of environment).

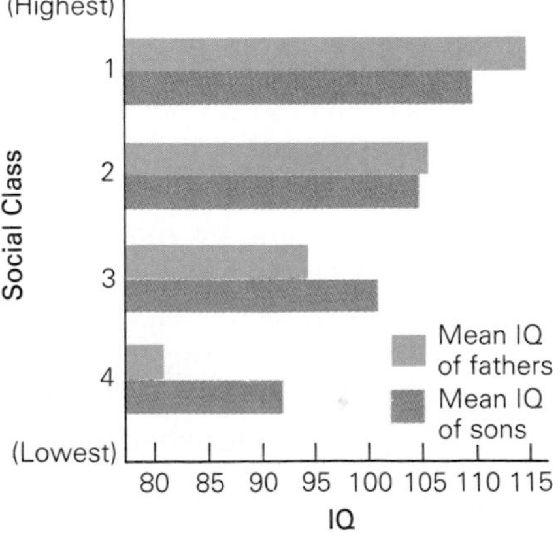

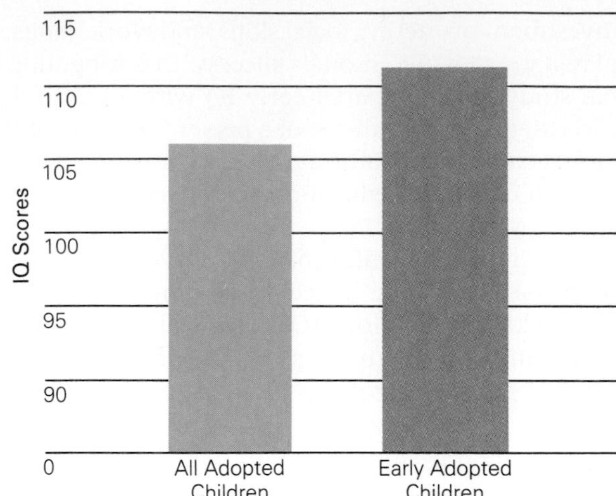

Figure 13.4 *IQ Scores of Black Children Adopted by White Families. (After Scarr & Weinberg, 1976)*

> *When black children were adopted by middle-class white families, their IQ scores became significantly above the average of 100. Those who were adopted at an earlier age (within the first year) into these transracial families had much higher IQ scores than those adopted later. Thus, when given access to an intellectually stimulating environment—likely to enhance componential intelligence of the kind IQ tests measure—black children perform similarly to their white peers (see* ***Figure 13.4****). (Scarr & Weinberg, 1976)*

In other studies IQ scores of children who had grown up under extreme conditions of deprivation were raised considerably by "enrichment" manipulations (Skeels, 1966), or by major changes in the circumstances of their lives (Heber, 1976).

Perhaps the best way to summarize these and other relevant findings is to say that *both* heredity and environment affect intelligence. Furthermore, the level of each at any given time affects the degree to which the other can influence intellectual functioning.

Sources of Bias in Intelligence Testing

Low IQ test scores are used to assign children to EMR classes (Educable Mental Retardation) that are "stigmatizing" and "dead-ends" academically. Because a disproportionate number of minority children, especially blacks and Hispanics, are assigned to such classes, the use of these test practices was challenged in a California court order (*Larry P.* v. *Wilson Riles*, 1979).

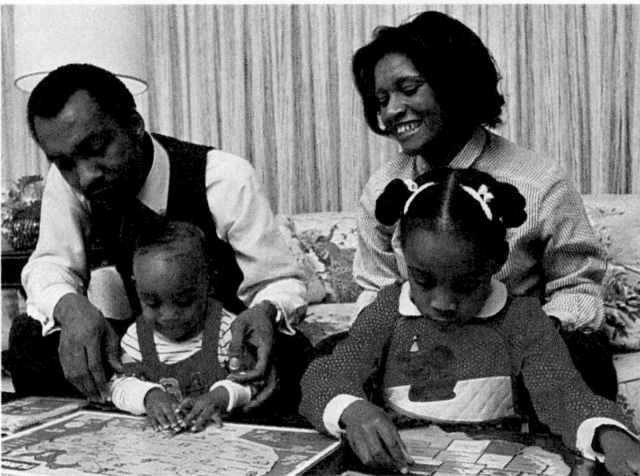

The environmental contrasts are sharp in these two photos. At left is a photo of an allegedly "separate but equal" Tennessee schoolroom for black children in the 1950s. At right, parents of today support their children in learning.

Intelligence tests are not "culture free," nor are school performance tests. Both reflect many variables such as cultural values, history, language usage, general test-taking skills or "sophistication," the conditions of test administration, and the test-taker's expectations of being effective or ineffective (Anastasi, 1982).

There are also biases in the content of most intelligence tests that will influence a person's scores because of his or her cultural, class, or language background. For example, one IQ test asks what you should do if you find a stamped, addressed envelope. "Mail it" is scored as the only correct answer. If you were poor and said, "Check it out for money before mailing," that would be scored wrong. Intellectually wrong or morally wrong? Similarly, if you were an urban ghetto child you might respond differently from one in the normative population to the IQ test item that asks what one should do if a same-sex, much younger child starts a fight.

Poverty can affect intellectual functioning in many ways. A mother's poor prenatal health, a child's poor nutrition, a lack of books and other materials for verbal stimulation, a "survival orientation" that leaves little time or energy for parents to play with and intellectually stimulate their children—all these can be detrimental to performance on tasks like those included in standard tests of IQ. In addition, there are differences between those who speak "standard English" at home and those who use dialects or "nonstandard English."

In a study designed to measure the effect of these language differences on IQ scores, the researchers enlisted the aid of black teachers and graduate students to translate the instructions of an IQ test into nonstandard English. The test they used was the Boehm Test of Basic Concepts *(BTBC), an IQ test that asks children to mark pictures matching concepts of time, space, or quantity. Their subjects were 890 black children attending kindergarten, first, or second grade. The children were carefully divided into two groups so that the ages, sexes, and grade levels of those in one group would match those of the children in the other. In addition, the researchers made sure that the children in the two groups had similar scores on other tests of intelligence.*

Then, one group was given the standard English version of the Boehm; the other group was given the nonstandard English version. The results?

The children who took the nonstandard version scored significantly higher *than those who took the same test with the standard instructions. What is surprising is that the nonstandard instructions did not seem to the* researchers *to be very different from the standard version. For example, the instructions on the standard version read* "behind *the* sofa," *while the nonstandard version read* "in back of *the* couch." *Nevertheless, when these seemingly minor differences in language were added up over the entire test, they had a major effect on the total IQ score a child earned. (Williams & Rivers, 1972)*

Although individual test scores are certainly affected at some age levels, overall these biases have been shown to have a relatively small statistical effect (Lambert, 1981). The major issue is not whether test scores are lowered by content bias but whether they can be *raised* by eliminating cultural disadvantages between groups in our society. It is possible that the term *IQ* soon will be dropped from a psychologist's vocabulary and maybe even from educational use. In its place will be terms that reflect intelligence as one's *current* level of functioning in academic or occupational settings rather than as a stamp of "mental worth." If so, the *conditions* that enhance or depress intellectual performance can be studied and environments manipulated accordingly.

Assessing Personality

There is much more to understanding people than knowing how intelligent they are. Think of all the other ways in which you differ from your best friend or sibling; what qualities attract you to some people and turn you off to others? Like you, psychologists wonder about the attributes that characterize an individual, set one person apart as unique from others, or distinguish between people in one group and those in another (for example, shy people from nonshy or paranoid individuals from "normals"). Personality assessment is the traditional approach to such questions.

Two assumptions are basic to these attempts at understanding and describing human personality: (1) the causes of behavior are intrapsychic—within a person—and (2) personality is a reflection of stable traits or states. In order to describe and explain personality functioning, psychologists use tests specially designed to reveal what these personal traits are, how they fit together in particular individual cases, and the dimensions of personality on which individuals differ. This knowledge may be used in psychological research aimed at a better understanding of human functioning. More often it is used as part of the data on which recommendations are made for personnel selection and career choice, or for treatment of mental problems.

Objective Tests

Objective tests of personality are those in which the scoring, like the administration, is relatively simple and follows objective rules. Some tests may be scored, and even interpreted, by computer programs. This means that objective tests do not require a skilled expert to interpret the results. The final score is usually a number along a single dimension (such as adjustment to maladjustment) or a set of scores on single traits (such as masculinity, dependency, or extroversion).

The most widely used objective personality test is the *Minnesota Multiphasic Personality Inventory*, known in brief as the MMPI (Dahlstrom et al., 1975). It is used in many clinical settings to aid in the diagnosis of patients and as a guide in their treatment. After reviewing its features and applications, we will briefly mention two other self-report inventories that are used widely with nonpatient populations—the *California Personality Inventory* (CPI), and the *Sixteen Personality Factor Questionnaire* (16PF).

Self-report Inventories

One type of objective personality test is the self-report inventory in which individuals answer a series of questions about their thoughts, feelings, and actions. One of the first self-report inventories focused on adjustment problems. The *Woodworth Personal Data Sheet* (written in 1917) asked questions such as "Are you often frightened in the middle of the night?" (see DuBois, 1970). Today, a person taking a **personality inventory** reads a series of statements and indicates whether they are true for himself or herself. On some inventories the person is also asked to assess how frequently each statement is true or how well each describes behavior, thoughts, or feelings.

The MMPI

The MMPI was developed at the University of Minnesota during the 1930s by Starke Hathaway, a psychologist, and J. R. McKinley, a psychiatrist. It was first published in the 1940s (Hathaway & McKinley, 1940, 1943). Its basic purpose was to diagnose individuals according to a set of psychiatric labels. Scales were developed that were relevant to the kinds of problems patients showed in psychiatric settings. Norms were established for both psychiatric patients and normal subjects (visitors to the University of Minnesota hospital).

The MMPI scales were unlike other existing personality tests of the time because they were developed using an *empirical* scale strategy rather than the usual *intuitive* approach. Items were included on a scale only if they clearly distinguished between the two groups—the mental patients and a normal comparison group. Each item had to demonstrate its validity by being answered similarly by members within each group, but differently between the two groups. The items were, thus, not selected on a rational, theoretical basis or according to what the content seemed to mean to experts.

The test consisted of 550 items, each answered simply true (for me), false (for me), or cannot say. Individual item answers were grouped into categories that formed several separate scales. Each item on a scale that was answered in the same direction as the clinical standardization group received one point. The higher one's scale score, the more he or she was like the clinical group and, thus, the less like the normal group. The more extreme the score, the less the likelihood that it was obtained by chance and the more probable it was that the person was within the norms established for the scale.

Table 13.1 MMPI Clinical Scales and Simulated PI Items

Clinical Scales	Simulated Items (Answered True)
Hypochondriasis (Hs) Abnormal concern with bodily functions	"At times I get strong cramps in my intestines."
Depression (D) Pessimism, hopelessness, slowing of action and thought	"I am often very tense on the job."
Conversion Hysteria (Hy) Unconscious use of physical and mental problems to avoid conflicts or responsibility	"Sometimes there is a feeling like something is pressing on my head."
Psychopathic Deviate (Pd) Disregard of social custom, shallow emotions, inability to profit from experience	"I wish I could do over some of the things I have done."
Masculinity-Femininity (Mf) Items differentiating between men and women	"I used to like to do the dances in gym class."
Paranoia (Pa) Abnormal suspiciousness, delusions of grandeur or persecution	"It distresses me that people have the wrong ideas about me."
Psychasthenia (Pt) Obsessions, compulsiveness, fears, guilt, indecisiveness	"The things that run through my head sometimes are horrible."
Schizophrenia (Sc) Bizarre, unusual thoughts or behavior, withdrawal, hallucinations, delusions	"There are those out there who want to get me."
Hypomania (Ma) Emotional excitement, flight of ideas, overactivity	"Sometimes I think so fast I can't keep up."
Social introversion (Si) Shyness, disinterest in others, insecurity	"I give up too easily when discussing things with others."

Originally the MMPI had 10 *clinical* scales, such as the ones outlined in **Table 13.1.** In addition to these 10 MMPI clinical scales, other scales, developed for both research and special clinical purposes, tap diverse aspects of personality—both personal problems and personal strengths. A unique feature of the MMPI is the inclusion of four scales to assess the validity of a person's responses. These *validity scales* check for dishonesty, carelessness, defensiveness, and evasiveness, any of which can bias a person's responses.

For example, some items are almost always answered in one direction (95 percent of all respondents say true, or 95 percent say false). If someone were to answer many of these items with an *unlikely response,* it is possible that he or she would be answering randomly or untruthfully or could not read. The tester would have to check these possibilities before interpreting the rest of the profile. The pattern of the scores—which ones are highest, how they differ, and so on—forms the "MMPI profile" (see **Figure 13.5**). Individual profiles are compared to those common for particular groups, such as paranoid individuals, felons, and gamblers.

There are two general strategies for interpreting MMPI data: clinical and actuarial. In *clinical interpretation* an expert examines each of the scale scores, the features of the profiles (such as extremity and clustering of certain high scale scores), and adds personal experience about patients of each profile type to make inferences about the problems and traits of the person. When an *actuarial interpretation* is made, a psychologist (or computer) merely checks codebooks of empirically established characteristics that describe each profile class or code type. The interpretation is based solely on statistical base rates and norms without ever adding any subjective, expert evaluation or personal knowledge of the patient (see ***Close-up*** on p. 475).

The popularity of the MMPI is seen in its current use in about 50 countries throughout the world and in the fact that it has been the subject of over 8000 books and articles (Butcher & Finn, 1983). This objective assessment technique has weathered criticism from both behaviorally oriented psychologists who advocate behavioral assessment and situational observations as superior and from psychodynamically oriented clinicians who argue for the

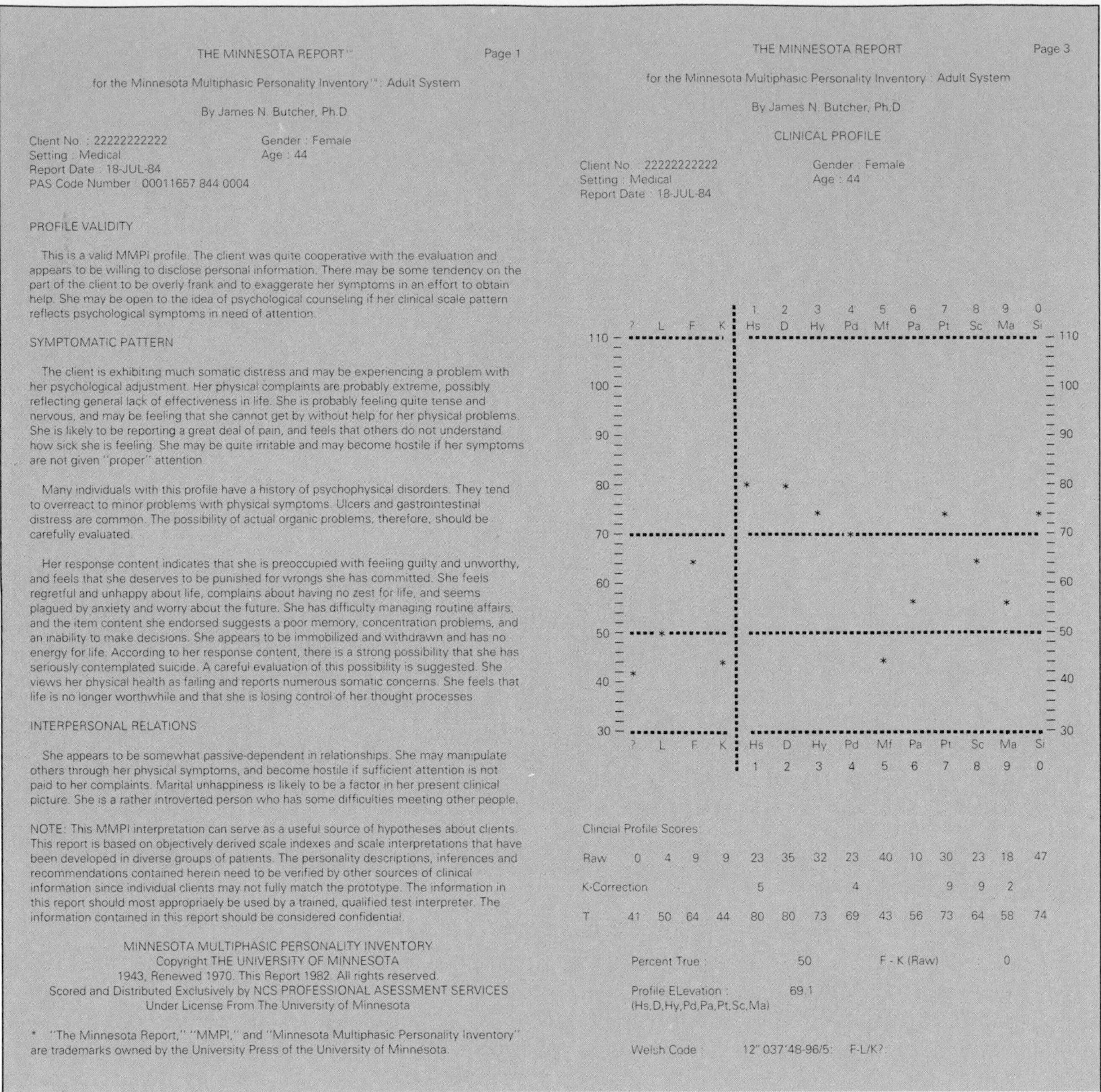

THE MINNESOTA REPORT™ Page 1

for the Minnesota Multiphasic Personality Inventory™: Adult System

By James N. Butcher, Ph.D

Client No. : 22222222222 Gender : Female
Setting : Medical Age : 44
Report Date : 18-JUL-84
PAS Code Number : 00011657 844 0004

PROFILE VALIDITY

This is a valid MMPI profile. The client was quite cooperative with the evaluation and appears to be willing to disclose personal information. There may be some tendency on the part of the client to be overly frank and to exaggerate her symptoms in an effort to obtain help. She may be open to the idea of psychological counseling if her clinical scale pattern reflects psychological symptoms in need of attention.

SYMPTOMATIC PATTERN

The client is exhibiting much somatic distress and may be experiencing a problem with her psychological adjustment. Her physical complaints are probably extreme, possibly reflecting general lack of effectiveness in life. She is probably feeling quite tense and nervous, and may be feeling that she cannot get by without help for her physical problems. She is likely to be reporting a great deal of pain, and feels that others do not understand how sick she is feeling. She may be quite irritable and may become hostile if her symptoms are not given "proper" attention.

Many individuals with this profile have a history of psychophysical disorders. They tend to overreact to minor problems with physical symptoms. Ulcers and gastrointestinal distress are common. The possibility of actual organic problems, therefore, should be carefully evaluated.

Her response content indicates that she is preoccupied with feeling guilty and unworthy, and feels that she deserves to be punished for wrongs she has committed. She feels regretful and unhappy about life, complains about having no zest for life, and seems plagued by anxiety and worry about the future. She has difficulty managing routine affairs, and the item content she endorsed suggests a poor memory, concentration problems, and an inability to make decisions. She appears to be immobilized and withdrawn and has no energy for life. According to her response content, there is a strong possibility that she has seriously contemplated suicide. A careful evaluation of this possibility is suggested. She views her physical health as failing and reports numerous somatic concerns. She feels that life is no longer worthwhile and that she is losing control of her thought processes.

INTERPERSONAL RELATIONS

She appears to be somewhat passive-dependent in relationships. She may manipulate others through her physical symptoms, and become hostile if sufficient attention is not paid to her complaints. Marital unhappiness is likely to be a factor in her present clinical picture. She is a rather introverted person who has some difficulties meeting other people.

NOTE: This MMPI interpretation can serve as a useful source of hypotheses about clients. This report is based on objectively derived scale indexes and scale interpretations that have been developed in diverse groups of patients. The personality descriptions, inferences and recommendations contained herein need to be verified by other sources of clinical information since individual clients may not fully match the prototype. The information in this report should most appropriaely be used by a trained, qualified test interpreter. The information contained in this report should be considered confidential.

THE MINNESOTA REPORT Page 3

for the Minnesota Multiphasic Personality Inventory : Adult System

By James N. Butcher, Ph.D

CLINICAL PROFILE

Client No : 22222222222 Gender : Female
Setting : Medical Age : 44
Report Date : 18-JUL-84

Clincial Profile Scores:

	?	L	F	K	Hs 1	D 2	Hy 3	Pd 4	Mf 5	Pa 6	Pt 7	Sc 8	Ma 9	Si 0
Raw	0	4	9	9	23	35	32	23	40	10	30	23	18	47
K-Correction					5			4			9	9	2	
T	41	50	64	44	80	80	73	69	43	56	73	64	58	74

Percent True : 50 F - K (Raw) : 0

Profile ELevation : 69.1
(Hs,D,Hy,Pd,Pa,Pt,Sc,Ma)

Welsh Code : 12" 037'48-96/5: F-L/K?:

Figure 13.5 *A Computerized Printout of an MMPI Profile*

need to understand the origins of personal conflicts and the meaning people attribute to their problem behavior. The continued use of the MMPI is attributed to factors of reliability, good standardization, established validity, ease and economy of administration, and usefulness in making decisions about patients and psychopathology.

Nevertheless, other critics have objected to the widespread use of the MMPI and similar personality inventories in our society (see APA, 1965). They argue, with justification, that tests like the MMPI were designed to provide rather rough screening tools to identify people who might need therapeutic counseling or who might be unable to perform certain job functions. Because of the way they were constructed, the MMPI and similar inventories should not be used as the sole source of information for such decisions. Even a large battery of test items cannot possibly capture the full richness and complexity of anyone's personality. The test can only reveal the particular aspects of personality for which it has valid items.

On the positive side, tests like the MMPI have proven to be very useful in many contexts (Hedlund, 1977). As with intelligence testing, the problem does not seem to lie so much with the tests as with those who use them (or abuse them) for purposes they were not designed to serve.

Close-up Clinical Versus Actuarial Prediction: Statistics Speak Louder Than Experts

On the basis of assessment information, predictions are made about some aspect of the lives of people who were tested—academic or job success, future maladjustment, homosexuality, marital conflict, criminal recidivism, parole violations, and more. The two methods of making these predictions rely either on expert clinical judgment or on statistical procedures based on actuarial tables and probability formulas (see Butcher, 1987). Which do you suppose is better?

An early survey of the evidence on the relative efficiency of these types of prediction was conducted by Paul Meehl (1954). Its results surprised many psychologists. The statistical approach was equal or superior to the clinical approach. Subsequently made comparisons confirm this conclusion (Meehl, 1965; Sawyer, 1966).

How can a prediction of human behavior by a "cold-blooded" statistical formula be better than one based on the judgment of a sensitive, skilled clinician who knows about people "in the flesh"? The picture is not as bleak for the human side of this controversy when we consider some of the limits on the comparisons made in the studies surveyed.

1. *The "clinicians" were not the best experts available, but varied widely in experience and skill.*
2. *Their individual "hit rates" were lost because they were averaged over the entire sample, so those predictions that were superior to the actuarial ones went unrecognized.*
3. *Most of the predictions were about specific outcomes, such as grades or vocational achievement, which usually do not concern clinicians.*
4. *The data the clinicians had to use was often derived from scales like the MMPI, designed for objective interpretation and not the kind of theoretically based data clinicians typically use.*

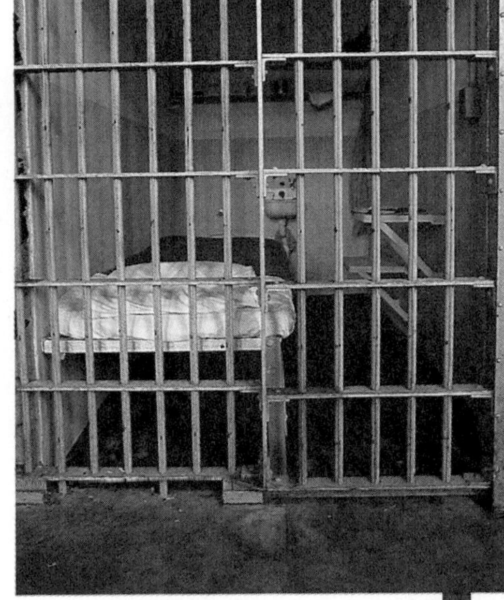

These and other criticisms restrict the simple conclusion of the relative inferiority of clinical predictions. They force us instead to restate the question in terms of the conditions for which each approach can be expected to provide the best prediction (Holt, 1970).

The following table summarizes the occasions and conditions when each of the approaches is most valuable (adapted from Phares, 1984).

Statistical Is Best	***Clinical Is Best***
When adequate norms on reliable, valid tests are available.	When no good tests are available.
For information combining.	For information gathering.
To predict average, typical cases.	To predict rare, atypical cases.
If the predicted event is *not* affected by any special circumstances.	If unforeseen conditions occur, making prediction idiosyncratic.
For specific, objective outcomes.	For global outcomes of patterns over time.
For large, heterogeneous samples.	For an individual case studied by an expert.
When the sample being predicted is same or similar to normative one used to derive formula.	
Where human judgment is biased by fatigue, boredom, or prejudice.	

Other Objective Inventories

The *California Personality Inventory* (CPI) is comparable to the MMPI in its empirical construction, the kinds of items used, and the use of special validity scales to assess test-taking attitudes (Gough, 1957). The major difference is that its purpose is to assess a variety of personality dimensions based on normal standardization groups, not psychiatric diagnosis based on patient groups. Its 18 scales measure traits such as self-control, sociability, flexibility, responsibility, and self-acceptance. The CPI is used widely to predict job success among police, airline stewardesses, dentists, student teachers, and others (Gynther & Gynther, 1976).

The *Sixteen Personality Factor Questionnaire* (16PF), developed by Raymond Cattell (1972), does not use the empirical criterion method of the MMPI and CPI. Instead, Cattell uses the mathematical technique of factor analysis to reduce a large pool of 1800 test items to about 100 that are statistically organized into 16 clusters or factors. Each factor is thought to reflect a basic underlying personality trait. The 16PF is often used in vocational and personal counseling.

Behavior Assessment

The MMPI and the inventories of Gough and Cattell have in common the premise that there are enduring qualities in a person that can be tapped by such instruments. A contrasting approach is that of **behavior assessment,** aimed at identifying a person's specific current, observable behaviors that can be changed. Behavior assessment generally uses judges' ratings.

In the 1960s and 1970s, with the rise of the behavior therapies (to be discussed in chapter 16), there arose a need to measure typical current, very specific behavior patterns, such as tantrum behavior or negative self-statements. It was assumed that problem behaviors were specific to the situation and were being maintained by conditions in the environment rather than conditions in the person. The best way to assess people seemed to be to observe directly how they behaved in the natural environments where the problem behavior occurred (Hartman et al., 1979).

Assessment is made of the rate or incidence of very specific problem behaviors before therapy starts, to provide a baseline, and then again after a period of therapy, to see whether the desired changes in behavior have occurred. Behavior assessment is now widely used and has had a remarkable record of usefulness and productivity (Haynes, 1983).

Projective Tests

Have you ever looked at a cloud and "seen" a face or the shape of an animal? If you asked your friends to look too, you may have discovered that they saw a reclining nude or a dragon or something else quite different. Psychologists rely on a similar phenomenon in their use of projective tests for personality assessment.

In a **projective test,** a person is given a series of stimuli that are purposely ambiguous, such as abstract patterns, incomplete pictures, and drawings that can be interpreted in several ways. The person may be asked to describe the patterns, finish the pictures, or tell stories about the drawings. Because the stimuli are vague, responses to them are determined partly by what the person brings to the situation—namely, inner feelings, personal motives, and conflicts from prior life experiences. These idiosyncratic aspects are projected, or "thrown outward," onto stimuli that permit various interpretations.

Projective tests were first used by psychoanalysts who hoped that such tests would reveal their patients' unconscious personality dynamics. For example, to uncover emotionally charged thoughts and fears, Carl Jung used **word associations** to a list of common words ("What is the first thing brought to mind by the word *house?*").

In addition to this technique of *associating* a verbal, auditory, or visual stimulus to its personal meaning, four other projective techniques have been used to assess personality (Lindzey, 1961). They are techniques of *construction*—making a story; *completion*—finishing a sequence of events in a story; *choice* or *ordering*—arranging materials in some order, ranking or choosing among alternatives; and *expression*—acting or performing some role, or expressing the self through art. Two of the more common projective tests are the Rorschach test and the Thematic Apperception Test (TAT).

The Rorschach

In the **Rorschach test,** developed by Swiss psychiatrist Hermann Rorschach in 1921, the ambiguous symmetrical stimuli are inkblots (Rorschach, 1942). Some are black and white, some are colored (see **Figure 13.6**). A respondent is shown an inkblot and asked, "Tell me what you see, what it might be to you. There are no right or wrong answers."

The tester records verbatim what is said, the time to the first response, total time taken per card, and how the card is handled. Then in a second phase of *inquiry,* the respondent is reminded of the

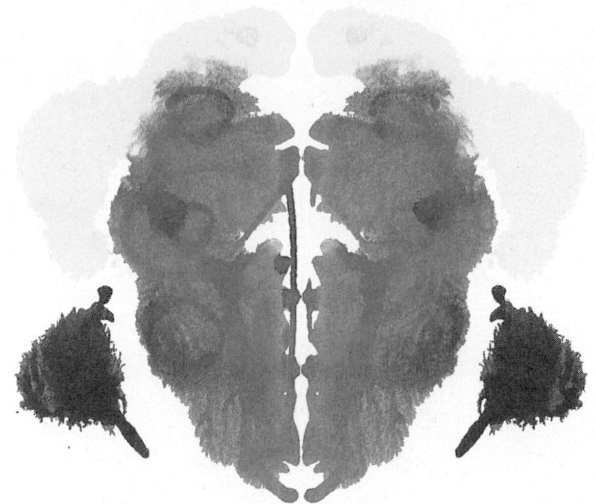

Figure 13.6 *A Sample Rorschach Inkblot*

previous responses and asked to elaborate on them: what prompted them, what location on the card they refer to, and so forth.

The responses are scored on three major dimensions: (a) the *location* of the responses on a card, whole stimulus or part response, size of details; (b) the *content* of the response in terms of the nature of the object and activities seen; and (c) the *determinants*—which aspects of a card (such as its color or shading) prompted the response. Some scorers also note whether responses are original and unique or popular, conforming ones.

Interpreting these scores into a coherent portrait of an individual's personality dynamics is a complex, highly subjective process that relies on clinical expertise and skilled intuition. Ideally, a tester uses these data as a source of hypotheses about a person that are then evaluated through other assessment procedures. Although the Rorschach has questionable reliability and validity, it is recommended as an indirect way to find areas of information, such as sexual interests or aggressive fantasies, that people may resent or lie about on objective tests, (Levy & Orr, 1959).

The TAT

In the **Thematic Apperception Test** (developed by American psychologist Henry Murray, 1938), respondents are shown pictures of ambiguous scenes and asked to generate stories about them, describing what the people in the scenes are doing and thinking, what led up to each event, and how each situation will end (see **Figure 13.7**). The person administering the TAT evaluates the structure and content of the stories, as well as the behavior of the individual in telling them, in an attempt to discover some of the respondent's major concerns and personality characteristics. For example, an examiner might evaluate a person as "conscientious" if the stories concerned people who lived up to their obligations and were told in a serious, orderly way. The test can be used with clinical patients to reveal emotional problems or with normal individuals to reveal dominant needs, such as needs for power, affiliation, and achievement (McClelland, 1961). We studied the achievement motive and its assessment by the TAT in chapter 11.

The Rorschach, TAT, and other projective tests have been widely used, especially in clinical settings. In fact, more articles have been published about the Rorschach than about any other psychological test (Buros, 1974). However, projective tests have been subject to a number of criticisms. A basic problem with these tests is that the interpretation of responses is very *subjective* and depends largely upon the skill and experience of the examiner. A clinician using these techniques listens to (or reads) a person's responses, observes the manner in which they are given, and, based on a series of guidelines, tries to put together a theory about the person's underlying needs, traits, motives, and problems. Because of difficulties with reliability and validity, some researchers have claimed that projective techniques are *not* actually very effective for revealing personality dynamics (Buros, 1978). These tests are best used in conjunction with other assessment techniques, since decisions based solely on projective test data lack the authority that comes with reliable, valid tests.

Figure 13.7 *A Sample Card from the TAT Test*

Assessing Creativity

Of those attributes that help define our humanity—language, tender emotions, a time sense, and abstract reasoning—none is more mysterious or desired than the "creative urge."

Millions of years ago, our ancestors did something no other animal species has ever done. They took time out from the rigors of trying to survive in environments beset with physical dangers from cold, heat, famine, drought, and powerful predators to paint pictures on the walls of their cave homes. Some murals seem to represent their desires for a successful hunt for food; others reflect more mystical ways of winning over stronger predators and adversaries. At some point these expressions of inner needs and feelings became redirected toward art that was purely decorative. Human creativity was channeled to produce objects that were aesthetically pleasing, whether or not they served any other function. In virtually every known civilization, men and women have put this distinctive imprint on anything that could be shaped, colored, textured, twisted, or made to be something beyond what it was originally.

When we think of creative people, great artists, inventors, scientists, and poets spring to mind—Michelangelo, Ludwig van Beethoven, William Shakespeare, Albert Einstein, Marie Curie, Emily Dickinson. However, ordinary, average people can be creative, even without public acclaim for their accomplishments. What can you infer about the background of a 10-year-old boy of average IQ from the variety of responses he gave to the question, "How many uses can you think of for a newspaper?"

> *You can read it, write on it, lay it down and paint a picture on it. If you didn't have covers, you could put it in your door for decoration, put it in the garbage can, put it on a chair if the chair is messy. If you have a puppy, you put newspaper in its box or put it in your backyard for the dog to play with. When you build something and you don't want anyone to see it, put newspaper around it. Put newspaper on the floor if you have no mattress, use it to pick up something hot, use it to stop bleeding, or to catch the drips from drying clothes. You can use a newspaper for curtains, put it in your shoe to cover what is hurting your foot, make a kite out of it, shade a light that is too bright. You can wrap fish in it, wipe windows or wrap money in it and tape it [so it doesn't make noise]. You put washed shoes on newspaper, wipe eyeglasses with it, put it under a dripping sink, put a plant on it, make a paper bowl out of it, use it for a hat if it is raining, tie it on your feet for slippers. You can put it on the sand if you had no towel, use if for bases in baseball, make paper airplanes with it, use it as a dustpan when you sweep, ball it up for the cat to play with, wrap your hands in it if it is cold. (Ward et al., 1972)*

This painting from the late Paleolithic Age (circa 28,000–10,000 B.C.) seems to suggest that the cave may have been used for the performance of hunting and religious rituals.

In evaluating the answers of this boy, you might say that he was very creative because he gave many responses that you would never have thought of. In fact, if you were to compare his answers to those of other 10-year-old children of average IQ, his performance might be even more impressive. Where does such an ability come from? Is it a general characteristic that he was born with, or is it something that he learned? If we look at this boy's answers again, we might guess that his *experience* has been an important factor. Clearly, the more often a person has had to use something in several ways, the more likely he or she is to think of other uses for it. Perhaps this child's responses would be considered less creative by other people with the same background. If so, this would imply that creativity is a relative quality that exists only when someone thinks it does. Many psychologists dispute such a viewpoint, however, and maintain that creativity can be reliably and objectively measured. (If you haven't guessed already, the 10-year-old boy with all the answers came from a New York City ghetto.)

What Qualifies as Creative?

The most widely used definition of **creativity** is that it is the occurrence of uncommon or unusual, but appropriate, responses. This assumption underlies most of the tests that have been developed to measure creativity.

Although originality is usually taken for granted as a major factor in creativity, the importance of *appropriateness* is not always recognized. However, this is the criterion that distinguishes between creative and nonsensical acts. Solutions to a problem that are unique but totally worthless or irrelevant are not considered creative; but, of course, "appropriate," like "desirable," involves a value judgment that may vary with a judge's background, a culture, or an era.

Creativity has several facets. First, there is a perceptual element—*heightened sensitivity* to features of the world that other people do not usually notice. Creativity also involves *synthesis*—the ability to make connections that relate observations or ideas in novel, meaningful ways. There is the ability to generate nonverbal images or special *internal representations* of a spatial or visual character. The creative *product* is the tangible "externalization" of these private images, whether in theories, inventions, or works of art (Shepard, 1978).

How can creative people be identified? What characteristics distinguish them from less creative people? Was Pablo Picasso more creative than Sigmund Freud? Is jazz trumpeter Miles Davis as creative as dance choreographer Martha Graham? Is a Mozart sonata more creative than comedian Robin Williams' monologue? Comparative assessments like these are difficult to make in any objective way, because they depend on both personal value judgments and social standards, and they mix creativity of different styles, types, and media. When psychologists assess creativity among "average" people, their goal is to determine how creative an individual is compared to a normative population of similar people.

As with intelligence, it is important to design *reliable* and *valid* measures. Unlike intelligence tests, however, creativity tests—by definition—cannot have a single right answer. A common approach to measuring creativity has been to assess evidence of **divergent thinking**—the ability to come up with unusual, but appropriate, responses to standard questions like "How many uses can you think of for a newspaper?" Divergent thinking moves away in various directions to encompass many aspects of different ideas. Such thinking is typically associated with creativity since it often generates novel ideas and fresh solutions to old problems. It contrasts with **convergent thinking,** thinking characterized by bringing together, or synthesizing, information and knowledge focused on identifying a single correct solution to a particular problem. Most intelligence tests, with their well-defined problems and objectively best answers, focus primarily on convergent thinking.

One technique for assessing creativity was adapted from the projective methods originally developed for personality assessment. As we have mentioned, projective tests have had questionable utility for their original purpose; however, they

What is more creative than to see beauty in other people's discarded objects? Get rid of a button, bead, or other bauble, and this sculptor may use it.

Common Responses
1. Smudges
2. Dark clouds

Uncommon Responses
1. Magnetized iron filings
2. A small boy and his mother hurrying along on a dark windy day, trying to get home before it rains

Common Responses
1. An African voodoo dancer
2. A cactus plant

Uncommon Responses
1. Mexican in sombrero running up a long hill to escape from rain clouds
2. A word written in Chinese

Common Responses
1. An ape
2. Modern painting of a gorilla

Uncommon Responses
1. A baboon looking at itself in a hand mirror
2. Rodin's "The Thinker" shouting "Eureka!"

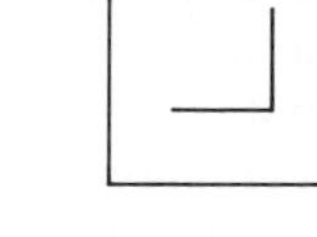

Common Response

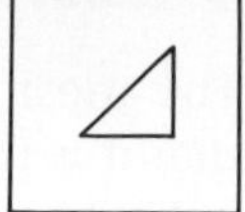

Uncommon Response

Figure 13.8

Two tests based on the methods of projective testing and used to distinguish between creative and noncreative individuals are shown. In an inkblot test, an individual must attribute order and meaning to vague configurations. An average individual is apt to concentrate on their simple, obvious features. A creative person is more likely to impose an elegant new order on the figure. In a drawing completion test, an average individual is satisfied with a simple figure that "makes sense" while a creative individual produces a more complex and meaningful drawing.

have provided useful means for assessing creativity. For example, in inkblot tests, the average individual is apt to concentrate on simple, obvious features. The creative person is more likely to impose an elegant new order on the figure. Where the task is to complete a drawing, an average individual is satisfied with a simple figure that "makes sense," while a creative individual produces a more complex and meaningful drawing (see **Figure 13.8**).

A different method of assessing creativity depends on behavior sampling and judges' ratings.

In a series of studies, college women were asked to make collages from pieces of lightweight paper or write Haiku poems. The products were then ranked for creativity—independent of their "technical goodness" or neatness or organization—by judges with some relevant expertise. This methodology resulted in considerable agreement among the judges, thus increasing our confidence that it was actually creativity—and not some other quality—being assessed.

This research also suggests that creativity is influenced by the social context in which a creative task is performed. Subjects who had been told their products would be evaluated by experts were later judged lower in creativity than those subjects who had not been forewarned of the evaluation. (Amabile, 1983)

Correlates of Creativity

Are there other qualities that creative people typically have? In general, studies have shown that creative persons are distinguished more by their interests, attitudes, and drives than by their intellectual abilities (Dellas & Gaier, 1970). The *lack* of a strong correlation between creativity and IQ may seem surprising, but research conducted so far has supported this conclusion (Barron & Harrington, 1981). For example, none of the many children with superior, "genius" level intelligence who were studied by Lewis Terman (described in chapter 3) had produced any outstanding creative works when they were restudied 40 years later (Terman & Oden, 1959). Therefore it is possible for intelligence and creativity to function independently; knowing about the one in any person tells us little about the other. This lack of association again questions why our society places so much emphasis on IQ and intellectual functioning—and so little on finding ways to enhance creativity.

Other cognitive variables *do* seem characteristic of creative people, however. One of the most distinctive of these is a cognitive preference for *complexity* rather than simplicity. This is revealed in a preference for drawings that are asymmetrical, dynamic, and even chaotic, rather than drawings that are regular, neat, and simple (see the ***Close-up*** on p. 481).

Much creativity research has been concerned with the personality characteristics of creative individuals. The results have pointed to a group of characteristics that includes independence, intuitiveness, high energy, and self-acceptance (Barron & Harrington, 1981). Architects and research scientists were remarkably similar in these personality traits, despite the differences in the content of their professional work (Gough, 1961; MacKinnon, 1961). Writers displayed a similar pattern of traits, although they showed greater originality and an emphasis on fantasy (Barron, 1963; see also Koestler, 1964). Creativity is also strongly related to the personality domain of "openness to new experience" (McCrae, 1987).

Close-up *The Mad Artist/Crazy Genius Controversy*

The popular view of the artist-as-mad and the creative genius-as-crazy has been around for a long time. As early as the first century A.D., the Roman philosopher Seneca wrote, "There is no great genius without some touch of madness."

There are, indeed, many examples of eminent creative people who have suffered serious psychological disorders, Most students are aware of the mental problems experienced by artist Vincent van Gogh, poets William Blake and Ezra Pound, and dancer Vaslov Nijinsky. The list of the mentally disturbed, based on various sources of evidence, includes many of the world's greatest creative artists and geniuses. Among them are Newton, Copernicus, Pascal, Darwin, Michelangelo, Beethoven, and Freud (see Karlsson, 1978; Prentky, 1980).

Such exemplars would seem to build a case for the popular association of creativity and madness, but what does the systematically collected research evidence tell us? Unfortunately, the data are mixed. Some research on creative people indicates that, as a group, they tend to have strong egos and constructive ways of handling problems (Cross et al., 1967). Hardly the seeds of madness there; but other research points to a similarity between schizophrenic individuals and creative people in their characteristic perceptual styles. Both groups "overinclude" loosely connected events and ideas, not excluding stimuli many "normal" people would judge as irrelevant (Hasenfus & Magaro, 1978).

Other analyses reveal that creative people commonly use thought processes that are intuitive, uncensored by socially acceptable ways of thinking. These directly experienced and expressed thoughts and feelings are called *primary process.* They are in contrast to those that are constrained by awareness of what is correct, desirable, or realistic, which are called *secondary process.* Loosening the inhibiting effects of secondary processes upon thinking can lead to original ideas and unusual associations that may then be labeled either as examples of creative genius or as deviant, strange thoughts characteristic of the mentally unbalanced (Becker, 1978). That decision rests, in part, on the values of an individual's society in assessing what is "art," "invention," or "discovery"; what its tolerance is for the nontraditional; and what its definition is of mental disorder.

We may conclude from the available evidence that (a) there are some similarities between

the thoughts and perceptual processes of creative and disturbed individuals; (b) many famous creative people have been mad; (c) we may think these cases are more common than they actually are because of their vividness and availability in our memories (recall the heuristic biases discussed in chapter 10); and (d) most creative people appear to be normal or even superior on several dimensions of psychological health.

Finally, a different perspective on the genius-madness association comes from Ezra Pound: "The concept of genius as akin to madness has been carefully fostered by the inferiority complex of the public" (1934, p. 82).

Assessment and You

Thus far we have presented some of the major features of assessment techniques and have discussed in detail certain approaches used to assess intelligence, personality, and creativity. As a college student, you may be struggling with decisions about the kind of job you would like to have when you finish school. In this section we will first discuss the role of assessment in vocational counseling. Then we will address some of the political and ethical issues posed by the widespread use of formal assessment procedures in our society today.

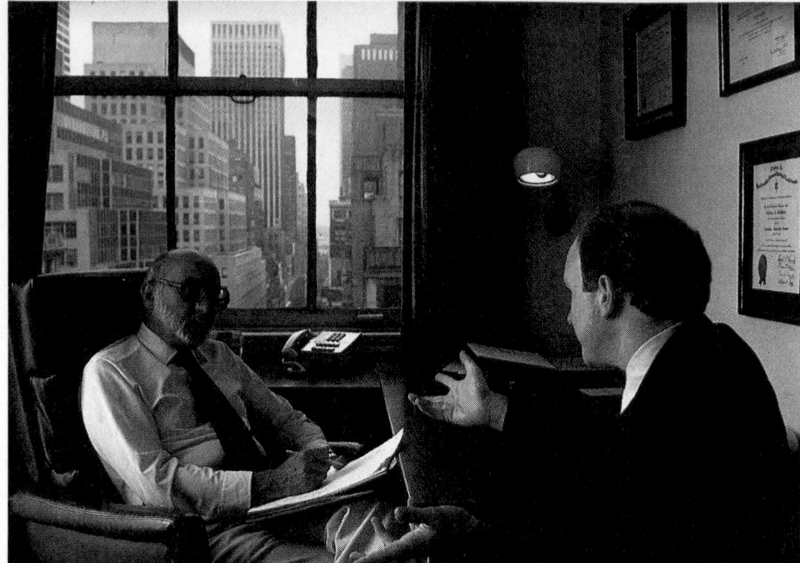

Individuals often need help to find out what their abilities really are and what fields they might be suited for. Career counselors are there to meet this need.

Vocational Interests and Aptitudes

Have you already decided what type of job you would like to have? Are you still undecided or perhaps thinking of leaving a job you are already in? No matter how you answer, much assessment activity in this country is aimed at people like you. Many assessment instruments have been developed to help people learn what vocations best fit their personalities, values, interests, and skills—or, in some cases, to show them before it's too late that the career they have chosen may not be the wisest choice.

Assessing Interests

Even if you do not yet know what jobs you might like best, you know you'd like to have a job that suits your interests. You'd like your job to involve activities you enjoy and to serve goals you consider worthwhile. However, you may be unsure about what your major interests and abilities are. Furthermore, you may have little idea of what people in many occupations actually do on the job and may not really know how these job activities relate to your personal situation. A number of tests have been designed to help you identify your major interests and abilities and to suggest the best career directions depending on your particular interest pattern.

The most widely used test to measure vocational interests is the *Strong-Campbell Interest Inventory,* which was constructed in 1927 by psychologist E. K. Strong. The test is based on an empirical approach similar to that used later for the MMPI. First, groups of men in different occupations answered items about activities they liked or disliked. Then the answers of those who were successful in particular occupations were compared with the answers of men in general. In this way, a set of items (norms) was determined that was representative of answers given by successful workers in each job category. Subsequent versions of the test have added norms relevant to women and to newer occupations. If you took this test, a vocational counselor could tell you what types of jobs are typically held by people with interests like yours. These are the jobs which are likely to appeal to you too.

Assessing Abilities

Even if the characteristics of a job appeal to you, and it suits your personality and fits your values and interests, you are unlikely to be satisfied with it unless you can do it well. And, of course, your employer is unlikely to be satisfied with you if you are unable to do the job for which you were hired.

In order to recommend a career path for you, a vocational counselor will want to assess your abilities as well as your interests. Ability has two components, aptitude and achievement, as we noted in the earlier discussions of intelligence. An **aptitude test** measures your potential for acquiring various skills—not necessarily how well you can perform tasks now but how well you will be at them in the future. An **achievement test,** on the other hand, measures your current level of competence. A test used to see how well you can speak a foreign language or how good you are at computer programming is an example of an achievement test.

Tests have been developed for assessing aptitude and achievement in many domains. With knowledge of not only what you like to do, but also what you can do well, a counselor is in a good position to predict your "fit" for different jobs (see Anastasi, 1976; Sundberg & Matarazzo, 1979; Tyler, 1974).

Tests of ability are also used by companies seeking new employees. If you apply for a specific job, you may be asked to take tests involving the abilities and skills required for that job. If a job involves typing, you may be given a timed typing test; if it involves hard physical labor, you may be given a test of strength. If managing other people will be an important part of the job, your tolerance for interpersonal stress and ability to assert yourself may be assessed. Again, the goal is to match people with the jobs for which they are best suited and, thus, to increase the satisfaction of both employees and their employers.

Assessing Jobs

The pay received for a job in an organization is usually determined by three primary factors: the nature and degree of *skill* required, the amount of *effort* demanded, and the extent of individual *responsibility* for decisions affecting company resources or personnel. Organizations invest much time and money in personnel selection to get the "right" person for the position. They rely not only on an assessment of an applicant's characteristics but also on a careful identification and analysis of the requirements of the job (Tenopyr & Oeltjen, 1982).

Job assessment is performed in many ways. Workers, supervisors, and specially trained job analysts are asked to provide information about the abilities required for doing particular jobs. Subject-matter experts may rate the relevance of various kinds of knowledge, skills, and abilities. An inventory of requirements, including the tasks and duties a worker must perform, can then be prepared for each occupation. One such inventory that has been developed—the *Occupational Analysis Inventory*—provides information about a wide spectrum of occupations and can be very helpful to a job seeker (Pass & Cunningham, 1978).

Some companies are supplementing other assessment methods with *realistic job previews.* They show applicants what will be expected of them on the job through films, tapes, employee checklists of most and least liked aspects of a job, and presentation of simulated "critical incidents" likely to arise (Wanous, 1980). This gives applicants a clearer picture of what will be expected of them if they take a job and helps them decide how well the job fits their abilities and interests.

Finally, how well a person does at a job often depends not only on *what that person knows* and *how hard he or she works* but also on variables not directly related to the abilities needed to do the work. Among them might be assertiveness, social skills, appearance, and general congruence or fit with a company's picture of its ideal supervisor, manager, or executive.

Political and Ethical Issues

The primary goal of psychological assessment is to reduce errors of judgment that bias accurate assessment of people. This is achieved by replacing subjective judgments of teachers, physicians, employers, and other evaluators with more objective measures that have been carefully constructed and are open to critical evaluation. This is the goal that motivated Alfred Binet in his pioneering work. We also saw that process work in the little Maria's trials and tribulations in the *Opening Case.* It was hoped that testing would help democratize society and minimize decisions based on arbitrary criteria of sex, race, nationality, or physical appearance. However, despite these lofty goals, there is no area of psychology more enmeshed in controversy than that of assessment. Testing has become big business in the United States. It is a multimillion dollar industry including companies that develop tests, publish tests, analyze tests, and recommend courses of action based on these tests. These companies constitute a powerful group interested in maintaining and extending the use of testing.

Test scores already form the basis for major decisions about people's lives—in the absence of the less economical, more inefficient evaluation of the whole person "in the flesh." In addition, as we have become a nation of test-takers, our test scores have become *reified,* as "special, personal things." They are invested with an absolute significance that is no longer limited by relative comparisons with appropriate norms. People too often think of themselves as "*being* IQs of 110," or "*being* B students," as if the scores were a label stamped on their foreheads. Such labels may become barriers to advancement. For people who are "negatively assessed" the scores may become self-imposed motivational limits that lower their sense of self-efficacy and restrict the risks taken and challenges willing to be faced.

A related criticism is that the use of test scores and arbitrary cut-off points to determine school admissions, job placements, and so forth gives an illusion of scientific legitimacy to decisions that eliminate those considered "socially undesirable." Sometimes people are evaluated on the basis of tests with norms that may be inappropriate. We have already mentioned this problem with respect to IQ tests, and it occurs with personality assessment too.

For example, although MMPI norms were based solely on mentally disturbed white patients, MMPI scores are being used to make decisions about both black and white students, job seekers, and other groups. Blacks who do not show mental disorders on other assessment instruments have relatively high scores on the MMPI scales that measure nonconformity, alienation, and impulsivity. Are blacks, then, more maladjusted than whites, or might their scores change comparatively if they were based on norms developed for black test-takers (Gynther, 1981)? It is likely that the revision of the MMPI—now in progress—will clear up some of these questions. However, until that time comes, courts, parole offices, and other agencies will continue to use existing test scores, norms, and published manuals to decide the fate of some of those in their charge.

It is easier to challenge another person's evaluation of your intelligence, personality, or psychopathology than to oppose a computerized printout that describes the supposed "real you" in statistically objective terms. It is as if the test added a postscript to the effect, "nothing personal, mind you, but this is just the way you are." Few people are willing to challenge the authoritative posture of test results even when such results may have an adverse impact on their lives.

Competency testing used in high schools, college-entrance examinations, job placement, and civil-service examinations is being challenged in the courts, and some states are passing laws to limit its use. The challenge comes from those who argue that the tests often do not provide accurate indexes of what they are intended to measure. Even where they are valid, they have other objectionable features. For example, some say that personnel selection is too often a one-way fit of people to available jobs. Instead, perhaps it might be better to change some job descriptions to fit the needs and abilities of the people.

Another problem of assessment is the pervasive assumption that intellectual abilities are inherited and the accompanying belief that those who do poorly on screening tests cannot learn to do better. This is an old issue that has centered on attempts to establish the degree to which IQ is influenced by nature versus nurture. Despite the obvious interaction of genetic endowment with learned experiences, advocates for both sides have attempted to minimize the contributions of the other type of input (Leowontin et al., 1984). Unfortunately, this difference in philosophy is not just a matter of personal opinion, but a difference that can influence public policy. Restrictive immigration laws, enforced sterilization programs, and resource cutbacks for educational enrichment programs (such as Head Start for minority children) have all been supported by those who believe mental abilities are inherited, unchangeable attributes—and opposed by those who believe in the importance of nurture in the realization of human potential. It is not an ivory-tower debate, but one in which the stakes are high—the basic understanding of our species—and the effects are widespread, influencing the quality of life for many in our society.

A final concern about the enterprise of traditional psychological assessment is its focus on locating traits, states, maladjustment, conflict, and pathology *within* an individual. This leads to thinking about "children as retarded" rather than about "educational systems that need to modify their programs to accommodate all their learners." It puts the spotlight on the deviant personality rather than on problems in the environment. Human assessors need to recognize that what people are now is a product of where they've been, where they think they are headed, and what situation is currently influencing their behavior. Such a view can help unite different assessment approaches as well as the social, behavioral, and dynamic approaches to understanding and dealing with personality on which they are based.

The next chapter treats a different kind of assessment by asking about the impact of environmental stressors on our functioning. How can we determine the effects of stress on our behavior, emotions, thoughts, and physiological responses? In addition, we will discover how we can better manage the stress we are heir to and prevent those stresses waiting in the wings, all-too-ready to get into our act.

Summary

- The purpose of psychological assessment is to describe or classify individuals in ways that will be useful for prediction or treatment.
- A useful assessment tool must be reliable and valid and must have been standardized. A reliable measure gives consistent results on different testings. A valid measure assesses the attributes for which the test was designed. Standardization of a measuring device includes establishing uniform procedures to administer and score it and obtaining norms by giving it to a large number of people, like those for whom it is intended.
- Formal assessment is carried out through interviews, life history and archival data, tests, and situational observations. Self-report measures and judges' ratings are sources of assessment information that come from an individual or from others.
- On self-report measures subjects answer questions or supply information about themselves. Self-report measures are convenient to administer, but may suffer from intentional or unwitting biases and inaccuracies.
- Judges' ratings may be biased by the halo and the stereotype effects; their reliability is enhanced by multiple judges and judgments tied to specific, observable actions.
- Objective, quantifiable intelligence testing began in France early in this century with the test by Binet. It was designed to identify and separate retarded from normal schoolchildren as a step in planning special training for the former. Scores were given in terms of mental ages.
- In the United States, intelligence testing was seized on as a way to solve the practical problems of classifying draftees and determining which immigrants would profit from what kinds of education. Unfortunately, early results were misinterpreted by some as evidence of the inferiority of certain groups.
- With the development of the Stanford revision of the Binet scale and the concept of the IQ, intelligence came to be seen as an inner, largely inherited, unchanging capacity.
- Because the Standford-Binet tests were standardized on white, English-speaking children, they often did not give accurate indications of the intelligence of non-English-speaking individuals. Tests developed by Wechsler, one for adults and one for children, provide separate scores for verbal and nonverbal items.
- Though an operational definition of intelligence is simply "what intelligence tests measure," there is general agreement today that intelligence includes verbal abilities and problem-solving abilities. It also involves adapting to new demands, learning from experience, and thinking abstractly.
- *Ability* is defined as the currently available power to perform, *aptitude* as the potential for performance after training, and *achievement* as the measure of success of performance.
- According to psychometric theories of intelligence, intelligence consists of a general g-factor, and a number of specific s-factors. One psychometric theory is Guilford's structure of intellect model, which classifies intellectual factors according to content, product, and operation.
- In contrast to psychometric theories are theories of intelligence based on cognitive science. Hunt's theory of cognitive processes defines intelligence in terms of the mental activities used to solve problems. Gardner proposes a culturally determined view, identifying intelligence as one of seven ways of looking at the world. Sternberg's theory distinguishes three aspects of intelligence—a componential aspect, an experiential aspect, and a contextual aspect.
- IQ scores are valid for predicting academic success and the status of one's occupation. Once in a profession, factors other than intelligence are more important in determining success.
- IQs of young children may change over time with several kinds of environmental change. IQs are relatively stable for older children, but individuals can show large changes. Both genetic and environmental factors contribute to the level of intelligence that an individual achieves, as does their interaction.
- No test is entirely culture free. Content and manner of administration are inevitably more appropriate for some groups than others, and cultural differences in habits, motivation, family encouragement, and relevant past experience all affect a child's test scores.
- Personality is assessed by both objective instruments and projective devices. The *Minnesota Multiphasic Personality Inventory* is an inventory that was developed to classify mental patients; it has several scales that were developed empirically to separate clinical populations from "normal" individuals. Responses can be scored and interpreted by a clinician or by a computer.
- The *California Personality Inventory,* too, was constructed empirically, but was based on a "normal" standardization group; it measures 18 personality dimensions and is widely used in vocational counseling. The *16 Factor Personality Test* was developed by factor analysis and measures 16 factors thought to reflect basic personality traits.

- Behavior assessment is a relatively new assessment approach in which specific behaviors are observed in a natural setting. It is used before and following behavior therapy, and grows out of behaviorists' interest in behaviors that can be changed rather than the ones that are enduring inner characteristics.
- Projective tests are devices in which subjects are asked to respond to purposely incomplete or ambiguous stimuli of various kinds, which leave considerable room for the "projection" of fantasies, motivations, and thoughts by an individual. Two well-known projective tests are the *Rorschach* and the *Thematic Apperception Test*.
- Most tests of creativity are designed to diagnose a person's ability to give unusual, but appropriate, responses. Creativity typically involves heightened sensitivity, synthesis of elements into new relationships, and the ability to translate private images into visible form. Projective devices, behavior sampling, and measures of divergent thinking have been used to test creativity. Creativity is not closely correlated with intelligence.
- Vocational assessment includes an assessment of an individual's interests, aptitudes, and current level of achievement. The *Strong-Campbell Interest Inventory* compares an individual's interests with those of people successful in various occupations. The *Occupations Analysis Inventory* provides information about the requirements of various jobs.
- Assessment is prevalent in many areas of our lives, but it also has become highly controversial. Though often useful for prediction and as an indication of present performance level, test results should not be used to limit an individual's opportunities for development and change.

14

Health, Stress, and Coping

It started out like most school days for the big-city college teacher—only bleaker. He was late because he had overslept, having set the clock-radio alarm to 7:00 P.M. instead of 7:00 A.M. (a Freudian wishful fantasy, no doubt); but he was still tired. He hadn't gone to sleep until almost 2:00 A.M., and he hadn't slept well—he had been worrying all night about his promotion decision, due to be handed down today by the senior faculty.

He skipped breakfast, checked to see if his socks were the same color, fly zipped, gathered his lecture notes together, and raced down the four flights of stairs to head off another parking ticket. He had already been tagged for over $200 worth, and he was determined not to get stung again; but with alternate street parking from 8:00 A.M. and overcongested traffic, it was a Mission Impossible situation.

7:58 and counting. But where was his car? He couldn't remember where he had parked it, because every night it was parked on a different street. He gambled on 71st Street—and lost. Running down 68th Street, he was just in time to see a police officer approaching his car. Too late; in an instant the ticket was issued and he owed the city another $15.00.

Outrage slowly turned to anger as he drove away and nearly ran a pedestrian down at the corner (she deserved to be frightened for walking so slowly). They exchanged obscenities. In no time he was stuck in the morning traffic jam in the tunnel—horns honking, exhaust fumes building up, tempers boiling.

Eleven minutes late to class, he begged departing students to return. Most did so resentfully. The lecture went badly; he

couldn't concentrate or get his emotions under sufficient control. He felt guilty for having forced the class to stay and promised himself to give a dynamite lecture tomorrow to make up for today's disaster (but that would mean working late again, and he was tired already).

During office hours, he had some doughnuts and coffee, and smoked a few cigarettes. His research assistant told him she had to leave school to work full-time because her father had died and she must support her family. She cried over the loss of her father and her education. He was distressed at the loss of his only reliable graduate assistant. He took some aspirin for the headache that got progressively worse during endless student counseling.

Afternoon mail a mixed bag. First letter told him his research article had been accepted for publication in a prestigious journal. Joy! Second letter told him he was overdrawn again at the bank—and it was ten days before payday. He wouldn't borrow from his kid brother again; too humiliating. What could he sell? He began to feel overwhelmed, depressed. There was no way out!

Finally he was invited into the Chairman's office. He wished he had not already finished his last pack of cigarettes. "We all respect the kind of work you've been doing . . . *but (but! but!)* some people feel you need more time to mellow . . . too brash."

Depressed: "I don't deserve it; I'm not any good."

Angry: "They're all wrong."

Result: more depressed; headache built up between his eyes. He gulped down a stiff drink from the bottle he kept in his desk.

Later in the day, he forgot to keep his doctor's appointment to check on the headaches and chest pain he'd been having. He got some candy bars and a soft drink from the vending machine, ignoring his secretary's pointed remarks about the extra weight he was gaining. Then he lost his temper with her for not finishing the typing he had given her yesterday. She cried and he apologized. He decided to call it a day.

He got stuck in the evening rush-hour traffic, as usual; but finally he got home—or, almost. He drove up 69th, down 70th, up 71st, down 72nd—in search of the elusive 10 × 4 feet of unoccupied asphalt in which to bury his car. The day ended like any other day—only much bleaker.

This account of the activities of one college professor is far removed from the serene life we imagine to exist in the "Ivory Tower" of academia. This stress-filled life-style is propelling this teacher—and many like him in other lines of work—away from well-being and toward illness. The choices he makes about eating, drinking, smoking, exercise, and commuting, as well as decisions regarding work and achievement, combine to create an unhealthy pattern of living that could be lethal. Even before this unhealthy life-style shortens the teacher's expected life span, it will spawn a variety of negative physical and psychological consequences that diminish the quality of his life. Moreover, because "no person is an island unto him or herself," as this teacher's stress builds, it spills over, negatively affecting the lives of those with whom he interacts. Thus he becomes a source of stress as well as its target.

In this chapter, we will see psychologists playing dual roles as scientists and advocates for health. As scientists engaged in one of psychology's newest research areas—health psychology—they investigate the ways in which psychological and social processes contribute to the development, treatment, and prevention of illness. As advocates, they are willing to apply their research findings and recommend strategies to help people get well and stay healthy. Moreover, they are able to utilize their methodological skills in the evaluation of medical and psychological interventions designed to promote health.

Health and Health Psychology

Health refers to the general condition of the body and mind in terms of their soundness and vigor. It is not simply the absence of illness or injury, but is more a matter of how well all the body's component parts are working. "To be healthy is to have the ability, despite an occasional bout of illness, to live with full use of your faculties and to be vigorous, alert, and happy to be alive, even in old age" (Insel & Roth, 1985, p. xvii).

The development of modern health care has rested largely on the biomedical model, which incorporates a dualistic conception of mind and body. The body alone—its changes and its pathology—has been the basis for the diagnosis and treatment of illness; the mind has been viewed as the province of philosophers and priests, not physicians. However, in recent years there has been a profound rethinking about the mind-body relationship. It is now recognized that the state of the body is linked in important ways to the state of the mind. For example, there is substantial research evidence that the mind can influence susceptibility and resistance to disease, apparently because of the physiological links between the brain, nervous system, and the immune system (Ornstein & Sobel, 1987).

Table 14.1 *Take Care of Yourself*

Research indicates that people who practice seven simple health habits feel better, have fewer illnesses, and are less likely to miss work or school because of health problems (Belloc & Breslow, 1972). How well are *you* following these basic rules for good health?

1. Do not smoke cigarettes.
2. Get some regular exercise.
3. Use alcohol moderately or not at all.
4. Get seven or eight hours of sleep nightly.
5. Maintain proper weight.
6. Eat breakfast.
7. Do not eat between meals.

In one set of studies, laboratory rats were subjected to stressful events. For some rats, the stress was uncontrollable; there was nothing they could do to change it. For other rats, the stress was under their control, because they learned to terminate the stressor by turning a wheel. This difference in the psychological factor of control was of critical importance. Although both groups of rats received exactly the same number of stressful events, the rats who lacked control showed decrements in their immune functioning. (Maier, 1984)

Psychological and social factors play a significant role in physical health, and the understanding of this point is leading to the development of a *biopsychosocial* model of health and illness. For example, a person is more likely to stay well if he or she practices good health habits, such as those listed in **Table 14.1;** but what determines whether these habits are carried out? They are certainly influenced by the person's beliefs and attitudes, cultural values, and the practice of these habits by family or friends. Psychological factors have also been clearly demonstrated to have a place in the development of many major illnesses (including heart disease, cancer, and stroke), as well as in such disorders as ulcers, high blood pressure, infectious diseases, migraine, low back pain, dermatitis, obesity, asthma, and diabetes. Furthermore, good health practices, such as those listed in Table 14.1, have been correlated with lower mortality rates (see **Figure 14.1**).

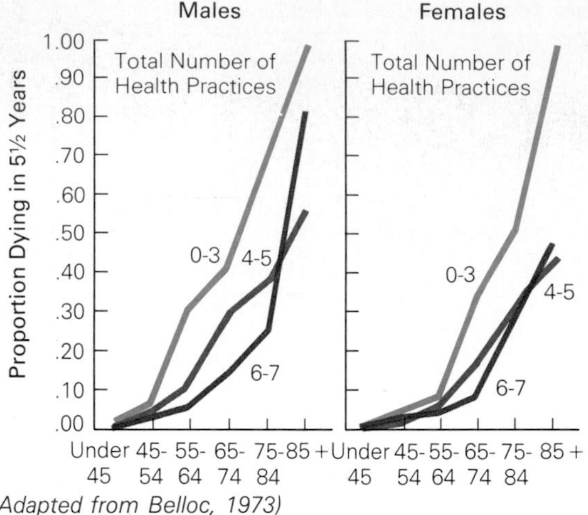

(Adapted from Belloc, 1973)

Figure 14.1 *Health Practices and Mortality*
Adults who followed most or all of the good health practices listed in Table 14.1 were found to be in better health than adults who followed few or none of the practices. A five and one-half year follow-up indicated a correlation between the health practices and longevity. The more of the seven practices followed, the lower were mortality rates at each age level.

The acknowledgment of the importance of psychological factors in health has spurred the growth of health psychology. **Health psychology** is devoted to understanding psychological influences on the way people stay healthy, the reasons they become ill, and the way they respond when they do get ill (Taylor, 1986). There are several different areas of concern for health psychologists: (a) health promotion and maintenance; (b) prevention and treatment of illness; (c) causes and correlates of health, illness, and dysfunction; and (d) improvement of the health care system and health policy information (Matarazzo, 1980).

There are several other fields that have focused on the study of psychology and medicine. How is health psychology related to them? *Behavioral medicine* had its origins in the psychological tradition of behaviorism (see chapter 1). As such, it dealt with overt health behaviors and the conditions that modified or maintained them. However, it has expanded beyond those early behaviorist boundaries. In addition to studying covert, as well as overt, behaviors, it draws on many other disciplines besides psychology, including immunology, neuroanatomy, epidemiology, anthropology, sociology, pharmacology, and public health (Miller, 1983). Thus, behavioral medicine is more an *interdisciplinary* field, whereas health psychology involves primarily the single discipline of psychology. Another related area is *psychosomatic medicine,* which, like health psychology, focuses on the relationship between psychological and somatic (bodily) processes; however, this area has developed within the field of psychiatry.

Other relevant disciplines in the social sciences are *medical sociology* and *medical anthropology,* which are also concerned with studying health and illness. The difference between them and health psychology lies in the unit of analysis. For psychology, the unit is the *individual;* for sociology, it is the larger *group;* and for anthropology, it is the *culture.* Thus, for instance, a medical sociologist might study the structure of a hospital or develop proposals for modifying its operation in order to provide better health care (Cockerham, 1978). A medical anthropologist might be concerned about cultural differences in the definition of health and illness, or cultural rituals for the treatment of disease (Foster & Anderson, 1978).

All of these medical fields are related to health psychology and share with it a reliance on the biopsychosocial model. However, health psychology has some unique contributions to make to our understanding of health and illness. In the following sections, we will get an overview of these contributions by looking at each of the major areas of health psychology.

Health Promotion and Maintenance

The first area focuses on the ways in which people can stay well and healthy and the methods that can be used to encourage such healthy behaviors. For example, it has been well established that regular exercise is an important factor in promoting and maintaining health. In particular, major improvements in health are gained from such exercises as bicycling, swimming, running, or jumping rope. These *aerobic* exercises are characterized by high intensity, long duration, and high endurance; and they lead to increased fitness of the heart and respiratory systems, improvement of muscle tone and strength, and many other health benefits. However, most people do not engage in such exercise in any consistent way. Researchers are now exploring the questions of who exercises regularly and why, as well as trying to determine what programs or strategies are most effective in getting people to start exercising and *continue* exercising (Dishman, 1982). One clear finding has been that people are more likely to exercise regularly if it is easy and convenient to do so. This is one reason why many companies are now providing exercise equipment, aerobics classes, or jogging tracks for their employees to use during their work breaks.

Joseph Matarazzo

Other examples of health-promoting behaviors are immunizations for childhood diseases and paying attention to diet (eating foods low in cholesterol and fats, eating regular meals, avoiding sugary snacks) and dental hygiene (brushing teeth regularly, using dental floss, having regular check-ups). Health psychologists must find ways to educate people about such health habits and motivate them to practice and maintain these habits. Psychologists have studied principles for changing attitudes and modifying behavior (as we shall see in chapter 17) and have applied these principles to techniques for therapy and for social change. Clearly, they can also apply them to the promotion of health.

Prevention and Treatment of Illness

Prevention of illness means to eliminate or reduce the risk that people will get sick. The prevention of illness in the 1980s poses a much different challenge than it did at the turn of the century (Matarazzo, 1984). In 1900 the primary cause of death was infectious disease. Health practitioners at that time launched the "first revolution" in American public health. Through the use of research, public education, the development of vaccines, and changes in public health standards (such as waste control and sewage), they were able to eradicate, or substantially reduce, such diseases as influenza, tuberculosis, polio, measles, and smallpox.

Today the primary cause of death is *life-style* (see **Table 14.2**). Smoking, being overweight, eating foods high in cholesterol, drinking too much alcohol, driving without seat belts, and leading stressful lives—all of these factors play a major role in heart disease, cancer, strokes, cirrhosis, accidents, and suicide (see the ***Close-up*** on preventing AIDS on p. 492). It is estimated that almost half of the deaths in the United States are the result of life-style factors, a statistic that led the U.S. Surgeon General to call for a "second revolution" in American public health (U.S. Department of Health, Education, and Welfare, 1979). In his report on the health of the nation, then-Secretary of Health, Education and Welfare Joseph Califano remarked:

> *We are killing ourselves by our own careless habits. We are killing ourselves by carelessly polluting the environment.*
>
> *We are killing ourselves by permitting harmful social conditions to persist—conditions like poverty, hunger and ignorance—which destroy health, especially for infants and children.*
>
> *You, the individual, can do more for your own health and well-being than any doctor, any hospital, any drug, any exotic medical device.* (1979, p. viii)

Table 14.2 *Major Causes of Death and Associated Risk Factors, United States, 1977*

Cause	Percentage of Deaths	Risk Factor
Heart Disease	37.8	Smoking, hypertension, elevated serum cholesterol, diet, lack of exercise, diabetes, stress, family history
Malignant Neoplasms (cancer)	20.4	Smoking, worksite carcinogens, environmental carcinogens, alcohol, diet
Stroke	9.6	Hypertension, smoking, elevated serum cholesterol, stress
Accidents Other Than Motor Vehicle	2.8	Alcohol, drug abuse, smoking (fires), product design, handgun availability
Influenza and Pneumonia	2.7	Smoking, vaccination status
Motor Vehicle Accidents	2.6	Alcohol, no seat belts, roadway design, vehicle engineering
Diabetes	1.7	Obesity
Cirrhosis of the Liver	1.6	Alcohol abuse
Arterio-sclerosis	1.5	Elevated serum cholesterol
Suicide	1.5	Stress, alcohol and drug abuse, gun availability

(Adapted from Harris, 1980)

Close-up Life-style Factors in Preventing AIDS

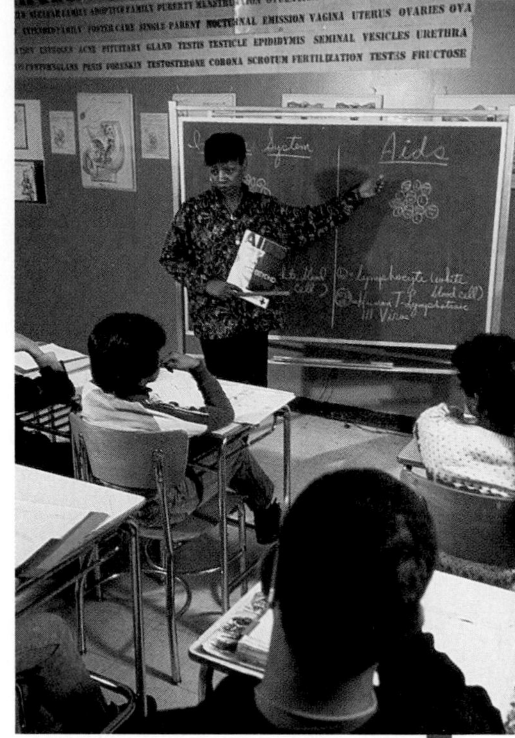

One of today's most frightening diseases is AIDS. Unheard of until a few years ago, it is now an epidemic: over 25,000 persons in the United States are known to have contracted AIDS, and, of these, about half have died. It is estimated that 1.5 million people are infected with the AIDS virus (although they may not yet be aware of it), and that all of them are capable of spreading the virus to others (U.S. Public Health Service, 1986).

AIDS is an acronym for Acquired Immune Deficiency Syndrome. The AIDS virus is known by several scientific names: HIV (Human Immunodeficiency Virus), HTLV-III (Human T-Lymphotropic Virus), or LAV (Lymphadenopathy Associated Virus). This virus attacks the white blood cells (T-Lymphocytes) in human blood, thus damaging a person's immune system and weakening his or her ability to fight other diseases. The person then becomes vulnerable to infection by a host of other viruses and bacteria, which can cause such life-threatening illnesses as cancer, meningitis, and pneumonia. The AIDS virus can be passed from one person to another primarily in one of two ways: (a) the exchange of semen and blood during sexual contact, and (b) the sharing of intravenous drug needles and syringes used for "shooting" drugs.

At the present time, *THERE IS NO CURE FOR AIDS.* Also, at the present time, *THERE IS NO VACCINE TO PREVENT AIDS.*

Who is at risk? *Everyone.* Although the initial discovery of AIDS in the United States was in the male homosexual community, the disease has spread. AIDS is being found among heterosexuals as well as homosexuals and among women, as well as men. It is predicted that AIDS will increase and spread throughout the general population, in just the same way as other sexually transmitted diseases like syphilis and gonorrhea—but with much more devastating consequences to the affected individuals and society. Given the escalating number of AIDS cases, the anticipated additional burden on the health care system will be unprecedented.

The only way to protect oneself from being infected with AIDS is to change those *life-style* factors that put one at risk. Basically, this means making changes in patterns of sexual behavior. The safest approach is either to abstain from sexual activity or to be faithful to one (noninfected) partner, who is also monogamous. However, where multiple sexual partners are involved, then the *only* way to prevent infection by the AIDS virus is to: (a) be tested for AIDS, and (b) practice "safe sex"—that is, use condoms during sexual contact.

At this time, *prevention* is the only protection against AIDS—and it is our only hope for stopping the AIDS epidemic.

For further information about AIDS, see Coates et al., 1984; Nungesser, 1986, and Temoshok et al., 1987. You can also call these toll-free telephone hotlines: Public Health Service AIDS Hotline (800/342-AIDS), Nationally Sexually Transmitted Diseases Hotline (800/221-7044).

This second revolution involves the necessity for Americans to modify their behavioral choices, which clearly have more effect on well-being and longevity than biological and genetic makeup or our exposure to viruses and bacteria. The U.S. government has become increasingly involved in establishing national goals for the prevention of disease and the protection and promotion of health (see **Table 14.3**).

What are prevention strategies in the "war on life-style"? One approach is to change or eliminate poor health habits. Programs to help people quit smoking, lose excess weight, or reduce alcohol intake are examples of this strategy.

A major study to prevent heart disease was conducted in three towns in California. The goals of the study were (a) to persuade people to reduce their cardiovascular risk via changes in smoking, diet, and exercise; and (b) to determine which method of persuasion was more effective. In one town a two-year campaign was conducted through the mass media, using television, radio, newspapers, billboards, and mailed leaflets. The second town received the same two-year media campaign plus *a personal instruction program on modifying health habits for high-risk individuals. The third town served as a control group and received no persuasive campaign. How successful were the campaigns in modifying life-style? The results showed that the townspeople who had gotten only the mass-media campaign were more knowledgeable about the links between life-style and heart disease, but they showed only modest changes in their own behaviors and health status; however, in the town where the media campaign was supplemented with personal instruction, people showed more substantial and long-lasting changes in their health habits, particularly reduced smoking. (Farquhar et al., 1984; Maccoby et al., 1977)*

Thus, the good news is that life-style factors *can* be modified. The bad news is that: (a) it is difficult and expensive to do so, and (b) mass media campaigns are not as effective in changing some health behaviors as had been hoped. They may, however, contribute to long-term changes in social attitudes that support life-style changes.

Another approach to prevention is to keep people from developing bad health habits in the first place. It is not easy to get people to stop a behavior that is well established, so it may be more effective in the long run to discover how to keep them from getting started. This issue is clearly illustrated by the habit of smoking, which has enormous societal costs and has been called the single greatest cause of preventable death in the United States. The severe economic costs to the nation associated with smoking are estimated to be nearly $54 billion a year, according to a team of five leading health economists quoted in the *Washington Post* (April 21, 1987). Their figures are as follows:

Direct Medical Costs	$23.3 billion
Salary Losses per Year	9.3
Lifetime Earning Losses of Smokers who Died in 1984	21.1
Total	$53.7 billion

In 1980 a total of 270,269 deaths were attributed to smoking—resulting in 3.9 million person-years lost. Smoking behavior is notoriously hard to change, despite a wide variety of programs and therapies (Leventhal & Cleary, 1980). Because smoking often starts in adolescence, some psychologists have tried to tackle the problem by studying ways to persuade teenagers *not* to try cigarettes. The programs that seem to be most successful provide antismoking information in formats that appeal to adolescents, portray a positive image of the nonsmoker as independent and self-reliant, and use peer group techniques—popular peers serve as nonsmoking role models—and instruction in ways to resist peer pressure (Evans et al., 1978). The principles developed from campaigns to teach people to "just say no" can be used to prevent the onset of drug use and other addictive behaviors.

Unlike prevention, *treatment* focuses on helping people adjust to their illnesses and recover from them. Pain is an aspect of many illnesses and injuries, and there are many psychological techniques of pain control, such as biofeedback, hypnosis, relaxation, and distraction (see our earlier discussion in chapter 5, p. 181). In addition to pain, emotional distress may be aroused by various medical procedures. Some people may be afraid of a dentist's drill or get upset at the idea of having surgery.

Researchers have found that patients who show the best recovery from surgery are those who received complete information before *their operations. This information prepared the patients for the aftereffects of the surgery, both physical and emotional, and gave them a greater sense of* psychological control. *Patients who received sufficient preoperative information showed better post-operative adjustment on a number of indexes: they experienced less psychological distress, they did not need as many narcotics to control pain, and they were able to leave the hospital sooner. (Janis, 1958; Johnson, 1983)*

Table 14.3 *Fifteen Specific, Measurable Objectives for Producing Better Health for Americans by 1990*

A. Preventive Health Services
1. Control of high blood pressure
2. Family planning
3. Pregnancy and infant health
4. Immunization
5. Sexually transmitted diseases

B. Health Protection
6. Control of toxic agents
7. Occupational safety and health
8. Accident prevention and injury control
9. Fluoridation and dental health
10. Surveillance and control of infectious diseases

C. Health Promotion
11. Smoking and health
12. Misuse of alcohol and drugs
13. Nutrition
14. Physical fitness and exercise
15. Control of stress and violent behavior

(From Matarazzo, 1984)

Often a treatment regimen, which might include medications, dietary changes, prescribed periods of bed rest and exercise, and follow-up procedures (such as return check-ups, rehabilitation training, or chemotherapy), will be established for patients. Inducing them to stick to these treatment plans (a problem known as patient adherence *or* compliance*) is a major issue for health care professionals and health psychologists. The communication between patient and practitioner is an important factor in patient adherence (and is also a factor in the rise of malpractice litigation). When practitioners communicate clearly, make sure that their patients understand what has been said, act courteously, and convey a sense of caring and supportiveness, patients will be more satisfied with their health care and will be more likely to adhere to the prescribed treatments (DiMatteo & DiNicola, 1982). Compliance-gaining strategies developed by social psychologists (described in chapter 17) help overcome the lack of cooperation between patients and practitioners.*

Type A people are always in a hurry, are unable to relax, and strive intensely for achievement.

Causes and Correlates of Health, Illness, and Dysfunction

Health psychologists are also interested in the *causes* (etiology) of illness and injury. Clearly, bad health habits are important causal factors, as noted earlier; however, personality or individual behavioral styles may also play a causal role.

A great deal of research attention has focused on a particular behavioral style called the **Type A behavior syndrome** that contributes to the chances of coronary heart disease. Type A people are always in a hurry, unable to relax, and are abrupt in their speech and gestures, frequently interrupting to finish what someone else is saying. They are highly competitive, insist on "going it alone," strive intensely for achievement, show a high level of hostility and impatience, and engage in compulsive activity. Some of these characteristics are valued in our society, but this is a very *dysfunctional* behavioral style. Type A businessmen, for example, are stricken with coronary heart disease more than twice as often as men in the general population (Friedman & Rosenman, 1974; Jenkins, 1976). In fact, many studies have shown that people manifesting the Type A behavior syndrome are at significantly greater risk for *all* forms of cardiovascular disease (Dembroski et al., 1978; Haynes & Feinleib, 1980). Unfortunately, Type A behavior patterns are now being seen among college and high-school students, and even among children in grade school (Thoresen & Eagleston, 1983).

Men have been much more likely than women to develop the Type A syndrome, evidently because our society has encouraged and reinforced those traits as essential for success in a competitive business enterprise (see **Close-up:** *The Masculine Sex Role Is Hazardous to Your Health,* p. 495). Alas, as more women enter top-level business positions, we are seeing more Type A behavior emerging among females, although there are twice as many Type A men under fifty who currently have coronary heart disease than Type A women of similar age. By contrast, among people who are clearly *not* Type A, the chances of such disease are equally low in both sexes.

Can Type A behaviors be modified to reduce the risk of heart disease? According to recent research, the answer is yes. When post-heart-attack patients were involved in an extensive 3-year program of counseling and behavior modification techniques, they showed fewer Type A behaviors, and they had a lower rate of repeat heart attacks (Friedman et al., 1984).

Health Care System and Health Policy Formation

A final focus of health psychology is on the delivery of health care. Health institutions, the health professionals who staff them, and the health policies that guide them have all been the focus of research. For example, studies have found distinct patterns in the use of health services. Social class is an important factor—the poor are more likely to be ill, but they have less money to spend on health care. Those who are poor are more likely to see a physician only for emergencies and not for any regular or preventive care, and they usually get treated in clinics rather than private offices (Herman, 1972). Other studies have found differences between eth-

Close-up "The Masculine Gender Role Is Hazardous to Your Health"

It has long been known that men, as a group in our society, die younger than women. In 1980, the average life span for males was about eight years shorter than that for females. In addition, there are striking sex differences in many of the major causes of death. As can be seen in the table, the death rate for males exceeds that for females for several types of disease. Moreover, the ratio of males to females is extremely large for homicide, suicide, and accidents. Analyses of this sex differential show clearly that the primary cause is *life-style*—even more than biological factors. More specifically, it is the behaviors which are learned as part of the masculine gender role that put males at greater risk (Harrison, 1978). "Each of these causes of death is linked to behaviors which are encouraged or accepted more in males than in females: using guns, drinking alcohol, smoking, working at hazardous jobs, and seeming to be fearless. Thus, the behaviors of males in our society make a major contribution to their elevated mortality" (Waldron, 1976, p. 2).

Major Causes of Death (1980 Data)

	Percentage of All Deaths	***Ratio of Males to Females (as a percentage)***
Heart Disease	38.3	1.2
Cancer	20.9	1.2
Cerebrovascular Disease	9.6	.7
Accidents	5.3	2.6
Pulmonary Disease (asthma, bronchitis, emphysema)	2.8	2.3
Influenza and Pneumonia	2.7	1.1
Diabetes Mellitus	1.8	.7
Cirrhosis, Liver Disease	1.5	1.9
Arteriosclerosis	1.5	.7
Suicide	1.4	3.4
Homicide	1.2	3.8
Certain Causes in Infancy	1.1	1.4

(U.S. National Center for Health Statistics, 1984)

nic groups in the interpretation of their symptoms and their readiness to seek medical treatment (Zola, 1973).

Providing health care can be enormously challenging and rewarding; however, dealing with pain, illness, and death can be so emotionally stressful that practitioners run the risk of "burnout." **Burnout** is a syndrome of emotional exhaustion, depersonalization, and reduced personal accomplishment. Health practitioners begin to lose their caring and concern for the patients, and may come to treat them in detached and even dehumanized ways. As they do so, they begin to feel bad about themselves and worry that they are failures. Burnout is correlated with greater absenteeism and turnover, impaired job performance, poor relations with coworkers, family problems, and poor personal health (Maslach, 1982).

Several social and situational factors affect the occurrence and level of burnout—and, by implication, suggest ways of preventing or minimizing it. For example, the quality of the patient-practitioner interaction is greatly affected by the number of patients for whom a practitioner is providing care; The greater the number, the greater the cognitive, sensory, and emotional overload. Another factor is the amount of direct contact with patients. Longer work hours in continuous direct contact with patients is correlated with greater burnout, especially when the nature of the contact is very difficult and upsetting (patients who are dying or who are verbally abusive). The emotional strain of such prolonged contact can be eased by a work schedule that provides chances for a practitioner to withdraw temporarily from such high-stress situations, while doing some other kind of work.

Issues of stress and coping have long been a central, core topic of health psychology. "Stress affects the lives of all people, everywhere. It is a cause of illness and accidents, producing stress in the victims and those who must care for them. Stress affects personality, modifying our perceptions, feelings, attitudes, and behavior, and it reaches beyond its immediate victims to affect the political, social, and work organizations whose activities they direct and carry out. . . . Growth and survival are very much related to . . . success in coping with stress" (Warshaw, 1979, p. 3).

In the remaining sections of this chapter, we will look at what psychologists mean by *stress*. Within this broad area of basic research and application, three general questions are of major concern to health psychologists: How does stress affect us physically and psychologically? How do common stressors in our society affect our health? How can we cope with stress more effectively?

The Concept of Stress

It should be obvious from the *Opening Case* why stress has been called a "disease of civilization." The rapid pace of our lives, overcrowded living conditions, too many demands on our time, interferences with our personal ambitions, and frustrating job conditions all contribute to the modern stress equation; but would we be better off without stress? That would be a life without challenge—no difficulties to surmount, no new fields to conquer, no reason to sharpen our wits or improve our abilities. Stress is an unavoidable part of living, because every organism faces challenges from its environment and from its own needs. These challenges are "problems" it must solve if it is to survive and thrive.

Stress is the pattern of specific and nonspecific responses an organism makes to stimulus events that disturb its equilibrium and tax or exceed its ability to cope. The stimulus events include a large variety of external and internal conditions that collectively are called stressors. A **stressor** is a stimulus event that places a demand on an organism for some kind of adaptive response. The stress response is composed of a diverse combination of reactions on several levels, including physiological, behavioral, emotional, and cognitive changes.

No doubt you have observed that some people experience one stressful event after another and do not break down, while others are seriously upset by even low-level stress. This happens because the effect of most stressors is not a direct one, but is determined partly by other conditions. These conditions are known as **moderator variables**—variables that change the effect of a stressor. The cognitive appraisal and evaluation of a stressor is one such moderator variable—is it viewed as a threat or a challenge? The resource that is available to deal with that stressor is another moderator variable. All of these elements of the stress process—stressors, stress, cognitive appraisal, resources, and stress response—are diagrammed in **Figure 14.2.**

The Role of Cognitive Appraisal

Before a stress response begins, a demand on the organism (stressor) must be recognized on some level and evaluated. **Cognitive appraisal** plays a central role in defining the situation—what the demand is, how big a threat it is, what resources one has for meeting it, and what strategies are appropriate. Some stressors, such as bodily injury or finding one's house on fire are seen as threats by almost anyone, but many other stressors can be defined in various ways, depending on our overall life situation, the relation of this particular demand to our central goals, our competence for dealing with it, and our assessment of our competence. The situation that causes acute distress for me may be all in a day's work for you.

Our appraisal of a stressor and of our resources for meeting it can be as important as the actual stressor in determining our conscious experience, what coping strategies we will see as appropriate, and how successful we will be. If we define a stressor as too much for us to deal with, we create a self-fulfilling prophecy: we are likely to fail even if objectively we are capable of dealing adequately with the demand. Doctors have long known that a patient's attitude can be as important as the physical condition in determining the course of the illness (see ***Close-up,*** p. 498).

Cognitive appraisal may define a stressor as an interesting new challenge that will be fun to test oneself against instead of as a threat. The experience may be one of exhilaration, of being "psyched up," anticipating achievement and increased self-esteem. Such a positive reaction to a stressor has been called **eustress** (*eu* means "good").

Richard Lazarus, a pioneer in recent stress research, has distinguished between two stages in our cognitive appraisal of demands. He uses the term **primary appraisal** for the primary evaluation of the seriousness of a demand. It starts with

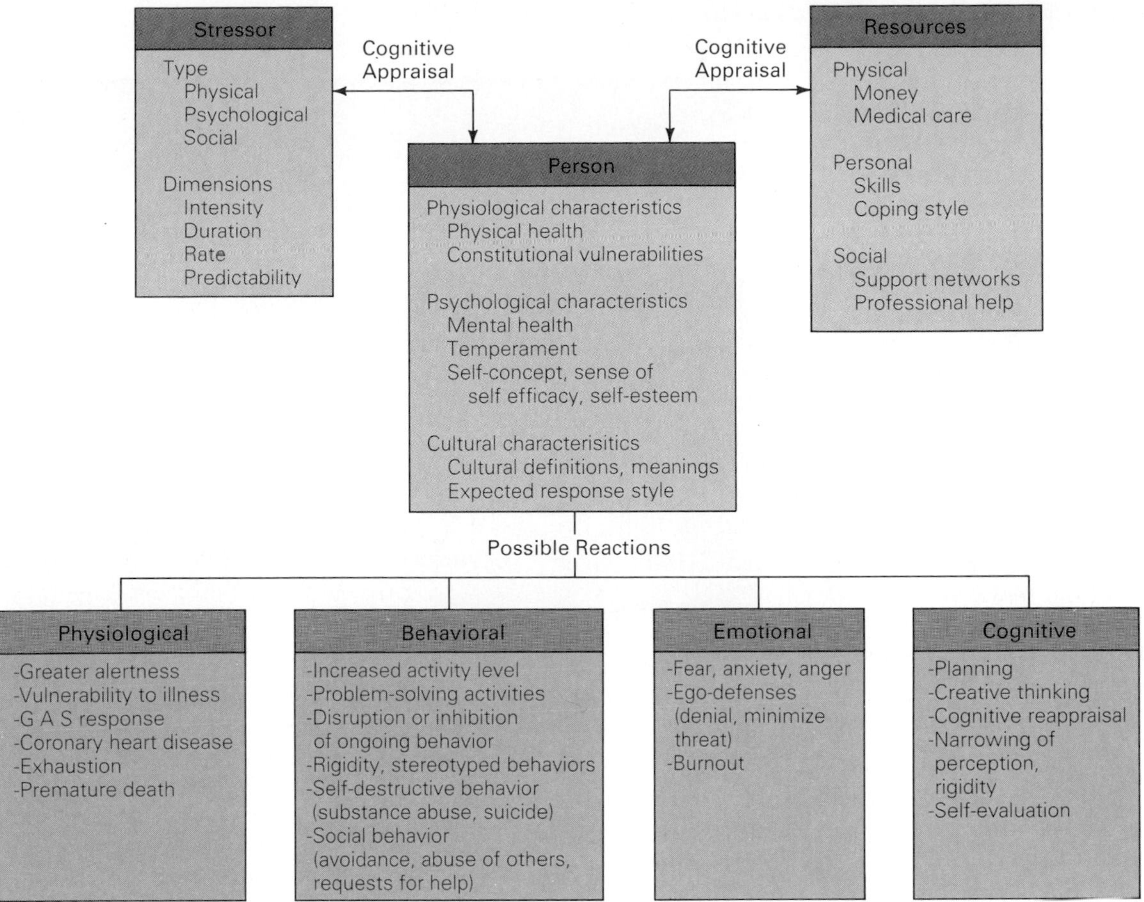

Figure 14.2 *A Model of Stress*

This chart summarizes the main relationships discussed in this chapter. Cognitive appraisal of the stress situation influences and is influenced by the stressor itself and the physical, social, and personal resources available for dealing with it. The person, embodying a unique combination of physiological, psychological, and cultural characteristics, reacts to threat in various possible ways, including physiological, behavioral, emotional, and cognitive responses, some adaptive and some maladaptive or even lethal.

the questions: What's happening? Is this thing good for me, stressful, or irrelevant? If the answer is *stressful,* an individual appraises the potential impact of the stressor by determining whether harm has occurred, or is likely to, and whether action is called for. Once a person decides something must be done, **secondary appraisal** begins. The person evaluates the personal and social resources that are available to deal with the stressful circumstance and the action that is needed (Lazarus, 1966). Then, as coping responses are tried, appraisal continues; if the first ones don't work and the stress persists, new responses are initiated. **Chronic stress** is defined as a state of arousal, continuing over time, in which demands are perceived by an individual as greater than the inner and outer resources available for dealing with them (Powell & Eagleston, 1983).

Physiological Stress Reactions

In chapter 4 we learned that the brain developed originally as a center for more efficient coordination of action. *Efficiency* meant flexibility of response to changing environmental requirements and also a quicker, often automatic response. One set of brain-controlled physiological stress responses occurs when an organism perceives an external threat (a predator, for example). Instant action and extra strength may be needed if the organism is to survive; a whole constellation of automatic mechanisms has evolved that meet this need. Another set of physiological stress reactions occurs when the danger is internal, and the stability and integrity of the organism are threatened by invading microbes or other disease agents that upset the normal physiological processes.

Close-up Voodoo Deaths

Captivating to the imagination are the sudden voodoo deaths described in anthropological reports. There are many documented cases in which healthy people who believed that they had transgressed sacred laws or had been the subjects of curses have died soon afterward. The following is an account of behavior observed in one tribe when a man discovered that a bone was being pointed at him in a certain way by an enemy.

He stands aghast, with his eyes staring at the treacherous pointer, and with his hands lifted as though to ward off the lethal medium, which he imagines is pouring into his body. His cheeks blanch and his eyes become glassy and the expression of his face becomes horribly distorted. . . . He attempts to shriek but usually the sound chokes in his throat, and all that one might see is froth at his mouth. His body begins to tremble and the muscles twist involuntarily. He sways backwards and falls to the ground, and after a short time appears to be in a swoon; but soon after he writhes as if in mortal agony, and, covering his face with his hands, begins to moan. . . . From this time onwards he sickens and frets, refusing to eat and keeping aloof from the daily affairs of the tribe. Unless help is forthcoming in the shape of a countercharm . . . his death is only a matter of a comparatively short time. (Basedow, 1925, cited in Cannon, 1942, p. 172)

Other reports tell of healthy people succumbing to sudden death upon discovering that they have transgressed against the supernatural world by eating forbidden food. In one case, the expectation of death—and hence the death itself—was delayed until long after the fateful act.

A young traveler, visiting a friend, was served a dish containing fowl. He asked if it was wild hen, a delicacy banned for the young, and ate it only when assured that it was not. A few years later, the friend admitted laughingly that it had, in fact, been wild hen. The young man began to tremble and within twenty-four hours was dead. (Pinkerton, 1814)

Reports such as these were thoroughly analyzed by the respected physiologist Walter Cannon (1942), who became convinced of the reality of the phenomenon, though, at the time, such reports were generally greeted with skepticism by sophisticated Westerners.

Two explanations for the "sudden death" phenomenon associated with extreme fright and feelings of hopelessness were advanced. According to Cannon's theory (1957), oversecretion of epinephrine could impair the capillary walls, allowing a passage of fluid to the surrounding tissues; the resulting reduction in the volume of the circulating blood could send the organism into a state of shock, leading to deterioration of the heart and nerve centers. Another researcher, who observed sudden death in wild rats placed under extreme, frightening stress, found that overstimulation of the parasympathetic nervous system was responsible (Richter, 1957). More recently, an anthropologist studying Australian aborigines has found evidence that victims of sorcery may actually die from dehydration when family and friends withdraw all life-support systems, including water (Eastwell, 1984).

Today we not only recognize the reality of the close interdependence of psychological and physiological processes, but are identifying the precise mechanisms by which emotions, attitudes, and beliefs can lead to physiological reactions that can become illness-inducing or life-threatening (see Lachman, 1983).

Emergency Reactions to External Threats

In the 1920s Walter Cannon, a Harvard University physiologist, outlined the first scientific description of the way animals and humans respond to external danger. He found that a sequence of activity was triggered in the nerves and glands to prepare the body for combat and struggle—or for running away to safety. Cannon called this basic dual stress response the **"fight-or-flight" syndrome.**

At the center of this primitive stress response is the *hypothalamus,* which, as we have seen, is involved in a variety of emotional responses. The hypothalamus has sometimes been referred to as the "stress center" because of its twin functions in emergencies: (a) it controls the autonomic nervous system, and (b) it activates the pituitary gland.

The autonomic nervous system (described briefly in chapter 4) regulates the activities of the body's organs. In conditions appraised as stressful, breathing becomes faster and deeper, heart rate increases, blood vessels constrict, and blood pressure rises. In addition to these internal changes, muscles open the passages of the throat and nose to allow more air into the lungs, while also producing facial expressions of strong emotion. Messages go to smooth muscles to stop certain bodily functions, such as digestion.

Another function of the autonomic nervous system during stress is to "get the adrenaline flowing." It signals the inner part of the adrenal glands, the adrenal medulla, to release two hormones, epinephrine and norepinephrine, which, in turn, signal a number of other organs to perform their specialized functions. The spleen releases more red blood corpuscles (to aid in clotting if there is an injury), while the bone marrow is stimulated to make more white corpuscles (to combat infection). The liver is stimulated to produce more sugar, which builds up body energy. It is believed that epinephrine (also called adrenaline) plays a more important role in fear reactions (and flight) while norepinephrine (also called noradrenaline) is more associated with rage reactions (and fight).

The pituitary gland responds to signals from the hypothalamus by secreting two hormones vital to the stress reaction. The **thyrotrophic hormone (TTH)** stimulates the thyroid gland which, in turn, makes more energy available to the body. The **adrenocorticotrophic hormone (ACTH)** stimulates the outer part of the adrenal glands, the adrenal cortex, resulting in the release of a group of hormones called *steroids,* which are important in metabolic processes and in release of sugar into the blood from the liver. ACTH also signals various organs of the body to release about thirty other hormones, each of which plays a role in the body's adjustment to this "call to arms." A summary of this physiological stress response is shown in **Figure 14.3.**

Figure 14.3 *The Body's Response to Stress*

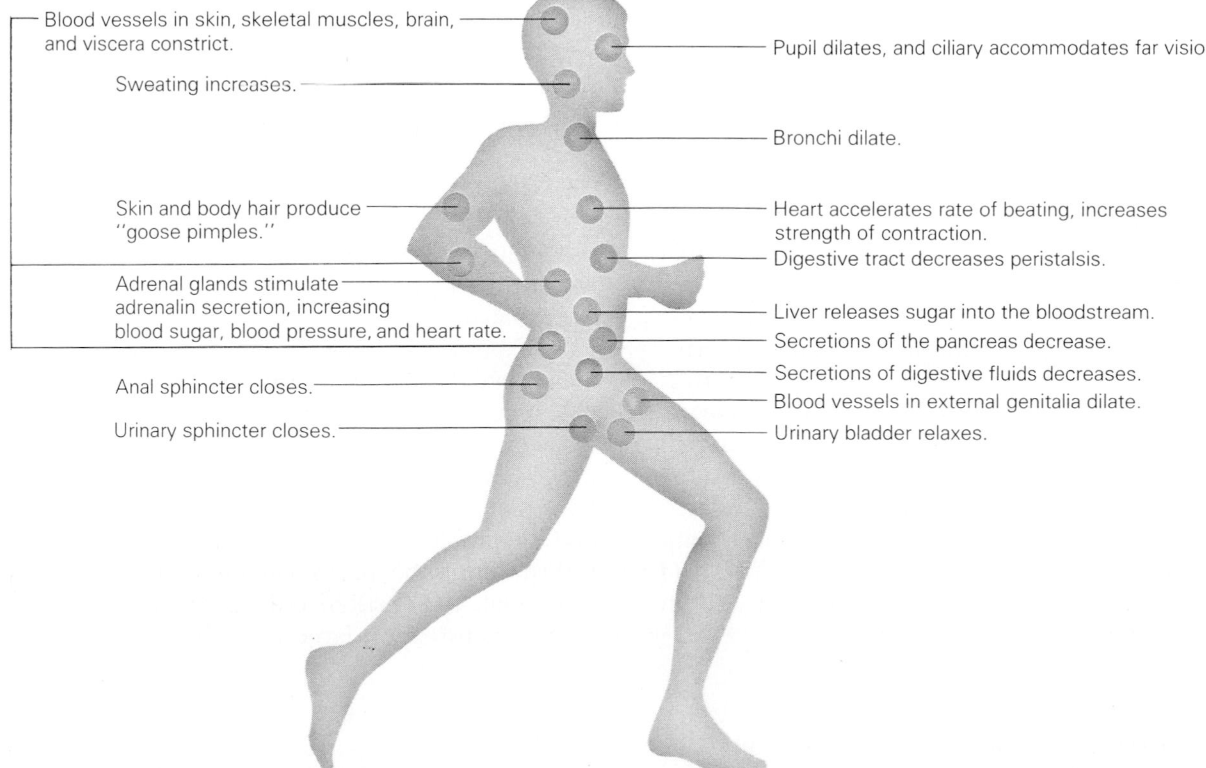
Blood vessels in skin, skeletal muscles, brain, and viscera constrict.
Sweating increases.
Skin and body hair produce "goose pimples."
Adrenal glands stimulate adrenalin secretion, increasing blood sugar, blood pressure, and heart rate.
Anal sphincter closes.
Urinary sphincter closes.
Pupil dilates, and ciliary accommodates far vision.
Bronchi dilate.
Heart accelerates rate of beating, increases strength of contraction.
Digestive tract decreases peristalsis.
Liver releases sugar into the bloodstream.
Secretions of the pancreas decrease.
Secretions of digestive fluids decreases.
Blood vessels in external genitalia dilate.
Urinary bladder relaxes.

A firefighter undergoes a physiological response to stress so that he or she can endure the physical strain.

It is obvious, then, that many bodily processes are activated by danger signals. Now let's consider their adaptive significance in two different stressful situations. When a call comes into a firehouse, the fire fighters respond with the physiological components of the stress response. Muscles tense, breathing speeds up, heart rate increases, adrenaline flows, extra energy becomes available, and the fire fighters become less sensitive to pain. They will need these responses in order to endure the physical strain of battling a potentially destructive, sometimes lethal, disaster. These built-in capacities to deal with *physical* stressors by mobilizing the body's active response systems have been valuable throughout the ages.

Now consider people working on a crisis "hot line," taking calls from potentially suicidal strangers. These workers undergo the same physiological stress responses as a result of the *psychological* stressors they face. In contrast to the fire fighters, their physiological response is not adaptive, because no physical activity is being demanded that might use the extra energy and strength. They must, instead, try to stay calm, concentrate on listening, and make thoughtful decisions. Unfortunately, these skills are not enhanced by the stress response, so what has developed in the species as an adaptive preparation for dealing with external danger is not the most adaptive pattern for dealing with many modern-day sources of stress. In fact, recurring or chronic arousal that is not dealt with by appropriate physical activity may, in time, lead to malfunctioning. (See also "The Way We Act" in *The Best of Science.*)

The General Adaptation Syndrome

The first modern researcher to investigate the effects of continued severe stress on the body was Hans Selye, a Canadian endocrinologist. Selye studied stressors that threatened the physical functioning of the body rather than stressors, like predators, that required behavioral responses. According to Selye's theory of stress, there are many kinds of stressors (including all diseases and many other physical and psychological conditions), but all call for adaptation by an organism to maintain or regain its integrity and well-being. (This is another aspect of homeostasis, mentioned in chapter 11.)

In addition to responses that are specific to a particular stressor (such as constriction of the blood vessels in response to cold), there is a characteristic pattern of *nonspecific* adaptational physiological mechanisms that occurs in response to continuing threat by almost any serious stressor. Selye called this pattern the **general adaptation syndrome (GAS).** He found a characteristic sequence of three stages in this syndrome: an alarm reaction, a stage of resistance, and a stage of exhaustion (Selye, 1956). These stages are diagrammed in **Figure 14.4:** "The General Adaptation Syndrome."

The *alarm reaction* consists of the physiological changes by which a threatened organism immediately moves to restore its normal functioning. Whether the stressor is physical (such as inadequate food, loss of sleep, disease, bodily injury) or psychological (such as loss of love or personal security), the alarm reaction consists of the same general pattern of bodily and biochemical changes. For example, people suffering from different illnesses all seem to complain of such symptoms as headache, fever, fatigue, aching muscles and joints, loss of appetite, and a general feeling of being unwell. Unlike the emergency mobilization for behavioral action against an external danger, discussed in the preceding section, the alarm reaction mobilizes the body's defenses for restoration of inner balance.

If exposure to the stress-producing situation continues, the alarm reaction is followed by the *stage of resistance,* in which an organism appears to develop a resistance to the stressor. Even though the disturbing stimulation continues, the symptoms that occurred during the first stage disappear, and the physiological processes that had been disturbed during the alarm reaction appear to return to normal. This resistance to the stressor seems to be accomplished, in large part, through increased

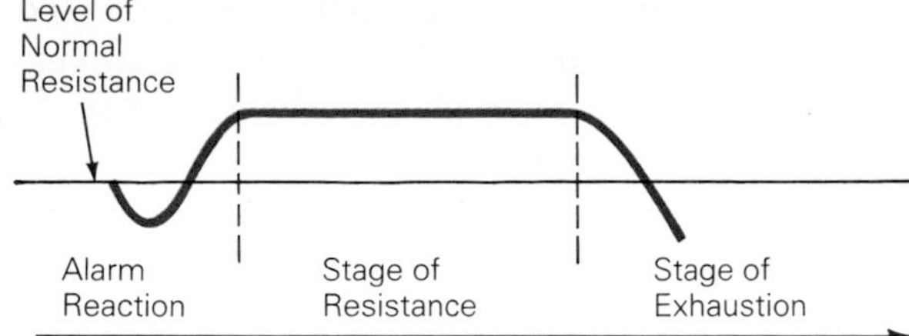

Figure 14.4 *The General Adaptation Syndrome*
On exposure to a stressor, the body's resistance is diminished until the physiological changes of the alarm reaction bring it back up to the normal level. Then, if the stressor continues, the defensive changes "overshoot" in the stage of resistance and the bodily signs characteristic of the alarm reaction virtually disappear; resistance to that stressor rises above normal, but is less to other stressors. Following prolonged exposure to the stressor, adaptation breaks down; in the stage of exhaustion, signs of the alarm reaction reappear, but now the stressor effects are irreversible, and the individual becomes ill and may die. (From Selye, 1956, p. 87)

secretions from the anterior pituitary and the adrenal cortex (ACTH and *cortin,* respectively).

Although there is *greater* resistance to the original stressor during this second stage, there is *reduced* resistance to other stressors. Even a weak stressor may now produce a strong response if it comes when the body's resources are engaged in resisting an earlier, more potent stressor. Some people find they get irritated more easily when getting over a cold, for example. General resistance to disease is reduced in this stage of resistance even though adaptation to the specific noxious agent is improved.

If exposure to the injurious stressor continues too long, a point is reached where an organism can no longer maintain its resistance. It then enters the third phase of Selye's general adaptation syndrome—the *stage of exhaustion.* The anterior pituitary and the adrenal cortex are unable to continue secreting their hormones at the increased rate. This means that the organism can no longer adapt to the chronic stress. Many of the symptoms of the alarm reaction now begin to reappear. If the stressor continues, destruction of bodily tissues, and even death, may occur.

The concept of the general adaptation syndrome has proven valuable to explain disorders that had baffled physicians. Within this framework, many disorders can be viewed as the results of the physiological processes involved in the body's long-continued attempts to adapt to a perceived dangerous stressor. The value of additional ACTH and cortisone in treating some of these diseases can also be understood: such treatment evidently helps the anterior pituitary and the adrenal cortex maintain the body's resistance to the stressor.

On the other hand, because Selye was a physician, and because his research focused on reactions to physical stressors among experimental animals, such as laboratory rats, his theory has had little to say about the importance of *psychological* aspects of stress in the case of human beings. In particular, Selye's critics believe he overstated the role of nonspecific, *systemic* factors in the production of stress-induced illness. (*Systemic* refers to the whole body as a system, not specific parts.) In work on animals, of course, there was no place for recognizing the importance of cognitive appraisal in human stress reactions, where the perceived *meaning* of a situation determines which physiological reactions occur (Lazarus, 1974; Mason, 1975). Selye himself came to examine similar concepts in his later writings (Selye, 1974). In any case, he is still recognized as the pioneering explorer of stress reactions; his insights and research have led to the creation of a whole new field of study.

Stress and Disease

Selye's original theory emphasized that the stress response occurs as a reaction to various stressors, including illness. The theory also shows how a long-continued stress reaction can itself lead to illness. In fact, stress is now believed to be a contributing factor in more than half of all cases of disease (Pelletier & Peper, 1977). For example, hypertension, a disease that increases the risk of heart attack and premature death, is a stress-related disease.

There are three ways in which stressors can be causal factors in illness. First, long-continued severe stress or chronic arousal resulting from perceived threat can, in time, lead to physiological malfunctioning and illness. In the case of the hotline workers, the emergency physiological arousal for dealing actively with perceived threat was not adaptive when action was not called for. This is true of most psychological stressors, yet the physiological arousal is automatic and keeps occurring anyway whenever people are anxious, feel threatened, or feel pressured. It is their personal appraisal of a situation, and not its objective reality, that matters.

Psychosomatic ("mind/body") **disorders,** also called *psychophysiologic disorders,* are physical disorders in which emotions and thought processes are believed to play a central role. Psychosomatic disorders are often called **diseases of adaptation,** because they have their roots in attempts to adapt to stressors. Stress-induced peptic ulcers or high blood pressure are classic examples of diseases of adaptation, although not all cases of these two disorders are induced by stress. Many disorders can have their origin in either physical or psychological factors or a combination of the two. For a chronic psychological stressor to lead to a physical disorder, a person must have a constitutional vulnerability in a particular bodily system and an ineffective style of dealing with a stressful situation. The person must be either unaware of the chronic emotional arousal or convinced that there is no better way to cope with the difficult situation.

Stressors can also cause illness when the complex physiological mechanisms of the general adaptation syndrome fail to function appropriately and themselves produce diseases. Defensive processes that normally are adaptive are used to excess or used unnecessarily; the body overreacts or reacts inappropriately to foreign invaders or other stressors that may threaten its stability. How does the body know which "invaders" are potentially harmful? The body does *not* always know, and sometimes it makes errors; sometimes, in fact, it responds to stimuli that are actually benign. Allergic reactions are the clearest example of this response. Ragweed pollen has no direct harmful effects on the body; we are best off ignoring its presence. For some people, however, ragweed pollen (or various other allergens) sets off an allergic response involving inflammation of nasal tissues and, often, a total body general adaptation syndrome. Allergies are true diseases of adaptation: if the body did not evaluate the stressor as a danger and create an unnecessary stress response, there would be no disease.

There is a third way in which stress is implicated in illness. The continuing process of adaptation, depleting an organism's store of adaptation energy and cumulatively damaging organ systems, can result in eventual illness. Each of us has a limited reserve of energy which can be used to adapt to stressors. When it has been exhausted, we can no longer fight stressors and will be overcome by disease. This is why all organisms eventually reach the "stage of exhaustion" in the general adaptation syndrome if the stressor is not removed. Although a person may lead an active, healthy life, successfully coping with specific stressors as they arise, each experience of stress uses up some adaptation energy. The thing to do, Selye argued, is to use our adaptation energy wisely, rather than squandering it by responding to civilization's "false alarms" that might better be ignored.

Selye believed that aging itself is primarily the result of loss of "adaptation energy" and of damage to organ systems incurred during a lifetime of stress responses. In his view, our bodies do not age at an even rate, according to some predetermined biological process. Rather, death occurs for each of us when our "weak link" gives out (assuming no special disease or accident). The "weak link" is determined partly by genetic vulnerability and partly by the stressors each of us has faced. It should be recognized that Selye's explanation of aging is far from complete, given the complexity of the aging process and the other causal factors involved (Timiras, 1978). However, there is general agreement that long-continued, severe stress hastens aging, and that reductions in severe stress can contribute to a longer and healthier life span.

Psychological Stress Reactions

Our physiological stress reactions are automatic and predictable, built-in responses over which we normally have no conscious control. Not so our psychological reactions. They are learned and are

The need for a bubble helmet illustrates how little we know about controlling allergies—the immune system's overreaction to harmless particles of pollen, dust, and animal dander.

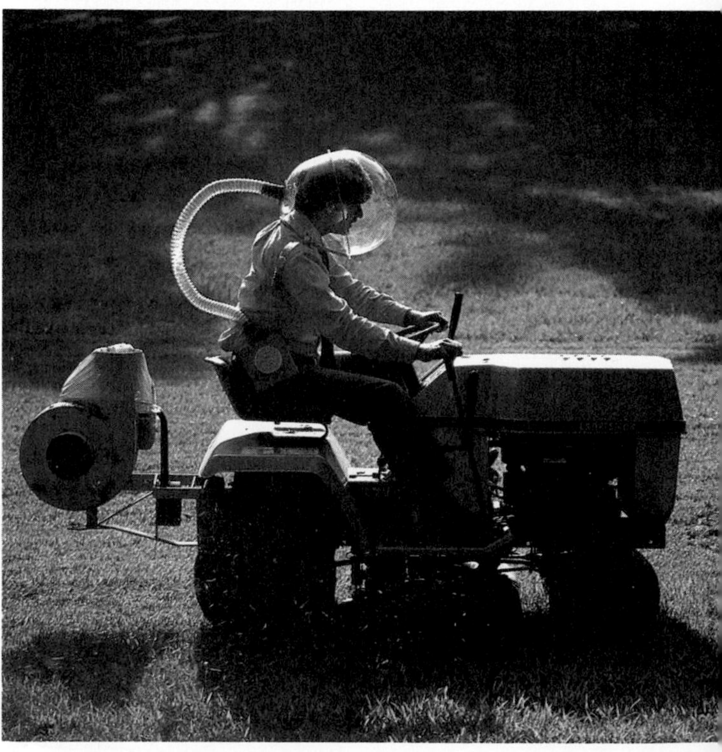

heavily dependent on our perceptions and interpretations of the world and of our capacity for dealing with it. They include behavioral, emotional, and cognitive aspects.

Behavioral Patterns

The behavior of a person under stress depends in part on the level of stress experienced. *Mild stress* activates and intensifies biologically significant behaviors, such as eating, aggression, and sexual behavior. Mild stress makes an organism more alert; energies are focused and performance may improve. Positive behavioral adjustments may occur, such as becoming better informed, becoming vigilant to sources of threat, seeking protection and support from others, and learning better attitudes and coping skills.

Continued unresolved stressors, such as those that beset the harried professor in our *Opening Case,* can accumulate to become more severe with time, causing maladaptive behavioral reactions such as increased irritability, poor concentration, lessened productivity, and chronic impatience. However, any of those stressors occurring only occasionally, or seen as within a person's capacity to control, causes no problem.

Moderate stress typically disrupts behavior, especially complex behavior requiring skilled coordination. Giving a speech or playing in a recital are familiar examples. For some people, overeating is a typical behavioral response to moderate levels of stress. Aggressive behavior can also occur, especially in response to frustration (we will learn more about the link between frustration and aggression in chapter 18). Moderate stress may also produce repetitive, stereotyped actions, such as pacing in circles or rocking back and forth. These repetitive responses have mixed effects. They are *adaptive* by reducing a high level of stressor stimulation and lessening an individual's sensitivity to the environment. At the same time, they are *nonadaptive* by being rigid and inflexible, and in persisting even when the environmental situation makes other responses more appropriate.

Severe stress inhibits and suppresses behavior and may lead to total immobility, as in the case of the dogs that learned helplessness after being shocked where no escape was possible (p. 268). It has been argued that immobility under severe stress may be a defensive reaction, representing "an attempt by the organism to reduce or eliminate the deleterious effects of stress . . . a form of self-therapy" (Antelman & Caggiula, 1980).

Emotional Aspects

The stress response includes a variety of emotional reactions ranging from exhilaration, in the cases where the stressor is seen as an exciting, manageable challenge, to the far more common negative emotions of irritation, anger, anxiety, discouragement, and depression. Most stress is acutely uncomfortable, producing only negative emotions and efforts to lessen the discomfort in direct or indirect ways.

Stressful life changes involving the loss or separation from friends and loved ones are frequent forerunners of *depression.* Being left behind when important others die or move away seems more likely to result in depression than a similar separation caused by one's own action (Paykel, 1973). Experiencing a cluster of stressful events is another predictor of emotional depression. We will examine the emotional reactions involved in depression when we review affective disorders in chapter 15.

Rape victims, survivors of plane crashes, combat veterans, and others who have experienced extremely traumatic events may react emotionally with a **posttraumatic stress disorder.** This reaction is characterized by involuntary reexperiencing of the traumatic event(s)—especially the original feelings of shock, horror, and fear—in dreams or "flashbacks." In addition, victims experience an emotional numbing in relation to everyday events, associated with feelings of alienation from other people. Finally, the emotional pain of this reaction can result in an increase of various symptoms, such as sleep problems, guilt about surviving, difficulty in concentrating, and an exaggerated startle response (see ***Close-up,*** p. 504.)

The emotional responses of posttraumatic stress can occur in an acute form immediately following a disaster and can subside over a period of several months. It can also persist, becoming a chronic syndrome called the **residual stress pattern** (Silver & Wortman, 1980). These emotional responses can also be delayed for months or even years. Clinicians are still discovering veterans of World War II and the Korean War who are displaying residual or delayed posttraumatic stress disorders (Dickman & Zeiss, 1982).

This delayed posttraumatic stress syndrome has been a special problem in the case of Vietnam war veterans (Blank, 1982). The problems of many of these former soldiers seemed to be made worse by feelings that they had been rejected by an unsympathetic American public and betrayed by their

Close-up The Aftershock of Rape

Two college women who had been sexually assaulted describe some of the enduring psychological dynamics generated by that extremely stressful episode.

Shock

Alice: I was in shock for a pretty long time. I could talk about the fact that I was a rape victim, but the emotions didn't start surfacing until a month later.

Beth: During the first two weeks there were people I had chosen to tell who were very, very supportive; but after two weeks, it was like, "Okay, she's over it, we can go on now." But the farther along you get, the more support you need, because, as time passes, you become aware of your emotions and the need to deal with them.

Denial

Alice: There is a point where you deny it happened. You just completely bury it.

Beth: It's so unreal that you don't want to believe that it actually happened or that it can happen. Then you go through a long period of fear and anger.

Fear

Alice: I'm terrified of going jogging. [Alice had been jogging when she was raped.] I completely stopped any kind of physical activity after I was raped. I started it again this quarter, but every time I go jogging I have a perpetual fear. My pulse doubles. Of course I don't go jogging alone any more, but still the fear is there constantly.

Beth: I've experienced some really irrational thoughts. I was home at Christmas riding in the car with my Dad—my Dad!—and the guy who attacked me was about 21 years old—and yet I got really afraid all of a sudden of my Dad. It's just something you have to work out. There's not anything anybody can do.

Betrayal and Loneliness

Alice: There's also a feeling of having all your friends betray you. I had a dream in which I was being assaulted outside my dorm. In the dream, everyone was looking out their windows—the faces were so clear—every one of my friends lined up against the windows watching, and there were even people two feet away from me. They all saw what was happening and none of them did anything. I woke up and had a feeling of extreme loneliness. Sometimes you just feel like there's nobody around.

Beth: I still feel very lonely [4 months later]. I didn't have any close friends when I got here. [Beth was raped at the start of her freshman year.] I felt betrayed by my family and friends from high school because they weren't here.

(Excerpted from the *Stanford Daily,* February 2, 1982, with permission. For a systematic analysis of psychological and social issues involved in rape, see Cann et al., 1981.)

---

government, and that they had spent important years of their lives in a wasted effort (Thienes-Hontos et al., 1982).

In a study of Vietnam veterans with combat experience, called the "Forgotten Warrior Project" (Wilson, 1980), it was found that:

1. *Their suicide rate was 23 to 33 percent higher than the national average.*
2. *Of those who had been married when they left the United States, 38 percent were divorced within six months after returning.*
3. *The rate of hospitalization for alcoholism or drinking problems was high and increasing.*
4. *About half of them still had some emotional problems related to adjustment to civilian life.*

Cognitive Effects

Once a stressor has been interpreted as threatening to one's well-being or self-esteem, a variety of intellectual functions may be adversely affected. In general, the greater the stress, the greater the reduction in cognitive efficiency and the interference with flexible thinking.

Because attention is a limited resource, a focus on the threatening aspects of a situation and on one's arousal reduces the amount of attention available for effective coping with the task at hand. Memory is affected too, because short-term memory is limited by the amount of attention given to new input, and retrieval of past relevant memories depends on smooth operation of the use of appropriate retrieval cues. Similarly, stress may interfere with problem solving, judging, and decision making by narrowing perceptions of alternatives and by substituting stereotyped, rigid thinking for more creative responding (Janis, 1982a).

A chronic feeling of threat can also be carried into ordinary situations, as happens when highly test-anxious students carry their anxiety into class discussions too. Finally, there is evidence that a high level of stress impairs children's intellectual development.

To test the hypothesis that stress affects competence and intelligence, researchers developed a stress index based on such variables as family problems and physical disorders. Stress indexes were calculated for over 4000 7-year-old children, and each child's intelligence was tested. The higher the stress index, the lower was the child's IQ. This was particularly true for children with eye problems and for lower-class black children. Children who were held back a year or were assigned to special education classes also showed greater intellectual deficits. The researchers concluded that the stress variables combined to influence the performance measured by the IQ test both in the immediate testing situation and also more generally, through interaction with other personal and social factors. (Brown & Rosenbaum, 1983)

Sources of Stress

Stress is a recurring problem. Naturally occurring changes are an unavoidable part of the lives of all of us. People close to us get sick, move away, die. We get new jobs, leave home, start college, succeed, fail, begin romances, get married, break up. In addition to the big life changes, there are also "life's little hassles"—frustrating traffic jams, snoring roommates, and missed appointments. Unpredictable, catastrophic events will occur for some of us, and for others, chronic societal problems will be important sources of stress.

Major Life Stressors

Sudden changes in our life situation are at the core of stressful life events for many of us. They may make it harder for us to act effectively or may make us physically ill. Even events that we welcome may require major changes in our routines and adaptation to new requirements; this, too, can be stressful.

The influence of major life changes on subsequent mental and physical health has been a source of considerable research. It started with the development of the Social Readjustment Rating Scale (SRRS), a simple scale for rating the degree of adjustment required by the various life changes that many people experience, including both pleasant and unpleasant changes. The scale was developed by asking adults, from all walks of life, to identify, from a list, all the life changes that applied to them and rate the amount of readjustment required by comparing each to marriage, which was arbitrarily assigned a value of 50 *life change units* (LCU). Researchers then calculated the total number of life change units an individual had undergone during that period, using it as a measure of the amount of stress the individual had experienced (Holmes & Rahe, 1967). A modification of this scale for college students is shown in **Table 14.4.**

Many studies have found that life change intensity, as measured by this scale, rises significantly before the onset of an illness. Life stress has been related to sudden cardiac death, tuberculosis, multiple sclerosis, diabetes, complications of pregnancy and birth, chronic illness, and many minor physical problems. It is believed that life stress increases a person's overall susceptibility to illness (Holmes & Masuda, 1974); but illness is itself a major stressor. As expected, LCU values are also high during an illness and for some time thereafter (Rahe & Arthur, 1977).

An improvement in measuring the effects of life events is provided in the Life Experiences Survey (LES), which has two special features. First, it provides scores for both increases *and* decreases in change, rather than increases only, as in the original scale. Second, its scores reflect individual assessments of the events and their desirability. For example, the death of an unloved spouse who left a big inheritance might be rated as quite desirable. Thus this scale goes beyond a mere count of the number of remembered life changes to measure the personal significance of each change (Sarason et al., 1978).

One problem with studies relating stressful life events to subsequent illness is that they tend to be *retrospective*. That is, both the stress measures and the illness measures are obtained by having subjects recall prior events. This presents an opportunity for distortion in memory to bias the results. For example, subjects who are sick may be more likely to remember past stressors than subjects who are well. More recently, however, *prospective* (looking ahead) studies have had similar findings. Life change scores on the *LES* have been obtained, and negative scores have been found to be significantly correlated with physical symptoms reported six months *later* (Johnson & Sarason, 1979). The message again is clear—too many stressful life events are bad for your health.

Table 14.4 *Student Stress Scale*

The Student Stress Scale represents an adaptation of Holmes and Rahe's Social Readjustment Rating Scale. Each event is given a score that represents the amount of readjustment a person has to make in life as a result of the change. People with scores of 300 and higher have a high health risk. People scoring between 150 and 300 points have about a 50–50 chance of serious health change within two years. People scoring below 150 have a 1 in 3 chance of serious health change. Calculate your score each month of this year and then correlate those scores with any changes in your health status.

Event	***Life Change Unit***
Death of a Close Family Member	100
Death of a Close Friend	73
Divorce Between Parents	65
Jail Term	63
Major Personal Injury or Illness	63
Marriage	58
Fired from Job	50
Failed Important Course	47
Change in Health of Family Member	45
Pregnancy	45
Sex Problems	44
Serious Argument with Close Friend	40
Change in Financial Status	39
Change of Major	39
Trouble with Parents	39
New Girl- or Boyfriend	38
Increased Workload at School	37
Outstanding Personal Achievement	36
First Quarter/Semester in College	35
Change in Living Conditions	31
Serious Argument with Instructor	30
Lower Grades than Expected	29
Change in Sleeping Habits	29
Change in Social Activities	29
Change in Eating Habits	28
Chronic Car Trouble	26
Change in Number of Family Get-togethers	26
Too Many Missed Classes	25
Change of College	24
Dropped More than One Class	23
Minor Traffic Violations	20
My Total	_____

(Adapted from Insel & Roth, 1985)

Life's Little Hassles

Life is filled with low-level frustrations. Your pencil breaks during an exam, you get stuck in traffic, or you forget to set your alarm clock for an important appointment. To what extent do these minor irritations pile up to become stressors that play havoc with your health? The answer is to a bigger extent than you might imagine.

A psychiatrist distributed 100 questionnaires to the faithful waiting for the 7:12 A.M. *''bullet'' train from Long Island into Manhattan. From the 49 completed questionnaires returned, it was determined that these average commuters had just gulped down their breakfast in less than 11 minutes, if at all; were prepared to spend 3 hours each day in transit; and in 10 years had logged about 7500 hours of rail time—assuming two-week vacations and no time off for illness. Two thirds of the commuters believed their family relations were im-*

paired by their commuting. Fifty-nine percent experienced fatigue, 47 percent were filled with conscious anger, 28 percent were anxious, and others reported headaches, muscle pains, indigestion, and other symptoms of the long-term consequences of beating the rat race in the city by living in the country. (F. Charaton, personal communication, Spring, 1973)

In another study, when a group of 100 white, middle-class, middle-aged men and women kept track of their daily hassles over a one-year period (along with a record of major life changes and physical symptoms), a clear relationship emerged between hassles and health problems: the more frequent and intense the hassles people reported, the poorer was their health, both physical and mental (Lazarus, 1981). This is only a correlational finding, however; the causal relationships are not clear.

Catastrophic Events

Dining and dancing in a beautiful setting on a Friday evening sounds like a prescription for relieving the stress of a hard week of work. Unfortunately it became, instead, a prescription for a disaster, creating great stress, when, in 1982, two aerial walkways collapsed into the lobby of a hotel in Kansas City, Missouri. Immediately affected were the 2000 people who were attending a tea dance, more than 300 of whom were killed or injured. Also experiencing stress were 1000 rescue workers, who worked more than 10 hours just to get through the rubble to all the victims. Another 5000 people were less directly affected: workers at the hotel, personnel at hospitals in the area, and friends and families of victims (Gist & Stolz, 1982). No count could be made of those who were affected in the immediate community and to television viewers across the nation, as people tried to deal with the senselessness of the event and the anxieties it created about the possibility of other such disasters elsewhere.

People's reactions when disaster strikes go through stages from shock to acceptance.

Research on the physical and psychological effects of catastrophic events has been prolific. However, it has followed a rather different research tradition from the one used in studies of personal stressors, and there is no scale assessing the relative impact of different kinds of natural disasters.

Researchers have found that five stages occur predictably in people's responses to disasters:

> *Typically, there is a period of shock and even "psychic numbness," during which people cannot fully comprehend what has happened. The next phase involves what has been called "automatic action"; people try to respond to the disaster and may behave adaptively, but with little awareness of their actions and poor later memory of the experience.*
>
> *In the next stage, people often feel great accomplishment and even a positive sense of communal effort for a shared purpose. Also in this phase, people feel weary and are aware that they are using up their reserves of energy. During the next phase, they experience a letdown; their energy is depleted and the impact of the tragedy is finally comprehended and felt emotionally. An extended period of recovery follows, as people try to rebuild and to adapt to the changes brought about by the disaster. (Cohen & Ahearn, 1980)*

Knowledge of these typical reaction stages provides a model that is helpful in predicting people's reactions when disaster strikes, enabling rescue workers to anticipate and help victims deal with the problems that arise. Responses to such varied events as floods, tornadoes, airplane crashes, and factory explosions have all been shown to fit this model of disaster reactions.

Chronic Societal Sources of Stress

What of environmental stressors that are part of the ongoing circumstances of life: overcrowding, economic recession, fear of nuclear war? What cumulative effect do such stressors have on us?

For today's children, the threat of nuclear war is a major source of stress. Studies of the nuclear fears of children since the mid-1960s have shown that children know and care about the threat of nuclear war and have a high degree of uncertainty about their own future. One of the early researchers concluded, "The profound uncertainty about whether or not mankind has a foreseeable future exerts a corrosive and malignant influence upon important development processes in normal and well-functioning children" (Escalona, 1965). Although this particular survey did not refer to the bomb or nuclear war, 70 percent of the children sampled mentioned spontaneously that their future would include nuclear weapons and destructive war.

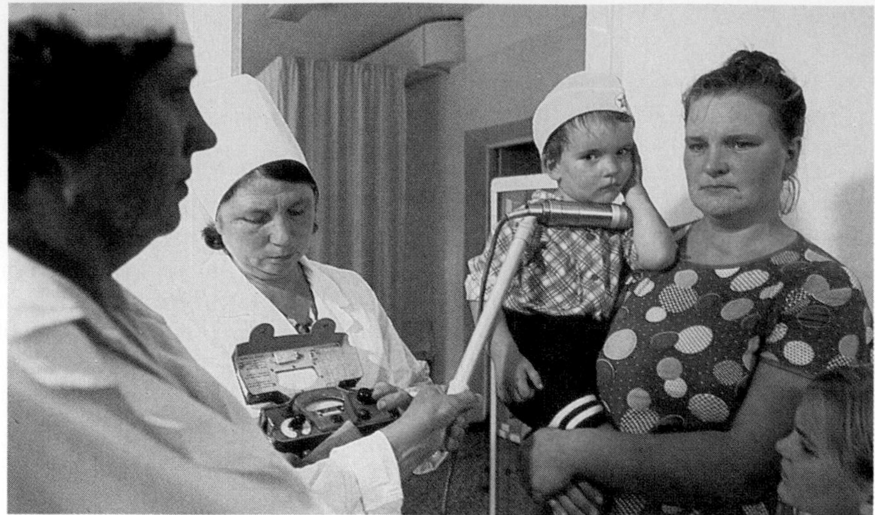

Twentieth-century technology has brought new frustrations into the lives of many Americans. The threat of nuclear war looms large in the minds of children as well as adults throughout the country. And chemical contamination of the environment has created a great deal of stress for individuals.

More recently, some psychiatrists made a detailed analysis of the attitudes of 1000 students in several parts of the country (Beardslee & Mack, 1983). They found a general disquiet and uneasiness about the future, with many students deeply disturbed. For example, a 10-year-old school child wrote to President Reagan:

> *I am 10 years old. I think nuclear war is bad because many innocent people will die. The world could even be destroyed. I don't want to die. I don't want my family to die. I want to live and grow up. Please stop nuclear bombs. (Yudkin, 1984, p. 24)*

Studies since 1983 have found a significant increase in the expression of fear, helplessness, and anger toward the adult generation, with many young people questioning whether it is worthwhile working hard to prepare for a future that they do not expect to have (Hanna, 1984; Yudkin, 1984).

Adults, too, are worried about nuclear disaster, but they are also affected by the more immediate problems of employment and economic security. Many stress-related problems increase when the economy is in a downswing. Admission to mental hospitals, infant mortality, suicide, and deaths from alcohol-related diseases and cardiovascular problems all increase (Brenner, 1976).

> *Psychologists found that unemployed men reported more symptoms, such as depression, anxiety, and worries about health than did those who were employed. Because these symptoms disappeared when they were subsequently reemployed, the researchers argued that the symptoms had been the results of being unemployed, rather than being indicators of more disturbed workers who had been particularly likely to lose their jobs. (Liem & Rayman, 1982)*

The pollution of our environment creates psychological stress as well as physical threats. The chemical miracles of our modern technology have led to unexpected contamination of whole areas where people have had to be evacuated, as at Love Canal, near Buffalo, New York, and Times Beach, Missouri. The malfunctioning and consequent release of radioactive steam at the Three Mile Island nuclear power plant in 1979 and the 1986 explosion of the Russian nuclear power factory in Chernobyl provided dramatic examples of environmental stressors. Those living in the area experienced considerable stress from fears about the immediate and long-term health consequences. In addition, widespread stress was experienced by citizens in other parts of the world, worried about other possible nuclear accidents. One consequence of the American nuclear accident was the U.S. Court of Appeals' decision to recognize the *legal status* of psychological stress as a necessary part of the environmental impact survey that must be carried out before the plant could be reopened.

Environmental sources of stress, as well as the others considered in this section, arise out of our imperfect human capacity to solve all the problems of a complex society. Such problems are not simply technological, but also political and psychological. Many modern day stressors will require solutions not at the individual level, but through cooperation within communities and even across nations. The clearest example of this international concern for combating shared environmental stressors is the "acid rain" pollution that is harming the Canadian environment, in part caused by emissions from factories in the United States.

Coping Strategies

If living is inevitably stressful, and if too much stress can disrupt our lives, and even kill us, we need to learn how to cope so that we can survive. **Coping** refers to attempts to meet environmental demands in order to prevent negative consequences (Lazarus & Folkman, 1984). There are many different coping techniques, some of which will be more effective than others for a given person in a given situation.

Because animals in the wild must adapt biologically to their environment, their mechanisms for coping are coded in their genes and limited by the slow timetable of evolutionary processes. Human beings have a tremendous potential for adapting not only biologically, over generations, but psychologically, within a lifetime—even within a short period of time if they decide they want to change.

In this final section of the chapter, we will look at a variety of strategies that people use to reduce the amount of stress they experience and to lessen its harmful effects. Some strategies are ones that most of us use naturally and habitually, whereas others are special techniques that can be learned. Some strategies are individual ones, to be done "on one's own"; in contrast, social strategies depend on the presence of other people.

Problem-focused Versus Emotion-focused Coping

Coping strategies can be grouped into two main types, depending on whether the goal is to *deal with the problem* (problem-focused) or to *lessen the discomfort of it* (emotion-focused). Several subcategories of these two basic approaches are shown in **Table 14.5.**

The first main approach includes any strategy to deal *directly* with the stressor, whether through overt action or through realistic problem-solving mental activities. We face up to a bully or run away; we try to win him or her over with bribes or other incentives. Taking martial arts training or notifying the "proper authorities" are other approaches that may prevent a bully from continuing to be a threat. In all these strategies, our focus is on the *problem* to be dealt with and on the agent that has induced the stress. We acknowledge the "call to action," we appraise the situation and our resources for dealing with it, and we undertake a response that is appropriate for removing or lessening the threat.

In the second approach, we do not look for ways of changing the stressful situation; instead we try to change our feelings and thoughts about it. This coping strategy is called *emotion regulation.* It is a remedial, rather than a problem-solving strategy, because it is aimed at relieving the emotional impact of stress to make us feel better, even though the threatening or harmful stressor is not changed. Relying on this approach, people may take alcohol or tranquilizers—and they may work for a while. On occasion, haven't you dealt with an unpleasant event by using consciously planned distractions such as going to a party or watching TV? Some-

Table 14.5 *Taxonomy of Coping Strategies*

Problem-focused Coping Change stressor or one's relationship to it through direct actions and/or problem-solving activities	Fight (destroy, remove, or weaken the threat) Flight (distance oneself from the threat) Seek options to fight or flight (negotiating, bargaining, compromising) Prevent future stress (act to increase one's resistance or decrease strength of anticipated stress)
Emotion-focused Coping Change self through "activities" that make one feel better but do not change the stressor	Somatically focused activities (use of drugs, relaxation, biofeedback) Cognitively focused activities (planned distractions, fantasies, thoughts about oneself) Unconscious processes that distort reality and result in intrapsychic stress

(Lazarus, 1975)

times, we confront our fears by "whistling a happy tune" or with laughter (see ***Close-up,*** p. 511). However, this approach to coping has its drawbacks.

> *One research study compared depressed and nondepressed middle-aged people over a one-year period. It was found that those who were depressed were using appraisals and coping patterns that created problems and perpetuated their depression. They were just as likely as the nondepressed to feel that something* could *be done about the situations they faced, and even to focus on problem solutions, but they diverged in their tendency to accentuate the negative. They worried more about not being stronger,* wished *they could change themselves and/or the situation, kept putting off action until they had more information, and spent more time seeking emotional support for their feelings of distress. What emerged was an indecisive coping style that was likely to promote a sense of personal inadequacy—which, in turn, was a source of more depression. (Coyne et al., 1981)*

The ego defense mechanisms discussed in chapter 12 (such as repression, denial of reality, and rationalization) are familiar emotion-regulating approaches. Undertaken unconsciously to protect us from the pain of inner anxieties, they enable us to appraise situations in less self-threatening ways. They lead to coping strategies that are essentially aimed at self-protection rather than at solving problems. At times, however, they cause us to distort reality and, when overused, can lead to maladaptive coping.

Altering Bodily Reactions

"Stress equals tension" for many people. This often means tight muscles, high blood pressure, constricted blood vessels in the brain, and chronic oversecretion of hormones. Fortunately, many of these tension responses can be controlled by a variety of techniques—some ages old, some quite new.

Relaxation

Relaxation through meditation has ancient roots in many parts of the world. For centuries in Eastern cultures, ways to calm the mind and still the body's tensions have been practiced. Today Zen discipline and Yoga exercises from Japan and India are part of daily life for many people both there and, increasingly, in the West. In our own culture, a growing number of people have been attracted to workshops and therapy in relaxation training and to various forms of meditation.

Just as stress is the nonspecific response of the body to any demand made on it, there is growing evidence that complete relaxation is a potent antistress response. The *relaxation response* is a condition in which muscle tension, cortical activity, heart rate, and blood pressure all decrease and breathing slows. There is reduced electrical activity in the brain, and input to the central nervous system from the outside environment is lowered. In this low level of arousal, recuperation from stress can take place. Four conditions are regarded as necessary to produce the relaxation response: (a) a quiet environment, (b) closed eyes, (c) a comfortable position, and (d) a repetitive mental device. The first three lower input to the nervous system, while the fourth lowers its internal stimulation (Benson, 1975).

Progressive relaxation is a technique that has been widely used in American psychotherapy. Designed by Edmund Jacobson (1970), the approach teaches people alternately to tense and relax their muscles. In this way they learn the experience of relaxation and discover how to extend it to each specific muscle. After several months of daily practice with progressive relaxation, people are able to achieve deep levels of relaxation. The relaxation response can also be produced by hypnosis. The beneficial effects of these relaxation training methods extend beyond the time when people are actively practicing them. For example, in one study hypertensive patients who learned to lower their blood pressure by relaxing continued to have lower blood pressure when they were asleep (Agras et al., 1980).

Biofeedback

Biological feedback, or *biofeedback,* was described briefly in chapter 8. Sophisticated recording devices and computers make it possible to provide this feedback by detecting small changes in a body process, amplifying them, and indicating they are present by means of a visual or auditory signal which is "on" whenever the change is occurring. Paradoxically, although individuals do not know how they do it, concentrating on the desired result in the presence of this signal produces change in the desired direction. Biofeedback is a self-regulatory technique being used for a variety of special applications, such as control of blood pressure, relaxation of forehead muscles (involved in tension headaches), and even overcoming extreme blushing. This method is also being used to induce nonspecific general relaxation (Birbaumer and Kimmel, 1979).

Close-up It's Not So Stressful When I Laugh

For decades the *Reader's Digest* has carried a feature of jokes entitled "Laughter, the Best Medicine." Is it? What is the relationship between laughter and stress? There are several lines of evidence to suggest that humor is used by children to handle stressful home life; that professional comedians and comedy writers tend to come from family backgrounds filled with tension, and that laughter may be good therapy for certain kinds of illness.

A longitudinal study examined the development of humor in young children during the first six years of their lives.

> *The elementary-school-age children who laughed most were those who had been exposed to "tough and potentially hazardous situations" and whose mothers had withheld help in solving problems. In contrast, children who had been "babied" and protected from conflict had a less developed sense of humor. (McGhee, 1979)*

This finding supports the view of Freud (1905/1960) that humor may develop as a means of coping with stressful situations or anxiety-arousing circumstances.

Humor as a "coping mechanism" is also revealed in two studies in which professional comedians and comedy writers were interviewed. Most professional humorists tended to be funny as children and continued this style of relating to people into adulthood (Fry & Allen, 1975). Their childhood typically showed a pattern of early stress and poor home adjustment. Their early lives were "marked by suffering, isolation, and feelings of deprivation. Humor offered a relief from their sufferings and a defense against inescapable panic and anxiety" (Janus, 1975, p. 174).

Carol Burnett, for example, had parents who were both alcoholics and fought frequently. She describes using humor as a way of gaining strength rather than "buckling under" in her tension-filled home. Humor created a playful state of mind for her as a child, deflected her attention away from its source onto the role of child-as-comedian, and dissipated some of the hostile feelings.

If a stressful childhood can promote the development of humor, maybe laughter can work to reduce adult stress. Norman Cousins, former editor of *The Saturday Review,* used such reasoning to help himself recover from a serious illness. He was hospitalized for a rare disease of the connective tissue, which is crippling and from which he was told he would not recover. Working with a cooperative physician, he checked out of the hospital and into a hotel room where for several months he supplemented massive injections of ascorbic acid (vitamin C) with a steady diet of old *Candid Camera* films and other belly-laugh-inducing movies. He completely recovered from his "incurable illness."

Fifteen years later, a high-pressure schedule of travel, speaking, and deadlines led to a heart attack and a diagnosis of damaged heart muscle and congested coronary arteries. Cousins was able to avoid a bypass operation by again confidently taking charge of his own recovery. Following a regimen of diet, gradually increasing exercise, writing, amateur photography, and *humor,* he was able to resume full-time work less than a year after his attack (Cousins, 1979, 1983). Allen Funt, the genius behind *Candid Camera,* is currently involved in a project to make available to patients funny scenarios from his library of classics and then to evaluate their effectiveness in coping with illness (from a personal communication, April 1987).

Modifying Cognitive Strategies

A powerful way to handle stress more adaptively is to change our evaluations of stressors and our self-defeating cognitions about the way we are dealing with them. We need to find a different way to think about a given situation, our role in it, and the causal attributions we make to explain the undesirable outcome.

Reappraising Stressors

The close connection between cognitive appraisal and the degree of autonomic nervous system arousal has been demonstrated in studies where the cognitive appraisal was systematically varied.

When subjects watched an upsetting film showing vivid circumcision rites in a primitive tribe, they were less *physiologically aroused when the film had a sound track that either denied the dangers or discussed them in an intellectual, detached way. (Speisman et al., 1964)*

In another study, subjects viewing a film of an industrial accident were less aroused if they were "emotionally inoculated" by being warned in advance that it was coming and given a chance to imagine the threatening scenes beforehand. As shown in Figure 14.5, this cognitive preparation, which gave them an opportunity to rehearse mentally both the stressful episode and their coping responses to it, was more successful than relaxation training in lowering arousal. (Folkins et al., 1968)

Learning to think differently about certain stressors, to relabel them, or to imagine them in a less threatening (perhaps even funny) context are forms of cognitive reappraisal that can reduce stress.

Restructuring Cognitions

Another way of managing stress better is intentionally changing what we are telling ourselves about stress and our handling of it. Such messages can lead to both cognitive restructuring and more effective coping. For example, depressed or insecure people often tell themselves that they are no good, that they'll do poorly, and—if something goes well—that it was a fluke.

Meichenbaum (1977) has proposed a three-phase process to intentionally change this self-fulfilling cycle. In Phase 1, people work to develop a greater awareness of their actual behavior, what instigates it, and what its results are. One of the best ways of doing this is to keep daily logs. By helping people redefine their problems in terms of their causes and results, they can increase their feelings of control.

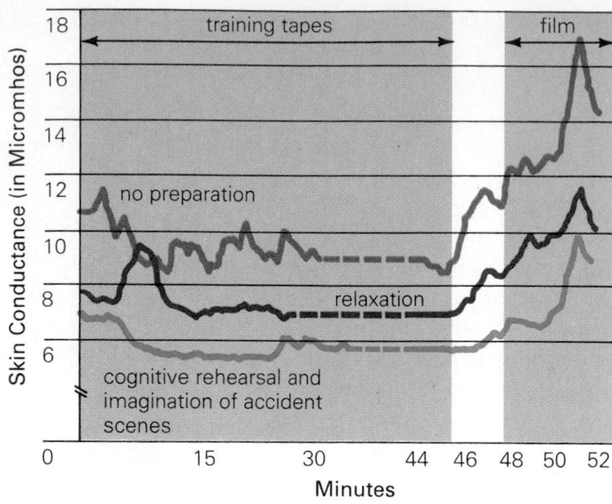

Figure 14.5

Stress induced by highly arousing films can be lowered to some extent by relaxation training. "Emotional inoculation" through cognitive rehearsal of the stressful scenes lowers the stress response even more. (Adapted from Folkins et al., 1968)

In Phase 2, they begin to identify new behaviors that negate the maladaptive, self-defeating behaviors—perhaps smiling at someone, offering a compliment, or acting assertively. In Phase 3, after adaptive behaviors are being emitted, individuals appraise their consequences, avoiding the former internal dialogue of put-downs. Instead of telling themselves "I was lucky the professor called on me when I happened to have read the text," they will say, "I'm glad I was prepared for the professor's question. It feels great to be able to respond intelligently in that class."

In sum, this approach means initiating responses and self-statements that are incompatible with previous defeatist cognitions. The people realize that they are changing and taking full credit for it—which promotes further successes. **Table 14.6** gives examples of the new kinds of self-statements that help at different stages in dealing with stressful situations.

Supportiveness of the Environment

Life in societies is the most powerful weapon in the struggle for life. . . . Thus it was that thousands of years before humans appeared, association [of animals in social units] was preparing the way for human society. (Chapin, 1913, p. 103)

We all cope with stress as individuals, but for a lifetime of effective coping and for the continued success of our species, it is necessary for us to band together with our families, friends, and neighbors (at home and throughout our small planet). Isola-

Table 14.6 *Examples of Coping Self-Statements*

Preparation
I can develop a plan to deal with it.
Just think about what I can do about it. That's better than getting anxious.
No negative self-statements, just think rationally.
Confrontation
One step at a time; I can handle this situation.
This anxiety is what the doctor said I would feel: it's a reminder to use my coping exercises.
Relax; I'm in control. Take a slow deep breath. Ah, good.
Coping
When fear comes just pause.
Keep focus on the present; what is it I have to do?
Don't try to eliminate fear totally; just keep it manageable.
It's not the worst thing that can happen.
Just think about something else.
Self-reinforcement
It worked; I was able to do it.
It wasn't as bad as I expected.
I'm really pleased with the progress I'm making.

(Adapted from Meichenbaum, 1975)

tion can lead to inadequate coping and is itself the cause of much stress. Much contemporary research points to the improvement in coping that can come from being part of a social support network and from living and working in a healthy environment.

Social Support Networks

Social support refers to the resources provided by other persons (Cohen & Syme, 1985). These resources can include material aid, socioemotional support (love, caring, esteem, sympathy, sense of group belonging), and informational aid (advice, personal feedback, information). The persons who can provide these resources for an individual are those with whom he or she has significant social relationships—such as family members, friends, coworkers, and neighbors.

There is now a sizable body of evidence showing that the presence of social support makes people less vulnerable to stress. When people have other people they can turn to, they are better able to handle job stressors, unemployment, marital disruption, serious illness, and other catastrophes, as well as their everyday problems of living (Gottlieb, 1981; Pilisuk & Parks, 1986).

> *Nearly 7000 adults were surveyed in 1965 to determine their health and health-related behaviors, as well as other background factors and the extent of their social relationships. From this information a* social network index *was computed for each person, based on the number and importance of social contacts in the person's life. Mortality (death rate) data were then collected for a 9-year period on 96 percent of this original sample.*
>
> *The social network index was significantly correlated with overall death rate and also with cause of death. For every age group and both sexes, there were more deaths among people who had few social contacts than among those with many connections. This effect was independent of their health status at the time of the initial survey and independent of their socioeconomic status. Furthermore, those who were socially isolated had been more likely to engage in poor health behaviors (smoking, drinking, overeating, irregular eating, inadequate sleep). Nevertheless the extent of their social contacts still predicted their mortality over and above the effects of any or all of these poor health practices. In fact, most of the deaths occurred among those who lacked social and community ties. It is clear that lack of a social support system increases one's vulnerability to disease and death. (Berkman & Syme, 1979)*

Other studies have found that socially unconnected people engage in more maladaptive ways of thinking and behaving than do those who share their concerns with other people (Silberfeld, 1978). *Decreases* in social support in family and work environments are related to *increases* in psychological maladjustment. This negative relationship was found even when the researchers looked at groups who had the same *initial* levels of support, maladjustment, and life change (Holohan & Moos, 1981).

Structure of the Physical Environment

Like the harried professor in our *Opening Case,* many of us are often coping with a succession of frustrating, stressful events—too often in ways that increase our stress still further. We need to give more thought to changing our unhealthy, stress-inducing *environments,* as well as developing more effective and satisfying behavior patterns.

In a study of residential care programs for the elderly, more cohesive, supportive groups developed where the environment provided such simple amenities as lounges and seating arrangements that were well grouped for conversation (Moos & Lemke, 1984). Likewise, the physical structure of a college dormitory influences the social climate among the students.

> *In one study, residents in dormitories with long corridors of many rooms had more difficulty developing a social support network than residents in dormitories with short corridors. The smaller areas helped define small friendship groups, while the extended areas created a greater sense of impersonality. (Baum & Valins, 1979)*
>
> *When the students on the long corridors felt that their living conditions were crowded, they developed coping patterns to deal with conflict situations that differed from the patterns developed by those living in short-corridor dormitories. On an experimental task in which it is possible either to cooperate or to compete, the residents of short corridors tended to be more cooperative. The students on the long corridors tended to be either more competitive or more likely to withdraw. (Baum et al., 1982)*

In addition to the physical structure of the environment, its social and psychological dimensions can be critically important in increasing or decreasing stress. For example, the perceived freedom of choice to either enter or not enter a particular environment may determine whether a person will adapt successfully to it. As we saw in chapter 2, elderly women who chose to go into a retirement home lived longer, as a group, than those who entered feeling they had no choice (Ferrare, 1962). Moreover, when residents of retirement homes felt that they had more choice and control over their environment, their health improved and they engaged in more activities (Rodin, 1983). Such research findings have important implications for policies and programs in institutional settings.

Stress Control and Your Mental Health

The harried professor in our *Opening Case* experienced many stressors, but several choices he had made contributed to his stress level and lack of good health—to eat poorly, to live in an overcrowded and noisy city, to own a car, to work at a competitive job, and to spend more than he earned. What choices are *you* making? Are they producing stress that is damaging to your health and well-being?

Instead of waiting for stress or illness to come and then reacting to it, we need to set goals and structure our lives and life-styles in ways most likely to bring us what we really want. The following ideas are presented as guidelines to encourage a more active role in taking charge of your own life and in creating a more positive psychological environment for yourself and others.

1. Look for the causes of your behavior in the current situation or in its relation to past situations, and *not* just in some defect in yourself. Understand the *context* of your behavior.
2. Compare your reactions, thoughts, and feelings with those of other comparable individuals in your current life environment so that you can gauge the appropriateness and relevance of your responses.
3. Have several close friends with whom you can share feelings, joys, and worries. Work at developing, maintaining, and expanding your social support networks.
4. Don't be afraid to risk showing others that you want to be their friend or even to give and accept love. Don't let rejection deter you from trying again—after "cleaning up your act."
5. Never say bad things about yourself, such as *stupid, ugly, uncreative, a failure.* Look for sources of your unhappiness in elements that can be modified by future actions—what can you do differently next time to get what you want?
6. Always take full credit for your successes and happiness (and share your positive feeling with other people).
7. Keep an inventory of all the things that make you special and unique, those qualities you have to offer others. For example, a shy person can offer a talkative person the gift of being an attentive listener. Know your sources of personal strength and the coping resources available to you.
8. When you feel you are losing control over your emotions (hyperexcited or depressed), distance yourself from the situation by: (a) physically leaving it; (b) role-playing the position of some other person in the situation or conflict; (c) projecting your imagination into the future to gain temporal perspective on what seems like an overwhelming problem now; or (d) talking to someone who is sympathetic.
9. Don't dwell on past misfortunes or sources of guilt, shame, and failure. The past is gone and thinking about it keeps it alive in memory. Nothing you have said or done is new under the sun.

10. Remember that failure and disappointment are sometimes blessings in disguise, telling you that your goals are not right for you or saving you from bigger letdowns later on. Learn from every failure experience. Acknowledge it by saying, "I made a mistake," and move on.
11. If you see someone you think is troubled, intervene in a concerned, gentle way to find out if anything is wrong and if you can help or get help. Often, listening to a friend's troubles is all the therapy needed, if it comes soon enough. Don't isolate the "stranger" and be tolerant of deviance—but, of course, respect your own need for personal safety as well.
12. If you discover you cannot help yourself or the other person in distress, seek the counsel of a trained specialist in your student health department. In some cases a problem that appears to be a psychological one may really be physical, as with glandular conditions.
13. Assume that anyone can be helped by an opportunity to discuss his or her problems openly with a mental health specialist; therefore, if you do go to one, there is no need to feel stigmatized.
14. Develop long-range goals; think about what you want to be doing five, ten, twenty years from now and about alternative ways of getting there. Always try to enjoy the process of getting there too; "travel hopefully" and you will arrive eventually and be more fulfilled.
15. Take time to relax, to meditate, to enjoy hobbies and activities that you can do alone and by means of which you can get in touch with yourself.
16. Think of yourself not as a passive object to which bad things just happen, but as an active agent who at any time can change the direction of your entire life. You are what you choose to be and you are seen by others in terms of what you choose to show them.
17. Remember that, as long as there is life, there is hope for a better life, and as long as we care for one another, our lives will get better.

Summary

- Health refers to more than the absence of illness or injury; it is concerned with the general soundness and vigor of the mind and body. The growing awareness of the role of psychological and social factors in physical health has led to the development of a biopsychosocial model of health and illness.
- Health psychology is devoted to understanding the influence of psychological factors on health, illness, and responses to illness. Behavioral medicine is an interdisciplinary field which focuses on overt health behaviors and the conditions that affect them. Psychosomatic medicine, which, like health psychology, studies the relationship between psychological factors and physical health, developed within the field of psychiatry. In the study of health and illness, medical sociology focuses on the group and medical anthropology focuses on the culture.
- The concerns of health psychology include the promotion and maintenance of health, the prevention and treatment of illness, and the study of the causes and correlates of health, illness, and dysfunction.
- Prevention of illness refers to reducing the risk that people will become ill. Today, prevention often focuses on changes in life-style, such as change or elimination of poor health habits. Treatment is concerned with helping people adjust to their illnesses and recover.
- Health psychologists study not only poor health habits as causes of illness, but also the influence of personality and individual behavioral styles, such as Type-A behavior syndrome, on health and illness. Type-A behavior is a competitive, hard-driving, hostile behavioral pattern associated with high risk for coronary heart disease. Most common in men, it is now being seen more in women and even in adolescents and children.
- Stress is the pattern of reactions an organism makes in response to stressors, stimulus events that tax its ability to cope.
- We do not react directly to a stressor, but to our perception and interpretation of it; thus our cognitive appraisal is a moderator variable: it moderates (changes) the effect of the stressor. Other moderator variables are our inner and outer resources for dealing with a stressor and our attitudes and coping patterns.
- Cognitive appraisal defines the demand; primary appraisal determines whether the demand is stressful, while secondary appraisal evaluates the available personal and social resources and the appropriate action. In chronic stress, demands over time are perceived as greater than resources.
- Physiological stress reactions are automatic mechanisms facilitating swift emergency action. They are regulated by the hypothalamus and include many emergency body changes, carried out through the action of the autonomic nervous system and the pituitary gland. They lessen sensitivity to pain and provide extra energy for fight or flight. They are useful to combat physical stressors, but can be maladaptive in response to psychological stressors, especially when stress is severe or chronic.

- The general adaptation syndrome is a three-stage pattern of physiological defenses against continuing stressors that threaten internal well-being. Following the alarm reaction, there is a stage of resistance in which psychological defenses are activated until adaptive resources fail in the stage of exhaustion.
- Psychosomatic diseases are physical diseases caused by chronic physiological stress reactions to perceived threats. Other diseases of adaptation occur when normal adaptive responses become excessive or are inappropriate. The "wear and tear" on the body brought about by continuing responses to stress is considered to be a factor in aging.
- Psychological stress reactions include behavioral, emotional, and cognitive elements. Mild stress can enhance performance and even be experienced as pleasant (eustress). Moderate stress disrupts behavior and may lead to repetitive, stereotyped actions. Severe stress suppresses behavior.
- Emotional stress reactions include irritation, anger, and depression. Posttraumatic stress disorders are emotional stress reactions that follow acutely stressful experiences, sometimes occurring months or years after the experience and including many behavioral, physiological, and emotional symptoms.
- Cognitive stress reactions include a narrowing of attention; rigidity of thought; and interference with judgment, problem solving, and memory.
- Psychological stressors are more common than physical stressors for most of us. Major life changes, even pleasant ones, can be stressful, as can the accumulation of everyday "hassles." Catastrophic events can be sources of severe stress, as can long-term environmental problems.
- Two basic coping strategies to deal with perceived threat are (a) treating the problem itself in some way (problem-focused coping), and (b) lessening the discomfort and anxiety we are feeling (emotion-focused coping).
- We can learn to manage stress better through: (a) changing health-threatening physiological reactions (relaxation and biofeedback), and (b) changing our cognitive strategies.
- Those most vulnerable to stress are individuals who lack a social support network and are in life situations in which they feel they have no control. Building and participating in positive social support groups is health promoting.

15

Abnormal Psychology

Jane is a 63-year-old woman who has been married for 40 years. Her husband, a very successful businessman, seems devoted to her. Jane has been very upset for the last few years, however. She has been having trouble getting out of bed in the morning and trouble getting to sleep at night. She has stopped doing any housework and sometimes doesn't even get dressed during the day. She feels guilty about her inaction, but just "can't get going." Nothing seems interesting or pleasant to her, and lately, she doesn't even feel like eating. She has another problem, too: she can't leave the house alone. If her husband or a friend is with her, she is fine, but when she's alone, she worries constantly that she'll leave the gas on or water running and cause a terrible accident. She repeatedly checks the house to make sure that everything is turned off, but when it comes time to leave, she has become too anxious to walk out the door. If someone else is with her, she trusts the report that everything will be okay, but she can't trust herself.

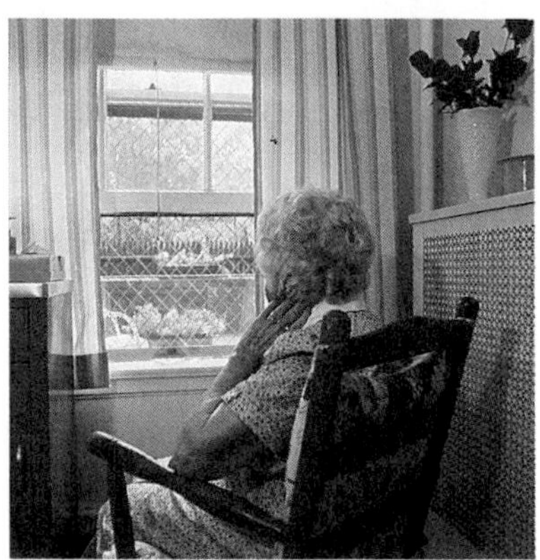

Sam is a 20-year-old college student. Lately he has been feeling fantastic. He has so much energy that he almost never needs to sleep, and he is completely confident that he is the top student at his school. He is bothered that everyone else seems so slow; they don't seem to understand the brilliance of his monologues, and no one seems able to keep up his pace. Sam has some exciting financial ideas and can't figure out why his friends aren't writing checks to get in on his schemes. He has been having problems lately with his bank, which is foolishly insisting that he not overdraw his account. It lacks the visionary wisdom, he is sure, to comprehend his financial wizardry, but its nervous concerns shouldn't be allowed to hold him back. Sam's other problem is that he is failing several of his courses, but he knows that is only because his professors are too dull to appreciate his brilliant contributions and too rigid about certain deadlines. Sam knows that he is just fine; his euphoria is not dimmed at all by his withdrawing friends, his sinking bank credit rating, and his failure in school.

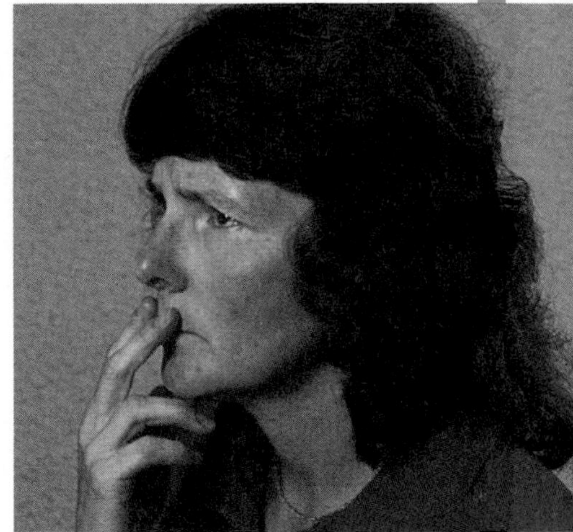

Ellen is a 28-year-old woman who has worked very hard to create a niche for herself in a highly competitive company. She lives in Los Angeles, far from her family and most of her friends. Ellen doesn't have time to make new friends, and besides, she's not sure if she can really trust any of the people she meets through her work. Ellen is ambitious and she's doing well, but, at least once a week, she experiences intense anxiety. Her heart pounds fast, she has trouble breathing, and she feels dizzy and unsteady. At the same time, she feels unreal, as if this couldn't really be happening. At these times, Ellen is terrified that she might be going crazy and worries about whether she might do something bizarre and uncontrollable during an attack. The attacks usually occur on weekends, when she is alone and has no plans. Lately she worries a lot about what would happen if she ever had an attack at work. What would people think? What would happen to her hard-won career?

What is happening to these people? In everyday language, they are having "nervous breakdowns." Although psychologists and other mental health workers do not use this term, because it is too vague to be of any value, they want to examine and understand the similarities and the differences among the psychological problems that afflict so many people in so many ways. One obvious reason to seek knowledge about these disorders of mind and behavior is to design treatments to alleviate them. In the next chapter we will examine some therapeutic approaches that have been developed to treat or prevent these disorders.

In this chapter our concern is to learn first what these disorders of thought, feeling, and action are. We want to know how they are diagnosed and classified by clinical psychologists and psychiatrists. Having surveyed a wide variety of the major categories, we will next try to understand how these disturbances come about and to discover what variables and processes may be implicated in the development and maintenance of abnormal psychological functioning.

Psychopathology is the broad area of mental disorders, studied by medical or psychological specialists. **Clinical psychology** is the field that specializes in the psychological treatment of individuals with mental and behavioral disorders. More psychologists specialize in clinical psychology than in any other subarea of psychology. Although most of them are practitioners who treat those with mental and behavioral disorders in hospitals, clinics, or private offices, others are engaged in diagnostic testing (discussed in chapter 13) or conduct research on psychopathology. Many students find the study of mental disorders and their treatment one of the most fascinating areas of psychology. (Indeed, more psychology majors enter this field of psychology than any other.) If you are one of those students, then as you read through this chapter, try to discover what it is about the topic that is so intellectually appealing while at the same time being so personally distressing—to learn about people who are suffering from the range of disorders we will review.

Before we look at the various forms that mental disorders take (and how the three *Opening Cases* relate to them), we need to put the phenomena in a broader prospective. Just how serious is the problem of mental disorder? And how do researchers and clinicians ever agree on a set of consistent terms to use in diagnosing mental disorders that can have so many different symptoms, yet be unique in any individual case?

The Problem of Mental Disorders

Have you ever: worried excessively, felt depressed and anxious without knowing why, been fearful of something you knew rationally could not harm you, felt someone was a threat to your well-being, believed you were not living up to your potential, thought about suicide as an escape, or abused alcohol and drugs to self-treat a psychological problem? It is the rare student who does not answer yes more than once to these questions.

As you might expect, the scope of this nation's problems with mental disorder is vast. It can be pervasive, touching the daily lives of many of us. It can be insidious, working its way into many situations that diminish our emotional and physical well-being. It can be devastating, destroying the effective functioning of individuals and their families, as well as creating an enormous financial burden through lost productivity and the high costs of prolonged treatment.

A **mental disorder** is defined as "a clinically significant behavioral or psychological syndrome or pattern that occurs in an individual and that is typically associated with either a painful symptom *(distress)* or impairment in one or more important areas of functioning *(disability)*" (DSM-III, 1980, p. 6).

How many people suffer from mental disorders? The dismal official picture in the United States can be seen in the figures in **Table 15.1.** Actually, these are only estimates based on readily identified populations such as patients in mental hospitals and other institutions, and clients in therapy. Such figures *underestimate* the true scope of the problem. Many disturbed people are privately treated at home, while others have learned to conceal their disturbances so that they don't act "crazy" in public. Still others act out their mental problems in ways that society does not judge as mentally disordered—perhaps joining "hate" groups or engaging in socially acceptable forms of violence. Just as unemployment statistics do not include all those who are chronically unemployed and have stopped looking for work, so, too, do statistics on mental disorders omit those who suffer in silence and all the "street people" living a marginal existence on the fringes of society.

For a greater appreciation of how serious and extensive the problem of mental disorder is, we might include all those who attempt suicide or commit violent crimes. Finally, consider the many people you know who, at some time in their lives,

Table 15.1 *Estimates of Mental Disorders in the United States*

30 million Americans (19–24 percent of the population) suffer some form of recent diagnosed mental disorder
14 million (8–15 percent) suffer anxiety/somatoform disorders, including phobias, panic, and obsessive disorders
10 million (6 percent) suffer substance abuse or dependence; most from alcohol-related problems
10 million (5–7 percent) suffer affective disorders
1.5 million (1 percent) suffer schizophrenic disorders
1.5 million (1 percent) suffer antisocial personality disorders
2 million (1–3 percent) suffer severe cognitive impairment

- During a six-month period, 16 to 24 percent of all visits by the adult population for general health or mental health care were for psychological problems.
- Prevalence of mental disorders is about the same for males and females. However, women are more likely to suffer depression and anxiety disorders, especially phobias, while men show a higher incidence of substance abuse and antisocial personality.
- The rate of mental disorders is twice as high for those under 45 years of age as it is for those who are older (excluding problems of cognitive impairment).
- Women are more likely to seek care for recent mental or emotional problems than are men. Young people 18–24 years of age are less likely than those 25–65 years to seek care for their mental problems.
- The majority of people suffering from a recent diagnosed mental disorder did not seek treatment, only about one out of every five people in need of mental health care utilized available care. In cities where the number of mental health specialists is relatively great, the percentage of the population seeking their services is much higher than where there are fewer such care providers per capita of the adult population.

(Data based on a recent, long-term survey of the National Institutes of Mental Health, reported in the Archives of General Psychiatry, Shapiro et al., 1984. The data are derived from samples of 3,000 to 3,500 adults living in each of three urban areas—New Haven, Baltimore, and St. Louis—with diagnosed disorders in the past six months.)

become their own worst enemies by letting fears control their actions or allowing distorted self-images to diminish their wills to try something new, to improve, to succeed. A tragic example of psychopathology-in-action is the case of Jim Backus, whom you probably know as the funny voice of Mr. Magoo.

Backus was a sociable humorist, a character comic in the TV series "Gilligan's Island," a writer, and a good golfer. He now is a recluse who refuses to see old friends and fears going into restaurants or working in front of a camera. He stopped writing and playing golf. An interviewer reported that: "The other day Backus sat in a chair in his home, a frightened, insecure man, contrasting tragically with the raucous extroverted Backus of old, needing reassurance that he wasn't, indeed, in the clutches of a life-threatening disease."

Backus suffered from an extreme case of hypochondria, believing he was afflicted with Parkinson's disease. Despite medical reassurances, his panic, depression, and fears got steadily worse. He told the interviewer: "I haven't been out of this house in almost six years. I was terrified when the doorbell rang. I'd run and hide. I'm trying to get over the acute panic right now as we talk. . . . Your mind can do this to you. You know it's doing it to you, but you're powerless to stop it." With the help of his wife, Backus has written the story of this living nightmare in a book entitled Backus Strikes Back *(1984). The book, in itself, is a positive sign of his being able to get well again. (adapted from Scott, 1984, p. 58)*

Statistics about the prevalence of mental disorders are likely to reveal only the tip of the abnormality iceberg. They underestimate the actual extent of the problem because they exclude many types of disordered, antisocial, self-destructive behaviors. They also don't reflect the total number of people suffering mental disorders because of the problems in defining and reporting cases. But statistics are just numbers; however large and impressive, they are always *impersonal.* Throughout this and the next chapter, as we talk about categories and processes and models, I would suggest you keep in mind also the *person*—someone like us, like the people in the *Opening Cases,* or like Jim Backus, who has lost personal control over thoughts, feelings, or actions.

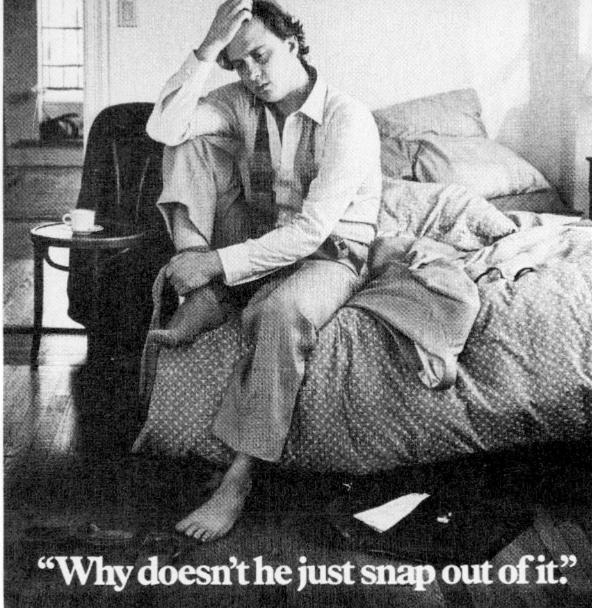

Classifying Mental Disorders

Imagine you are a physician and a patient reports headaches, pains, dizziness, palpitations, and weakness. You will likely examine a set of physical evidence from blood and urine tests, X-rays, and other sources in search of the problem's organic basis. The pattern of these tests results will help you diagnose the problem and begin to plan a treatment. Now suppose all tests prove negative, and you find no physical evidence to support or justify the reported disturbances and debilitation. What will you do? "Most physicians either send these patients away after telling them there is nothing wrong or prescribe a sedative, and then forget the whole matter or blame the patient by labeling him a 'crock'—medical slang for a neurotic complainer" (Pitts, 1969, p. 60). Between 8 and 15 percent of the population of the United States—nearly 14 million Americans—are estimated to have anxiety symptoms with no *organic* cause. An organic cause is one found in a bodily, physical function—in our genes, hormones, and brains. A mental disorder, in the absence of an organic cause, is called a *functional disorder,* based on impairment of psychological functions.

The evidence a clinical psychologist or psychiatrist must rely on to make a diagnosis is usually based on observations of a person's speech and actions—a patient's behavior and also what others report about that behavior. The first general decision to be made is whether to label the behavior *abnormal.* Once it is determined that there is something wrong with a person's behavior or personality, the next decision becomes how to judge the specific ways in which the person is abnormal. This judgment results in a diagnosis or classification of the person as belonging to one or more established categories of mental disorder. We need to know: What is abnormal, and also, what is the system that professionals use to classify abnormality into specific categories that reliably distinguish among different types of abnormal functioning?

What Is Abnormal?

What are some of the conditions under which a person might be labeled *abnormal?* We can readily generate a half dozen criteria. The person is *suffering* and acts in ways that are *maladaptive,* that do not contribute to his or her well-being. The person's behavior is *irrational;* it does not seem to make sense or be comprehensible. The person behaves *unpredictably* from situation to situation or over time, as if there were a *loss of control.* In appearance of actions, the person is *unconventional,* deviating from commonly acceptable standards. At times, the person does things that are *morally unacceptable,* violating social standards of what is right and just to do. Finally, it is more likely that a person will be labeled abnormal if he or she creates *observer discomfort,* making others feel threatened or distressed (see Rosenhan & Seligman, 1984).

It should be obvious that any one of these elements of abnormality could fit you or your friends at times. The problem is that none of them is a *necessary* condition shared by all cases of abnormality. None constitutes a *sufficient* condition that distinguishes all cases of abnormal behavior from normal variations in behavior. A solution has been to judge what is abnormal *not* as a difference in *kind* between two distinct types of people or acts, but as a difference in the *degree* to which it resembles a set of agreed upon criteria of abnormality.

A useful analogy is the "family resemblance" of children to parents; while everyone does not look exactly alike, there often are enough similar characteristics to judge that each belongs to the same family. So, too, with what is abnormal. We can use the concept of family resemblance in two ways, general and specific. First, we decide on the general resemblance of a person's characteristics to the family of characteristics we consider to be abnormal. Then we make more detailed family resemblance matches with the specific ways in which abnormal behavior is expressed.

The woman shown here is a tragic example of the dangerous effects of labeling. It took 42 years to discover that she was not mentally retarded.

DSM-III

Why do clinical psychologists and psychiatrists use labels that separate the abnormal from the normal and then distinguish among different types of abnormality? There are at least four reasons for this diagnostic labeling process (although it is abnormal *functioning,* and not *people,* that should be labeled). Labeling is for legal purposes, insurance claims, therapeutic treatment, and research uses.

The legal determination of psychological abnormality as "insanity" carries with it serious implications regarding a defendant's competence to stand trial and be held responsible for criminal indictments. It also can deprive a defendant of the right to administer his or her own estate, and it can be the basis for an involuntary commitment to a mental hospital for further evaluation and court-ordered care. Payments by insurance and health plans for mental disability and its treatment require that the disorder be diagnosed and labeled by a mental health specialist. The kinds of therapy recommended in all cases of mental disorders are always specific to a particular kind of disorder; some being ineffective or even harmful if given for the "wrong" condition. Finally, researchers studying different aspects of psychopathology or evaluating the effectiveness of treatment programs must agree on the disorder they are observing. They need to share a common set of criteria to make reliable diagnoses from the same behavioral data.

By classifying problems into useful categories professionals can design research studies to find out about the causes or the natural course of different kinds of psychological problems. Only with a good classification scheme can individuals be diagnosed reliably and studies be designed to determine the treatment programs that are most helpful for different kinds of problems.

Mental health workers have long sought to develop and agree on a common classification scheme that can be used to *diagnose* the problem of any specific individual. The currently accepted scheme is one developed by the American Psychiatric Association and set forth in a diagnostic manual for clinicians and researchers. It classifies, defines, and describes over 200 mental disorders. The complete name for this manual is the *Diagnostic and Statistical Manual of Mental Disorders, 3rd Edition* (1980), but it is known more simply as **DSM-III.** Using its carefully developed diagnostic language, clinicians can identify clinical disorders more reliably and report them in a uniform way, making possible more precise evaluation studies of the treatment that works best in a specific case.

How DSM-III Works

The attempt to classify disorders is complex and controversial. Any classification is influenced by the theory one holds about mental problems, and no one theoretical approach is shared by all workers in the field of mental health. It is unlikely, therefore, that any diagnostic scheme will ever be universally accepted, and DSM-III certainly has its critics (see, for example, Smith & Kraft, 1983). It is an improvement over earlier diagnostic approaches however. A minor revision, DSM-III-R, has just been published in response to the new research evidence generated by DSM-III and in response to problems found in the previous edition.

DSM-III tries, in particular, to minimize former differences between the basic approaches of *psychiatry* (which emphasizes concepts of disease, illness, and a medical interpretation of mental disorders) and *psychology* (which emphasizes the causal role of anxiety and learning). It does so in the following ways:

- Behavior syndromes (patterns) rather than people are classified and described. (DSM-III never refers to "schizophrenics" but rather to "people who show schizophrenia.")
- Terminology acceptable to both psychologists and psychiatrists is used, such as *mental health professionals* or *clinicians* instead of *psychiatrists*. Likewise, *mental disorder* is used instead of *mental illness*.
- When the **etiology**—the *causes* or factors related to the development of a disorder—is not known, then only *descriptive* statements are made in DSM-III; theoretical statements about the way the disturbances come about are avoided. This is important because, as we shall discuss later in this chapter, there is considerable disagreement about the causes of most mental disorders. The descriptive terms allow clinicians to develop a common language to *describe* problems, while leaving opportunity for disagreement and continued research about the best models to *explain* and *treat* the problems.

For most of the DSM-III categories, the criteria were based on the *clinical judgments* of a panel of about 100 psychiatrists and psychologists. The *reliability* of these diagnostic categories was then established by having over 800 clinicians test them in field settings where they worked—to demonstrate that different judges would use the categories in the same way. However, the *validity* of these DSM-III categories—the extent to which the differentiations and descriptions accurately represent mental disorders—remains to be tested.

In this context, validity is a complex concept. One validity question of interest is whether disorders that are regarded as unrelated might be better regarded as similar—and vice versa. For example, are all the subtypes of depression best thought of as variants of one basic kind of problem, or are there very different kinds of depression that have different causes and require different treatment? Validity studies are ongoing (Spitzer, 1981; Stangler & Printz, 1980), but determining the validity of all of DSM-III is clearly going to be a difficult task.

DSM-III does more than just put an individual into a category or pigeonhole. It differs from earlier schemes of diagnostic evaluation by requiring a clinician to assess every case of five different classes of information. Only the first three classes of information, or axes, constitute the official diagnostic evaluation (see **Table 15.2**); however, mental disorders are exclusively described on either Axis I or II. The disorders listed in Axis II consist of the personality disorders and the specific developmental disorders. The remainder of mental disorders and conditions are listed on Axis I. A clinician using this *multiaxial evaluation system* must consider the possible presence of personality traits and disorders frequently overlooked during more conventional evaluations.

Axes IV and V provide for supplemental information which can be useful when planning an individual's treatment or assessing the prognosis for improvement. The presence of a stressor associated with the onset of the mental disorder favors a positive outcome and a speedier return to the individual's standard level of functioning. Thus, a clinician assesses the severity of psychological stressors on Axis IV and the highest level of adaptive functioning in the past year on Axis V for each case.

Neurosis and Psychosis

You are probably familiar with the term *neurosis* (and its adjective *neurotic*). In earlier editions of the DSM, neurosis had been a formal diagnostic category; in the DSM-III, however, such is no longer the case. The reasoning underlying this change was that, over the years the frequent use of *neurosis* as a label had so broadened its meaning that it had become virtually useless as a reliable or valid category. As such, disorders that used to be considered under the "family name" of neuroses are now further delineated into the categories of anxiety, somatoform, and dissociative disorders; and some are also included in affective and psychosexual disorders. Even so, many people continue to feel that the term *neurosis* is a useful one, and, of course, research carried out prior to DSM-III used such categorization. You will no doubt come across it in your reading so we will take a moment to review it.

In traditional usage, **neurosis** has represented a mental disorder in which there are one or more symptoms, such as phobias or compulsions, that are ineffective attempts to deal with anxiety. There is no clear-cut organic problem, no violation of basic social norms, and no loss of orientation to reality, but an individual shows a lifelong pattern of self-defeating and inadequate coping strategies aimed more at reducing anxiety than at solving life problems. By one means or another, a neurotic person proves to others that he or she is impotent in the face of a threatening world.

Table 15.2 *The Five Axes of DSM-III-R*

Axis	Classes of Information	Description
Axis I	a) Clinical Syndromes	These mental disorders present symptoms or patterns of behavioral or psychological problems that typically are painful (distress) or impair an area of functioning (for example, being able to do schoolwork).
	b) "V Codes"	Conditions worthy of clinical interventions, not attributable to a mental disorder (for example, an academic problem, a marital problem, a phase of life problem).
Axis II	a) Personality Disorders	These are the dysfunctional strategies of perceiving and responding to the "world." Personality characteristics or traits can also be noted on this axis when *no* personality disorder exists.
	b) Developmental Disorders	Developmental disorders in children in such specific skills as reading, language, and articulation that are unrelated to any mental disorder.
Axis III	Physical Disorders and Conditions	Physical problems relevant to understanding or managing an individual's mental problems.
Axis IV	Severity of Psychosocial Stressors	On this axis the clinician rates the amount and degree of stressor(s) contributing to the current disorder. The coding of the stressor(s) goes from none or minimal to extreme or catastrophic. This judgment takes into account the sociocultural values and responsiveness of an "average" person.
Axis V	Global Assessment of Functioning	The highest level of functioning achieved in three life areas (social, work, and leisure activity) during the past year. Usually the previous level can be used as the comparison for recovery from the presenting problem.

(Based on DSM-III-R, 1987)

There is no clear dividing line between neurotic and normal individuals; the difference is one of degree. Neurotic symptoms are only rarely severe enough to require hospitalization, but they are distressing to an individual who recognizes them as personally unacceptable and alien.

Neurotic behavior patterns vary considerably, but all share a common mechanism for limiting anxiety by an avoidance of direct confrontation with its source and by an inability to consider any other way to cope with the problem. Those who suffer from the high costs of maintaining a neurotic life-style see "no exit" from life's problems and no choices among alternative ways of being. They are confined in a psychological prison in which the mind is both the jailer and the prisoner. Theologian Paul Tillich once said, "Neurosis is the way of avoiding nonbeing by avoiding being" (1952, p. 66).

The continuum from normal to neurotically abnormal breaks with the step across to psychosis. Psychotic disorders differ in kind and quality from neurotic ones, not just in their greater severity. Psychosis is the general category for a number of severe mental disorders in which perception, thinking, and emotion are impaired. A person characterized as *psychotic* is one who is suffering from a major organic or psychological dysfunction that causes him or her to feel, think, and/or act in very deviant ways. These extremely abnormal reactions may cause the person to lose contact with reality, requiring intensive treatment and perhaps hospitalization.

Some psychotic conditions result from organic brain damage which makes it impossible for a person to meet the ordinary demands of life. The **functional psychoses** consist of subgroups which are *not* attributable to brain damage, though, in some cases, subtle biochemical abnormalities may be involved.

We turn now to consideration of the major categories of mental disorders that are currently recognized by psychologists and psychiatrists. After describing the kinds of problems people experience, we will examine a number of attempts to explain these disorders and then see how the explanations can combine to give us a deeper understanding of one of the most complex mental disorders—schizophrenia.

Major Types of Mental Disorders

Although we will discuss a few of the personality disorders listed on Axis II, our focus will be primarily on major mental disorders found on Axis I of the DSM-III. We will emphasize those that are most prevalent and illustrative of the range of mental problems that humans can experience.

Three main categories must be excluded, simply because of space limitations. The first is the set of *organic mental disorders,* psychological or behavioral abnormalities associated with temporary or permanent brain damage or malfunction. They may be because of aging of the brain, disease, accidents, or excessive ingestion of substances such as alcohol, lead, and many types of pharmacological agents (such as barbiturates, amphetamines, and opiates, as discussed in chapter 7). The second category is *substance-use disorders,* which includes both dependence on, and abuse of, alcohol and drugs. We discussed many of the issues surrounding the use of drugs in the broader context of states of consciousness. The third diagnostic category is the *group of disorders that typically arise in infancy or childhood,* such as retardation, stuttering, or childhood behavior problems. Nor will we discuss the group of disorders referred to as eating disorders of adolescence and adulthood. However, there is one disorder in this category that is relevant to college women and is described in the ***Close-up:*** *A Preoccupation with Weight* on page 526.

Our discussion in this section will focus on what the various disorders look like to observers and feel like to those afflicted. That is, we will focus on *description.* In most cases, we will hold off on attempts at *explanation* until the second half of the chapter, by which time you will have a better idea of the range of disorders that are involved. Consideration of *treatment* and *prognosis* (outlook) for such problems will be the subject of the next chapter.

Personality Disorders

Personality disorders consist of long-standing (chronic), inflexible, maladaptive patterns of perceiving, thinking, or behaving. They can seriously impair an individual's ability to function in social or work settings, or cause significant distress. In DSM-III, there are twelve types of personality disorders grouped into three broad clusters of behavior that is (a) "odd or eccentric"; (b) "dramatic, emotional, erratic"; or (c) "anxious or fearful." We will discuss three of the better known personality disorders—*narcissistic* and *antisocial personality disorders,* in the second cluster, and *compulsive personality disorder,* in the third cluster.

While we all know people who seem particularly impressed with themselves, specific criteria must be met before such a pattern constitutes **narcissistic personality disorder.** People with this type of disorder have a grandiose sense of self-importance, preoccupation with fantasies of success or power, and a need for constant attention or admiration. These people have inappropriate responses to criticism or defeat, either by an apparent indifference to criticism or a marked overreaction to it. Finally, they have problems in interpersonal relationships, feeling entitled to special favors with no reciprocal obligations, exploiting others to indulge themselves, having relationships that vary between overevaluation and complete rejection, and lacking empathy for the feelings of others.

Some of these attributes may remind you of the *Opening Case* of Sam, the euphoric student. In some ways he sounds narcissistic, but other features of his problems don't fit—for example, his lack of need for sleep and his constantly euphoric mood. Later we will come to a diagnostic category that fits Sam's behavior much better.

Individuals with **compulsive personality disorder** are task-oriented perfectionists, overly devoted to their work to the exclusion of pleasure. Individuals showing this disorder often display an inability to express warm and tender emotions, along with a stubborn insistence that others do

Close-up A Preoccupation with Weight

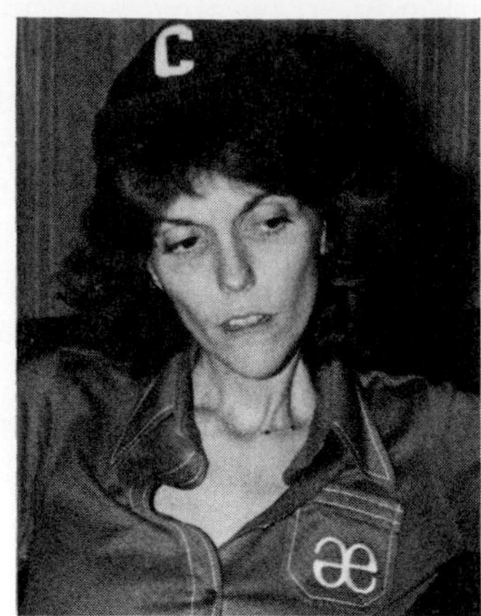

Over the past 20 years, there has been a dramatic increase in the frequency of two eating disorders, *anorexia nervosa* and *bulimia.* These disorders can cause serious health damage to an afflicted individual; in some cases, they can be fatal. Popular singer Karen Carpenter was a victim of such a disorder, dying in 1983 of cardiac arrest caused by metabolic imbalance and loss of essential proteins from severe weight loss. Although eating disorders can occur at any age, they are most commonly seen among teenagers. Furthermore, most of the victims (over 90 percent) are female. It is estimated that 5 to 15 percent of adolescent females suffer from eating disorders.

Anorexia nervosa is an eating disorder of compulsive self-starvation. It often begins when a young woman becomes self-conscious about changes in her body around puberty, or when someone suggests that she watch her weight. The woman's dieting behavior eventually gets out of control, to the point where she loses more than 25 percent of her original body weight. The woman develops an intense fear of becoming obese, even though she is underweight. Indeed, there may be a disturbance in her image of her own body—she may see herself as being "too fat" even when she is emaciated. Some of the effects of this "relentless pursuit of thinness" (or "weight phobia") are absence of menstrual periods, gastrointestinal problems, low blood pressure and pulse rate, and cardiac arrhythmia. The anorectic often denies that she has a problem, even while she is wasting away. She may eventually become so weak that she is bedridden and must be fed intravenously to prevent death from starvation.

The paradox of anorexia is that it usually strikes young women who appear to have everything going for them—they get good grades in school, they are attractive and bubbling over with energy, they have not experienced much turbulence in their adolescent years, and their family may appear to be "the perfect family." Behind this perfect facade, however, lie depression, low self-esteem, emotional conflicts, and family dysfunction.

Bulimia is an eating disorder of recurrent episodes of binge eating. A binge occurs within a short time period and involves the consumption of an excessive amount of high-calorie, easily digested foods. Following the binge, the bulimic individual will often try to purge the food she has consumed, by forced vomiting, laxative abuse, enemas, diuretics, or other means. She is aware that her eating is abnormal and often fears that she will be unable to control or stop a binge. Unlike anorexia, bulimia can occur in people of all body weights, from thin to obese. Bulimic behavior is usually done in private and is very secretive—consequently, it is often hard to detect.

Signs of bulimia include erosion of tooth enamel from stomach acids, abrasions on fingers and knuckles from vomiting, frequent disappearance of food from a household, and shoplifting of food. There are many medical complications, including chronic diarrhea, dehydration, ruptures of the esophagus or stomach, kidney failure, and electrolyte imbalances that can lead to heart failure. Like the anorectic, the bulimic individual is often suffering from major depression.

Anorexia and bulimia are not just cases of women trying to be thin. The disturbed pattern of eating is not the problem per se; it is merely the tip of the iceberg—a symptom of deeper underlying emotional conflicts. Thus, treatment requires both medical and psychological care (Andersen, 1985; Swift et al., 1986).

Anorexia and bulimia are obsessive—most victims cannot stop their self-destructive behavior without professional help. To get that professional attention, they may need *your* help first. Notice when a classmate loses a great deal of weight in a short time and express your concern. Your indifference may only serve to increase her depression. ATTEND AND CARE.

things their way. They get preoccupied with rules, roles, and trivia, while missing the big picture and ignoring the needs of others. Typically, they either avoid or postpone making decisions or completing projects; that is, they are often "all talk but little show." If this sounds like a classmate you know, it is more likely to be a male than a female, according to a survey of students seeking outpatient services in a large university clinic (Stangler & Printz, 1980).

People with **antisocial personality disorders** often create trouble for all of us. They start early in life disrupting class, getting into fights, running away from home, having promiscuous sexual experiences, never keeping their jobs. Their history of continuous and chronic antisocial actions typically includes violating the rights of others and refusing to accept social norms with respect to lawful behavior. They may break the law, develop a criminal life-style, and wind up in jail. In fact, approximately 80 percent of all criminals are diagnosed as antisocial personalities (Guze et al., 1969).

We should also note several other commonly found features among those with an antisocial personality disorder. They do not experience shame or intense emotion of any kind; thus, they can "keep their cool" in situations that would make other people emotionally aroused and upset. They also reveal an *absence* of conscience as well as of a sense of responsibility to others. These inadequately socialized individuals are also termed *sociopaths*. Although they can be found among street criminals and "con artists," we find them well represented among successful politicians and business people who put career, money, and power above everything and everyone.

You were probably able to recognize many familiar qualities in the descriptions of these three personality disorders. Most of us have some human frailties that appear among these criteria. It is important, however, to remember that to be diagnosable, they must be the predominant characteristics of a person. Few people meet *all* the criteria necessary for a formal diagnosis of personality disorder. This is also true of the more serious disorders we discuss next: some of the criteria may seem to apply to you or those you know (your "family resemblance"); others may sound very strange or even bizarre.

Personality disorders are the least reliably judged of all the mental disorders and are also the most controversial. Psychologists even disagree about whether personality disorders can be said, truly and reliably, to exist. The only *exception* is antisocial personality disorder, in which the reliability of judging its presence in any given instance is reasonably high. There is controversy about evaluating these lifelong behavior patterns independent of the *contexts* in which they developed. Economic, social, family, and cultural factors may provide better explanations of the observed symptoms of a given patient than do explanations based on a diagnosis of personality disorder. This diagnosis runs into trouble with those researchers who argue against the existence of personality traits, as you will recall from our discussion in chapter 12.

An example is seen in the current battle between psychiatrists and feminists over the label "masochistic personality disorder," a brand-new entry proposed for the revised DSM-III manual (see Franklin, 1987). Masochism is currently diagnosed as part of the psychosexual disorders in which sexual gratification requires being hurt or humiliated. Psychiatrists wanted it to be included as a more pervasive personality disorder in which a person *seeks* failure on the job, at home, or in relationships, rejects opportunities for pleasure, and engages in excessive self-sacrifice, along with other characteristics. Feminist therapists and researchers argued that such a label was biased against women and perpetuated the myth of women's masochism (Caplan, 1985). After a year-long debate the label was changed to "self-defeating personality disorder" and put in the appendix of the revised manual. Nevertheless, the political and ideological implications of diagnosing certain behavior patterns as mental disorders is clearly illustrated by this example.

In any case, beware of the natural human tendency to apply labels or categories to people. As you are no doubt aware, the labels of abnormal psychology can be very powerful and very damaging if abused. Any labeling should be left to the professionals who are trained and licensed to help individuals suffering from behavioral and mental problems. Any other use is name-calling, pure and simple. With that in mind, we shall turn now to some of the Axis I disorders, beginning with problems that are less serious and moving toward increasing levels of severity and more abnormal functioning.

Anxiety Disorders

Anxiety problems are common in the United States. Millions of people in the general population have, at some time, experienced the symptoms that psychiatric classification terms *anxiety disorders*.

All the **anxiety disorders** include physiological arousal (changes in heart rate, respiration,

A person suffering from a bridge phobia would not have been able to participate in the fiftieth anniversary of the Golden Gate Bridge.

muscle tension, dizziness) and feelings of tension, tremor, shaking, and intense apprehension without reason. Such anxiety, having no known cause, is called **free-floating anxiety.** Not knowing why the reaction is occurring, a person becomes even more upset at the feeling of losing control—"for no good reason."

There are two major subcategories of anxiety disorders: *phobic disorders* and *anxiety states.* The latter is further subdivided into generalized anxiety disorder, panic disorder, obsessive-compulsive disorder, and posttraumatic stress disorder. Physiological arousal and free-floating anxiety occur in all of them, but there are differences in a person's experience of anxiety, in the situations in which it is felt, and in the particular symptoms that develop.

Phobic Disorders

Fear is a rational reaction to an objective, identified external danger (such as a fire in one's home or being mugged on the street) and may involve flight or attack in self-defense. In contrast, a person with a **phobic disorder** recognizes that he or she is suffering from a persistent and irrational fear of some specific object, activity, or situation (the *phobic stimulus*) that causes a compelling desire to avoid it (the *phobic reaction*).

Sometimes, the phobic stimulus may not be the "real" or sufficient cause of the phobic disorder. For example, a bridge phobia (gephyrophobia) might really represent a fear of increased responsibility. A phobic person may even know this, but will still focus on the external stimulus—the bridge—that triggers the internal feelings of anxiety. At other times, a phobia is exactly what it appears to be—a bridge phobia may quite simply be a fear of bridges collapsing.

Since many fears are shared across cultures, it has been proposed that, at one time in the past, they enhanced the chances of survival for our ancestors. Perhaps humans are born with a predisposition to fear certain things which are related to objects and situations that were sources of serious danger in the distant past. This *preparedness hypothesis* suggests we carry around an evolutionary tendency to respond quickly and "thoughtlessly" to once feared stimuli (Seligman, 1971).

However, this hypothesis has difficulty explaining the many "exotic" brands of phobia that have little apparent survival value, among them:

autophobia	fear of oneself;
hypergiaphobia	fear of responsibility;
tropophobia	fear of moving or making changes;
gamophobia	fear of marriage;
blennophobia	fear of slime.

Many of us have irrational fears of spiders or snakes (or even multiple-choice tests). Such fears become phobic disorders only when they interfere with our adjustment, cause significant distress, or inhibit necessary action.

Edith is afraid of writing her name in public. She is terrified when placed in a situation where she might be asked to sign her name, and she gets the common anxiety symptoms: muscle tension, rapid heart rate, and apprehension. This phobia has far-reaching effects on her life. She can't go shopping if she needs to sign a check or credit card slip. She no longer can play golf because she can't sign the golf register. She can't go to the bank unless all transactions are prepared ahead of time in her home. She can't sign her Diner's Card at a restaurant, she can't sign any papers that require approval of a notary public, and she can't vote because she can't sign the voting register.

So even a very specific simple phobia can have a great impact on one's whole life.

Almost any stimulus can come to generate a phobic avoidance reaction (see **Table 15.3**); many hundreds are reported in the clinical literature

Table 15.3 *The Common Phobias*

	Approximate Percent of All Phobias	Sex Difference	Typical Age of Onset
Agoraphobias (fear of places of assembly, crowds, open spaces)	10–50	Large majority are women.	Early adulthood
Social Phobias (fear of being observed doing something humiliating	10	Majority arc women.	Adolescence
The Specific Phobias			
Animals Cats (ailurophobia) Dogs (cynophobia) Insects (insectophobia) Spiders (arachnophobia) Birds (avisophobia) Horses (equinophobia) Snakes (ophidiophobia) Rodents (rodentophobia)	5–15	Vast majority are women.	Childhood
Inanimate Objects Dirt (mysophobia) Storms (brontophobia) Heights (acrophobia) Darkness (nyctophobia) Closed spaces (claustrophobia)	20	None	Any age
Illness-Injury (nosophobia) Death phobia (thanatophobia) Cancer (cancerophobia) Venereal disease (venerophobia)	15–20	None	Middle age

(From Rosenhan & Seligman, 1984)

(Melville, 1977). Some phobias are much more common than others. We shall discuss two of them: agoraphobia and social phobia.

The extreme fear of being in public places or open spaces from which one cannot escape is the essential feature of **agoraphobia.** It deprives agoraphobic individuals of their freedom; in extreme cases they become prisoners in their own homes. It is not possible for them to hold a job or carry on normal daily activities because their fears constrict contact with the outside world. Agoraphobia is the most commonly cited phobic disorder among people who seek psychiatric or psychological treatment. About half of all those with phobias who are being treated in clinics suffer from this disorder. Between 2.7 percent and 5.8 percent of American adults are estimated to suffer from agoraphobia (NIMH, 1986). Most of them are women for whom the phobia begins in early adulthood, often with an extreme anxiety attack. In addition to their fear of going out into public places, agoraphobics have more psychological problems, such as anxiety, depression, and obsessive-compulsive symptoms, than do other phobic individuals. Like others with extreme anxiety, they may abuse alcohol and drugs in an effort to suppress the emotional arousal.

When the anticipation of a public appearance (speaking, writing, performing artistically, or eating in public) causes a persistent, irrational fear, a **social phobia** is operating. The person recognizes that the fear is excessive and unreasonable, yet feels compelled to avoid the phobic stimulus for fear of being humiliated or embarrassed by his or her unacceptable or inappropriate performance. The social phobic generally has no psychological problem other than this excessive performance anxiety.

A vicious cycle may develop that supports a self-fulfilling prophecy. A person so fears the scrutiny and rejection of others who will judge his or her performance that enough anxiety is created to impair the performance—"See, I told you so. I was right to avoid trying to do that in the first place." Brilliant students with social phobias have been known to drop out of law school, for example, when they discovered that public oral performance was regularly expected of them. (For a complete review of current research and treatment of social phobia and shyness see Jones et al., 1986.)

Anxiety States

Because anxiety is the chief characteristic in *all* the anxiety disorders, it may seem strange for a subcategory to be named **anxiety states.** The diagnosis of this syndrome is made when anxiety attacks occur in the *absence* of specific phobias. We will review three major kinds of anxiety states: *generalized anxiety disorder, panic disorder,* and *obsessive-compulsive disorder.* The fourth disorder that fits in the category of anxiety states is *posttraumatic stress disorder* which has already been reviewed in the last chapter.

Generalized anxiety disorder. When anxiety persists for at least a month and is generalized, without any of the specific symptoms of the other anxiety disorders, it is diagnosed as a **generalized anxiety disorder.** The anxiety itself is the principal problem. The way this anxiety is expressed varies from person to person. For a formal DSM-III diagnosis, symptoms must be from at least three of the following four categories:

1. *Motor tension* (jitters, trembling, tension, aches, fatigue, twitches, inability to relax);
2. *Autonomic hyperactivity* (heart pounding or racing, shallow breathing, sweating, dizziness, upset stomach, diarrhea, other signs of physiological overreaction);
3. *Apprehensive expectation* (continuous anxiety, worry, anticipation of some misfortune for self or others);
4. *Vigilance and scanning* (hyperattentiveness to environmental events and to one's own internal reactions, leading to distractibility, poor concentration, "edginess," and sleep difficulties).

Despite all this, a chronically anxious person continues to function with only mild impairment of his or her social life or job. The constant physical and psychological drain, however, takes a toll that may show up in greater susceptibility to many common illnesses, such as colds and flu, headaches, infections, and heart attacks.

Researchers have found that anxious patients may contribute to the *maintenance* of their anxiety by employing cognitive biases that highlight threatening stimuli.

> *Clinically anxious (but not depressed) subjects were compared to normal controls on a task that measured* attention *to a visual display of 48 threat-related or neutral words (such as* injury, agony, failure, lonely). *The words were presented in pairs for a brief duration, either a neutral word paired with a threat word or two neutral words. On a random one third of 288 trials, a dot of light (a probe) appeared in the area where one of the two words had just been flashed. The subjects pressed a button as quickly as possible when this probe appeared. The dependent variable was the speed with which the probe was detected when it replaced neutral versus threat-related words.*
>
> *The highly anxious subjects were faster than the controls in detecting the presence of the probe when it appeared in the vicinity of threat words. They shifted their* attention *toward* threatening stimuli, *while normal control subjects shifted attention away from such material. In this way, anxious patients may use an encoding bias mechanism that makes them more susceptible to noticing threatening stimuli in their environment. (MacLeod et al., 1986).*

Panic disorders. In a **panic disorder,** there are episodes of full-blown anxiety and intense feelings of unpredictability, usually lasting only minutes but recurring at least once a week, on the average. This panic attack includes symptoms of autonomic hyperactivity, dizziness, faintness, choking or smothering sensations, and feelings of unreality, terror, and impending doom. An attack can occur at times other than during physical exertion or actual threats to one's life.

Panic disorder, which tends to run in families, afflicts some 1.2 million Americans. Most often the panic attacks begin between the ages of 15 and 19, during high school and college days. Researchers have not discovered what causes panic attacks, although biological origins seem at least partially involved in panic and agoraphobia, while early learning may influence simple phobias.

The following excerpts taken during a panic attack, will help you appreciate the panic being experienced:

> *"Uh, I'm not going to make it, I can't get help, I can't get anyone to understand the feeling . . . it's like a feeling that sweeps over from the top of my head to the tip of my toes. And I detest the feeling. I'm very frightened."*
>
> *"It feels, I just get all, like hot through me, and shaky, and my heart just feels like it's pounding and breathing really really quick. . . . It feels like I'm going to die or something." (Muskin & Fyer, 1981, p.81)*

Because of the random nature of these "hit and run" attacks, *anticipatory anxiety* develops as an added complication. The dread of the "next attack" and of being helpless and suddenly out of control often leads a person to avoid public places—yet fear being alone. You might recognize the beginnings of this pattern if you look back to the *Opening Case* of Ellen, who fits all the criteria for panic disorder.

Obsessive-compulsive disorders. A thought, image, or impulse that recurs or persists is called an **obsession;** it is an unwanted invasion of consciousness, seems to be senseless or repugnant, and is unacceptable to the person experiencing it. It is difficult or impossible to ignore or suppress, though the person may try to resist it.

You probably have had some sort of mild obsessional experience, such as the intrusion of petty worries, "Did I really lock the door?" or "Did I turn off the oven?" or the persistence of a haunting melody you simply could not stop from running through your mind. Neurotic obsessive thoughts are much more compelling, cause much distress, and may interfere with your social or role functioning.

An obsessional *thought* might be "Am I the one who really killed John Lennon?" An obsessional *impulse* might be to expose one's genitals in class. An obsessional *image* might be the view of someone who disagrees with you being violently destroyed. A content analysis of the obsessions of 82 obsessional neurotics yielded 5 broad categories of obsessions, in the following order of frequency: (a) dirt and contamination, (b) aggression, (c) the orderliness of inanimate objects, (d) sex, and (e) religion (Akhtar et al., 1975).

A **compulsion** is a repetitive act carried out in a stereotyped ritual that seems to follow certain rules: a person feels compelled to engage in this excessive or exaggerated behavior. At least initially he or she resists carrying it out, but, though it appears senseless to the compulsive person when he or she is calm, it provides a release of tension when anxiety is high. In addition, preoccupation with carrying out a minor ritualistic task often leaves the compulsive individual with no time or energy to carry out the impulsive action that is unconsciously being guarded against. In some cases, a compulsive ritual seems designed to undo guilt feelings for real or imagined sins; an example is repetitive hand washing—a kind of Lady Macbeth reaction.

Obsessions and compulsions may occur separately, but they go together so often that they are considered two aspects of a single disorder. In one study of 150 hospitalized obsessional patients, nearly 70 percent had both obsessions and compulsions. Of the rest, most had only obsessions (Welner et al., 1976).

Compulsions can grow so out of proportion that they virtually enslave a person (Rachman & Hodgson, 1980). This happened with Jane, the woman in the *Opening Case* who couldn't leave her house. She had both obsessive thoughts and compulsive rituals. You should notice, though, that Jane had another problem as well which was not an anxiety problem, but involved fatigue, loss of interest, and sleep problems. This second syndrome is one we will discuss later.

"HOW CAN I RELAX WHEN I KNOW THIS COUCH WOULD LOOK SO MUCH BETTER IN THE OPPOSITE CORNER OF THE ROOM?"

Somatoform Disorders

When physical complaints suggest a physical disorder, but no organic probiems are found, the reaction is assumed to reflect psychological conflicts. Such reactions are termed **somatoform disorders** (*soma* means "body").

A mild form of turning a psychological reaction into a physical one can be seen in young children, who will point to a sudden bodily pain that justifies their crying when, in fact, they are emotionally distressed—rejected by a playmate or reprimanded by a parent, perhaps. In its neurotic form, such concern about health is a central preoccupation, with recurring and persisting complaints about illness and assorted pains. A person with this disorder seeks medical attention frequently and may spend a great deal of money on unnecessary treatment and hospitalization, including surgery for suspected tumors. We will discuss briefly two forms of this transformation of mental problems into somatic complaints—*hypochondriasis* and *conversion disorder*.

Hypochondriasis

The preoccupation, despite medical reassurance, with bodily sensations as possible signs of serious disease is called **hypochondriasis.** Individuals suffering from this disorder are often said to "enjoy poor health," for their greatest satisfaction seems to be in finding bodily symptoms that confirm their dire predictions. Their supposed ailments not only prevent active engagement in life—with its risk of failure—but also may bring attention, sympathy, and service from others. These "secondary gains" or their symptoms are powerful sources of reinforcement. For some, the choice may seem to be between "being ill" and "going crazy": Better to have a concrete physical ailment that is making them ill than a vague emotional problem for which they are somehow held personally responsible. Isn't it easier to get sympathy for a tumor in the brain than for free-floating anxiety in the mind? As we saw in the case of Jim Backus, the long-term consequences of hypochondriasis can be devastating however.

Conversion Disorder

In this extreme abnormal reaction, there is a loss of a specific sensory or motor function—a person suddenly goes blind or is paralyzed, for example—without any organic cause. The "conversion" of a working, healthy part of the body into a nonfunctional state is a **conversion disorder.**

Conversion symptoms are reinforced in two ways. An individual gets the "primary gain" of being removed from a threatening situation in a way that keeps a serious internal conflict out of awareness. The symptom usually has a symbolic value that represents at least a partial solution to that emotional conflict. Thus, a soldier who sees a wounded buddy in need of help, but is himself under heavy fire and feels unable to offer help, may express his conflict as "blindness."

Conversion reactions—and other types of mental disorders too—also achieve the "secondary gain" of extra sympathy and social support that might not otherwise be forthcoming. Such benefits, in turn, further reinforce the reactions and contribute to maintaining them. Interestingly, conversion reactions are more common in areas where the education level is low; they become rarer as the level of education increases. The disorder serves little purpose when one's symptoms violate generally available medical knowledge—and are then not "acceptable."

In a dramatic case of conversion disorder, a married, middle-aged salesman entered the hospital with what appeared to be recurring seizures that paralyzed half of his body while they were going on. Before his brain was to be operated upon, the staff made a routine psychological assessment. From the man's responses on several different tests, the consulting psychologist (Seymour Sarason of Yale University) detected a pattern that suggested a severe conflict over sexual identity. Sodium amytal was administered, and the patient was interviewed under the influence of this so-called "truth serum." His seizures disappeared while he recounted a recent (his first) homosexual exploit with a sailor he had picked up while on a sales trip. He felt enormous guilt over what he considered a "sinful act," as well as anxiety and confusion over his "manhood." Psychotherapy, rather than surgery, alleviated the conversion symptoms and helped him deal directly with his emotional and sexual problems.

Dissociative Disorders

Have you ever forgotten an appointment you really did not want to keep? Unpleasant, feared situations can be avoided by such convenient slips of memory. "Forgetting" keeps you away from a situation where your self-esteem or well-being might be threatened, but you cannot be blamed for avoiding the situation—you just forgot. Carried to an extreme, this normal mechanism can result in a sudden, temporary alteration of consciousness in the form of a severe memory loss, loss of personal identity, or even the disturbed motor behavior of wandering away from home. These are the main features of a **dissociative disorder.**

It is important for us to see ourselves basically in control of our behavior—including our emotions, thoughts, and actions. Essential to this perception of self-control is the sense of selfhood—the consistency of different aspects of the self and the continuity of our identity over time and place. Psychologists believe that, in dissociated states, individuals escape from their conflicts by giving up this precious consistency and continuity—in a sense, disowning part of themselves. We will discuss three dissociative disorders: *psychogenic amnesia, psychogenic fugue,* and *multiple personality.*

Psychogenic Amnesia

The sudden extensive inability to recall important personal material (not caused by neurological disorders) constitutes **psychogenic amnesia**—mentally caused blocking out of certain memories. Its most common form is *localized amnesia* in which

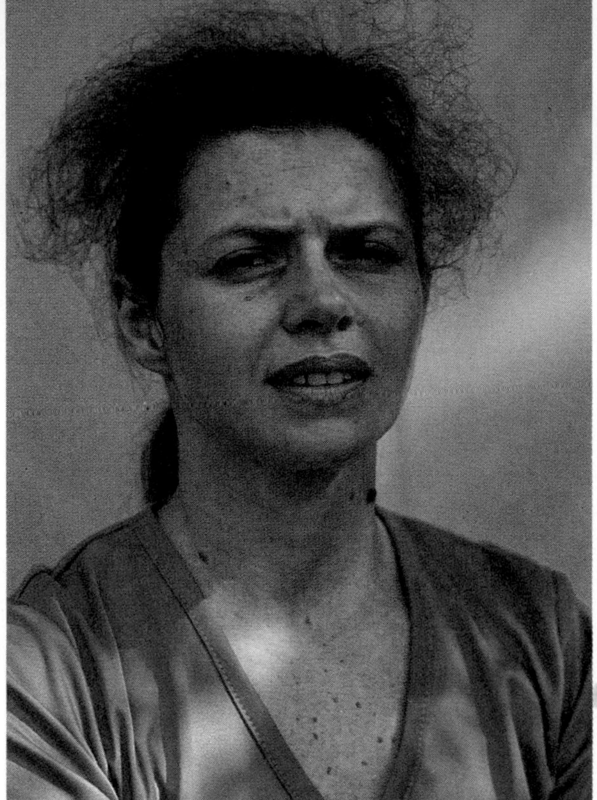

When found in a Florida park in September 1980, this woman was emaciated, incoherent, and near death. Dubbed "Jane Doe" by authorities, she was suffering from a rare form of psychogenic amnesia in which she had lost the memory of her name, her past, and her ability to read and write.

all events, usually involving some traumatic experience, during a given period of time are forgotten. A rape victim, for example, may recall nothing from the time she was approached until she wandered into a police station. In *selective amnesia* only some of the traumatic events are forgotten. The victim might remember what the rapist looked like, but have no apparent memory of the details of the violent act itself.

A brilliant scholar who experienced a series of traumatic incidents within a few months—rape, sudden death of her mother, and the breakup of her marriage—developed almost total amnesia. She remembered only the two things in her life associated with joy—her son and English literature. She had no idea of her own identity, her past, and her mother's death. She showed no recognition of those she had known for many years—her father, husband, or colleagues. She even forgot that she was always dieting and ate with a great appetite. Having put her grief and anxieties "out of mind," this young woman was typically full of very positive emotions, until over a period of several months, the repressed memories began to return, and she had to "face the reality."

Psychogenic Fugue

Often an amnesic person who has given up an old identity may actually travel to some other place, either a familiar place that was emotionally supportive at some earlier time or a completely new one. This is called a **psychogenic fugue,** from the Latin word meaning "to flee." Once in a new place, the person may assume a new identity and create a new life-style, dissociated psychologically, temporally, and geographically from his or her prior unacceptable life. Cases have been reported in which such persons were rediscovered several years after their disappearances. We do not know how many remain undiscovered and lead the rest of their lives as their "recycled" selves.

Multiple Personality

One of the most dramatic forms of a radically altered consciousness occurs in people who develop multiple personalities. **Multiple personality** is a dissociative mental disorder in which two or more distinct personalities exist within the same individual. At any particular time one of these personalities is dominant in directing the individual's behavior. Although the original personality is unaware of the other personalities, *they* are conscious of *it.* Each of the emerging other personalities contrasts in some significant way with the "true" self, perhaps by being outgoing if the person is shy, tough if the original personality is weak, sexually assertive if the other is fearful and sexually naive. Each personality has a unique identity, name, relationship, behavior pattern, and even characteristic brain-wave activity. In some cases, dozens of different characters emerge to help the person deal with a difficult life situation. The emergence of these alternate personalities, each with its own consciousness, is sudden, precipitated by stressful experiences.

Multiple personality disorders have been popularized in books and movies, such as *The Three Faces of Eve* (Thigpen & Cleckley, 1957) and *Sybil* (Schreiber, 1973). Patients experiencing the disorder typically respond best to treatment that centers on hypnotherapy. Under hypnosis, the alternate selves "come out," and a therapist can assist the patient in eliminating some of them while integrating others into a more effective single self.

Patients with multiple personalities are typically women who were severely abused physically or sexually for extended periods during childhood by parents, relatives, or close friends. They may have been beaten or locked up by those who were supposed to love them, those on whom they were so dependent that they could not fight back or run away. They have fled symbolically through dissociation. They protect their vulnerable self by creating more hardy internal actors and actresses to help cope with the traumatic situation. Somehow these abused children create an alternate reality and enter it so fully that it comes to substitute for their actual reality.

Until recently, the data on multiple personality disorders have come from single cases treated over an extended period of time. However, newer research with the collaboration of many investigators is enabling clinicians to get a more complete picture of this remarkable disorder that puts too many actors on stage for any one director to manage (see Putnam, 1984).

One study obtained questionnaire data from 450 clinicians who had treated cases of multiple personality disorders and also major depressions, for comparative purposes. As can be seen in **Table 15.4,** *the dominant features of the 355 cases of multiple personality are almost universal incidence of being abused among these mostly female patients who show high intelligence and creativity. The majority had imaginary companions and more than three fourths became alternate personalities. (R. Shultz, personal communication, Aug. 20, 1986)*

Sexual Disorders

Through sexual experiences, we are attracted to others, share deep levels of intimacy, enjoy sensuous pleasure, and may discover romantic love. These benefits of sex are learned through experience, daily observations, literature, and the mass media. On the other hand, a contrary message is also being communicated: sex is dangerous. Sex can be a weapon by which people can reject, abuse, and violate us—or we can harm others. Society provides both powerful temptations *for* and strong deterrents *against* sexual impulses and actions—thereby making sex a conflict-filled experience for many people. Sexual taboos still prevent open discussion of things sexual in many families and in schools, allowing ignorance and false myths to go unchecked.

Sexual disorders center around problems of: *sexual inhibitions and dysfunctions* and *sexual deviations.* Before going on it is important to note that there are marked individual differences within the normal range of functioning when it comes to any aspect of sexual behavior and attitudes. Many college students are often too ready to become concerned by reading "disorder" into their own sexual reactions when "different" is the appropriate descriptor.

Table 15.4 *Characteristics of Multiple Personality Disorders*

	Percentage of Patients with Multiple Personality Disorder (n = 355)	***Percentage of Patients with Major Depression (n = 235)***
Abuse		
Incidence	98	54
Types		
Physical	82	24
Sexual	86	25
Psychological	86	42
Neglect	54	21
All of the above	47	6
Physical and sexual	74	14
Gender: Female	90	73
IQ: 111 > 140	80	39
Incidence of Creativity	81	39
Imaginary Companion Phenomenon Incidence		
All ages	60	12
After age 6	49	10
Percentage Became Alternate Personalities	79	—

(From R. Schultz, personal communication, August 20, 1986)

Sexual Inhibitions and Dysfunctions

There are three stages of the normal sexual response cycle where *sexual inhibitions* may disturb one's sense of sexual pleasure, desire, or objective performance. Initial sexual desire may be inhibited so that a person does not have any fantasies or thoughts about the pleasurable nature of sexual activity. During foreplay, sexual excitement may be inhibited. Finally, during the act of sex, psychological problems can result in no orgasm or one that comes too soon or is delayed. When such inhibitions occur regularly in a setting appropriate for sexual activity, they are regarded as psychosexual disorders.

Once a therapist determines that such disorders are *not* the result of physiological or situational factors, such as trying to perform sexually when under the influence of alcohol, drugs, tension, or fatigue, then the causal focus turns toward social psychological factors. A therapist may find, for example, that a couple's relationship is troubled, or something about the sexual performance, perceived excessive demands, or lack of appropriate responsiveness of a patient's partner may be playing an inhibitory role.

Sexual Deviance

For other people, the sexual cycle presents no problem, but sexual arousal is possible only in the context of unusual sexual practices or when accompanied by bizarre imagery. Their deviation from the norm is in the thoughts or acts to which they are attracted.

Para- means *beyond; -philia* means *like* or *love.* To an individual with a **paraphilia** disorder, sexual excitement necessarily and involuntarily demands the presence of nonconventional sexual objects, sexual practices, or sexual circumstances. Pedophilia, fetishism, masochism, and sadism are some of the paraphilias. **Pedophilia** is a paraphilia that involves an adult's action or fantasy about sexual activity with young children. In **fetishism,** sexual excitement is achieved repeatedly with the aid of nonliving objects (fetishes). A fetish may be an article of clothing or other objects associated with someone with whom the individual had an intimate involvement (real or imagined).

What makes paraphilias mental disorders rather than just "kinky, odd-ball" preferences is that individuals with paraphilia disorders cannot be aroused sexually *except* in the presence of specific objects. **Voyeurism** is a paraphilia in which one's preferred means of sexual arousal is observing others disrobing, nude, or engaged in sexual activity—without their awareness of being observed. A voyeur does not derive the same pleasure from strip-tease shows, public nudity, or viewing pornography.

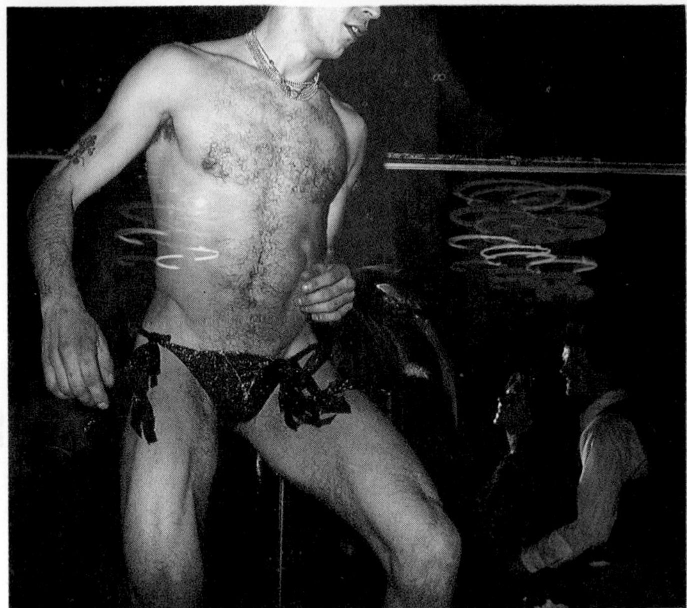
A voyeur will not get the same pleasure from watching a stripper as from watching someone getting undressed without their awareness.

The time, energy, planning, risks, and negative consequences associated with sexual deviance are illustrated in the recent case of a middle-age voyeur and panty thief.

> *Upon being paroled from prison on convictions of burglary, theft, and lewd conduct, Darrell F. won his request for the judge to return more than 300 pairs of unclaimed panties and other lingerie that he had stolen while working as a tree trimmer. He would ask to use the restroom and then steal the female employer's undergarments. Darrell F. also advertised for women to live in his house as housekeepers. He would then videotape them, through a two-way mirror, while they were bathing. The judge ruled that a parole officer would keep the man's two-way mirror. (Associated Press, September 13, 1986)*

Consider that the significance of these fetish objects to the man was great enough to "go public" to get them back—and become a wire service news item.

Masochism and **sadism** both involve sexual excitement through the experience of personal suffering. Sexual masochists prefer arousal that comes from being humiliated, bound, or beaten. They are unable to achieve adequate sexual arousal without the fantasy or actuality of their own pain, abuse, and suffering (sometimes self-inflicted). Sexual sadists are all too willing to wield the whips against masochists. They get sexual excitement from inflicting injury or humiliation on others—with or without their informed consent. When the disorder becomes severe, sadists may rape, torture, or kill their victims. Not all rapists, however, are sexual sadists—only those whose motivation is to inflict suffering in order to become sexually excited.

How do paraphilias develop? One explanation suggests that they are the results of an abnormal first sexual experience. Another suggests that the sexual deviance may arise from *conditioning* based on an imagined sexual fantasy or a memory of early sexual arousal. A young man masturbates repeatedly, using the context of a fantasy or remembered contact as the arousal stimulus, and the orgasm he achieves powerfully reinforces this activity. Over time, this imagined sexual stimulus becomes the only one capable of inducing sexual arousal. Thus a middle-aged pedophiliac person may have masturbated to the memory of his first prepubertal sexual encounter—he aged, but his fantasy partners remained children.

One's theory or knowledge about the origins of paraphilias has implications for treatment. In the case of the middle-aged pedophiliac reconditioning procedures would be appropriate (Marquis, 1970; McGuire et al., 1965).

Affective Disorders

Affective disorders are mood disturbances in which a person is either excessively depressed or excessively elated (manic), or in some cases both, in turn, without organic cause. The person's behavior is exaggerated and self-defeating, but he or she is not out of touch with reality. In some cases the disorder is severe enough to be labeled *psychotic.*

During a **manic episode,** the mood is one of elation, expansiveness, or irritability. Accompanying this highly charged mood state (lasting for at least a week) are restless activity; a flight of ideas; pressure to talk fast, loud, and often; and an inflated, grandiose sense of self-esteem. Typically there is a decreased need for sleep, and the person is easily distractible. Caught up in this manic mood, the person shows unwarranted optimism, takes unnecessary risks, promises anything, and may give away everything. You may recognize that we have defined a syndrome which almost exactly captures the problems of Sam, the young man described in the *Opening Case.* Almost always, those who have manic episodes will also have a history of periodic depressive episodes.

At the other extreme of the mood continuum is a **depressive episode,** in which there is a loss of interest or pleasure. This disturbance is usually coupled with feelings of sadness, discouragement, and dissatisfaction, and usually occurs with other symptoms, such as feelings of worthlessness or guilt, decreased energy, and suicidal thoughts, as shown in **Table 15.5.** Looking at these, you probably recognize Jane, the woman described earlier. We have already pointed out the obsessive-compulsive pattern she displayed; in addition, she was experiencing a major depression. It is not uncommon for people to meet the criteria for more than one of the problem categories in the DSM-III classification. Just as they can have the flu and a bladder infection at the same time, it is quite possible, especially in the milder forms of affective disorder, to be both abnormally depressed and anxious at the same time.

The more severely disturbed patients tend to show only a depressive pattern—called *unipolar depression,* or some alternate between manic and depressive periods, often in some regular cycle—called *bipolar depression.* With or without treatment, an episode typically runs its course (perhaps in a few weeks or months) and then subsides—but can recur later if not treated. Between episodes there are often long periods of normal functioning.

Depression has been called the "common cold of psychopathology." Of all forms of pathology described in this chapter, it is the one most students are likely to have already experienced. We have all,

Table 15.5 *Characteristics of Clinical Depression*

Characteristic	Example
Dysphoric Mood	Sad, blue, hopeless; loss of interest or pleasure in almost all usual activities
Appetite	Poor appetite; significant weight loss
Sleep	Insomnia or hypersomnia (sleeping too much)
Motor Activity	Markedly slowed down (motor retardation) or agitated
Guilt	Feelings of worthlessness; self-reproach
Concentration	Diminished ability to think or concentrate; forgetfulness
Suicide	Recurrent thoughts of death; suicidal ideas or attempts

at one time or another, been depressed at the loss or separation from a loved one, at the failure to achieve a desired goal, or from chronic frustration and stress.

This "garden variety" depression that most of us experience sometime in our lives is one end of a continuum. At the opposite pole are the depressive disorders. The mood, thought, motivational, and physical deficits associated with depressive disorders are more severe, but not qualitatively different from ordinary depressive symptoms. Also the biological and psychosocial correlates of both the "ordinary" and "pathological" forms of depression have been found to be similar (Hirschfeld & Cross, 1982). Estimates of the prevalence of affective disorders reveal that about 20 percent of females and 10 percent of males have a major depression at some time in their lives. Bipolar depression is much more rare, occurring among about 1 percent of adults. Bipolar disorder is influenced by genes, shown in studies of identical twins where there is an 80-percent *concordance* rate, (rate at which the twin pair shares a trait) and in adoption studies where the rates of the disorder among adoptees correlate with their biological parents, not their adoptive parents.

The toll that major depressive disorders take on those afflicted, their families, and society is enormous. One European study found that those with recurrent depression spend a fifth of their entire adult lives hospitalized, while another 20 percent are totally disabled by their symptoms and do not ever work again (Holder, 1986). In the United States, depression accounts for the majority of all mental hospital admissions, but it is still underdiagnosed and undertreated (Bielski & Friedel, 1977). According to a 1983 NIMH survey, 80 percent of those suffering from clinical depression never receive treatment. Because of the cyclical nature of clinical depression, 85 percent of those who have been hospitalized *relapse* and require treatment again.

Symptoms of Unipolar Depression

There are four categories of symptoms seen in those suffering from unipolar depression.

- *Mood:* sadness is the dominant emotion, accompanied by crying, loss of joy in any activity, and feelings of anxiety, shame and guilt.
- *Thought:* a sense of low self-esteem comes from thinking of oneself as a failure, as an incompetent who deserved to be blamed for troubles. There is also a pessimistic belief in an unchangeable, hopeless future.
- *Motivation:* a "paralysis of the will" sets in, which inhibits initiating and responding. This prevents a patient from working, engaging in hobbies, or even from making love. Decision making also falls victim to this suspension of motivation (Hammer & Padesky, 1977).
- *Physical symptoms:* There is a loss of appetite for food, and for sex; difficulties in sleeping and a general state of weakness and fatigue. It is also common to observe the depressed person in a slumping posture.

An inventory of depressive symptoms has been developed by Aaron T. Beck (1967) to assess the number of these symptoms a person is experiencing and their severity. The Beck Depression Inventory is widely used in depression research with college students. (See also "Depression at an Early Age" in *The Best of Science.)*

Bad News View Versus Reality Appraisal

One current view of depression centers on the theme of negative cognitive distortions. Aaron Beck (1976) has argued that a depressed person shows three specific cognitive distortions, which he calls, "the cognitive triad" of depression: a negative world view, a negative self-conception, and a negative appraisal of the future. The depressed person anticipates failure, readily accepts blame for it, and misattributes success to chance or luck rather than skill. The sense of a hopeless future is shown in reactions of hospitalized depressives to experimental tasks of skill and of luck. When comparison subjects (nondepressed or schizophrenics) succeeded on skill tasks, their expectations for future

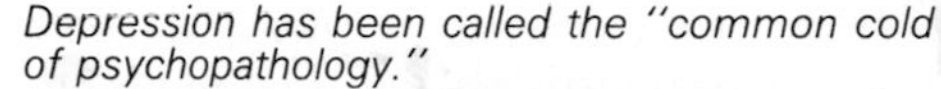

Depression has been called the "common cold of psychopathology."

success went up but were lowered by failing. Not so with depressed patients—success on skilled tasks did *not* "go to their heads," nor did failure have an effect. They simply assumed that their responses had a noncontingent effect on future success (Abramson et al., 1978). However, other research paints a different picture of depression as an accurate source of self-appraisal. One study compared self-ratings and observer ratings of depressed patients with those of patients suffering from other disorders and those of normal individuals.

> *As expected, the depressed group rated themselves less positively on social competencies than did either of the nondepressed groups. Unexpected results were found in the discrepancies between the way patients rated themselves and the way observers rated them. Judged by their agreement with observer ratings, the depressed patients were the* most realistic *in their self-perceptions, while the nondepressed controls distorted their self-perceptions in a* positive *direction. This "illusory glow" of perceived competence helped perpetuate positive self-attributions among the nondepressed and also made them likely to attend to and remember more positive than negative events. (Lewinsohn et al., 1980)*

A realistic, depressed person "sees it like it is"—if it is negative feedback. Support for this intriguing new look at the cognitively "wiser but sadder" world of the depressed person comes from another study in which depressed and nondepressed students were confronted with a series of problems that they had to deal with.

> *The problems varied in the degree of* contingency *between the performer's responding and the outcomes obtained—the extent to which the person's behavior actually influenced the outcomes. Nondepressed students selectively distorted the situation. They overestimated the degree of contingency when they experienced the desired outcomes, while underestimating it when the outcomes were not what they wanted—thus giving themselves more credit than they were due when things went well and less blame than they deserved for undesired results. In contrast, the depressed students gave accurate judgments of the degree of contingency that really existed between their responses and the outcomes in both cases. (Alloy & Abramson, 1979)*

Another study confirmed the first finding—nondepressed subjects took more credit than they were due for successes on an achievement test and less blame for failures, blaming them on "bad luck." However, the depressed subjects also showed distortion in both cases—in the *opposite direction,* attributing successes to just "luck," while attributing failures to their lack of ability (Barthe & Hammen, 1981). It is not yet clear how far we can generalize the results of these studies using mildly depressed college students to depressive disorders that require hospitalization.

Sex Differences in Depression

Many explanations have been advanced to account for the greater incidence of unipolar depression in women (Boyd & Weissman, 1981). Although each of them has some empirical support, none can account for the magnitude of sex differences in depression. A new proposal points to the response styles of men and women once they begin to experience negative moods (Nolen-Hoeksema, 1987). According to this view, women accentuate the negative, while men distract themselves from it.

Socialization training of women encourages them to pay attention to their moods, to experience them, talk about them, but not actively try to cope with them. For men, the rule is never feel bad, never show it, and do whatever is necessary to get over depressed feelings. Paying attention to one's negative moods can increase thoughts of negative events and cycle back to increase negative feelings. Thus, the more active male response of engaging in distracting physical and cognitive activities may be more adaptive in general than the female response of thinking about moods and thus amplifying them.

Depression and Youth Suicide

The most extreme consequence of any psychological disorder is suicide. While most depressed people do not commit suicide, most suicides are attempted by those who are suffering from depression (Schneidman, 1985). They commit suicide at a rate 25 times higher than nondepressed comparison groups (Flood & Seager, 1968). In the general population, some estimates of the number of suicidal deaths run as high as 100,000 per year. Since depression occurs more frequently in women, it is, therefore, not surprising that they *attempt* suicide about three times more often than do men; but men's attempts are more successful—they tend to use guns, while women use less potentially lethal means, such as overdoses of sleeping pills (Perlin, 1975).

One of the most alarming social problems in recent decades is the rise of youth suicide. Every 9 minutes a teenager attempts suicide, and every 90 minutes a teenager succeeds. In one week, 1000 teenagers will try suicide and 125 will succeed in killing themselves. In the last two decades the suicide rate among American teenagers has jumped by 300 percent (Coleman, 1987).

A suicide hot line can save a teenager from committing suicide. It can provide emotional backup to youths who feel lost in today's society of highly mobile families, divorcing parents, peers exerting pressure, and less available people.

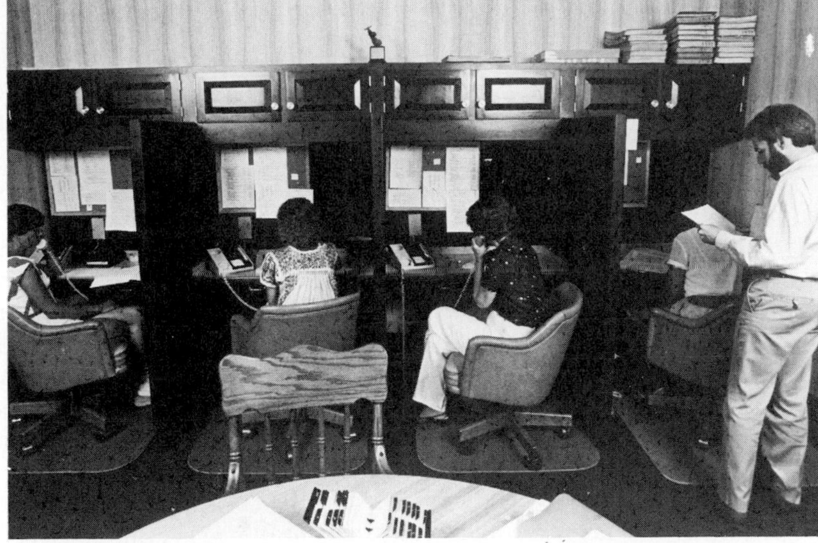

What life-style patterns are found most commonly to be associated with youth suicides? Among males the majority of suicides are found with those who have conduct disorders (aggressive, abusive, unruly behavior) mixed with drug abuse. The next most common pattern is the hard-driving male perfectionist who is socially inhibited and overly anxious about many social or academic challenges. Among females, depression ranks as the primary predictor of youth suicide. These symptoms reflect serious emotional disorders in the lives of suicidal youths that go unrecognized or not treated.

Youth suicide is not a spur-of-the-moment impulsive act, but typically occurs as the final stage in a period of inner turmoil and outer distress. The majority of young suicide victims have talked about their intentions to others or written about them. Thus, talk of suicide should always be taken seriously (Shafii et al., 1985). In addition to long-standing psychological problems of maladjustment, there are several precipitating factors that can trigger suicidal actions. The breakup of a close relationship is the leading traumatic incident for both sexes. Other significant causal antecedents that create shame and guilt which overwhelm immature egos are being assaulted, beaten up, raped, or arrested for the first time. Suicide is an extreme reaction to these acute stressors, especially when adolescents feel unable to cry out to others for help.

Girls and boys parallel their adult counterparts in the way they go about committing suicide. Boys are more likely to use guns—and to succeed. Girls are more likely to try suicide, but, because girls are more often part of a social support network than are boys, they are more able to confide in others about their distress (Holden, 1986a, 1986b). What suicide makes apparent is the interplay of social-environmental forces and individual psychological processes. Recognizing the signs of suicidal thinking and the experiences that can start or intensify such destructive thoughts is a first step toward prevention. Edwin Shneidman (1987), a psychologist who has studied and treated people with suicidal tendencies for almost 40 years concludes that: "Suicide is the desperate act of a perturbed and constricted mind, in seemingly unbearable and unresolvable pain. . . . The fact is that we can relieve the pain, redress the thwarted needs and reduce the constriction of suicidal thinking" (p. 58). Being sensitive to signs of suicidal intentions and caring enough to intervene are essential for saving lives of youthful and mature people who have come to see "no exit" for their troubles except total self-destruction. (See also "Suicide Signals" in *The Best of Science*.)

Paranoid Disorders

Paranoid disorders are among the more fascinating and frightening of all the forms of psychopathology. There is only one major symptom in a paranoid disorder: a persistent delusion. A **delusion** is a rigidly held belief that persists despite contradictory information about its content and lack of social support for its truth. Paranoid delusions typically consist of scenarios in which individuals are sure that some person or group is posing a serious personal threat. Recall that hallucinations, which characterize schizophrenic disorders, differ from delusions in being false visual or auditory perceptions.

There are four types of paranoid delusions:

1. *Delusions of Persecution:* Individuals feel that they are constantly being spied on and plotted against and are in mortal danger of attack. Delusions of persecution may accompany delusions of grandeur—an individual is a great person, but is continually opposed by evil forces.
2. *Delusional Jealousy:* Individuals become convinced—*without* due cause—that, for example, their mate is unfaithful. "Data" are contrived to fit the theory and prove the "truth" of the delusion.
3. *Delusions of Grandeur:* Individuals believe they are important or exalted beings, such as millionaires or great inventors.
4. *Delusions of Reference:* Individuals misconstrue chance happenings as being directly aimed at them. A paranoid individual who sees two people in earnest conversation immediately concludes that he or she is being talked about. Even lyrics in popular songs or words spoken by radio or TV actors are perceived as having some special message for the individual, often exposing some personal secret.

In the early stages of a paranoid disorder, the ideas that make up the delusional belief often do not fit together well and even contain elements that are inconsistent. Over time, as the tale is retold and practiced, it becomes more coherent, logical, and systematized. The accusations seem more rational, and other people—especially strangers—may sympathize with the individual's plight or even offer support in this "struggle against the forces of evil." A paranoid disorder is classified as *paranoia* when the persecutory delusional system lasts for at least six months.

Another curious aspect of this disorder is the relatively high intelligence and economic level of paranoid people compared to those suffering from all other psychological disorders. Paranoid individuals can usually function for some time without others realizing their need for treatment and hospitalization. Except for the highly specific delusion, there are often no other signs of pathology. Their personalities are intact; they usually maintain jobs and go through daily functions without impairment. However, social and marital adjustments are typically poor, in part because people close to them are either the targets of the delusions or "safe" listeners who are forced to hear the sorry story constantly (Meisner, 1978).

Paranoid reactions are often precipitated by nonsocial external events that do, in fact, threaten a person's sense of self-esteem, security, and autonomy. These include threats to life (from disease, illness, major surgery, and war), impaired sensory functions, social isolation, senility, or abrupt change of status because of immigration, unemployment, or demotion (see ***Close-up,*** p. 541). Many of us react to such threats to our self-esteem by *introjecting* (internalizing) them, blaming ourselves, and feeling self-reproach. In paranoid disorders, by contrast, they are *externalized:* blame is turned outward onto external agents.

Paranoia can be frightening to the community when its suspicion turns into overt hostility and frequent law suits—or worse, when the paranoid delusional system is shared by several individuals. In this case, a persuasive paranoid person, such as Charles Manson or cult leader Jim Jones, may recruit other people into a campaign to rid the world of some threat embodied in people that fit a given category. When three or more share the delusion, it can become an ideology, protected by the free speech amendments of our constitution. In this way, bizarre social movements may arise.

Schizophrenic Disorders

There is an underlying continuum between normal reactions and most other disorders; everyone knows what it is like to be depressed or anxious, even though most of us never experience these feelings at the degree of severity that constitutes a disorder. Schizophrenia seems to represent a qualitatively different experience. Schizophrenic people do not necessarily pass through a neurotic stage, nor do very disturbed neurotic individuals eventually become schizophrenic. In fact, whereas *anxiety* is often predominant in the disorders presented up to now, anxiety tends to be *absent* or at least peripheral in schizophrenia. Neurotic individuals seem to be "too much" in contact with their worlds (of guilt, frustration, fear, and rejection). In contrast, schizophrenic individuals have minds that seem to have been "loosed from their moorings"—to be sailing off to far-away worlds of their own.

The **schizophrenic disorders** constitute a severe form of psychopathology in which personalities seem to disintegrate, perception is distorted, emotions are blunted, thoughts are bizarre, and language is strange. The person with a schizophrenic disorder is the one we conjure up when we think about "real" mental disorder, "madness," psychosis, or insanity.*

*Schizophrenia is *not* a "split personality" as popularly described. It is a disordered, disintegrated personality, while *split personality* better describes cases of multiple personality disorder.

Close-up *Why Are You Whispering About Me?*

What is madness? To have erroneous perceptions and to reason correctly from them.

Voltaire, 1764

Elderly people seem especially prone to paranoid thinking. This tendency was originally thought to be traced to circulation disorders in brain functioning brought on by senility which, in turn, created the disordered thought processes of paranoia. However, it has recently been discovered that many older patients hospitalized for paranoia have had unrecognized hearing deficits (Cooper, 1976).

If people cannot properly hear what other people are saying and do not realize that the problem is their own sensory impairment, there is a good likelihood that they will find a social cause for the problem. In trying to make sense of the unusual perceptual experience (people are moving their mouths in apparent conversation, but little sound is heard), a hearing impaired person may reasonably assume they are whispering. If confronted with this accusation, the others deny it (because they aren't), but then they become "liars" (because the person sees what they are doing). In other scenarios, not recognizing one's hearing loss can result in perceived lack of respect on the part of others who are seen as "turning their back." Because the polite "good-bye" or the request to "please wait while I check on it" is not heard, the older person reacts with anger—to the dismay and irritation of others.

Does this mean that paranoia may simply reflect perfectly rational cognitive processes in the service of explaining an unrecognized perceptual disorder—as Brendan Maher (1974) has hypothesized? The following study was designed to find out.

Normal, healthy male college students were induced to experience the perceptual disorder found in many older paranoid patients—namely, deafness without awareness. A hearing deficit was induced through hypnotic suggestion in these subjects, along with amnesia for its source. Each subject was brought to a social situation in a laboratory where he was to work on some tasks with two other students. They were actually confederates of the experimenter, who enacted a standard script of recalling a funny party where they had met. Several solitary and group tasks followed, during which the confederates spoke often to each other, but only occasionally to the subject—creating the opportunity to feel excluded.

Across a variety of measures, these young subjects acted as if they were paranoid. They were suspicious, irritated, angry, and hostile (in their self-ratings and according to ratings by the confederates). On the MMPI and other personality tests designed to assess paranoia, they changed significantly toward paranoia after this experience. They were significantly more paranoid on all assessment measures than either of two control groups, one in which subjects had been hypnotized to be temporarily deaf, but with awareness of the deafness and its source, and the other in which subjects were given a different posthypnotic suggestion, but with no hypnotically induced deafness. (Zimbardo et al., 1981)

Copyright, 1976, Universal Press Syndicate. Reprinted with permission. All rights reserved.

This finding lends support to the theory that a cognitive-social process underlies the development of paranoid delusions in some cases. It points to the importance of full medical checkups for older people (and others, too) before a psychiatric diagnosis is made of apparently abnormal behavior. For the elderly paranoid person found to be suffering from an undetected hearing disorder, the first recommended therapy consists of simply providing a hearing aid. It should also make us more aware of how easy it is to be unaware of the source of some personal perception of reality that differs from that of others—and thus use perfect logic to reason incorrectly from that false initial premise to a "crazy" conclusion.

Between two and three million living Americans at one time or another have suffered from this most mysterious and tragic mental disorder. Half of the beds in this nation's mental institutions are currently occupied by schizophrenic patients. Overall, it is estimated that 2 percent of the population will have episodes of schizophrenia during their lives. This estimate is much higher for college students (Koh & Peterson, 1974) and for the urban poor (Dohrenwend & Dohrenwend, 1974). The first occurrence of a schizophrenic episode more commonly occurs for men *before* they are 25 and for women after 25 but before they are 45 years old (Lewine et al., 1981).

Mark Vonnegut, son of novelist Kurt Vonnegut, was in his early twenties when the first symptoms of schizophrenia appeared. While pruning some fruit trees, he recalled hallucinating, distorting the reality that was there, and creating a reality that wasn't:

> *I began to wonder if I was hurting the trees and found myself apologizing. Each tree began to take on personality. I began to wonder if any of them liked me. I became completely absorbed in looking at each tree and began to notice that they were ever so slightly luminescent, shining with a soft inner light that played around the branches. And from out of nowhere came an incredibly wrinkled, iridescent face. Starting as a small point infinitely distant, it rushed forward, becoming infinitely huge. I could see nothing else. My heart had stopped. The moment stretched forever. I tried to make the face go away but it mocked me . . . I was holding my life in my hands and was powerless to stop it from dripping through my fingers. I tried to look the face in the eyes and realized I had left all familiar ground. (1975, p. 96)*

During the next weeks, young Vonnegut's behavior went out of control more often and more extremely. He cried without reason. Terror would evaporate into periods of ecstasy, with no corresponding change in his life situation. "There were times when I was scared, shaking, convulsing in excruciating pain and bottomless despair." For 12 days he ate nothing and did not sleep. While visiting friends in a small town, he stripped and ran naked down the street. Suicidal despair nearly ended his young, once promising life. In Eden Express *(1975), Mark Vonnegut tells the story of his break with reality, its forms, and his eventual recovery after being hospitalized twice for "acute schizophrenia."*

Some people do *not* recover from the acute episodes, but instead go on to become chronically schizophrenic. Observing such chronic patients, one typically sees social withdrawal, eccentric behavior, illogical or incoherent speech, and seemingly inappropriate affect (mood and emotion). These patterns can go on and on, associated with impaired personal grooming and hygiene and a failure to follow social rules of appropriate behavior. Whether such people are internally experiencing the thoughts and feelings described by Mark Vonnegut we cannot know—but their suffering is usually all too apparent.

In this final section on mental disorders, we shall examine the main types of schizophrenic reactions and the psychological processes that are distorted when a person is drawn into this "other reality." It will be apparent why schizophrenic reactions represent mental disorders of a different kind and not merely a difference of degree of deviance from normal, optimal functioning (see Bellak, 1979).

Schizophrenic Reaction Types

Imagine all the things that possibly could go wrong with a person's mental life: with that view, welcome to the world of schizophrenia. *Thinking* becomes illogical; the normal associations among ideas are remote or without apparent pattern. *Language* may become incoherent—a "word salad" of unrelated words—or an individual may become mute. *Hallucinations* occur, involving imagined sights or sounds (usually voices) that are assumed to be real. A person may hear a voice that keeps a running commentary on his or her behavior, or may hear several voices in conversation.

Delusions are common; often a person believes that he or she is persecuted or a person of great importance. A person can also experience delusions of jealousy, bodily processes, religion, or death and destruction—for example, someone might believe that his or her brain is rotting away. Some delusions are absurd, without possible factual basis, such as the belief that one's thoughts are being broadcast, controlled, or taken away by alien forces.

Emotions may be flat or inappropriate to the situation. *Psychomotor behavior* may be disorganized (grimaces, strange mannerisms), or posture may become rigid. Even when only some of these symptoms are present, there will certainly be deteriorated functioning in work, social relations, and self-care.

There is also a current trend toward viewing schizophrenia not as a single or unitary disorder, but as a cluster of disorders—the schizophrenias—and thus as a heterogeneous concept (Haier, 1980). In this thinking, clinical subtypes are defined on the basis of biological, genetic, or neurophysiological variables rather than by "classic" symptoms, such as hallucinations and delusions. For example, when two groups of schizophrenic

Table 15.6 *Types of Schizophrenic Disorder*

Type of Schizophrenia	***Major Symptoms***
Disorganized (formerly Hebephrenia)	Inappropriate behavior and emotions; incoherent language
Catatonic	Motor behavior is frozen, rigid, or excitable
Paranoid	Delusions of persecution or grandeur with hallucinations
Undifferentiated	Mixed set of symptoms with thought disorders and features from other types

(Based on DSM-III-R, 1987)

patients were compared—one with and the other without a family history of schizophrenia—the two groups were found to differ consistently in their brain wave response to electrical stimulation although they were not distinguishable on the basis of clinical symptoms (Asarnow et al., 1978).

Reliably diagnosing schizophrenia has been a problem for clinicians trying to understand and treat this disorder. The DSM-III classification deals directly with this problem by using explicitly defined operational criteria, summarized in the chart of types in **Table 15.6,** and by narrowing the boundaries between types of disorders.

In the *disorganized type,* a person shows severe disorganization of emotional responding, language, and social behavior. Affect is blunted (no high or low degrees of emotion), inappropriate to an emotional stimulus, and often silly (giggling "at nothing"). Language is so incoherent, full of unusual words and incomplete sentences, that communication with others breaks down. Delusions are disorganized, not coherently structured around a theme. Mannerisms are unusual, odd, and childish; hypochondriacal complaints are frequent; and social withdrawal is extreme. This is a chronic disorder that rarely shows remission once it starts in adolescence.

Mr. F. B. was a hospitalized mental patient in his late twenties when he was interviewed and given a battery of psychological tests (by the author). When asked his name, he said he was trying to forget it because it made him cry whenever he heard it. He then proceeded to cry vigorously for several minutes. Then when asked about something serious and sad, Mr. F. B. giggled or laughed. More striking was his disorganized speech production, evidenced in his answers to interview questions, sentence completions, and proverb interpretations, a few examples of which follow.

Q: What sort of mood have you been in for the past few days?

A: If the world moved, the world moved.

Q: Has anyone been unfair to you?

A: At home a person misses what they are deprived of and don't get, don't see. Something that one person cooks best no one knows where it comes from.

I regret: a person is taking away another person's feelings and giving him their own.

A mother: is a mother, becomes a mother. No one knows why a mother is a mother, they know in their hearts. They know why they criticize.

I like: filling myself and not caring nothing.

Proverb: "When the cat's away the mice will play."

Interpretation: Takes less place. Cat didn't know what mouse did and mouse didn't know what cat did. Cat represented more on the suspicious side than the mouse. Dumbo was a good guy. He saw what the cat did, put himself with the cat so people wouldn't look at them as comedians.

Mr. F. B.'s mannerisms, depersonalized, incoherent speech, and delusions are the hallmarks of the *disorganized* or *hebephrenic* type of schizophrenia.

In the *catatonic type,* a person seems frozen in a stupor, with little or no reaction to anything in the environment. The person is also mute. Rigidity of posture occurs despite efforts to get the person to move. Negativism is displayed in the form of motionless resistance to instructions. Sometimes a catatonic's negativity takes the form of doing the opposite of what is requested, sitting when told to stand or standing when asked to sit. Posturing is inappropriate or bizarre positions are voluntarily assumed. When someone moves a catatonic, he or she will "freeze" in the new position with the body assuming a "waxy flexibility" like that of a soft plastic toy. Excitement sometimes alternates with the stupor; then motor activity is agitated, apparently purposeless, and not influenced by external stimuli.

In the *paranoid type* of schizophrenia, a person's delusions are persecutory, grandiose, or jealous. Hallucinations occur that are filled with voices or images of people organized around themes of persecution or grandiosity. A paranoid patient's anger, unfocused anxiety, and argumentativeness can lead to violence. Gender identity confusion can lead to fear of homosexuality. Onset tends to be later in life than other schizophrenic types. Unlike other types of schizophrenia, the paranoid type rarely displays obviously disorganized behavior. Instead it is more likely that behavior will be intense, quite formal, and focused on specific themes around which the delusions are organized.

In the *undifferentiated type,* a person exhibits prominent delusions, hallucinations, incoherent speech, or grossly disorganized behavior that fit the criteria of more than one other type—or no clear type. This type is thus a hodgepodge of symptoms not clearly differentiating among various schizophrenic reactions.

Schizophrenic Process

A number of intriguing characteristics of the schizophrenic process are being discovered through controlled psychological research. Schizophrenic patients, as a group, exhibit a greater sensitivity to sensory stimuli than normal subjects. This hypersensitivity results in a "flooding" by external stimulation and great distractibility, making it difficult for the person to find constancy in the sensory environment. Disturbed thought patterns may thus be the consequence of an inability to give sustained selective attention to particular events or processes that are taking place.

In order to think, a person may attempt to shut out external stimulation, yet the attempt is not completely successful and the immediate stimulus situation keeps intruding. Not being able to filter out and ignore irrelevant stimuli results in a confusion of "signals" and "noise." Not surprisingly, a schizophrenic patient shows a loss of abstract thinking in favor of concrete thinking. Improved experimental studies of the biology and psychology of attention, comparing normal and schizophrenic individuals, are needed to enhance our understanding of the way the world of schizophrenia becomes so different from ours (see Garmezy & Matthysse, 1977).

A schizophrenic patient's speech seems to be under the control of immediate stimuli. Distracted from complete expression of a simple train of thought by constantly changing sensory input and vivid inner reality, a schizophrenic speaker does not make sense to a listener. The incomprehensibility of schizophrenic speech is due, in part, to bizarre intrusions by thoughts that are irrelevant to the statement being uttered—intrusions that the person cannot suppress. Normal speaking requires that a speaker remember what has just been said (past), monitor where he or she is (present), and direct the spoken sentence toward some final goal (future). This coherence between past, present, and future is not possible for a schizophrenic individual; thus he or she cannot maintain long interconnected strings of words.

It has been argued that bizarre schizophrenic speech is a particular brand of nonsense in which there is a deviation from normal whenever a person comes to a "vulnerable" word—one that has multiple meanings to him or her. At that point, a personally relevant, but semantically inappropriate, word is used. For example, a patient may say, "Doctor, I have pains in my chest and hope and wonder if my box is broken and heart is beaten." *Chest* is a vulnerable word; it can mean a respiratory cage or a container like a *hope* chest. *Wonder* could mean *Wonder Bread,* kept in a bread *box.* Similarly hearts *beat* and are *broken* (Maher, 1968). By carefully listening to schizophrenic speech, it is often possible for a clinician to decode the sense in what appears at first to be pure nonsense (Forest, 1976).

Psychotic patients often lump together "what is" and "what ought to be." They may dissociate effects from their causes, actions from thoughts, feelings from actions, conclusions from premises, or truth from evidence. It has been suggested that whereas most of us evaluate the reality of our inner worlds against criteria in the external world, psychotic individuals *reverse* this usual reality-testing procedure. Their inner experience is the criterion against which they test the validity of outer experience (Meyer & Ekstein, 1970). Theirs is a world in which thinking it makes it so. Thus, it may be that what appears to us as bizarre, inappropriate, and irrational behavior follows from the creation of a closed system that is self-validating and internally consistent.

With her arm raised in a rigid, uncomfortable pose, a woman diagnosed as catatonic schizophrenic stands silent and motionless, seemingly oblivious to her surroundings.

Understanding Mental Disorders

In examining the specific categories of disorder, we have come from the vague popular conception of "nervous breakdown" to more precise descriptions of disorders that include aspects of cognitive, emotional, and behavioral functioning. However, when the question is not *how* mental disorders afflict individuals, but instead *why* they do, then we find little agreement.

In this final section we shift our focus to examine a diversity of viewpoints that attempt to explain the "why" of mental illness. First, we will consider explanations that have been popular at different historical periods and in other cultures. Then we'll see how several current scientific models account for these phenomena and how, together, they can add to our understanding of the causes of schizophrenia—that most puzzling of all challenges to scientist, physician, and lay person. Finally, we will look briefly at the role of judgment in the decision that someone is mentally disordered and at the problem of public stigmatizing of the mentally ill in our society.

Major Models of Mental Disorder

In every age, in every known society, there has been some explanation for mental disorders that was in accord with the dominant, accepted view of the causes of good and evil, health and sickness. In some instances, these models have begun by assuming that the disorder is not logically explicable. In other cases, the disorder has been seen not as an unrelated event but as a special case of broader phenomena that are understood. Only in the last hundred years have we begun to have models based on scientific research, whose predictions can be checked by further research.

In earlier times, when religious views were very influential, abnormal behavior was assumed to be caused by *demonic possession,* the devil's take-over of someone's body and mind. During the Renaissance (about 1350–1630 A.D.) when intellectual and artistic enlightenment flourished, so did the Inquisition, which found untold thousands of people guilty of being bewitched—and sentenced them to death. One symptom of demonic possession was "sudden loss of reason" (see ***Close-up*** on p. 546 for a modern view of the causes of one's becoming "bewitched").

Culture and "Madness"

All cultures establish certain rules (norms) to be followed and roles to be enacted if people are to be considered normal and acceptable members. Each culture also maintains more general belief systems about the forces that determine life and death, health and sickness, success and failure. This means that there is some *cultural relativity* in what is judged as "mad" or abnormal in different societies: what one sees as abnormal, another may see as appropriate (such as wearing your mother's skull around your neck to ward off evil spirits). It also means that some styles of mental disorder are more likely than others to be seen in a particular society (see Triandis & Draguns, 1980). Thus our view of the origins and manifestations of psychopathology are broadened by taking a cross-cultural perspective (see Mezzich & Berganza, 1984).

On the other hand, all known cultures consider people abnormal if they (a) exhibit unpredictable behavior or (b) do not communicate with others. Some symptoms of mental disorder appear to be *universal* manifestations of affliction and are regarded as pathological in all cultural settings. In such distinctly contrasting groups as the Eskimos of northwest Alaska and the Yorubas of rural tropical Nigeria, we find descriptions of a disorder in which beliefs, feelings, and actions are thought to come from a person's mind over which he or she has lost control. This pattern resembles what is diagnosed as schizophrenia in the United States (Murphy, 1976).

In many cultures—not only preliterate ones but "developed" ones too—folk beliefs about the causes of mental illness are part of a more general world view about unexpected personal disasters—sudden illness, infertility, crop failure, and premature deaths of loved ones. These discontinuities in life's drama are attributed to the operation of "evil magic." Unnatural effects are induced by supernatural influences through spells and hexes of one person on another who is envied or resented for some success. Thus some human enemy calls upon a malign agency to bring down the unsuspecting victim or a family member. This view is seen in the witchcraft theories of West Africa, in sorcery among Cree Indians of Canada, in the voodoo practices of Haitians, and in the "evil eye" beliefs still common among most Mediterranean peoples (Wintrob, 1973).

In many cultures, notably those of some African groups and of the southwestern American Indians,

Close-up Salem Witchcraft: Possession, Mental Disorder, or Food Poisoning

In the year 1692, the New England colony of Salem, Massachusetts, was swept by an outbreak of public hysteria that resulted in the execution of many people accused of witchcraft. Most of the people accusing others were young women who had been behaving in strange, unexplained ways. The victims suffered convulsions and reported sensations of being pinched, pricked, or bitten. Many became temporarily blind or deaf; others reported visions and sensations of flying through the air. Many reported feeling nauseated and weak; they also experienced other physical problems, such as swollen faces.

When someone's behavior suddenly deviates from the normal, others always seek an explanation. For the people of Salem, who accepted without question the prevailing explanatory model of that time, the explanation was clear: the women were victims of witches in the community. To the modern mind, other explanations seem more reasonable. Some have argued that the women were probably suffering from conversion disorders, others that they may have been schizophrenic. These explanations share the assumption that the symptoms reflected some sort of mental disorder.

More recently, a new hypothesis has been proposed—that the "bewitched" were victims of poisoning from ergot fungus, which had contaminated their rye crop, the primary grain source at that time (Caporeal, 1976). This hypothesis of a physical cause for the strange symptoms has been investigated by historian Mary Matossian (1982), who has traced court records, agricultural records, weather records, and medical literature to pull together a picture of the way the outbreak could have occurred.

The weather preceding 1692 provided perfect, cool, damp conditions for the growth of the fungus. Young women are more susceptible to ergot poisoning, and all the households affected by the "witchcraft" symptoms farmed land which most favored the growth of ergot-infected rye. The symptoms of ergot poisoning closely fit the available behavioral records: convulsions, sensations of crawling or pinching on the skin, spasms of facial muscles and tongue, and so on. In addition, ergot is the source of lysergic acid diethylamide (LSD), a potent hallucinogen. Even cows grazing on land near the affected households were reported to show similarly strange symptoms (for a critique of the hypothesis, see Spanos & Gottlieb, 1976).

We will probably never know for certain what happened in Salem in 1692; records are too limited to validate or refute the ergot hypothesis completely. We do know it was the only place and the only time in the United States where "witchcraft" broke out. We, in the 1980s, looking back on our ancestors of almost 300 years ago, have very different models to explain the bizarre behavior they observed. Our descendants in 2280 may look back on our explanations as equally naive and inappropriate, but they will undoubtedly share the need to find a satisfactory explanation when others behave in a deviant, mystifying fashion.

mental disorder is seen not as something in an individual, but as part of an *ecological relationship:* it is a sign of *disharmony* in the relationship of tribal members to their earthly environment and spiritual reality. Treatment, in this view, consists of communal rituals that renew the vitality of the bonds among an afflicted individual, his or her society, and the natural habitat in which he or she lives (Nobles, 1972).

If these cross-cultural beliefs about mental disorder as disharmony in a person's social relationships seem "quaint" and unscientific, consider that, to the extent that an individual feels *isolated* from a meaningful social context or is not part of a social support network, he or she is, in fact, "at risk" for a variety of pathological conditions, as you saw in the preceding chapter. Isolation plays a primary causal role in many cases of depression, suicide, mass murder, rape, child-abuse, paranoia, and psychotic states. *Social isolation is perhaps the best single predictor variable of most pathological reactions.*

Biological Theories

In sharp contrast to the views that emphasize social and environmental factors in the development of mental disorders are the predominantly biological theories. Theories about the biology of schizophrenia point to different factors that play key roles in an individual's bodily functioning. Among them are genetic factors, hormonal imbalances, altered brain dopamine systems, and structural abnormalities in the brain (Nasrallah & Weinberger, 1986). It is generally agreed that the brain is a biochemical organ whose elements are held in delicate balance. A number of conditions can disrupt this balance, predisposing a person to mental disorder.

One way abnormal brain functioning can be brought about is through faulty heredity. Some interpret schizophrenia as a hereditary disease because people genetically related to schizophrenic individuals have a greater likelihood of becoming affected than those with no schizophrenic relatives (Kessler, 1980). We will review some of this evidence a little later.

In recent years, rapid advances in the field of neurobiology (biology of the brain) have linked certain mental disorders with specific abnormalities in biochemical processes (as we noted in chapter 4). Biochemical interpretations of disorder have also been encouraged by studies showing the ways in which drugs can alter the normal reality of the mind, as well as by the proven success of chemical therapy in alleviating certain pathological symptoms (Bowers, 1980). In addition, mental disorders have been linked with severe malnutrition, brain injury, lead poisoning, oxygen deficiency, and pathology of the metabolic activity of brain cells.

According to the traditional **medical model,** mental illness was the result of a disease of the nervous system. Patients so afflicted were to be treated by "curing the disease" rather than by merely working to eliminate the symptoms of strange behavior.

A medical model implies that a disturbed person is a passive victim of disease processes. It also minimizes the importance of environmental stress, personal conflict, maladaptive learning patterns, and distressed interpersonal relationships in the development of mental disorder. Current biological theories, however, are going beyond this to a much broader view of the subtle ways in which neurochemical processes can change our processing of information and our interactions with those around us.

An unusual example of a biological approach to understanding some kinds of mental disorder comes from an experiment that sheds new, bright light on depression. Some people regularly become depressed during the winter, especially in the long Scandinavian winters. In most species, including humans, the level of *melatonin* (secreted by the pineal gland into the blood) rises after dusk and falls at or before dawn. Melatonin is implicated in sleep processes as well as circadian (24-hour) rhythms that set the body's biological clock.

> *When depressed patients and normal control subjects were exposed to bright light in the morning, melatonin onset was advanced (occurred earlier) and it was delayed by evening light. Bright morning light also reduced the symptoms of depression in those patients who regularly suffered from seasonal patterns of recurring winter depression. It appears that these patients may be effectively treated by a biological intervention that "resets" their abnormal circadian rhythm. (Lewy et al., 1987)*

Psychological Approaches

Psychological models recognize that some mental disorders are *organic,* with a physical, biochemical basis, but assume that most mental disorders are caused by psychosocial variables. The key is unusual experiences and learning that occur in the absence of brain pathology. Within the overall psychological approach, different models have been developed with their own accounts of the way a normal person is transformed into one who functions abnormally. Of the many psychological models of abnormality, we will outline three dominant ones—the psychodynamic, the behavioristic, and the cognitive models—those we have used throughout our journey to help make sense of the various phenomena encountered.

Freud's psychodynamic model. Sigmund Freud rejected the view of a suffering individual as a passive victim of either demons or disease. He proposed a more dynamic view in which an individual was seen as an active—though unknowing—agent in creating his or her mental anguish.

As we noted in earlier chapters, Freud thought that unconscious motivation and the repression of unacceptable impulses accounted for much that was abnormal. He developed psychoanalytic theory so that it rationally explained much apparently irrational and senseless neurotic behavior. His ideas profoundly changed our basic conception of human nature; he believed that neurotic disorders were simply an extension of "normal processes" that we all experience in psychic conflict and ego defense. In his classic work *The Psychopathology of Everyday Life,* written in 1904, Freud tried to demonstrate that, at times, all human beings experience distortions of thinking and feeling which are *similar in kind* to those of an emotionally disturbed neurotic individual—but just not so severe.

Freud was a neurologist whose theory was really an extension of the medical model. His psychodynamic theory of neurosis assumed an inner core of psychic functioning, disturbed by an inability to handle excessive inner conflict. From this disease core spring the manifest symptoms that we can observe (Freud, 1949). However, a patient is unaware of the connection between the symptoms and their underlying origin and thus perceives them as irrational.

Freud's plan envisioned a model of mental functioning that would ultimately integrate the biology of the brain with the psychology of the mind (Pribram & Gill, 1976). His vision also provided a foundation for a whole new psychological approach in which learning, thought processes, and social relationships play key roles.

Behaviorist models. Freudian notions gained ready acceptance among American clinical psychologists and psychiatrists. However, you will recall that American research psychology from the 1930s to the early 1970s was dominated by a behavioristic orientation. To those who insisted on observable responses as the only acceptable psychological data, psychodynamic processes were too vague to be useful. Recasting them in the language of behavioral learning theory was one step toward integrating some of the theoretical richness of Freud's concepts into an empirically based view of the way people learn—maladaptive as well as adaptive behavior patterns (Dollard & Miller, 1950).

Current behavioral approaches to understanding maladaptive behaviors typically examine people's inadequate coping strategies. Often behavior is inhibited or ineffective, not because a person is intellectually unaware of what to do, but because high levels of anxiety are causing rigidity or interfering with the translation of plans into meaningful actions. Behavior might also be affected if an individual has learned self-defeating strategies. By discovering the environmental contingencies that maintain any undesirable, abnormal behavior, an investigator can recommend treatment to change those aspects of the *situation.* Sometimes changing the situation will positively affect a person's behavior (see Franks & Barbrack, 1983).

Cognitive models. Over the past decade, a cognitive view of human nature has replaced the strictly behavioristic view. It suggests that we should *not* expect to discover the origins of mental disorders in the objective reality of stimulus environments, reinforcers, and overt responses. Rather, what is important in disordered—as well as in ordered—functioning is what we *perceive* or *think* about ourselves and about our relations with other people and our environment. Among the cognitive variables that can guide—or misguide—our adaptive responding are our self-esteem, our perceived degree of control over important reinforcers, and our beliefs in our own efficacy to change the way we act to cope with threatening events.

This newest approach assumes that emotional upsets are caused not directly by events, but by the mediating processes of our perceptions and interpretations of events. Psychological problems are seen to be a result of our reality distortions about a situation or ourselves or to be based on faulty reasoning, misattributions, or poor problem solving.

None of us can get past our perceptions and interpretations to see the world directly; we have only our perceptions to go by, bolstered by the context of conceptions, generalizations, and meanings we have built up through our experiences so far. Sometimes our conceptions help us and sometimes they harm us; either way, they are our own per-

These four genetically identical women each experiences a schizophrenic disorder, which would seem to suggest a hereditary role in the development of schizophrenic disorder. For each of the Genain quadruplets, the disorder was different in severity, duration, and outcome.

sonal way of dealing with the complexities and uncertainties of everyday life.

> *Man creates his own gods to fill in gaps in his knowledge about a sometimes terrifying environment, creating at least an illusion of control which is presumably comforting. Perhaps the next best thing to being the master of one's fate is being deluded into thinking that he is. (Geer et al., 1970, pp. 737–38)*

None of these broad models is adequate for a complete account of all mental disorders. Some fare well for certain disorders—such as the psychodynamic approach to understand some anxiety disorders, the learning approach to understand phobias, or the cognitive approach to understand depression. Similarly, some models are helpful in illuminating one facet of a disorder, but do not offer an adequate causal analysis. When we come to the puzzle of schizophrenia, none of them seems adequate, although several contribute important pieces of a solution.

Using the Models to Make Sense of Schizophrenia

> *Despite thousands of scientific publications and innumerable psychiatric theories, no one is yet certain as to what is fundamental in the schizophrenic process. (Snyder, 1974, p. 73)*

The same conclusion can be drawn about the etiology of this severe mental disorder. We do not yet know what causes a person to take the twisted path in life that can lead to the cul-de-sac of schizophrenia.

Different models point to quite different initial causes of schizophrenia, different pathways by which it develops, and different modes of treatment (as we shall see in the next chapter). Biologically oriented researchers look for problems with brain mechanisms caused by *inherited disorders* or *biochemical malfunctioning.* From a psychodynamic view, schizophrenia is a *regression to an infantile stage* of functioning caused by an inability to handle id/ego sexual impulses. This leads to an erosion of the boundaries between the internal ego and external reality. To a behaviorist, the origins of schizophrenia can be traced to *social reinforcements* for behaving abnormally. The cognitive model emphasizes *attentional* and *perceptual problems.* Let's look further at the contributions several of these models can make to our understanding of the way a person may become a patient with a schizophrenic disorder.

Genetic Predisposition

It has long been known that schizophrenia tends to run in families (Bleuler, 1978; Kallmann, 1946); thus, the possibility of genetic transmission of some predisposition for schizophrenia is a likely causal candidate. Three independent lines of research—family studies, twin studies, and adoption studies—point to a common conclusion: persons "genetically at risk" for schizophrenia (related genetically to someone who has been schizophrenic) are more likely to become affected than those who are not (Kessler, 1980). A large body of empirical research supports the notion that a *potential* for schizophrenia may be transmitted genetically (Gottesman & Shields, 1976).

In the general population about one percent will become schizophrenic at some time in their lives. When both parents are schizophrenic, the schizophrenia risk for their offspring is about 40 percent. Where either parent is normal, the risk for the offspring drops sharply to about 14 percent. It is greater with first-degree relatives (siblings and children), greater in families with many affected relatives, and greater where schizophrenic reactions are severe (Hanson et al., 1977). In fact, for all close relatives of a diagnosed "index case" of schizophrenia, the risk factor may be as great as 46 times higher than the average risk for schizophrenia in the general population (see **Figure 15.1**).

However, the genetics of schizophrenia are not clear-out. Critics of the genetic hypothesis of schizophrenia argue that the available evidence is weak for all types of schizophrenia except for chronic forms of the disorder. They point to the fact that 90 percent of the relatives of schizophrenics do not have schizophrenia according to current DSM-III criteria (reported by Barnes, 1987).

Just "running in families" does not prove that the cause of a behavior is hereditary, because family members share the same environment as well as the same heredity. To separate the influence of heredity from that of learned components in schizophrenia, researchers study twins and adopted children. Where one member of a pair of *identical twins* is schizophrenic, the chances that the other will also be affected are 4 to 5 times greater than among pairs of fraternal twins, though in both cases the twins usually have shared the same general environments. Put technically, among monozygotic (identical) twins the **concordance rates** for schizophrenia (rates for cases in which both twins are affected) far exceed the concordance rates among dizygotic (fraternal) twins. Yet environmental factors also play a role, as shown by the fact that the concordance rates among identical twins are far from perfect: in many cases where one member of the pair develops schizophrenia, the other one never does.

The most compelling evidence for the role of genetic factors in the etiology of schizophrenia comes from adoption studies. When the offspring of a schizophrenic parent are reared by a normal parent in a foster home, they still have the same risk for the disorder as if they had been brought up by the biological parent (Heston, 1970; Rosenthal et al., 1975). In addition, adoptees who are schizophrenic have significantly more biological relatives with schizophrenic disorders than adoptive relatives with the disorder (Kety et al., 1975). Another study showed that adopted children of biologically normal parents raised by schizophrenic individuals were much less likely to be diagnosed later in life as schizophrenic than were children born of schizophrenic parents who were raised by normal, adoptive parents (Wender, 1972).

Figure 15.1 *Genetic Risk for Schizophrenic Disorder*
Out of a sample of 100 children of schizophrenic parents, from 10 to 50 percent will have the genetic structure that can lead to schizophrenia. Of these, about 5 percent will develop schizophrenia early and 5 percent later in life. It is important to note that as many as 40 percent of the high-risk subjects will not become schizophrenic. (Adapted from Hanson et al., 1977)

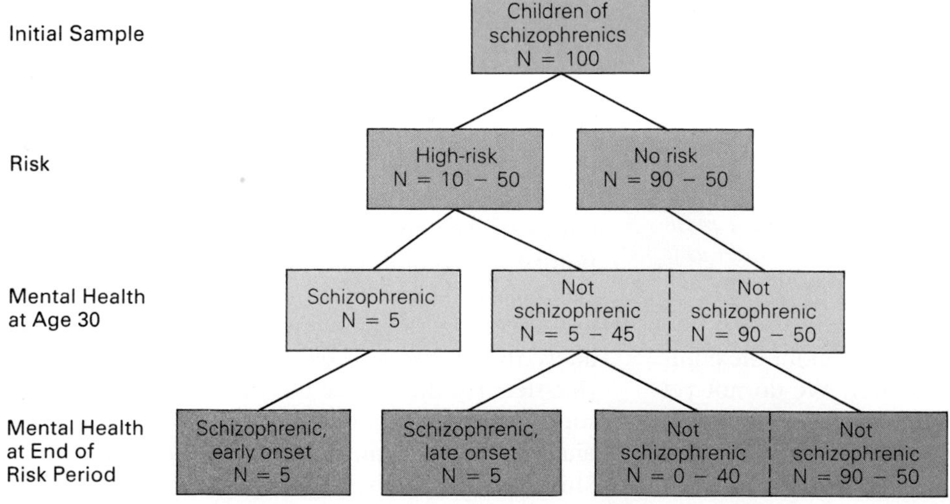

In some cases, a physiological—or medical—problem can affect the way a person is treated by others—which, in turn, can either minimize or exacerbate the person's problems. Even where physiological abnormalities are present, it can be useful to look also at the social context in which mental disorders occur.

> *A study of pairs of twins in which only one twin was schizophrenic found that those who became schizophrenic had been smaller or weaker at birth or had been less healthy as young children. These fragile twins then had become the objects of intense worry and attention on the part of concerned adults. When these twins became older and faced adulthood, with its accompanying demands for autonomy and separation from parents and home, they were overwhelmed, and symptoms of schizophrenia appeared. (Yahraes, 1975)*

In these cases biology, social environment, and personal experiences had interacted to set the stage for a full-blown schizophrenic reaction.

Biochemical Processes

"For every twisted thought there is a twisted molecule" is one assumption of a biochemical model of schizophrenia. Particular biochemical materials and processes in the brain are viewed as essential for the production—and reduction—of schizophrenic reactions. This viewpoint gained support in the 1950s with the development of new "miracle drugs" (the Phenothiazine tranquilizers) that altered certain schizophrenic disorders in dramatic ways.

The success of drug therapy has led medical researchers to search for the natural biochemical processes that influence the development or remission of schizophrenia. The most promising biochemical research today is focused on specific blood substances, neurotransmitters in the central nervous system, and opiate receptors in the brain.

Dopamine is one neurotransmitter that may be responsible for both the abnormalities in movement found in Parkinson's disease and the rigid catatonic postures and other motor symptoms seen in schizophrenia. The **dopamine hypothesis** holds that schizophrenia is associated with a relative excess of dopamine at specific receptor sites in the central nervous system (Carlsson, 1978). This view states that schizophrenic symptoms may be the result of the relative increase in the activity of neurons that use dopamine as their neurotransmitter. Researchers are studying the relationships between drugs that alter the availability or reception of dopamine and changes in patterns of movement and other symptoms of schizophrenic disorders. Rather than higher levels of the neurotransmitter itself, there may be an increased number of receptors for dopamine in the brains of schizophrenics, according to new data from several medical laboratories. Although the dopamine hypothesis is the most tenable one concerning the biochemical mechanisms for schizophrenia, the evidence is circumstantial and not yet compelling. There is also the possibility that dopamine availability may be one factor in the sequence of development of schizophrenia, but not the elusive central factor.

It is unlikely that one biological "silver bullet" will ever be found that will explain the origins of the wide range of schizophrenic symptoms. There is no question, however, that increasingly refined methodology will clarify our understanding of the biochemical processes at work in schizophrenia.

Family Interaction

If it is difficult to prove that a highly specific biological factor is a *sufficient* cause of schizophrenia, it is equally hard to prove that a vague general psychological one is a *necessary* condition. At best, what we can expect to discover is the relative contributions of each of a complex of variables that together produce a schizophrenic reaction pattern. Just as genetic factors can make an individual biologically vulnerable, so environmental factors (such as parental rejection or overprotection, excessive or inconsistent discipline, or extreme insecurity) can psychologically predispose some individuals to mental disorder. Studies of the family structure of schizophrenic patients, as well as of other features of their social context, reveal the extent to which functional psychosis may represent learned ways of attempting to cope with chronic stress and unresolvable conflicts (Liem, 1980).

One of the most reliable predictors of schizophrenic development is a pattern of *social isolation* during adolescence, in which an individual withdraws from interacting with others. This may be a consequence of feeling different or "abnormal" in some way, or of not having learned how to relate to other people in a positive and meaningful way, or both.

Sociologists, family therapists, and psychologists have all studied family role relationships in the development of schizophrenia; generally, these studies have been guided by psychodynamic theory (Lidz et al., 1965). Many such studies show that one of the most abnormal things about the backgrounds of schizophrenic children is the use of the

All adolescents like some time to themselves, but if there is a pattern of social isolation, it could be a predictor of schizophrenic development.

child by unhappy parents in working out their own feelings of frustration and hostility. Often the child is cast in the role of "buffer" or mediator and made to feel responsible for the continuation or failure of the marriage.

Another finding has been that the basic *power structure* in families with children at risk for schizophrenia differs from that of families with low-risk children. For example, in the families of schizophrenic children (or children who later become schizophrenic), parents often tend to form coalitions that exclude the child. The schizophrenic patient's failure to differentiate between self and external world may also be traced to an early, intense *symbiotic attachment* between mother and child in which the two failed to differentiate themselves from each other, were highly dependent on one another, intruded in each other's lives, and had difficulty separating (Mahler, 1979).

Studies of disordered family communication show less responsiveness and less interpersonal sensitivity in the speech patterns of families with a schizophrenic member than in normal families. In families with a disturbed offspring, the members do not listen to each other nor spend as much time in information exchange as do normal families. Members of families with withdrawn adolescents are less able to predict each other's responses in a test situation (see Goldstein & Rodnick, 1975).

The disordered communication in these families can "drive the child crazy" by distorting his or her reality through concealing or denying the true meaning of an event, or by injecting a substitute meaning that is confusing (Wynne et al., 1979). **Double bind** is the term for a situation in which a child receives multiple messages from a parent that are contradictory and cannot all be met. A mother may complain that a son is not affectionate, yet reject his attempts to touch her. Torn between these different verbal and nonverbal meanings, between demands and feelings, a child's grip on reality testing may begin to slip. The result may be that the child will see his or her feelings, perceptions, and self-knowledge as unreliable indicators of the way things are "really like" (Bateson et al., 1956).

These interesting studies of deviance in family communication styles have treated the family as a *closed system.* Current research is examining the family as a functional unit in a larger social context, a unit that is influenced by many context factors, including available resources, the state of the economy, extended family relationships, social class, occupations, and other "macro" variables (see Bronfenbrenner, 1977).

Cognitive Processes

Among the hallmarks of schizophrenia are deficits in attention, thought, memory, and language. Some psychologists argue that, instead of being consequences of schizophrenia, these deficits may play a role in causing the disorder. "The crucial behavior, from which other indicators of schizophrenia may be deduced, lies in the extinction of attention to social stimuli to which 'normal' people respond" (Ullmann & Krasner, 1975, p. 375). Attentional deficits may involve ignoring important environmental or cultural cues that most people use to socially regulate or "normalize" their behavior. They may lead a person to notice remote, irrelevant thought or word associations while thinking or talking, thereby confusing these distracting peripheral ideas and stimuli with the main points or central themes.

Schizophrenic thought disorder is in part a result of an inability to focus or sustain attention on relevant task features. This impaired selective attention then causes poor performance across a variety of perceptual and cognitive tasks (Garmezy, 1977; Place & Gilmore, 1980). What is the nature of this attentional disorder? Results of a recent neurophysiological study support the hypothesis that schizophrenic attentional deficits are because of an inability to control and maintain an effective selective processing strategy, rather than a general slowness of information processing or an absence of attentional selectivity.

> *On the basis of evoked brain potentials (see chapter 4) measured during dichotic listening tasks that required attention to auditory signals in one or the other ear (or in both together), researchers found that schizophrenic subjects* can *focus their attention selectively on information in different ears, but only under certain conditions. They perform well in the early stages of selecting one channel of information based on some physical stimulus characteristic (such as its pitch). They are poor at processing information that requires a response to a stimulus target that has been detected. They also perform much worse than a normal comparison group of subjects when* divided attention *is required to select information coming into both ears at the same time. Thus, their disorder appears to be in the cognitive mechanism that controls the strategy for selectively attending to certain kinds of information. (Baribeau-Braun et al., 1983)*

It is clear that genetic predispositions, biochemical processes, family structure and communication, and cognitive-behavioral processes have all been identified as playing roles in at least some cases of schizophrenia, but their roles are interactive ones. No *one* of them explains schizophrenia in every case. Much of the mystery remains for creative researchers and clinicians to solve.

Making Judgments About Individuals

Even with a carefully worked out classification system, the task of actually putting a person into the group called "mentally disordered" remains a matter of human judgment. All human judgments are subject to bias and error, and all judgments about a person are likely to have significance for both the judge and the person judged. How objective are these judgments likely to be and how does being called "mentally disordered" affect a person's self-image and interactions with other people?

The Problem of Objectivity

Who declares a person to be mentally disordered, and how objective is the process? In our society today, we generally make such a decision on the basis of some combination of the following evidence: (a) the person is under psychiatric care; (b) influential members of the community (teachers, judges, parents, spouses, priests) agree that the person's behavior represents a dangerous degree of maladjustment; (c) a psychiatrist or clinical psychologist diagnoses mental disturbance; (d) the person's test scores on psychological self-report inventories deviate by a specified extent from scores of individuals designated as normal; (e) the person declares himself or herself to be "mentally sick" by applying this term directly or by expressing feelings such as unhappiness, anxiety, depression, hostility, or inadequacy extreme enough to be associated with emotional disturbance; (f) the person behaves publicly in ways dangerous to himself or herself (suicidal threats or gestures, inability to care for themselves) or to others (aggressive or homicidal impulses or gestures).

The decision to declare someone mentally disordered or *insane* (the legal term) is always a *judgment about behavior.* It is a judgment made by one or more people about the behavioral functioning of another individual—often one of less political power or socioeconomic status. Because psychiatric diagnoses are only *judgments* and are validated only by agreement with other judgments rather than by the kinds of objective, impersonal evidence used to validate medical diagnoses, they are susceptible to many sources of judgmental bias—bias based on expectation, status, gender, prejudice, and other factors.

Research has uncovered a "double standard" used by clinicians in assessing the maladjustment of male versus female "target" persons. Both male and female clinicians ascribed more positive characteristics to males and less desirable ones as typical of normal, healthy females. Characteristics ascribed to females resembled the symptoms of the hysterical or masochistic personality (Broverman et al., 1972). Other research showed that clinicians tend to judge females as maladjusted or "sick" when they show behaviors that are incongruent with their gender role. When women act like men—use foul language, abuse alcohol, or exhibit uncontrollable temper—they are seen as "neurotic" or "self-destructive." Moreover, clinicians reflect the biases of their society in regarding masculinity as more important than femininity. Male gender-role incongruent behavior was rated as a more serious violation of a man's "personhood" than was female gender role incongruity for a woman (Page, 1987).

We have seen throughout our study of psychology that the *meaning* of behavior is jointly determined by its *content* and the *context* in which it occurs. The same act in different settings conveys very different meanings. A man kisses another man; it may mean a homosexual advance, ritual greeting (in France), or Mafia "kiss of death" (in Sicily). Unfortunately, the diagnosis of a behavior as psychotic can also depend on where the behavior occurs: even professionals' judgments may be influenced not only by the behavior itself but by its context.

In a classic study by David Rosenhan, he and seven other sane people gained admission to different psychiatric hospitals by pretending to have a single symptom—hallucinations. All eight of these pseudopatients were diagnosed on admission as either "paranoid schizophrenic" or "manic-depressive."

Once admitted, they behaved normally; but when a sane person is in an insane place, he or she is likely to be judged insane. The context of the mental hospital ward biased the diagnosis. The pseudopatients remained on the wards for almost three weeks, on the average, and not one was identified by the staff as sane. When they were finally released—with the help of spouses or colleagues—their discharge diagnosis was still "schizophrenia" but "in remission" *(symptoms not active). (Rosenhan, 1973, 1975; see also criticisms by Fleischman, 1973; Lieberman, 1973)*

This research challenged the former system of classifying mental disorders, but it also raises basic issues about the validity of judgments of "abnormality" in other people and how dependent such judgments may be on factors other than behavior.

In the view of psychiatrist Thomas Szasz, in fact, clinical judgments are all there is. "Mental illness" does not even exist—it is a "myth" (1961, 1977). Szasz argues that the symptoms used as evidence of mental illness are merely medical labels that sanction professional intervention into what are social problems—people violating social norms. Once labeled, these people can be treated either benignly or harshly for their problem "of being different," with no threat to our status quo. British psychiatrist R. D. Laing (1967) goes further yet—proposing that labeling people as mad often suppresses the creative, unique probing of reality by individuals who are questioning their social context.

Few clinicians would go this far, but the problem of the dependence on judgment when one person labels another "mentally disordered" remains a very real one. In some cases prevailing stereotypes can influence the judgments of those with the power to label others.

An outrageous example of the "medicalization of deviance" in the United States is found in an 1851 report in a medical journal on "The Diseases and Physical Peculiarities of the Negro Race." Its author, Samuel Cartwright, M.D., had been appointed by the Louisiana Medical Association to chair a committee to investigate the strange practices of Negro slaves. "Incontrovertible scientific evidence" was amassed to justify the accepted practice of slavery. In the course of doing so, several "diseases" previously unknown to the white race were discovered. One finding was that Negroes allegedly suffered from a sensory disease that made them insensitive "to pain when being punished" (thus no need to spare the whip).

The classic misuse of the medical model was the committee's invention of the new disease drapetomania*—a mania to seek freedom—a mental illness that caused certain slaves to run away from their masters. Runaway slaves needed to be caught so that their illness could be properly treated! (see Chorover, 1981)*

The Problem of Stigma

From a sociological point of view, the mentally disordered are people who are "deviant"—who deviate from the rest of us; but "deviance" and "abnormality" are rarely used in a value-free statistical sense when other people's behavior is being judged. In practice, being "deviant" connotes moral inferiority and brings social rejection. In addition, the term *deviant* implies that the whole person "is different in kind from ordinary people and that there are no areas of his personality that are not afflicted by his 'problems' " (Scott, 1972, p. 14).

It has been proposed that each society defines itself negatively by pointing out what is *not*—rather than what *is*—appropriate, thereby setting boundaries on what is socially acceptable. Deviants, since they clarify these boundaries, serve to make the rest of the society feel more normal, healthy, moral, and law abiding—by contrast (Ericksen, 1966). In any case, there is little doubt that, in our society, to be "mentally disordered" is to be publicly degraded and personally devalued. Society extracts costly penalties from those who deviate from its norms of right and "normal" (see **Figure 15.2**).

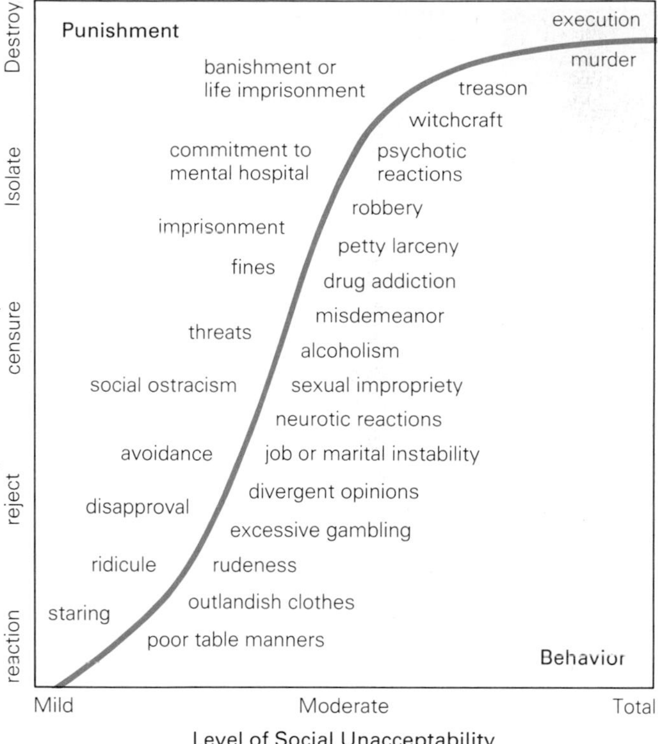

Figure 15.2 *"Let the Punishment Fit the Crime"*
This figure illustrates a continuum of behaviors that are deemed increasingly unacceptable and are responded to with increasing severity. Basically, all these reactions are punishments for deviance; thus, behavior toward those who behave neurotically or psychotically can be seen to resemble that toward criminals and other antisocial deviants. (Adapted from Haas, 1965)

Those who are mentally disordered are stigmatized in ways that most physically ill people are not. *Stigma* means a mark or brand of disgrace; in this context it means a set of negative attitudes about a person that sets him or her apart as unacceptable (Clausen, 1981). Such a negative attitude toward the mentally disturbed come from many sources. Prominent among them are mass media portrayals of the mentally deranged as violent criminals, "sick jokes" that we hear and laugh at, family denial of the mental distress of one of its members, fear of loss of employment if others discover one is distressed or has received mental health care, and legal terminology that stresses mental incompetence (see Rabkin et al., 1980). The stigmatizing process not only marks a target as deviating from an acceptable norm, but discredits a person as "flawed" (see E. Jones et al., 1984).

"For me, the stigma of mental illness was as devastating as the experience of hospitalization itself," writes a recovered patient. She describes her personal experience in vivid terms:

> *Prior to being hospitalized for mental illness, I lived an enviable existence. Rewards, awards, and invitations filled my scrapbook. My diary tells of many occasions worth remembering. . . . The crises of mental illness appeared as a nuclear explosion in my life. All that I had known and enjoyed previously was suddenly transformed, like some strange reverse process of nature, from a butterfly's beauty into a pupa's cocoon. There was a binding, confining quality to my life, in part chosen, in part imposed. Repeated rejections, the awkwardness of others around me, and my own discomfort and self-consciousness propelled me into solitary confinement.*
>
> *My recovery from mental illness and its aftermath involved a struggle—against my own body, which seemed without energy and stamina, and against a society that seemed reluctant to embrace me. It seemed that my greatest needs—to be wanted, needed, valued—were the very needs which others could not fulfill. (Houghton, 1980, pp. 7–8)*

At a recent (1986) congressional hearing, the director of the National Institute of Mental Health reported several aspects of the national neglect of schizophrenia. Although 1 in every 100 Americans will be diagnosed as a sufferer of this insidious disease, only $17.00 per year in federal funds is spent on research per schizophrenic victim, in comparison to the $300.00 spent for each cancer victim. Nearly 60 percent of all schizophrenia sufferers receive no known treatment.

At the hearing, actress Trish Van Devere, whose younger brother is afflicted, reported the human side of the disease. She said: "It steals. It murders. It leaves bereft. It takes away hope, promise and joy. It leaves despair, emptiness and desolate recall of what might have been. There is nothing more cruel . . . yet it is spoken of in hushed tones—if at all" (*San Francisco Chronicle,* 1986, November 30, p. 1).

When it becomes difficult to continue the usual interpersonal relations with an individual who is acting odd, upset, or "plain ornery," others begin to perceive him or her as unreliable, untrustworthy, a threat. They change the quality of their relationship to try to avoid and exclude the person. In response, the distressed person further isolates him- or herself, thereby cutting him- or herself off from both social support and social checks on reality (Lemert, 1962).

Our negative attitudes toward the mentally disturbed bias our perceptions of and actions toward

Although 1 in every 100 Americans will be diagnosed as a sufferer of schizophrenia, 60 percent will receive no treatment. Only seventeen dollars a year in federal funds will be spent on research.

them and also influence their behavior toward us. A series of experiments conducted in laboratory and naturalistic settings demonstrates the unfavorable influences of the social situation on both the behavior of a person perceived to be a mental patient (even when not so) and that of the person making that judgment.

> *When one member of a pair of male college students was (falsely) led to believe the other had been a mental patient, he perceived the pseudo ex-patient to be inadequate, incompetent, and not likable. By making one of a pair of interacting males* falsely *believe he was perceived by the other as stigmatized, he behaved in ways that actually caused the other naive subject to reject him. (Farina, 1980; Farina et al., 1971)*

There seem to be clear sex differences, too, in the tendency to stigmatize those who are former mental patients or believed to be. Men behave more harshly and are more rejecting than women. Women have been found to be more generous in their overall reactions to those who have been afflicted by mental disorder (Farina & Hagalauer, 1975).

Our growing understanding of mental disorder does more than enable society to reclaim its "familiar strangers." In making sense of mental disorder, we are forced to come to grips with basic conceptions of normality, reality, and social values. A mind loosed from its stable moorings does not just go on its solitary way; it bumps into other minds, sometimes challenging their stability. In discovering how to treat and prevent mental disorders, we not only help those unfortunates who are suffering, but we also expand our basic understanding of our own human nature. How do psychologists and psychiatrists intervene to "right" minds gone wrong, to modify behavior that doesn't work? We shall see in the next chapter.

Summary

- Psychopathology is a broad study of mental disorders by medical or psychological specialists. Clinical psychology is the field of psychology that specializes in the psychological treatment of individuals with mental disorders.
- A mental disorder is a clinically significant behavioral or psychological pattern that is associated with an individual's distress and/or impairment of functioning.
- Statistics about the incidence of mental disorders underestimate the actual extent of the problem, covering only those who are treated in public institutions and not including many types of antisocial and self-defeating behavior.
- The judgment that a person is suffering from a mental disorder is made on the basis of several kinds of evidence, including suffering, behaving in maladaptive ways, irrationality, unpredictability, loss of control, moral unacceptability, or making other people uncomfortable.

- A good classification scheme permits reliable diagnosis of individual cases and enables researchers to make studies of the way particular problems develop and the treatment programs that will be most effective.
- The currently used classification scheme, DSM-III, describes behavior syndromes instead of labeling individuals, uses terminology acceptable to both psychiatrists and psychologists, and uses only descriptive statements where causal factors are not known. DSM-III is a multiaxial system, with three axes to assess symptoms and two to rate the stress situation and the individual's overall recent functioning.
- Most of the disorders formerly covered in a category called *neurosis* are now delineated into anxiety, somatoform, and dissociative disorders, as well as some of the affective and psychosexual disorders. In neurotic behavior patterns there is no clear-cut organic problem and no loss of orientation to reality, but an individual does show a lifelong pattern of inadequate coping strategies designed to reduce anxiety by avoiding direct confrontation with it.
- Psychosis is a general category for a number of severe disorders in which perception, thinking, and emotion are so impaired that a person loses contact with reality, requiring intensive treatment and perhaps hospitalization. Some psychoses result from brain damage; others, known as *functional psychoses,* are not attributable to organic causes, though, in some cases, biochemical abnormalities may be involved in addition to presumed psychological and social factors.
- Personality disorders are long-standing, inflexible, maladaptive patterns of perceiving, thinking, or behaving which seriously impair an individual's functioning or cause significant distress. Three of the better known personality disorders are narcissistic personality disorder, compulsive personality disorder, and antisocial personality disorder. Some psychologists reject the diagnosis of a personality disorder, preferring instead to base explanations for behavior on situational factors.
- Anxiety disorders affect millions of people in the United States. They involve physiological arousal and free-floating anxiety—intense feelings of apprehension without any known cause. Two major subcategories are phobic disorder, characterized by a specific fear that a person recognizes is irrational, and four types of anxiety states, including generalized anxiety disorder, panic disorder, obsessive-compulsive disorder, and posttraumatic stress disorder.
- Somatoform disorders include hypochondriasis and conversion disorder, in which there are physical symptoms in the absence of an organic basis sufficient to account for them. Dissociative disorders are patterns with extreme alterations of consciousness in the form of memory loss (psychogenic amnesia), sometimes accompanied by wandering away from home (psychogenic fugue), and loss of identity (multiple personality).
- Psychosexual disorders center on problems of inhibition and dysfunction, and deviance in expression. These disorders reflect the conflicting temptations for and deterrents against sexual impulses and actions in our society.
- Affective disorders are disturbances of mood, with episodes of excessive elation or excessive depression or both, which may be severe enough to be called psychotic. Episodes tend to run their course with or without treatment, but may recur. Bipolar depression, an alternation of manic and depressive periods, is much rarer than unipolar depression, in which only a depressive pattern is shown.
- One explanation for the greater incidence of depression in women centers on socialization training which encourages women to think about their moods, but not try actively to cope with them. While most depressed people do not commit suicide, most suicides are attempted by those suffering from depression. More women than men attempt suicide, but men's attempts are more often completed using guns. An alarming social trend in recent years is the increase in youth suicide.
- The major symptom in a paranoid disorder is a delusion, a false belief that persists despite contradictory information. Paranoid delusions are of four types: persecution, jealousy, grandeur, or reference. Such individuals typically feel under serious threat of some kind.
- Schizophrenic disorders are a group of psychotic disorders in which perception is distorted, emotions are blunted, thoughts are bizarre and fragmented, and language is strange and disjointed; hallucinations and delusions are common, and expressive mannerisms are odd. Four types of schizophrenia are the disorganized type, the catatonic type, the paranoid type, and the undifferentiated type. Schizophrenic patients as a group seem to be hypersensitive to external stimuli and highly distractible; coherence between past, present, and future is lost in thought and speech, though the individual may have created a closed, inner, self-validating system.

- Widely differing views of mental disorders have been held, reflecting differing cultural and religious beliefs and world views. Certain symptoms, such as unpredictability and lack of communication with others are seen as abnormal in all known cultures. In some cultures a mental disorder is seen as a breakdown not in an individual, but in the individual's relation with the community and environment.
- Biologically oriented theories have classified mental disorders as diseases of the nervous system or linked them to genetic factors, abnormalities of biochemical processes, or structural abnormalities. Psychological explanations have included psychodynamic models, such as Freud's, that emphasize inner conflicts and defense mechanisms, behaviorist explanations based on learning through reinforcement, and cognitive models that emphasize an individual's perceptions and interpretations of experience.
- Evidence for the cause of schizophrenia has been found in genetic factors, biochemical abnormalities, family interactions, and faulty cognitive processes; several of these may contribute in a given case.
- The decision that someone is mentally disordered is always based on human judgment and will depend on both the behavior being judged and the context in which it occurs, as well as on the beliefs of the observer. Too often a person identified as mentally disordered suffers stigma, which then distorts both that person's behavior and the subsequent behavior of others toward him or her.

16

Therapies for Personal Change

Gary was a college freshman who sought treatment for a mental problem that was ruining his life. His case provides us with some interesting clues about the way a psychological disorder may develop and be treated successfully, if therapy begins early enough.

Like most people seeking professional treatment for a mental disorder, Gary came with *presenting symptoms,* problem reactions that made him feel distressed and unable to function effectively in school, on the job, or in social settings. Gary had three presenting symptoms, and they were all major. He appeared to be developing anorexia nervosa, sexual dysfunction, and paranoid obsessional delusions. Any one of these problems was enough to occupy most of his attention, leaving little energy for schoolwork. The triad—which all had begun about the same time—was simply overwhelming everything else in his life. Unless some remedy could be found soon, Gary knew he would have to drop out of college and maybe even be hospitalized.

It was fortunate that Gary came to see a therapist soon after his problems began. Most people wait months or years after their first abnormal symptoms appear before they seek treatment. Typically, the delay increases their suffering and makes more difficult the road to mental health.

After lengthy discussion with Gary, his therapist came up with an interpretation of his problems that could account for all three of the difficulties he was experiencing. The interpretation also suggested that a particular therapeutic approach would be most helpful. (See how soon in this case you can detect where the analysis is headed.)

Because Gary's symptoms were all of recent vintage, the therapist was able to get him to fix the onset of each one within approximately a week's time. Gary recalled:

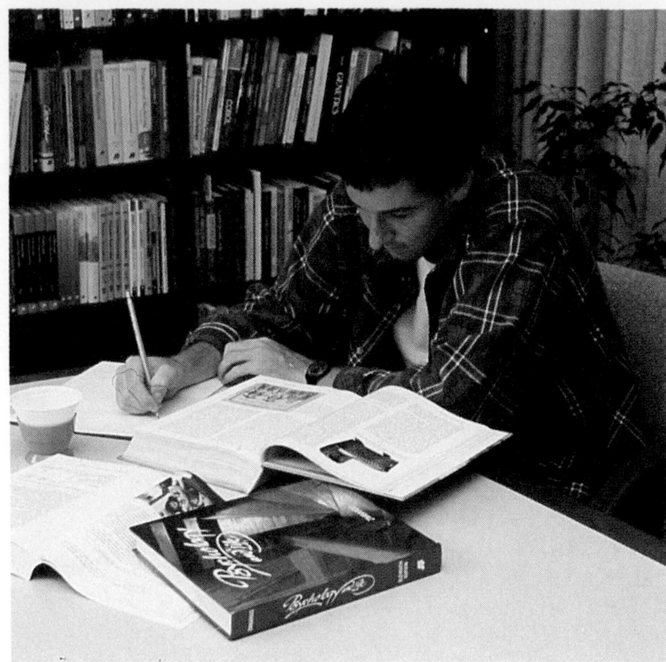

I started vomiting up most of the food I ate in the dorm cafeteria about mid-January, and just couldn't eat without feeling sick. I've been losing about 5 pounds a week. A little later, I noticed I couldn't maintain an erection when out on a heavy date or when looking at sexy magazine photos. I couldn't study because I was weak, dizzy, and worried about these things happening to me; *but then an even worse punishment started happening. I had these thoughts, sometimes vivid images, of people I knew who were in bloody accidents or committing suicide—whenever they disagreed with me about anything. I couldn't shake these horrible thoughts; they kept occurring. I'm gonna flunk out—all these problems are causing me to mess up my studying. This has never happened to me, ever; you see, I'm a straight A student. I've always been 'perfect'—academically* perfect. *I need help with these emotional problems, or else I'm never going to graduate with honors.*

What is cause and what is effect in Gary's problems and symptoms? Gary argues persuasively that the syndrome of symptoms is causing cognitive and emotional problems which, in turn, result in poor grades; but have you considered the *timing* of the onset of his symptoms and the alternative reasons why this freshman might be getting poor grades at a major university even without any mental disorder to disrupt studying? Might it be possible that the poor grades were the cause, and not the effect, of the psychological problems? With Gary's permission, this alternative scenario was checked out with his teachers. The therapist discovered that Gary already knew he was getting low grades in his courses *before* his first symptom appeared!

This "perfect" student had been confronted with the reality that he was only average when competing with classmates who were *all* high-school "hot shots." It was such a blow to his self-image to acknowledge an *ability deficiency* that he developed a set of psychological problems to justify and explain the sudden discontinuity he was experiencing as an "A student" who was getting just ordinary grades. He could not ask for help to make him smarter (nor was he yet aware of help available at his college to improve study habits and test-taking skills). What Gary *could* ask for was psychological help for temporary emotional, motivational problems—and get some sympathy in the bargain.

The therapeutic help for Gary consisted of facilitating his: (a) acknowledgement of the proper sequence of timing between poor grades and symptom onset; (b) awareness of the error he was making in thinking his average (not perfect) performance was because of psychological problems rather than increased competition; (c) admitting that "perfection" was a burden imposed by his parents' unrealistic expectations for him, as well as an impossibility for anyone to maintain in an imperfect world; (d) acceptance of the reality that he was a good student who could graduate from a good school and recognition that no one would ever ask him for his G.P.A. after graduation (he was planning to go into business); (e) seeking assistance to improve his study and test-taking skills; and finally (f) enjoyment of the discovery that he could now learn for the sake of learning, not just for A grades. Once he could accept that, he would not have to be so grade-conscious; he would probably have more time to socialize and enjoy his college years.

In Gary's case, this brief therapy was extremely helpful. Gary's triad of symptoms vanished over the next few weeks, and he did not develop any new symptoms. Four years later he received his B.A. degree, and he now has a good job.

Such "sudden cures" are rare in psychology and psychiatry. It would not have been possible to pinpoint the crucial timing variable had Gary been treated much later. Even a year later, his memory would probably have been too vague about the onset of the symptoms and the deterioration of his grades for a therapist to formulate the causal hypothesis linking them. For many people there is usually a long delay between the time their first symptoms appear and they decide to seek professional treatment.

One person suffering from a psychological affliction that has no origin in physical illness goes to a native shaman seeking a remedy or curative ritual, while another seeks counseling from a parish priest. A hospitalized mental patient, unable to function "normally," is administered electroshocks, while another patient, as a treatment of "last resort" for his serious emotional disorder, is operated upon to sever connections between the frontal lobes and the rest of the brain. Less dramatic is the example of a person who deals with psychological problems by "talking it out" on the couch, sharing anxieties with others in a group, or is coached in practicing new behavioral skills that will enable more effective functioning.

Treatments for mental illness and behavior disorders are almost as plentiful and varied as are the types of psychopathologies that we reviewed in the previous chapter. The task before us is to appreciate the way psychotherapies represent the practical application and "operational testing" of theoretical conceptions regarding the origins of abnormal functioning. How has the treatment for psychological disorders been influenced by historical, cultural, and social forces? What is the relationship between theory, research, and practice in this area where

psychology confronts its most imposing adversary—the human suffering caused by "madness" in its many manifestations? What can be done to change a mind ungoverned by ordinary reason, to modify behavior uncontrolled by usual contingencies, to alter emotions unchecked by situational appropriateness, or to intervene into the workings of the brain and even the genes themselves to correct their abnormality?

A cross-cultural perspective shows that communally oriented societies—for example, American Indians and many African tribes—treat cases of behavior pathology within a social group context. By contrast, societies with more individualistic values, such as ours, have therapies that generally reflect those dominant values. Most treatment for mental and behavioral problems in our society is typically conducted in an environment alien to the patient, in a one-on-one interaction with an "expert-stranger" who is paid to try to improve a client's well-being.

Within the field of psychology the largest category of professionals is health care providers—more specifically, clinical psychologists. This chapter surveys the different types of treatments in progress: psychoanalysis, behavior modification, cognitive restructuring, and humanistic therapies, along with drug therapies that revolutionized the treatment of patients with severe mental disorders. We want to know not only *how* they work, but also, *do* they work? What is the evidence supporting the validity of claims regarding the efficacy of one therapy over another, or for that matter, for any therapy over the placebo of *time* "which heals all wounds"? This chapter will provide some general advice about when and how to seek professional help for the psychological problems we all have—all of us who are not "crazy" but troubled, unable to come up with solutions on our own.

The Therapeutic Context

Therapy involves a helping relationship. Someone with a mental or medical problem is given help by someone who is designated by society as a helper for that kind of problem. There are different types of therapy for mental disorders and many reasons why someone seeks help (and why others who need it do not). In addition, the purposes or goals of therapy are varied, as are the settings in which it occurs and the kinds of people who are the therapeutic helpers. Despite any differences between therapies they are all *interventions* into a person's life, designed to change that person's functioning in some way.

At the risk of being obvious, it is well to point out that mental problems vary in their severity, just as physical illnesses do; their treatment is similarly dependent on the nature of the illness. Some, like cancer or a major schizophrenic episode, are so serious that they require long-term treatment by highly trained professionals in special institutional settings. At the other end of the continuum are relatively minor problems, a noticeable wart, a mild phobia of escalators, for example, for which only a small number of us will seek treatment. In between, are a range of problems that may be intense, but not long-lasting; mild, but disturbingly repetitive; and varying in the degree of discomfort they cause and their interference with life-style.

Overview of Kinds of Therapy

Using a computer analogy, mental problems may occur either in the "hardware" of the defective human computer or in the "software" of the instructions that program its actions. Correspondingly, the two main kinds of therapy for mental disorders focus on one or the other. **Biomedical therapies** focus on changing the hardware—the mechanisms that run the central nervous system, endocrine system, or metabolism. They try to alter brain functioning by chemical or physical interventions, including surgery, electric shock, and drugs. Psychological therapies, collectively called **psychotherapy,** focus on changing the software—the faulty behaviors we have learned and the words, thoughts, interpretations, and feedback that direct our strategies for living.

The four major types of psychotherapy, in turn, are the psychodynamic, behavior, cognitive, and existential-humanistic therapies. The *psychodynamic* approach—more commonly called a *psychoanalytic* approach—views adult neurotic suffering as the outer symptom of inner, unresolved childhood traumas and conflicts. *Psychoanalysis* treats mental disorder with words. It is a "talking cure" in which a therapist helps a person develop insights about the relation between the overt symptoms and the unresolved hidden conflicts that presumably caused them.

Behavior therapies treat the behaviors themselves as disturbances that must be modified. Disorders are viewed as learned behavior patterns rather than as the tip of an iceberg of mental disease. For behavior therapists, changing the problem behavior corrects the disorder. This is done in many ways, including changing reinforcement contingencies for desirable and undesirable responding, extinguishing conditioned fear responses, and providing models of effective problem solving.

Cognitive therapies try to restructure the way a person thinks about him- or herself. They do so by helping to alter the often distorted self-statements a person is making about the causes of the problem and the chances of alleviating it. Often the difficulties a person has can be coped with by changing the way they are defined and explained.

Therapies that have emerged from the *existential-humanistic* tradition emphasize the *values* of patients. Existential-humanistic therapies are directed toward self-actualization, psychological growth, forming more meaningful interpersonal relationships, and enhancing freedom of choice. They tend to focus more on improving the functioning of essentially healthy people than on correcting the symptoms of seriously disturbed individuals.

We will look in some detail a little later at several kinds of biomedical intervention and at each of these four major kinds of psychotherapy. Before we examine these "schools" of therapy, let's start at the beginning of the process with a person about to seek therapy. (See also the article "The Shrinking of George" in *The Best of Science.*)

Entering Therapy

Why does anyone go into therapy? As with physical illness, it is not easy to specify the reasons people decide to seek professional help for their psychological problems. Optimally, we expect that people will enter therapy when their everyday functioning violates societal criteria of normality and/or their own sense of adequate adjustment. People with problems may seek therapy on their own initiative or may do so on the advice of others.

Many people who might benefit from therapy do not seek professional help. Sometimes it is inconvenient to do so. All of us put off doing some useful things that might involve a hassle or loss of time and money. We do not get our car tuned as often as we should or go for regular physical and dental checkups. In the case of mental disorder, if a person's behavior is judged dangerous to self or others, he or she can be involuntarily committed by a state court to a mental institution for treatment (see Wexler, 1976).

Whether someone seeks "outside professional help" depends on many factors in addition to inconvenience, personal distress, and experience of disability. Someone who can benefit from such treatment is less likely to be in therapy because of any or all of the following factors: lack of accessible mental health facilities, ignorance of available resources, lower socioeconomic class, older age group, fear of stigmatization for being in therapy, and value systems that minimize the need or worth of going to psychologists for help with personal problems—be they religious, cultural, or masculine role values.

Some psychological problems themselves affect one's ability to make constructive life choices. The agoraphobic person finds it hard, even impossible, to leave home to seek therapy; a paranoid person will not trust mental health professionals or institutions. In many communities, it is still much easier to get help from a medical doctor for physical health problems than it is to find a qualified, affordable mental health worker who has time to provide needed psychological help.

People who do enter therapy are usually referred to as either patients or clients. The term *patients* is used more by professionals who take a biomedical approach to the treatment of psychological problems and professionals who view problems as symptoms of underlying mental illnesses that must be treated by getting at underlying roots of the illness. Those who use the term *clients* are usually professionals who think of psychological disorders as "problems in living" (Szasz, 1961). We will try to use the preferred term for each approach as we present its views: *patient* for biomedical and psychoanalytic therapies and *client* for other therapies.

Goals and Settings

The therapeutic process can involve four tasks: (a) reaching a *diagnosis* about what is wrong, possibly putting a psychiatric label on the problem and classifying the disorder; (b) proposing a probable *etiology* (cause of the problem), identifying the probable origins of the disorder and the functions being served by the symptoms; (c) making a *prognosis* or estimate of the course the problem will take with and without any treatment; and finally, (d) prescribing and carrying out some form of *treatment,* therapeutic intervention designed to minimize or eliminate the troublesome symptoms and, perhaps, also their sources. We will see, however, that some psychological models of treatment do not accept all of these four tasks or goals.

Despite the differences in theory, most therapeutic interventions have the same purpose—to reduce a patient's or client's suffering and increase his or her sense of well-being, which usually means helping a person develop more effective means of coping with everyday demands and stresses. The goal is to replace psychological problems or inadequate functioning with improved psychological health and effective coping styles.

Healers and Therapists

When psychological problems arise, most of us seek out "informal counselors" who operate in more familiar settings. Many people turn to family members, close friends, personal physicians, lawyers, or favorite teachers for support, guidance, and counsel. Others get advice and a chance to "talk it out" by "opening up" to neighborhood bartenders, beauticians, cab drivers—or other people willing to listen. These informal therapists carry the bulk of the daily burden of relieving human suffering.

Although more people seek out therapy now than in the past, usually it is only when their psychological problems become severe or persist after some form of informal therapy that trained mental health professionals are called upon. When they do, the four types of therapists they turn to are counseling psychologists, psychiatric social workers, and either clinical psychologists or psychiatrists.

The term **counseling psychologist** describes the general category of professional psychologists who specialize in providing guidance in areas such as vocational selection, school problems, drug abuse, or marital conflict. Typically, they will work in community settings related to the problem areas—within a business, school, prison, military service, or neighborhood clinic—and use interviews, tests, guidance, and advising to help individuals solve specific problems and make decisions about future options. **Psychiatric social workers** are also mental health professionals whose specialized training in a school of social work prepares them to work in collaboration with psychiatrists and clinical psychologists. Unlike the latter care providers, their training emphasizes the importance of the social context of people's problems, so they may also involve other family members, or at least become acquainted with clients' homes or work settings.

Clinical psychologists have earned a Ph.D. degree in which their major graduate school training was in the assessment and treatment of psychological problems. In addition, they have completed a supervised internship in a clinical setting. They tend to have a broader background in psychology, assessment, and research than do psychiatrists. **Psychiatrists** have completed all medical school training for an M.D. degree and also have completed some postdoctoral specialty training in dealing with mental and emotional disorders. Their training lies more in the biomedical base of psychological problems, and only they can prescribe medications or convulsive therapy. **Psychoanalysts** are therapists with either an M.D. or a Ph.D. degree who have completed specialized postgraduate training in the Freudian approach to understanding and treating mental disorders.

From this general overview of the therapeutic context we shall proceed—first turning to the past to consider the way therapy was delivered in earlier times, then returning to the present to examine the strategies and tactics involved in the major forms of contemporary therapy.

Historical and Cultural Contexts

What kind of treatment might you have received in past centuries if you were suffering from psychological problems? It all depends on when and where you lived.

Several events occurred in fourteenth-century western Europe that dramatically affected the treatment of psychological problems—for the worse. Population increases, coupled with migration to big cities, created unemployment, poverty, and alienation in many countries. Special institutions arose to warehouse society's three main categories of misfits—the poor, the criminals, and the mentally disturbed. In 1403, St. Mary of Bethlehem, a London hospital for the poor, admitted its first patient with psychological problems. *Bedlam* (a corruption of Bethlehem) came to stand for the chaotic confusion of this place and the dehumanized treatment of its patients. For the next 300 years, people were chained, tortured, and exhibited like animals in zoos for the amusement of the public, who paid admission to see the mad beasts perform their antics (Foucault, 1975).

Meanwhile, in fifteenth-century Germany, mental disorders began to be labeled as witchcraft; the mad were assumed to be possessed by the Devil who deprived them of reason. As the Inquisition and its "persecutory mania" spread throughout Europe, symptoms of mental disturbances were "cured" by some form of painful death.

The view that people with psychological problems were just *sick* emerged in eighteenth-century Europe. During this age of enlightenment and revolution, the French physician, Philippe Pinel described the new concept of "mental illness." "The mentally ill," wrote Pinel in 1801, "far from being guilty people deserving of punishment are sick people whose miserable state deserves all the consideration that is due to suffering humanity. One should try with the most simple methods to restore their reason" (in Zilboorg & Henry, 1941, pp. 323–24).

In eighteenth-century America psychologically disturbed citizens were physically removed from society and confined for their own protection and that of the community—but given no treatment. By the mid-nineteenth century, when psychology was emerging as a respectable way to understand human nature, a "cult of curability" swept the country. Insanity was thought to be related to the environmental stresses brought on by the turmoil of living in newly developing cities. When the confinement of the mentally ill assumed a new *rehabilitative* goal, the *asylum* became the central fixture of this social-political movement. The disturbed were confined to these asylums in the rural countryside, far from the stress of the city, not just for protection, but to be treated (Rothman, 1971).

Below is a famous engraving depicting the conditions that existed in the 1730s at a London mental institution known as Bedlam. At the right is a patient, William Norris, in his cell at Bedlam.

The idea that mental illness could be cured helped transform people's view of the disturbed. No longer were they seen as animal-like "madmen"; instead they were "sick patients" not personally responsible for their illnesses, deserving of the same quality of medical treatment and scientific analysis that society extended to the physically ill. Unfortunately, many of these asylums rapidly became overcrowded. The humane goal of rehabilitation soon was replaced by an emphasis on the *warehousing* of the mentally ill.

The disease view of psychological problems has contributed to the alliance of political institutions (enacting laws) with the mental health profession (attempting cures). This alliance is neither wholly positive nor wholly negative, but it is certainly important in the current systems by which both psychotherapy and biomedical therapy are delivered to disturbed people.

One of the founders of modern psychiatry, German psychiatrist J. C. Heinroth, helped provide the conceptual and moral justification for the disease view. Heinroth wrote, in 1818, that madness was a complete loss of inner freedom or reason depriving those afflicted of any ability to control their lives. Others who "know best" what is good for these patients must therefore care for them. Heinroth maintained that it was the duty of the state to cure mentally ill patients of the disease that forced them to be burdensome to society (cited in Szasz, 1979). From Heinroth's time to the present, "in this alliance between psychology and state, the state's protective power to confine the mentally ill has been transformed into a power of the state to treat, through its agent the mental health profession, the mental disorder thought to be the basis of the problem" (White & White, 1981, p. 954).

You can learn much about the values of a society and the thinking within an historical epoch from its dominant views on the way to deal with the problem of those citizens who don't fit in with the rest of the population—the poor, the criminal, the insane, the aliens, and deviants. This historical overview barely gives you a flavor of the changing conceptions of treatment of the mentally ill across time. You may find it to be a really fascinating project to study that history, even if you limit your research to your own country over the past hundred years.

In reviewing these historical trends, it is important to note that, so far, we have presented only Western views. The movement from trying to exorcise demons to trying to cure sickness or other problems within an individual seems less profound in Western culture when contrasted with the historical trends in other cultures.

The European and American world view emphasizes individuality, uniqueness, competition, independence, survival of the fittest, a mastery over nature, and personal responsibility for success and failure. Both demonology and the disease model are consistent with this emphasis, regarding mental disorder as something that happens *inside* a person. This view is not universally shared. In the African world view we see, instead, an emphasis on groupness, commonality, cooperation, interdependence, tribal survival, unity with nature, and collective responsibility (Nobles, 1976). It is *contrary* to the therapeutic practices in many non-European cultures to treat mentally ill individuals by removing them from society.

Among the Navajo and in African cultures, healing is a matter that always takes place in a social context and involves a distressed person's beliefs, family, work, and life environment. Recently the African use of group support in therapy has been expanded into a procedure called "network therapy," where a patient's entire network of relatives, coworkers, and friends becomes involved in the treatment (Lambo, 1978).

One therapeutic practice used in a number of healing ceremonies is *dissociation of consciousness,* induced in a distressed person or in a faith healer *(shaman).* In the Western view, dissociation is itself a symptom of mental disorder to be prevented or corrected; but, in other views, evil spirits are exorcised and good spirits communicated with as consciousness is altered. This use of ceremonial alteration of consciousness can be seen today among the cult of Puerto Rican *Espiritistas* in New York City, whose healing ceremonies involve communication with good spirits that are believed to exist outside a person's skin (Garrison, 1977). Some of these views from other cultures have begun to work their way into Western practices. The social-interactive concept and the focus on a person *in a family context* and *a supportive community* have become particularly influential in our newer therapeutic approaches.

From this general background, we are ready to move to the central focus of the chapter—an analysis of the major forms of psychological and medical therapies. We will examine four general kinds of psychotherapy that have evolved from the alternative conceptual orientations we have studied earlier. We will add a fifth therapeutic approach that emerges from the biological orientation to mental illness.

Psychodynamic Therapies

Psychodynamic therapies assume that a patient's problems have been caused by the psychological tension between unconscious impulses and the constraints of his or her life situation. These therapies locate the core of the disturbance inside the disturbed person, accepting a general model of a disease core that shows up in symptoms. However, their emphasis is on ongoing, intense psychological processes rather than physical imbalances.

Freudian Psychoanalysis

Psychoanalytic therapy, as developed by Freud, is the premier psychodynamic therapy. It is an intensive and prolonged technique for exploring unconscious motivations and conflicts in neurotic, anxiety-ridden individuals. The major goal of psychoanalysis is "to reveal the unconscious." According to the president of the American Psychoanalytic Institute:

> *We believe an unconscious exists in all humans and that it dictates much of our behavior. If it is a relatively healthy unconscious, then our behavior will be healthy, too. Many who are plagued by symptoms from phobias, depression, anxiety, or panic may have deposits of unconscious material that are fostering their torment. Only the psychoanalyst is qualified to probe the unconscious. . . . (Theodore Rubin, quoted in Rockmore, 1985, p. 71)*

As we saw in our earlier discussion of Freudian theory, neurotic disorders are viewed as inabilities to resolve adequately the inner conflicts between the unconscious, irrational impulses of the *id* and the internalized social constraints imposed by the *superego.* As an individual progresses through the biologically determined stages from infancy to adulthood, according to Freudian theory, his or her particular psychological experiences at each stage determine whether there will be a fixation at an immature stage or progress to a more mature level of development. The goal of psychoanalysis is the establishment of intrapsychic harmony that expands one's awareness of the forces of the *id,* reduces overcompliance with the demands of the *superego,* and strengthens the role of the *ego.*

Of central importance to a therapist is the understanding of the way a patient uses the process of *repression* to handle conflicts, by pushing unacceptable urges and feelings out of consciousness. Symptoms are considered to be messages from the unconscious that something is wrong; thus a psychoanalyst's task is to help a patient bring repressed thoughts to consciousness and gain insight into the relation between the current symptoms and the repressed conflicts from years gone by. In this psychodynamic view, therapy works and patients recover when they are "released from repression" established in early childhood (Munroe, 1955). Because a central goal of a therapist is to guide a patient toward discovering insights between present symptoms and past origins, psychodynamic therapies are often called *insight therapies.* Other therapies we will discuss do not have insight as a goal; rather they focus on the present, on behavior, or on giving direct advice.

The goals of psychoanalysis are ambitious. They involve not just the elimination of neurotic symptoms, but a total personality reorganization. When psychoanalysis overcomes barriers to self-awareness and to freedom of thought and communication, a person can achieve more intimate human associations as well as more intellectual creativity Because traditional psychoanalysis is an attempt to reconstruct long-standing repressed memories and then work through painful feelings to an effective resolution, it is a therapy that takes a long time (several years at least, with one to five sessions a week). It also requires introspective patients who are verbally fluent, highly motivated to remain in therapy, and willing and able to undergo considerable expense. Some of the newer forms of psychodynamic therapy try to deal with some of these drawbacks, especially attempting to make therapy briefer in total duration.

Psychoanalysts use several techniques to bring repressed conflicts to consciousness and to help a patient resolve them. These include free association, analysis of resistance, dream analysis, and analysis of transference and countertransference (see the ***Close-up*** on page 568).

Free Association

The principal procedure used in psychoanalysis to probe the unconscious and release repressed material is called **free association.** A patient, sitting comfortably in a chair or lying in a relaxed position on a couch, lets his or her mind wander freely, giving a running account of thoughts, wishes, physical sensations, and mental images as they occur. The patient is encouraged to reveal every thought or feeling, no matter how personal, painful, or seemingly unimportant.

Freud maintained that free associations are *predetermined,* not random. The task of an analyst is to track the associations to their source and identify

Close-up Anna O. and the Talking Cure

Modern psychotherapy began in 1880 with the case of Fraulein Anna O. and her famous physician, Joseph Breuer. This bright, personable, attractive 21-year-old Viennese woman became incapacitated and developed a severe cough while nursing her ill father. When the physician began to treat her "nervous cough," he became aware of many more symptoms that seemed to have a psychological origin. Anna squinted, had double vision, and experienced paralysis, muscle contractions, and anesthesias (loss of sensitivity to pain stimuli).

Breuer told a young physician, Sigmund Freud, about this unusual patient. Together they coined the term *hysterical conversion* for the transformation of her blocked emotional impulses into physical symptoms (Breuer & Freud, 1895/1955). This case of Anna O. is the first detailed description of physical symptoms resulting from psychogenic causes—a hysterical illness. It was Anna O. herself who devised her own treatment, with Breuer as therapist. She referred to the procedures as a "talking cure," or jokingly as "chimney sweeping."

In the context of hypnosis, Anna O. talked freely, giving full reign to her imagination ("free associations"). Once she was able to express herself in an open and direct fashion to her therapist, she no longer needed to use the indirect and disguised communication of physical symptoms. According to Breuer, her "complexes were disposed of by being given verbal expression during hypnosis."

Breuer and Freud's analysis of Anna O.'s disorder was in terms of internal psychodynamic forces (instincts and impulses). What they failed to acknowledge fully were the external social obstacles that limited the ambitions of all women for a professional career at that time and place. Some of her symptoms may have stemmed from repressed rage, while the intellectual and emotional involvement with her therapist helped break the monotony of her existence. After a year of nearly daily treatment, Breuer terminated the psychotherapy.

Anna O. went on to become a pioneer of social work, a leader in the struggle for women's rights, a playwright, and a housemother of an orphanage. Her true name was Bertha Pappenheim (Rosenbaum & Muroff, 1984).

The importance of Anna O.'s role in the development of modern psychotherapy is considerable.

Before the invention of the talking cure, hypnosis was used mainly for suggestion and the physician was a doer. With the shift to catharsis, the physician became a listener. This step may seem trivial today, but in its time it was monumental. As a result of it, Breuer could state that his patient's life became known to him in a way that one person's life is seldom known to another. It also shifted the focus from biology to psychology. Instead of asking what caused the disease *labeled hysteria, the physician now asked about the emotional antecedents of the disorder. Thus, Breuer's treatment of Anna O. started us on the road that would lead to definitive forms of psychotherapy. It led the way, too, to the giant steps taken by Breuer's young friend [Freud], who was so profoundly impressed when he heard about this remarkable case. (Hollender, 1980, p. 500)*

In a provocative new view of Anna O.'s illness, E. M. Thornton (1984) casts doubt on the original diagnosis—even if the subsequent treatment did pave the way for the talking cure that was to become central in psychoanalytic therapy. A reasonably good alternative diagnosis is that her symptoms were those associated with *tuberculous meningitis,* which she might have contracted from her father who probably was dying from a form of tuberculosis himself. After Anna O. had terminated her treatment with Breuer, she entered a sanatorium from which she was later discharged relatively recovered from her illness. It is likely that many, or all, of her "hysterical conversion" reactions were of organic, not psychological, origin. On the other hand, she may still have experienced considerable suppressed rage and guilt over having to be her father's nurse for so long and not being given outlets for her considerable talents because of sexual discrimination that was so pervasive in her time.

the significant patterns that lie beneath the surface of what is apparently "just words." Throughout, a patient is encouraged to express strong feelings, usually toward authority figures, that have been repressed for fear of punishment or retaliation. Any such emotional release, by this or other processes, is termed **catharsis.**

Resistance

During the process of free association, a patient will, at times, show **resistance**—an inability or unwillingness to discuss certain ideas, desires, or experiences. Resistances prevent the return to consciousness of repressed material that is especially painful to recall, material often related to an individual's sexual life (which includes all things pleasurable) or to hostile, resentful feelings toward parents. Sometimes resistance is shown by a patient coming late to therapy or "forgetting" it altogether. When the repressed material is finally brought into the open, a patient generally claims that it is too unimportant, too absurd, too irrelevant, or too unpleasant to be discussed.

A psychoanalyst attaches particular importance to subjects that a patient does *not* wish to discuss. Such resistances are conceived of as *barriers* between the unconscious and the conscious. The aim of psychoanalysis is to break down resistances and enable the patient to face these painful ideas, desires, and experiences. Breaking down resistances is a long and difficult process considered to be essential if the underlying problem is to be brought to consciousness where it can be resolved.

Dream Analysis

Psychoanalysts believe that dreams are an important source of information about a patient's unconscious motivations. When a person is asleep, the superego is presumably less on guard against the unacceptable impulses originating in the id, so a motive that cannot be expressed in waking life may find expression in a dream.

Some motives are so unacceptable to the conscious self that they cannot be revealed openly, even in dreams, but must be expressed in disguised or symbolic form. As we saw in chapter 7, a dream has two kinds of content. Its *manifest* (openly visible) content is what we remember and report upon awakening. Beneath this manifest content is the *latent* (hidden) content—the actual motives that are seeking expression, but are so painful or unacceptable to us that we do not want to recognize their existence. Therapists attempt to uncover these hidden motives by using **dream analysis,** a therapeutic technique that examines the content of a person's dreams to find the underlying or disguised motivations and symbolic meanings of significant life experiences and desires.

Consider the following dream and the therapist's analytic interpretation.

> *"I am in a gym, performing various exercises, with some other men. They are arranged in a line, in which they perform the exercises. I try to join the line at the head, but am rejected; I then try for the second place and am rejected again; I try one place after the other till coming to the end of the line, and am rejected from every one of them."*
>
> *At first the dreamer has difficulty associating to the dream. The analyst points out that the dream seems to involve men only. The dreamer then realizes that the men in the dream were actually boys from his all-male Catholic primary school, a place dominated by "oughts" and "shoulds." With this come unpleasant memories of the gym class, which the dreamer hated passionately. The only reason he attended was because he was forced to; had it been left up to him he would not have shown up at any of the classes. As an afterthought, he adds that his mother also thought that "it was good for you." The imagery of the dream is direct and clear—the dreamer is being rejected from the line; he does not belong there. (Kaufmann, 1984, p. 124)*

However, the latent content of the dream may also involve ambivalence about his homosexual feelings when seeing other boys naked before or after gym class. In addition, it may reflect inferiority feelings over his imagined small penis size—not being able to meet the requirements.

Transference and Countertransference

During the course of the intensive therapy of psychoanalysis a patient usually develops an emotional reaction toward the therapist. Often the therapist is identified with a person who has been at the center of an emotional conflict in the past, most often a parent or a lover. This emotional reaction is called **transference.** The transference is called *positive transference* when the feelings attached to the therapist are those of love or admiration; *negative transference* when the feelings consist of hostility or envy. Often a patient's attitude is *ambivalent,* including a mixture of positive and negative feelings.

An analyst's task in handling transference is a difficult and dangerous one because of the patient's emotional vulnerability; however, it is a crucial part of treatment. A therapist helps a patient to interpret the present transferred feelings by understanding their original source in earlier experiences and attitudes.

Personal feelings are also at work in a therapist's reactions to a patient. **Countertransference,** in which a therapist comes to like or dislike a patient because the patient is perceived as similar to significant people in the therapist's life, may occur. In working through countertransference, a therapist may discover some unconscious dynamics of his or her own. The therapist becomes a "living mirror" for his patient, and the patient, in turn, for the therapist. Failure by the therapist to recognize the operation of countertransference interferes with the effectiveness of therapy (Little, 1981).

Margaret Mahler (1897–)

Beyond Freud

Changes have been made in both psychoanalytic theory and practice by some of Freud's followers, who retain many of his basic ideas but modify one or another principle. In general, these neo-Freudians place more emphasis than Freud did on (a) a patient's *current* social environment (less on the past); (b) the continuing influence of life experiences (not just infantile fixations); (c) the role of social motivation and interpersonal relations of love (rather than on biological instincts and selfish concerns); (d) the significance of ego functioning and development of the self-concept (less on the conflict between *id* and *superego*); and (e) the possibility of using psychoanalytic therapy with psychotic disorders (not just neurotic ones). To get a flavor of the more contemporary psychodynamic approaches of the neo-Freudians, we sample two of them in the work of Harry Stack Sullivan and Margaret Mahler.

Sullivan supported the significance of social interaction. He felt that Freudian theory and therapy did not recognize the importance of social relationships or a patient's needs of acceptance, respect, and love. Mental disorders, he insisted, involve not only traumatic intrapsychic processes, but troubled interpersonal relationships and even strong societal pressures. A young child needs to feel secure, to be treated by others with caring and tenderness. Anxiety and other mental ills arise out of insecurities in relations with parents and "significant others." In Sullivan's view, a self-system is built up to hold anxiety down to a tolerable level. This self-system is derived from a child's interpersonal experiences and is organized around conceptions of the self as the "good-me" (associated with the mother's tenderness), the "bad-me" (associated with the mother's tensions), and the "not me" (a dissociated self that is unacceptable to the rest of the self).

Therapy based on this interpersonal view involves observing a *patient's feelings* about the *therapist's attitudes.* The therapeutic interview is seen as a social setting in which each party's feelings and attitudes are influenced by the other's. The patient is gently provoked to state his or her assumptions about the therapist's attitudes—and other assumptions as well. Misunderstandings are corrected without humiliation by use of various therapeutic tactics. Above all, the therapeutic situation, for Sullivan, was one where the therapist learned and taught lovingly (Sullivan, 1953; Wallach & Wallach, 1983).

Margaret Mahler was one of the first psychoanalysts to recognize and treat childhood schizophrenia. She traced a child's fragmentation of ego and retreat from reality to sources of disharmony in the mother-child relationship. The normal development of an independent ego requires a process of gradual separation of the mother and child, along with an emerging sense of *individuation,* a unique, stable identity. A child's development can be skewed toward mental disorder by the pathology of the mother, a need on her part not to separate from her child, or a re-engulfing of the separated child into an infantile dependency. Mahler also saw a mother's lack of "emotional availability" as a contributor to abnormal development.

To help such a child, a therapist must treat the disturbed parent-child relationship as well as the disturbed child, being sensitive to the conflict over separation-individuation and to the process by which the "dual unity" of mother and child needs to be differentiated into distinct selves. The therapy works through the phases of this process toward the goal of forming a stable sense of personal identity in the patient (Mahler, 1979).

Psychodynamic therapies continue to evolve with a varying emphasis placed on Freud's constructs. Although they have been widely criticized (as we shall see in a final section where different therapeutic approaches are evaluated), there is still considerable enthusiasm by supporters, especially in many western European countries and in large urban centers in the United States.

Behavior Therapies

Behavior therapies apply the principles of conditioning and reinforcement to modify undesirable behavior patterns associated with mental disorders. Fundamental to this orientation is a *rejection* of the medical model and of assumptions about "mentally sick" people suffering from "mental illness." Behavior therapists argue that abnormal behaviors are acquired in the same way as normal behaviors: through a learning process. They assert that all pathological behavior, except where there is established organic causation, can be best understood and treated by focusing on the behavior itself, rather than by attempting to alter any underlying "disease core." The term *behavior* is used by contemporary behavior therapists to include all reactions that are influenced by learning variables—thoughts and feelings, as well as overt actions.

The therapies that have emerged from the theories of conditioning and learning are grounded in a pragmatic, empirical research tradition. The central task of all living organisms is to learn how to adapt to the demands of their current social and physical environment. When organisms do not learn how to cope effectively, their maladaptive reactions can be overcome by therapy based on principles of learning (or relearning). The unique aspect of this treatment is that it is directed toward a modification of *behavior,* rather than a cure of something within an individual.

Many people go through SOAR therapy to overcome their fear of flying.

Mary Cover Jones

Behavior modification is defined as "the attempt to apply learning and other experimentally derived psychological principles to problem behavior" (Bootzin, 1975). The terms *behavior therapy* and *behavior modification* are often used interchangeably. Both refer to the systematic use of principles of learning to increase the frequency of desired behaviors and/or decrease that of problem behaviors. The range of deviant behaviors and personal problems that typically are treated by behavior therapy is extensive, including fears, compulsions, depression, addictions, aggression, and delinquent behaviors.

The target behavior is not assumed to be a symptom of any underlying process. Change the problem behavior and the problem is changed, argue the behaviorists. Psychodynamic therapists predicted that treating only the outer behavior without confronting the true, inner problem would result in *symptom substitution,* the appearance of a new physical or psychological problem, but this has not happened. Research has shown that when pathological behaviors are eliminated by behavior therapy, new symptoms are *not* substituted (Kazdin, 1982). "On the contrary, patients whose target symptoms improved often reported improvement in other, less important symptoms as well" (Sloane et al., 1975, p. 219).

The earliest recorded use of behavior therapy was carried out by Mary Cover Jones in 1924. She showed how fears, learned through conditioning, could be unlearned. In a sense she followed up on the demonstration by John Watson who showed that strong fears could be learned (the case study of little Albert in chapter 8). Her subject was Peter, a 3-year-old boy who was afraid of rabbits. The technique was simply to feed Peter at one end of a room while the rabbit was brought in at the other end. Over a series of sessions, the rabbit was gradually brought closer until finally all fear disappeared and Peter played freely with the rabbit. In essence, the procedure is identical to the technique of "systematic desensitization," which we will cover shortly.

Behavior therapies today are more sophisticated, but still are based on classical conditioning or operant conditioning—or a combination of the two (see chapter 8 if you need a refresher on these two types of conditioning). The development of neurotic fears and other undesirable *emotional* reactions is assumed to follow the paradigm of classical conditioning. Therapy to change these negative responses uses principles of *counterconditioning* to substitute a new response for the inadequate one. Operant conditioning principles are applied when the therapeutic task is to increase the frequency of desired actions or decrease undesired habits. *Contingency management* refers to the general treatment strategy of changing behavior by modifying (managing) its consequences. Special adaptations have also been developed for *social learning* and for generalizing to life situations new responses learned in therapy. Our information about behavior therapy is organized around these basic approaches to conditioning and learning.

Counterconditioning

Why does someone become anxious when faced with a harmless stimulus, such as a fly, a nonpoisonous snake, an open space, or a social contact? We know that *any* neutral stimulus may acquire the power to elicit strong conditioned reactions on the basis of prior association with an unconditioned stimulus. If an unconditioned stimulus has some special evolutionary significance to an individual, or is intense, physically painful, or emotionally traumatic, conditioning can occur with a single pairing.

Strong emotional reactions that disrupt a person's life "for no good reason" are often conditioned responses that the person does not recognize as having been learned. To weaken the strength of negative learned associations, behavior therapists use the techniques of systematic desensitization, implosion, and aversive learning.

Systematic Desensitization and Implosion

It is difficult—but not impossible—to be both happy and sad, or relaxed and anxious, at the same time. This principle is applied in the **systematic desensitization** technique developed primarily by Joseph Wolpe (1958, 1973). Since anxiety is assumed to be a major cause of maladaptive avoidance, a client is taught to prevent the arousal of anxiety by relaxing.

Desensitization therapy involves three major steps. It begins by identifying the stimuli that provoke anxiety in a client and arranging them in a *hierarchy* ranked from weakest to strongest. For example, a student suffering from severe test anxiety constructed the hierarchy in **Table 16.1.** Note that she rated immediate anticipation of an examination as more stressful than taking the exam itself.

Then the client is trained in a system of progressive deep-muscle relaxation. Relaxation training requires several sessions in which the client learns to distinguish between sensations of tension and relaxation, and "to let go of tension" in order to achieve a state of physical and mental relaxation.

Finally, the actual process of desensitization begins. The client, in a relaxed state, is told to imagine, as vividly as possible, the *weakest* anxiety stimulus on the list. If anxiety reactions occur, the client stops and concentrates on relaxing again. When the weakest stimulus can be visualized without discomfort, the client goes on to the next stronger one. Great care is taken not to arouse anxiety during this process of gradually approaching the "unthinkable" stimulus. If anxiety is evoked, the therapist terminates the imagery production, gets the client to relax again, and goes back to a weaker stimulus. After a number of sessions, the most distressing situations on the list can be imagined without anxiety—even situations that could not be faced originally.

Table 16.1 *Hierarchy of Anxiety-Producing Stimuli for a Test-Anxious College Student*

1. On the way to the university on the day of an examination.
2. In the process of answering an examination paper.
3. Before the unopened doors of the examination room.
4. Awaiting the distribution of examination papers.
5. The examination paper face down.
6. The night before an examination.
7. One day before an examination.
8. Two days before an examination.
9. Three days before an examination.
10. Four days before an examination.
11. Five days before an examination.
12. A week before an examination.
13. Two weeks before an examination.
14. A month before an examination.

(Adapted from Wolpe, 1973)

As in other conditioning, stimulus generalization operates. Once anxiety to a particular stimulus is extinguished, there is a *generalization* of this effect to related stimuli. Thus desensitization works both directly, by replacing anxiety with a particular stimulus through relaxation, and indirectly, through generalization of anxiety reduction to similar stimuli.

Desensitization is ideally suited for treatment of specific phobic reactions. These "irrational" behaviors have been maintained (reinforced) by the relief experienced when the anxiety-producing stimuli were avoided or escaped. Desensitization has also been successfully applied to a diversity of other human problems, including such generalized fears as test anxiety, stage fright, impotence, and frigidity (Kazdin & Wilcoxin, 1976; Paul, 1969).

Another technique, **implosion,** uses an opposite approach from systematic desensitization. Instead of experiencing a gradual, step-by-step progression, a client is exposed at the start to the most frightening stimuli at the top of the anxiety hierarchy—but in a "safe" setting.

The rationale for this procedure begins with the recognition that neither anxiety nor the neurotic behavior will ever extinguish as long as the person is allowed to deny, avoid, or otherwise escape from experiencing the anxiety-arousing stimulus situations. The person must discover that contact with the stimulus does not actually have the anticipated negative effects (Stampfl & Levis, 1967).

One way to extinguish an irrational fear is to force a client to experience a full-blown anxiety reaction without suffering any harm. The therapeutic situation is arranged so that the frightening stimulus occurs in circumstances where the client cannot run away. The therapist *describes* an extremely frightening situation relating to the client's fear and urges the client to *imagine* being in it, experiencing it through all the senses as intensely as possible. In this way the client is *flooded* with a rapid exposure to anxiety-eliciting sensations.

Such imagining is assumed to cause an explosion of panic. Since this explosion is an inner one, the process is called *implosion;* hence the term *implosion therapy.* As this happens again and again, and no harm is forthcoming, the stimulus loses its power to elicit anxiety. When anxiety no longer occurs, the maladaptive neurotic behavior previously used to avoid it disappears. Flooding has proven to be superior to systematic desensitization in the treatment of some behavior problems, such as agoraphobia. Treatment gains are shown to be enduring for most clients (Emmelkamp & Kuipers, 1979).

Aversion Therapy

Implosion and desensitization therapies help clients deal directly with stimuli that are not really harmful; but what can be done to help those who are *attracted* to stimuli that *are* harmful or illegal? Drug addiction, sexual perversions, and uncontrollable violence are human problems in which deviant behavior is elicited by "tempting stimuli." **Aversion therapy** uses counterconditioning procedures of aversive learning to pair these stimuli with strong noxious stimuli (such as electric shocks or nausea-producing drugs). In time, through conditioning, the same negative reactions are elicited by the conditioned tempting stimuli, and the person develops an aversion for them.

Why would anyone submit to such a therapy that is, in effect, a kind of torture? Usually people do so only because they realize that the long-term consequences of continuing their behavior pattern will destroy their health or ruin their lives. They may also be coerced to do so by institutional pressures, as has happened in some prison treatment programs.

This man has realized that the only way to overcome his alcohol problem is to submit to aversion therapy. He will receive an electric shock every time he takes a drink.

Many critics are concerned that the painful procedures in aversion therapy give too much power to a therapist, can be more punitive than therapeutic, and are most likely to be used in situations where people have least freedom of choice about what is done to them. The movie *Clockwork Orange*, from Anthony Burgess' novel, depicted aversion therapy as an extreme form of mind control in a police state. In recent years, use of aversive therapy in institutional rehabilitation programs has become more regulated by state laws and ethical guidelines for clinical treatment. In essence, the hope is that, under these restrictions, when used, it will be a therapy of choice rather than coercion.

Contingency Management

The operant conditioning approach to developing desirable behavior is simple: find the reinforcer that will maintain a desired response, apply that reinforcer—contingent upon the response—and evaluate its effectiveness. This approach has been applied to modify behavior in the classroom, in mental hospitals, in homes for the aged, and in many other settings. Even patients who have been totally mute for many years, but are physically capable of speech, have been trained to speak by the use of operant techniques (Sherman, 1963). The two major techniques of contingency management in behavior therapy are *positive reinforcement* and specific *extinction strategies*.

Positive Reinforcement Strategies

When a response is followed immediately by a reward, the response will tend to be repeated and will increase in frequency over time. That central principle of operant learning becomes a therapeutic strategy when it is applied to modifying the frequency of emission of a "desirable" response.

Dramatic success has been obtained in the application of positive reinforcement procedures to the behavior problems of children with psychiatric disorders. Two examples were cited in chapter 8—the case of the little boy who would not wear his glasses and the use of running and screaming in a preschool as reinforcement for sitting still first.

Positive reinforcement procedures have been extended to many other settings and problems. In mental hospitals, token economies have been established to reward positive behavior. In a token economy, patients are tangibly rewarded for socially constructive activities such as maintaining personal cleanliness, arriving on time for meals, and performing assigned tasks. Payment consists of tokens (such as poker chips) that may be used later to "purchase" such luxuries as more elegant dining facilities, increased television time, private sleeping accommodations, and weekend passes (Kazdin, 1980).

Hospital administrators have found that token economies can often be quite effective in eliciting desired behaviors, even on the part of rather severely disturbed patients; but the system works only when the "learners" have no other means of obtaining the things that the tokens will purchase. Some critics have argued that the result is that such a "materialist" system of behavior control gets used primarily with poor, deprived, institutionalized adults and children.

Behavior therapists have generally agreed with this criticism, but they have wanted to maintain the obvious benefits of positive reinforcement systems. One resolution to the problem has been to involve individuals directly in their own contingency management. A **behavioral contract** is an explicit agreement (often in writing) that states the consequences of specific behaviors. Such contracts are often required by behavior therapists working with clients on obesity or smoking problems. The contract may specify what the client is expected to do (client's obligations) and what, in turn, the client can expect from the therapist (therapist's obligations).

Behavioral contracting facilitates therapy by making both parties responsible for achieving the agreed-upon changes in behavior. Treatment goals are spelled out, as well as the specific rewards that are associated with meeting planned responsibilities and reaching desired subgoals. The therapeutic situation becomes more structured in terms of what each party can reasonably expect as appropriate content and acceptable interpersonal behavior. The person with less status and power (patient or child, for example) benefits if a condition for third-party arbitration of alleged contract violation is included (Nelson & Mowrey, 1976).

It is not reasonable to expect all individuals to be able to collaborate on behavioral contracts; hospitalized psychotic patients may not be able to understand the complicated steps and mutual commitments involved, for example; however, the idea of engaging the client or patient in a joint decision-making effort about the way to use positive reinforcement to change behaviors is a step forward from the original institutional use of token economies. Some parents have found that contracts with their teenagers have brought more acceptable behavior while greatly improving the emotional climate of the home; reinforcements, in fact, often include more reasonable parental behaviors and both people benefit (Stuart, 1971).

Extinction Strategies

Why do people continue to do something that causes pain and distress when they are capable of doing otherwise? The answer is that many forms of behavior have multiple consequences—some negative, some positive. Often subtle positive reinforcements keep a behavior going despite its obvious negative consequences. Children punished for misbehaving may continue to misbehave if punishment is the only form of attention they can earn.

Extinction is useful in therapy when neurotic behaviors have been maintained by unrecognized reinforcing circumstances. Those reinforcers are identified by a careful situational analysis, and then a program is arranged to withhold them in the presence of the undesirable response. When this approach is possible, the behavior becomes less frequent and is eventually extinguished.

Even psychotic behavior can be maintained and encouraged by unintentional reinforcement. It is standard procedure in many mental hospitals for the staff to ask patients frequently how they are feeling. This may suggest to the patients that the "appropriate" behavior is to be thinking and talking about one's feelings, unusual symptoms, hallucinations, and so on. In fact, the more bizarre the symptoms and verbalizations, the more attention the staff members may show in their efforts to understand the "dynamics" of the case.

Dramatic decreases in psychotic behavior sometimes have been observed when the staff was simply instructed to ignore the psychotic behavior and to give attention to the patients only when they were behaving normally (Ayllon & Michael, 1959). Just as positive reinforcement can increase the incidence of a behavior, the *lack* of desirable consequences can make it less likely to occur. With a "time-out from reinforcement" the target behavior stops being followed by its usual consequence—and should begin to extinguish.

Punishment

We have not mentioned a most obvious, traditional form of behavior modification—"a good spanking for doing bad things." *Punishment* is not used by most therapists, because it is counterproductive to the long-term goal of all treatment programs, namely, the person's future *self-regulation* of behavior in his or her natural environment. Punishment "works" to stop ongoing behavior, suppressing it in the presence of the punishing agent. On the "cost" side of the ledger punishment generates many negative side effects that are beneficial neither to the punished person nor to the interpersonal relationship with the punisher (as we noted in chapter 8).

Punishment is most typically used in a treatment setting in response to a patient's self-injurious behavior, but then it is used in combination with shaping an appropriate behavior. This is the case with some autistic children who must be kept in restraints continuously because they bang their heads against the walls or crib. Electric shocks stop the self-destructive behavior, allow them to be free from "straightjackets" and able to be reinforced for new behaviors (Lovaas, 1977).

Are there circumstances when punishment can be used to good effect by parents, teachers, and therapists as part of their arsenal of strategies for behavior modification? Yes, according to many experts, as long as the message it conveys is that it is simply a means to achieve an end seen to be in the best interest of the person being punished. It loses its potential for changing undesirable behavior if it is perceived as a hostile reaction of a frustrated punishing agent rather than as a reasoned strategy for controlling a specific behavior that has not been responsive to other reinforcement contingencies. Instead of using physical abuse, punishment tactics can more effectively employ time outs from, and restricted access to, desired activities, curfews, and other limitations on behavioral freedoms. There are no conditions when public humiliation is ever justified as "therapeutic" for an individual being punished, although it may serve as a deterrent to others engaging in similar behaviors. The dictum is "punish the undesirable response, but not the person—who should never be made to feel that he or she is undesirable, as well."

Social Learning Therapy

Behavior therapies have been given an expanded focus by social learning theorists who point out that humans learn—for better or worse—by observing the behavior of other people. Often we learn and apply rules to understand new experiences, not just through direct participation, but also through symbolic means, such as watching other people's experiences in life, in a movie, or on TV. Social learning therapy is based on observing others; it has been of special value in overcoming phobias and building social skills. We have noted in earlier chapters that this social learning approach was largely developed by Albert Bandura (1977a, 1986).

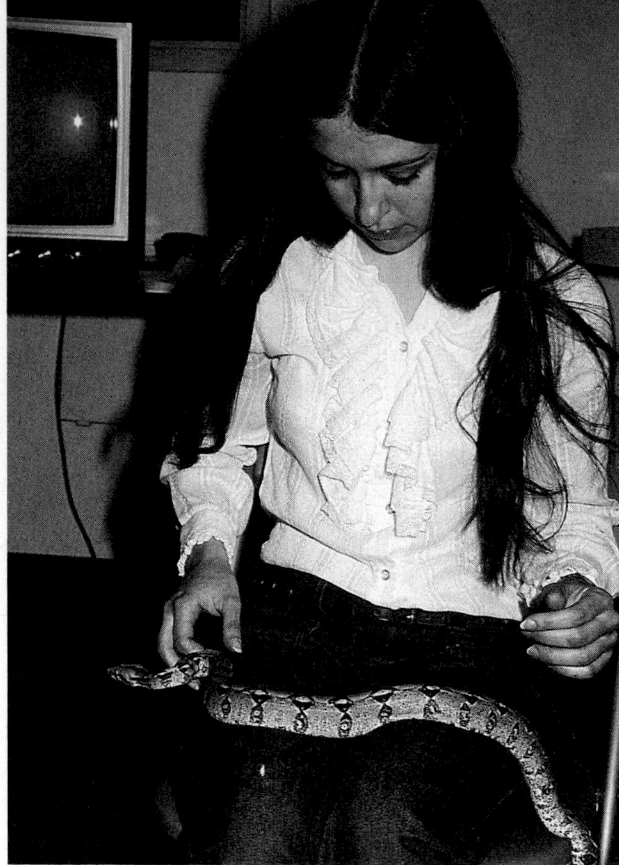

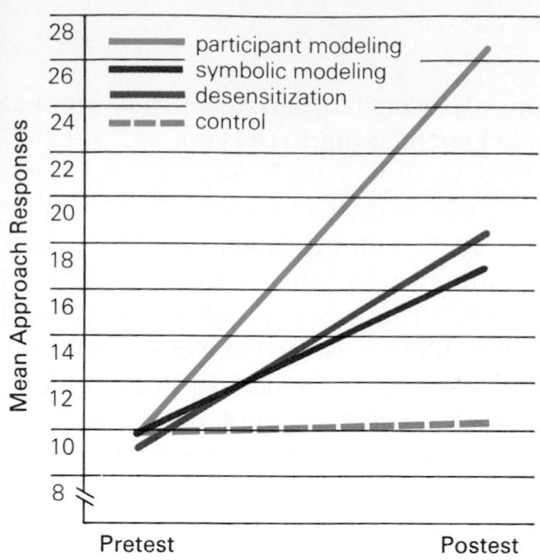

Figure 16.1
The subject shown in the photo first watched a model make a graduated series of snake-approach responses and then repeated them herself. She eventually was able to pick up the snake and let it crawl about on her. The graph compares the number of approach responses made by subjects before and after receiving participant modeling therapy with the behavior of those exposed to two other therapeutic techniques and a control group. (Adapted from Bandura, 1970)

Imitation of Models

Before desired responses can be reinforced, they must occur. Many new responses, especially complex ones, can be acquired more readily if a person can observe and imitate another person (model) who performs the desired behavior and is reinforced for doing so.

In treating a phobia of snakes, a therapist using this method will first demonstrate fearless approach behavior at a relatively minor level, perhaps approaching a snake's cage or touching a snake. The client is aided, through demonstration and supportive encouragement, to imitate the modeled behavior. Gradually the approach behaviors are shaped so that the client can pick the snake up and let it crawl freely over him or her. At no time is the client forced to perform any behavior. Resistance at any level is overcome by having the client return to a previously successful, less threatening approach behavior.

The power of this form of **participant modeling** can be seen in research comparing the participant modeling technique just described with symbolic modeling, desensitization, and a control condition (see **Figure 16.1**). In symbolic modeling therapy, subjects who had been trained in relaxation techniques watched a film in which several models fearlessly handled snakes; the subjects could stop the film and relax themselves whenever a scene made them feel anxious. In the control condition, no therapeutic intervention was used. Participant modeling was clearly the most successful of these techniques. Snake phobia was eliminated in eleven of the twelve subjects in the participant modeling group (Bandura, 1970).

Imitation of models has also been used to teach autistic, mute children to talk. The children were first reinforced for making sounds resembling those of the model-therapist, then only for duplicating his words. Finally, reinforcement was contingent upon being more socially responsive. Although the process is long, tedious, and requires much patience by the therapist, it reveals that such behavior change tactics *do* work where all others fail. (Lovaas, 1968).

Social Skills Training

A major therapeutic innovation encouraged by social learning therapists is training people with inadequate social skills to be more effective (Hersen & Bellack, 1976). Many difficulties arise for someone with a psychotic or neurotic disorder, or even just an everyday problem, simply because he or she is socially inhibited, inept, or unassertive. *Social skills* are sets or responses that enable a person to be effective when approaching or interacting with others. They include knowing *what* to say and do in given situations (content) in order to elicit a desired response (consequences), as well as *how* (style) and *when* (timing) to do so. One of the most common social skill problems is lack of assertiveness, inability to state one's own thoughts or wishes in a clear, direct, nonaggressive manner (Bower & Bower, 1976). To overcome such a problem, many social learning therapists recommend **behavioral rehearsal.** This includes all the procedures used to establish and strengthen any basic skill, from personal hygiene to work habits to social interactions. It is accomplished through a combination of modeling, instruction, behavioral contracting, and repeated practice of what to say and do with specific feedback. Behavioral rehearsal procedures are being widely used in social skills training programs with many different populations (Yates, 1985).

One application of this approach modified abusive verbal outbursts in pyschiatric patients. They were taught to handle interpersonal disagreements, not by their usual strategies of avoidance, intimidation, or violence, but by learning to make appropriately assertive responses in those situations. (Foy et al., 1975; Frederiksen et al., 1976)

It has been found that adult pathology has often been preceded by deficits in social skills in childhood (Oden & Asher, 1977). A considerable amount of research and therapy is currently directed at building competence in shy and withdrawn disturbed children (Conger & Keane, 1981; Zimbardo & Radl, 1981).

One study demonstrated that preschool-age children diagnosed as "social isolates" could be helped to become sociable in a short training period.

Twenty-four subjects were randomly assigned to one of three play conditions: with a same-age peer, with a peer 1 to 1½ years younger, or a control condition with no partner. The pairs were brought together for ten play sessions, each only 20 minutes long, over a period of about a month. Their classroom behavior before and after this treatment was recorded and revealed a strong effect of the intervention.

The opportunity to play with a younger playmate doubled the frequency with which the former social isolates interacted later on with other classmates—bringing them up to the average level of the other children. Playing with a same-age peer also increased children's sociability, but not nearly so much. The researchers concluded that the one-on-one play situation had offered the shy children safe opportunities to be socially assertive. They were allowed to practice leadership skills that were likely to be approved by the nonthreatening, younger playmates. (Furman et al., 1979)

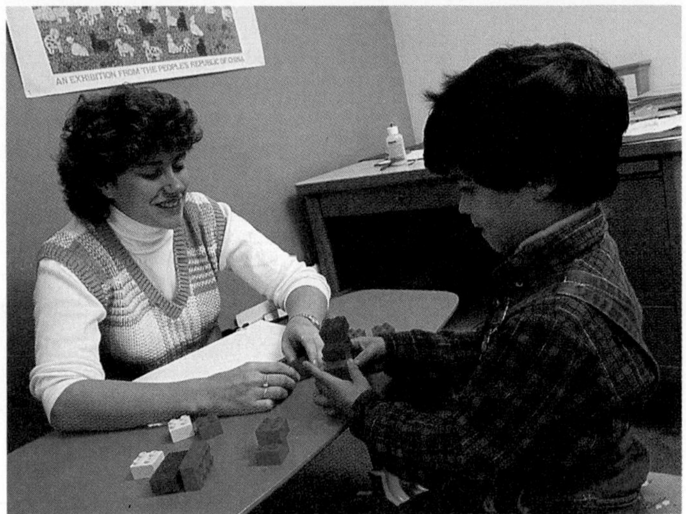

A shy child can develop social skills by interacting with a therapist through play therapy.

In another study, social skills training with a group of hospitalized emotionally disturbed children changed both verbal and nonverbal components of their behavior in social settings. The children were taught to give appropriate verbal responses in various social situations (giving help or compliments, making requests). They were also taught to display appropriate affect (for example, to smile while giving a compliment) and to make eye contact and use proper body posture (face the person being talked to).

These improved social skills were generalized to "untreated" situations outside of training. The children also put them into practice on their own when on the ward. These good effects were found to continue even months later. (Matson et al., 1980)

Generalization Techniques

An issue of concern for behavior therapists is whether new behavior patterns generated in a therapeutic setting will actually be used in the everyday situations faced by clients. This question is important for all therapies, and any measure of treatment effectiveness must include maintenance of long-term changes that go beyond a therapist's couch, a clinic, or a laboratory.

When essential aspects of a client's real-life setting are absent from the therapy program, behaviors that have been modified by therapy can be expected to deteriorate over time when therapy terminates. To prevent this loss, it is becoming common practice to build *generalization techniques* into the therapeutic procedure itself. These techniques attempt to *increase* the similarity of target behaviors, reinforcers, models, and stimulus demands between therapy and real-life settings.

For example, behaviors are taught that are likely to be reinforced naturally in a person's environment, such as showing courtesy or consideration. Rewards are given on a partial reinforcement schedule so their effect will be maintained when rewards are not always forthcoming in the real world. The dependence of token-economy patients on tangible token rewards is gradually *faded out* while social approval and more naturally occurring consequences are introduced. Opportunities are provided for patients to practice new behaviors under the supportive guidance of staff members during field trips away from the institution. Halfway houses also help to transfer new behaviors from the institution to the community setting (Fairweather et al., 1969; Orlando, 1981). Careful attention to ways of increasing the generalizability of treatment effects will enhance the long-term success of behavior therapy (Marks, 1981).

Before turning to cognitive therapies, take a few minutes to review the major differences between the two dominant psychotherapies—the psychoanalytical and the behavioral—as summarized in **Table 16.2.** Not mentioned in the table is the time course of these therapies. While psychoanalysis is both intensive and long in duration (daily for several years or more) behavioral therapies are typically time-limited to a specific number of treatments or to achieving a specific behavioral goal, often in less than a year.

Table 16.2 *Comparison of Psychoanalytic and Behavioristic Approaches to Psychotherapy*

Issue	***Psychoanalysis***	***Behavior Therapy***
Basic Human Nature	Biological instincts, primarily sexual and aggressive, press for immediate release, bringing people into conflict with social reality.	Like other animals, people are born only with the capacity for learning, which follows similar principles in all species.
Normal Human Development	Growth occurs through resolution of conflicts during successive stages. Through identification and internalization, mature ego controls and character structures emerge.	Adaptive behaviors are learned through reinforcement and imitation.
Nature of Psychopathology	Pathology reflects inadequate conflict resolutions and fixations in earlier development, which leave overly strong impulses and/or weak controls. Symptoms are defensive responses to anxiety.	Problematic behavior derives from faulty learning of maladaptive behaviors. The "symptom" is the problem; there is no "underlying disease."
Goal of Therapy	Psychosexual maturity, strengthened ego functions, reduced control by unconscious and repressed impulses are attained.	"Symptomatic" behavior is removed by eliminating it and replacing it with adaptive behaviors.
Psychological Realm Emphasized	Motives and feelings, fantasies and cognitions are experienced.	Therapy involves behavior and observable feelings and actions.
Time Orientation	The orientation is discovering and interpreting past conflicts and repressed feelings in light of the present.	There is little or no concern with early history or etiology. Present behavior is examined and treated.
Role of Unconscious Material	This is primary in classical psychoanalysis, somewhat less emphasized by neo-Freudians.	There is no concern with unconscious processes or with subjective experience even in conscious realm.
Role of Insight	Insight is central; emerges in "corrective emotional experiences."	Therapy is irrelevant and/or unnecessary.
Role of Therapist	The therapist functions as a *detective,* searching basic root conflicts and resistances; detached and neutral, to facilitate transference reactions.	The therapist functions as a *trainer,* helping patients unlearn old behaviors and/or learn new ones. Control of reinforcement is important; interpersonal relation is minor.

(Adapted from Korchin, 1976)

Cognitive Therapies

Cognitive therapies attempt to change problem feelings and behaviors by changing the way a client thinks about significant life experiences. Underlying this approach is the assumption that abnormal behavior patterns and emotional distress start with problems in *what* we think (cognitive content), and *how* we think (cognitive process).

Remember the case of Gary, the "nearly perfect student" in the *Opening Case?* His problems were treated by changing the way he thought about himself, his expectations about academic performance, and the image he presented to others. He was given a brief exposure to a therapy designed to alter his current thoughts about these major problem areas in his life.

The increasing numbers of cognitive therapies focus on different types of cognitive processes and different methods for "cognitive restructuring." The two major approaches are those that involve cognitive behavior modification (including "self-efficacy") and those that try to alter false belief systems (including "rational-emotive therapy" and cognitive therapy for depression).

Cognitive Behavior Modification

We are what we tell ourselves we can be, and we are guided by what we believe we ought to do. That is a starting assumption of **cognitive behavior modification.** This therapeutic approach combines the cognitive emphasis on the importance of thoughts and attitudes to influence motivation and response with the focus of behaviorism on performance that is changed by modifying reinforcement contingencies. Unacceptable behavior patterns are modified by changing a person's negative self-statements into constructive coping statements.

You learned Donald Meichenbaum's (1977) three-phase process for changing behavior patterns in chapter 14. The sequence includes (a) *cognitive preparation* in which therapist and client discover how the client thinks about and expresses the problem for which therapy is sought; (b) *skill acquisition* and *rehearsal,* which involve learning new self-statements that are constructive, while minimizing the use of self-defeating ones (anxiety-eliciting or esteem reducing); and, finally, (c) *application* and *practice* of the new learning in actual situations, starting with easy ones and graduating to those more difficult.

For example, for the negative self-statement "I was really boring at that party; they'll never ask me back" a more positive one is substituted. "Next time, if I want to appear interesting, I will plan some provocative opening lines, practice telling a good joke, and be responsive to the host's stories." Someone "feeling overwhelmed" by a fear of tests can rehearse as follows:

1. "I've studied carefully and know enough of the information";
2. "I will take some deep breaths, pause, and be ready to do my best";
3. "I will focus on the present, attend only to the test materials";
4. "I will answer the questions I know first to increase my confidence";
5. "My fear may rise when I don't recall something; that's OK, I can manage it and use that energy to help me search my memory for the missing information";
6. "I can do (am doing) a good job on this test";
7. "It seems like a big deal now, but it will be over shortly and whatever happens will itself be just a memory when I look back on it in the future";
8. "I will reward myself for my studying and concentration with a movie tonight and two new albums if I do as well as I now think I will."

Building *expectations of being effective* increases the likelihood of behaving effectively. It is through setting attainable goals, developing realistic strategies for attaining them, and evaluating feedback realistically that people develop a sense of mastery and self-efficacy (Bandura et al., 1980).

Changing False Beliefs

Some cognitive behavior therapists emphasize the important role of thoughts, but still use many behavioral assumptions—such as the rewarding or punishing function of thoughts. Other cognitive therapists put less emphasis on behavioral processes. Their primary targets for change in psychotherapy are beliefs, attitudes, and habitual thought patterns, or "schemas." These cognitive therapists argue that many psychological problems arise because of the way we think about ourselves in relation to other people and events we face. Faulty thinking can be based on: (a) unreasonable attitudes ("Being perfect is the most important trait for a student to have"), (b) false premises ("If I do everything they want me to, then I'll be popular"), or (c) rigid rules that put behavior on "automatic pilot," so that prior patterns are repeated even when they have not worked ("I must obey authorities"). Emotional distress is seen as caused by misunderstandings and by failing to distinguish between current reality and one's imagination (or expectations).

Cognitive Therapy for Depression

A cognitive therapist induces a patient to correct faulty patterns of thinking by applying more effective problem-solving techniques. Aaron Beck has successfully pioneered cognitive therapy for the problem of depression. He states the formula for treatment in simple form: "The therapist helps the patient to identify his warped thinking and to learn more realistic ways to formulate his experiences" (1976, p. 20). For example, depressed individuals may be instructed to write down negative thoughts about themselves, figure out why these self-criticisms are unjustified, and come up with more realistic (and less destructive) self-cognitions.

Beck believes that depression is maintained because depressed patients are unaware of the negative "automatic thoughts" that they habitually say to themselves, thoughts such as "I will never be as good as my brother"; "Nobody would like me if they really knew me"; "I'm not smart enough to make it in this competitive school." A therapist then uses four tactics to change the cognitive foundation that supports the depression: (1) reality testing is conducted and the evidence the patient has for and against these automatic thoughts is evaluated; (2) blame is reattributed to situational factors rather than to the patient's incompetence; (3) alternative solutions to the problem are openly discussed; and (4) basic assumptions are made explicit and challenged, such as Gary's that "In order to be accepted, I must be perfect" (Beck et al., 1979).

Rational-Emotive Therapy

One of the earliest forms of cognitive therapy was the *rational-emotive therapy* developed by Albert Ellis (1962, 1977). It is a comprehensive system of personality change based on changing irrational beliefs that are causing undesirable, highly charged emotional reactions, such as severe anxiety. Clients may have core values *demanding* that they succeed and be approved, *insisting* that they be treated fairly, or *dictating* that the universe be more pleasant. A therapist teaches clients how to recognize the shoulds, oughts, and musts that are controlling their actions and preventing them from choosing the life they want.

A therapist attempts to break through a client's "closed-mindedness" by showing that an emotional reaction which follows some event is really because of unrecognized beliefs about the event. For example, failure to achieve orgasm during intercourse (event) is followed by an emotional reaction of depression and self-derogation. The belief that is causing the emotional reaction is likely to be "I am sexually inadequate and may be impotent, or frigid, because I failed to perform as expected." This belief (and others) is openly disputed through rational confrontation and examination of alternative reasons for the event, such as fatigue, too much alcohol, false notions of sexual "performance," or really not wanting to engage in intercourse at that time. This technique is followed by a variety of others—those used in behavior modification, humor, and role-playing to replace dogmatic, irrational thinking with rational, situationally appropriate ideas.

Rational-emotive therapy aims at increasing an individual's sense of self-worth and the potential to be self-actualized by getting rid of the system of faulty beliefs that block personal growth. As such, it shares much with humanistic therapies, which we consider after first examining a therapy that is a "newcomer" for Westerners, one which has its origins in a different cultural tradition—Morita therapy.

Morita Therapy

In the early twentieth century a Japanese contemporary of Freud, Dr. Shoma Morita, developed a character-building process which aimed at overcoming certain neuroses, such as shyness, procrastination phobias, and feelings of inferiority. This system which has its roots in Eastern thought, notably Zen Buddhism, focuses on a wholly pragmatic and action-centered approach to solving these problems. Morita therapy assists a distressed person to "get on with the business of life" in the face of personal problems.

The leading practitioner and advocate for Morita psychotherapy in the United States, David Reynolds (1980, 1984), uses the term *constructive living* to categorize the principles of this "path" to mental health. Constructive living is a way of approaching life *mindfully* with attention to what is controllable and what is not. The credo of this work is "Do what needs to be done." Three principles underlie Morita therapy: (a) Emotions or feelings of all kinds, like weather, are natural to the human condition, but arise quite independent of will. Feelings cannot be controlled, but can be and should be accepted simply as they are. We are not responsible for our feelings. (b) Behavior *is* controllable regardless of the feelings that precede or accompany it; therefore, the essence of Morita treatment is found in focusing on specific actions to be taken. (c) Understanding the dynamics of this intricate and complex dance between feeling and behavior comes from the personal experience of living responsibly and "doing what needs to be done" rather than from intellectual constructs.

In Morita therapy no time is spent trying to understand one's feelings, nor their origins or causes. All too often even vivid insight into the cause of a feeling such as shyness or depression has no influence on a person's actual behavior. Morita therapy runs counter to many Western psychological theories and treatment models, especially Freudian, since it asserts that insight may feel satisfying intellectually, but provokes no life change.

The Morita therapist acts as a "guide," giving clear and practical feedback to help patients separate issues of feeling from those of behavior. This "work" is done through assignments based on patients' actual life problems and schedules to help them begin to develop concrete, daily strategies for getting on with the responsibilities and commitments of life even in the face of contrary or nonsupportive feelings. Negative feelings, according to these therapists, often have a way of simply disappearing when people are engaged in purposeful action—without action, these feelings may dominate.

> Client: You see, doctor, I'm just so depressed. I just can't seem to get it together. My parents are hassling me about my grades and my girlfriend is leaving and I just don't feel like studying.
>
> Therapist: You mean you didn't study.
>
> Client: That's what I said.
>
> Therapist: No, you said you didn't *feel* like studying. Feelings are one thing. What you do is another. Did you go to class today? Have you been in the library? Did you read any assignments, write anything? Did you make a list of what is required for school tomorrow?
>
> Client: You don't seem to understand how bad I feel.
>
> Therapist: I do care that you are hurting. I care so much that I want you to do what will bring you the greatest payoff in your life. Doing what needs to be done will have an impact on your feelings, too.

This philosophy and treatment form, also called a "lifeway," is practiced widely in Japan. Interest in these ideas and their application to modern life has spread recently to the United States (see Reynolds, 1986).

Existential-Humanistic Therapies

Among the primary symptoms for which many college students seek therapy are general dissatisfaction, feelings of alienation, and failure to achieve all they feel they should. Problems in everyday living, the lack of meaningful human relationships, and the absence of significant goals to strive for are thought of as "existential crises" by proponents of humanism and existentialism. These orientations have contributed to a therapy that addresses itself to basic problems of existence common to all human beings.

The humanistic movement has been called a "third force" in psychology, because it grew out of a reaction to the two dominant forces with the pessimistic view of human nature offered by early psychoanalytic theory and the mechanistic view offered by early radical behaviorism. At the time the humanistic movement was forming in the United States, similar viewpoints, which came to be known collectively as *existentialism,* had already gained acceptance in Europe.

At the core of both humanistic and existential therapies is the concept of a whole person in the continual process of changing and of becoming. Although environment and heredity place certain restrictions on the process of becoming, we remain always free to choose what we will become by creating our own values and committing ourselves to them through our decisions. Along with this *freedom to choose,* however, comes the burden of responsibility. Since we are never fully aware of all the implications of our actions, we experience anxiety and despair. We also suffer from guilt over lost opportunities to achieve our full potential.

Psychotherapies that apply the principles of this general theory of human nature attempt to help clients define their own freedom, value their experiencing selves and the richness of the present moment, cultivate their individuality, and discover ways of realizing their fullest potential (self-actualization). Of importance in the existential perspective is the current life situation experienced by individuals (their phenomenological views).

Client-centered Therapy

As pioneered by Carl Rogers, this humanistic approach to treating people with problems has had a significant impact on the way many different kinds of therapists define their relationship to their clients. Its primary goal is promoting the healthy psychological growth of the individual (Rogers, 1951). This approach begins with the assumption that all people share the basic tendency of human nature toward self-actualization—that is, to realize one's potentialities (discussed in chapter 12). Rogers believed that, "It is the inherent tendency of the organism to develop all its capacities in ways which seem to maintain or enhance the organism" (1959, p. 196). Mature, well-adjusted people make judgments based on their own evaluations of what is intrinsically satisfying and actualizing. This healthy development is hindered by faulty learning patterns in which a person accepts the evaluations of others in place of those provided by his or her own mind and body. A conflict between one's naturally positive self-image and negative external criticisms creates anxiety and unhappiness. This conflict, or *incongruence,* may function outside of one's awareness so that a person experiences feelings of unhappiness and low self-worth without knowing why.

The task of Rogerian therapy is to create a therapeutic environment that allows a client to become able again to evaluate how best to behave in order to contribute to self-enhancement and self-actualization. Since a person is assumed to be basically good, the therapist's task is helping to remove barriers that limit the expression of this natural positive tendency. The basic therapeutic strategy is to recognize, accept, and clarify a client's feelings. This is done within an atmosphere of *unconditional positive regard*—nonjudgmental acceptance and respect for the client, with no strings attached, no performance evaluations to be met. The emotional style and attitude of the therapist empowers the client to attend once again to the true sources of personal conflict and begin to remove the distracting influences that suppress self-actualization. A consequence is the stripping away of the client's defenses that were erected to deal with criticism and rejection. The therapist is tuned in to his or her own feelings and thoughts, and allows them to be transparent to the client. In addition to this *genuineness,* the therapist tries to experience the client's feelings. Such total empathy rests upon a caring for the client as a worthy, competent individual who is not to be evaluated or judged but is to be assisted in discovering his or her individuality (Meador & Rogers, 1979).

Client-centered therapy strives to be *nondirective* by having the therapist merely facilitate the patient's search for self-awareness and self-acceptance, never to direct it. Unlike other therapies, in which the therapist interprets, gives answers, or instructs, the therapist is a supportive listener who reflects, and, at times, restates, the client's evaluative statements and feelings. An example of the way a client-centered therapy interaction might proceed is as follows:

> Client: My boyfriend really bugs me. He never likes my friends or whatever I try to do to get my career started. I'm fed up with it.
>
> Therapist: You sound angry with him.
>
> Client: You bet! I am just trying my best, but I guess it's not good enough for him. He's got impossibly high standards that I always fail to meet.
>
> Therapist: Which makes you feel what?
>
> Client: Dumb, silly, and frustrated, like a kid.
>
> Therapist: Maybe you are not just angry with him?
>
> Client: No I'm upset that I can't stand up for what I believe is best for me. Now that I think of it, it's like when I was younger and my dad was always laying down the "shoulds" and "oughts" I had to follow to be accepted. . . .

The key ingredient in this therapeutic exchange is the patient's honest talk about her emotions and self-evaluations. Rogers believes that once freed to relate to others openly and to accept themselves, individuals have the potential to lead themselves back to psychological health. This optimistic view and the "humane" relationship between therapist-as-caring-expert and client-as-person has influenced many practitioners (see Smith, 1982).

Human Potential Movement

The source of the "human potential movement" that sprang up in the United States in the late 1960s is to be found in the general perspective of the existential-humanistic therapies. The human potential movement encompasses all those practices and methods that release the potential of the average human being for greater levels of performance and greater richness of experience. Therapy for growth, personal enrichment, increased interpersonal sensitivity, and greater joy in sex is the modern offspring of existential and humanistic views of human nature. Thus, therapy originally intended for the mentally disturbed has been extended to well, normal people who want to be more effective, productive, and happier human beings. This is one of the major changes in the direction of psychotherapy in the past few decades. It has also spilled out of the confines of therapists' offices into the popular culture with large group activities where hundreds of people are brought together for intensive weekend "encounter" sessions, as in EST, Lifespring, and other self-help businesses. Although these brief, relatively impersonal sessions, can help many people they must be viewed with caution since there is no systematic follow-up to learn about and deal with any adverse reactions of the participants.

Group therapy can be designed to accommodate a variety of goals.

Group Therapies

All the treatment approaches outlined thus far are primarily designed to be "one-on-one" relationships between a patient or client and a therapist. There are many reasons why therapy in groups has begun to flourish and may even be more effective than individual therapy in some cases. Group therapy (a) is less expensive to participants; (b) better utilizes limited mental health personnel; (c) is a less threatening power situation for many people; (d) allows powerful group processes to be used to influence individual maladaptive behavior, such as group consensus, commitment, and modeling; and (e) provides opportunity to observe and practice interpersonal skills.

The use of group processes as a medium for personal change is common to an extraordinarily diverse range of groups, with varied goals and philosophies. Recent estimates put the number of Americans who have participated in some form of encounter group for personal growth at over 5 million. Untold others participate in self-help groups (such as those for weight reduction, alcoholism, or consciousness raising), and many are involved in more formal varieties of group psychotherapy that share some of the basic views of the humanist and existentialist approaches (Lieberman, 1977).

Group therapies have some basic premises that differ from those of individual therapy. The social setting provides an opportunity to learn how one "comes across" to others, how the self-image that is projected differs from the one that is intended or personally experienced. In addition, the group provides confirmation that one's symptoms, problems, and "deviant" reactions are not unique, but often are quite common. Since we tend to conceal from others the negatives about ourselves, it is possible for many people with the same problem to believe "it's only me." The shared group experience can help to dispel this *pluralistic ignorance.* In addition, the group of peers "who all have been there" can provide social support outside of the therapy setting, as the members of Alcoholics Anonymous do in virtually any city an individual member visits.

When group therapy is effective, what variables seem to account for its curative value? Some of the general variables include:

- feelings of belonging and acceptance;
- opportunities to observe, imitate, and be socially rewarded;
- experiencing the universality of human problems, weaknesses, and strengths;
- recreating analogues to the primary family group which enables corrective emotional experiences to take place (Klein, 1983).

Two group therapy approaches that have developed special techniques now used by other therapists are Gestalt therapy and transactional analysis. After we examine these techniques, we will see what is unique about new therapies for couples and families.

Gestalt Therapy

Gestalt therapy focuses on ways to unite mind and body to make a person whole. (Recall the orientation of Gestalt psychologists to the study of perception, described in chapter 6.) Its goal of self-awareness is reached by learning to express pent-up feelings in a group and to recognize "unfinished business" from past conflicts that is carried into new relationships. Fritz Perls (1969), its originator, asked participants to act out fantasies concerning conflicts and strong feelings, and also to recreate their dreams, which were seen as repressed parts of personality. He said, "We have to *re-own* these projected, fragmented parts of our personality, and re-own the hidden potential that appears in the dream" (1967, p. 67).

Transactional Analysis

In transactional analysis, as developed by Eric Berne (1972), group members are encouraged to describe the "games" they play in their interpersonal relationships and also to enact them. By doing so, they become aware of the habitual patterns of manipulation they impose on others.

One typical status manipulation is termed the "Why Don't You—Yes But" game of "one-upmanship." One person assumes a docile, low status role of soliciting advice from another person: "Why don't you try to find a solution to my problem?" Whatever the advice offered, the person counters with "Yes, but—you haven't considered . . ." all the things which make the advice worthless, or stupid. If the would-be helper continues to try to help, there is always another, "Yes but," until the helper quits and the "victim" achieves victory and an illusory boost in status. Removing these deceptive strategies in therapy opens the possibility of achieving more honest, meaningful relationships with other people.

Support Groups for the Terminally Ill

A new development in group therapy is the application of psychological group therapy techniques as interventions with patients who have terminal illnesses, such as cancer and AIDS. The goals of such therapy are to help patients live as fulfilling lives as possible during their illnesses; to cope realistically with impending death; and to help them and their families adjust optimally to the terminal illness as a central component of overall quality care of mind and body (Adams, 1979; Yalom & Greaves, 1977). Objective evidence for the psychological benefit of supportive group intervention for terminally ill patients was demonstrated in a controlled experiment with women who had metastatic (spreading) cancer of the breast.

> *Eighty-six women patients with breast cancer were randomly assigned to a control or year-long treatment program of weekly supportive group meetings. The groups focused on problems faced by terminal illness, improving relationships with family, friends, and staff, and living as fully as possible in the face of death. Evaluations done at four-month intervals revealed that the treatment group members were less anxious, confused, fatigued, and fearful than the controls. Their moods were significantly less distressed, and they showed fewer maladaptive coping responses. (Spiegel et al., 1981).*

Marital and Family Therapy

Much group therapy involves strangers who come together periodically to form a temporary association from which they may benefit. However, some people's troubles come from their association with others they are familiar with—spouses and family members.

Couples counseling for marital problems seeks to clarify the typical communication patterns of the

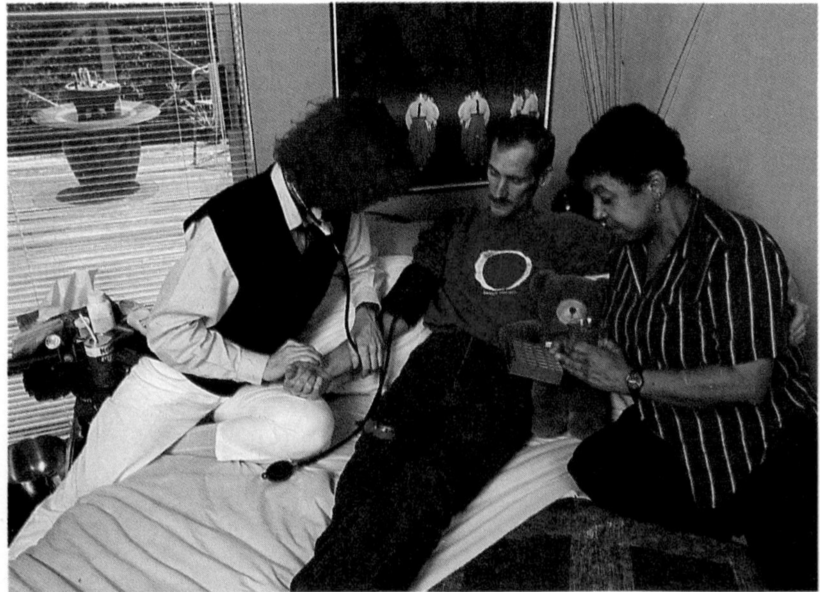

Home care and outpatient programs must absorb the caseload of people with AIDS and ARC, AIDS-Related Complex. Hospice workers visit the victims, giving them physical and emotional support.

partners and then to improve the quality of their interaction. By seeing a couple together, and often videotaping and playing back their interactions, a therapist can help them appreciate the verbal and nonverbal styles they use to dominate or control each other. Each party is taught how to reinforce desirable responding in the other and withdraw reinforcement for undesirable reactions; they are also taught nondirective listening skills to help the other person clarify and express feelings and ideas. Couples therapy is more effective to resolve marital problems than is individual therapy for only one partner, and it has been shown to reduce marital crises and keep marriages intact (Cookerly, 1980; Gurman & Kniskern, 1978).

In family therapy, the client is a whole nuclear family, treated as members of a system of relationships. A family therapist works together with troubled family members to help them perceive *what* is happening among them that is creating problems for one or more of them. The focus is on altering the "spaces" between people and their relationships, rather than on changing processes within maladjusted individuals (Foley, 1979).

Family therapy can reduce tensions within a family and improve the functioning of individual members. The therapist plays many roles, acting as an interpreter and clarifier of the interactions that are taking place in the therapy session, and as influence agent, mediator, and referee. Most family therapists assume that the problems brought into therapy represent *situational* difficulties between people, problems of social interaction. These difficulties may develop over time as members are forced into or accept unsatisfying roles (Satir, 1967). Nonproductive communication patterns may be set up in response to natural transitions in a family system—loss of a job, a child's going to school, starting to date, getting married, having a new baby, and so forth.

In a *structured family therapy* approach, the family is seen as the system that is creating disturbances in the individuals rather than the other way around (Minuchin, 1974). The therapist focuses on the way the family interacts in the present in order to understand its organizational structure, power hierarchy, channels of communication, and who gives and gets blame for what goes wrong. As a consultant to an organization might do, a family therapist actively—but not always directly—tries to help the family "system" reorganize its structure and function better to meet the needs of its members and the demands imposed on it.

Biomedical Therapies

The ecology of the mind is held in delicate balance. It can be upset by mishaps in the workings of our genes, hormones, enzymes, metabolism, and other biochemical events. Behavior and affect (emotional tone) are end-products of brain mechanisms. When something goes wrong with the brain, we see the consequences in abnormal patterns of behavior and peculiar emotional reactions. Similarly, environmental, social, or behavioral disturbances can alter brain chemistry, as we know from the effects of certain kinds of pollution, drugs, and violence.

One approach to correcting these wrongs has been to change the functioning of the brains of disturbed people. This has been accomplished by means of surgically destroying specific areas in the brain or by administering to the brain electroshock of sufficient intensity to cause a temporary coma and, presumably, disruption of the brain's own electrical activity. These extreme, irreversible approaches have been used less as our understanding of the biochemical bases of nervous system functioning has become more precise.

The newer interventions have been guided by research discoveries from many fields of neuroscience. The most dramatic modern therapeutic approach emerging from this research is *chemotherapy*—the use of drugs that alter mood and mental states—for a range of mental disorders. In addition, a growing awareness of the genetic involvement in certain kinds of mental disorder is likely to encourage applications of "genetic engineering" to make direct alterations in genes identified as causally linked to particular mental disorders (see the ***Close-up*** on page 586).

Psychosurgery and Electroconvulsive Therapy

Two of the most direct interventions for changing thought and mood disorders have involved cutting parts of the brain or subjecting the whole brain to intensive electrical stimulation. The best-known form of psychosurgery is the prefrontal lobotomy, an operation that severs the nerve fibers connecting the frontal lobes of the brain with the thalamus, but removes no brain tissue. The procedure was developed by neurologist Egas Moniz, who, in 1949, won a Nobel Prize for it. Prefrontal lobotomy soon

Close-up Genetic Engineering for Mental Disorders

When we say that some mental condition is inherited, we mean that its probability of being transmitted from parents to offspring is increased because of the action of a specific gene located on one of the 23 human chromosomes that contain the entire human genetic code. Genes manifest themselves in heredity by controlling the development of enzymes, which are the basis of all chemical reactions in the body. Enzymes, in turn, influence the synthesis of proteins, such as those protein chains that play a vital role in the neurotransmitter systems responsible for nerve impulse transmission in the human brain (described in chapter 4). A goal of current researchers in molecular biology is to catalog the functions controlled by each of the more than 40,000 genes in the human genetic makeup.

Once genes that encode a particular process can be isolated and characterized, the gene products can be recreated in the laboratory through the powerful, new technology of *recombinant DNA.* Recall that the DNA molecule, the "building block of life," forms the basis for the genetic organization of plant and animal life. Genes that are found to carry the codes for a given abnormal functioning of the brain or nervous system may be modified through genetic engineering techniques. However even before this ambitious goal can be achieved, recognition of the role of molecular abnormalities in mental retardation and mental illness can be used in *genetic counseling.* Prospective parents can be screened for the presence of the defective gene in question and counseled about the likelihood of any genetically based disorder that they might pass on to their offspring. At a more conceptual level, identification of the genetic basis of any mental disorder points up its biological origin. However, this "biological biasing" may be expressed in behavior only when an individual is under prolonged or intense stress—an interaction of heredity and environment (Barchas et al., 1975).

Research has established a genetic basis for some kinds of mental retardation, chronic schizophrenia, at least one type of depression, and Alzheimer's disease, which causes mental impairment through degeneration of brain cells. Of the more than 100 diseases involving errors of metabolism, several dozen result in mental retardation.

In one kind of mental retardation, *phenylketonuria (PKU),* a recessive genetic defect is inherited (from both parents) in which a simple liver enzyme is missing (see Depue & Monroe, 1983). This enzyme is essential for breaking down the amino acid *phenylalanine,* which is found in many foods. If a child with PKU eats foods with phenylalanine, the substance builds up in the blood, and brain damage results. "Prevention" of PKU damage includes early detection through routine urine and blood tests or when any of the manifest symptoms first appear (intellectual retardation, lack of pigmentation, musty odor, vomiting, convulsions). Then, basic treatment for individuals with PKU consists of avoiding foods with phenylalanine, such as lettuce or the artificial sweetener aspartame (Equal and Nutrasweet). Recently, genetic researchers have discovered that another genetic defect is the direct cause of an even more destructive type of mental disorder called *Lesch-Nyhan syndrome* (see Vogel & Motulsky, 1982). Young people with this disorder become uncontrollably violent and mutilate themselves. Mental retardation follows, and they die prematurely. In families with a history of this syndrome, pregnant mothers can be tested (from samples of amniotic fluid) for the presence of the defective gene and genetic counseling provided.

Evidence for a biological cause of depression comes from

---

became a popular "operation of last resort" in the United States and England, because it could be performed quickly and simply in a physician's office.

The ideal candidates for a lobotomy were agitated schizophrenic patients, as well as patients who were compulsive and anxiety-ridden. The effects of neurosurgery were dramatic: a "new personality" emerged, one without intense emotional arousal and, thus, no longer overwhelmed by anxiety, guilt, or anger. In part, this positive effect occurred because the operation disconnected present functioning from memory for past traumas and conflicts, and also from future concerns.

Unfortunately, the immediate benefits of psychosurgery in altering undesirable mood states and disrupting undesirable behavior patterns were off-

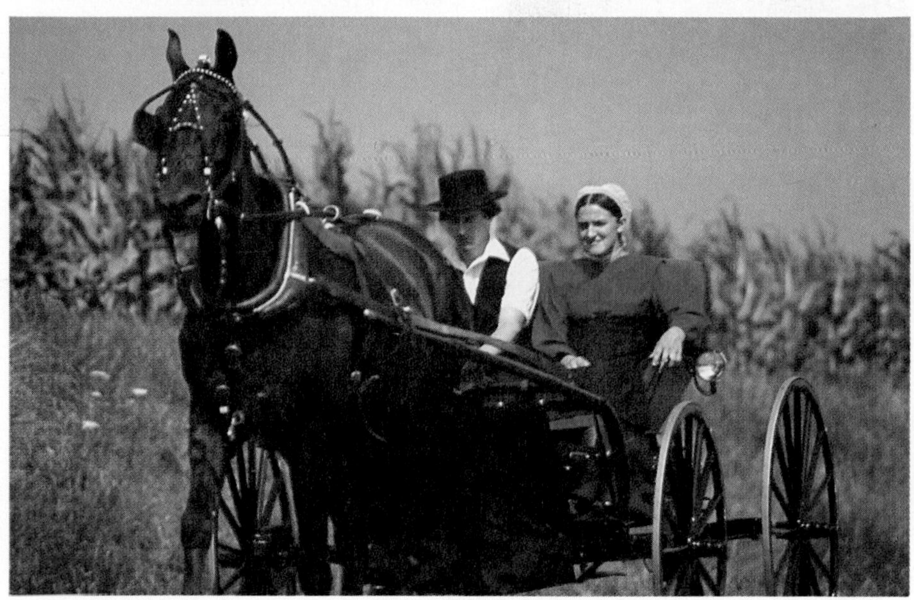

a study that demonstrated an abnormally high number of receptor sites for the neurotransmitter acetylcholine among manic depressive patients (Nadi et al., 1984). This indicates an oversensitivity to acetylcholine that can be the basis for abnormal behavior; but more direct evidence for the biology of some forms of mental illness, along with new hopes for its treatment, comes from a recent study that linked depression to a specific gene. This is the first time in history that a major mental disorder has been traced to a defective gene. A team of researchers from three universities, headed by Dr. Janice Egeland, studied the pattern of transmission of manic depressive psychosis across many generations among the Amish community in Pennsylvania (Egeland et al., 1987).

Although the rate of clinical depression is about the same for the Amish as for the general population (one in a hundred), they could be systematically studied over an extended time period because they are a closed community with complete genealogical records and few behavioral factors, such as alcoholism or violence, that could confuse the diagnosis. A piece of DNA was isolated that was common in all manic depressive members of one extended Amish family. The defective gene was passed on to children half the time, and of those who received it, 80 percent had at least one manic depressive episode in their lives. Not all who had the genetic vulnerability became depressed, perhaps because of the interaction with other biological or psychological variables. The implicated gene was found on chromosome 11. Now researchers are experimenting to discover what this gene does chemically to create manic depressive reactions and how they might turn off its genetic trigger.

As biomedical researchers discover more about inborn genetic errors in metabolic and central nervous system disorders, new treatments can be developed. This suggests that certain mental disorders can be treated, or prevented, by alterations in the defective genetic material. There is good reason to be optimistic about new breakthroughs in genetic engineering, whereby defective genes that control specific metabolic or neural functions will be identified and then "corrected" by innovative biogenetic techniques; but we must be cautious not to overgeneralize the extent to which all, or even most, mental and behavioral disorders are potentially treatable medically.

set by the most disheartening side effects. A lobotomized patient lost something—the unique flavor of the personality. Specifically, the psychological changes caused by the lobotomy were evident in the patient's inability to plan ahead, indifference to the opinions of others, childlike actions, and the intellectual and emotional flatness of a person without a coherent sense of self. Because the effects of psychosurgery are permanent, its negative effects severe and common, and its positive results less certain, its continued use is limited to special cases.

Electroconvulsive therapy (ECT) is a "shock" treatment designed to produce upheaval in the central nervous system by the application of electric current to a patient's temples for a fraction of a second. The patient loses consciousness, has a

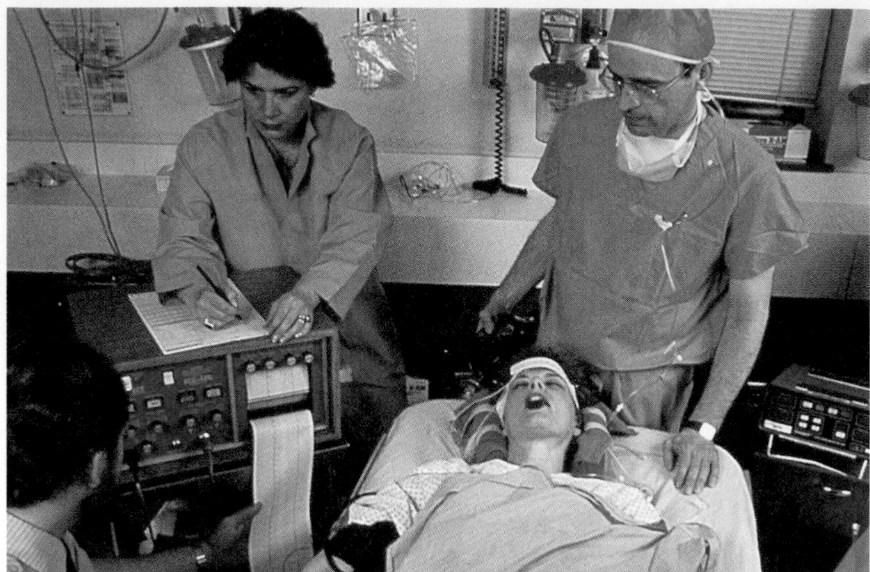

Electroconvulsive therapy (ECT) has been especially effective in cases of severe depression. However, there is considerable controversy about its therapeutic value.

convulsion similar to that in an epileptic seizure, and then falls into a comalike sleep for some minutes. Following this coma, the patient tends to be calmer and more susceptible to psychotherapy. In the past, similar shocks to the nervous system were produced by other forms of convulsive therapy.

The effects of electroconvulsive therapy were initially hailed as "unparalleled" in the history of psychiatry. It has been especially effective in cases of severe depression; but no one knows why it works. It may be because of some aspect of the coma itself, to physiological changes in nervous system circuits, or even to a strong psychological reaction, such as determination to avoid another treatment or feeling sufficiently punished to get rid of guilt over an imagined wrong (Fink, 1979).

Methodologically sound evaluation studies indicate that electroconvulsive therapy also seems to have some beneficial effect with some types of schizophrenic patients, especially those with more recent onset of symptoms; but while it reduces some of the bizarre symptoms of schizophrenia, such as catatonic posturing, it does not change the problems of cognitive processing that seem central to schizophrenic pathology (Salzman, 1980).

There are many critics of this extreme form of biomedical therapy (see Breggin, 1979). An early review pointed to poorly conducted evaluation studies that lacked standardized procedures, diagnostic information on the types of patients, and reliable measures of patient response to treatment, using vague criteria for "improvement" and "cure." It found that immediate positive effects were not lasting: treated patients left the mental institution after short stays, but were soon readmitted. More serious, a patient's language and memory became impaired. Familiar knowledge—both declarative and procedural—was lost, damaging the self-esteem of a person who couldn't recall important information or perform routine tasks. In a patient given extensive series of electroconvulsive treatments, signs of personality deterioration became apparent. The individual became dull, listless, and without concern for personal needs (Group for the Advancement of Psychiatry, 1950).

Even today, the debate continues between those who argue that it is the only effective treatment for some suicidally depressed patients and opponents who claim that it is used indiscriminately in understaffed, large state institutions; has permanently damaging effects to the brains of many patients; and is often used as a threat or punishment. In 1982, the citizens of Berkeley, California, voted to ban the use of electroconvulsive shock in any of their community mental health facilities. Though the action was later overturned on legal grounds, it exemplifies the public's ability to organize an effective protest against an established form of treatment for mental disorders. In part, the opposition underscored a theme in Ken Kesey's novel, *One Flew Over the Cuckoo's Nest* (1962)—be wary of any "therapy" that might be a disguised form of suppressing dissent, making it easier for managers to manage social deviants.

Chemotherapy

In the history of the treatment of mental disorder, nothing has ever rivaled the "revolution" created by the discovery of drugs that could calm anxious patients, restore reality contact in withdrawn patients, and suppress hallucinations in psychotic patients. This new therapeutic era began in 1953–1954 with the introduction of tranquilizing drugs, notably *chlorpromazine* (American brand name, Thorazine) into mental hospital treatment programs.

Chemotherapy is the use of drugs to treat mental and behavioral disorders. The new scientific field of psychopharmacology gained almost instant recognition and status as a chemically based therapy for transforming patient behavior. Unruly, assaultive patients became cooperative, calm, and sociable. Those absorbed only in their delusions and hallucinations began to be responsive to the physical and social environment around them. No longer was there the need for staff to act as guards, putting patients in seclusion or straitjackets. Staff morale improved as rehabilitation became a reality that replaced mere custodial care of the mentally ill (see Swazey, 1974).

Another profound aspect of the chemotherapy revolution was its impact on the nation's mental hospital population. Over half a million Americans were living in mental institutions in 1955, staying an average of several years—some for an entire lifetime. The steadily increasing numbers were stopped and reversed by the introduction of chlorpromazine and other drugs. By the early 1970s, it was estimated that less than half the country's mental patients actually resided in mental hospitals and that those who did were institutionalized for an average of only a few months.

In human terms, these statistics mean that, "since the introduction of these [antipsychotic] drugs, the 'snake pit' atmosphere of mental hospitals' back wards, with walls and floors covered with human excrement, and filled twenty-four hours a day with terror-laden shrieking, essentially exist no more" (Snyder, 1974, p. 20).

Those who benefited most from psychopharmacology were younger patients who were suffering from acute, rather than chronic, psychoses and who had had recent, few, and short periods of institutionalization. Older, chronic patients who had been hospitalized for more than five years were not as affected by chemotherapy, but still it reduced their hallucinations and delusions.

Three major categories of drugs are used today in chemotherapy programs: *antipsychotic, antidepressant,* and *antianxiety* compounds. As their names suggest, these drugs chemically alter specific brain functions that are responsible for psychotic symptoms, depression, and extreme anxiety, respectively.

Antipsychotic Drugs

The psychotic symptoms of delusion, hallucinations, social withdrawal, and occasional agitation are altered by antipsychotic drugs. Although they are chemically different from each other, all the antipsychotic drugs have similar effects on particular aspects of brain functioning. Patients become calm and tranquil, but remain alert. With many such patients, psychotherapy becomes possible for the first time.

Chlorpromazine is the "miracle" antipsychotic drug that is derived from the compound *phenothiazine.* Another remarkable antipsychotic drug is a simple salt, the extract of a rock, which can influence the uniquely subtle property of mind that regulates our moods. *Lithium salt* is a chemical proven to be effective in the treatment of manic disorders. People who experience uncontrollable periods of hyperexcitement, during which their energy seems timeless and their behavior extravagant and flamboyant, are brought down from this state of manic excess by doses of lithium.

Seven or eight of every ten manic patients treated with lithium have a good chance to recover—even where other treatments have failed (NIMH, 1977). Furthermore, regular maintenance doses of lithium can help break the cycle of recurring episodes of mania and/or depression. When used in this way, lithium regulates extreme mood swings; it also allows a person to be alert and creative (Ehrlich & Diamond, 1980). One negative side effect of long-term administration of antipsychotic drugs is the development of an unusual disturbance of motor control, especially of the facial muscles, called tardive dyskinesia.

Antidepressant Drugs

Depressed patients given antidepressant drugs often show significant improvement. The two basic antidepressants are the *tricyclics* and the *monoamine oxidase (MAO) inhibitors.* The tricyclics (such as Tofranil and Elavil) are the more widely used of the two because they are less toxic, do not require dietary restrictions, and seem to be more potent therapeutically.

In the case of many drugs, we know that patients taking them appear to get better, but we do not know why or how the drugs work. In the case of the antidepressants, however, the chemical and the physiological effects are better understood. These drugs change the emotional state of a chronically depressed person (they are not appropriate for transient depression) by prolonging the action of two neurotransmitters, *serotonin* and *norepinephrine.* Affective disorders appear to be associated with a reduced availability of these chemicals at transmission points in the brain. Tricyclics increase their availability by preventing them from being reabsorbed so quickly by the neurons that release them; thus, they keep circulating and are more available. MAO inhibitors produce the same effect through a different mechanism. Monoamine oxidase itself ordinarily alters serotonin and norepinephrine, thus stopping their effects on nerve receptors. MAO inhibitors allow these substances to remain in their effective states longer. Thus, both tricyclics and MAO inhibitors allow neurotransmitters that are in limited supply in the brains of depressed individuals to have greater impact on nerve transmission. As a consequence, these individuals feel—and act—less depressed.

Antianxiety Drugs

To cope with the "garden variety" of everyday hassles, untold millions of Americans "pop pills" that reduce tension and suppress anxiety. In general, these antianxiety drugs are tranquilizers that work by sedating. The three classes of antianxiety compounds are *barbiturates, propanediols,* and *benzodiazepines.*

Barbiturates have a general relaxing effect, but can be dangerous if taken in excess or in combination with alcohol. Propanediol drugs (such as Miltown and Equanil) reduce the tension that accompanies agitated anxiety. As tense muscles relax, a person experiences a general calming, soothing effect. Benzodiazepine drugs (Valium and Librium are two examples) are effective in reducing generalized fears and anxiety without affecting a person's ability to pay attention or process information.

Because these tranquilizers work so well, it is easy to become psychologically dependent on them or physically addicted to all three. When faced with conflicts or sources of emotional distress, many people are taking the mellow, low road of coping chemically rather than actively confronting the problems, trying to solve them, or accepting pain and grief as part of the human experience. In addition, there is considerable evidence that these drugs are physiologically addicting.

Since 1975 when Valium was the most frequently prescribed drug in the United States, its sales have fallen. However, the 8 to 9 million Americans who still take it daily make it the nation's most popular tranquilizer. A medicinal marvel to those for whom it controls stress, anxiety, and pain, Valium has a high potential for being abused and being overly relied upon to handle the "emotional chores" of modern life. Critics point to it as the symbol of the pill-for-anything-that-ails-you mentality. They argue that it is self-defeating to acknowledge that the pill, and not the person, controls the stress. In addition, drug therapy is often given in place of, and not as an adjunct to, the psychotherapy a person may need to cope with life's recurring hassles.

Some cautions about tranquilizers, which students are most likely to take among the drugs outlined in this section: The benzodiazepines should not be taken to relieve anxieties that are part of the ordinary stresses of everyday life. They should not be taken for more than four months at a time, and their dosage should be gradually reduced by a physician. Abrupt cessation of these "minor tranquilizers" can lead to withdrawal symptoms, such as convulsions, tremors, abdominal and muscle cramps, sweating, and vomiting. Because they depress the central nervous system, they can impair driving, operating machinery, and tasks that require alertness. Finally, in combination with alcohol, which also is a central nervous system depressant, benzodiazepines can lead to unconsciousness and even death (Hecht, 1986).

Does Therapy Work?

Do these therapies work? That is *THE* question. The answer is not so easy to come by. You can begin to appreciate the difficulties by trying to formulate an answer to the comparable question: Does college education work? Are you asking about all people who enter college, those who complete it, or those who are motivated to make it work while exposed to it? Does it depend on which kind of college (or type of therapy) you're examining, or on the particular teachers (therapists) involved? Do you want to know only to what extent the original goals are achieved (getting a B.A., or symptom relief), or are you interested in new goals, added with experience but never attained once and for all (enjoying learning for its own sake, wanting to have an integrated, effective, personal style)? Should the effects of a college education be compared with those of other experiences requiring equal investments of time and money in order to decide if it was "worth it"? And finally, when should that decision be made, and by whom—at graduation or some years after, by you, parents, or teachers?

Parallel issues and problems plague any easy attempts to assess whether any given therapy is effective or is more effective than other forms of treatment. Certain factors seem related to the success of therapy, however, and some of these are listed in **Table 16.3.**

Therapeutic Effectiveness

British psychologist Hans Eysenck created a furor some years ago (1952) by reporting a study showing that people receiving no therapy had just as high a cure rate as those receiving psychoanalysis or other forms of insight therapy. How could that be?

For unknown reasons, some percentage of mental patients improve without any professional intervention. This *spontaneous recovery effect* is the *baseline* against which the "cure rate" of therapies must be assessed. Simply put, doing something must be shown to lead to a significantly greater percentage of improved cases than doing nothing, or just letting time pass. As is often the case with physical ailments, many psychological problems improve because "time heals all (or a reasonable proportion of) wounds."

Placebo therapy must also be distinguished from substantive therapeutic effects if we are to determine whether client improvement results from specific clinical procedures or just from "being in therapy." Some psychologists believe that a patient's *belief* that therapy will help and a therapist's social influence in conveying this suggestion are key placebo ingredients in the success of any therapy (Fish, 1973).

While most psychotherapy researchers agree with Eysenck that it is important to show that psychotherapy is more effective than spontaneous recovery or client expectations, they criticized his findings because of many methodological problems in his study. A later evaluation of about a hundred therapy outcome studies (of "reasonable" quality) found that psychotherapy *did* lead to greater improvement than spontaneous recovery in 80 percent of the cases (Meltzoff & Kornreich, 1970). Thus, it seems safe to conclude that the therapeutic experience itself is a useful one.

One of the well-controlled studies compared patients who had undergone psychoanalytic or behavior therapy with patients who had simply been on the "waiting list." It was found that both types of therapy were beneficial, with behavior therapy leading to the greatest overall improvement. The researchers also concluded that the improvement of patients in therapy was "not entirely

Table 16.3 *Factors Affecting the Success of Psychotherapy*

	Positive (Success more likely)	***Negative (Success less likely)***
Disorder	Neurotic, especially anxiety	Schizophrenic, paranoid
Pathology	Short duration, not severe	Serious disturbance
Ego Strength	Strong, good	Weak, poor
Anxiety	Not high	High
Defenses	Adequate	Lacking
Patient's Attitudes	Motivated to change	Indifferent
	Realistic expectations for therapeutic change	Unrealistic expectations for change or none at all
Patient's Activity in Therapy	Actively collaborates, involved, responsible for problem solving	Passive, detached, makes therapist solely responsible
Therapeutic Relationship	Mutual liking and attraction	Unreciprocated attraction
Therapeutic Characteristics	Personally well adjusted, experienced	Poorly adjusted
No differences in outcome, or inconsistent findings, were found for these factors: age, sex, social class, and race of patient.		

(Adapted, with permission, from the Annual Review of Psychology, *Volume 29, Copyright © 1978 by Annual Reviews, Inc.)*

due either to spontaneous recovery or to the placebo effect of the nonspecific aspects of therapy, such as arousal of hope, expectation of help, and an initial cathartic interview" (Sloane et al., 1975, p. 224). Because of such findings, current researchers are less concerned about asking *whether* psychotherapy works and more concerned about asking *why* it works and whether any one treatment is most effective for any particular problem.

All the therapies presented in this chapter (and dozens more that we did not examine) have devoted defenders. What can be said about their comparative effectiveness? The answer, of course, is not simple.

In one exemplary attempt to find an answer, 375 controlled studies of therapy outcome were surveyed, using a sophisticated measure of relative improvement to calculate the degree of improvement for patients in each study for each kind of psychotherapy. Not all therapies were represented in their review; in particular, the current expansion of cognitive therapies was not reflected. Nevertheless, the survey provides a useful summary of relative effectiveness for most major psychotherapies, as shown in **Table 16.4** (Smith & Glass, 1977).

In this survey the most effective approach was systematic desensitization; however, it is important to recognize that this approach is not suitable for the majority of clinical problems. It is particularly designed for anxiety problems, especially when there is a clear, known stimulus for the anxiety. Relative improvement for behavioral therapies as a group was greater than for the three major nonbehavioral therapies. The difference was not large, however, and numerous factors make it difficult to know how confident we should be about that finding. For example, follow-up times were longer in the nonbehavioral studies and therapist experience varied. Problems like these are common in conducting therapy outcome studies. Differences in the severity and types of patient difficulties, the kinds of outcome measures used, the fit between a patient's expectations and the type of therapy offered, and a host of other crucial variables make the study of psychotherapy outcome a very complex business.

In a similar subsequent study, the same investigators found cognitive behavior modification to be the most effective (Smith et al., 1980). They are in agreement with Jerome Frank that no one theoretical approach can be considered clearly superior for all types of problems. As Frank had said, quoting from *Alice in Wonderland*, "*Everybody* has won, and *all* must have prizes" (1979).

Table 16.4 *Which Therapy Works Best?*

	Number of Studies Surveyed	***Index of Average Relative Improvement***
Traditional Psychodynamic	96	.59
Behavioral:		
Systematic Desensitization	223	.91
Implosion	45	.64
Behavior Modification	132	.76
Cognitive Rational-Emotive	35	.77
Existential-Humanistic: Client-centered	94	.63
Other Therapies		
Eclectic	70	.48
Gestalt	8	.26

(Adapted from Smith & Glass, 1977)

After distributing the prizes, many questions remain. Are some therapies clearly superior for some problems, but inferior for others? Are there underlying similarities across all psychotherapies that cause their effectiveness (despite differences in their "brand name" labels)? Are the human qualities of the therapist and the personal relationship between therapist and client more important than the theory that guides the technique (see Kazdin & Wilson, 1980; Smith et al., 1980)? (See also "Testing the Talking Cure" in *The Best of Science*.)

NIMH Treatment Evaluation Study

The first collaborative research program to assess the outcome of psychotherapy in treating a specific mental disorder, depression, has been completed recently. The long-term evaluation study was coordinated and funded by NIMH. Its special features include: (a) comparisons of the effectiveness of two different forms of brief psychotherapy, an antidepressant drug treatment, and placebo control; (b) careful definition and standardization of the treatments by training 28 therapists in each of the four treatment conditions, with each treatment delivered at three different institutions; (c) random assignment of 240 outpatients who met standard diagnostic criteria for definite major depressive disorder; (d) standardized assessment procedures to monitor both the process of the therapy (by analysis of therapy session videotapes, for example) as well as a battery of outcome measures administered before treatment began, during the 16-week treatment period, at termination, and again at a follow-up 18 months later; and (e) independent assessment of the results at an institution separate from any involved in the training or treatment phases of the study (Elkin et al., 1985).

The psychotherapies evaluated were two that had been developed, or modified, especially for the treatment of depression for people outside a hospital setting. The methods were also sufficiently standardized to be transmitted to other clinicians in training manuals. Cognitive behavior therapy (described on page 579), and interpersonal psychotherapy, which is a psychodynamically oriented therapy that focuses on a patient's current life and interpersonal relationships, were compared (Klerman et al., 1979). Imipramine, a tricyclic antidepressant, and a placebo control were administered in a double-blind procedure. For ethical reasons, the placebo patients received more than just an inert pill. They were seen weekly by a psychiatrist who provided minimal supportive therapy along with the placebo. Although the massive data analysis and follow-up are not yet completed, some initial results can be summarized from this model program of therapy outcome.

1. Depressive symptoms were significantly reduced in all four conditions. This general effect was found for patients who were moderately depressed. The placebo treatment was not effective for more severely depressed patients, produced fewer patients showing full recovery, and had more patients who dropped out of the study.
2. The therapeutic effects of the active drug were significantly greater than the placebo on many measures. Its effects occurred sooner than that of the psychotherapies, which caught up with it by the end of the study. In addition, these effects were more consistent across the different sites than the other therapies.
3. Improvement was found across a broad range of measures and was not limited to specific areas of patient functioning.
4. The social-psychodynamic therapy appears to have been more effective than the cognitively based behavior therapy; the effectiveness of the latter varied considerably across the different sites.
5. Patient characteristics, such as marital status, expectation of improvement, and daily functioning, also contributed to the success of the two psychotherapy treatments. The relationship of those predictor variables to patient response within each therapy is being analyzed. (Elkin et al., 1986).

The complex analysis of the treatments to discover which one will most benefit different kinds of patients is one of the important contributions of this innovative evaluative research. It serves as a model for the way scientifically sound research can be conducted to evaluate the claims of other therapeutic approaches. While various therapists disagree with certain aspects of this clinical comparison study, the program of rigorous, systematic evaluations of the specific treatments is definitely welcome. Not only can such collaborative research compare the effectiveness of different therapies, it can do a much more valuable service by giving us a new understanding of the complex interaction between therapist, treatment, symptoms, patient, and the process of change.

Therapeutic Pros and Cons

It is important to recognize the limitations, as well as the special contributions, of any particular therapeutic approach in evaluating its effectiveness. Psychodynamic therapy typically is expensive, takes a long time, can only be conducted by a professional expert, and is geared toward patients with a relatively high level of verbal fluency, intelligence, affluence, and motivation to persist in therapy. Like all one-on-one, long-term treatments, it is not "cost effective" for the society, since a therapist is limited to treating only a small number of patients at any one time. Because the goals of psychodynamic therapy involve global changes in personality and adjustment, the criteria for evaluating its success are not precise and are difficult to assess.

Short-term therapy of a fixed duration, usually of 10 to 20 sessions, is becoming more popular for the practical and economic advantages it offers patients and society. Such brief therapy is better suited to acute, rather than chronic, problems, for crisis intervention, and for modifying specific behaviors rather than general personality patterns. This symptom-oriented approach focuses on a present situation and not on its past origins. Brief therapy is not possible within a traditional psychoanalytic perspective. However, brief approaches have been found to be useful in other therapies, especially behaviorally oriented ones and family or marital therapy with a existential-humanistic focus (Weakland et al., 1974).

Behavior therapies have, in addition to their economy of time and cost, the advantages of specifying concrete objectives that can be more readily assessed within rigorous experimental paradigms. They can also be administered by trained professionals and not just by specialists. However, while they work well for distinct types of behavior problems, such as phobias, they are not as suitable for broader classes of problems associated with motivation, mood, or thought disorders.

Cognitive approaches have supplemented the behavioral processes. They are not as useful, however, where disturbed behavior is influenced by unconscious processes or where an individual's problem involves deficits in social or action skills that require practice and feedback.

Like the psychodynamic, existential-humanistic therapy works best for a selected group of verbal, intelligent, motivated individuals. The offshoots of this general approach into group therapies that each address a particular type of problem—such as interpersonal power or faulty communication patterns in married couples—have increased the practical utility of this usually abstract, indirect approach.

Biomedical therapies remain quite controversial, especially among many psychologists. They are seen as having both enormous promise and potential harm. Psychosurgery and ECT have equivocal success for certain types of extreme disorders, but can also have highly undesirable side effects. Chemotherapy certainly has been a boon in the treatment of institutionalized mental patients, as well as outpatients with previously severe disorders. Among the hazards of long-term chemotherapy are (a) an overreliance on drug therapy in place of "human contact" therapies; (b) some serious physical side effects, including the syndrome of *tardive dyskinesia* (involuntary, stereotyped body and face movements); and (c) the development of a psychological dependence on drugs as a way to avoid developing adequate behavior patterns to cope with life's problems (Davison & Valins, 1969).

The problem of evaluating the effectiveness of chemotherapy is illustrated by the *revolving door phenomenon.* There is now a higher discharge rate from mental hospitals, but an even higher return rate of mental patients.

There is no question that biomedical interventions can change behavior and mental processes, both directly and indirectly—dramatically so in the case of some psychoses. To the extent that normal behavior and reactions depend on an intact brain and nervous system functioning smoothly, physical agents that restore or maintain such functioning will provide physical readiness for healthy adjustment; but to the extent that effective behavior depends also on learning in a social setting, one can expect that relearning and social interaction will also need to be part of therapy if new behavioral patterns are to be acquired. If effective adjustment depends on a perception of one's own control over one's destiny, therapy must increase that perception of self-regulation and autonomy. Dependence on pills or other external physical agents is likely to work in the other direction.

Insanity and Commitment

Up to now we have been assuming that a person suffering psychological distress has chosen voluntarily to undergo one or another type of therapy. However, many people judged to be legally insane are involuntarily committed to mental hospitals by the state "for their own good," often without due process. The criteria for involuntary hospitalization generally include some evidence that the person is suffering from a psychological disability, shows impaired judgment, needs treatment, and poses a danger to self or others. The evaluation of potential danger is scientifically difficult and usually not possible, but it is made on subjective, moral and political grounds by representatives of the state who may use coerced commitment and extreme forms of treatment to stifle those who are *dissidents* or "troublemakers." This form of political psychiatry has been used in the Soviet Union as a weapon against sane people who are seen as threats to the political system (Bloch & Reddaway, 1977).

Former Red Army Major General Pyotr Grigorenko was committed by Soviet psychiatrists twice because he was a dissident.

Since democratic societies are on record opposing deprivation of their citizens' liberty, the courts have been involved in determining the standards of proof necessary for involuntary commitment, as well as patients' rights to appropriate treatment once hospitalized. Judge David Bazelon affirmed this right to treatment: "The purpose of involuntary hospitalization is treatment, not punishment . . . absent treatment, the hospital is transform[ed] . . . into a penitentiary where one could be held indefinitely for no convicted offense" (*Rouse* v. *Cameron*, 1966, p. 453). In a later decision, Judge Frank Johnson affirmed the constitutional right to adequate treatment, to individualized treatment plans, privacy, and dignity (*Wyatt* v. *Stickney*, 1971, 1972). Unfortunately, one consequence of this legal doctrine has been for states to release many mental patients from their wards rather than face the increased expenses of providing the required, more expensive psychiatric care. Some of those released are aided by patient self-help groups or community mental health outpatient clinics, but all too many simply have become part of the homeless masses that live anonymously in the underground world found in our large urban centers. Weighing the toll to them and to society of this new "freedom" against the loss of liberty by involuntary confinement is a difficult task that has not been confronted by the state or mental health professionals. (For an excellent analysis of the legal, moral, and political issues surrounding society's response to the treatment of psychopathology, see Rosenhan and Seligman, 1984).

For a practical guide to therapy, see the ***Close-up*** on page 596.

Promoting Mental Health

Two friends were walking on a riverbank when a child swept by downstream in the current, screaming and drowning. One of the pair jumped in and rescued the child. They had just resumed their stroll when another child appeared in the water, also struggling for air. The rescuer jumped in again and pulled the victim to safety. Soon a third drowning child came by. The still-dry friend began to trot up the riverbank. The rescuer yelled, "Hey, where are you going? Here's another one." The dry one replied, "I'm going to get the bastard that's throwing them in." (Wolman, 1975, p. 3)

The moral of this little story is clear: *preventing* a problem is the best solution. All traditional therapies have in common the focus of changing a person who is already distressed or disabled. They begin to do their work *after* the problem behaviors show up and *after* the suffering starts—too often *long* after, by which time the mental disorder has settled in.

The goal of *preventing* psychological problems is being put into practice by a number of community mental health centers under the general direction of the National Association for Mental Health. The first step toward this goal is the recognition that systematic efforts toward combating psychological problems can take place at any of three levels:

1. reducing the *severity* of existing disorders (using traditional therapies);
2. reducing the *duration* of disorders by means of new programs for early identification and prompt treatment;
3. reducing the *incidence* of new cases among the unaffected, normal population that is potentially "at risk" for a particular disorder. (Klein & Goldston, 1977)

The development of this three-stage model has signaled a "new look" in mental health care with major shifts in focus—in basic paradigms—in this field. The most important of these "paradigm shifts" are (a) supplementing treatment with prevention; (b) going beyond a medical disease model to a public health model; (c) focusing on "at risk" situations, and away from "at risk" people; (d) looking for current precipitating factors in life settings rather than long-standing predisposing factors in people; (e) not just preventing problems, but promoting positive mental health (see Albee & Joffe, 1977; Price et al., 1980).

Where the medical model is concerned with treating people who are afflicted, a public health model includes identifying and eliminating the sources of disease and illness that exist in the environment. In this approach, an affected individual is seen as the host or carrier—the end-product of an existing process of disease. Change the conditions that breed illness and there will be no need to change people later, with expensive, extensive treatments. The dramatic reduction of many contagious and infectious diseases, such as tuberculosis, smallpox, and malaria, has come about through this approach. With psychopathology, too, many sources of environmental or organizational stress can be identified; plans can then be made to alleviate them, thus reducing the number of people who will be exposed by them.

Some of our emotional problems undoubtedly stem from early life experiences, such as unresolved conflicts and inappropriate learning. Never-

Close-up A Practical Guide to Therapy

Many of us have developed (or been taught) the feeling that we ought to be able to work out our own problems and not burden others with them. It somehow seems a sign of weakness to admit that we might need help. There is little doubt, however, that almost everyone sometimes experiences feelings of depression, loneliness, or inability to cope. Numerous life experiences have the potential of inducing such personal crises. It is important to realize that everyone faces such crises at one time or another and that there is nothing wrong or unusual about reacting to them emotionally. Seeking help at such times may not be easy, but it is preferable to muddling through alone.

When our usual emotional supports, such as parents or close friends, are absent or unavailable, we should not hesitate to seek help from other sources. For most people, the duration of a crisis is usually short (from 4 to 6 weeks) and contains both the danger of increased psychological vulnerability and the opportunity for personal growth. The outcome seems to depend on the availability of appropriate help and on one's own attitude and definition of the "problem."

In terms of prevention, however, it makes better sense to know about sources of help before they are needed. An interesting and worthwhile project is to identify the various sources of psychological support available to you now. First of all, list the available sources of help outside the mental health profession, such as family, friends, teachers, clergy, "rap centers," and so on. Perhaps visiting a local church or drop-in center would help you decide whether one or both of these places can be of help to you. You can simply explain that you are trying to identify sources of emotional support in the community (as a class project). Also, find out about the mental health facilities at your college as part of your growing knowledge of psychology in your life. Later on, if you need help or someone asks you for help, you will know where to find it.

Most problems are, in fact, minor ones that go away in time and diminish in intensity; but the process of working them through helps us get in touch with ourselves and perhaps reduces the stress of similar problems later. However, there are also times when you or a friend might become severely depressed, seriously contemplate suicide, or begin to develop paranoid feelings of persecution, hallucinations, or other signs of major psychological stress. For such problems you should go at once to an accredited professional therapist. Go early, before the symptoms themselves become problems (causing poor grades or disrupting friendships).

It is not unreasonable to talk ahead of time about the "therapeutic contract"—what you get for what you give. If you think it appropriate, you might want to explore the therapist's view of human nature and the causes of emotional and behavioral disturbance. Of course, feeling comfortable with the therapist and being able to develop feelings of trust are more important than knowing his or her philosophy. This can best be accomplished through sharing your problems and concerns, and gauging the helpfulness of the response you get. Remember, though, that many therapists refrain from giving direct advice, seeking instead to help clients achieve their own resolutions to problems. You may judge for yourself whether this is what you need. Also, at first, a therapist must learn about you and your "problems," so in the early session(s), he or she may do more listening than advising or informing.

Therapy is an intimate social exchange in which you pay for a service. If you feel the service is not benefiting you, discuss this openly with the therapist; expose the possibility that the failure of the therapy represents the *therapist's failure* as well as your own. Discuss criteria for successful termination of therapy—when will the two of you know that you are "really" better? Also discuss the issue of terminating therapy if you are unsatisfied with it or think it has given you what you needed. This may, itself, be a positive step toward self-assertion. Professionals understand that no therapist relates well to everyone, and a good one will sometimes suggest that a client might do better with another therapist.

Two additional points should be mentioned. Even when you are terminating therapy that has "worked," you might still want to arrange for some future "booster sessions" with the therapist or therapy group should you feel they are needed. Finally, be willing to listen to others who may need your help. This course has not prepared you to be a therapist, but it should increase your sensitivity to other people's psychological concerns and your willingness to give up a little of your time and patience to reaffirm the human connection by being "there" when someone asks for your help.

theless, as we have seen, major sources of the stress we face are in the conditions under which we live our daily lives. The newer approaches, directing attention toward *precipitating* factors in a person's current environment, deal in practical ways with changing *what is* rather than reinterpreting *what was*. They recognize that certain situations are likely to foster psychopathology—when people are made to feel anonymous, rejected, isolated, or abused. They try to avoid psychopathology by involving people in learning how to avoid or change these kinds of situations.

We know that a large portion of the population suffers from debilitating fears and anxieties in response to a variety of situations. Prevention strategies can be developed for routinely training children and adults to cope more effectively with commonly experienced stressful situations (starting school, leaving home, marrying, bearing and rearing children, retiring, and so forth). Such training in coping skills can be administered by paraprofessionals in schools, via cable TV, or through other means of wide-scale delivery. This training can be provided at critical periods in adolescence and adulthood to prevent recurring interpersonal problems that are centered around issues such as heterosexual contact, public speaking, relating to authority, and being evaluated (Barrios & Shigetomi, 1980).

To prevent mental disorders is a complex and difficult task. It involves not only understanding the relevant causal factors, but overcoming individual and institutional resistance to change. A major reeducation effort is necessary to demonstrate the long-range utility of prevention and a community mental health approach to psychopathology and to justify the necessary expense in the face of other pressing problems demanding solutions.

An associated task facing professionals in the new field of health psychology, and all of us, is how to foster the attitude that mental health should be promoted rather than treated or even prevented. We need to set our sights on the way to realize the human potential better and on ways to make the human connection stronger. Our mental health will be enhanced by our strong sense of self-worth and self-efficacy. One personal translation of a mental health philosophy can be phrased as follows; "If it is to be, it is up to me to do it. If I choose to try, I'll enjoy my success, learn from my failure, and always continue to grow in the process of becoming a unique individual, interdependent with others in meaningful social networks." In our next chapter, we will examine the person within the social context.

Summary

- Treatments for psychological problems vary widely and include several quite different kinds of psychological therapies, as well as biomedical therapies. The goal of all of these therapies is to replace psychological problems with improved psychological health and more effective coping styles.
- The term *counseling psychologist* refers to a professional psychologist who specializes in providing guidance in a particular area. A psychiatric social worker has received training in a school of social work. A clinical psychologist has earned a Ph.D. degree in assessment and treatment of psychological problems. A psychiatrist is a medically trained professional with expertise in mental and emotional diseases. A psychoanalyst is a therapist with either an M.D. or a Ph.D. whose training is in the Freudian approach.
- Treatment of those with mental disorders has changed with changes in attitudes and understanding, and has ranged from persecution to kindness to attempts at rehabilitation. Treatment also varies from culture to culture. Western tradition emphasizes individuality and personal responsibility, while non-Western cultures often emphasize the group and communal responsibility. In these cultures healing of the mentally ill often takes place in a social context. Today in our society some disorders are attributed to physiological factors and treated medically, while others are recognized as psychological problems requiring psychological treatment.
- Freudian psychoanalysis is an intensive, prolonged technique for exploring unconscious motivations and conflicts in neurotic, anxiety-ridden individuals. Its goal is to establish intrapsychic harmony among id, superego, and ego. Through free association, dream analysis, and analysis of resistances, a therapist seeks to uncover repressed conflicts; these are worked through, in part, by transference and counter-transference.
- Psychodynamic therapies since Freud have put more emphasis on continuing life experiences, the current social environment, social motivations, and the importance of ego functioning. Two neo-Freudians are Harry Stack Sullivan, who emphasized interpersonal influences and the self-system, and Margaret Mahler, an important contributor to work on childhood schizophrenia.

- Behavior therapies involve applications of conditioning principles to the modification of specific behaviors. Counterconditioning is used in systematic desensitization and in aversion therapy; extinction is used in implosive therapy. Contingency management has been widely used in schools and other institutions to produce and maintain desired behavior through positive reinforcement and specific extinction strategies; token economies are often a part of contingency management and, in some cases, behavioral contracts are successful. Punishment is not often used in therapy, because it is counterproductive to the goal of self-regulation of behavior. Punishment, when used, is most often used to control self-injurious behavior that has not been responsive to other strategies.
- Social learning techniques include imitation of models and participant modeling, as well as specific social skills training, including behavioral rehearsal. Generalization techniques are ways of getting new knowledge applied beyond the therapy setting to a person's natural life settings.
- Cognitive therapies are aimed at changing problem feelings and behaviors by changing an individual's perceptions and thoughts. Cognitive behavior modification combines reinforcement of positive self-statements with new constructive actions; seeing one's successes and taking credit for them changes one's cognitions about oneself and creates expectations of personal effectiveness.
- Other cognitive therapies focus on correcting faulty thought patterns. In cognitive therapy for depression, a therapist attempts to help a patient change the underlying negative automatic thoughts that support the depression. Rational-emotive therapy is a comprehensive system based on changing irrational beliefs that are causing undesirable emotional reactions. Morita therapy, which originated in Japan and is based on Eastern thought, focuses on specific actions to be taken and minimizes the role of emotions.
- Existential-humanistic therapies seek to replace feelings of dissatisfaction and alienation with commitment to positive values and willingness to take responsibility for one's life. Their focus is on psychological growth and self-actualization rather than the correction of deficiencies or disorders. The goal of client-centered therapy is to promote the psychological growth of the client in a therapeutic environment characterized by unconditional positive regard and genuineness. The humanistic-existential perspective is at the center of the human potential movement.
- Therapy in groups can sometimes be more effective and cost-efficient than traditional one-on-one therapies. Types of group therapy include encounter groups, self-help groups, Gestalt therapy, transactional analysis, and marital and family therapy. Support groups for the terminally ill also use group psychotherapy techniques.
- Biomedical therapies include psychosurgery, now rarely used, and electroconvulsive therapy; the latter produces a period of calmness and greater susceptibility to therapy. It seems to have beneficial effects for severe depression and some kinds of schizophrenia (for reasons unknown), but the effects do not last, memory is impaired, and personality deterioration may develop.
- Chemotherapy has revolutionized the treatment of mental patients and reversed the mounting numbers of people needing hospitalization. There are less than half as many mental patients hospitalized today as there were prior to the discovery of antipsychotic drugs.
- Antipsychotic drugs include chlorpromazine, helpful in treating schizophrenia, and lithium, which regulates manic swings. Antidepressant drugs are effective with chronic, serious depression. Antianxiety drugs are used by millions of Americans to reduce tension, but may be addicting. These drugs, however, do not cure mental problems, may have unwanted side effects, and may prevent more active attempts to develop better coping patterns.
- Spontaneous recoveries and patients' beliefs that therapy will help them complicate attempts to assess the effectiveness of therapy. In general, studies indicate that the therapeutic experience is valuable. No one approach can be considered clearly superior for all types of problems. With more sophisticated evaluation studies, we can expect to learn more about the special benefits of particular therapies for particular problems.
- As a result of the legal dilemma over involuntary commitment, many former mental patients have been released from mental institutions. Some get assistance from patient self-help groups or from community mental health centers, but others simply have no place to go.
- Preventing a problem is the best solution. Three levels of prevention of mental disorders include reducing the rate of new cases, reducing the duration of disorders that occur through early recognition and prompt treatment, and reducing the severity of these disorders through therapy. Identification and elimination of environmental sources of problems is as important as looking for causes in individuals.

17

Social Processes

I never imagined that the color of a shirt could define a person's identity—until the redness of a shirt I wore defined mine. For a few days, that red shirt was "me," and I wore it with pride. It made me feel special and, yes, even superior to the other people who saw me wear it. So why did I feel so relieved when I finally decided to surrender it and, with it, my uniqueness?

It all started with a traffic accident. I, along with other members of the faculty, was en route to the downtown campus when the university's limousine crashed head-on into another car. Screams, moans, blood, silence. Compared to the injuries suffered by the driver and the other passengers, my mild concussion deserved little attention. At least that's what I thought while I was waiting to be X-rayed—and then I passed out.

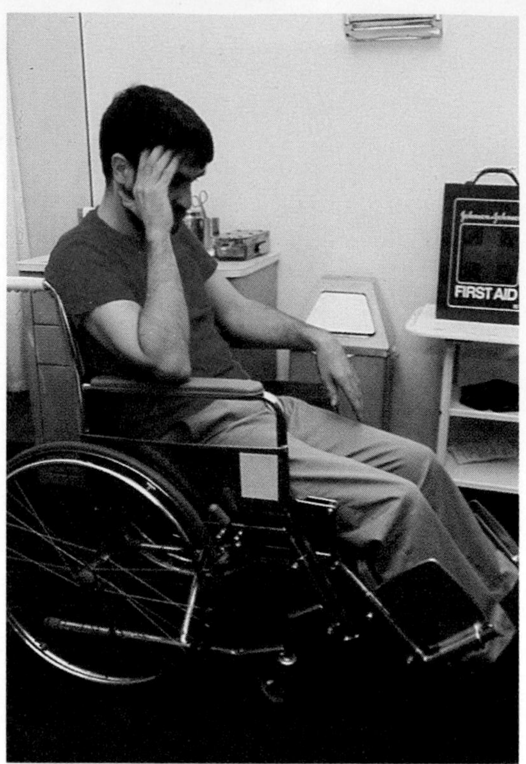

After a prolonged unconsciousness, I awakened to find myself in the trauma ward of a local charitable hospital. Strapped into bed and fed through the veins in my arm, I had a head that throbbed and a neck that ached. As my vision sharpened, I saw what looked like the set for a movie about prison. The ward had deteriorated beyond repair, and so had the lives of the patients it sheltered. They were the misfits of society: old alcoholics who had fallen into some hole, derelicts beaten for their only quarter, the skid-row crew whose eyes you try to avoid when you're walking down the street. The men wore grubby green pajamas. The only thing that set me apart from them was my red shirt.

"Say, Red," summoned the nurse, "you're sure lucky. That other Italian, the driver, he didn't make it. You're gonna be just fine once we get some hot soup and cold jello into you. But don't doze off! That's a bad sign for someone with a concussion. Stay awake and talk to the other guys, why don't you?"

Talk to the other guys? About what? What did we have in common? My red shirt said it all. I didn't belong there with the "greenies." I was not one of the boys. I was the man in the red shirt—and the others knew it. No one talked to the red shirt. No one asked the red shirt to pass along the newspaper. No one pestered the red shirt to share the sugar or butter taken from the kitchen cart. The other patients wanted nothing to do with me, and my red shirt was the silent conspirator. It erected a visual barrier that separated the likes of me from the likes of them.

After a few days, I felt a curious impulse to remove the red shirt. "How silly to keep wearing a dirty old red shirt that never was a favorite anyway." So I took it off. Only minutes after I had exchanged my red shirt for the communal greens, all kinds of social activities erupted around my bed. The heavy silence was shattered. A newspaper was offered, someone came by to tell a joke, and someone else offered me advice. There were concerns about my condition and questions about the fatal accident. We played poker, made obscene comments about the staff and worse still about the food. It felt good to laugh again. It felt even better to hear the burly leader of the "Trauma Tigers" exclaim: "I knew you wuz one of da bunch, a regular guy after all."

"Thanks, I'm glad we're gonna be buddies," I had replied, feeling the pride of having won their friendship and of having been accepted into their group—*our group.* The trauma ward was no longer traumatic for me—not home, mind you, but not so bad as it might have looked to an "outsider," such as that fellow in the red shirt who, just days ago, I thought was "me."

My interactions with the Trauma Tigers illustrates the major focus of social psychological research and theory: the nature of social influence. *Social psychologists* examine the way the perceptions, thoughts, feelings, and actions of an individual are influenced by other people. More formally, **social psychology** is the subfield within psychology that explores the way people are affected by their social context.

Social context is defined broadly. It includes not only (a) the presence of *other individuals*—whether real, imagined, or symbolic—but also (b) the *interactions* between individuals; (c) the *setting* in which these interactions take place; (d) the *activities* that occur in these settings; and (e) the set of *unwritten rules* and *expectations* that govern how people relate to each other—for example, "Don't interrupt others as they speak, and take what they say as the truth" (C. Sherif, 1981).

There are many different processes studied in social psychology, as you might expect from a *social context* that includes so much. Some occur *within an individual,* such as my perception of the "greenies" and my need (or affiliation motivation) to befriend them. Some occur *between individuals,* such as those that cause people to become friends or remain strangers, become lovers and then grow apart. Finally, some occur *within and between groups* of individuals. I was punished with the "silent treatment" while I insisted on being different from the others on the trauma ward; then I was treated warmly when I began to look and act like one of the gang. "Our gang" was a group whose rules and perceptions of Ward C were obviously different from those of the group of nurses who were in charge.

We will begin this chapter by examining what is unique about the social psychological approach. Then we will sample research and theory on each of the three kinds of social processes just described: within individuals, between individuals, and those operating at the group level. In the final chapter, we will broaden our perspective to consider contemporary social problems—such as violence and blind obedience to authority—that the social psychological approach helps us to understand.

The Social Psychological Approach

John Donne's famous line "No [hu-]man is an island, entire of itself; every [hu-]man is a piece of the continent" concisely states the major assumption social psychologists make about human behavior: all humans are social beings whose development, functioning, and even identities are shaped by their relationships to others. Social psychologists investigate how events and experiences outside a person (the *external situation*) come to influence his or her behavior. This theme, unifying the many processes studied in social psychology, adds much to what has been psychology's more dominant theme—that human behavior is best understood by *person-centered* variables, such as a person's physiological, cognitive, and motivational states, and personality traits. True, behavioral psychologists have also stressed the importance of environmental stimuli in causing behavior, but their research has centered on physical stimuli rather than social stimuli. They have assumed a passive organism, controlled by these stimuli. In contrast, social psychologists have stressed an active organism, a person who assigns a social meaning to environmental events. For example, the statement "Nice lecture" is an environmental event that can have an emotional effect on a professor. Whether the professor feels pride or anger *depends* on the social meaning he or she assigns to the phrase: does the professor hear it as a compliment or as a ploy to be "buttered up." That, in turn, *depends* on the person saying it and the circumstances under which it is said. Social psychology occupies a unique place in the study of human nature. It recognizes the value of personal and situational variables in the explanation, prediction, and control of human thought, feeling, and behavior.

The Person in the Social Environment

Research in psychology has focused on psychological processes in a social *vacuum,* as though the individual alone were the sole determinant of behavior. In this respect, psychology is similar to religion, law, and psychiatry, disciplines in which an individual is held personally responsible for sin, crime, and even mental illness. Success, too, is seen, in our culture, as the result of individual initiative; it is taken as a sign that a person is able to stand apart from, or above, the rank and file.

This central role of the individual emerged relatively recently in the history of Western culture. It was encouraged by two interrelated social movements in Europe—the Protestant Reformation and the Industrial Revolution which brought with it the rise of capitalism. Calvinism gave individualism a significant place by stressing a person's relationship to God. Capitalism advanced an economic system that rewarded labor directed toward personal profit and individual success. This work orientation meshed with the stern, self-denying aspects of the Calvinist life-style, as first described by sociologist Max Weber in his classic work, *The Protestant Ethic and the Spirit of Capitalism* (1904–5/1958). By contrast, in many Asian, African, and Native American cultures, the group was the figure and the individual was the background. Individuals were viewed as causal agents only when they had deviated from some community standard of behavior.

Social psychology has been nurtured by both non-Western and Western traditions. On the one hand, it shares the perspective of non-Western cultures by recognizing the important causal role of groups and of social situations more generally. On the other hand, it has acquired, from the West, a belief that, to understand an individual's behavior, one must understand the individual's personal interpretation of social situations.

The Social Situation

No description of behavior is complete without a description of the circumstances surrounding the behavior. Who else is present, and what are they doing that might influence what is taking place? Social psychologists find these descriptions of a current situation essential for understanding an individual's behavior, even more essential than is knowledge of an individual's past. For example, suppose a prison guard accuses an inmate of an "unprovoked" assault. The guard is claiming that there is nothing in the situation that would cause aggression. The cause is to be found within the prisoner—in his aggressive personality. Suppose we were to examine the situation, however, to see whether the guard's allegations were valid. In an actual incident, a guard, monitoring the shower room, turned off the water after two minutes. An inmate, who was still soaped up, pleaded for just enough water to rinse off. When the guard refused, the inmate attacked him. Now that you have these additional details about the situation, would you say that the assault was "unprovoked"? Assaulting the guard may have been an overreaction on the inmate's part, but it was a *reaction,* caused, in part, by the situation—factors outside the prisoner. It was not entirely by his alleged aggressive personality. The same prisoner would probably not have attacked a guard who had let him rinse off.

Personal Interpretations

To a social psychologist, a situation means more than just the physical setting in which people behave. What's more important than mere setting is the *meaning* that people assign to the events taking place. Indeed, it is not at all unusual to find that no two people interpret events in the same way, that each person in the same physical location has a unique **phenomenological perspective:** that is, each person may perceive a situation, his or her own actions, and those of others differently.

In the prison example, the facts were that the guard turned off the shower after two minutes and then the inmate attacked him. How did the actors perceive these facts? From the guard's point of view, the incident was brought about by the inmate, who defied the two-minute rule because of a hostile nature and a desire to show off. Of course, that's not what happened as seen from the phenomenological perspective of the inmate. To him, a reasonable request for water was denied because the guard wanted to flaunt his arbitrary power and thought he could do so by humiliating the inmate in front of the other prisoners. Because these views of the event contradict one another, one or both of them has to be wrong. The social psychologist would, nevertheless, treat each point of view as "real" because of the real consequences each had. In this case, not only did the actors' interpretations influence their immediate behavior and subsequent relationship, but, if the guard's views were accepted by his superiors, it could have meant a longer sentence for the prisoner or perhaps solitary confinement.

Once again, we see that a person and a situation together determine behavior, and so it is best not to focus on either alone. Focus only on a person without regard to the situation and you will find that there is no person who behaves the same in all situations. Focus only on a situation without regard to the person and you will find that there is no situation that brings out the same behavior in all persons. The most adequate accounts of behavior are those that consider both the facts of the situation and an individual's subjective interpretation of these facts.

The Importance of Social Reality

In many circumstances, people coordinate their actions with others and work together as a group. Social psychologists assume that when individuals act as a group, as when they act alone, they respond to their subjective interpretation of a situation rather than to the situation's objective details. Furthermore, just as subjective interpretations differ from one person to the next, so can we assume that they will differ from one group to the next. Indeed, these differences among groups in defining reality help to explain why different groups respond differently to the same event or situation.

For example, the objective event defined by "a bright light moving rapidly across the sky" may be seen as "an alien invasion" by one group of perceivers and as "Halley's Comet" by another. The first group may respond by tossing crude weapons at the sky, while the second may take sophisticated astrophysical measurements. In this example, each group responds not to the objective reality of the situation, but to its subjective or social reality.

Social reality refers to the phenomenological perspective of a group—whether a small group of friends or an entire nation. When members of a group reach a common interpretation of an event, an activity, or a person, they come to regard their "interpretation" as the "truth." As the saying goes, "There's truth in numbers."

Individuals want to see the world as it is seen by the groups they care about; they are less attuned to the social reality of groups that do not matter to them. They are uncomfortable if their viewpoint is not the viewpoint of a group that is important to them. They are upset because they know the fate of those whose social reality has differed from that of the group; these nonconformists are subject to psychological harassment, physical abuse, and outright expulsion. To escape this fate, there is a strong pressure to adopt the views of the group or perhaps get the group to adopt theirs.

For example, while I was wearing my red shirt in the trauma ward, I assumed that the "greenies" had an outlook on life that was different from my own, an outlook that was probably all wrong. My "smug attitude" eventually gave way to my need for human company, which the greenies wouldn't satisfy as long as I was different from them. Once I took off my red shirt, however, I found myself wanting to agree with the others and actually did agree with them about the staff, the food, and other aspects of our social context. As a group, we shared the same social reality and chose to look at the world from the same perspective—temporarily, at least.

Sometimes social reality is formally mandated—stated by law or official policy. It is part of the social reality of Americans that individuals have certain inalienable rights the government is constitutionally forbidden to take away. Our social reality with regard to the abilities and rights of women is currently undergoing a major change, reflected in current legal decisions.

More often, however, social reality emerges informally. One person's casual remark to a friend about a mutual acquaintance can evolve first to gossip, then to a spreading rumor, and before long to a ruined reputation. You can imagine what the prison guard at the shower told the other guards about "that troublemaker" or what the prisoner told other inmates about that "hostile guard." Social reality is, for the most part, the product of our everyday communications with others (Shotter, 1984).

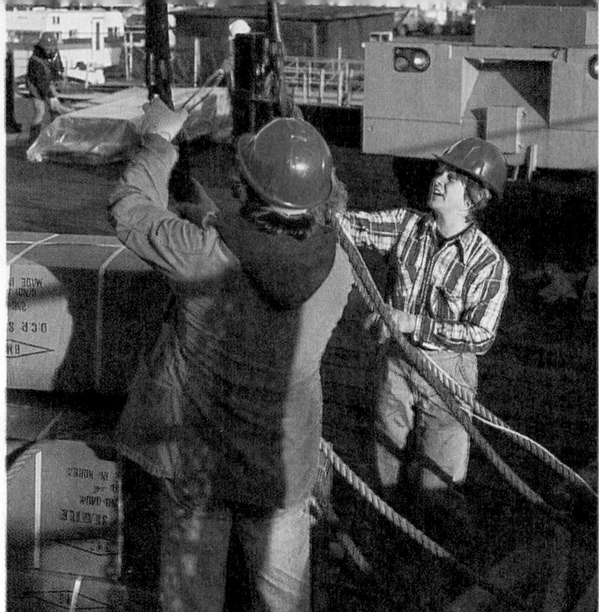

Female stevedores are a sign of our changing attitudes about women.

It is usually very difficult to shatter a belief that has become part of a group's social reality, even if objective evidence is presented against it. Once people expect certain events to occur or certain people to act in specified ways, they will typically see what they expect to see and find evidence for their view in nearly any outcome. To illustrate, recall from chapter 3 that parents hold their sons to one set of standards and expectations and their daughters to another. It has been shown that these sex-typed expectations affect the way parents perceive, and then behave toward, their own children.

> *When parents of newborn infants (less than 24 hours old) were asked to describe their babies, they gave very different descriptions depending on the baby's sex. Compared to sons, daughters were rated softer, smaller, weaker, more delicate, and more awkward. Objective measurements were then made of the infants' weight, length, state of health, and other attributes relevant to the subjective descriptions. According to these objective criteria, there were no actual differences between the boys and the girls. (Rubin et al., 1974)*

> *In a controlled experiment, parents viewed a videotape of a baby playing with a Jack-in-the-box toy. When the figure popped up, the baby was startled, cried a bit, and showed mixed emotions as it continued to explore the toy. These behaviors were seen as the overt signs of* anger *by parents who were told that the baby's name was David, but of* fear *by parents who were told that the baby's name was Diane. (Condry & Condry, 1976)*

These studies suggest that the sexist aspect of our culture's social reality may bear on our lives from the very start. Within 24 hours of our birth, parents and others have already begun to distort what we do and how we look so that they see "what is supposed to be," not necessarily "what is." One can only imagine how much these sex-typed *beliefs*—applied to children—must be reinforced by the many physical differences introduced by puberty to create two such "different" sexes. Systematic analysis of psychological differences between males and females reveals very *few* reliable effects of biological sex on behavioral variables (Maccoby & Jacklin, 1974).

Much of what has been found in research about the sexist aspects of social reality has been found in studies about the racist aspects as well. People find ways to distort what others do to make these actions conform to their racist beliefs and prejudices.

College students viewed a videotape of two men working on a task. The tape was interrupted after one man "shoved" the other man. The shove was described as "playful" or "dramatic" by most of the subjects who viewed a white man shove a black man. The same action was described as "violent" or "aggressive" by most of the subjects who viewed a black man shove a white man. (Duncan, 1976)

In another study, grade-school children looked at cartoons of two children interacting. All were shown the same cartoons, except that one character—the "shover"—was white for some subjects and black for the rest. As hypothesized, the shove was considered more aggressive when done by the black character. Even more interesting: the bias against the black character was shown by the black subjects at least as much as it was shown by the white subjects! (Sagar & Schofield, 1980)

These studies broaden the conclusions about sex-typing in a number of ways. First, they provide additional evidence that people distort "what is" to make it conform to "what is supposed to be." Second, they show that these distortions apply not only to beliefs about sex, but to beliefs about race as well. Indeed, virtually any dimension of the human experience can be distorted by social reality which defines the way individuals *should* perceive and interpret the actions of other people. Third, there is evidence that, from a very early age, racism, as well as sexism, affects the way we are perceived: the characters in the cartoons, after all, were only children. Fourth, because racist judgments of these cartoon characters were also made by children, children must learn racist aspects of social reality very early in life. Of course, sexism is learned early too; it is an easy lesson to derive from the differences between the toys, names, and clothes of little girls and little boys.

Social reality is also affected by **self-fulfilling prophecies** (see Merton, 1957). In the textbook case individuals first made a prediction about the way someone would act, a prediction that affected how they acted themselves. Their action then produced in the other person a reaction much like the action they had predicted in the first place. This *behavioral confirmation,* mentioned in chapter 12, typically works because it solicits only selected kinds of information about the "target person" through questions and nonverbal actions. This process is more likely to get back the behavioral evidence that tends to confirm the original hypothesis of that person as sociable or shy, dominant or submissive, or possessing any of a variety of personal traits (Snyder, 1984).

Subjects took part in a "getting to know you" study to determine a major aspect of strangers' personalities on the basis of their answers to a set of 12 questions. Half the subjects had been randomly assigned to find out if the target people were extraverted, while the other subjects' task was to discover if the target individuals were introverted. The questions they selected were those most likely to reveal what they expected to find. Thus, those looking for extraverts would ask, "What would you do to liven up a party?" while those searching for introverted personalities would ask, "What factors make it hard for you to really open up to people?" Then they had an opportunity to interact with their targets, who also were randomly assigned to the two conditions and were not really assigned to a group because of their extraverted or introverted natures. However, those who were hypothesized to be extraverts actually presented themselves in more extraverted fashion than did the targets expected to be introverted. These behavioral differences, induced in the target people by the particular kinds of questions they were asked, were also detectable by naive raters listening only to tape recordings of their answers. In this and many similar studies, personality and other attributes that are perceived to be "in" someone else are shown to be "put there" by this process of beliefs creating behavior that, in turn, creates reality. (Kulik, 1983; Snyder & Swann, 1978)

Naturally, there are limitations to the power that expectancies have on the control of others' behavior. When the expectancy pertains to a skill not easily altered, believing is not necessarily seeing: a friend will not run the mile in 4 minutes merely because you have come to believe that she can. However, if your expectancy is not too far off target, it can have a noticeable effect on performance.

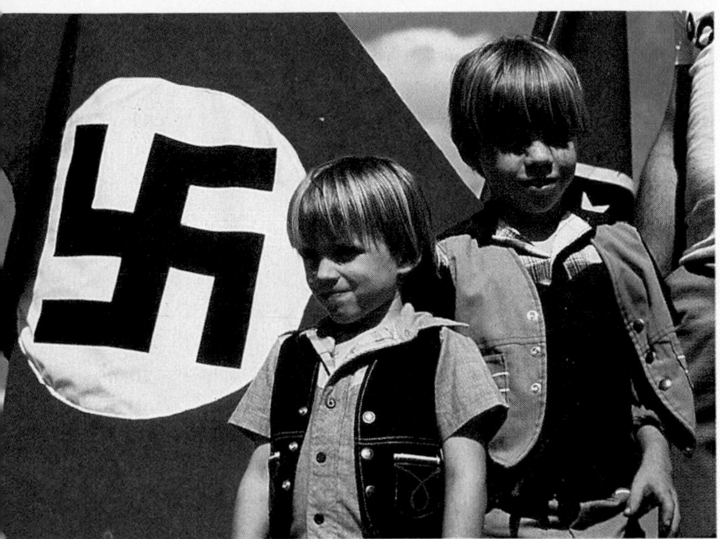

Children can easily learn racist aspects of social reality. These ideas can distort their perceptions of other people.

A little encouragement may be all that's needed to turn a certain "slow learner" into a competitive student.

> *Each student in a group of grade-schoolers, selected at random from a larger pool, was described to his or her teacher as "a late bloomer about to blossom." Compared to a control group—grade-schoolers not so described—the "bloomers" were given more attention, challenges, and encouragement by their teachers. Although the two groups of children had the same average IQ before the study began, the students expected to improve had higher scores on a posttest than did the other children. The posttest difference was the result of a significant improvement by the "bloomers" and no change in IQ in the control group. (Rosenthal & Jacobsen, 1968a)*

Whether an expectancy is self-fulfilled also depends on whether it is detected by the person to whom it is applied. People do not always let others get away with negative expectancies involving a lack of intelligence, maturity, or sincerity. When people detect these unflattering expectancies, they may do all they can to prove the expectancy-holder wrong. However, when they accept as truth the false beliefs about their abilities and personal attributes, they are likely to try hard to live up to them—if positive—or sadly, down to them—if negative. In this way, social reality exerts a profound influence not only on the way people see the world around them, but more importantly, on the way they ultimately see themselves. To a large extent, that self-perception determines "who they really are," and what they really do.

Social Applications

An additional difference between social psychology and other areas should be mentioned. Many social psychologists are strongly motivated by psychology's fifth goal—to improve the human condition. This concern is expressed in two major ways. First, the knowledge obtained from the laboratory is used to explain phenomena and attempt to remedy problems in the real world (Deutsch & Hornstein, 1975). Second, studies by social psychologists are often carried out in *natural field settings,* as well as in laboratory analogies of those natural settings—in housing projects, at dances, in nursing homes, in factories, or "wherever the action is" (see Rodin, 1985).

Kurt Lewin, whom many consider the *founder* of modern social psychology, believed that theory and research must be integrated with practical application for psychology to make its greatest contribution. "No action without research, no research without action" was his dictum (1948).

During World War II, ordinary meats were scarce and had to be rationed; highly nutritional visceral meats—such as hearts and kidneys—were plentiful but unpopular. Lewin's objective was to find an effective way to change the purchasing habits of American housewives. Some in his group of housewives—those whose habits were of interest—heard a lecture on the positive effects of serving these glandular meats to their families—the usual means recommended to influence the public-at-large. Other women subjects met in small discussion groups to discuss the issue and consider ways to make the undesirable meats appealing to their families. These women then made a public commitment to follow through. They were far more likely to make the socially beneficial move to buy, prepare, and feed the visceral meats to their families than were those who received the same information in a lecture format (Lewin, 1947).

A missed opportunity to apply social psychology, especially what was known about the dynamics of small groups from research done by Lewin and his students, has come back to haunt Americans. Studies conducted in factories during the 1950s showed that workers who were given an active role in making decisions about production performed far better on the job than did passive workers, who were told what to do and got paid for doing only what "the man ordered." The active decision makers surpassed the passive laborers on measures of productivity, efficiency, morale, and satisfaction (Coch & French, 1948; Pelz, 1955/

1965). These results were brought to the attention of many American executives, but few decided to implement the recommended procedures because they objected to the idea of a group as a unit of democratic decision making and behavior. This did not conform to the American ethic of individualism and bore a superficial resemblance to "socialism." The recommendations were put to productive use in another part of the world, though: in Japan, where societal norms are favorable to group-based behavior. One can only speculate about the course of economic history if American executives had accepted social psychology's empirically based advice that people work better when they participate in group decisions that affect their lives at work. Would America's position at the top of the industrialized nations have diminished as much as it has, especially relative to Japan's?

Social Perception

Social psychology was introduced at the start of this chapter as the study of social influence: an examination of an individual's thoughts, feelings, and actions shaped by the real or imagined presence of others. It has probably already occurred to you that, whereas some people influence your behavior a lot, others may try to, but do not. Not just anyone can persuade you to accept a particular viewpoint, and not all people can get you to sign a petition. Before you agree with others' opinions or say yes to their requests, you may ask, "Do these people have the attributes I look for? Are they honest, or biased and insincere? Are they knowledgeable about the topic or grossly ill-informed? Are they altruistic in their motives or selfish and corrupt?" Having posed these questions about others, how do you go about finding the answers? What in their behavior or appearance is the key that opens the door to their inner character? These are the questions of **social perception:** the process by which you come to know or perceive the personal attributes of yourself and other people.

Social psychologists assume that an individual observes others carefully as they act, wants to know why they act as they do, and tries to infer from action something about their personalities. This social perception, occurring within an individual, is almost identical to the job description for a psychologist, who makes a living explaining human behavior and making inferences about personality. Because of this similarity, social psychologists have formulated a model that portrays an individual as an *intuitive psychologist* who has an interest in determining what people are like and what causes their behavior (Ross, 1977). This can serve a very useful function: to identify, for that person, a way to act depending on the attributes of the other person. For example, it is a good idea to determine if an acquaintance is trustworthy in order to avoid discussing intimate matters with a person who might pass your secrets on to others.

Let us look more closely at this model of the intuitive psychologist and consider an important theory that is based on it—attribution theory. Then we shall see that, although intuitive judgment is often insightful, it is prey to many errors that the scientific method of the professional psychologist was designed to avoid.

The Intuitive Psychologist

Throughout this book, we have encountered many theories of human behavior. They included Freud's psychoanalytic theory, the behavioristic model of Watson and Skinner, and the humanistic doctrines of Rogers and Maslow. Fritz Heider (1944, 1958), a German-born psychologist who came to the United States shortly before World War II, took a different approach to the task of psychology. Rather than proposing a theory of his own, Heider suggested that psychologists listen to the theories of those they studied—"ordinary, average people." His basic argument was that people act according to their own beliefs about the causes and effects of

Someone who spreads gossip would not be a good person to confide in.

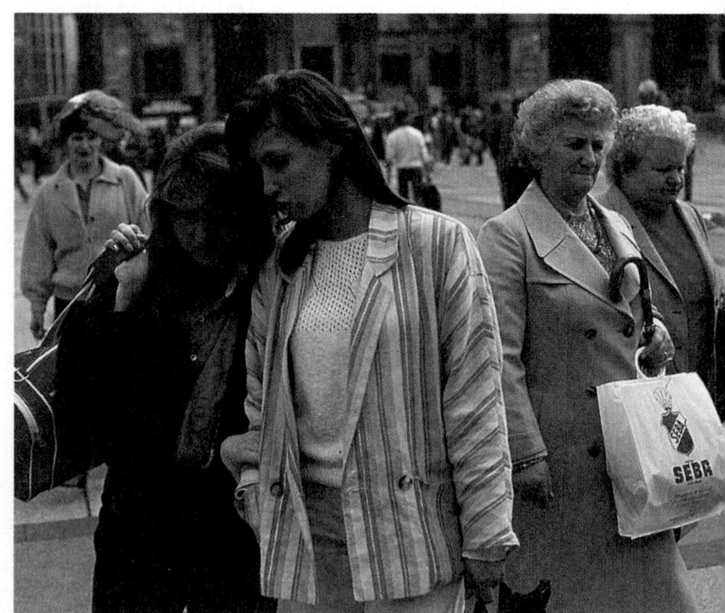

behavior, not according to the beliefs of Freud, Skinner, or anyone else. Heider believed that psychologists would do a better job of explaining and predicting behavior if they would attend to the layperson's ideas rather than only to the theoretical ideas of one another.

Read these two paragraphs, first *A* and then *B*, and ask a friend to read them in the *reverse* order—first *B* and then *A*. Compare your impressions of what Jim is really like (Luchins, 1957). This task is relevant to a study discussed on page 608.

A. Jim left the house to get some stationery. He walked out into the sun-filled street with two of his friends, basking in the sun as he walked. Jim entered the stationery store, which was full of people. Jim talked with an acquaintance while he waited for the clerk to catch his eye. On his way out, he stopped to chat with a school friend who was just coming into the store. Leaving the store, he walked toward school. On his way out he met the girl to whom he had been introduced the night before. They talked for a short while, and then Jim left for school.

B. After school Jim left the classroom alone. Leaving the school, he started on his long walk home. The street was brilliantly filled with sunshine. Jim walked down the street on the shady side. Coming down the street toward him, he saw the pretty girl whom he had met on the previous evening. Jim crossed the street and entered a candy store. The store was crowded with students, and he noticed a few familiar faces. Jim waited quietly until the counterman caught his eye and then gave his order. Taking his drink, he sat down at a side table. When he had finished his drink he went home.

Imagine that, for two months, you have been having difficulty falling asleep at night. Neither your body nor mind has been getting the rest it needs, and no immediate end to the problem is in sight. You have decided that the time has come to take action, but you don't know what action to take. A common solution begins by identifying the cause, for this is the factor to be fought. For example, if you suspect it is coffee that has been keeping you awake at night, you may switch to a decaffeinated brand or to tea. If you believe that the problem is the result of anxiety, you may shop for a therapist or talk to a friend. Alternatively, you might decide that your mattress is to blame, which may be just the excuse you needed to buy that waterbed you've always wanted.

This example illustrates Heider's point that no theory of behavior can predict your responses to events as reliably as your own. In this situation, it is your *theory* of insomnia that matters, your beliefs about the causes of sleepless nights. The causal attribution you make—excessive caffeine, unbridled anxiety, or an uncomfortable mattress—will often affect the action you take—switch to decaffeinated, see a therapist, or purchase a waterbed.

Heider's ideas laid the foundation for attribution theory, which has shaped much of the research in social psychology for the past 25 years. It is different from the other theories we have considered because it is concerned with *your hypotheses* about behavior, not those of psychologists. **Attribution theory** focuses on the attempts of an ordinary person to make sense of events that he or she perceives are occurring either internally or in an external situation. "Making sense" involves seeking causes for actions, generating inferences about inner dispositions from observed behavior, and assigning responsibility or blame for one's actions and those of others. Research on attribution is designed to identify the rules people use and the thought processes they engage in when they are trying to determine why an action or an outcome occurred. In the preceding example, investigators might study the processes that led you to attribute insomnia to caffeine, anxiety, the mattress, or perhaps some other cause. Most social psychologists would concur with Heider that these processes ought to be understood, because attributions may be among the most important factors that influence human action.

Impression Formation

Besides affecting your actions and responses to various situations, attributions also play an important role in **impression formation:** the process of knowing other people and of determining their traits, abilities, and attitudes. The following two stories, taken from the newspapers, illustrate the relationships between causal attribution and impression formation.

> *Sadie Lee Carter confessed to shooting her husband, Edward, as he slept. Although Sadie admitted that the murder was premeditated, she was sentenced to 5 years probation for the crime rather than to jail. Judge David Borden opted for leniency because he thought Sadie's husband may have driven her too far. There was evidence that Edward forced their daughter to have sex with him and that he beat Sadie brutally on a regular basis—even once after she had just returned home from having surgery. In the judge's words, "[The situation] was too much for her, it pushed her beyond the breaking point." Because the judge attributed Sadie's action to an abusive situation, he did not find her dangerous or homicidal, characteristics that a different attribution for her behavior would suggest. (Associated Press, 1982)*

*A contrasting case is that of a 15-year-old boy named Kenneth Holloway. Kenneth pleaded guilty to the fatal shooting of a woman he robbed for 75 cents. Although he claimed to have shot the woman to prevent her later testimony, the evidence suggested an additional motive. It was revealed that, even though he robbed the woman from behind, he walked around and shot her in the chest. What makes this action noteworthy is that he could have silenced the woman by shooting her from behind—where he already was. Because he made a point of facing the woman before firing, people infer that he must have sought a ''thrill'' from watching her expression of terror and pain. Unlike Judge Borden, who went easy on Sadie, Judge Dennis Rigg chose the maximum penalty in Kenneth's case: for a minor, 6 years in the state Youth Authority. The judge, who had wanted a stiffer penalty, lamented that, ''In this case, the community is not being protected.'' (*San Francisco Examiner, *1982, Nov. 21)*

If we attribute one person's action to one intention and another person's same action to a different intention, we are likely to form very different impressions of their personalities (Jones & Davis, 1965). Sadie Lee Carter and Kenneth Holloway performed the same action—they both shot and killed another human being. Their actions were attributed to very different intentions, however. Sadie was thought to have acted in self-defense to terminate the abusive treatment she and her daughter suffered. In contrast, Kenneth appeared as a person who killed because he enjoyed watching others die.

Snap Judgments and Stereotypes

The attributions we make about a person's behavior may sometimes be biased by an impression based on the person's looks. In many circumstances, we may just take a glance at a stranger and immediately make a snap judgment about what the person is probably like (Schneider et al., 1979). A person's appearance is frequently all we need to get a ''gut level'' idea about his or her most likely attitudes and abilities, and even about whether we would like the person.

In some cases, a snap judgment can be quite reasonable. An individual's build may be related to athletic ability; the person's clothing may be a clue to political orientation. Unfortunately, many snap judgments are based on racial, sexual, and other group stereotypes that are either false or gross distortions of the truth. A **social stereotype** reflects the beliefs people have about the personality traits and abilities commonly found among individual members of a particular social group.

Stereotypes play a large role in forming first impressions; we usually learn about an individual's group memberships before we learn anything else. Characteristics such as sex, race, and age are apparent to the naked eye. They serve a generally useful cognitive function to provide mental shortcuts to judgments and decisions based on a quick review of a limited amount of information, like others we discussed in chapter 10. Problems arise when the inferences made on the basis of the stereotype are, in fact, ''quick *and dirty.*'' Others then may suffer because our minds are programmed to use such simplifying cognitive strategies. In one study observers, believing that a student came from a low socioeconomic background, rated her performance more poorly than did observers who believed she was from a high socioeconomic background.

Observers watching on videotape a student taking a test of academic ability, were given false information about her social class. Those who thought she was from a high social class evaluated her abilities well above *grade level, while the other observers, who had prior information about her* low *social class, judged her to be* below *grade level. As you might expect by now, both of the groups of raters ''found'' behavioral evidence to support their false hypotheses generated by the stereotypic information about the student's socioeconomic background. (Darley & Gross, 1983)*

Our mistaken first impressions about a person generally stay that way, even if the person's later behavior can be taken as evidence against them. As many studies have shown, the first things we learn about others have greater impact than do later bits of information, a phenomenon known as the **primacy effect.** In a classic study by Luchins (1957), for example, subjects read the two paragraphs about Jim on page 607. Some subjects read the paragraphs in the order shown (A, then B) and some read them in the reverse order (B, then A). This procedure ensured that all subjects would get the same set of total information about Jim. Still, he was considered ''friendly'' by 78 percent of subjects who first read paragraph A, which features a socially active Jim, but only 18 percent of those who first read paragraph B, which features Jim's solitary side. The results suggested that the interpretation of a person's behavior (Jim's conduct in the second paragraph) may depend upon judgments already made (those learned in the first paragraph).

Why are our first impressions often lasting impressions? Part of the answer has already surfaced in the discussion of social reality. People can find

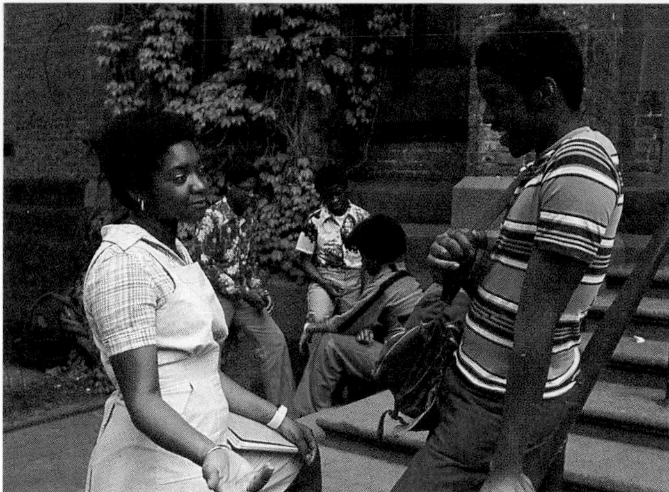

First impressions have greater impact on a relationship than do later ones.

evidence for their beliefs, whether true or false by (a) distorting a person's action so that "what is" conforms to "what is supposed to be," and (b) influencing the way others behave, thus creating a self-fulfilling prophecy. Another process that leads to primacy effects is the tendency to attribute to temporary or external causes those behaviors that challenge a first impression. For example, we may attribute the low grades of a "smart" person to an unfair exam and regard the kind gestures of a "selfish" person as a ploy to bait some sucker—thus making it only an "exception to the rule." Primacy effects are especially common for negative first impressions. Individuals are *avoided* after being labeled dangerous, incompetent, or dumb, and so they find very few chances to prove the labels wrong. This mechanism sheds light on why prejudice—a negative impression about a whole group of people—persists in spite of efforts to combat it. Civil rights, in other words, has always been a struggle to guarantee "equal opportunity for all"—despite prevailing stereotypes.

When the attributes of an individual cannot be inferred from group membership, they might be inferred from behavior. Judgments based on behavior are, in many ways, superior to prejudgments based on group membership. We shall now see, though, that people have preconceptions about behavior, as well as about groups, and behavioral preconceptions can also bias the way an individual is perceived.

Like personality characteristics, causes cannot be seen. All our attributions of cause are inferences based on our interpretations of what we observe (see **Figure 17.1**). How do we make the inferences we do about causes of behavior?

Causal Theories

For any behavior, some causal hypotheses appear more plausible and are remembered more readily than others. For example, how can the following statement be completed: "Bill did poorly on the exam because ____________________." Most people find acceptable such endings as, "he isn't very intelligent," "he didn't study very hard," "the test was difficult," and "he had bad luck." In contrast, people find rather bizarre an ending like, "the exam was given in April." It isn't immediately clear to them what the month of the year has to do with an individual's performance on an exam.

These different degrees of acceptability illustrate a common causal theory of intuitive psychologists; namely, *performance depends on ability, effort, difficulty,* and *luck.* Social psychologists use the term **causal theory** to refer to the beliefs people have about which factors can bring about a particular outcome and which factors cannot. In most people's theory of performance, for example, lack of ability is considered a better explanation for failure than is the month of the year or which political party is in the majority.

The major advantage of having causal theories is that they limit to a manageable size the number of factors to be considered when an outcome needs to be explained. Without a causal theory about insomnia, for example, where would we begin to look for an explanation about our lack of sleep? Exploring every possibility would prove so time-consuming that the problem would never be

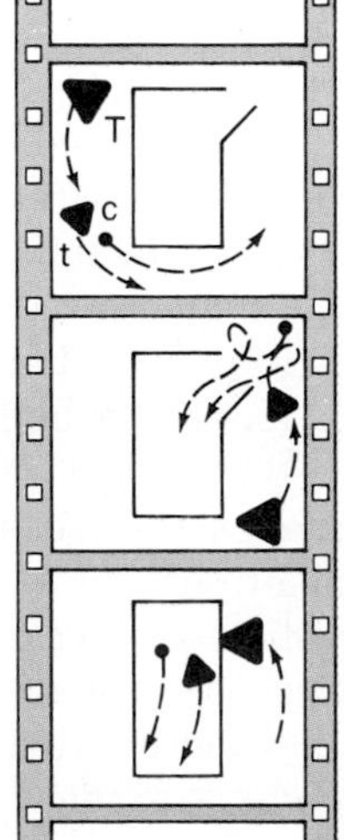

Figure 17.1
These geometric figures were stimuli in a convincing demonstration of the fact that we infer rather than observe personal characteristics and causes. When subjects were shown a film in which the geometrical forms simply moved in and out of the large rectangle at different speeds and in different patterns, they attributed underlying "motivations" to the "characters." They often "saw" the triangles as two males fighting over a female (the circle). The large triangle was "seen" as being aggressive, the small triangle as being heroic, and the circle as being timid. In the sequence shown here, most observers reported seeing T chase t and c into the house and close the door (Heider & Simmel, 1944).

solved. It is much more useful to have at hand a theory that identifies a small set of likely causal candidates—caffeine, anxiety, and the mattress—than it is to engage in an endless search for "the truth."

This advantage, however, can backfire. Sometimes an outcome's real cause may be completely overlooked because its causal effects have yet to be recognized. For example, many people do not know that exercising before bed will delay the onset of sleep—in fact, some believe that it hastens sleep. Consequently, people may be taking a lot of needless and potentially harmful drugs to induce sleep when all they need to do is exercise a few hours earlier.

It is senseless to catalog all causal theories, for these will vary from person to person and from outcome to outcome. Instead, investigators have tried to identify properties shared by most, if not all, causal theories. One fundamental property is that each factor in a causal theory can usually be categorized as an internal cause or as an external cause. For example, consider the theory that performance is a product of ability, effort, difficulty, and luck. Which of these causal factors would you say are internal and which external? Most people consider ability and effort the internal causes, reflecting "something about the person." That is, ability refers to intelligence, creativity, or some other skill people have, and effort measures their motivation to succeed. Difficulty, though, is considered an external cause, because it stipulates that "something about the task" was responsible for success or failure. Luck is usually regarded as external to the person, but sometimes we may believe that there are people who are characteristically "lucky" or "unlucky."

The distinction between internal and external causation has a number of important consequences. For example, an individual's emotional responses to success and failure depend on whether the outcome is attributed to "something about me" or "something about the situation or task." When tests measure an internal cause like ability, for example, the successes feel better and the failures feel worse than when they reflect an external cause like luck (Weiner et al., 1971). Also affected by internal versus external attributions are decisions about rewards and punishments. Recall that Sadie Carter did not go to prison because the judge attributed her behavior to the abusive conduct she suffered—a cause external to Sadie—rather than to an antisocial personality on her part—the internal cause that got young Holloway a stiff sentence. Recall in our discussion of *attributional styles* in chapter 12 that the inferred causes for one's successes and failures can have a major impact on self-esteem and subsequent willingness to perform on certain tasks (Seligman's theory in Trotter, 1987).

Another property shared by nearly all causal theories is that they are subject to a **discounting principle** (Kelley, 1971). This principle states that, as the number of possible causes for an outcome increases, the attributor discounts—that is, becomes less confident about—the causal role played by each. For example, suppose you hear one person telling another that he or she favors laws prohibiting abortion. You ordinarily have no reason to doubt that the speaker is sincere, but suppose you learn that the speaker is running for public office and that the listener is a voter opposed to abortion. Because you know that politicians may be less sincere when looking for votes, you have grounds to question whether the speech should be taken at face value. The motive to win a vote discounts the role of sincerity as an explanation for the statement.

A causal theory may include not only the factors that promote an outcome, but also the factors that work against it. For example, if you think that

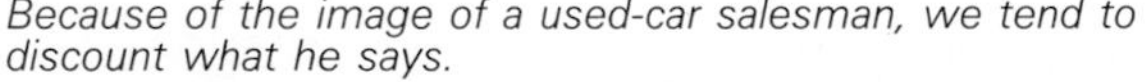
Because of the image of a used-car salesman, we tend to discount what he says.

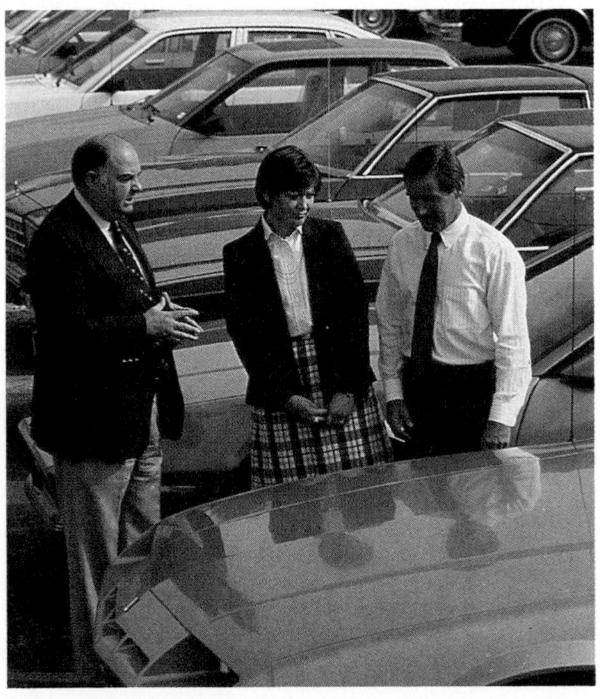

earning a college degree is difficult enough as it is, imagine the additional difficulties faced by those who are blind or deaf. In view of these difficulties, what impression do you form of Adeline Becht, a woman who, despite being both blind and deaf, still earned a doctorate in clinical and counseling psychology? Most people attribute Dr. Becht's achievements to very high intelligence and motivation. What is remarkable about her story is that people who are usually quite impressed just to learn that someone attained a doctoral degree attribute even more intelligence and motivation to Dr. Becht because of her handicaps. She is seen as having all it takes to earn a Ph.D.—and then some. That something extra illustrates the **augmentation principle** (Kelley, 1971). The principle states that, if an outcome occurred despite factors working against it, the causes that produced it are seen as particularly powerful, more so than if no obstacles had to be overcome.

Covariation Principle

So far our intuitive psychologist—you—has made no assumptions about the way an actor whose behavior is being analyzed behaved in the past or the way others behaved in the actor's situation. Having this additional information may affect inferences about the actor's present behavior. The **covariation principle** (Kelley, 1967) attributes that behavior to a causal factor if the factor was present whenever the behavior occurred and was absent whenever the behavior did not occur.

To illustrate, consider the insomnia example. To identify the cause, think of the nights when sleeping was most problematic and the nights when it was least problematic. What did you do, where did you go, and how did you feel during the days that preceded the sleepless nights and the restful nights? Do you detect any differences between the two groups of days? If so, a casual factor may be at hand. For example, suppose the restful nights all fell on Thursdays, days you got together with your closest friends. Then the cause of your insomnia may be anxiety-maintained loneliness or a need to affiliate more than you do. This attribution follows from the covariation principle: insomnia occurs when you have spent the day away from friends and it does not occur when you have had a few hours of their company.

People find the covariation principle especially useful when they need to know whether they would respond to a situation the same way someone else responded. For example, suppose someone advises you to take a certain course. To ascertain whether you would like the course as much as the person who recommends it, it is reasonable to find out whether the advice reflects "something about the course"—its objective merits—or "something about the person"—he or she has personal tastes that you may not share. Harold Kelley (1967) has derived three criteria from the covariation principle to describe the way people would address this question: distinctiveness, consensus, and consistency.

1. **Distinctiveness** is based on the way a person responded to similar situations in the past. If an advisor's recommendation is high in distinctiveness—unique to a particular course and few others—we can attribute her reaction to the course and infer that it is probably worth taking. If she gives the "thumbs up" response to all courses, regardless of worth, we see it as a less persuasive appeal. It suggests a personal bias, a kind of "yea saying" that is not very discriminating. As an aid, reword "high distinctiveness" as follows: a positive reaction occurs in the advisor in the presence of this course, but a positive reaction does not occur in the absence of this course. From these data, the covariation principle's high distinctiveness would point to the course as the probable cause of the positive reaction.
2. **Consensus** is based on the way other people responded to the same situation. If the advisor reacted to the course's objective merits, then others who took the course should have reacted favorably too: her response should be high in consensus in order for us to attribute it to the entity being judged. High consensus makes her response a part of social reality; once again, there's social truth in numbers. A personal bias, though, would mean that few people responded as she did (low consensus), her response being found only among those who shared her personal biases.
3. The **consistency** of a response is its reliability. Suppose the advisor shows little consistency, praising the course one day and condemning it the next. Then you wouldn't have any idea whether she actually liked it or hated it, let alone whether the cause of her response was internal or external. You might attribute her reaction on either day to her shifting mood or anything else that varied over time. Only when she consistently said the same good things about the course would you find it worth your while to use distinctiveness and consensus to determine the reason.

Errors and Biases in Social Perception

Professional psychologists use the scientific method so that the science of psychology is not hindered by their personal biases, as we noted in chapter 2. Because intuitive psychologists use the rules of ordinary thought instead of the rules of science, their impressions about others are open to error and subject to bias. In this section, we consider some of the most common shortcomings encountered in social perception when laypeople develop and use causal theories to make sense of their social world. The general theme is similar to that encountered in the study of social biases in chapter 10. These rules of judgment and decision making usually work well; however, under some circumstances, they may mislead us into premature, false beliefs and wrong actions.

The Fundamental Attribution Error

In our discussion of causal theories, we saw that causal factors are usually thought of as internal (for example, ability) or as external (for example, difficulty). Although people make attributions to both kinds of causal factors, they tend to favor internal causes to explain a person's behavior and to overlook the power of a situation. This bias favoring internal over external attributions has been found so often and it tends to be so strong that it has earned the label the **fundamental attribution error** (Ross, 1977).

Examples of the fundamental error can be detected in our own daily lives. All of us have noticed that what we do depends on who we are with. We tend to act one way with our parents, another way with our professors, another way with our closest friends, and yet another way with a romantic partner. We know that these variations do not mean that our behavior is random or capricious; rather different people and different situations bring out different aspects of our personalities as they demand somewhat different responses. Do people recognize the role they play in shaping our behavior? Do they know that we behave in other situations differently from the way we behave in their presence? The answer is generally no. Our parents, for example, may be convinced they know us, having no idea how different we really are when they are not around. In other words, they usually attribute our behavior to internal factors—our dispositions to behave the same across situations—rather than to the external factors created by their very presence, the norms of the situation we share with them, the rules and roles that are in effect.

On a societal level, the fundamental attribution error can be seen in the tendency "to blame the victim" (Ryan, 1976). People tend to hold the victims of poverty and racial discrimination personally responsible for their plights. Unemployment among minorities leads to the attribution "they're lazy," squalid living conditions to "they're filthy," and high rates of crime to "they're bad." Somehow, the external societal variables that foster these conditions are largely overlooked, and, instead, the consequences of poverty are blamed on the personal deficits of the poor. Similarly, people often blame rape on its victims—as if the unfortunate person invited the assault—and aloneness on lonely people—as if the problem is a result of social laziness. Beyond these anecdotal illustrations, there have been many experimental demonstrations of the fundamental attribution error, also known as FAE.

A classroom of college students wrote essays on various issues, one of which was socialized medicine. They wrote these essays having no choice about the opinions they expressed: some subjects were told to support the proposition and the rest were told to oppose it. All subjects were given a sample of arguments they could use if they so desired. The essays were collected and then handed out so that each student read an essay written by someone else. When asked to infer the real attitude of the people who wrote the essays, subjects were overly influenced by the positions taken: they attributed an essay in favor of a proposition to someone who had a favorable attitude; they attributed an essay against a proposition to someone who had that attitude. They did not make appropriate adjustments for the no choice instructions *to which they themselves, as well as the writers of the essays they read, had been subjected. (Snyder & Jones, 1974)*

In another study, subjects watched a videotape that was lacking a sound track of a woman being interviewed about her vacation plans. Some subjects were told she was asked questions about her sex life and the rest were told the questions concerned her political views. Because "people saw what they expected to see," they rated her behavior during the interview as more anxious when they thought the topic was sex instead of politics. Subjects were then asked to infer how anxious the woman was "in general," across all situations. Although they all saw the same tape, those who thought the topic was sex inferred that the woman was, in general, more anxious than those who thought the topic was politics. In other words, subjects failed to take into account the nature of the situation (sex or politics) which was responsible for her level of anxiety they perceived initially. (Snyder & Frankel, 1976)

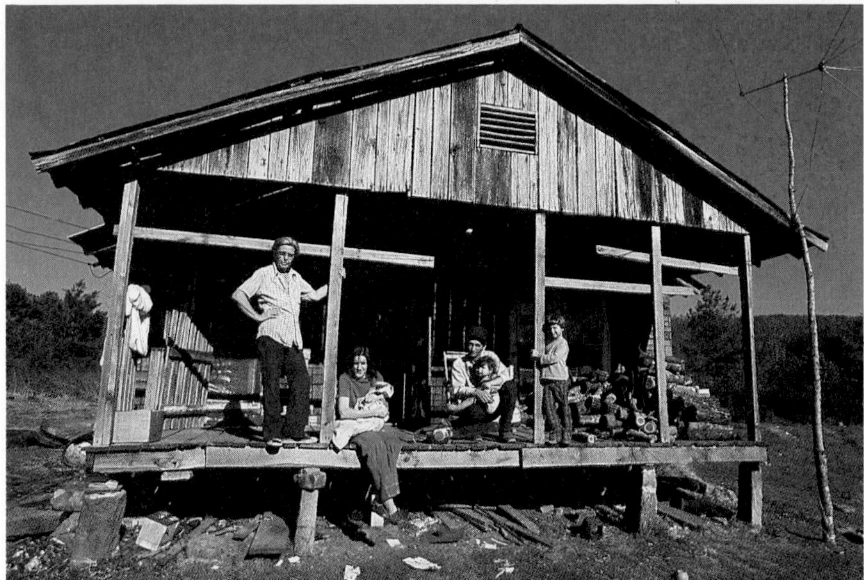

People tend to blame the homeless for their plight. This example of the fundamental attribution error ignores the situation, while holding the individual wholely responsible.

Why is there this general tendency to perceive persons rather than situations as causes for behavior? Part of the reason concerns the social reality of our culture. In Western cultures individuals are held personally responsible for their actions, whereas in other cultures the role of groups and situations is given greater emphasis. Language also contributes to the error. In English, for example, there are over 18,000 trait-like terms that describe an individual's personality, yet how many terms can you think of that describe a situation?

Because of the social reality and language of our culture we are much more likely to think it is "something about the person" rather than "something about the situation" when we are asked or ask ourselves why someone acted in a particular way. In Heider's terms, we are more prone to form a "causal unit" linking behavior to a person rather than to a situation. The implication is that, by encouraging people to form a "situation/act unit," we can undermine the fundamental attribution error and perhaps even reverse it by focusing the observer's attention on that link. Thus, in the study involving essays, people might guess whether writers were provided more affirmative or more negative arguments when they were preparing their essays. Having more affirmative arguments is an external cause that explains favorable essays; having more negative arguments explains negative essays. In fact, this is exactly what subjects did in a study that focused their attention on the situation/act unit (Quattrone, 1982). Even when subjects knew the writers took positions consistent with their own opinions, the subjects attributed the position of the essays not to the writers' attitudes, but to the situational factors. These results indicate that people can sometimes mistakenly give too much weight to a situation rather than recognize that a person's attitude is a sufficient explanation for behavior. However, under most circumstances, people in our culture are more likely to form an actor/act unit than a situation/act unit, and so errors will more often involve giving too much weight to a person, not to a situation. Put differently, when people are uncertain about the relative contributions of situational (external) and dispositional (internal) tendencies as causes for things they observe, they err by overemphasizing the influence of the dispositional and underestimating the influence of the situational. Some possible reasons for the fundamental attribution error are summarized in **Table 17.1.**

Table 17.1 *Reasons for the Fundamental Attribution Error*

Information: Social realities in the situation (norms, power relationships) may be unknown to the observer.
Ideology: People tend to accept the doctrine of personal responsibility for their actions.
Perception: To observers, actors are figures that stand out against the background of the situation.
Language: Western languages have many more terms for describing personality than for describing situations.

Actor-Observer Bias

Other reasons for the fundamental attribution error are best understood by comparing the attributions made by actors to those made by observers (Jones & Nisbett, 1972). Earlier, we saw that, although our actions depend on the situation and whom we are with, others are unlikely to recognize their effect on us; they assume we always act as they observe us to act. The difference between our perceptions of our reasons for acting and others' is one example of an attributional difference shown in many studies. In general, we attribute our own actions to external factors—the situation or other persons present—but observers are likely to attribute the same actions to internal factors, such as our traits, attitudes, and abilities. The tendency to make such attributions is known as the **actor-observer bias.** Observers make the fundamental attribution error, not actors themselves.

One reason for this difference between actors and observers involves differences in the information each has. When you think about your own action, you can compare it to other actions you have undertaken in other situations. You know that your conduct in the presence of a professor is quite different from your conduct elsewhere; it is high in distinctiveness, and, therefore, you can attribute your behavior to the nature of the student/professor situation. The professor, though, has not observed you elsewhere; indeed, his or her presence alone adds constancy to the subjective situation, whatever the physical setting might be. If the professor has observed you several times and you have acted in a consistent manner over these occasions, although all other students in the professor's presence have not, your behavior, from the professor's perspective, is high in consistency and low in consensus. Therefore it should be attributed to your internal characteristics. Hence, if people had the opportunity to observe others across many situations, not just physical settings, then the fundamental attribution error would be less prevalent than it is, and differences between actors and observers would not be so common.

A second reason for the difference is so obvious it is easy to ignore. When an actor behaves in the presence of an observer, what is each person looking at? An observer is usually looking at the actor, whose behavior is the salient, moving, dynamic figure set against the stable, unchanging background. The actor's eyes, however, are not well-located for self-observation, but are aimed at objects and persons other than him- or herself. It seems intuitive that a person may attribute behavior to whatever stimulus he or she looks at. The stimulus for an observer is the actor and for an actor it is the situation. If this intuitive hypothesis is correct, we should be able to reverse the usual actor-observer difference. In fact, if before making attributions, actors are shown their own behavior on a videotape and observers are shown the situation as seen through the actor's eyes, actors see themselves as the causal agent, and observers point to the situation (Storms, 1973).

The location of our eyes is not the only factor that affects whether we attend to a stimulus—whether we find the stimulus salient. In general, any property that makes a person or thing unusual, distinct, or different from other stimuli in the setting is a property that will draw attention. For example, being a "solo"—the only black in a group of whites, the only woman in a group of men—makes a person salient. As it happens, solos receive more credit for a group's positive outcomes and more blame for its negative outcomes than do less salient members of the group (Taylor, 1982). It is rather disturbing that credit and blame should be biased in this manner, and who knows how many people have been treated unfairly because of trivial qualities that made them stand out.

Motivational Biases

The fundamental attribution error, and the actor-observer bias refer to general cognitive biases and tendencies found in attribution. There are exceptions, as there are to all rules. One very important exception involves our tendency to think well of ourselves—to maintain a *self-serving bias.* For example, we usually take much more credit for our successes and make many more excuses for our failures than we would if we were perfectly objective and not motivated to maintain a positive self-image.

Think about an exam you took recently on which you did very well. Was this exam a fair test, in which performance was based on ability and effort rather than luck? Now think of a test on which you performed below par. How fair was this exam, and how did its fairness compare to the fairness of the test you aced? Research has shown that the same test that is considered fair—by people who did well—is also judged unfair and picky—by people who did less well. Analyses of college students' emotions and appraisals before and after a psychology midterm examination revealed that those who did poorly when they had expected to do well felt angry, guilty, and fearful. Their anger was correlated with their appraisals of the exam as unfair (Smith & Ellsworth, 1987). (Recall also our earlier discussion in chapter 12 of the phenomenon of self-handicapping in which people protected themselves from a "fall from grace" by building into their performances excuses that shifted the blame away from lack of ability and put it anywhere else. (See Arkin & Baumgardner, 1985.)

The tendency to think well of ourselves is shown in other ways, some of which are quite amusing. On insurance claims, for example, drivers are asked to explain the events leading up to accidents. One driver wrote, "An invisible car came out of nowhere, struck my car, and vanished." Another explained, "The pedestrian walked into the street up to my car and then went under it."

When people rank themselves relative to others, their motive to look good may lead to logically impossible outcomes. For example, each of the 800,000 + high-school students taking the SAT some years ago was asked to indicate how he or she compared to the rest in terms of "ability to get along with others" (College Board, 1976–1977). One fourth put themselves in the top 1 percent. An additional 65 percent put themselves in the top 10 percent, and the remaining 10 percent indicated merely that they were above average, in the fiftieth percentile. If everyone is above average, is anyone left to be average, let alone below?

There are exceptions to this self-serving bias, and, like the other exceptions we considered, they are instructive in helping us to understand the principle. For each of the 8 negative conditions in Table 17.2, indicate your chances of someday having the problem: below, above, or equal to the chances of others reading this chapter. After you have done this, go back and select the 4 problems that are most under your control—afflictions you can bring on yourself—and the 4 least controllable—afflictions that can just happen to you.

Most people rate the even-numbered items (obesity, alcoholism, lung cancer, suicide) as highly controllable, and they rate the odd-numbered items low (pneumonia, arthritis, car accident, laryngitis). If you look back at your ratings, you will probably find that you considered your chances for the controllable situations to be below average and for the uncontrollable problems to be average or above average. The self-serving bias—indicated by below average ratings given the negative nature of the outcomes—is found primarily for outcomes perceived under your control.

The importance of control actually makes sense when you consider why people even make attributions at all. Recall that you make attributions to be in control of your life—to know how to treat insomnia and whether you should trust your secrets to others. This perception of being in control is very important; in fact, the need to be in control may be what is really behind the self-serving bias. That is, to attribute success to ability implies that you can use that ability in the future, to serve your interests when the need arises again. If you attribute failure to low ability, though, you will abandon that sense of control; it's better to blame failure on something in the situation—an unfair exam—because situations always change. Abilities do not. Consequently, when the element of control is removed from an outcome, as it was in the odd-numbered items of Table 17.2, the self-serving bias is also removed from attributions about the outcome. Indeed, the need to be in control may foster a bias of its own: the *illusion of control.* Ellen Langer (1975) has shown that, in many circumstances, people try to introduce elements of skill and, therefore, control into outcomes determined purely by chance. For example, before throwing a pair of dice, people often blow into their hands and speak to the dice as if they could encourage the inanimate objects to land auspiciously. People manifest the illusion of control in other ways as well.

Table 17.2 *Expectations of Personal Health Problems*

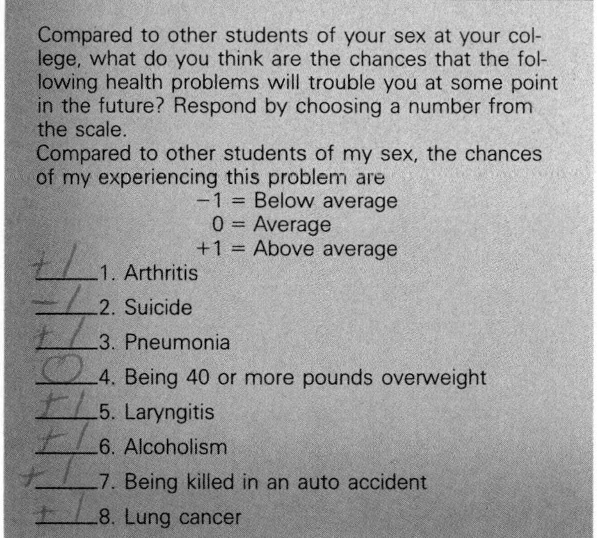

Compared to other students of your sex at your college, what do you think are the chances that the following health problems will trouble you at some point in the future? Respond by choosing a number from the scale.

Compared to other students of my sex, the chances of my experiencing this problem are

−1 = Below average
0 = Average
+1 = Above average

____ 1. Arthritis
____ 2. Suicide
____ 3. Pneumonia
____ 4. Being 40 or more pounds overweight
____ 5. Laryngitis
____ 6. Alcoholism
____ 7. Being killed in an auto accident
____ 8. Lung cancer

(From Weinstein, 1980)

> *Subjects, buying lottery tickets for a dollar, were either handed tickets or selected them from several offered. Buyers understood that the winning ticket would be determined from the spin of a barrel containing all entries; therefore, selecting tickets rather than being handed them was irrelevant to their chances of win-*

ning. On the morning of the lottery, the experimenter tried to buy the tickets back. Subjects who were handed tickets held out for a bid of $1.96. In contrast, those who had selected their own tickets did not sell until the average bid was raised to as much as $8.67. It is as if subjects believed that they could somehow pick *"hot" tickets and had less control over the "hotness" of the tickets handed to them. (Langer, 1975)*

Why is there an illusion of control and a self-serving bias? Evidence suggests that these biases may actually help us cope better, live longer, and adjust more adequately. People suffering from depression, for example, do not show these biases: they see themselves as helpless rather than as in control, and they tend to take no more personal credit for their successes than for their failures. Ordinarily, clinically "abnormal" persons are assumed to be somewhat out of touch; for example, it has been assumed that the depressed must be unduly harsh on themselves. It turns out, though, as we noted in chapter 15, that the depressed may actually be more accurate than nondepressed persons in their appraisals of social situations. That is, unlike most of us, who tend to overestimate the favorability of others' impressions of us, the depressed tend to be right on the mark; they don't filter their social perceptions through rose-colored, biased glasses (Alloy & Abramson, 1980; Lewinsohn et al., 1980). However, then the depressed behave in ways that make others avoid or respond negatively to them—further creating a depressing social reality (Coyne, 1976).

Other evidence about the beneficial aspects of biases and control come from nursing homes. Elderly people who are well cared for at the "better" institutions are freed of having to make personal decisions or of having any responsibility for their own lives. Given the value people place on personal control, these good intentions may backfire in fatal ways, as revealed in a now classic study by social psychologists Ellen Langer and Judith Rodin (1976).

On one floor of a high-quality nursing home in Connecticut, residents were encouraged to exercise control and responsibility over the humdrum activities of everyday life: when to get up in the morning; what to have for breakfast; on which day to see a movie; which plants to place in their rooms. They had to care for the plants if they accepted these gifts. On another floor, it was business as usual. These decisions and responsibilities were made by the institutional staff, including care of gift plants. The experimental procedures were designed by the researchers and carried out operationally by the usual staff personnel. The control experienced by the former group (the responsibility condition) was somewhat illusory, for their activities and treatments were actually not much different from those in the latter group (the nurturance condition). For example, although residents in the responsibility condition could choose when to wake up in the morning, they actually did not get up any earlier or later than did residents in the nurturance condition.

Older people still need to feel responsible for and in control of their lives. They will live better and longer lives if they have some control over what happens to them.

Comparisons between the two groups made 3 weeks and 18 months following the experimental intervention were striking. Residents in the responsibility condition were more satisfied with life than were respondents in the nurturance condition; they were rated by the staff as more alert; they were more active in contests, attending movies, and socializing; and they were judged by physicians to be medically healthier. Most dramatic of all, 30 percent of the residents in the nurturance condition had died by the 18-month follow-up. In the responsibility condition, the figure was only half as large—15 percent. Again, caution is advised when trying to generalize from these findings, for too much control and responsibility may be a burden that carries its high costs for some people not able to cope with it. Nonetheless, these studies show how social psychological principles can be applied to the fields of mental and medical health. These health psychology topics are among the "hottest" in contemporary social psychology, as you saw in chapter 14 (see Rodin, 1985).

Attitudes and Persuasion

Long before cognitively oriented psychologists emphasized the important functions of schemas, social psychologists studied another inferred mental process, social attitudes. **Attitudes** are predispositions to react in a particular way. They are learned judgments about the actions that are appropriate toward certain types of people or issues. Although an individual's attitudes are relatively stable attributes, they are considered more modifiable by experience than personality traits (Allport, 1968).

While social psychologists attempt to understand how attitudes are formed and changed, hosts of would-be persuaders are interested in attitude change for the more practical reason of social control. **Persuasion** is human communication designed by one source to influence other people by modifying their attitudes or one or more of the components that make up their attitudes. Parents, teachers, employers, politicians, advertisers, and many others expend a great amount of effort trying to influence attitudes in order to change behavior. They want us to think, feel, and be inclined to act in certain directions rather than others. George Orwell's novel *1984* made us aware of obvious government attempts at attitude change that were so extreme and coercive that they were labeled "mind control." Big Brother comes packaged in many forms, however; often we are least aware of the most powerful forms (Schrag, 1978).

In this section, we will explore the nature of attitudes along with some principles and strategies of persuasion. Though attitudes are intra-individual processes, they link people to a social world of people, activities, and issues—and to all those who are active in helping to form or change their attitudes.

The Nature of Attitudes

Attitudes are based on three components: (a) *beliefs*, which are judgments about what is true or about relationships that are probable; (b) *affects*, which are feelings of attraction or repulsion, and (c) *behavior dispositions*, which are predispositions or intentions toward action (Bem, 1970; Fishbein & Ajzen, 1975). Related to attitudes, and influencing behavior with them, are values. *Values* are judgments about the abstract qualities of experience; what is moral, important, beautiful, desirable, and so on.

Beliefs, formed from experience, are judgments about the truth or probability of *propositions*, which are statements about reality. They describe our physical and social world in ways that enable us to construct our personal realities. Our realities correspond to those of others to form a shared social reality. Beliefs are, in principle, subject to proof of their truth or accuracy. Given new, reliable information that proves a given belief to be wrong, a person should change the belief.

"Capital punishment deters serious crime" is a widely held belief, which should be modified by data to the contrary. When it does not, then something more than that belief is operating on the attitude regarding capital punishment. It is likely that strongly held values are at work, values that information alone does not change. "Murder is immoral; the world would be a better place if murderers were eliminated" are values that would sustain a belief in capital punishment despite information of its falsity. When a belief resists change in the face of contradictory evidence, the belief (and the person holding it) is judged to be *dogmatic*. This dogmatic attitude is common in the thought processes of both prejudiced persons and those with paranoid delusions.

A person's attitudes help determine what the person will notice, value, remember, and act upon. A social setting that might be positively valued by a college student might be perceived as dangerous and threatening by an elderly person who has developed a negative attitude about novel, dimly lit places with a lot of people and loud music. Attitudes offer justifications (reasons) for feelings, give emotional meaning to beliefs, and provide purposes for actions.

To make these abstract distinctions concrete, try rating your attitude toward the Equal Rights Amendment (ERA), a proposed (and defeated) constitutional amendment aimed at eliminating economic and political discrimination based on sex. First indicate the extent of your feelings in favor of or in opposition to the amendment (affective evaluation).

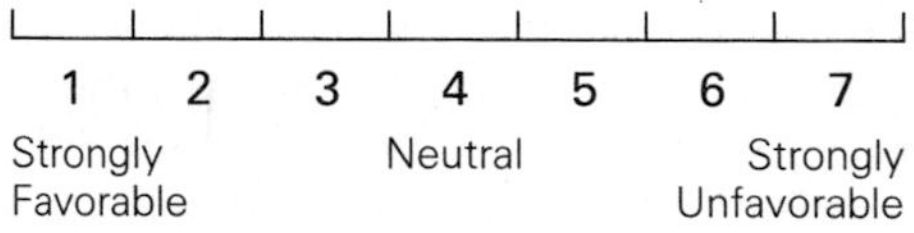

Then list your beliefs as a set of propositions about the ERA, such as: "The ERA is long overdue in a democratic country that claims equality of all its citizens," or "The ERA will disrupt family life by encouraging women to work." You will find that many of your values are involved, such as the place and worth of women relative to men.

Based on your affect, beliefs, and values, what action will you take? Will you donate money or time to a campaign in favor of or opposing the ERA? Will you argue publicly for or against it, or support political candidates who would?

Your specific attitude about the ERA may be part of a more general attitude about women's liberation. So too your attitude toward "safe and sane" highway driving speeds may be part of a general attitude about energy conservation or a general attitude about individual freedom from government restriction.

When an attitude is a *generalized* predisposition, it may exert control over many specific behaviors. By changing such a central attitude, we are likely to produce changes in a variety of specific actions. Changing attitudes toward energy conservation can result in slower driving, less use of heat and tap water, more recycling, and litter pick-up (Stern & Aronson, 1984). Research has indeed found that knowing a person's general environmental attitude predicts a wide pattern of behaviors toward the environment (Weigel & Newman, 1976). Where the attitude-behavior link is strong, we can expect that attitude change will lead to behavior change.

The Attitude-Behavior Link

The seemingly obvious assumption of consistency between attitudes and behavior has *not* been confirmed by research (Wicker, 1969). What people believe and feel about issues often differs from the way they behave toward them. Is there a strong relationship between your attitude toward the ERA and what you have done to support or oppose it? If not, what might account for the discrepancy? Researchers who are reluctant to abandon the theory that attitudes predict behavior have proposed a number of explanations for the low correlation between the two (Kleinke, 1984; Rokeach, 1968).

The most general reason for the discrepancy comes under the heading of *situational contexts.* When there is a difference between the situation in which an attitude is measured and that in which behavior is assessed, discrepancies can be expected. In one classic study, people who said they would not serve customers of a differing ethnic group (attitude) actually did so when "real-live" people of that group showed up (behavior), perhaps because the actual people differed from their abstract conceptions (La Piere, 1934). The context may function to constrain someone from acting on his or her private attitude. It would be difficult to donate to a cause if your friends were ridiculing it or to express anger at an offensive joke if your boss expected you to laugh at it. Situations like these have strong *demand characteristics* that determine the behavior of most people in that setting regardless of their personal attitudes or other attributes.

In these cases we learn about the power of those situational forces when an individual's attitudes are *not* reflected in his or her behavior. On the other hand, an attitude *is* likely to predict behavior when the attitude includes a specific behavioral intention (Fishbein & Ajzen, 1975), when both attitude and behavior are very specific (Ajzen & Fishbein, 1977), and when the attitude is based on first-hand experience. Knowing a heavy smoker who dies from cancer is more likely to affect one's smoking behavior than reading statistics about the effects of smoking on cancer (Fazio & Zanna, 1981).

A field study on the Cornell University campus was conducted after a housing shortage had forced some of the incoming freshmen to sleep on cots in the dorm lounges. All freshmen were asked about their attitudes toward the housing crisis and were then given an opportunity to take some related actions (such as signing a petition or joining a committee of dorm residents). While all of the respondents expressed the same attitude about the crisis, those who had had more direct experience with it (were actually sleeping in a lounge) showed a greater consistency between their expressed attitudes and their subsequent behavioral attempts to alleviate the problem. (Regan & Fazio, 1977)

Apparently, direct experience with an attitude object produces an attitude that is more vivid, better defined, and held with greater confidence. If you really know what your position is, you will be more likely to act in ways consistent with it.

The Behavior-Attitude Connection

Have you ever done something that did not really fit your beliefs or was contrary to your values or feelings? Perhaps you can recall such an incident done as a favor or to make a good impression, maybe for some anticipated reward or to avoid punishment. What happens to private attitudes in the face of undeniable behavioral evidence of such public deeds? Saluting the flag, reciting the Pledge of Allegiance, and singing the National Anthem are acts that increase patriotic attitudes even among children who do not know what the words of these selections mean. There is a strong link between public behavior and subsequent attitudes: *the act alters the attitude.* It does so when a special motivational state, called *cognitive dissonance,* is aroused.

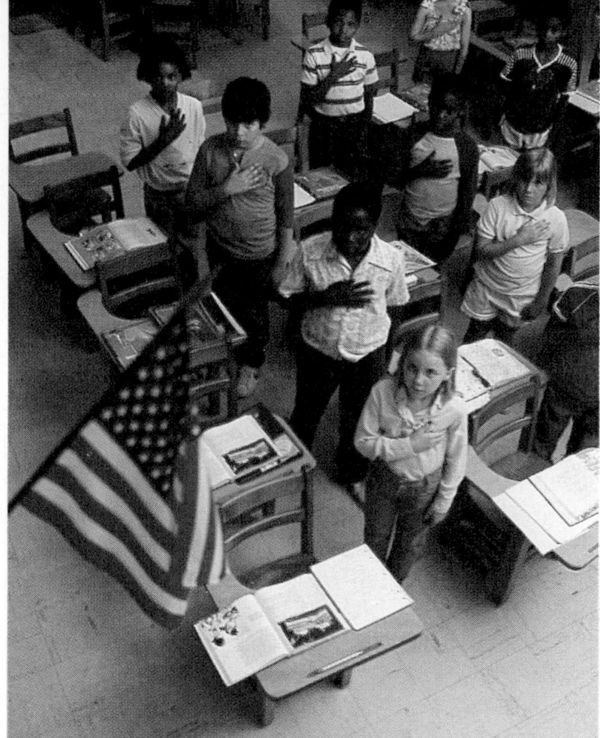

Pledging allegiance to the flag, if done consistently, may increase the patriotic attitudes of these children.

Cognitive dissonance is the term and general theory developed by Leon Festinger (1957) to account for the state of conflict someone experiences after making a decision, taking an action, or being exposed to information that contradicts prior beliefs, feelings, or values. It is assumed that when cognitions about one's behavior and relevant attitudes are discrepant, one experiences distress and is then motivated to reduce it. Dissonance-reducing activities modify this unpleasant state and achieve consonance among one's cognitions.

For example, suppose the two dissonant cognitions are some self-knowledge ("I smoke") and a belief about smoking ("Smoking causes lung cancer"). To reduce the dissonance involved one could: *change one's belief* ("The evidence that smoking causes lung cancer is not very convincing"); *change one's behavior* (stop smoking); *reevaluate the behavior* ("I don't smoke very much"); or *add new cognitions* ("I smoke low-tar cigarettes") that make the inconsistency less serious. (The latter works until you learn that smoking low-tar cigarettes has *not* lowered cancer risk.)

Cognitive dissonance produces a motivation to make discrepant behavior seem more rational, following "naturally" and logically from your attitudes. If you can't deny that you took an action, you may assert that it was actually in keeping with your attitudes. "I did it because I like it—I've always liked it—sort of." The attitude change is then internalized to make acceptable what otherwise appears to be "irrational behavior"—doing something you don't believe in when you had the choice to do otherwise and in the absence of sufficient external force to justify the action. Hundreds of experiments and field studies have shown the power of cognitive dissonance to change attitudes (Wicklund & Brehm, 1976).

In the classic dissonance experiment, lying for a small, rather than a large, reward was shown to change attitudes toward the object of the lie.

> *Subjects participated in a very dull task and were then asked (as a favor to the experimenter) to lie to another subject by saying that the task had been fun and interesting. Half the subjects were paid $20 to tell the lie, while the others were paid only $1. The first group saw the $20 payment as sufficient external justification for lying, but the second group saw the $1 payment as an inadequate reason for telling the lie. The members of the second group were left with two dissonant cognitions: "The task was dull" and "I chose to tell another student it was fun and interesting even though I had no good reason for doing so." To reduce their dissonance, these subjects changed their evaluations of the task. They later expressed the belief that "it really was fun and interesting—I might like to do it again." In comparison, the subjects who lied for $20 did not change their evaluations—the task was still a bore, even though they had lied "for the money." (Festinger & Carlsmith, 1959)*

On the basis of much research using this dissonance paradigm, a basic principle of social influence has emerged. Attitude change following dissonant public compliance is greatest when: (a) the behavioral commitment is elicited with *minimal justification,* the least amount of pressure necessary to get the compliance, and (b) a person's "illusion of free choice" to behave differently is emphasized. Under these circumstances, an individual engages in self-persuasion, feeling responsible for the consequences of his or her decision and thereby becoming his or her own most convincing persuader.

Persuasive Communications

Aristotle, in his philosophical analysis of *rhetoric,* distinguished three factors that made a communication persuasive: *ethos* (communicator characteristics), *logos* (message features), and *pathos* (emotional nature of the audience). Rhetoric, as the study of persuasion, was considered by the Greeks to be a vital tool of democracy. It was the instrument with which a common citizen might influence others by the force of argument, instead of by the power of rank and noble birth. The scientific study of communication effectiveness has followed Aristotle's lead by investigating *who* says *what* to *whom* with *what* effect (Lasswell, 1948). However, the first systematic large-scale program of persuasion was carried out not by researchers, but by a practitioner—Adolf Hitler. The Nazi dictator established a ministry of propaganda to produce materials that would modify the attitudes of enemy forces against resistance and turn the German people against the Jews. This was the first wide-scale use of film as a tool of persuasion: powerful images and symbols were used to evoke strong emotions such as fear, disgust, and resignation.

A little later, the United States developed its own "psychological warfare" program, to build up nationwide patriotic support to enter the war. It produced films to explain the reasons for fighting and to bolster the morale of the armed forces. Social psychologists began to study the impact of these mass communications on attitude change in general. After the war, psychologist Carl Hovland created the first center for research on attitude change at Yale University (Hovland et al., 1949). For the next few decades, attitude and change was one of the major topics in social psychology (Hovland et al., 1953; McGuire, 1985). For a current example of research in this area, see the ***Close-up*** on page 621.

Communicator Credibility

Typical of this laboratory-based study of persuasion was the investigation of the *credibility* of the message source as a factor in attitude change. Credible communicators are perceived to have expertise about a topic and/or to be trustworthy. A given communication is more effective if it appears to come from a highly credible source, compared to one of lower credibility (Hovland & Weiss, 1951). Source credibility has been shown to affect attitude change even when a position very different from that of the subjects is being advocated.

> *In one study students first ranked their preferences for nine stanzas from obscure modern poems. Then they read an essay expressing a favorable opinion for a stanza that they had ranked next to the bottom (poor quality). One group was told that the essay had been written by T. S. Eliot, a highly credible source. Another group was told that the source was Agnes Stearns, a college student who was studying to become a high-school English teacher, a mildly credible source.*
>
> *Three degrees of discrepancy between the subjects' original judgments and the new opinion were presented: Some of the subjects were told that the poem was the best example of a certain poetic style (extreme discrepancy). Others were told either that the stanza was "superior to all but two of the others" (moderate discrepancy) or that it was "just average" (mild discrepancy).*
>
> *As you can see in* ***Figure 17.2,*** *the more credible communicator was the more persuasive—produced more attitude change—at every level of discrepancy even though the content of the messages from the two sources was identical. (Aronson et al., 1963)*

Over time, however, credible communications lose some of their persuasive impact. This weakening of communicator credibility effects over a period of time is known as the *sleeper effect.* Later on, subjects are less likely to associate the message with the source from which it came and may even forget the source entirely. In addition, they may critically evaluate the message and argue against it, something they did not do earlier because of the prestige effect of the credible source. Over time the message from the highly credible communicator has *less* impact on attitudes and that from the less credible source has more impact than it did originally (Gillig & Greenwald, 1974).

Social Compliance

Often persuasion works not only through formal written communications and speeches, but in a more informal fashion that does not rely as much on cognitive evaluation of new information. We may be persuaded to change our attitudes or modify our behavior by emotional appeals used in advertising. We may be influenced unknowingly by the subtle manipulation of the situational context, which can make us feel guilty, important, insecure, or grateful.

Figure 17.2 *Communicator Credibility*
The graph shows both predicted and actual effects of communication from two sources, varying in three degrees of discrepancy from the subjects' original opinions. When the less credible source advocated an extremely discrepant view, there was an even greater difference in relative persuasive power (Aronson et al., 1963).

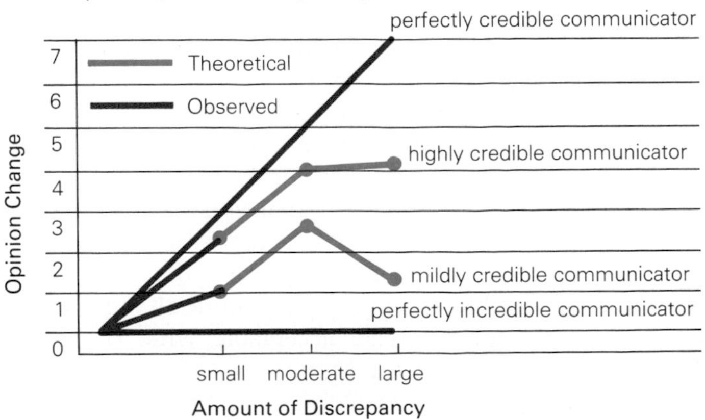

Close-up Nuclear Fears Don't Fuel Activism

Suppose you want to persuade people to quit smoking, wear seat belts, or support nuclear arms control. What is the most effective strategy you can use? Will it work to shock and frighten them, to show graphic pictures of a cancerous lung, an automobile accident, or the effects of nuclear weapons?

According to Seymour Feshbach and his colleagues, the answer is a qualified no. Fear appeals tend to be effective only when an audience is convinced that something very bad is about to happen and that the feared event is more likely to occur if a suggested specific course of action is ignored (Leventhal, 1970). There is a trade-off, though. The more convincing the fear appeal is, the more likely people are to respond defensively by denying the threat or refusing to think about it.

This trade-off may have taken place when *The Day After,* a graphic movie portraying the effects of nuclear war, was nationally broadcast on American television in 1983. Although the percentage of people who regard nuclear war as "a real threat and worry about it a lot" increased from 26 percent before the film to 88 percent afterward, opinion polls immediately preceding and following the broadcast revealed no major shifts in favor of nuclear arms control or decreased defense spending (Collins, 1984; McFadden, 1983). Fear induced by the film did not translate into support for arms control.

Nor is fear of nuclear war usually associated with arms control support. Feshbach and White (1986) have found, for example, that the degree of destructiveness people fear from a nuclear conflict is unrelated to their support for a nuclear freeze, their support for a test moratorium, or their inclination toward activism. In many cases, opponents of arms control are just as concerned and just as fearful of nuclear war as active supporters of nuclear arms control. What distinguishes opponents of arms control, according to Feshbach and White, is that they tend to harbor a greater distrust of the Soviet Union and tend to know less about nuclear issues than arms control supporters. Also, there is some evidence indicating that arms control supporters value children more highly than opponents of arms control, though the relationship reported by Feshbach and White is weak.

These findings imply that direct fear appeals may not succeed in changing attitudes about arms control. As Oliver Wendell Holmes once remarked, however, "Every person's feelings have a front door and a side door through which they may be entered." The work of Feshbach and others suggests that arms control may be effectively promoted by strengthening public education and improving Soviet-American relations.

Sometimes a minimal communication in the form of a request for a small favor can result later in a surprisingly big consequence. This is what happened in the following case study.

> *When a group of homeowners were asked to allow a big, ugly public service billboard reading "Drive Carefully" to be installed on their front lawns, most (83 percent) refused. Seventy-six percent of a second group agreed to this extreme request. Why the difference?*
>
> *Two weeks earlier most of those in the second group had readily agreed to a small request—either to put a three-inch square sign reading "Be a Safe Driver" in their windows or to sign a petition "to keep California beautiful." Two weeks later, a different person came to their door with the big request for the "Drive Carefully" billboard installation—unrelated to the earlier commitment. They were more receptive to the request than was the control group, who had made no earlier commitment. (Freedman & Fraser, 1966)*

Apparently getting involved in taking a public action, however small and trivial, may create this "foot-in-the-door" phenomenon. We become vulnerable to big requests we would reject by agreeing to a small commitment that, in a way, changes our self-image. The subjects in the second group saw themselves as "civic minded," while those in the control group did not (Eisenberg et al., 1987).

The dissonance research on attitude and behavior change following compliance focused on variables that affected the magnitude of dissonance experienced *after* a person agreed to engage in the dissonant activity—such as lying. In other studies, college student subjects *complied* with a researcher's requests to go hungry, thirsty, take electric shocks, eat fried grasshoppers—and more (see Zimbardo, 1969). Why did they comply? **Compliance** involves behaving in ways that other people suggest, request, or command. Often such compliance benefits us, as when we follow parental requests to forego smoking or to eat healthful foods. However, we are bombarded with other requests that may not be in our best interests—by TV ads inviting children to eat sugar-saturated cereals, by car salespeople selling us "lemons," or by cult recruiters inviting students to spend a week at their camp in a rural area. Are there any common principles that these and other influence agents employ in their *compliance-gaining strategies?*

It appears that there are a limited number of basic principles used "across the board" to get us to comply with almost any imaginable request. They were uncovered not by laboratory research, but by "going to the source" and observing first-hand the way successful influence agents operate. Social psychologist Robert Cialdini (1985) sold vacuum cleaners, encyclopedias, used cars, advertisements, and interviewed political lobbyists, military recruiters, police bunko (fraud) squads, and others. He found that the *psychological context* in which a request is made is all-important for the compliance principle to work.

Influence agents put the targets of their compliance attempts in a specific type of psychological context that encourages compliance. For example, the dissonance researchers and those who used the "foot-in-the-door" technique created a context of commitment to a public action. The principle of *consistency* is invoked by such commitment. We try to be consistent in our public actions because we are motivated to maintain images of personal consistency. Knowing this, influence agents elicit from us, the "targets," small initial commitments of our time, effort, or money, or make us "go on the record" agreeing publicly with some point of view. Having done so, we are primed for increasingly greater levels of commitment. A summary of these six basic principles of influence is outlined in **Table 17.3.** We are persuadable not because we are naive or gullible but because we are social beings who are generally responsive to and attracted to other people—our next topic.

Interpersonal Attraction

Does "absence make the heart grow fonder," or is it "out of sight, out of mind"? Do "birds of a feather flock together," or does "familiarity breed contempt"? Was Shakespeare right when he wrote, "They do not love that do not show their love," or when he wrote, "Love looks not with the eyes, but with the mind"? There seem to be quotations, folk wisdom, and down-home good sense to handle all outcomes—as long as you select the one that suits the occasion and you conveniently ignore its contradiction.

Early psychologists attributed social attraction to a supposed "gregarious instinct"—until it was demonstrated that individuals (animal or human) with no early experience of being with their kind did not show this supposedly universal sociability. Since then, psychologists have been trying to distill the flowery verse and common sense beliefs about sociability, liking, and loving into testable hypotheses. In this section we will learn what social psychological research tells us about the situational variables involved in social relationships that become increasingly intense as we go from affiliation to friendship to love.

Reasons for Affiliation

Gregarious instinct or no, human beings are clearly social animals, choosing overwhelmingly to live with or near other people and to spend time with them. The survival value of group life was mentioned earlier, but what motivates people to seek the company of others, rather than choose a solitary existence? When they choose to affiliate, what factors determine their choice of companions?

Interacting with other people satisfies some of our most important psychological needs. The importance of other people in *consensual validation,* in which we affirm each other's constructions of reality, was mentioned in chapter 7. In constructing our personal social realities, we evaluate what is

Table 17.3 *Compliance-Gaining Strategies: Six Influence Contexts and Principles*

1. *Commitment-Consistency*
   Public commitment engages needs to be or appear consistent with others and/or oneself.
2. *Authority-Credibility*
   Conferring authority status on others by virtue of their roles, appearances, or symbolic signs of power simplifies information processing by believing in their expertise and trustworthiness—the credibility component of persuasive communicators.
3. *Obligation-Reciprocity*
   When someone does us a favor or gives us a gift or compliment, a context of obligation is created, which induces a social need to respond positively—to reciprocate.
4. *Scarcity-Competition*
   When anything is perceived as scarce, in short supply, demand for it escalates. We want things that are scarce, exclusive, not for everyone, and will compete to get them against potential rivals.
5. *Social Validation-Consensus*
   We use the behavior of similar others as guidelines for what to do, especially in novel or ambiguous situations. In contexts where we are unsure of what is correct or appropriate we seek social validation by going along with the majority, agreeing with the consensus of others present.
6. *Friendship-Liking*
   Contexts that encourage the perception of familiarity and similarity with an influence agent increase liking and attraction toward him or her. The more liked, the more effective that influence agent will be.

correct, appropriate, even desirable in terms of those evaluations made by most others whom we respect and refer to for behavioral standards. What is right or true, then, is often a matter of validation by consensus, by mutual agreement—often implicit. Several other benefits of social interaction are *attention,* recognition of our existence, needs, unique identity; *soothing,* relief from hurt, pain, disappointment; *praise,* rewards for successful efforts; *stimulation,* competition, constructive feedback, teaching; *sharing,* cooperative activities and accomplishments; *affection,* giving and receiving trust, touch, and tenderness; and *social comparison,* a measuring stick for evaluating ourselves against other people (Buss, 1980). The importance of all but the last is probably obvious to you.

Affiliating for Social Comparison

According to **social comparison theory,** affiliating with other people enables us to evaluate our own strengths and weaknesses, resources, and biases. Especially when there is no clear physical or objective standard of correctness for us to use, other people become our subjective yardsticks, against which we assess ourselves (Festinger, 1954). Is this how other people feel? Do other people think the same way I do? Am I normal? How much better can they do this task that I can?

Such comparisons can be useful when we compare ourselves with people who are fairly similar to us in ability. If we want to know how good we are at tennis, we don't compare ourselves with champions like John McEnroe or Martina Navratilova—or with our 7-year-old cousins—but with acquaintances who have had similar amounts of experience. When we use other people to gauge the correctness of our ideas or behavior, there is no inherent reason to assume they are more correct than we, but we often tend to do so, doubting our own judgment, especially if the others have higher status than we do.

Research has shown that people who are fearful of something that may happen to them in a novel situation prefer being with someone else, even a total stranger, to being alone (Schachter, 1959). Why should fear produce this desire for company? One possibility is that people can get some more information about what is likely to happen. Perhaps they think that being with someone else will distract them and take their mind off their fear; or, as predicted by social comparison theory, they may want to find out how other people are feeling to determine the appropriateness of their own reactions. If given a choice, anxious subjects prefer to wait with others who are likely to be going through the same experience rather than with those who have completed it. Apparently, misery does not love just *any* sort of company. Rather, *misery loves miserable company* (Zimbardo & Formica, 1963).

There is also a general social phenomenon in which people who are feeling frustrated or anxious, or have suffered a misfortune, look for others who are *worse off*—a *downward* type of comparison. It seems comforting to compare their own bad situations with the "disaster" faced by someone even less fortunate (Wills, 1981).

Being alone does not always mean that a person is lonely.

Being Alone

To say that people are social animals does not mean that they always want to socialize. Often they seek quiet situations with no one to disturb them to carry out activities that require a great deal of thought and attention. They may seek solitude for periods of personal thought and reflection, to sort out what's happening in their lives, gain new insights, be creative, meditate, or pray. In such cases, being alone can serve the positive functions of personal growth, healing, and renewal (Suedfeld, 1980).

Sometimes, however, the choice to be alone may have a negative basis. If we are worried that people will not like us or will laugh at us, then we will avoid contact with them. If we think that social comparison may reveal something unpleasant or upsetting about our reactions, we may avoid it by choosing to be alone.

Although there are times when we choose to be alone, sometimes isolation is imposed on us against our will. Society recognizes the powerful need humans have for affiliation and punishes some prisoners by isolating them from human contact in solitary confinement.

A more common type of negative experience is simple loneliness. **Loneliness** is the perception of being unable to achieve the level of affiliation that we would like. Two types of loneliness have been identified. One is *social isolation,* which occurs when we feel cut off from the social support network of family and friends that we are used to. This happens to most of us when we move away from our "old neighborhood" as children or later when we leave home for college, a job, or even marriage. We feel like strangers in an alien land—until we can establish new sources of social contact.

A second type of loneliness is *emotional isolation,* in which we feel the absence of a close, intimate relationship with another person. Even though surrounded by many acquaintances, people will feel lonely without emotionally meaningful connections (Weiss, 1973; 1987). Students who drop out of college after their freshman year are more likely to decorate their dorm rooms with many items showing their close ties to their life at home. Those who do not drop out tend to decorate their rooms with more items related to their new environment (Brown, 1984).

The way in which we interpret our state of loneliness affects our feelings and shapes our subsequent interactions with other people. Those who focus on the situation ("People are too busy to be friendly") are more likely to keep trying than those who blame their loneliness on their own personal inadequacies ("I'm ugly and stupid"). The latter attributions tend to use ineffective strategies, leading to pessimism, depression, and more loneliness (Peplau et al., 1982).

> *Most college freshmen feel lonely during the first weeks of the term, but usually new social contacts develop and loneliness decreases over the year. Not so for the new students who are shy: their initial loneliness does not go away as they grow more familiar with the new environment. Even by the end of the school year they are still more lonely than their non-shy peers. The shy freshmen tend to have lower self-esteem and to blame their loneliness on their own social undesirability. They are then less ready to risk failure by putting out the effort needed to meet others and make friends. (Cheek & Busch, 1981)*

The most constructive way to view one's loneliness is to see it as an event or experience that you have control over and can change by your actions—and then take some constructive action. Social psychologists propose that "person-centered" approaches to modifying loneliness be supplemented by interventions that are designed to modify features of social settings (Rook, 1984). Existing opportunities for social contact can be restructured to promote more friendly interaction. This goal can be achieved by redesigning college dormitories, schools, nursing homes, hospitals, supermarkets, and shopping malls, and public settings to reduce the alienating aspects and increase their "user friendliness." Social psychologists support the conclusion of the President's Commission on Mental Health (1978) that puts the responsibility on society, not just the individual, for the social integration of people: "a healthy society provides opportunities for people to be connected in (meaningful) ways . . . and provides special help for those unable to avail themselves of such opportunities" (p. 144).

Liking

We all need to like and be liked in return, but why do we like some people more than others? Basically, it seems to depend on how rewarding the relationship is—which, in turn, is determined by several factors.

Factors Fostering Friendship

In general, we like people whose attitudes, values, and beliefs are similar to ours. *Similarity* is rewarding because it makes a relationship more pleasant and harmonious. We have more to share and are less likely to have upsetting encounters. We also gain a sense of personal validation, since a similar person makes us feel that our attitudes are, indeed, the right ones. Recent research has shown that *dissimilarity* in attitudes between strangers leads to strong *repulsion*—especially if the target person is also physically unattractive (Rosenbaum, 1986).

Sometimes we may be attracted to a person with attributes that complement our own. *Complementary* traits enable us to broaden our perspective and learn new ways of behaving. A quiet person may find an assertive friend more appealing than someone who is similarly quiet and withdrawn. Overall, however, similarity is a more important factor in whom we like than is complementarity.

Another ingredient in our liking someone is *reciprocal liking*—the perception that the other person likes us and is genuinely interested in us. We look for evidence that people are attracted to us and that we are special to them.

Neighbors tend to like one another because they are exposed to one another often and share common problems.

A number of studies have demonstrated that we tend to like *physically attractive* people more than unattractive ones. The rewards associated with beauty appear to derive from the stereotype that "what is beautiful is good." We think beautiful people are more desirable as good friends and perceive them as more intelligent, more successful, more pleasant, and happier than other people—even when there is no objective basis for these judgments. We even perceive children to have different personality and behavioral characteristics depending on their physical attractiveness. Children themselves react the same way: they like physically attractive children best (Dion et al., 1972). The power of good looks is convincingly demonstrated by a series of studies conducted by psychologists Elaine Hatfield and Ellen Berscheid in the context of computer-arranged dating for a college dance.

> *Freshmen at the University of Minnesota were told their dates were matched by computer, but in fact, dates were randomly assigned. When the subjects purchased their tickets, the researchers assessed their intelligence and personality using standardized tests and made ratings of their attractiveness. At the intermission in the dance, the members of the 400 couples attending the dance were interviewed by the research team to find out what they thought of their dates. Subjects were also asked 6 months later to follow-up what happened to their "dream blind dates."*
>
> *The results were clear. Beauty mattered more than high IQs, good social skills, or "good personalities." Virtually all of the college freshmen (and women) wanted good-looking dates. Only those matched by chance with beautiful or handsome blind dates "wanted to pursue the dream." Regardless of the males' looks, they pursued the women who were prettiest—not the smartest. (see Berscheid & Walster, 1978; Hatfield & Sprecher, 1986)*

Other things being equal, we tend to like people who live closer to us *(proximity)*. Perhaps you have noticed that students in adjacent dorm rooms are likely to become friends, or that the most popular students have rooms near such social crossroads as the lounge or the hall bathroom. Why are we more attracted to people whose paths cross often with ours? Familiarity may be one answer. According to research on the **mere exposure effect,** repeated exposure to the same stimulus produces greater attraction toward that stimulus (Zajonc, 1968). Since we are exposed more often to people who are in closer proximity, we come to like them more. (For a summary of the qualities judged most important for friendship, see the ***Close-up*** on page 626.)

Close-up Ten Friendship Ingredients

What are the qualities you feel are most important in a friend? In a survey of the opinions of over 40,000 readers of *Psychology Today* magazine (Parlee, 1979) the most prized qualities of a friend were loyalty and the ability to keep confidences (not spread secrets). Warmth, affection, and the feeling that the other person was supportive were also important. The top ten ingredients of friendship and the percentage of respondents who rated each as "important" or "very important" are listed. How does your list compare with these norms? Would the ingredients change if you were judging qualities of a potential life partner?

Top Ten Friendship Qualities

	Percentage
1. Keep confidences	89
2. Loyalty	88
3. Warmth, affection	82
4. Supportiveness	76
5. Frankness	75
6. Sense of humor	72
7. Willing to make time for me	62
8. Independence	61
9. Good conversationalist	59
10. Intelligence	57

From Psychology Today, *October 1979, Reader Survey of about 40,000 respondents, self-selected, primarily white, single, female, college-educated students and professional occupations.*

Theories of Liking

As researchers have learned more about the factors that affect liking, they have tried to pull them together into a comprehensive theory. The concept of rewards is a key element in any such model. Indeed, some researchers have proposed a *reinforcement theory* of attraction, arguing that we like people who reward us and dislike people who punish or fail to reward us (Byrne, 1971).

This reinforcement principle is incorporated and developed further in **social exchange theory** (Kelley & Thibaut, 1978). It conceives of social interaction in economic terms as exchanges between people, having both benefits and costs. Whenever two people interact, they each size up the costs and benefits. In general, if the benefits outweigh the costs, they will feel attracted to one another and will continue in the relationship. However, this cost-benefit ratio is also evaluated in terms of the *comparison level* of other possibilities. If an individual has been in other relationships where the overall gains were greater, then he or she will be dissatisfied with the present relationship (even if its benefits do outweigh its costs). On the other hand, a person may remain in a relationship with an unfavorable cost-benefit ratio because the available alternatives are seen as even less rewarding.

Building on these reinforcement and exchange principles, another model of liking has been developed. **Equity theory** deals with the *ratio* of inputs to outcomes for both participants in a relationship. An equitable relationship is defined as one in which the participants' outcomes are proportional to their inputs. If someone puts a lot into a relationship (the costs), that person should get a lot out of it (the benefits); but if the person contributes very little, he or she should only get a little in return. Note that the outcomes to the partners are evaluated *relative* to the investment of each, not in absolute terms according to the amount each gained from the relationship.

According to equity theory, people feel happiest and are most attracted to their partners in equitable relationships. They are most distressed in inequitable relationships. They will get upset if they think they are getting *less* from the relationship than they are putting into it. This may seem obvious, but equity theory also makes the surprising prediction that they will be dissatisfied if they are getting *more* than they deserve, since this is also an instance of inequity. When a relationship is perceived as inequitable by one or both partners, attempts will be made to restore equity. Restoration of equity can take two forms: actual and psychological. People can make actual changes in their inputs or outcomes (such as reducing the number of gifts they give to someone who is providing little affection), or, they can distort reality and convince themselves that they really are getting a good outcome (such as reinterpreting hostile criticism as an expression of concerned frankness).

Another theoretical contribution to our understanding of attraction concerns the *pattern* or sequence of rewards we get from someone, rather than their absolute number. According to a pure reinforcement perspective, we will like a person who always says nice things about us better than one who says some nice things and some bad things. However, research has shown that when comments are in a *gain* pattern (negative comments first, nice ones later), we will like that person more than one who has been consistently favorable. Conversely, when the feedback is in a *loss* pattern (first positive, then negative), we will like that person less than someone who consistently says negative things. These results have led to the hypothesis of a **gain-loss principle of attraction:** our feeling of attraction toward someone is influenced more by the direction of change, than by the level of his or her evaluation (Aronson, 1969).

Loving

Given the importance of love in promoting happiness and making the world go 'round, it may seem surprising that psychologists have only recently begun systematic research on this topic. Partly this was because of the popular belief that to study love scientifically would strip it of its romance and wonder. This view was publicly stated by Senator William Proxmire (1975) in criticizing the National Science Foundation for using taxpayers' money to fund research on romantic attraction:

> *I believe that 200 million other Americans want to leave some things in life a mystery, and right at the top of things we don't want to know is why a man falls in love with a woman and vice versa. . . . Here, if anywhere, Alexander Pope was right when he observed, ''if ignorance is bliss, 'tis folly to be wise.''*

Another reason for the relative scarcity of research on love even today is the difficulty in defining it. One of the important questions has centered on the distinction between love and liking: is the difference a *quantitative* one, with love simply a more intense form of liking? Or is there a *qualitative* difference between liking and loving, making the two experiences different in kind? Most researchers have argued for the qualitative position, pending further evidence.

> *One attempt to study both love and liking involved the development of scales to measure these two concepts. The Love Scale included three components: affiliative and dependent needs, predisposition to help, and exclusiveness and absorption. The Liking Scale had items assessing variables such as perceived similarity, maturity, adjustment, and intelligence. The two scales were filled out by 182 dating couples at the University of Michigan. Results indicated that dating partners both liked and loved each other more than they liked or loved their friends. Women tended to express a greater liking for their companions than did men and were also more loving and liking toward friends of the same sex.*

The researcher was also curious to know if a couple's scores on the love scale were related to their actual behavior toward one another.

> *To see if their behavior showed the absorption with each other that their scores indicated, he unobtrusively watched couples who were sitting alone waiting for the experiment to begin. He found that couples who had high scores on the love scale were indeed more likely to gaze into each other's eyes than couples with low love scores. On a questionnaire about their relationship filled out six months later, those with high love scores were more likely to report that their relationship had made progress toward permanence. (Rubin, 1973)*

Triangular Theory of Love

Understanding the complex nature of love that underlies intimate relationships has long inspired poets, philosophers, and dramatists. A new psychological theory attempts to reduce this complexity to three components: emotional, motivational, and cognitive (Sternberg, 1986c). The *amount* of love you experience depends on the *absolute* strength of these three aspects, while the *kind* of love experienced is a function of their strengths *relative* to each others.

The *emotional* component of love includes all feelings of closeness, bondedness, and intimacy in loving relationships. The *motivational* component refers to the drives that move someone toward romance, physical attraction, and sexual pleasure with a loved partner. The *cognitive* component of the love triangle adds cool thinking to hot feelings and drives. It encompasses conscious decisions that one loves the other person with adequate personal justification for doing so. In the long term a commitment to maintain a loving relationship is also a cognitive activity.

In this model, *liking* results when only the emotional component is experienced. *Infatuation* is the motivational arousal component in the absence of the other two. *Empty love* is found when there is a commitment to maintain a love relationship, but no other investment of emotion or motivation. It occurs at the end of stagnant relationships or at the beginning of "arranged" marriages in other cultures. *Romantic lovers* are drawn together by the emotional and motivational aspects of love, as in *Romeo and Juliet.* When emotional and cognitive aspects are combined without the motivational, then we have *companionate love.* When all three are combined, the ideal of *consummate love* is reached.

Self-Disclosure and Trust

What is the process by which two people move from a superficial acquaintance to a close relationship? According to one theory of social penetration processes, intimacy develops as a result of mutual *self-disclosure,* in which each person reveals personal and private information about him- or herself to the other (Taylor & Altman, 1987). Initially, the information that is disclosed is rather limited and nonrevealing, but, over time, more private thoughts and feelings are shared. Revealing intimate information about oneself can be a risky thing to do, so when someone shares such information with us, we infer that he or she likes and trusts us. As noted earlier in this chapter, we like those who like us. Consequently, we are likely to reciprocate with intimate disclosures about ourselves, and so the relationship will deepen and continue.

Group Processes

A **group** is defined as two or more persons who are engaged in interaction such that each influences and is influenced by the other(s). A group becomes a *team* when the contributions of two or more individuals are coordinated for the good of successfully accomplishing a common objective or mission (Emurian et al., 1984). Throughout your life you can expect to belong to many different groups and be a member of various teams. This collective participation will exert powerful influences on your perceptions, feelings, and actions—often even more influence than your own personal attitudes will be able to exert.

> *Success, recognition, and conformity are the bywords of the modern world where everyone seems to crave the anesthetizing security of being identified with the majority.*
>
> *Martin Luther King, Jr.,* Strength to Love, *1963*

In this section we will look at the way groups form and function, the way group influence develops, and some basic processes that develop in relationships between groups.

Group Form and Function

Groups usually have a particular structure, leader, and communication network. Often there is a common goal that unites the members, implies cooperative effort, and also produces identification with the group and the potential for considerable social influence.

Reasons for Joining a Group

Why do people choose to become part of a group? At the most basic level, it is to satisfy personal needs. They may be seeking fun and excitement, or emotional comfort and companionship, or status. The group may provide an opportunity to acquire information, learn new skills, gain prestige, earn a living, or achieve other goals. Different individuals may have different reasons for joining the same group: one student joins a drama club to learn how to act, another to meet some nonconventional people. The motives that bring a person into a group are important because they will influence how much he or she "invests"—and also how vulnerable he or she will be to its pressures.

The tendency for humans and animals to "herd together" also satisfies more primitive survival needs. Groups offer greater protection from predators for individuals, especially young, old, weak, and vulnerable ones. They also allow a diversity of functions to be carried out by different group members, which benefits both the individuals and the groups. Recent ecological studies also show that gregarious grazers eat better (see R. Lewin, 1985). Studies of great herds of buffalo, zebra, and wildebeest on East African plains have found that their systematic patterns of grazing enhances the concentration and nutritional quality of the food available. This positive effect, reported by ecologists, occurs because the plants that survive after the passage of a grazing herd have genetic characteristics to produce new lower, bushier, more dense foliage than was originally present.

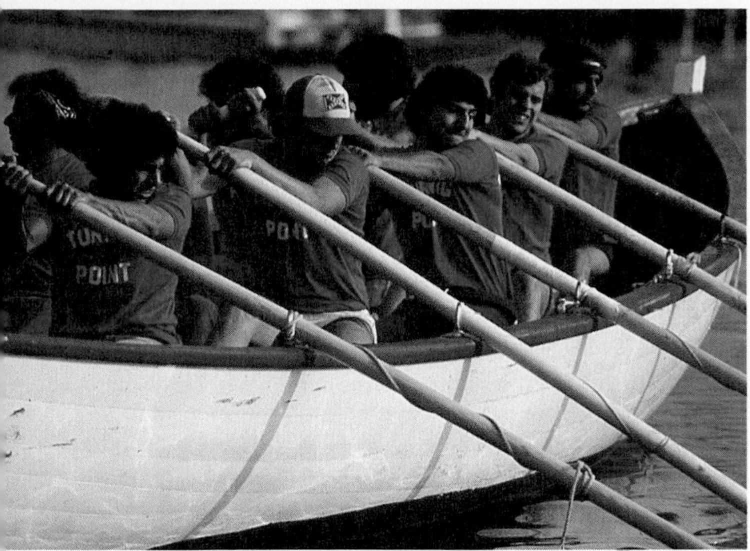
Each member of this crew has a specific role.

Group Structure and Roles

As you watch a sports team in action, you can see clearly that each member has a specific position to play. Each position is characterized by a certain set of behaviors and is related in various ways to all of the other positions. Certain communication patterns are also apparent. In baseball, for example, a catcher will signal the pitcher about the type of pitch to throw; coaches will signal the fielders where to position themselves or will signal the batters when to try to hit and when to wait. Although some outcomes depend only on individual performance, many others depend on a highly coordinated effort among team members. This can be seen in the baton pass from one relay runner to the next or the scoring of a goal when one player passes a hockey puck rather than shooting it.

This pattern of functional relationships among the various positions group members play constitutes the *group structure.* In most groups the rules and relationships are not as well defined as they are in a team sport, but they are a central part of all groups. The rules about *who* does *what* and *when* shape the interaction among the group members and provide expectations about the actions of each person.

A **role** is a socially defined pattern of behavior that is expected of a person who has a certain function in a group. Professors are expected to lecture, answer questions, and give exams, while students are expected to listen, ask questions, and take exams. Some role behaviors (such as the formal duties of the club treasurer) are explicit requirements, while others (such as who is expected to make the coffee before the meeting) may be based on implicit assumptions.

Roles are largely independent of the particular individuals who occupy them. The expected behaviors are the same, regardless of the personal characteristics of the role-player. A judge is expected to be fair and impartial, even when the decision is contrary to his or her personal values.

Although we *know* that these expectations guide a person's behavior, we sometimes are insensitive to the constraints that accompany a role and, thus, misinterpret role-directed behavior as reflecting a person's own traits or choices. We tend to ignore that the behavior is a result of a "role-driven script" and assume that the person is acting out a "person-driven script" (see chapter 10).

Pairs of students played the roles of questioner and contestant in a "college bowl" quiz game. The questioner had to think of ten difficult questions to ask the contestant, the contestant had to try to answer them, and the questioner then had to indicate whether the contestant's answers were correct. Both the students and the audience knew that students had been randomly *assigned to one role or the other. Nevertheless, the audience consistently judged the questioners to be smarter than the contestants. Even the contestants thought that people who asked difficult questions were more knowledgeable than the people who could not answer them.*

In making these judgments, they were all failing to take account of the inherent advantage of the questioner role and disadvantage of the contestant role. A questioner could choose any question for which he or she knew the answer, but the contestant had no choice about the material that would be covered. Even though the questioners were actually no smarter than the contestants, their performances were more impressive because their roles *allowed them to control the situation to their advantage. Nevertheless, everyone attributed the more impressive performance of the questioners to greater knowledge. (Ross et al., 1977)*

This is another variation of the fundamental attribution error, in which causes of behavior are attributed to a person instead of to a situation. In this case, people failed to *discount* the influence of the arbitrarily assigned roles in determining the expertise of the people playing each role. (See also "The Holy Ghost People" in *The Best of Science.*)

Group Influence

Have you ever done anything in a group that you would not ordinarily do by yourself? Have you ever been at a football rally, fraternity or sorority initiation, beach party, or *The Rocky Horror Picture Show,* where usual standards of civilized decorum were suspended? Were you ever not your "real self" in the presence of a date's parents, on a job interview, or with strangers in an elevator? If so, you are aware of some of the ways in which behavior is influenced when individuals are in group settings.

The power of other people to influence us is more common and more subtle than we generally realize. In this section we shall first consider how the mere presence of others can have a facilitating effect on our individual performance. Next we will examine the way a group's standards or norms exert pressure on its members to conform or be rejected. Finally, we will ask the "revolutionary" question: how can a minority change the views of the group majority?

Social Facilitation

The first study about the impact the *mere presence* of others has on individual behavior was published in 1897. It has the historical significance of being the first social psychological experiment.

> *The researcher, an avid bicyclist, had noticed that bicycle racers had faster times when they were racing with other people than when they were racing against a clock. To determine whether this effect held true for other activities, he had children perform the task of winding fishing reels. Sure enough: the children performed faster when another child was present in the room than when they were alone. (Triplett, 1897)*

This result was not simply the result of competition, because other studies found that it occurred when an individual performed in front of an audience. It also occurred in a *co-acting group*—a group of people engaged in the same behavior, but not interacting with each other, such as when several people play carnival games side-by-side, but separately. This improvement of individual performance brought about by the mere presence of other people is called **social facilitation.**

The social facilitation effect turns out not to be as straightforward as it seemed at first, however. Subsequent researchers found that sometimes the presence of others *interfered* with performance, rather than facilitating it. Standing up before an audience, for example, may cause stage fright rather than a stellar performance. One explanation for these apparently contradictory findings is that the presence of other people has the general effect of increasing an individual's level of arousal, or drive. This high drive will facilitate performance when a person is engaging in behavior that is well-learned; but, if the responses are relatively new and not well-learned, then the increased drive can be disruptive. An individual will become tense and the drive will interfere with optimal performance (Zajonc, 1976).

The social facilitation (and interference) effect demonstrates the power of even the most minimally social situation—the mere presence of other people. Most groups, however, involve more dynamic and direct interactions among their members. What sort of influence do these groups have on an individual?

Social Loafing

Have you ever been less productive when working on a team project than when toiling alone? It seems that there are times when being in a group encourages "goofing off," not performing as well as in its absence. The phenomenon is called **social loafing,** defined as the unconscious tendency to slack off when performing in a group, regardless of whether the task is interesting and meaningful (Latane, 1981). The negative effects of "social loafing" are that people not only work less, but they take less responsibility for what they're doing.

"Social loafing" has been found to be greater as the size of a group increases, perhaps because there is reduced self-attention when the *ratio* of others present to the total size of the group decreases. When there is just you and a buddy, the ratio is 1:2; when it's you and a task force from your school, it might be 9:10, 49:50, 99:100, or a *smaller* ratio. As self-attention diminishes, the regulatory controls of self-surveillance are weakened, and people become less concerned about matching their behavior to salient standards of appropriate behavior (Carver & Scheier, 1981; Mullen & Baumeister, 1987). What do you think are the reasons that social loafing is found to be greater among men than among women working in groups (see also Hunt, 1985)?

Social Norms

Besides the expectations regarding role behaviors, mentioned earlier, groups develop many expectations for their members regarding appropriate behavior and attitudes. These group expectations are called **social norms.** In some instances group norms are clear and explicit standards that function almost like laws.

Often, however, expectations of what members should or should not do to be "socially acceptable" are not spelled out. Rather, they serve as informal, covert regulators of behavior. New members become aware of their operation only gradually by observing two phenomena: uniformities in the behavior of all or most other members and the negative consequences of behaving "undesirably"—in nonnormative ways. We see these unwritten norms in action when codes of dress are subtly enforced to make everyone in a group look alike, whether in a group of business people, a gang of bikers, a fan club, or almost any type of permanent group.

Norms serve several indispensable functions. Awareness of the norms operating in a given group situation helps orient and regulate social interaction. Each participant can anticipate the way others will enter the situation (for example, what they will wear) and what they are likely to say and do, as well as what behavior on his or her own part will be expected and approved. Some *tolerance for deviating* from the standard is also part of the norm—wide in some cases, narrow in others. Members usually can estimate how far they can go before experiencing the coercive power of the group in the form of the three deadly R's: *ridicule, repression,* and *rejection.*

Adhering to the norms of a group is the first step in establishing *identification* with it. Such identification allows an individual to have the feeling of sharing in whatever prestige and power the group possesses. The social control carried out by group norms influences us almost from birth as part of the socialization process discussed in chapter 3.

Norms emerge in a new group through two processes: *diffusion* and *crystallization*. When people first enter a group, they bring with them their own expectations, previously acquired through other group memberships and life experiences. These various expectations are diffused and spread throughout the group as the members communicate with each other. As people talk and carry out activities together, their expectations begin to converge or crystallize into a common perspective.

The classic experiment that demonstrated norm crystallization was cited in chapter 6. It involved having subjects judge the amount of movement of a light that was actually stationary, but appeared to move when viewed in the darkness with no reference points—the *autokinetic effect.* Originally, the subjects' judgments varied widely, but when they made their judgments in a group, their estimates converged; individual subjects then followed the group norm even when they made judgments alone (Sherif, 1935).

Once norms are established in a group, they tend to perpetuate themselves. Current group members exert social pressure on incoming members to adhere to the norms, and they, in turn, put pressure on successive newcomers. Thus, norms can be transmitted from one generation of group members to the next and can continue to influence people's behavior long after the original group which created the norm exists (Insko et al., 1980).

Group norms have a strong impact on an individual's behavior as long as the member values that group. If the person comes to value and identify with a new group, then he or she will change to follow the norms of the new group. The formal or informal groups from which an individual derives attitudes and standards of acceptable and appropriate behavior and to which the individual refers for information, direction, and support for life-style are called **reference groups.**

Often the process of being influenced by group norms is so gradual and so subtle that an individual does not perceive what is happening; but it is the rare cucumber who can emerge from the vinegar vat as anything but a pickle. Some insights into this process of becoming the kind of person valued by the group are provided by a classic study conducted in a small New England college for women.

> *The prevailing norm at Bennington College was one of political and economic liberalism. On the other hand, most of the women had come from conservative homes and brought conservative attitudes with them. The question studied was what impact this "liberal atmosphere" would have on the attitudes of individual students.*
>
> *The conservatism of the freshmen class steadily declined as it progressed through college. By their senior year most students had been "converted" to a clearly liberal position. This seemed to be the result of both faculty and upper-class social approval for expression of liberal views and to the greater availability of politically oriented information in the college community.*
>
> *The students who had* resisted *this pervasive norm and retained their conservatism fell into two categories. Some, part of a small, close-knit group, simply had been unaware of the conflict between their conservatism and the prevailing campus attitudes. Others had maintained strong ties with their conservative families and continued to conform to the family standards. (Newcomb, 1943)*
>
> *Twenty years later, the marks of the Bennington experience were still evident. Most women who had left as liberals were still liberals; those who had resisted had remained conservatives. For the most part, both had married men with values like their own, thus creating a supportive home environment. Of those who left college as liberals, but married conservative men, a high proportion had returned to their freshmen-year conservatism. (Newcomb, 1963)*

Group norms, then, have the power to produce fundamental changes in our attitudes and behavior. In fact, the more we rely on social rewards from a group for our sense of self-worth and legitimacy, the greater will be the social pressure that it can bring to bear on us.

Conformity Versus Independence

In the norm crystallization experiment described earlier, in which the subjects' individual judgments of perceived motion became more like the group norm, the group's influence on the subject's judgment may not have seemed very relevant to real-life situations. After all, the perception of motion was an illusion in the first place, and the situation was so ambiguous that there was no physical reality on which an individual could depend. Later research showed convincingly, however, that group norms can sway the judgments of individuals even when the stimuli being judged are very clear and can be perceived very accurately.

Ironically, this investigation by Solomon Asch (1955) began as an attempt to show that, under conditions where physical reality was clear, individuals would *not* be swayed by social reality. Instead, it has become the classic illustration of *conformity*. **Conformity** is the tendency for people to adopt the behavior and opinions of other group members.

Groups of seven to nine male college students were shown cards with three lines of differing lengths and were asked to indicate which of the three lines was the same length as a line on a standard card (see ***Figure 17.3A****). The lines were different enough so that mistakes would ordinarily be made less than 1 percent of the time. In the experiment, however, all but one of the members of each group were confederates of the researcher. The confederates were unanimous in the incorrect answers they gave on 12 of the 18 trials. For example, they might all report that line 1 was the same length as line* A. *When it finally became the turn of the real subject to judge the lines, the subject yielded to the majority's wrong judgments in 37 percent of the trials.*

This figure is misleading, however, for individual differences were marked. Of the 123 subjects, about 30 percent nearly always yielded, while another 25 percent never did so. All who yielded underestimated the influence of the social pressure and the frequency of their conformity; some even claimed that they really had seen the lines as the same.

Next, the design of the experiment was changed slightly to investigate the effects of the size of the opposing majority. Pitted against just one person giving an incorrect judgment, a subject exhibited some uneasiness but did not conform. When as many as 3 opposed the subject, errors rose to 32 percent. In contrast, when one other person agreed *with the subject's perception, the effects of the majority were weakened: errors decreased to one fourth of what they had been with no agreeing partner. Significantly, this effect of a supportive "deviant" lasted even after the partner left (see the graph in* ***Figure 17.3****). (Asch, 1955)*

Numerous studies of conformity have confirmed these results. The power of the group majority depends on its unanimity. Once it is broken—in any way—the rate of conformity drops dramatically. A person is also more likely to conform when: (a) a judgment task is difficult or ambiguous; (b) a group is a highly cohesive one to which an individual feels attracted: (c) the group members are perceived as competent and the person feels incompetent; and (d) a person's responses are made known to others in the group.

Minority Influence and Nonconformity

Given the power of the majority to control resources and reinforcements, it is not surprising to observe the extent of conformity that exists at all levels of our society. What is remarkable is how anyone escapes this group domination or how anything new—counternormative—ever comes about. How do revolutions against the status quo emerge? Are there any conditions under which a small minority can turn the majority around and create new norms?

An example in which this occurred was cited in chapter 6. A third of the subjects who judged color slides followed the lead of the minority, who consistently said "green" whenever a blue slide appeared (Moscovici & Faucheux, 1972).

Researchers have also studied minority influence in the context of simulated jury deliberations, where a disagreeing minority prevented unanimous acceptance of the majority point of view. The minority group was never well liked, and its persuasiveness, when it occurred, was not immediate, but appeared only gradually over time. The minority was most influential when it took a consistent position and seemed confident in doing so. Eventually, the power of the many may be undercut by the conviction of the few. (Nemeth, 1979)

These findings show that conflict between a group and an individual does not have to destroy the person's integrity. Rather, such conflict is an essential precondition of innovations that can lead to positive social change. An individual is constantly engaged in a two-way exchange with society. The individual adapts to its norms, roles, and status prescriptions, but also can act upon it to reshape those norms (Moscovici, 1985). Perhaps the greatest challenge for social psychologists is to understand the dynamics of this interplay of group forces that influence an individual's behavioral and mental processes and those individual factors that maintain or change group functioning.

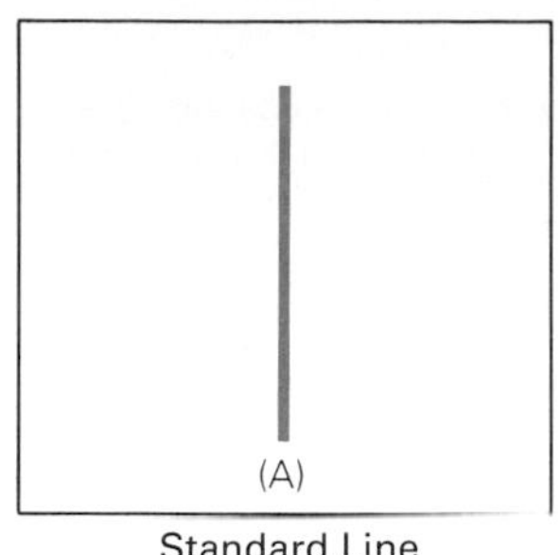

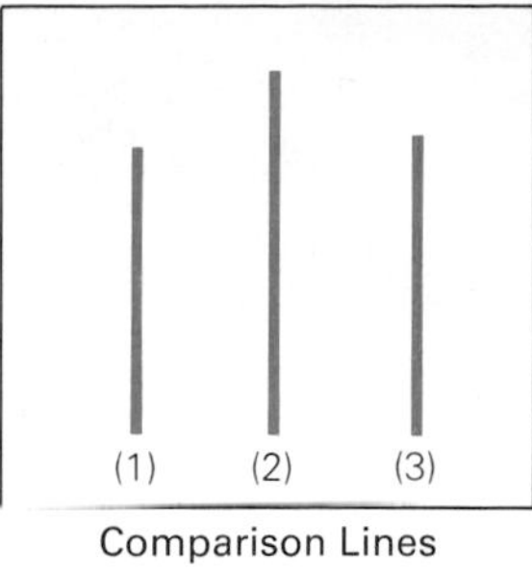

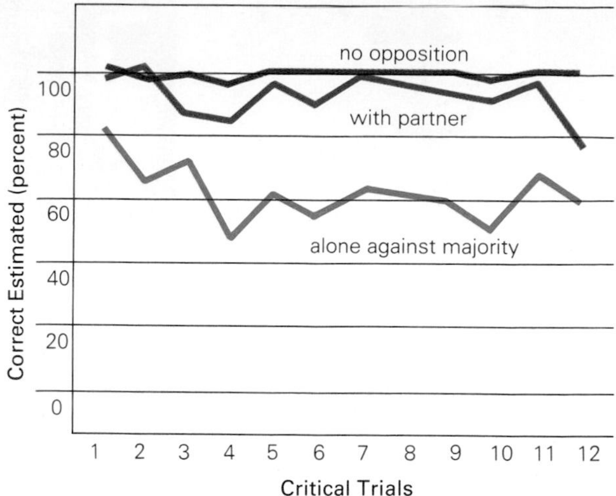

Figure 17.3
The graph compares the average number of correct judgments under normal circumstances with those made under social pressure both with and without a supporting partner.

Intergroup Relations

Some social psychologists are interested in social influence *between* groups rather than within them. They are concerned with the dynamics of intergroup relations, competition and cooperation, and conflict resolution.

When one group of people is differentiated from another, members of both groups develop a "we-feeling" about their own group, the **in-group,** and a "they-feeling" about the others, the **out-group.** Not only are distinctions made between "us" and "them," but there is a clear bias toward evaluating "us" as better (Brewer, 1979). This bias in favor of one's own group is called an *in-group bias.* It takes surprisingly little to produce it.

In a series of experiments, subjects were randomly divided into two groups: a "blue" group and a "green" group. The groups were given blue or green pens and wrote on blue or green paper; they were addressed by the experimenter in terms of their group color. Even though these color categories had no intrinsic psychological significance and assignment to the groups was completely arbitrary, subjects gave a more positive evaluation of their own group than of the other. Furthermore, this in-group bias, based on their color identification, appeared even before *the group members began to work together. (Rabbie, 1981)*

Apparently merely categorizing people into different groups under totally arbitrary pretexts is sufficient to cause a change in attitudes. People begin to favor their own "in-group" as superior and they develop a hostile attitude toward the "out-group," which is perceived to be inferior (Allen & Wilder, 1975; Rabbie & Wilkens, 1971; Tajfel, 1970). Furthermore, anything that leads to a perception of a "we-they" dichotomy then induces the members of each group to try to increase the extent and significance of the perceived difference, however trivial (Wilder, 1978).

An arbitrary assignment into a group labeled "inferior" can make children perform below their usual level, while average children, led to believe they are in a "superior" group, act more in keeping with their designated group category. A powerful demonstration of this effect was devised in a remarkable experiment by a third-grade class teacher, Jane Elliott, who wanted her pupils from an all-white, rural community to experience what prejudice and discrimination felt like.

One day she arbitrarily designated brown-eyed children as "superior" to the "inferior" blue-eyed children. The superior, allegedly more intelligent, "brown-eyes" were given special privileges, while the inferior "blue-eyes" had to obey rules that enforced their second-class status.

The blue-eyed children immediately began to do more poorly in their schoolwork and became depressed, sullen, and angry. They described themselves as "sad," "bad," "stupid," "dull," and "mean." One boy said he felt like a "vegetable." Of the brown-eyed superiors, the teacher reported, "what had been marvelously cooperative, thoughtful, children became nasty, vicious, discriminating little third-graders . . . it was ghastly."

To show how arbitrary and irrational intergroup prejudice and its rationalizations were, Mrs. Elliott told the class on the next school day that she had been wrong, that it was really the blue-eyed children who were superior and the brown-eyed ones who were inferior. The brown-eyes now switched from their previously "happy," "good," "sweet," and "nice" self-labels to derogatory ones similar to those used the day before by the blue-eyes. Their academic performance deteriorated, while that of the new ruling class improved. Old friendship patterns between children temporarily dissolved and were replaced with hostility until the experiment was called off. (Elliott, 1977)

Besides the observable changes in the children's overt behavior toward each other and in their schoolwork under the two conditions of the experiment, Jane Elliott obtained measures of their feelings under each condition by having them draw pictures of how they felt. The picture shown was drawn by a child who felt "on top," competent, and capable.

This experience of being in a disadvantaged out-group can have the positive effect of enabling people to develop greater empathy for members of groups that are discriminated against in society. In a replication of Mrs. Elliott's study, psychologists found that, weeks later, the children who had participated held less prejudiced beliefs than did a comparison group without this experience (Weiner & Wright, 1973). The paradigm of categorizing people by arbitrary cues of differentness—eye color—was equally effective with the adult groups that Mrs. Elliott instructed. The effects were also long-lasting. A ten-year follow-up of her original grade-school students revealed that, as young adults, they were quite *tolerant* of group differences and were actively *anti-prejudice.*

The ease with which people can divide their social world into "us" and "them" and their immediate preference for the in-group have many important consequences for their behavior toward other people. They may be more sociable and helpful to someone who is "one of us" even if that individual is a stranger. Conversely, they may be more ready to act in negative ways toward any member of an out-group. There is also a general tendency to perceive one's own groups as being quite variable in their attributes whereas out-groups are seen in stereotypic ways, with all members perceived as being pretty much alike. This is true regardless of the amount of exposure we have to the out-groups and despite contrary experience with their individual members—of the other sex, college, occupation, race, or any other out-group category (Park & Rothbart, 1982; Quattrone, 1985).

Given the prevalence of this favoritism for the in-group, we can expect that there will often be a great deal of rivalry and competition between groups and sometimes mutual hostility and overt aggression. Is this inevitable? What factors aggravate conflict between groups and what factors would promote cooperation instead? Some answers are provided in a classic study by social psychologist Muzafer Sherif at his Robber's Cave summer camp for boys, described in the ***Close-up*** on page 635.

Clearly this study with boys has implications for reducing the bitterness between antagonistic adult groups within our own society as well as between national groups. The task is to discover superordinate goals that will be perceived by these groups to be in their best interest, but achievable only through cooperation with each other. What might some superordinate goals be for labor and management? For Russians and Americans? For Arabs and Israelis?

This dual potential of groups—either to bring out the best in people or to create some of the worst crimes against humanity—will be one of our major concerns in the next chapter, as we examine several social issues, problems, and potential solutions. (See also "The Delicate Sex" in *The Best of Science.*)

Summary

- The central focus of social psychology is the study of social influence. Psychologists study this influence within individuals, in interactions between people, and in groups and intergroup relations.
- In social psychological research individual behavior in the current social context is the unit of study. Ideally what is studied is the interaction of person and situation variables on a given behavior.
- Social reality is created out of the phenomenological perspective of the participants in a situation. The shared social reality may be formally or informally defined. The social reality provides powerful schemas that shape a person's perceptions, expectations, and behavior, and create self-fulfilling prophecies.

Close-up The Rattlers vs. the Eagles

Friction was generated between two groups of boys at a summer camp. It was later overcome as the groups worked toward common goals. In the beginning, the experimenters assigned the groups to different bunkhouses and kept them separate for daily group activities. By the end of this part of the experiment, the two groups had acquired definite group structures, including leaders, names (Rattlers and Eagles), private signals, and other identification symbols.

Next, rivalry between the groups was stimulated by a series of competitive events. As predicted, this increased in-group solidarity had produced unfavorable stereotypes of the out-group and its members. After losing a tug-of-war, the Eagles burned the Rattlers' flag. The Rattlers retaliated, and a series of bunkhouse raids ensued, accompanied by name calling, fist fights, and other expressions of hostility. During the conflict, a physically daring leader emerged to replace the less aggressive boy who had led the "peacetime" Eagles, explaining how relations with other groups can cause changes within a group and the emergence of new leaders.

An attempt was then made to break down the hostility and induce the two groups to cooperate. First, the rival groups were brought into close contact in pleasant activities—such as eating and shooting off firecrackers. The groups refused to intermingle, however, and the activities merely provided them with further opportunities for expressions of hostility. Intergroup contact did not in itself decrease tension.

Situations were then contrived to bring about interaction of the groups to achieve *superordinate goals*—that is, important goals that required the combined efforts of both groups. The most striking episode in this period was one in which the tug-of-war rope, formerly the central object in a most antagonistic situation, served as a tool. On an overnight trip, a truck that was to bring their food "stalled," and the boys decided to use the rope to pull the vehicle. After looping the rope through the bumper, the two groups pulled on different ends, but the next day, when the truck "stalled" again, members of the two groups intermingled on the two lines, eliminating group divisions. The groups also worked together to solve the problem when the camp's water supply stopped.

Further evidence of the change in the boys' attitudes was obtained from friendship choices made at the end of the period of intense competition and again at the close of the experiment. Rattlers' choices of Eagles as friends went up from 6 to 36 percent of their total friendship choices. Eagles' choices of Rattlers went up from 8 to 23 percent. The boys were also asked to rate each other on six characteristics designed to reveal the presence of stereotyped images. During the period of antagonism, Eagles received few favorable ratings from Rattlers, and Rattlers few from Eagles, but at the close of the experiment there was no significant difference in the ratings of in-group or out-group members (Sherif et al., 1961; Sherif & Sherif, 1979).

- A much studied social process *within* individuals is social perception—the way we form impressions of other people and explain their behavior. Some attributions about behavior are based on stereotypes and snap judgments. First impressions are more influential than later information. Causal theories attempt to identify the internal and external factors that account for behavior.
- In attributing causes to people's behavior, we tend to use the discounting principle—to discount situational factors if there are personality factors adequate to account for a behavior. We also use the covariation principle and its three criteria of distinctiveness, consensus, and consistency. We use these criteria to judge whether an action was caused by factors in an individual or in a situation.

- Common errors in attribution of causes are the fundamental attribution error and the actor-observer bias. Motivational biases include the self-serving bias and the illusion of control.
- Attitudes are learned predispositions to react in a particular way to certain stimuli. They include beliefs, affects, and behavioral dispositions. Attitudes help determine what a person will notice, value, remember, and act upon. An attitude is most likely to predict behavior when it includes a specific behavioral intention, when both attitude and behavior are very specific, and when it is based on first-hand experience.
- When one is induced to act in a way contrary to one's attitude for minimal justification, cognitive dissonance is experienced; this dissonance is arousing, motivating actions to reduce it, often by changing attitudes to make them more consistent with the behavior.
- Systematic study of attitude change began following Hitler's massive and successful use of propaganda. Such studies investigated the role of the source of a message, features of the message itself, and audience characteristics in producing attitude change.
- Compliance is behaving in ways that other people suggest, request, or command. Sometimes compliance is in our best interest, but often it is not. A psychological context that encourages compliance is important for compliance to work, as seen in everyday compliance-gaining strategies of salespeople and others.
- Affiliation with others provides opportunities for consensual validation, praise, stimulation, sharing affection, and social comparison, giving us a measuring stick to evaluate ourselves against others. People who are fearful in a novel situation often prefer to be with others, whereas those who are anxious and do not know why may avoid affiliation.
- Loneliness may involve social isolation or emotional isolation or both. Lonely people who blame the situation for their loneliness are more likely to try to change it than those who blame their own inadequacies.
- Liking depends on how mutually rewarding a relationship is; this, in turn, is influenced by similarity, presence of complementary traits, reciprocity, physical attractiveness, and proximity. Theories of liking include reinforcement theory, social exchange theory, equity theory, and the gain-loss principle, according to which attraction is influenced by the direction of change in rewards received.
- Though there has been little research on love, one means of studying loving has involved a self-report Love Scale. It has successfully predicted continuation and progress in the loving relationships of dating couples. The triangular theory of love proposes three components of love: emotional investment, motivational arousal, and cognitive commitment. The amount of love depends on the absolute strength of each component; the kind of love on the relative strength of each.
- Our group memberships may influence our perceptions, feelings, and actions even more than our attitudes. Groups usually have a structure, leader, communication network, set of rules, and common goal; all these help to induce a sense of identification with the group on the part of the members and provide the potential for social influence.
- Group influence occurs through the mere presence of other people, but most strongly through group norms that members are expected to follow. Those who identify strongly with a group come to share its attitudes and values. Recent research on the phenomenon of social loafing indicates that people in groups work less and take less responsibility for the work.
- Pressure toward conformity is felt strongly by those who depend on a group to meet their personal needs. Conformity may represent only external compliance, uncritical identification with, or internalization of, a group position. Under some conditions, a consistent, confident, deviant minority can change the position of the majority.
- When two groups are differentiated from each other, members of both develop "we-feelings" toward the in-group and "they-feelings" toward the out-group. These feelings are accompanied by a conviction of their own superiority and efforts to accentuate the perceived differences.
- Rivalry increases these "we" and "they" distinctions and may lead to hostility and intergroup aggression. Working toward a superordinate goal of importance to all can lessen these antagonisms and lead to new ways of constructively relating to former enemies.

18

Exploring Social Issues

Tommy Whitlow liked to relax on summer Sundays doing nothing more serious or intellectual than to watch a ball game on TV. His serenity was shattered one Sunday morning by a screeching siren as the city police arrived to arrest him at his home. They swept through the college town, rounding up nine students in a surprise mass arrest. Each was charged with a felony, warned of his constitutional rights, searched, handcuffed, and carted off to the police station for booking. After fingerprinting and paperwork were completed, each prisoner was blindfolded and transported to the "Stanford County Prison." Here he was stripped naked and issued a smock-type uniform with his I.D. number on front and back. At this point, Tommy lost his name and became only Prisoner 647.

Orders were shouted at Prisoner 647, and he was pushed around by the guards if he didn't comply quickly enough. The guards all wore khaki uniforms. They, too, were not identified by name, and their anonymity was furthered by reflector sunglasses, which made eye contact with them impossible. Most of the youthful prisoners sat on cots in their barren cells, dazed and shocked by the unexpected events that had transformed their lives so suddenly. Just what kind of prison was this? Prisoner 647 and the others soon found out.

The guards insisted that their prisoners blindly obey all institutional rules, without question or hesitation. Failure to do so would lead to the loss of a privilege. At first, privileges were opportunities to read, write, or talk to other inmates. Later, however, the slightest disobedience was punished by loss of the "privilege" of eating, sleeping, or washing. Punishment also included menial, mindless work, such as cleaning toilets with bare hands, doing push-ups, and spending time in solitary confinement.

Every guard Prisoner 647 encountered engaged in abusive, authoritarian behavior at some time. Many appeared to enjoy the elevated status that accompanied putting on the guard uniforms, which transformed their routine, everyday existence into one where they had virtually total control over other people. The guards were always devising new strategies to make the prisoners feel worthless, depriving them not only of basic freedoms, but even of a sense of humanity and individuality.

Less than 36 hours after the mass arrest, one of the prisoners began to cry uncontrollably. He also experienced fits of rage, disorganized thinking, and severe depression. Three more prisoners developed similar symptoms on successive days. A fifth prisoner developed a psychosomatic rash over his body when the Parole Board rejected his appeal.

After lights were out, Prisoner 647 tried hard to remember what Tommy was like before becoming a prisoner. He also tried to imagine what his tormentors did before they became guards. He reminded himself that he was a college student who had answered an ad to be a subject in a two-week-long experiment on prison life. He had volunteered in order to make some money and to have some fun doing something unusual.

The guards were college students, too. In fact, everyone in that strange prison had been selected from a large pool of volunteers because he was a normally healthy, average, middle class college student! On the basis of extensive personality tests and clinical interviews, they had all been judged to be law-abiding, emotionally stable, physically healthy, and "normal-average." This was not a prison run by the state, but a mock prison experiment run by psychologists.

Assignment of the participants to the condition of "guard" or "prisoner" had been *randomly determined* by the flip of a coin. The assignment to these roles was the independent variable. At the start of the study, then, there were no measurable differences between the mock "guards" and the "prisoners."

The experimenters ended the planned two-week simulation study after just six days, because of the dramatic emotional

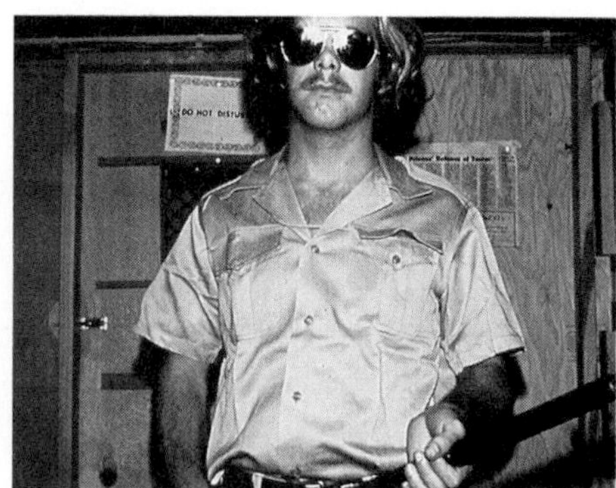

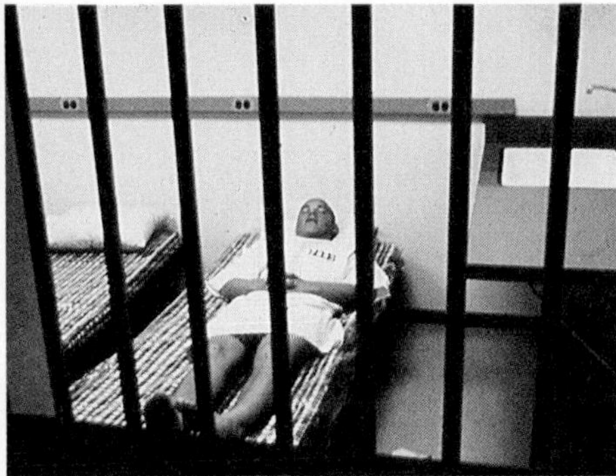

and behavioral effects it was creating. (Those prisoners who seemed especially distressed had been released even sooner.) Students who were pacifists had become sadistic when they were in their "guard" roles; psychologically stable students had behaved pathologically as prisoners confined in this total environment. The power of this simulated prison situation had become strong enough to create a new *social reality*—it was a real prison in the minds of the jailers and the captives.

Tommy Whitlow said later that he wouldn't want to go through it again, but valued the experience because he learned so much about himself and about human nature. He and the other students were so basically healthy that they readily bounced back from that powerful situation and follow-ups revealed no lasting negative effects. Guards and prisoners alike had learned an important lesson: never underestimate the power of an evil situation to overwhelm the personalities and good upbringing of even the best and brightest among us (Haney & Zimbardo, 1977; Zimbardo, 1975; replicated in Australia by Lovibond et al., 1979).

What is the nature of human nature? Are we molded in the images of Jesus and Buddha as loving, caring beings? Or are we really self-centered animals, driven to inflict suffering on others without any compassion? Does society curb our instinctively evil nature, or is society the corrupting force that perverts our basic goodness?

In this final stage of our journey through the realm of psychology, we will consider some of these "big" questions. Our focus will be on the bonds between individuals and society, on the way the social-psychological processes described in the last chapter operate in life situations to pull us upward toward divinity or draw us downward toward destruction. Some of the themes in the story of Tommy's imprisonment that we will look at include human aggression, obedience to authority, the loss of individuality, and dehumanization.

We will end the chapter with a look at new areas of interest for social psychologists, including the relationship between people and their physical environment. We will see why ecological issues are often "people problems" that need people-centered solutions. Finally, we will examine the role of psychology to maintain peace and prevent nuclear war.

Human Potential and Social Influence

Perhaps the most basic question in psychology is "What is the nature of human nature?" How are we to understand what people are all about, what they are capable of doing, being, or becoming? Is the influence of society on the individual beneficial or harmful? Are we programmed by our past, which we bring to new situations, or controlled by the social context of the present?

The Puzzle of Human Nature

According to some views, people do not "go wrong"; they basically *are* wrong. In other words, people are evil by nature and will naturally hurt one another and engage in destructive acts—unless strong forces are present to restrain them. Among the most negative views of human nature is this excerpt from Jonathan Swift's *Gulliver's Travels:*

> *[The historical account of humans is a] heap of conspiracies, rebellions, murders, massacres, revolutions, banishments, the very worst effects that avarice, faction, hypocrisy, perfidiousness, cruelty, rage, madness, hatred, envy, lust, malice, and ambition could produce. . . . I cannot but conclude the bulk of your natives to be the most pernicious race of little odious vermin that nature ever suffered to crawl upon the surface of the earth.*

If we are basically so evil, than how can it be that we often do good? Why do we sometimes care for one another, form friendships, and act in ways that seem to benefit all involved? One answer (strongly stated by philosopher Thomas Hobbes) is that, although we are naturally driven by base desires, appetites, and impulses, proper education can transform us into responsible, law-abiding human beings. Then, firm and well-meaning authorities can control our behavior.

In contrast to this view of natural depravity is the idea that people are basically good, but that they are the victims of corrupting social forces. As we saw in chapter 3, this theme was developed by the philosopher Jean Jacques Rousseau, who envisioned human beings as noble, primitive savages diminished by contact with society. To recapture and preserve their essential goodness, then, individuals must escape from civilization. For Americans, Henry Thoreau's isolated cabin at Walden Pond, Massachusetts, has become symbolic of a solitary "natural life," an escape from the bonds of social convention and community-controlled lifestyle.

Where do *you* stand in this argument? Are people born good and corrupted by an evil society, or born evil and redeemed by a good society? Is it that some people are basically good, while others are basically bad? Before casting your ballot, consider an alternative perspective. Maybe each of us has the capacity to be a saint *or* a sinner, altruistic *or* selfish, gentle *or* cruel, dominant *or* submissive. Perhaps human nature is a *capacity* for learning, for adapting, for constantly changing. Perhaps each person is born with that capacity to adapt and can learn many possible realities and alternative ways of being.

Human Potentials for Good and Evil

The preceding chapters have documented the complex development and supreme refinement of human capacities that have resulted from untold millions of years of evolution, growth, and adaptation. We have become the rulers of this planet, controlling other animals and the physical matter of the earth for our survival, comfort, and happiness. This reign is currently being extended to life beneath the oceans as well as to outer space. We have reached this position because of our capacity to learn new relationships, to remember old ones, to reason, invent, and plan new action strategies. We have developed both natural and computer languages to manipulate symbols and transmit thoughts and information to others. Our perceptual, cognitive, and motor skills allow us to see, reflect, and act in countless intricate ways to avoid pain, gain pleasure, and change our surroundings to suit ourselves.

Each of these unique attributes can also become cancerous, however. Implanted in the very potential for perfectibility are the seeds of perversion and breakdown. A partial catalog of human traits and attributes and their possible positive and negative consequences is given in **Table 18.1.** Which way they develop is influenced by the interaction of the psychological processes with processes at economic, political, historical, and cultural levels. As we develop, cultural and social forces make certain options more available to us than others, certain potentialities more likely to be expressed. Equally important, though our past has shaped us, we can change at any moment as a result of a chance encounter or immersion in a new, powerful social reality (see Bandura, 1982a).

Table 18.1 Ways We Can Go Wrong: Perverting Perfection

Attribute	Enables Us to	Can Also Lead Us to
Memory	Profit from past mistakes Develop and use complex concepts Relate present to past Distinguish novel events from previously experienced ones	Carry grudges, suffer from former conflicts and past traumatic events Lose spontaneity of behavior because of commitment and obligations Feel excessive remorse or sense of loss
Time sense	Develop a history and sense of continuous self Relate present behavior to the future Distinguish between transience and permanence	Fear change, live in the past, feel guilt Dread an unknown future, become anxious Experience disappointments from unfulfilled expectations Concentrate on past or future, ignoring the present
Ability to associate elements and infer unseen events	Create, imagine events not experienced Generalize from partial data Construct theories, hypotheses	Form negative, crippling associations Misperceive self or others, develop stereotypic and delusional thinking
Perception of choice	Not be stimulus bound, be independent See ourselves as responsible agents Hope, build for future	Experience conflicts, indecision Suffer from inability to act when action is necessary
Responsiblity, self-evaluation	Take pride in accomplishments Delay gratification, undertake difficult or unpopular tasks Be concerned about effects of our actions on others	Feel inadequate Feel guilt for not living up to standards or for letting someone down Feel constrained by obligations
Competence motivation	Do work well, set high standards Gain benefits of hard work Advance technologically, use resources to meet our needs	Fear failure, suffer feelings of inadequacy Be anxious about tests of our ability Work for self-aggrandizement, to be "number one," to beat others down
Ability to use language and other symbols	Communicate with others, present and absent, for information, comfort, pleasure, planning, social control	Circulate and be prey to rumors and falsehoods; conceal true feelings Mistake the symbol for the reality
Susceptibility to social influence	Follow group standards Learn and transmit values Cooperate; establish community	Overconform, sacrifice integrity Reject innovation and stifle creativity in ourselves and others
Love	Experience tender emotions Nurture growth and independence of others Support, encourage, comfort others Feel wanted and special	Become jealous, vengeful Possessively limit another person's freedom Become depressed and suicidal from loss of love

Situationism and Social Reality Revisited

The central theme of social psychology, which comes from the Lewinian tradition, is that social situations matter—more than we recognize or believe they possibly could. Stated more formally, social situations exert significant control over individual behavior, often dominating personality and a person's past history of learning, values, and beliefs. More than we suspect, our actions are determined by forces and constraints in behavior settings rather than by personal qualities, intentions, or well-laid plans. Thus, situational aspects that appear trivial to observers—words, labels, signs, rules, roles, the mere presence or number of other people—can powerfully influence how we behave, sometimes without awareness of their determining force.

The situations in which we live and move determine the roles available to us. They also help define the social meaning that each role will have. Thus situations can be powerful agencies to change us—or keep us from changing.

In the simulated prison experiment, the guards and the prisoners, at the end of the study, were different from one another in virtually every observable way; yet just a week before, they had been very similar. Chance, in the form of random assignment, decided their roles, and these roles created status and power differences which, in turn, led to all the other differences in how they thought, felt, and acted (see **Figure 18.1**).

No one taught them to play their roles. We have to assume that each of the students had the capacity to become either a prisoner or a guard by calling upon stored knowledge structures about those roles. Without ever visiting a real prison or speaking with prison staff or inmates, we have all learned these roles (Banuazizi & Movahedi, 1975).

In our schemas and scripts, a guard limits the freedom of prisoners to manage their behavior more easily. This task is aided by the use of coercive rules. Prisoners can only *react* to the structure created by others. Rebellion or compliance are their primary options; the first gets punished, while the second takes away their sense of autonomy and dignity. The student participants had already experienced such power differences in many previous interactions: parent-child; teacher-student; doctor-patient; boss-worker; traditional male-female. They merely refined and intensified their scripts for this particular setting.

Too often, we limit our own freedom by sticking with the traditional roles we find operating in our groups, even though our human nature gives us the potential to learn new roles and expand our repertoire in almost any direction. We need to seek out those situations that will help us change in ways we want to change, while avoiding or altering situations that can change us in destructive ways.

Social psychologists have attempted to demonstrate the power of a situation by experiments that reveal the ease with which smart, independent, rational, good people can be led into behaving in ways that are dumb, compliant, irrational, and evil. In this chapter we will witness some of the most extreme transformations of personality induced by situational variables.

Although social psychologists have shown the serious consequences of such situational power, it is equally possible to demonstrate this principle with humor. Indeed, Allen Funt's "Candid Camera" scenarios have been doing so for over 40 years. Recall the clips in which a person stopped eating a hamburger whenever the "Don't Eat" light flashed; people stopped at a red street light even when it was above the sidewalk on which they were walking; highway drivers turned back when faced with a sign that read "Delaware Closed"; and how about the person riding the elevator (who was manipulated like a puppet attached to our "situational strings") who faced the rear, the right, the left, or wherever in response to the contrived actions of the other passengers (confederates) in that "Candid Camera" elevator?

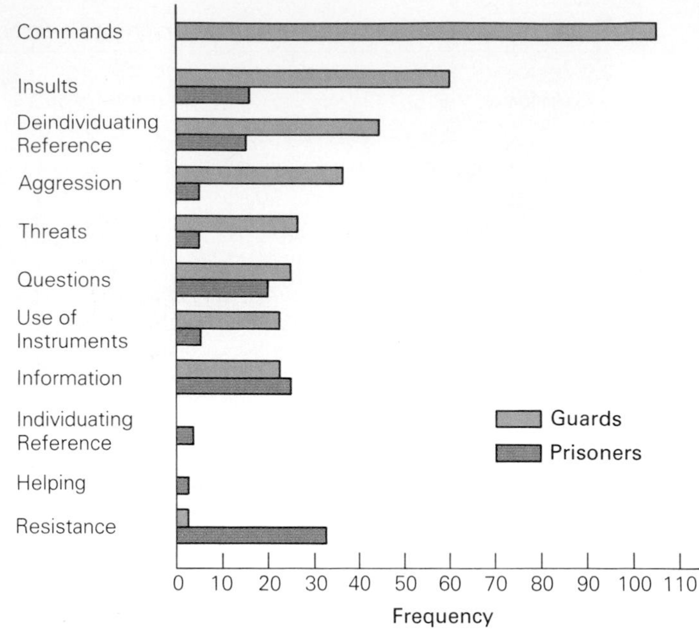

Figure 18.1
This interaction profile shows guard and prisoner behavior across 25 occasions over 6 days in the simulated prison environment.

We see in these slice-of-life episodes the minimal conditions needed to elicit certain behaviors in people. We laugh, because people who appear much like us are behaving so foolishly and acting so irrationally in response to small features of their situations. We implicitly distance ourselves from them by assuming, "I would not act like that!"

The humble lesson learned from much social psychological research is to assume that whatever anyone has done in a given situation you might also do if your behavior was affected by the same situational forces. The wise reply to someone asking how you would have acted if you were in some situation where a tragic event took place or where people behaved in evil, foolish, or irrational ways, is, "I don't know; it depends on how powerful the situation is and whether I can resist or overcome its controlling variables."

Added to the Lewinian principle of the power of a situation is a related central theme. To understand *how* a situation matters, we need to discover how the behavioral setting looks to those in it, how they interpret it, and what meanings they attribute to its various components. We must discover the nature of the *social reality* that they construct from a situation's objective features. Why? Because the way an actor views a situation can engage psychological processes that change the situation so that it comes to fit the actor's perception. The actor's beliefs can create new realities, his or her expectations can become self-fulfilling prophesies. We learn of the enormous power of "cognitive control" to transform the givens of biology, motivation, personality, and environment into manageable matters of mental manipulation.

When these two fundamental principles are taken together, they lead to a very important conclusion: People are basically similar in all their basic biological and psychological processes. Whenever this principle is violated—*they* seem or act different from *us*—we should base our subsequent actions on the awareness that (a) their situation is different from ours or has changed in some way we don't notice, or (b) their perception of the situation we are sharing is different in some important way.

The source of much human misunderstanding as well as social conflict between groups, and even nations, is the belief that *we*, as reasonable people, perceive the world or some vital part of it accurately—the only way it could be rationally seen—while *they*, the other side who see it differently, are wrong. These differences go beyond merely point-of-view variations when *we* attribute to *us* personal characteristics that justify this difference in terms of our wisdom, goodness, or righteousness, and to *them* stupidity, foolishness, or inadequacies. Obviously, however, "we are they to them." Each side attributes negative dispositions to the other and positive ones to itself, all the while ignoring the situational determinants of the differences that, if changed, can reverse its perceptions and actions.

The error that individuals and societies make by overemphasizing such personal or dispositional determinants of behavior while simultaneously underestimating the situational or contextual factors that are operating can have serious consequences. This *fundamental attribution error* often leads to policy decisions to deal with social problems by changing those who are "different" through re-education, therapy, conversion, segregation, imprisonment, sterilization, or execution. The social psychological wisdom here does not excuse "evil deeds" by demonstrating their situational determinants; rather, it makes salient that the best way to change problem behaviors is by changing *problem situations*.

This final phase of our journey widens the breadth of psychological inquiry to encompass several fundamental issues that all societies must resolve if they are to survive. We begin by applying situationism and the construction of social reality to the investigation of aggression and violence within our society and among nations.

Human Aggression and Violence

Aggression can be defined as physical or verbal behavior with the intent to injure or destroy. We have daily reminders of its prevalence in our society and world. Each year in the United States, about 6 percent of the nation's households have at least one member who is the victim of a violent crime—that is about five million people (U.S. Department of Justice Bulletin, June 1983). We get a frightening reminder of our own vulnerability with a daily diet of violent lead stories in the morning papers and in the evening TV news. Paradoxically, however, America as a nation seems to be fascinated by violence as evidenced by the popularity of violent themes in cartoons, movies, and on TV. **Violence** is aggression in its most extreme and socially unacceptable form. It may be directed against people or property and usually is an expression of hostility and rage at an individual level, but of planned destruction of "enemies" at an institutional level.

The aggression of individuals against other individuals pales by comparison to the aggression that occurs at the international level of world conduct. In 1986, the nations of the world spent nearly $1 trillion on military weapons—more than the total incomes of half the human race. U.S. military expenditures, which have increased by over 100 percent since 1980, amounted to a trillion dollars in the past five years. The Soviet Union spends one seventh of its total resources for military purposes. Even the poorest nations are spending more for arms than for food and agriculture (Gilliam, 1986). In 1986, declared the "Year of Peace" by the United Nations, about 5 million people died in 36 wars and armed conflicts fought by 41 nations (Deutshe & Presse-Agentur, 1987, June 18).

Research evidence on aggression has been drawn from a wide variety of sources, including physiological studies, clinical observations, and studies of aggressive interactions in both the laboratory and the "real world" of homicides and war. An excellent summary of the methodological issues in the experimental study of human aggression is found in Koněcni (1984). In this section we will review theories that have been proposed to account for aggressiveness: aggression as an inborn part of human nature or caused by physiological mechanisms or environmental conditions, aggression as a response to frustration, aggression as simply an impulsive response to external stimuli, and aggression as a socially learned behavior pattern.

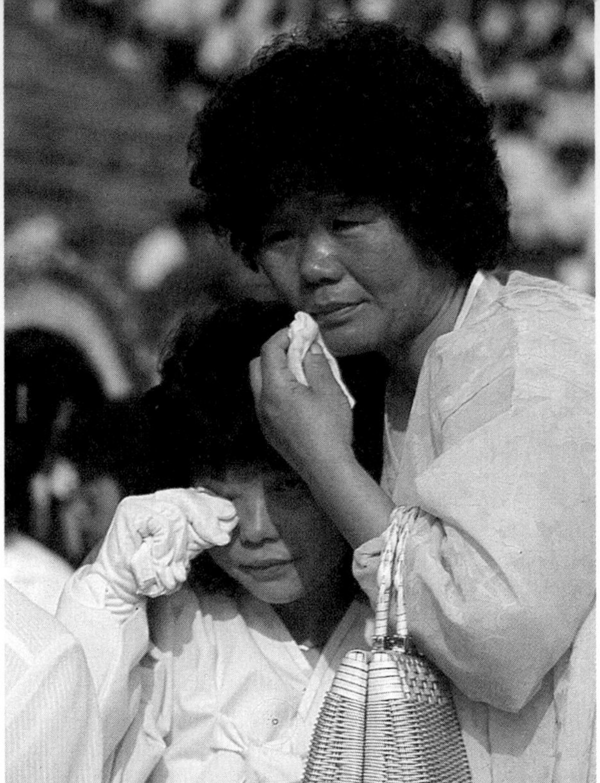

Grieving has a cathartic effect for these mourners who lost relatives in the crash of a Korean airliner, KAL 007.

Aggression as Inborn

In his famous essay "Leviathan," Hobbes argued that people are naturally selfish, brutal, and cruel toward other people. He expressed this concept using the phrase *Homo homini lupus*—"Man is [like] a wolf to [his fellow] man." Although the wolf is unjustly maligned by this phrase (wolves are actually quite gentle with others of their own species), it expresses a common belief that human beings are instinctively aggressive animals. Freud thought so, and so do others who believe in the "animal instinct" side of human nature. (See also "Infanticide" in *The Best of Science.*)

Freud's Death Instinct and Catharsis

As we have seen, Freud believed that, from the moment of birth, a person possessed two opposing instincts: a life instinct *(Eros),* which provided energy for growth and survival, and a death instinct *(Thanatos),* which worked toward an individual's self-destruction. He believed that the death instinct was often redirected outward against the external world in the form of aggression toward others.

According to Freud, energy for the death instinct was constantly being generated within the body. Freud visualized this energy as water accumulating in a reservoir. If it was not released in small amounts and in socially acceptable ways, it would accumulate and eventually spill over in some extreme and socially unacceptable form.

One hypothesized way of draining off this energy is *catharsis* (a Greek word meaning purification or cleansing). In **catharsis,** emotions are expressed in their full intensity through crying, words, symbolic means, or other direct acts. Aristotle first used this concept to explain the way in which good drama first builds up and then purges an audience's feelings of intense emotion. As we saw in chapter 16, catharsis is an important part of psychoanalytic therapy.

Limited experimental support for Freud's hypothesis of aggressive energy and catharsis is found in a study by Robert Sears (1961).

> *Male children high in aggressiveness at age 5 were also high at age 12, some still overtly and antisocially aggressive. Other boys, however, showed low* antisocial *aggression, but high* prosocial *aggression (aggression for socially acceptable purposes, such as law enforcement or punishing others for rule-breaking). This second group also showed more* self-aggression *than did the boys who were still highly antisocial aggressors. Furthermore, the prosocial aggressors were more anxious and fearful of antisocial aggression than the antisocial—extremely directed—aggressors.*

This finding was interpreted to mean that the same inner aggressive energy was simply finding different forms of expression in the two groups of children.

In spite of some supporting evidence, however, Freud's theory has been criticized by psychologists for failing to specify any factors that can be used to *predict* either the occurrence of aggression or the direction or form it will take. It has a lovely literary, after-the-fact, descriptive quality, but little scientific utility to predict or control behavior. Indeed, in his later writings Freud himself abandoned reliance on this death instinct, although others have continued to incorporate some version of it into their conception of human nature. The bulk of the evidence on catharsis of aggressive feelings suggests that an emotional release of hostile feelings by *talking* about them may decrease subsequent aggression, but the opportunity "to cathart" by overt aggressive acts does the opposite, by increasing aggressiveness (see discussion on pp. 649–50).

The Aggressive Instinct

Another theory stressing the innateness of aggression is that of ethologist Konrad Lorenz (1966). On the basis of animal studies, Lorenz argues that aggression is a spontaneous, innate readiness to fight, which is critical to an organism's survival. In most species, however, displays of aggressiveness between individuals rarely involve actual injury or death because one animal will eventually "signal" appeasement or submission. According to Lorenz, human beings have somehow lost this pacification strategy to inhibit aggression while retaining the instinct to aggress. They have become killers of their own kind—in part because they can kill at a distance.

Ardrey (1966) goes beyond Lorenz to argue that aggression results from **territoriality,** which is an innate drive to gain and defend property—the "territorial imperative." Animals of some species mark off their living area by various means, such as urination. Other members of the species then respond to these territorial markers by withdrawing from the area. If they do not and violate the turf, they risk aggressive confrontation with the owner.

Evidence for this instinct-based theory is not clear-cut. Not all species display territorial behavior (Crook, 1973). Animals' responses to "appeasement gestures" are in fact quite variable, much as with humans (Barnett, 1967). Moreover, many instances of within-species killing among animals have been observed (E. Wilson, 1973). Even relatively peaceful and sociable chimpanzees have been observed to gang up on other chimps—beating them and, in some cases, killing infants (Goodall, 1986). While territorial issues may well be the reason for some human conflicts, there is no need to assume that all aggression derives from an innate drive rather than from learned needs for power and security.

The Aggressive Temperament

In the past decade researchers in psychology and biology have become increasingly interested in discovering the extent to which traits such as aggressiveness are influenced by genetic factors. The primary method for assessing the heritability of individual differences involves correlating scores on a given behavioral trait with the degree of relatedness of individuals within a family (as described for intelligence in chapter 13). In this classic twin research paradigm, the trait scores of identical (monozygotic) twins who share 100 percent of their genes are compared with scores of fraternal (dizygotic) twins who share only 50 percent of their genes. When their environment is comparable, then higher correlations on the trait scores of identical twins is taken as evidence of the operation of genetic influences on the trait in question. From the size of the correlations it is possible to estimate the extent of the trait's heritability (see Plomin et al., 1980).

Recent evidence points to a significant contribution of genetic factors to aggressiveness, as well as to altruism (to be discussed later).

> *Hundreds of adult twin pairs completed questionnaires that measured aggressiveness, along with other traits. Among 179 same-sex dizygotic twin pairs scores on aggressiveness were uncorrelated (r = .04). However, for the 286 monozygotic twin pairs the correlation of aggressiveness scores was highly significant (r = .40). The researchers estimate that approximately 50 percent of the variation in the aggressiveness trait is because of genetic influences. Further, they conclude from other evidence that very little of the twins' aggressive tendencies are the result of their shared environment. What is not related to genetic influences is the specific environment that each separate twin experienced. Altruism, which also showed a similar temperamental basis, was greater among women, while aggressiveness was greater among men in this sample (Rushton, et al., 1986).*

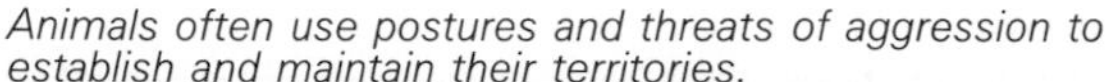
Animals often use postures and threats of aggression to establish and maintain their territories.

Genes can influence behavior only indirectly by coding for the production of specific proteins which function in the brain and nervous system and can affect behavior directly. This type of research on the aggressive temperament points to the importance of studying the role of hormonal and neurotransmitter influences on aggression. One obvious limitation of this research is the self-report, questionnaire measure of aggressivity and its uncertain relationship to overt acts of physical aggression.

Physiological Bases of Aggression

In the summer of 1966, Charles Whitman killed his wife and mother, and then climbed to the top of a tower at the University of Texas. Armed with a high-powered hunting rifle equipped with a telescopic sight, he shot 38 people, killing 14, before he himself was gunned down. A postmortem examination of Whitman's brain revealed a malignant tumor the size of a walnut in the area of the amygdala (Sweet et al., 1969).

The *amygdala* (part of the limbic system) was mentioned in chapter 4 as being involved in aggressive behavior. Recall also the pattern of aggressive behavior in Keith (chapter 11), whose pituitary tumor activated a hormonal imbalance. Brain disease of the limbic system or temporal lobe has sometimes been found in persons exhibiting a *dyscontrol syndrome,* characterized by senseless brutality, pathological intoxication, sexual assault, or repeated serious automobile accidents.

In both humans and animals, males appear to be more aggressive than females—in part the result of the early influence of sex hormones on the brain. Female animals that have been injected with male sex hormones often display increased aggressive behavior (Edwards, 1971).

> *Some years ago, progestins (steroid hormones) were given to many women to help prevent miscarriages. It turned out that both males and females exposed as fetuses to small amounts of these hormones showed a significantly higher potential for physical aggression than their unexposed siblings (see* ***Figure 18.2****). About 10 million people in our country, alive today, were exposed to these drugs during the critical period of their development. (Reinisch, 1981)*

Although hormones have a direct influence on behavior in animals, they appear to work indirectly on humans, in whom personality factors are added to the behavioral tendencies. In humans the relationship between any physiological factors and aggression is far more complex than in other species because of the greater importance of learning and experience in the direction and control of human behavior (Moyer, 1976).

Researchers are discovering a number of different neurotransmitters that play a role in the expression of aggression. For example, intermale aggression in animals is higher when their level of catecholamines (such as dopamine) is high, but it is lower when serotonin level is high. The physiological regulation of aggression clearly involves a complex interaction of neurochemical and neuroendocrine systems (Whalen & Simon, 1984).

So many more young men than women commit both interpersonal and self-directed acts of aggression that some researchers assume biological factors must be involved. Sex is a "biological reality" with a clear connection to violent behavior, but whether it is causally related or only correlationally linked is not known. Those who postulate a biological predisposition to violence look to male hormones and other factors within the body that put men "at risk" for violence (Herrnstein & Wilson, 1985). Obviously, those researchers who emphasize the role of nurture in aggression, rather than nature, argue that it is the gender-role demands and life-style of males, rather than male biology, that is the culprit.

The Environment and Aggression

Since biology and environment interact in many aspects of human behavior, why shouldn't they interact in aggression, as well? We mentioned in chapter 8 the impact of publicized suicide stories on subsequent suicide imitations (Phillips, 1979). This

Figure 18.2
This bar graph shows the effect of exposure to progestins during fetal life for both males and females. It also shows characteristically higher aggression scores for males both with and without this exposure. (Adapted from Reinisch, 1981.)

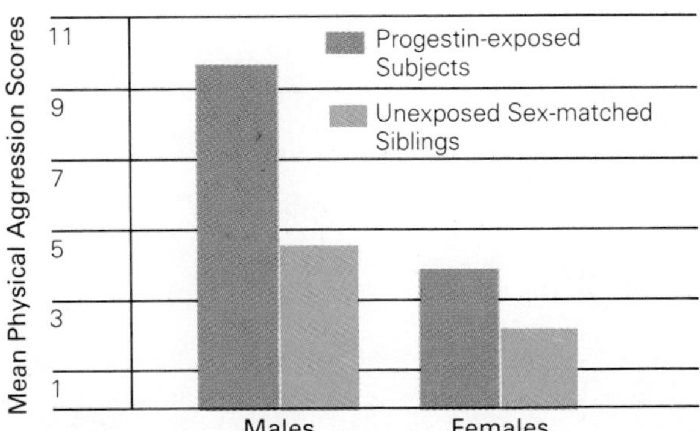

Figure 18.3

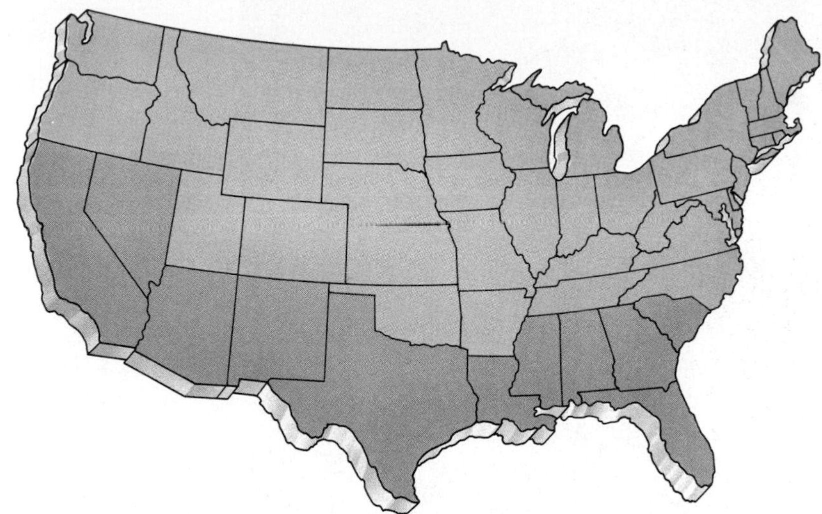

suggestive "imitation" effect also extends to homicides, which are shown to increase following mass media exposure of particularly violent events, such as prize fights (Phillips, 1983, 1986). Because of the high incidence of violence in the United States and the possibility of a "contagion" effect, the Center for Disease Control in Atlanta has recently begun to study violence as a special kind of "disease"—to examine statistical patterns of violent behavior as a function of geographical area, season, and other variables. Their researchers act as **epidemiologists,** experimenters who examine diseases, their distributions within different populations, and their environmental impacts. They argue that violence is a public health issue to be treated within the perspective of the medical model (discussed in chapter 15 and 16) as a contagious disease. They have found that violence seems to "breed" in certain geographic areas, notably the southern "homicide belt" that runs across 11 states in the southern United States (see **Figure 18.3**)

One factor that may contribute to this "homicide belt" is *heat.* Some researchers believe that neuroendocrine pathways may be activated by higher temperatures, thus propelling individuals toward aggressive acts. A number of studies do report associations between violence and aspects of climate. Rape and other violent assaults rise with the temperature in the summer months (Michael & Zumpe, 1983). Since attacks on women in their homes also are higher as outdoor temperature rises, this effect is *not* simply because there are more people outdoors, thus increasing opportunities for violence. There is also more violent behavior when temperatures and air pollution are high. Family disturbances (in one city that was studied) were highest when ozone levels were high and were low when windy, humid conditions were recorded (Rotton & Frey, 1984, 1985). These ideas are provocative, but challenged by psychologists who reject both the basic notion of violence as a contagious disease and the causal inferences from these loosely correlated data. However, recent carefully controlled research continues to point to a link between uncomfortable heat and violent crime (Anderson, 1987).

The Frustration-Aggression Hypothesis

Almost 20 years after Freud proposed the existence of a death instinct, a group of academic psychologists at Yale University formally presented an alternative view of aggression called the *frustration-aggression hypothesis* (Dollard et al., 1939). Their hypothesis was that aggression was a learned (not instinctive) drive acquired in response to frustration. **Frustration** was defined as a natural and inevitable condition that existed when an ongoing response toward a goal was blocked. The greater the present and accumulated frustration, the stronger the resulting aggressive response.

It soon became obvious, however, that not every act of aggression was preceded by frustration and that not every frustration resulted in aggression. The original frustration-aggression hypothesis was revised to state that every frustration produced an instigation to aggression, but that this instigation may be too weak to elicit actual aggressive behavior (N. Miller, 1941). These theorists agreed with Freud that the aggressive drive would increase if it

This is certainly one *way to alleviate frustration!*

were not expressed (if frustration continued). However, they saw the origin of aggressive behavior in *external* factors (accumulated frustrating situations) rather than in an aggressive "instinct." Recently it has been recognized that a person's *perception* of frustration helps to determine that person's response (Berkowitz, 1982).

When frustration occurs, the first and strongest aggressive impulse is toward its source. If a child wants a piece of candy, but is prevented from having it by a parent, the child is most strongly motivated to be aggressive toward the parent. Because of the threat of punishment, however, such aggression may be inhibited and displaced onto a safer target, perhaps a younger sibling or the family pet. Other favorite targets of displaced aggression are minorities, children, and women, who are already in vulnerable positions and, thus, are not likely to retaliate. Displacing anger and aggression onto members of less powerful groups who are not responsible for an aggressor's frustration is called **scapegoating.**

According to the frustration-aggression hypothesis, the less similar the target is to the source of the frustration, the weaker is the displaced aggression and the less complete the cathartic effect. Some research has suggested, however, that displaced aggression can be as strong as aggression directed at the source of frustration, and that it can reduce subsequent tendencies toward aggressive behavior (Konĕcni & Doob, 1972). Frustration is most likely to lead to aggression when aggressing has *instrumental value* to modify the frustration (Buss, 1971).

Aggression as Provoked Readiness

A revision of the frustration-aggression hypothesis proposes an interaction between emotional states and environmental cues. Leonard Berkowitz (1982) maintains that frustration creates a *readiness* for aggressive acts, as does being previously reinforced for acting aggressively. Whether this readiness gets translated into overt aggression depends on the presence of a second factor—stimulus cues in the environment that are associated with aggression. For example, the presence of a *weapon* appears to serve as a *cue* that has been previously associated with the emotion of anger.

Berkowitz believes that much aggression is not planned or anticipated, but erupts impulsively in response to provocative environmental stimuli. Aggression may also be stimulated by events or conditions in the environment that arouse intense sexual or hostile emotions or that have aggressive elements (seeing a prize-fight, war movie, or international soccer match).

Interpersonal violence is rarely a case of one person acting aggressively against a totally passive individual. More typically, both people are involved in an escalating interaction.

> *One analysis of 344 arrest reports found that, in the cases where violent incidents occurred,* both *parties were reacting to what they perceived as threats against their integrity and self-esteem. Often the encounter began with an officer's request for information or identification or an order to "move on," "break it up." In 60 percent of the episodes, the civilian reacted negatively to the officer's approach and failed to cooperate, perceiving the request as unwarranted or discourteous or as an expression of personal hostility. The officer viewed this uncooperativeness as irrational, disrespectful, and perhaps concealing criminal activity. A chain of events was then set off in which both parties contributed to the spiraling potential for violence. (Toch, 1969)*

Violence may also be provoked by societal influences. An analysis of criminal violence statistics drawn from 110 nations over a decade reveals that homicides by citizens increase in a nation that has just fought a war. This is especially true if it has won that war. Other worldwide data from this ambitious archival research effort show that citizens of a country are not deterred from murder by the death penalty. To the contrary, homicide rates decline slightly after the death penalty has been abolished (Archer & Gartner, 1984).

Aggression as Socially Learned

Another answer to the "why" of aggression is that it is learned just like many other kinds of behavior, through experience with rewards, punishments, models, and social norms. Albert Bandura (1973) is the leading proponent of this view of the socially learned basis of human aggression.

Consequences, Learned or Anticipated

According to social-learning theory, any kind of aversive experience (not only frustration) produces a general state of emotional arousal. This arousal can then lead to a number of different behaviors, depending on an individual's prior learning history. People whose aggression has been rewarded in the past may become aggressive; others may withdraw, ask for help, or engage in constructive problem solving, depending on what has worked for them in the past.

Aggression, like other responses, can also occur in the absence of emotional arousal if an individual feels that it will lead to some desired outcome (when an older child hits a younger one in order to get a toy). Boys who have been reinforced for aggressive responses in one situation tend to respond aggressively in other situations even when no rewards are provided (Horton, 1970).

Children in wartorn countries are familiar, from a very early age, with aggression.

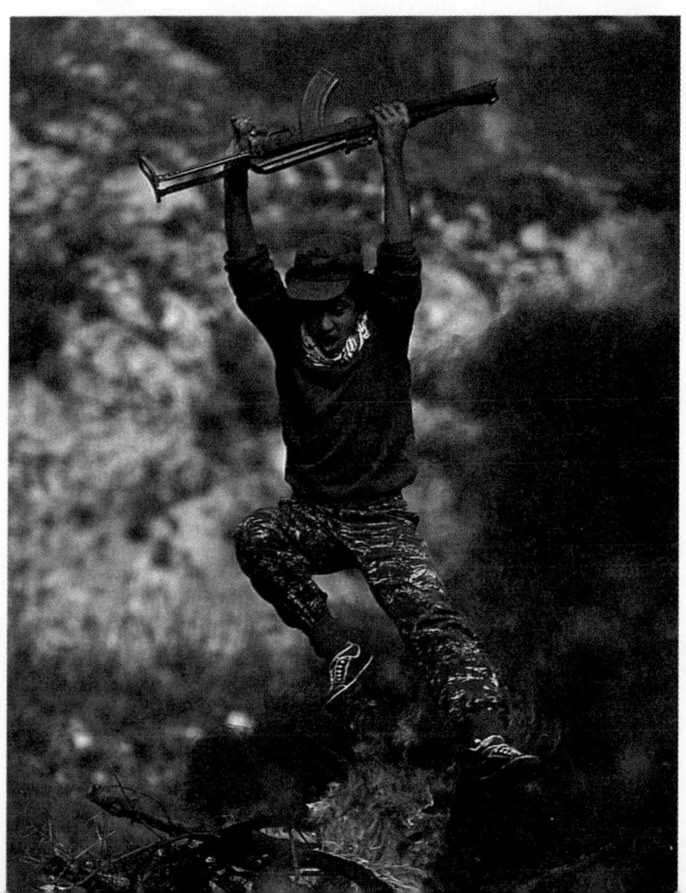

Models and Norms

Aggression can also be learned by watching others behave aggressively. As we saw in chapter 8, nursery-school children who watched adults or filmed models hitting, kicking, and punching a large inflated balloon doll later performed these actions themselves (Bandura et al., 1963).

> *In a subsequent study, children performed fewer imitative aggressive acts when they saw the model being punished. Evidently even though the aggressive act had been learned, so had the knowledge that such an act was inappropriate. Later, however, when the experimenter offered each child a prize for doing just what the model had done, all the children readily performed the actions they had seen. When the payoff was changed, the act was performed. (Bandura, 1965)*

Other research has shown that children who are emotionally aroused (when they are participating in competitive games, for example) are more likely to imitate a model's behavior whether the model is displaying aggressive or nonaggressive behavior (Christy et al., 1971).

The social group and broader culture, too, can encourage violent behavior. If a person's community or reference groups provide aggressive models, and give approval and prestige for violent acts, an individual—especially a young one—is likely to feel under pressure to conform to the aggressive norm.

These same pressures may affect aggression indirectly through group pressure to use alcohol or other drugs. A study using American students as subjects found opposite effects for alcohol and marijuana.

> *Research on the relationship of alcohol and marijuana to aggression (shocks delivered in a competition against a partner) revealed that the two substances had opposite effects. As the dose of alcohol was increased (from .5 to 1.5 ounces per 40 pounds of body weight), the amount of aggression more than doubled. In contrast larger doses of marijuana decreased the amount of shock administered to the other person (see* ***Figure 18.4****). (Taylor et al., 1976)*

Does Catharsis Reduce Aggression?

Social-learning theory challenges the Freudian prediction about catharsis and aggression makes the opposite prediction: that expressing aggressive impulses or watching aggressiveness in others will *increase* the probability of future aggression. Which view does research support?

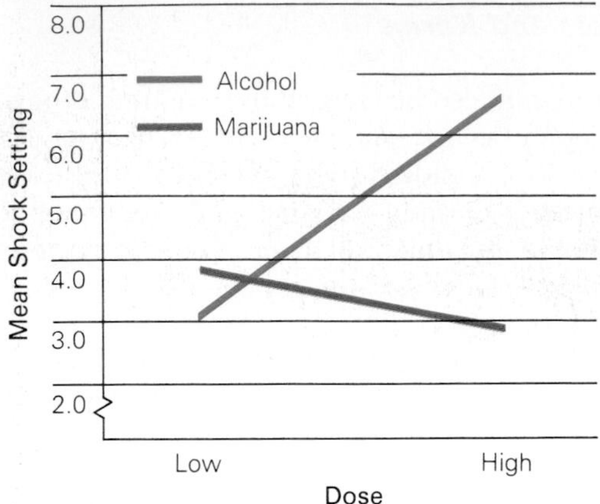

Figure 18.4
The figure shows the mean shock setting as a function of high and low doses of alcohol and marijuana. Increasing the amount of alcohol in the system leads to greater aggression in the laboratory setting, while marijuana tends to have the opposite effect. (Adapted from S. P. Taylor et al., 1976.)

Confirmation of the social-learning hypothesis comes from studies which show that aggression increases after exposure to aggressive models. In addition, it has been demonstrated that expressing aggressive feelings in a permissive setting maintains the feelings at their original level, instead of reducing them.

> *Subjects were exposed to an anger-arousing antagonist; then half of them were allowed to express their anger and hostility to a sympathetic interviewer. The other subjects did not have such an interview, but merely sat for a while. Later, subjects who had experienced the cathartic interview disliked the antagonist even more (rather than less) and remained more physiologically aroused than the control subjects. (Kahn, 1966)*

These results suggest that therapies encouraging a person to express or act out aggressive feelings for cathartic purposes may have an effect opposite to the intended one.

Such findings seem to run counter to the common-sense notion that it is good to "let off steam" and "get it all off one's chest." It may help us to understand this contradiction if we make a distinction between *expressing emotional feelings* and *acting aggressively* or *watching aggressive actions*. Giving vent to our feelings (crying, laughing, or talking to others) may make us feel better or relieve our anxiety; but *expressing aggression* against our enemies, verbally or in overt action, directly or vicariously, is *not* likely to reduce our tendencies toward aggression. Learning how to negotiate conflicts verbally, however, can reduce the need for physical aggression against others.

TV Violence: Catharsis or Release?

Anyone who watches American television is very likely to see both drama and comedy episodes in which people are killed or injured in a wide variety of ingenious ways, cartoons with lovable but sadistic characters, and news programs with on-the-spot coverage of wars, assassinations, riots, and "crime in the streets." If children engage in aggressive actions after a few minutes of watching aggressive models in the laboratory, what do they learn from their extended consumption of violence on TV? Given their estimated viewing time of between 20 and 45 hours per week, their views of social reality become very negative ones, according to one documented analysis (Gerbner, 1981).

From portrayals on TV children learn that violence is frequent, rewarded, thought to be justified, clean, fun, imaginative, and more appropriate for males than for females. They also begin to exaggerate the real threat of violence in their daily lives—which, in turn, makes them fearful and suspicious of strangers. A national survey of American children between the ages of 7 and 11 indicates that the heavy TV viewers report more fears than the light viewers "that somebody bad might get into your house" or that "when you go outside somebody might hurt you" (Peterson & Zill, 1981).

Well-designed psychological studies suggest a clear link between viewing and doing. Although the causal connection cannot be firmly established, the correlations imply a direction of influence from violent content to aggressive deeds.

> *One large-scale, ten-year, longitudinal study of children showed that preferences for violent TV programs in the third grade were correlated significantly with aggressive behavior in the thirteenth grade. The reverse was not true: children's early aggressiveness was not related to a later preference for watching violent TV. (Eron et al., 1972)*

Although there have been some studies claiming that media violence is cathartic and decreases children's tendencies toward overt aggression, major methodological flaws have reduced their credibility. Better controlled research has supported the opposite conclusion: boys who view movie violence become *more* aggressive than boys who are similar in other ways, but see nonviolent films (Parke et al., 1977).

Not only are children more prone to act aggressively after viewing violence, but they become more tolerant of aggressive behavior in others. They are less likely to take responsible action and intervene, for example, in a fight between two

younger children (Drabman & Thomas, 1974). Similar effects have been found in studies that examine television viewing among adults (Gorney, 1976).

One challenge to the bulk of evidence that causally links media violence to aggressive behavior concludes, "There is little convincing evidence that viewing violence on television in *natural settings* causes an increase in subsequent aggressiveness" (Freedman, 1984, p. 243). The critic argues that the convincing demonstrations of aggression caused by viewing televised violence are found in laboratory studies, not field studies. However, this negative conclusion is not justified when additional recent field study data are examined (see Huesmann et al., 1986; Singer et al., 1984).

Another way to test hypothesized cause-effect relationships is through the use of intervention studies which attempt to change the causal variable and note consequences on the dependent variable. In such a "real-world" intervention study, when violence viewing was modified by an attitude change procedure, aggressiveness of high violence viewers decreased, while there was no change in a comparable control group (Huesmann et al., 1983).

Seeing violence routinely, often combined with humor, also has a "psychic numbing" effect, a dulling of both sensitivity to and moral outrage at real-life violence. One of the strongest counterforces to aggression is being part of a community that cares about victimized individuals. Anything that reduces this concern and compassion indirectly contributes to violence.

U.S. Surgeon General Everett Koop has suggested that the body of available research provides a strong link between television violence and the epidemic of violent behavior in our country. He argues that a nation's political and social health is endangered "whenever any of our citizens feel unjustly threatened and withdraw in fear from casual human contact" (United Press, quoted in *San Francisco Chronicle,* February 6, 1984, p. 39).

However, regardless of what "psychological research shows" about the adverse effects of exposure to mass media violence, television networks continue to use violent programming to boost their ratings, according to Senator Paul Simon of Illinois. He points to systematic data collected over the past two decades by researchers from the Annenberg School of Communications (of the University of Pennsylvania). Violence, defined as "overt and explicit physical threats, hurting or killing in any context," erupts in prime-time evening programs at the rate of eight incidents per hour. The level of violence in children's weekend programs is even higher than that found for weeknight prime-time violence. This is shown in **Figure 18.5.** (Associated Press, 1986, September 2).

The Violence of Pornography

The number of reported forcible rapes in the United States nearly doubled in the last decade. In 1982 nearly 78,000 women were raped—about one every seven minutes (U.S. Bureau of the Census, 1984). This social problem has many causes, but some researchers believe exposure to pornography contributes to the violence of men against women. *Erotic* films are explicit portrayals of passionate love and sexual activities. By contrast, *pornographic* films present images of violence and dehumanization as sexual entertainment. What is the evidence social psychologists have collected that popular pornography is implicated in aggressive reactions toward women?

Laboratory Studies

The typical research paradigm involves college students viewing films with content that is either neutral, nonaggressive-erotic, or aggressive-erotic. Afterwards they are given an opportunity to engage in aggressive behavior and to report their feelings and beliefs about rape and other issues (Donnerstein, 1983; Malamuth & Donnerstein, 1982).

Several consistent patterns of results emerge from such experiments. First, men are sexually aroused by aggressive-erotic films, become more accepting of rape myths such as "women really want to be sexually dominated," and even admit to the greater possibility of committing rape themselves. In addition, viewing sexual violence can increase the amount of aggression subsequently displayed toward women. Men paired with a male partner administered a somewhat higher level of shock after either the erotic or the aggressive-erotic film than after a neutral film. They did so within the context of a study allegedly about stress, learning, and physiology in which subjects were to reward or punish their partners (confederates) with varying amounts of shock. However, those paired with a female partner administered no higher shock after the nonaggressive-erotic film, but a very much higher level of shock following the aggressive-erotic one, as shown in **Figure 18.6.** (Donnerstein, 1980).

Figure 18.6 Pornography and Aggression
Aggression was higher following aggressive-erotic films than following either neutral or nonaggressive-erotic films only by men against women, not by men against other men. (Adapted from Donnerstein, 1980)

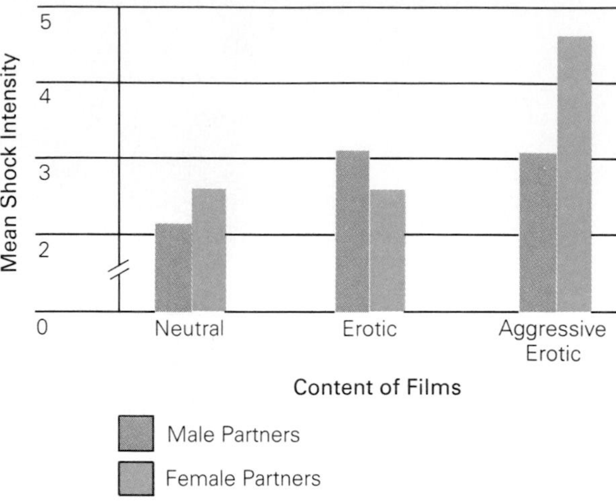

Figure 18.5 Level of Violence in Children's vs. Family Prime-time Television Programming

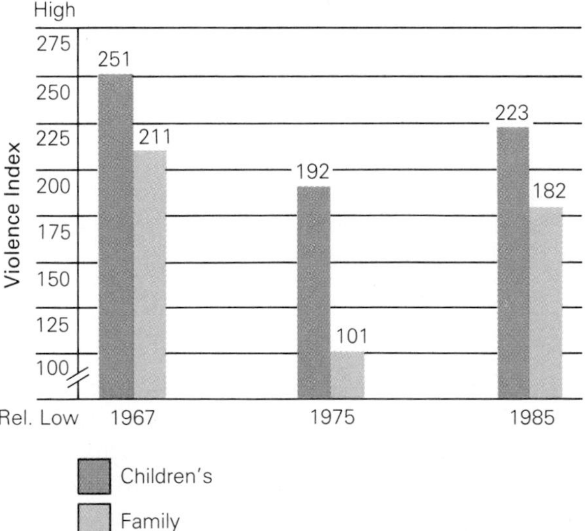

Note: The 1975 drop was the result of violence reduction put into effect temporarily by CBS.

Media Images of Sex and Violence

The report of the U.S. Attorney General's Commission on Pornography, issued in July 1986, concluded that pornography has a causal relationship to sexual violence. Policy recommendations included ways to restrict pornography in our society. There is little question about the prevalence of and accessibility to pornographic materials, largely in the form of "adult" movies, magazines, and videos that constitute a multibillion-dollar industry. However, despite the references in the commission's report to alleged supporting psychological research (such as that of Malamuth and Donnerstein, 1984), there is *not* scientifically sound evidence for asserting a causal link between exposure to pornography and sexual violence.

> *A content analysis of the leading erotic/pornographic magazine identified over 2000 child-related visual images in cartoons, pictures, and advertisements among nearly 700 copies of the magazines sampled, About 75 percent of these images depicted children as either the recipient or initiator of violent or sexual activities. (Reisman, 1986)*
>
> *Another content analysis of pornography by a Canadian researcher compared sexual and aggressive depictions in both adult and "triple-x" videos. As expected,*

there was a signficantly greater number of sex scenes in the triple-x videos, and they were rated as much more explicit than the adult videos. However, in these commercially available videos, there was an unexpected difference in depictions of aggression. There was significantly more aggression shown in the adult videos than in the triple-x ones. About a fourth of all coded scenes in adult videos were judged to be aggressive. Moreover, the adult videos showed more sexually aggressive scenes (rape, bondage, humiliation, and coercion). Of special note was the unbalanced, unidirectional nature of this sexual aggression. In adult videos, men were the perpetrators nearly 70 percent of the time, while women were victims in over 70 percent of the scenes. (Palys, 1986)

Despite the data on aggressive content in pornography, there is not yet reliable evidence that viewing pornographic materials *causes* changes in attitudes and behavior. Already callous attitudes of men toward women and rape may be *strengthened,* but not necessarily induced, by their selectively exposing themselves to pornography.

Several psychologists whose experimental research was wrongly alleged to demonstrate the causal relationship between pornography and sexual violence argue forcefully that *violence,* and not sex or erotica, is the central issue. Summarizing the results of a series of studies by psychologists, they conclude, "Taken together, these studies strongly suggest that violence against women need not occur in a pornographic or sexually explicit context to have a negative effect upon viewer attitudes and behavior. But even more importantly, it must be concluded that violent images, rather than sexual ones, are most responsible for people's attitudes about women and rape" (Donnerstein & Linz, 1986, p. 59).

Despite accumulating evidence that pornography fosters both general downgrading of women and specific tendencies toward violence against them, the right to exhibit such propaganda is a constitutionally guaranteed freedom in our country. Therein lies a major social and political problem—beyond the scope of psychologists except through their continued concern about documenting the destructive mental and behavioral effects of pornography.

Obedience to Authority

When you think of the long and gloomy history of man, you will find more hideous crimes have been committed in the name of obedience than have been committed in the name of rebellion.

C. P. Snow, 1961, p. 3

What made Adolf Eichmann and other Nazis willing and able to send millions of Jews to the gas chambers? Did some character defect lead them to carry out orders blindly, even if the orders violated their own values and beliefs? How can we best explain the mass suicide-murders of the members of the People's Temple who engaged in the ultimate act of obedience? Hundreds willingly took their children's lives and their own because their leader, Reverend Jim Jones, told them to.

We are asking again the question raised in earlier chapters about dispositional versus situational causes of behavior. If we blame the individuals who did these terrible things, we are making the *fundamental attribution error* by underestimating the possible influence of the social situation while overestimating dispositional influences. Doing so is comforting because it creates a psychological distance between *us* ("good" people) and *them* ("bad" people). It also takes society and social conditions "off the hook" as contributors to the problem. The alternative is to acknowledge that *we* might be capable of these terrible actions.

How about *you?* Could *you* imagine being part of a company of American soldiers who massacred innocent women, children, and elderly citizens in the Vietnamese village of My Lai (Hersh, 1971; Opton, 1970, 1973)? Are there any conditions under which *you* would blindly obey an order from your religious leader to give poison to your family and then commit suicide? Would you obey a command to electrocute a stranger? Your answers—as mine used to be—are all most likely, "*No!* What kind of person do you think I am?" After reading this next section, you may be more willing to answer, "Maybe. I don't know for sure." Depending on the power of the social forces operating to distort your moral judgment and weaken your will to resist, might even you do what other human beings have done in that situation, however horrible and alien to your way of thinking when you're outside that setting?

Milgram's Obedience Paradigm

To separate the variables of personality and situation, which are always entangled in natural settings, we need a controlled experiment. Social psychologist Stanley Milgram (1965, 1974) devised an effective and dramatic paradigm to demonstrate the power of situational forces to induce obedience to authority in people like you and me. We'll take a close look at the procedures and processes involved in his studies, because they tell us some things about human nature that you may find personally relevant and socially significant. This research is one of the most controversial in psychology both because of the ethical issues it raises and the implications for real world phenomena (see A. G. Miller, 1986).

Milgram's first experiments were conducted using Yale college students as paid volunteers. In later variations, Milgram put his "obedience laboratory" into the community. He set up a storefront research unit in Bridgeport, Connecticut, recruiting through newspaper ads a broad cross-section of the population varying widely in age, occupation, and education. In all, over 2000 subjects participated in a dozen studies using variations of this obedience paradigm.

The basic experimental paradigm involved having subjects deliver a series of what they thought were extremely painful electric shocks to another subject. They did so not because they were sadistic, but because they were participating in a worthwhile cause—or so they believed. In their *roles* as "teachers" they were to punish errors made by a "learner." They were led to believe that the purpose of the study was to discover how punishment affects memory so that learning and memory could be improved through the proper balance of reward and punishment. The major *rule* they were told to follow was to increase the level of shock by a certain amount each time the learner made an error. The experimenter acted as the legitimate *authority* figure: he presented the rules, arranged for the assignment of roles (by a rigged drawing of lots), and ordered the "teachers" to do their jobs whenever they hesitated or dissented.

An experimenter instructs a "teacher" in the use of the shock generator. How would you behave if you were in the subject's place?

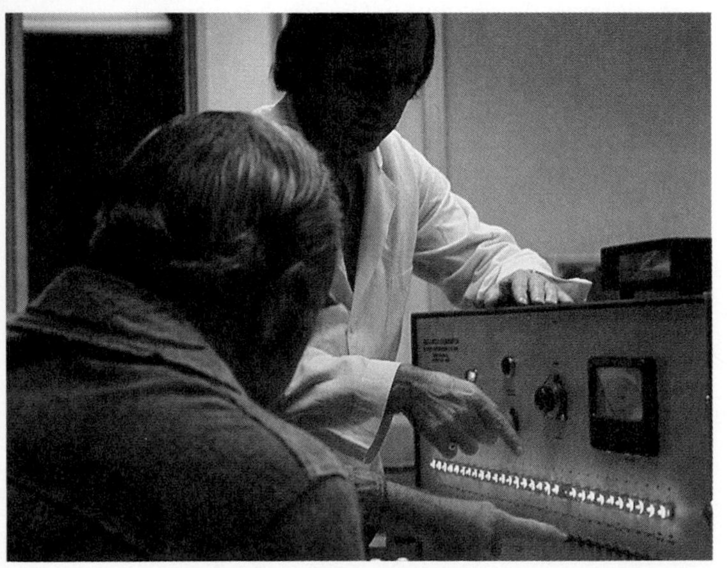

The *dependent variable* was the final level of shock a "teacher" gave before refusing to continue to obey the authority. The initial study was simply a demonstration of the phenomenon of obedience; there was *no* manipulation of an independent variable. Later versions did study the effect of varying factors such as the physical distance between the authority and "teacher," and also between "teacher" and "learner." Milgram did not use a formal no-treatment control or comparison group in this study—as was also true of the Stanford Prison Study. In both these demonstrations, the comparison group is comprised of other "observers" with a belief about the way they would behave under such circumstances—you and other ordinary citizens.

Staging the Research

The study was staged to make a subject think that, by following orders, by being obedient, the subject was causing pain and suffering—and perhaps even killing an innocent person. The "learner" was a pleasant, mild-mannered man about 50 years old, who mentioned something about a heart condition, but was willing to go along with the procedure. He was strapped into an "electric chair" in the next room and communicated with the "teacher" via an intercom. His task was to memorize pairs of words, giving the second word in a pair when he heard the first one. The "learner" soon ran into difficulty and began making errors.

A "teacher" was to punish each error by pressing a switch on a shock generator. The 30 switches were marked in 15-volt units from slight shock (15 volts) to Danger: Severe Shock XXX (450 volts). Each teacher had been given a sample shock of about 75 volts to feel the amount of pain it caused.

The protests of the victim rose with the shock level. At 75 volts, he began to moan and grunt; at 150 volts he demanded to be released from the experiment; at 180 volts he cried out that he could not stand the pain any longer. At 300 volts he insisted that he would no longer take part in the experiment and must be freed. He yelled out about his heart condition and screamed. If a subject hesitated or protested delivering the next shock, the experimenter told him, "Teacher, you have no other choice; you must go on! Your job is to punish the learner's mistakes."

As you might imagine, the situation was not an enjoyable one for the subjects. Most subjects complained and protested. They insisted they could not go on with their jobs. That the experimental situation produced considerable conflict in the subjects is readily apparent from their protests:

180 volts delivered: "He can't stand it! I'm not going to kill that man in there! You hear him hollering? He's hollering. He can't stand it. What if something happens to him? . . . I mean, who is going to take the responsibility if anything happens to that gentleman?" (The experimenter accepts responsibility.) "All right."

195 volts delivered: "You see he's hollering. Hear that. Gee, I don't know." (The experimenter says: "The experiment requires that you go on.")—"I know it does, sir, but I mean—huh—he don't know what he's in for. He's up to 195 volts." . . .

240 volts delivered: "Aw, no. You mean I've got to keep going up with that scale? No sir, I'm not going to kill that man! I'm not going to give him 450 volts!" (1965, p. 67)

When the "learner" stopped responding, some subjects called out to him to respond, urging him to get the answer right so they would not have to continue shocking him, all the while protesting loudly to the experimenter, but the experimenter insisted that the "teacher" go on. Rules are rules! So even when there was only silence from the "learner's" room, the "teacher" was ordered to keep shocking him more and more strongly. Did he? Did they? Would you? (Stop! Before reading further, think about what your response would have been, then answer the following questions.)

How far do you think the average subject in Milgram's experiment actually went in administering the shocks? Suppose for a moment that you were the subject-teacher. How far up the scale would you go? Which of the levels of shock would be the absolute limit beyond which you would refuse to continue? Indicate your estimates below.

1. The average subject probably stopped at _____ volts.
2. I would refuse to shock the other person beyond voltage level (circle one number):

0	15	30	45	60
75	90	105	120	135
150	165	180	195	210
225	240	255	270	285
300	315	330	345	360
375	390	405	420	435
450				

To Shock or Not to Shock?

When 40 psychiatrists were asked to predict the performance of subjects in this experiment, they estimated that most would not go beyond 150 volts. In their professional opinions, fewer than 4 percent of the subjects would still be obedient at 300 volts and only about 0.1 percent would continue to 450 volts. The psychiatrists presumed that only those few individuals who were *abnormal* in some way would blindly obey orders to harm another person in an experiment. How close are your predictions to theirs?

In fact, these professionals were quite wrong. They fell into the trap of the fundamental attribution error—overestimating the role of personality while being unaware of the power of the situation. The *majority* of the subjects obeyed! Nearly two thirds delivered the 450 volts to the subject. They followed orders, giving the maximum punishment possible. No subject who got within five switches of the end ever refused to go all the way. By then, their resistance was broken; they had resolved their own conflict—and just tried to get it over with as quickly as possible. They *dissented* verbally, but they did not *disobey.*

Through later research we know that this obedience effect becomes even *stronger* when: (a) the "victim" is more physically remote; (b) a subject is under direct surveillance by the authority; and (c) a subject acts as an *intermediary* assisting another person who actually delivers the shock.

Attributions for Blind Obedience

Maybe the personalities of the obedient majority were different from those of the rebellious minority? Personality tests administered to the subjects did *not* reveal any traits that differentiated those who obeyed from those who refused or any psychological disturbance or abnormality in the obedient "punishers."

Maybe the subjects did not really believe the "cover story" of the experiment? Perhaps they figured out that the "victim" was really a confederate of the experimenter whose protests were tape recorded. Maybe they just "went along for the ride." To test this possibility, other researchers replicated the conceptual design of Milgram's study while making the effects more vivid and direct.

College students were asked to train a puppy on a discrimination task by punishing it with increasing levels of shock whenever it made an error. They could see it jumping around on an electrified grid when they pressed a switch. Actually, the puppy received only a low level of shock—just enough to make it squeal. The students dissented and complained. They said they were upset, they did not want to do it. Some even cried.

At a given point, an odorless, colorless anesthetic was secretly released into the puppy's enclosed chamber. The dog wobbled and finally fell asleep. The subjects thought they had killed that cuddly puppy, but the experimenter reminded them of the rule: failure to respond is a punishable error; they must continue to give shocks. Would anyone really do so?

Three fourths of all students did. They delivered the maximum shock. Every one of the female subjects proved to be totally obedient despite their tearful dissent. (Sheridan & King, 1972)

Maybe subjects who knew they were in a "scientific experiment" were obeying out of a "higher" need to help science? In real life then, people would not obey an authority whose orders put someone's life in danger—or would they? A team of psychiatrists and nurses performed the following field study to test the power of obedience in a real-life hospital setting.

A nurse (the subject) received a call from a staff doctor whom she had not met. He told her to administer some medication to a patient so that it could take effect by the time he arrived. He'd sign the drug order after he got to the ward. He ordered a dose of 20 milligrams of a drug called Astroten.

The label on the container of Astroten stated that 5 milligrams was the usual dose and warned that the maximum dose was 10 milligrams. Would a nurse actually administer an excessive dose of a drug on the basis of a telephone call from an unfamiliar person? To do so would be contrary to standard medical practice.

When this dilemma was described *to 12 nurses, 10* said *they would disobey. When actually in the situation, however, almost every nurse obeyed! Twenty-one of 22 had started to pour the medication (actually a harmless substance) before a physician researcher stopped them. (Hofling et al., 1966)*

Sadly, a similar scenario was recently enacted, but not as part of an experiment—with tragic results. A nurse followed the telephone order of someone posing as an AIDS patient's physician to administer a particular drug. She did, and shortly after the patient died *(Los Angeles Times,* 1986, September 28).

Like the prison study, this obedience research challenges the myth that evil lurks in the minds of evil people—the *them* who are different dispositionally from the *us* who would never do such things. The purpose in recounting these findings is not to diminish human nature, but to make clear the human potential for frailty in the face of strong social forces in the situation, even for normal, well-meaning individuals.

Five conditions can be distinguished that lead to blind obedience to authority in violation of one's self-image and moral values:

1. Obedience is nurtured by the presence of a *legitimate authority* whom we trust and see as a valid representative of society or who controls significant reinforcers. We feel freer to act when an authority assumes responsibility for the consequences of our action. Identification with a strong authority may also help us overcome feelings of personal weakness and insignificance.
2. Obedience is nurtured by the establishment of a *role relationship* in which we are subordinated to another person. In this role we do not feel as responsible for our behavior since we are not spontaneously initiating it, but merely carrying out orders. Other research has shown that if subjects see people defy commands and refuse to accept their roles, then the majority of subjects *disobey* (Rosenhan, 1969).
3. Obedience is nurtured by the presence of *social norms* that specify socially acceptable behaviors. These norms come to govern and constrain what is perceived as possible and appropriate, and people feel embarrassed and apologetic about not conforming to the expected. One subject in the original Milgram study said to the experimenter, *"I don't mean to be rude, sir,* but shouldn't we look in on him? He has a heart condition and may be dying." It is important to note that even among the heroic band of *disobedient* subjects, not one spontaneously got up to check on the "victim," even after having *quit* the experiment. In that sense, obedience was 100 percent.
4. Obedience is nurtured by the *redefinition of evil as good.* Those who engage in evil deeds rarely, if ever, see them as evil. Instead, they see the deeds as not only reasonable, but necessary. This, again, is the paradox of human perfection—the same minds that can comprehend the most profound philosophical and metaphysical truths can distort and redefine reality in ways that eliminate inconsistency and maintain self-esteem. The prison guards were "keeping order"; Milgram's subjects were being "concerned teachers"; the Inquisition and seventeenth-century witch burnings were defined as "saving souls." The physicians who assist jailors in the torture of political prisoners in many countries define their behavior as "doing their duty to their government" (Amnesty International, 1983). To appreciate how it is possible to

attribute the most horrible deeds to noble causes, consider Hitler's statement:

> *Thus, if we review all the causes of the German collapse, the final and decisive one is seen to be the failure to realize the racial problem and, more especially, the Jewish menace . . . . Thus do I now believe that I must act in the sense of the Almighty creator: by fighting against the Jews, I am doing the Lord's work. (Hitler, 1933, p. 25)*

5. Obedience is nurtured in *situations that are ambiguous* and in which it is easy to take the first, small steps, but difficult to know how to quit, escape, or disobey "going all the way." Milgram's subjects, like those in life's real obedience situations, perceived "no exit," no clear channel for disobeying the rules or violating the contract. They were not able to muster the motivation or the mental strategy for disengaging from this intense, confusing scenario.

Authority Systems, Disobedience, and You

Milgram's subjects did not learn obedience to authority in the psychology laboratory. The research described merely demonstrates the extent to which we all have been taught "the obedience lesson" in many socializing environments, especially in grade school: "Do as you're told and there won't be any trouble." "Stay in your seat and don't complain." "Don't talk back."

Obedience must exist at some optimal level in society if the best interests of all are to be met. The danger arises when we let the values prescribed by the situation replace our individual values.

Authority relations do not always involve only a leader and a follower. *Authority systems* emerge when people transfer or delegate the rights over their actions to agents of the primary authority or to an organization. An authority system exists when they pledge allegiance to a nation-state and thereby to all its government officials or when they are employed by a corporation with its hierarchy of authorities.

Consider the statements made by the bombardier who released the first atomic bomb over Hiroshima. He was not told what his "payload" was, but from the special preparations, he "put two and two together and figured it was radioactive. I'd flown so many missions by then that it was mostly a job to do." The power of authority systems over individuals as well as the naive belief in dispositional control, even when faced with overwhelming evidence of situational control, is loud and clear in the bombardier's self-analysis 25 years later:

> *I don't believe in everything we do, but if I'm in the military, I've got to support the government. I may not agree, but if ordered I'll sure do it. I think everyone has enough sense never to use the bomb again.* (Newsweek, *August 10, 1970)*

Are *you* that certain no one will ever order you to press THE button, and would you or wouldn't you press it? (For more on resistance to obedience pressures, see the ***Close-up*** on p. 658).

Deindividuation and Dehumanization

Have you ever "stepped out of character" and behaved in ways that were alien to you? Said or done things that simply were not the "real you" talking or acting? Obviously, this was one of the post-experimental reactions experienced by subjects in the obedience studies. It is disturbing to have the illusion of self-knowledge challenged by the possibility of being controlled by external situational forces rather than directed by personality.

Social psychological researchers have shown that there are a number of circumstances that contribute to altering the usual ways in which behavior is consciously regulated. Such conditions include those that make us *less* concerned about *social evaluation*—not monitoring or caring about what other people think of us—and about *self-attention*—not monitoring our thoughts, feelings, or actions. When that happens, we are more likely to lose our sense of individuation and humanity—to become deindividuated and dehumanized.

Individuation

A clear demonstration that the same individuals have the potential for both prosocial and antisocial behavior, depending on the social setting, has been provided by research on the effects of individuation and deindividuation. **Individuation** is both the psychological *state* and the *process* in which a person is differentiated from the other people in a given social context. An individual stands out and is unique and identifiable both to others and in his or her own perceptions (Snyder & Fromkin, 1980; Ziller, 1964). For example, a person is individuated

Close-up Send Your Child to Disobedience School

Sarah McCarthy, a former public school teacher, believes that Milgram's results reflect the intense training for uncritical obedience that takes place daily in our schools, churches, and throughout society. Her concern is not, as is so often the case, with getting Johnny to be more compliant, but rather with why Johnny can't disobey when disobedience is called for.

Along with worrying about the S.A.T. scores and whether Johnny can read, we must begin to question seriously whether Johnny is capable of disobedience. . . . We must stop equating sanity with conformity, eccentricity with craziness, and normalcy with number. We must get in touch with our own liberating ludicrousness and practice being harmlessly deviant. . . .

It seems that the best armor is a rational mind. We must insist that all authorities account for themselves, and we need to be as wary of false prophets as we are of false advertising. Leaders, political and spiritual, must be subjected to intense scrutiny, and we must insist that their thought processes and proclamations measure up to reasonable standards of rational thought. Above all, we must become skilled in activating our inner resources toward rebellion and disobedience, when this seems reasonable. . . .

Little notice is taken of the legions of overly obedient children in the schools; yet, for every overly disobedient child, there are probably twenty who are obeying too much. There is little motivation to encourage the unsqueaky wheels to develop as noisy, creative, independent thinkers who may become bold enough to disagree. Conceivably, we could administer modified Milgram obedience tests in the schools which detect hyper-obedience, just as we test for intelligence, visual function, vocational attributes and tuberculosis. When a child is found to be too obedient, the schools should mobilize against this psychological crippler with the zeal by which they would react to an epidemic of smallpox. In alcoholism and other mental disturbances, the first major step toward a reversal of the pathology is recognition of the severity of the problem. Obedience should be added to the list of emotional disturbances requiring therapy. Disobedience schools should be at least as common as military schools and reform schools. (McCarthy, 1979, p. 34)

This same theme was echoed in recent Congressional testimony by an F.B.I. agent working on cases of sexual molestation of children (of which nearly 75,000 were reported in a one-year period). This investigator called for education programs that teach children "they have the right to say no" to adults. On the basis of his experience, children become more vulnerable to adult child molesters because they have overlearned the lesson of blindly obeying authority figures (United Press, April 12, 1984).

Even our nation's leaders are subject to the pressures applied to those who disobey the wishes of the "team." When the Iranscam was exposed, former director of the National Security Council, Robert McFarlane, testified before a Congressional in-

---

when he or she is called by name, when the person's special features or contributions are recognized, and when the person's actions are rewarded by others. Individuation acts to inhibit socially undesirable behaviors and to promote norm-appropriate acts (Ickes et al., 1978).

Other research has found that the extent to which people will *individuate* themselves, by behaving in distinctive ways, is a function of the potential rewards and punishments in the environment. If there is the possibility of a positive outcome (acclaim, prizes, recognition), then people will try to call attention to themselves and their unique characteristics. However, if negative consequences are anticipated (ridicule, attack, a burdensome assignment), then people will try to melt into the crowd and not look different from the rest of the group (Maslach, 1974). Recall how you and your elementary-school classmates acted when the teacher asked an easy question ("Call on me!") versus a hard one ("I want to be invisible").

The sense of distinctiveness associated with being individuated can have negative as well as positive consequences. Those perceived as "differ-

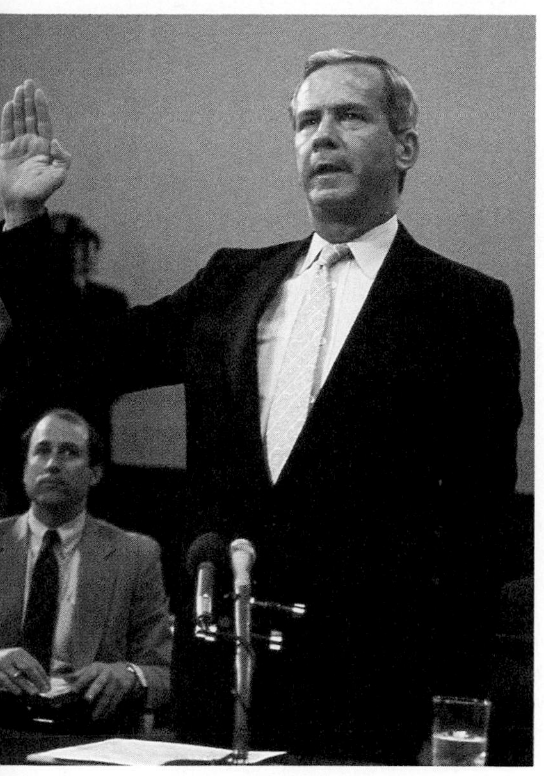

vestigating committee that he was part of the attempt by the White House to deceive Congress. He said he "didn't have the guts" to tell the President that he thought the method for achieving their goal was wrong. Why not? "To tell you the truth, probably the reason I didn't is because if I'd done that, Bill Casey [former CIA Director], Jeane Kirkpatrick [former U.N. ambassador], and Cap Weinberger [Defense Secretary] would have said I was some kind of Commie, you know" (*Newsweek*, May 25, 1987).

How does all this apply to you? What can you, as an adult, do to resist being obedient to unjust authority or to unjust demands of just authority? These suggestions may help:

1. *Don't let others define the situation for you without your questioning the premises, methods, and ends. For example, why was the "teacher" even necessary in the Milgram study; why couldn't the experimenter give the shocks if the true purpose was to study learning and not the "teacher's" reaction?*
2. *Be sensitive to small, initial, trivial steps that can escalate into big commitments; don't let the little foot in the door.*
3. *Separate the message from the communicator's characteristics so that you will evaluate what is said without the biasing influence of the age, position, sex, dress, title of the authority.*
4. *Remember you are not the role you play in various life dramas; be prepared to step out of it and evaluate what you are doing from other perspectives, especially that of a critic.*
5. *Be able to admit you made a mistake, were wrong, so you do not have to continue to do the unacceptable deed just to be consistent.*
6. *When in doubt, never make action-decisions in the influence situation; don't sign on the dotted line, take time out to reflect and to check with independent sources.*
7. *Remember the fundamental attribution error and reverse it to evaluate better how you might be operating a mental vehicle under the influence of social control intoxicants (see also Andersen & Zimbardo, 1980; Sabini & Silver, 1983).*

ent" become "deviants," and are more likely to be rejected, avoided, or mistreated (Freedman & Doob, 1968; Goffman, 1963). On the other hand, the different person in a group is more salient, and, if competent, will be judged to be more influential (S. E. Taylor et al., 1979). An individuated person becomes so, not merely in the perception of others, but also as a result of a greater self-awareness, of an attentional focus on the self (Duval & Wicklund, 1972). When people focus on their self-concepts, they tend to perceive them in terms of the distinctive and peculiar characteristics that make them "information rich" and thus differentiated from others in their social environment (McGuire et al., 1978).

People vary in their willingness to be individuated, to act in ways which make them stand out from the crowd. Those high on a self-reported scale of individuation were found to be more likely to have high self-esteem, unique nicknames, distinctive styles of hair, dress, signatures, and ways of introducing themselves. They also made more controversial statements than those low on this individual difference variable (Maslach et al., 1985).

Deindividuation

Deindividuation is a psychological process in which a set of antecedent variables reduces one's identifiability and self-awareness. Under such circumstances normally inhibited social acts (among them, aggressive behavioral outcomes) are released. The antecedent variables fall into two classes: accountability cues and attention modifiers (Prentice-Dunn & Rogers, 1983).

Accountability cues are those variables which cue a person that he or she will not be held accountable for what is done. When responsibility is diffused, potential victims cannot retaliate and authority figures cannot identify the source of the behavior. As a result, the probability of antisocial and inhibited acts increases. People do things they normally wouldn't do because they perceive they can get away with it, nobody knows . . . or cares.

The second postulated variables induce a state of deindividuation by modifying one's attentional and perceptual processes. Suspended are the usual cognitive processing of input relevant to self-standards, moral values, personal commitments, and projected utility of alternative courses of action. When that happens, the output behavior is high in intensity, present-oriented, situationally focused, and without internally directed constraints.

Deindividuation is also the label used for the subjective state a person experiences during the process of transforming attention away from self. This state can be induced by conditions in which a person feels anonymous or without responsibility; by conditions in which a person is immersed in the immediate present and does not think about the past or future; and by conditions in which sensory overload, drugs, strong emotions, or physical activity overwhelm rational, cognitive processing. The deindividuated person then becomes more likely to act without first thinking, to let feelings instead of conscience be a guide. Let's examine how deindividuation functions.

Varying Accountability Cues

Sure, this robe of mine doth change my disposition.

Shakespeare, The Winter's Tale

The term *deindividuation* was first used by Leon Festinger and his colleagues (1952) to label the process by which a person's feelings of social responsibility and fear of punishment were weakened by that person's anonymity in a group. They theorized that when a person cannot be identified or judged by others, emotions and impulses that are usually held in check are more likely to be expressed. "You don't know who I am and I don't care who you are." Such perceived anonymity interferes with identifying and remembering who said what.

Since this early research, several studies have investigated the effects of deliberately created anonymity (Diener, 1979; Prentice-Dunn & Rogers, 1982; Singer et al., 1965). In one series of studies some of the subjects were made anonymous while others were clearly individuated. The amount of aggressive behavior of both groups was observed. As in the prison study, the subjects were all the same at the start; any differences in aggressiveness would be the result of the difference in induced anonymity rather than existing personality differences.

> *Anonymity was created by having women, who were tested in groups of four, wear baggy lab coats and hoods that covered their faces. In addition, they sat in a darkened room and were never referred to by name. In other identifiable groups the women wore name tags, were frequently called by name, and saw the faces of the others in their group. All subjects were led to believe that they would be giving electrical shocks to each of two volunteer students as part of a supposed study of their empathy and the volunteers' ability to perform under stress.*
>
> *The subjects listened to a taped interview with each "victim" before watching her twist, squirm, and jump in reaction to each "shock" they gave her (actually, she was a confederate who received no shock). In one condition the victim was portrayed in the interview as obnoxious, prejudiced, and "bitchy"; in the other, as sweet, warm, and altruistic.*
>
> *As predicted, the anonymous subjects shocked the victims more (twice as long) than did the identifiable subjects. Furthermore, the aggression by the anonymous subjects did not vary as a function of the characteristics of the victim: they shocked the victim more and more over time, regardless of her portrayal as nice or obnoxious. In contrast, there was a positive correlation between the identifiable subjects' ratings of the target victims and the duration of shock they gave them: more shock as the victim was more obnoxious. (Zimbardo, 1970)*

Subsequent research supports the basic conclusion of this study. Conditions that foster anonymity lead people to act aggressively or to behave in other antisocial ways when they are given the opportunity to do so. College student subjects were more likely to cheat or steal from the research professor's office when they were treated as anonymous "guinea pigs" than when they were treated humanely as individuals (Kiernan & Kaplan, 1971).

Anonymity increases aggression even when it "costs" the aggressor the loss of tangible rewards.

In one experiment eight children were invited to a Halloween party where they were allowed to play aggressive or nonaggressive games in which they could win tokens. They were told that these tokens could be exchanged for attractive toys at an auction held at the end of the party. Playing the aggressive games involved physical competition (pushing and shoving) and took more time, thus earning fewer tokens. The aggressive and nonaggressive games were similar in content. For example, a child could compete with another to retrieve a single bean bag from a tunnel or could be timed while retrieving it alone.

*At first, the children played these games in their normal street clothes with name tags (condition A); then they were dressed in Halloween costumes that made them appear anonymous (condition B); finally, they were unmasked and wore their regular clothing again (condition A). As you can see in **Figure 18.7**, the children were more aggressive when they were anonymous than when they were identifiable. They chose more aggressive games when they were anonymous, even though it cost them valuable tokens to do so. It appears that there were intrinsic awards associated with being deindividuated and acting aggressively that were more powerful than the desire to earn tokens. The within-subjects, A-B-A design used in this study provided a powerful demonstration of anonymity manipulation to alter behavior, holding constant the personalities and other attributes of the subjects. (Fraser, 1974)*

The link between anonymity and aggression has been demonstrated in vastly different social settings. In some societies men prepare for war by putting on masks or painting their bodies. In other societies, there is no such process of changing one's appearance prior to becoming a warrior. Which of the two social groups do you predict would exhibit most aggression in combat?

To answer this question, data from 23 different cultures were examined. The striking results can be seen in ***Table 18.2.*** Of the 15 societies in which warriors changed their appearance, 12 were high on the index of "killing, torturing, or mutilating the enemy," while only 1 of the 8 with unchanged appearances were so aggressive (Watson, 1973).

Another study of extreme aggression in lynch mobs found that the extent of the atrocities committed was a function of mob size relative to the number of the victims (Mullen, 1986). As lynchers were more numerous, their individual anonymity was greater, and accountability cues lessened. The result was more savage attacks on their victims.

Does deindividuation always bring out the worst side of human nature, as these studies seem to suggest? Not necessarily. Conditions that minimize concern for social accountability lower the threshold for expressing other ordinarily inhibited behaviors too—for example, expressing intimate feelings and crying in public by males.

Figure 18.7 *Aggression Versus Rewards*
The effects of simply being made anonymous are dramatic. Aggression was much higher in the anonymous condition even though the children earned far fewer tokens when they chose the aggressive games. (Based on Fraser, 1974.)

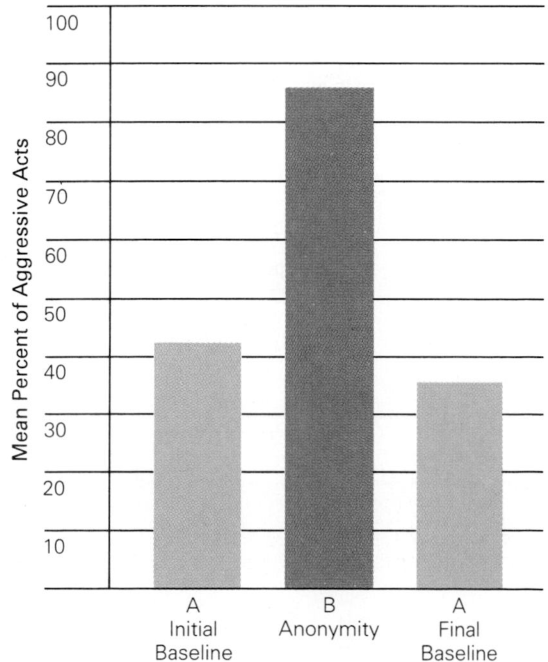

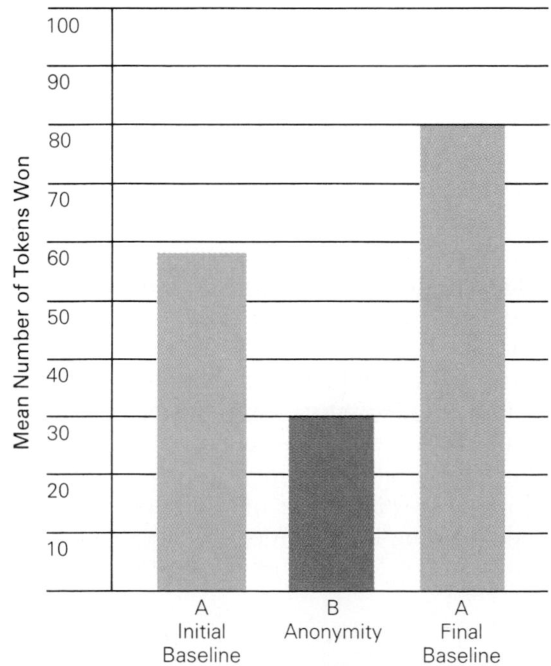

In some societies, men prepare for war by painting their faces to change their appearances. This preserves their anonymity.

> *Research subjects brought into a dark room to spend an hour with a group of strangers of both sexes behaved differently from others in a lighted room. Those in the anonymous setting talked more about personally significant things and were more openly affectionate, touching and hugging others. The darkness provided an opportunity to "liberate" feelings of intimacy that were suppressed in usual situations. (Gergen et al., 1973; see also Johnson & Downing, 1979)*

Attention Modifiers

Usual cognitive regulators of behavior can be dampened by heightened emotional arousal, physical involvement in task activities, and alterations in states of consciousness through drugs, hypnosis, repetitive chanting, and ritual dancing. While the accountability cues reduce public self-awareness, these attention modifiers reduce private self-awareness (Buss, 1980).

The subjective state of deindividuation is produced only by reduced *private* self-awareness. When subjects are made to focus attention externally rather than internally, they score higher on measures of altered experience and lower on self-awareness—the two components of the deindividuated state (Prentice-Dunn & Rogers, 1981). "Altered experience" includes time distortion, feelings of greater cohesiveness to the present group, altered thinking, and emotional arousal. When in this deindividuated state, research subjects (college students) act more aggressively and engage in socially inappropriate behaviors that are available in the situations—playing in mud, writing obscenities, and sucking baby bottles (Diener, 1980)

Emergent Norms

When collections of individuals are exposed to the deindividuating antecedent conditions (outlined previously) while also witnessing socially sanctioned aggression, as in soccer or hockey games, their potential for violent outbursts can be lethal. Another psychological process adds to that of deindividuation. Within such groups, norms emerge that stimulate, encourage, and reward aggression toward out-group members. These *emergent norms* also make other antisocial behaviors, such as vandalism and gang rape, acceptable to the group at that time and place (Rabbie, 1985; Turner & Killian, 1972).

Dehumanized Relationships

Would you ever deliberately humiliate, embarrass, or degrade another person? Can you imagine turning down a poor family's request for food or clothing if you could authorize it just by signing your name? Is it conceivable that you would ever decide that certain groups were unfit and order their extermination? What would it take to make *you* kill another person?

These and other antisocial behaviors become possible for normal, morally upright, and idealistic people under conditions in which they stop perceiving others as having the same feelings, thoughts, and purposes in life that they do. Such a psychological erasure of human qualities is called **dehumanization.** It is a particular type of psychic defense mechanism used to protect a person from painful or overwhelming emotions in dealing with others. It leads to misperceiving certain other people as "subhuman" (animallike), or as "nonhuman" objects.

Table 18.2 *A Cross-Cultural Study of Anonymity and Aggression*

	Appearance		
	Changed	Unchanged	Total
High Aggression	12	1	13
Low Aggression	3	7	10
Total Number of Societies	15	8	23

(Based on Watson, 1973)

When one is not responding to the human qualities of other persons, the golden rule may become "Do unto others as you would." The genocide of millions of people by governments and their military agents throughout the world has been carried out with the same efficiency as occurs daily at animal slaughterhouses—by the simple expedient of perceiving these fellow human beings as inferior forms of animal life—as "worms" to would-be torturers (Gibson & Haritos-Fatouros, 1986).

In a laboratory experiment on dehumanization, college student subjects were led to believe that researchers were studying the effects of punishment on decision making. They supervised the work of a group of male students and had the option of punishing them with electric shock whenever inadequate decisions were made. Some of the subjects overheard the experimenter describe the students as perceptive and understanding. Other subjects overheard a dehumanizing characterization of the students as an animalistic, rotten bunch. Control subjects received neither positive nor negative descriptions of the potential victims.

Subjects who thought of their "victims" in dehumanized terms chose much higher levels of shock as punishment. (No shock was actually delivered.) They also felt less personal responsibility for the consequences of their punitive actions. Subjects given a humanized description of the victims showed less *aggression against them than did the controls (see* **Figure 18.8***). Finally, even the way the subjects justified their decisions to administer the shocks differed depending on the humanization or dehumanization of their victims. (Bandura et al., 1975)*

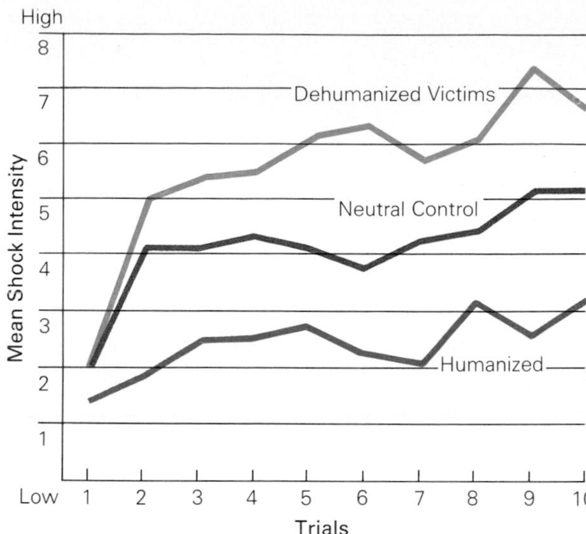

Figure 18.8

"Overhead" cues that humanized or dehumanized performers affected the intensity of shocks that subjects administered to them. Victims who were described in humanized terms were shocked less than the neutral control group, while the dehumanized subjects categorized as "animals" were shocked the most—and increasingly so over the ten trials. (Adapted from Bandura et al., 1975.)

Dehumanization may be (a) imposed in self-defense, (b) socially imposed, or (c) rationalized as the necessary means toward some noble end. While this psychological process may serve to temporarily help cope with a difficult situation, it always results in more negative than positive consequences.

Socially Imposed Dehumanization

Dehumanization can occur in various work situations. Some jobs encourage workers to dehumanize other people because large numbers of people have to be "processed" efficiently—college students during registration, subway commuters during rush hour, prisoners or mental patients during mealtime. Administrators of institutions often become concerned with minimizing disruptions and "managing the flow." Once the number of individuals requiring a given service becomes too great, they stop being seen or treated as individuals.

In other cases, the jobs themselves dehumanize workers by allowing no expression of personal feelings or unique abilities. Examples are assembly-line jobs that are repetitive, boring, and tedious. Workers feel no meaningful relationship to the product of their labors—and are, in fact, being gradually replaced by a new breed who never complain about dehumanized work settings: industrial robots.

Dehumanization in Self-defense

Individuals in many health and service professions work in situations that ordinarily arouse intense emotional feelings, elicit painful empathy, and/or involve "taboo" behaviors, such as invasion of privacy or violation of a human body. Dehumanizing their patients or clients may help these individuals handle such jobs. Treating people as "cases" in an objective, detached way enables them to perform necessary interviews and operations with minimal emotional involvement. This self-protective "detachment" can become extreme, however.

Sometimes dehumanization is the result of emotional "burnout," as described in chapter 14. The psychological stress and strain of a job become so severe that a person loses all human feeling for the people being served. They may become just "case loads" to social workers, "dockets" to lawyers, "crocks" to physicians—and burdens to all care givers who have "burned out." (Maslach, 1982).

Dehumanization as a Means to an End

At many times in history people have viewed a particular group as obstacles to the achievement of their goals. By perceiving such people as "the enemy," "the masses," "a threat to national security," or "inferior," it becomes easier to take action against them in the name of some great cause, such as peace, liberty, or "God's will." Their suffering, injury, or destruction is then justified as a means toward a "noble" end. Many examples of such dehumanization come to mind, including the dropping of the atomic bomb on the residents of Hiroshima in order to "bring peace," the mass killing of Jews by the Nazis because "they are unfit," and the denial of medical treatment to black men afflicted with syphilis (the control group in a controversial study in Tuskegee, Alabama) in order to "study the course of the disease."

Essential to the process of transforming civilians into soldiers who must be willing and able to kill when necessary during war, is the creation of the "enemy" as a nonhuman object of hate. This is accomplished by politicians who define an enemy and justify the need to destroy that enemy. They are aided and abetted by the media, and especially cartoonists, who provide the visual images that arouse fear, unconscious anxieties, and a hostile imagination. (See the photos at the bottom of this page for some good examples.) "A variety of dehumanizing faces is superimposed over the enemy to allow him to be killed without guilt. The problem of military psychology is how to convert the act of murder into patriotism. . . . Wars come and go, but—strangely amid changing circumstances—the hostile imagination has a certain standard repertoire of images it uses to dehumanize the enemy" (Keen, 1986, p. 12–13).

These are the "faces of the enemy" as seen through the eyes of cartoonists. Notice the characterization and the dehumanization of all these creations.

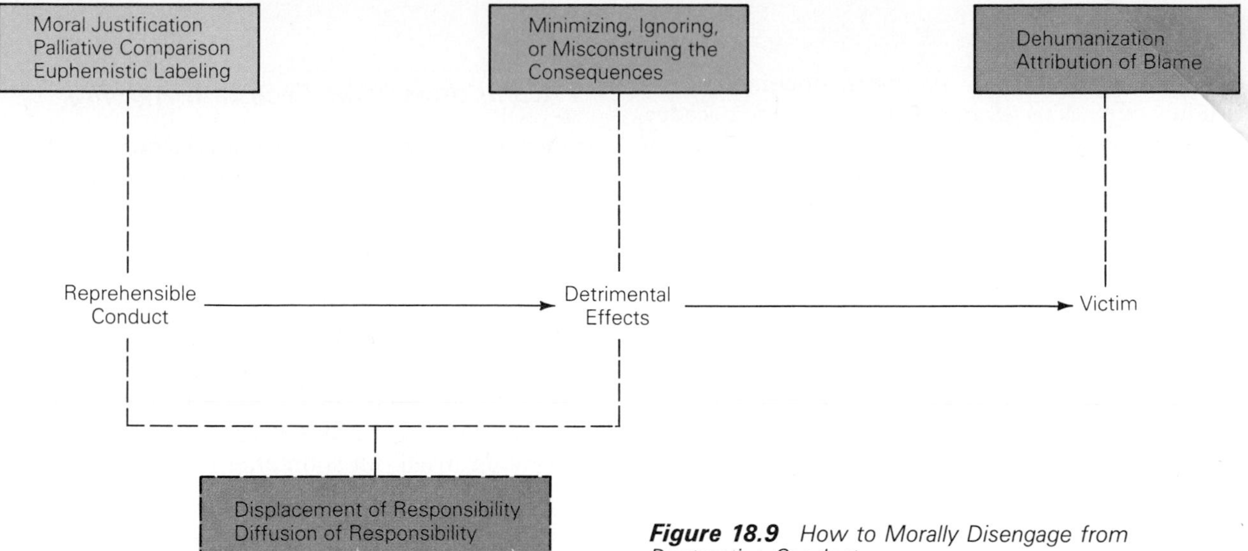

Figure 18.9 *How to Morally Disengage from Destructive Conduct*

The ease with which people can be induced to adopt a dehumanized view of others was demonstrated in a 1974 study using college students.

> *The researcher brought together a large group of students and introduced a ''professor'' who asked for their assistance in a project ''designed to eliminate the mentally and emotionally unfit.'' The idea was convincingly presented as high-minded and scientifically sound, beneficial for humanity, and actually even a kindness to those who would be eliminated. The students themselves were praised as being intelligent and educated, with high ethical values. In case they had any lingering misgivings, they were assured that careful research would be carried out before any actions were taken. A questionnaire was then administered to the students. A startling degree of acceptance of the proposed ''final solution'' was found. The students agreed that some people were not fit to survive and should be eliminated as painlessly as possible (Mansson, 1972). In a later replication of this study, a surprising 29 percent even supported the suggested measures when applied to their own families. (Carlson & Wood, 1974)*

This study of the "final solution" shows how little effort might be necessary to translate these "artificial" experimental findings into the same nightmare of reality that occurred in Germany in World War II—and in other places and other times both before and since that time.

Moral Disengagement

To engage in political and military violence against individuals and groups requires more than dehumanizing a victim. Terrorists, for example, use violent strategies designed to promote desired outcomes by instilling fear in the public (Bassiouni, 1981). To transform socialized citizens into terrorists does not require personality change, merely a restructuring of their cognitive-moral framework into one that approves violence. This is accomplished by techniques that disconnect reprehensible conduct and its detrimental effects from the usual moral standards and internal controls that prohibit such inhumane behavior (Bandura, 1987).

Figure 18.9 outlines the steps in the process of moral disengagement from destructive conduct. Reprehensible conduct can be *morally justified* in many ways: it can be essential for "freedom," "national security," or in "God's will." *Palliative comparisons* can make deplorable deeds righteous by comparing them with a more extreme practice or historical example. *Euphemistic labels* can be used to make evil deeds seem benign—soldiers "waste" or "eliminate" enemies rather than "murder" them; violent terrorists become "freedom fighters."

The detrimental effects of one's actions can be cognitively distorted, reinterpreted, or disregarded through strategies of self-deception. The link between conduct and consequence is weakened when responsibility is displaced onto others. Finally, the dehumanized victims become "animal-others," blamed for bringing destruction on themselves because "that's the way they wanted it." Social-political structures that allow or encourage such strategies of moral disengagement can induce the worst excesses of human destructiveness imaginable. Once these structures are removed, the "evil-doers" return to their former lives as model citizens with little or no noticeable carryover of these situation-specific transgressions. This return to "behavior-as-usual" has been documented in studies of ex-Nazi SS members over three decades (Steiner, 1980).

Since war begins
In the minds of men
It is in the minds of men
That we have to erect
The ramparts of peace.

UNESCO Charter

Bystander Intervention

In a big city one is surrounded by literally hundreds of thousands of people, hears them on radio, sees them on television, eats with them in restaurants, sits next to them in movies, waits in line with them, gets pushed around in subways with them, touches them—but remains unconnected, as if they did not exist.

For a woman in Queens, they did not exist, when she most needed them.

> *For more than half an hour, thirty-eight respectable, law-abiding citizens in Queens [New York] watched a killer stalk and stab a woman in three separate attacks in Kew Gardens. Twice the sound of their voices and the sudden glow of their bedroom lights interrupted him and frightened him off. Each time he returned, sought her out, and stabbed her again. Not one person telephoned the police during the assault; one witness called the police after the woman was dead. (*New York Times*, 1964, March 13)*

This newspaper account of the murder of Kitty Genovese shocked a nation that could not accept the idea of such apathy on the part of its responsible citizenry. Only a few months later there was an even more vivid and chilling depiction of how alienated and out of contact one can be in the midst of people. An 18-year-old secretary was beaten, choked, stripped, and raped in her office. She finally broke away from her assailant and, naked and bleeding, ran down the stairs of the building to the doorway screaming, "Help me! Help me! He raped me!" A crowd of 40 persons gathered on the busy street and watched passively as the rapist dragged her back upstairs. Only the chance arrival of passing police prevented her further abuse and possible murder (*New York Times*, 1964, May 6).

Would *you* have called the police if you had lived in Kew Gardens? Would you have intervened to help the woman being raped? Will you (when your chance comes) do anything but "your own thing"?

Conditions That Facilitate Helping

Since the murder of Kitty Genovese our city streets have become increasingly unsafe by night and sometimes even by day. The failure of bystanders to intervene is certainly not the cause of crimes that occur; but a higher likelihood that observers would help might deter an attacker. In any case, it could improve a victim's chances of survival.

Why don't bystanders help in cases like these? What would make them more likely to do so? A classic study of the bystander intervention problem was carried out soon after the Kitty Genovese murder.

> *Two social psychologists ingeniously created in the laboratory an experimental analog of the bystander-intervention situation. A college student, placed in a room by himself, was led to believe that he was communicating with other students via an intercom. During the course of a discussion about personal problems, he heard what sounded like one of the other students having an epileptic seizure and gasping for help.*
>
> *During the "seizure" it was impossible for the subject to talk to the other students or to find out what, if anything, they were doing about the emergency. The dependent variable was the speed with which he reported the emergency to the experimenter. The major independent variable was the number of people he thought were in the discussion group with him.*
>
> *It turned out that the likelihood of intervention depended on the number of bystanders he thought were present. The more there were, the slower he was in reporting the seizure, if he did so at all. As you can see in* **Figure 18.10,** *everyone in a two-person situation intervened within 160 seconds, but nearly 40 percent of those in the larger group never bothered to inform the experimenter that another student was seriously ill. Personality tests showed no significant relationship between particular personality characteristics and speed or likelihood of intervening. (Darley & Latané, 1968)*

Related studies have since shown that if you are a victim in an emergency, your chances of being helped are better if the bystanders:

a. are black rather than white;
b. are men rather than women;
c. have witnessed a model similar to themselves helping someone else (but not if they have witnessed people like themselves *not* helping);
d. see the situation as a clear emergency;
e. see that you are trying to help yourself; and
f. do not perceive the situation to be a formal, structured one.

Figure 18.10 *Bystander Intervention in an Emergency*

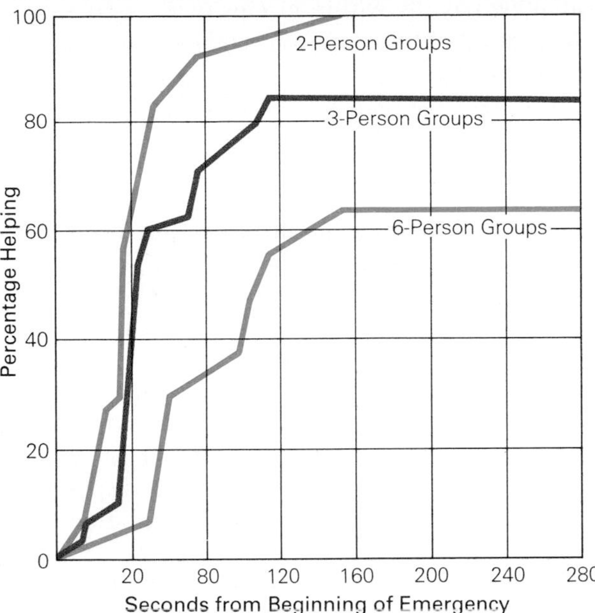

Darley and Latané "Bystander Intervention in Emergencies: Diffusion of Responsibilities." Journal of Personality and Social Psychology, 1968, 8(4), 377-384. Copyright 1968 by the American Psychological Association. Reprinted by permission.

Help and Hope in the Real World

When similar investigations are carried out in field situations, a victim's chances of getting help are quite a bit better. For example, compare the following field experiment with those of Darley and Latané.

> *A man on a moving New York subway train suddenly collapsed and fell to the floor. This event was witnessed by a number of bystanders. The experimenters manipulated the situation by varying the characteristics of the "victim"—an invalid with a cane, a drunk smelling of liquor, or, in a companion study, an invalid seemingly bleeding (or not bleeding) from the mouth. They then unobtrusively recorded the bystander responses to these emergency situations.*
>
> *Despite the newspaper stories of the "callous" city folk, one or more persons responded directly to almost every emergency (81 out of 103) and did so with little hesitation. Help was slower when the apparent cost of intervening was higher (that is, slower for a bloody victim than for a simple collapse), but still it came, even if it was indirect, by asking if there was a doctor on the train. (Piliavan & Piliavan, 1972; Piliavan et al., 1969)*

Why the difference? Helping may be inhibited in the laboratory setting for the following reasons: (a) the college student subjects have already adopted the *passive* role of "the subject"; (b) they assume that the experimenter in charge is ultimately responsible for everything that occurs during an experimental session, which itself is an artificial situation; (c) they often do not actually see the victim-in-distress; and (d) their physical locomotion is severely restricted by obedience to an unstated rule of the laboratory setting—"You stay in your seat; you stay put and follow instructions until told otherwise." In unstructured, informal settings none of these conditions hold, and the decision to intervene is probably based more on an observer's weighing the personal costs of interventions.

Despite the higher rate of help in field studies, however, the fact remains that many people do *not* help and that some settings render help less likely than others. For example, when a man on crutches put on his act in an airport, the percentage of those who helped was much lower than in the subway—41 percent compared with 83 percent. The important factor seemed to be familiarity with the environment: the subway riders felt more at home on the subway, dirty and noisy as it was, and thus were more likely to deal with the trouble that arose (Latané & Darley, 1970).

A victim has a better chance to be helped if the bystanders see the situation as a clear emergency and if they are familiar with the environment.

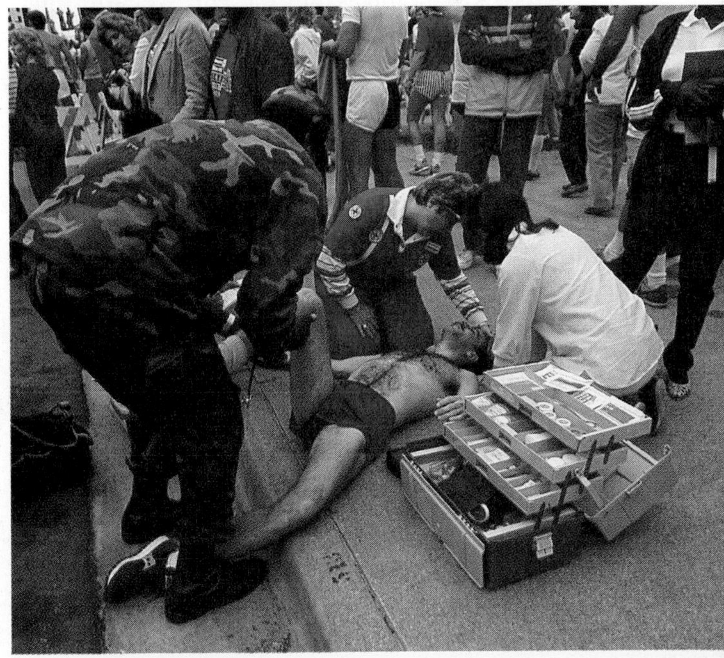

Altruism

We began this chapter by considering the ways in which the human species has the potential for virtually all imaginable behaviors. Our extended analysis of aggression and "the psychology of evil" was designed to focus attention on a major social problem of our time and to stimulate your thinking about possible remedies. It is apparent that while we hurt, abuse, and kill others, we also risk our own lives to come to the aid of strangers, to give sanctuary to "enemies of the state," or even to sacrifice ourselves to save the life of another person.

Although their behavioral manifestations are quite different, aggression and altruism share enough similarities in their development and sources of influence that investigators are beginning to synthesize conceptual and methodological approaches to these formerly divergent domains of behavior (see Olweus, et al., 1986; Zahn-Waxler, et al., 1986). Our review of the evidence indicates that both biological and cultural factors are involved in altruistic and aggressive behaviors. We humans are somewhat good and somewhat evil by nature and by nurture. Biologically and culturally based dispositions may either counteract or complement one another. Original sin and natural-goodness positions emphasize the conflict between nature and nurture, but the complementarity may be more significant for some types of behavior [such as aggression and altruism] (Krebs & Miller, 1985, p. 27–28).

Altruism involves putting the welfare, interests, and survival of others above one's own. In practice, altruism means behaving in risk situations in ways that increase the safety, interests, or lives of others while possibly jeopardizing one's own. It is possible to study altruism (and aggression) from multiple perspectives at different levels of analysis. The determinants of altruism can function at three broad levels: the biological and cultural; the personal and situational; and the affective and cognitive. This organization corresponds to an analysis from most molar and abstract to molecular and proximal.

Biology and Culture

Sociobiologists have argued that the development of both prosocial and antisocial behavior is genetically based in the evolution of the species (Trivers, 1983; Wilson, 1975). While the disposition to behave aggressively evolved as one strategy of competition, its high costs to individuals within the same group tended to limit it to outgroup aggression. The evolutionary strategies that had the most adaptive payoffs within groups were cooperation, the sharing of resources, division of labor, and caring of the young.

Altruism is biologically adaptive when helping behavior increases the probability of future reciprocal assistance from the person for whom the sacrifice is made. This implies that a person killed in the line of duty cannot be altruistic. However, even that ultimate sacrifice can be adaptive if it increases the fitness of the individual's net genetic representation in future generations—which can be achieved by altruistic deeds toward one's kin and those who resemble kin. Evolutionary evidence also suggests that altruistic dispositions should be greatest in women who are the primary caregivers for offspring, and that the aggressive dispositions derived from hunting and defense should be more adaptive for men. Recall the recent evidence (p. 645) from modern twin research that supports this view. Altruism was greater among women than men, while aggression was higher among men (Rushton, et al., 1986).

Culture adds to biological experiences that occur within the lifespan of a single individual. The selfishness of an individual is constrained by cultural norms and prescriptions about ideal, socially appropriate ways of behaving. Norms of reciprocity, equity, and justice become internalized through socialization practices within family, community, and school systems. Altruistic behavior is shaped by reinforcement, by observing models who exhibit prosocial behaviors, by hearing specific exhortations or preaching, and by conditions that heighten self-awareness (or minimize deindividuation) in the presence of socially desirable norms.

Personality and Situational Factors

Is there an altruistic personality type? At present the question remains unanswered because of the failure to demonstrate cross-situational consistency in altruistic behavior, or in most personality traits, for that matter (as discussed in chapter 12). It is possible to characterize people who generally behave altruistically (such as community mental health volunteers) and then identify the pattern of personality traits that distinguishes them from other people. However, paper-and-pencil personality trait tests to assess altruism typically show low validity.

Altruistic behavior is influenced by situations that provide salient cues to act in a prosocial way, by the presence of rules, roles, and contingencies that support helping and caring of others. Much of what we have said in this and the previous chapter has emphasized the potential power that situational variables can exert on individual and group behavior. But in the world beyond the psychological laboratory, people actively select the situations they enter, if they are free to do so. This choice of situations is affected by the characteristics of the person, a variable which also influences the way a situation is interpreted and structured. It becomes impossible to separate what is attributable to aspects of the person and what is attributable to aspects of the situation.

Affective and Cognitive Mediators

When people see someone in distress, they experience physiological arousal which may mediate their helping reaction. Help comes faster and is greater as this distress-contingent arousal is higher. Where there is a genuine concern for the suffering of others, arousal may get labeled as empathy or sympathy, two emotions that should lead to more pervasive and intense involvement with the other people's plights.

Altruistic reactions have been shown to be mediated by a variety of cognitive factors that result in inferences about the need to help, the appropriateness of taking action, attributions about a victim's deserving help, one's sense of responsibility, and expected costs and consequences. Necessary conditions for helping are the clear perception that another person needs aid and the decision that the situation is compelling enough to warrant giving help. Beyond that, what is required are inferences about the appropriateness of intervening, which often are affected by the evaluations of others who are present. In addition, the likelihood of helping is increased when a person is perceived as deserving aid—the need is evaluated as legitimate.

All these cognitive mediators will not activate helping unless an individual feels personally responsible for rendering assistance. A hedonistic model of altruism proposes that prosocial acts become more probable as the anticipated costs are less than the prospective gain to the helper. Nevertheless, people do intervene spontaneously in life-threatening situations, with "pure" altruistic, prosocial acts, apparently without calculating their cost/benefit ratio. However, it is impossible to scientifically and precisely study the affective or cognitive mediators of such impulsive altruism because it occurs suddenly and unexpectedly, before researchers can assess what is going on in the minds or guts of the good Samaritan prior to the decision to do good for another human being.

Psychology Beyond the Individual

The social problems presented in this chapter and the suggestions for dealing with them move us a long way beyond the traditional view of psychology as the study of individual actions and mental processes. We become aware of the person as only one level in a complex system that includes social groups, institutions, cultural values, historical circumstances, political and economic realities, and specific situational forces. Modern social psychologists have expanded the domain of their inquiry to include this broader network of interacting elements. Many new areas of application have opened up to both the curious investigator and the social change agent (see Fisher, 1982).

Psychological knowledge is applied in many different areas, holding the potential for enriching all concerned. In addition, this expansion of psychology's relevance to life problems provides greater opportunities and challenges to psychologists just beginning their professional careers (perhaps *you* in the near future?).

Among the new liaisons are psychology and law; psychology and education; psychology and health care; psychology and politics (international relations, terrorism, conflict, public policy); psychology and the consumer; psychology and business; the union of psychology and environmental issues; and a field of importance to everyone on the planet, peace psychology. In this final phase of our journey, we will briefly examine a selection of these areas of application (see Oskamp, 1984 and Rodin, 1985 for more applications of social psychology to everyday life).

Areas of Application

Three areas in which psychological knowledge is now being applied to the study of social problems are psychology and law, psychology and education, and environmental psychology. We discussed the first of these areas in chapter 9 (see the ***Close-up*** on pp. 328–29). In this section we examine the other two areas.

Psychology and Education

Much that occurs in the educational process involves the psychology of the classroom. Peer interactions, teacher-student relationships, and the expectations of both teachers and students affect the amount of learning that takes place and the feelings of students about the learning process. Students as learners respond to the ecology of the classroom, to pressures toward competition, to curriculum design, to educational technology, and to a school's organizational goals and strategies. Psychology's contributions to education should go well beyond a concern for simply reinforcing correct responding and improving basic skills (see Glaser, 1984).

One of the new discoveries that will eventually affect learning in the classroom is the finding that different psychological principles affect different kinds of learning outcomes: intellectual skills (procedural knowledge), verbal information (declarative knowledge), cognitive strategies, motor skills, and attitudes (Gagne, 1984). The next step will be to systematically study the procedures that can best foster each of these five kinds of outcomes in natural settings, rather than to treat them all as variations of a common educational theme as teachers now do. Another current focus of research is to find a way to incorporate the new technologies represented by microcomputers and the instant feedback of video games into the instructional process (Malone & Lepper, 1987).

Psychologists are well aware of the importance of the classroom climate to educate the whole person; social, cognitive, and developmental psychologists are all working on ways to develop better classroom climates (Bar-Tal & Saxe, 1978). Too often, a school environment fosters interpersonal competition and provides a breeding ground for envy, jealousy, hostility, and self-derogation.

Elliot Aronson and his colleagues (1978) reasoned that, by creating conditions in which students must depend on one another for learning required material, teachers would be able to overcome some of the unnecessary conflicts that often exist in classrooms.

> *Working with fifth-graders, they developed a "jigsaw" technique to promote cooperation. Each pupil was given part of the total material to master and then share with other group members. Performance was evaluated on the basis of the overall group presentation. Thus every member's contribution was essential and valued. Pupils were made to feel like team workers rather than competitors, and those in desegregated settings discovered the advantages of sharing knowledge (and friendship) with "equal and interdependent" peers—regardless of race, creed, or sex.*

This method of changing classroom climate has had positive results in a number of schools. It has improved student and teacher morale as well as providing a better level of academic performance. In addition, interracial conflict has decreased in classes where jigsawing united formerly hostile students in a "common fate" (Gonzales, 1983).

"Jigsawing" promotes cooperation and teamwork.

Another school problem for which psychologists are contributing solutions is that of vandalism. Hundreds of millions of dollars are spent annually to repair the damage done to our schools by "vandals." Efforts aimed at identifying and punishing these elusive destroyers of public property have not lessened the problem.

> *Working on the assumption that school vandalism is a symptom of student dissatisfaction with the school, a team of psychologists set out to transform those negative feelings into positive ones. They trained teachers in 18 different schools to praise and positively reinforce appropriate behavior instead of punishing and ridiculing unacceptable behavior as they usually did. As the teachers began to accentuate the positive, the students started to eliminate the negative. Hitting, throwing objects, lack of attention, and uncompleted assigned projects declined. Teachers were happier and so were more students. This improved atmosphere carried over into other classrooms where the teachers had not received special reinforcement training. What effect did all these good vibrations have on vandalism? Over a three-year period, school costs because of vandalism decreased by 75 percent. (Mayer et al., 1983)*

Environmental Psychology

Systematic study of the effects of the larger environment on behavior (in contrast to specific stimuli) began in the 1950s with studies of behavior in psychiatric wards, where different physical arrangements seemed to produce different behavior on the part of the patients. Such studies have led to the new field of *environmental psychology* (Proshansky, 1976). Environmental psychologists study the relationships between psychological processes and physical environments, both natural and humanmade (Darley & Gilbert, 1985).

Environmental psychologists use an *ecological approach* to study the way people and environments affect each other. The ecological approach emphasizes the reciprocity and mutual influence in an organism-environment relationship. Organism and environment influence each other, and both keep changing as a result. We see a circular pattern; humans change the natural environment and create physical and social structures. These, in turn, confine, direct, and change us, encouraging certain behaviors, while discouraging or preventing others, often in unanticipated ways.

Environmental psychology is oriented not so much toward past determinants as toward the future that is being created. This means, in turn, that it has to be concerned with values. Some environments are more nourishing for us than others, and some uses of the environment, as we have discovered, are destructive. This new psychology is concerned with identifying what makes environments supportive and what human behaviors will create those environments—while not trespassing on the health of the ecosystem that makes life possible in the first place (see Russell & Ward, 1982).

Environmental psychologists use an ecological approach to make a city more liveable for its inhabitants.

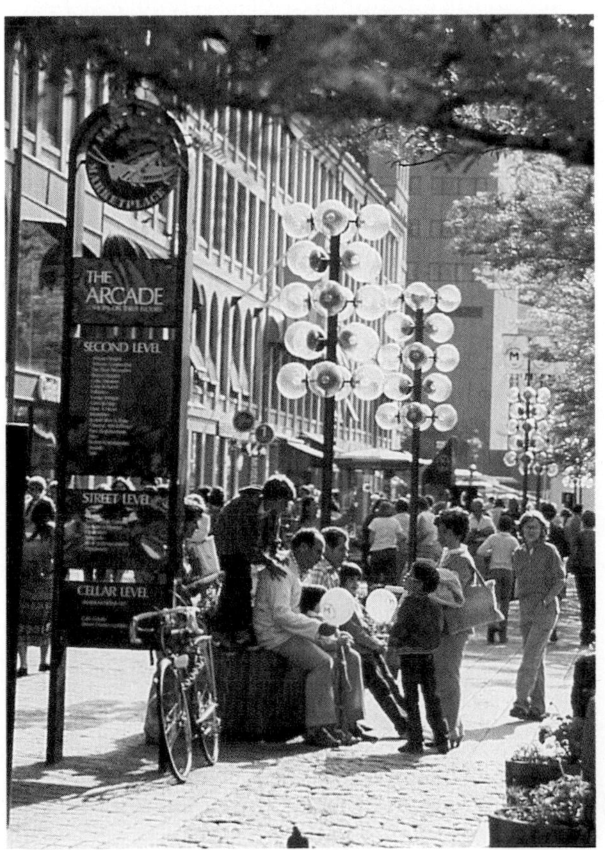

There is ample evidence of the influence of physical design on psychological activities and processes. Different physical arrangements have been studied in hospital settings, work places, homes, and whole cities. Different moods, self-images, and overt behaviors are consistently found to be related to these physical differences.

The way space is partitioned can help bring people together or isolate them. The type of windows in an apartment house can encourage residents to look out at activities on their streets and "keep an eye on the neighborhood" or, if they are small and high, can cut off such "people watching." An architect can design space to appeal to snobbery, to invite informality, or to induce confusion (Altman, 1976).

Can we make our cities more livable? What features of the environment encourage vandalism and crime? Does crowding cause physical and social pathology? What is the impact of uncontrollable levels of noise in the work place or the home? Can psychological knowledge contribute to energy conservation programs? These are among the intriguing questions being studied by environmental psychologists. By reformulating massive social issues into smaller, less overwhelming problems, social psychologists are beginning to get small wins that can add up to big victories (Weick, 1984).

Peace Psychology

Psychologists for Social Responsibility is an organization of psychologists who not only study various aspects of the complex issues involved in war and peace, but conduct educational programs on these topics for professionals, schoolchildren, and the lay public. In addition, they try to have input to relevant political decision-making policies at state and national levels. This is just one example of the dual roles that many psychologists have chosen to play: as dedicated, objective scientists and, at other times, as committed, impassioned advocates of social-political action based on knowledge and personal values.

How to help resolve the dilemmas of superpower competition—or, for that matter, many of the domestic and international problems that we now face—poses challenges that psychology is uniquely equipped to study. **Peace psychology** represents an interdisciplinary approach to prevention of nuclear war and maintenance of peace (see Plous, 1987). Psychologists committed to contributing their talents and energies to this area so vital to our future draw upon the work of investigators in many areas. Among them are political scientists, economists, physicists, mathematicians, computer scientists, anthropologists, climatologists, and physicians.

Some of these psychologists are conducting research that examines the basis for false beliefs, misperceptions, and erroneous attributions on issues germane to nuclear arms, military strength, risk, and national security. Fears of children and anxieties of adults about nuclear war are also being studied. Exploring some of the individual and cultural forces that create war and promote peace involves studies of propaganda and images of the enemy through content and fantasy analysis of violence and war themes in the media. Terrorism is being studied as a political-psychological phenomenon; it is also being examined from a psychohistorical perspective.

A Peace Psychology Sampler

Psychologists from many different orientations are working to promote peace through their research efforts that foster a better understanding of relevant aspects of human behavior. We will examine four of the directions being taken by some peace psychologists. For quite some time, social scientists have been investigating simulated arms negotiations, international crisis management, and conflict resolution strategies. They have been developing experimental gaming studies to test the utility of different models of the nuclear arms race between the United States and the Soviet Union. These studies use the beliefs and strategies of individual protagonists as the behavioral data that might ultimately motivate the political decisions of national leaders. Personality analyses of these people suggest that their drive for power may be the impetus for nuclear arms race. Finally, many researchers are studying psychological aspects of nuclear war—its fears, concerns, and basis for citizen action or failure to become involved.

Arms negotiations or international crises are simulated to resemble hypothetical or historical situations. Participants are divided into bilateral or multilateral teams, often with internal decision hierarchies and "domestic" constraints on their bargaining positions (Guetzkow et al., 1963). By varying factors such as the opening position, the presence or absence of an intermediary, or the amount of emphasis on verification, parallel negotiations can be compared by the patterns of cooperation or competition they produce. These simulations also generate new negotiating strategies and techniques for crisis management.

A similar approach has been to analyze the historical record of actual negotiations and crises. One such project, directed by psychologist Irving Janis and political scientist Richard Ned Lebow, has led to some interesting preliminary results. Janis and Lebow categorized the quality of decision making in 19 major international crises since World War II. Characterizing these decisions along seven independent dimensions, the researchers found a strong relationship between the way decisions were made and whether or not international conflict intensified. Janis and Lebow also found that "defective decision making" predominated in more than a third of the crises, and they suggested various safeguards to ensure better decision making in future crises (Fisher, 1985).

Some psychologists believe that to affect policy making toward nuclear war, it is necessary to study the way those in authority have handled nuclear crises, the most feared events that are least well understood by those in charge of nuclear weapons. By learning how decision makers have made sense of events that could have led to nuclear war, psychologists may be in a position to offer more fully formed decision rules that minimize cognitive and motivational biases of policy makers. The goal is to prevent future crises through an understanding of past and current crises management (Blight, 1987).

Yet another major area of psychological peace research involves experimental gaming. "Games" do not refer to light-hearted play, but to strategic interactions between individuals or groups. With respect to the nuclear arms race, the game that has been studied most extensively is the "Prisoner's Dilemma."

In its original form, the Prisoner's Dilemma describes a situation in which two criminals are caught and put into separate cells. The prisoners are told that if they inform on their partner, they will be released and their counterpart will be severely sentenced. Conversely, if they are silent while their partner confesses, they will be heavily sentenced and their partner will go free. If both prisoners confess, each will receive a moderate sentence, and if neither talk, they will each be sentenced lightly. The dilemma is that each prisoner is better off by confessing—regardless of what the partner does—but if both confess, the outcome is worse than if both remain silent.

When modeled as a Prisoner's Dilemma, the nuclear arms race is typically cast as a conflict solely between the United States and the Soviet Union. Each superpower has two choices: (a) to continue arming (a competitive choice equivalent to turning informant in the original Prisoner's Dilemma), or (b) to initiate some form of disarmament (a cooperative choice equivalent to remaining silent). As in the case of the prisoners, each side will do better by competing, yet if both countries arm, neither will do as well as if both disarm. Unfortunately, if one side recognizes the problem and moves to cooperate, it must not only disarm unilaterally until the other country reciprocates, but, in the very act of disarming, it must allow the other side to pursue unilateral armament—thereby removing any immediate incentive for the other side to cooperate. Because of the way these payoffs are structured, mutual cooperation is usually very difficult to achieve.

A more hopeful model of the nuclear arms race is the Perceptual Dilemma. Originally based on survey research with U.S. senators, the Perceptual Dilemma portrays the present arms race primarily as a consequence of misperception rather than conflicting interests (Plous, 1985). In a Perceptual Dilemma, both sides prefer mutual disarmament to all other outcomes, but because each *believes* that the other side prefers unilateral armament, neither is willing to initiate disarmament. Unlike a Prisoner's Dilemma, a Perceptual Dilemma can be resolved when either country realizes that its preference for peace is shared by the other side. Once either side in a Perceptual Dilemma begins to disarm clearly and consistently, it is in the other side's interest to follow suit shortly thereafter.

From a psychodynamic perspective, the impetus for the nuclear arms race is the drive for personal power among national leaders (Frank, 1987). Some of their errors of judgment are seen as deriving from the constellation of personality traits which characterize most superpower leaders—toughness, persuasiveness, suspiciousness, optimism, and competitiveness. Faced with the difficulty of changing the very traits that make the leaders successful in many aspects of their jobs, psychologists stress the need to promote awareness of superordinate goals that leaders can agree upon, such as destruction of the ozone layer of the atmosphere by pollutants. Also there is a need to provide effective alternatives for violence as the ultimate expression of power.

Finally, many researchers are focusing their attention on the sociopsychological effects of nuclear war—how people perceive and respond to its threat and why citizens who are fearful of nuclear destruction do not get involved in activities to promote peace (Allen, 1985; Fiske, 1987). Nuclear concern is lowest among men and greatest among children, women, and college students, according to a review of more than 50 studies since 1945. However, nuclear fears have been found to exert little impact on either political preferences or political behavior despite the belief that nuclear war is not survivable.

Why are reasonable fears not translated into responsible action and what can be done to increase the nuclear concerns of young and middle-aged men? Psychological analysis indicates that nuclear war should be presented in terms of human suffering, not abstract aspects of material losses, as it is typically portrayed. Individuals also feel ineffective and without means of control over this fearful outcome which they perceive to be in the hands of remote leaders making political decisions. The anxiety-arousing aspects of messages about nuclear destruction must be balanced against some concrete proposals for politically effective action that ordinary citizens can take. By making national leaders more responsive to the concerns of the electorate, nuclear war decisions can become political decisions shared by the public, not the exclusive province of the few world leaders entrusted with the survival of the planet. (See also "Nice Guys Finish First" in *The Best of Science.*)

Future Promises

This new brand of psychology is quite different from that envisioned by Wilhelm Wundt in his little brass-instrument laboratory in Leipzig over 100 years ago. Today we are witnessing a curious merger between scientific understanding and humanistic involvement, between dispassionate analysis and social advocacy. It is only when these elements coalesce, fusing to form one discipline, that "psychology and life" are truly integrated. In a peace-filled world, psychology is poised to make great strides toward understanding human nature and enhancing human potential. Unless conditions can be created that avert war and the debilitating effects of its constant threat, psychology can do little more than prepare us for the inevitability of life lived in the flickering light of fall-out shelters. An optimistic psychologist looks up while a pragmatic psychologist tries to prevent any backsliding; together both hold out the promise of a future where bombs will not destroy our rainbows. ***Psychology and Life*** ends on this somber note of idealism with the hope that any new understanding of human nature gained from research and the practice of psychology will enrich our lives and contribute to the healthy, peaceful longevity of individuals and their nations.

Summary

- The same perceptual, cognitive, motor, and other potentials that enable us to create, solve problems, and relate constructively to each other also enable us to destroy and cause pain to ourselves and others. We all have potentials for both prosocial and antisocial behavior; for altruism and aggression.
- Freud saw aggression as inborn and instinctive, with catharsis as necessary to release pent-up aggressive feelings. Ethologists argue that the territoriality observed in animals is the basis for human aggression. There is new evidence that aggressiveness and altruism are partly inherited temperaments. Physiological psychologists cite the effects of tumors and other brain events to produce aggressive behavior. Other psychologists postulate a link between physical environmental conditions and aggressive behavior.
- Aggression has also been seen as a natural response to frustration, though, in some cases, practical realities prevent overt aggression or lead to displacement of the aggression onto safe targets. Cues in the situation, such as the presence of weapons, combined with an inner readiness to be aggressive, play an important role in triggering hostile actions.
- Aggressive behavior may be learned through reinforcement, social norms, or by imitating the aggressive behavior of others. Though catharsis—expression of emotional feelings—may lessen such feelings, expressing aggressive impulses or watching aggressive behavior in others increases the probability of future aggression.
- From watching violence on TV, children develop a negative view of social reality, seeing violence as acceptable, exaggerating the threat of violence in their own lives, and becoming more fearful and less likely to intervene to stop violence by others.
- Despite the conclusions of the U.S. Attorney General's Commission on Pornography, there is no evidence of a *causal* relationship between pornography and sexual violence. However, previously existing negative attitudes may be strengthened by exposure to pornographic materials.
- We tend to believe that atrocities are the work of evil people, failing to realize the power of the social situation and the strength of our habit of obedience. Milgram's research demonstrated that most people will obey a recognized authority despite the belief that they are causing suffering and perhaps death to another person; they may dissent, but most will not disobey.
- Obedience is fostered by the presence of a legitimate authority, a relationship in which one is in a subordinate position, the presence of social norms supporting it, the redefinition of the evil acts as good, and a situation which is ambiguous.
- Aggression and other antisocial behavior increase under conditions of deindividuation. Deindividuation lowers an individual's inhibitions against both antisocial behavior and prosocial forms of emotional expression. Diffusion of responsibility lowers public self-awareness and increases the probability of antisocial behavior. Reduced private self-awareness, through heightened emotional arousal or alteration in states of consciousness, also increases the probability of more aggressive and socially inappropriate behavior.
- Dehumanization may be imposed as a coping strategy by individuals or groups in self-defense; it may be socially imposed by those in political or economic power; or it may be rationalized as a means to an end. Through the process of moral disengagement, reprehensible conduct and its destructive effects are disconnected from the moral standards and internal controls that usually regulate behavior.
- A number of incidents have demonstrated that victims of assault often go unaided by bystanders. Studies of this phenomenon indicate that bystanders are more likely to intervene to help if they have previously seen someone in a similar situation giving aid, see the situation as a clear emergency, believe that the victim is trying to help him- or herself, and are familiar with the surroundings.
- Altruism involves behaving in ways that increase the interests, safety, or survival of others at the risk of sacrificing one's own interests, safety, or survival. Biological perspectives suggest an evolutionary adaptiveness of altruism within groups. Other determinants of altruism that are being studied are cultural, personality, situational factors as well as affective and cognitive mediators.
- Applications of psychology are occurring in many fields today. Among these are the use of psychological principles in the educational system to improve teaching methods and climates for learning, studies of the way people and environments affect each other, and strategies to maintain peace and prevent nuclear war. Techniques used in the study and promotion of peace psychology include analysis of historical records, interviews, and questionnaire studies of fears about nuclear war, simulations of arms negotiations and crisis management, and experimental gaming.

A Postscript: Psychology and You

Well, you've come a long way on this journey that has introduced you to the field of psychology. A lot of words have passed between us. Now is the time to reflect upon what in all this study of human nature is of significance to you.

You will soon be given your final examination to test your memory for definitions, facts, concepts, experiments, and extensions of the information contained in this book. After the examination, will you do a "memory dump"? Will you erase that information base so you'll have room for new input? I hope not. I'd like to believe instead that you have come to realize what is behind all the fancy definitions, abstract concepts, and fascinating little experiments. It is *YOU!* Psychology is the study of the way *you* think, the way *you* feel, and the way *you* act. What motivates you to do what you do? Why do you hold the attitudes and values you do? What makes you become depressed? On what are your decisions and attributions based—and biased? Can you change a troublesome aspect of your life-style? How can you best relate to other people?

Psychology can help answer these questions. Read some more; there is a sizable reference list at the back of this book. Take some more psychology courses. Which topics did you find most interesting? If you liked a particular chapter best, you can probably take a whole course that expands upon it. While you're at it, why not consider the possibility of taking a minor or co-major in psychology? Psychology complements virtually every field of knowledge and every career, including art, business, medicine, education, law, architecture, psychiatry, and politics.

If you are really "turned on" about the prospect of becoming a professional psychologist and would like to be able to design and conduct original research, treat patients, counsel clients, administer tests, or teach psychology to others, you should seek advice from the psychology department at your school. Someone there can tell you about the advantages and procedures for majoring in psychology. Whatever the state of the economy, there are always good positions available to creative, curious thinkers and energetic contributors to psychological knowledge.

Psychology has been a constant source of joy to me during the many years since I first declared my major at Brooklyn College. The more I learned in graduate school at Yale University, the more and better questions I was able to ask. Since then, my students at New York University and Stanford University have been helping me find some of the answers we've shared in *Psychology and Life.*

Psychology poses intriguing challenges and returns enormous rewards, both intellectual and emotional, to those who accept them. What could be more exciting and satisfying than discovering the neural basis of memory, the way to treat schizophrenia or depression, to cope with stress, to reduce violence, to promote health, to find out how to help people love their neighbors and to like themselves? These challenges await *you*—if you choose to continue on the next phase of your journey into more advanced levels of psychology.

Playwright Tom Stoppard reminds us that "Every exit is an entry somewhere else." In exiting from *Psychology and Life,* I hope you will begin a new journey better prepared for life because of what you have learned and better able to put new life into the psychology everywhere that makes up the essence of human nature.

Phil Zimbardo

Glossary

References

Acknowledgments

Name Index

Subject Index

Glossary

A

Absolute Threshold The minimum amount of physical energy needed to reliably produce a sensory experience (p. 145)

Accommodation A process of restructuring or modifying cognitive structures so that the new information can fit more easily into them; also, the process by which the ciliary muscles change the thickness of the lens to permit variable focusing for near and distant objects (p. 77; 152)

Achievement Tests Standardized tests designed to measure an individual's current level of competence in a given area (p. 483)

Acquired Drives Learned motivational states (p. 382)

Action Potential A nerve impulse activated in an axon when the graded potential that reaches the axon is above a certain threshold (p. 114)

Actor-Observer Bias The tendency of actors in a situation to attribute the causes of their own behavior to situational influences while observers tend to attribute the same actions to dispositional influences (p. 614)

Addiction A physical state in which the body requires the presence of a certain drug and withdrawal symptoms occur if the drug is not present (p. 248)

Adolescence A stage of life commonly defined as beginning at the onset of puberty when sexual maturity or the ability to reproduce is attained (p. 91)

Adrenocorticotrophic Hormone (ACTH) A pituitary hormone which stimulates the adrenal cortex to release hormones important in metabolic processes and in physiological reactions to prolonged stress (p. 499)

Affect Emotion or mood state (p. 71)

Affective Disorders Disorders in which the primary symptoms are associated with mood disturbances such as excessive depression, excessive elation, or both (p. 536)

Afterimage A visual sensation occurring after a stimulus has ended (p. 156)

Age Regression A technique used during hypnosis in which a hypnotized individual receives suggestions that he or she is "returning" to an earlier period in life (p. 246)

Aggression Physical or verbal behavior with the intent to injure or destroy (p. 643)

Agoraphobia A type of phobia in which there is a fear of being in public places or away from familiar surroundings (p. 529)

Algorithm A rote procedure for solving problems in which every possible solution is tried; guaranteed to lead to a correct solution eventually if there is one (p. 360)

All-or-None Principle Property of axon firing in which a uniform action potential is generated when a threshold has been reached, and no nerve impulse is generated when it has not been reached (p. 114)

Altruism Putting the welfare, interests, and survival of others above one's own (p. 668)

Amoral Lacking in understanding of people's responsibilities to each other; neither moral nor immoral (p. 87)

Amplitude The physical property of strength of a sound wave, as measured by its peak-to-valley height (p. 167)

Amygdala Portion of the limbic system; brain center for aggression (p. 131)

Anal Stage Second of Freud's psychosexual developmental stages; during this stage (approximately 2 years of age) gratification comes primarily from the elimination process (p. 89)

Anterograde Amnesia A type of amnesia in which there is a loss of the ability to form memories for newly presented facts (p. 332)

Antisocial Personality Disorder Personality disorder in which the symptoms include an absence of conscience and a sense of responsibility to others (p. 527)

Anxiety An intense emotional response caused by the preconscious recognition that a repressed conflict is about to emerge into consciousness (p. 435)

Anxiety Disorders Mental disorders marked by physiological arousal and feelings of tension, tremor, shaking, and intense apprehension without reason (p. 527)

Anxiety States Neurotic disorders in which anxiety occurs in the absence of specific phobias (p. 530)

Apparent Motion A movement illusion in which one or more stationary lights going on and off in succession are perceived as a single moving light; also called the *phi phenomenon* (p. 202)

Appetitive Conditioning Classical conditioning procedures in which the unconditioned stimulus is of positive value to the organism (p. 266)

Applied Research Research undertaken with the explicit goal of finding solutions to practical problems (p. 11)

Aptitude Tests Tests designed to measure an individual's potential for acquiring various skills (p. 482)

Archetype In Jungian personality theory, a universal, inherited, primitive, symbolic representation of a particular experience or object; part of the collective unconscious (p. 436)

Archival Research A research method in which an investigator uses previously published findings or data already existing in documents, books, or cultural artifacts in order to determine the relationship between certain variables (p. 46)

Artificial Intelligence (AI) "Computer thought"; computer programs that can make the kinds of judgments humans make (p. 364)

Assimilation A process whereby new cognitive elements are fitted; the new elements may be modified to fit more easily (p. 77)

Association Psychology View associated with John Locke and other seventeenth-century British philosophers which emphasizes the role of experience of mental growth by holding that most knowledge and abilities are determined by experience (p. 259)

Associationism The view, developed by the British empirical philosophers, that ideals arose from sensory experiences and that thought and memory were composed of chains of these ideas (p. 12)

Attachment A close emotional relationship between a child and the regular caregiver; inferred from behaviors that elicit and maintain nearness between the two (p. 82)

Attention A state of focused awareness accompanied by sensory clearness and a central nervous system readiness to response (p. 224)

Attitude A learned, relatively stable tendency to respond to people, concepts, and events in an evaluative way (p. 268; 617)

Attribution Theory A cognitive approach that is influential in understanding individual and social behavior which emphasizes inferences about the causes of behavior (p. 607)

Audition The sensation of hearing (p. 167)

Auditory Cortex Area of the temporal lobes of the cerebral hemisphere which receives and processes auditory signals (p. 132; p. 170)

Auditory Nerve The nerve that carries impulses from the cochlea to the cochlear nucleus of the brain (p. 170)

Augmentation Principle Principle which states that, if an outcome occurred despite powerful factors working against it, the causes that produced the outcome are seen as particularly powerful (p. 611)

Authoritarian Parenting A style of parenting characterized by restrictive control without warmth or open parent-child dialogue (p. 85)

Authoritative Parenting Style of parenting in which firm parental control is combined with warmth, open communication, and shared decisions (p. 85)

Autohypnosis The practice of inducing a hypnotic state in oneself (p. 244)

Autokinetic Effect A visual illusion in which a stationary point of light in a dark room appears to move slowly from its initial position (p. 202)

Automaticity In information processing, an apparently effortless, involuntary process triggered without a person's supporting intention to engage in it (p. 228)

Autonomic Nervous System The part of the peripheral nervous system that governs activities not normally under voluntary control, such as processes of bodily maintenance (p. 123)

Availability Heuristic A heuristic for estimating probabilities, based on dependence on one's personal experience (p. 353)

Aversion Therapy A type of behavioral therapy used for individuals attracted to harmful stimuli in which procedures of aversive learning are used to pair a presently attractive substance with other noxious stimuli in order to elicit a negative reaction in the presence of the target substance (p. 573)

Aversive Conditioning Classical conditioning procedures in which an unconditioned stimulus is of negative value to an organism (p. 266)

Axon Extended fiber of a neuron in which nerve impulses occur; transmits signals from the soma to the terminal buttons (p. 111)

B

Backward Conditioning Temporal pattern in classical conditioning in which a conditioned stimulus comes on after an unconditioned stimulus (p. 264)

Backward Masking A phenomenon in which a sensory stimulus presented within a certain time interval after another similar stimulus has already been presented erases or masks the perception or processing of the first stimulus (p. 306)

Barbiturates A group of drugs classified as depressants and used in low doses to reduce anxiety and in higher doses for sleep induction (p. 250)

Base Rate A statistic that identifies the normally occurring frequency of a given event (p. 9)

Basic Level The optimal level of categorization for thinking about an object; it is the level that can be accessed from memory most quickly and used most efficiently (p. 346)

Basic Research Research undertaken to study a phenomenon or processes for accurate and comprehensive knowledge initially without regard to later practical applications (p. 10)

Basilar Membrane A membrane in the cochlea which, when set into motion, stimulates hair cells which produce the neural effects of auditory stimulation (p. 170)

Behavioral Contingency Conditioning approach of B. F. Skinner in which, by systematic variation of stimulus conditions, all the ways that various kinds of experience affect the probability of responses are discovered (p. 274)

Behavioral Contract An explicit agreement (often in writing) that states the consequences of specific behaviors (p. 574)

Behavioral Rehearsal All the procedures used to establish and strengthen any basic skills; often used in social skills training programs (p. 577)

Behavior Assessment A method of personality assessment in which specific, current, observable behaviors are identified and rated by judges to yield a personality profile (p. 476)

Behavior Genetics A field of research that attempts to identify genetic components in behavioral traits (p. 66)

Behaviorism A scientific approach formulated by John B. Watson that views measurable or observable behavior as psychology (p. 18)

Behavioristic Model A psychological model that is primarily concerned with visible behavior and its relationships to environmental stimulation. Behaviorally oriented investigators attempt to understand the way particular environmental stimuli control certain kinds of behavior (p. 18)

Behavior Modification A behavioral psychotherapeutic approach that involves the use of operant and classical conditioning procedures to eliminate unwanted responses and reinforce desired ones (p. 571)

Bias An unwanted systematic source of error in scientific results and conclusions as a result of factors not related to the variables being studied or measured (p. 31)

Binocular Disparity The displacement between the horizontal positions of corresponding images in the two eyes (p. 203)

Biofeedback Training A procedure by which an individual acquires voluntary control over nonconscious biological processes by receiving information about successful changes (p. 284)

Biological Constraint on Learning Any limitation on an organism's capacity to learn that is caused by the inherited sensory, response, or cognitive capabilities of members of a given species (p. 288)

Biomedical Therapies The group of therapies used to treat psychological disorders that focus on changing biological or physical mechanisms that may be associated with specific disorders (p. 563)

Bipolar Cells Nerve cells that combine impulses from many receptors and send the results to ganglion cells (p. 153)

Blindsight Visually guided behavior that is not consciously occurring in individuals whose visual cortex has been removed (p. 154)

Blind Spot Region of the retina which contains no photoreceptor cells because it is the place where the optic nerve leaves the eye (p. 153)

Blocking A phenomenon in which the ability of a new stimulus to signal an unconditioned stimulus is not learned when it is presented simultaneously with a stimulus that is already effective as a signal (p. 290)

Blood-Brain Barrier A semipermeable membrane that keeps foreign substances in the bloodstream from flowing into the brain (p. 112; 248)

Body Image One's subjective experience of the way one's body looks (p. 94)

Bottom-up Processes Processes in perception in which incoming stimulus information is interpreted as coming from sensory data and sent upward to the brain for extraction and analysis of relevant information (p. 188)

Bradykinin The most potent pain-producing chemical known, involved in the body's sensation of pain (p. 178)

Brain Stem Hindbrain structure in front of the cerebellum which contains the reticular activating system (RAS) and structures involved in the control of basic life processes (p. 130)

Brightness The dimension of color space that captures the intensity of light (p. 156)

Burnout A syndrome of emotional exhaustion in which an individual loses concern and emotional feeling as a result of continuing emotional arousal and stress (p. 495)

C

Cardinal Trait A trait around which a person organizes his or her life (p. 426)

Case Studies Extensive biographies of selected individuals; many kinds of data may be collected from a variety of sources (p. 45)

Catch Trial Trial on which no stimulus is presented; a technique used to determine whether response biases are operating in sensory detection tasks (p. 147)
Catharsis The process and beneficial effect of expressing strongly felt, but usually inhibited, emotions (p. 569; 644)
Causal Theory Beliefs people have about which factors can bring about a particular outcome and which factors cannot (p. 609)
Cell Assemblies Term for groups of neurons acting together as a consequence of particular, repeated stimulation; theory proposed by Donald Hebb (p. 109)
Central Nervous System (CNS) The part of the nervous system consisting of the brain and spinal cord (p. 122)
Central Sulcus A vertical groove that serves to divide the cerebral hemispheres into lobes (p. 132)
Central Trait A major characteristic of a person that is assumed to be basic to an understanding of the individual (p. 426)
Centration A thought pattern common during the beginning of the preoperational stage of cognitive development; characterized by the inability of a child to take more than one perceptual factor into account at the same time (p. 78)
Cerebellum A structure under the back of the cerebrum which controls balance and motor coordination (p. 130)
Cerebral Cortex See *cerebrum.*
Cerebral Dominance The tendency for one cerebral hemisphere to play a more dominant role than the other in controlling particular functions (p. 232)
Cerebral Hemispheres The two halves of the cerebrum, connected by the corpus callosum (p. 131)
Cerebrum The upper part of the brain; covered by the cerebral cortex, the outer surface of folds and deep grooves (p. 131)
Chaining An operant procedure in which many different responses in a sequence are reinforced until an effective chain of behaviors has been learned (p. 281)
Chemotherapy The use of drugs to treat mental and behavioral disorders (p. 589)
Chromosomes Large molecules consisting of double strands of DNA and proteins, which contain the genes responsible for hereditary traits. Every human cell contains 46 chromosomes except the germ cells which contain only 23 (p. 66)
Chronic Stress A state of arousal, continuing over time, in which an individual perceives demands as greater than the inner and outer resources available for dealing with them (p. 497)
Chronological Age (CA) The number of months or years since birth (p. 63; 462)
Chunk A meaningful unit of information (p. 308)
Chunking The process of taking single items of information and recoding them by grouping on the basis of similarity or some other organizing principle (p. 308)
Ciliary Muscles Structures attached to the edge of the lens which control its shape (p. 151)
Circadian Rhythm The consistent pattern of cyclical body activities that lasts approximately 24 hours and is determined by an internal "biological clock" (p. 239)
Classical Conditioning A form of learning in which behavior (conditioned response) comes to be elicited by a stimulus (conditioned stimulus) that has acquired its power through an association with a biologically significant stimulus (unconditioned stimulus); also called *Pavlovian* or *respondent conditioning* (p. 261)
Classification Processes which identify and label perceptual objects as members of meaningful categories (for example, *cars, trees,* or *people*) (p. 186)
Clinical Psychologist An individual who has earned a doctorate in psychology and whose training is in the assessment and treatment of psychological problems; unlike a psychiatrist, a psychologist cannot prescribe medications or physical treatments (p. 564)
Clinical Psychology The field of psychology specializing in the psychological treatment of individuals with mental and behavioral disorders (p. 519)
Closure A perceptual organizing process as a result of which one tends to see incomplete figures as complete (p. 197)
Cochlea A fluid-filled organ in the inner ear that is the primary organ of hearing (p. 170)
Cognition The processes of knowing, including attending, remembering, and reasoning; also the content of these processes, such as concepts and memories (p. 337)
Cognitive Appraisal Recognition and evaluation of a stressor by which one assesses what the demand is, the size of the threat, the resources available for dealing with it, and the strategies which are appropriate (p. 496)
Cognitive Behavior Modification Therapeutic approach combining the cognitive emphasis on the importance of thoughts and attitudes to influence motivation and response with the behavioral focus on changing performance through modification of reinforcement contingencies (p. 579)
Cognitive Bias A systematic way of thinking that generally works but may result in errors in drawing inferences or making decisions or judgments when an individual fails to discriminate between appropriate and inappropriate conditions for its use (p. 353)
Cognitive Development The development of processes of knowing including imagining, perceiving, reasoning, and problem solving (p. 76)
Cognitive Dissonance A tension-reduction theory about the motivating effects of discrepant or incongruous cognitions and about the ways individuals attempt to reduce this tension (p. 619)
Cognitive Map A mental representation of physical space (p. 295; 349)
Cognitive Model A psychological model that emphasizes and studies the mental processes intervening between stimulus input and overt responses (p. 19)
Cognitive Psychology The study of the higher mental processes and structures (p. 337)
Cognitive Science An interdisciplinary field, a broad approach to studying systems and processes which manipulate information (p. 338)
Cognitive Therapies Psychotherapeutic treatments that attempt to change problem feelings and behaviors by changing the way a client thinks about or perceives significant life experiences (p. 579)
Cohort A group of individuals defined as similar in some way (for example, a birth cohort, individuals born the same year) (p. 61)
Collective Unconscious In Jungian personality theory, that part of an individual's unconscious which is inherited, evolutionarily developed, and common to all members of the species (p. 436)
Color Blindness An inability to distinguish between some or all of the colors in the color solid (p. 158)
Color Space A three-dimensional model for describing color experience in terms of hue, saturation, and brightness (p. 155)
Complementary Colors Colors opposite each other on the color circle (p. 156)
Compliance Conforming one's outward behavior to that of others in order to avoid punishment or rejection by members of a valued group (p. 622)
Compulsion An undesired repetitive act carried out in stereotypic, ritualistic fashion and one which the individual feels compelled to act out (p. 531)
Compulsive Personality Disorder Personality disorder marked by an excessive concern with rules, roles, trivia, and work, and an inability to express warm and tender emotions (p. 525)
Concepts Mental representations of kinds or categories of things; formed through experience with the world (p. 344)
Concordance Rate The extent to which both members of a set of twins share a particular characteristic or trait used in assessing heritability (p. 550)
Concrete Operational Stage Third of Piaget's cognitive developmental stages (from 7–11 years); characterized by un-

derstanding of conservation and readiness for other mental operations involving concrete objects (p. 79)

Conditioned Reinforcer In instrumental conditioning, a formerly neutral stimulus that has become a reinforcer (p. 278)

Conditioned Response (CR) In classical conditioning, a response elicited by some previously neutral stimulus; occurs as a result of pairing the neutral stimulus with an unconditioned stimulus (p. 263)

Conditioned Stimulus (CS) In classical conditioning, the previously neutral stimulus which comes to elicit a conditioned response (p. 263)

Conditioning Trial In classical conditioning, the pairing of a neutral, to-be-conditioned stimulus with an unconditioned stimulus (p. 263)

Cones Photoreceptors concentrated in the center of the retina which are responsible for visual experience under normal viewing conditions and for all experiences of color (p. 153)

Conformity The tendency for people to adopt the behavior, attitudes, and values of other members of a reference group (p. 632)

Confounding Variable Something that changes a subject's behavior other than the variable an experimenter explicitly introduces into a research setting (p. 33)

Consciousness The state of awareness of internal events and of the external environment (p. 221)

Consensual Validation Mutual affirmation of views of reality (p. 216; 222)

Consensus Criterion A criterion used when deciding whether an action should be attributed to situational or dispositional factors; it involves deciding whether most people would have behaved in a similar or dissimilar fashion in the same situation (p. 611)

Conservation The understanding that physical properties do not change when nothing is added or taken away, even though appearances may change; also, the principle that many aspects of biological mechanisms are similar across species—it permits studies of systems in lower animals to be valid and informative for understanding of human functioning (p. 79; 105)

Consistency Criterion Criterion used when deciding whether an action should be attributed to situational or dispositional factors; involves deciding whether an action is a reliable one for a particular person (p. 611)

Consolidation The process by which learned information is gradually transformed from a fragile short-term memory code to a more durable, long-term memory code (p. 332)

Constitutional Factors Basic physical and psychological characteristics; shaped by genetic and early environmental influences, they remain fairly consistent throughout a person's life (p. 69)

Construct Validity The degree to which scores on a test based on the defined variable correlate with scores of other tests, judges' ratings, or experimental results already considered valid indicators of the characteristic being measured (p. 456)

Continuity A theoretical view in developmental psychology which holds that development is essentially continuous and occurs through the accumulation of quantitative changes in behaviors (p. 63)

Control Group The group of subjects in a controlled experiment who share all of the characteristics and procedures of the experimental group except exposure to the independent variable being studied (p. 41)

Controlled Experiment A research method in which observations are made of specific behaviors under systematically varied conditions (p. 41)

Controlled Procedures Consistent procedures for giving instructions, scoring responses, and for holding all other variables constant except for those being systematically varied (p. 41)

Convergence Binocular depth cue in which the two eyes turn inward toward the nose as they fixate on a object that is relatively close (p. 203)

Convergent Thinking An aspect of creativity in which one uses knowledge and logic to eliminate possibilities and reach the best solution to a problem (p. 479)

Conversion Disorder A type of psychological disorder in which there is a loss of a specific sensory or motor function in the absence of any physiological or organic cause (p. 532)

Coping Means of dealing with a situation perceived to be threatening (p. 509)

Cornea Transparent bulge at the front of the eye filled with a clear liquid, the aqueous humor (p. 151)

Corpus Callosum A bundle of myelinated axons that connects the two cerebral hemispheres (p. 131)

Correlation A measure of the degree to which two variables are related or covary systematically (p. 34)

Correlation Coefficient A statistic which indicates the degree of relationship between two variables (p. 52)

Correlational Study A research design which assesses the degree of relationship between variables (p. 45)

Cortex See *neocortex.*

Counseling Psychologist Term for the general category of professional psychologists who specialize in providing guidance in areas such as vocational selection, school problems, drug abuse, or marital conflict (p. 564)

Countertransference The process in which a psychoanalyst develops personal feelings about a client because of perceived similarity of the client to significant people in the therapist's life (p. 570)

Covariation Principle A postulated social judgment rule regarding the way inferences about the cause of an event are often made in relation to the conditions that vary with the event (p. 611)

Coverant A covert operant response that is influenced by the consequences it produces (p. 441)

Covert Behaviors The unseen psychological processes such as thoughts, images, or feelings, or physiological reactions that cannot be directly observed (p. 8)

Creativity The uninhibited, imaginative thought processes involved in the act of creating; the occurrence of uncommon or unusual, but appropriate, responses to situations (p. 479)

Criterion Validity The degree to which test scores indicate a result on a specific measure that is consistent with some other criterion of the characteristic being assessed (p. 455)

Critical Features Attributes that are necessary and sufficient conditions for a concept to be included in a category (p. 345)

Critical Period A sensitive time during development when an organism is optimally ready to acquire a particular behavior if the proper stimuli and experiences occur; also, the period of most rapid biochemical change for a given structure of the brain and nervous system (p. 63; 127)

Cross-cultural Research Research designed to discover whether some behavior found in one culture also occurs in other cultures (p. 46)

Cross-sectional Design A research method in which groups of subjects of different chronological ages are observed and compared (p. 61)

Cutaneous Senses The skin senses, which produce sensations of pressure, warmth, and cold (p. 176)

Cytoplasm Substance in the cell in which most of a cell's biochemical reactions take place and in which metabolism occurs (p. 110)

D

Dark Adaptation A process in which the eyes get more sensitive to light under conditions of low illumination (p. 165)

Data Reports of observations (p. 7)

Daydreaming A mild form of consciousness alteration in which attention is temporarily shifted away from a response to external stimulation toward responding to an internal stimulus (p. 238)

Decentration The ability to take into account two or more physical dimensions at the same time (p. 78)
Decision making The process of choosing between alternatives, selecting and rejecting among available options (p. 351)
Deficiency Motivation Motivation in which individuals seek to restore physical or psychological equilibrium (p. 384)
Dehumanization A type of defense mechanism in which the human qualities and values of other people are psychologically erased or cancelled (p. 662)
Deindividuation The subjective states and the process in which a person does not feel differentiated from others (p. 660)
Delayed Forward Conditioning Temporal pattern in classical conditioning in which the conditioned stimulus stays on (is delayed) until the unconditioned stimulus comes on (p. 264)
Delta Sleep A stage during the sleep cycle in which electrical brain activity is characterized by large, slow waves (p. 240)
Delusions False beliefs maintained despite contrary evidence and lack of social support; they may arise from unconscious sources and appear to serve personal needs, such as relieving guilt or bolstering self-esteem (p. 190; 539)
Dendrites Branched fibers of a neuron which receive incoming signals (p. 111)
Dependence A process in which the body or mind becomes adjusted to and dependent on the ingestion of a certain substance (p. 248)
Dependent Variable The response whose form or amount is expected to vary with changes in the independent variable (p. 41)
Depressants A group of drugs including alcohol, barbiturates, and opiates which slows down mental and physical activities by reducing or inhibiting the transmission of nerve impulses in the central nervous system (p. 249)
Depressive Episodes Recurrent periods characterized by a loss of interest or pleasure in most activities together with feelings of sadness, discouragement, dissatisfaction, worthlessness, guilt, and decreased energy (p. 536)
Descriptive Statistics Collections of data that are used to describe sets of scores collected from different groups of subjects and to describe relationships among variables (p. 48)
Developmental Age The chronological age at which most children show a particular level of physical or mental development (p. 63)
Developmental Psychology A branch of psychology that is concerned with interaction between physical and psychological processes and stages of growth from conception across the life span (p. 59)
Developmental Stage A period during which physical, mental, or behavioral functioning is different from times before and after it (p. 63)
Dichotic Listening An experimental technique in which a different auditory stimulus is simultaneously sent to each ear (p. 225)
Diencephalon The lower part of the forebrain (p. 128)
Difference Threshold The smallest physical difference between two stimuli that will be recognized as a difference; also known as the *just noticeable difference* (p. 149)
Direct Observation An observation that can be made with the naked eye and easily recorded in writing or on videotape (p. 38)
Discontinuity A theoretical view in developmental psychology which holds that development is discontinuous, qualitatively different behaviors at different life periods (p. 63)
Discounting Principle The tendency for people to consider certain causes as less likely explanations of behavior to the extent that other plausible causes are present (p. 610)
Discriminative Stimuli Stimuli which act as predictors of reinforcement signaling when a particular behavior will result in positive reinforcement (p. 276)
Diseases of Adaptation Diseases that have their roots in attempts to adapt to stressors (p. 501)
Dishabituation Recovery from habituation (p. 80)
Display Rules Social norms governing the public expression or display of emotions (p. 416)
Dispositional Theories Those personality theories that focus on innate qualities within a person as the main force influencing behavior (p. 437)
Dissociation Functioning of consciousness at different levels (p. 247)
Dissociative Disorder A type of psychological reaction in which an individual experiences a sudden, temporary alteration of consciousness in the form of a severe memory loss or loss of personal identity (p. 532)
Distal Stimulus The object in the environment, the source of stimulation, as contrasted with the *proximal stimulus* (p. 188)
Distinctiveness Criterion A criterion used when deciding if an action should be attributed to situational or dispositional factors that involves determining if an action is unusual and atypical for a particular person (p. 611)
Divergent Thinking An aspect of creativity characterized by an ability to produce unusual, but appropriate, responses to standard questions (p. 479)
Dominant Genes Genes that are expressed in an individual's development (p. 66)
Dopamine Hypothesis A theory proposing a relationship between many of the symptoms associated with schizophrenia and a relative excess of the neurotransmitter dopamine at specific receptor sites in the central nervous system (p. 551)
Double Bind A situation hypothesized to contribute to schizophrenic reactions in which a child receives, from a parent, multiple messages that are contradictory and cannot be met (p. 552)
Dream Analysis The psychoanalytic technique involving the interpretation of dreams in order to gain insight into a person's unconscious motives or conflicts (p. 569)
Drive Term used to describe motivation that is biologically instigated (p. 376)
DSM-III The current diagnostic and statistical manual of the American Psychiatric Association that classifies, defines, and describes over 200 mental disorders; the 1987 revision of the manual is known as DSM-III-R (p. 522)
Dual-code Model of Memory A theoretical view about the nature of the coding system in memory which proposes that both visual and verbal codes are used to store information in memory, not only verbal codes (p. 318)
Dual Hypothalamic Theory of Hunger The theory that the lateral hypothalamus and ventromedial hypothalamus control the starting and stopping of feeding (p. 387)
Dualism The belief that the mechanistic body and brain act separately from the spiritual soul and ephemeral mind (p. 107)
Duplex Theory of Memory A theory about the structure of the memory system that postulates qualitatively different systems for short- and long-term memory (p. 322)

E

Echo An auditory memory lasting several seconds (p. 305)
Ecological Optics A theory of perception that emphasizes the richness of the stimulus information and the perceiver as an active explorer of the environment (p. 195)
Ectomorph A somatotype characterized by a body build that is thin, long, and fragile in appearance (p. 424)
EEG See *electroencephalogram.*
Ego In Freudian theory, that aspect of the personality involved in self-preservation activities and in directing instinctual drives and urges into appropriate channels (p. 433)
Egocentrism An aspect of centrism that refers to a preoperational child's difficulty in imagining a scene from someone else's perspective (p. 78)

Ego Defense Mechanism A Freudian concept referring to a mental strategy (conscious or unconscious) used by the ego to defend itself from the conflicts experienced in the normal course of life (p. 434)
Ego Ideal In Freudian theory, an individual's view of the kind of person he or she should strive to become (p. 433)
Eidetic Imagery An uncommon memory phenomenon in which a few individuals seem to be able to store detailed, whole images of scenes or complex patterns for a relatively long period of time (p. 319)
Elaborative Rehearsal Repetition of incoming information in which new information is analyzed and related to already stored knowledge (p. 310)
Electroconvulsive Therapy (ECT) "Shock" treatment in which electric current is applied to a patient's temples for a fraction of a second in order to produce upheaval in the central nervous system (p. 587)
Electroencephalogram (EEG) Recording of electrical activity of the brain at the scalp (p. 135)
Electromagnetic Spectrum An energy spectrum which includes X-rays, microwaves, radio waves, TV waves, and visible light waves (p. 155)
Electrode A thin wire through which small amounts of electric current can pass; used in recording electrical activity in the brain (p. 134)
Emotion A complex pattern of changes, including physiological arousal, feelings, cognitive processes, and behavioral reactions, made in response to a situation perceived to be personally significant (p. 405)
Empirical Evidence Evidence obtained through the careful observation of perceivable events or phenomena (p. 6)
Encoding Conversion of information into a code capable of being conveyed in a communication channel (p. 302)
Encoding Specificity Principle The assumption about the close relationship between encoding, storage, and retrieval of information in which subsequent retrieval of information is enhanced if cues received at the time of recall are consistent with those present at the time of encoding (p. 315)
Endocrine System A glandular system transferring information between cells in different parts of the body by way of hormonal messengers (p. 124)
Endomorph A somatotype characterized by a body build that is full, round, or soft in appearance (p. 424)
Endorphins A class of neurotransmitters involved in many reactions to pleasure and pain (p. 118)
Engram General term for the coding of acquired information in the brain; also called *memory trace* (p. 331)
Episodic Memory That component of long-term memory which stores autobiographical information in conjunction with some type of coding designating a time frame for past occurrences (p. 316)
Equity Theory Cognitive theory of work motivation which proposes that workers are motivated to maintain fair and equitable relationships with other relevant persons; also, a model addressing factors influencing attraction and satisfaction within social relationships which postulates that equitable relationships are those in which the participants' outcomes are proportional to their inputs (p. 402; 626)
ERG Theory Need theory of work motivation which proposes that workers are motivated by three sets of needs—existence needs, relatedness needs, and growth needs; also assumes that higher-level needs can become activated before lower-level needs are met (p. 402)
Erogenous Zones Areas of the skin surface that are especially sensitive to stimulation and which give rise to erotic or sexual sensations (p. 176)
Eros A concept of Freudian theory referring to the life instinct which provides energy for growth and survival (p. 432)
Estrogen A female hormone essential to triggering the release of eggs from the ovaries (p. 126)
Ethology The observational study of animal behavior patterns in an animal's natural environment (p. 290; 381)
Etiology The causes or factors related to the development of a disorder (p. 523)
Eustress A positive reaction to a stressor defined as a challenge rather than a threat (p. 496)
Evaluation Research A type of research in psychology that focuses on evaluating whether a particular social program or type of therapy achieves previously specified goals and whether it is cost effective (p. 46)
Evoked Potentials The patterns of brain activity caused by specific stimuli (p. 137; 343)
Excitation Stimulation that increases the activity or "firing rate" of a nerve cell (p. 109)
Existentialism A philosophy which emphasizes an individual's responsibility and potentiality for existence fully through choice (p. 20; 438)
Expectancy Theory Cognitive theory of work motivation which proposes that workers are motivated when they expect their effort and job performance to result in desired outcomes (p. 403)
Experimental Analysis of Behavior Skinnerian approach to operant conditioning which systematically varies stimulus conditions to discover the ways that various kinds of experience affect the probability of responses; makes no inferences about inner states or nonobservable bases for behavioral relationships demonstrated in the laboratory (p. 273)
Experimental Group The subjects in a controlled experiment for whom the independent variable or treatment variables are systematically altered (p. 41)
Extinction In conditioning, the weakening of a conditioned association in the absence of a reinforcer or unconditioned stimulus (p. 264; 276)
Extrinsic Motivation Motivation to engage in an activity for some outside consequence (p. 398)

F

Face Validity The degree to which test takers can figure out what a test is supposed to measure (p. 456)
Faculty Psychology Rationalistic view associated with Immanuel Kant which assumed that the mind had built-in structures for its development that did not depend on experience (p. 259)
Feature-detection Model The theory that cells at different levels in the visual system detect different features of the stimulus (p. 163)
Feature Detectors Cells in the visual cortex which respond when specific patterns are present in their receptive fields (p. 163)
Fechner's Law The assertion that the strength of a sensation is proportional to the logarithm of physical stimulus intensity (p. 150)
Fetish A nonsexual object that becomes capable of producing sexual arousal through conditioning (p. 393)
Fetishism Paraphilia in which sexual excitement is achieved with the aid of nonliving objects (p. 535)
Fetus The label given to the developing embryo eight weeks after conception until birth (p. 68)
Fight-or-Flight Syndrome The sequence of internal activities triggered when an organism is faced with a threat; prepares the body for combat and struggle or for running away to safety (p. 499)
Figural Goodness Perceptual organizational process in which a figure is seen according to perceived simplicity, symmetry, and regularity (p. 199)
Figure Objectlike regions of the visual field (p. 197)
Fixation According to Freudian theory, arrested psychosexual development in which a child does not progress to the next stage because of excessive frustration or overgratification during the current stage (p. 89)
Fixed Action Pattern An unlearned response released by a specific environmental event or object (p. 381)

Fixed Interval Schedule (FI) In operant conditioning, a procedure in which reinforcement is delivered for the first response made after a fixed amount of time has elapsed (p. 287)
Fixed Ratio Schedule (FR) In operant conditioning, a procedure in which reinforcement is delivered only after a fixed number of responses (p. 286)
Formal Operational Stage Fourth of Piaget's cognitive developmental stages; characterized by abstract thinking and conceptualization (p. 79)
Forward Conditioning Temporal pattern in classical conditioning in which the conditioned stimulus comes on before the unconditioned stimulus (p. 264)
Fovea Area of the retina which contains densely packed cones and forms the point of sharpest vision (p. 153)
Free Association Principal procedure used in psychoanalysis to probe the unconscious in which a patient gives a running account of thoughts, wishes, physical sensations, and mental images as they occur (p. 567)
Free-floating Anxiety Anxiety not focused on any particular agent or not associated with any known cause (p. 528)
Frequency The number of cycles a wave completes in a given amount of time (p. 167)
Frequency Distribution An array of individual scores arranged in order from highest to lowest (p. 49)
Frequency Theory The theory that neural firing rate is determined by a tone's frequency (p. 171)
Frustration A state of an organism assumed to exist when goal-directed activity is blocked in some manner (p. 647)
Functional Fixedness An inhibition in perceiving a new use for an object previously associated with some other purpose; adversely affects problem solving and creativity (p. 359)
Functionalism A perspective on studying mind and behavior that focused on examination of the intact organism interacting with its environment; study of the contents of consciousness (p. 14; 144)
Functional Psychoses A group of psychotic disorders, not attributable to brain damage or organic factors, that includes affective disorders, paranoid states, and the schizophrenias (p. 525)
Function Words Words like *the, and,* or *of* which help express relationships between other words (p. 74)
Fundamental Attribution Error The dual tendency of observers to underestimate the impact of situational factors on an actor's behavior and to overestimate the influence of dispositional factors (p. 612)

G

Gain-Loss Principle of Attraction Principle which states that our feelings of attraction toward someone are influenced more by the direction of change of his or her attitude toward us than by the level of the evaluation (p. 627)
Ganglion Cells Cells which integrate impulses from many bipolar cells into a single firing rate (p. 153)
Gate-control Theory Theory about pain modulation which proposes that certain cells in the spinal cord act as gates to interrupt and block some pain signals while sending others on to the brain (p. 179)
Gender A psychological phenomenon; refers to learned sex-related behaviors and attitudes of males and females (p. 86)
Gender Identity One's sense of "maleness" or "femaleness"; usually includes an awareness and acceptance of one's biological sex (p. 86)
Gender Role The set of behaviors and attitudes defined by society that are associated with being male or female and are expressed publicly by the individual (p. 86)
General Adaptation Syndrome (GAS) A pattern of nonspecific adaptational physiological mechanisms that occurs in response to continuing threat by almost any serious stressor (p. 500)
Generalized Anxiety Disorder A disorder in which an individual experiences anxiety that persists for at least one month and is not focused on a specific object or situation (p. 530)
Genes Ultramicroscopic areas of DNA within a chromosome; the basic unit of hereditary transmission (p. 66)
Genital Development Development of genital tissue (p. 69)
Genital Stage Fifth and final stage of psychosexual development proposed by Freud (from puberty throughout adulthood); during this period an individual moves from autoeroticism to gaining sexual gratification from others and also learns socially appropriate channels for the expression of sexual impulses (p. 89)
Genotype The genetic constitution of an organism; many genes are not expressed in an individual's development (p. 66)
Germ Cells In humans, the spermatozoa in the male and the ova in the female; the cells which carry and transmit the genetic information of the parents to the offspring (p. 66)
Gestalt German word meaning "whole configuration," from which is derived *Gestaltism,* the theoretical approach to perception that emphasizes whole configurations and emergent properties (p. 198)
Glial Cells (Glia) Cells which hold neurons close together and facilitate neural transmission by forming a sheath that insulates the axons of some neurons, thereby speeding conduction of electrochemical impulses; they also function in removal of damaged and dead neurons and prevent poisonous substances in the blood from reaching the brain by forming the blood-brain barrier (p. 112)
Goal-setting The intention to work toward an explicit goal, a primary motivating force in work behavior as goals direct and focus attention, mobilize effort, and increase persistence (p. 403)
Graded Potential Spreading activity along a dendrite or cell body membrane produced by stimulation from another neuron (p. 113)
Ground Background areas of the visual field, against which figures stand out (p. 197)
Group Two or more persons who are engaged in interaction so that each influences and is influenced by the other(s) (p. 628)
Grouping A perceptual organizing process through which one tends to see independent items grouped together; such grouping follows the laws of proximity, common fate, and similarity (p. 198)
Growth Motivation Motivation in which individuals seek to develop themselves beyond what they have been and done in the past (p. 384)
Gustation The sensation of taste (p. 172)

H

Habituation A decrease in strength of responding when a stimulus is presented repeatedly (p. 80; 119)
Hallucinations False sensory perceptions produced by a variety of conditions such as mental disorders, brain diseases, or intoxication from various drugs (p. 190; 243)
Hallucinogens The group of psychoactive drugs that are capable of producing altered states of awareness in which visual, auditory, or other sensory hallucinations occur (p. 251)
Halo Effect A bias in which an observer judges a liked person favorably on most or all dimensions (p. 461)
Hawthorne Effect Type of bias in which the psychological effect of participating in an experiment affects physical variables being manipulated (p. 33)
Health Psychology A field in psychology that focuses on understanding the psychological influences on the way people stay healthy, the reasons they become ill, and the way they respond when they do become ill (p. 490)
Hertz (Hz) A unit of sound frequency expressed in cycles per second (p. 167)
Heuristics Cognitive strategies, or "rules of thumb," often used as shortcuts in solving complex inferential tasks (p. 353)

Hidden Observer A term referring to the part of the self which maintains an intellectual awareness of, and contact with, reality even under altered states of awareness such as hypnosis (p. 247)

Hippocampus Part of the limbic system involved in memory (p. 131)

Historical Approach Research design in which time is the primary independent variable in the study of development (p. 62)

Holistic Approach A theoretical approach in which separate actions are explained in terms of a person's entire personality (p. 437)

Homeostasis Constancy or equilibrium of the internal conditions of the body; the tendency of organisms to maintain equilibrium and resist change (p. 125)

Hormones Substances secreted into the bloodstream from specialized cells located in various glands; are carried in the blood until they attach themselves to the surface of a target tissues (p. 124)

Hue The dimension of color space that corresponds to the light's wavelength (p. 155)

Human Sexuality The physical characteristics and capacities for specific sex behaviors together with the psychosexual learning, values, norms, and attitudes about these behaviors (p. 391)

Humanistic Model A psychological model that emphasizes an individual's phenomenal world and inherent capacity for making rational choices and developing to maximum potential (p. 20)

Hypnosis An altered state of awareness induced by a variety of techniques and characterized by deep relaxation, susceptibility to suggestions, and changes in perception, memory, motivation, and self-control (p. 244)

Hypnotic Induction A preliminary set of activities that precedes and prepares a participant for the altered awareness state of hypnosis (p. 245)

Hypnotizability The degree to which an individual is responsive to standardized hypnotic suggestions (p. 245)

Hypochondriasis A pathological condition characterized by a preoccupation with bodily sensations as possible signs of a serious disease despite medical reassurance (p. 532)

Hypothalamus A structure below the thalamus that regulates processes such as eating, drinking, body temperature, and hormonal activity (p. 130)

Hypothesis A tentative and testable explanation of the relationship between two (or more) events or variables; often stated as a prediction that a certain outcome will result from specific conditions (p. 6)

I

Icon A visual memory lasting about half a second (p. 305)

Id In Freudian theory, the primitive, unconscious part of the personality which operates irrationally and acts on impulse (p. 433)

Identity Sense of self; includes the perception of one's self as distinct from other people and of other things as related to one's self or alien to one's self (p. 445)

Idiographic Approach A methodological approach to the study of personality processes in which emphasis is placed on understanding the unique aspects of each individual's personality rather than on common dimensions on which all individuals can be measured (p. 422)

Illusion Experience of a stimulus pattern in a manner that is demonstrably incorrect (p. 190)

Immediate Memory Span Refers to the limited, brief storage capacity of short-term memory that seems to be between five and nine chunks of information (p. 308)

Implosion A behavioral therapeutic technique that exposes a client to stimuli previously rated by the client as most anxiety-provoking in an attempt to extinguish the anxiety associated with the stimuli (p. 573)

Impression Formation The process of knowing other people and of determining their traits, abilities, and attitudes (p. 607)

Imprinting A primitive form of learning in which an infant animal physically follows and forms an attachment to the first moving object it sees and/or hears (p. 82)

Incentive Motivation Motivation aroused by external stimuli (p. 383)

Independent Variable In a controlled experiment, the stimulus that, when varied, is expected to change some behavior (the dependent variable) (p. 41)

Index Variable A variable that is itself not causal but is a manifest sign of an underlying causal variable (p. 63)

Individuation The psychological state in which a person is differentiated from other people in a given social context (p. 657)

Induced Motion An illusion in which a stationary point of light within a moving reference frame is seen as moving and the reference frame is perceived as stationary (p. 201)

Infancy Period In humans, the period from birth to 18 months; from the Latin word for "incapable of speech" (p. 70)

Inference A logical assumption made on the basis of some evidence other than direct observation about something that is happening inside an organism; the reasoning process of drawing a conclusion on the basis of a sample of evidence or on the basis of prior beliefs and theories (p. 8; 351)

Inferential Statistics Measures that allow researchers to know what conclusions can legitimately be drawn from data (p. 52)

In-group Term used by members for their own group, when one group of people is differentiated from another (p. 633)

In-group Bias A tendency for a person to evaluate more positively the groups he or she is a member of (p. 633)

Inhibition Stimulation that decreases activity or the "firing rate" of a nerve cell (p. 109)

Initiation Rite Ritual in many nonindustrial societies which takes place around puberty and serves as public acknowledgment of the passage from childhood to adulthood; also called *rites of passage* (p. 91)

Insight A phenomenon in problem-solving tasks in which learning results from an understanding of relationships (often sudden) rather than from blind trial and error (p. 296)

Instinct An unlearned behavior pattern that appears in the same form in every member of the species at a certain point in its development (p. 380)

Instinctual Drift The tendency for learned behavior to drift toward instinctual behavior over time (p. 288)

Instrumental Conditioning Type of learning in which the relationship that is learned is between a response and its consequences; see also *operant conditioning* (p. 271)

Intelligence The global capacity to profit from experience and to go beyond given information about the environment (p. 461)

Intelligence Quotient (IQ) An index of intelligence derived from sources on standardized intelligence tests; obtained by dividing an individual's mental age by chronological age and then multiplying by 100 (p. 464)

Interaction The joint effect of two independent variables on a behavior that could not have been predicted from the separate effect of each on the dependent measure (p. 44)

Interneurons Neurons providing communication between other neurons; make up the bulk of nerve cells in the brain (p. 111)

Interposition A depth cue present when one object blocks off the view of part of another object; also known as *occlusion* (p. 204)

Intervening Variable A condition or event whose existence is inferred in order to explain a link between some observable input and a measurable response output (p. 8)

Interview A face-to-face conversation between a researcher and a respondent for the purpose of gathering detailed information about the respondent (p. 40)

Intrinsic Motivation Motivation to engage in an activity for its own sake (p. 398)
Introspection A method of gathering data in which trained subjects report their current conscious experience as accurately as possible (p. 19)
Introversion-Extraversion A personality dimension that describes people by the degree to which they need other people as sources of rewards and cues to appropriate behaviors (p. 425)
Invariants Things in the environment that do not change their identities though they change appearances (p. 78)
Invulnerable Term for those children who can withstand extreme stress, deprivation, or disadvantage, and emerge unscathed, showing normal personality functioning (p. 65)
Ion Channels Excitable membrane molecules that produce and transduce signals in living cells (p. 114)
Ions Electrically charged particles that flow through the membrane of a cell, changing its polarity and thereby its capacity to conduct electrochemical signals (p. 112)
Iris A muscular disk that surrounds the pupil and expands and contracts to control the amount of light entering the eye (p. 151)

J

James-Lange Theory Theory of emotion stating that an eliciting stimulus triggers a behavioral response which sends different sensory and motor feedback to the brain and creates the feeling of a specific emotion (p. 408)
Job Design Research design in work motivation in which the goal is to identify the characteristics of work that make it enjoyable and motivating and then to use this information in designing or redesigning jobs (p. 403)
Judgment The process by which we form opinions, reach conclusions, and make critical evaluations of events and people based on available material; also the product of that mental activity (p. 351)
Just Noticeable Differences See *difference threshold.*

K

Kinesthetic Sense The sense concerned with bodily position and movement of the body parts relative to each other (p. 175)

L

Latency Stage Fourth of Freud's psychosexual developmental stages (from age 6 to puberty); during this stage satisfaction is gained primarily through the exploration and development of skills and interests and exploration of the environment (p. 89)
Latent Content In Freudian dream analysis, the hidden, actual content of a dream (p. 242)
Latent Learning Associations learned from experience and observation in which there is no change in behavior at the time (p. 260)
Lateral Geniculate Nucleus Relay point in the thalamus through which impulses pass when going from the eye to the occipital cortex (p. 154)
Lateral Inhibition Tendency for a receptor excited by an intense amount of light to suppress neighboring receptors receiving less intense light (p. 162)
Lateral Sulcus A deep horizontal groove that serves to divide the cerebral hemispheres into lobes (p. 132)
Law of Association Doctrine which holds that we acquire knowledge through associating ideas—mental events that originate in sensory information from the environment (p. 259)
Law of Common Fate Law of grouping which states that elements moving in the same direction at the same rate are grouped together (p. 198)
Law of Effect A basic law of learning which states that the power of a stimulus to evoke a response is strengthened when the response is followed by a reward and weakened when it is not followed by a reward (p. 272)
Law of Forward Conduction The principle stating that neurons transmit information in only one direction—from the axon of one neuron to the dendrites or soma of the next (p. 111)
Law of Proximity Law of grouping which states that the nearest, or "most proximal," elements are grouped together (p. 198)
Law of Similarity Law of grouping which states that the most similar elements are grouped together (p. 198)
Law of Specific Nerve Energy The principle that all nerve impulses are virtually identical and that the quality of sensory experience is determined by the type of receptor stimulated (p. 109)
Learned Helplessness The general pattern of nonresponding in the presence of noxious stimuli which often follows after an organism has previously experienced noncontingent, inescapable aversive stimuli (p. 285)
Learning A process that results in a relatively permanent change in behavior or behavioral potential based on experience (p. 260)
Lens A structure behind the iris through which light travels before reaching the central chamber of the eye (p. 151)
Lesion The careful destruction of a particular brain area by surgical removal, the cutting of connections, or the destruction of brain tissue (p. 135)
Levels of Processing Theory A theory regarding the structure and characteristics of the memory system; it postulates a single system of memory in which the only differentiation is in the levels of processing applied to incoming information (p. 322)
Libido In Freudian theory, the psychic energy that drives individuals toward sensual pleasures of all types, including sexual (p. 432)
Limbic System Area at the upper end of the old brain which contains centers for emotional behavior and basic motivational urges (p. 130)
Linear Perspective A depth cue based on the illusion that parallel lines converge to a point on the horizon as they recede into distance (p. 204)
Locus of Control A generalized belief about the causes for outcomes of our actions—whether they are caused by what we do or by events outside our control (p. 386)
Loneliness The perception of being unable to achieve the level of affiliation that a person desires (p. 624)
Longitudinal Design Research design in which the same subjects are observed repeatedly, sometimes over many years (p. 61)
Longitudinal Study A method of scientific investigation in which selected measurements and observations of the same individuals are taken repeatedly over time (p. 46)
Long-term Memory Those memory processes associated with the preservation of information for retrieval at any later time, and, theoretically, having the characteristics of unlimited capacity (p. 304)

M

Magnitude Estimation A method of constructing psychophysical scales by having observers scale their sensations directly into numbers (p. 150)
Main Effect In a 2×2 research design, the effect that one independent variable has on the dependent variable, regardless of the other independent variable (p. 44)
Maintenance Rehearsal Active repetition of information in order to enhance subsequent access to it (p. 310)

Manic Episode A psychotic reaction characterized by a recurring period of extreme elation, unbounded euphoria without sufficient reason, and grandiose thoughts or feelings about personal abilities (p. 536)
Manifest Content In Freudian dream analysis, the surface content of a dream that is remembered; assumed to mask the real meaning of a dream (p. 242)
Masochism A type of psychosexual disorder involving sexual excitement derived from the experience of personal suffering (p. 535)
Materialism See *monism.*
Maturation Continuing influence of heredity during development and later life; important in age-related physical and behavioral changes characteristic of the species (p. 67)
Mean The most commonly used measure of central tendency of a distribution; the average value for a group of scores (p. 50)
Mechanistic Approach The belief that complex behavior can be reduced to its underlying physical basis (p. 107)
Median A measure of central tendency of a distribution; the score within a group of observations for which half of the remaining scores have values less than and half have values greater than this number (p. 50)
Mediated Observation Observation which requires the use of special equipment or instrumentation (p. 38)
Medical Model A paradigm which defines and studies psychological abnormality in a way analogous to that used to study and treat physical illness (p. 547)
Medulla Area of the brain stem responsible for controlling repetitive processes such as breathing and heartbeat (p. 130)
Memory The mental capacity to store and later recognize or recall events that were previously experienced (p. 301)
Memory Trace See *engram.*
Mental Age (MA) In Binet's measure of intelligence, the age at which a child is performing intellectually, expressed in terms of the average age at which normal children achieve a particular score (p. 462)
Mental Disorder A clinically significant behavioral or psychological syndrome or pattern that occurs in an individual and that is typically associated with either a distressing symptom or impairment in one or more important areas of functioning (p. 519)
Mental Operation The mental manipulation of information; depends on concepts of objects rather than direct perceptual information (p. 79)
Mental Set A tendency to respond to a new problem in the manner used on a previous problem (p. 359)
Mere Exposure Effect The ability of repeated exposures to the same stimulus to produce greater attraction toward that stimulus, a preference that develops without necessarily being aware of the cognitions involved (p. 625)
Mesomorph A somatotype characterized by a body build that is muscular, rectangular, and strong (p. 424)
Metabolism The breakdown of nutrients into body energy (p. 110)
Metacognition Thinking about thinking (p. 81)
Metacognitive Knowledge The awareness of what you know and how well you are comprehending a situation (p. 364)
Mnemonics Special strategies or devices used during the encoding of new information that use already familiar items to enhance subsequent access to the information in memory (p. 314)
Mode A measure of central tendency of a distribution; the score occurring most frequently among the observations (p. 50)
Model A conceptual framework which provides a simplified way of thinking about the basic components in a field of knowledge (p. 15)
Moderator Variables Conditions in a situation and in an individual's functioning that can change the effect of a stressor (p. 496)
Molar Level of Analysis A level of analysis in which the behavior of the whole functioning organism in a complex environment is the focus of study (p. 15)
Molecular Level of Analysis A level of analysis in which precisely defined units of behavior are the focus, but the units are somewhat larger than at the micro level (p. 15)
Monism The view that mind and brain are aspects of a single reality; also called *materialism* (p. 108)
Morality A system of beliefs and values which ensures that individuals will act to keep their obligations to others in the society and will behave in ways that do not interfere with the rights and interests of others (p. 87)
Motherese Special form of speech with an exaggerated and high-pitched intonation that adults use to speak to infants and young children (p. 73)
Motivation General term for the process of starting, directing, and maintaining physical and psychological activities; includes mechanisms involved in preferences for one activity over another and the vigor and persistence of responses (p. 376)
Motive Term used to refer to psychologically and socially instigated motivation, assumed to be at least in part learned (p. 376)
Motor Cortex Area of the cerebral cortex located along the front of the central sulcus, devoted to sending messages to the muscles; also known as the *motor projection area* (p. 132)
Motor Neurons Neurons that carry messages from the central nervous system to the muscles or glands (p. 111)
Motor Projection Area See *motor cortex.*
Multiple Personality A dissociative disorder in which different aspects of a personality function independently of one another, creating the appearance of two or more distinct personalities within the same individual (p. 533)
Myelin Sheath A covering, made up of glial cells, that insulates some axons, speeding the conduction of nerve impulses (p. 112)

N

Narcissistic Personality Disorder Personality disorder marked by a grandiose sense of self-importance, preoccupation with fantasies of success and power, and a need for constant attention or admiration (p. 525)
Naturalistic Observation Observation of naturally occurring behaviors with no attempt to change or interfere with them; data collection without laboratory controls or the manipulation of variables (p. 38)
Nature-Nurture Controversy A debate in psychology concerning the relative importance of heredity (nature) and learning or experience (nurture) in determining development and behavior (p. 69)
Needs Hierarchy Sequence from most "primitive" to most "human" (p. 384)
Negative Reinforcement The condition following a response of not receiving or escaping an aversive stimulus that increases the probability of the response (p. 275)
Negative Reinforcer A stimulus, not received (terminated or avoided) after a response, that increases the probability of that response occurring (p. 275)
Neocortex The outer layer of the cerebrum, necessary for precise perception and conscious thought; also known as the *cortex* (p. 131)
Neonate The newborn infant; in humans, from birth to one month old (p. 70)
Neural Substrate Basis of thoughts, feelings, and actions sought by neuropsychologists in the activity of the brain and nervous system (p. 105)
Neuron A nerve cell specialized to provide rapid communication within and between adjacent cells (p. 111)
Neuron Doctrine Theory advanced by Ramon y Cajal which states that all parts of the brain are composed of specialized cells called neurons (p. 109)

Neuropsychology Branch of physiological psychology which studies the foundations of behavior and mental processes as functions of the activity of the brain and nervous system (p. 105)
Neuroscience Branch of the life sciences that deals with the anatomy, physiology, and biochemistry of the brain and nervous systems mechanisms involved in the production of normal and abnormal behavior (p. 106)
Neurosis A mental disorder in which there are one or more symptoms related to ineffective attempts to deal with anxiety (p. 523)
Neurotransmitters Chemical messengers released from neurons which cross the synapse and interact with receptors on the postsynaptic cell membrane (p. 116)
Nomothetic Approach A methodological approach to the study of personality processes in which emphasis is placed on identifying universal trait dimensions or lawful relationships between different aspects of personality functioning (p. 423)
Nonconscious Processes Processes involving information that is not represented in either consciousness or memory, such as the organization of incoming stimuli into figure and ground (p. 231)
Normal Curve A symmetrical distribution where, in the ideal case, the mean, median, and mode have the same value (p. 52)
Normative Investigations Research efforts designed to describe what is characteristic of a specific age or developmental stage (p. 59)
Norms Standards based on measurements of a large group of people; used for comparing the score of an individual with those of others within a well-defined group (p. 39; 59; 456)
Nucleus Area of the cell that contains DNA and directs activities in the cytoplasm through the production of nucleic acids (p. 110)

O

Object Permanence Recognition that objects exist independently of an individual's action or awareness (p. 78)
Observational Learning The process of learning new responses by watching the behavior of another (p. 292; 443)
Obsession A persistent and unwanted thought, image, or impulse that is difficult to ignore or suppress (p. 531)
Occlusion. See *Interposition.*
Olfaction The sensation of smell (p. 172)
Operant Any behavior emitted by an organism that can be characterized in terms of the observable effects it has on the environment (p. 274)
Operant Conditioning Type of learning in which the probability or ratio of a response is changed by a change in its consequences; see also *instrumental conditioning* (p. 274)
Operational Definition A definition of a variable or condition in terms of the specific operations an investigator uses to determine its presence (p. 30)
Opiates A group of drugs derived from the opium poppy and classified as depressants (p. 249)
Opponent-process Theory The theory that all color experiences arise from three systems, each of which include two "opponent" elements: red vs. green, blue vs. yellow, and black vs. white (p. 159)
Optic Chiasma Region of the brain at which messages from the inner half of each retina cross over to the opposite hemisphere (p. 154)
Optic Nerve The axons of the ganglion cells, which carry information from the eye back toward the brain (p. 153)
Oral Stage First and most primitive of Freud's psychosexual developmental stages, during which the mouth region is the primary source of gratification from nourishment, stimulation, and making contact with the environment (p. 89)
Organismic Factors Term used by those who study only human behavior to refer to dispositional factors such as traits, states, status characteristics, and time (p. 30)
Orientation Constancy Ability to perceive the actual orientation of objects in the world despite their orientation in the retinal image (p. 208)
Orienting Reaction A physiological and behavioral response that maximizes sensitivity to environmental input and prepares the body for emergency action (p. 119)
Orienting Response A general response of attention to the source of novel stimulation (p. 263)
Out-group Term used by members of one group for another group, when one group of persons is differentiated from another (p. 633)
Oval Window Structure at the base of the cochlea against which the footplate of the stirrup vibrates (p. 170)
Overregularization A grammatical error usually appearing during early language development in which rules of the language are applied too widely, resulting in incorrect linguistic forms (p. 74)
Overt Behaviors Responses that are visible to an observer (p. 8)

P

Pain The body's response to noxious stimuli that are intense enough to cause, or threaten to cause, tissue damage (p. 177)
Panic Disorder An anxiety disorder in which an individual experiences recurrent episodes of intense anxiety and feelings of unpredictability that usually last for a few minutes and include symptoms of autonomic hyperactivity (p. 530)
Paradigm A symbolic model in research that represents the essential features of a process being investigated (p. 262)
Paranoid Disorders A group of psychotic disorders characterized by well-developed, systematized, intricate delusions (p. 539)
Paraphilia A type of psychosexual disorder in which sexual excitement necessarily and involuntarily demands the presence of nonconventional sexual objects, practices, or circumstances (p. 535)
Parasympathetic Division The division of the autonomic nervous system that deals with internal monitoring and regulation of various bodily functions (p. 123)
Partial Reinforcement Effect The behavioral principle that responses acquired under intermittent reinforcement are more difficult to extinguish than those acquired with continuous reinforcement (p. 285)
Partial-report Procedure An experimental technique used in memory studies in which subjects presented with a pattern containing several individual stimuli are subsequently asked to recall just a portion of the pattern instead of all the information presented (p. 305)
Participant Modeling Therapeutic technique in which a therapist demonstrates the desired behavior and a client is aided, through demonstration and supportive encouragement, to imitate the modeled behavior (p. 576)
Patterns of Reinforcement In operant conditioning, the patterns of delivering or withholding reinforcement that determine the timing and spacing of consequences (p. 285)
Payoff Matrix Detection matrix for estimating gains and losses in a detection trial (p. 148)
Peace Psychology An interdisciplinary approach to the prevention of nuclear war and the maintenance of peace (p. 671)
Pedophilia A paraphilia that involves an adult's action with or fantasy about sexual activity with young children (p. 535)
Percept What a perceiver experiences (p. 196)
Perception Processes that organize information in the sensory image and interpret it as having been produced by properties of objects in the external, three-dimensional world (p. 185)
Perceptual Constancy An ability to retain an unchanging percept of an object despite variations in the retinal image (p. 205)
Perceptual Defense A hypothesized perceptual process which protects a person from identifying stimuli that are unpleasant or anxiety provoking (p. 213)

Perceptual Organization Processes that put sensory information together to give the perception of a coherent scene over the whole visual field (p. 196)

Perceptual Set A readiness to detect a particular stimulus in a given context (p. 212)

Peripheral Nervous System (PNS) The part of the nervous system outside of the central nervous system (p. 122)

Permissive Parenting Style of parenting characterized by little parental structure (p. 85)

Personal Construct In Kelly's theory, a person's interpretation of reality, his or her beliefs about the way two things are similar to each other and different from a third (p. 442)

Personality The unique psychological qualities of an individual that influence a variety of characteristic behavior patterns (both overt and covert) across different situations and over time (p. 422)

Personality Disorder A chronic, inflexible, maladaptive pattern of perceiving, thinking, and behaving that seriously impairs an individual's ability to function in social or other settings (p. 525)

Personality Inventory A self-report questionnaire used for personality assessment that includes a series of items about personal thoughts, feelings, and behaviors (p. 472)

Personality Psychology A field of psychology in which all aspects of an individual's normal and abnormal functioning are studied by the use of an integrative approach; the whole person is the unit of observation (p. 422)

Persuasion Systematic attempts to influence another person's thoughts, feelings, or actions by means of communicative arguments (p. 617)

Phallic Stage Third of Freud's psychosexual developmental stages (from 3–5 years) during which satisfaction is gained primarily through genital manipulation and exploration; according to Freud, a strong attraction develops for the opposite-sex parent during this stage (p. 89)

Phenomenological Approach An approach in personality psychology which attempts to understand a person by understanding his or her view of reality (p. 437)

Phenomenological Perspective A person's subjective view and interpretation of a situation or environment (p. 602)

Phenotype The observable set of characteristics of an organism resulting from the interaction of genotype and the environment (p. 66)

Pheromones Chemical signals released by organisms to communicate with other members of the species (p. 82; 174)

Phi Phenomenon See *apparent motion.*

Phobia A maladaptive avoidance response that interferes with normal functioning (p. 285)

Phobic disorder A neurotic pattern of behavior in which anxiety is associated with some specific external environmental object or situation (p. 528)

Photon A single, indivisible unit of electromagnetic energy (p. 155)

Photoreceptors Receptor cells in the retina which are sensitive to light (p. 153)

Physiological Psychology The branch of psychology that studies the physical and chemical factors or processes involved in behavior and mental processes (p. 105)

Physiological Zero An intermediate temperature point at which one feels neither warmth nor cold (p. 177)

Pitch The sound quality of "highness" or "lowness," primarily dependent upon the frequency of the sound wave (p. 167)

Pituitary Gland A gland located in the brain that secretes a variety of hormones which influence growth and the secretion of other hormones by other glands (p. 126)

Place Theory The theory that different frequencies produce maximum activation at different locations along the basilar membrane, with the result that pitch can be coded by the place where activation occurs (p. 171)

Placebo Controls Control procedures used in cases where placebo effects might occur (p. 33)

Placebo Effect A clinically significant response to a stimulus or treatment that occurs independent of its physiological effect (p. 32)

Polarity The electrical state (positive or negative) of the membrane of a cell (p. 113)

Polygenic A human characteristic dependent on a combination of several genes (p. 66)

Pons Areas of the brain stem involved in dreaming and waking from sleep (p. 130)

Positive Reinforcement The condition of receiving a stimulus, following a response, that increases the rate or probability of the response (p. 275)

Positive Reinforcer A stimulus, received after a response, that increases the probability of that response occurring (p. 275)

Positron Emission Tomography (PET) A technique for obtaining detailed pictures of activity in the living brain; involves injecting a radioactive substance which is taken up by the active neurons (p. 137)

Postsynaptic Membrane Membrane of the dendrite on the receiving side of the synapse (p. 116)

Posttraumatic Stress Disorder A reaction in which an individual involuntarily reexperiences the emotional, cognitive, and behavioral aspects of past trauma (p. 503)

Premack Principle Principle, formulated by David Premack, that a more preferred activity can be used to reinforce a less preferred one (p. 280)

Prenatal The period of development prior to birth (p. 68)

Preoperational Stage Second of Piaget's stages of cognitive development (from 2–7 years); characterized by centrism, discovery of qualitative identity, and increasing use of symbols but continued dependence on appearances (p. 78)

Presynaptic Membrane Membrane of the axon on the sending side of a synapse (p. 116)

Primacy Effect The phenomenon that the first information we learn about others has greater impact that does later information (p. 608)

Primary Appraisal A term used in stress research referring to the first stage in the cognitive appraisal of a potentially stressful situation; an individual evaluates the seriousness of a demand or potentially stressful situation (p. 496)

Primary Drives Motivational states induced by biological needs and not dependent on learning (p. 382)

Principle of Adaptive Hedonism Principle associated with Jeremy Bentham that individuals act in ways that provide pleasure and avoid ways that result in pain; used as explanation of basic source of human motivation (p. 259)

Proactive Interference A memory phenomenon in which previously stored information interferes with the learning of new, but similar information (p. 328)

Procedural Memory That component of long-term memory which stores the way in which we remember how things get done and how perceptual, cognitive, and motor skills are acquired, retained, and utilized (p. 315)

Projective Test A method of personality assessment in which an individual is presented with a standardized set of ambiguous, abstract stimuli and asked to interpret the meaning of the stimuli; responses are assumed to reveal inner feelings, motives, and conflicts (p. 476)

Proposition An abstract unit of meaning that expresses a relationship between concepts, objects, or events (p. 318)

Prototype The most representative example of a category (p. 345)

Proximal Stimulus The image on the retina, as contrasted with the *distal stimulus* (p. 188)

Psychiatric Social Worker A mental health professional who has received specialized training in a school of social work and whose training emphasizes the importance of the social context of people's problems (p. 564)

Psychiatrist An individual who has completed all medical school training for the M.D. degree and also has completed some postdoctoral specialty training in dealing with mental and emotional disorders; a psychiatrist may prescribe medications for the treatment of psychological disorders (p. 564)

Psychoactive Drugs Chemicals which affect mental processes and behavior by changing conscious awareness of reality (p. 248)

Psychoanalyst An individual who has earned either a Ph.D. or an M.D. and has completed postgraduate training in an institute that offers specialized training in the Freudian approach to understanding and treatment of mental disorders (p. 564)

Psychoanalytic Therapy Psychodynamic therapy developed by Freud; an intensive and prolonged technique for exploring unconscious motivations and conflicts in neurotic, anxiety-ridden individuals (p. 567)

Psychodynamic Model A psychological model in which behavior is explained in terms of past experiences and motivational forces. Actions are viewed as stemming from inherited instincts, biological drives, and attempts to resolve conflicts between personal needs and social requirements (p. 16)

Psychogenic Amnesia A type of amnesia not caused by any physical damage or neurological disorder in which there occurs a sudden inability to recall important personal information and which is precipitated by psychological distress (p. 532)

Psychogenic Fugue An amnesic state during which an individual travels to a new place and assumes a new identity and life-style (p. 533)

Psychological Assessment The use of specified procedures to evaluate the abilities, behaviors, and personal qualities of people (p. 453)

Psychological Test A measuring instrument used to assess an individual's standing relative to others on some mental or behavioral characteristic (p. 40)

Psychology The scientific study of the behavior and mental processes of organisms (p. 5)

Psychometric Function A graph that plots the percentage of detections of a stimulus (on the vertical axis) for each stimulus intensity (on the horizontal axis) (p. 145)

Psychometrics Field of psychology that specializes in mental testing (p. 466)

Psychopathology The study of mental or emotional disorders by medical or psychological specialists; also the general term for psychological abnormalities (p. 519)

Psychophysics The study of the correspondence between psychological experience and physical stimulation (p. 144)

Psychophysiological Model A paradigm based on the assumption that the functioning of an organism is best explained in terms of the biological or physical structures and processes that make it work (p. 16)

Psychosexual Disorders A group of psychological disorders centering on problems of sexual inhibitions and dysfunctions and sexual deviations (p. 534)

Psychosexual Stages Freud's stages of sexual development in a child which involve successive ways of satisfying instinctual biological urges through stimulation of different areas of the body: the mouth, anus, and the genitals (p. 89)

Psychosis A severe mental disorder in which a person experiences impairments in reality-testing manifested through thought, emotional, or perceptual difficulties (p. 524)

Psychosocial Stages Successive developmental stages proposed by Erik Erikson that focus on an individual's orientation toward the self and others; these stages incorporate both sexual and social aspects of a person's development and social conflicts that arise from the interaction between an individual and the social environment (p. 90)

Psychosomatic Disorder A physical disorder aggravated by, or primarily attributable to, prolonged emotional stress or other psychological causes (p. 501)

Psychotherapy The group of therapies used to treat psychological disorders that focus on changing faulty behaviors, thoughts, perceptions, and emotions that may be associated with specific disorders (p. 563)

Puberty The attainment of sexual maturity, indicated for girls by menarche, the onset of menstruation, and for boys by the production of live sperm accompanied by the ability to ejaculate (p. 92)

Pubescent Growth Spurt Physical growth spurt that is the first concrete indicator of the end of childhood (p. 92)

Punishment The condition of receiving an aversive stimulus, which decreases the probability of the preceding response (p. 276)

Pupil An opening in the iris that allows light to enter the eye (p. 151)

Pure Tone A sound produced by a single sine wave (p. 167)

Q

Questionnaire A written set of questions (p. 40)

R

Random Assignment Assignment of subjects to either the experimental or control groups by a chance procedure so that each subject has an equal change of being placed in either group (p. 41)

Range The difference between the highest and the lowest scores in a frequency distribution; the simplest measure of variability (p. 51)

Rationalism The view, associated with Plato and Descartes, that the human mind came prepared with certain basic ideas that ordered all sensory experience (p. 12)

Reaction Time The elapsed time between a stimulus presentation and a designated response; used as a measure of the time required for mental processes (p. 109; 340)

Recall A method of retrieval in which an individual is required to reproduce the information previously presented (p. 321)

Receptive Field The visual area from which a given ganglion cell receives messages (p. 162)

Recessive Genes Genes that are expressed in an individual's development only when paired with similar genes (p. 66)

Reciprocal Determinism A concept of Bandura's social learning theory referring to the notion that a complex reciprocal interaction exists between factors of an individual, behavior, and environmental stimuli, with each of these components affecting the others (p. 442)

Recognition A method of retrieval in which an individual is required to identify present stimuli as having been experienced before (p. 321)

Reductionism The belief that observable phenomena at one level of analysis can be accounted for by more fundamental laws at a lower or more basic level (p. 108)

Redundancy Duplication in a cellular system, providing a "margin of safety" to guarantee that a specific job will get done even if some cells are damaged (p. 110)

Reference Frame Spatial or temporal context (p. 200)

Reference Groups The formal or informal groups from which a person derives attitudes and standards of acceptability and appropriateness and to which a person refers for information, direction, and support for life-style (p. 631)

Reflex A reaction in which an external stimulus leads to a physical response; an unlearned response elicited by specific stimuli which have biological relevance for an organism (p. 107; 262)

Reflex Arc Neural circuit including nerve pathways carrying incoming sensory information and pathways carrying outgoing motor signals (p. 118)

Refractory Period Period of rest during which a nerve impulse cannot be activated (p. 114)

Reinforcers Stimuli occurring after a response that change its rate or probability (p. 275)

Relative Motion Parallax A source of information about depth in which the relative distances of objects from a viewer determine the amount and direction of their relative motion in the retinal image (p. 204)
Releaser An environmental cue that evokes a specific response pattern in every member of a species (p. 380)
Reliability The degree to which individuals earn the same relative scores each time they are measured (p. 33; 455)
REM Sleep A stage during the sleep cycle in which electrical brain activity is characterized by erratic, low-voltage patterns similar to those observed during the waking state and during which there are bursts of rapid eye movements; also known as *paradoxical sleep* (p. 240)
Replication Repetition of an experiment under similar conditions in order to see if the same results will be obtained; usually conducted by an independent investigator (p. 29)
Representativeness Heuristic A cognitive strategy that assigns something to a category on the basis of a few characteristics regarded as representative of the category (p. 355)
Repression In Freudian theory, a defense mechanism by which painful or guilt-producing thoughts, feelings, or memories are excluded from conscious awareness (p. 434)
Research Design Conditions under which an investigator measures behavior (p. 41)
Residual Stress Pattern Chronic syndrome in which the emotional responses of posttraumatic stress persist over time (p. 503)
Resistance Inability or unwillingness of a patient in psychoanalysis to discuss certain ideas, desires, or experiences (p. 569)
Response Any behavior of organisms in reaction to a stimulus (p. 7)
Response Bias A systematic tendency, as a result of nonsensory factors, for an observer to favor responding in a particular way (p. 146)
Reticular Activating System (RAS) A long structure in the middle of the brain stem through which sensory messages pass on their way to higher centers of the brain (p. 130)
Retina The layer at the back of the eye which contains photoreceptors (p. 151)
Retrieval The recovery of stored information from memory at a later time (p. 302)
Retrieval Cues Internally or externally generated stimuli available to help with the retrieval of a memory (p. 320)
Retroactive Interference A memory phenomenon in which the learning of new information interferes with the memory of a previously stored similar item (p. 328)
Retrograde Amnesia A type of amnesia in which there is loss of memory for events experienced prior to the event that precipitated the amnesia (p. 332)
Rites of Passage See *initiation rite.*
Rods Photoreceptors that are concentrated in the periphery of the retina, are most active for seeing in dim illumination, and do not produce sensations of color (p. 153)
Role A socially defined pattern of behavior that is expected of a person who has a certain function within a group or setting (p. 629)
Rorschach Test Projective test in which the ambiguous symmetrical stimuli are inkblots (p. 476)
Round Window Structure which absorbs wave motion circulating through the cochlea (p. 170)
Rule Behavioral guideline to act in a certain way in certain situations (p. 294)
Rule Learning Recognition of the behavioral implications of rules, the contexts in which they are relevant, and the perception of reinforcing contingencies for obeying or violating rules (p. 294)

S

Sadism A type of psychosexual disorder involving sexual excitement derived from inflicting pain, suffering, or humiliation on others (p. 535)
Saturation The dimension of color space that captures the "purity" and "vividness" of color sensations (p. 155)
Savings Term for phenomenon by which a conditioned response which has been extinguished, with further acquisition training, gains strength more rapidly than it did initially (p. 265)
Scapegoat A target other than the original source of frustration onto which aggression is displaced (p. 648)
Schedules of Punishment In operant conditioning, the pattern of delivering punishment (p. 285)
Schedules of Reinforcement In operant conditioning, the pattern of delivering and withholding reinforcement (p. 285)
Schema An integrated cluster of knowledge organized around a topic; includes expectations (p. 211; 324; 346)
Scheme A term first used by Piaget to denote a cognitive structure that relates means to ends; guides sensorimotor sequence such as sucking with little or no "thought" (p. 77)
Schizophrenic Disorders A group of psychotic disorders characterized by the breakdown of integrated personality functioning, withdrawal from reality, emotional distortions, and disturbed thought processes (p. 540)
Schwann Cells Specialized glial cells that wrap themselves around the axons forming the myelin sheath (p. 112)
Scientific Method A set of attitudes and procedures for gathering and interpreting objective information in a way that minimizes sources of error and yields dependable generalizations (p. 28)
Script A cluster of knowledge about a sequence of interrelated specific events and actions that are expected to occur in a certain way in particular settings (p. 347)
Secondary Appraisal A term used in stress research to refer to the second stage in the cognitive appraisal of a potentially stressful situation in which an individual evaluates the personal and social resources available to deal with the stressful circumstance and determines the needed action (p. 497)
Secondary Trait A characteristic that is not crucial to an understanding of an individual but nevertheless provides some information about enduring qualities of the person (p. 426)
Second Messenger Chemical substance released by the sensor portion of an ion channel when it detects a sensory stimulus (p. 116)
Second-order Conditioning A classical conditioning procedure in which a neutral stimulus is paired with a conditioned stimulus rather than an unconditioned stimulus; also called *higher-order conditioning* (p. 268)
Selective Attention Refers to the ability to be aware of only part of the available sensory input (p. 307)
Self In humanistic psychology, the irreducible unit out of which the coherence and stability of a personality emerge (p. 445)
Self-actualization A concept in personality psychology referring to a person's constant striving to realize his or her potential and to develop inherent talents and capabilities; many humanistic psychologists see the need for self-actualization as the most basic human need (p. 385; 438)
Self-concept An individual's awareness of his or her continuing identity as a person (p. 445)
Self-deception The mind's tendency to filter out information that is threatening to a person's self-esteem (p. 190)
Self-efficacy A belief that a person can perform adequately in a particular situation (p. 397; 443)
Self-esteem A generalized evaluative attitude toward the self that influences both moods and behavior (p. 445)
Self-fulfilling Prophecy The notion that a hypothesis or expectation about the way someone will act exerts a subtle influence on the person to act in the expected way or for the perceiver to "see" what is expected (p. 604)
Self-report Method An often used research technique in which a personality assessment is achieved through respondents' answers to a series of questions (p. 460)
Semantic Memory That aspect of long-term memory which stores the basic meaning of words and concepts (p. 316)

Semicircular Canals Fluid-filled canals in the inner ear which provide vestibular sense information (p. 174)

Sensation Processes that analyze physical energy in the world (for example, light and sound waves) and convert it into neural activity that codes simple information about the way the receptor organs are being stimulated (p. 143; 185)

Sensorimotor Stage First of Piaget's stages of cognitive development (from about 0–2 years); characterized by improvement and coordination of sensorimotor sequences, object permanence, and the beginning of internal symbolic representation (p. 78)

Sensory Adaptation A phenomenon in which visual receptors cells lose their power to respond after a period of unchanged stimulation (p. 164)

Sensory Gating A brain-directed process in which information in one sensory channel may be enhanced while information in another is suppressed or disregarded (p. 305)

Sensory Memory Those memory processes involved in the momentary preservation of fleeting impressions of sensory stimuli; also called *sensory register* (p. 304)

Sensory Neurons Neurons that carry messages from the cells in the periphery toward the central nervous system (p. 111)

Sensory Physiology The study of the way biological mechanisms convert physical events into neural events (p. 144)

Sensory Preconditioning The learning of an association between two paired stimuli prior to any pairing of either one with an unconditioned stimulus (p. 292)

Sensory Register See *sensory memory.*

Sequential Design A research approach in which a group of subjects spanning a small age range are grouped according to year of birth and are observed repeatedly over several years; design combines some features of both the cross-sectional and longitudinal approaches (p. 61)

Serial Position Effect A characteristic of retrieval in which the recall of beginning and end items on a list is better than memory for items appearing in the middle (p. 323)

Set A temporary readiness to perceive or react to a stimulus in a particular way (p. 212)

Sex The biologically based characteristics that distinguish males from females (p. 86)

Sexual Arousal The motivational state of excitement and tension brought about by physiological and cognitive reactions to erotic stimuli (p. 391)

Sexual Scripts Socially learned programs of sexual responsiveness (p. 393)

Shape Constancy Ability to perceive the true shape of an object despite variations in the size of the retinal image (p. 208)

Shaping The operant learning technique in which a new behavior is produced by reinforcing successive approximations of the final behavior desired (p. 281)

Short-term Memory Those memory processes associated with the preservation of events or experiences recently perceived; short-term memory is of limited capacity and stores information for only a short length of time without rehearsal (p. 304)

Significant Difference A statistical correlation showing that the difference between groups or conditions is probably not caused by chance (p. 54)

Simultaneous Conditioning Temporal pattern in classical conditioning in which a conditioned stimulus and an unconditioned stimulus are presented at the same time (p. 264)

Size Constancy Ability to perceive the true size of an object despite variations in the size of its retinal image (p. 206)

Social Comparison Theory A concept postulating a need for individuals to seek out and make subjective comparisons to certain other people in order to assess their own abilities, opinions, and emotions. (p. 623)

Social Context The part of the total environment that includes other people, both real and imagined, interactions, the setting in which the interactions take place, and unwritten rules and expectations that govern the way people relate to each other (p. 601)

Social Exchange Theory A hypothesis about social interactions that conceives of them in economic terms as exchanges between people having both benefits and costs (p. 626)

Social Facilitation The facilitating effect that the presence of other people sometimes has on individual performance (p. 630)

Socialization The lifelong process whereby an individual's behavioral patterns, values, standards, skills, attitudes, and motives are shaped to conform to those regarded as desirable in a particular society (p. 82)

Social Loafing The unconscious tendency to slack off when performing in a group (p. 630)

Social Norms Expectations that a group has for its members regarding acceptable and appropriate attitudes and behavior (p. 630)

Social Perception The process by which a person comes to know or perceive the personal attributes of him- or herself and other people (p. 606)

Social Phobia A type of phobia in which an individual experiences an irrational fear of speaking, writing, performing artistically, or eating in public (p. 529)

Social Psychology The branch of psychology that studies the effect of social variables on individual behavior, attitudes, perceptions, and motives; it also studies group and intergroup phenomena (p. 601)

Social Reality The phenomenological perspective and norms of the group which define reality for its members (p. 603)

Social Referencing Process of searching for emotional information as a behavioral regulator (p. 413)

Social Stereotype The beliefs people have about the personality traits and abilities commonly found among individual members of a particular social group (p. 608)

Social Support Resources, including material aid, socioemotional support, and informational aid, provided by others to help a person cope with stress (p. 513)

Sodium and Potassium Pump Transport mechanism which pushes sodium out of a cell and potassium back into it, thus returning it to resting potential (p. 115)

Soma The cell body of a neuron; contains the nucleus and cytoplasm of the cell (p. 111)

Somatic Nervous System The part of the peripheral nervous system that controls the skeletal muscles of the body (p. 123)

Somatoform Disorders A group of disorders characterized by bodily (somatic) complaints in the absence of any known organic problems that is assumed to reflect psychological conflicts (p. 531)

Somatosensory Area Area of the parietal lobes that receives sensory input from various body areas (p. 132)

Somatotype A descriptive category that classifies a person on the basis of a few salient physical characteristics with the hope of relating these to personality characteristics (p. 424)

Sound Spectrum A graph of all the frequencies, with their amplitudes, present in a sound (p. 168)

Spatial Frequency The number of dark-light cycles in a pattern over a given distance of visual space (p. 164)

Spatial-frequency Model The theory that the visual system analyzes complex stimuli into spatial frequencies (p. 164)

Spinal Cord The nerve tract in the spinal column between the brain and the peripheral nervous system (p. 122)

Split-span Task An experimental task requiring recall of simultaneous input to the two ears (p. 226)

Spontaneous Recovery The reappearance of an extinguished conditioned response after a rest period (p. 265)

Standard Deviation A measure of the variability of scores in a distribution indicating the average difference between scores and their mean (p. 51)

Standardization Uniform procedures for treating each participant or for recording data; in test construction, includes giving the test to a large number of representative individuals to establish norms (p. 31; 456)

Standardized Measuring Device A measuring device that has been administered to a large group of subjects who are representative of the group for which the device is intended, thus yielding statistical standards or norms to be used for comparisons (p. 456)

Standford-Binet Intelligence Test The most widely used children's intelligence test; a version of the Binet written intelligence test using age-level subtests, in which subjects are tested individually (p. 463)

State-dependent Learning A characteristic of the memory system in which retrieval is better if the psychological or physical state present at the time of learning is similar to that present at the time of retrieval (p. 315)

Statistics Mathematical tool used by researchers to help them describe their findings in an objective, uniform way; provides a sound standard for inferring whether the results are real or chance occurrences (p. 48)

Stereochemical Theory A theory of smell which suggests that receptor sites in odor-sensitive cells have distinctive sizes and shapes corresponding to those of the chemical molecules which stimulate them (p. 174)

Stereotype Effect A bias sometimes occurring in ratings or observations in which judges' beliefs about the qualities of most people who belong to a certain category influence the perception of an observed individual who belongs to that particular category (p. 461)

Stimulants Drugs that increase the transmission of impulses in the central nervous system and tend to speed up mental and physical activity (p. 250)

Stimulus An environmental condition that elicits a response from an organism (p. 7)

Stimulus Control Control of the occurrence of a response by means of a dependable signal (a discriminative stimulus) indicating a reinforcer is available (p. 276)

Stimulus Discrimination A conditioning process in which an organism learns to respond differently to stimuli that are different from the conditioned stimulus on some dimension (p. 266)

Stimulus Generalization The automatic extension of conditioned responding to similar stimuli that have never been paired with the unconditioned stimulus (p. 265)

Storage The retention of encoded material over time involving neurophysiological changes in certain synapses (p. 302)

Stress The pattern of specific and nonspecific responses an organism makes to stimulus events that disturb its equilibrium and tax or exceed its ability to cope (p. 496)

Stressors Internal or external events or stimuli that induce stress (p. 496)

Structuralism The view, associated with Wundt and Titchener and based on the presumption that all human mental experience can be understood as the combination of simple events or elements, that the underlying structure of the human mind can be revealed by analyzing all the basic elements of sensation and other experience which forms an individual's mental life; the study of the how and why of experience (p. 14; 144)

Subconscious Processes Mental processes involving material not currently in consciousness but retrievable by special recall procedures (p. 231)

Subject A participant in an experiment whose behavior is being observed (p. 41)

Superego In Freudian theory, that aspect of personality representing the internalization of society's values, standards, and morals; the inner conscious (p. 433)

Superior Colliculus Cluster of nerve cell bodies in the midbrain region of the brain stem involved in the integration of sensory input of different type (p. 154)

Survey A method of gathering information from a large number of people; self-report information is gathered in response to a list of questions that follow a fixed format (p. 40)

Sympathetic Division The division of the autonomic nervous system that deals with emergency responding (p. 123)

Synapse The gap between one neuron and the next; it is filled with a fluid that does not permit electrical activity to pass across (p. 116)

Synaptic Vesicles Tiny sacs in the terminal button of the axon which release precisely measured amounts of transmitter chemicals into the synaptic gap (p. 116)

Systematic Desensitization Behavioral therapy technique in which a client is taught to prevent the arousal of anxiety by relaxing (p. 572)

T

Tabula Rasa Term associated with the philosophical view of John Locke that, at birth, individuals are born with a "blank slate" and that all knowledge comes from experience (p. 13)

Taste Aversion Learning Biological constraint on learning in which an organism learns to avoid a food whose ingestion is followed by illness (p. 289)

Taste Buds The receptors for taste, located primarily on the upper side of the tongue (p. 173)

Telegraphic Speech The speech pattern of a normal child 2–3 years of age that consists of short, simple sentences with many nouns and verbs but lacks tense endings, plurals, and function words (p. 74)

Teleology The view that an immaterial, purposeful mind gives behavior its direction by acting on a passive, mechanistic brain (p. 108)

Temporal Contiguity The principle stating that sensations, movements, or ideas occurring closely in time become associated with one another (p. 13)

Tension Reduction The reinforcing state that follows from the reduction of unpleasant sensations which occur as a result of unsatisfied drives (p. 439)

Terminal Buttons Swollen, bulblike structures at the branched endings of axons that transmit impulses to the next neuron in the chain (p. 111)

Territoriality An innate drive to gain and defend property (p. 645)

Testosterone A male hormone secreted by the testes; responsible for sex-linked characteristics such as facial hair and deep voice (p. 126)

Test-retest Reliability A measure of the correlation between the scores of the same people on the same test given on two different occasions (p. 455)

Texture Gradient Change in apparent texture when a uniform textured surface is slanted away from an observer (p. 195)

Thalamus Structure below the corpus callosum that serves as a relay station for all incoming sensory information (p. 130)

Thanatos In Freudian theory, the death instinct, assumed to drive people toward aggressive and destructive behavior (p. 432)

Thematic Apperception Test (TAT) A type of projective test in which pictures of ambiguous scenes are presented to an individual who is encouraged to generate stories about the stimuli (p. 477)

Theory of Signal Detection A theory that all perceptual judgments combine sensory and decision-making processes (p. 147)

Theory X View of human nature which assumes that people are basically lazy, ignorant, selfish, prone to error, and motivated solely by money (p. 400)

Theory Y View of human nature which assumes that people are basically creative, responsible, and intrinsically motivated to do good work to the extent that the work is challenging (p. 400)

Think-aloud Protocols Reports of mental processes and strategies made by experimental subjects while working on a task (p. 339)

Threshold The minimum stimulus energy sufficient to excite a neuron and nerve impulse (p. 113)

Thyrotrophic Hormone (TTH) A hormone released from the pituitary gland which stimulates the thyroid gland to make more energy available to the body during a stress reaction (p. 499)

Timbre A dimension of auditory sensation which reflects the complexity of a sound wave (p. 168)

Time Perspective The way we partition the flow of perceived events and experiences into the frames of past, present, and future (p. 398)

Token Economy A technique of positive reinforcement in which individuals are rewarded for socially constructive behaviors by tokens which may later be exchanged for privileges (p. 280)

Tolerance Lessened effect of a drug following continued use (p. 248)

Top-down Processes Perceptual processes in which information from an individual's past experience, knowledge, expectations, motivations, and background feed down to influence the way a perceived object is interpreted and classified (p. 188)

Trace Forward Conditioning Temporal pattern in classical conditioning in which a conditioned stimulus goes off before the onset of an unconditioned stimulus, but presumably some form of memory trace bridges the gap between the offset of the conditioned stimulus and the onset of the unconditioned stimulus (p. 264)

Trait Enduring and continuous quality or attribute which influences behavior because it acts as a generalized action tendency (p. 426)

Trance Logic Denial at one level of information processing occurring at another level (p. 246)

Transactional Perception Theory of "perception as hypotheses" which stresses the importance of transactions with the environment as the basis for developing hypotheses (p. 195)

Transduction Transformation of one form of energy into another; for example, chemical energy into physical energy or light into neural impulses (p. 110; 144)

Transference The process by which a person in psychoanalysis attaches to a therapist feelings formerly held toward some significant person who figured in a past emotional conflict (p. 569)

Trichromatic Theory The theory that there are three types of color receptors producing the psychologically "primary" color sensations: red, green, and blue (p. 158)

Two-factor Theory of Emotion The theory that emotion is the joint effect of two central processes: physiological arousal and cognitive appraisal (p. 410)

Tympanic Membrane A thin membrane in the ear set into motion by the pressure variations of sound waves; also known as the *eardrum* (p. 170)

Type A distinct pattern of personality characteristics (p. 424)

Type-A Behavior Pattern Competitive, compulsive, and hostile behavior characteristic of a particular style of coping with stress; assumed to increase the risk of coronary heart disease (p. 494)

U

Unconditioned Response (UR) In classical conditioning, the response which is elicited by an unconditioned stimulus without prior training or learning (p. 263)

Unconditioned Stimulus (US) In classical conditioning, the stimulus which elicits an unconditioned response and the presentation of which acts as reinforcement (p. 263)

Unconscious Inference Helmholtz' term for perception, so called because it took place outside the conscious awareness (p. 195)

Unconscious Processes In Freudian theory, mental processes that are not directly observable or subject to verification by self-report, but whose existence is inferred from effects on observable behaviors (p. 231)

V

Validity The extent to which a test measures what it was intended to measure (p. 33; 455)

Variable A factor that varies in amount or kind (p. 6)

Variable Interval Schedule (VI) In operant conditioning, a schedule in which reinforcement is delivered after differing lengths of time, regardless of the number of correct responses that have occurred (p. 287)

Variable Ratio Schedule (VR) In operant conditioning, a schedule in which reinforcement is given after a changing number of responses (p. 286)

Verbal Report Measurement technique in which subjects provide answers to questions (p. 39)

Vestibular Sense The sense that tells us how our bodies are oriented in the world with respect to gravity (p. 174)

Violence The expression of hostility and rage directed against people or property (p. 643)

Visual Cortex Area at the back of the brain, in the occipital lobes, where visual information is processed (p. 132; 154)

Volley Principle An extension of frequency theory which proposes that when peaks in a sound wave come too frequently for a single neuron to fire at each peak, several neurons as a group could fire at the frequency of the stimulus tone (p. 172)

Voyeurism Paraphilia in which the preferred means of sexual arousal is observation of others disrobing, nude, or engaged in sexual activity—without their awareness of being observed (p. 535)

W

Wavelength A physical property of waves measured in units of distance along the wavelike propagation; wavelength is the only property that distinguishes one photon from another (p. 155)

Weber's Law The assertion that the size of a difference threshold is proportional to the intensity of the standard stimulus (p. 149)

Whole-report Procedure An experimental technique used in memory studies in which subjects presented with a pattern containing several stimuli are subsequently asked to recall as many of the individual stimuli as possible (p. 305)

Withdrawal Symptoms Painful physical symptoms experienced when the level of a drug to which physical addiction has occurred is decreased or eliminated (p. 248)

Word Association A technique of personality assessment using an individual's responses to a list of common words to identify unconscious personality dynamics (p. 476)

References

A

Abelson, R. P. (1981). Psychological status of the script concept. *American Psychologist, 36,* 715–729.

Abramson, L. Y., Garber, J., Edwards, N., & Seligman, M. E. P. (1978). Expectancy changes in depression and schizophrenia. *Journal of Abnormal Psychology, 87,* 102–109.

Abramson, L. Y., Seligman, M. E. P., & Teasdale, J. D. (1978). Learned helplessness in humans: Critique and reformulation. *Journal of Abnormal Psychology, 87,* 49–74.

Adams, J. (1979). Mutual-help groups: Enhancing the coping ability of oncology clients. *Cancer Nursing, 2,* 95–98.

Adams, J. A. (1987). Historical review and appraisal of research on the learning, retention, and transfer of human motor skills. *Psychological Bulletin, 101,* 41–74.

Adams, J. L. (1979). *Conceptual blockbusting* (2d ed.). New York: Norton.

Adams, J. S. (1965). Inequity in social exchange. In L. Berkowitz (Ed.), *Advances in experimental social psychology* (Vol. 2, pp. 267–99). New York: Academic Press.

Ader, R. (1981). A historical account of conditioned immunobiologic responses. In R. Ader (Ed.), *Psychoneuroimmunology.* New York: Academic Press.

Ader, R., & Cohen, N. (1981). Conditioned immunopharmacological responses. In R. Ader (Ed.), *Psychoneuroimmunology* (pp. 281–319). New York: Academic Press.

Adler, A. (1929). *The practice and theory of individual psychology.* New York: Harcourt, Brace & World.

Agras, W. S., Taylor, C. B., Kraemer, H. C., Allen, R. A., & Schneider, J. A. (1980). Relaxation training: Twenty-four-hour blood pressure changes. *Archives of General Psychiatry, 37,* 859–863.

Ainsworth, M. D. S. (1973). The development of infant-mother attachment. In B. M. Caldwell & H. N. Ricciuti (Eds.), *Review of child development research* (Vol. 3). Chicago: University of Chicago Press.

Ajzen, I., & Fishbein, M. (1977). Attitude-behavior relations: A theoretical analysis and review of empirical research. *Psychological Bulletin, 84,* 888–918.

Akhtar, S., Wig, N. H., Verma, V. K., Pershod, D., & Verma, S. K. (1975). A phenomenological analysis of symptoms in obsessive-compulsive neurosis. *British Journal of Psychiatry, 127,* 342–348.

Akil, H. (1978). Endorphins, beta-LPH and ACTH: Biochemical pharmacological and anatomical studies. *Advances in Biochemical Psychopharmacology, 18,* 125–139.

Alba, J. W., & Hasher, L. (1983). Is memory schematic? *Psychological Bulletin, 93,* 203–231.

Albee, G. W., & Joffe, J. M. (Eds.). (1977). *Primary prevention of psychopathology: Vol. 1. Issues.* Hanover, NH: University Press of New England.

Albuquerque, E. X., Aguayo, L. G., Warnick, R. K., Ickowicz, R. K., & Blaustein, M. P. (1983, June). Interactions of phencyclidine with ion channels of nerve and muscle: Behavioral implications. *Federation Proceedings, 42(9),* 2584–2589.

Alderfer, C. (1972). *Existence, relatedness, and growth.* New York: Free Press.

Alker, H., & Poppen, P. J. (1973). Ideology in university students. *Journal of Personality, 41,* 653–671.

Allen, B. P. (1985). After the missiles: Sociopsychological effects of nuclear war. *American Psychologist, 40,* 927–937.

Allen, V. L., & Wilder, D. A. (1975). Categorization, belief, similarity, and intergroup competition. *Journal of Personality and Social Psychology, 32,* 971–977.

Allison, T., & Cicchetti, D. (1976). Sleep in mammals: Ecological and constitutional correlates. *Science, 194,* 732–734.

Alloy, L. B., & Abramson, L. Y. (1979). Judgment of contingency in depressed and nondepressed students: Sadder but wiser? *Journal of Experimental Psychology: General, 108,* 441–485.

Alloy, L. B., & Abramson, L. Y. (1980). The cognitive component of human helplessness and depression. In J. Garber & M. E. P. Seligman (Eds.), *Human helplessness: Theory and applications.* New York: Academic Press.

Allport, G. W. (1937). *Personality: A psychological interpretation.* New York: Holt, Rinehart & Winston.

Allport, G. W. (1960). *Personality and social encounter.* Berkeley, CA: Beacon Press.

Allport, G. W. (1961). *Pattern and growth in personality.* New York: Holt, Rinehart & Winston.

Allport, G. W. (1965). *Letters from Jenny.* New York: Harcourt, Brace & World.

Allport, G. W. (1966). Traits revisited. *American Psychologist, 21,* 1–10.

Allport, G. W. (1968). The historical background of modern social psychology. In G. Lindzey & E. Aronson (Eds.), *The handbook of social psychology* (2d ed.). Reading, MA: Addison-Wesley.

Allport, G. W., & Postman, L. J. (1947). *The psychology of rumor.* New York: Holt, Rinehart & Winston.

Almli, C. R. (1978). The ontogeny of feeding and drinking behavior: Effects of early brain damage. *Neuroscience and Behavioral Reviews, 2,* 281–300.

Altman, I. A. (1976). Environmental psychology and social psychology. *Personality and Social Psychology Bulletin, 2,* 96–113.

Amabile, T. M. (1983). *The social psychology of creativity.* New York: Springer-Verlag.

American Psychological Association. (1965). Special issue: Testing and public policy. *American Psychologist, 20,* 857–993.

Ames, A. (1951). Visual perception and rotating trapezoidal window. *Psychological Monographs, 324.*

Amoore, J. E. (1965). Psychophysics of odor. *Cold Springs Harbor symposia in quantitative biology, 30,* 623–637.

Amnesty International. (1983). *Chile: Evidence of torture.* London: Amnesty International Publications.

Anastasi, A. (1976). *Psychological testing* (4th ed.). New York: Macmillan.

Anastasi, A. (1982). *Psychological testing* (5th ed.). New York: Macmillan.

Andersen, A. (1985). *Practical and comprehensive treatment of anorexia nervosa and bulimia.* Baltimore: Johns Hopkins University Press.

Andersen, S. M., & Zimbardo, P. G. (1980, November). Resisting mind control. *U.S.A. Today,* 44–47.

Anderson, C. A. (1987). Temperature and aggression: Effects on quarterly, yearly, and city rates of violent and nonviolent crime. *Journal of Personality and Social Psychology, 52,* 1161–1173.

Anderson, J. R. (1976). *Language, memory, and thought.* Hillsdale, NJ: Erlbaum.

Anderson, J. R. (1978). Arguments concerning representations for mental imagery. *Psychological Review, 85,* 249–277.

Anderson, J. R. (1980). *Cognitive psychology and its implications.* San Francisco: Freeman.

Anderson, J. R. (Ed.). (1981). *Cognitive skills and their acquisition.* Hillsdale, NJ: Erlbaum.

Anderson, J. R. (Ed.). (1981). *Cognitive skills and their acquisition.* Hillsdale, NJ: Erlbaum.

Anderson, J. R. (1982). Acquisition of cognitive skill. *Psychological Review, 89,* 369–406.

Anderson, J. R., & Bower, G. H. (1973). *Human associative memory.* Washington, DC: Winston & Sons.

Angier, R. P. (1927). The conflict theory of emotion. *American Journal of Psychology, 39,* 390–401.

Antelman, S. M., & Caggiula, A. R. (1980). Stress-induced behavior: Chemotherapy without drugs. In J. M. Davidson & R. J. Davidson (Eds.), *The psychobiology of consciousness* (pp. 65–104). New York: Plenum.

Antelman, S. M., Rowland, N. E., & Fisher, A. E. (1976). Stimulation bound ingestive behavior: A view from the tail. *Physiology and Behavior, 17,* 743–748.

Ardrey, R. (1966). *The territorial imperative.* New York: Atheneum.

Archer, D., & Gartner, R. (1984). *Violence and crime in cross-national perspective.* New Haven, CT: Yale University Press.

Arkin, R. M., & Baumgardner, A. H. (1985). Self-handicapping. In J. H. Harvey & G. Weary (Eds.), *Attribution: Basic issues and applications* (pp. 169–202). New York: Academic Press.

Arnold, M. B. (1970). Perennial problems in the field of emotion. In M. B. Arnold (Ed.), *Feelings and emotions: The Loyola symposium* (pp. 169–85). New York: Academic Press.

Aronson, E. (1969). Some antecedents of interpersonal attraction. In W. J. Arnold & D. Levine (Eds.), *Nebraska symposium on motivation.* Lincoln: University of Nebraska Press.

Aronson, E., Blaney, N., Stephan, C., Sikes, J., & Snapp, M. (1978). *The jigsaw classroom.* Beverly Hills, CA: Sage.

Aronson, E., Turner, J. A., & Carlsmith, J. M. (1963). Communicator credibility and communication discrepancy as determinants of opinion change. *Journal of Abnormal and Social Psychology, 67,* 31–36.

Asarnow, R. F., Cromwell, R. L., & Rennick, P. M. (1978). Cognitive and evoked response measures of information processing in schizophrenics with and without a family history of schizophrenia. *The Journal of Nervous and Mental Disease, 166,* 719–730.

Asch, S. E. (1955). Opinions and social pressure. *Scientific American, 193(5),* 31–35.

Aserinsky, E., & Kleitman, N. (1953). Regularly occurring periods of eye mobility and concomitant phenomena during sleep. *Science, 118,* 273–274.

Ashley, W. R., Harper, R. S., & Runyon, D. L. (1951). The perceived size of coins in normal and hypnotically induced economic states. *American Journal of Psychology, 64,* 564–572.

Ashton, P. T., & Webb, R. B. (1986). *Making a difference: A teacher's sense of efficacy and student achievement.* New York: Longman.

Atkinson, J. W., & Birch, D. (1970). *The dynamics of action.* New York: Wiley.

Atkinson, R. C., & Shiffrin, R. M. (1968). Human memory: A proposed system and its control processes. In K. W. Spence & J. T. Spence (Eds.), *The psychology of learning and motivation: Advances in research and theory* (Vol. 2). New York: Academic Press.

Averbach, I., & Coriell, A. S. (1961). Short-term memory in vision. *Bell System Technical Journal, 40,* 309–328.

Averill, J. R. (1969). Autonomic response patterns during sadness and mirth. *Psychophysiology, 5,* 399–414.

Averill, J. R. (1976). Emotion and anxiety: Sociocultural, biological, and psychological determinants. In M. Zuckerman & C. O. Spielberger (Eds.), *Emotion and anxiety: New concepts, methods and applications* (pp. 87–130). Hillsdale, NJ: Erlbaum.

Ayllon, T., & Azrin, N. H. (1965). The measurement and reinforcement of behavior of psychotics. *Journal of Experimental Analysis of Behavior, 8,* 357–383.

Ayllon, T., & Azrin, N. H. (1968). *The token economy: A motivational system for therapy and rehabilitation.* New York: Appleton-Century-Crofts.

Ayllon, T., & Michael, J. (1959). The psychiatric nurse as a behavioral engineer. *Journal of the Experimental Analysis of Behavior, 2,* 323–334.

Azrin, N. H., & Fox, R. M. (1976). *Toilet training in less than a day.* New York: Pocket Books.

Azrin, N. H., & Holz, W. C. (1966). Punishment. In N. K. Honig (Ed.), *Operant behavior* (pp. 380–447). New York: Appleton-Century-Crofts.

B

Bachman, J. G., O'Malley, P. M., & Johnston, J. (1979). *Adolescence to adulthood: Change and stability in the lives of young men.* Ann Arbor, MI: Institute for Social Research.

Backus, J., & Backus, H. (1984). *Backus strikes back.* Briarcliff Manor: Stein and Day.

Baddeley, A. D. (1982). *Your memory, a user's guide.* New York: Macmillan.

Baddeley, A. D., & Hitch, G. (1974). Working memory. In G. H. Bower (Ed.), *The psychology of learning and motivation* (Vol. 8). New York: Academic Press.

Baillargeon, R. (1986). Representing the existence and the location of hidden objects: Object permanence in 6- and 8-month-old infants. *Cognition, 23,* 21–42.

Baillargeon, R., Spelke, E. S., & Wasseman, S. (1985). Object permanence in five-month-old infants. *Cognition, 20,* 191–208.

Baker, A. A., & Thorpe, J. G. (1957). Placebo response. *AMA Archives of Neurology and Psychiatry, 78,* 57–60.

Bales, R. F. (1958). Task roles and social roles in problem-solving groups. In E. E. Maccoby, T. M. Newcomb, & E. L. Hartley (Eds.), *Readings in social psychology* (3d ed.). New York: Holt, Rinehart & Winston.

Balsam, P. D., & Tomie, A. (Eds.). (1985). *Context and learning.* Hillsdale, NJ: Erlbaum.

Baltes, P. B., Reese, H. W., & Lipsitt, L. P. (1980). Life-span developmental psychology. In M. Rosenzweig & L. Porter (Eds.), *Annual review of psychology.* Palo Alto, CA: Annual Reviews Press.

Bandura, A. (1965). Influence of models' reinforcement contingencies on the acquisition of imitative responses. *Journal of Personality and Social Psychology, 1,* 589–595.

Bandura, A. (1970). Modeling therapy. In W. S. Sahakian (Ed.), *Psychopathology today: Experimentation, theory and research.* Itasca, IL: Peacock.

Bandura, A. (1973). *Aggression: A social learning analysis.* Englewood Cliffs, NJ: Prentice-Hall.

Bandura, A. (1977a). *Social learning theory.* Englewood Cliffs, NJ: Prentice-Hall.

Bandura, A. (1977b). Self-efficacy. *Psychological Review, 84,* 191–215.

Bandura, A. (1981a). In search of pure unidirectional determinants. *Behavior Therapy, 12,* 30–40.

Bandura, A. (1981b). Self-referent thought: A developmental analysis of self-efficacy. In J. H. Flavell & L. Ross (Eds.), *Social cognitive development: Frontiers and possible futures.* Cambridge: Cambridge University Press.

Bandura, A. (1982a). The psychology of chance encounters and life paths. *American Psychologist, 37,* 747–755.

Bandura, A. (1982b). Self-efficacy mechanism in human agency. *American Psychologist, 37,* 122–147.

Bandura, A. (1986). *Social foundations of thought and action: A social cognitive theory.* Englewood Cliffs, NJ: Prentice-Hall.

Bandura, A. (1987, March). *Mechanisms of moral disengagement.* Washington, DC: Woodrow Wilson International Center for Scholars. Paper presented at the Conference, Psychology of Terrorism: Behaviors, World-Views, States of Mind.

Bandura, A., Adams, N. E., Hardy, A. B., & Howells, G. N. (1980). Tests of the generality of self-efficacy theory. *Cognitive Therapy and Research, 4,* 39–66.

Bandura, A., & Mischel, W. (1965). Modification of self-imposed delay of reward through exposure to live and symbolic models. *Journal of Personality and Social Psychology, 2,* 698–705.

Bandura, A., Ross, D., & Ross, S. A. (1963). Imitation of film-mediated aggressive models. *Journal of Abnormal and Social Psychology, 66,* 3–11.

Bandura, A., Underwood, B., & Fromson, M. E. (1975). Disinhibition of aggression through diffusion of responsibility and dehumanization of victims. *Journal of Research in Personality, 9,* 253–269.

Banuazizi, A., & Movahedi, S. (1975). Interpersonal dynamics in a simulated prison: A methodological analysis. *American Psychologist, 30,* 152–160.

Banyai, E. I., & Hilgard, E. R. (1976). Comparison of active-alert hypnotic induction with traditional relaxation induction. *Journal of Abnormal Psychology, 85,* 218–224.

Barber, T. X. (1969). *Hypnosis: A scientific approach.* New York: Van Nostrand.

Barber, T. X. (1976). *Hypnosis: A scientific approach.* New York: Psychological Dimensions.

Barchas, J. D., Ciaranello, R. D., Kessler, S., & Hamburg, D. A. (1975). Genetic aspects of catecholamine synthesis. In R. R. F. Eve, D. Rosenthal, & H. Brill (Eds.), *Genetic research in psychiatry* (pp. 27–62). Baltimore: Johns Hopkins University Press.

Baribeau-Braun, J., Dicton, T. W., & Gosselin, J. Y. (1983). Schizophrenia: A neurophysiological evaluation of abnormal information processing. *Science, 219,* 874–876.

Barker, L. M., Best, M. R., & Domjan, M. (Eds.). (1978). *Learning mechanisms in food selection.* Houston: Baylor University Press.

Barland, G., & Raskin, D. C. (1976). *Validity and reliability of polygraph examinations of criminal suspects* (Report No. 76-1, Contract 75-NI-99-0001). Washington, DC: U.S. Department of Justice.

Barlow, H. B., Hill, R. M., & Levick, W. R. (1964). Retinal ganglion cells responding selectively to direction and speed of image motion in the rabbit. *Journal of Physiology (London), 173,* 377–407.

Barnes, D. (1987). Defect in Alzheimer's is on Chromosome 21. *Science, 235,* 846–847.

Barnes, D. M. (1987). Biological issues in schizophrenia. *Science, 235,* 430–433.

Barnett, S. A. (1967). Attack and defense in animal societies. In C. D. Clemente & D. B. Lindsley (Eds.), *Aggression and defense.* Los Angeles: University of California Press.

Barrios, B. A., & Shigetomi, C. C. (1980). Coping skills training: Potential for prevention of fears and anxieties. *Behavior Therapy, 11,* 431–439.

Barron, F. X. (1963). *Creativity and psychological growth: Origins of personal vitality and creative freedom.* Princeton, NJ: Van Nostrand.

Barron, F., & Harrington, D. M. (1981). Creativity, intelligence, and personality. *Annual Review of Psychology, 32,* 439–476.

Bar-Tal, D., & Saxe, L. (Eds.). (1978). *Social psychology of education: Theory and research.* Washington, DC: Hemisphere.

Barthe, D. G., & Hammen, C. L. (1981). The attributional model of depression: A naturalistic extension. *Personality & Social Psychology Bulletin, 7(1),* 53–58.

Bartlett, F. C. (1932). *Remembering: A study in experimental and social psychology.* Cambridge: Cambridge University Press.

Bassiouni, M. C. (1981). Terrorism, law enforcement, and the mass media: Perspectives, problems, proposals. *The Journal of Criminal Law and Criminology, 72,* 1–51.

Bateson, G., Jackson, D. D., Haley, J., & Weakland, J. H. (1956). Toward a theory of schizophrenia. *Behavioral Science, 1,* 251–264.

Baum, A., Calesnick, L. E., Davis, G. E., & Gatchel, R. J. (1982). Individual differences in coping with crowding: Stimulus screening and social overload. *Journal of Personality and Social Psychology, 43,* 821–830.

Baum, A., & Valins, S. (1979). Architectural mediation of residential density and control: Crowding and the regulation of social contact. In L. Berkowitz (Ed.), *Advances in experimental social psychology* (Vol. 12). New York: Academic Press.

Baumrind, D. (1967). Child care practices anteceding three patterns of preschool behavior. *Genetic Psychology Monographs, 75,* 43–88.

Baumrind, D. (1973). The development of instrumental competence through socialization. In A. Pick (Ed.), *Minnesota Symposium in Child Development* (Vol. 7). Minneapolis: University of Minnesota Press, 1973.

Baumrind, D. (1986). Sex differences in moral reasoning: Response to Walker's (1984) conclusion that there are none. *Child Development, 57,* 511–521.

Bavelas, A., Hastorf, A. H., Gross, A. E., & Kite, W. R. (1965.) Experiments on the alteration of group structure. *Journal of Experimental and Social Psychology, 1,* 55–70.

Bayley, N. (1956). Individual patterns of development. *Child Development, 27,* 45–74.

Bayley, N. (1969). *Bayley Scales of Infant Development.* New York: The Psychological Corporation.

Baylor, D. (1987). Photoreceptor signals and vision. *Investigative Opthalmology and Visual Science. 28,* 34–49.

Beach, F. A. (1955). The descent of instinct. *Psychological Review, 62,* 401–410.

Beardslee, W. R., & Mack, J. E. (1983). Adolescents and the threat of nuclear war: The evolution of a perspective. *Yale Journal of Biological Medicine, 56(2),* 79–91.

Beck, A. T. (1967). *Depression: Clinical, experimental, and theoretical aspects.* New York: Harper & Row.

Beck, A. T. (1976). *Cognitive therapy and emotional disorders.* New York: International Universities Press.

Beck, A. T., Rush, A. J., Shaw, B. F., & Emery, G. (1979). *Cognitive therapy of depression.* New York: Guilford Press.

Beck, J. (1972). Similarity groupings and peripheral discriminability under uncertainty. *American Journal of Psychology, 85,* 1–20.

Becker, G. (1978). *The mad genius controversy: A study in the sociology of deviance.* Beverly Hills, CA: Sage.

Beecher, E. (1972). *Licit and illicit drugs.* Boston: Little, Brown.

Beecher, H. K. (1956). Relationship of significance of wound to the pain experienced. *Journal of the American Medical Association, 161,* 1609–1613.

Beecher, H. K. (1959). *Measurement of subjective responses.* New York: Oxford University Press.

Begg, I., & Paivio, A. V. (1969). Concreteness and imagery in sentence meaning. *Journal of Verbal Learning and Behavior, 8,* 821–827.

Bekerian, D. A., & Bowers, J. M. (1983). Eyewitness testimony: Were we misled? *Journal of Experimental Psychology: Learning, Memory, and Cognition, 9,* 139–145.

Békésy, G. von. (1960). *Experiments in hearing.* New York: McGraw-Hill.

Békésy, G. von. (1961). Concerning the fundamental component of periodic pulse patterns and modulated vibrations observed in the cochlear model with nerve supply. *Journal of the Acoustical Society of America, 33,* 888–896.

Bell, R. R. (1974). Female sexual satisfaction as related to levels of education. In L. Gross (Ed.), *Sexual behavior* (pp. 3–11). Flushing, NY: Spectrum.

Bellak, L. (Ed.). (1979). *Disorders of the schizophrenic syndrome.* New York: Basic Books.

Belloc, N. B. (1973). Relationship of health practices and mortality. *Preventive Medicine, 2,* 67–81.

Belloc, N. B., & Breslow, L. (1972). Relationship of physical health status and family practices. *Preventive Medicine, 1,* 409–421.

Bellugi, U., Klima, E. S., & Siple, P. A. (1975). Remembering in signs. *Cognition, 3:* 93–125.

Bem, D. J. (1970). *Beliefs, attitudes, and human affairs.* Belmont, CA: Brooks/Cole.

Bem, D. J., & Allen, A. (1974). On predicting some of the people some of the time: The search for cross-situational consistencies in behavior. *Psychological Review, 81(6):* 506–20.

Bem, S. L. (1974). The measurement of psychological androgyny. *Journal of Consulting and Clinical Psychology, 42:* 155–62.

Bem, S. L. (1981a). *The Bem Sex Role Inventory: Professional manual.* Palo Alto, CA: Consulting Psychology Press.

Bem, S. L. (1981b). Gender schema theory: A cognitive account of sex typing. *Psychological Review, 88,* 354–364.

Bem, S. L. (1984). Androgyny and gender schema theory: A conceptual and empirical integration. In T. B. Sonderegger (Ed.), *Nebraska Symposium on Motivation, 1984: The Psychology of Gender.* Lincoln: University of Nebraska Press.

Benedict, R. (1938). Continuities and discontinuities in cultural conditioning. *Psychiatry, 1,* 161–167.

Benedict, R. (1959). *Patterns of culture.* Boston: Houghton Mifflin.

Bennett, H. L. (1983). Remembering drink orders: The memory skills of cocktail waitresses. *Human Learning, 2,* 157–169.

Benson, H. (1975). *The relaxation response.* New York: Morrow.

Berglas, S., & Jones, E. E. (1978). Drug choice as a self-handicapping strategy in response to noncontingent success. *Journal of Personality and Social Psychology, 36,* 405–417.

Berkman, L. F., & Syme, S. L. (1979). Social networks, host resistance, and mortality: A nine-year follow-up study of Alameda County residents. *American Journal of Epidemiology, 109,* 186–204.

Berkowitz, L. (1982). Aversive conditions as stimuli to aggression. *Advances in Experimental Social Psychology, 15,* 249–288.

Berlyne, D. E. (1960). *Conflict, arousal, and curiosity.* New York: McGraw-Hill.

Berlyne, D. E. (1967). Reinforcement and arousal. In O. Levine (Ed.), *Nebraska Symposium on Motivation, 1966.* Lincoln: University of Nebraska Press.

Bernard, L. L. (1924). *Instinct.* New York: Holt, Rinehart & Winston.

Berndt, T. J. (1979). Developmental changes in conformity to peers and parents. *Developmental Psychology, 15,* 608–616.

Berne, E. (1972). *What do you say after you say hello?* New York: Grove Press.

Berry, J. W. (1967). Independence and conformity in subsistence level societies. *Journal of Personality and Social Psychology, 7,* 415–418.

Berscheid, E., & Peplau, L. A. (1983). The emerging science of relationships. In H. H. Kelley, E. Berscheid, A. Christensen, J. Harvey, T. Huston, G. Levinger, E. McClintock, L. A. Peplau, & D. R. Peterson, *Close relationships.* San Francisco: Freeman.

Berscheid, E., & Walster, E. H. (1978). *Interpersonal attraction* (2d ed.). Reading, MA: Addison-Wesley.

Betz, E. L. (1982). Need fulfillment in the career development of women. *Journal of Vocational Behavior, 20,* 53–66.

Bielski, R. J., & Friedel, R. O. (1977). Subtypes of depression, diagnosis and medical management. *Western Journal of Medicine, 126,* 347–352.

Bigelow, H. J. (1850). Dr. Harlow's case of recovery from the passage of an iron bar through the head. *American Journal of Medical Science, 20,* 13–22.

Binet, A. (1894). *Psychologie des grandes calculateurs et joueurs d'echecs.* Paris: Hachette.

Binet, A. (1911). *Les idées modernes sur les enfants.* Paris: Flammarion.

Binkley, S. (1979). A timekeeping enzyme in the pineal gland. *Scientific American, 204*(4), 66–71.

Birbaumer, N., & Kimmel, H. (Eds.). (1979). *Biofeedback and self-regulation.* Hillsdale, NJ: Erlbaum.

Bird, O. A. (1974). Humanities. *Encyclopaedia Brittanica (Macropaedia),* Vol. 8, 1179–1183.

Bitner, R. (1983). Awareness during anesthesia. In F. Orkin & L. Cooperman (Eds.), *Complications in anesthesiology* (pp. 349–54). Philadelphia: Lippincott.

Bitterman, M. E. (1975) The comparative analysis of learning. *Science, 188,* 699–709.

Blake, R., & Hirsch, H. V. B. (1975). Deficits in binocular depth perception in cats after altering monocular deprivation. *Science, 190,* 1114–1116.

Blakemore, C., & Campbell, P. W. (1969). On the existence of neurons in the human visual system selectively sensitive to the orientation and size of retinal images. *Journal of Physiology, 203,* 237–260.

Blank, A. A., Jr. (1982). Stresses of war: The example of Vietnam. In L. Goldberger & S. Breznitz (Eds.), *Handbook of stress* (pp. 631–643). New York: Free Press/Macmillan.

Bleuler, M. (1978). The long-term course of schizophrenic psychoses. In L. C. Wynne, R. L. Cromwell, & S. Mattysse (Eds.), *The nature of schizophrenia: New approaches to research and treatment* (pp. 631–636). New York: Wiley.

Blight, J. G. (1987). Toward a policy-relevant psychology of avoiding nuclear war: Lessons for psychologists from the Cuban missile crisis. *American Psychologist, 42,* 12–19.

Bloch, S., & Reddaway, P. (1977). *Psychiatric terror: How Soviet psychiatry is used to suppress dissent.* New York: Basic Books.

Block, A. (1980). An investigation of the response of the spouse to chronic pain behavior. *Pain, 9,* 243–252.

Block, J. H. (1983). Differential premises arising from differential socialization of the sexes: Some conjectures. *Child Development, 54,* 1335–1354.

Blodgett, R. (1986, May). Lost in the stars: Psychics strike out (again). *People Expression,* 32–35.

Blos, P. (1967). The second individuation process of adolescence. *Psychoanalytic Study of the Child, 22,* 162–188.

Bolles, R. C., & Faneslow, M. S. (1982). Endorphins and behavior. *Annual Review of Psychology, 33,* 87–101.

Bongiovanni, A. (1977). *A review of research on the effects of punishment in the schools.* Paper presented at the Conference on Child Abuse, Children's Hospital National Medical Center, Washington, DC.

Bootzin, R. R. (1975). *Behavior modification and therapy: An introduction.* Cambridge, MA: Winthrop.

Boring, E. G. (1950). *A history of experimental psychology* (2d ed.). New York: Appleton-Century-Crofts.

Boring, E. G., Langfeld, H. S., & Weld, H. P. (1948). *Foundations of psychology.* New York: Wiley.

Borke, H. (1975). Piaget's mountains revisited: Changes in the egocentric landscape. *Developmental Psychology, 11,* 240–243.

Bourguignon, E. (1973). Introduction: A framework for the comparative study of altered states of consciousness. In E. Bourguignon (Ed.), *Religion, altered states of consciousness, and social change.* Columbus: Ohio State University Press.

Bower, G. H. (1972). A selective review of organizational factors in memory. In E. Tulving & W. Donaldson (Eds.), *Organization of memory.* New York: Academic Press.

Bower, G. H. (1981). Mood and memory. *American Psychologist, 36.* 129–148.

Bower, S. A., & Bower, G. H. (1976). *Asserting yourself.* Reading, MA: Addison-Wesley.

Bowers, K. S. (1976). *Hypnosis for the seriously curious.* New York: Norton.

Bowers, M. B., Jr. (1980). Biochemical processes in schizophrenia: An update. In S. J. Keith & L. R. Mosher (Eds.), *Special Report: Schizophrenia, 1980.* Washington, DC: U.S. Government Printing Office.

Bowlby, J. (1969). *Attachment and loss, Vol. 1: Attachment.* New York: Basic Books.

Bowlby, J. (1973). *Attachment and loss: Vol. 2. Separation, anxiety and anger.* London: Hogarth.

Boyd, J. H., & Weissman, M. M. (1981). Epidemiology of affective disorders: A reexamination and future directions. *Archives of General Psychiatry, 38,* 1039–1046.

Brackbill, Y. (1979). Developmental psychology. In M. E. Meyer (Ed.), *Foundation of contemporary psychology* (pp. 468–487). New York: Oxford University Press.

Braginsky, B., & Braginsky, D. (1967). Schizophrenic patients in the psychiatric interview: An experimental study of their effectiveness at manipulation. *Journal of Consulting Psychology, 31,* 543–547.

Braginsky, B., Braginsky, D., & Ring, K. (1969). *Methods of madness: The mental hospital as a last resort.* New York: Holt, Rinehart & Winston.

Braine, M. D. S. (1976). Children's first word combinations. *Monographs of the Socity for Research in Child Development, 41* (Serial No. 164).

Bransford, J. D., & Franks, J. J. (1971). The abstraction of linguistic ideas. *Cognitive Psychology, 2,* 331–350.

Bransford, J. D., & Johnson, M. K. (1972). Contextual prerequisites for understanding: Some investigations of comprehension and recall. *Journal of Verbal Learning and Verbal Behavior, 11, 17–21.*

Bransford, J. D., & Johnson, M. K. (1973). Considerations of some problems of comprehension. In W. G. Chase (Ed.), *Visual information processing.* New York: Academic Press.

Bransford, J., Sherwood, R., Vye, N., & Reiser, J. (1986). Teaching, thinking and problem solving. *American Psychologist, 41,* 1078–1089.

Bray, C. W. (1948). *Psychology and military proficiency.* Princeton: Princeton University Press.

Breggin, P. R. (1979). *Electroshock: Its brain disabling effects.* New York: Springer.

Breland, K., & Breland, M, (1951). A field of applied animal psychology. *American Psychologist, 6,* 202–204.

Breland, K., & Breland, M. (1961). A misbehavior of organisms. *American Psychologist, 16,* 681–684.

Brenner, M. H. (1976). *Estimating the social costs of national economic policy: Implications for mental and physical health and criminal violence.* Report prepared for the Joint Economic Committee of Congress, Washington, DC: U.S. Government Printing Office.

Breuer, J., & Freud, S. (1955). Studies on hysteria. In J. Strachey (Ed. and Trans.), *The standard edition of the complete psychological works of Sigmund Freud* (Vol. 2). London: Hogarth Press. (Original work published 1895)

Brewer, M. B. (1979). In-group bias in the minimal intergroup situation: A cognitive-motivational analysis. *Psychological Bulletin, 86,* 307–324.

Bridgeman, B. (1983). Independent evidence for neural systems mediating blindsight. *The Behavioral and Brain Sciences, 6,* 450–451.

Brim, O. G., & Kagan, J. (1980). *Constancy and change in human development.* Cambridge,: Harvard University Press.

Brislin, R. W. (1981). *Cross-cultural encounters: Face-to-face encounters.* New York: Pergamon.

Broadbent, D. E. (1954). The role of auditory localization in attention and memory span. *Journal of Experimental Psychology, 47,* 191–196.

Broadbent, D. E., (1958). *Perception and communication.* London: Pergamon Press.

Broadbent, D. E. (1971). *Decision and stress.* New York: Academic Press.

Broadbent, D. E., & Gregory, M. (1967). Perception of emotionally toned words. *Nature, 215,* 581–584.

Brody, E. B., & Brody, N. (1976). *Intelligence: Nature, determinants, and consequences.* New York: Academic Press.

Brody, R. V. (1986). Pain management in terminal disease. *Focus: A Review of AIDS Research, 1:* 1–2

Broman, S. H., Nichols, P. I., & Kennedy, W. A. (1975). *Preschool IQ: Prenatal and early developmental correlates.* Hillsdale, NJ: Erlbaum.

Bronfenbrenner, U. (1977). Toward an experimental ecology of human development. *American Psychologist, 32,* 513–531.

Brown, A. L., & De Loache, J. L. (1978). Skills, plans, and self-regulation. In R. S. Siegler (Ed.), *Children's thinking: What develops?* (pp. 3–35). Hillsdale, NJ: Erlbaum, 1978.

Brown, B., & Rosenbaum, L. (1983, May). *Stress effects on IQ.* Paper presented at the meeting of the American Association for the Advancement of Science, Detroit.

Brown, J. S. (1961). *The motivation of behavior.* New York: McGraw-Hill.

Brown, R., et al. (1962). *New directions in psychology.* New York: Holt, Rinehart and Winston.

Brown, R., & Hanlon, C. (1970). Derivational complexity and order of acquisition. In J. R. Hayes (Ed.), *Cognition and the development of language.* New York: Wiley.

Brown, R. W., & McNeil, D. (1966). The "tip-of-the tongue" phenomenon. *Journal of Verbal Learning and Verbal Behavior, 5,* 325–337.

Bruner, J. (1986). *Actual minds, possible worlds.* Cambridge, MA: Harvard University Press.

Bruner, J. S. (1973). *Beyond the information given.* New York: Norton.

Bruner, J. S., & Goodman, C. C. (1947). Value and need as organizing factors in perception. *Journal of Abnormal and Social Psychology, 42,* 33–44.

Bruner, J. S., Olver, R. R., & Greenfield, P. M. (1966). *Studies in cognitive growth.* New York: Wiley.

Brunswick, A. F. (1980). *Smoking and health: A report of the Surgeon General.* Washington, DC: U.S. Department of Health, Education & Welfare.

Buchsbaum, M. S. (1980). The two brains. In *1981 Yearbook of sciences and the future* (pp. 138–53). Chicago: Encyclopaedia Britannica.

Buczek, R. (1979, July 30). Too old to be hired—so he just died. *Chicago Sun-Times.*

Bullock, M., & Gelman, R. (1979). Preschool children's assumptions about cause and effect: Temporal coding. *Child Development, 50,* 89–96.

Bullock, T. H., Orkand, R., & Grinnell, A. (1977). *Introduction to the nervous system.* San Francisco: Freeman.

Buros, O. K. (Ed.). (1974). *Tests in print: II.* Highland Park, NJ: Gryphon Press.

Buros, O. K. (Ed.). (1978). *The eighth mental measurements yearbook.* Highland Park, NJ: Gryphon Press.

Burrows, G. D., & Dennerstein, L. (Eds.). (1980). *Handbook of hypnosis and psychosomatic medicine.* New York: Elsevier/North Holland Biomedical Press.

Buss, A. H. (1971). Aggression pays. In J. L. Singer (Ed.), *The control of aggression and violence.* New York: Academic Press.

Buss, A. H. (1980). *Self-consciousness and social anxiety.* San Francisco: Freeman.

Butcher, J. N., & Finn, S. (1983). Objective personality assessment in clinical settings. In M. H. Jersen, A. E. Kazdin, & A. S. Bellock (Eds.), *The clinical psychology handbook* (pp. 329–44). New York: Pergamon.

Butler, M. J., & Rice, L. N. (1963). Audience, self-actualization, and drive theory. In J. M. Wepman & R. W. Heine (Eds.), *Concepts of personality* (pp. 79–110). Chicago: Aldine.

Butler, R. A., & Harlow, H. F. (1954). Persistence of visual exploration in monkeys. *Journal of Comparative and Physiological Psychology, 47,* 258–263.

Buzan, T. (1976). *Use both sides of your brain.* New York: Dutton.

Bykov, K. M. (1957). *The cerebral cortex and the internal organs.* New York: Academic Press.

Byrne, D. (1971). *The attraction paradigm.* New York: Academic Press.

Byrne, D. (1981, August). *Predicting human sexual behavior.* G. Stanley Hall Lecture, presented at the meeting of the American Psychological Association, Los Angeles.

C

Cairns, R. B., & Valsinger, J. (1984). Child psychology. *Annual Review of Psychology, 35,* 553–577.

Calkins, M. W. (1893). Statistics of dreams. *American Journal of Psychology, 5,* 311–343.

Cameron, P., Frank, R., Lifter, M., & Morrissey, P. (1968, September). *Cognitive functionings of college students in a general psychology class.* Paper presented at the meeting of the American Psychological Association, San Francisco.

Campbell, F. W., & Robson, J. G. (1968). Application of Fourier analysis to the visibility of gratings. *Journal of Physiology, 197,* 551–566.

Campion, J., Latto, R., & Smith, Y. M. (1983). Is blindsight an effect of scattered light, spared cortex, and near threshold vision? *The Behavioral and Brain Sciences, 6,* 423–486.

Cann, A., Calhoun, L. G., Selby, J. W., Kin, H. E. (Eds.). (1981). Rape. *Journal of Social Issues, 37* (whole no. 4).

Cannon, W. B. (1927). The James-Lange theory of emotion: A critical examination and an alternative theory. *American Journal of Psychology, 39,* 106–124.

Cannon, W. B. (1929). *Bodily changes in pain, hunger, fear and rage* (2d ed.). New York: Appleton-Century-Crofts.

Cannon, W. B. (1934). Hunger and thirst. In C. Murchison (Ed.), *A handbook of general experimental psychology.* Worcester, MA: Clark University Press.

Cannon, W. B. (1942). "Voodoo" death. *American Anthropologist, 44,* 169–181.

Cannon, W. B. (1957). "Voodoo" death. *Psychosomatic Medicine, 19,* 182–190.

Cannon, W. B., & Washburn, A. L. (1912). An explanation of hunger. *American Journal of Physiology, 29,* 441–454.

Cantor, N., & Mischel, W. (1979). Traits as prototypes: Effects on recognition memory. *Journal of Personality and Social Psychology, 35,* 38–48.

Caplan, G. (1969, November). A psychiatrist's casebook. *McCall's:* 65.

Caporeal, L. R. (1976). Ergotism: The satan loosed in Salem? *Science, 192,* 21–26.

Carey, S. (1978). The child as word learner. In M. Halle, J. Bresnan, & G. A. Miller (Eds.), *Linguistic theory and psychological reality* (pp. 265–93). Cambridge, MA: MIT Press.

Carlsmith, J. M., Lepper, M. R., & Landauer, T. K. (1974). Children's obedience to adult requests: Interactive effects of anxiety arousal and apparent punitiveness of adults. *Journal of Personality and Social Psychology, 30,* 822–828.

Carlson, J. G., & Wood, R. D. (1974). *Need the final solution be justified?* Unpublished manuscript, University of Hawaii.

Carlsson, A. (1978). Antipsychotic drugs, neurotransmitters, and schizophrenia. *American Journal of Psychiatry, 135,* 164–173.

Carmichael, L. (1926). The development of behavior in vertebrates experimentally removed from the influence of external stimulation. *Psychological Review, 33,* 51–58.

Carmichael, L. (1970). The onset and early development of behavior. In P. H. Mussen (Ed.), *Carmichael's manual of child psychology* (3rd ed.) (Vol. 1). New York: Wiley.

Carpenter, G. C. (1973). Differential response to mother and stranger within the first month of life. *Bulletin of the British Psychological Society, 16,* 138.

Carrell, M. R., & Dittrich, J. E. (1978). Equity theory: The recent literature, methodological considerations, and new directions. *Academy of Management Review, 3,* 202–210.

Cartwright, R. D. (1978). *A primer on sleep and dreaming.* Reading, MA: Addison-Wesley.

Cartwright, R. D. (1982). The shape of dreams. In *1983 Yearbook of science and the future.* Chicago: Encyclopaedia Britannica.

Cartwright, S. (1851, May). The diseases and physical peculiarities of the negro race. *New Orleans Medical and Surgical Journal.*

Carver, C. S., & Scheier, M. P. (1981). *Attention and self-regulation: A control theory approach to human behavior.* New York: Springer-Verlag.

Case, R. S. (1985). *Intellectual development: A systematic reinterpretation.* New York: Academic Press.

Cattell, R. B. (1971). *Abilities: Their structure and growth.* Boston: Houghton Mifflin.

Cattell, R. B. (1972). The 16 PF and basic personality structure: A reply to Eysenck. *Journal of Behavioral Science, 1,* 169–187.

Cattell, R. B. (1982). *The inheritance of personality and ability: Research methods and findings.* New York: Academic Press.

Catterall, W. A. (1984). The molecular basis of neuronal excitability. *Science, 223,* 653–661.

Center for Disease Control. (1985). *Suicide surveillance report, United States, 1970–1980.* Atlanta: Department of Health and Human Services.

Cermak, L. S., & Craik, F. I. M. (1979). *Levels of processing In human memory.* Hillsdale, NJ: Erlbaum.

Cervone, D., & Peake, P. K. (1986). Anchoring, efficacy, and action: The influence of judgmental heuristics on self-efficacy judgments. *Journal of Personality and Social Psychology, 50,* 492–501.

Chapin, S. F. (1913). *Introduction to the study of social evolution.* New York: Century.

Chapman, R. M., McCrary, J. W., & Chapman, J. A. (1978). Short-term memory: The "storage" component of human brain responses predicts recall. *Science, 202,* 1211–1213.

Chase, W. G., & Ericsson, K. A. (1981). Skilled memory. In J. R. Anderson (Ed.). *Cognitive skills and their acquisition.* Hillsdale, NJ: Erlbaum.

Chase, W. G., & Simon, H. A. (1973). Perception in chess. In W. G. Chase (Ed.), *Visual information processing* (pp. 215–81). New York: Academic Press.

Cheek, D. (1979, November). *Awareness of meaningful sounds under general anesthesia: Consideration and a review of the literature 1959 to 1979.* Paper presented at the annual meeting of the American Society of Clinical Hypnosis.

Cheek, J. M., & Busch, C. M. (1981). The influence of shyness on loneliness in a new situation. *Personality and Social Psychology Bulletin, 7,* 572–577.

Cheney, D. L., & Seyfarth, R. (1985). Vervet monkey alarm calls: Manipulation through shared information. *Behavior, 4,* 150–166.

Cherkin, A., & Harrour, P. (1971). Anesthesia and memory processes. *Anesthesiology, 34,* 469–474.

Cherry, E. C. (1953). Some experiments on the recognition of speech, with one and with two ears. *Journal of the Acoustical Society of America, 25,* 975–979.

Chi, M. T. H., Feltovich, P. J., & Glaser, R. (1981). Categorization and representation of physics problems by experts and novices. *Cognitive Science, 5,* 121–152.

Chi, M. T. H. & Koeske, R. D. (1983). Network representation of a child's dinosaur knowledge. *Developmental Psychology, 19,* 29–39.

Chilman, C. S. (Ed.). (1979). *Adolescent sexuality in a changing American society: Social and psychological perspectives* (Dhew Publications No. 79–1426). Washington, DC: National Institute of Health.

Chilman, C. S. (1983). *Adolescent sexuality in a changing American society* (2d ed.). New York: Wiley.

Chomsky, N. (1957). *Syntactic structures.* The Hague: Mouton.

Chomsky, N. (1965). *Aspects of a theory of syntax.* Cambridge, MA: MIT Press.

Chomsky, N. (1975). *Reflections on language.* New York: Pantheon Books.

Chomsky, N. (1984). *Modular approaches to the study of the mind.* San Diego, CA.: San Diego University Press.

Chomsky, N. (1986). *Knowledge of language: Its nature, origin, and use.* New York: Praeger.

Chorover, S. (1981, June). *Organizational recruitment in "open" and "closed" social systems: A neuropsychological perspec-*

tive. Conference paper presented at the Center for the Study of New Religious Movements, Berkeley, CA.

Christy, P. R., Gelfand, D. M., & Hartman, D. P. (1971). Effects of competition-induced frustration on two classes of modeled behavior. *Developmental Psychology, 5,* 104–111.

Church, R. M., Getty, D. J., & Lerner, N. D. (1976). Duration discrimination by rats. *Journal of Experimental Psychology: Animal Behavior Processes, 2,* 303–312.

Cialdini, R. B. (1985). *Influence: Science and practice.* Glenview, IL: Scott, Foresman.

Ciminero, A. R., Calhoun, K. S., & Adams, H. E. (Eds.). (1977). *Handbook of behavioral assessment.* New York: Wiley.

Clancey, M., & Robinson, M. J. (1985). General election coverage: Part 1. *Public Opinion, 7,* 49–54, 59.

Claparede, E. (1928). Feelings and emotions. In M. L. Reymert (Ed.), *Feelings and emotions: The Wittenberg symposium* (pp. 124–39). Worcester, MA: Clark University Press.

Clark, E. V. (1928). Feelings and emotions. In M. L. Reymert (Ed.), *Feelings and emotions: The Wittenberg symposium* (pp. 124–39). Worcester, MA: Clark University Press.

Clark, E. V. (1973). What's in a word? On the child's acquisition of semantics in his first language. In T. E. Moore (Ed.), *Cognitive development and the acquisition of language.* New York: Academic Press.

Clark, H. H., & Clark, E. V. (1977). *Psychology and language: An introduction to psycholinguistics.* New York: Harcourt Brace Jovanovich.

Clarke-Stewart, K. A. (1978). Recasting the lone stranger. In J. Glick & K. A. Clarke-Stewart (Eds.), *The development of social understanding.* New York: Gardner Press.

Clausen, J. A. (1981). Stigma and mental disorder: Phenomena and mental terminology. *Psychiatry, 44,* 287–296.

Clausen, T. (1968). Perspectives on childhood socialization. In J. A. Clausen (Ed.), *Socialization and society.* Boston: Little, Brown.

Coates, T. J., Temoshok, L., & Mandel, J. (1984). Psychosocial research is essential to understanding and treating AIDS. *American Psychologist, 39,* 1309–1314.

Coch, L., & French, J. R. P., Jr. (1948). Overcoming resistance to change. *Human Relations, 1,* 512–532.

Cockerham, W. C. (1978). *Medical sociology.* Englewood Cliffs, NJ: Prentice-Hall.

Cohen, B. S., & Nagel, E. (1934). *An introduction to logic and scientific method.* New York: Harcourt Brace Jovanovich.

Cohen, L. B., & Gelber, E. R. (1975). Infant visual memory. In L. Cohen & P. Salapatek (Eds.), *Infant perception: From sensation to cognition, Vol. 1: Basic visual processes* (pp. 347–403). New York: Academic Press.

Cohen, R. E., & Ahearn, F. L., Jr. (1980). *Handbook for mental health care of disaster victims.* Baltimore: Johns Hopkins University Press.

Cohen, S., & Syme, S. L. (Eds.). (1985). *Social support and health.* Orlando, FL: Academic Press.

Coleman, J. C. (1980). Friendship and the peer group in adolescence. In J. Adelson (Ed.), *Handbook of adolescent psychology.* New York: Wiley.

Coleman, R. M. (1986). *Wide awake at 3:00 A.M.: By choice or by chance?* New York: Freeman.

College Board. (1976–1977). *Student descriptive questionnaire.* Princeton, NJ: Educational Testing Service.

Collier, G., Hirsch, E., & Hamlin, P. (1972). The ecological determinants of reinforcement. *Physiology and Behavior, 9, 705–716.*

Collins, G. (1984, June 19). "Day After" fades, but debate on effects lingers. *New York Times,* 8.

Conant, J. B. (1958). *On understanding science: An historical approach.* New York: New Amsterdam Library.

Condry, J., & Condry, S. (1976). Sex differences: A study in the eye of the beholder. *Child Development, 47,* 812–819.

Conger, J. J. (1977). *Adolescence and youth: Psychological development* (2d ed.). New York: Harper & Row.

Conger, J. C., & Keane, S. P. (1981). Social skills intervention in the treatment of isolated or withdrawn children. *Psychological Bulletin, 90,* 478–495.

Conrad, R. (1964). Acoustic confusions in immediate memory. *British Journal of Psychology, 55,* 75–84.

Conrad, R. (1972). Short-term memory in the deaf: A test for speech coding. *British Journal of Psychology, 63,* 173–180.

Cookerly, J. R. (1980). Does marital therapy do any lasting good? *Journal of Marital and Family Therapy, 6,* 393–397.

Cooper, A. F. (1976). Deafness and psychiatric illness. *British Journal of Psychiatry, 129,* 216–26.

Cooper, L. A., & Shepard, R. N. (1973). The time required to prepare for a rotated stimulus. *Memory and Cognition, 1,* 246–250.

Coren, S., & Girgus, J. S. (1978). *Seeing is deceiving: The psychology of visual illusions.* Hillsdale, NJ: Erlbaum.

Coren, S., Porac, C., & Ward, L. M. (1978). *Sensation and perception.* New York: Academic Press.

Cornsweet, T. N. (1970). *Visual perception.* New York: Academic Press.

Corsini, R. J. (1977). *Current theories of personality.* Itasca, IL: Peacock.

Cousins, N. (1979). *The anatomy of an illness as perceived by a patient: Reflections on healing and rejuvenation.* New York: Norton.

Cousins, N. (1983). *The healing heart.* New York: Norton.

Cowles, J. T. (1937). Food tokens as incentives for learning by chimpanzees. *Comparative Psychology Monographs, 74,* 1–96.

Coyne, J. C. (1976). Toward an interactional description of depression. *Psychiatry, 39,* 28–40.

Coyne, J. C., Aldwin, C., & Lazarus, R. S. (1981). Depression and coping in stressful episodes. *Journal of Abnormal Psychology, 90,* 439–447.

Craik, F. I. M., & Lockhart, R. S. (1972). Levels of processing; A framework for memory research. *Journal of Verbal Learning and Verbal Behavior, 11,* 671–684.

Craik, K. (1943). *The nature of explanation.* Cambridge: Cambridge University Press.

Crapo, L. (1985). *Hormones: The messengers of life.* Stanford, CA: Stanford Alumni Association Press.

Crick, F. H. C. (1979, September). Thinking about the brain. *Scientific American, 247,* 219–232.

Cronbach, L. J., & Meehl, P. E. (1955). Construct validity in psychological tests. *Psychological Bulletin, 52,* 281–302.

Crook, J. H. (1973). The nature and function of territorial aggression. In M. F. A. Montague (Ed.), *Man and aggression* (2d ed.). New York: Oxford University Press.

Crosby, F. J. (1982). *Relative deprivation and working women.* New York: Oxford University Press.

Cross, P. G., Cafiell, R. B., & Butcher, H. J. (1967). The personality patterns of creative artists. *British Journal of Educational Psychology, 37,* 292–299.

Crowder, R. G., & Morton, J. (1969). Precategorical acoustic storage (FAS). *Perception and Psychophysics, 8,* 815–820.

Csikszentmihalyi, M., Larson, R., & Prescott, S. (1977). The ecology of adolescent activity and experience. *Journal of Youth and Adolescence, 6,* 281–294.

Curtiss, S. (1977). *Genie: A psycholinguistic study of a modern-day "wild child."* New York: Academic Press.

Cutler, W. B., Preti, G., Krieger, A., Huggins, G. R., Ramon Garcia, C., & Lawley, H. J. (1986). Human axillary secretions influence women's menstrual cycles: The role of donor extract from men. *Hormones and Behavior, 20,* 463–473.

Cutting, J. E. (1987). Perception and information. *Annual Review of Psychology, 38,* 61–90.

Cynader, M. N., & Chernenko, G. (1976). Abolition of directional sensitivity in the visual cortex of the cat. *Science, 193,* 504–505.

Czeisler, C. A., Allan, J. S., Strogatz, S. H., Ronda, J. M., Sanchez, R., Dios, C. D., Freitag, W. O., Richardson, G. S., & Kronauer, R. E. (1986). Bright light resets the human circadian pacemaker independent of the timing of the sleep-wake cycle. *Science, 233,* 667–670.

D

Dackman, L. (1986). Everyday illusions. *Exploratorium Quarterly, 10,* 5–7.

Dahlstrom, W. G., Welsh, H. G., & Dahlstrom, L. E. (1975). *An MMPI handbook, Vol. 1: Clinical interpretation.* Minnesota: University of Minnesota Press.

Darley, J., & Gilbert, D. T. (1985). Social psychological aspects of environmental psychology. In G. Lindzey & E. Aronson (Eds.), *Handbook of social psychology* (2d ed., Vol. 2, pp. 949–92). New York: Random House.

Darley, J. M., & Goethals, G. R. (1980). People's analysis of the causes of ability-linked performances. In L. Berkowitz (Ed.), *Advances in experimental social psychology* (Vol. 13, pp. 1–37). New York: Academic Press.

Darley, J. M., & Gross, P. H. (1983). A hypothesis-confirming bias in labeling effects. *Journal of Personality and Social Psychology, 44,* 20–33.

Darley, J., & Latané, B. (1968). Bystander intervention in emergencies: Diffusion of responsibility. *Journal of Personality and Social Psychology, 8,* 377–383.

Darwin, C. (1965). *The expression of emotions in man and animals.* Chicago: University of Chicago Press. (Originally published 1872)

Darwin, C. J., Turvey, M. T., & Crowder, R. G. (1972). The auditory analogue of the Sperling partial report procedure: Evidence for brief auditory stage. *Cognitive Psychology, 3,* 255–267.

Davidson, J. M. (1980). The psychobiology of sexual experience. In J. M. Davidson & R. J. Davidson (Eds.), *The psychobiology of consciousness* (pp. 271–331). New York: Plenum.

Davidson, R. J. (1983). Affect, repression, and cerebral asymmetry. In L. Temoshok, C. Van Dyke, & L. S. Zegans (Eds.), *Emotions in health and illness: Theoretical and research foundations* (pp. 123–35). New York: Grune & Stratton.

Davis, I. P. (1985). *Adolescents: Theoretical and helping perspectives.* Boston: Kluwer-Nijhoff Publishing.

Davison, G. C., & Valins, S. (1969). Maintenance of self-attributed and drug-attributed behavior change. *Journal of Personality and Social Behavior, 11,* 25–33.

Daw, N. W., & Wyatt, H. J. (1976). Kittens reared in a unidirectional environment: Evidence for a critical period. *Journal of Physiology, 257,* 155–170.

Day, R. S. (1986, November). *Ways to show it: Cognitive consequences of alternative representations.* Paper presented at the meeting of the Psychonomic Society, New Orleans.

D'Azevedo, W. L. (1962). Uses of the past in Gola discourse. *Journal of African History, 3,* 11–34.

de Bono, F. (1970). *Lateral thinking.* New York: Harper.

De Charms, R., & Moeller, G. (1962). Values expressed in American children's readers: 1800–1950. *Journal of Abnormal and Social Psychology, 64,* 136–142.

De Charms, R. C., & Muir, M. S. (1978). Motivation: Social approaches. *Annual Review of Psychology, 29,* 91–113.

Deci, E. L. (1975). *Intrinsic motivation.* New York: Plenum.

De Fries, J. C., & Decker, S. N. (1982). Genetic aspects of reading disability: The Colorado family reading study. In P. G. Aaron & H. Malatesha (Eds.), *Reading disorders: Varieties and treatments* (pp. 255–79). New York: Academic Press.

DeGroot, A. D. (1965). *Thought and choice in chess.* The Hague: Mouton.

Dellas, M., & Gaier, E. L. (1970). Identification of creativity: The individual. *Psychological Builletin, 73,* 55–73.

Dembroski, T. M., Weiss, S. M., Shields, J. L., et al. (1978). *Coronary-prone behavior.* New York: Springer-Verlag.

Dement, W. C. (1976). *Some watch while some must sleep.* San Francisco: San Francisco Book Co.

Dement, W. C., & Kleitman, N. (1957). Cyclic variations in EEG during sleep and their relations to eye movement, body mobility and dreaming. *Electroencephalography and Clinical Neurophysiology, 9,* 673–690.

Dennett, D. C. (1978). *Brainstorms.* Cambridge, MA: Bradford Books.

Depue, R. A., & Monroe, S. M. (1983). Psychopathology research. In M. Hersen, A. E. Kazdin, & A. S. Bellack (Eds.), *The clinical psychology handbook* (pp. 239–64). New York: Pergamon Press.

Deregowski, J. B. (1980). *Illusions, patterns and pictures: A cross-cultural perspective* (pp. 966–77). London: Academic Press.

Descartes, R. (1911). Traitées de l'homme. In E. S. Haldane & G. T. Ross (Trans.), *The philosophical works of Descartes.* New York: Dover. (Original work published 1642)

Descartes, R. (1951). The passions of the soul. In E. S. Haldane & G. T. Ross (Trans.), *The philosophical works of Descartes.* New York: Dover. (Original work published 1646)

Deutsch, M., & Hornstein, H. A. (1975). *Applying social psychology.* Hillsdale, NJ: Erlbaum.

De Valois, R. L., & De Valois, K. K. (1980). Spatial vision. *Annual Review of Psychology,* 80.

De Valois, R. L., & Jacobs, G. H. (1968). Primate color vision. *Science, 162,* 533–540.

DeVries, R. (1969). Constancy of generic identity in the years three to six. *Society for Research in Child Development Monographs, 34* (Serial No. 127), 3.

Diamond, M. J. (1974). Modification of hypnotizability: A review. *Psychological Bulletin, 81,* 180–198.

Dickinson, A. (1980). *Contemporary animal learning theory.* Cambridge: Cambridge University Press.

Dickman, H., & Zeiss, R. A. (1982). *Incidents and correlates of post-traumatic stress disorder among ex–Prisoners of War of World War II.* Manuscript in progress. Palo Alto, CA.: Veterans Administration.

Diener, E. (1979). Deindividuation, self-awareness, and disinhibition. *Journal of Personality and Social Psychology, 37,* 1160–1171.

Diener, E. (1980 Deindividuation: The absence of self-awareness and self-regulation in group members. In P. Paulus (Ed.), *The psychology of group influence* (pp. 209–42). Hillsdale, NJ: Erlbaum.

Diener, E., & Crandall, R. (1978). *Ethics in social and behavioral research.* Chicago: University of Chicago Press.

DiMatteo, M. R., & DiNicola, D. D. (1982). *Achieving patient compliance: The psychology of the medical practitioner's role.* New York: Pergamon.

Dion, K. L., Berscheid, E., & Walster, E. (1972). What is beautiful is good. *Journal of Personality and Social Psychology, 24,* 285–290.

Dishman, R. K. (1982). Compliance/adherence in health-related exercise. *Health Psychology, 1,* 237–267.

Dixon, N. F. (1971). *Subliminal perception: The nature of a controversy.* London: McGraw Hill.

Dohrenwend, B. P., & Dohrenwend, B. S. (1974). Social and cultural influences on psychopathology. *Annual Review of Psychology, 25,* 417–452.

Dollard, J., Doob, L. W., Miller, N., Mower, O. H., & Sears, R. R. (1939). *Frustration and aggression.* New Haven, CT: Yale University Press.

Dollard, J., & Miller, N. E. (1950). *Personality and psychotherapy.* New York: McGraw-Hill.

Donchin, E. (1975). On evoked potentials, cognition, and memory. *Science, 790:* 1004–5.

Donchin, E. (1985). *Can the mind be read in brain waves?* Presentation at a Science and Public Policy Seminar. Washington, DC: Federation of Behavioral, Psychological, and Cognitive Sciences.

Donnerstein, E. (1980). Aggressive-Erotica and violence against women. *Journal of Personality and Social Psychology, 39,* 269–277.

Donnerstein, E. (1983). Erotica and human aggression. In R. G. Green & E. Donnerstein (Eds.), *Aggression: Theoretical and empirical reviews, Vol. 2: Issues in research.* New York: Academic Press.

Donnerstein, E. I., & Linz, D. G. (1986, December). The question of pornography. *Psychology Today:* 56–59.

Dooling, D. J., & Lachman, R. (1971). Effects of comprehension on retention of prose. *Journal of Experimental Psychology, 88,* 216–222.

Dorfman, D. D. (1965). Esthetic preference as a function of pattern information. *Psychonomic Science, 3,* 85–86.

Dowling, W. F. (1973). Job redesign on the assembly line: Farewell to the blue-collar blues. *Organizational Dynamics, 2,* 51–67.

Drabman, R. S., & Thomas, M. H. (1974). Does media violence increase children's tolerance of real-life aggression? *Developmental Psychology, 10,* 418–421.

DSM-III. (1980). *Diagnostic and statistical manual of mental disorders* (3d ed.). Washington, DC: American Psychiatric Association.

DuBois, P. H. (1970). *A history of psychological testing.* Boston: Allyn and Bacon.

Duba, R. O., & Shortliffe, E. H. (1983). Expert systems research. *Science, 220,* 261–268.

Dudycha, G. J. (1936). An objective study of punctuality in relation to personality and achievement. *Archives of Psychology, 204,* 1–53.

Dugdale, R. L. (1912). *The Jukes* (4th ed.). New York: Putnam's Sons.

Dumont, J. P. C., & Robertson, R. M. (1986). Neuronal circuits: An evolutionary perspective. *Science, 233,* 849–853.

Dumont, J. P. C., & Wine, J. J. (1986). The telson flexor neuromuscular system of the crayfish. III. The role of feedforward inhibition in shaping a stereotyped behaviour pattern. *Journal of Experimental Biology, 127,* 295–311.

Duncan, B. L. (1976). Differential social perception and attribution of intergroup violence: Testing the lower limits of stereotyping of blacks. *Journal of Personality and Social Psychology, 34,* 590–598.

Duncker, K. (1945). On problem solving. *Psychological Monographs, 58* (No. 270).

Duval, S., & Wicklund, R. A. (1972). *A theory of objective self awareness.* New York: Academic Press.

Dweck, C. S. (1975). The role of expectations and attributions in the alleviation of learned helplessness. *Journal of Personality and Social Psychology, 31,* 674–685.

E

Eastwell, H. D. (1984). Death watch in East Arnhem, Australia. *American Anthropologists, 86,* 119–121.

Ebbinghaus, H. (1913). *Memory.* New York: Columbia University. (Original work published 1885, Liepzig: Altenberg)

Edwards, A. E., & Acker, L. E. (1962). A demonstration of the long-term retention of a conditioned galvanic skin response. *Psychosomatic Medicine, 24,* 459–463.

Edwards, B. (1979). *Drawing on the right side of the brain.* Los Angeles: J. P. Tarcher.

Edwards, D. A. (1971). Neonatal administration of androstenedione, testosterone, or testosterone propionate: Effects on ovulation, sexual receptivity, and aggressive behavior in female mice. *Physiological Behavior, 6,* 223–228.

Egeland, J. A., Gerhard, D. S., Pauls, D. L., Sussex, J. N., Kidd, K. K., Allen, C. R., Hostetter, A. M., & Housman, D. E. (1987). Bipolar affective disorder linked to DNA markers on chromosome 11. *Nature, 325,* 783–787.

Ehrhardt, A. A., & Baker, S. W. (1974). Fetal androgens, human central nervous system differentiation, and behavior sex differences. In R. C. Friedman, R. M. Richart, & R. L. Vande Wiele (Eds.), *Sex differences in behavior.* New York: Wiley.

Ehrlich, B. E., & Diamond, J. M. (1980). Lithium, membranes, and manic-depressive illness. *Journal of Membrane Biology, 52,* 187–200.

Eisenberg, N., Cialdini, R. B., McCreath, H., & Shell, R. (1987). Consistency-based compliance: When and why do children become vulnerable? *Journal of Personality and Social Psychology, 52,* 1161–1173.

Ekman, P. (1972). Universal and cultural differences in facial expressions of emotion. In J. Cole (Ed.), *Nebraska Symposium on Motivation.* Lincoln: University of Nebraska Press.

Ekman, P. (1983). Cross cultural studies of emotion. In P. Ekman (Ed.), *Darwin and facial expression: A century of research in review* (pp. 169–222). New York: Academic Press.

Ekman, P. (1984). Expression and the nature of emotion. In K. R. Scherer, & P. Ekman, (Eds.), *Approaches to emotion.* Hillsdale, NJ: Erlbaum.

Ekman, P. (1985). *Telling lies: Clues to deceit in marketplace, politics and marriage.* New York: Norton.

Ekman, P., & Friesen, W. V. (1971). Constants across cultures in the face and emotion. *Journal of Personality and Social Psychology, 17,* 124–129.

Ekman, P., & Friesen, W. V. (1986). A new pan-cultural facial expression of emotion. *Motivation and Emotion, 10:* 159–168.

Ekman, P., Sorenson, E. R., & Friesen, W. V. (1969). Pancultural elements in facial displays in emotion. *Science, 764,* 86–88.

Elkin, I., Parloff, M. B., Hadley, S. W., & Autrey, J. H. (1985). NIMH treatment of depression collaborative research program. *Archives of General Psychiatry, 42,* 305–316.

Elkin, I., Shea, T., Imber, S., Pilkonis, P., Sotsky, S., Glass, D., Watkins, J., Leber, W., & Collins, J. (1986, May). *NIMH treatment of depression collaborative research program: Initial outcome findings.* Paper presented to the Association for the Advancement of Science.

Elliott, J. (1977). The power and pathology of prejudice. In P. G. Zimbardo & F. L. Ruch, *Psychology and life* (9th ed., Diamond Printing). Glenview, IL: Scott, Foresman.

Ellis, A. (1962). *Reason and emotion in psychotherapy.* New York: Lyle Stuart.

Ellis, A. (1977). The treatment of a psychopath with rational therapy. In S. J. Morse & R. I. Watson (Eds.), *Psychotherapies: A comparative casebook.* New York: Holt, Rinehart & Winston.

Eme, R., Maisiak, R., & Goodale, W. (1979). Seriousness of adolescent problems. *Adolescence, 14,* 93–99.

Emmelkamp, P. M. G., & Kuipers, A. (1979). Agoraphobia: A follow-up study four years after treatment. *British Journal of Psychology, 134,* 352–355.

Emurian, H. H., Brady, J. V., Ray, R. L., Meyerhoff, J. L., & Mougey, E. H. (1984). Experimental analysis of team performance. *Naval Research Reviews* (Office of Naval Research), *36,* 3–19.

Endler, N. S. (1983). Interactionism: A personality model, but not yet a theory. In M. M. Page (Ed.), *Nebraska symposium on motivation, 1982: Personality—current theory and research* (pp. 155–200). Lincoln: University of Nebraska Press.

Epstein, S. (1979). The stability of behavior: 1. On predicting most of the people much of the time. *Journal of Personality and Social Psychology, 37,* 1097–1126.

Epstein, W. (1961). The influence of syntactical structure on learning. *American Journal of Psychology, 74,* 80–85.

Erdelyi, M. H. (1974). A new look at the New Look: Perceptual defense and vigilance. *Psychological Review, 87,* 1–25.

Ericksen, C. W. (1966). Cognitive responses to internally cued anxiety. In C. D. Spielberger (Ed.), *Anxiety and behavior.* New York: Academic Press.

Ericsson, K. A., Chase, W. G., & Falcoon, S. (1980). Acquisition of a memory skill. *Science, 208,* 1181–1183.

Ericsson, K. A., & Chase, W. G. (1982). Exceptional memory. *American Scientist, 70,* 607–615.

Erikson, E. H. (1963). *Childhood and society* (2d. ed.). New York: Norton.

Erikson, E. H. (1968). *Identity: Youth and crisis.* New York: Norton.

Eron, L. D., Huesmann, L. R., Lefkowitz, M. M., & Walder, L. O. (1972). Does television violence cause aggression? *American Psychologist, 27,* 253–263.

Escalona, S. (1965). Children and the threat of nuclear war. *Behavioral Science and Human Survival.* California: Science and Behavior Books.

Evans, R. I., Rozelle, R. M., Mittelmark, M. B., Hansen, W. B., Bane, A. L., & Havis, J. (1978). Deterring the onset of smoking in children: Knowledge of immediate physiological effects and coping with peer pressure, media pressure, and parent modeling. *Journal of Applied Social Psychology, 8,* 126–135.

Eysenck, H. J. (1952). The effects of psychotherapy: An evaluation. *Journal of Consulting Psychology, 16,* 319–324.

Eysenck, H. J. (1970). *The structure of human personality* (3d ed.). London: Methuen.

Eysenck, H. J. (1973). *The inequality of man.* London: Temple Smith.

Eysenck, H. J. (1975). *The inequality of man.* San Diego, CA: Educational and Industrial Testing Service.

Eysenck, H. J., & Kamin, L. (1981). *The intelligence controversy: H. J. Eysenck vs. Leon Kamin.* New York: Wiley-Interscience.

F

Fagot, B. I. (1978). The influence of sex of child on parental reactions to toddler children. *Child Development, 49,* 459–465.

Fairweather, G. W., Sanders, D. H., Maynard, R. F., & Cresler, D. L. (1969). *Community life for the mentally ill: Alternative to institutional care.* Chicago: Aldine.

Fantz, R. L. (1963). Pattern vision in newborn infants. *Science, 140,* 296–297.

Farah, M. J. (1984). The neurological basis of mental imagery: A componential analysis. *Cognition, 18,* 245–272.

Farina, A. (1980). Social attitudes and beliefs and their role in mental disorders. In J. G. Rabkin, L. Gelb, & J. B. Lazar (Eds.), *Attitudes toward the mentally ill: Research perspectives* (pp. 35–37). Rockville, Md.: National Institute of Mental Health.

Farina, A., Gliha, D., Boudreau, L. A., Allen, J. G., & Sherman, M. (1971). Mental illness and the impact of believing others know about it. *Journal of Abnormal Psychology, 77,* 1–5.

Farina, A., & Hagalauer, H. D. (1975). Sex and mental illness: The generosity of females. *Journal of Consulting and Clinical Psychology, 43,* 122.

Farquhar, J. W., Maccoby, N., & Solomon, D. S. (1984). Community applications of behavioral medicine. In W. D. Gentry (Ed.), *Handbook of behavioral medicine* (pp. 437–78). New York: Guilford Press.

Farr, M. J. (1984). Cognitive psychology. *Naval Research Reviews, 36,* 33–36.

Fass, P. S. (1980). The IQ: A cultural and historical framework. *American Journal of Education, 88,* 431–458.

Fazio, R. H., & Zanna, M. P. (1981). Direct experience and attitude-behavior consistency. In L. Berkowitz (Ed.), *Advances in experimental social psychology* (Vol. 14). New York: Academic Press.

Fechner, G. T. (1860). *Elemente der psychophysik.* Germany: Breitkopf und Hartel.

Fechner, G. T. (1966). *Elements of psychophysics* (Vol. 1) E. G. Boring & D. H. Howes, (Eds.); H. E. Adler, (Trans.). New York: Holt, Rinehart & Winston. (Originally published 1860)

Feigenbaum, E. A., & McCorduck, P. (1983). *The fifth generation.* Reading, MA: Addison-Wesley.

Fernald, A. (1985). Four-month-old infants prefer to listen to motherese. *Infant Behavior and Development, 8:* 118–195.

Fernald, D. (1984). *The Hans legacy.* Hillsdale, NJ: Erlbaum.

Ferrare, N. A. (1962). *Institutionalization and attitude change in an aged population.* Unpublished doctoral dissertation, Western Reserve University.

Ferster, C. B., Culbertson, S., & Perron Boren, M. C. (1975). *Behavior principles* (2d ed.). Englewood Cliffs, NJ: Prentice-Hall.

Ferster, C. B., & Skinner, B. F. (1957). *Schedules of reinforcement.* New York: Appleton-Century-Crofts.

Feshbach, S., & White, M. J. (1986). Individual differences in attitudes toward nuclear arms policies: Some psychological and social policy considerations. *Journal of Peace Research, 23,* 129–138.

Festinger, L. (1954). A theory of social comparison processes. *Human Relations, 7,* 117–140.

Festinger, L. (1957). *A theory of cognitive dissonance.* Stanford, CA: Stanford University Press.

Festinger, L., & Carlsmith, J. M. (1959). Cognitive consequences of forced compliance. *Journal of Abnormal and Social Psychology, 58,* 203–211.

Festinger, L., Pepitone, A., & Newcomb, T. (1952). Some consequences of deindividuation in a group. *Journal of Abnormal Social Psychology, 47,* 382–389.

Fink, M. (1979). *Convulsive therapy: Theory and practice.* New York: Raven Press.

Fish, J. M. (1973). *Placebo therapy.* San Francisco: Jossey-Bass.

Fishbein, M. & Ajzen, I. (1975). *Belief, attitude, intention, and behavior: An introduction to theory and research.* Reading, MA: Addison-Wesley.

Fisher, K. (1985). Attitude, logic keys to nuclear survival. *APA Monitor: 24.*

Fisher, R. J. (1982). *Social psychology: An applied approach.* New York: St. Martin's Press.

Fisher, S., & Greenberg, R. P. (1985). *The scientific credibility of Freud's theories and therapy.* New York: Columbia University Press.

Fiske, S. (1987). People's reactions to nuclear war: Implications for psychologists. *American Psychologist, 42,* 207–217.

Fiske, S. T., & Pavelchak, M. A. (1986). Category-based versus piecemeal-based affective response: Developments in schema-triggered affects. In R. M. Sorrentino & E. T. Higgins (Eds.), *The handbook of motivation and cognition: Foundations of social behavior* (pp. 167–203). New York: Guilford Press.

Fitts, P. M., & Posner, M. (1967). *Human performance.* Belmont, CA.: Brooks/Cole.

Fitzgerald, R., & Ellsworth, P. C. (1984). Due process vs. crime control: Death qualification and jury attitudes. *Law and Human Behavior, 8,* 31–51.

Five more teenagers kill themselves in Japan. (1986, April 23). *The Guardian.*

Flavell, J. H. (1977). *Cognitive development.* Englewood Cliffs, NJ: Prentice-Hall.

Flavell, J. H. (1979). Metacognition and cognitive monitoring: A new area of cognitive-developmental inquiry. *American Psychologist, 34,* 906–911.

Flavell, J. H. (1981). Cognitive monitoring. In W. P. Dickson (Ed.), *Children's oral communication skills* (pp. 35–60). New York: Academic Press.

Flavell, J. H. (1985). *Cognitive development* (2d ed.). Englewood Cliffs, NJ: Prentice-Hall.

Fleischman, P. R. (1973). Letter to *Science* concerning "On being sane in insane places." *Science, 180,* 356.

Fletcher, H. (1929). *Speech and hearing.* New York: Van Nostrand.

Floderus-Myrhed, B., Pedersen, N., & Rasmussen, I. (1980). Assessment of heritability for personality, based on a short form of the Eysenck Personality Inventory: A study of 12,898 twin pairs. *Behavior Genetics, 10,* 507–520.

Flood, R. A., & Seager, C. P. (1968). A retrospective examination of psychiatric case records of patients who subsequently committed suicide. *British Journal of Psychiatry, 114,* 433–450.

Foley, V. D. (1979). Family therapy. In R. J. Corsini (Ed.), *Current psychotherapies* (2d ed.) (pp. 460–69). Itasca, IL: Peacock.

Folkins, D. H., Lawson, K. D., Opton, E. M., Jr., & Lazarus, R. S. (1968). Desensitization and the experimental reduction of threat. *Journal of Abnormal Psychology, 73,* 100–113.

Fong, G. T., & Markus, H. (1982). Self-schemas and judgments about others. *Social Cognition, 1,* 191–204.

Fontaine, G. (1974). Social comparison and some determinants of expected personal control and expected performance in a novel situation. *Journal of Personality and Social Psychology, 29,* 487–496.

Ford, C. S., & Beach, F. A. (1951). *Patterns of sexual behavior.* New York: Harper & Row.

Fordyce, W. E. (1973). An operant conditioning method for managing chronic pain. *Postgraduate Medicine, 53,* 123–128.

Forest, D. V. (1976). Nonsense and sense in schizophrenic language. *Schizophrenia Bulletin, 2,* 286–381.

Forgas, J. P. (1982). Episodic cognition: Internal representation of interaction routines. In L. Berkowitz (Ed.), *Advances in experimental social psychology* (Vol. 5). New York: Academic Press.

Foster, G. M., & Anderson, B. G. (1978). *Medical anthropology.* New York: Wiley.

Foucault, M. (1975). *The birth of the clinic.* New York: Vintage Books.

Fouts, R. S., Bouts, D., & Schoenfeld, D. (1984). Sign language conversational interactions between chimpanzees. *Sign Language Studies, 41,* 1–12.

Fouts, R. S., & Rigby, R. L. (1977). Man-chimpanzee communication. In T. A. Sebeok (Ed.), *How animals communicate.* Bloomington: University of Indiana Press.

Fowler, H. (1965). *Curiosity and exploratory behavior.* New York: Macmillan.

Fox, M. W. (1974). *Concepts in ethology: Animal and human behavior.* Minneapolis: University of Minnesota Press.

Foy, D. W., Eisler, R. M., Pinkston, S. (1975). Modeled assertion in a case of explosive rages. *Journal of Behavioral Therapy and Experimental Psychiatry, 6,* 135–137.

Fraisse, P. (1968). Les emotions. In P. Fraisse & J. Piaget (Eds.), *Traite de psychologie experimentale* (Vol. 5). Paris: Presses Universitaires.

Frank, J. D. (1979). The present status of outcome studies. *Journal of Consulting and Clinical Psychology, 47,* 310–316.

Frank, J. (1987). The drive for power and the nuclear arms race. *American Psychologist, 42,* 337–344.

Franks, C. M., & Barbrack, C. R. (1983). Behavior therapy with adults: An integrative perspective. In M. Hersen, A. E. Kazdin, & A. S. Bellack (Eds.), *The clinical psychology handbook* (pp. 507–23). New York: Pergamon Press.

Fraser, S. C. (1974). *Deindividuation: Effects of anonymity on aggression in children.* Unpublished mimeograph report. University of Southern California.

Frederiksen, L. W., Jenkins, J. O., Foy, D. W., & Eisler, R. M. (1976). Social-skills training to modify abusive verbal outbursts in adults. *Journal of Applied Behavior Analysis, 9,* 117–125.

Freedman, J. L. (1984). Effect of television violence on aggressiveness. *Psychological Bulletin, 96,* 227–246.

Freedman, J. L., & Doob, A. N. (1968). *Deviancy: The psychology of being different.* New York: Academic Press.

Freedman, J. L., & Fraser, S. C. (1966). Compliance without pressure: The foot-in-the-door technique. *Journal of Personality and Social Psychology, 4,* 195–202.

Freeman, F. R. (1972). *Sleep research: A critical review.* Springfield, IL: Charles C. Thomas.

Freud, A. (1946). *The Ego and the mechanisms of defense.* New York: International Universities Press.

Freud, A. (1958). Adolescence. *Psychoanalytic Study of the Child, 13,* 255–278.

Freud, S. (1900). *The interpretation of dreams.* In J. Strachey (Ed. and Trans.), *The standard edition of the complete psychological works of Sigmund Freud* (Vol. 5). London: Hogarth Press.

Freud, S. (1914). *The psychopathology of everyday life.* New York: Macmillan. (Original work published 1904)

Freud, S. (1915). Instincts and their vicissitudes. In S. Freud, *The collected papers.* New York: Collier.

Freud, S. (1923). *Introductory lectures on psycho-analysis.* (J. Riviera, Trans.). London: Allen & Unwin.

Freud, S. (1925). The unconscious. In S. Freud, *The collected papers* (Vol. 4). London: Hogarth.

Freud, S. (1949). *A general introduction to psychoanalysis.* New York: Penguin Books.

Freud, S. (1960). *Jokes and their relation to the unconscious.* New York: Norton. (Original work published 1905)

Freud, S. (1976). Totem and taboo. In J. Strachey (Ed. and Trans.), *The standard edition of the complete psychological works of Sigmund Freud.* (Vol. 13). London: Hogarth Press. (Original work published 1913)

Freud, S. (1976). Three essays on the theory of sexuality. In J. Strachey (Ed. and Trans.), *The standard edition of the complete psychological works of Sigmund Freud.* (Vol. 7). London: Hogarth Press. (Original work published 1905)

Frey, W. H., II, Hoffman-Ahern, C., Johnson, R. A., Lydden, D. T., & Tuason, V. B. (1983). Crying behavior in the human adult. *Integrative Psychiatry, 1,* 94–98.

Frey, W. H., & Langseth, M. (1986). *Crying: The mystery of tears.* New York: Winston Press.

Fridlund, A. J., & Gilbert, A. N. (1985, November 8). Emotions and facial expression [Letter to the editor]. *Science, 230,* 607–608.

Friedman, M., & Rosenman, R. F. (1974). *Type A behavior and your heart.* New York: Knopf.

Friedman, M., Thoresen, C. E., Gill, J. J., Powell, L. H., Ulmer, D., Thompson, L., Price, V. A., Rabin, D. D., Breall, W. S., Dixon, T., Levy, R., & Bourg, E. (1984). Alteration of Type A behavior and reduction in cardiac recurrences in postmyocardial infarction patients. *American Heart Journal, 108,* 237–248.

Frisby, J. P. (1980). *Seeing.* Oxford: Oxford University Press.

Fromkin, V. A. (Ed.). (1980). *Errors in linguistic performance: Slips of the tongue, pen, and hand.* New York: Academic Press.

Fromm, E. (1947). *Man for himself.* New York: Holt, Rinehart & Winston.

Fromm, E., & Shor, R. E. (Eds.) (1979). *Hypnosis: Developments in research and new perspectives* (2d ed.). Hawthorne, NY: Aldine.

Frumkin, B., & Anisfeld, M. (1977). Semantic and surface codes in the memory of deaf children. *Cognitive Psychology, 9,* 475–493.

Fry, W. F., & Allen, M. (1975). *Make 'em laugh.* Palo Alto, CA: Science and Behavior Books.

Fuller, J. L. (1982). Psychology and genetics: A happy marriage? *Canadian Psychology, 23,* 11–21.

Furman, W., Rahe, D., & Hartup, W. W. (1979). Rehabilitation of socially withdrawn preschool children through mixed-aged and same-sex socialization. *Child Development, 50,* 915–922.

Furstenberg, F., Jr. (1985). Sociological ventures in child development. *Child Development, 56,* 281–288.

G

Gagné, R. M. (1984). Learning outcomes and their effects: Useful categories of human performance. *American Psychologist, 39,* 377–385.

Gagnon, J. H. (1977). *Human sexualities.* Glenview, IL: Scott, Foresman.

Galaburda, A. M., LeMay, M., Kemper, T. L., &

Geschwind, N. (1978). Right-left asymmetries in the brain. *Science, 199,* 852–856.

Galanter, E. (1962). Contemporary psychophysics. In R. Brown et al., (Eds.), *New directions in psychology.* New York: Holt, Rinehart & Winston.

Gallagher, J. M., & Reid, D. K. (1981). *The learning theory of Piaget and Inhelder.* Monterey, CA: Brooks/Cole.

Galton, F. (1884). Measurement of character. *Fortnightly Review, 42,* 179–185.

Garcia, J., & Garcia y Robertson, R. (1985). Evolution of learning mechanisms. In B. L. Hammonds (Ed.), *Psychology and learning: 1984 Master Lecturers* (pp. 187–243). Washington, DC: American Psychological Association.

Garcia, J., & Koelling, R. A. (1966). The relation of cue to consequence in avoidance learning. *Psychonomic Science, 4, 123–124.*

Gardner, B. T., & Gardner, R. A. (1972). Two-way communication with an infant chimpanzee. In A. M. Schrier & F. Stollnitz (Eds.), *Behavior of nonhuman primates* (Vol. 4). New York: Academic Press.

Gardner, H. (1983). *Frames of mind.* New York: Basic Books.

Gardner, H. (1985). *The mind's new science: A history of the cognitive revolution.* New York: Basic Books.

Gardner, L. I. (1972). Deprivation dwarfism. *Scientific American, 227* (7), 76–82.

Garland, H. (1984). Relation of effort-performance expectancy to performance in goal setting experiments. *Journal of Applied Psychology, 69,* 79–84.

Garmezy, N. (1976). Vulnerable and invulnerable children: Theory, research, and intervention. *Journal Abstract Supplement Service. Catalog of Selected Documents in Psychology, 6,* 96.

Garmezy, N. (1977). The psychology and psychopathology of Allen Head. *Schizophrenia Bulletin, 3,* 360–369.

Garmezy, N., & Mattysse S. (Eds.). (1977). Special issue on the psychology and psychopathology of attention. *Schizophrenic Bulletin: 3*(3).

Garner, W. R. (1974). *The processing of information and structure.* Potomac, Md.: Lawrence Erlbaum Associates.

Garrison, V. (1977). The "Puerto Rican syndrome" in psychiatry and Espiritismo. In V. Crapanzano & V. Garrison (Eds.), *Case studies in spirit possession.* New York: Wiley Interscience.

Gates, D. W. (1971). Verbal conditioning, transfer, and operant level "speech style" as functions of cognitive style. (Doctoral dissertation, City University of New York, 1971). *Dissertation Abstracts International, 32,* 3634B. (University Microfilms No. 71–30, 719)

Gazzaniga, M. (1970). *The bisected brain.* New York: Appleton-Century-Crofts.

Gazzaniga, M. (1980). *Psychology.* New York: Harper & Row.

Gazzaniga, M. S. (1985). *The social brain.* New York: Basic Books.

Geer, J. H., Davidson, G. C., & Gatchel, R. I. (1970). Reduction of stress in humans through nonveridical perceived control of aversive stimulation. *Journal of Personality and Social Psychology, 16,* 731–738.

Geldard, F. A. (1972). *The human senses* (2d ed.). New York: Wiley.

Gelman, R. (1979). Preschool thought. *American Psychologists, 34,* 900–905.

Gelman, R., & Baillargeon, R. (1983). A review of Piagetian concepts. In J. Flavell & E. Markman (Eds.), *Handbook of child psychology* (Vol. 3, pp. 167–230). New York: Wiley.

Gerbner, G. (1981, April). Television: The American school child's national curriculum day in and day out. *PTA Today,* 3–5.

Gerbner, G., Gross, L., Signorielli, N., & Morgan, M. (1986, September). *Television's mean world: Violence profile No. 14–15.* Philadelphia: University of Pennsylvania, The Annenberg School of Communication.

Gergen, K. J., Gergen, M. M., & Barton, W. (1973, October). Deviance in the dark. *Psychology Today,* 129–130.

Geschwind, N. (1979). Specializations of the human brain. *Scientific American, 241*(3), 180–199.

Gevarter, W. B. (1982, May). *An overview of artificial intelligence and robotics: Vol. 3, Expert systems.* (NBSIR 82-2505). Washington, DC: National Bureau of Standards.

Gevins, A. S., Morgan, N. H., Bressler, S. L., Cutillo, B. A., White, R. M., Illes, J., Greer, D. S., Doyle, J. C., & Zeitlin, G. M. (1987). Human neuroelectric patterns predict performance accuracy. *Science, 235,* 580–585.

Gevins, A. S., Shaffer, R. E., Doyle, J. C., Cutillo, B. A., Tannehill, R. S., & Bressler, S. L. (1983). Shadows of thought: Shifting lateralization of human brain electrical potential patterns during brief visuo-motor task. *Science, 220,* 97–99.

Gibbs, J. C. (1977). Kohlberg's stages of moral judgment: A constructive critique. *Harvard Educational Review, 47,* 43–61.

Gibbs, J. C., Arnold, K. D., & Burkhart, J. E. (1984). Sex differences in the expression of moral judgment. *Child Development, 55,* 1040–1043.

Gibson, J. J. (1950). *The perception of the visual world.* New York: Houghton-Mifflin.

Gibson, J. J. (1966). *The senses considered as perceptual systems.* New York: Houghton-Mifflin.

Gibson, J. J. (1979). *An ecological approach to visual perception.* New York: Houghton-Mifflin.

Gibson, J. T., & Haritos-Fatouros, M. (1986, November). The education of a torturer. *Psychology Today,* 50–58.

Gilliam, H. (1986, July 6). Fencing out world prosperity. *San Francisco Chronicle:* 18.

Gillig, P. M., & Greenwald, A. G. (1974). Is it time to lay the sleeper effect to rest? *Journal of Personality and Social Psychology, 29,* 132–139.

Gilligan, C. (1982). *In a different voice: Psychological theory and women's development.* Cambridge, MA: Harvard University Press.

Gist, R., & Stolz, S. B. (1982). Mental health promotion and the media: Community response to the Kansas City hotel disaster. *American Psychologist, 37,* 1136–1139.

Glanzer, M., & Cunitz, A. R. (1966). Two storage mechanisms in free recall. *Journal of Verbal Learning and Verbal Behavior, 5,* 351–360.

Glaser, R. (1984). Education and thinking: The role of knowledge. *American Psychologist, 39,* 93–104.

Glass, A. L., Holyoak, K. J., & Santa, J. L. (1979). *Cognition.* Reading, MA: Addison-Wesley.

Glassman, R. B. (1983). Free will has a neural substrate: Critique of Joseph F. Rychlak's *Discovering free will and personal responsibility. Zygon, 18,* 67–82.

Glucksberg, S., & Danks, J. H. (1975). *Experimental psycholinguistics.* Hillsdale, NJ: Erlbaum.

Goddard, H. H. (1914). *The Kallikak family, a study of the heredity of feeble-mindedness.* New York: Macmillan.

Goffman, E. (1959). *The presentation of self in everyday life.* New York: Doubleday.

Goffman, E. (1963). *Stigma.* Englewood Cliffs, NJ: Prentice-Hall.

Gold, P. E. (1984). Memory modulation: Neurobiological contexts. In G. Lynch, J. L. McGaugh, & N. M. Weinberger (Eds.), *Neurobiology of learning and memory* (pp. 374–82). New York: Guilford Press.

Gold, P. E. (1987). Sweet memories. *American Scientist, 75,* 151–155.

Golding, S. L. (1977). The problem of construal styles in the analysis of person-situation interactions. In D. Magnusson & N. E. Endler (Eds.), *Personality at the crossroads* (pp. 401–08). Hillsdale, NJ: Erlbaum.

Goldman, R. B. (1976). *A work experiment: Six Americans in a Swedish plant.* New York: Ford Foundation.

Goldstein, E. B. (1980). *Sensation and perception.* Belmont, CA: Wadsworth.

Goldstein, M., & Rodnick, E. H. (1975). The family's contribution to the etiology of schizophrenia: Current status. *Schizophrenia Bulletin, 14,* 48–63.

Goleman, D. (1987). Who are you kidding? *Psychology Today:* 24–30.

Gomes-Schwartz, B., Hadley, S. W., & Strupp, H. H. (1978). Individual psychotherapy and behavior therapy. *Annual Review of Psychology, 29,* 435–471.

Gonzalez, A., & Zimbardo, P. G. (1985, March). Time in perspective. *Psychology Today,* 20–26.

Goodall, J. (1986). *The chimpanzees of Gombe: Patterns of behavior.* Cambridge, MA: Harvard University Press.

Goodman, D. A. (1978). Learning from lobotomy. *Human Behavior,* 7(1), 44–49.

Goodman, L. S., & Gilman, A. (1970). *The pharmacological basis of therapeutics* (4th ed.). New York: Macmillan.

Gordon, C., & Gergen, K. J. (1968). *The self in social interaction* (Vol. 1). New York: Wiley.

Gorman, B. S., & Wessman, A. E. (1977). *The personal experience of time.* New York: Plenum.

Gorney, R. (1976, September). Paper presented at annual meeting of the American Psychiatric Association.

Gottesman, I. I. (1963). Genetic aspects of intelligent behavior. In N. Ellis (Ed.), *Handbook of mental deficiency: Psychological theory and research.* New York: McGraw-Hill.

Gottesman, I. I., & Shields, J. (1972). *Schizophrenia and genetics: A twin study vantage point.* New York: Academic Press.

Gottesman, I. I., & Shields, J. (1976). A critical review of recent adoption, twin, and family studies of schizophrenia: Behavioral genetics perspective. *Schizophrenia Bulletin, 2,* 360–401.

Gottlieb, B. H. (Ed.). (1981). *Social networks and social support.* Beverly Hills, CA.: Sage.

Gough, H. G. (1957). *California Psychological Inventory Manual.* Palo Alto, CA.: Consulting Psychology Press.

Gough, H. G. (1961). Techniques for identifying the creative research scientist. In *Conference on the creative person.* Berkeley: University of California, Institute of Personality Assessment & Research.

Gould, J. L. (1985). How bees remember flower shapes. *Science, 227,* 1492–1494.

Gould, J. L., & Marler, P. (1984). Ethology on the natural history of learning. In P. Marler & H. Terrace (Eds.), *The biology of learning* (pp. 47–74). Berlin: Springer-Verlag.

Gould, S. J. (1981). *The mismeasure of man.* New York: Norton.

Gray, C. R., & Gummerman, K. (1975). The enigmatic eidetic image: A critical examination of methods, data, and theories. *Psychological Bulletin, 82,* 383–407.

Green, D. M., & Swets, J. A. (1966). *Signal detection theory and psychophysics.* New York: Wiley.

Greenberg, J., & Ornstein, S. (1983). High status job title as compensation for underpayment: A test of equity theory. *Journal of Applied Psychology, 68,* 285–297.

Greenfield, P. M., & Smith, J. H. (1976). *The structure of communication in early language development.* New York: Academic Press.

Greening, T. (Ed.). (1984). Special peace issue. *Journal of Humanistic Psychology: 23*(3).

Greeno, C. G., & Maccoby, E. E. (1986). How different is the "different voice"? *Signs, 11,* 310–316.

Griffin, D. R. (1984). Animal thinking. *American Scientist, 72,* 456–464.

Grossman, S. P. (1979). The biology of motivation. *Annual Review of Psychology, 30,* 209–242.

Group for the Advancement of Psychiatry. (1950). *Revised electro-shock therapy report, special volume: Report No. 15,* 1–3.

Guerra, F., & Aldrete, J. (1980). *Emotional and psychological responses to anesthesia and surgery.* New York: Grune & Stratton.

Guetzkow, H., Alger, C. F., Brody, R. A., Noel, R. C., & Snyder, R. C. (1963). *Simulation in international relations.* Englewood Cliffs, NJ: Prentice-Hall.

Guilford, J. P. (1961). *Psychological Review, 68,* 1–20.

Guilford, J. P. (1967). *Crystalized intelligences: The nature of human intelligence.* New York: McGraw-Hill.

Guilford, J. P. (1973). Theories of intelligence. In B. B. Wolman (Ed.), *Handbook of general psychology.* Englewood Cliffs, NJ: Prentice-Hall.

Gummerman, K., Gray, C. R., & Wilson, J. M. (1972). An attempt to assess eidetic imagery objectively. *Psychonomic Science, 28,* 115–118.

Gur, R. C., & Gur, R. E. (1974). Handedness, sex and eyedness as moderating variables in the relation between hypnotic susceptibility and functional brain asymmetry. *Journal of Abnormal Psychology, 83,* 635–643.

Gur, R. C., Gur., R. E., Obrist, W. D., Hungerbuhler, J. P., & Younken, D. (1982). Sex and handedness differences in cerebral blood flow during rest and cognitive activity. *Science, 217,* 659–661.

Gurman, A. S., & Kniskern, D. P. (1978). Research in marital and family therapy: Progress, perspective, and prospect. In S. L. Gafield & A. E. Bergan (Eds.), *Handbook of psychotherapy and behavior change* (pp. 817–904). New York: Wiley.

Guze, S., Goodwin, D., & Crane, J. (1969). Criminality and psychiatric disorders. *Archives of General Psychiatry, 20,* 583–591.

Gynther, M. D. (1981). Is the *MMPI* an appropriate assessment device for blacks? *Journal of Black Psychology, 7,* 67–75.

Gynther, M. D., & Gynther, R. A. (1976). Personality inventories. In I. B. Weiner (Ed.), *Clinical methods in psychology.* New York: Wiley-Interscience.

H

Haas, H., Fink, H., & Hartfelder, G. (1959). *Das placeboproblem. Fortschritte der Arzneimittleforchung, 1:* 279–454. Translated in *Psychopharmacology Service Center Bulletin,* 1963, *8:* 1–65. U.S. Department of Health, Education and Welfare, Public Health Service.

Haas, K. (1965). *Understanding ourselves and others.* Englewood Cliffs, NJ: Prentice-Hall.

Habot, T. B., & Libow, L. S. (1980). The interrelationship of mental and physical status and its assessment in the older adult: Mind-body interaction. In J. E. Birren & R. B. Sloane (Eds.), *Handbook of mental health and aging* (pp. 701–16). Englewood Cliffs, NJ: Prentice-Hall.

Hackman, J. R., & Oldham, G. R. (1980). *Work redesign.* Reading, MA: Addison-Wesley.

Haier, R. J. (1980). The diagnosis of schizophrenia: A review of recent developments. In S. J. Keith & L. R. Mosher (Eds.), *Special report: Schizophrenia, 1980* (pp. 2–13). Washington, DC: U.S. Government Printing Office.

Hale, R. L. (1983). Intellectual assessment. In M. Hersen, A. E. Kazdin, & A. S. Bellack (Eds.), *The clinical psychology handbook* (pp. 345–76). New York: Pergamon.

Hall, G. S. (1904). *Adolescence: Its psychology and its relations to physiology, anthropology, sociology, sex, crime, religion and education* (Vols. 1 and 2). New York: D. Appleton.

Halpin, A., & Winer, B. (1952). *The leadership behavior of the airplane commander.* Ohio State University Research Foundation.

Hamill, R., Wilson, T. D., & Nisbett, R. E. (1980). *Ignoring sample bias: Inferences about populations from atypical cases.* Unpublished manuscript, University of Michigan, Ann Arbor.

Hamilton, D. L., Katz, L. B., & Leirer, V. O. (1980). Memory for persons. *Journal of Personality and Social Psychology, 39,* 1050–1063.

Hammer, D. L., & Padesky, C. A. (1977). Sex differences in the expression of depressive responses on the Beck Depression Inventory. *Journal of Abnormal Psychology, 86,* 609–614.

Haney, C. (1984). On the selection of capital juries: The biasing effects of the death-qualification process. *Law and Human Behavior, 8,* 121–132.

Haney, C., & Zimbardo, P. G. (1977). The socialization into criminality: On becoming a prisoner and a guard. In J. L. Tapp

& F. L. Levine (Eds.), *Law, justice and the individual in society: Psychological and legal issues* (pp. 198–223). New York: Holt, Rinehart & Winston.

Hanna, S. D. (1984). *The psychosocial impact of the nuclear threat on children.* Unpublished manuscript. (Available from Physicians for Social Responsibility, 639 Massachusetts Ave., Cambridge, MA 02139)

Hanson, D., Gottesman, I., & Meehl, P. (1977). Genetic theories and the validation of psychiatric diagnosis: Implications for the study of children of schizophrenics. *Journal of Abnormal Psychology, 86,* 575–588.

Hareven, T. (1985). Historical changes in the family and the life course: Implications for child development. *Monographs of the Society for Research in Child Development, 50* (Serial No. 211), 8–23.

Harlow, H. F. (1965). Sexual behavior in the rhesus monkey. In F. Beach (Ed.), *Sex and behavior.* New York: Wiley.

Harlow, H. F., & Harlow, M. K. (1966). Learning to love. *American Scientist, 54,* 244–272.

Harlow, H. F., & Zimmerman, R. R. (1958). The development of affectional responses in infant monkeys. Proceedings of the *American Philosophical Society, 102,* 501–509.

Harner, M. J. (1973). The sound of rushing water. In M. J. Harner (Ed.), *Hallucinogens and shamanism* (pp. 15–27). Oxford: Oxford University Press.

Harris, P. R. (1980). *Promoting health—preventing disease: Objectives for the nation.* Washington, DC: U.S. Government Printing Office.

Harrison, J. (1978). Male sex role and health. *Journal of Social Issues, 34*(1), 65–86.

Harshman, R. A., Crawford, H. J., & Hecht, E. (1976). Marijuana, cognitive style, and lateralized hemispheric functions. In S. Cohen & R. C. Stillman (Eds.), *The therapeutic potential of marijuana* (pp. 205–54). New York: Plenum.

Hart, R. A., & Moore, G. I. (1973). The development of spatial cognition: A review. In R. M. Downs & D. Stea (Eds.), *Image and environment.* Chicago: Aldine.

Hartmann, D. P., Roper, B. L., & Bradford, D. (1979). Some relationships between behavioral and traditional assessment. *Journal of Behavioral Assessment, 1,* 3–21.

Hartmann, E. L. (1973). *The functions of sleep.* New Haven, CT: Yale University Press.

Hartshorne, H., & May, M. A. (1928). *Studies in the nature of character, Vol. 1: Studies in deceit.* New York: Macmillan.

Hartshorne, H., & May, M. A. (1929). *Studies in the nature of character, Vol. 2: Studies in service and self-control.* New York: Macmillan.

Harvey, O. J., & Consalvi, C. (1960). Status and conformity in informal groups. *Journal of Abnormal and Social Psychology, 60,* 182–187.

Hasenfus, N., & Magaro, P. (1976). Creativity and schizophrenia: An equality of empirical constructs. *British Journal of Psychiatry, 129,* 346–349.

Hass, A. (1979). *Teenage sexuality: A survey of teenage sexual behavior.* New York: Macmillan.

Hatfield, E. (1986). *Mirror, mirror: The importance of looks in everyday life.* Albany: State University of New York Press.

Hatfield, E., & Sprecher, S. (1986). *Mirror, mirror . . . The importance of looks in everyday life.* New York: State University of New York Press.

Hathaway, S. R., & McKinley, J. C. (1940). A multiphasic personality schedule (Minnesota): I Construction of the schedule. *Journal of Psychology, 10,* 249–254.

Hathaway, S. R., & McKinley, J. C. (1943). *The Minnesota Multiphasic Personality Schedule.* Minneapolis: University of Minnesota Press.

Hauri, P. (1977). *The sleep disorders.* Kalamazoo, MI: Upjohn.

Hayes, C. (1951). *The ape in our house.* New York: Harper.

Hayes-Roth, B., & Hayes-Roth, F. (1979). A cognitive model of planning. *Cognitive Science, 3,* 275–310.

Haynes, S. G., & Feinleib, M. (1980). Women, work, and coronary heart disease: Prospective findings from the Framingham Heart Study. *American Journal of Public Health, 70,* 133–141.

Haynes, S. N. (1983). Behavioral assessment. In M. Hersen, **A. E. Kazdin, & A. S. Bellack** (Eds.), *The clinical psychology handbook* (pp. 397–425). New York: Pergamon.

Haynes, S. N., & Wilson, C. C. (1979). *Behavioral assessment: Recent advances in methods and concepts.* San Francisco: Jossey-Bass.

Hebb, D. O. (1949). *The organization of behavior: A neuropsychological theory.* New York: Wiley.

Hebb, D. O. (1955). Drives and the CNS (conceptual nervous system). *Psychological Review, 62,* 243–254.

Hebb, D. (1974). What is psychology about? *American Psychologist, 29,* 71–79.

Heber, R. (1976, June). *Sociocultural mental retardation: A longitudinal study.* Paper presented at the Vermont Conference on the Primary Prevention of Psychopathology.

Hecht, A. (1986, April). A guide to the proper use of tranquilizers. *Healthline Newsletter,* pp. 5–6.

Hedlund, J. L. (1977). MMPI clinical scale correlated. *Journal of Consulting and Clinical Psychology, 45,* 739–750.

Heider, F. (1958). *The psychology of interpersonal relationships.* New York: Wiley.

Heider, F., & Simmel, M. (1944). An experimental study of apparent behavior. *American Journal of Psychology, 57,* 243–259.

Heider, R. (1944). Social perception and phenomenal causality. *Psychological Review, 51,* 358–374.

Helmholtz, H. von. (1962). Treatise on physiological optics (Vol. 3). J. P. Southall, (Ed.) and (Trans.). New York: Dover Press. (Original work published 1866)

Henderson, N. D. (1980). Effects of early experience upon the behavior of animals: The second twenty-five years of research. In E. C. Simmel (Ed.), *Early experiences and early behavior: Implications for social development* (pp. 39–77). New York: Academic Press.

Henning, H. (1916). Die Qualitatenreihe des Gasmachs. *Z. Psychol., 74,* 203–219.

Hensel, H. (1968). Electrophysiology of cutaneous thermoreceptors. In D. R. Kenshalo (Ed.), *The skin senses* (pp. 384–99). Springfield, IL: Charles C Thomas.

Hering, E. (1861–1864). *Beitrage zur physiologie.* Leipzig: W. Engelmann.

Herman, M. (1972). The poor: Their medical needs and the health services available to them. *Annals of the American Academy of Political and Social Science, 399,* 12–21.

Herrnstein, R. J., Nickerson, R. S., Sanchez, M. de, & Swets, J. A. (1986). Teaching thinking skills. *American Psychologist, 41,* 1279–1289.

Herrnstein, R. J., & Wilson, J. Q. (1985). *Crime and human nature.* New York: Simon & Schuster.

Hersen, M., & Bellack, A. J. (1976). Assessment of social skills. In A. R. Ciminero, K. R. Calhoun, & H. E. Adams (Eds.), *Handbook of behavioral assessment* (pp. 509–54). New York: Wiley.

Hersh, S. M. (1971). *My Lai 4: A report on the massacre and its aftermath.* New York: Random House.

Hess, E. H. (1972). Pupillometrics: A method of studying mental, emotional, and sensory processes. In N. E. Greenfield & R. A. Steinbach (Eds.), *Handbook of psychophysiology.* New York: Holt, Rinehart & Winston.

Hess, W., & Akert, K. (1955). Experimental data on the role of hypothalamus in the mechanism of emotional behavior. *Archives of Neurological Psychiatry, 73,* 127–129.

Heston, L. L. (1970). The genetics of schizophrenia and schizoid disease. *Science, 112,* 249–256.

Hetherington, E. M., & Parke, R. D. (1975). *Child psychology: A contemporary viewpoint.* New York: McGraw-Hill.

Hilgard, E. (1965). *Hypnotic susceptibility.* New York: Harcourt Brace Jovanovich.

Hilgard, E. R. (1968). *The experience of hypnosis.* New York: Harcourt Brace Jovanovich.

Hilgard, E. R. (1973). The domain of hypnosis with some comments on alternative paradigms. *American Psychologist, 28,* 972–982.

Hilgard, E. R. (1977). *Divided consciousness:Multiple controls in human thought and action.* New York: Wiley.

Hilgard, E. R. (1980). Consciousness in contemporary psychology. *Annual Review of Psychology, 31,* 1–26.

Hilgard, E. R. (1986). *Psychology in America: A historical survey.* San Diego CA: Harcourt Brace Jovanovich.

Hilgard, E. R., & Hilgard, J. R. (1974, Spring-Summer). Hypnosis in the control of pain. *The Stanford Magazine,* 58–62.

Hilgard, J. R. (1970). *Personality and hypnosis: A study of imaginative involvement.* Chicago: University of Chicago Press.

Hilgard, J. R. (1979). *Personality and hypnosis: A study of imaginative involvement* (2d ed.). Chicago: University of Chicago Press.

Hille, B. (1984). *Ionic channels of excitable membranes.* Sunderland, MA: Sinauer Associates.

Hillis, W. D. (1985). *The connection machine.* Cambridge, MA: MIT Press.

Hinton, G. F., & Anderson, J. A. (1981). *Parallel models of associative memory.* Hillsdale, NJ: Erlbaum.

Hirsch, H. V. B., & Spinelli, D. N. (1970). Visual experience modifies distribution of horizontally and vertically oriented receptive fields in cats. *Science, 168,* 869–871.

Hirschfield, R. M. A., & Cross, C. K. (1982). Epidemiology of affective disorders: Psychosocial risk factors. *Archives of General Psychiatry, 39:* 35–46.

Hitler, A. (1933). *Mein Kampf.* Cambridge, MA: Riverside.

Hobson, J. A., & McCarley, R. W. (1977). The brain as a dream state generator: An activation-synthesis hypothesis of the dream process. *American Journal of Psychiatry, 134,* 1335–1348.

Hochberg, J. (1968). In the mind's eye. In R. N. Haber (Ed.), *Contemporary theory and research in visual perception.* New York: Holt, Rinehart & Winston.

Hockett, C. F. (1960). The origin of speech. *Scientific American, 203:* 89–96.

Hofer, M. (1981). *The roots of human behavior: An introduction to the psychobiology of early development.* San Francisco: Freeman.

Hofling, C. K., Brotzman, E., Dalrymple, S., Graves, N., & Pierce, C. M. (1966). An experimental study in nurse-physician relationships. *Journal of Nervous and Mental Disease, 143*(2), 171–180.

Hofstede, G. (1980). *Culture's consequences: International differences in work-related values.* Beverly Hills, CA: Sage.

Holahan, C. J., & Moos, R. (1981). Social support and psychological distress: A longitudinal analysis. *Journal of Abnormal Psychology, 90,* 365–370.

Holden, C. (1978). Patuxent: Controversial prison clings to belief in rehabilitation. *Science, 199,* 665–668.

Holden, C. (1986a). Depression research advances, treatment lags. *Science, 233,* 723–725.

Holden, C. (1986b). Youth suicide: New research focuses on a growing social problem. *Science, 233,* 839–841.

Holen, M. C., & Oaster, T. R. (1976). Serial position and isolation effects in a classroom lecture simulation. *Journal of Educational Psychology, 68,* 293–296.

Holland, P. C., & Rescorla, R. A. (1975). Second-order conditioning with food unconditioned stimulus. *Journal of Comparative and Physiological Psychology, 88,* 459–467.

Hollender, M. H. (1980). The case of Anna O.: A reformulation. *American Journal of Psychiatry, 137,* 797–800.

Holmes, T. H. & Masuda, M. (1974). Life change and stress susceptibility. In B. S. Dohrenwend & B. P. Dohrenwend, (Eds.), *Stressful life events: Their nature and effects* (pp. 45–72). New York: Wiley.

Holmes, T. H., & Rahe, R. H. (1967). The social readjustment rating scale. *Journal of Psychosomatic Research, 11*(2), 213–218.

Holt, R. R. (1970). Yet another look at clinical and statistical prediction: Or is clinical psychology worthwhile? *American Psychologist, 25,* 337–349.

Homme, L. E. (1965). Control of coverants, the operants of mind. *Psychological Record, 15,* 501–511.

Homme, L. E., de Baca, P. C., Devine, J. V., Steinhorst, R., & Rickert, E. J. (1963). Use of the Premack principle in controlling the behavior of nursery school children. *Journal of the Experimental Analysis of Behavior, 6,* 544.

Honzik, M. P. (1984). Life-span development. *Annual Review of Psychology, 35,* 309–331.

Hooper, J., & Teresi, D. (1986). *The three-pound universe.* New York: Macmillan.

Hopson, J. L. (1979). *Scent signals: The silent language of sex.* New York: Morrow.

Horney, K. (1939). *New ways in psychoanalyses.* New York: Norton.

Horton, L. E. (1970). Generalization of aggressive behavior in adolescent delinquent boys. *Journal of Applied Behavior Analysis, 3,* 205–211.

Horvath, F. S. (1977). The effects of selected variables on the interpretation of polygraph records. *Journal of Applied Psychology, 62,* 127–136.

Hosobuchi, Y., Rossier, J., Bloom, F. E., & Guillemin, R. (1979). Stimulation of human periaqueductal gray for pain relief increases immunoreactive B-endorphin in ventricular fluid. *Science, 203,* 279–281.

Houghton, J. (1980). One personal experience: Before and after mental illness. In J. G. Rabkin, L. Gelb, & J. B. Lazar (Eds.), *Attitudes toward the mentally ill: Research perspectives* (pp. 7–14). Rockville, MD: National Institute of Mental Health.

Hovland, C. I., Janis, I. L., & Kelley, H. H. (1953). *Communication and persuasion.* New Haven, CT: Yale University Press.

Hovland, C., Lumsdain, A., & Sheffield, F. (1949). *Experiments on mass communication.* Princeton, NJ: Princeton University Press.

Hovland, C., & Weiss, W. (1951). The influence of source credibility on communication effectiveness. *Public Opinion Quarterly, 15,* 635–650.

Howard, D. T. (1928). A functional theory of emotions. In M. L. Reymert (Ed.), *Feelings and emotions: The Wittenberg symposium* (pp. 140–49). Worcester, MA: Clark University Press.

Howarth, E., & Eysenck, H. J. (1968). Extroversion, arousal, and paired associate recall. *Journal of Experimental Research in Personality, 3,* 114–116.

Hubel, D. H. (1979). The brain. *Scientific American, 241*(9), 45–53.

Hubel, D. H., & Wiesel, T. N. (1959). Receptive fields of single neurons in the cat's striate cortex. *Journal of Physiology (London), 148,* 574–591.

Hubel, D. H., & Wiesel, T. N. (1962). Receptive fields, binocular interaction, and functional architecture in the cat's visual cortex. *Journal of Physiology (London), 160,* 106–154.

Hubel, D. H., & Wiesel, T. N. (1979). Brain mechanisms of vision. *Scientific American, 241*(9), 150–168.

Huesmann, L. R., Eron, L. D., Berkowitz, L., & Chafee, S. (1986). *Effect of television violence on aggression: A reply to Freedman.* Unpublished paper, University of Illinois, Chicago.

Huesmann, L. R., Eron, L. D., Klein, R., Brice, P., & Fischer, P. (1983). Mitigating the imitation of aggressive behaviors by children's attitudes about media violence. *Journal of Personality and Social Psychology, 44,* 899–910.

Huesmann, L. R., & Malamuth, N. M. (Eds.). (1986). Media violence and antisocial behavior. *Journal of Social Issues, 42,* Whole issue.

Hughes, J., Smith, T. W., Kosterlitz, H. W., Fotergill, L. A., Morgan, B. A., & Morris, H. R. (1975). Identification of two related pentapeptides from the brain with potent opiate antagonist activity. *Nature, 258,* 577–579.

Hull, C. L. (1943). *Principles of behavior: An introduction to behavior theory.* New York: Appleton-Century-Crofts.

Hull, C. L. (1952). *A behavior system: An introduction to behavior theory concerning the individual organism.* New Haven, CT: Yale University Press.

Humphrey, N. K. (1976). The social function of intellect. In P. P. G. Bateson & R. A. Hinde (Eds.), *Growing points in ethology* (pp. 303–317). Cambridge, MA: Cambridge University Press.

Humphrey, T. (1970). The development of human fetal activity and its relation to postnatal behavior. In H. W. Reese & L. P. Lipsitt (Eds.), *Advance in child development and behavior* (Vol. 5). New York: Academic Press.

Hunt, E., (1983). On the nature of intelligence. *Science, 219,* 141–146.

Hunt, E. (1984). Intelligence and mental competence. *Naval Research Reviews, 36,* 37–42.

Hunt, M. (1982). *The universe within: A new science explores the human mind.* New York: Simon & Schuster.

Hunt, M. (1985). *Profiles of social research: The scientific study of human interactions.* New York: Russell Sage Foundation.

Hunter, F., & Youniss, J. (1982). Changes in functions of three relations during adolescence. *Developmental Psychology, 18,* 806–811.

Hurlburt, R. T. (1979). Random sampling of cognitions and behavior. *Journal of Research in Personality, 13,* 103–111.

Hurvich, L. M., & Jameson, D. (1957). An opponent process theory of color vision. *Psychological Review, 64,* 384–404.

Huston, A. (1985). *Television and human behavior.* Transcript of a Science and Public Policy Seminar. Washington, DC: Federation of Behavioral, Psychological, and Cognitive Sciences.

Hutchins, D. (1961). The value of suggestion given under anesthesia. *American Journal of Clinical Hypnosis, 4,* 106–114.

Hyman, I. A., McDowell, E., & Raines, B. (1977). Corporal punishment and alternatives in the schools: An overview of theoretical and practical issues. In J. H. Wise (Ed.), *Proceedings: Conference on corporal punishment in the schools* (pp. 1–18). Washington, DC: National Institute of Education.

I

Ickes, W., Layden, M. A., & Barnes, R. D. (1978). Objective self-awareness and individuation: An empirical link. *Journal of Personality, 46,* 146–161.

Inglis, J., & Lawson, J. S. (1981). Sex differences in the effects of unilateral brain damage on intelligence. *Science, 212,* 693–695.

Insel, P. L., & Roth, W. T. (1985). *Core concepts in health.* Palo Alto, CA: Mayfield.

Insko, C. A., Thibaut, J. W., Moehle, D., Wilson, M., Diamond, W. D., Gilmore, R., Solomon, M. R., & Lipsitz, A. (1980). Social evolution and the emergence of leadership. *Journal of Personality and Social Psychology, 39,* 431–448.

Isen, A. M., Horn, N., & Rosenhan, D. L. (1973). Effects of success and failure on children's generosity. *Journal of Personality and Social Psychology, 27,* 239–247.

Itani, J. (1961). The society of Japanese monkeys. *Japan Quarterly, 8*(4), 421–430.

Itard, J. M. G. (1962). *The wild boy of Averyron* (G. & M. Humphrey, Trans.). New York: Appleton-Century-Crofts.

Iversen, L. L. (1979). The chemistry of the brain. *Scientific American, 241*(9), 134–149.

Izard, C. (1971). *The face of emotion.* New York: Appleton-Century-Crofts.

Izard, C. E. (Ed.). (1982). *Measuring emotions in infants and children.* New York: Cambridge University Press.

Izard, C. E. (1985). Emotions and facial expression [Letters to the editor]. *Science, 230,* 608.

J

Jacob, F. (1977). Evolution and tinkering. *Science, 196,* 161–166.

Jacobs, B. L., & Trulson, M. E. (1979). Mechanisms of action of L.S.D. *American Scientist, 67,* 396–404.

Jacobson, E. (1970). *Modern treatment of tense patients.* Springfield, IL: Charles C Thomas.

James, W. (1884). What is an emotion? *Mind, 9,* 188–205.

James, W. (1890). *The principles of psychology* (2 vols.). New York: Holt, Rinehart & Winston.

Janis, I. L. (1958). *Psychological stress.* New York: Wiley.

Janis, I. L. (1972). *Victims of groupthink: A psychological study of foreign-policy decisions and fiascoes.* Boston: Houghton Mifflin.

Janis, I. L. (1982a). Decisionmaking under stress. In L. Goldberger & S. Breznitz (Eds.), *Handbook of stress* (pp. 69–87). New York: Free Press.

Janis, I. L. (1982b). *Groupthink: Psychological studies of policy decisions and fiascoes* (2d ed.). Boston: Houghton Mifflin.

Janis, I. L. (1985). International crisis management in the nuclear age. *Applied Social Psychology Annual, 6,* 63–86.

Janowitz, H. D., & Grossman, M. I. (1950). Hunger and appetite: Some definitions and concepts. *Journal of The Mount Sinai Hospital, 16,* 231–240.

Janus, S. S. (1975). The great comedians: Personality and other factors. *American Journal of Psychoanalysis, 3,* 169–174.

Jenkins, C. D. (1976). Recent evidence supporting psychologic and social risk factors for coronary disease. *New England Journal of Medicine, 294,* 987–994, 1033–1038.

Jenkins, J. G., & Dallenbach, K. M. (1924). Oblivescence during sleep and waking. *The American Journal of Psychology, 35,* 605–612.

Jenni, D. A., & Jenni, M. A. (1976). Carrying behavior in humans: Analysis of sex differences: *Science, 194,* 859–860.

Jensen, A. R. (1962). Spelling errors and the serial position effect. *Journal of Educational Psychology, 53,* 105–109.

Jensen, A. R. (1973). *Educability and group differences.* New York: Harper & Row.

Jervis, R., Lebow, R. N., & Stein, J. G. (1985). *Psychology and deterrence.* Baltimore: Johns Hopkins University Press.

Jessor, R. (1982, May). Problem behavior and developmental transition in adolescence. *Journal of School Health,* pp. 295–300.

John, E. R., et al. (1977). Neurometrics. *Science, 196,* 1393–1410.

Johnson, G. B. (1966). Penis envy or pencil hoarding? *Psychological Reports, 19,* 758.

Johnson, J. E. (1983). Psychological interventions and coping with surgery. In A. Baum, S. E. Taylor, & J. E. Singer (Eds.), *Handbook of psychology and health* (Vol. 4). Hillsdale, NJ: Erlbaum.

Johnson, J. H., & Sarason, I. B. (1979). Recent developments in research on life stress. In V. Hamilton & D. M. Warburton (Eds.), *Human stress and cognition: An information processing approach* (pp. 205–33). Chichester, England: Wiley.

Johnson, R. D., & Downing, L. L. (1979). Deindividuation and valence of cues: Effects on prosocial and antisocial behavior. *Journal of Personality and Social Psychology, 37,* 1532–1538.

Johnson, T. D., & Gottlieb, G. (1981). Visual preferences of imprinted ducklings are altered by the maternal call. *Journal of Comparative and Physiological Psychology, 95*(5), 665–675.

Johnson-Laird, P. (1983). *Mental models.* Cambridge, England: Cambridge University Press.

Johnston, L. D., Bachman, J. G., & O'Malley, P. M. (1982). *Student drug use, attitudes and beliefs: National trends 1975–1982.* Rockville, MD: National Institute on Drug Abuse.

Jones, E. (1953). *The life and works of Sigmund Freud.* New York: Basic Books.

Jones, E. E. (1985). Major developments in social psychology during the last five decades. In G. Lindzey & E. Aronson

(Eds.), *The handbook of social psychology* (Vol. 1, pp. 47–107). New York: Random House.

Jones, E. E., & Berglas, S. (1978). Control of attributions about the self through self-handicapping strategies: The appeal of alcohol and the role of underachievement. *Personality and Social Psychology Bulletin, 4,* 200–206.

Jones, E. E., & Davis, K. E. (1965). From acts to dispositions: The attribution process in person perception. In L. Berkowitz (Ed.), *Advances in experimental social psychology* (Vol. 2). New York: Academic Press.

Jones, E. E., Farina, A., Hastod, A. H., Markus, H., Miller, D. T., & Scott, R. A. (1984). *Social stigma: The psychology of marked relationships.* New York: Freeman.

Jones, E. E., & Nisbett, R. E. (1972). The actor and the observer: Divergent perceptions on the causes of behavior. In E. E. Jones et al. (Eds.), *Attribution: Perceiving the causes of behavior.* Morristown, NJ: General Learning Press.

Jones, E. E., & Pittman, T. (1982). Toward a general theory of strategic self-presentation. In J. Suls (Ed.), *Psychological perspectives on the self* (pp. 231–262). Hillsdale, NJ: Erlbaum.

Jones, M. C. (1924). A laboratory study of fear: The case of Peter. *Pedagogical Seminary and Journal of Genetic Psychology, 31,* 308–315.

Jones, R. (1978). The third wave. In A. Pines & C. Maslach (Eds.), *Experiencing social psychology.* New York: Knopf.

Jones, W., Cheek, J. M., & Briggs, S. R. (1986). *Shyness: Perspectives on research and treatment.* New York: Plenum.

Julesz, B. (1981). Textons, the elements of texture perception and their interaction. *Nature, 290,* 91–97.

Jung, C. G. (1959). The concept of the collective unconscious. In *The archetypes and the collective unconscious, collected works* (Vol. 9, Part 1, pp. 54–74). Princeton, NJ: Princeton University Press. (Original work published 1936)

Jung, C. G. (1973). *Memories, dreams, reflections* (rev. ed.) (A. Jaffe, Ed.). New York: Pantheon Books.

Just, H. A., & Carpenter, P. A. (1981). Cognitive processes in reading: Models based on reader's eye fixations. In C. A. Prefetti & A. M. Lesgold (Eds.), *Interactive processes and reading.* Hillsdale, NJ: Erlbaum.

K

Kagan, J., & Klein, R. E. (1973). Cross-cultural perspectives on early development. *American Psychologist, 28,* 947–961.

Kahn, M. (1966). The physiology of catharsis. *Journal of Personality and Social Psychology, 3,* 278–286.

Kahneman, D. (1973). *Attention and effort.* Englewood Cliffs, NJ: Prentice-Hall.

Kahneman, D., Slovic, P., & Tversky, A. (Eds.). (1982). *Judgment under uncertainty: Heuristics and biases.* Cambridge, MA: Cambridge University Press.

Kahneman, D., & Treisman, A. (1984). Changing views of attention and automaticity. In R. Parasuraman, D. R. Davies, & J. Beatty (Eds.), *Varieties of attention* (pp. 29–61). New York: Academic Press.

Kahneman, D., & Tversky, A. (1973). On the psychology of prediction. *Psychological Review, 80,* 237–251.

Kalat, J. W. (1974). Taste salience depends on novelty, not concentration in taste-aversion learning in the rat. *Journal of Comparative and Physiological Psychology, 86,* 47–50.

Kalat, J. W. (1984). *Biological psychology.* (2d ed.). Belmont, CA: Wadsworth.

Kallmann, F. J. (1946). The genetic theory of schizophrenia: An analysis of 691 schizophrenic index families. *American Journal of Psychiatry, 103,* 309–322.

Kamin, L. J. (1969). Predictability, surprise, attention, and conditioning. In B. A. Campbell & R. M. Church (Eds.), *Classical conditioning: A symposium.* New York: Appleton-Century-Crofts.

Kamin, L. J. (1974). *The science and politics of IQ.* Potomac, MD: Erlbaum.

Kandel, D. (1973). Adolescent marijuana use: Role of parents and peers. *Science, 181,* 1067–1070.

Kandel, E. R. (1976). *The cellular basis of behavior.* San Francisco: Freeman.

Kandel, E. R. (1979). Cellular insights into behavior and learning. *The Harvey Lectures,* Series 73, 29–92.

Kanigel, R. (1981). Storing yesterday. *Johns Hopkins Magazine, 32,* 27–34.

Kaplan, J. (1983). *The hardest drug: Heroin and public policy.* Chicago: University of Chicago Press.

Karlsson, J.L. (1978). *Inheritance of creative intelligence.* Chicago: Nelson-Hall.

Kaufman, L., & Rock, I. (1962). The moon illusion. *Scientific American, 207*(7), 120–130.

Kaufmann, Y. (1984). Analytical psychotherapy. In R. J. Corsini & Contributors (Eds.), *Current psychotherapies* (3d ed.) (pp. 108–126). Itasca, IL: Peacock.

Kaushall, P. I., Zetin, M., & Squire, L. R. (1981). A psychological study of chronic, circumscribed amnesia: Detailed report of a noted case. *Journal of Nervous and Mental Disorders, 169,* 383–389.

Kazdin, A. E. (1980). *Behavior modification in applied settings* (2d ed). Homewood, IL: Dorsey.

Kazdin, A. E. (1982). The token economy: A decade later. *Journal of Applied Behavior Analysis, 15,* 431–445.

Kazdin, A. E., & Wilcoxin, L. A. (1976). Systematic desensitization and nonspecific treatment effects: A methodological evaluation. *Psychological Bulletin, 83,* 729–758.

Kazdin, A. E., & Wilson, G. T. (1980). *Evaluation of behavior therapy: Issues, evidence, and research strategies.* Lincoln: University of Nebraska Press.

Keen, S. (1986). *Faces of the enemy: Reflections of the hostile imagination.* New York: Harper & Row.

Keesey, R. E., & Powley, T. L. (1975). Hypothalamic regulation of body weight. *American Scientist, 63,* 558–565.

Kelley, H. H. (1967). Attribution theory in social psychology. In D. Levine (Ed.), *Nebraska symposium on motivation* (Vol. 15). Lincoln: University of Nebraska Press.

Kelley, H. H. (1971a). *Attribution: Perceiving the causes of behavior.* New York: General Learning Press.

Kelley, H. H. (1971b). Attribution in social interaction. In E. E. Jones, D. E. Kanouse, H. H. Kelley, R. E. Nisbett, S. Valins, & B. Weiner (Eds.), *Attribution: Perceiving the causes of behavior.* New York: General Learning Press.

Kelley, H. H., & Thibaut, J. W. (1978). *Interpersonal relations: A theory of interdependence.* New York: Wiley-Interscience.

Kellogg, W. N., & Kellogg, L. A. (1933). *The ape and the child.* New York: McGraw-Hill.

Kelly, G. A. (1955). *A theory of personality: The psychology of personal constructs* (2 vols.). New York: Norton.

Keniston, K. (1971). Psychological development and historical change. *Journal of Interdisciplinary History, 2,* 329–345.

Kennedy, G. C. (1953). The role of depot fat in the hypothalamic control of food intake in the rat. *Proceedings of the Royal Society, 140* (Series B), 578–592.

Kesey, K. (1962). *One flew over the cuckoo's nest.* New York: Viking Press.

Kessen, S., & Cahan, E. D. (1986). A century of psychology: From subject to object to agent. *American Scientist, 74,* 640–649.

Kessler, S. (1980). The genetics of schizophrenia: A review. In S. J. Keith & L. R. Mosher (Eds.), *Special report: Schizophrenia, 1980* (pp. 14–26). Washington, DC: U.S. Government Printing Office.

Kett, J. F. (1977). *Rites of passage: Adolescence in America, 1790 to present.* New York: Basic Books.

Kety, S. S., Rosenthal, D., Wender, P. H., Schulsinger, F., & Jacobsen, B. (1975). Mental illness in the biological and adoptive families of adopted individuals who have become schizophrenic: A preliminary report based on psychiatric interviews. In R. R. Fieve, D. Rosenthal, & H. Brill (Eds.), *Ge-*

netic research in psychiatry (pp. 147–65). Baltimore: The Johns Hopkins University Press.

Kiernan, R. J., & Kaplan, R. M. (1971, April). *Deindividuation, anonymity, and pilfering.* Paper presented at the Western Psychological Association meeting, San Francisco.

Kihlstrom, J. F., & Harackiewicz, J. M. (1982). The earliest recollection: A new survey. *Journal of Personality, 50,* 134–148.

Kimmel, D. C., & Weiner, I. B. (1985). *Adolescence: A developmental transition.* Hillsdale, NJ: Erlbaum.

King, R. J. (1986). Motivational diversity and mesolimbic dopamine: A hypothesis concerning temperaments. In R. Plutchik & H. Kellerman (Eds.), *Emotion: Theory, research, and experience: Biological foundations of emotions* (Vol. 3, pp. 363–380). Orlando, FL: Academic Press.

King, R. J., Mefford, I. N., Wang, C., Murchison, A., Caligari, E. J., & Berger, P. A. (1986). CSF dopamine levels correlate with extraversion in depressed patients. *Psychiatry Research, 19,* 305–310.

Kinsey, A. C., Martin, C. E., & Pomeroy, W. B. (1948). *Sexual behavior in the human male.* Philadelphia: Saunders.

Kinsey, A. C., Pomeroy, W. B., Martin, C. E., & Gebhard, R. H. (1953). *Sexual behavior in the human female.* Philadelphia: Saunders.

Kintsch, W. (1974). *The representation of meaning in memory.* Hillsdale, NJ: Erlbaum.

Kintsch, W. (1981). Semantic memory: A tutorial. In R. S. Nickerson (Ed.), *Attention and performance* (Vol. 8). Hillsdale, NJ: Erlbaum.

Klatzky, R. (1980). *Human memory: Structures and processes* (2d ed.) San Francisco: Freeman.

Klein, D. C., & Goldston, S. E. (Eds.). (1977). *Primary prevention: An idea whose time has come.* Washington, DC: U.S. Government Printing Office.

Klein, G. (1970). *Perception, motives, and personality.* New York: Knopf.

Klein, G. S., & Schlesinger, H. J. (1949). Where is the perceiver in perceptual theory? *Journal of Personality, 18,* 32–47.

Klein, R. H. (1983). Group treatment approaches. In M. Hersen, A. E. Kazdin, & A. S. Bellack (Eds.), *The clinical psychology handbook.* New York: Pergamon Press.

Kleinginna, P. R., & Kleinginna, A. M. (1981). A categorized list of motivation definitions with a suggestion for a consensual definition. *Motivation and Emotion, 5,* 263–291.

Kleinke, C. L. (1984). Two models for conceptualizing the attitude-behavior relationship. *Human Relations,* 37, 333–350.

Kleinke, C. L. (1986). Gaze and eye contact: A research review. *Psychological Bulletin, 100,* 78–100.

Kleinmuntz, B., & Szucko, J. J. (1984). Lie detection in ancient and modern times: A call for contemporary scientific study. *American Psychologist, 39,* 766–776.

Klinnert, M. D., Campos, J. J., Sorce, J. F., Emde, R. N., & Svejda, M. (1983). Emotions as behavioral regulators: Social referencing in infancy. In R. Plutchik & H. Kellerman (Eds.), *Emotion: Theory, research, and experience* (Vol. 2, pp. 57–86). New York: Academic Press.

Knox, V. J., Morgan, A. H., & Hilgard, E. R. (1974). Pain and suffering in ischemia: The paradox of hypnotically suggested anesthesia as contradicted by reports from the "hidden observer." *Archives of General Psychiatry, 30,* 840–847.

Kobre, K. R., & Lipsitt, L. P. (1972). A negative contrast effect in newborns. *Journal of Experimental Child Psychology, 2,* 81–91.

Koch, S., & Leary, D. E. (1985). *A century of psychology as science.* New York: McGraw-Hill.

Koestler, A. (1964). *The act of creation.* London: Hutchinson.

Koffka, K. (1935). *Principles of Gestalt psychology.* New York: Harcourt Brace.

Koh, S. O., & Peterson, R. A. (1974). A perceptual memory for numerousness in "nonpsychotic schizophrenics." *Journal of Abnormal Psychology, 83,* 215–226.

Kohlberg, L. (1964). Development of moral character and moral ideology. In M. L. Hoffman & L. W. Hoffman (Eds.), *Review of child development research* (Vol. 1). New York: Russell Sage Foundation.

Kohlberg, L. (1966). A cognitive-developmental analysis of children's sex-role concepts and attitudes. In E. E. Maccoby (Ed.), *The development of sex differences.* Stanford, CA: Stanford University Press.

Kohlberg, L. (1967). Moral and religious education and the public schools: A developmental view. In T. Sizer (Ed.), *Religion and public education.* Boston: Houghton Mifflin.

Kohlberg, L. (1969). Stage and sequence: The cognitive-developmental approach to socialization. In D. A. Goslin (Ed.), *Handbook of socialization theory and research.* Chicago: Rand McNally.

Kohlberg, L. (1981). *The philosophy of moral development.* New York: Harper & Row.

Köhler, W. (1925). *The mentality of apes.* New York: Harcourt Brace Jovanovich.

Köhler, W. (1947). *Gestalt psychology.* New York: Liveright.

Kolata, G. (1985). Why do people get fat? *Science, 227,* 1327–1328.

Kolata, G. (1986). Maleness pinpointed on Y chromosomes. *Science, 234,* 1076–1077.

Kolb, L. C. (1973). *Modern clinical psychiatry.* Philadelphia: Saunders.

Konĕcni, V. J. (1984). Methodological issues in human aggression research. In R. M. Kaplan, V. J. Konĕcni, & R. W. Navaco (Eds.), *Aggression in children and youth* (pp. 1–43). The Hague: Martinus Nijhoff Publishers.

Konĕcni, V. J., & Doob, A. N. (1972). Catharsis through displacement of aggression. *Journal of Personality and Social Psychology, 23,* 379–387.

Konĕcni, V. J., & Ebbesen, E. B. (1984). The mythology of legal decision making. *International Journal of Law and Psychiatry, 7,* 5–18.

Konĕcni, V. J., & Ebbesen, E. B. (1986). Courtroom testimony by psychologists on eyewitness identification issues: Critical notes and reflections. *Law and Human Behavior, 10,* 117–126.

Konner, M. J. (1977). Research reported in Greenberg, J. The brain and emotions. *Science News, 112,* 74–75.

Korchin, S. J. (1976). *Modern clinical psychology.* New York: Basic Books.

Korn, J. W. (1985). Psychology as a humanity. *Teaching of Psychology, 12,* 188–193.

Kosecoff, J. B., & Fink, A. (1982). *Evaluation basics: A practitioner's manual.* Beverly Hills, CA: Sage Publications.

Koslow, S. H. (1984). Preface. In *The neuroscience of mental health: A report on neuroscience research* (DHHS Publication No. ADM 84–1363). Rockville, MD: National Institute of Mental Health.

Kosslyn, S. M. (1980). *Image and mind.* Cambridge, MA: Harvard University Press.

Kosslyn, S. M. (1983). *Ghosts in the mind's machine: Creating and using images in the brain.* New York: Norton.

Kosslyn, S. M. (1985). Computational neuropsychology: A new perspective on mental imagery. *Naval Research Reviews, 37,* 30–50.

Kosslyn, S. M., Holtzman, J. D., Farah, M. J., & Gazzaniga, M. S. (1985). A computational analysis of mental image generation: Evidence from functional dissociations in split-brain patients. *Journal of Experimental Psychology: General, 114,* 311–341.

Kramer, J. C. (1969). Introduction to amphetamine abuse. *Journal of Psychedelic Drugs, 2,* 1–16.

Krasner, L. (1985). Applications of learning theory in the environment. In B. L. Hammonds (Ed.), *Psychology and learning: 1984 Master Lecturers* (pp. 51–93). Washington, DC: American Psychological Association.

Kübler-Ross, E. (1969). *On death and dying.* Toronto: Macmillan.

Kuffler, S. W., Nicholls, J. G., & Martin, A. R. (1984). *From neuron to brain: A cellular approach to the function of the nervous system* (2d ed.). Sunderland, MA: Sinauer Associates.

Kuhn, T. S. (1970). *The structure of scientific revolutions* (2d ed.). Chicago: University of Chicago Press.

Kulik, J. A. (1983). Confirmatory attribution and the perpetuation of social beliefs. *Journal of Personality and Social Psychology, 44,* 1171–1181.

Kupfermann, I., et al. (1974). Local, reflex, and central commands controlling gill and siphon movements in *Aplysia. Journal of Neurophysiology, 37,* 996–1019.

Kurtines, W., & Greif, E. B. (1974). The development of moral thought: Review and evaluation of Kohlberg's approach. *Psychological Bulletin, 8,* 453–470.

Kutas, M., & Hillyard, S. A. (1980) Reading senseless sentences: Brain potentials reflect semantic incongruity. *Science, 207,* 203–205.

L

LaBerge, S. P. (1980). Lucid dreaming as a learnable skill. *Perceptual and Motor Skills, 51,* 1039–1042.

LaBerge, S. (1986). *Lucid dreaming.* New York: Valentine Books.

LaBerge, S. P., Nagel, L. E., Dement, W. C., & Zarcone, V. P., Jr. (1981). Evidence for lucid dreaming during REM sleep. *Sleep Research, 10,* 148.

Lachman, R., Lachman, J. L., & Butterfield, E. C. (1979). *Cognitive psychology and information processing: An introduction.* Hillsdale, NJ: Erlbaum.

Lachman, R., & Naus, M. (1984). The episodic/semantic continuum in an evolved machine. *Behavioral and Brain Sciences, 7,* 244–246.

Lachman, S. (1983). The concept of learning: Connectioning and selectioning. *Academic Psychology Bulletin, 5,* 155–166.

Lachman, S. J. (1983). A physiological interpretation of voodoo illness and voodoo death. *Omega, 13*(4), 345–360.

Laing, R. D. (1967, February 3). Schizophrenic split. *Time,* p. 56.

Lambert, N. M. (1981). Psychological evidence in Larry P. versus Wilson Riles. *American Psychologist, 36,* 937–952.

Lambo, T. A. (1978). Psychotherapy in Africa. *Human Nature, 1*(3), 32–39.

Landsberger, H. A. (1958). *Hawthorne revisited.* Ithaca, NY: Cornell University Press.

Lane, H. (1976). *The wild boy of Aveyron.* Cambridge, MA: Harvard University Press.

Lane, H. (1986). The wild boy of Aveyron and Dr. Jean-Marc Itard. *History of Psychology, 17,* 3–16.

Lang, P. J. (1979). A bio-informational theory of emotional imagery. *Psychophysiology, 16,* 495–512.

Langer, E. J. (1975). The illusion of control. *Journal of Personality and Social Psychology, 32,* 311–328.

Langer, E. (1978). Rethinking the role of thought in social interaction. In J. H. Harvey, W. J. Ickes, & R. F. Kidd (Eds.), *New directions in attribution research* (Vol. 2) (pp. 35–38). Hillsdale, NJ: Erlbaum.

Langer, E. J., & Rodin, J. (1976). The effects of choice and enhanced personal responsibility for the aged: A field experiment in an institutional setting. *Journal of Personality and Social Psychology, 34,* 191–198.

Langlois, J. H., & Downs, A. C. (1980). Mothers, fathers and peers as socialization agents of sex-typed play behaviors in young children. *Child Development, 51,* 1237–1247.

Lanzetta, J. T., Sullivan, D. G., Masters, R. G., & McHugo, G. J. (1985). Viewers' emotional and cognitive responses to televised images of political leaders. In S. Kraus & R. M. Perloff (Eds.), *Mass media and political thought: An information processing approach* (pp. 50–67). Beverly Hills, CA: Sage.

La Piere, R. (1934). Attitudes versus actions. *Social Forces, 13,* 230–237.

Lashley, K. S. (1929). *Brain mechanisms and intelligence.* Chicago: University of Chicago Press.

Lashley, K. S. (1950). In search of the engram. In *Physiological mechanisms in animal behavior: Symposium of the Society for Experimental Biology.* New York: Academic Press.

Lasswell, H. D. (1948). The structure and function of communication in society. In L. Bryson (Ed.), *Communication of ideas.* New York: Harper.

Latané, B. (1981). The psychology of social impact. *American Psychologist, 36,* 343–356.

Latané, B. & Darley, J. M. (1970). *The unresponsive bystander: Why doesn't he help?* New York: Appleton-Century-Crofts.

Latham, G. P., & Yukl, G. A. (1975). A review of research on the application of goal setting in organizations. *Academic Management Journal, 18,* 824–845.

Lazarus, R. S. (1966). *Psychological stress and the coping process.* New York: McGraw-Hill.

Lazarus, R. S. (1975). A cognitively oriented psychologist looks at biofeedback. *American Psychologist, 30,* 553–561.

Lazarus, R. S. (1981, July). Little hassles can be hazardous to your health. *Psychology Today,* pp. 58–62.

Lazarus, R. S. (1984). On the primacy of cognition. *American Psychologist, 39,* 124–129.

Lazarus, R. S. (1987). *A relational and cognitive theory of emotion.* Unpublished manuscript, University of California, Berkeley.

Lazarus, R. S. (in press). Constructs of the mind in adaptation. In M. Stein, B. Leventhal, & T. Trabasso (Eds.), *Psychological and biological approaches to emotion.* Hillsdale, NJ: Erlbaum.

Lazarus, R. S., & Folkman, S. (1984). *Stress, appraisal, and coping.* New York: Springer.

Leask, J., Haber, R. N., & Haber, R. B. (1969). Eidetic imagery in children: II, Longitudinal and experimental results. *Psychonomic Monograph Supplements, 3* (3, Whole No. 35).

LeBon, G. (1960). *The crowd.* New York: Viking Press. (Originally published 1895)

Le Doux, J. E., Wilson, D. H., & Gazzaniga, M. S. (1977). A divided mind: Observations on the conscious properties of the separated hemispheres. *Annals of Neurology, 2,* 417–421.

Lee, M., Zimbardo, P., & Bertholf, M. (1977, November). Shy murderers. *Psychology Today,* pp. 68–70, 76, 148.

Leeper, R. W. (1948). A motivational theory of emotion to replace "emotions as disorganized response." *Psychological Review, 55,* 5–21.

Leff, H. (1984). *Playful perception: Choosing how to experience your world.* Burlington, VT: Waterfront Books.

Lemert, E. M. (1962). Paranoia and the dynamics of exclusion. *Sociometry, 25,* 2–20.

Lenneberg, E. H. (1962). Understanding language without ability to speak: A case report. *Journal of Abnormal and Social Psychology, 65,* 415–419.

Lenneberg, E. H. (1969). On explaining language. *Science, 164,* 635–643.

Leowontin, R. C., Rose, S., & Kamin, L. J. (1984). *Not in our genes: Biology, ideology, and human nature.* New York: Pantheon.

Lepper, M. R. (1981). Intrinsic and extrinsic motivation in children: Detrimental effects of superfluous social controls. In U. A. Collins. (Ed.), *Aspects of the development of competence: The Minnesota Symposium on Child Psychology* (Vol. 14, pp. 155–214). Hillsdale, NJ: Erlbaum.

Lepper, M. R., & Greene, D. (Eds.). (1978). *The hidden costs of reward.* Hillsdale, NJ: Erlbaum.

Lepper, M. R., Greene, D., & Nisbett, R. E. (1973). Undermining children's intrinsic interest with extrinsic reward: A test of the overjustification hypothesis. *Journal of Personality and Social Psychology, 28*(1), 129–137.

Lerner, R. M., Orlos, J. R., & Knapp, J. (1976). Physical attractiveness, physical effectiveness and self-concept in adolescents. *Adolescence, 11,* 313–326.

Lettvin, J. Y., Maturana, H. R., McCulloch, W. S., & Bitts, W. H. (1959). What the frog's eye tells the frog's brain. *Proceedings of the Institute of Radio Engineers, 47,* 1940–1951.

Leventhal, H. (1970). Findings and theory in the study of fear communications. In L. Berkowitz (Ed.), *Advances in experimental social psychology* (Vol. 5, pp. 120–86). New York: Academic Press.

Leventhal, H. (1984). A perceptual motor theory of emotion. In K. R. Scherer & P. Ekman (Eds.), *Approaches to emotion* (pp. 271–291). Hillsdale, NJ: Erlbaum.

Leventhal, H., & Cleary, P. D. (1980). The smoking problem: A review of the research and theory in behavioral risk modification. *Psychological Bulletin, 88,* 370–405.

Levine, J. D., et al. (1978, August). Paper presented at the World Congress on Pain, Montreal.

Levine, M. (1987, April). *Effective problem solving.* Englewood Cliffs, NJ: Prentice-Hall.

Levine, M. W., & Shefner, J. M. (1981). *Fundamentals of sensation and perception.* Reading, MA: Addison-Wesley.

Levinger, G. (1980). Toward the analysis of close relationships. *Journal of Experimental Social Psychology, 16,* 510–544.

Levinson, B. W. (1967). States of awareness during general anesthesia. In J. Lassner (Ed.), *Hypnosis and psychosomatic medicine* (pp. 200–207). New York: Springer-Verlag.

Levinson, D. L. (1978). *The seasons of a man's life.* New York: Knopf.

Levy, J., & Trevarthen, C. (1976). Metacontrol of hemispheric function in human split brain patients. *Journal of Experimental Psychology: Human perception and performance, 2,* 299–312.

Levy, L. H., & Orr, T. B. (1959). The social psychology of Rorschach validity research. *Journal of Abnormal and Social Psychology, 58,* 79–83.

Lewin, K. (1936). *Principles of topological psychology.* New York: McGraw-Hill.

Lewin, K. (1947). Group decision and social change. In T. N. Newcomb & E. L. Hartley (Eds.), *Readings in social psychology.* New York: Holt, Rinehart & Winston.

Lewin, K. (1948). *Resolving social conflicts.* New York: Harper.

Lewin, R. (1985). Gregarious grazers eat better. *Science, 228,* 567–568.

Lewin, R. (1987). The origin of the modern human mind. *Science, 236,* 668–670.

Lewine, R. R., Strauss, J. S., & Gift, T. E. (1981). Sex differences in age at first hospital admission for schizophrenia: Fact or artifact? *American Journal of Psychiatry, 138,* 440–444.

Lewinsohn, P. M., Mischel, W., Chapline, W., & Barton, R. (1980). Social competence and depression: The role of illusory self-perceptions. *Journal of Abnormal Psychology, 89,* 203–212.

Lewis, C. (1981). The effects of parental firm control: A reinterpretation of findings. *Psychological Bulletin, 90,* 547–563.

Lewis, J. W., Cannon, J. T., & Liebeskind, J. C. (1980). Opiod and nonopiod mechanisms of stress analgesia. *Science, 208,* 623–625.

Lewy, A. J., Sack, R. L., Miller, S., & Hoban, T. M. (1987). Antidepressant and circadian phase-shifting effect of light. *Science, 235,* 352–354.

Leyland, C. M., & Mackintosh, NJ: (1978). Blocking of first and second-order autoshaping in pigeons. *Animal Learning and Behavior, 6,* 391–394.

Li, P. (1975). *Path analysis: A primer.* Pacific Grove, CA: The Boxwood Press.

Lidz, T., Fleck, S., & Cornelison, A. R. (1965). *Schizophrenia and the family.* New York: International University Press.

Lieberman, L. R. (1973, April 3). Letter to *Science* concerning "On being sane in insane places." *Science, 179.*

Lieberman, M. A. (1977). Problems in integrating traditional group therapies with new forms. *International Journal of Group Psychotherapy, 27,* 19–32.

Liebert, R. M., & Spiegler, M. D. (1982). *Personality: Strategies and issues.* Homewood, IL: Dorsey Press.

Liem, J. H. (1980). Family studies of schizophrenia: An update and commentary. In S. J. Keith & L. R. Mosher (Eds.), *Special report: Schizophrenia, 1980* (pp. 82–108). Washington, DC: U. S. Government Printing Office.

Liem, R., & Rayman, P. (1982). Health and social costs of unemployment: Research and policy considerations. *American Psychologist, 37,* 1116–1123.

Lindsay, P. H., & Norman, D. A. (1977). *Human information processing* (2d ed.). New York: Academic Press.

Lindsley, D. B. (1951). Emotion. In S. S. Stevens (Ed.), *Handbook of experimental psychology.* New York: Wiley.

Lindzey, G. (1961). *Projective techniques and cross-cultural research.* New York: Appleton-Century-Crofts.

Linton, M. (1975). Memory for real-world events. In D. Norman & D. Rumelhart (Eds.), *Explorations in cognition* (pp. 376–404). San Francisco, CA: Freeman.

Lipsitt, L. P., & Reese, H. W. (1979). *Child development.* Glenview, IL: Scott, Foresman.

Lipsitt, L. P., Reilly, B., Butcher, M. G., & Greenwood, M. M. (1976). The stability and interrelationships of newborn sucking and heart rate. *Developmental Psychobiology, 9,* 305–310.

Little, M. I. (1981). *Transference neurosis and transference psychosis.* New York: Jason Aronson.

Locke, E. A. (1982). *A new look at work motivation: Theory V.* (Technical Report GS-12). Arlington, VA: Office of Naval Research.

Locke, E. A., Shaw, K. N., Saari, L. M., & Latham, G. P. (1981). Goal setting and task performance: 1969–1980. *Psychological Bulletin, 90,* 125–152.

Locke, J. (1690). *An essay concerning human understanding.*

Loehlin, J. C., Lindzey, G., & Spuhler, J. N. (1975). *Race differences in intelligence.* San Francisco: Freeman.

Loftus, E. F. (1979). *Eyewitness testimony.* Cambridge, MA: Harvard University Press.

Loftus, E. F. (1984). The eyewitness on trial. In B. D. Sales & A. Alwork (Eds.), *With liberty and justice for all.* Englewood Cliffs, NJ: Prentice Hall.

Logan, F. A. (1960). *Incentive.* New Haven, CT: Yale University Press.

Loomis, A. L., Harvey, E. N., & Hobart, G. A. (1937). Cerebral status during sleep as studied by human brain potentials. *Journal of Experimental Psychology, 21,* 127–144.

Lorenz, K. (1937). Imprinting. *The AUK, 54,* 245–273.

Lorenz, K. (1966). *On aggression.* New York: Harcourt Brace Jovanovich.

Lott, B., & Lott, A. J. (1985). Learning theory in contemporary social psychology. In G. Lindzey & E. Aronson (Eds.), *The handbook of social psychology* (3d ed.). (Vol. 1, pp. 109–135). Hillsdale, NJ: Erlbaum.

Lovaas, O. I. (1968). Learning theory approach to the treatment of childhood schizophrenia. In *California Mental Health Research Symposium: No. 2 Behavior theory and therapy.* Sacramento, CA: Department of Mental Hygiene.

Lovaas, O. I. (1977). *The autistic child: Language development through behavior modification.* New York: Halsted Press.

Lovibond, S. H., Adams, M., & Adams, W. G. (1979). The effects of three experimental prison environments on the behavior of nonconflict volunteer subjects. *Australian Psychologist, 14,* 273–285.

Luborsky, L., Blinder, B., & Schimek, J. G. (1965). Cooking, recalling and GSR as a function of defense. *Journal of Abnormal Psychology, 70,* 270–280.

Lubow, R. E., Rifkin, B., & Alex, M. (1976). The context effect: The relationship between stimulus preexposure and environmental preexposure determines subsequent learning. *Journal of Experimental Psychology: Animal Behavior Processes, 2,* 38–47.

Luchins, A. S. (1942). Mechanization in problem solving. *Psychological Monographs, 54*(No. 248).

Luchins, A. S. (1957). Primacy-recency in impression formation. In C. I. Hovland (Ed.), *The order of presentation in persuasion* (pp. 34–35). New Haven, CT: Yale University Press.

Ludwig, A. M. (1966). Altered states of consciousness. *Archives of General Psychiatry, 15,* 225–234.

Luker, K. C. (1975). *Taking chances: Abortion and the decision not to contracept.* Berkeley: University of California Press.

Lunde, A. S. (1981). Health in the United States. *Annals of the American Academy of Political and Social Science, 453,* 28–69.

Lykken, D. T. (1979). The detection of deception. *Psychological Bulletin, 86,* 47–53.

Lykken, D. T. (1981). *A tremor in the blood: Uses and abuses of the lie detector.* New York: McGraw-Hill.

Lykken, D. T. (1984). Polygraphic interrogation. *Nature, 307,* 681–684.

Lynch, G. (1986). *Synapses, circuits, and the beginnings of memory.* Cambridge, MA: MIT Press.

Lyons, N. (1983). Two perspectives: On self, relationships, and morality. *Harvard Educational Review, 53,* 125–146.

M

Maccoby, E. E. (1980). *Social development: Psychological growth and the parent-child relationship.* San Diego, CA: Harcourt Brace Jovanovich.

Maccoby, E. E., & Jacklin, C. N. (1974). *The psychology of sex differences.* Stanford, CA: Stanford University Press.

Maccoby, E. E., & Jacklin, C. N. (1987). Gender segregation in childhood. In H. Reese (Ed.), *Advances in child behavior and development* (Vol. 20). New York: Academic Press.

Maccoby, E. E., & Martin, J. A. (1983). Socialization in the context of the family: Parent-child interaction. In P. H. Mussen (Ed.), *Carmichael's manual of child psychology.* New York: Wiley.

Maccoby, N., Farquhar, J. W., Wood, P. D., & Alexander, J. K. (1977). Reducing the risk of cardiovascular disease: Effects of a community-based campaign on knowledge and behavior. *Journal of Community Health, 3,* 100–114.

Mace, W. M. (1977). James J. Gibson's strategy for perceiving: Ask not what's inside your head, but what your head's inside of. In R. Shaw & J. Bransford (Eds.), *Perceiving, acting, and knowing.* Hillsdale, NJ: Erlbaum.

Machlowitz, M. (1980). *Workaholics: Living with them, working with them.* Reading, MA: Addison-Wesley.

MacKinnon, D. W. (1961). The study of creativity and creativity in architects. In *Conference on the creative person.* Berkeley: University of California, Institute of Personality Assessment and Research.

Mackintosh, NJ: (1975). A theory of attention. *Psychological Review, 82,* 276–298.

MacLean, P. (1977). On the evolution of three mentalities. In S. Arieti & G. Chrzanowki (Eds.), *New directions in psychiatry: A world view* (Vol. 2). New York: Wiley.

MacLeod, C., Mathews, A., & Tata, P. (1986). Attentional bias in emotional disorders. *Journal of Abnormal Psychology, 95,* 15–20.

Magnusson, D., & Endler, N. S. (1977). Interactional psychology: Present status and future prospects. In D. Magnusson & N. S. Endler (Eds.), *Personality at the crossroads: Current issues in interactional psychology.* Hillsdale, NJ: Erlbaum.

Maher, B. A. (1968, November). The shattered language of schizophrenia. *Psychology Today,* pp. 30ff.

Maher, B. A. (1974). Delusional thinking and cognitive disorder. In M. London & R. E. Nisbett (Eds.), *Thought and feeling: Cognitive alteration of feeling states.* Chicago: Aldine.

Mahler, M. S. (1979). *The selected papers of Margaret S. Mahler* (2 vols.). New York: Jason Aronson.

Mahoney, M. J. (1974). *Cognition and behavior modification.* Cambridge, MA: Ballinger.

Maier, N. R. F. (1931). Reasoning in humans: II. The solution of a problem and its appearance in consciousness. *Journal of Comparative Psychology, 12,* 181–194.

Maier, S. (1984, March). Stress: Depression, disease and the immune system. *Science and public policy seminars.* Washington, DC: Federation of Behavioral, Psychological, and Cognitive Sciences.

Maier, S. F., & Seligman, M. E. P. (1976). Learned helplessness: Theory and evidence. *Journal of Experimental Psychology, 105,* 3–46.

Majewska, M. D., Harrison, N. L., Schwartz, R. D., Barker, J. L., & Paul, S. M. (1986). Steroid hormone metabolites are barbiturate-like modulators of the GABA receptor. *Science, 232,* 1004–1007.

Malamuth, N. E., & Donnerstein, E. (1982). The effects of aggressive-pornographic mass media stimuli. *Advances in Experimental Social Psychology, 15,* 103–136.

Malamuth, N. E., & Donnerstein, E. (1984). *Pornography and sexual aggression.* New York: Academic Press.

Malone, T. W., & Lepper, M. R. (in press). Making learning fun: A taxonomy of intrinsic motivations for learning. In R. E. Snow & M. J. Farr (Eds.), *Aptitude, learning, and instruction: III, Cognitive and affective process analysis* (pp. 223–253). Hillsdale, NJ: Erlbaum.

Maloney, M. P., & Ward, M. P. (1976). *Psychological assessment: A conceptual approach.* New York: Academic Press.

Mandler, G. (1972). Organization and recognition. In E. Tulving & W. Donaldson (Eds.), *Organization and memory.* New York: Academic Press.

Mandler, G. (1975). *Mind and emotion.* New York: Wiley.

Mandler, G. (1984). *Mind and body: The psychology of emotion and stress.* New York: Norton.

Manfredi, M., Bini, G., Cruccu, G., Accornero, N., Beradelli, A., & Medolago, L. (1981). Congenital absence of pain. *Archives of Neurology, 38,* 507–511.

Mann, L. (1979). *On the trail of progress: A historical perspective on cognitive processes and their training.* New York: Grune & Stratton.

Mansson, H. H. (1972). Justifying the final solution. *Omega, 3,* 79–87.

Marcel, A. J. (1983). Conscious and unconscious perception: An approach to the relation between phenomenal experience and perceptual processes. *Cognitive Psychology, 15,* 238–300.

Marek, G. R. (1975). *Toscanini.* London: Vision Press.

Markman, E. M., Cox, B., & Machida, S. (1981). The standard object-sorting task as a measure of conceptual organization. *Developmental Psychology: 17,* 115–117.

Marks, I. (1981). *Cure and care of neuroses: Theory and practice of behavioral psychotherapy.* New York: Wiley.

Marks, R. (1976–1977). Providing for individual differences: A history of the intelligence testing movement in North America. *Interchange, 1,* 3–16.

Marlatt, G. A. (1978). Behavioral assessment of social drinking and alcoholism. In G. A. Marlatt & P. E. Nathan (Eds.), *Behavioral approaches to alcoholism.* New Brunswick, NJ: Rutgers Center for Alcohol Studies.

Marler, P. R., & Hamilton, W. J. (1966). *Mechanisms of animal behavior.* New York: Wiley.

Marquis, J. N. (1970). Orgasmic reconditioning: Changing sexual object choice through controlling masturbation fantasies. *Journal of Behavior Therapy and Experimental Psychiatry, 1,* 263–271.

Marr, D. (1982). *Vision.* San Francisco: Freeman.

Marshall, G. D., & Zimbardo, P. G. (1979). Affective consequences of inadequately explained physiological arousal. *Journal of Personality and Social Psychology, 37,* 970–988.

Martin, C. L., & Halverson, C. F. (1981). A schematic processing model of sex typing and stereotyping in children. *Child Development, 52,* 1119–1134.

Martin, G., & Pear, J. (1983). *Behavior modification: What it is and how to do it* (2d ed.). Englewood Cliffs, NJ: Prentice-Hall.

Martin, J. A. (1981). A longitudinal study of the consequences of early mother-infant interaction: A microanalytic approach. *Monographs of the Society for Research in Child Development, 46* (203, Serial No. 190).

Maslach, C. (1974). Social and personal bases of individuation. *Journal of Personality and Social Psychology, 29,* 411–425.

Maslach, C. (1979). Negative emotional biasing of unexplained arousal. *Journal of Personality and Social Psychology, 37,* 953–969.

Maslach, C. (1982). *Burnout: The cost of caring.* Englewood Cliffs, NJ: Prentice-Hall.

Maslach, C., Stapp, J., & Santee, R. T. (1985). Individuation: Conceptual analysis and assessment. *Journal of Personality and Social Psychology, 49,* 729–738.

Maslow, A. H. (1970). *Motivation and personality* (rev. ed.). New York: Harper & Row.

Mason, J. W. (1975). An historical view of the stress field: Parts 1 & 2. *Journal of Human Stress, 1,* 6–12, 22–36.

Mason, W. A., & Kenney, M. D. (1974). Reduction of filial attachments in Rhesus monkeys: Dogs as mother surrogates. *Science, 183,* 1209–1211.

Masters, J. C. (1981). Developmental psychology. *Annual Review of Psychology, 32,* 117–151.

Masters, W. H., & Johnson, V. E. (1966). *Human sexual response.* Boston: Little, Brown.

Masters, W. H., & Johnson, V. E. (1970). *Human sexual inadequacy.* Boston: Little, Brown.

Masters, W. H., & Johnson, V. E. (1979). *Homosexuality in perspective.* Boston: Little, Brown.

Matarazzo, J. D. (1972). *Wechsler's measurement and appraisal of adult intelligence* (5th ed.). Baltimore: Williams & Wilkins.

Matarazzo, J. D. (1980). Behavioral health and behavioral medicine: Frontiers for a new health psychology. *American Psychologist, 35,* 807–817.

Matarazzo, J. D. (1984). Behavioral immunogens and pathogens in health and illness. In B. L. Hammonds & C. J. Scheirer (Eds.), *Psychology and health: The Master Lecture Series, Vol. 3* (pp. 9–43). Washington, DC: American Psychological Association.

Matas, L., Arend, R. A., & Sroufe, L. A. (1978). Continuity of adaptation in the second year: The relationship between quality of attachment and later competence. *Child Development, 49,* 547–556.

Matossian, M. (1982). Ergot and the Salem witchcraft affair. *American Scientist, 70,* 355–357.

Matson, J. L., Esveldt-Dawson, K., Andrasik, F., Ollendick, T. H., Petti, T., & Hersen, M. (1980). Direct, observational, and generalization effects of social skills training with emotionally disturbed children. *Behavior Therapy, 11,* 522–531.

Maugh, T. H. (1982). Sleep-promoting factor isolated. *Science, 216,* 1400.

Maugh, T. H., II. (1985, August 18). The chimpanzee-human dialogue. *San Francisco Examiner-Chronicle,* pp. 19–20.

May, R. (1975). *The courage to create.* New York: Norton.

Mayer, G. R., Butterworth, T., Nafpaktitis, M., & Sulzer-Azaroff, B. (1983). Preventing school vandalism and improving discipline: A three-year study. *Journal of Applied Behavior Analysis, 16,* 355–369.

Mayer, J. (1955). Regulation of energy intake and body weight: the glucostatic theory and lipostatic hypothesis. *Annals of the New York Academy of Sciences, 63,* 15–43.

Mayer, R. E. (1981). *The promise of cognitive psychology.* San Francisco: Freeman.

Mayo, E. (1946). *Human problems of an industrial civilization* (2d ed.). New York: Macmillan.

McAdams, D. P., & Vaillant, G. E. (1982). Intimacy motivation and psychosocial adjustment: A longitudinal study. *Journal of Personality Assessment, 46,* 586–593.

McCall, R. B. (1977). Childhood IQs as predictors of adult education and occupational status. *Science, 197,* 483–485.

McCarthy, S. J. (1979, September). Why Johnny can't disobey. *The Humanist,* pp. 30–33.

McClelland, D. C. (1955). Some social consequences of achievement motivation. In M. R. Jones (Ed.), *Nebraska symposium on motivation* (Vol. 3). Lincoln: University of Nebraska Press.

McClelland, D. C. (1961). *The achieving society.* Princeton, NJ: Van Nostrand.

McClelland, D. C. (1971). *Motivational trends in society.* Morristown, NJ: General Learning Press.

McClelland, D. C., Atkinson, J. W., Clark, R. A., & Lowell, L. (1953). *The achievement motive.* New York: Appleton-Century-Crofts.

McClelland, D. C., Atkinson, J. W., Clark, R. A., & Lowell, E. L. (1976). *The achievement motive* (2d ed.). New York: Irvington.

McClintock, M. K. (1971). Menstrual synchrony and suppression. *Nature, 229,* 244–245.

McCloskey, M., & Egeth, H. E. (1983). Eyewitness identification: What can a psychologist tell a jury? *American Psychologist, 38,* 550–563.

McCormick, D. A., & Thompson, R. F. (1984). Cerebellum: Essential involvement in the classically conditioned eyelid response. *Science, 223,* 296–299.

McCrae, R. R. (1982). Consensual validation of personality traits: Evidence from self-reports and ratings. *Journal of Personality and Social Psychology, 43,* 293–303.

McCrae, R. R. (1987). Creativity, divergent thinking, and openness to new experience. *Journal of Personality and Social Psychology, 52,* 1258–1265.

McCrae, R. R., & Costa, P. T., Jr. (1987). Validation of the five-factor model of personality across instruments and observers. *Journal of Personality and Social Psychology, 56,* 81–90.

McCrae, R. R., Costa, P. T., Jr., & Busch, C. M. (1986). Evaluating comprehensiveness in personality systems: The California Q-Set and the five factor model. *Journal of Personality, 54,* 430–446.

McDougall, W. (1908). *An introduction to social psychology.* London: Methuen.

McFadden, R. D. (1983, November 22). Atomic war film spurs nationwide discussion. *New York Times,* p. A27.

McGaugh, J. L. (1983). Hormonal influences on memory. *Annual Review of Psychology, 34,* 297–323.

McGaugh, J. L., & Herz, M. J. (1972). *Memory consolidation.* San Francisco: Albion.

McGaugh, J. L., Weinberger, N. M., Lynch, G., & Granger, R. H. (1985). Neural mechanisms of learning and memory: Cells, systems and computations. *Naval Research Reviews, 37,* 15–29.

McGhee, P. E. (1979). *Humor: Its origin and development.* San Francisco: Freeman.

McGinnies, E. (1949). Emotionality and perceptual defense. *Psychological Review, 56,* 244–251.

McGregor, D. (1960). *The human side of enterprise.* New York: McGraw-Hill.

McGuire, R. J., Carlise, J. M., & Young, B. G. (1965). Sexual deviations as conditioned behavior: A hypothesis. *Behavioral Research and Theory, 12,* 185–190.

McGuire, W. J. (1972). Attitude change: The information-processing paradigm. In C. G. McClintock (Ed.), *Experimental social psychology.* New York: Holt, Rinehart & Winston.

McGuire, W. J., McGuire, C. V., Child, P., & Fujioka, T. A. (1978). Salience of ethnicity in the spontaneous self-concept as a function of one's ethnic distinctiveness in the social environment. *Journal of Personality and Social Psychology, 36,* 511–520.

McKean, K. (1986, October). Pain. *Discover,* pp. 82–92.

McLearn, G. E., & De Fries, J. C. (1973). *Introduction to behavioral genetics.* San Francisco: Freeman.

McNeil, B. J., Pauker, S. G., Sox, H. C., Jr., & Tversky, A. (1982). On the elicitation of preferences for alternative therapies. *New England Journal of Medicine, 306,* 1259–1262.

Mead, M. (1928). *Coming of age in Samoa.* New York: Morrow.

Mead, M. (1939). *From the South Seas: Studies of adolescence and sex in primitive societies.* New York: Morrow.

Meador, B. D., & Rogers, C. R. (1979). Person-centered therapy. In R. J. Corsini (Ed.), *Current psychotherapies* (2d ed.) (pp. 131–184). Itasca, IL: Peacock.

Meehl, P. E. (1954). *Clinical versus statistical prediction.* Minneapolis: University of Minnesota Press.

Meehl, P. E. (1965). Seer over sign; The first good example. *Journal of Experimental Research in Personality, 1,* 27–32.
Mehrabian, A. (1971). *Silent messages.* Belmont, CA: Wadsworth.
Meichenbaum, D. (1975). A self-instructional approach to stress management: A proposal for stress innoculating training. In D. C. Spielberger & I. G. Sarason (Eds.), *Stress and anxiety* (Vol. 1, pp. 237–63). New York: Wiley.
Meichenbaum, D. (1977). *Cognitive-behavior modification: An integrative approach.* New York: Plenum.
Meisner, W. W. (1978). *The paranoid process.* New York: Jason Aronson.
Meltzoff, J., & Kornreich, M. (1970). *Research in psychotherapy.* New York: Atherton.
Melville, J. (1977). *Phobias and obsessions.* New York: Penguin Books.
Melzack, R. (1973). *The puzzle of pain.* New York: Basic Books.
Melzack, R. (1980). Psychological aspects of pain. In J. J. Bonica (Ed.), *Pain.* New York: Raven.
Menzel, E. M. (1978). Cognitive mapping in chimpanzees. In S. H. Hulse, H. Fowler, & W. K. Honzig (Eds.), *Cognitive processes in animal behavior* (pp. 375–422). Hillsdale, NJ: Erlbaum.
Meredith, M. A., & Stein, B. E. (1985). Descending efferents from the superior colliculus relay integrated multisensory information. *Science, 227,* 657–659.
Merton, R. K. (1957). *Social theory and social structures.* New York: Free Press.
Mervis, C. B., & Rosch, E. (1981). Categorization of natural objects. *Annual Review of Psychology, 32,* 89–115.
Meyer, M. M., & Ekstein, R., (1970). The psychotic pursuit of reality. *Journal of Contemporary Psychotherapy, 3,* 3–12.
Michael, R., & Zumpe, D. (1983). Annual rhythms in human violence and aggression in the United States and the role of temperature. *Journal of Social Biology, 30,* 263–278.
Milavsky, J. R., Kessler, R. C., Stipp, H. H., & Rubens, W. S. (1982). *Television and aggression: Results of a panel study.* New York: Academic Press.
Milgram, S. (1965). Some conditions of obedience and disobedience to authority. *Human Relations, 18,* 56–76.
Milgram, S. (1974). *Obedience to authority.* New York: Harper & Row.
Milgram, S., & Jodelet, D. (1976). Psychological maps of Paris. In H. M. Proshansky, W. H. Ittleson, & L. G. Rivlin, (Eds.), *Environmental psychology.* New York: Holt, Rinehart & Winston.
Millar, K., & Watkinson, N. (1983). Recognition of words presented during general anesthesia. *Ergonomics, 26,* 585–594.
Miller, A. G. (1986). *The obedience paradigm: A case study in controversy in social science.* New York: Praeger.
Miller, B. E. (1978). Biofeedback and visceral learning. *Annual Review of Psychology, 29,* 373–404.
Miller, G. A. (1956). The magic number seven plus or minus two: Some limits on our capacity for processing information. *Psychological Review, 63,* 81–97.
Miller, G. A. (1962). Some psychological studies of grammar. *American Psychologist, 17,* 748–762.
Miller, N. E. (1941). The frustration-aggression hypothesis. *Psychological Review, 48,* 333–342.
Miller, N. E. (1948). Fear as an acquired drive. *Journal of Experimental Psychology, 38,* 89–101.
Miller, N. E. (1983). Behavioral medicine: Symbiosis between laboratory and clinic. *Annual Review of Psychology, 34,* 1–31.
Miller, P. Y., & Simon, W. (1980). The development of sexuality in adolescence. In J. Adelson (Ed.), *Handbook of adolescent psychology.* New York: Wiley.
Milner, B. (1966). Amnesia following operation on the temporal lobes. In C. W. Whitty & O. L. Zangwill (Eds.), *Amnesia* (pp. 109–33). London: Butterworth.
Milojkovic, J. D. (1982). Chess imagery in novice and master. *Journal of Mental Imagery, 6,* 125–144.
Minuchin, S. (1974). *Families and family therapy.* Cambridge, MA: Harvard University Press.
Mischel, W. (1968). *Personality and assessment.* New York: Wiley.
Mischel, W. (1973). Toward a cognitive social learning reconceptualization of personality. *Psychological Review, 80,* 252–283.
Mischel, W. (1976). *Introduction to personality* (2d ed.). New York: Holt, Rinehart & Winston.
Mischel, W. (1979). On the interface of cognition and personality; Beyond the person-situation debate. *American Psychologist, 34,* 740–754.
Mischel, W. (1984). Convergences and challenges in the search for consistency. *American Psychologist, 39,* 351–364.
Mischel, W., Mischel, H. N. (1973). A cognitive social learning approach to morality and self-regulation. In T. Lickona (Ed.), *Men and morality.* New York: Holt, Rinehart & Winston.
Mischel, W., & Mischel, H. N. (1977). *Essentials of psychology.* New York: Random House.
Mischel, W., & Peake, P. (1982). Beyond déja vu in the search for cross-situational consistency. *Psychological Review, 89*(6), 730–755.
Misgeld, V., Deisz, R. A., Dodt, H. U., & Lux, H. D. (1986). The role of chloride transport in postsynaptic inhibition of hippocampal neurons. *Science, 232,* 1413–1415.
Mishkin, M. (1982). A memory system in the monkey. *Philosophical Transactions of the Royal Society of London, 298,* 85–95.
Mishkin, M., Malamut, B., & Backevalier, J. (1984). Memories and habits: Two neural systems. In G. Lynch, J. L. McGaugh, & N. M. Weinberger (Eds.), *The neurobiology of learning and memory* (pp. 65–77). New York: Guilford Press.
Mitchell, T. R. (1974). Expectancy models of job satisfaction, occupational preference, and effort: A theoretical, methodological, and empirical appraisal. *Psychological Bulletin, 81,* 1053–1077.
Miyake, K., Chen, K., & Campos, J. J. (1985). Infant temperament, mother's mode of interaction, and attachment in Japan: An interim report. In I. Bretherton & E. Waters (Eds.), *Growing points of attachment theory and research. Monographs of the Society for Research in Child Development, 50* (1–2, Serial No. 209), 276–297.
Moar, I. (1980). The nature and acquisition of cognitive maps. In D. Cantor & T. Lee (Eds.), *Proceedings of the international conference on environmental psychology.* London: Architectural Press.
Moncrieff, R. W. (1951). *The chemical senses.* London: Leonard Hill.
Money, J., Hampson, J. G., & Hampson, J. L. (1957). Imprinting and the establishment of gender role. *AMA Archives of Neurology and Psychiatry, 77,* 333–336.
Moniz, E. (1973). Prefrontal leucotomy in the treatment of mental disorders. *American Journal of Psychiatry, 93,* 1379–1385.
Monson, T. C., Hesley, J. W., & Chernick, L. (1982). Specifying when personality traits can and cannot predict behavior: An alternative to abandoning the attempt to predict single-act criteria. *Journal of Personality and Social Psychology, 43,* 385–399.
Montague, W. E., Adams, J. A., & Kiess, H. O. (1966). Forgetting and natural language mediation. *Journal of Experimental Psychology, 72,* 829–833.
Moore, B. S., Underwood, B., & Rosenhan, D. L. (1973). Affect and altruism. *Developmental Psychology, 9,* 99–104.
Moos, R. (1979). *Evaluating educational environments.* San Francisco: Jossey-Bass.
Moos, R., & Lemke, S. (1984). Supportive residential settings for older people. In I. Altman, M. P. Lawton, & J. F. Wohlwill (Eds.), *Elderly people and the environment* (pp. 159–90). New York: Plenum.
Moran, J., & Desimone, R. (1985). Selective attention gates visual processing in the extrastriate cortex. *Science, 229,* 782–785.
Morgan, A. H., Hilgard, E. R., & Davert, E. C. (1970). The

heritability of hypnotic susceptibility of twins: A preliminary report. *Behavior Genetics, 1,* 213–224.

Morgan, A. H., Johnson, D. L., & Hilgard, E. R. (1974). The stability of hypnotic susceptibility: A longitudinal study. *International Journal of Clinical and Experimental Hypnosis, 22,* 249–257.

Morris, C., & Hackman, J. (1969). Behavioral correlates of perceived leadership. *Journal of Personality and Social Psychology, 13,* 350–361.

Morris, J. J., & Clarizio, S. (1977). Improvement in IQ of high risk, disadvantaged preschool children enrolled in a developmental program. *Psychological Reports, 41*(1), 111–114.

Moscovici, S. (1976). *Social influence and social change.* New York: Academic Press.

Moscovici, S., & Faucheux, C. (1972). Social influence, conformity bias, and the study of active minorities. In L. Berkowitz (Ed.), *Advances in experimental social psychology* (Vol. 6). New York: Academic Press.

Moskowitz, B. A. (1978). The acquisition of language. *Scientific American, 239*(11), 92–108.

Motley, M. T. (1987, February). What I meant to say. *Psychology Today,* pp. 24–28.

Mowrer, O. (1960). *Learning theory and symbolic processes.* New York: Wiley.

Moyer, K. E. (1976). *The psychobiology of aggression.* New York: Harper & Row.

Mullen, B. (1986). Atrocity as a function of lynch mob composition: A self-attention perspective. *Personality and Social Psychology Bulletin, 12,* 187–197.

Mullen, B., & Baumeister, R. F. (1987). Group effects on self-attention and performance: Social loafing, social facilitation, and social impairment. In C. Hendrick (Ed.), *Review of personality and social psychology.* Beverly Hills, CA: Sage.

Mullin, B., Futrell, D., Stairs, D., Tice, D. M., Baumeister, R. F., Dawson, K. E., Riordan, C. A., Radloff, C. E., Goethals, G. R., Kennedy, J. G., & Rosenfeld, P. (1986). Newscasters' facial expressions and voting behavior of viewers: Can a smile elect a president? *Journal of Personality and Social Psychology, 51,* 291–295.

Munroe, R. L. (1955). *Schools of psychoanalytic thought.* New York: Dryden.

Munsterberg, H. (1927). *On the witness stand: Essays on psychology and crime.* New York: Clark Boardman. (Original work published New York: Doubleday, 1908)

Murphy, J. M. (1976). Psychiatric labeling in cross-cultural perspective. *Science, 191,* 1019–1028.

Murray, H. A. (1938). *Explorations in personality.* New York: Oxford University Press.

Muskin, P. R., & Fyer, A. J. (1981). Treatment of panic disorder. *Journal of Clinical Psychopharmacology, 1,* 81–90.

Mussen, P. H., Honzik, M. P., & Eichorn, D. H. (1982). Early adult antecedents of life satisfaction at age 70. *Journal of Gerontology, 37,* 316–322.

Myers, R. E., & Sperry, R. W. (1958). Interhemispheric communication through the corpus callosum: Mnemonic carryover between the hemispheres. *Archives of Neurology and Psychiatry, 80,* 298–303.

N

Nadi, S. N., Nurnberger, J. I., & Gershon, E. S. (1984). Muscarinic cholinergic receptors on skin fibroblasts in familial affective disorder. *New England Journal of Medicine, 311*(4), 225–230.

Nasrallah, H. A., & Weinberger, D. W. (1986). *The neurology of schizophrenia: Handbook of schizophrenia, Vol. 1.* Amsterdam: Elsevier.

Nathans, J., Thomas, D., & Hogness, D. S. (1986). Molecular genetics of human color vision: The genes encoding blue, green, and red pigments. *Science, 232,* 193–202.

National Assessment of Educational Progress. (1983). *The third national mathematics assessment: Results, trends, and issues* (13-MA-01). Denver, CO: Educational Commission of the States.

National Institute on Drug Abuse. (1982). *Student drug use, attitudes, and beliefs: National trends 1975–1982.* Washington, DC: U. S. Government Printing Office.

National Institutes of Mental Health. (1977). *Lithium and the treatment of mood disorders* (DHEW Publication No. ADM 77–73). Washington, DC: U. S. Government Printing Office.

National Institutes of Mental Health. (1982). *Television and behavior: Ten years of scientific evidence and implications for the eighties: Vol. 1. Summary report.* Washington, DC: U. S. Government Printing Office.

National Institutes of Mental Health. (1986). *Useful information on phobias and panic* (DHHS Publication No. ADM 86–1472). Washington, DC: U. S. Government Printing Office.

Natsoulas, T. (1978). Consciousness. *American Psychologist, 33* (10), 906–914.

Natsoulas, T. (1981). Basic problems of consciousness. *Journal of Personality and Social Psychology, 41,* 132–178.

Nauta, W. J. H., & Feirtag, M. (1979). The organization of the brain. *Scientific American, 241*(9), 88–111.

Navon, D., & Gopher, D. (1979). On the economy of the human processing system. *Psychological Review, 86,* 214–255.

Neale, M. A., & Bazerman, M. H. (1985). Perspectives for understanding negotiation: Viewing negotiation as a judgmental process. *Journal of Conflict Resolution, 29,* 33–55.

Neisser, U. (1967). *Cognitive psychology.* New York: Appleton-Century-Crofts.

Nelson, K. E. (1971). Accommodation of visual tracking patterns in human infants to object movement patterns. *Journal of Experimental Child Psychology, 16,* 180–196.

Nelson, K. E. (1974). Short-term progress toward one component of object permanence. *Merrill–Palmer Quarterly, 20,* 3–8.

Nelson, Z. P., & Mowrey, D. D. (1976). Contracting in crisis intervention. *Community Mental Health Journal, 12,* 37–43.

Nemeth, C. (1979). The role of an active minority in intergroup relations. In W. Austin & S. Worchel (Eds.), *The social psychology of intergroup relations.* Monterey, CA: Brooks/Cole.

Nesselroade, J. R., & Baltes, P. B. (1974). Adolescent personality development and historical change: 1970–1972. *Monographs of the Society for Research in Child Development, 39.*

Neugarten, B. L. (1976). *The psychology of aging: An overview.* Master lectures on developmental psychology. Washington, DC: American Psychological Association.

Newcomb, T. M. (1929). *The consistencey of certain extrovert-introvert behavior traits in 50 problem boys.* New York: Columbia University, Contributions to Education, No. 382.

Newcomb, T. M. (1943). *Personality and social change.* New York: Holt.

Newcomb, T. M. (1963). Persistence and regression of changed attitudes: Long-range studies. *Journal of Social Issues, 19,* 3–4.

Newell, A., Shaw, J. C., & Simon, H. A. (1958). Elements of a theory of human problem solving. *Psychological Review, 65,* 152–166.

Newell, A., & Simon, H. A. (1972). *Human problem solving.* Englewood Cliffs, NJ: Prentice-Hall.

Newton, I. (1671–72). New theory about light and colors. *Philosophical Transactions of the Royal Society of London, 80,* 3075–87. In D. L. MacAdam (Ed.) (1970). *Sources of color science.* Cambridge, MA: MIT Press.

Nguyen, T., Heslin, R., & Nguyen, M. L. (1975). The meanings of touch: Sex differences. *Journal of Communication, 25,* 92–103.

Nideffer, R. M. (1976). Altered states of consciousness. In T. X. Barber, *Advances in altered states of consciousness and human potentialities* (Vol. 1, pp. 3–35). New York: Psychological Dimensions.

Nisbett, R. E. (1972). Hunger, obesity and the ventromedial hypothalamus. *Psychological Review, 79,* 433–453.

Nisbett, R. E., Fong, G. T., Lehman, D., & Cheng, P. (1987). *Teaching reasoning.* Unpublished manuscript, University of Michigan.

Nisbett, R. E., & Ross, L. (1980). *Human inference: Strategies and shortcomings of social judgment.* Englewood Cliffs, NJ: Prentice-Hall.

Nisbett, R. E., & Wilson, T. D. (1977). Telling more than we can know: Verbal reports on mental processes. *Psychological Review, 84,* 231–259.

Nobles, W. W. (1972). African psychology: Foundations for black psychology. In. R. L. Jones (Ed.), *Black psychology.* New York: Harper & Row.

Nobles, W. W. (1976). Black people in white insanity: An issue for black community mental health. *Journal of Afro-American Issues, 4,* 21–27.

Nolen-Hoeksema, S. (1987). Sex differences in unipolar depression: Evidence and theory. *Psychological Bulletin, 101,* 259–282.

Nomi, M. (1971). *Good combinations of blood types.*

Norman, D. A. (1968). Toward a theory of memory and attention. *Psychological Review, 75,* 522–536.

Norman, D. A. (1981). Categorization of action slips. *Psychological Review, 88,* 1–15.

Norman, D. A. (1983). Design rules based on analyses of human error. *Communications of the Association for Computing Machinery, 26,* 254–258.

Norman, D. A., & Rumelhart, D. E., (1975). *Explorations in cognition.* San Francisco: Freeman.

Nungesser, L. G. (1986). *Epidemic of courage: Facing AIDS in America.* New York: St. Martin's Press.

Nuttin, J. (1985). *Future time perspective and motivation: Theory and research method.* Hillsdale, NJ: Erlbaum.

O

Oden, S., & Asher, S. R. (1977). Coaching children in social skills for friendship making. *Child Development, 48,* 495–506.

Offer, D., & Offer, J. B. (1975). *From teenage to young manhood.* New York: Basic Books.

Offer, D., Ostrov, E., & Howard, K. I. (1981a). *The adolescent: A psychological self-portrait.* New York: Basic Books.

Offer, D., Ostrov, E., & Howard, K. I. (1981b). The mental health professional's concept of the normal adolescent. *AMA Archives of General Psychiatry, 38,* 149–153.

Oldham, D. G. (1978a). Adolescent turmoil: A myth revisited. In S. C. Feinstein & P. L. Giovacchini (Eds.), *Adolescent psychiatry* (Vol. 6). Chicago: University of Chicago Press.

Oldham, D. G. (1978b). Adolescent turmoil and a myth revisited. In A. H. Esman (Ed.), *The psychology of adolescence.* New York: International University Press.

Olds, J. (1973). Commentary on positive reinforcement produced by electrical stimulation of septal areas and other regions of rat brain. In E. S. Valenstein (Ed.), *Brain stimulation and motivation: Research and commentary.* Glenview, IL: Scott, Foresman.

Olds, J., & Milner, P. (1954). Positive reinforcement produced by electrical stimulation of septal area and other regions of the rat brain. *Journal of Comparative and Physiological Psychology, 47,* 419–427.

Olson, J. M., & Zanna, M. P. (1979). A new look at selective exposure. *Journal of Experimental Social Psychology, 15,* 1–15.

Olton, D. S. (1979). Mazes, mazes, and memory. *American Psychologist, 34,* 583–596.

Olweus, D., Block, J., & Radke-Yarrow, M. (Eds.). (1986). *The development of anti-social and pro-social behavior: Research, theories, and issues.* New York: Academic Press.

Oppel, J. J. (1854–55). Ueber geometrisch-optische Tauschungen. *Jahresbericht des physikalischen Vereins zu Frankfurt a. M.,* 34–47.

Opton, E. M. (1970). Lessons of My Lai. In N. Sanford & C. Comstock (Eds.), *Sanctions for evil.* San Francisco: Jossey-Bass.

Opton, E. M., Jr. (1973). "It never happened and besides they deserved it." In W. E. Henry & N. Sanford (Eds.), *Sanctions for evil* (pp. 49–70). San Francisco: Jossey-Bass.

Orlando, N. J. (1981). Mental patient as therapeutic agent—self-change, power, and caring. *Psychotherapy: Theory, Research, and Practice, 7,* 58–62.

Orne, M. T. (1972). On the stimulating subject as a quasi-control group in hypnosis research: What, why, and how? In E. Fromm & R. E. Shor (Eds.), *Hypnosis: Research developments and perspectives* (p. 399–443). Chicago: Aldine.

Orne, M. T. (1980). Hypnotic control of pain: Toward a clarification of the different psychological processes involved. In J. J. Bonica (Ed.), *Pain* (pp. 155–72). New York: Raven Press.

Ornstein, P. A., & Naus, M. J. (1978). Rehearsal processes in children's memory. In P. A. Ornstein (Ed.), *Memory development in children.* Hillsdale, NJ: Erlbaum.

Ornstein, R. E. (1972). *The psychology of consciousness.* San Francisco: Freeman.

Ornstein, R. E. (1975). *The psychology of consciousness.* New York: Penguin Books.

Ornstein, R. E. (1986a). *Multimind: A new way of looking at human behavior.* Boston: Houghton-Mifflin.

Ornstein, R. E. (1986b). *The psychology of consciousness* (rev. ed.). New York: Penguin Books.

Ornstein, R., & Sobel, D. (March, 1987). The healing brain. *Psychology Today,* pp. 48–52.

Oskamp, S. (1984). *Applied social psychology.* Englewood Cliffs, NJ: Prentice-Hall.

Oskamp, S. (Ed.). (1985). International conflict and national public policy issues. *Applied Social Psychology Annual, 6.*

Ouchi, W. (1981). *Theory Z: How American business can meet the Japanese challenge.* Reading, MA: Addison-Wesley.

P

Page, S. (1987). On gender roles and perception of maladjustment. *Canadian Psychology, 28,* 53–59.

Paivio, A. (1983). The empirical case for dual coding. In J. C. Yuille (Ed.), *Imagery, memory and cognition* (pp. 307–32). Hillsdale, NJ: Erlbaum.

Paivio, A. (1986). *Mental representations: A dual coding approach.* New York: Oxford University Press.

Palmer, S. E. (1975). The effects of contextual scenes on the identification of objects. *Memory and Cognition, 3,* 519–526.

Palmer, S. E. (1984). The psychology of perceptual organization: A transformational approach. In A. Rosenfeld & J. Beck (Eds.), *Human and machine vision.* New York: Academic Press.

Palys, T. S. (1986). Testing the common wisdom: The social content of video pornography. *Canadian Psychology, 27,* 22–35.

Park, B., & Rothbart, M. (1982). Perception of out-group homogeneity and levels of social categorization: Memory for the subordinate attributes of in-group and out-group members. *Journal of Personality and Social Psychology, 42,* 1051–1068.

Park, R. D., & Walters, R. H. (1967). Some factors influencing the efficacy of punishment training for inducing response inhibition. *Monographs of the Society for Research in Child Development, 32* (1, Whole No. 109).

Parke, R. D., Berkowitz, L., Leyens, J. P., West, S. G., & Sebastian, R. J. (1977). Some effects of violent and nonviolent movies on the behavior of juvenile delinquents. In L. Berkowitz (Ed.), *Advances in experimental social psychology* (Vol. 10). New York: Academic Press.

Parke, R. D., & Sawin, D. B. (1976). The father's role in infancy. *Family Coordinator, 25,* 265–371.

Parlee, M. B. (1979, October). The friendship bond. *Psychology Today,* pp. 43–45.

Parpal, M., & Maccoby, E. E. (1985). Maternal responsiveness and subsequent child compliance. *Child Development, 56,* 1326–1334.

Parrott, J., & Gleitman, H. (1984, April). *The joy of peekaboo: Appearance or reappearance?* Paper presented at the meeting of the Eastern Psychological Association, Baltimore.

Parsons, H. M. (1974). What happened at Hawthorne? *Science, 183,* 922–932.

Pass, J. J., & Cunningham, J. W. (1978). Occupational clusters based on systematically derived work dimensions: Final report. *Journal of Supplemental Abstract Service.* Catalogue of selected documents. Psychology (Vol. 8, pp. 22–23).

Patterson, F. G. (1986). The mind of the gorilla: Conversation and conservation. In K. Benirschke (Ed.), *Primates: The road to self-sustaining populations* (pp. 933–47). New York: Springer-Verlag.

Patterson, F. G., Patterson, C. H., & Brentari, D. K. (1987). Language in child, chimp, and gorilla. *American Psychologist, 42,* 270–272.

Paul, G. L. (1969). Outcome of systematic desensitization: II, Controlled investigations of individual treatment technique variations, and current status. In C. M. Franks (Ed.), *Behavior therapy: Appraisal and status.* New York: McGraw-Hill.

Pavlov, I. P. (1927). *Conditioned reflexes* (G. V. Anrep, Trans.). London: Oxford University Press.

Pavlov, I. P. (1928). *Lectures on conditioned reflexes: Twenty-five years of objective study of higher nervous activity (behavior of animals)* (Vol. 1) W. H. Gantt (Trans.). New York: International Publishers.

Paykel, E. S. (1973). Life events and acute depression. In J. P. Scott & E. C. Senay (Eds.), *Separation and depression* (pp. 215–236). Washington, DC: American Association for the Advancement of Science.

Pear, T. H. (1927). Skill. *Journal of Personnel Research, 5,* 478–489.

Pearson, R. E. (1961). Response to suggestions given under general anesthesia. *American Journal of Clinical Hypnosis, 4,* 106–114.

Pelletier, K. R., & Peper, E. (1977). Developing a biofeedback model: Alpha EEG feedback as a means for main control. *The International Journal of Clinical and Experimental Hypnosis, 25,* 361–371.

Pelletier, L., & Herold, E. (1983, May). *A study of sexual fantasies among young single females.* Paper presented at the meeting of the World Congress of Sexuality, Washington, DC.

Pelz, E. B. (1965). Some factors in "Group decision." In H. Proshansky & B. Seidenberg (Eds.), *Basic studies in social psychology* (pp. 437–44). New York: Holt, Rinehart, & Winston. (Originally published 1955)

Penfield, W., & Baldwin, M. (1952). Temporal lobe seizures and the technique of subtotal lobectomy. *Annals of Surgery, 136,* 625–634.

Penfield, W., & Perot, P. (1963). The brain's record of auditory and visual experience. *Brain, 86,* 596–696.

Pennick, S., Smith, G., Wienske, K., & Hinkle, L. (1963). An experimental evaluation of the relationship between hunger and gastric motility. *American Journal of Physiology, 205,* 421–426.

Penrose, L. S., & Penrose, R. (1958). Impossible objects: A special type of visual illusion. *British Journal of Psychology, 49.*

Peplau, L. A., Miceli, M., & Morasch, B. (1982). Loneliness and self-evaluation. In L. A. Peplau & D. Perlman (Eds.), *Loneliness.* New York: Wiley.

Perenin, M. T., & Jeannerod, M. (1975). Residual vision in cortically blind hemiphields. *Neuropsychologia, 13,* 1–7.

Perlin, S. (Ed.). (1975). *A handbook for the study of suicide.* New York: Oxford University Press.

Perlmutter, M., & Hall, E. (1985). *Adult development and aging.* New York: Wiley.

Perls, F. S. (1967). Group vs. individual therapy. *ECT: A Review of General Semantics, 34,* 306–312.

Perls, F. S. (1969). *Gestalt therapy verbatim.* Lafayette, CA: Real People Press.

Peters, T. J., & Waterman, R. H., Jr. (1983). *In search of excellence: Lessons from America's best-run companies.* New York: Warner.

Peterson, J. L., & Zill, N. (1981). Television viewing in the United States and children's intellectual, social, and emotional development. *Television and Children, 2,* 21–28.

Peterson L. R., & Peterson, M. J. (1959). Short-term retention of individual verbal items. *Journal of Experimental Psychology, 58,* 193–198.

Petit, C. (1987, April 9). San Francisco doctors find brain damage in 2 of 10 cocaine users. *San Francisco Chronicle,* p. 8.

Pfaffman, C. (1959). The sense of taste. In J. Field (Ed.), *Handbook of physiology: Section 1. Neurophysiology* (Vol. 1). Washington, DC: American Physiological Society.

Pfefferbaum, A. (1977). Psychotherapy and psychopharmacology. In J. D. Barchas, P. A. Berger, R. D. Ciacanello, & G. R. Elliott (Eds.), *Psychopharmacology: From theory to practice* (pp. 481–92). New York: Oxford University Press.

Pfungst, O. (1911). *Clever Hans (the horse of Mr. Von Osten)* (R. Rosenthal, Trans.). New York: Holt, Rinehart & Winston.

Phares, E. J. (1984). *Clinical psychology: Concepts, methods, and professionals* (rev. ed.). Homewood, IL: Dorsey.

Phelps, M. E., & Mazziotta, J. C. (1986). Positron emission tomography: Human brain function and biochemistry. *Science, 228,* 799–809.

Phillips, D. P. (1979). Suicide, motor vehicle fatalities, and the mass media: Evidence toward a theory of suggestion. *American Journal of Sociology, 84,* 1150–1174.

Phillips, D. P. (1983). The impact of mass media violence on U. S. homicides. *American Sociological Review, 48,* 560–568.

Phillips, D. P. (1985a). The found experiment: A new technique for assessing the impact of mass media violence on real-world aggressive behavior. In G. Comstock (Ed.), *Public communication and behavior.*

Phillips, D. P. (1985b). Natural experiments on the effects of mass media violence on fatal aggression: Strengths and weaknesses of a new approach. In L. Berkowitz (Ed.), *Advances in experimental social psychology* (Vol. 19, pp. 207–50). Orlando, FL: Academic Press.

Piaget, J. (1954). *The construction of reality in the child.* New York: Basic Books.

Piaget, J. (1960). *The moral judgment of the child.* New York: Free Press.

Piaget, J. (1977). *The development of thought: Equilibrium of cognitive structures.* New York: Viking Press.

Piaget, J., & Inhelder, B. (1967). *The child's conception of space.* New York: Norton.

Piccione, C., Hilgard, E. J., & Zimbardo, P. G. (1987). *On the consistence of measured hypnotizability over a 25-year period.* Unpublished manuscript, Stanford University.

Piliavin, I. M., Rodin, J., & Piliavin, J. A. (1969). Good Samaritanism: An underground phenomenon? *Journal of Personality and Social Psychology, 13,* 289–300.

Piliavin, J. A., & Piliavin, I. M. (1972). Effect of blood on reactions to a victim. *Journal of Personality and Social Psychology, 23,* 353–361.

Pilisuk, M., & Parks, S. H. (1986). *The healing web: Social networks and human survival.* Hanover, NH: University Press of New England.

Pines, M. (1983, November). Can a rock walk? *Psychology Today,* pp. 46–54.

Pinkerton, J. (Ed.). (1814). *A general collection of the best and most interesting voyages and travels in all parts of the world, 1808–1814.* London: Longman, Hurst, Rees, & Orne.

Pitts, F. N. (1969). The biochemistry of anxiety. *Scientific American, 220*(2), 69–75.

Place, E. J. S., & Gilmore, G. C. (1980). Perceptual organization in schizophrenia. *Journal of Abnormal Psychology, 89,* 409–418.

Plomin, R., & Daniels, D. (1987). Genetics and shyness. In W. W. Jones, J. M. Cheek, & S. R. Briggs (Eds.), *Shyness: Perspectives on research and treatment* (pp. 63–80). New York: Plenum.

Plomin, R., DeFries, J. C., & McClearn, G. E. (1980). *Behavioral genetics: A primer.* San Francisco: Freeman.

Plous, S. (1985). Perceptual illusions and military realities: A social-psychological analysis of the nuclear arms race. *Journal of Conflict Resolution, 29,* 363–389.

Plous, S. (1986, February). *The effects of anchoring on subjective probability estimates of an imminent nuclear war.* Paper presented at the meeting of the California State Psychological Association, San Francisco.

Plous, S. (in press). Disarmament, arms control, and peace in the nuclear age: Political objectives and relevant research, *Journal of Social Issues.*

Plous, S. & Zimbardo, P. G. (1984, November). The looking glass war. *Psychology Today,* pp. 48–59.

Plutchik, R. (1980). *Emotion: A psychoevolutionary synthesis.* New York: Harper & Row.

Plutchik, R., Kellerman, H., & Conte, H. Q. (1979). A structural theory of ego defenses and emotions. In C. Izard, (Ed.), *Emotions and psychopathology* (pp. 229–57). New York: Plenum.

Poppel, E. (1977). Midbrain mechanisms in human vision. In E. Poppel, R. Held, & J. E. Downing (Eds.), *Neurosciences research program bulletin: Vol. 15. Neuronal mechanisms in visual perception* (pp. 335–43). Cambridge, MA: MIT Press.

Porter, L. W., & Lawler, E. E. (1968). *Managerial attitudes and performance.* Homewood, IL: Irwin.

Posner, J. K. (1982). The development of mathematical knowledge in two West African societies. *Child Development 53,* 200–208.

Posner, M. I. (1978). Cumulative development of attentional theory. *American Psychologist, 37,* 168–179.

Posner, M. I., & Snyder, C. R. R. (1974). Attention and cognitive control. In R. L. Solso (Ed.), *Information processing and cognition: The Loyola Symposium* (pp. 55–88). Potomac, MD: Erlbaum.

Posner, M. I., & Snyder, C. R. (1975). Facilitation and inhibition in the processing of signals. *Journal of Experimental Psychology: General, 109,* 160–174.

Post, F. (1980). Paranoid, schizophrenic-like, and schizophrenic states in the aged. In J. E. Birren & R. B. Stone (Eds.), *Handbook of mental health and aging* (pp. 591–615). Englewood Cliffs, NJ: Prentice-Hall.

Postman, L., & Phillips, L. (1965). Short-term temporal changes in free recall. *Quarterly Journal of Experimental Psychology, 17,* 132–138.

Pound, E. (1934). *The ABC of reading.* New York: New Directions Publishing Co.

Powell, L. H., & Eagleston, J. R. (in press). The assessment of chronic stress in college students. In E. M. Altmaier (Ed.), *Helping students manage stress—new directions for student services* (Vol. 21, pp. 23–41). San Francisco: Jossey-Bass.

Powley, T. L. (1977). The ventromedial hypothalamic syndrome, satiety, and a cephalic phase hypothesis. *Psychological Review, 84,* 89–126.

Premack, D. (1965). Reinforcement theory. In D. Levine (Ed.), *Nebraska symposium on motivation* (pp. 128–80). Lincoln: University of Nebraska Press.

Premack, D. (1976). *Intelligence in ape and man.* Hillsdale, NJ: Erlbaum.

Premack, D. (1983). The codes of man and beasts. *The Behavioral and Brain Sciences, 6,* 125–167.

Prentice-Dunn, S., & Rogers, R. W. (1982). Effects of public and private self-awareness on deindividuation and aggression. *Journal of Personality and Social Psychology, 42,* 503–513.

Prentice-Dunn, S., & Rogers, R. W. (1983). Deindividuation in aggression. In R. G. Green & E. I. Donnerstein (Eds.), *Aggression: Theoretical and empirical reviews* (Vol. 2, pp. 155–71). New York: Academic Press.

Prentky, R. A. (1980). *Creativity and psychopathology.* New York: Praeger.

President's Commission on Mental Health. (1978, February). Report of the Task Panel on Community Support Systems. Washington, DC: U. S. Government Printing Office.

Preti, G., Cutler, W. B., Garcia, G. R., Huggins, & Lawley, J. J. (1986). Human axillary secretions influences women's menstrual cycles: The role of donor extract from females. *Hormones and Behavior.*

Pribram, K. H. (1979). Behaviorism, phenomenology and holism in psychology: A scientific analysis. *Journal of Social and Biological Sciences, 2,* 65–72.

Pribram, K. H., & Gill, M. M. (1976). *Freud's "Project" reassessed.* New York: Basic Books.

Price, R. H., Ketterer, R. F., Bader, B. C., & Monahan, J. (Eds.). (1980). *Prevention in mental health: Research, policy, and practice* (Vol. 1). Beverly Hills, CA: Sage.

Pritchard, R. D., Dunnette, M. D., & Jorgenson, D. O. (1972). Effects of perceptions of equity and inequity on worker performance and satisfaction. *Journal of Applied Psychology, 56,* 75–94.

Proshansky, H. M. (1976). Environmental psychology and the real world. *American Psychologist, 31,* 303–310.

Proxmire, W. (1975). Quote on the National Science Foundation.

Putnam, F. W. (1984, March). The psychophysiologic investigation of multiple personality disorder (Symposium on Multiple Personality). *The Psychiatric Clinics of North America, 7*(1), 31–40.

Q

Quattrone, G. A. (1982). Overattribution and unit formation: When behavior engulfs the person. *Journal of Personality and Social Psychology, 42,* 593–607.

Quattrone, G. A., Lawrence, C. P., Warren, D. L., Souza-Silva, K., Finkel, S. E., & Andrus, D. E. (1984). *Explorations in anchoring: The effects of prior range, anchor extremity, and suggestive hints.* Unpublished manuscript, Stanford University.

Quattrone, G. A., & Tversky, A. (1984). Causal versus diagnostic contingencies: On self-deception and on the voter's illusion. *Journal of Personality and Social Psychology, 46,* 337–348.

R

Rabbie, J. M. (1981). The effects of intergroup competition and cooperation on intra- and intergroup relationships. In J. Grzelak & V. Derlega (Eds.), *Living with other people: Theory and research on cooperation and helping.* New York: Academic Press.

Rabbie, J. M. (1985, December 16). *Anonymity and group aggression.* Paper presented at University College, Galway, Ireland.

Rabbie, J. M., & Wilkens, G. (1971). Intergroup competition and its effect on intragroup and intergroup relations. *European Journal of Psychology, 1,* 215–234.

Rabkin, J. G., Gelb, L., & Lazar, J. B. (Eds.). (1980). *Attitudes toward the mentally ill: Research perspectives* (Report of an NIMH workshop). Rockville, MD: National Institutes of Mental Health.

Rachman, S. (1966). Sexual fetishism: An experimental analogue. *Psychological Record, 6,* 293–296.

Rachman, S., & Hodgson, R. (1980). *Obsessions and compulsions.* Englewood Cliffs, NJ: Prentice-Hall.

Rahe, R. H., & Arthur, R. J. (1977). Life-change patterns surrounding illness experience. In A. Monat & R. S. Lazarus, (Eds.), *Stress and coping* (pp. 36–44). New York: Columbia University Press.

Raiffa, H. (1982). *The art and science of negotiation.* Cambridge, MA: Harvard University Press.

Rakic, P. (1985). Limits of neurogenesis in primates. *Science, 227,* 1054–1057.

Rasmussen, G. L., & Windle, W. F. (1960). *Neural mechanisms of the auditory and vestibular systems.* Springfield, IL: Charles C Thomas.

Ray, W. J., & Cole, H. W. (1985). EEG alpha activity reflects attentional demands, and beta activity reflects emotional and cognitive processes. *Science, 228,* 750–752.

Regan, D. T., & Fazio, R. (1977). On the consistency between attitudes and behavior: Look to the method of attitude formation. *Journal of Experimental Social Psychology, 13,* 28–45.

Reid, T. (1785/1850). *Essays on the intellectual powers of man.* Cambridge: J. Bartlett.

Reinisch, J. M. (1981). Prenatal exposure to synthetic progestions increases potential for aggression in humans. *Science, 211,* 1171–1173.

Reisenzein, R. (1983). The Schachter theory of emotion: Two decades later. *Psychological Bulletin, 94,* 239–264.

Reisman, J. (1986, January 16). *A content analysis of Playboy, Penthouse, and Hustler magazines with special attention to the portrayal of children, crime, and violence.* Supplementary testimony given to the United States Attorney General's Commission on Pornography, New York.

Reiterman, T., & Jacobs, J. (1983). *Raven: The untold story of Jim Jones and his people.* New York: Dutton.

Rescorla, R. A. (1972). Information variables in Pavlovian conditioning. In G. Bower (Ed.), *The psychology of learning and motivation* (Vol. 6). New York: Academic Press.

Rescorla, R. A. (1980). *Pavlovian second-order conditioning: Studies in associative learning.* Hillsdale, NJ: Erlbaum.

Rescorla, R. A., & Wagner, A. R. (1972). A theory of Pavlovian conditioning: Variations in the effectiveness of reinforcement and nonreinforcement. In A. H. Black & W. F. Prokasy (Eds.), *Classical conditioning. II: Current research and theory* (pp. 64–94). New York: Appleton-Century-Crofts.

Rest, J. R., & Thoma, S. J. (1976). Relation of moral judgment development to formal education. *Developmental Psychology, 21,* 709–714.

Reston, NJ: (1986, December 24). Questions about the President's memory. *New York Times.*

Reuters. (1982, January 1). Tiny superman fans making fatal dives. *Kota Kinabalu,* Malaysia.

Reynolds, D. (1980). *The quiet therapies.* Honolulu: University of Hawaii Press.

Reynolds, D. (1984). *Constructive living.* Honolulu: University of Hawaii Press.

Reynolds, D. (1986). *Even in summer the ice doesn't melt.* New York: Morrow.

Rheingold, H. L., & Cook, K. V. (1975). The contents of boys' and girls' rooms as an index of parents' behavior. *Child Development, 46,* 459–463.

Richter, C. P. (1957). On the phenomenon of sudden death in animals and man. *Psychosomatic Medicine, 19,* 191–198.

Richter, C. P. (1965). *Biological clocks in medicine and psychiatry.* Springfield, IL: Charles C Thomas.

Riddle, D., & Morin, S. (1977). Removing the stigma from individuals. *American Psychological Association Monitor, 16,* 28.

Riggs, J. M., & Cantor, N. (1981). *Information exchange in social interaction: Anchoring effects of self-concepts and expectancies.* Unpublished manuscript, Gettysburg College.

Riskind, J. H. (1984). They stoop to conquer: Guiding and self-regulatory functions of physical posture after success and failure. *Journal of Personality and Social Psychology, 47,* 479–493.

Robbins, L. C. (1963). The accuracy of parental recall of aspects of child development and of child rearing practices. *Journal of Abnormal and Social Psychology, 66,* 261–270.

Roberts, T. B. (1973). Maslow's human motivation needs hierarchy: A bibliography. *Research in Education.* (ERIC Document Reproduction Service No. ED 069 591)

Robinson, M. J. (1985). Jesse Helms take stock: Study shows Rather bears no liberal bias. *Washington Journalism Review, 7,* 14–17.

Rock, I. (1975). *An introduction to perception.* New York: Macmillan.

Rockmore, M. (1985, March 5). Analyzing analysis. *American Way,* pp. 71–75.

Rodin, J. (1983, April). Behavioral medicine: Beneficial effects of self control training in aging. *International Review of Applied Psychology, 32,* 153–181.

Rodin, J. (1985). The application of social psychology. In G. Lindzey & E. Aronson (Eds.), *Handbook of social psychology* (3d ed.) (Vol. 2, pp. 805–82). New York: Random House.

Roediger, H. L., & Crowder, R. G. (1976). A serial position effect in recall of United States presidents. *Bulletin of the Psychonomic Society, 8,* 275–278.

Roethlisberger, F. J., & Dickson, W. J. (1939). *Management and the worker.* Cambridge, MA: Harvard University Press.

Roffwarg, H. P., Munzio, J. N., & Dement, W. C. (1966). Ontogenetic development of the human sleep-dream cycle. *Science, 152,* 604–619.

Rogers, C. R. (1947). Some observations on the organization of personality. *American Psychologist, 2,* 358–368.

Rogers, C. R. (1951). *Client-centered therapy: Its current practice, implications and theory.* Boston: Houghton-Mifflin.

Rogers, C. R. (1959). A theory of therapy, personality, and interpersonal relationships, as developed in the client-centered framework. In S. Koch (Ed.), *Psychology: A study of a science* (Vol. 3). New York: McGraw-Hill.

Rogers, C. R. (1977). *On personal power: Inner strength and its revolutionary impact.* New York: Delacorte.

Rokeach, M. (1968). *Beliefs, attitudes and values.* San Francisco: Jossey-Bass.

Rook, K. (1984). Promoting social bonding: Strategies for helping the lonely and socially isolated. *American Psychologist, 37,* 1389–1407.

Rorschach, H. (1942). *Psychodiagnostics: A diagnostic test based on perception.* New York: Grune & Stratton.

Rosch, E. H. (1973). Natural categories. *Cognitive Psychology, 4,* 328–350.

Rosch, E. H. (1978). Principles of categorization. In E. Rosch & B. B. Lloyd (Eds.), *Cognition and categorization* (pp. 27–48). Hillsdale, NJ: Erlbaum.

Rosch, E. H., Mervis, C. B., Gray, W. D., Johnson, D. M., & Boyes-Braem, P. (1976). Basic objects in natural categories. *Cognitive Psychology, 8,* 382–439.

Rose, S. (1973). *The conscious brain.* New York: Knopf.

Roseman, I. J. (1984). Cognitive determinants of emotions: A structural theory. In P. Shaver (Ed.), *Review of personality and social psychology: Vol. 5. Emotions, relationships, and health* (pp. 11–36). Beverly Hills, CA: Sage.

Rosenbaum, M., & Muroff, M. (Eds.). (1984). *Fourteen contemporary reinterpretations.* New York: Free Press.

Rosenbaum, M. E. (1986). The repulsion hypothesis: On the nondevelopment of relationships. *Journal of Personality and Social Psychology, 51,* 1156–1166.

Rosenbaum, R. M. (1972). *A dimensional analysis of the perceived causes of success and failure.* Unpublished doctoral dissertation, University of California, Los Angeles.

Rosenblith, W. A. (1961). *Sensory communication.* Boston: MIT Press.

Rosenhan, D. (1969). Some origins of concern for others. In P. Mussen, J. Langer, & M. Covington (Eds.), *Trends and issues in developmental psychology.* New York: Holt, Rinehart & Winston.

Rosenhan, D. L. (1973). On being sane in insane places. *Science, 179,* 250–258.

Rosenhan, D. L. (1975). The contextual nature of psychiatric diagnoses. *Journal of Abnormal Psychology, 84,* 462–474.

Rosenhan, D. L., & Seligman, M. E. P. (1984). *Abnormal Psychology.* New York: Norton.

Rosenthal, D. (Ed.). (1963). *The Genain quadruplets.* New York: Basic Books.

Rosenthal, D., Wender, P. H., Kety, S. S., Schulsinger, F., Weiner, J., & Rieder, R. (1975). Parent-child relationships and psychopathological disorder in the child. *Archives of General Psychiatry, 32,* 466–476.

Rosenthal, R. (1966). *Experimenter effects in behavioral research.* New York: Appleton-Century-Crofts.

Rosenthal, R., & Jacobson, L. F. (1968a). *Pygmalion in the classroom.* New York: Holt.

Rosenthal, R., & Jacobson, L. F. (1968b). Teacher expectations for the disadvantaged. *Scientific American, 218*(4), 19–23.

Rosenweig, M., & Leiman, A. L. (1982). *Physiological psychology.* Lexington, MA: D. C. Heath.

Rosenzweig, M. R. (1984). Experience, memory, and the brain. *American Psychologist, 39,* 365–376.

Ross, L. (1977). The intuitive psychologist and his shortcomings. In L. Berkowitz (Ed.), *Advances in experimental social psychology* (Vol. 10). New York: Academic Press.

Ross, L. (1978). Some afterthoughts on the intuitive psychologist. In L. Berkowitz (Ed.), *Cognitive theories in social psychology.* New York: Academic Press.

Ross, L., Amabile, T., & Steinmetz, J. (1977). Social roles, social control and biases in the social perception process. *Journal of Personality and Social Psychology, 37,* 485–494.

Ross, L., & Lepper, M. R. (1980). The perseverance of beliefs: Empirical and normative considerations. In R. A. Shweder & D. Fiske (Eds.), *New directions for methodology of behavioral science: Fallible judgments in behavioral research* (pp. 17–36). San Francisco: Jossey-Bass.

Ross, R. T., Begab, M. J., Dandis, E. M., Giannipiccolo, J. S., Jr., & Meyers, C. E. (1986). *Lives of the mentally retarded.* Stanford, CA: Stanford University Press.

Rossi, A. (1984). Gender and parenthood. *American Sociological Review, 49,* 1–19.

Roth, J. D., Le Roith, D., & Shiloach, J. (1982). The evolutionary origins of hormones, neurotransmitters, and other extracellular chemical messengers. *New England Journal of Medicine, 306,* 523–527.

Rothman, D. J. (1971). *The discovery of the asylum: Social order and disorder in the new republic.* Boston: Little, Brown.

Rotter, J. B. (1954). *Social learning and clinical psychology.* Englewood Cliffs, NJ: Prentice-Hall.

Rotton, J., & Frey, J. (1984). Psychological costs of air pollution: Atmospheric conditions, seasonal trends, and psychiatric emergencies. *Population and Enviroment: Behavioral and Social Issues, 7,* 3–16.

Rotton, J., & Frey, J. (1985). Air pollution, weather, and violent crimes: Concomitant time-series analysis of archival data. *Journal of Personality and Social Psychology, 49,* 1207–1220.

Rovee-Collier, C. K., Sullivan, M. W., Enright, M., Lucas, D., & Fagen, J. W. (1980). Reactivation of infant memory. *Science, 208,* 1159–1161.

Rozin, P. (1976). The evolution of intelligence and access to the cognitive unconscious. In J. M. Sprague & A. A. Epstein (Eds.), *Progress in psychobiology and physiological psychology* (pp. 245–80). New York: Academic Press.

Rozin, P., & Kalat, J. W. (1971). Specific hungers and poison avoidance as adaptive specializations of learning. *Psychological Review, 78,* 459–486.

Rubin, J. Z., Provenzano, F. J., & Luria, Z. (1974). The eye of the beholder: Parents' views on sex of newborns. *American Journal of Orthopsychiatry, 44,* 512–519.

Rubin, L. B. (1976, October). The marriage bed. *Psychology Today,* pp. 44–50, 91–92.

Rubin, Z. (1973). *Liking and loving.* New York: Holt, Rinehart & Winston.

Rudy, J. W., & Wagner, A. R. (1975). Stimulus selection in associative learning. In W. K. Estes (Ed.), *Handbook of learning and cognition* (Vol. 2). Hillsdale, NJ: Erlbaum.

Rumbaugh, D. M. (Ed.). (1977). *Language learning by a chimpanzee: The Lana project.* New York: Academic Press.

Rumelhart, D. E., & McClelland, J. L. (1986). *Parallel distributed processing: Explorations in the microstructure of cognition* (2 vols.). Cambridge, MA: MIT Press.

Rushton, J. P., Fulker, D. W., Neale, M. C., Nias, D. K. B., & Eysenck, H. J. (1986). Altruism and aggression: The heritability of individual differences. *Journal of Personality and Social Psychology, 50,* 283–305.

Russell, B. (1948). *Human knowledge, its scope and limits.* New York: Simon & Schuster.

Russell, J. A., & Ward, L. M. (1982). Environmental psychology. *Annual Review of Psychology, 33,* 651–688.

Rutter, M. (1979). Maternal deprivation, 1972–1978: New findings, new concepts, new approaches. *Child Development, 50,* 283–305.

Ryan, W. (1976). *Blaming the victim.* (rev. ed.). New York: Vintage Books.

Rychlak, J. (1979). *Discovering free will and personal responsibility.* New York: Oxford University Press.

Rylsky, M. (1986, February). A town born of the atom. *Soviet Life,* p. 8.

S

Sabini, J., & Silver, M. (1982). *Moralities of everyday life.* New York: Oxford University Press.

Sacks, O. (1973). *Migraine: Evolution of a common disorder.* Berkeley: University of California Press.

Sachs, O. (1985). *The man who mistook his wife for a hat and other clinical tales.* New York: Summit.

Saegert, S., & Hart, R. (1976). The development of sex differences in the envionmental competence of children. In P. Burnett (Ed.), *Women in society.* Chicago: Maarouta.

Saks, M. J. (1977). *Jury verdicts: The role of group size and social decision rule.* Lexington, MA: Lexington Books.

Salovey, P., & Rodin, J. (1985). Cognitions about the self: Connecting feeling states and social behavior. In L. Wheeler (Ed.), *Review of Personality and Social Psychology* (Vol. 6, pp. 143–67). Beverly Hills, CA: Sage.

Salzman, C. (1980). The use of ECT in the treatment of schizophrenia. *American Journal of Psychiatry, 137,* 1032–1041.

Sanders, R. S., & Reyhen, J. (1969). Sensory deprivation and the enhancement of hypnotic susceptibility. *Journal of Abnormal Psychology, 74,* 375–381.

Sarason, I. G., Johnson, J. H., & Siegel, J. M. (1978). Assessing the impact of life changes: Development of the Life Experiences Survey. *Journal of Consulting and Clinical Psychology, 46,* 932–946.

Sarbin, T. R., & Coe, W. C. (1972). *Hypnosis: A social psychological analysis of influence communication.* New York: Holt, Rinehart & Winston.

Sarnoff, I., & Corwin, S. M. (1959). Castration anxiety and the fear of death. *Journal of Personality, 27,* 374–385.

Satir, V. (1967). *Conjoint family therapy* (rev. ed.). Palo Alto, CA: Science and Behavior Books.

Sattler, J. M. (1982). *Assessment of children's intelligence and special abilities.* Boston: Allyn & Bacon.

Savage, C. W. (1970). *The assessment of sensation.* Berkeley: University of California Press.

Sawyer, J. (1966). Measurement and prediction, clinical and statistical. *Psychological Bulletin, 66,* 178–200.

Scammon, R. E. (1930). The measurement of the body in childhood. In J. Harris, C. M. Jackson, D. G. Patterson, & R. E. Scammon (Eds.), *The measurement of man.* Minneapolis: University of Minnesota Press.

Scardamalia, M., & Bereiter, C. (1985). Fostering the development of self-regulation in children's knowledge processing. In S. F. Chapman, J. W. Segall, & R. Glaser (Eds.), *Thinking and learning skills: Research and open questions, Vol. 2* (pp. 563–77). Hillsdale, NJ: Erlbaum.

Scarr, S. (1981). *Race, social class, and individual differences in IQ.* Hillsdale, NJ: Erlbaum.

Scarr, S., & Weinberg, R. A. (1976). I. Q. test performance of black children adopted by white families. *American Psychologist, 31,* 726–739.

Schachter, S. (1959). *The psychology of affiliation.* Stanford, CA: Stanford University Press.

Schachter, S. (1971). *Emotion, obesity and crime.* New York: Academic Press.

Schachter, S. (1982). Recidivism and self-cure of smoking and obesity. *American Psychologist, 37,* 436–444.

Schachter, S., Goldman, R., & Gordon, A. (1968). The effects of fear, food deprivation, and obesity on eating. *Journal of Personality and Social Psychology, 10,* 91–97.

Schachter, S., & Singer, J. (1962). Cognitive, social and physiological determinants of emotional state. *Psychological Review, 69,* 379–399.

Schaie, K. W. (1980). Intelligence and problem solving. In J. E. Birren & R. B. Sloan, (Eds.), *Handbook of mental health and aging* (pp. 262–84). Englewood Cliffs, NJ: Prentice-Hall.

Schank, R. C., & Abelson, R. (1977). *Scripts, plans, goals and understanding: An inquiry into human knowledge and structures.* Hillsdale, NJ: Erlbaum.

Scherer, K. R. (1984). On the nature and function of emotion: A component process approach. In K. R. Scherer & P. Ekman (Eds.), *Approaches to emotion* (pp. 293–317). Hillsdale, NJ: Erlbaum.

Schneider, D. J., Hastorf, A. H., & Ellsworth, P. C. (1979). *Person perception* (2d ed.). Reading, MA: Addison-Wesley.

Schneider, G. E. (1969). Two visual systems. *Science, 163,* 895–902.

Schneider, W. (1984). Developmental trends in the meta-memory-memory behavior relationship. In D. L. Forrest-Pressley, G. E. Mackinnon, & P. G. Waller, (Eds.), *Metacognition, cognition, and human performance.* New York: Academic Press.

Schneider, W., & Shiffran, R. M. (1977). Controlled and automatic information processing: 1. Detection, search, and attention. *Psychological Review, 84,* 1–66.

Schneidman, E. S. (Ed.). (1976). *Deaths of man.* New York: Quadrangle.

Schrag, P. (1978). *Mind control.* New York: Delta.

Schreiber, F. (1973). *Sybil.* New York: Warner Books.

Schwartz, B. (1984). *Psychology of learning and behavior* (2d ed.). New York: Norton.

Schwartz, B., & Lacey, H. (1982). *Behaviorism, science, and human nature.* New York: Norton.

Schwartz, G. E., Brown, S. L., & Ahern, G. L. (1980). Facial muscle patterning and subjective experience during affective imagery: Sex differences. *Psychophysiology, 17,* 75–82.

Schwartz, P., & Strom, D. (1978). The social psychology of female sexuality. In J. Sherman & F. L. Denmark (Eds.), *Psychology of women: Future directions of research* (pp. 149–77). New York: Psychological Dimensions.

Schwartz, S. (1986). *Classic experiments in psychology.* Palo Alto, CA: Mayfield Press.

Scott, J. P. (1963). The process of primary socialization in canine and human infants. *Monographs of the Society for Research in Child Development 28,* 1–47.

Scott, J. P., Stewart, J. M., & De Ghett, V. J. (1974). Critical periods in the organization of systems. *Developmental Psychobiology, 7,* 489–513.

Scott, R. A. (1972). A proposed framework for analyzing deviance as a property of social order. In R. A. Scott & J. D. Douglas (Eds.), *Theoretical perspectives on deviance.* New York: Basic Books.

Scott, V. (1984, June 13). A six-year nightmare for Jim Backus [United Press]. *San Francisco Chronicle,* p. 58.

Sears, P., & Barbee, A. H. (1977). Career and life situations among Terman's gifted women. In J. C. Stanley, W. C. George, & C. H. Solano (Eds.), *The gifted and the creative: A fifty-year perspective* (pp. 28–65). Baltimore: Johns Hopkins University Press.

Sears, R. R. (1961). Relation of early socialization experiences to aggression in middle childhood. *Journal of Abnormal and Social Psychology, 63,* 466–492.

Sears, R. R. (1977). Sources of life satisfactions of the Terman gifted men. *American Psychologist, 32,* 119–128.

Sebeok, T. A., & Rosenthal, R. (1981). The clever Hans phenomenon. *Annals of the New York Academy of Sciences,* Whole Vol. 364.

Selfridge, O. G. (1955). Pattern recognition and modern computers. *Proceedings of the Western Joint Computer Conference.* New York: Institute of Electrical and Electronics Engineers.

Seligman, M. E. P. (1971). Preparedness and phobias. *Behavior Therapy, 2,* 307–320.

Seligman, M. E. P. (1975). *Helplessness: On depression, development, and death.* San Francisco: Freeman.

Seligman, M. E. P., & Maier, S. F. (1967). Failure to escape traumatic shock. *Journal of Experimental Psychology, 74,* 1–9.

Selman, R. (1980). *The growth of interpersonal understanding.* New York: Academic Press.

Selye, H. (1956). *The stress of life.* New York: McGraw-Hill.

Selye, H. (1974). *Stress without distress.* New York: New American Library.

Shafii, M., Carrigan, S., Whittinghill, J. R., & Derrick, A. (1985). Psychological autopsy of completed suicide in children and adolescents. *American Journal of Psychiatry, 142,* 1061–1064.

Shapiro, A. K. (1960). A contribution to a history of the placebo effect. *Behavioral Science, 5,* 109–135.

Shapiro, S., Skinner, E. A., Kessler, L. G., Korff, M. Von, German, P. S., Tischler, F. L., Leaf, P. J., Benham, L., Cottler, L., & Regier, D. A. (1984). Utilization of health and mental health services. *Archives of General Psychiatry, 41,* 971–978.

Shatz, M., Wellman, H. M., & Silber, S. (1983). The acquisition of mental verbs: A systematic investigation of the first reference to mental state. *Cognition, 14,* 301–321.

Sheehy, G. (1976). *Passages: Predictable crises of adult life.* New York: Dutton.

Sheffield, F. D. (1966). New evidence on the drive-induction theory of reinforcement. In R. N. Haber (Ed.), *Current research in motivation* (pp. 111–22). New York: Holt.

Sheffield, F. D., & Roby, T. B. (1950). Reward value of a non-nutritive sweet taste. *Journal of Comparative and Physiological Psychology, 43,* 471–481.

Sheingold, K., & Tenney, Y. J. (1982). Memory for a salient childhood event. In U. Neisser (Ed.), *Memory observed.* San Francisco: Freeman.

Sheldon, W. (1942). *The varieties of temperament: A psychology of constitutional differences.* New York: Harper.

Shepard, R. N. (1978). Externalization of mental images and the act of creation. In B. S. Randhawa & W. E. Coffman (Eds.), *Visual learning, thinking, and communicating.* New York: Academic Press.

Shepard, R. N., & Cooper, L. A. (1982). *Mental images and their transformations.* Cambridge, MA: MIT Press.

Shepard, R. N., & Jordan, D. S. (1984). Auditory illusions demonstrating that tones are assimilated to an internalized musical scale. *Science, 226,* 1333–1334.

Sheridan, C. L., & King, R. G. (1972). Obedience to authority with an authentic victim. *Proceedings of the 80th Annual Convention, American Psychological Association, Part 1, 7,* 165–166.

Sherif, C. W. (1981, August). *Social and psychological bases of social psychology.* The G. Stanley Hall Lecture on social psychology, presented at the annual convention of the American Psychological Association, Los Angeles.

Sherif, M. (1935). A study of some social factors in perception. *Archives of Psychology, 27* (187).

Sherif, M., Harvey, O. J., White, B. J., Hood, W. E., & Sherif, C. W. (1961). *Intergroup conflict and cooperation: The Robber's Cave experiment.* Norman: University of Oklahoma Press.

Sherif, M., & Sherif, C. W. (1979). Research on intergroup relations. In W. G. Austin & S. Worchel (Eds.), *The social psychology of intergroup relations* (pp. 7–18). Monterey, CA: Brooks/Cole.

Sherman, J. A. (1963). Reinstatement of verbal behavior in a psychotic by reinforcement methods. *Journal of Speech and Hearing Disorders, 28,* 398–401.

Sherman, S. M. (1979). The functional significance of x and y cells in normal and visually deprived cats. *Trends in Neuroscience, 2,* 192–195.

Sherrington, C. S. (1906). *The integrative action of the nervous system.* New York: Scribner.

Sherrod, K., Vietze, P., & Friedman, S. (1978). *Infancy.* Monterey, CA: Brooks/Cole.

Shiffman, S. S., & Erickson, R. P. (1971). A theoretical review: A psychophysical model for gustatory quality. *Physiology and Behavior, 7,* 617–633.

Shirley, M. M. (1931). *The first two years.* Minneapolis: University of Minnesota Press.

Shneidman, E. (1987, March). At the point of no return. *Psychology Today,* pp. 55–59.

Shortliffe, E. H. (1983). Medical consultation systems: Designing for doctors. In M. S. Sime & M. J. Coombs (Eds.), *Designing for human computer communication* (pp. 209–38). London: Academic Press.

Shotter, J. (1984). *Social accountability and selfhood.* Oxford: Blackwell.

Siegel, S. (1977). Morphine tolerance acquisition as an associative process. *Journal of Experimental Psychology: Animal Behavior Processes, 3,* 1–13.

Siegel, S. (1979). The role of conditioning in drug tolerance and addiction. In J. D. Keehn (Ed.), *Psychopathology in animals: Research and clinical applications* (pp. 143–67). New York: Academic Press.

Siegler, R. S. (1983). Information processing approaches to cognitive development. In W. Kessen (Ed.), *Handbook of child psychology: History, theory, and methods* (Vol. 1). New York: Wiley.

Siegman, A. W., & Feldstein, S. (1985). *Multichannel integrations of nonverbal behavior.* Hillsdale, NJ: Erlbaum.

Silberfeld, M. (1978). Psychological symptoms and social supports. *Social Psychiatry, 13,* 11–17.

Silver, R., & Wortman, E. (1980). Coping with undesirable life events. In J. Garber & M. E. P. Seligman (Eds.), *Human helplessness: Theory and application.* New York: Academic Press.

Silverman, L. H. (1976). Psychoanalytic theory: "The reports of my death are greatly exaggerated." *American Psychologist, 31,* 621–637.

Simmel, E. C. (1980). *Early experiences and early behavior: Implications for social development.* New York: Academic Press.

Simon, H. (1955). A behavioral model of rational choice. *Quarterly Journal of Economics, 69,* 99–118.

Simon, H. (1973). The structure of ill-structured problems. *Artificial Intelligence, 4,* 181–202.

Simon, H. (1985). *Using cognitive science to solve human problems.* Presentation at a Science and Public Policy Seminar. Washington, DC: Federation of Behavioral, Psychological, and Cognitive Sciences.

Simon, H. A., & Gilmartin, K. (1973). A simulation of memory for chess positions. *Cognitive, Psychology, 5,* 29–46.

Simpson, E. E. L. (1974). Moral development research: A case study of scientific cultural bias. *Human Development, 17,* 81–106.

Sinclair, J. D. (1983, December). The hardware of the brain. *Psychology Today,* pp. 8, 11, 12.

Singer, C. (1958). *From magic to science: Essays on the scientific twilight.* New York: Dover.

Singer, J. E., Brush, C., & Lublin, S. C. (1965). Some aspects of deindividuation: Identification and conformity. *Journal of Experimental Social Psychology, 1,* 356–378.

Singer, J. L. (1966). *Daydreaming: An introduction to the experimental study of inner experience.* New York: Random House.

Singer, J. L. (1975). Navigating the stream of consciousness: Research in daydreaming and related inner experience. *American Psychologist, 30,* 727–739.

Singer, J. L. (1976). Fantasy: The foundation of serenity. *Psychology Today, 10,* pp. 32ff.

Singer, J. L. (1978). Experimental studies of daydreaming and the stream of thought. In K. S. Pope & J. L. Singer (Eds.), *The stream of consciousness: Scientific investigations into the flow of human experience* (pp. 187–223). New York: Plenum.

Singer, J. L., & McCraven, V. J. (1961). Some characteristics of adult daydreaming. *Journal of Psychology, 51,* 151–164.

Singer, J. L., Singer, D. G., & Rapaczynski, W. S. (1984). Family patterns and television viewing as predictors of children's beliefs and aggression. *Journal of Communication, 34*(2), 73–89.

Sjoberg, B. M., & Hollister, L. F. (1965). The effects of psychotomimetic drugs on primary suggestibility. *Psychopharmacologia, 8,* 251–262.

Skeels, H. M. (1966). Adult status of children with contrasting early life experiences. *Monographs of the Society for Research in Child Development, 31*(3).

Skinner, B. F. (1953). *Science and human behavior.* New York: Macmillan.

Skinner, B. F. (1957). *Verbal behavior.* New York: Appleton-Century-Crofts.

Skinner, B. F. (1966). What is the experimental analysis of behavior? *Journal of the Experimental Analysis of Behavior, 9,* 213–218.

Skolnick, A. (1986). Early attachment and personal relationships across the life course. In P. B. Baltes, D. M. Featherman, & R. M. Lerner (Eds.), *Lifespan development and behavior* (Vol. 7, pp. 173–206). Hillsdale, NJ: Erlbaum.

Sloane, R. B., Staples, F. R., Cristol, A. H., Yorkston, NJ:, & Whipple, K. (1975). *Psychotherapy versus behavior therapy.* Cambridge, MA: Harvard University Press.

Slobin, D. (1979). *Psycholinguistics* (2d ed.). Glenview, IL: Scott, Foresman.

Solvic, P. (1984). *Facts vs. fears: Understanding perceived risk.* Presentation at a Science and Public Policy Seminar. Washington, DC: Federation of Behavioral, Psychological, and Cognitive Sciences.

Smart, M. S., & Smart, R. C. (1973). *Adolescents: Development and relationships.* New York: Macmillan.

Smith, C. A. (1986). *The information structure of the facial expression of emotion.* Dissertation, Stanford University.

Smith, C. A., & Ellsworth, P. C. (1985). Patterns and cognitive appraisal in emotion. *Journal of Personality and Social Psychology, 48,* 813–838.

Smith, C. A., & Ellsworth, P. C. (1987). Patterns of appraisal and emotion related to taking an exam. *Journal of Personality and Social Psychology, 52,* 475–488.

Smith, D. (1982). Trends in counseling and psychotherapy. *American Psychologist, 37,* 802–809.

Smith, D., & Kraft, W. A. (1983). DSM-III: Do psychologists really want an alternative? *American Psychologist, 38,* 777–785.

Smith, E. E., & Medin, D. L. (1981). *Cognitive Science Series: 4. Categories and concepts.* Cambridge, MA: Harvard University Press.

Smith, M. L., & Glass, G. V. (1977). Meta-analysis of psychotherapy outcome studies. *American Psychologist, 32,* 752–760.

Smith, M. L., Glass, G. V., & Miller, T. I. (1980). *The benefits of psychotherapy.* Baltimore: Johns Hopkins University Press.

Smith, S. M., Brown, H. O., Toman, J. E. P., & Goodman, L. S. (1947). The lack of cerebral effects of d-tubercurarine. *Anesthesiology, 8,* 1–14.

Smuts, A. B., & Hagen, J. W. (1985). History and research in child development. *Monographs of the Society for Research in Child Development, 50*(Serial No. 211), 4–5.

Snow, C. P. (1961, January 7). In the name of obedience. *Nation,* 3.

Snowden, C. T. (1969). Motivation, regulation and the control of meal parameters with oral and intragastric feeding. *Journal of Comparative and Physiological Psychology, 69,* 91–100.

Snyder, C. R., & Fromkin, H. L. (1980). *Uniqueness: The human pursuit of difference.* New York: Plenum.

Snyder, C. R., & Smith, T. (1982). Symptoms as self-handicapping strategies: The virtue of old wine in new bottles. In G. Weary & H. Mirels (Eds.), *Integrations of clinical and social psychology.* New York: Oxford University Press.

Snyder, M. (1984). When beliefs create reality. In L. Berkowitz (Ed.), *Advances in experimental social psychology, Vol. 18* (pp. 247–305). New York: Academic Press.

Snyder, M., & Frankel, A. (1976). Observer bias: A stringent test of behavior engulfing the field. *Journal of Personality and Social Psychology, 34,* 857–864.

Snyder, M., & Jones, E. E. (1974). Attitude attribution when behavior is constrained. *Journal of Experimental Social Psychology, 10,* 585–600.

Snyder, M., & Swann, W. B., Jr. (1978a). Behavioral confirmation in social interaction: From social perception to social reality. *Journal of Experimental Social Psychology, 14,* 148–162.

Snyder, M., & Swann, W. B., Jr. (1978b). Hypothesis-testing processes in social interaction. *Journal of Personality and Social Psychology, 36,* 1202–1212.

Snyder, S. H. (1974). Catecholamines as mediators of drug effects in schizophrenia. In F. O. Schmitt & F. G. Worden (Eds.), *The neurosciences: Third study program* (pp. 721–732). Cambridge, MA: MIT Press.

Snyder, S. H., & Childers, S. R. (1979). Opiate receptors and opioid peptides. *Annual Review of Neurosciences, 2,* 35–64.

Snyder, S. H., & Mattysse, S. (1975). *Opiate receptor mechanisms.* Cambridge, MA: MIT Press.

Sorce, J. F., Emde, R. N., Campos, J., & Klinnert, M. D. (1985). Maternal emotional signaling: Its effect on the visual cliff behavior of 1-year-olds. *Developmental Psychology, 21,* 195–200.

Sorenson, R. C. (1973). *Adolescent sexuality in contemporary America.* Cleveland: World.

Spanos, N. P., & Gottlieb, J. (1976). Ergotism and the Salem village witch trials. *Science, 194,* 1390–1394.

Speisman, J. C., Lazarus, R. S., Mordkoff, A. M., & Davison, L. A. (1964). The experimental reduction of stress based on ego-defense theory. *Journal of Abnormal and Social Psychology, 68,* 367–380.

Spelke, E., Hirst, W., & Neisser, U. (1976). Skills of divided attention. *Cognition, 4,* 215–230.

Spence, D. P. (1967). Subliminal perception and perceptual defense: Two sides of a single problem. *Behavioral Science, 12,* 183–193.

Sperling, G. (1960). The information available in brief visual presentations. *Psychological Monographs, 74,* 1–29.

Sperling, G. (1963). A model for visual memory tasks. *Human Factors, 5,* 19–31.

Sperry, R. W. (1952). Neurology and the mind-brain problem. *American Scientist, 40,* 291–312.

Sperry, R. W. (1968). Mental unity following surgical disconnection of the cerebral hemispheres. *The Harvey Lectures,* Series 62. New York: Academic Press.

Spiegel, D., Bloom, J. R., & Yalom, I. (1981). Group support for patients with metastatic cancer. *Archives of General Psychiatry, 38,* 527–533.

Spiro, R. J. (1977). Remembering information from text: The "state of schema" approach. In R. C. Atkinson, R. J. Spiro, & W. E. Montague (Eds.), *Schooling and the acquisition of knowledge.* Hillsdale, NJ: Erlbaum.

Spitz, R. A., & Wolf, K. (1946). Anaclitic depression. *Psychoanalytic Study of Children, 2,* 313–342.

Spitzer, R. (1981, October). Nonmedical myths and the DSM-III. *APA Monitor.*

Springer, S. P., & Deutsch, G. (1984). *Left brain, right brain* (2d ed.). San Francisco: Freeman.

Squire, L. R. (1986). Mechanisms of memory. *Science, 232,* 1612–1619.

Squire, L. R., & Slater, P. C. (1975). Forgetting in very long-term memory as assessed by an improved questionnaire technique. *Journal of Experimental Psychology: Human Learning and Memory, 104,* 50–54.

Squires, S. (1985, August 19). It's hard to tell a lie. *San Francisco Chronicle, This World,* p. 9.

Staats, A. W., Gross, M. C., Guay, P. F., & Carlson, C. C. (1973). Personality and social systems and attitude-reinforcer-discriminative theory: Interest (attitude) formation, function, and measurement. *Journal of Personality and Social Psychology, 26,* 251–261.

Staats, A. W., Minke, K. A., Martin, C. H., & Higa, W. R. (1972). Deprivation-satiation and strength of attitude conditioning: A test of attitude-reinforcer-discriminative theory. *Journal of Personality and Social Psychology, 24,* 178–185.

Staats, A. W., & Staats, C. K. (1958). Attitudes established by classical conditioning. *Journal of Abnormal and Social Psychology, 57,* 37–40.

Stampfl, T. G., & Levis, D. J. (1967). Essentials of implosive therapy: A learning theory-based psychodynamic behavioral therapy. *Journal of Abnormal Psychology, 72,* 496–503.

Stanford Daily. (1982, February 2). pp. 1, 3, 5.

Stangler, R. S., & Printz, A. M. (1980). DSM–III: Psychiatric diagnosis in a university population. *American Journal of Psychiatry, 137,* 937–940.

Stanley, J. (1976). The study of the very bright. *Science, 192,* 668–669.

Stanovich, K. (1986). *How to think straight about psychology.* Glenview, IL: Scott, Foresman.

Stapp, J., & Fulcher, R. (1981). The employment of APA members. *American Psychologist, 36,* 1263–1314.

Stayton, D., Hogan, R., & Ainsworth, M. D. S. (1971). Infant obedience and maternal behavior: The origins of socialization reconsidered. *Child Development, 42,* 1057–1069.

Steers, R. M., Porter, L. W. (1974). The role of task-goal attributes in employee performance. *Psychological Bulletin, 81,* 434–452.

Steiner, J. (1980). The SS yesterday and today: A sociopsychological view. In J. E. Dimsdale (Ed.), *Survivors, victims, and perpetrators: Essays on the Nazi holocaust* (pp. 405–56). Washington, DC: Hemisphere Publishing.

Steininger, M., Newell, J. D., & Garcia, L. T. (1984). *Ethical issues in psychology.* Homewood, IL: Dorsey.

Stellar, E. (1954). The physiology of motivation. *Psychological Review, 61,* 5–22.

Stern, P., & Aronson, E. (Eds.). (1984). *Energy use: The human dimension.* New York: Freeman.

Stern, R. M., & Ray, W. J. (1977). *Biofeedback.* Chicago: Dow Jones-Irwin.

Stern, W. (1914). The psychological methods of testing intelligence. *Educational Psychology Monographs* (No. 13).

Stern, W. C., & Morgane, P. S. (1974). Theoretical view of REM sleep function: Maintenance of catecholomine systems in the central nervous system. *Behavioral Biology, 11,* 1–32.

Sternbach, R. A., & Tursky, B. (1965). Ethnic differences among housewives in psychophysical and skin potential responses to electric shock. *Psychophysiology, 1,* 241–246.

Sternberg, R. (Ed.). (1982). *Handbook of human intelligence.* Cambridge, MA: Cambridge University Press.

Sternberg, R. (1985). *Beyond IQ.* Cambridge, MA: Cambridge University Press.

Sternberg, R. (1986a). Inside intelligence. *American Scientist, 74,* 137–143.

Sternberg, R. (1986b). *Intelligence applied.* San Diego, CA: Harcourt Brace Jovanovich.

Sternberg, R. (1986c). A triangular theory of love. *Psychological Review, 93,* 119–135.

Sternberg, R. J., Conway, B. E., Ketron, J. L., & Bernstein, M. (1981). People's conceptions of intelligence. *Journal of Personality and Social Psychology, 41,* 37–55.

Sternberg, S. (1966). High-speed scanning in human memory. *Science, 153,* 652–654.

Sternberg, S. (1969). Memory-scanning: Mental processes revealed by reaction time experiments. *American Scientist, 57,* 421–457.

Stevens, C. F. (1979). The neuron. *Scientific American, 241*(9), 54–65.

Stevens, S. S. (1961). To honor Fechner and repeal his law. *Science, 133,* 80–86.

Stevens, S. S. (1962). The surprising simplicity of sensory metrics. *American Psychologist, 17,* 29–39.

Stevens, S. S. (1975). In G. Stevens (Ed.), *Psychophysics: Introduction to Its perceptual, neutral, and social Prospects.* New York: Wiley.

Storms, M. (1973). Videotape and the attribution process: Reversing actors' and observers' points of view. *Journal of Personality and Social Psychology, 27,* 165–175.

Storms, M. D. (1980). Theories of sexual orientation. *Journal of Personality and Social Psychology, 38,* 783–792.

Storms, M. D. (1981). A theory of erotic orientation development. *Psychological Review, 88,* 340–353.

Strack, S., & Coyne, J. C. (1983). Social confirmation of dysphoria: Shared and private reactions to depression. *Journal of Personality and Social Psychology, 50,* 149–167.

Straub, E. (1974). Helping a distressed person: Social, personality, and stimulus determinants. In L. Berkowitz (Ed.), *Advances in experimental and social psychology* (Vol. 7). New York: Academic Press.

Stromeyer, D. F., Psotka, J. (1970). The detailed texture of eidetic images. *Nature, 225,* 346–349.

Strong, E. K. (1927). Differentiation of certified public accountants from other occupational groups. *Journal of Educational Psychology, 18,* 227–238.

Stroop, J. R. (1935). Studies of interference in serial verbal reactions. *Journal of Experimental Psychology, 18,* 643–662.

Stuart, R. B. (1971). Behavioral contracting with families of delinquents. *Journal of Behavior Therapy and Experimental Psychiatry, 2,* 1–11.

Suedfeld, P. (1980). *Restricted environmental stimulation: Research and clinical applications.* New York: Wiley.

Sullivan, H. S. (1953). *The interpersonal theory of psychiatry.* New York: Norton.

Sundberg, N. D. (1977). *Assessment of persons.* Englewood Cliffs, NJ: Prentice-Hall.

Sundberg, N. D., & Matarazzo, J. D. (1979). Psychological assessment of individuals. In M. E. Meyer (Ed.), *Foundations of contemporary psychology* (pp. 580–617). New York: Oxford University Press.

Swann, W. B., Jr. (1985). The self as architect of social reality. In B. Schlenker (Ed.), *The self and social life* (pp. 100–26). New York: McGraw-Hill.

Swazey, J. P. (1974). *Chlorpromazine in psychiatry: A study of therapeutic innovation.* Cambridge, MA: MIT Press.

Sweet, W. H., Ervin, F., & Mark, V. H. (1969). The relationship of violent behavior to focal cerebral disease. In S. Garattini & E. Sigg (Eds.), *Aggressive behavior.* New York: Wiley.

Swift, W. J., Andrews, D., & Barklage, N. E. (1986). The relationship between affective disorders and eating disorders: A review of the literature. *American Journal of Psychiatry, 143,* 290–299.

Szasz, T. S. (1961). *The myth of mental illness.* New York: Harper & Row.

Szasz, T. S. (1977). *The manufacture of models.* New York: Dell.

Szasz, T. S. (1979). *The myth of psychotherapy.* Garden City, NY: Doubleday.

T

Tajfel, H. (1970). Experiments in intergroup discrimination. *Scientific American, 223,* 96–102.

Tanner, J. M. (1962). *Growth at adolescence* (2d ed.). Oxford: Blackwell Scientific Publications.

Tapp, J. L. (1976). Psychology and the law: An overture. *Annual Review of Psychology, 27,* 359–404.

Targ, R., & Harary, K. (1984). *The mind race: Understanding and using psychic abilities.* New York: Villard Books.

Tarpy, R. M. (1982). *Principles of animal learning and motivation.* Glenview, IL: Scott, Foresman.

Tart, C. T. (1969). *Altered states of consciousness.* New York: Wiley.

Tart, C. T. (1971). *On being stoned: A psychological investigation of marijuana intoxication.* Palo Alto, CA: Science and Behavior Books.

Taylor, D. A., & Altman, I. (1987). Communication in interpersonal relationships: Social penetration processes. In M. Roloff & G. Miller (Eds.), *Exploration in interpersonal communication* (2d ed.). Beverly Hills, CA: Sage.

Taylor, F. W. (1911). *Principles of scientific management.* New York: Harper & Row.

Taylor, J. A. (1951). The relationship of anxiety to the conditioned eyelid response. *Journal of Experimental Psychology, 41,* 81–92.

Taylor, S. E. (1980). The interface of cognitive and social psychology. In J. H. Harvey (Ed.), *Cognition, social behavior, and the environment* (pp. 189–211). Hillsdale, NJ: Erlbaum.

Taylor, S. E. (1982). The availability bias in social perception and interaction. In D. Kahneman, P. Slovic, & A. Tversky (Eds.), *Judgment under uncertainty: Heuristics and biases* (pp. 190–200). Cambridge: Cambridge University Press.

Taylor, S. E. (1986). *Health psychology.* New York: Random House.

Taylor, S. E., Crocker, J., Fiske, S. T., Sprinzen, M., & Winkler, J. D. (1979). The generalizability of salience effects. *Journal of Personality and Social Psychology, 39.*

Taylor, S. P., Vardaris, R. M., Rawtich, A. B., Gammon, C. B., Cranston, J. W., & Lubetkin, A. I. (1976). The effects of alcohol and delta-9-tetrahydrocannabinol on human physical aggression. *Aggressive Behavior, 2,* 153–161.

Taylor, W., Pearson, J., Mair, A., & Burns, W. (1965). Study of noise and hearing in jute weaving. *Journal of the Acoustical Society of America, 38,* 113–120.

Teitelbaum, P. (1966). The use of operant methods in the assessment and control of motivational states. In W. K. Honig (Ed.), *Operant behavior.* New York: Appleton-Century-Crofts.

Teitelbaum, P. (1977). The physiological analysis of motivated behavior. In P. Zimbardo & F. L. Ruch, *Psychology and Life* (9th ed., Diamond Printing). Glenview, IL: Scott, Foresman.

Tellegen, A., & Atkinson, S. (1974). Openness to absorbing and self-altering experiences ("absorption"), a trait related to hypnosis. *Journal of Abnormal Psychology, 83,* 268–277.

Temoskok, L. (1987, in press). Psychoimmunology and AIDS. *Clinical Immunology Newsletter.*

Temoshok, L., Sweet, M. D., & Zick, J. (1987, in press). A three city comparison of the public's knowledge and attitudes about AIDS. *Psychology and Health: An International Journal.*

Tenopyr, M. L., & Oeltjen, P. D. (1982). Personnel selection and classification. *Annual Review of Psychology, 33,* 581–618.

Terman, L. M. (1916). *The measurement of intelligence.* Boston: Houghton-Mifflin.

Terman, L. M. (1925). *Genetic studies of genius: Vol 1. Mental and physical traits of a thousand gifted children.* Stanford, CA: Stanford University Press.

Terman, L. M., & Merrill, M. A. (1937). *Measuring intelligence.* Boston: Houghton-Mifflin.

Terman, L. M., & Merrill, M. A. (1960). *The Stanford-Binet intelligence scale.* Boston: Houghton-Mifflin.

Terman, L. M., & Merrill, M. A. (1972). *Stanford-Binet intelligence scale—manual for the third revision, Form L–M.* Boston: Houghton-Mifflin.

Terman, L. M., & Oden, M. H. (1947). The gifted child grows up. *Genetic studies of genius* (Vol. 4). Stanford, CA: Stanford University Press.

Terman, L. M., & Oden, M. H. (1959). The gifted group at mid-life. *Genetic studies of genius: Vol. 5.* Stanford, CA: Stanford University Press.

Terrace, H. (1979). *Nim: A chimpanzee who learned sign language.* New York: Knopf.

Terrace, H. (1985). In the beginning was the "name." *American Psychologist, 40,* 1011–1028.

Thienes-Hontos, P., Watson, C. G., & Kucala, T. (1982). Stress-disorder symptoms in Vietnam and Korean War veterans. *Journal of Consulting and Clinical Psychology, 50,* 558–561.

Thigpen, C. H., & Cleckley, H. A. (1957). *Three faces of Eve.* New York: McGraw-Hill.

Thompson, D. A., & Campbell, R. G. (1977). Hunger in humans induced by 2-Deoxy-D-Glucose: Glucoprivic control of taste preference and food intake. *Science, 198,* 1065–1068.

Thompson, J. A. (1985). *Psychological aspects of nuclear war.* Chichester: The British Psychological Society.

Thompson, M. J., & Harsha, D. W. (1984, January). Our rhythms still follow the African sun. *Psychology Today,* 50–54.

Thompson, P. (1980). Margaret Thatcher: A new illusion. *Perception, 9,* 483–484.

Thompson, R. F. (1972). Sensory preconditioning. In R. F. Thompson & J. F. Voss (Eds.), *Topics in learning and performance.* New York: Academic Press.

Thompson, R. F. (1975). *Introduction to physiological psychology.* New York: Harper & Row.

Thompson, R. F. (1984, February 4), Searching for memories: Where and how are they stored in your brain? *Stanford Daily.*

Thompson, R. F. (1986). The neurobiology of learning and memory. *Science, 233,* 941–944.

Thoresen, C. E., & Eagleston, J. R. (1983). Chronic stress in children and adolescents. *Theory into Practice, 22,* 48–56. [Special edition: Coping with stress.]

Thorndike, E. L. (1898). Animal intelligence. *Psychological Review Monograph Supplement, 2* (4, Whole No. 8).

Thorndyke, P. W., & Hayes-Roth, B. (1979). *Spatial knowledge acquisition from maps and navigation.* Paper presented at the Psychonomic Society Meeting, San Antonio, TX.

Thornton, E. M. (1984). *The Freudian fallacy: An alternative view of Freudian theory.* New York: The Dial Press/Doubleday.

Tillich, P. (1952). *The courage to be.* New Haven, CT: Yale University Press.

Timiras, P. S. (1978). Biological perspectives on aging. *American Scientist, 66,* 605–613.

Titchener, E. B. (1898). The postulates of structural psychology. *Philosophical Review, 7,* 449–453.

Tizzard B., & Hodges, J. (1978). The effect of early institutional rearing on the development of eight-year-old children. *Journal of Child Psychology and Psychiatry, 19,* 99–118.

Toch, H. (1969). *Violent men.* Chicago: Aldine.

Tolman, E. C. (1948). Cognitive maps in rats and men. *Psychological Review, 55,* 189–208.

Tolman, E. C., & Honzik, C. H. (1930). "Insight" in rats. *University of California Publications in Psychology, 4,* 215–232.

Tomkins, S. (1962). *Affect, imagery, consciousness* (Vol. 1). New York: Springer.

Tomkins, S. (1981). The quest for primary motives: Biography and autobiography of an idea. *Journal of Personality and Social Psychology, 41,* 306–329.

Tourangeau, R., & Ellsworth, P. C. (1979). The role of facial response in the experience of emotion. *Journal of Personality and Social Psychology, 37,* 1519–1531.

Townsend, J. T. (1972). Some results concerning the identifiability of parallel and serial processes. *British Journal of Mathematical and Statistical Psychology, 25,* 168–199.

Tranel, D., & Damasio, A. R. (1985). Knowledge without awareness: An autonomic index of facial recognition by prosopagnosics. *Science, 228,* 1453–1454.

Treisman, A. (1960). Contextual cues in selective listening. *Quarterly Journal of Experimental Psychology, 12,* 242–248.

Treisman, A. (1986). Features and objects in visual processing. *Scientific American, 254,* 114–125.

Triandis, H. C., & Draguns, J. G. (Eds.). (1980). *Handbook of cross-culture psychology: Vol. 6. Psychopathology.* Boston: Allyn & Bacon.

Triplett, N. (1897). The dynamagenic factors in pacemaking and competition. *American Journal of Psychology, 9,* 507–533.

Trivers, R. L. (1983). The evolution of cooperation. In D. L. Bridgeman (Ed.), *The nature of pro-social behavior.* New York: Academic Press.

Tronick, E., Als, H., & Brazelton, T. B. (1980). Moradic phases: A structural description analysis of infant-mother face to face interaction. *Merrill-Palmer Quarterly, 26,* 3–24.

Trotter, R. J. (1987, February). Stop blaming yourself. *Psychology Today,* pp. 30–39.

Tryon, W. W. (1979). The test-trait fallacy. *American Psychologist, 34,* 402–406.

Tucker, O. M. (1981). Lateral brain functions, emotion, and conceptualization. *Psychological Bulletin, 89,* 19–46.

Tulving, E. (1972). Episodic and semantic memory. In E. Tulving & W. Dondaldson (Eds.), *Organization of memory. New York: Academic Press.*

Tulving, E. (1983). *Elements of episodic memory.* Oxford: Clarendon Press.

Tulving, E. (1985). Memory and consciousness. *Canadian Psychology, 26,* 1–12.

Tulving, E., & Pearlstone, Z. (1966). Availability versus accessibility of information in memory for words. *Journal of Verbal Learning and Verbal Behavior, 5,* 381–391.

Turnbull, C. (1962). *The forest people.* New York: Simon & Schuster.

Turner, R. H., & Killian, L. M. (1972). *Collective behavior* (2d ed.). Englewood Cliffs, NJ: Prentice-Hall.

Tversky, A., & Kahneman, D. (1973). Availability: A heuristic for judging frequency and probability. *Cognitive Psychology, 5,* 207–232.

Tversky, A., & Kahneman, D. (1980). Causal schemata in judgments under uncertainty. In M. Fishbein (Ed.), *Progress in social psychology.* Hillsdale, NJ: Erlbaum.

Tversky, A., & Kahneman, D. (1986). Rational choice and the framing of decisions. *Journal of Business, 59,* S251–S278.

Tversky, B. (1981). Distortions in memory for maps. *Cognitive Psychology, 13,* 407–433.

Twain, M. [S. L. Clemens]. (1923). *Mark Twain's speeches.* New York: Harper & Row.

Tyler, L. E. (1965). *The psychology of human differences* (3d ed.). New York: Appleton-Century-Crofts.

Tyler, L. E. (1974). *Individual differences.* Englewood Cliffs, NJ: Prentice-Hall.

Tzeng, O. J. L., & Wang, W. S. Y. (1983). The first two R's. *American Scientist, 71,* 238–243.

U

Ullmann, L. P., & Krasner, L. (1975). *Psychological approach to abnormal behavior* (2d ed.). Englewood Cliffs, NJ: Prentice-Hall.

Ultan, R. (1969). Some general characteristics of interrogative systems. *Working Papers in Language Universals, 1,* 41–63.

Underwood, B. J. (1948). Retroactive and proactive inhibition after five and forty-eight hours. *Journal of Experimental Psychology, 38,* 28–38.

Underwood, B. J. (1949). Proactive inhibition as a function of time and degree of prior learning. *Journal of Experimental Psychology, 39,* 24–34.

United Press International. (1984, April 12). Testimony on child molesting. (Press Release, Washington, DC: Senate Judiciary Subcommittee hearings on Child Molesting.)

U. S., Bureau of the Census. (1983). *American in transition: An aging society* (Current Population Reports, Series P–23, No., 128). Washington, DC: U. S. Government Printing Office.

U. S., Bureau of the Census. (1984a). *Educational attainment in the United States: March 1981 and 1980* (Current Population Reports, Series P-20, No. 390). Washington, DC: U. S. Government Printing Office.

U. S., Bureau of the Census. (1984b). *Population characteristics* (Current Population Reports, Series P-20, No. 394). Washington, DC: U. S. Government Printing Office.

U. S., Bureau of the Census. (1985a). *Marital status and living arrangements: March 1984* (Current Population Reports, Series P-20, No. 399). Washington, DC: U. S. Government Printing Office.

U. S., Bureau of the Census. (1985b). *Statistical abstract of the United States: 1986* (106th ed.). Washington, DC: U. S. Government Printing Office.

U. S., Bureau of the Census. (1986a). *Demographic and socioeconomic aspects of aging in the United States* (Current Population Reports, Series P-23, No. 138). Washington, DC: U. S. Government Printing Office.

U. S., Bureau of the Census. (1986b). *Money income and poverty status of families and persons in the United States: 1985* (Current Population Report, Series P-60, No. 154). Washington, DC: U. S. Government Printing Office.

U. S., Department of Health, Education, and Welfare. (1979). *Healthy people: The Surgeon General's report on health promotion and disease prevention* (USPHS Publication No. 79–55071). Washington, DC: U. S. Government Printing Office.

U. S., National Center for Health Statistics. (1984). *Vital statistics of the United States.* Quoted in U. S., Department of Commerce, Bureau of the Census, *Statistical Abstract of the United States* (104th ed.). Washington, DC: U. S. Government Printing Office.

U. S. Public Health Service. (1986). *Surgeon General's report on Acquired Immune Deficiency Syndrome.* Washington, DC: U. S. Government Printing Office.

"U. S. Women Today." (1983). *New York Times* poll taken Nov. 11–20, 1983, reported in *International Herald Tribune.*

V

Vaillant, G. E. (1977). *Adaptation to Life.* Boston: Little, Brown.

Valle, V. A., & Frieze, I. H. (1976). Stability of causal attributions as a mediator in changing expectations for success. *Journal of Personality and Social Psychology, 33,* 579–587.

Van Wagener, W., & Herren, R. (1940). Surgical division of commissural pathways in the corpus callosum. *Archives of Neurology and Psychiatry, 44,* 740–759.

Vasari, G. (1967). *Lives of the most eminent painters.* New York: Heritage.

Vaughan, E. (1977). Misconceptions about psychology among introductory psychology students. *Teaching of Psychology, 4,* 138–141.

Vaughan, E. (1986). *Some factors influencing the nonexperts' perception and evaluation of environmental aids.* Unpublished doctoral dissertation, Stanford University, CA.

Vogel, F., & Motulsky, A. G. (1982). *Human genetics.* New York: Springer-Verlag.

von Hofsten, C., & Lindhagen, K. (1979). Observations on the development of reaching for moving objects. *Journal of Child Psychology, 28,* 158–173.

Vonnegut, M. (1975). *The Eden express.* New York: Bantam.

Von Wright, J. M., Anderson, K. & Stenham, U. (1975). Generalization of conditioned GSRs in dichotic listening. In P. M. A. Rabbit & S. Dornic (Eds.), *Attention and performance* (pp. 194–204). New York: Academic Press.

Vroom, V. H. (1964). *Work and motivation.* New York: Wiley.

W

Wahba, M. A., & Bridwell, L. G. (1976). Maslow reconsidered: A review of research in the need hierarchy theory. *Organizational Behavior and Human Performance, 15,* 212–240.

Waldron, I. (1976, March). Why do women live longer than men? *Journal of Human Stress,* 2–13.

Waldron, T. P. (1985). *Principles of language and mind: An evolutionary theory of meaning.* Boston: Routledge and Kegan Paul.

Waldrop, M. M. (1984). Artificial intelligence: I. Into the world (research news). *Science, 223,* 802–805.

Waldvogel, S. (1948). The frequency and affective character of childhood memories. *Psychological Monographs, 62* (Whole No. 291).

Walker, L. (1984). Sex differences in the development of moral reasoning: A critical review. *Child Development, 55,* 667–691.

Wallach, M. A., & Wallach, L. (1983). *Psychology's sanction for selfishness.* San Francisco: Freeman.

Waller, J. H. (1971). Achievement and social mobility: Relationships among IQ score, education, and occupation in two generations. *Social Biology, 18,* 252–259.

Wallis, C. (1984, June 11). Unlocking pain's secrets. *Time,* pp. 58–66.

Walsh, R. N., & Vaughan, F. (Eds.), (1980). *Beyond ego: Transpersonal dimensions in psychology.* Los Angeles: Tarcher.

Walster, E., & Walster, G. W. (1978). *A new look at love.* Reading, MA: Addison-Wesley.

Walters, C. C., & Grusec, J. E. (1977). *Punishment.* San Francisco: Freeman.

Walters, R. G. (1974). *Primers for prudery: Sexual advice to Victorian America.* Englewood Cliffs, NJ: Prentice-Hall.

Walton, R. E. (1977). Successful strategies for diffusing work innovations. *Journal of Contemporary Business, 6,* 1–22.

Wanous, J. P. (1980). *Organizational entry: Recruitment, selection, and socialization of newcomers.* Reading, MA: Addison-Wesley.

Ward, W. C., Kogan, N., & Pankove, E. (1972). Incentive effects in children's creativity. *Child Development, 43*(2), 669–676.

Warden, C. J. (1931). *Animal motivation: Experimental studies on the albino rat.* New York: Columbia University Press.

Warshaw, L. (1979). *Managing stress.* Reading, MA: Addison-Wesley.

Watson, J. B. (1913). Psychology as the behaviorist views it. *Psychological Review, 20,* 158–177.

Watson, J. B. (1919). *Psychology from the standpoint of a behaviorist.* Philadelphia: Lippincott.

Watson, J. B. (1926). *Behaviorism.* New York: Norton.

Watson, J. B. (1930). *Behaviorism.* New York: Norton.

Watson, J. B., & Rayner, R. (1920). Conditioned emotional reactions. *Journal of Experimental Psychology, 3,* 1–14.

Watson, R. I., Jr. (1973). Investigation into deindividuation using a cross-cultural survey technique. *Journal of Personality and Social Psychology, 25,* 342–345.

Weakland, J. H., Fish, R., Watzlawick, P., & Bodin, A. M. (1974). Brief therapy: Focused problem resolution. *Family Process, 13,* 141–168.

Webb, W. B. (1974). Sleep as an adaptive response. *Perceptual and Motor Skills, 38,* 1023–1027.

Webb, W. B. (1981). The return of consciousness. In L. T. Benjamin, Jr. (Ed.), *The G. Stanley Hall lecture series* (Vol. 1). Washington, DC: American Psychological Association, *100,* 133–152.

Weber, E. H. (1834). *De pulsu, resorptione, auditu et tactu: Annotationes anatomical et physiological.* Leipzig: Koehler.

Weber, M. (1958). *The Protestant ethic and the spirit of capitalism* (T. Parsons, Trans.). New York: Scribners. (Originally published 1904–5)

Wechsler, D. (1974). *Wechsler intelligence scale for children—revised.* New York: Psychological Corp.

Wechsler, D. (1981). *Manual for the Wechsler Adult Intelligence Scale—revised.* New York: Psychological Corp.

Weick, K. E. (1984). Small wins: Redefining the scale of social problems. *American Psychologist, 39,* 40–49.

Weigel, R. H., & Newman, L. S. (1976). Increasing attitude-behavior correspondence by broadening the scope of the behavioral measure. *Journal of Personality and Social Psychology, 33,* 793–802.

Weil, A. T. (1977). The marriage of the sun and the moon. In N. E. Zinberg (Ed.), *Alternate states of consciousness* (pp. 37–52). New York: Free Press.

Weiner, B. (1980). *Human motivation.* New York: Holt, Rinehart & Winston.

Weiner, B., Frieze, I., Kukla, A., Reed, L., Rest, S., & Rosenbaum, R. M. (1971). Perceiving the causes of success and failure. In E. E. Jones et al. (Eds.), *Attribution: Perceiving* *the causes of behavior.* Morristown, NJ: General Learning Press.

Weiner, B., Russell, D., & Lerman, D. (1978). Affective consequences of causal ascriptions. In J. H. Harvey, W. J. Ickes, & R. F. Kidd (Eds.), *New directions in attribution research* (Vol. 2). Hillsdale NJ: Erlbaum.

Weiner, M. J., & Wright, F. E. (1973). Effects of undergoing arbitrary discrimination upon subsequent attitudes toward a minority group. *Journal of Applied Social Psychology, 3,* 94–102.

Weins, A. N., & Matarazzo, J. D. (1983). Diagnostic interviewing. In M. Hersen, A. E. Kazdin, & A. S., Bellack (Eds.), *The clinical psychology handbook* (pp. 309–28). New York: Pergamon.

Weinstein, N. D. (1980). Unrealistic optimism about future life events. *Journal of Personality and Social Psychology, 39,* 806–820.

Weisenberg, M. (1977). Cultural and racial reactions to pain. In M. Weisenberg (Ed.), *The control of pain.* New York: Psychological Dimensions.

Weiskrantz, L., Warington, E. K., Sanders, M. D., & Marshall, J. (1974). Visual capacity in the hemianopic field following a restricted occipital ablation. *Brain, 97,* 709–728.

Weiss, B., & Laties, V. G. (1962). Enhancement of human performance by caffeine and amphetamines. *Pharmacological Review, 14,* 1–27.

Weiss, R. F., Buchanan, W., Alstatt, L., & Lombardo, J. P. (1971). Altruism is rewarding. *Science, 171,* 1262–1263.

Weiss, R. S. (1973). *Loneliness: The experience of emotional and social isolation.* Cambridge, MA: MIT Press.

Weiss, R. S. (1987). Reflections on the present state of loneliness research. *Journal of Behavior and Personality, 2*(2), 1–16.

Welker, R. L., & Wheatley, K. L. (1977). Differential acquisition of conditioned suppression in rats with increased and decreased luminance levels as CS + S. *Learning and Motivation, 8,* 247–262.

Welner, A., Reish, T., Robbins, I., Fishman, R., & van Doren, T. (1976). Obsessive-compulsive neurosis. *Comprehensive Psychiatry, 17,* 527 539.

Wender, P. H. (1972). Adopted children and their families in the evaluation of nature-nurture interactions in the schizophrenic disorders. *Annual Review of Medicine, 23,* 255–372.

Werner, E. E., & Smith, R. S. (1982). *Vulnerable but invincible: A longitudinal study of resilient children and youth.* New York: McGraw-Hill.

Wertheimer, M. (1923). Untersuchungen zur lehre von der gestalt, II. *Psychologische Forschung, 4,* 301–350.

Wever, E. G. (1949). *Theory of hearing.* New York: Wiley.

Whalen, R., & Simon, N. G. (1984). Biological motivation. *Annual Review of Psychology, 35,* 257–276.

White, B. W., Saunders, F. A., Scadden, L., Bach-Y-Rita, P., & Collins, C. C. (1970). Seeing with the skin. *Perception & Psychophysics,* 7(1), 23–27.

White, G. L., Fishbein, S., & Rutstein, J. (1981). Passionate love and the misattribution of arousal. *Journal of Personality and Social Psychology, 41,* 56–62.

White, M. D., & White, C. A. (1981). Involuntarily committed patients' constitutional right to refuse treatment. *American Psychologist, 36,* 953–962.

White, R. K. (1952). *Lives in progress.* New York: Dryden Press.

Whorf, B. L. (1956). *Language, thought, and reality.* Cambridge, MA: MIT Press.

Wickelgren, W. A. (1974). *How to solve problems.* San Francisco: Freeman.

Wicker, A. W. (1969). Attitudes versus actions: The relationship of verbal and overt behavioral responses to attitude objects. *Journal of Social Issues, 25*(4), 41–78.

Wicklund, R. A., & Brehm, J. W. (1976). *Perspectives on cognitive dissonance.* Hillsdale, NJ: Erlbaum.

Wiggins, J. S. (1973). *Personality and prediction: Principles of personality assessment.* Reading, MA: Addison-Wesley.

Wilcoxon, H. G., Dragoin, W. B., & Kral, P. A. (1971). Illness-induced aversions in rat and quail: Relative salience of visual and gustatory cues. *Science, 171,* 826–828.

Wilder, D. A. (1978). Reduction of intergroup discrimination through individuation of the out-group. *Journal of Personality and Social Psychology, 36,* 1361–1374.

Williams, J. H. (1983). *The psychology of women* (2d ed.). New York: Norton.

Williams, R. L., & Rivers, L. W. (1972, September). *The use of standard and nonstandard English in testing black children.* Paper presented at the meeting of the American Psychological Association, Honolulu, HI.

Wills, T. A. (1981). Downward comparison principles in social psychology. *Psychological Bulletin, 90,* 245–271.

Wilson, E. D., Reeves, A., & Culver, C. (1977). Cerebral commissurotomy for control of intractable seizures. *Neurology, 27,* 708–715.

Wilson, E. O. (1973). The natural history of lions. *Science, 179,* 466–467.

Wilson, J. P. (1980). Conflict, stress, and growth: The effects of war on the psychosocial development of Vietnam veterans. In C. R. Figley & S. Leventman (Eds.), *Strangers at home: Vietnam veterans since the war* (pp. 123–65). New York: Praeger.

Wing, C. W., & Wallach, M. A. (1971). *College admissions and the psychology of talent.* New York: Holt, Rinehart & Winston.

Wingfield, A. (1973). Effects of serial position and set size in auditory recognition memory. *Memory and Cognition, 1,* 53–55.

Wingfield, A., & Byrnes, D. L. (1981). *The psychology of human memory.* New York: Academic Press.

Winton, W. M., Putnam, L. E., & Krauss, R. M. (1984). Facial and autonomic manifestations of the dimensional structure of emotions. *Journal of Experimental Social Psychology, 20,* 196–216.

Wintrob, R. M. (1973). The influence of others; Witchcraft and root-work as explanations of behavior disturbances. *Journal of Nervous and Mental Diseases, 156,* 318–326.

Wispé, L. G., & Drambarean, N. C. (1953). Physiological need, word frequency, and visual duration threshold. *Journal of Experimental Psychology, 46,* 25–31.

Witkin, H. A., Dyk, R. B., Faterson, H. F., Goodenough, D. R., & Karp, S. A. (1962). *Psychological differentiation.* New York: Wiley.

Witkin, H. A., & Goodenough, D. R. (1977). Field dependence and interpersonal behavior. *Psychological Bulletin, 84,* 661–689.

Witkin, H. A., Moore, C. A., Goodenough, D. R., & Cox, P. W. (1977). Field-dependent and field-independent cognitive styles and their educational implications. *Review of Educational Research, 47,* 1–64.

Wolf, M., Risley, T., & Mees, H. (1964). Application of operant conditioning procedures to the behavior problems of an autistic child. *Behavior Research and Therapy, 1,* 305–312.

Wolitzky, D. L., & Wachtel, P. L. (1973). Personality and perception. In B. J. Wolman (Ed.), *Handbook of general psychology* (pp. 826–57). Englewood Cliffs, NJ: Prentice-Hall.

Wolman, C. (1975). Therapy and capitalism. *Issues in Radical Therapy, 3*(1).

Wolpe, J. (1958). *Psychotherapy by reciprocal inhibition.* Stanford, CA: Stanford University Press.

Wolpe, J. (1973). *The practice of behavior therapy* (2d ed.). New York: Pergamon.

Woods, D. L., Hillyard, S. A., Courchesne, E., & Galambos, R. (1980). Electrophysiological signs of split-second decision making. *Science, 207,* 655–657.

Woodworth, R. S. (1918). *Dynamic psychology.* New York: Columbia University Press.

Woodworth, R. S., & Schlossberg, H. (1954). *Experimental psychology* (rev. ed.). New York: Holt.

Woolridge, D. E. (1963). *The machinery of the brain.* New York: McGraw-Hill.

Worthington, E. L., Jr., Martin, G. A., Shumate, M., & Carpenter, J. (1983). The effect of brief Lamaze training and social encouragement on pain endurance in a cold pressor task. *Journal of Applied Social Psychology, 13,* 223–233.

Wundt, W. (1907). *Outlines of psychology* (7th ed.) (C. H. Judd,

Trans.). Leipzig: Englemann. (Originally published 1896)

Wurtman, R. J. (1982). Nutrients that modify brain functions. *Scientific American, 246*(4), 50–59.

Wylie, R. C. (1974). *The self concept.* Lincoln: University of Nebraska Press.

Wynne, L. C., Roohey, M. L., & Doane, J. (1979). Family studies. In L. Bellak (Ed.), *The schizophrenic syndrome.* New York: Basic Books.

Y

Yahraes, H. (1975). *Research in the service of mental health: Summary report of the research task force of the National Institutes of Mental Health (V-5).* Washington, DC: U. S. Government Printing Office.

Yalom, I. D., & Greaves, C. (1977). Group therapy with the terminally ill. *American Journal of Psychiatry, 134,* 396–400.

Yarrow, L. (1975). *Infant and environment: Early cognitive and motivational development.* New York: Halsted.

Yates, B. T. (1980). *Improving effectiveness and reducing costs in mental health.* Springfield, IL: Charles C Thomas.

Yates, B. (1985). *Self-management.* Belmont, CA: Wadsworth.

Yerkes, R. M. (1921). Psychological examining in the United States Army. In R. M. Yerkes (Ed.), *Memoirs of the National Academy of Sciences: Vol. 15.* Washington, DC: U. S. Government Printing Office.

Young, P. T. (1961). *Motivation and emotion.* New York: Wiley.

Young, T. (1807). On the theory of light and colours. In *Lectures in natural philosophy* (Vol. 2, pp. 613–32). London: William Savage.

Yudkin, M. (1984, April). When kids think the unthinkable. *Psychology Today,* pp. 18–20, 24–25.

Z

Zajonc, R. B. (1968). Attitudinal effects of mere exposure. *Journal of Personality and Social Psychology, Monograph Supplement, 9*(2, Part 2), 1–27.

Zajonc, R. B. (1976). Family configuration and intelligence. *Science, 192,* 227–236.

Zajonc, R. B. (1980). Feeling and thinking: Preferences need no inferences. *American Psychologist, 35,* 151–175

Zajonc, R. B. (1984). On the primacy of affect. *American Psychologist, 39,* 117–129.

Zajonc, R. B. (1985a). Emotion and facial efference: A theory reclaimed. *Science, 228,* 15–21.

Zajonc, R. B. (1985b). Emotions and facial expression: Reply to letters to the editor. *Science, 230,* 609, 610, 687.

Zanchetti, A. (1967). Subcortical and cortical mechanisms in arousal and emotional behavior. In G. C. Quarton, T. Melnechuk, & F. O. Schmitt (Eds.), *The neurosciences: A study program.* New York: Rockefeller University Press.

Zborowski, M. (1969). *People in pain.* San Francisco: Jossey-Bass.

Zelnik, M., Kim, Y. J., & Kantner, J. F. (1979). Probabilities of intercourse and conception among U. S. teenage women, 1971–1976. *Family Planning Perspectives, 11,* 177–183.

Zilboorg, G., & Henry, G. W. (1941). *A history of medial psychology.* New York: Norton.

Ziller, R. C. (1964). Individuation and socialization. *Human Relations, 17,* 341–360.

Zimbardo, P. G. (1970). The human choice: Individuation, reason, and order versus deindividuation, impulse, and chaos. In W. J. Arnold & D. Levine (Eds.), *Nebraska symposium on motivation, 1969.* Lincoln: University of Nebraska Press.

Zimbardo, P. G. (1975). On transforming experimental research into advocacy for social change. In M. Deutsch & H. Hornstein (Eds.), *Applying social psychology: Implications for research, practice and training.* Hillsdale, NJ: Erlbaum.

Zimbardo, P. G., Andersen, S. M., & Kabat, L. G. (1981). Induced hearing deficit generates experimental paranoia. *Science, 212,* 1529–1531.

Zimbardo, P. G., & Formica, R. (1963). Emotional comparison and self-esteem as determinants of affiliation. *Journal of Personality, 31,* 141–162.

Zimbardo, P. G., & Montgomery, K. D. (1957). The relative strengths of consummatory responses in hunger, thirst, and exploratory drive. *Journal of Comparative and Physiological Psychology, 50,* 504–508.

Zimbardo, P. G., & Radl, S. (1981). *The shy child.* New York: McGraw-Hill.

Zola, I. K. (1973). Pathways to the doctor—from person to patient. *Social Science and Medicine, 7,* 677–689.

Zubeck, J. P., Pushkar, D., Sansom, W., & Gowing, J. (1961). Perceptual changes after prolonged sensory isolation (darkness and silence). *Canadian Journal of Psychology, 15,* 83–100.

Zucker, R. S., & Lando, L. (1986). Mechanism of transmitter release: Voltage hypothesis and calcium hypothesis. *Science, 231,* 574–579.

Zuckerman, M. (1979). Sensation seeking and risk taking. In C. E. Izard (Ed.), *Emotions in personality and psychopathology.* New York: Plenum.

Acknowledgments

Illustration Credits

Lewis E. Calver: Figures 4.5, 4.7, 4.8, 4.10, 4.12, 4.13, 4.14, 4.15, 5.6, 5.32, 7.6, 9.13
Sara Forbes Woodward: Figures 4.1, 4.2, 4.3, 4.4, 4.6, 4.11, 5.7, 5.8, 5.29, 5.30
Candace Haught: Figures 7-H, 14.3
Precision Graphics: Figures 3.7, 5.9, 5x, 6.1, 6.2, 6.24, 7.7, 7-x, 8.4, 8.5, 9.1, 10.2, 11.3, 13.2, 18.3
Peter Fraterdeus: Calligraphic Alphabet

Photo Credits

All photographs not credited are the property of Scott, Foresman.
Cover: James L. Ballard

Chapter 1

2 UPI/Bettmann Newsphotos
3 Tony Tomsic/SPORTS ILLUSTRATED © Time Inc.
4 Kojo Tanaka
5 Zentralbibliothek Zurich, Ms. C 54 f. 34v-36r
7,xii "Senecio," 1922 by Paul Klee. Kunstmuseum, Basel, © COSMOPRESS, Geneva/SPADEM, Paris/ARS, New York, 1987
8 Marcia Weinstein
11 Mark Tuschman © DISCOVER Magazine 6/84
13 (l) Giraudon/Art Resource, NY (r) Darwin Museum
14 (both) The Bettmann Archive
16 California Institute of Technology
17 (t) Ira Wyamn/Sygma (b) UPI/Bettmann Newsphotos
18 UPI/Bettmann Newsphotos
19 REPRINTED FROM PSYCHOLOGY TODAY MAGAZINE Copyright © 1986 American Psychological Association
20 (both) The Bettmann Archive

Chapter 2

26 (t) Pictorial Parade (b) Wide World
27 Sidney Harris
29 Rick Browne/Stock, Boston
31 Jerry Howard/Positive Images
32 Sidney Harris
37 Richard Wood/The Picture Cube
38 Rick Friedman/Black Star
39 Christopher Springmann
42 Jim Pickerell/Click/Chicago
46 Sidney Harris

Chapter 3

58 Bibliothèque Nationale, Paris
64 Carolina Art Association/Gibbes Art Gallery, Charleston, S. C.
69 Carlo Bevilacqua/CEDRI
71 Vic Bider/Click/Chicago
73 James D. Wilson/Woodfin Camp & Assoc.
77 (l) Peter Menzel/Stock, Boston (c) George Godwin/ Monkmeyer (r) Robert Mayer/Click/Chicago
79 (all) Marcia Weinstein
84 Martin Rogers/Stock, Boston
92 Jason Lauré
96 Cenzus/Click/Chicago
98 Harley Schwadron
100 Renate Hiller/Monkmeyer

Chapter 4

106 Roe Di Bona
107 The Bettmann Archive
109 (l) Culver Pictures (r) The Bettmann Archive
120 (both) J.P. Laffont/Sygma
127 Wide World
134 Montreal Neurological Institute
136 Warren Anatomical Museum, Harvard Medical School
137 Brookhaven National Laboratory and State University of New York, Stony Brook
138 Dan McCoy/Rainbow

Chapter 5

143 Stephen Dalton/Photo Researchers
157 Figure 5.10. Courtesy of Munsell Color, Baltimore, Maryland
160 Figure 5.14. MacMillan Science Co., Inc.
162 Figure 5.17. Dr. Phillip G. Zimbardo
165 Figure 5.20. The Kobal Collection. From Frisby, J., *Seeing: Illusion, Brain, and Mind.* Oxford University Press, 1980.
166 Figure 5.22. From Carlson, N. R., *Physiology of Behavior*, 3rd ed. Boston: Allyn and Bacon, 1986
169 Andrew Dalsimer/Bruce Coleman Inc.
175 Louis Psihoyos
180 Marcia Weinstein

Chapter 6

184 Drawing by Chas. Addams; © 1983, The New Yorker Magazine, Inc.
193 "Gestalt Bleue" by Victor Vasarely. Courtesy of the artist.
194 (l) © M.C. Escher Heirs c/o Cordon Art-Baarn, Holland. Collection of C. V. S. Roosevelt, Washington, D.C. (r) "Slave Market with the Disappearing Bust of Voltaire," oil, 1940. The Salvador Dali Museum, St. Petersburg, Florida
195 Figure 6.7. Earth Scenes/Holt Studios
201 Figure 6.17B. Earth Scenes/Esao Hashimoto
207 Figure 6.23. Susan Schwartzenberg/The Exploratorium for Scott, Foresman
209 Figure 6.25. Dr. Peter Thompson, University of York, England

Chapter 7

220 SIU Biomedical Communications/Photo Researchers
223 (l) Linda Koebner/Bruce Coleman Inc. (r) Jeff Foott
225 Alan Carey/The Image Works
227 Joe Sohm/The Image Works
228 Peter Fronk/Click/Chicago
231 Donald Smetzer/Click/Chicago
239 Norman R. Thompson/Taurus Photos, Inc.
240 Figure 7.8. DREAMSTAGE Scientific Catalog © 1977 J. Allan Hobson and Hoffmann-La Roche Inc.
242 "The Far Side" cartoon is reprinted by permission of Chronicle Features, San Francisco
244 Otto Muller Verlag, Salzburg

246 Randa Bishop/DPI
249 Figure 7.12. Marcia Weinstein
250 (1) P. Chock/Stock, Boston (r) R. D. Ullman/Taurus Photos, Inc.
251 National Child Safety Council
252 Collection of Ronald K. Siegel

Chapter 8

261 Jerry Howard/Positive Images
262 The Bettmann Archive
267 From John Watson's 1919 film *Experimental Investigation of Babies*, courtesy of Prof. Ben Harris
268 Vloo/Stockphotos, Inc.
270 Tannenbaum/Sygma
272 The Granger Collection, New York
274 Joe McNally/Wheeler Pictures
275 (1) Hank Morgan © DISCOVER Magazine 10/85
278 Malcolm Hancock
280 Yerkes Primate Research Center, Emory University
281 Bill Gallery/Stock, Boston
282 Barbara Van Cleve/Click/Chicago
283 Flip Nicklin
284 REPRINTED FROM PSYCHOLOGY TODAY MAGAZINE Copyright © 1985 American Psychological Association
289 Animal Behavior Enterprises, Inc.
293 Focus On Sports
296 (all) Norman Baxley © DISCOVER Magazine 5/84

Chapter 9

300 Don & Pat Valenti
301 Ellis Herwig/The Picture Cube
308 LRN/Southern Light
313 Ellis Herwig/The Picture Cube
316 Sidney Harris
321 Milt & Joan Mann/Cameramann International, Ltd.
324 Figure 9.12. Cartoon from *Transactions of the New York Academy of Sciences*, Vol. 8, No. 2, Fig. 1, p. 66, G. W. Allport and L. J. Postman. Copyright The New York Academy of Sciences, 1945. Reprinted by permission.
326 (both) Pete Souza/The White House
327 Sidney Harris
329 William Hubbell/Woodfin Camp & Assoc.

Chapter 10

336 From Krall, *Denkende Tiere*, 1912
337 © 1985, BLOOM COUNTY, Washington Post Writers Group. Reprinted with permission.
338 (1) Yves De Braine/Black Star (r) Stephen Sherman
341 © 1976 by B. Kliban. Reprinted from *Never Eat Anything Bigger than Your Head*. By permission of The Workman Publishing Co., New York.
342 The museum of Modern Art/Film Stills Archive
345 Jean-Claude Lejeune
350 Chad Slattery
355 Ellis Herwig/The Picture Cube
364 Joe Feingersh/Tom Stack & Assoc.
371,xii Paul Fusco/Magnum

Chapter 11

374 Focus On Sports
377 (both) Rich Clarkson/SPORTS ILLUSTRATED © Time Inc.
381 Robert P. Carr
385 Spencer Swanger/Tom Stack & Assoc.
387 John Sanderson
391 (both), **xviii** (6) (both) Wolfgang Bayer
393 © 1983, Punch Publs. Ltd. Reprinted with permission, Los Angeles Times Syndicate
401 John Feingersh/Tom Stack & Assoc.
402 REPRINTED FROM PSYCHOLOGY TODAY MAGAZINE Copyright © 1986 American Psychological Association
405, xvii George H. Harrison
412 (all) © 1975, 1986 Paul Ekman, Ph.D.
413 Enrico Ferorelli/Dot
415 Pete Souza/The White House

Chapter 12

428 John Anderson/Click/Chicago
432 Lawrence Manning/Click/Chicago
433 Ellis Herwig/Taurus Photos, Inc.
437, xviii Robert Frerck/Odyssey Productions, Chicago
438 Mikki Ansin/Taurus Photos, Inc.
443 REPRINTED FROM PSYCHOLOGY TODAY MAGAZINE Copyright © 1986 American Psychological Association
448 Focus On Sports

Chapter 13

459 Bruce Roberts/Photo Researchers
465 REPRINTED FROM PSYCHOLOGY TODAY MAGAZINE Copyright © 1985 American Psychological Association
467, xix Gus Giordano Dance Co.; Jon Randolph/WTTW-TV
469 Brown Brothers
471 (1) Edward Clark, LIFE Magazine © 1949 Time Inc. (r) Terry Parke/Gamma-Liaison
475 Peter Fronk/Click/Chicago
477 Figure 13.7. Reprinted by permission of the publishers from THEMATIC APPERCEPTION TEST, by Henry A. Murray, Cambridge, Massachusetts: Harvard University Press, Copyright © 1943 by the President and Fellows of Harvard College; © 1971 by Henry A. Murray.
478 Alex Greely/Alpha
479 Louis Psihoyos
481 Giraudon/Art Resource, NY
482 REPRINTED FROM PSYCHOLOGY TODAY MAGAZINE Copyright © 1985 American Psychological Association

Chapter 14

488 Bohdan Hrynewych/Southern Light
491 Courtesy of Dr. Joseph Matarazzo
492 Robert McElroy/Woodfin Camp & Assoc.
494 Richard Kalvar/Magnum
498 Randy Taylor/Black Star
500 Thomas McInnes/The Picture Cube
502 Martha Cooper/Peter Arnold, Inc.
504 Frank Siteman/The Picture Cube
507 Bob Daemmrich/Stock, Boston
508 (t) Frederique Hibon/Sygma (b) Drawing by Christine Blas, age 10, Duncan, B. C. From *Dear World: The Canadian Children's Project*. Copyright © 1986 Global Ed/Med Supplies (Canada) Inc. Methuen Publications, Ontario, Canada.
511 Steve Schapiro/Sygma

Chapter 15

518 (t,c) Don & Pat Valenti (b) Jack Spratt/The Image Works
521 Courtesy of The Advertising Council Inc. and the American Mental Health Fund
522 Wide World
526 (1) Michael Ochs Archives/Venice, CA (r) Bonnie Schiffman/Gamma-Liaison
528 Doug Menuez/Picture Group
531 Harley Schwadron
533 Susan Greenwood/Gamma-Liaison
535 Charles Gatewood/The Image Works
537 Jim McNee/Tom Stack & Assoc.
539 Ben Weaver/Camera 5
544 Elinor S. Beckwith/Taurus Photos, Inc.

546 Courtesy of the Essex Institute, Salem, MA
549 NIMH
552 Meri Houtchens-Kitchens/The Picture Cube
556 Ethan Hoffman/Archive

Chapter 16

562 Copyright © 1985 S. Gross
565 (l) The Trustees of Sir John Soane's Museum (r) National Library of Medicine
568 Historical Pictures Service, Chicago
570 Dr. Margaret S. Mahler
571 (t) G. Paul Bishop (b) Rick Friedman/Black Star
573 Curt Gunther/Camera 5
576 Figure 16.1. Dr. Philip G. Zimbardo
577 Rick Friedman/Black Star
583 Bohdan Hrynewych/Southern Light
584 James D. Wilson/Woodfin Camp & Assoc.
587 Obremski/The Image Bank
588 James D. Wilson/Woodfin Camp & Assoc.
594 Bob Adelman

Chapter 17

603 Janice Fullman/The Picture Cube
605 Ethan Hoffman/Archive
606 Michael Philip Manheim/Southern Light
609 Harry Wilks/Stock, Boston
610 Charles Gupton/Stock, Boston
613 J. P. Laffont/Sygma
616 Ellis Herwig/Taurus Photos, Inc.
619 Charles Gupton/Southern Light
621 UPI/Bettmann Newsphotos
624 Lenore Weber/Taurus Photos, Inc
625 Sam Sweezy/Stock, Boston
629 Philip Jon Bailey/The Picture Cube
634 (both) Courtesy of Mrs. Jane Elliott and ABC Television. Photos by Charlotte Button
635 (both) Courtesy of Dr. Muzafer Sherif, from *An Outline of Social Psychology*, revised edition by Muzafer Sherif and Carolyn W. Sherif. Copyright 1948, 1956 by Harper and Row Publishers, Inc.

Chapter 18

638-639 (all) Dr. Philip G. Zimbardo
644 Baldev/Sygma
645 Lynn M. Stone
648 Frank Siteman/Taurus Photos, Inc.
649 J. P. Laffont/Sygma
651 Reprinted by permission: Tribune Media Services
654, xxi Dr. Philip G. Zimbardo
659 Sygma
662 Dr. Philip G. Zimbardo
664 (all), **xii** (tc) (all) From Keen, S., *Faces of the Enemy: Reflections of the Hostile Imagination*. Copyright © 1986 by Sam Keen. All rights reserved. Harper & Row Publishers, Inc., New York.
667 Charles Gupton/Southern Light
671 Courtesy of The Rouse Company

Literary Credits

Chapter 1

7 From "Misconceptions about Psychology among Introductory Psychology Students." *Teaching Psychology*, 1977, 4, 138–141. Copyright © 1977 by Division Two of the American Psychological Association. Excerpt reprinted by permission.

12 Figures 1.1 & 1.2. Data from "The Employment of APA Members" by Joy Stapp and Robert Fulcher, *American Psychologist*, November 1981. Copyright © 1981 by the American Psychological Association, Inc. Reprinted by permission of the authors.

Chapter 3

60 Table 3.1. From *Child Development* by L. P. Lipsitt and H. W. Reese, p. 18. © 1979 Scott, Foresman and Company.

62 Figure 3.1. From "Adolescent Personality Development and Historical Change: 1970-1972" by J. R. Nesselroade and P. B. Baltes, *Monographs of the Society for Research in Child Development*, 1974, 39 (1, Whole No. 154). © The Society for Research in Child Development, Inc. Reprinted by permission.

68 Figure 3.3. From *The First Two Years* by Mary M. Shirley, by permission of University of Minnesota Press.

70 Figure 3.5. From "Carrying Behavior in Humans: Analysis of Sex Differences" by D. A. Jenni and M. A. Jenni, *Science*, November 19, 1976, Vol. 194, pp. 859-860. Copyright © 1976 by the American Association for the Advancement of Science. Reprinted by permission of the American Association for the Advancement of Science and the authors.

80 Figure 3.7. From "Representing the existence and the location of hidden objects: Object permanence in 6- and 8-month-old infants" by Renee Baillargeon, *Cognition*, 23(1986) 21-41. Reprinted by permission of North-Holland Publishing Company and the author.

83 Table 3.4. From *Perspectives on Childhood Socialization* by J. Clausen. Copyright © 1968 by Little, Brown and Company. Reprinted by permission of the author.

93 From *The Adolescent: A Psychological Self-Portrait*, by Daniel Offer, Eric Ostrov, and Kenneth I. Howard. Copyright © 1981 by Basic Books, Inc. Reprinted by permission of the publisher.

99 Table 3.7. From *Adaptation to Life* by George Vaillant. Copyright © 1977 by George E. Vaillant. By permission of Little, Brown and Company.

Chapter 4

117 Table 4.1. From "Some Synaptic Transmitters and Transmitter Candidates" from *Physiological Psychology* by Mark Rosenzweig and A. L. Leiman. Copyright © 1982 by D. C. Heath and Company. Adapted by permission.

121 Figure 4.6. From "Local, Reflex, and Central Commands Controlling Fill and Siphon Movements in Aplysia" by I. Kupfermann, et al., *Journal of Neurophysiology*, Vol. 37, pp. 996-1019. Copyright © 1974 by American Physiological Society. Reprinted by permission of the publisher.

125 Figure 4.10 & p. 126 Table 4.2. From *Hormones: The Messengers of Life* by Lawrence Crapo. Copyright © 1985 by Lawrence Crapo, M.D. Reprinted with the permission of W. H. Freeman and Company.

128 Figure 4.11. Adaptation of illustration "Three Brains in One" from *Biological Psychology*, 2nd Edition by James W. Kalat. Copyright © 1984, 1981 by Wadsworth, Inc. Used by permission of the publisher.

128 Figure 4.12. From "Development of Human Brain 3 Weeks to Birth, Lateral View," *Introduction to Physiological Psychology* by Richard F. Thompson, Harper & Row, Publishers, 1975, adapted from figures 203 and 206 in *Human Embryology*, second edition by Bradley M. Patten, McGraw-Hill Book Company, 1953.

137 Figure 4.16. From Wilder Penfield, M.D. and Herbert Jasper, M.D., *Epilepsy and the Functional Anatomy of the Human Brain*, p. 188. Copyright 1954 Wilder Penfield and Herbert Jasper. Reprinted by permission of Little, Brown and Company.

Chapter 5

145 Table 5.1. Reprinted by permission from *The Encyclopedic Dictionary of Psychology*, 3rd Edition, p. 254. Copyright © 1986 by The Dushkin Publishing Group, Inc., Guilford, Connecticut.

146 Table 5.2. From *New Directions in Psychology* by Roger Brown, et al. Copyright © 1962 by Holt, Rinehart and Winston, Inc. Reprinted by permission of the author.

150 Figure 5.5. From *Sensory Communication* by W. A. Rosenblith. Copyright © 1961 by The Massachusetts Institute of Technology. Reprinted by permission.

154 Figure 5.8. Adapted from *Seeing: Illusion, Brain and Mind* by John P. Frisby. Copyright © 1979 by John P. Frisby. Reprinted by permission of Oxford University Press.

161 Figure 5.16. From *Sensation and Perception* by Stanley Coren, Clare Porac and Lawrence M. Ward. Copyright © 1979 by Harcourt Brace Jovanovich, Inc. Reprinted by permission of the publisher.
From *Visual Perception* by Tom N. Cornsweet. Copyright © 1970 by Harcourt Brace Jovanovich, Inc. Reprinted by permission of the publisher.

164 Figure 5.19. From *Fundamentals of Sensation and Perception* by Michael W. Levine and Jeremy M. Shefner. Reprinted by permission of Michael W. Levine.

170 Figure 5.25 (top). From *The Science of Musical Sound* by D. C. Miller, MacMillan Company 1926. Reprinted by permission of Case Western Reserve University.

172 Figure 5.27B. From *Experiments in Hearing* by Georg von Békésy, translated and edited by E. G. Wever. Copyright © 1960 by the McGraw-Hill Book Company, Inc. Adapted by permission.

172 Figure 5.28. From *Theory of Hearing* by Ernest Glen Wever. Copyright 1949 by John Wiley & Sons, Inc. Reprinted by permission of the author.

Chapter 6

195 Figure 6.7. James J. Gibson: *The Perception of the Visual World.* Copyright 1950, renewed 1977 by Houghton Mifflin Company. Used with permission.

201 Figure 6.16. From "Impossible Objects: A Special Type of Visual Illusion" by L. S. Penrose and R. Penrose, *The British Journal of Psychology*, Vol. 49, 1958. Reprinted by permission.

203 Figure 6.19. From *The Ames Demonstrations in Perception* by W. H. Ittelson. Reprinted by permission of the author.

203 Figure 6.20. From *Sensation and Perception* by Stanley Coren, Clare Porac, Lawrence M. Ward. Copyright © 1979 by Harcourt Brace Jovanovich, Inc. Reprinted by permission of the publisher.

204 Figure 6.21. Adapted from James J. Gibson: *The Perception of the Visual World.* Copyright 1950, renewed 1977 Houghton Mifflin Company. Adapted with permission.

Chapter 7

226 Figure 7.1. From *Cognitive Psychology and Information Processing: An Introduction* by Roy Lachman, Janet L. Lachman and Earl C. Butterfield. Reprinted by permission of Lawrence Erlbaum Associates, Inc. and the authors.

229 Figure 7.4. From "Features and Objects in Visual Processing" by Anne Triesman in *Scientific American.* Copyright © 1986 by Scientific American, Inc. All rights reserved. Reprinted by permission.

230 Figure 7.5. From "Features and Objects in Visual Processing" by Anne Triesman in *Scientific American.* Copyright © 1986 by Scientific American, Inc. All rights reserved. Reprinted by permission.

235 Figure 7.7. From R. W. Sperry from The Harvey Lectures, Series 62, 1968. New York: Academic Press, Inc. Reprinted by permission.

237 Figure from *Psychology* by Michael S. Gazzaniga. Copyright © 1980 by Michael S. Gazzaniga. Reprinted by permission of Harper & Row, Publishers, Inc.

240 Figure 7.8. From *The Sleep Disorders* by Peter Hauri. Copyright © 1977 The Upjohn Company. Reprinted by permission from Scope® Pubications, the Upjohn Company and the author.

241 Figure 7.9. From "Ontogenetic Development of the Human Sleep-Dream Cycle" by H. P. Roffwarg, et al., *Science,* April 1966, 152 (9), pp. 604-619. Copyright © 1966 by the American Association for the Advancement of Science. Reprinted by permission of the American Association for the Advancement of Science.

245 Figure 7.10. Based on Ernest R. Hilgard, *Hypnotic Susceptibility.* Copyright © 1965 by Harcourt Brace Jovanovich, Inc. Reprinted by permission of the publisher.

249 Figure 7.12. Kandel, D. "Adolescent Marijuana Use: Role of Parents and Peers," *Science*, Vol. 181, pp. 1067-1070, Fig. 1. September 14, 1973. Copyright © 1973 by the American Association for the Advancement of Science. Reprinted by permission of the Association and the author.

Chapter 8

264 Figure 8.2. From *Principles of Animal Learning and Motivation* by R. M. Tarpy, p. 51. © 1982 Scott, Foresman.

289 Figure 8.7. From *Psychonomic Science*, 1966, 4, 123-124. Reprinted by permission of Psychonomic Society, Inc.

295 Figure 8.10. From "Degrees of Hunger, Reward and Nonreward, and Maze Learning in Rats" by E. C. Tolman and C. H. Honzik, *University of California Publications in Psychology*, Vol. 4, No. 16, December 1930. Reprinted by permission.

Chapter 9

306 Figure 9.2. From "The Information Available in Brief Visual Presentations" by George Sperling, *Psychological Monographs: General and Applied*, Vol. 174, No. 11, Whole No. 498, 1960. Copyright © 1960 by the American Psychological Association, Inc. Adapted by permission of the publisher and the author.

306 Figure 9.3. From "Short Term Memory in Vision" by E. Averbach and A. S. Coriell in *The Bell System Technical Journal*, January 1961. Copyright © 1961 by AT&T. Reprinted with permission from the AT&T Technical Journal.

310 Figure 9.4. From "Short-Term Retention of Individual Verbal Items" by Lloyd R. Peterson and Margaret Jean Peterson, *Journal of Experimental Psychology*, September 1959, Vol. 58, No. 3. Copyright © 1959 by the American Psychological Association, Inc. Reprinted by permission of the publisher and the authors.

311 Figure 9.5. From "High Speed Scanning in Human Memory," Sternberg, S., *Science*, Vol. 153, pp. 652-654, Fig. 1, August 5, 1966. Copyright © 1966 American Association for the Advancement of Science. Reprinted by permission of the American Association for the Advancement of Science and the author.

323 Figure 9.11. From "Two Storage Mechanisms in Free Recall" by Murray Glanzer and Anita R. Cunitz, *Journal of Verbal Learning and Verbal Behavior*, 1966. Reprinted by permission of Academic Press, Inc. and the author.

333 Figure 9.14. From "Mechanisms of Memory" by L. R. Squire in *Science*, Vol. 232, No. 4758, June 27, 1986. Copyright © 1986 American Association for the Advancement of Science. Reprinted by permission.

Chapter 10

348 Figure 10.1. From *Mental Images and Their Transformations* by Roger N. Shepard and Lynn A. Cooper. Copyright © 1982 by The Massachusetts Institute of Technology. Reprinted by permission.

349 Figure 10.2. From "Scanning Visual Images: Some Structural Implications" by Stephen Michael Kosslyn in *Perception and Psychophysics*, Vol. 14, No. 1, 1973, pp. 90–94. Reprinted by permission of Psychonomic Society, Inc.

362 Figure 10.5. From "Acquisition of a Memory Skill," K. Anders Ericsson, et al., *Science*, Vol. 208, p. 1181, Fig. 1,6, June 1980. Copyright © 1980 American Association for the Advancement of Science. Reprinted by permission of the American Association for the Advancement of Science and the author.

369 Figure 10.7. From "The First Two R's" by Ovid J. L. Tzeng and William S. Y. Wang in *American Scientist*, Vol. 71, May–June 1983, p. 241. Reprinted by permission.

Chapter 11

380 From Warden, C. J. *Animal Motivation: Experimental Studies on the Albino Rat*, 1931. Reprinted by permission of Columbia University Press.

389 Figure 11.4. From "Hunger in Humans Induced by 2-Deoxy-D-Glucose: Glucoprivic Control of Taste Preference and Food Intake," Thompson, D. A. and Campbell, R. G., *Science*, December 9, 1977, Vol. 198, pp. 1065-1067, Copyright © 1977 American Association for the Advancement of Science. Reprinted by permission.

392 Figure 11.5. From *Human Sexualities* by J. H. Gagnon, p. 207. © 1977 Scott, Foresman and Company.

396 Figure 11.8. From *Human Motivation* by Bernard Weiner. Copyright © 1980 by Bernard Weiner. Reprinted by permission.

397 Table 11.2. Adapted from *Human Motivation* by Bernard Weiner. Copyright © 1980 by Holt, Rinehart and Winston. Reprinted by permission of CBS College Publishing.

410 Figure 11.11. Reprinted by permission of the publisher and the author from "Crying Behavior in the Human Adult" by William H. Frey, II, Ph.D., et al., *Integrative Psychiatry*, September/October 1983. Copyright © 1983 by Elsevier Science Publishing Co., Inc.

411 Figure 11.12. From "The Schachter Theory of Emotion: Two Decades Later" by Rainer Reisenzein, *Psychological Bulletin*, 1983, Vol. 94, No. 2. Copyright © 1983 by the American Psychological Association, Inc. Reprinted by permission of the publisher and the author.

Chapter 12

423 Table 12.1. Reproduced by permission of the publisher, F. E. Peacock Publishers, Inc., Itasca, Illinois. From Raymond J. Corsini, *Current Personality Theories*. Copyright © 1977, pp. 2 and 3.

425 Figure 12.2. From *The Inequality of Man* by H. J. Eysenck. Copyright © 1973 Hans J. Eysenck. Reprinted by permission of the author.

Chapter 13

464 Figure 13.1. From *Wechsler's Measurement and Appraisal of Adult Intelligence* by J. D. Matarazzo. Copyright © 1972 by Oxford University Press, Inc. Reprinted by permission.

466 Figure 13.2. From *Way Beyond the IQ: Guide to Improving Intelligence and Creativity*, page 161, by J. P. Guilford, Buffalo, New York: Barely Limited, 1977. Reprinted by permission of the author.

470 Figure 13.3. From "Achievement and Social Mobility: Relationships among IQ Score, Education, and Occupation in Two Generations" by Jerome H. Waller, *Social Biology*, Vol. 18, September 1971, No. 3. Copyright © 1971 by The American Eugenics Society, Inc.

470 Figure 13.4. From "I. Q., Test Performance of Black Children Adopted by White Families" by S. Scarr and R. A. Weinberg in *American Psychologist*, 1976, 31, 726–739. Copyright 1976 by the American Psychological Association. Adapted by permission of the author.

473 Table 13.1. From *Minnesota Multiphasic Personality Inventory*. Copyright The University of Minnesota 1943, renewed 1970. Reprinted by permission of the University of Minnesota Press.

474 Figure 13.5. From *Minnesota Multiphasic Personality Inventory*. Copyright The University of Minnesota 1943, renewed 1970. Reprinted by permission of the University of Minnesota Press.

475 Table based on material from pp. 350-351 from *Clinical Psychology: Concepts, Methods, and Profession*, Rev. Ed. by E. Jerry Phares. (The Dorsey Press, Homewood, Illinois © 1984). Reprinted by permission.

Chapter 14

499 Figure 14.3. From Core Concepts of Health by Paul M. Insel and Walton T. Roth, page 31, 1985. Reprinted by permission of Mayfield Publishing Company.

501 Figure 14.4. From *Stress Without Distress* by Hans Selye, M.D., J. B. Lippincott Company. Copyright © 1974 by Hans Selye, M.D. Reprinted by permission of Harper & Row, Publishers, Inc.

504 Excerpts from "The Aftershock of Rape," *The Stanford Daily*, February 2, 1982. Reprinted by permission.

506 Table 14.4. "The Social Readjustment Rating Scale" reprinted with permission from *Journal of Psychosometic Research* 11: 213-218, 1967, T. H. Holmes and R. H. Rahe, Copyright © 1967, Pergamon Press, Inc. and T. H. Holmes.

512 Figure 14.5. From "Desensitization and the Experimental Reduction of Threat" by Carlyle H. Folkins, et al., *Journal of Abnormal Psychology*, 1968, 73 Copyright © 1968 by the American Psychological Association, Inc. Reprinted by permission of the publisher and the authors.

513 Table 14.6. From D. Meichenbaum. "A Self-Instructional Approach to Stress Management: A Proposal for Stress Innoculating Training." In D. C. Spielberger and I. G. Sarason, (Eds.), *Stress and Anxiety*, Vol. 1. New York: Wiley, 1975, 237-263. Copyright © 1975 by Hemisphere Publishing Corporation. Reprinted by permission.

Chapter 15

519 Excerpt from *Diagnostic and Statistical Manual of Mental Disorders* (Third Edition). Copyright © 1980, The American Psychiatric Association. Reprinted by permission.

520 Excerpt from "A Six-Year Nightmare for Jim Backus" by Vernon Scott. Reprinted with permission of United Press International, Inc. Copyright © 1984.

524 Table 15.2. Reprinted with permission from the *Diagnostic and Statistical Manual of Mental Disorders* (Third Edition, revised). Copyright © 1987, The American Psychiatric Association.

530 Material based on *Diagnostic and Statistical Manual of Mental Disorders* (Third Edition). Copyright © 1980, The American Psychiatric Association. Reprinted by permission.

543 Table 15.6. Reprinted with permission from the *Diagnostic and Statistical Manual of Mental Disorders* (Third Edition, revised). Copyright 1987, The American Psychiatric Association.

550 Figure 15.1. From "Genetic Theories and the Validation of Psychiatric Diagnosis: Implications for the Study of Children of Schizophrenics" by Daniel R. Hanson, et al., *Journal of Abnormal Psychology*, 1977, 86. Copyright © 1977 by the American Psychological Association, Inc. Reprinted by permission of the publisher and the authors.

555 Figure 15.2. From Haas, K. "Let the Punishment Fit the Crime." *Understanding Ourselves and Others*, 1965. Reprinted by permission of Prentice-Hall, Inc. Englewood Cliffs, New Jersey.

Chapter 16

568 Excerpt from "The Case of Anna O.: A Reformulation" by Marc H. Hollender, M.D., *The American Journal of Psychiatry*, vol. 137: 7, p. 800, 1980. Copyright © 1980, the American Psychiatric Association.

569 Excerpt from Yoram Kaufmann, "Analytical Psychotherapy." Reproduced by permission of the publisher, F. E. Peacock Publishers, Inc., Itasca, Illinois. From Raymond J. Corsini and Contributors, *Current Psychotherapies* (Third Edition). Copyright © 1984, p. 124.

572 Table 16.1. Reprinted with permission from *The Practice of Behavior Therapy*, 2nd Edition by J. Wolpe, Copyright © 1973 Pergamon Books Ltd.

576 Figure 16.1. From "Modeling Therapy" by Albert Bandura. Reprinted by permission of the author.

578 Table 16.2. Adapted from *Modern Clinical Psychology: Principles of Intervention in the Clinic and Community* by Sheldon J. Korchin. Copyright © 1976 by Sheldon J. Korchin. Reprinted by permission of Basic Books, Inc., Publishers.

592 Table 16.4. From "Meta-Analysis of Psychotherapy Outcome Studies" by Mary Lee Smith and Gene V. Glass, *American Psychologist*, Vol. 32, September 1977, No. 9. Copyright © 1977 by the American Psychological Association, Inc. Adapted by permission of the publisher and the authors.

Chapter 17

607 Excerpt from "Primacy-Recency in Impression Formation" by A. S. Luchins, *The Order of Presentation in Persuasion*, C. I. Hovland (Ed.). Copyright © 1957 Yale University Press, Inc. Reprinted by permission.

609 Figure 17.1. From "An Experimental Study of Apparent Behavior" by F. Heider and M. Simmel, *American Journal of Psychology*, Vol. 57, 1944, pp. 243-259. Reprinted by permission of the University of Illinois Press.

620 Figure 17.2. From "Communicator Credibility and Communication Discrepancy as Determinants of Opinion Change" by Eliot Aronson, Judith A. Turner and J. Merrill Carlsmith, *Journal of Abnormal and Social Psychology*, 1963, Vol. 67, No. 1. Copyright © 1963 by the American Psychological Association, Inc. Reprinted by permission of the publisher and the authors.

626 Table from "The Friendship Bond" by Mary Brown Parlee and the Editors of *Psychology Today*, October 1979. Copyright © 1979 American Psychological Association. Reprinted by permission.

Chapter 18

646 Figure 18.2. From "Prenatal Exposure to Synthetic Progestins Increases Potential for Aggression in Humans" by June M. Reinisch, *Science*, Vol. 211,13, March 1981, pp. 1171-1173. Copyright © 1981 American Association for the Advancement of Science. Reprinted by permission of the American Association for the Advancement of Science and the author.

650 Figure 18.4. From "The Effects of Alcohol and Delta-9-Tetrahydrocannabinol on Human Physical Aggression" by Stuart P. Taylor, et al., *Aggressive Behavior*, Volume 2, pages 153-161. Copyright © 1976 Alan R. Liss, Inc. Adapted by permission.

652 Figure 18.6. From "Aggressive Erotica and Violence Against Women" by Edward Donnerstein, *Journal of Personality and Social Psychology*, August 1980, Vol. 39, No. 2. Copyright © 1980 by the American Psychological Association, Inc. Adapted by permission of the publisher and the author.

658 Excerpt from "Why Johnny Can't Disobey" by Sarah J. McCarthy, *The Humanist*, September/October 1979. Copyright © 1979 by The Humanist. Reprinted by permission.

663 Figure 18.8. From "Disinhibition of Aggression Through Diffusion of Responsibility and Dehumanization of Victims" by Albert Bandura, et al., *Journal of Research in Personality*, 1975, 9, pp. 253-269. Copyright © 1975 by Academic Press, Inc. Reprinted by permission of the publisher and the author.

665 Figure 18.9. From "Mechanisms of Moral Disengagement," a paper presented at the conference "Psychology of Terrorism: Behaviors, World-Views, States of Mind," March 1987 by Albert Bandura. Reprinted by permission of the author.

667 Figure 18.10. Darley and Latané, "Bystander Intervention in Emergencies: Diffusion of Responsibilities." *Journal of Personality and Social Psychology*, 1968, 8(4), 377–384. Copyright © 1968 by the American Psychological Association. Adapted by permission of the publisher and author.

Name Index

C

D

E

F

G

N

O

T

Subject Index

D

E

I

J

K

L

M

N

O

P

S

T

U

V

W

Y